CASES AND MATERIALS ON

EMPLOYMENT LAW

Third edition

Richard W. Painter, LLB, MA

Professor of Law and Dean of the Law School,
Staffordshire University

Ann E. M. Holmes, BA, M.Phil,
Pg.D (Occupational Health and Safety)

Associate Dean of the Law School, Staffordshire University

Stephen D. Migdal, BA (Hons)

Barrister at Law of the Inner Temple and
Victoria Chambers Birmingham

BLACKSTONE
PRESS LIMITED

First published in Great Britain 1995 by Blackstone Press Limited,
Aldine Place, London W12 8AA. Telephone (020) 8740 2277
www.blackstonepress.com

© R. W. Painter, A. Holmes and S. Migdal, 1995

First edition, 1995
Second edition, 1996
Third edition, 2000

ISBN: 1 85431 882 9

British Library Cataloguing in Publication Data
A CIP catalogue record for this book is available from the British Library

Typeset by Style Photosetting Ltd, Mayfield, East Sussex
Printed by Ashford Colour Press, Gosport, Hampshire

CONTENTS

I Contexts and approaches — II The institutional framework of employment law — III The International Labour Organisation — IV European Community law

I Employee status — II Continuity of Employment — III Constructing the contract of employment: express terms — IV Collective bargaining — V Constructing the contract of employment: implied terms — VI Constructing the contract of employment: characteristic or imposed terms — VII Constructing the contract of employment: work rules — VIII Constructing the contract of employment: custom and practice — IX Constructing the contract of employment: statutory implied terms — X The characteristic rights and obligations of the employer and employee

PREFACE

The need for a third edition of this collection of cases and materials within four years of the publication of the first edition is yet a further illustration of the dynamic and controversial nature of Employment Law.

In preparing the new edition we have had to take on board the Employment Rights (Dispute Resolution) Act 1998, the Public Interest Disclosure Act 1998, the Human Rights Act 1998, the National Minimum Wage Act 1998 and the Working Time Regulations 1998. We have also been able to provide coverage on the latest EC Directives on Burden of Proof in Discrimination Cases, the European Works Councils, Parental Leave and Part-time Work. Most importantly, the timing of the publication of the new edition has allowed us to monitor the implementation of the proposals contained in the White Paper, Fairness at Work, via the Employment Relations Act 1999.

In the midst of all this legislative activity, there have some important developments in case law, particularly in relation to the implied term of trust and confidence, discrimination on the grounds of disability, the definition of redundancy, and transfers of undertakings.

All these and many other developments are fully represented in this book. As with the first edition, our intention has been to provide students with a 'laptop labour law library': a collection of statutory and case law extracts linked by questions and commentary. We have attempted to state the law as at 1 January 2000.

Stephen Migdal was not able to join us in the preparation of this new edition but we are pleased to acknowledge his contribution to two of the chapters in the first two editions. The authors would like to express their gratitude to all those at Blackstone Press who have provided encouragement and patient support throughout the duration of the project. We would also like to gratefully acknowledge the contribution of our colleagues, Keith Puttick for the commentary on the National Minimum Wage Act 1998 and Alison Pope, Senior Law Tutor Librarian, for assistance with researching a number of areas. Finally, our thanks to Enka Hegewald, our PA, who not only word-processed our revisions to the manuscript with such speed and accuracy but also sought to ensure that we managed to complete the new edition with our sanity (relatively) intact.

This new edition is dedicated to our children – Adam, Daniel and James.

Richard W. Painter
Ann E. M. Holmes
Stoke-on-Trent, Staffordshire
January 2000

ACKNOWLEDGMENTS

The authors and publishers would like to thank the following for permission to reproduce copyright material:

ACAS
The Controller of Her Majesty's Stationery Office

Extracts from *The Law Reports, The Weekly Law Reports* and *The Industrial Cases Reports* are reproduced with the permission of the Incorporated Council of Law Reporting for England and Wales.

Extracts from the *All England Reports* are reproduced with the permission of Butterworths Law Publishers Ltd.

Extracts from the *Industrial Relations Law Reports* are reproduced with the permission of Eclipse Group Ltd.

ABBREVIATIONS

ACAS	Advisory, Conciliation and Arbitration Service
CA	Court of Appeal
CAC	Central Arbitration Committee
CRE	Commission for Racial Equality
CROTUM	Commissioner for the Rights of Trade Union Members
DDA	Disability Discrimination Act
EA	Employment Act (1980–1990)
EAT	Employment Appeal Tribunal
ECJ	European Court of Justice
EOC	Equal Opportunities Commission
EPA	Equal Pay Act 1970
EPCA	Employment Protection (Consolidation) Act 1978
ERA	Employment Rights Act
ETA	Employment Tribunals Act
GOQ	Genuine Occupational Qualification
HASAWA	Health and Safety at Work etc. Act 1974
HSC	Health and Safety Commission
HSE	Health and Safety Executive
ICFTD	In contemplation and furtherance of a trade dispute
ILO	International Labour Organisation
IT	Industrial Tribunal
NIRC	National Industrial Relations Court
NMWA	National Minimum Wage Act 1988
NMWR	National Minimum Wage Regulations 1999
PRP	Pay reference period
RRA	Race Relations Act 1976
SDA	Sex Discrimination Act 1975
TULRA	Trade Union and Labour Relations Act 1974
TULR(C)A	Trade Union and Labour Relations (Consolidation) Act 1992
TURERA	Trade Union Reform and Employment Rights Act 1993

TABLE OF CASES

TABLE OF STATUTES

Statutes, and sections thereof, which are set out in full or in part are shown in heavy type. The page at which the statute or section is printed is shown in heavy type.

TABLE OF STATUTORY INSTRUMENTS

Statutory instruments, and rules and regulations thereof, which are set out in full or in part are shown in heavy type. The page at which the statutory instrument is printed is shown in heavy type.

1 INTRODUCTION TO EMPLOYMENT LAW

I Contexts and Approaches

A: The Traditional Approach

O. Kahn Freund, in Flanders and Clegg (eds), *The System of Industrial Relations in Great Britain* (1954) p. 44

There exists something like an inverse correlation between the practical significance of legal sanctions and the degree to which industrial relations have reached a state of maturity. The legal aspect of those obligations on which labour-management relations rests is, from a practical point of view, least developed where industrial relations are developed most satisfactorily. There is, perhaps, no major country in the world in which the law has played a less significant role in the shaping of these relations than in Great Britain and in which today the law and the legal profession have less to do with labour relations. In the writer's opinion this is an indication that these relations are fundamentally healthy.

Note
This description of the State's traditional approach to the conduct of British industrial relations, known variously as legal abstentionism, voluntarism or collective *laissez-faire*, was by the 1970s, in need of considerable modification. The droplets of legal intervention discernible in the 1960s assumed torrential proportions during the following decade.

The Labour Government of 1974–79, as part of the 'Social Contract' between the Government and the TUC, enacted a 'statutory floor' of employment rights, originally brought together by the Employment Protection (Consolidation) Act 1978, and now contained in the Employment Rights

Act 1996; legislation on sex and race discrimination (Sex Discrimination Act (SDA) 1975; Equal Pay Act (EPA) 1970; Race Relations Act (RRA) 1976) and a statutory regime regulating occupational safety (Health and Safety at Work etc. Act 1974).

While the enactment of a range of minimum individual employment rights was perceived as a way of protecting those workers not covered by collective bargaining, the Labour Administration still retained the traditional policy of legal abstentionism in relation to collective labour law. Collective bargaining was perceived to be the best way of conducting labour relations and the 'Social Contract' legislation, while providing a degree of support for union organisation and collective bargaining, eschewed intervention in strikes and other forms of industrial conflict. It was felt that the dangers of departing from the traditional abstentionist model were evident from the brief currency of the Industrial Relations Act (1971–74) which was a failed attempt to introduce a comprehensive legal regulation of employment relations in line with the North American model.

B: The Alternative Approach

F.A. Hayek, *1980s Unemployment and the Unions* (1980) p. 58 and p. 52

There can be no salvation for Britain until the special privileges granted to the trade unions three-quarters of a century ago are revoked. Average real wages of British workers would undoubtedly be higher and their chances of finding employment better, if the wages paid in different occupations were again determined by the market, and if *all limitations* on the work an individual is allowed to do were removed . . . [The] legalised powers of the unions have become the biggest obstacle to raising the living standards of the working class as a whole . . . They are the prime source of unemployment. They are the main reason for the decline of the British economy in general.

Notes
1.   The writings of F.A. Hayek appear to have had a significant effect on the direction of Conservative Government policy post-1979. For arguments in favour of this link, see Lord Wedderburn, 'Freedom of Association and Philosophies of Labour Law', (1989) 18 ILJ 1; McCarthy, W., 'The Rise and Fall of Collective Laissez Faire' in William McCarthy (ed.), *Legal Intervention in Industrial Relations: Gains and Losses* (Oxford: Basil Blackwell, 1992), Ch. 1; and Fosh, P., Morris, H., Martin, R., Smith, P., and Undy, R., 'Politics Pragmatism and Ideology: The "Wellsprings" of Conservative Union Legislation (1979–92)' (1992) 22 ILJ 14. By contrast, Simon Auerbach is critical of the thesis that the theories of the 'new right' were so influential on Government policy, arguing that the content of legislation had less to do with the ideological thinking of Hayek and others than the reaction of the Government to particular political and industrial events in the 1970s and 1980s (Auerbach, S., *Legislating for Conflict* (Oxford: Clarendon Press, 1990). But, as Wedderburn observes, 'Hayek did not of course write the "step-by-step" programme of labour law for 1980–1988; but one would need to be

juridically tone deaf not to pick up the echoes of his philosophy in recent policies and pronouncements' (ibid., p. 15)

2. In radical contrast to the 1974–79 period, the legislation of the 1980s and 1990s – the Employment Acts (EA) 1980 to 1990, the Trade Union Act 1984, the Wages Act 1986, the Trade Union Reform and Employment Rights Act (TURERA) 1993 – aimed to deregulate so far as employment protection and collective bargaining are concerned, but imposed major legal restrictions on trade unions.

This legislation aimed to place major obstacles in the way of the organisation of industrial action. Strike organisers and trade unions were exposed to court orders and damages by the narrowing of the statutory immunities from judge-made liabilities. In this way, secondary industrial action, solidarity and political strikes, picketing away from the pickets' own workplaces and official action not preceded by ballot were, in effect, made unlawful. In addition, the reduction of strikers' dependants' entitlement to supplementary benefit and the widening of the employer's freedom to sack strikers without incurring the risk of liability for unfair dismissal, were put in place in order to make individual workers think twice before withdrawing their labour.

3. In addition to the civil law, the Public Order Act 1986 redefined and expanded some of the criminal law offences which were extensively used against pickets in the 1984/85 miners' dispute. (For an excellent discussion of this area see Lewis, R., 'The Role of Law in Employment Relations', in Lewis, R., (ed.), *Labour Law in Britain* (Oxford: Basil Blackwell, 1986) and Lewis, R. 'Reforming Labour Law: Choices and Constraints', (1987) *Employee Relations*, vol. 9, No. 4, pp. 28–31.)

4. Whilst the logic of the 'free market' points to the legal restriction of trade unions, it requires that most of the burdens of State intervention are lifted from employers. According to free market theory, such legal and bureaucratic controls deter employers, especially small employers, from recruiting labour. Landmarks in the deregulatory process included:

(a) the abolition of the procedure under the Employment Protection Act 1975 and the Fair Wages resolution, measures designed to establish the 'going-rate' of pay and other conditions in particular industries and fair wages in companies awarded government contracts;

(b) the removal of persons under the age of 21 from the protection of the Wages Council system, followed by abolition of the Wages Council's system altogether in 1993;

(c) the repeal of the Truck Acts 1831–1940, a series of statutes which, albeit in a somewhat complicated, anachronistic and piecemeal manner, offered groups of workers a measure of legal protection against arbitrary deductions from pay and the right to payment in cash;

(d) the removal of restrictions on working hours and conditions of women. The SDA 1986, s. 7 removed all major restrictions on women working shifts and at night, overtime restrictions and maximum hours limitations;

(e) the quadrupling of the qualification period for workers before they could claim unfair dismissal – from 26 weeks in 1979 to two years in 1985;

(f) a weakening of maternity rights. In particular, firms employing five or fewer employees being given complete exclusion from employees having a right to return to work after maternity leave.

5. The Conservative Administration claimed that the employment protection legislation had a negative employment effect. However, surveys of management attitudes and responses suggest that the legislation has had only a minor impact in discouraging recruitment. It has induced, however, a greater care in selection in order to ensure the right quality of recruits rather than reducing quantity (see Daniel, W.W., and Stilgoe, E. *The Impact of the Employment Protection Laws* (London: PSI, 1978); Clifton, A., and Tatton-Brown, C., *The Impact of Employment Protection on Small Firms*, Department of Employment Research Paper 7 (London: HMSO, 1979)). Later research found that only 8 per cent of firms surveyed expressed reluctance to recruit additional staff on account of the law of unfair dismissal (Evans, Goodman and Hargreaves, *Unfair Dismissal Law and Employment Practice in the 1980s*, DES Research Paper 53 (London: HMSO, 1985)). The most recent survey does no more than confirm the previous findings (Wood, D., and Smith, P., *Employers' Labour Use Strategies: First Report on the 1987 Survey*, Department of Employment Research Paper 63 (London: HMSO, 1989)).

6. The policy of deregulation, though significant, has been subject to certain constraints or countervailing pressures.

The curtailment of statutory rights did not prevent, and may have even encouraged, resort to alternative remedies provided by the common law. For example, recent developments have seen the courts display a greater willingness to grant injunctions in order to halt dismissals which take place in breach of a contractually incorporated disciplinary procedure, or to prevent a breach of the employer's other obligations under the contract (see *Irani* v *Southampton & SW Hampshire HA* [1985] ICR 590, discussed in Chapter 5). Other cases have seen courts upholding claims for breach of contract against employers based on terms incorporated into the contract of employment from a collective agreement (see *Rigby* v *Ferodo Ltd* [1987] IRLR 516, also discussed in Chapter 5).

Furthermore, Conservative governments of the 1980s and 1990s were forced, mainly on account of pressures from Europe, actually to introduce new measures such as the Transfer of Undertakings Regulations 1981, Equal Pay (Amendment) Regulations 1983, the Data Protection Act 1984, the SDA 1986 and the pregnancy and employment documentation provisions of TURERA 1993. EC membership means that UK law is subordinate to the provisions of the Treaty of Rome, the Single European Act and the regulations and directives made under the Treaty. This conflict between the Conservative Government's policies of deregulation and the interventionist stance adopted by the European Commission is discussed in more detail later in this chapter.

C: A Conclusion on the Previous Conservative Government's Employment Relations Strategy

P. Fosh, H. Morris, R. Martin, P. Smith and R. Undy, 'Politics, Pragmatism and Ideology: The "Wellsprings" of Conservative Union Legislation (1979–92)' (1993) 22 ILJ 14

The Conservatives appear to have had twin aims in their legislative activity for the reform of industrial relations and the reshaping of the labour market. These were the deregulation of the labour market (regulation of terms conditions by statute or by collective bargaining must be reduced as a 'burden on business') and individual freedom (the individual must be free to enter into those contracts which seem to him/her appropriate or necessary), often summarised as 'ideological individualism'.

There are, however, a number of apparent contradictions contained within the Conservative Government's twin aims: (i) if the individual is free, then he/she is free to form unions with others and organise them how they wish, and the operations of these unions, if efficient, can prevent the deregulation of the labour market; (ii) the massive legislative programme mounted by the Conservatives since 1979 seems as much focused on regulating unions' internal affairs, as on restricting unions' activities in collective bargaining. In introducing so much legislation, the Conservatives have now *reregulated* the labour market.

Question
Do you accept that there is a contradiction here?

D: A Third Way?

Foreword by the Prime Minister, *Fairness at Work*, (CM 3968), May 1998

This White Paper is part of the Government's programme to replace the notion of conflict between employers and employees with the promotion of partnership. It goes along with our emphasis on education and skills – not overburdensome regulation – in the labour market, as the best means of equipping business and people for a modern economy. It complements our prudent economic management and our proposals for encouraging small businesses and stimulating long-term investment.

The White Paper steers a way between the absence of minimum standards of protection at the workplace, and a return to the laws of the past. It is based on the rights of the individual, whether exercised on their own or with others, as a matter of their choice. It matches rights and responsibilities. It seeks to draw a line under the issue of industrial relations law.

There will be no going back. The days of strikes without ballots, mass picketing, closed shops and secondary action are over. Even after the changes we propose, Britain will have the most lightly regulated labour market of any leading economy in the world. But it cannot be just to deny British citizens basic canons of fairness – rights to claim unfair dismissal, rights against discrimination for making a free choice of being a union member, rights to unpaid parental leave – that are a matter of course elsewhere.

These proposals, together with the introduction of a minimum wage – set sensibly, implemented sensibly – put a very minimum infrastructure of decency and fairness around people in the workplace. They have been extensively consulted upon with business and industry. They offer the right way forward for the future.

Note

Following the election of the new Labour Government in May 1997, there was a flurry of legislative activity in the field of employment law. Legislation was introduced for a national minimum wage below which pay would not fall. The Government also supported Richard Shepherd's Private Member's Bill on public interest disclosure, or 'whistleblowing'. The Public Interest Disclosure Act 1998 provides protection against dismissal or victimisation for employees who responsibly raise concerns about criminal offences, failures to meet legal obligations, miscarriages of justice, health, safety and environmental dangers and 'covers up' of these matters. The Government also supported the Employment Rights (Dispute Resolution) Act 1998, introduced by Lord Archer of Sandwell. This Act improves and streamlines the procedures of employment tribunals, encourages the use of internal procedures and promotes a new voluntary arbitration scheme, developed by ACAS, to settle unfair dismissal claims.

However, the most significant package of reforms to employment and trade union law were outlined in the Government's White Paper, *Fairness at Work*, published in May 1998 (Cm 3968) and developed in the light of consultation. The three main elements of the *Fairness at Work* framework are:

(a)   provisions for the basic fair treatment of employees;
(b)   new procedures for collective representation at work;
(c)   policies that enhance family life while making it easier for people – both men and women – to go to work.

Fairness at Work (Cm 3968), May 1998

New Rights for Individuals

The government *proposes* to:
1.   reduce the qualifying period for unfair dismissal claims to one year
2.   abolish the maximum limit on awards for unfair dismissal
3.   introduce a legislation to index-link limits on statutory awards and payments 'subject to a maximum rate'.

The government *invites views* on:
4.   whether the limits on 'additional' and 'special' awards should be retained; and whether tribunals should be able to award 'aggravated' damages
5.   possible options for changing the law allowing employees with fixed-term contracts to waive their right to claim unfair dismissal, and receive statutory redundancy payments
6.   whether further action should be taken to address the potential abuse of 'zero hours' contracts and, if so, how to take this forward without undermining labour market flexibility
7.   whether legislation is needed to extend the coverage of some or all existing employment rights by regulation to all those who work for another person.

Collective Rights

The government *proposes* to:

8. enable employees to have a trade union recognised by their employer, but only where the majority of the relevant workforce wishes it. Statutory procedures for both recognition and derecognition, where currently there are few rules (or limitations on employers), will be introduced.

9. change the law so that, in general, those dismissed for taking part in lawfully organised official action should have the right to complain to a tribunal of unfair dismissal

10. make it unlawful to discriminate by omission on grounds of trade union membership, non-membership or union-related activities

11. prohibit blacklisting of trade unionists

12. amend the law on ballots before industrial action and notice to make clear that, while the union's notice to the employer should still identify as accurately as reasonably practicable the group or category of employees concerned, it need not give names

13. create a legal right to be accompanied by a fellow employee or trade union representative of their choice during grievance and disciplinary procedures

14 abolish the Commissioner for the Rights of Trade Union Members (CRTUM) and Commissioner for the Protection Against Unlawful Industrial Action (CPAUIA), and give new powers to the Certification Officer, to hear complaints involving most aspects of the law where CRTUM is currently empowered to provide assistance

15. make funds available which would contribute to the training of managers and employee representatives in order to assist and develop partnerships at work;
and the government *invites views* on:

16. whether training should be among the matters automatically covered by an award of trade union recognition

17. how procedures for derecognition should work

18. how protection against dismissal for those taking part in lawfully organised industrial action should be implemented

19. simplifying the law, and Code of Practice, on industrial action ballots and notice.

Family-friendly Policies

The government *proposes* to:

20. extend the right to maternity leave to 18 weeks and to align it with maternity pay

21. give employees rights to extended maternity leave; and parental leave, but only after one year's service

22. provide for the contract of employment to continue during the whole period of maternity or parental leave (unless it is expressly determined by either party, by dismissal, or resignation)

23. provide similar rights to employees to return to their jobs after parental leave, as apply under present arrangements after maternity absence

24. provide three months' parental leave for adoptive parents

25. provide a right to 'reasonable time off' for family emergencies, applicable to all employees regardless of length of service

26. ensure that employees are protected against dismissal (or 'detriment') if they exercise rights to parental leave and time off for 'urgent family reasons';
and *invites views* on:

27. simplifying notice requirements relating to maternity leave

28.   its options for framing legislation to comply with the Parental Leave Directive
29.   the difficulties small firms could face in complying with the Directive on parental leave.

Notes
1.   Following publication of *Fairness at Work*, the Government consulted on a number of proposals. In some instances, the consultation process resulted in legislation not being pursued ('zero hours' contracts, for example). In others, it led to the proposals being modified. On 17 December 1998, for example, the Secretary of State for Trade and Industry announced that there would be a limit on the compensatory award (£50,000 from the current £12,000 rather than abolition of the limit). The Government also diluted its original proposal that a union should be automatically recognised where it had at least 50 per cent membership within a particular bargaining unit. The revised proposal allowed the CAC to conduct a ballot in such circumstances where it was satisfied that it was 'in the interests of good industrial relations' or there was evidence that a significant number of the union members with the bargaining unit did not want the union to conduct collective bargaining on their behalf. The *Fairness at Work* package, as revised, was implemented by the Employment Relations Act 1999.
2.   These legislative changes do not mean that we have seen a complete return to the voluntary policies of the post-war years. In *Fairness at Work*, the Labour Government confirms that it does not intend radically to change the highly restrictive laws governing lawful industrial action introduced by the previous Conservative administration. Also, the Government has distanced itself from a clear commitment given by its former party leader, John Smith, to give all workers basic employment rights 'on the first day of employment'.
3.   A notable feature of the *Fairness at Work* legislation is that it leaves a substantial amount of the detail to regulations. In practical terms this will mean that consultation will undoubtedly continue behind the scenes in the lead up to specific regulations being made. By subjecting large areas of employment law to a new enabling system under which modifications can readily (and at short notice) be made by regulations (rather than keeping basic entitlements and responsibilities in primary legislation), there is obviously scope in the future for developing them further. Equally, there is increased scope for rolling back entitlements, and with the minimum of Parliamentary debate and prior consultation, under such a system.
4.   Bob Simpson offers the following critique of the *Fairness at Work* package:

In making an overall assessment of *Fairness at Work* it is necessary to place the White Paper in the context of other action taken by the government during its first year in office. From this broader picture it appears that there is some ambiguity in its attitude towards collective labour rights. While it appears to be anxious to ensure that the basic right to freedom of association is enjoyed by all members of the labour force, except those groups which can legitimately be excluded in accordance with international standards, the restrictive terms on which union membership rights were restored to workers at GCHQ, the minimalist approach to reversing the effect of the House of Lords decision in *Wilson/Palmer* and the uncertain scope of both the right to union representation in grievance and disciplinary proceedings and the proposal to outlaw blacklisting of union members call the strength of the government's commitment on this issue into question. The proposed new recognition procedure is more clearly equivocal since it is not backed by any government endorsement of collective bargaining such as underpinned the Donovan report's proposal for permanent machinery to resolve recognition disputes made 30 years ago and government initiatives in pursuit of that proposal over the following decade. Instead the government relies on 'the development of strong partnerships at work . . . as the best way of improving fairness at work' and this '[w]ithin Britain's flexible and efficient labour market' (para. 1.8). From this perspective recognition is to be supported only where it is the 'choice' of the relevant workforce; in a telling echo of the previous government's 1992 White Paper *People, Jobs and Opportunity* (Cm 1810 London: HMSO), *Fairness at Work* accepts that 'many employers and employees will continue to choose direct relationships without the involvement of third parties' (para. 1.9). If the choice of parties to an unequal bargaining relationship is to be the overriding consideration, it is wholly unsurprising that the government has few proposals for amending the highly restrictive legal framework which now surrounds the right to strike and that the White Paper twice expressly endorses key elements of the labour legislation of the previous government (para. 2.15 and footnote to para. 4.8).

The focus on individual employment rights, to which the national minimum wage will be a radical addition, is heavily qualified by the government's evident deference to the view that social rights for workers are a part of employers' labour costs which must be minimised in the interests of maintaining their ability to compete in increasingly global markets – even for public sector employers – for goods and services. The repeated references to the benefits of a 'flexible and efficient' labour market in the first two chapters of the White Paper can be seen to explain the extremely qualified and cautious way in which, for example, the proposals and matters for consultation in relation to widening the range of workers who have access to 'the right not to be unfairly dismissed' (Employment Rights Act 1996, s. 94(1)) are presented.

It may be that the government lacks any clear vision of how it would like labour relations to evolve and the role of the law in that process. Or it may be that its vision is blurred by an inability or unwillingness to try to resolve two dilemmas for a Labour government anxious to appear different from its predecessors yet seeking to carry with it at least the mainstream of the labour movement to which the Labour Party owes its origins. These are first whether to promote collective labour relations founded on effective collective bargaining which can only be based on strong trade unions, or whether to encourage the progressive dilution of 'bargaining' in favour of the more ambiguous 'information and consultation 'standards which now underpin a number of EC social policy initiatives, including the European Works Council Directive, the extension of which to the United Kingdom is welcomed (para. 4.4). The second dilemma is to determine the extent to which it is legitimate to qualify management prerogatives, which some employers would like to exercise subject to little or no restriction, by individual employment rights. On this issue it appears from *Fairness at Work* that the government feels more enthusiastic about extending social rights where change can be subsumed under another label – 'Family-friendly Policies' – which resonates of a different debate in which the government feels more comfortable in defending its position. (Simpson, R., (1998) 27 ILJ 245, at pp. 252–3)

(For a radical manifesto for Labour law reform, see Ewing, K., *Working Life: A New Perspective on Labour Law* (London: The Institute of Employment Rights, Lawrence and Wishart, 1996).)

II The Institutional Framework of Employment Law

A: *The Advisory, Conciliation and Arbitration Service*

The Advisory, Conciliation and Arbitration Service (ACAS) was established in 1974 and put on a statutory basis by the Employment Protection Act 1975. The constitution of ACAS is now to be found in the Trade Union and Labour Relations (Consolidation) Act (TULR(C)A) 1992, ss. 247–253. Its functions are set out in ss. 209–214 of the Act.

Trade Union and Labour Relations (Consolidation) Act 1992

209. General duty to promote improvement of industrial relations
It is the general duty of ACAS to promote the improvement of industrial relations . . .

210. Conciliation
(1) Where a trade dispute exists or is apprehended ACAS may, at the request of one or more parties to the dispute or otherwise, offer the parties to the dispute its assistance with a view to bringing about a settlement.

(2) The assistance may be by way of conciliation or by other means, and may include the appointment of a person other than an officer or servant of ACAS to offer assistance to the parties to the dispute with a view to bringing about a settlement.

(3) In exercising its functions under this section ACAS shall have regard to the desirability of encouraging the parties to a dispute to use any appropriate agreed procedures for negotiation or the settlement of disputes.

211. Conciliation officers
(1) ACAS shall designate some of its officers to perform the functions of conciliation officers under any enactment (whenever passed) relating to matters which are or could be the subject of proceedings before an industrial tribunal.

(2) References in any such enactment to a conciliation officer are to an officer designated under this section.

212. Arbitration
(1) Where a trade dispute exists or is apprehended ACAS may, at the request of one or more of the parties to the dispute and with the consent of all the parties to the dispute, refer all or any of the matters to which the dispute relates for settlement to the arbitration of—
(a) one or more persons appointed by ACAS for that purpose (not being officers or employees of ACAS), or
(b) the Central Arbitration Committee.

(2) In exercising its functions under this section ACAS shall consider the likelihood of the dispute being settled by conciliation.

(3) Where there exist appropriate agreed procedures for negotiation or the settlement of disputes, ACAS shall not refer a matter for settlement to arbitration under this section unless—
(a) those procedures have been used and have failed to result in a settlement, or

(b)   there is, in ACAS's opinion, a special reason which justifies arbitration under this section as an alternative to those procedures.

(4)   Where a matter is referred to arbitration under subsection (1)(a)—

(a)   if more than one arbitrator or arbiter is appointed, ACAS shall appoint one of them to act as chairman; and

(b)   the award may be published if ACAS so decides and all the parties consent.

(5)   Part I of the Arbitration Act 1950 (general provisions as to arbitration) does not apply to an arbitration under this section.

213.   Advice

(1)   ACAS may, on request or otherwise, give employers, employers' associations, workers and trade unions such advice as it thinks appropriate on matters concerned with or affecting or likely to affect industrial relations.

ACAS may also publish general advice on matters concerned with or affecting or likely to affect industrial relations.

214.   Inquiry

(1)   ACAS may, if it thinks fit, inquire into any question relating to industrial relations generally or to industrial relations in any particular industry or in any particular undertaking or part of an undertaking.

(2)   The findings of an inquiry under this section, together with any advice given by ACAS in connection with those findings, may be published by ACAS if—

(a)   it appears to ACAS that publication is desirable for the improvement of industrial relations, either generally or in relation to the specific question inquired into, and

(b)   after sending a draft of the findings to all parties appearing to to be concerned and taking account of their views, it thinks fit.

Notes

1.   Prior to its amendment by TURERA 1993, s. 209 read as follows:

It is the general duty of ACAS to promote the improvement of industrial relations, and in particular to encourage the extension of collective bargaining and the development and, where necessary, reform of collective bargaining machinery.

This ostensibly minor change perfectly encapsulated the Conservative Government's policy of disestablishing collectivism. It is also significant that the new Labour Government did not see fit to reinstate ACAS's original duty as part of *Fairness at Work* reforms.

2.   ACAS's role in individual conciliation 'has been one of strong and steady growth, with the number of claims (i.e. jurisdiction) rising year-on-year between 1994 and 1998, from 79,332 to 113,636 (an increase of 43 per cent). This expansion is a direct consequence of the extension of individual employment rights over the period and a growing number of cases involving multiple jurisdictions. Other factors include changes in the economic climate and a greater willingness by individuals to seek redress for their grievances'. (ACAS Annual Report, 1998.) In line with the trend in recent years, 73 per cent of cases were either settled or withdrawn before reaching an employment tribunal hearing.

'In the area of dispute resolution, there has been a generally stable level of demand for ACAS collective conciliation. In 1994, there were 1,313 requests, and in each of the next four years the volume varied below or above this figure by at most 32 cases, to stand at 1,301 in 1998.' (ACAS Annual Report, 1998.) As in previous years, pay issues provided the most fertile ground for disagreement representing 48 per cent of ACAS's workload in this area. Conciliation was unsuccessful in only 104 cases.

B: The Central Arbitration Committee

The Central Arbitration Committee (CAC) is a permanent arbitral body which was established by the Employment Protection Act 1975 and replaced the Industrial Arbitration Board. Rules governing its composition, etc. are set out in TULR(C)A 1992, ss. 259–265, as amended.

Under the 1975 Act, the CAC had a wide-ranging jurisdiction which included recognition disputes, and also where it was claimed that an employer was not observing 'the going rate' established by collective bargaining for that trade or industry. Both functions were repealed by the EA 1980 as the CAC became one of the first victims of the new Conservative Government's industrial relations reforms.

Until the passage of the Employment Relations Act 1999, the only statutory functions which CAC retained were in relation to disputes over disclosure of information to recognised trade unions for the purposes of collective bargaining (TULR(C)A 1992, ss. 181–185; discussed in Chapter 8). Section 1 and Sch. 1 of the 1999 Act confer new functions on the CAC to administer the statutory recognition and derecognition scheme and determine cases brought under it (see Chapter 8 for a detailed discussion).

C: The Certification Officer

Trade Union and Labour Relations (Consolidation) Act 1992

254.   The Certification Officer
(1)   There shall continue to be an officer called the Certification Officer.

(2)   The Certification Officer shall be appointed by the Secretary of State after consultation with ACAS.

. . .

(5)   ACAS shall provide for the Certification Officer the requisite staff (from among the officers and servants of ACAS) and the requisite accommodation, equipment and other facilities.

. . .

258.   Annual report and accounts
(1)   The Certification Officer shall, as soon as reasonably practicable after the end of each calendar year, make a report of his activities during the year to ACAS and to the Secretary of State.

The Secretary of State shall lay a copy of the report before each House of Parliament and arrange for it to be published.

(2)   The accounts prepared by ACAS in respect of any financial year shall show separately any sums disbursed to or on behalf of the Certification Officer in consequence of the provisions of this Part.

Notes

1. The Certification Officer is an independent statutory officer originally appointed under the Employment Protection Act 1975. He has taken over the powers of the Chief Registrar of Friendly Societies. Although finance and staff are provided by ACAS, the Certification Officer is formally independent of the Service and of the Government.

2. Under TULR(C)A 1992, the Certification Officer must maintain a list of all organisations which fall within the statutory definition of 'trade union' and which apply for listing. In addition, the Certification Officer has the power to determine whether a trade union should be granted a certificate of independence. As we shall see in Chapter 8, achieving the status of independence has important legal implications for trade unions as it is a pre-condition for claiming a number of statutory rights. The decisions of the Certification Officer in respect of listing and independence are subject to appeal to the Employment Appeal Tribunal (EAT) on both law and fact.

3. The other jurisdictions of the Certification Officer include: monitoring the annual returns which unions are legally obliged to provide; hearing complaints of union members regarding the conduct of ballots to set up a political fund, to elect members of the union executive or to approve trade union amalgamations; determining whether there has been a breach of the rules relating to the operation of a union's political fund; and hearing applications from members that the union has failed to compile or maintain a register of members' names and addresses.

4. Section 29 of the Employment Relations Act 1999 gives effect to Sch. 6, which amends the statutory powers of the Certification Officer (CO), as set out in the 1992 Act. The overall effect is to widen the scope for trade union members to make complaints to the CO of alleged breaches of trade union law or trade union rules, thereby enlarging the CO's role as an alternative to the courts as a means to resolve disputes. It achieves this by giving the CO order-making powers in areas of trade union law where previously he could only make declarations, and by extending his powers to make declarations and orders into areas where previously he had no competence to hear complaints and issue such orders.

D: The Commission for Racial Equality/Equal Opportunities Commission

The Equal Opportunities Commission (EOC) and the Commission for Racial Equality (CRE) have broadly similar duties in their respective spheres of operation. The statutory role and powers of the EOC are set out below, while the equivalent provisions for the CRE are to be found in the RRA 1976, Pt VII.

Sex Discrimination Act 1975

PART VI   EQUAL OPPORTUNITIES COMMISSION

53.   Establishment and duties of Commission
    (1)   There shall be a body of Commissioners named the Equal Opportunities Commission, consisting of at least eight but not more than fifteen individuals each

appointed by the Secretary of State on a full-time or part-time basis, which shall have the following duties—

(a)   to work towards the elimination of discrimination,

(b)   to promote equality of opportunity between men and women generally, and

(c)   to keep under review the working of this Act and the Equal Pay Act 1970

and, when they are so required by the Secretary of State or otherwise think it necessary, draw up and submit to the Secretary of State proposals for amending them.

(2)   The Secretary of State shall appoint—

(a)   one of the Commissioners to be chairman of the Commission, and

(b)   either one of two of the Commissioners (as the Secretary of State thinks fit) to be deputy chairman or deputy chairmen of the Commission.

(3)   . . .

54.   Research and education

(1)   The Commission may undertake or assist (financially or otherwise) the undertaking by other persons of any research, and any educational activities, which appear to the Commission necessary or expedient for the purposes of section 53(1).

(2)   The Commission may make charges for educational or other facilities or services made available by them.

55.   Review of discriminatory provisions in health and safety legislation

(1)   Without prejudice to the generality of section 53(1), the Commission, in pursuance of the duties imposed by paragraphs (a) and (b) of that subsection—

(a)   shall keep under review the relevant statutory provisions in so far as they require men and woman to be treated differently, and

(b)   if so required by the Secretary of State, make to him a report on any matter specified by him which is connected with those duties and concerns the relevant statutory provisions.

Any such report shall be made within the time specified by the Secretary of State, and the Secretary of State shall cause the report to be published.

(2)   Whenever the Commission think it necessary, they shall draw up and submit to the Secretary of State proposals for amending the relevant statutory provisions.

(3)   The Commission shall carry out their duties in relation to the relevant statutory provisions in consultation with the Health and Safety Commission.

(4)   In this section 'the relevant statutory provisions' has the meaning given by section 53 of the Health and Safety at Work etc. Act 1974.

56.   Annual reports

(1)   As soon as practicable after the end of each calendar year the Commission shall make to the Secretary of State a report on their activities during the year (an 'annual report').

(2)   Each annual report shall include a general survey of developments, during the period to which it relates, in respect of matters falling within the scope of the Commission's duties.

56A.   Codes of practice

(1)   The Commission may issue codes of practice containing such practical guidance as the Commission think fit for either or both of the following purposes, namely—

(a)   the elimination of discrimination in the field of employment;

(b)   the promotion of equality of opportunity in that field between men and women.

(2) When the Commission propose to issue a code of practice, they shall prepare and publish a draft of that code, shall consider any representations made to them about the draft and may modify the draft accordingly.

(3) In the course of preparing any draft code of practice for eventual publication under subsection (2) the Commission shall consult with—

(a) such organisations or associations of organisations representative of employers or of workers; and

(b) such other organisations, or bodies,

as appear to the Commission to be appropriate.

(4) If the Commission determine to proceed with the draft, they shall transmit the draft to the Secretary of State who shall—

(a) if he approves of it, lay it before both Houses of Parliament; and

(b) if he does not approve of it, publish details of his reasons for withholding approval.

. . .

57. Power to conduct formal investigations

(1) Without prejudice to their general power to do anything requisite for the performance of their duties under section 53(1), the Commission may if they think fit, and shall if required by the Secretary of State, conduct a formal investigation for any purpose connected with the carrying out of those duties.

(2) The Commission may, with the approval of the Secretary of State, appoint, on a full-time or part-time basis, one or more individuals as additional Commissioners for the purposes of a formal investigation.

58. Terms of reference

(1) The Commission shall not embark on a formal investigation unless the requirements of this section have been complied with.

(2) Terms of reference for the investigation shall be drawn up by the Commission or, if the Commission were required by the Secretary of State to conduct the investigation, by the Secretary of State after consulting the Commission.

(3) It shall be the duty of the Commission to give general notice of the holding of the investigation unless the terms of reference confine it to activities of persons named in them, but in such a case the Commission shall in the prescribed manner give those persons notice of the holding of the investigation.

(3A) Where the terms of reference of the investigation confine it to activities of persons named in them and the Commission in the course of it propose to investigate any act made unlawful by this Act which they believe that a person so named may have done, the Commission shall—

(a) inform that person of their belief and of their proposal to investigate the act in question; and

(b) offer him an opportunity of making oral or written representations with regard to it (or both oral and written representations if he thinks fit);

and a person so named who avails himself of an opportunity under this subsection of making oral representations may be represented—

(i) by council or a solicitor; or

(ii) by some other person of his choice, not being a person to whom the Commission object on the ground that he is unsuitable.

(4) The Commission or, if the Commission were required by the Secretary of State to conduct the investigation, the Secretary of State after consulting the Commission may from time to time revise the terms of reference; and subsections (1),

(3) and (3A) shall apply to the revised investigation and terms of reference as they applied to the original.

59. Power to obtain information

(1)   For the purposes of a formal investigation the Commission, by a notice in the prescribed form served on him in the prescribed manner,—

(a)   may require any person to furnish such written information as may be described in the notice, and may specify the time at which, and the manner and form in which, the information is to be furnished;

(b)   may require any person to attend at such time and place as is specified in the notice and give oral information about, and produce all documents in his possession or control relating to, any matter specified in the notice.

(2)   Except as provided by section 69, a notice shall be served under subsection (1) only where—

(a)   service of the notice was authorised by an order by or on behalf of the Secretary of State, or

(b)   the terms of reference of the investigation state that the Commission believe that a person named in them may have done or may be doing acts of all or any of the following descriptions—

(i)   unlawful descriminatory acts,

(ii)   contraventions of section 37,

(iii) contraventions of section 38, 39, or 40, and

(iv) acts in breach of a term modified or included by virtue of an equality clause, and confine the investigation to those acts.

(3)   A notice under subsection (1) shall not require a person—

(a)   to give information, or produce any documents, which he could not be compelled to give in evidence, or produce, in civil proceedings before the High Court or the Court of Sessions, or

(b)   to attend at any place unless the necessary expenses of his journey to and from that place are paid or tendered to him.

(4)   If a person fails to comply with a notice served on him under subsection (1) or the Commission has reasonable cause to believe that he intends not to comply with it, the Commission may apply to a county court for an order requiring him to comply with it or with such directions for the like purpose as may be contained in the order; and section 84 (penalty for neglecting witness summons) of the County Courts Act 1959 shall apply to failure without reasonable excuse to comply with any such order as it applies in the case there provided.

(5)   . . .

(6)   A person commits an offence if he—

(a)   wilfully alters, suppresses, conceals or destroys a document which he has been required by a notice or order under this section to produce, or

(b)   in complying with such a notice or order, knowingly or recklessly makes any statement which is false in a material particular, and shall be liable on summary conviction to a fine not exceeding level 5 on the standard scale.

(7)   . . .

60. Recommendations and reports on formal investigations

(1)   If in the light of any of their findings in a formal investigation it appears to the Commission necessary or expedient, whether during the course of the investigation or after its conclusion—

(a)   to make to any persons, with a view to promoting equality of opportunity between men and women who are affected by any of their activities, recommendations for changes in their policies or procedures, or as to any other matters, or

(b)   to make to the Secretary of State any recommendations, whether for changes in the law or otherwise,

the Commission shall make those recommendations accordingly.

(2)   The Commission shall prepare a report of their findings in any formal investigations conducted by them.

(3)   If the formal investigation is one required by the Secretary of State—

(a)   the Commission shall deliver the report to the Secretary of State, and

(b)   the Secretary of State shall cause the report to be published,

and unless required by the Secretary of State the Commission shall not publish the report.

(4)   If the formal investigation is not one required by the Secretary of State, the Commission shall either publish the report, or make it available for inspection in accordance with subsection (5).

(5)   Where under subsection (4) a report is to be made available for inspection, any person shall be entitled, on payment of such fee (if any) as may be determined by the Commission—

(a)   to inspect the report during ordinary office hours and take copies of all or any part of the report, or

(b)   to obtain from the Commission a copy, certified by the Commission to be correct, of the report.

. . .

75. Assistance by Commission

(1)   Where, in relation to proceedings or prospective proceedings either under this Act or in respect of an equality clause, an individual who is an actual or prospective complainant or claimant applies to the Commission for assistance under this section, the Commission shall consider the application and may grant it if they think fit to do so on the ground that—

(a)   the case raises a question of principle, or

(b)   it is unreasonable, having regard to the complexity of the case or the applicant's position in relation to the respondent or another person involved or any other matter, to expect the applicant to deal with the case unaided,

or by reason of any other special consideration.

(2)   Assistance by the Commission under this section may include—

(a)   giving advice;

(b)   procuring or attempting to procure the settlement of any matter in dispute;

(c)   arranging for the giving of advice or assistance by a solicitor or counsel;

(d)   arranging for representation by any person including all such assistance as is usually given by a solicitor or counsel in the steps preliminary or incidental to any proceedings, or in arriving at or giving effect to a compromise to avoid or bring to an end any proceedings,

(e)   any other form of assistance which the Commission may consider appropriate,

but paragraph (d) shall not affect the law and practice regulating the descriptions of persons who may appear in, conduct, defend and address the court in, any proceedings.

. . .

Notes

1. The Commissions may conduct a general investigation or an investigation into the activities of a particular person or body. They must conduct an investigation if so required by the Secretary of State. There are very detailed procedural rules regulating the steps to be followed in conducting a formal investigation. These requirements have been made more stringent as a result of judicial interpretations, the cumulative effect of which unnecessarily restrict the Commissions' role.

A formal investigation cannot take place until terms of reference have been drawn up and notice has been given of the investigation. In the case of a 'general' formal investigation, general notice is sufficient, but in the situation where the investigation relates to named person, the Commissions must notify those named. In addition, in a named person investigation, where the Commissions believe that unlawful discrimination is present, the named person has the right to make oral or written representations and to be supported by legal representation.

Since the judgment of the House of Lords in *R v CRE ex parte Prestige Group plc* [1984] IRLR 355, the power of the EOC and CRE to carry out formal investigations has been considerably narrowed. The Lords held that the CRE could not investigate a named person or organisation unless it believed that such a person or organisation might be acting in breach of the law. The effect of the *Prestige* judgment is to require the Commission to have sufficient evidence to found such a belief before it can commence a named person investigation. The limiting effects of this requirement have been described by the EOC as follows:

There are many situations which give rise to concern that equality of opportunity is being denied, for example where a high degree of job segregation between men and women occurs, but where, in advance of an investigation, there is no evidence as to the reasons why this has come about on which a belief relating to unlawful acts could be based. This is particularly likely to be the case where indirect discrimination is occurring as a result of certain practices and procedures. It is also important to note that, where a particular institution has a monopoly or near monopoly position, the Commission could not conduct a general investigation and is thus precluded from investigating its activities at all unless it can form a belief that unlawful acts may have occurred. (Equal Treatment for Men and Women: Strengthening the Acts (London: EOC, 1988).)

In the circumstances, therefore, it is hardly surprising the both the EOC and CRE have argued for a legislative amendment so as to overturn the *Prestige* decision.

Once the formal investigation is underway, whether or not the Commission has any power to compel the attendance of witnesses and the production of evidence depends on whether it is a general or a named person investigation. In the former case, the Commission only has the power to serve notice requiring information where it is authorised by the Secretary of State. In a named person investigation, each Commission has the power to require information and evidence and this can be enforced by court order.

On completion of investigation, the Commissions are required to prepare a report of their findings which must be published or made available for inspection. They are also obliged to make recommendations which appear necessary in the light of their findings. These recommendations may be directed at any person with a view to promoting equality of opportunity; or at the Secretary of State relating to changes in the law.

2. If, in the course of a formal investigation, the Commission is satisfied that a person is committing an unlawful discriminatory act, the Commission must issue a non-discrimination notice (RRA 1976, s. 58; SDA 1975, s. 67).

A notice lasts for five years. The Commission can stop further ('persistent') discrimination within these five years by obtaining an injunction (see below).

A notice can be issued if someone has:

(a) committed an act of direct or indirect discrimination;
(b) applied an actual or a potential discriminatory practice;
(c) published an unlawful advertisement;
(d) issued instructions to discriminate;
(e) put pressure on an employer to discriminate.

A non-discrimination notice requires the recipient:

(a) not to commit any discriminatory acts;
(b) to change his or her practices in order to comply with (a);
(c) to inform the Commission that he or she has made the changes and what they consist of;
(d) to take reasonable steps, as specified in the notice, to tell people concerned about the changes;
(e) to provide information so that the Commission can verify that the notice has been complied with; and
(f) to give information in a specified form and by a certain date.

Before it issues a non-discrimination notice, the Commission must tell the proposed recipient of its intention, give its reasons, give him or her at least 28 days to make written and/or oral representations, and take these into account.

After a non-discrimination notice has been served on him or her, the recipient has six weeks to appeal to an industrial tribunal. It was originally assumed that the appeal was an appeal against the specific requirements of the notice, rather than an opportunity to reopen the case. However, in *CRE v Amari Plastics Ltd* [1986] IRLR 252, the Court of Appeal took the view that the recipient is entitled not only to contest the Commission's requirements as set out in the notice, but also any of the facts relied upon by the Commission. This re-run of the case merely adds to an already unduly cumbersome and lengthy procedure. Lord Denning was moved to remark that the legislative provisions were 'a spider's web spun by Parliament, from which there is little hope of escaping'.

3. If, within five years of a non-discrimination notice becoming final, it appears to the Commission that unless restrained the person concerned is likely to commit more unlawful acts of discrimination, it may apply to a county court for an injunction restraining that person from doing so. However, if the employer has not appealed against the non-discrimination notice, the employer must first test the legality of the notice before an employment tribunal. This is a final tortuous twist in a massively cumbersome procedure. The complexities surrounding the formal investigation process go some way to explaining why the Commissions have made relatively limited use of their powers.

E: Employment Tribunals

Employment Tribunals Act 1996

PART I EMPLOYMENT TRIBUNALS

Introductory

1. Employment tribunals
    (1) The Secretary of State may by regulations make provision for the establishment of tribunals to be known as employment tribunals.
    (2) Regulations made wholly or partly under section 128(1) of the Employment Protection (Consolidation) Act 1978 and in force immediately before this Act comes into force shall, so far as made under that provision, continue to have effect (until revoked) as if made under subsection (1) . . .

Jurisdiction

2. Enactments conferring jurisdiction on employment tribunals
Employment tribunals shall exercise the jurisdiction conferred on them by or by virtue of this Act or any other Act, whether passed before or after this Act.

Notes
1. Employment tribunals were formerly known as industrial tribunals. The change of title was made by the Employment Rights (Dispute Resolution) Act 1998 s. 1(1), with effect from 1 August 1998. According to Lord Archer of Sandwell, the Bill's sponsor, the term 'employment tribunals', as opposed to 'industrial tribunals', 'conveys more clearly what the function of these tribunals is intended to be'. (Hansard HL 25 July 1997, col. 1583). The 1998 Act also renamed the Industrial Tribunals Act 1996 accordingly.
2. Employment tribunals were created in 1964 in order to resolve disputes regarding training levies on employers under the Industrial Training Act of that year. From this very limited beginning, their jurisdiction has expanded to embrace virtually every statutory employment right. Until recently, they had no jurisdiction over breach of contract claims. However, the ministerial power, now contained in ETA 1996, s. 3, to transfer jurisdiction in order to give employment tribunals the right to determine contract claims was eventually exercised in 1994.

Employment Tribunals Act 1996

3. Power to confer further jurisdiction on employment tribunals

(1) The appropriate Minister may by order provide that proceedings in respect of—

(a) any claim to which this section applies, or

(b) any claim to which this section applies and which is of a description specified in the order,

may, subject to such exceptions (if any) as may be so specified, be brought before an employment tribunal.

(2) Subject to subsection (3), this section applies to—

(a) a claim for damages for breach of a contract of employment or other contract connected with employment,

(b) a claim for a sum due under such a contract, and

(c) a claim for the recovery of a sum in pursuance of any enactment relating to the terms or performance of such a contract,

if the claim is such that a court in England and Wales or Scotland would under the law for the time being in force have jurisdiction to hear and determine an action in respect of the claim.

(3) This section does not apply to a claim for damages, or for a sum due, in respect of personal injuries.

The Employment Tribunals Extension of Jurisdiction (England and Wales) Order 1994

. . .

Extension of jurisdiction

3. Proceedings may be brought before an employment tribunal in respect of a claim of an employee for the recovery of damages or any other sum (other than a claim for damages, or for a sum due, in respect of personal injuries) if—

(a) the claim is one to which [ETA 1996, s. 3(2)] applies and which a court in England and Wales would under the law for the time being in force have jurisdiction to hear and determine;

(b) the claim is not one to which article 5 applies; and

(c) the claim arises or is outstanding on the termination of the employee's employment.

4. Proceedings may be brought before an employment tribunal in respect of a claim of an employer for the recovery of damages or any other sum (other than a claim for damages, or for a sum due, in respect of personal injuries) if—

(a) the claim is one to which [ETA 1996, s. 3(2)] applies and which a court in England and Wales would under the law for the time being in force have jurisdiction to hear and determine;

(b) the claim is not one to which article 5 applies;

(c) the claim arises or is outstanding on the termination of the employment of the employee against whom it is made; and

(d) proceedings in respect of a claim of that employee have been brought before an employment tribunal by virtue of this Order.

5. This article applies to a claim for breach of a contractual term of any of the following descriptions—

(a)   a term requiring the employer to provide living accommodation for the employee;

(b)   a term imposing an obligation on the employer or the employee in connection with the provision of living accommodation;

(c)   a term relating to intellectual property;

(d)   a term imposing an obligation of confidence;

(e)   a term which is a covenant in restraint of trade.

In this article, 'intellectual property' includes copyright, rights in performances, moral rights, design right, registered designs, patents and trade marks.

Manner in which proceedings may be brought

6.   Proceedings on a contract claim may be brought before an employment tribunal by presenting a complaint to an employment tribunal.

Time within which proceedings may be brought

7.   An employment tribunal shall not entertain a complaint in respect of an employee's contract claim unless it is presented—

(a)   within the period of three months beginning with the effective date of termination of the contract giving rise to the claim, or

(b) · where there is no effective date of termination, within the period of three months beginning with the last day upon which the employee worked in the employment which has terminated, or

(c)   where the tribunal is satisfied that it was not reasonably practicable for the complaint to be presented within whichever of those periods is applicable, within such further period as the tribunal considers reasonable.

8.   An employment tribunal shall not entertain a complaint in respect of an employer's contract claim unless—

(a)   it is presented at a time when there is before the tribunal a complaint in respect of a contract claim of a particular employee which has not been settled or withdrawn;

(b)   it arises out of a contract with that employee; and

(c)   it is presented—

(i)   within the period of six weeks beginning with the day, or if more than one the last of the days, on which the employer (or other person who is the respondent party to the employee's contract claim) received from the tribunal a copy of an originating application in respect of a contract claim of that employee; or

(ii)   where the tribunal is satisfied that it was not reasonably practicable for the complaint to be presented within that period, within such further period as the tribunal considers reasonable.

Question

Which claims are excluded by the Order?

Notes

1.   Tribunals sit in most local centres of population in Great Britain. An employment tribunal is composed of three members: a legally qualified chair (a barrister or solicitor of seven years' standing) and two lay members, drawn from both sides of industry. The lay members are full members of the tribunal and can outvote the legal chair, though over 90 per cent of decisions are reached unanimously. As a result of amendments introduced under

TURERA 1993 and now embodied in the ETA 1996, s. 4, as amended by the Employment Rights (Dispute Resolution) Act 1998, s. 3, chairs may sit alone in certain cases, including claims relating to unauthorised wage deductions; unauthorised deduction of union subscriptions; interim relief for trade union and health and safety representative dismissals; redundancy payments; breach of contract claims; uncontested claims and where the parties have consented in writing. Appeals in these cases, and appeals from interlocutory tribunal decisions, will usually be heard by an Employment Appeal judge sitting alone (ETA 1996, s. 28(4)).

2.   The aim of conferring jurisdiction on tribunals was to provide a decision-making forum which was less formal, more accessible, quicker and less expensive than the ordinary courts. However, the law the tribunals have to apply has become increasingly more complex, and therefore it is not surprising that around one-third of applicants and over one-half of respondent employers are legally represented at tribunal hearings (see Hawes, W.R., and Smith, G., Patterns of representation of the parties in unfair dismissal cases: a review of the evidence, D.E. Research Paper No. 22 (London: Department of Employment, 1981); Genn, H., and Genn, Y., *The Effectiveness of Representation at Tribunals*, London: Lord Chancellor's Department, 1989).

3.   The fact that the procedure is adversarial means that the onus is on the parties to present their own evidence. This can result in major injustice if one party can afford legal representation and the other cannot. A recent survey found that it was only the employer's side which had some form of representation in about one-quarter of all cases, and unrepresented applicants faced legally represented employers in about 12 per cent of cases surveyed (see Genn, ibid.). Furthermore, a series of studies has shown that there is a clear causal relation between legal and other forms of representation and a successful outcome of the case (see Kumar, V.C., *Industrial Tribunal Applicants under the Race Relations Act 1976* (London: CRE, 1986); Leonard, A., *The First Eight Years: A Profile of Applicants to the Industrial Tribunals under the Sex Discrimination Act 1975 and the Equal Pay Act 1970* (Manchester: EOC, 1986) and Dickens, L., et al., *Dismissed: A Study of Unfair Dismissal and the Industrial Tribunal System* (Oxford: Blackwell, 1985). This situation has brought forward calls for legal aid to be extended to cover representation before industrial tribunals.

4.   A review of the employment tribunal system by a committee appointed by JUSTICE, concluded that in 90 per cent of all unfair dismissal and redundancy payment cases an investigative (or inquisitorial) approach by the tribunal is the most suitable, offering the optimum in terms of accessibility, informality and speed and the most efficient return on costs to both litigants and the public purse (*Industrial Tribunals, A Report by JUSTICE* (Chairman of Committee: Bob Hepple), London: JUSTICE, 1987). Other commentators have argued that a system of voluntary private arbitration would be cheaper, quicker and generally much less formal and legalistic (see Dickens et al., *op. cit.*; Lewis R. and Clark, J., *The Case for Alternate Dispute Resolution* (London: Institute of Employment Rights, 1993).

5.   Employment tribunals are now constituted by ETA 1996, ss. 4 and 5 and their procedure is regulated primarily by the Employment Tribunals (Constitution and Rules of Procedure) Regulations 1993. An award made by an employment tribunal now attracts interest, after 42 days from the date when the decision has been sent to the parties. Interest is not payable on any costs awarded. Interest remains payable if the tribunal's decision is subject to appeal or review (Employment Tribunals (Interest) Order 1990).

6.   Unlike in the courts, costs are not usually awarded in employment tribunal proceedings. A costs award may be made where one of the parties has acted 'frivolously, vexatiously, or otherwise unreasonably'.

Costs may be payable in cases where there has been a pre-hearing review. In an attempt to filter out the number of claims proceeding to full tribunal hearing, the pre-hearing assessment was introduced in 1980. This could be ordered on the application of either party, or by a Chairman of tribunals on his or her own motion. A fully constituted tribunal considered the contents of the originating application and the notice of appearance, any representations in writing and oral arguments advanced by the parties. If the tribunal considered that the originating application or any contentions of a party had no reasonable prospect of success, the party concerned could be warned that if he or she continued with the case or persisted in the contention it could result in an award of costs against him or her at full hearing. If the case proceeded after a costs warning it would be before a different tribunal. The warning was not referred to until after the result of the case, when costs could be considered.

Research by Wallace and Clifton ('Pre-hearing assessments in unfair dismissal cases' [1985] *Employment Gazette* 65, highlighted the following defects in the pre-hearing assessment procedure:

(a)   the regional inconsistencies in deciding which cases should be subject to a pre-hearing assessment;

(b)   a pre-hearing assessment was useless in cases of disputed facts which could only be resolved at full hearing;

(c)   the parties were subject to the cost and inconvenience of an additional appearance at the tribunal;

(d)   where the tribunal does not issue a costs warning, the case is more likely than usual to proceed to hearing because the party may infer from this – rightly or wrongly – that he or she has a good chance of success;

(e)   the use of pre-hearing assessments may harden attitudes and delay the conciliation process.

It was for these reasons that the report by JUSTICE (ibid.) proposed that the pre-hearing assessment procedure should be repealed. However, unsurprisingly, the Government has not accepted this advice and, instead, has attempted to reinforce the 'filter' process. Under the EA 1989, s. 20, pre-hearing 'reviews' are made available. The procedure is controversial because it allows employment tribunals to require deposits of up to £150 to be paid by parties as a condition of continuing a claim. Such a requirement could obviously be a powerful disincentive to continue, especially as there will also be a risk of paying costs if these exceed the deposit amount.

The pre-hearing review and deposit rules are contained in the Employment Tribunals (Constitution and Rules of Procedure) Regulations 1993 and came into force on December 1993. These rules completely replace the previous rules on pre-hearing assessments, which no longer exist.

7. In July 1996, the Government published a new consultation document containing draft legislation on industrial tribunals and the resolution of employment rights disputes.

The Employment Rights (Dispute Resolution) Act contains provisions designed to implement those aspects of the Green Paper, *Resolving employment rights disputes: options for reform* (CM 2707, 1994), which attracted wide support and which required primary legislation.

The most significant change under the Act is to grant ACAS power to fund and provide an arbitration scheme for unfair dismissal claims (see TULR(C)A 1992, s. 212A). This will be available as an alternative to an employment tribunal hearing and would be voluntary on both sides. ACAS produced a consultation document containing a draft scheme in July 1998 and intends to introduce the new scheme on a phased basis, starting in Greater London during 1999 and moving to a national basis in early 2000.

8. The number of applications to an employment tribunal rose 14 per cent in 1998–99 to 92,000. About two-thirds of all cases registered in 1997–99 were conciliated or withdrawn without the need for a hearing.

The percentage of cases relating to unfair dismissal has continued the decline shown in the last reporting period (1994–96) and has fallen steadily from 59 per cent in 1994–95 to 44 per cent in 1998–99. Nearly a third of all unfair dismissal cases proceeding to a hearing were upheld by the tribunal in 1998–99.

The Employment Tribunals Service (ETS) exceeded and improved its performance against targets in 1998–99. The Service has targets of bringing 85 per cent of single employment tribunal cases to a hearing within 26 weeks of receipt, and of issuing 85 per cent of decisions within four weeks. In 1998–99 the ETS exceeded both targets (89 per cent and 86 per cent respectively), improving in each case its performance over the previous year. (See 'Employment Tribunal and Employment Appeal Tribunal Statistics 1997–98 and 1998–99', *Labour Market Trends*, September 1999, pp. 493–97.)

F: The Employment Appeal Tribunal

Employment Tribunals Act 1996

Jurisdiction

21.   Jurisdiction of Appeal Tribunal

(1)   An appeal lies to the Appeal Tribunal on any question of law arising from any decision of, or arising in any proceedings before, an employment tribunal under or by virtue of—

(a)   the Equal Pay Act 1970,
(b)   the Sex Discrimination Act 1975,
(c)   the Race Relations Act 1976,
(d)   the Trade Union and Labour Relations (Consolidation) Act 1992,
(e)   the Disability Discrimination Act 1995,
(f)   the Employment Rights Act 1996,
(ff)   the National Minimum Wage Act 1998,
(fg)   the Tax Credits Act, 1999, or
(g)   this Act,
or under the Working Time Regulations 1998.

(2)   No appeal shall lie except to the Appeal Tribunal from any decision of an employment tribunal under or by virtue of the Acts listed in subsection (1).

(3)   Subsection (1) does not affect any provision contained in, or made under, any Act which provides for an appeal to lie to the Appeal Tribunal (whether from an employment tribunal, the Certification Officer or any other person or body) otherwise than on a question to which that subsection applies.

Note

Appeal from a tribunal decision lies to the Employment Appeal Tribunal (EAT). The EAT was originally constituted by the Employment Protection Act 1975 and is now governed by ETA 1996, ss. 22–28. It consists of a High Court judge and two – though sometimes four – lay members providing equal representation from both sides of industry. As with employment tribunals, the judge may be outvoted by the lay members.

The EAT is a superior court of record and its decisions are binding on employment tribunals. The EAT hears all appeals from the employment tribunals, in England and Wales and in Scotland. In general, appeal lies to the EAT on *a point of law only*. The only exceptions to this are an appeal from the decision of the Certification Officer on the question of registration or certification as an independent trade union, or on an appeal in a claim for unreasonable exclusion or expulsion from a union where appeal may be on law or fact.

Neale v Hereford and Worcester County Council
[1986] IRLR 168
Court of Appeal

Mr Neale was head of the music department at one of the appellant county council's schools. He was dismissed following an incident which occurred while he was invigilating pupils sitting an 'A' level examination. An industrial tribunal dismissed Mr Neale's complaint of unfair dismissal. While critical of some procedural aspects of the case, the industrial tribunal concluded that such procedural defects could not lead to the conclusion that, in the circumstances, the dismissal was outside the band of reasonable responses open to a reasonable employer.

The EAT allowed Mr Neale's appeal against that finding and ruled that this was one of the exceptional cases where the industrial tribunal's decision fell to be reversed, because it was one which no reasonable tribunal could have reached. The Court of Appeal allowed the county council's appeal and restored the decision of the industrial tribunal.

MAY LJ: . . . An industrial tribunal has been described as an 'industrial jury', and so in many ways it is. It knows its area; it comprises a lawyer, a representative of employees and a representative of employers within that district; each has substantial experience of industrial relations problems and they are hearing this type of case regularly. Their job is to find the facts, to apply the relevant law and to reach the conclusion to which their findings and experience lead them. It will not, in my opinion, be often that when an industrial tribunal has done just that, and with the care clarity and thoroughness which the Industrial Tribunal in the present case displayed, that one can legitimately say that their conclusion 'offends reason', or that their conclusion was one to which no reasonable industrial tribunal could have come. Deciding these cases is the job of industrial tribunals and when they have not erred in law neither the EAT nor this Court should disturb their decision unless one can say in effect: 'My goodness, that was certainly wrong'.

Piggott Brothers & Co. Ltd v *Jackson*
[1991] IRLR 309
Court of Appeal

LORD DONALDSON MR: The EAT, in unanimously allowing the employers' appeal, reminded itself of the limitations upon its own jurisdiction in the following passage in the judgment delivered by Knox J.:

> We were very properly reminded by Miss Warren that the jurisdiction of this tribunal is limited to questions of law by [what is now ETA 1996, s. 21], that it is not right that questions of fact should be dressed up as points of law so as to encourage appeals or to go through the reasoning of Industrial Tribunals with a fine-tooth comb to see if some error can be found here or there. See *Hollister* v *NFU* [1979] IRLR 238 at 241, 17 per Lord Denning MR. In that judgment there is also a quotation from Lord Russell of Killowen's judgment in *Retarded Children's Aid Society Ltd* v *Day* [1978] IRLR 128 at p. 130, 9 where he said:

> > The function of the Employment Appeal Tribunal is to correct errors of law where one is established and identified. I think care must be taken to avoid concluding that an experienced Industrial Tribunal by not expressly mentioning some point or breach has overlooked it, and care must be taken to avoid, in a case where the Employment Appeal Tribunal members would on the basis of the merits and the oral evidence have taken a different view from that of the Industrial Tribunal, searching around with a fine-tooth comb for some point of law.

In short, it is not for us on a question of reasonableness to substitute our view for that of the Industrial Tribunal.

There are, however, three categories of case where it is the duty of the EAT to interfere. They are stated by Lord Donaldson MR in *British Telecommunications* v *Sheridan* [1990] IRLR 27 at p. 30 as follows:

> The Employment Appeal Tribunal can indeed interfere if it is satisfied that the Tribunal (scil. the Industrial Tribunal) has misdirected itself as to the applicable law, or if there is no evidence to support a finding of fact, since the absence of

evidence to support a finding of fact has always been regarded as a pure question of law. It can also interfere if the decision is perverse, as has been explained by May LJ in *Neale* v *Hereford & Worcester CC* [1986] IRLR 168 at p. 173, 44.

This last is an allusion to the now very familiar sentence at p. 173, 45:

> Deciding these cases is the job of Industrial Tribunals and when they have not erred in law neither the appeal tribunal nor this Court should disturb their decision unless one can say in effect. 'My goodness, that was certainly wrong'.

I accept, as I must, the exposition of May LJ Indeed, it has the added authority of, I think, being derived, albeit expressed in more homely terms, from the speech of Lord Diplock in *R* v *Secretary of State for Foreign and Commonwealth Affairs ex parte Council of Civil Service Unions* [1985] IRLR 28 at p. 36, 49 where he said that a decision which was plainly wrong could found an application for judicial review and that it was no longer necessary to resort to Viscount Radcliffe's explanation in *Edwards* v *Bairstow* [1956] AC 14 of irrationality as raising an inference of an unidentifiable mistake of law.

Nevertheless, it is an approach which is not without its perils. A finding of fact which is unsupported by *any* evidence clearly involves an error of law. The Tribunal cannot have directed itself, as it should, that findings of fact need *some* evidence to support them. The danger in the approach of May LJ is that an appellate court can very easily persuade itself that, as it would certainly not have reached the same conclusion, the Tribunal which did so was 'certainly wrong'. Furthermore, the more dogmatic the temperament of the judges concerned, the more likely they are to take this view. However, this is a classic non sequitur. It does not matter whether, with whatever degree of certainty, the appellate court considers that it would have reached a different conclusion. What matters is whether the decision under appeal was a permissible option. To answer that question in the negative in the context of employment law, the EAT will almost always have to be able to identify a finding of fact which was unsupported by *any* evidence or a clear self-misdirection in law by the Industrial Tribunal. If it cannot do this, it should re-examine with the greatest care its preliminary conclusion that the decision under appeal was not a permissible option and has to be characterised as 'perverse'.

Note

These decisions reflect the Court of Appeal's concern relating to excessive legalism and the proliferation of appeals from employment tribunals. In a series of rulings, the Court has adopted a two-pronged strategy designed to reverse the trend and reduce the number of cases coming through on appeal from employment tribunals to the EAT.

First, it has ruled that many issues in employment law are ultimately questions of fact and not questions of law. Given that appeal to the EAT *must* involve a claim that the employment tribunal misdirected itself in law, this is clearly an attempt to return decision-making to the tribunals. The following are examples of this policy of classifying issues as question of fact and thus limiting the possibility of appeals: whether a worker is an 'employee'; whether a 'constructive dismissal' has taken place; whether an employee resigned or was forced to do so; whether it was reasonably practicable to present an unfair dismissal claim on time.

The second element of the strategy against legalism has been the Court of Appeal's rejection of the EAT's practice of laying down guidelines for tribunals to follow when confronted with major problem areas of unfair dismissal law, e.g redundancy procedure, suspected dishonesty, long-term sickness absence. The nature of the Court of Appeal's attack on what was seen as the EAT's unduly interventionist role is clearly illustrated by the following statement of Lawton LJ in *Bailey* v *BP Oil (Kent Refinery) Ltd* [1980] IRLR 287:

Each case must depend on its own facts. In our judgement it is unwise for this court or the Employment Appeal Tribunal to set out guidelines, and wrong to make rules and establish presumptions for industrial tribunals to follow or take into account.

While the concern of the Court of Appeal to rid the law of unfair dismissal of excessive legal technicality is understandable, it may be that the Court has taken matters too far and that the attack on legalism and the proliferation of appeals may be achieved at the cost of certainty and consistency. In the absence of established guidelines and precedent, it becomes extremely difficult for legal or personnel practitioners to offer the advice on any particular case. For example, if the question of 'employee' status is classified a question of fact, there is every prospect that employment tribunals in different parts of the country can come to diametrically opposed conclusions in cases involving identical facts, and with little or no prospect of the EAT resolving the matter on appeal.

Concern about the restricted role of the EAT is clearly evident in the next extract.

East Berkshire Health Authority v *Matadeen*
[1992] IRLR 336
Employment Appeal Tribunal

WOOD J. (PRESIDENT): The law as it stands seems to me to indicate that the EAT can only interfere with a decision of the 'industrial jury', i.e. the Industrial Tribunal if, first, there is ex facie an error of law, a misdirection or a misapplication of the law. Secondly, that there is a material finding of fact relied upon by the Tribunal in the decision, which was unsupported by any evidence or contrary to the evidence before them. Thirdly, and as a free-standing basis in law, there is a finding of perversity. It is likely to be a very rare occasion upon which the Employment Appeal Tribunal can interfere on this ground and it should caution itself against so doing and in particular to be careful not merely to substitute its own view for that of the Industrial Tribunal.

The fact that perversity, properly understood, is a free-standing basis in law is also supported by a passage in the speech of Lord Fraser of Tullybelton in *Melon* v *Hector Powe Ltd* [1980] IRLR 477 where at p. 479, 12 he says:

It is common ground that the appeal from the Industrial Tribunal to the Employment Appeal Tribunal and thence to the courts is open only on a question of law. The appellate tribunals are therefore only entitled to interfere with the decision of the Industrial Tribunal if the appellants can succeed in showing, as they seek to do, that it has either misdirected itself in law or reached a decision which no reasonable

Tribunal, directing itself properly on the law, could have reached (or it has gone fundamentally wrong in certain other respects, none of which is here alleged). The fact that the appellate tribunal would have reached a different conclusion on the facts is not a sufficient ground for allowing an appeal.

Thus, even on factual findings of an Industrial Tribunal, the EAT can interfere if the members are completely satisfied in the light of their own experience and of the sound practices in the industrial field that the decision is 'not a permissible option' per Lord Donaldson of Lymington MR: 'a conclusion which offends reason or is one to which no reasonable Industrial Tribunal could come' or 'so very clearly wrong that it just cannot stand' per May LJ, or to paraphrase Lord Diplock in the *GCHQ* case, the decision was 'so outrageous in its defiance of logic or of accepted standards of industrial relations that no sensible person who had applied his mind to the question and with the necessary experience could have arrived at it.' It is also interesting to note that Lord Diplock continues at p. 36, 49:

> Whether a decision falls within this category is a question that judges by their training and experience should be well equipped to answer or else there would be something badly wrong with our judicial system.

I would respectfully add that there is something wrong with our system and with this Appeal Tribunal if those industrial members who are appointed to it, with their vast experience of industry, were not able to recognise a decision which fell within this category.

I have cautioned the members against interfering with decisions of Industrial Tribunals. They cannot interfere merely because they disagree. They cannot interfere even if they feel strongly that the result is unjust, though in this latter case it may be that on a careful analysis of the true reason lying behind such a view the decision flies in the face of properly informed logic.

III   The International Labour Organisation

The International Labour Organisation (ILO) was established in 1919. It is based in Geneva and, as an agency of the United Nations, is charged with setting universal labour standards. It is a tripartite body composed of representatives of governments, employers and workers.

ILO standards are set by the International Labour Conference – convened annually – in the form of Conventions and Recommendations. There are now some 168 Conventions, of which the most significant include Convention No. 87 on Freedom of Association and Protection of the Right to Organise (1949) and Convention No. 98 on the Right to Organise and Collective Bargaining (1949). If a State ratifies a Convention, it undertakes to ensure that its domestic law conforms with the Convention's standards. Since 1979, the UK Government has denounced four of the Conventions which it had previously ratified. Those include Convention No. 94 (Labour Clauses (Public Contracts) (1949)), allowing the Government to rescind the Fair Wages Resolution of 1946, and Convention No. 95 (Protection of Wages Convention (1949)), enabling the Government to enact the Wages Act 1986 and to repeal the Truck Act which required wages to be paid in cash rather than in kind.

For further discussions of these issues see Ewing, K.D., *Britain and the ILO* (London: Institute of Employment Rights, 1989); Brown, D., and McColgan, A., 'UK Employment Law and the International Labour Organisation: The Spirit of Co-operation?' (1989) 21 ILJ 265.

IV European Community Law

A: Historical Background

When the Treaty of Rome was signed by the UK in 1972, the prospects for using it as a vehicle for improvements in labour law protections were not readily apparent. The primary idea behind the Treaty was the benefits which would flow from liberalisation of trade and the expansion of the market for goods and services. With the exceptions of Article 119 (now 141) (dealing with equal pay) and Articles 48 to 51 (now 39 to 42) (requiring free movement of workers), the references to social policy issues were extremely vague with little indication as to how improvements would be achieved. Indeed, the Articles on equal pay and free movement were inserted primarily on the basis of an economic – as opposed to a social – rationale (see Davies, P.L., 'The Emergence of European Labour Law', in William McCarthy (ed.), *Legal Intervention in Industrial Relations: Gains and Losses* (Oxford: Basil Blackwell, 1992), Ch. 10).

By 1972, there was an emerging view amongst the heads of government of the Member States that the Community should adopt a policy of more rigorous action in the social field. This led to the Social Action Programme which was adopted by the Council of Ministers in 1974. However, 'the argument for a social policy was still one that made social policy subordinate to economic goals, but it was now accepted that economic growth through closer European economic integration would require the support of a *Community* social policy, both to ensure that the benefits of growth were adequately diffused throughout Europe and to help socialise the costs of economic growth' (Davies, *op. cit.*, at p. 326).

The Social Action Programme produced a series of directives which were adopted between 1974–79 and which constitute the main body of Community labour law. These are as follows:

- The Equal Pay Directive 75/117/EEC
- The Directive on Collective Redundancies 75/129/EEC
- The Equal Treatment Directive 76/207/EEC.
- The Transfer of Undertakings Directive 77/187/EEC
- The Social Security Directive 79/7/EEC
- The Directive on Insolvency 80/987/EEC.

The 'legal base' for these measures was generally Article 100 (now 94), though, on occasion, Article 235 (now 308) was employed. Both Articles require a unanimous vote in the Council of Ministers. Following this flurry of activity, little else was achieved until the late 1980s. The election of a

Conservative administration in 1979, determined to free the labour market from control imposed by legislation or collective bargaining, meant that all but the most innocuous measures, generally concerned with health and safety, were vetoed. Among the measures which were blocked by the UK, were draft directives on parental leave, temporary and part-time work. Also moves by the EEC to finalise draft directives on company law and on information and consultation procedures (the 'Vredling' Directive) were strongly opposed, and this has left the process of introducing EC legislation on worker rights of participation temporarily in limbo.

During the 1980s, it was accepted that the completion of the single internal market required amendments to the Treaty of Rome. This was achieved by the passage of the Single European Act, which came into force in July 1987. Under the Act, certain Community legislation can be adopted by qualified majority voting (QMV) rather than by requiring the agreement of all Member States. This included measures relating to the establishment or functioning of the internal market but, significantly, specifically excluded provisions 'relating to the rights and interests of employed persons' (Article 100a (now 95) of the Treaty of Rome). On the other hand, provisions on 'improvements, especially in the working environment, as regards the health and safety of workers' were covered by QMV (Article 118a (now 138)). Under the QMV procedure, Council members' votes are weighted according to the size of their State's population.

While the UK Government was pursuing its policy of deregulation during the 1980s, the EC was following a different path. In 1989 the European Commission published its Charter of Fundamental Social Rights. The Charter represented principles on the future of European workplace policy, and proposed a number of social and employment rights for EC citizens. These included, for example, a right to 'fair remuneration' and annual paid leave, the right to belong to a trade union and rights in relation to working time.

Other aspects of the Charter, for example, those establishing rights to 'equal treatment' and 'participation' in decision-making processes and in redundancy situations were, of course, anathema to the UK Government.

The Commission's hope was that the Charter would be unanimously adopted by the Council of Ministers. It would then form the basis of an 'action programme' which would be binding on Member States if adopted.

The then United Kingdom Government strongly opposed the Charter, and continues to resist much of the detailed legislation designed to implement it, on the ground that it will lead to excessive regulation and will impede rather than foster the creation of jobs. Indeed, Mrs Thatcher described the Charter as 'inspired by the values of Karl Marx and the class struggle'. It was, therefore, unsurprising when at the meeting of the European Council in Strasbourg in December 1989 the UK was the only dissenting voice amongst 'the twelve' on the question of the adoption of the Charter.

At the Maastricht summit in December 1991, the UK strongly resisted the expansion of EC legislative activity in the area of social policy. The Treaty on

European Union which resulted from the negotiations was signed by the Heads of the then 12 Member States at Maastricht on 7 February 1992. However, the accompanying protocol and agreement which extended the scope of the qualified voting procedure into new areas of social policy covered only 14 of the 15 current Member States – the UK being in a minority of one. In July 1993, after a bitter and prolonged parliamentary struggle and culminating in a vote of confidence in the Major Government, the Social Protocol was not incorporated in the Act approving the Maastricht Treaty.

The Social Policy Agreement (SPA) extended the areas in which directives can be enacted by qualified majority to include health and safety; working conditions; the information and consultation of workers; equality of treatment with regard to labour market opportunities and treatment at work; and the 'integration' of people excluded from the labour market. It continues to require unanimity for: social security and social welfare; representation and collective defence of workers; conditions of employment for non-EU nationals; financing job promotion and creation. The basis of the protocol was that all Member States apart from the UK 'wish to continue along the path laid down in the 1989 Social Charter'.

The UK's situation was further complicated by the fact that the Commission retained its powers within the framework of the EC of 15 to propose and press for directives in the social field on the basis of the EC Treaty, i.e. Articles 118a (now 138), 100a (now 95) and 100 (now 94). This caused immediate problems in relation to measures the EC was keen to enact using those provisions. Not least of these was the Directive on Working Hours and Holidays (Directive 93/104/EC concerning the organisation of working time), which had been adopted by the EC Commission in 1990 and was based on Article 118a (now 138). This was not unreasonable given the co-relation between excessive hours of work and accidents, and the recognised effects of stress at work. It was not, however, how the UK Government saw things, and in a belated attempt to block progress on the measure it launched an unsuccessful action in the European Court of Justice against the Directive (see *Council of the European Union* [1997] IRLR 30.

During the five years of the British opt-out from the Social Policy Protocol (SPP) only two pieces of legislation were adopted – the European Works Council (EWC) Directive 94/95 and the Directive on Parental Leave (96/34/EC). As Barnard wryly observes: 'It seems that despite the avowed intention in the SPP "to continue along the path laid down in the 1989 Social Chapter" they have done so with little enthusiasm in the absence of their recalcitrant brother.' (Barnard, C., 'The United Kingdom, The "Social Chapter" and the Amsterdam Treaty', (1997) 26 *ILJ* 275, at p. 279)

With the election of the new Labour Government in May 1997 came a marked change of policy in the UK towards the social dimension of the European Union. Within days of its election, the Government formally announced its commitment to 'sign up' to the Social Chapter. The new, more positive UK approach towards the European Union was further underlined with the signing of the Treaty of Amsterdam in October 1997. The Treaty contains an amended chapter on social policy, incorporating into a single chapter (and revising) both Articles 136–144 (ex 117–121) of the EC Treaty and the Agreement on Social Policy. This received the required ratification in all 15 Member States and entered into force on 1 May 1999.

Treaty Establishing the European Economic Community

TITLE XI (ex Title VIII)   SOCIAL POLICY, EDUCATION, VOCATIONAL TRAINING AND YOUTH

CHAPTER 1   SOCIAL PROVISIONS

Article 136 (ex Article 117)
The Community and the Member States, having in mind fundamental social rights such as those set out in the European Social Charter signed at Turin on 18 October 1961 and in the 1989 Community Charter of the Fundamental Social Rights of Workers, shall have as their objectives the promotion of employment, improved living and working conditions, so as to make possible their harmonisation while the improvement is being maintained, proper social protection, dialogue between management and labour, the development of human resources with a view to lasting high employment and the combating of exclusion.

To this end the Community and the Member States shall implement measures which take account of the diverse forms of national practices, in particular in the field of contractual relations, and the need to maintain the competitiveness of the Community economy.

They believe that such a development will ensue not only from the functioning of the common market, which will favour the harmonisation of social systems, but also from the procedures provided for in this Treaty and from the approximation of provisions laid down by law, regulation or administrative action.

Article 137 (ex Article 118)
1.   With a view to achieving the objectives of Article 136, the Community shall support and complement the activities of the Member States in the following fields:
—improvement in particular of the working environment to protect workers' health and safety;
—working conditions;
—the information and consultation of workers;
—the integration of persons excluded from the labour market, without prejudice to Article 150;
—equality between men and women with regard to labour market opportunities and treatment at work.

2.   To this end, the Council may adopt, by means of directives, minimum requirements for gradual implementation, having regard to the conditions and technical rules obtaining in each of the Member States. Such directives shall avoid imposing administrative, financial and legal constraints in a way which would hold back the creation and development of small and medium-sized undertakings.

The Council shall act in accordance with the procedure referred to in Article 251 after consulting the Economic and Social Committee and the Committee of the Regions.

The Council, acting in accordance with the same procedure, may adopt measures designed to encourage cooperation between Member States through initiatives aimed at improving knowledge, developing exchanges of information and best practices, promoting innovative approaches and evaluating experiences in order to combat social exclusion.

3.   However, the Council shall act unanimously on a proposal from the Commission, after consulting the European Parliament, the Economic and Social Committee and the Committee of the Regions in the following areas:

—social security and social protection of workers;

—protection of workers where their employment contract is terminated;

—representation and collective defence of the interests of workers and employers, including co-determination, subject to paragraph 6;

—conditions of employment for third country nationals legally residing in Community territory;

—financial contributions for promotion of employment and job creation, without prejudice to the provisions relating to the Social Fund.

4.   A Member State may entrust management and labour, at their joint request, with the implementation of directives adopted pursuant to paragraphs 2 and 3.

In this case, it shall ensure that, no later than the date on which a directive must be transposed in accordance with Article 249, management and labour have introduced the necessary measures by agreement, the Member State concerned being required to take any necessary measure enabling it at any time to be in a position to guarantee the results imposed by that directive.

5.   The provisions adopted pursuant to this Article shall not prevent any Member State from maintaining or introducing more stringent protective measures compatible with this Treaty.

6.   The provisions of this Article shall not apply to pay, the right of association, the right to strike or the right to impose lock-outs.

Article 138 (ex Article 118a)

1.   The Commission shall have the task of promoting the consultation of management and labour at Community level and shall take any relevant measure to facilitate their dialogue by ensuring balanced support for the parties.

2.   To this end, before submitting proposals in the social policy field, the Commission shall consult management and labour on the possible direction of Community action.

3.   If, after such consultation, the Commission considers Community action advisable, it shall consult management and labour on the content of the envisaged proposal. Management and labour shall forward to the Commission an opinion or, where appropriate, a recommendation.

4.   On the occasion of such consultation, management and labour may inform the Commission of their wish to initiate the process provided for in Article 139. The duration of the procedure shall not exceed nine months, unless the management and labour concerned and the Commission decide jointly to extend it.

Article 139 (ex Article 118b)

1.   Should management and labour so desire, the dialogue between them at Community level may lead to contractual relations, including agreements.

2.   Agreements concluded at Community level shall be implemented either in accordance with the procedures and practices specific to management and labour and the Member States or, in matters covered by Article 137, at the joint request of the signatory parties, by a Council decision on a proposal from the Commission.

The Council shall act by qualified majority, except where the agreement in question contains one or more provisions relating to one of the areas referred to in Article 137(3), in which case it shall act unanimously.

Article 140 (ex Article 118c)
With a view to achieving the objectives of Article 136 and without prejudice to the other provisions of this Treaty, the Commission shall encourage cooperation between the Member States and facilitate the coordination of their action in all social policy fields under this chapter, particularly in matters relating to:
—employment;
—labour law and working conditions;
—basic and advanced vocational training;
—social security;
—prevention of occupational accidents and diseases;
—occupational hygiene;
—the right of association and collective bargaining between employers and workers.
To this end, the Commission shall act in close contact with Member States by making studies, delivering opinions and arranging consultations both on problems arising at national level and on those of concern to international organisations.
Before delivering the opinions provided for in this Article, the Commission shall consult the Economic and Social Committee.

Article 141 (ex Article 119)
1.   Each Member State shall ensure that the principle of equal pay for male and female workers for equal work or work of equal value is applied.
2.   For the purpose of this Article, 'pay' means the ordinary basic or minimum wage or salary and any other consideration, whether in cash or in kind, which the worker receives directly or indirectly, in respect of his employment, from his employer.
Equal pay without discrimination based on sex means:
   (a)   that pay for the same work at piece rates shall be calculated on the basis of the same unit of measurement;
   (b)   that pay for work at time rates shall be the same for the same job.
3.   The Council, acting in accordance with the procedure referred to in Article 251, and after consulting the Economic and Social Committee, shall adopt measures to ensure the application of the principle of equal opportunities and equal treatment of men and women in matters of employment and occupation, including the principle of equal pay for equal work or work of equal value.
4.   With a view to ensuring full equality in practice between men and women in working life, the principle of equal treatment shall not prevent any Member State from maintaining or adopting measures providing for specific advantages in order to make it easier for the under-represented sex to pursue a vocational activity or to prevent or compensate for disadvantages in professional careers.

Article 142 (ex Article 119a)
Member States shall endeavour to maintain the existing equivalence between paid holiday schemes.

Article 143 (ex Article 120)
The Commission shall draw up a report each year on progress in achieving the objectives of Article 136, including the demographic situation in the Community. It shall forward the report to the European Parliament, the Council and the Economic and Social Committee.
The European Parliament may invite the Commission to draw up reports on particular problems concerning the social situation.

Article 144 (ex Article 121)
The Council may, acting unanimously and after consulting the Economic and Social Committee, assign to the Commission tasks in connection with the implementation

of common measures, particularly as regards social security for the migrant workers referred to in Articles 39 to 42.

Article 145 (ex Article 122)
The Commission shall include a separate chapter on social developments within the Community in its annual report to the European Parliament.

The European Parliament may invite the Commission to draw up reports on any particular problems concerning social conditions.

B: What's Next?

(i) EC proposals for employment laws adopted as directives but not yet in force in the UK

- **Posted Workers Directive (adopted 24 September 1996)** This seeks to give workers temporarily sent to work in another Member State (posted workers) the right to receive the minimum pay and conditions applicable to that State's own nationals. Implementation date: 24 September 1999.
- **Parental Leave Directive 96/34/EC (adopted June 1996)** Allows parents the right to take at least three months' unpaid parental leave. The Employment Relations Act 1999 provides the Secretary of State with the power to make regulations designed to regulate parental leave. The proposed regulations, as amended in the light of consultation, will be implemented by 15 December 1999.
- **Part-time Work Directive 97/81/EC (adopted May 1997)** Provides for 'the removal of discrimination against part-time workers and to improve the quality of part-time work' and 'to facilitate the development of part-time work'. The Employment Relations Act 1999, s. 19 provides the Secretary of State with the power to make regulations designed to implement the Directive. The UK is required to implement the Directive by 7 April 2000.
- **European Works Councils Directive 94/45/EEC (adopted 22 September 1994)** This envisages the setting up of bodies for the informing and consulting of employees within Community-scale undertakings above a certain size. The UK has to give effect to this law by December 1999.
- **Burden of Proof in Sex Discrimination Cases Directive 97/80/EC (adopted 15 December 1997, extended to the UK by Directive 98/52)** This requires Member States to take measures to ensure that the burden of disproving discrimination shifts to the employer when facts from which it may be presumed that there has been direct or indirect discrimination have been established. The Directive also contains a definition of indirect discrimination and defines the justification which is needed to defeat a claim of indirect discrimination. The Directive must be implemented by the UK by 13 July 2001.

(ii) Other proposals not yet adopted as directives

- **European Company Law Statute** This proposal would, *inter alia*, require that if workers are not actually elected as part of the supervisory board of a company, then a body representing workers would have specific legal rights to receive regular reports on the progress of the company's business. This proposal is controversial and has been blocked by disagreement for over 20 years.

- **National-level Information and Consultation** This proposal – adopted by the Commission in November 1998 – would require any organisation with 50 or more employees to inform and consult its workforce on recent and foreseeable developments in the enterprise's activities, financial situation, changes in employment and substantial changes in work organisation and contractual relations. Again this measure is controversial and is opposed by the European private sector employers' organisation UNICE. It is argued that the proposed directive breaches the principle of subsidiarity. The UK Government is also opposed.
- **Fixed-term Contracts** Discussions between the social partners on a measure to restrict the use of fixed-term contracts are currently suspended.
- **Working Time** This proposal would extend the original legislation to cover sectors and activities currently excluded from the legislation. It is likely to be several years before this measure is implemented.

C: The Relationship Between Community Law and Domestic Law

The general rule is that the articles of the Treaty of Rome cannot be enforced directly by the individual citizen against a Member State. The citizen must wait for the Government to legislate and transform its international treaty obligation into domestic law. In relation to the Treaty of Rome, this was accomplished by the European Communities Act 1972.

European Communities Act 1972

2. (1) All such rights, powers, liabilities and restrictions from time to time created or arising by or under the Treaties, and all such remedies and procedures from time to time provided for by or under the Treaties, as in accordance with the Treaties are without further enactment to be given legal effect or used in the United Kingdom shall be recognised and available in law, and be enforced, allowed and followed accordingly; and the expression 'enforceable Community right' and similar expressions shall be read as referring to one to which this subsection applies.

Note
Where Community legislation has been enacted, there are limits to the extent to which any Member State has the freedom to avoid its obligations. Under Article 226 (ex 169), if the Commission considers that a Member State has failed to fulfil an obligation under Community law, it may bring infringement proceedings against the State before the ECJ and obtain a declaration obliging the Member State to end that violation. Moreover, the UK is subject to the interpretation given to EC law by the Court of Justice, particularly in response to references from the courts of Member States under Article 234 (ex 177).

(i) Supremacy

R v Secretary of State for Transport, ex parte Factortame Ltd (No. 2)
(Case C-213/89) [1991] 1 All ER 70
European Court of Justice

DECISION: 17. It is clear from the information before the court, and in particular from the judgment making the reference and, as described above, the course taken by the proceedings in the national courts before which the case came at first and second instance, that the preliminary question raised by the House of Lords seeks essentially to ascertain whether a national court which, in a case before it concerning Community law, considers that the sole obstacle which precludes it from granting interim relief is a rule of national law must disapply that rule.

18. For the purpose of replying to that question, it is necessary to point out that in its judgment in *Amministrazione delle Finanze dello Stato v Simmenthal SpA* Case 106/77 [1978] ECR 629 at 643 (paras 14, 17) the court held that directly applicable rules of Community law—

> must be fully and uniformly applied in all the Member States from the date of their entry into force and for so long as they continue in force [and that] in accordance with the principle of the precedence of Community law, the relationship between provisions of the Treaty and directly applicable measures of the institutions on the one hand and the national law of the Member States on the other is such that those provisions and measures . . . by their entry into force render automatically inapplicable any conflicting provision of . . . national law . . .

19. In accordance with the case law of the court, it is for the national courts, in application of the principle of co-operation laid down in art 5 of the EEC Treaty, to ensure the legal protection which persons derive from the direct effect of provisions of Community law (see, most recently, the judgments in *Amministrazione delle Finanze dello Stato v Ariete SpA* Case 811/79 [1980] ECR 2545 and *Amministrazione delle Finanze dello Stato v Sas Mediterranea Importazione Rappresentanze Esportazione Commercio (MIRECO)* Case 826/79 [1980] ECR 2559).

20. The court has also held that any provision of a national legal system and any legislative, administrative or judicial practice which might impair the effectiveness of Community law by withholding from the national court having jurisdiction to apply such law the power to do everything necessary at the moment of its application to set aside national legislative provisions which might prevent, even temporarily, Community rules from having full force and effect are incompatible with those requirements, which are the very essence of Community law (see the *Simmenthal* case Case 106/77 [1978] ECR 629 at 644 at (paras 22–23)).

21. It must be added that the full effectiveness of Community law would be just as much impaired if a rule of national law could prevent a court seised of a dispute governed by Community law from granting interim relief in order to ensure the full effectiveness of the judgment to be given on the existence of the rights claimed under Community law. It follows that a court which in those circumstances would grant interim relief, if it were not for a rule of national law, is obliged to set aside that rule.

22. That interpretation is reinforced by the system established by art 177 [now 234] of the EEC Treaty, whose effectiveness would be impaired if a national court, having stayed proceedings pending the reply by the Court of Justice to the question referred to it for a preliminary ruling, were not able to grant interim relief until it delivered its judgment following the reply given by the Court of Justice.

23.   Consequently, the reply to the question raised should be that Community law must be interpreted as meaning that a national court which, in a case before it concerning Community law, considers that the sole obstacle which precludes it from granting interim relief is a rule of national law must set aside that rule.

(ii)   Direct Effect

Kowalska v *Freie und Hansestadt Hamburg*
[1990] IRLR 447
European Court of Justice

. . . Article 119 [now 141] of the EEC Treaty is sufficiently precise to be relied upon by an individual before a National Court in order to have any national provision set aside, which may include a collective agreement, which is contrary to that Article.

Note

The Treaty of Rome is supplemented by directives made by the Council of Ministers. Under Article 249 (ex 189) of the Treaty, a directive is 'binding as to the result to be achieved' but the form and method of achieving the result is left to the individual Member State.

In certain circumstances, however, a directive may be held to be directly enforceable. In *Van Duyn* v *Home Office* [1975] 3 All ER 190, it was held that a directive *could* be enforceable by an individual, and this depended on whether the directive was 'clear, precise, admitted of no exceptions, and therefore of its nature needed no intervention by the national authorities'.

Unlike provisions of the Treaty which may be enforceable against private individuals and organisations and have, therefore, a 'horizontal direct effect', directives can only have a direct effect against the Member State itself as an employer (i.e. a vertical direct effect); they are not enforceable against a private sector employer.

Marshall v *Southampton and South-West Hampshire Area Health Authority (Teaching)*
[1986] IRLR 140; [1986] ECR 723
European Court of Justice

The facts of this case are set out at p. 254.

DECISION: It is necessary to recall that, according to a long line of decisions of the Court (in particular its judgment of 19.1.82 in Case 8/81, *Becker* v *Finanzamt Munster-Innenstadt* [1982] ECR 53), wherever the provisions of a Directive appear, as far as their subject-matter is concerned, to be unconditional and sufficiently precise, those provisions may be relied upon by an individual against the State where that State fails to implement the Directive in national law by the end of the period prescribed or where it fails to implement the Directive correctly.

That view is based on the consideration that it would be incompatible with the binding nature which Article 189 [now 249] confers on the Directive to hold as a matter of principle that the obligation imposed thereby cannot be relied on by those concerned. From that the Court deduced that a Member State which has not adopted the implementing measures required by the Directive within the prescribed period may not plead, as against individuals, its own failure to perform the obligations which the Directive entails. . . .

With regard to the argument that a directive may not be relied upon by an individual, it must be emphasised that according to Article 189 [now 249] of the EEC Treaty the binding nature of a directive, which constitutes the basis for the possibility of relying on the directive before a national court, exists only in relation to 'each Member State to which it is addressed'. It follows that a directive may not of itself impose obligations on an individual and that a provision of a directive may not be relied upon as against such a person.

Notes

1. Whilst it is clear that directives can be enforced only against bodies which are 'organs or emanations of the State', there was, until recently, some doubt as to the scope of this phrase. In *Foster* v *British Gas* [1990] IRLR 354, the House of Lords referred the matter to the European Court for a ruling. The ECJ was prepared to give a wide definition to these terms. It held that a directive which has direct effect may be relied upon in a claim against a body, whatever its legal form, which has been made responsible for providing a public service under the control of the State and has for that purpose special powers beyond those which result from the normal rules applicable in relations between private individuals. This broad approach means that local government, universities and colleges, and nationalised industries all clearly now fall within the potential scope of direct effect.

2. The limitation on the enforceability of directives is perhaps less important than it would be given the ruling of the ECJ in *Francovich* v *Italian Republic* [1992] IRLR 84. In *Francovich* the ECJ ruled that when an individual suffers damage as a result of a Member State's failure correctly to implement a directive which confers rights for the benefit of the individual, the individual can sue the State directly under European law for the damage suffered by the State's failure. This ruling considerably strengthens the position of private sector workers.

In more recent judgments, the ECJ has elaborated upon the criteria for State liability. In *R* v *HM Treasury ex parte British Telecommunications plc* [1996] IRLR 300, the ECJ held that where a Member State incorrectly transposes a Community Directive into national law the following conditions apply: the rule of law infringed must be intended to confer rights on individuals; the breach must be sufficiently serious; and there must be a direct causal link between the breach of the obligation resting on the State and the damage sustained by the injured parties.

A breach is 'sufficiently serious' where, in the exercise of its legislative powers, an institution or a Member State has manifestly and gravely disregarded the limit on the exercise of its powers. Factors which the competent court may take into account include the clarity and precision of the rule breached (see also (1) *Brasserie du Pêcheur SA* v *Federal Republic of Germany* and (2) *R* v *Secretary of State for Transport ex parte Factortame Ltd and others (No. 3)*, [1996] IRLR 267, ECJ).

(iii)   Indirect Effect

Litster v Forth Dry Dock Engineering Co. Ltd
[1989] 1 All ER 1134
House of Lords

This case is concerned with the interpretation of the Transfer of Undertakings (Protection of Employment) Regulations 1981 in the light of the EC Employee Rights on Transfer of Business Directive 77/187. This aspect of the case is discussed at p. 578.

LORD TEMPLEMAN: In *von Colson and Kamann* v *Land Nordrhein-Westfalen* (Case 14/83) [1984] ECR 1891, 1909 the European Court of Justice dealing with Directive (76/207/EEC), forbidding discrimination on grounds of sex regarding access to employment, ruled that:

> the Member States' obligation arising from a Directive to achieve the result envisaged by the Directive and their duty under Article 5 [now 10] of the Treaty to take all appropriate measures, whether general or particular, to ensure the fulfilment of that obligation, is binding on all the authorities of Member States including, for matters within their jurisdiction, the courts. It follows that, in applying the national law and in particular the provisions of a national law specifically introduced in order to implement Directive [(76/207/EEC)], national courts are required to interpret their national law in the light of the wording and purpose of the Directive in order to achieve the result referred to in the third paragraph of Article 189 [now 249].

Thus the courts of the United Kingdom are under a duty to follow the practice of the European Court in giving a purposive construction to directives and regulations issued for the purpose of complying with directives. In *Pickstone* v *Freemans plc* [1988] IRLR 357, this House implied words in a regulation designed to give effect to Directive (75/117/EEC) dealing with equal pay for women doing work of equal value. If this House had not been able to make the necessary implication, the Equal Pay (Amendment) Regulations 1983 would have failed their object and the United Kingdom would have been in breach of its treaty obligations to give effect to Directives.

Duke v GEC Reliance Ltd
[1988] IRLR 118
House of Lords

The complainant alleged sex discrimination when she had been required to retire at the age of 60, while men could work on to 65. Because she was not a State employee, she could not rely on EC law as interpreted in *Marshall* (above). Further, her case was brought before changes introduced by the SDA 1986 took effect. Her argument was based on interpreting the SDA 1975, s. 6(4) (a provision which allowed for differential retirement ages based on gender) in accordance with the Equal Treatment Directive. The argument was rejected by the House of Lords.

LORD TEMPLEMAN: Section 2(4) of the European Communities Act 1972 does not in my opinion enable or constrain a British court to distort the meaning of a

British statute in order to enforce against an individual a Community directive which has no direct effect between individuals. . . . It would be most unfair to the respondent to distort the construction of the 1975 Sex Discrimination Act in order to accommodate the Equal Treatment Directive as construed by the European Court in the 1986 *Marshall* case. As between the appellant and respondent the Equal Treatment Directive did not have direct effect and the respondent could not be reasonably expected to appreciate the logic of Community legislators in permitting differential retirement ages. The respondent is not liable to the appellant under Community law. I decline to hold that liability under British law attaches to the respondent or any other private employer to pay damages based on wages which women over 60 and under 65 did not earn before the amending Sex Discrimination Act 1986 for the first time and without retrospective effect introduced the statutory tort of operating differential retirement ages.

Notes
1. The correctness of this approach was acknowledged recently by the House of Lords in *Webb* v *EMO Air Cargo (UK) Ltd* [1993] IRLR 27, HL. However, there is a strong argument that the House of Lord's view that it cannot construe a national Act purposively where it was enacted prior to the relevant directive flies in the face of EC law. In *Marleasing SA* v *La Commercial Internacional di Alimentacion* Case 106/89 (13 November 1990), the ECJ stated:

It followed from the obligation on Member States to take all measures appropriate to ensure the performance of their obligations to achieve the results provided for in Directives, that in applying national law, whether it was a case of provisions prior to or subsequent to the Directive, the national court called on to interpret it was required to do so as far as possible in the light of the wording and purpose of the Directive in order to achieve the result sought by the Directive.

2. Other Community measures include:
   (a) Recommendations: In *Grimaldi* v *Fonds des Maladies Professionelles* [1990] IRLR 400, the ECJ ruled that national courts must take such non-binding measures into account, in particular to clarify the interpretation of other provisions of national and Community law.
   (b) Regulations: Under Article 249 (ex 189) of the Treaty of Rome, a regulation is stated to be of general application, binding in its entirety and directly applicable in all Member States.

2 THE NATURE AND CONTENT OF THE CONTRACT OF EMPLOYMENT

As we saw in Chapter 1, the individual employment relationship was altered quite radically by the legislation of the 1970s which created the statutory floor of employment rights and a specialised system of industrial tribunals through which disputes over these rights are adjudicated. Does this mean that the law of contract no longer provides the foundation of employment law? Is possession of the status of 'employee' the all-important issue, given that it is that status and not contract which attracts the rights bestowed by statute? To accept this view would be going too far, however, for a number of reasons.

First, today there are still many situations for which statute has not legislated, and it is then up to the law of contract to fill the gap and supply the answers to questions such as whether there is a right to receive wages when absent through sickness (see *Mears* v *Safecar Security Ltd* [1982] 2 All ER 865).

Secondly, even when it comes to adjudicating statutory rights, the courts and tribunals will often look to the guidance of contractual theories in reaching a decision, e.g. in the context of unfair dismissal, whether an employee's repudiation of the contract requires acceptance by the employer in the form of a dismissal or whether the repudiation automatically brings the contract to an end.

Thirdly, the law of industrial action and possible immunity from the economic torts is often influenced by whether or not a breach of contract has occurred.

Lastly, as was seen in the introduction, the perceived weakness of the 'statutory floor of employment rights' has caused workers to look towards contractual remedies as a more effective form of job protection.

As Anderman observes, 'a thorough understanding of the characteristics of the contract of employment is a virtual precondition to an understanding of the subject of labour law' (Anderman, S.D., *Labour Law: Management Decisions & Workers' Rights*, 3rd ed. 1998 at p. 34).

I Employee Status

The distinction between contracts of employment and self-employment is of fundamental importance, because only 'employees' qualify for employment protection rights such as unfair dismissal, redundancy payments, minimum notice on termination, etc. Wider protection is provided under the Health and Safety at Work etc. Act 1974, and the discrimination and equal pay legislation which applies to those both under a contract of service and a contract 'personally to execute any work or labour' includes the self-employed.

Given the fundamental importance of the distinction, it is unfortunate that the formulation of the test of employee status has come from the courts and tribunals rather than from statute. The only guidance on the question in the legislation is so completely circular as to be absolutely useless.

Employment Rights Act 1996

230. Employees, workers, etc.

(1) In this Act 'employee' means an individual who has entered into or works under (or, where the employment has ceased, worked under) a contract of employment.

(2) In this Act 'contract of employment' means a contract of service or apprenticeship, whether express or implied, and (if it is express) whether oral or in writing.

Note

The case law on this subject is confusing and contradictory. Historically, the leading approach was to apply the test of 'control', i.e. could the employer control how, when and where the worker was to work? If he could, that worker was his employee. However, as nowadays many employees possess skills not held by their employer, control as the sole determinant of status had been rejected. Along the way the test of 'integration' was floated, i.e. whether the worker was fully integrated into the employing organisation, but the test was never widely adopted. The modern approach has been to abandon the search for a single test and adopt a multifactorial test, weighing up all the factors for and against the existence of a contract of employment to determine whether the worker is 'in business on his own account'.

Ready Mixed Concrete (South East) Ltd v *Minister of Pensions and National Insurance*
[1968] 2 QB 497
Queen's Bench Division

The Minister claimed that the plaintiff company was liable to pay national insurance contributions in respect of a driver employed by it to transport concrete. The contract between the driver and the company stated that he was an independent contractor (self-employed) and provided that, for a fixed period, he would carry nothing but the company's concrete in a vehicle which he would hire purchase from the company. He was to wear the company's uniform and the vehicle was to be painted with the company's colours and insignia. Repairs to the vehicle could be required by the company, the driver being responsible for all running and repair costs. If, at any time, the driver was unable to carry out the company's requirements because of illness, he could hire another driver for the vehicle.

MACKENNA J: A contract of employment exists if these three conditions are fulfilled. (i) The servant agrees that, in consideration of a wage or other remuneration, he will provide his own work and skill in the performance of some service for his master. (ii) He agrees, expressly or impliedly, that in the performance of that service he will be subject to the other's control in a sufficient degree to make that other master. (iii) The other provisions of the contract are consistent with its being a contract of service. . . . I have shown that [the driver] must make the vehicle available throughout the contract period. He must maintain it . . . in working order, repairing and replacing worn parts when necessary. He must hire a competent driver to take his place if he should be for any reason unable to drive at any time when the company requires the service of the vehicle. He must do whatever is needed to make the vehicle (with a driver) available throughout the contract period. He must do all this, at his own expense, being paid a rate per mile for the quantity which he delivers. These obligations are more consistent, I think, with a contract of carriage than with one of service. The ownership of the assets, the chance of profit and the risk of loss in the business of carriage are his and not the company's.

A: A Checklist

Market Investigations v *Minister of Social Security*
[1969] 2 QB 173
Queen's Bench Division

COOKE J: No exhaustive list can be compiled of the considerations which are relevant to [the] question, nor can strict rules be laid down as to the relevant weight which the various considerations should carry in particular cases. The most that can be said is that control will no doubt always have to be considered, although it can no longer be regarded as the sole determining factor; and that factors which may be of importance are such matters as whether the man performing the services provides his own equipment, whether he hires his own helpers, what degree of financial risk he takes, what degree of responsibility for investment and management he has, and whether and how far he has an opportunity of profiting from the sound management of his task.

Notes
1.   The business test, together with the checklist set out above, received the approval of the Privy Council in *Lee* v *Chung and Shun Sing Construction and Engineering Co. Ltd* [1990] IRLR 236. More recently the Court of Appeal has warned against a mechanistic application of Cooke J's checklist (see *Hall (HM Inspector of Taxes)* v *Lorimer* [1994] IRLR 171). While the checklist

should not be regarded as laying down an all-purpose definition, it does offer valuable guidance in many cases.

2. In the next case, the Court of Appeal utilised the traditional tests to provide a liberal interpretation of the concept of 'employee' on policy grounds.

Lane v Shire Roofing Co. Ltd
[1995] IRLR 493
Court of Appeal

The plaintiff was a roofer who traded as a one-man firm and was categorised as self-employed for tax purposes. In 1986, he was hired by the defendants, a newly established roofing business which had not wanted to take on direct labour, and so had taken on the plaintiff on a 'payment-by-job' basis. While re-roofing a porch of a house, he fell off a ladder, suffering serious injuries. The central question in the case was whether the defendants owed the plaintiff a duty of care. In the High Court, Judge Hutton held the defendants were not liable for the injuries sustained because Mr Lane was doing the work as an independent contractor, not as an employee, and that accordingly the defendants owed him no duty of care.

The Court of Appeal allowed the appeal and awarded damages of £102,500.

HENRY LJ: We were taken through the standard authorities on this matter: *Ready Mixed Concrete (South-East) Ltd* v *Minister of Pensions and National Insurance* [1968] 2 QB 497; *Market Investigations* v *Minister of Social Security* [1969] 2 QB 173; and *Ferguson* v *Dawson & Partners (Contractors) Ltd* [1976] IRLR 346, to name the principal ones. Two general remarks should be made. The overall employment background is very different today (and was, though less so, in 1986) than it had been when those cases were first decided. First, for a variety of reasons there are more self-employed and fewer in employment. There is a greater flexibility in employment, with more temporary and shared employment. Second, there are perceived advantages for both workman and employer in the relationship between them being that of independent contractor. From the workman's point of view, being self-employed brings him into a more benevolent and less prompt taxation regime. From the employer's point of view, the protection of employees' rights contained in the employment protection legislation of the 1970s brought certain perceived disincentives to the employer to take on full-time long-term employees. So even in 1986 there were reasons on both sides to avoid the employee label. But, as I have already said, there were, and are, good policy reasons in the safety at work field to ensure that the law properly categorises between employees and independent contractors.

That line of authority shows that there are many factors to be taken into account in answering this question, and, with different priority being given to those factors in different cases, all depends on the facts of each particular case. Certain principles relevant to this case, however, emerge.

First, the element of control will be important: who lays down what is to be done, the way in which it is to be done, and the time when it is done? Who provides (i.e. hires and fires) the team by which it is done, and who provides the materials, plant and machinery and tools used?

But it is recognised that the control test may not be decisive – for instance, in the case of skilled employees, with discretion to decide how their work should be done. In such cases the question is broadened to whose business was it? Was the workman carrying on his own business, or was he carrying on that of his employers? The American Supreme Court, in *United States of America* v *Silk* [1946] 331 US 704, asks the question whether the men were employees 'as a matter of economic reality'. The answer to this question may cover the same ground as the control test (such as whether he provides his own equipment and hires his own helpers) but may involve looking to see where the financial risk lies, and whether and how far he has an opportunity of profiting from sound management in the performance of his task (see *Market Investigations* v *Minister of Social Security*, supra).

And these questions must be asked in the context of who is responsible for the overall safety of the men doing the work in question. Mr Whittaker, of the respondents, was cross-examined on these and he agreed that he was so responsible. Such an answer is not decisive (though it may be indicative) because ultimately the question is one of law and he could be wrong where the legal responsibility lies (see *Ferguson* v *Dawson*, supra, at 1219G).

Note

The policy orientated approach adopted in this case is to be welcomed (see the case note by McKendrick in (1996) 25 ILJ 136). However, the question arises whether it would have been decided in the same way if it had been an unfair dismissal claim, where the courts have a tendency to focus on whether there was a *general* long-term employment relationship involving mutuality of obligation. The following two cases illustrate this point.

B: *Mutuality of Obligation*

O'Kelly and others v *Trusthouse Forte plc*
[1983] IRLR 369
Court of Appeal

Messrs O'Kelly, Pearman and Florent all worked as 'regular casuals' for Trusthouse Forte in the Banqueting Department at the Grosvenor House Hotel. They complained to an industrial tribunal that they had been unfairly dismissed by the company for being members of a trade union and for taking part in the activities of that union. They applied to the tribunal for interim relief under what is now TULR(C)A 1992, s. 161.

As a preliminary point, the industrial tribunal considered whether or not the claimants were 'employees' of the company within the meaning of what is now ERA 1996, s. 230(1), which is a prerequisite for a claim under the interim relief provisions. In determining this question, the industrial tribunal directed itself in accordance with the following test: 'What we derive from the authorities is that the tribunal should consider all aspects of the relationship, no single feature being in itself decisive and each of which may vary in weight and direction, and having given such balance to the factors as seems appropriate, to determine whether the person was carrying out business on his own account.'

On the facts of the case, the industrial tribunal found the following factors to be consistent with the regular casuals being employed under a contract of employment as opposed to a contract for services:

(a) The applicants provided their services in return for remuneration for work actually performed. They did not invest their own capital or stand to gain or lose from the commercial success of the functions organised by the Banqueting Department.

(b) They performed their work under the direction and control of the respondents.

(c) When the casual workers attended at functions they were part of the respondents' organisation and for the purpose of ensuring the smooth running of the business they were represented in the staff consultation process.

(d) When working they were carrying on the business of the respondents.

(e) Clothing and equipment were provided by the respondents.

(f) The applicants were paid weekly in arrear and were paid under deduction of income tax and social security contribution.

(g) Their work was organised on the basis of a weekly rota and they required permission to take time off from rostered duties.

(h) There was a disciplinary and grievance procedure.

(i) There was holiday pay or an incentive bonus calculated by reference to past service.

The tribunal then found that the following additional factors in the relationship were not inconsistent with a contract of employment:

(j) The applicants were paid for work actually performed and did not receive a regular wage or retainer. The method of calculating entitlement to remuneration is not an essential aspect of the employment relationship.

(k) Casual workers were not remunerated on the same basis as permanent employees and did not receive sick pay and were not included in the respondents' staff pension scheme and did not receive the fringe benefits accorded to established employees. There is, however, no objection to employers adopting different terms and conditions of employment for different categories of employee (e.g. different terms for manual and managerial staff).

(l) There were no regular or assured working hours. It is not a requirement of employment that there should be 'normal working hours'.

(m) Casual workers were not provided with written particulars of employment. If it is established that casual workers are employees there is a statutory obligation to furnish written particulars.

Five factors, however, were found to be inconsistent with the relationship being that of employer and employee. These were:

(n)   The engagement was terminable without notice on either side.

(o)   The applicants had the right to decide whether or not to accept work, although whether or not it would be in their interest to exercise the right to refuse work is another matter.

(p)   The respondents had no obligation to provide any work.

(q)   During the subsistence of the relationship it was the parties' view that casual workers were independent contractors engaged under successive contracts for services.

(r)   It is the recognised custom and practice of the industry that casual workers are engaged under a contract for services.

The majority of the industrial tribunal then went on to say that whilst the relationship did have many of the characteristics of a contract of employment, there was one important ingredient missing – mutuality of obligation.

On this basis, together with the finding that the intention of the parties in the light of the known custom and practice in the industry was not to create an employment relationship, the industrial tribunal dismissed the claim. This view was ultimately upheld by the Court of Appeal.

ACKNER LJ: It was submitted that the industrial tribunal, having found that in practice 'regular' casuals on the list had priority in the offer of available work and a reciprocal practical requirement to do the work once rostered (because failure to do the work could lead to possible suspension and subsequent removal from the list) the right conclusion to draw was that there was a contractual obligation on Trusthouse Forte to offer work to 'regulars' in priority and on 'regulars' to do the work when offered. It was therefore contended that factors (o) and (p) in paragraph 23 of the industrial tribunal's reasons should not have been placed in the balance against there being a contract of employment. On the contrary, 'the one important ingredient' (namely, mutuality of obligation) which the industrial tribunal found to be missing was indeed present. . . . I do not think this is right. The 'assurance of preference in the allocation of any available work' which the 'regulars' enjoyed was no more than a firm expectation in practice. It was not a contractual promise. The appellants, of course, expected the respondents to accept engagements rostered, but to suggest that a failure to accept amounted to a breach of contract is going too far. They were entitled to choose whether or not to attend, and however irritating it might have been to Trusthouse Forte if faced with a refusal it would have been quite unreal to conclude that either party would have thought it was a breach of contract.

Notes

1.   The implications of the 'mutuality of obligation' test for workers with irregular working patterns are highly disadvantageous – at least if it is applied in a strict sense. The sort of narrow reasoning seen in *O'Kelly* is also to be found in the judgment of the EAT in *Wickens* v *Champion Employment* [1984] ICR 365, where 'temps' engaged by a private employment agency were not accorded employment status because of the lack of binding obligation on the part of the agency to make bookings for work and the absence of any obligation by the worker to accept them. (Cf. *McMeecham* v *Secretary of State*

for Employment [1997 IRLR 353, where the Court of Appeal held that a temporary worker can have the status of employee of an employment agency in respect of each assignment actually worked, notwithstanding that the same worker may not be entitled to employee status under his general terms of engagement.)

2.   In neither *O'Kelly* nor *Wickens* is there any recognition of the policy considerations of protecting workers from anti-union employers (*O'Kelly*) or providing job protection rights for 'marginal' workers (*Wickens*). A more liberal approach can be seen in the next case.

Nethermere (St Neots) Ltd v Taverna and Gardiner
[1984] IRLR 240
Court of Appeal

Mrs Taverna and Mrs Gardiner were at one time both employed at the appellants' garment factory but later became 'home workers'. Mrs Taverna began working at home at the beginning of 1978. The sewing machine that she used for the work was provided by the appellants. She had no fixed hours for doing the work and for a number of weeks she did no work at all. She was paid weekly according to the number of garments she did. Mrs Gardiner ceased working at the factory in 1976. In September 1979, the appellants asked if she would do work at home and she agreed. At first she used her own machine but was then supplied with one by the appellants. She normally put 200 pockets onto trousers each day. If she wanted less work she would tell the driver who delivered the materials to her. The only stipulation was that it had to be sufficient to make it worthwhile for the driver to call.

When these arrangements came to an end in 1981 following a dispute about holiday pay, Mrs Taverna and Mrs Gardiner complained that they had been unfairly dismissed. As a preliminary issue, the industrial tribunal were asked to decide whether the two women were employees of the company within the meaning of what is now ERA 1996, s. 230(1) – i.e. that they were employed under a contract of service – or whether they were self-employed under a contract for services. The tribunal held that the women were employed under a contract of service and were eligible therefore to complain of unfair dismissal.

Both the Employment Appeal Tribunal and the Court of Appeal dismissed the employer's appeal against the industrial tribunal's decision.

DILLON LJ: For my part I would accept that an arrangement under which there was never any obligation on the outworkers to do work or on the company to provide work could not be a contract of service. But the mere facts that the outworkers could fix their own hours of work, could take holidays and time off when they wished and could vary how many garments they were willing to take on any day or even to take none on a particular day, while undoubtedly factors for the industrial tribunal to consider in deciding whether or not there was a contract of service, do not as a matter of law negative the existence of such a contract.

I see no reason in law why the existence of a contract of service may not be inferred from a course of dealing, continued between the parties over several years, as in *Airfix*. This is indeed a line with the decision in *Brogden v Metropolitan Railway Company*, (1877) 2 AC 666. The fact that machines were supplied by the company to each of the applicants indicates at the least an expectation on both sides that the applicants would be doing work for the company which was provided for them by the company, and I find it unreal to suppose that the work in fact done by the applicants for the company over the not inconsiderable periods which I have mentioned was done merely as a result of the pressures of market forces on the applicants and the company and under no contract at all.

Mr Weisfeld's evidence that it was up to the home workers to decide how much work they did subject to making it worthwhile for van drivers to call, is capable of being read as importing an obligation on the outworkers to take a reasonable amount of work once they have agreed to act as outworkers for the company. Conversely the statement of Mr Weisfeld that it was the van driver's duty to be as fair as he could is capable of being read as importing an obligation on the company to provide a reasonable share of work for each outworker whenever the company had more work available than could be handled by the factory.

There was a regular course of dealing between the parties for years under which garments were supplied daily to the outworkers, worked on, collected and paid for. If it is permissible on the evidence to find that by such conduct a contract had been established between each applicant and the company. I see no necessity to conclude that that contract must have been a contract for services and not a contract of service.

In my judgment there was material to support the view of the industrial tribunal in paragraph 11 and it was entitled to reach the conclusion that a contract of employment had been created between the parties and both the applicants were employees. Thus the court is not entitled to interfere with that conclusion and so I would dismiss this appeal.

STEPHENSON LJ: . . . I cannot see why well founded expectations of continuing homework should not be hardened or refined into enforceable contracts by regular giving and taking of work over periods of a year or more and why outworkers should not thereby become employees under contracts of service like those doing similar work at the same rate in the factory.

KERR LJ (*Dissenting*): . . . A course of dealing can be used as a basis for implying terms into individual contracts which are concluded pursuant thereto, but I can find no authority for the proposition that even a lengthy course of dealing can somehow convert itself into a contractually binding obligation – subject only to reasonable notice – to continue to enter into individual contracts, or to be subject to some 'umbrella' contract. The nearest analogy appears to be *Brogden v Metropolitan Railway*, (1877) 2 AC 666. But the parties in that case had concluded a contract in principle which only lacked formal signature, and their course of dealing within its terms was treated as an acceptance of its terms by conduct. There is nothing of a similar nature in the present case.

Express and Echo Publications Ltd v Tanton
[1999] IRLR 367
Court of Appeal

Mr Tanton worked for the appellants as an employee until he was made redundant. He was then re-engaged as a driver on an ostensibly self-employed basis. Clause 3.3 of his contract provided that: 'In the event that the contractor is unable or unwilling to perform the services personally, he shall arrange at his own expense entirely for another suitable person to perform the service.' Mr Tanton found the agreement unacceptable and refused to sign it. However, he continued to work in accordance with its terms and, on the odd occasion, utilised the right to provide a substitute driver. He later brought a claim to an employment tribunal complaining that he had not been provided with a written statement of particulars – effectively asking for his status as an employee to be confirmed. The employment tribunal chairman approached the case on the basis of what actually had occurred, rather than what the document recorded as being the obligations of the parties. Having carried out a balancing exercise, he concluded that the factors pointing to Mr Tanton being an employee outweighed the factors which pointed to contractor status. Mr Tanton was required to follow a set route, wear a uniform provided by the company and drive a vehicle from the company's pool. The chairman regarded those requirements and the degree of control exercised by the company as suggesting a contract of employment. According to the chairman, the provision enabling Mr Tanton to provide a substitute driver which, on his own evidence, he had used from time to time, was only one factor of many; and though there might come a point at which the provision of a substitute was so frequent as to change the whole nature of the arrangement, there was no evidence that that point had been approached. The EAT (Judge Clark presiding) dismissed an appeal against this decision at a preliminary hearing on the ground that it raised no arguable point of law. Both the tribunal chair and the EAT considered that the substitution clause was not fatal to there being a contract of employment, either in law or in fact. However, the Court of Appeal ruled that the right to provide a substitute is 'inherently inconsistent' with employment status. A contract of employment must necessarily contain an obligation on the part of the employee to provide services personally. Without such an 'irreducible minimum' of obligation, it cannot be said that there is a contract of employment, according to the Court of Appeal.

PETER GIBSON LJ: . . . Clause 3.3, to my mind vividly illustrates the difficulty in approaching the identification of the terms of the agreement by concentrating on what actually occurred rather than looking at the obligations by which the parties were bound. Of course, it is important that the industrial tribunal should be alert in this area of the law to look at the reality of any obligations. If the obligation is a sham, it will want to say so. But to concentrate on what actually occurred may not elucidate the full terms of the contract. If a term is not enforced, that does not justify a conclusion that such a term is not part of the agreement. The obligation could be temporarily waived. If there is a term that is inherently inconsistent with the existence of a contract of employment, what actually happened from time to time may not be decisive, given the existence of that term. For example, if, under an agreement, there is a provision enabling, but not requiring, the worker to work, and enabling, but not requiring, the person for whom he works to provide that work, the fact that work is from time to time provided would not mean that the contract was a contract of service, consider *Clark* v *Oxfordshire Health Authority* [1998] IRLR 125. For my part, therefore, I think that the chairman went wrong at that point in concentrating on what occurred rather than seeking to determine what were the mutual obligations. . . .

In these circumstances, it is, in my judgment, established on the authorities that where, as here, a person who works for another is not required to perform his services personally, then as a matter of law the relationship between the worker and the person for whom he works is not that of employee and employer. Mr Tanton has submitted to us that, though the personal service to the appellant was a highly material consideration, it was not conclusive. I am afraid that the proposition cannot stand in the light of the authorities.

In my judgment, on the facts this is a plain case. One starts with the common intention of the parties that Mr Tanton should not be an employee but should be a self-employed contractor. The terms which the chairman found to be pointers to a contract of service are in no way inconsistent with a contract for services, and, as the chairman himself recognised, some of the facts which he found are pointers to the relationship being one of contractor and client, for example the absence of holiday pay and sickness pay. But, for the reasons which I have given, clause 3.3 entitling Mr Tanton not to perform any service personally, is a provision wholly inconsistent with the contract of service which the chairman found the contract to be. In my judgment, therefore, the chairman and the Employment Appeal Tribunal erred in law.

Notes

1. Rubenstein offers the following criticism of the above decision:

A number of points can be made, but the most important of them is that this decision carries with it the real danger of abuse. It opens the possibility for employers and their advisers to draft contracts which will negate employment status for certain workers by including a substitution clause in their contracts. It is by no means clear from Lord Justice Peter Gibson's decision precisely what error of law the tribunal chair is held to have made. It is said that he went wrong 'in concentrating on what occurred rather than seeking to determine what were the mutual obligations', but whether that is seen as a misdirection or as a perverse conclusion makes a difference to how this case is regarded. In determining the right to be given the decision, it should also be pointed out that the appellant was not legally represented. Most of the leading authorities on employment status are from the Court of Appeal. *Carmichael* v *National Power* is soon to be heard by the House of Lords, and it is to be hoped that they will take the opportunity of a general review of the case law. (Rubenstein, M., 'Highlights', [1999] IRLR 337).

2. The employment status of workers on 'zero hours' contracts has yet to be authoritatively clarified. In their pure form, such contracts require workers to be on call but specify no hours of work and no work is guaranteed. A variant arrangement is the 'min-max' contract where minimum and maximum hours are specified. Such arrangements have gained in prevalence in recent years and are most likely to be found in sectors such as retail, banking and the public sector, including health and local authorities. A recent survey of selected organisations in the private and public sectors found that just over a fifth used 'something which could be described as zero-hours contracts' (see Katherine E. Cave, *Zero Hours Contracts: A Report into the Incidence and*

Implications of Such Contracts, Huddersfield: University of Huddersfield 1997). The report (p. 23) discussed two then unreported cases (*Clark* v *Oxfordshire Area Health Authority* (1996) and *Carmichael and Leese* v *National Power plc* (1996)) where employee status was found in one (a bank nurse) but not the other (a 'casual as required' tourist guide). Subsequently, the Court of Appeal overruled both decisions thus underlying the uncertainties and inconsistencies pervading this area (see [1998] IRLR 125 and [1998] IRLR 301 respectively).

In *Carmichael*, the Court of Appeal held that a 'casual as required' contract had the requisite mutuality of obligations between the parties to be regarded as an umbrella contract of employment because there was an implied term in the contract that the applicants would take on a reasonable amount of work and a corresponding implied term that the employers would provide a reasonable share of such guiding work as it became available. However, no such implied term was found to exist between the parties in *Clark*. While the reasoning and decision in *Carmichael* offer enhanced protection for casual workers, it is not difficult for employers to avoid a similar outcome by drafting terms which expressly exclude a requirement to undertake specified levels of work (or on the employer to provide work when available).

3.   In the light of this confusion, the Government considered it desirable to clarify the coverage of the employment protection legislation and to reflect better the diversity of working relationships in the modern labour market. Consequently, s. 23 of the Employment Relations Act 1999 gives the Secretary of State the power, by order subject to the affirmative resolution procedure, to extend to individuals who do not at present enjoy them the employment rights under TULR(C)A 1992, ERA 1996 and the 1999 Act itself. The Government envisages using this new power to ensure that all workers other than the genuinely self-employed enjoy the minimum standards of protection that the legislation is intended to provide, and that none is excluded simply because of the technicalities relating to the type of contract or other arrangement under which they are engaged.

Indeed, a recent trend has been to extend the scope of the newer employment protection rights to a broader category of 'workers': see s. 43K of the ERA 1996 (encompassing the changes introduced by the Public Interest Disclosure Act 1998); the Working Time Regulations 1998, regs 2 and 36; and the National Minimum Wage Act 1998, ss. 1(2), 34, 35, 41.

Richard W. Painter and Keith Puttick, with Ann Holmes, 'The Gateway To Employment Rights', in *Employment Rights*, (1998) 2nd edn

The employment protection legislation was drafted principally with full-time, permanent employees – so-called core workers – in mind. The legislation of the mid 1970s which established the 'statutory floor of employment rights' effectively excluded millions of workers from its protections because they were considered to be self-employed, or failed to qualify through lack of continuity of employment. Indeed, it may well be argued that, if the policy behind the legislation was to protect those workers which collective bargaining could not reach, the groups who were excluded – the peripheral workers' – were the ones in greatest need of protection.

It is a paradox that at the very moment the contemporary structure of labour law was erected, the labour market started a rapid transformation, both in terms of composition and structure, leaving even more workers engaged, for instance, as part-timers, casuals, homeworkers, or as part of a government training scheme on the margins of employment protection.

Part-time workers constitute the largest group of peripheral workers. Trends in the UK labour market in recent years show a marked increase in part-time work as full-time work has declined. Labour Force surveys show that about 6 million people (25 per cent of all employees) now work less than 30 hours a week, women constituting around 90 per cent of this total and married women accounting for some three-quarters of all part-timers. Most of the growth in the number of part-time jobs and the increase in part-timers as a proportion of the workforce has resulted from changes in the structure of the labour market. Manufacturing, traditionally employing few part-timers, has declined, while the services sector, which has always engaged a relatively large number, has grown.

While the increase in part-time working since the 1960s may be explained by appreciation by employers of the benefits in terms of lower overheads, increased productivity and greater flexibility engendered by the use of part-time labour, there are serious disadvantages from the worker's point of view, not least the low rate of pay relative to full-time employment. A House of Lords committee which examined the problems of part-time workers made this comment on the part-time worker's vulnerability:

Part-time employees, while contributing significantly to the development of the economy and to the flexibility of the productive system, are as a group still behind their full-time colleagues in regard to wage rates, access to training and the promotion and the provision of other benefits. This is both economically self-defeating and socially unacceptable, not least when it reinforces other types of discrimination such as that between male and female employees [House of Lords Select Committee on the European Communities, 'Voluntary Part-time Work' Session 1981–82, 19th Report, HMSO, London 1982].

As will be seen, this economic vulnerability is compounded by the status and continuous service requirements of our employment protection law, with the result that a significant number of part-timers will be excluded from rights to redundancy pay, minimum notice periods, statutory guarantee payments, maternity leave, maternity pay or protection against unfair dismissal.

As the use of part-timers increased in the 1980s, this was also paralleled by a marked, though less spectacular, growth in the use of temporary and casual workers. The definition of a temporary employee covers a number of arrangements: fixed-term contracts; agency temping; casual work; seasonal work. Research by the Institute of Employment Studies [P. Heather, J. Rick, J. Atkinson and S. Morris, 'Employers' Use of Temporary Workers', *Labour Market Trends*, September 1996, pp. 403–11] suggests that three-quarters of employers in most industrial sectors hire temporary workers. Just over one million employees were temporary workers in 1985, compared with over one and a half million in 1996. Of these, 720,000 worked part-time. Whilst women make up 48 per cent of all employees, 55 per cent of temporary workers are women. It was found that the proportion had grown since 1980 and was on a rising trend. It appears that newer rationales for the engagement of temporary workers (associated with 'flexible manning' policies) are increasingly seen by employers to be important, though traditional rationales (holiday, sickness and absence cover, etc.) still exist.

As with part-time work, the vast majority of 'temps' are women (two-thirds) and are concentrated in personal services, semi- and unskilled manual occupations. However, the survey does suggest that a small but growing proportion of temporary workers is to be found in managerial, technical and professional work.

In legal terms, temporary workers are at least as, and perhaps more, vulnerable than their part-time counterparts. Once again, problems of employment status and continuity present themselves, while those engaged on fixed-term contracts may lawfully be required to sign away redundancy and unfair dismissal rights should the employer not renew the contract [see ERA 1996, s. 197].

Notes

1.   For a detailed analysis of these issues and a programme for reform see Linda Dickens, *Whose Flexibility? Discrimination and equality issues in atypical work*, The Institute of Employment Rights: London (1992).

2.   The legal protection available to part-time and temporary workers has been significantly increased as a result of the judgment of the House of Lords in *R v Secretary of State for Employment ex parte EOC* [1995] 1 AC 1, HL (discussed at p. 59); see also *R v Secretary of State for Employment ex parte Seymour-Smith and Perez* c-167/97 [1999] IRLR 253, ECJ (discussed at p. 63).

3.   The EC has been concerned for some while to ensure that part-time workers receive no less favourable treatment than full-time workers. There are a number of policy considerations for this, including recent rapid increases in part-time and 'atypical' working within Member States; and the need to promote labour market objectives of 'employability', and conditions generally in which workers are going to remain in employment rather than leave work to take up out-of-work State benefits. The principles of equal treatment in respect of terms and conditions of employment and the application of statutory employment protection is recognised in most other European Member States (see, for example, the French *Code du Travail*, Article L212–4-2). However, the translation of this principle into an EC directive was, for many years, opposed by the UK Government on the grounds of the negative employment effect it would allegedly create.

The Directive on Part-time Work (EC Directive 97/81) was the result of an earlier Framework Agreement between the 'social partners' (employers, unions and public sector employers). Concerns among employers that have been expressed in EC social partner forums have tended to focus on the instability of part-time working, and what they perceive as a need to coordinate approaches between State support for working (primarily through the tax and benefits systems Member States operate) and the occupational provision made by employers. Unions and other interest groups have generally sought to improve the working conditions of this increasingly important section of the labour market (where pay and other employment terms can be significantly worse than for full-time workers). Unions representing workers in both the private and public sector now seek to recruit, and retain in membership, part-time workers – and collective agreements have started to cover such workers in increasing numbers. (For a critical analysis of the Directive, see Jeffery, M., "'Not Really Going to Work?' Of the Directive on Part-Time Work, "Atypical Work and Attempts to Regulate It"' (1998) 27 ILJ 193.)

A Commission study in February 1999 indicated that State support measures for integrating part-time workers (both in the labour market and in society in general) vary greatly. In particular, it concluded, States' policies to enhance income and occupational welfare are very inconsistent. In the UK, part-time work will be supported by the end of 1999 by a variety of measures, including tax credits (replacing family credit and the disability working allowance), in-work benefits like income support and the jobseeker's allowance (for those working below the 16-hour threshold), and the national minimum wage. Both the EC Commission and the UK Government have indicated that further employment measures will follow.

The new provisions in ss. 19 to 21 of the Employment Relations Act 1999 are the first step in implementing this policy. The Government has confirmed that it is committed to implementing Directive 97/81 (largely by making regulations under these new enabling powers) by the end of 2000.

The power provided in s. 19(i) is wide-ranging. It simply says:

The Secretary of State *shall* make regulations for the purpose of securing that persons in part-time employment are treated, *for such purposes and to such extent as the regulations may specify*, no less favourably than persons in full-time employment. (emphasis added)

It clearly goes further than pay-related issues, which was why such legislation was considered necessary. This was because Directives made for the purposes of implementing the Framework Agreement cannot deal with 'pay'. UK policy, however, is to use regulation-making powers to supplement other measures in primary legislation, including the National Minimum Wage Act 1998 and the Tax Credits Act 1999. The Government has undertaken to publish draft regulations before they are made, and subject them to what may prove to be lengthy consultations.

There is provision in ss. 20 and 21 for Codes of Practice to be issued, and these will contain guidance for the purpose of eliminating discrimination, as well as facilitating flexible working and the organisation of working time. The Codes would be admissible in employment tribunal proceedings, and s. 20(4)(b) says that a Code 'shall be taken into account . . . in any case in which it appears to the tribunal to be relevant'. This could clearly become relevant in a range of proceedings, including unfair dismissal cases, where procedures have not been followed in a way which would have been applicable to full-time staff.

Current practice in many workplaces does indicate that practices on termination of part-time arrangements (and making other changes in conditions) may need to be extensively revised. Part-time staff can, in some workplaces, receive substantially worse treatment than their 'full-time' counterparts; and this can be at most stages of the employment relationship, from when they are recruited through to termination, dismissal or redundancy. When regulations are made under s. 19 employers may well need to ask their legal advisers to review their employment practices, from the recruitment stage through to termination.

C: Employee Status: A Question of Law or Fact?

1. Chung and 2. Shun Shing Lee v Construction & Engineering Co. Ltd
[1990] IRLR 236
Privy Council

LORD GRIFFITHS: Whether or not a person is employed under a contract of service is often said in the authorities to be a mixed question of fact and law. Exceptionally, if the relationship is dependent solely upon the true construction of a written document it is regarded as a question of law: see *Davies* v *Presbyterian Church of Wales* [1986] IRLR 194. But where, as in the present case, the relationship has to be determined by an investigation and evaluation of the factual circumstances in which the work is performed, it must now be taken to be firmly established that the question of whether or not the work was performed in the capacity of an employee or as an independent contractor is to be regarded by an appellate court as a question of fact to be determined by the trial court. At first sight it seems rather strange that this should be so, for whether or not a certain set of facts should be classified under one legal head rather than another would appear to be a question of law. However, no doubt because of the difficulty of devising a conclusive test to resolve the question and the threat of the appellate courts being crushed by the weight of appeals if the many borderline cases were considered to be questions of law, it was held in a series of decisions in the Court of Appeal and in the House of Lords under the English Workmen's Compensation Acts that a finding by a county court judge that a workman was, or was not, employed under a contract of service was a question of fact with which an appellate court could only interfere if there was no evidence to support his finding: see *Smith* v *General Motor Cab Company* [1911] AC 188, *Bobbey* v *Crosbie* [1915] 114 LT 244 and *Easdown* v *Cobb* [1940] 1 All ER 49. More recently, in *O'Kelly* v *Trusthouse Forte* [1983] IRLR 369 the Court of Appeal, despite a powerful dissenting judgment by Ackner LJ, held that whether or not a waiter was employed under a contract of employment within the meaning of the Employment Protection (Consolidation) Act 1978 was a question of mixed fact and law, and that the finding of an industrial tribunal on this issue, from which an appeal lay on a point of law only, could only be impugned if it could be shown that the tribunal correctly directing itself on the law could not reasonably have reached the conclusion under appeal. Lord Donaldson pointed out that this was a heavy burden on an appellant and concluded by saying: 'I would have thought that all this was trite law, but if it is not, it is set out with the greatest possible clarity in *Edwards* v *Bairstow* [1956] AC 14'.

In *Edwards* v *Bairstow* the question that fell to be decided was whether the General Commissioners were right in their finding that the respondents had not entered into 'an adventure in the nature of trade'. Whether or not persons have entered into 'an adventure in the nature of trade' is a decision of a like nature to whether or not a person is employed under a contract of service or, to state the question in modern language, under a contract of employment. The decision will depend upon the evaluation of many facts and there will be many borderline cases in which similarly instructed minds may come to different conclusions. It is in such situations that an appeal court must not interfere and it is in this sense that the decision is said to be one of fact. But an appellate court must not abdicate its responsibility and it is worth bearing in mind the works with which Lord Radcliffe concluded his speech in *Edwards* v *Bairstow* at pp. 38 and 39:

> I think it possible that the English courts have been led to be rather over-ready to treat these questions as 'pure questions of fact' by some observations of Warrington and Atkin LJJ. in *Cooper* v *Stubbs* [1925] 2 KB 753. If so, I would say, with very great respect, that I think it a pity that such a tendency should persist. As I see it, the reason why the courts do not interfere with commissioners' findings or determinations when they really do involve nothing but questions of fact is not any supposed advantage in the commissioners of greater experience in matters of business or any other matters. The reason is simply that by the system that has been set up the commissioners are the first tribunal to try an appeal, and in the interest of the efficient administration of justice their decisions can only be upset on appeal if they have been positively wrong in law. The court is not a second opinion, where there is reasonable ground for the first. But there is no reason to make a mystery about the subjects that commissioners deal with or to invite the courts to impose any exceptional restraints upon themselves because they are dealing with cases that arise out of facts found by commissioners. Their duty is no more than to examine those facts with a decent respect for the tribunal appealed from and if they think that the only reasonable conclusion on the facts found is inconsistent with the determination come to, to say so without more ado.

Note

See also *Clifford* v *Union of Democratic Mineworkers* [1991] IRLR 518, CA.

Question

If the question of employee status is held to be largely a question of fact, is there not a risk of inconsistency in outcome in cases involving similar facts?

D: Self-description

Young and Woods Ltd v *West*
[1980] IRLR 201
Court of Appeal

West, a sheet metal worker, requested that he be treated as self-employed. This was accepted by his employer and, although there was no difference between his working conditions and the 'employees' he worked alongside, doing the same job and under the same level of supervision, he was paid gross of tax. When West's job was terminated, he claimed that he was an employee after all and therefore entitled to claim unfair dismissal. The Court of Appeal held that, despite West's arrangement with his employer, he was really an employee and the industrial tribunal had jurisdiction to hear the complaint.

STEPHENSON LJ: Mr Clifford [counsel for the employer] has submitted that, though a party cannot alter the true relationship, if the parties genuinely and expressly intend to establish a person (on the employer's books) to do a job as a self-employed person, then he cannot make a claim as an employee for the purpose of getting compensation for unfair dismissal. Either, he says, the parties cannot resile from the position which they have deliberately and openly taken up in any circumstances or, if that is putting the matter too high, the presumption created by their deliberately and openly chosen relationship is rebuttable, but not easily rebuttable.

I am satisfied that the parties can resile from the position which they have deliberately and openly chosen to take up and that to reach any other conclusion would be, in effect, to permit the parties to contract out of the [Employment Rights] Act [1996] and to deprive, in particular, a person who works as an employee within the definition of the Act under a contract of service of the benefits which this statute confers upon him. If I consider the policy of the Act I can see the dangers, pointed out by Lord Justice Ackner in the course of the argument, of employers anxious to escape from their statutory liabilities under this legislation or the Factories Acts offering this choice to persons whom they intend to employ, as Mr West was employed, as employees within the definition of the Act and pressing them to take that employment – it may be even insisting upon their taking that employment – on the terms that it shall not be called that employment at all, but shall be called a contract for services with a self-employed person I, therefore, reject Mr Clifford's submission in its extreme form.

II Continuity of Employment

Even where part-time or casual workers could establish their status as employees, many were excluded from employment law protections either because they did not work sufficient hours per week, or because their employment was intermittent or of a short duration. Generally, the law required employees to have worked for the employer for at least 16 hours per week for a minimum of two calendar years before they could mount a claim for unfair dismissal or redundancy payments. Those who worked between 8 and 16 hours per week had to have five years' service in order to bring a complaint. Only in exceptional cases was no period of qualification required, e.g., dismissals relating to union membership and activities or to non-unionism and sex and race discrimination. Recent, EC inspired case law has brought about a dramatic change to the situation.

A: Continuity: Hours of Work

R v Secretary of State for Employment ex parte Equal Opportunities Commission and another
[1995] 1 AC 1
House of Lords

On 21 March 1990, the Equal Opportunities Commission (EOC) wrote to the Secretary of State for Employment referring to the provision of the EPCA 1978 concerning redundancy pay and compensation for unfair dismissal, and expressing the view that the hours thresholds for these rights constituted indirect discrimination against women employees, contrary to Community law. The EOC argued that, as nearly 90 per cent of employees working fewer than 16 hours are women, the statutory provisions were contrary to Article 119 (now 141) of the Treaty of Rome, which lays down the principle of equal pay for equal work; the 'Equal Pay' Directive (75/117/EEC), which provides further detail on the right to equal pay; and the 'Equal Treatment' Directive (76/207/EEC), which prohibits discrimination in working conditions, including the conditions governing dismissal.

On 23 April 1990, the Minister replied, stating that he did not accept that the legislation was in breach of EC law and had no plans to change the statutory thresholds. The EOC applied to the High Court for judicial review.

The High Court held that statutory redundancy pay and unfair dismissal compensation fell within the definition of pay under EC law, and that the provisions were indirectly discriminatory because of their adverse effect on women. However, it was held that the Government was able to justify the provisions on grounds of social policy. The Court accepted the Government's argument that to remove or reduce the hours threshold would place additional burdens on employers and lead to fewer job opportunities for those wishing to work less than 16 hours per week. The EOC's appeal against this decision was rejected by a majority of the Court of Appeal, on the grounds that the EOC did not have standing to bring proceedings against the Secretary of State and that judicial review was not the appropriate mechanism for determining whether the UK is in breach of EC law. In the Court's view what the EOC should do is support test cases in industrial tribunals. The House of Lords allowed the EOC's appeal. Having decided, *inter alia*, that the EOC had *locus standi* to bring the proceedings, their Lordships held that the hours threshold was not capable of objective justification.

LORD KEITH OF KINKEL: The original reason for the threshold provisions of the Act of 1978 appears to have been the view that part time workers were less committed than full time workers to the undertaking which employed them. In his letter of 23 April 1990 the Secretary of State stated that their purpose was to ensure that a fair balance was struck between the interests of employers and employees. These grounds are not now founded on as objective justification for the thresholds. It is now claimed that the thresholds have the effect that more part time employment is available than would be the case if employers were liable for redundancy pay and compensation for unfair dismissal to employees who worked for less than 8 hours a week or between 8 and 16 hours a week for under five years. It is contended that if employers were under that liability they would be inclined to employ less part time workers and more full time workers, to the disadvantage of the former.

The bringing about of an increase in the availability of part time work is properly to be regarded as a beneficial social policy aim and it cannot be said that it is not a necessary aim. The question is whether the threshold provisions of the Act of 1978 have been shown, by reference to objective factors, to be suitable and requisite for achieving that aim. As regards suitability for achieving the aim in question, it is to be noted that the purpose of the thresholds is said to be to reduce the costs to employers of employing part time workers. The same result, however, would follow from a situation where the basic rate of pay for part time workers was less than the basic rate for full time workers. No distinction in principle can properly be made between direct and indirect labour costs. While in certain circumstances an employer might be justified in paying full time workers a higher rate than part time workers in order to secure the more efficient use of his machinery (see *Jenkins* v *Kingsgate (Clothing Production) Ltd* [1981] ICR 715) that would be a special and limited state of affairs. Legislation which permitted a differential of that kind nationwide would present a very different aspect and considering that the great majority of part time workers are women would surely constitute a gross breach of the principle of equal pay and could not possibly be regarded as a suitable means of achieving an increase in part time employment. Similar considerations apply to legislation which reduces the indirect cost of employing part time labour. Then as to the threshold provisions being requisite to achieve the stated aim, the question is whether on the evidence before the Divisional Court they have been proved actually to result in greater availability of part time work than would be the case without them. In my opinion that question must be answered in the negative. The evidence for the Secretary of State consisted principally of an affidavit by an official in the Department of Employment which set out the views of the Department but did not contain anything capable of being regarded as factual evidence demonstrating the correctness of these views. One of the exhibits to the affidavit was a report with draft Directives prepared by the Social Affairs Commissioner of the European Commission in 1990. This covered a wide range of employment benefits and advantages, including redundancy pay and compensation for unfair dismissal, but proposed a qualifying threshold for those benefits of 8 hours of work per week. The basis for that was stated to be the elimination of disproportionate administrative costs and regard to employers economic needs. These are not the grounds of justification relied on by the Secretary of State. The evidence put in by the EOC consisted in large measure in a Report of the House of Commons Employment Committee in 1990 and a Report of the House of Lords Select Committee on the European Communities on Part-Time and Temporary Employment in 1990. These revealed a diversity of views upon the effect of the threshold provisions on part time work, employers' organisations being of the opinion that their removal would reduce the amount available with trade union representatives and some employers and academics in the industrial relations field taking the opposite view. It also appeared that no other member state of the European Community, apart from the Republic of Ireland, had legislation providing for similar thresholds. The Republic of Ireland, where statute at one time provided for an 18-hour per week threshold, had recently introduced legislation reducing this to 8 hours. In the Netherlands the proportion of the workforce in part time employment was in 1988 29.8 per cent and in Denmark 25.5 per cent, neither country having any thresholds similar to those in the Act of 1978. In France legislation was introduced in 1982 providing for part time workers to have the same rights as full time, yet between 1983 and 1988 part time work in that country increased by 36.6 per cent, compared with an increase of 26.1 per cent over the same period in the United Kingdom. While various explanations were suggested on behalf of the Secretary of State for these statistics, there is no means of ascertaining whether these explanations have any validity. The fact is, however, that the proportion of part time employees in the national workforce is much less than the proportion of full time employees, their weekly remuneration is necessarily much lower, and the number of them made redundant or unfairly dismissed in any year is not likely to be unduly large. The conclusion must be that no objective justification for the thresholds in the Act of 1978 has been established.

A subsidiary issue of substance in the appeal is whether or not compensation for unfair dismissal is 'pay' within the meaning of Article 119 [now 141] of the Treaty and the Equal Pay Directive. The definition of 'pay' in Article 119 [now 141] has been set out above. In *Arbeiterwohlfahrt der Stadt Berlin ev v Bötel* [1992] IRLR 423, at p. 425, the European Court of Justice said:

> 12. According to the case law of the court . . . the concept of 'pay' within the meaning of article 119 of the Treaty comprises any consideration whether in cash or in kind, whether immediate or future, provided that the employee receives it, albeit indirectly, in respect of his employment from his employer, whether under a contract of employment, legislative provisions or made ex gratia by the employer.

In *Barber* v *Guardian Royal Exchange Assurance Group* [1990] ICR 616 the Court held that redundancy pay was 'pay' within the meaning of Article 119 [now 141] on the ground (paragraph 18 of the judgment at p. 668) that receipt of it arose 'by reason of the existence of the employment relationship'. There is much to be said in favour of the view that compensation for unfair dismissal is of a comparable nature, but the European Court of Justice has not yet pronounced upon this issue, and there may be a question whether the answer to it can properly be held to be acte clair, or whether resolution of it would require a reference to the European Court under Article 177 [now 234] of the Treaty.

Such a reference is in any event, however, unnecessary for the disposal of the present appeal. Discrimination as regards the right to compensation for unfair dismissal, if not objectively justified, is clearly in contravention of the Equal Treatment Directive.

In the light of the foregoing I am of the opinion that the appeal by the EOC should be allowed and that declarations should be made in the following terms:

1.　That the provisions of the Employment Protection (Consolidation) Act 1978 whereby employees who work for fewer than sixteen hours per week are subject to different conditions in respect to qualification for redundancy pay from those which apply to employees who work for sixteen hours per week or more are incompatible with Article 119 [now 141] of the Treaty of Rome and the Council Directive 75/117/EEC of 10 February 1975.

2.　That the provisions of the Employment Protection (Consolidation) Act 1978 whereby employees who work for fewer than sixteen hours per week are subject to different conditions in respect of the right to compensation for unfair dismissal from those which apply to employees who work for sixteen hours per week or more are incompatible with the Council Directive 76/207/EEC of 9 February 1976.

It remains to note that the EOC proposed that the House should grant a declaration to the effect that the Secretary of State is in breach of those provisions of the Equal Treatment Directive which require Member States to introduce measures to abolish any laws contrary to the principle of equal treatment. The purpose of such a declaration was said to be to enable part time workers who were employed otherwise than by the State or an emanation of the State, and who had been deprived of the right to obtain compensation for unfair dismissal by the restrictive thresholds in the Act of 1978, to take proceedings against the United Kingdom for compensation, founding upon the decision of the European Court of Justice in *Francovich* v *Italian Republic* [1992] IRLR 84. In my opinion it would be quite inappropriate to make any such declaration. If there is any individual who believes that he or she has a good claim to compensation under the *Francovich* principle, it is the Attorney-General who would be defendant in any proceedings directed to enforcing it, and the issues raised would not necessarily be identical with any of those which arise in the present appeal.

Note

As a consequence of the above judgment, the Government was forced to introduce the Employment Protection (Part-time Employees) Regulations 1995, which came into force on 6 February 1995. The Regulations repeal various provisions of what was sch. 13 of EPCA 1978 so that periods of part-time service will now count in computing the employee's continous employment under the legislation. This ensured that employees working fewer than 16 hours per week had only to complete two years' service with their employer before they qualified for the right to claim unfair dismissal and redundancy pay.

The then Secretary of State, Michael Portillo MP, made it clear that, while accepting the Lords' decision, the Government remained committed to the view that the legislation must strike 'an appropriate balance between the rights of employees and the burdens on business which discourage job creation'. He therefore stated that the Government would carefully monitor the effects of the changes in order to assess their impact on business and employment opportunities, and would reconsider the position if any objective evidence of adverse effects emerged.

Nevertheless, the pressure from Europe is relentless, and this is spectacularly illustrated by the following case:

R v Secretary of State for Employment ex parte Seymour-Smith and Another
(Case C-167/97) [1999] IRLR 253
Court of Justice of the European Communities

Ms Seymour-Smith was employed by Christo and Co. from 1 February 1990 until her dismissal on 1 May 1991. Ms Perez was employed by Matthew Stone Restoration Ltd from 19 February 1990 until her dismissal on 25 May 1991. Both sought to complain to an employment tribunal that they had been unfairly dismissed, but they were unable to register their applications because they lacked the two years' continuous service required by what is now s. 94 of the Employment Rights Act (then the Employment Protection (Consolidation) Act).

They sought judicial review of the Unfair Dismissal (Variation of Qualifying Period) Order 1985, which increased the qualifying period from one year to two years. They claimed that the proportion of women who could comply with the two-year qualifying period is considerably smaller than the proportion of men, so as to amount to prima facie indirect sex discrimination against women. Therefore, they argued that the two-year qualifying period, unless justified, was contrary to the EC Equal Treatment Directive.

In 1985, 77.4% of men had two or more years of service at the requisite 16 hours or more per week with their current employer necessary to qualify to bring an unfair dismissal complaint, compared with 68.9% of women. Over the period from 1985 to 1991, the proportion of men who had two or more years of service at 16 hours or more per week with their current employer ranged from 72.0% to 77.4%. The proportion of women in this category ranged between 63.8% and 68.9%. The female percentage as a percentage of the male percentage averaged 89.1. In 1991, it was 90.5. It was accepted that the differences found in the impact of the requirement on the sexes were statistically significant, in that it could be said with confidence that they were due to social facts rather than to chance.

The applicants sought an order of certiorari to quash the 1985 Order. The Divisional Court [1994] IRLR 448 rejected the application. The Divisional Court held that even if the applicants could succeed on the merits, an order of certiorari would not be appropriate. In any event, the Divisional Court held that the applicants had failed to show that the effect of the two-year qualifying period prima facie discriminated against women, in that the proportion of qualifying women was not considerably smaller than the proportion of qualifying men. The Divisional Court went on to hold, however, that if adverse impact had been shown to have resulted from the two-year service requirement, the Secretary of State could not be held to have discharged the onus of establishing objective justification.

The applicants appealed, and were given leave to include a contention that the right to compensation for unfair dismissal constitutes 'pay' for the purposes of Article 119 [now 141] of the EC Treaty and that by making and maintaining in force the 1985 Order, the UK was in breach of its obligations under Article 119. The Secretary of State cross-appealed against the Divisional Court's conclusion that objective justification had not been established.

The Court of Appeal [1995] IRLR 464, allowing the appeal in part, held as follows:

— The applicants had standing to bring proceedings for judicial review relying on the Equal Treatment Directive to challenge the 1985 Order.

— The question whether compensation for unfair dismissal is 'pay' for the purpose of Article 119 [now 141] is not acte clair.

— The two-year qualification period had a disparate adverse impact on women which was incompatible with the principle of equal treatment enshrined in the Equal Treatment Directive. It had been demonstrated that for the period leading up to when the applicants sought to complain of unfair dismissal, there had been and continued to be a considerable and persistent difference between the numbers and percentages of men and women in the groups that did comply and the groups that did not comply with the two-year qualifying period.

— The Secretary of State had failed to establish objective justification for the discriminatory impact of the two-year qualifying period. There was no empirical evidence which enabled the inference to be drawn that the increase in the threshold period had led to an increase in employment opportunities.

— An order to quash the 1985 Order would be inappropriate. However, the applicants were entitled to a declaration that the two-year qualifying period was indirectly discriminatory at the time they were dismissed and that there was no objective justification for that discrimination.

The Secretary of State appealed against the grant of the declaration. The House of Lords (1997] IRLR 315 discharged the declaration made by the Court of Appeal and referred the following questions to the European Court of Justice:

1. Does an award of compensation for breach of the right not to be unfairly dismissed under national legislation such as the Employment Protection (Consolidation) Act 1978 constitute 'pay' within the meaning of Article 119 [now 141] of the EC Treaty?

2. If the answer to question 1 is 'yes', do the conditions determining whether a worker has the right not to be unfairly dismissed fall within the scope of Article 119 [now 141] or that of Directive 76/207?

3. What is the legal test for establishing whether a measure adopted by a Member State has such a degree of disparate effect as between men and women as to amount to indirect discrimination for the purposes of Article 119 [now 141] of the EC Treaty unless shown to be based upon objectively justified factors other than sex?

4. When must this legal test be applied to a measure adopted by a Member State? In particular at which of the following points in time, or at what other point in time, must it be applied to the measure:

(a) When the measure is adopted?

(b) When the measure is brought into force?

(c) When the employee is dismissed?

5. What are the legal conditions for establishing the objective justification, for the purposes of indirect discrimination under Article 119 [now 141], of a measure adopted by a Member State in pursuance of its social policy? In particular, what material need the Member State adduce in support of its grounds for justification?

DECISION: . . .

Question 1

By its first question, the national court is asking whether a judicial award of compensation for breach of the right not to be unfairly dismissed constitutes pay within the meaning of Article 119 [now 141] of the Treaty.

The applicants in the main proceedings and the Commission maintain that compensation awarded for unfair dismissal does constitute pay within the meaning of Article 119 [now 141] of the Treaty. According to the Commission, it is compensation for loss of earnings in terms of salary and other benefits connected with the employment.

The United Kingdom Government, on the other hand, argues that this case concerns allegedly unequal working conditions within the meaning of Directive 76/207, as regards specifically the right not to be unfairly dismissed. The compensation which an industrial tribunal might award does not constitute remuneration for work carried out by the employee but compensation for the employer's breach of a working condition. Consequently, the principal feature of pay, namely that it constitutes remuneration for work done, is absent in this case.

According to settled case law, the concept of pay, within the meaning of the second paragraph of Article 119 [now 141], comprises any other consideration, whether in cash or in kind, whether immediate or future, provided that the worker receives it, albeit indirectly, in respect of his employment from his employer (see, in particular, case 12/81 *Garland* v *British Rail Engineering* [1982] IRLR 111, paragraph 5, and case C-262/88 *Barber* [1990] IRLR 240, paragraph 12).

The Court has also held that the fact that certain benefits are paid after the termination of the employment relationship does not prevent them from being in the nature of pay, within the meaning of Article 119 [now 141] of the Treaty (*Barber*, cited above, paragraph 12).

As regards, in particular, the compensation granted by an employer to an employee on termination of his employment, the Court has already stated that such compensation is a form of deferred pay to which the worker is entitled by reason of his employment but which is paid to him on termination of the employment relationship with a view to enabling him to adjust to the new circumstances arising from such termination (see *Barber*, cited above, paragraph 13, and case C-33/89 *Kowalska* [1990] IRLR 447, paragraph 10).

In this case, the compensation awarded to an employee for unfair dismissal, which comprises a basic award and a compensatory award, is designed in particular to give the employee what he would have earned if the employer had not unlawfully terminated the employment relationship.

The basic award refers directly to the remuneration which the employee would have received had he not been dismissed. The compensatory award covers the loss sustained by him as a result of the dismissal, including any expenses reasonably incurred by him in consequence thereof and, subject to certain conditions, the loss of any benefit which he might reasonably be expected to have gained but for the dismissal.

It follows that compensation for unfair dismissal is paid to the employee by reason of his employment, which would have continued but for the unfair dismissal. That compensation therefore falls within the definition of pay for the purposes of Article 119 [now 141] of the Treaty.

The fact that the compensation at issue in the main proceedings is a judicial award made on the basis of the applicable legislation cannot, of itself, invalidate that conclusion. As the Court has already stated in this connection, it is irrelevant that the right to compensation, rather than deriving from the contract of employment is, for instance, a statutory right (see, to that effect, *Barber*, cited above, paragraph 16).

In the light of the foregoing, the answer to the first question must be that a judicial award of compensation for breach of the right not to be unfairly dismissed constitutes pay within the meaning of Article 119 [now 141] of the Treaty.

Question 2

By its second question the national court is asking, essentially, whether the conditions determining whether an employee is entitled, where he has been unfairly dismissed, to obtain reinstatement or re-engagement, or else compensation, fall within the scope of Article 119 [now 141] of the Treaty or that of Directive 76/207.

Since this case concerns pay falling within the scope of Article 119 [now 141], the applicants claim that Directive 76/207, concerning equal treatment, is inapplicable. The law cannot prevent an employee who is entitled to compensation for unfair dismissal as part of the right to equal pay under Article 119 [now 141] from relying on that provision to ensure that his employer does not apply to him discriminatory conditions which, if applied, would result in a denial of the principle of equal pay.

The United Kingdom Government maintains that even if the compensation awarded for breach of the right not to be unfairly dismissed were to be regarded as pay within the meaning of Article 119 [now 141], any alleged breach of the principle of equal treatment in the conditions determining enjoyment of the right, including financial compensation, must be governed by Directive 76/207 rather than by Article 119 [now 141].

In support of that argument, it relies on case 149/77 *Defrenne (No. 3)* [1978] ECR 1365, in which the Court held, at paragraph 21, that the fact that the fixing of certain working conditions may have pecuniary consequences is not sufficient to bring such conditions within the scope of Article 119 [now 141], which is based on the close connection which exists between the nature of the services provided and the amount of remuneration.

On that point it should be noted, as the Commission was right to point out, that where the claim is for compensation, the condition laid down by the disputed rule concerns access to a form of pay to which Article 119 [now 141] and Directive 75/117 apply.

In this case, the proceedings brought by Ms Seymour-Smith and Ms Perez before the industrial tribunal do not relate to the possible consequences of a working condition, namely the right not to be unfairly dismissed, but seek compensation as such, which is a matter falling under Article 119 [now 141] of the Treaty rather than Directive 76/207.

It would be otherwise if the dismissed employee were to seek reinstatement or re-engagement. In such a case, the conditions laid down by national law would concern working conditions or the right to take up employment and would therefore fall under Directive 76/207.

In the latter case, in the context of an application for judicial review of the variation of s. 64(1) of the 1978 Act by the 1985 Order brought against the Secretary of State for Employment, the applicants in the main proceedings would be entitled to object to discrimination on grounds of sex in reliance on Directive 76/207 rather than Article 119 [now 141] of the Treaty.

As the Court has consistently held, wherever the provisions of a Directive appear, as far as their subject-matter is concerned to be unconditional and sufficiently precise, those provisions may be relied upon by individuals against the State (see, in particular, case C-188/89 *Foster and others* [1990] IRLR 353, paragraph 16).

With regard to Article 5(1) of Directive 76/207, which prohibits any discrimination on grounds of sex with regard to working conditions, including the conditions governing dismissal, the Court has already held it to be sufficiently precise to be relied upon by an individual as against the State and applied by a national court in order to prevent the application of any national provision which is inconsistent with Article 5(1) (see case 152/84 *Marshall (No. 1)* [1986] IRLR 140, paragraphs 52 and 56).

Accordingly, the answer to the second question must be that the conditions determining whether an employee is entitled, where he has been unfairly dismissed, to obtain compensation fall within the scope of Article 119 [now 141] of the Treaty. However, the conditions determining whether an employee is entitled, where he has been unfairly dismissed, to obtain reinstatement or re-engagement fall within the scope of Directive 76/207.

Question 4

By its fourth question, which it is appropriate to answer at this stage, the national court asks essentially, whether the legality of a rule of the kind at issue must be assessed as at the time of its adoption, the time when it entered into force or the time when the employee is dismissed.

The applicants in the main proceedings maintain that, where there is an intrinsic risk that a measure to be adopted and/or brought into force by a Member State will have a disparate effect on pay as between men and women, that Member State will act in breach of the EC Treaty if it proceeds with that measure, unless its introduction can be shown to be based upon objectively justified factors unrelated to sex. Moreover, the Treaty requires Member States periodically to monitor measures which affect employees' pay and to disapply a measure if they find that any of the obligations imposed in that respect by the Treaty have been infringed.

The United Kingdom Government, however, considers that the correct time at which to consider the impact of the measure is the date of the employee's dismissal. That is the date at which the disputed rule produces the effect complained of by the employees, namely preventing them from making a complaint of unfair dismissal. The discriminatory or non-discriminatory character of a measure is not 'fixed' at the time of the enactment or introduction of a measure, but depends on the circumstances prevailing at the time of the effect complained of.

It should be noted at the outset that the requirements of Community law must be complied with at all relevant times, whether that is the time when the measure is adopted, when it is implemented or when it is applied to the case in point.

However, the point in time at which the legality of a rule of the kind at issue in this case is to be assessed by the national court may depend on various circumstances, both legal and factual.

Thus, where the authority which adopted the act is alleged to have acted ultra vires, the legality of that act must, in principle be assessed at the point in time at which it was adopted.

On the other hand, in circumstances involving the application to an individual situation of a national measure which was lawfully adopted, it may be appropriate to examine whether, at the time of its application, the measure is still in conformity with Community law.

With regard, in particular, to statistics, it may be appropriate to take into account not only the statistics available at the point in time at which the act was adopted, but also statistics compiled subsequently which are likely to provide an indication of its impact on men and on women.

Accordingly, the answer to the fourth question must be that it is for the national court, taking into account all the material legal and factual circumstances, to determine the point in time at which the legality of a rule of the kind at issue is to be assessed.

Question 3

By its third question, the national court seeks to ascertain the legal test for establishing whether a measure adopted by a Member State has disparate effect as between men and women to such a degree as to amount to indirect discrimination for the purposes of Article 119 [now 141] of the Treaty.

Article 119 [now 141] of the Treaty sets out the principle that men and women should receive equal pay for equal work. That principle excludes not only the application of provisions leading to direct sex discrimination, but also the application of provisions which maintain different treatment between men and women at work as a result of the application of criteria not based on sex where those differences of treatment are not attributable to objective factors unrelated to sex discrimination (see joined cases C-399/92, C-409/92, C-425/92, C-34/93, C-50/93 and C-78/93 *Helmig and others* [1994] IRLR 216, paragraph 20).

It is common ground that the disputed rule does not entail direct sex discrimination. It must therefore be considered whether the rule may constitute indirect discrimination incompatible with Article 119 [now 141] of the Treaty.

The applicants in the main proceedings maintain that where there is an intrinsic risk that a measure adopted by a Member State will have a disparate effect on pay as between men and women, and/or such disparate effect is actually demonstrated by reliable and significant statistics, Article 119 [now 141] of the EC Treaty is infringed unless that measure can be shown to be based upon objectively justified factors unrelated to sex.

In particular, they claim that where there are statistics which are significant, cover the entire workforce, and demonstrate long-term phenomena that cannot be explained as fortuitous, anything more than a minimal difference in impact would infringe the obligation to give effect to the principle of equal treatment.

According to the United Kingdom Government, the terms used by the Court in its case law on indirect discrimination clearly show that it has in mind a markedly different impact.

For its part, the Commission proposes a 'statistically significant' test, whereby statistics must form an adequate basis of comparison and the national court must ensure that they are not distorted by factors specific to the case. The existence of statistically significant evidence is enough to establish disproportionate impact and pass the onus to the author of the allegedly discriminatory measure.

As regards the establishment of indirect discrimination, the first question is whether a measure such as the rule at issue has a more unfavourable impact on women than on men.

Next, as the United Kingdom Government was right to point out, the best approach to the comparison of statistics is to consider, on the one hand, the respective proportions of men in the workforce able to satisfy the requirement of two years' employment under the disputed rule and of those unable to do so, and, on the other, to compare those proportions as regards women in the workforce. It is not sufficient to consider the number of persons affected, since that depends on the number of working people in the Member State as a whole as well as the percentages of men and women employed in that State.

As the Court has stated on several occasions, it must be ascertained whether the statistics available indicate that a considerably smaller percentage of women than men is able to satisfy the condition of two years' employment required by the disputed rule. That situation would be evidence of apparent sex discrimination unless the disputed rule were justified by objective factors unrelated to any discrimination based on sex.

That could also be the case if the statistical evidence revealed a lesser but persistent and relatively constant disparity over a long period between men and women who satisfy the requirement of two years' employment. It would, however, be for the national court to determine the conclusions to be drawn from such statistics.

It is also for the national court to assess whether the statistics concerning the situation of the workforce are valid and can be taken into account, that is to say, whether they cover enough individuals, whether they illustrate purely fortuitous or short-term phenomena, and whether, in general, they appear to be significant (see case C-127/92 *Enderby* [1993] IRLR 591, paragraph 17). It is, in particular, for the national court to establish whether, given the answer to the fourth question, the 1985 statistics concerning the respective percentages of men and women fulfilling the requirement of two years' employment under the disputed rule are relevant and sufficient for the purposes of resolving the case before it.

In this case, it appears from the order for reference that in 1985, the year in which the requirement of two years' employment was introduced, 77.4% of men and 68.9% of women fulfilled that condition.

Such statistics do not appear, on the face of it, to show that a considerably smaller percentage of women than men is able to fulfil the requirement imposed by the disputed rule.

Accordingly, the answer to the third question must be that in order to establish whether a measure adopted by a Member State has disparate effect as between men and women to such a degree as to amount to indirect discrimination for the purposes of Article 119 [now 141] of the Treaty, the national court must verify whether the statistics available indicate that a considerably smaller percentage of women than men is able to fulfil the requirement imposed by that measure. If that is the case, there is indirect sex discrimination, unless that measure is justified by objective factors unrelated to any discrimination based on sex.

Question 5
By its fifth question, the national court seeks to ascertain the legal criteria for establishing the objective justification, for the purposes of indirect discrimination under Article 119 [now 141] of the Treaty, of a measure adopted by a Member State in pursuance of its social policy.

In that respect, the first point to note is that it is ultimately for the national court, which has sole jurisdiction to assess the facts and interpret the national legislation, to determine whether and to what extent a legislative provision, which, though applying independently of the sex of the worker, actually affects a considerably higher percentage of women than men, is justified by objective reasons unrelated to any discrimination on grounds of sex (case 171/88 *Rinner-Kühn* [1989] IRLR 493, paragraph 15).

However, although in preliminary ruling proceedings it is for the national court to establish whether such objective factors exist in the particular case before it, the Court of Justice, which is called on to provide answers of use to the national court, may provide guidance based on the documents in the file and on the written and oral observations which have been submitted to it, in order to enable the national court to give judgment (case C-278/93 *Freers and Speckmann* [1996] ECR I-1165, paragraph 24).

It is settled case law that if a Member State is able to show that the measures chosen reflect a necessary aim of its social policy and are suitable and necessary for achieving that aim, the mere fact that the legislative provision affects far more women than men at work cannot be regarded as a breach of Article 119 [now 141] of the Treaty (see, in particular, case C-444/93 *Megner and Scheffel* v *Innungskrankenkasse Vorderpfalz* [1996] IRLR 236, paragraph 24, and *Freers and Speckmann*, cited above, paragraph 28).

In this case, the United Kingdom Government contends that the risk that the exposure of employers to proceedings for unfair dismissal brought by employees who had only fairly recently been engaged is a deterrent to recruitment, so that extension of the qualifying period for protection against dismissal would stimulate recruitment.

It cannot be disputed that the encouragement of recruitment constitutes a legitimate aim of social policy.

It must also be ascertained, in the light of all the relevant factors and taking into account the possibility of achieving the social policy aim in question by other means, whether such an aim appears to be unrelated to any discrimination based on sex and whether the disputed rule as a means to its achievement, is capable of advancing that aim.

In that connection, the United Kingdom Government maintains that a Member State should merely have to show that it was reasonably entitled to consider that the measure would advance a social policy aim. It relies to that end on case C-317/93 *Nolte* [1996] IRLR 225.

It is true that in paragraph 33 of the *Nolte* case the Court observed that, in choosing the measures capable of achieving the aims of their social and employment policy, the Member States have a broad margin of discretion.

However, although social policy is essentially a matter for the Member States under Community law as it stands, the fact remains that the broad margin of discretion available to the Member States in that connection cannot have the effect of frustrating the implementation of a fundamental principle of Community law such as that of equal pay for men and women.

Mere generalisations concerning the capacity of a specific measure to encourage recruitment are not enough to show that the aim of the disputed rule is unrelated to any discrimination based on sex nor to provide evidence on the basis of which it could reasonably be considered that the means chosen were suitable for achieving that aim.

Accordingly, the answer to the fifth question must be that if a considerably smaller percentage of women than men is capable of fulfilling the requirement of two years' employment imposed by the disputed rule, it is for the Member State, as the author of the allegedly discriminatory rule, to show that the said rule reflects a legitimate aim of its social policy, that that aim is unrelated to any discrimination based on sex, and that it could reasonably consider that the means chosen were suitable for attaining that aim.

. . .

Notes

1. In *Davidson v City Electrical Factors* [1998] IRLR 108, the EAT in Scotland held that employment tribunals should adjourn all unfair dismissal complaints from employees with between one year's and two years' service pending resolution of *Seymour-Smith* in order to preserve their position. This rightly rejects the practice of many tribunal regions which have listed such claims for hearing, or even dismissed them for want of jurisdiction.

Unfortunately, the ECJ's decision does not provide clear guidance as to how the case should be determined so as to allow the adjourned cases to be resolved. The crucial question for the House of Lords will be to determine whether the difference in the impact of the two-year qualifying period was sufficiently significant so as to establish discrimination against females. In this regard, the ECJ reiterated the established test of whether 'a considerably smaller percentage of women than men is able to satisfy the condition of two years' employment required by the disputed rule'. In 1985, when the qualifying period was increased, 77.4 per cent of males and 68.9 per cent of females could comply with the two-year rule. Interestingly, the Court offers the view: 'Such statistics do not appear, on the face of it, to show that a considerably smaller percentage of women than men is able to fulfil the requirement imposed . . .' If that view carries weight with the House of Lords then the applicants will lose. However, the ECJ offers an alternative test whereby sex discrimination can also be shown 'if the statistical evidence revealed a lesser but persistent and relatively constant disparity over a long period between men and women who satisfy the requirement of two years' employment'. On this basis, it could be argued that a disparate impact persisted from 1985 to 1991 when the applicants were dismissed, and has retained statistical significance ever since, even though the disparity has reduced during the 1990s.

2.   If the qualifying period, as applied to these employees, is ultimately held to contravene Article 141 (ex 119) then the applicants will be able to rely on this ruling against their private sector employers so as to circumvent the two-year threshold since, unlike a Directive, Article 141 (ex 119) has direct effect against all employers, whether in the public or private sector.

3.   Even if upheld, *Seymour-Smith* will not necessarily result in the removal of the two-year service threshold. The reason for this is that any declaratory relief may still be restricted to May 1991, and since that date the disparity between men and women who can meet the two-year qualifying period appears to have narrowed significantly. The implications are clear in the decision in *R v Secretary of State for Trade and Industry, ex parte Unison and others* [1996] IRLR 438, where it was held that the introduction of a two-year qualifying period, pursuant to reg. 8 of the Collective Redundancies and Transfer of Undertakings (Protection of Employment) (Amendment) Regulations 1995 (SI 1995/2587), for bringing an unfair dismissal claim in respect of a dismissal as a result of a transfer of an undertaking, was not unlawful because the available evidence for 1995 did not show a disparate adverse impact on women contrary to EC law.

4.   Note the ECJ's robust approach in rejection of the UK Government's argument in relation to justification.

5.   In the light of the *EOC* case and the possibility of the applicants ultimately being successful in *Seymour-Smith*, the complex issue is raised of retrospective complaints by those whose unfair dismissal and redundancy claims had been previously excluded by virtue of the hours thresholds and service qualification rules. In *Biggs* v *Somerset County Council* [1996] IRLR 203, CA, the applicant was seeking to challenge her dismissal which had taken place in August 1976. Because she worked only 14 hours (rather than the 21 hours then required), she lacked the relevant continuous service to bring an unfair dismissal claim under the law then in force. However, within three months of the decision of the House of Lords in *R v Secretary of State for Employment, ex parte EOC*, Mrs Biggs made a complaint to an industrial tribunal.

Upholding the decision of the EAT, the Court of Appeal held that the applicant could not argue that it was not reasonably practicable to have brought her claim in 1976. The decision of the House of Lords in the *EOC* case was declaratory of what the law has always been ever since the primacy of Community law was established by s. 2 of the European Communities Act 1972. When the applicant's employment came to an end in 1976, therefore, there was no legal impediment preventing someone who claimed to be unfairly dismissed from presenting a claim and contending that the restriction on claims by part-time workers was indirectly discriminatory, even though, at that time, the fact that UK legislation might have to yield to Community law was fully appreciated by only a comparatively small number of people.

Demonstrating an acute awareness of the policy considerations in this case, Neill LJ stated that it would be contrary to the principle of legal certainty to allow past transactions to be re-opened and limitation periods to be circumvented because the existing law at the relevant time had not been understood. (See also *Barber* v *Staffordshire County Council* [1996] IRLR 209, CA, for a similarly strict approach to retrospective claims).

6. The discriminatory effect of the service qualification will be reduced with the introduction of the requirement for one year's continuous service for unfair dismissal applicants (though it will remain at two years for redundancy payments claims). The period of continuous employment is relevant not only for determining whether an employee is *qualified* to make claim for unfair dismissal, redundancy payments, etc., but also for calculating the *amount* of compensation. The statutory provisions attempt to ensure that 'continuity' is preserved despite certain changes of employer and certain periods where the employee is away from work.

B: Continuity: Periods away from Work

Employment Rights Act 1996

212. Weeks counting in computing period
(1) Any week during the whole or part of which an employee's relations with his employer are governed by a contract of employment counts in computing the employee's period of employment.

(2) Any week (not within subsection (1)) during an employee's period of absence from work occasioned wholly or partly by pregnancy or childbirth after which the employee returns to work in accordance with section 79, or in pursuance of an offer described in section 96(3), counts in computing the employee's period of employment.

(3) Subject to subsection (4), any week (not within subsection (1)) during the whole or part of which an employee is—
(a) incapable of work in consequence of sickness or injury,
(b) absent from work on account of a temporary cessation of work,
(c) absent from work in circumstances such that, by arrangement or custom, he is regarded as continuing in the employment of his employer for any purpose, or
(d) absent from work wholly or partly because of pregnancy or childbirth, counts in computing the employee's period of employment.

(4) Not more than twenty-six weeks count under subsection (3)(a) or (subject to subsection (2)) subsection (3)(d) between any periods falling under subsection (1).

Ford v Warwickshire County Council
[1983] IRLR 126
House of Lords

Mrs Ford was a teacher who had been employed by the County Council under a series of consecutive short-term contracts, each for an academic year, for a total of eight years. There was, therefore, a break between the end of one contract and the beginning of the next. The House of Lords held that [what is now ERA 1996, s. 212(3)(b)] could apply in order to preserve the continuity of her employment and allow her claim for unfair dismissal and a redundancy payment to be heard.

LORD DIPLOCK: My Lords since [s. 212(3)] only applies to an interval of time between the coming to and end of one contract of employment and the beginning of a fresh contract of employment, the expression 'absent from work', where it appears in [ERA 1996, s. 212(3)(b), (c) and (d)], must mean not only that the employee is not doing any actual work for his employer but that there is no contract of employment subsisting between him and his employer that would entitle the latter to require him to do any work. So in this context the phrase 'the employee is absent from work on account of a temporary cessation of work' as descriptive of a period of time, as it would seem to me must refer to the interval between (1) the date on which the employee who would otherwise be continuing to work under an existing contract of employment is dismissed because for the time being his employer has no work for him to do, and (2) the date on which work for him to do having become again available, he is re-engaged under a fresh contract of employment to do it; and the words 'on account of a temporary cessation of work' refer to the reason why the employer dismissed the employee, and make it necessary to inquire what the reason for the dismissal was. The fact that the unavailability of work had been foreseen by the employer sufficiently far in advance to enable him to anticipate it by giving to the employee a notice to terminate his contract of employment that is of sufficient length to satisfy the requirements of [ERA 1996, s. 86] (which may be as long as 12 weeks), cannot alter the reason for the dismissal or prevent the absence from work following upon the expiry of the notice from being 'on account of a temporary cessation of work'.

. . .

My Lords, I am quite unable to be persuaded that [s. 212(3)] is *not* applicable to cases where a contract of employment for a fixed term has expired and upon expiry has not been renewed by the employer, in exactly the same way as it is applicable to contracts of employment of indefinite duration which are terminated by the employer by notice. One looks to see what was the reason for the employer's failure to renew the contract on the expiry of its fixed term and asks oneself the question: was that reason 'a temporary cessation of work', within the meaning of that phrase in [s. 212(3)(b)]?

. . .

From the fact that there is no work available for the employee to do for the employer during the whole of the interval between the end of one fixed-term contract of employment and the beginning of the next, and that this was the reason for his non-employment during that interval, it does not necessarily follow that the interval constitutes a '*temporary* cessation of work.' In harmony with what this House held in *Fitzgerald* v *Hall, Russell & Co. Ltd* [1970] AC 984, [s. 212(3)(b)], in cases of employment under a succession of fixed-term contracts of employment with intervals in between, requires one to look back from the date of the expiry of the fixed-term contract in respect of the non-renewal of which the employee's claim is made over the whole period during which the employee has been intermittently employed by the same employer, in order to see whether the interval between one fixed-term contract and the fixed-term contract that next preceded it was short in duration relative to the combined duration of those two fixed-term contracts during which work had continued; for the whole scheme of the Act appears to me to show that it is in the sense of 'transient', i.e. lasting only for a relatively short time, that the word 'temporary' is used in [ERA 1996, s. 212(3)(b)]. So, the continuity of employment for the purposes of the Act in relation to unfair dismissal and redundancy payments is not broken unless and until, looking backwards from the date of the expiry of the fixed term contract on which the employee's claim is based, there is to be found between one fixed-term contract and its immediate predecessor an interval that cannot be characterised as short relatively to the combined duration of the two fixed-term contracts. Whether it can be so characterised is a question of fact and degree and so is for decision by an Industrial Tribunal rather than by the Employment Appeal Tribunal or an appellate court of law.

. . .

In the instant case, however, it is conceded by the Council that each of the intervals between Mrs Ford's successive fixed-term contracts could properly be characterised as 'temporary'. I would therefore allow the appeal and remit Mrs Ford's claims to the Industrial Tribunal to decide such other matters, if any, as may remain in dispute between her and the Council.

My Lords, as I indicated at the outset, the length of successive fixed-term contracts on which part-time lecturers are employed and the intervals between them vary considerably with the particular course that the part-time lecturer is engaged to teach: so it by no means follows that a similar concession would be made or would be appropriate in each of their cases. It also follows from what I have said that successive periods of seasonal employment of other kinds under fixed-term contracts, such as employment in agriculture during harvest-time or in hotel work during the summer season will only qualify as continuous employment if the length of the period between two successive seasonal contracts is so short in comparison with the length of the season during which the employee is employed as properly to be regarded by the Industrial Tribunal as no more than a *temporary* cessation of work in the sense that I have indicated.

Note

This approach is undoubtedly of benefit to many workers, such as part-time or temporary teachers, and makes it much more difficult for employers to avoid the employment protection laws by offering a succession of fixed-term contracts. However, it may not be appropriate where patterns of employment are not regular, as they were in Ford's case, but are subject to fluctuation. To look only at a particular period of unemployment and to compare that period with the combination of the periods either side could lead to some unjust results. This issue was addressed by the Court of Appeal in the next case.

Flack v *Kodak Ltd*
[1986] IRLR 258
Court of Appeal

Mrs Flack had been employed by Kodak in their photo-finishing department over a number of years for periods which fluctuated markedly. Following her final dismissal, she and the other 'seasonal employees' claimed redundancy payments. An industrial tribunal, purporting to follow what Lord Diplock had said in *Ford* with regard to temporary cessation, rejected their claim. In coming to this conclusion, the tribunal confined itself to a purely mathematical comparison of the gap in employment falling within the two years preceding the final dismissal with the period of employment immediately before and after that gap. Both the EAT and the Court of Appeal thought that this was the wrong approach in the context of this particular case. They were of the view that the correct approach was to take into account all the relevant circumstances and, in particular, consider the length of the period of employment as a whole.

WOOLF LJ: Where the pattern of employment is a regular pattern of the type that existed in the *Ford* case, then it may be of little assistance to look at more than one period of dismissal. However, where the periods of dismissal are irregular, to look only at a particular period of dismissal and to compare that period with the combination of the periods either side, in the manner which was adopted by the Industrial Tribunal in this case, could lead to a wrong result.

The word 'temporary' in [s. 212(3)(b)] is not being used in the sense of something which is not permanent, since otherwise in every case where employment is resumed where there has been a dismissal on account of cessation of work, para. 9(1)(b) would apply. It is, as stated by Lord Diplock, being used in the sense of 'lasting only for a relatively short time'. (I myself would not use the word 'transient', however, I would stress the word *relatively*.)

What is a short time in one employment is not necessarily a short time in another employment. In deciding what is relatively a short time in a particular employment, it is now clearly established that it is necessary to look at the period of dismissal with hindsight – looking backwards as to the circumstances from the date of the final dismissal. In doing this, the period of dismissal relative to the period of employment is of the greatest importance. However, it is the whole period of employment which is relevant. In the case of irregular employment, if the periods of employment either side of the dismissal are only looked at, a most misleading comparison would be drawn.

Notes

1. It has been suggested that the 'mathematical approach' used in *Ford* should apply where the gaps in employment are regular, whereas the 'broad-brush' approach seen in *Flack* should be adopted where the pattern of employment is irregular (see *Sillars* v *Charrington Fuels Ltd* [1989] IRLR 152, CA).

2. Absence from work 'in circumstances such that, by arrangement or custom . . .' (ERA 1996, s. 212(3)(c)). It would appear that in order to fall within this provision, the arrangement or understanding must be established before or at the time the absence commences (see, for example, *Murphy* v *A. Birrell & Sons* [1978] IRLR 458; *Booth* v *United States of America* [1999] IRLR 16, EAT). The absences that might be encompassed could be leave of absence arrangements, employees placed upon a 'reserve list' to be called upon as necessary, and employees on secondment. A number of commentators argue that the EAT's broad application of the sub-paragraph in *Lloyds Bank Ltd* v *Secretary of State for Employment* [1979] IRLR 41 is no longer good law following the judgments of their Lordships in *Ford*. In the *Lloyds* case, the EAT held that where an employee works on a one week on and one week off basis, the weeks which she does not work count towards continuity by virtue of what is now s. 212(3)(c). In the *Lloyds* case a contract did exist throughout the period of employment. In the *Ford* case, the House of Lords placed considerable emphasis on the requirement that there be no subsisting contract before what is now s. 212(3) could operate. On that basis, the authority of the *Lloyds* case looks extremely suspect.

C: *Strikes and Lockouts*

Employment Rights Act 1996

216. Industrial disputes

(1) A week does not count under section 212 if during the week, or any part of the week, the employee takes part in a strike.

(2) The continuity of an employee's period of employment is not broken by a week which does not count under this Chapter (whether or not by virtue only of subsection (1)) if during the week, or any part of the week, the employee takes part in a strike; and the number of days which, for the purposes of section 211(3), fall within the intervening period is the number of days between the last working day before the strike and the day on which work was resumed.

(3) The continuity of an employee's period of employment is not broken by a week if during the week, or any part of the week, the employee is absent from work because of a lock-out by the employer; and the number of days which, for the purposes of section 211(3), fall within the intervening period is the number of days between the last working day before the lock-out and the day on which work was resumed.

Notes

1. The effect of s. 216 is that the period of the industrial dispute does not count towards continuity, but it does not break it.

2 For the rules governing continuity of employment on a change of employer, see Chapter 7.

III Constructing the Contract of Employment: Express Terms

Only in exceptional cases must the contract be in writing, e.g. contracts under the Merchant Shipping Act 1970, contracts of apprenticeship. However, since 1963 most employees have possessed the right to receive a written statement of some of the most important terms.

Employment Rights Act 1996

PART I EMPLOYMENT PARTICULARS

Right to statements of employment particulars

1. Statement of initial employment particulars

(1) Where an employee begins employment with an employer, the employer shall give to the employee a written statement of particulars of employment.

(2) The statement may (subject to section 2(4)) be given in instalments and (whether or not given in instalments) shall be given not later than two months after the beginning of the employment.

(3) The statement shall contain particulars of—
  (a) the names of the employer and employee,
  (b) the date when the employment began, and
  (c) the date on which the employee's period of continuous employment began (taking into account any employment with a previous employer which counts towards that period).

(4) The statement shall also contain particulars, as at a specified date not more than seven days before the statement (or the instalment containing them) is given, of—
  (a) the scale or rate of remuneration or the method of calculating remuneration,
  (b) the intervals at which remuneration is paid (that is, weekly, monthly or other specified intervals),
  (c) any terms and conditions relating to hours of work (including any terms and conditions relating to normal working hours),
  (d) any terms and conditions relating to any of the following—
    (i) entitlement to holidays, including public holidays, and holiday pay (the particulars given being sufficient to enable the employee's entitlement, including any entitlement to accrued holiday pay on the termination of employment, to be precisely calculated),
    (ii) incapacity for work due to sickness or injury, including any provision for sick pay, and
    (iii) pensions and pension schemes,
  (e) the length of notice which the employee is obliged to give and entitled to receive to terminate his contract of employment,
  (f) the title of the job which the employee is employed to do or a brief description of the work for which he is employed,
  (g) where the employment is not intended to be permanent, the period for which it is expected to continue or, if it is for a fixed term, the date when it is to end,
  (h) either the place of work or, where the employee is required or permitted to work at various places, an indication of that and of the address of the employer,
  (j) any collective agreements which directly affect the terms and conditions of the employment including, where the employer is not a party, the persons by whom they were made, and
  (k) where the employee is required to work outside the United Kingdom for a period of more than one month—
    (i) the period for which he is to work outside the United Kingdom,
    (ii) the currency in which remuneration is to be paid while he is working outside the United Kingdom,
    (iii) any additional remuneration payable to him, and any benefits to be provided to or in respect of him, by reason of his being required to work outside the United Kingdom, and
    (iv) any terms and conditions relating to his return to the United Kingdom.

(5) Subsection (4)(d)(iii) does not apply to an employee of a body or authority if—
  (a) the employee's pension rights depend on the terms of a pension scheme established under any provision contained in or having effect under any Act, and
  (b) any such provision requires the body or authority to give to a new employee information concerning the employee's pension rights or the determination of questions affecting those rights.

2. Statement of initial particulars: supplementary

(1) If, in the case of a statement under section 1, there are no particulars to be entered under any of the heads of paragraph (d) or (k) of subsection (4) of that section, or under any of the other paragraphs of subsection (3) or (4) of that section, that fact shall be stated.

(2) A statement under section 1 may refer the employee for particulars of any of the matters specified in subsection (4)(d)(ii) and (iii) of that section to the provisions of some other document which is reasonably accessible to the employee.

(3) A statement under section 1 may refer the employee for particulars of either of the matters specified in subsection (4)(e) of that section to the law or to the provisions of any collective agreement directly affecting the terms and conditions of the employment which is reasonably accessible to the employee.

(4) The particulars required by section 1(3) and (4)(a) to (c), (d)(i), (f) and (h) shall be included in a single document.

(5) Where before the end of the period of two months after the beginning of an employee's employment the employee is to begin to work outside the United Kingdom for a period of more than one month, the statement under section 1 shall be given to him not later than the time when he leaves the United Kingdom in order to begin so to work.

(6) A statement shall be given to a person under section 1 even if his employment ends before the end of the period within which the statement is required to be given.

3. Note about disciplinary procedures and pensions

(1) A statement under section 1 shall include a note—

(a) specifying any disciplinary rules applicable to the employee or referring the employee to the provisions of a document specifying such rules which is reasonably accessible to the employee,

(b) specifying (by description or otherwise)—

(i) a person to whom the employee can apply if dissatisfied with any disciplinary decision relating to him, and

(ii) a person to whom the employee can apply for the purpose of seeking redress of any grievance relating to his employment,

and the manner in which any such application should be made, and

(c) where there are further steps consequent on any such application, explaining those steps or referring to the provisions of a document explaining them which is reasonably accessible to the employee.

(2) Subsection (1) does not apply to rules, disciplinary decisions, grievances or procedures relating to health or safety at work.

(3) The note need not comply with the following provisions of subsection (1)—

(a) paragraph (a),

(b) in paragraph (b), sub-paragraph (i) and the words following subparagraph (ii) so far as relating to sub-paragraph (i), and

(c) paragraph (c),

if on the date when the employee's employment began the relevant number of employees was less than twenty.

(4) In subsection (3) 'the relevant number of employees', in relation to an employee, means the number of employees employed by his employer added to the number of employees employed by any associated employer.

(5) The note shall also state whether there is in force a contracting-out certificate (issued in accordance with Chapter I of Part III of the Pension Schemes Act 1993) stating that the employment is contracted-out employment (for the purposes of that Part of that Act).

Notes

1.   Prior to the passage of TURERA 1993, the statement had to be provided within 13 weeks of entering employment. An employee had to work for 16 hours or more a week in order to qualify unless he or she had been continuously employed for five years under a contract of employment requiring him or her to work eight hours or more per week. The adoption of the EC Directive on proof of an employment relationship (91/533) requires that 'essential aspects of the contract or employment relationship should be given to all employees, except where the Member State is able to justify excluding those working less than eight hours a week, or those who have been employed for less than a month, or those whose work is of a casual and/or specific nature'. The necessary information must be provided within two months of the beginning of the employment. In terms of the type of information which is required, in many areas UK law already went further than the Directive. But there were certain aspects where our law was lacking. TURERA 1993 was designed to comply with the Directive (see now ERA 1996, Part I).

2.   Under the TURERA 1993 amendments, employers have now to give the following information in addition to that already required:

(a)   the place of work;

(b)   where the employee is required (or permitted) to work in various places, an indication of that fact and the address of the employer;

(c)   any collective agreement which directly affects the terms and conditions of employment of the individual employee (including the identity of the parties by whom such collective agreements were made);

(d)   where the employment is not intended to be permanent, the period of the expected duration of the contract;

(e)   where the employee is to work outside the UK for a period of one month certain additional information.

The employers have to give this written statement no later than two calendar months after the beginning of employment. In addition, all employees are entitled to this as of right, unless their contract involves fewer than eight hours a week.

3.   Under the previous law, instead of giving a written statement of particulars in statutory form to each employee, the statement could merely refer the employee to some other document which the employee had reasonable opportunities of reading in the course of employment, or which was made reasonably accessible to the employee. Secondly, while any changes in terms had to be communicated to the employee within one month of the alteration, the employer could indicate that any future changes in the document to which the employee was referred would be made in that document within the permissible period.

TURERA 1993 tightened up the law in a number of important respects. It is no longer sufficient to refer employees to another document (e.g. a collective agreement) for details of their hours of work, pay or holiday entitlement. These must be given in the statement of terms itself. However, it is still permissible to refer the employee to other reasonably accessible documents for sickness and pension provisions, and to the law or a collective agreement for details regarding notice rights. It is also still possible to cross-refer in relation to disciplinary rules and procedures.

With these exceptions, all the other required particulars now have to be supplied directly to the employee. Previously, it is was not necessary for a written statement to be given if an employer gave a written contract or made a copy reasonably accessible, and the written contract might be scattered across a number of documents.

Some particulars must be set out in one document, known as the 'principal statement'. These particulars are the ones listed by the following provisions: s. 1(3); s. 1(4)(a)–(c), (d)(i), (f) and (h). The remaining particulars set out in s. 1 must be given to the employee, but can be given in instalments so long as this is done no later than two months after the start of the employment.

If there is a change to any of the terms about which particulars must be provided or referred to in the document, the employer now has to notify employees individually in writing. This notice must be given at the earliest opportunity, and, in any event, no later than one month after the change. Where the change results from the employee being required to work outside the UK for a period of more than one month, the change must be notified no later than the time the employee leaves the UK, if that is earlier. The statement of change may refer the employee to other reasonably accessible documents, or to the law or a collective agreement as appropriate, *but only in respect of changes to sickness, pension, notice and disciplinary provisions.*

4. By virtue of ERA 1996, s. 11, the employee can complain to an employment tribunal if he or she is provided with no statement at all, or an incomplete statement or a complete but inaccurate statement. The tribunal is empowered to determine what particulars ought to have been provided, or to amend inaccurate particulars (see *Mears v Safecar Security Ltd* [1982] IRLR 183, CA).

5. Given the weakness of the remedy it is not surprising that research has shown that many employers do not keep their employees informed in writing of their principal terms of employment (see Leighton, P., and Dumville, S., 'From Statement to Contract' (1977) 6 ILJ 133). Any new employee who successfully complained to an employment tribunal that he or she had not received the statutory statement may well have achieved a 'Pyrrhic' victory. The employer's response may have been to dismiss what he saw as an 'employment protection rip-off artist' who will have insufficient continuity to claim unfair dismissal. Fortunately, as a result of amendments introduced by TURERA 1993, it is automatically unfair to dismiss an employee for asserting a statutory right, including failure to supply written particulars (see ERA 1996, s. 104; discussed at p. 439).

6. The statement is not a contract itself.

Gascol Conversions Ltd v *Mercer*
[1974] IRLR 155
Court of Appeal

Mr Mercer was employed as a gas inspector. He worked a 54-hour week, calculated on the basis of 40 hours basic and 14 hours overtime. He was then asked to sign a document which was entitled 'Non-Staff Employees' Contract of Employment', which stated his normal working week to be 40 hours. When he was dismissed for redundancy, he claimed that his normal working week should have been 54 hours as opposed to the 40 hours which was used to calculate his compensation. The industrial tribunal and the National Industrial Relations Court (NIRC) supported Mercer's claim but the Court of Appeal allowed the employer's appeal.

LORD DENNING MR: . . . In February 1972 the Industrial Relations Act 1971 came into operation. By Schedule 2, Part II, the employer was bound to give to the employee a written statement specifying among other things 'any terms and conditions relating to hours of work (including any terms and conditions relating to normal working hours)'. In pursuance of that statutory obligation, the employers, Gascol Conversions Ltd, on 25.2.72 sent a new contract of employment to each of their men. One was sent to Mr Mercer. He sent it back signed on 21.3.72. He was given a copy of it for himself to keep. He agreed to it by a document in these terms which he signed himself

I confirm receipt of a new Contract of Employment dated 25.2.72 which sets out, as required under the Industrial Relations Act (1971), the terms and conditions of my employment.
Signed JW Mercer Date 21.3.72.

That was clearly a binding contract. Being reduced into writing, it is the sole evidence that is permissible of the contract and its terms. Turning to the terms themselves, the opening words are clear. They follow the very words of the national agreement:

The normal working week consists of 40 hours which shall be worked Monday to Friday, five days of eight hours, at times specified by the Department concerned.
Overtime: Employees will be expected to work overtime where necessary for completion of the conversion work. You will be paid at the rate of $1\frac{1}{2}$ times the basic hourly rate on week days, and at double time on Sundays.

That agreement seems to me to be conclusive. There is no possible ground for setting it aside. There was no mistake, misrepresentation or misunderstanding of any kind. It shows that the normal working week was 40 hours and the employers were not bound to provide any more. Even the employees were not bound to work more. They were only 'expected' to work extra hours when necessary.
. . .

In the Industrial Court, Sir Hugh Griffiths was more concerned about the written contract of March 1972. He spoke of it as 'a most formidable point'. But in the end, that Court held that 'the Tribunal was entitled to look, as it did, at the reality of the situation and to conclude that it was not intended by either party that the mutual obligation to provide and work 54 hours a week should be altered by the written contract of employment'. I am afraid that observation goes against the general law. It is well settled that where there is a written contract of employment, as there was here, and the parties have reduced it to writing, it is the writing which governs their relations. It is not permissible to say they intended something different.

I would only add this: it is a very great advantage to the men to have short working hours of 40 hours a week – on basic rates – with considerable overtime work – on overtime rates. It means a great increase in the take-home pay. It means also that they can take industrial action – by banning overtime – without thereby being in breach of their contracts of employment. Those conditions can carry however with them this disadvantage: when a man is made redundant, his redundancy payment is less because his normal working hours are only 40 hours. No doubt the union feel that the advantages outweigh the disadvantage. The men cannot have it both ways. Having committed themselves by written agreement to normal working hours of 40, they cannot go back on it.

Systems Floors (UK) Ltd v *Daniel*
[1982] ICR 54
Employment Appeal Tribunal

Mr Daniel commenced work for the employers in September 1979 as an agency worker. In November he requested to work directly for the employers and was told to start on 26 November. When he was provided with his statutory statement, this stated that his employment had commenced on 19 November. Mr Daniel signed for this, to acknowledge receipt. He was dismissed on 14 November 1980 and, when he made a claim for unfair dismissal, the question arose as to whether he had the requisite length of continuous service (at that time 52 weeks). The EAT held that the employer could adduce evidence to show that the commencement date expressed in the statutory statement was not the actual starting date.

BROWNE-WILKINSON J: The first issue is whether the industrial tribunal was right in holding the statement was a contract and fell within *Gascol Conversions Ltd* v *Mercer* [1974] ICR 420. The statement was served under the statutory provisions now included in [ERA 1996, Part I]. Under section [1(3)(b)], an employer is required, in a statement which must be served under that section, to specify the date when the employment began.

There is some authority as to the effect of the statutory particulars of the terms of employment. In *Turriff Construction Ltd* v *Bryant* [1967] 2 KIR 659, the Divisional Court had to consider for the purposes of redundancy payment what effect was to be given to the number of hours worked specified in a statutory statement. Speaking of the statutory predecessor of section 1 of the Act of 1978, Lord Parker CJ, giving the decision of the court, said, at p. 662:

It is, of course, quite clear that the statement made pursuant to section 4 of the Act of 1963 is not the contract; it is not even conclusive evidence of the terms of a contract.

Again, the Divisional Court in *Parkes Classic Confectionery Ltd* v *Ashcroft* (1971) 8 ITR 43 overruled the decision of an industrial tribunal which had held that where the terms of the contract of employment had been varied, but the employers had failed to serve particulars of the changes in the terms in accordance with what is now section 4 of the [Act of 1996], the employers were not entitled to rely on the varied contract. The Divisional Court held that notwithstanding the failure to serve the necessary statutory statement and notwithstanding that that might be a criminal offence, there was nothing in the Act to provide that a change of contractual terms should be ineffectual between the parties merely because the employer had failed to give written notice of the change.

It seems to us, therefore, that in general the status of the statutory statement is this. It provides very strong prima facie evidence of what were the terms of the contract between the parties, but does not constitute a written contract between the parties. Nor are the statements of the terms finally conclusive: at most, they place a heavy burden on the employer to show that the actual terms of contract are different from those which he has set out in the statutory statement.

Against that background we turn to consider the decision of the Court of Appeal in *Gascol Conversions Ltd v Mercer* [1974] ICR 420, which was the basis of the industrial tribunal's decision in this case. In that case there was an agreed variation in the terms on which the employees were engaged. When the Industrial Relations Act 1971 came into operation the employers became bound to give a written statement of particulars, and in pursuance of that obligation the employers sent a new contract of employment to each of their men. Each man was given a copy to keep, and he was required to sign a document in these terms: 'I confirm receipt of a new contract of employment dated February 25, 1972, which sets out, as required under the Industrial Relations Act 1971, the terms and conditions of my employment.' Mr Mercer signed such a document. The Court of Appeal held that in those circumstances the document constituted a binding written contract and that accordingly no evidence was admissible to show that the terms of the contract were otherwise.

In our view that case does not cover the present case. In that case Mr Mercer had signed a document which he confirmed was a new contract of employment and that it set out the terms and conditions of his employment. The Court of Appeal treated that as being a contract in writing, as indeed it was, having been signed by both parties. But in the case of an ordinary statutory statement served pursuant to the statutory obligation, the document is a unilateral one merely stating the employer's view of what those terms are. In the absence of an acknowledgment by the parties that the statement is itself a contract and that the terms are correct, such as that contained in the *Mercer* case, the statutory statement does not itself constitute a contract in writing.

In the present case, all that the employee did was to sign an acknowledgment that he had received the statement. In no sense did he sign it as a contract or acknowledge the accuracy of the terms in it. We, therefore, think that the industrial tribunal erred in law in treating the date of commencement mentioned in the statement as decisive because it was a contractual term. In our view the statement is no more than persuasive, though not conclusive, evidence of the date of commencement.

Notes

1. In *Gascol Conversions Ltd v Mercer* the written statement was actually described as the 'new contract of employment', so it was not simply a case of signing a receipt to say that the document had been received by the employee. If the latter was the case, it would not be so easy to construe it as a written contract.

This was the view taken by the EAT in *System Floors (UK) Ltd v Daniel*, which distinguished *Gascol* on the basis that it involved a signed contract of employment, whereas in the instant case Daniel was merely signing to acknowledge he had received the statement. The approach adopted by the EAT was subsequently adopted by the Court of Appeal in *Robertson* v *British Gas Corporation* [1983] ICR 351 (see below).

2.   While a statutory statement on its own cannot bring about a contractual variation, where the employee continues to work without protest under the changed terms, this may be held to amount to an implied agreement to the change. However, where the alleged variation is not one which has an immediate impact, like a change in pay or hours, it is asking too much of the 'ordinary employee to require him either to object to an erroneous statement of his terms of employment . . . or be taken to have assented to the variation' (per Browne-Wilkinson J in *Jones* v *Associated Tunnelling Co. Ltd* [1981] IRLR 477). (See also *Aparau* v *Iceland Frozen Foods plc* [1996] IRLR 119, an extract appears at p. 393.)

IV   Collective Bargaining

Trade Union and Labour Relations (Consolidation) Act 1992

Enforceability of collective agreements

179.   Whether agreement intended to be a legally enforceable contract
(1)   A collective agreement shall be conclusively presumed not to have been intended by the parties to be a legally enforceable contract unless the agreement—
(a)   is in writing, and
(b)   contains a provision which (however expressed) states that the parties intend that the agreement shall be a legally enforceable contract.
(2)   A collective agreement which does satisfy those conditions shall be conclusively presumed to have been intended by the parties to be a legally enforceable contract.
(3)   If a collective agreement is in writing and contains a provision which (however expressed) states that the parties intend that one or more parts of the agreement specified in that provision, but not the whole of the agreement, shall be a legally enforceable contract, then—
(a)   the specified part or parts shall be conclusively presumed to have been intended by the parties to be a legally enforceable contract, and
(b)   the remainder of the agreement shall be conclusively presumed not to have been intended by the parties to be such a contract.
(4)   A part of a collective agreement which by virtue of subsection (3)(b) is not a legally enforceable contract may be referred to for the purpose of interpreting a party of the agreement which is such a contract.

A: Methods of Incorporation

(i)   *Agency*

Burton Group Ltd v Smith
[1977] IRLR 361
Employment Appeal Tribunal

Mr Smith volunteered for redundancy under a scheme negotiated by his union and was due to leave sometime between October and December. On

24 October, the union and employer agreed that the terminations would take place on 26 December. Mr Smith died before he could be informed of the agreed date. His right to a redundancy payment depended on him being under notice of dismissal when he died. It was argued, on behalf of Mr Smith's personal representative, that the union received notice of his dismissal on his behalf as agent by agreeing the date with the employer. This contention was rejected by the EAT.

ARNOLD J: There is no reason at all why, in a particular case, union representatives should not be the agents of an employee to make a contract, or to receive a notice, or otherwise effect a binding transaction on his behalf. But that agency so to do does not stem from the mere fact that they are union representatives and that he is a member of the union; it must be supported in the particular case by the creation of some specific agency, and that can arise only if the evidence supports the conclusion that there was such an agency. It is sufficient to say that in this case there was no evidence before the tribunal of the existence of such an agency.

Note

For two cases which seem to approve the agency argument see *Singh* v *British Steel Corporation* [1974] IRLR 131 and *Land* v *West Yorkshire Metropolitan County Council* [1979] ICR 452. The decision in both cases is based on the premise that a worker who has resigned from union membership cannot be bound by a variation in terms which was collectively agreed subsequent to his or her resignation.

Question

What is the main disadvantage of basing incorporation of collective agreements on the concept of agency?

(ii)   Express Incorporation

National Coal Board v *Galley*
[1958] 1 WLR 16
Court of Appeal

In 1949, the defendant, a pit deputy, entered into a written contract of employment with the Board which provided that his wages should be 'regulated by such national agreement and county wages agreement for the time being in force and that this contract of service shall be subject to those agreements and to any other agreements relating to or in connection with or subsidiary to the wages agreement and to statutory provisions for the time being in force affecting the same'.

In 1952 revised national terms were agreed between the Board and the union. This agreement contained a clause that required pit deputies to work 'such days or part days in each week as may reasonably be required'.

In June 1956, Galley and other pit deputies at his colliery gave notice that they intended to ban Saturday working. The Court of Appeal held that Galley had broken his contract.

PEARCE LJ: The judge thought that, since one of the objects of NACODS [the union] was to negotiate the wages and conditions of all members and the defendant was a member of the local trade union which was itself a member of NACODS the defendant was individually bound by the NACODS agreement. But in any event, by the defendant's personal contract his wages were to be regulated by national agreements for the time being in force and the contract was to be subject to those agreements; and therefore, since the NACODS agreement was a national agreement, the defendant was bound by it. 'He has' continued the judge 'in fact accepted it and worked under it. He has taken the advantages of it and accepted the responsibilities of it for a period of some four years before this particular trouble arose. On the point that the agreement itself was not properly made, I think the complete answer would be that it is expressly admitted in the defence that the Coal Board, the plaintiffs, and the union did enter into an agreement which in fact contains the vital matters which are in dispute here'.

[Defendant's counsel] contends that the judge was wrong in holding that the defendant was personally bound by the NACODS agreement. If that point fell to be decided it might well be a matter of some difficulty. But, as the judge said, it is clear that the defendant's personal contract of service is regulated by the NACODS agreement, and the defendant by working on the terms of the NACODS agreement has entered into an agreement which contains the term now in dispute.

Robertson v *British Gas Corporation*
[1983] IRLR 302
Court of Appeal

In 1970, the offer letter to men appointed as meter readers/collectors stated that 'Incentive bonus scheme conditions will apply to meter reading and collecting work'. At this time, there was in existence a collective agreement made between the employers and the union which regulated the amounts payable under the bonus scheme. In 1977, the men received a s. 1 statement, which stated:

The provisions of the agreement of the National Joint Council for Gas Staffs relating to remuneration will apply to you. Any payment which may, from time to time, become due in respect of incentive bonuses will be calculated in accordance with the rules of the scheme in force at the time.

In 1981, the employers gave the union notice that they were terminating the bonus aspect of the agreement at the end of the year. Robertson and another successfully sued British Gas in the county court for the loss of what amounted to a third of their wages.

Before the Court of Appeal the employers argued that the men's contracts were to be found in the 1977 s. 1 statement, which on their understanding was to be interpreted as meaning that if there was no bonus scheme in force then no bonus was payable.

The Court of Appeal disagreed with the employers' interpretation of the 1977 statement but were of the view that, even if it were correct, the s. 1 statement could not be used as an interpretation of the 1970 letter which was the contract itself (approving the view of the status of the statement adopted in *System Floors (UK) Ltd* v *Daniel* – see above).

KERR LJ: It is true that collective agreements such as those in the present case create no legally enforceable obligation between the trade union and the employers. Either side can withdraw. But their terms are in this case incorporated into the individual contracts of employment, and it is only if and when those terms are varied collectively by agreement that the individual contracts of employment will also be varied. If the collective scheme is not varied by agreement, but by some unilateral abrogation or withdrawal or variation to which the other side does not agree, then it seems to me that the individual contracts of employment remain unaffected. This is another way of saying that the terms of the individual contracts are in part to be found in the agreed collective agreements as they exist from time to time, and, if these cease to exist as collective agreements, then the terms, unless expressly varied between the individual and the employer, will remain as they were by reference to the last agreed collective agreement incorporated into the individual contracts.

Notes

1.   For a similar approach, see *Gibbons* v *Associated British Ports* [1985] IRLR 376 and *Whent* v *T. Cartledge Ltd* [1997] IRLR 153, EAT.

2.   The question of incorporation is not always so straightforward and, as Wedderburn has observed, 'if a term of a collective agreement is incorporated into the employment contract with legal effect, it may still profit the worker nothing if, on its proper construction, the employer is entitled unilaterally to deprive him of its benefit' (*The Worker and The Law*, 3rd edn, p. 336). This observation was prompted by the next case.

Cadoux v *Central Regional Council*
[1986] IRLR 131
Court of Session

Mr Cadoux's letter of appointment stated that: 'The post is subject to the Conditions of service laid down by the National Joint Council for Local Authorities' Administrative, Professional, Technical and Clerical Services (Scottish Council) and as supplemented by the Authorities' Rules and as amended from time to time'. These rules provided Mr Cadoux with a non-contributory life assurance scheme. Subsequently, however, the employers unilaterally withdrew the scheme.

The Scottish Court of Session dismissed Mr Cadoux's claim for breach of contract.

LORD ROSS: In my opinion, the reference to the authorities' rules as amended from time to time shows that it was in the contemplation of the parties that the defenders' rules might be altered. The rules contain no express provision regarding amendment, and the clear inference from the fact that they are the defenders' rules is that the defenders have power to alter them, the only obligation being to enter the amendments in the rules or otherwise record them for the pursuer to refer to within a stipulated period.

Notes

1.   *Robertson* was distinguished on the basis that, in that case, a collective agreement had been made between an employer and a trade union, whereas in *Cadoux* there was no agreement but merely 'local arrangements entered into after consultation'.

2. The *Cadoux* decision has been subject to the following criticisms by Napier:

B. Napier, 'Incorporation of Collective Agreements' (1986) 15 ILJ 52, p. 53

Two comments can be made about this disposal of the issue. In the first place it would appear to run quite contrary to the general position in contract law, which does not allow there to be departure by unilateral act from an entitlement which has acquired contractual status. An employer cannot, for example, alter rates of pay once these have acquired contractual status – even if these rates of pay were introduced by his unilateral act in the first place. It is, with respect, not convincing to reply to this point by stating that here it was within the contemplation of the parties that the defender's rules might be changed at his will. Such a finding is inherently incompatible with the earlier determination that there was a contractual right to receive non-contributory life assurance. It is a strange variety of contractual obligation under which one party remains free to alter or cancel altogether any part of his indebtedness to another. The very idea of obligation is opposed to the notion that one party has complete licence to behave as he likes, and any assertion to the contrary is open to the charge of empty conceptualism.

The second comment relates to the reason used by Lord Ross to support his conclusion on this point. The fact that the life assurance scheme was not founded in any 'agreement' between the employer and the trade union but only in consultations, meant that no collective agreement could be identified here, and decisions such as *Robertson* v *British Gas Corporation* [1982] ICR 351, taking a restrictive view of the employer's power to alter the contract by unilateral declaration, distinguished. By pursuing this line of argument, however, Lord Ross has arguably taken the same approach as Lord Denning did in *Gascol* v *Mercer* [1974] IRLR 155 in that he too has made a link between questions of substantive rights within the employment relationship and the legal nature of the source from which incorporation is alleged to proceed. Why should it make any difference to the employee's position in law that the contractual entitlement to life assurance arose following consultation and not agreement with the trade union? Yet such is the substance of Lord Ross's reasoning. It is respectfully submitted that, whether or not this reasoning is properly classified as a restatement of the heresies to be found in *Gascol Ltd* v *Mercer*, it is unwelcome on policy grounds and should not be followed.

Notes
1. See *Airlie* v *City of Edinburgh District Council* [1996] IRLR 516, where the Scottish EAT adopted similar reasoning to that utilised in *Cadoux*.
2. The Court of Appeal's reasoning in the next case is in line with the approach advocated by Napier.

Marley v *Forward Trust Ltd*
[1986] IRLR 369
Court of Appeal

Marley's contract of employment with Forward Trust Group Ltd expressly incorporated the terms of a collective agreement which had been negotiated with the trade union, ASTMS, and was subject to modifications to that agreement. There had always been a 'mobility clause' in his contract of employment which obliged him to work in any department of the company to which he might be posted.

Early in 1983, the union negotiated an amendment to the collective agreement which introduced certain provisions as to redundancy. These provided that, in the event of redundancy, employees who were offered significant changes to the terms of their employment such as location would have the right to a six-month trial period. If at the end of this trial period, they rejected the job, their right to an agreed scheme of redundancy payments would be preserved.

At the end of 1983, the employer, faced with redundancies, closed the Bristol office where Marley was employed and he was transferred to London. Marley, having tried the job, was unhappy and decided to leave and claim under the redundancy agreement. The company resisted his claim because in their view he had been transferred under the mobility clause and not under the redundancy agreement. Further, the redundancy clause did not have the force of law because the collective agreement was expressed to be 'binding in honour only'. This argument was accepted by both the industrial tribunal and EAT.

The Court of Appeal allowed Marley's appeal and remitted the case to the industrial tribunal.

LAWTON LJ: There has been a long judicial history to the problem of incorporation of the terms of collective agreements into contracts of personal service. The judicial history goes back to the days when there were arguments as to whether collective agreements were enforceable in law. All that line of argument has now been rendered otiose by the provisions of s. 18 of the Trade Union and Labour Relations Act 1974 as amended by subsequent Acts [see now TULR(C)A 1992, s. 179]. No collective agreement now is enforceable as between the parties to it save in special circumstances and in ways specifically agreed by the parties. So there was not much point, as Mr McMullen has pointed out, in the union putting in clause 11 when they negotiated this collective agreement with the respondents. But, since 1974, the courts on a number of occasions have had to consider whether, when there is an unenforceable collective agreement incorporated into a contract of personal service, the terms of it, or some of them, can be incorporated into that contract of personal service. We found it unnecessary to go into all the cases because, as recently as 1983, this Court considered the problem in *Robertson v British Gas Corporation* [1983] IRLR 302. This Court decided that such terms can be incorporated into contracts of personal service and, when they are so incorporated, they are enforceable.

(iii)   Incorporation by Conduct

This is sometimes called implied incorporation or, in the words of Kahn-Freund, 'crystallised custom', and will operate where, in the absence of express agreement, collectively bargained terms and conditions are uniformly observed for a group of workers of which the employer is a member.

B: Inappropriateness of Collective Terms

On occasion, the question arises as to whether certain terms of a collective agreement are appropriate for inclusion in the individual contract of employment. This is very much a 'grey' area, compounded by the fact that the courts have never developed a test for what makes a particular clause 'appropriate'. The most that can be said is that much will depend on whether the particular clause is seen as relating to collective rather than individual relationships, such as union recognition (*Gallagher* v *The Post Office* [1970] 3 All ER 712), or redundancy planning (*British Leyland (UK) Ltd* v *McQuilken* [1978] IRLR 245) or dispute resolution (*National Coal Board* v *National Union of Mineworkers* [1986] IRLR 439).

Alexander v *Standard Telephone & Cables Ltd (No. 2)*
[1991] IRLR 286
Queen's Bench Division

The plaintiff employees were seeking to rely on seniority provisions in the redundancy procedure of the relevant collective agreement, which they said had been breached by their employers when dismissing them. On an application for an interim injunction, the High Court – assuming a breach of contract – had refused to grant the order on the basis that trust and confidence had broken down. Subsequently, the plaintiffs brought an action for damages for breach of contract. Their actions failed because Hobhouse J held that the redundancy procedure was not incorporated into their individual contracts of employment. Their statement of terms and conditions clearly referred to the collective agreement, but it was held that this particular part of the agreement was inappropriate for incorporation, thus remaining in the collective sphere and therefore unenforceable.

HOBHOUSE J: In the case *National Coal Board* v *National Union of Mineworkers* [1986] IRLR 439, to which some individual employees were also parties, Mr Justice Scott reviewed the authorities on incorporation at pp. 453 and following. In that case there was an express provision in the individual contracts of employment that the employees' 'wages and conditions of service shall be regulated by and subject to such national, district and pit agreements as are for the time being in force'. The question was the application of that clear contractual intent: the question in the action therefore was: what was the extent of the resultant incorporation? He drew a distinction which was derived from the argument of Mr Dehn before him, at p. 454 (151).

He seeks, however, to draw a distinction between the terms of a collective agreement which are of their nature apt to become enforceable terms of an individual's contract of employment and terms which are of their nature inapt to become enforceable by individuals. Terms of collective agreements fixing rates of pay, or hours of work, would obviously fall into the first category. Terms . . . dismissing an employee also would fall into the first category. But conciliation agreements setting up machinery designed to resolve by discussions between employers' representatives and union representatives, or by arbitral proceedings, questions arising within the industry, fall, submitted Mr Dehn, firmly in the second category. The terms of conciliation schemes are not intended to become contractually enforceable by individual workers whether or not referred into the individual contracts of employment.

. . .

A collective agreement between an employer and a union providing machinery for collective bargaining and for resolving industrial disputes may be of very great importance to each and every worker in the industry. But it is not likely to be an agreement intended to be legally enforceable as between employer and union, and it is almost inconceivable to my mind that it could have been intended to become legally enforceable at the suit of an individual worker. In the procedures laid down by the 1946 Scheme, for instance, no part is played by an individual mineworker. The machinery is designed to be invoked and operated either by the NCB or by the NUM with the co-operation of the other. It simply does not lend itself at all to enforceability at the suit of an individual mineworker.

Therefore, even in a case which involved wide express words of incorporation the court considered it necessary to look at the content and character of the relevant parts of the collective agreement in order to decide whether or not they were incorporated into the individual contracts of employment.

The principles to be applied can therefore be summarised. The relevant contract is that between the individual employee and his employer; it is the contractual intention of those two parties which must be ascertained. In so far as that intention is to be found in a written document, that document must be construed on ordinary contractual principles. In so far as there is no such document or that document is not complete or conclusive, their contractual intention has to be ascertained by inference from the other available material including collective agreements. The fact that another document is not itself contractual does not prevent it from being incorporated into the contract if that intention is shown as between the employer and the individual employee. Where a document is expressly incorporated by general words it is still necessary to consider, in conjunction with the words of incorporation, whether any particular part of that document is apt to be a term of the contract; if it is inapt, the correct construction of the contract may be that it is not a term of the contract. Where it is not a case of express incorporation, but a matter of inferring the contractual intent, the character of the document and the relevant part of it and whether it is apt to form part of the individual contract is central to the decision whether or not the inference should be drawn.

In the present cases I have concluded that the wording of the only document directly applicable to the individual plaintiffs, the statutory statements, is not sufficient to effect an express incorporation of the provisions relating to redundancy in the collective agreements: accordingly it is a matter of considering whether or not to *infer* that the selection procedures and the principle of seniority have been incorporated into the individual contracts of employment and this has to be decided having regard to the evidence given and an evaluation of the character of the relevant provisions in the collective agreements.

Note

The judge went on to hold that there could be no inference that the redundancy selection clause was intended to form part of the individual contract because the clause happened to be situated in an agreement containing other provisions incapable of incorporation, i.e. statements of policy.

Do you agree with the judge's reasoning? As Rubenstein observes:

It requires no great expertise to appreciate that some terms of collective agreements are suitable for incorporation and others are not. That much of a given collective agreement is not apt to be incorporated into individual contracts is the starting point for legal analysis, we would submit, not the finish line. I doubt whether there are many labour lawyers reading this commentary who, if called upon to advise the firm, would not have recommended that the wording of the redundancy selection clause should be qualified by reference to additional criteria if avoiding enforceability was intended (and that is just what the employers subsequently did). ('Highlights', [1991] IRLR 282)

(Cf. Anderson v Pringle of Scotland [1997] IRLR 208.)

C: 'No-Strike Clauses'

Trade Union and Labour Relations (Consolidation) Act 1992

180. Effect of provisions restricting right to take industrial action

(1) Any terms of a collective agreement which prohibit or restrict the right of workers to engage in a strike or other industrial action, or have the effect of prohibiting or restricting that right, shall not form part of any contract between a worker and the person for whom he works unless the following conditions are met.

(2) The conditions are that the collective agreement—

(a) is in writing,

(b) contains a provision expressly stating that those terms shall or may be incorporated in such a contract,

(c) is reasonably accessible at his place of work to the worker to whom it applies and is available for him to consult during working hours, and

(d) is one where each trade union which is a party to the agreement is an independent trade union;

and that the contract with the worker expressly or impliedly incorporates those terms in the contract.

(3) The above provisions have effect notwithstanding anything in section 179 and notwithstanding any provision to the contrary in any agreement (including a collective agreement or a contract with any worker).

V Constructing the Contract of Employment: Implied Terms

A: Subjective or Objective Tests

Although an increasing role has been played by statutory obligations which cannot be contracted out of by the employer, the common law implied terms of employment are still of considerable importance.

The judges of the common law laid down two, or probably one combined, test/s to determine whether a term should be implied into the contract. These tests allow the court to imply a term 'of which it can be predicated that "it goes without saying", some term not expressed but necessary to give to the transaction such business efficacy as the parties must have intended' (per Lord Wright in *Luxor (Eastbourne) Ltd v Cooper* [1941] AC 108, at p. 137).

This subjective basis for implication always had an air of unreality about it, given, as Kahn-Freund has observed. 'It is . . . sheer utopia to postulate a common interest in the substance of labour relations' (*Labour and the Law*, 3rd edn, 1983, p. 28). Also, as we shall see, the courts have long been willing to hold that at common law there are certain terms which will be implied to most if not all employments, not on the basis of the intention of the parties but because they were a 'necessary condition of the relation of master and man' (per Viscount Simonds in *Lister* v *Ramford Ice Co.* [1957] AC 555, at p. 576). Lastly, in recent years we have witnessed a distinct shift away from a subjective test as the basis for incorporation towards an objective test which questions whether it is 'necessary' to imply a term.

Mears v *Safecar Security Ltd*
[1982] 2 All ER 865
Court of Appeal

Other aspects of this case are discussed at p. 118.

STEPHENSON LJ: I am of the opinion that when, in exercising its statutory jurisdiction under [ERA 1996, s. 12] an industrial tribunal has to imply and insert missing terms, it is not tied to the requirements of the test propounded by Lord Justice Scrutton, a test for commercial contracts which goes back to *The Moorcock* (1889) 14 Probate Division 64 but can and should consider all the facts and circumstances of the relationship between the employer and employee concerned, including the way in which they had worked the particular contact of employment since it was made in order to imply and determine the missing term which ought to have been particularised by the employer and so to complete the contract.

. . . We can treat as an agreed term a term which would not have been at once assented to by both parties at the time when they made the contract, e.g. where one party would at once have assented to it and the other would have done so after it had been made clear to him that unless he did so there would be no contract – which is, I think, this case.

B: Factual Implied Terms: Some Examples

Jones v *Associated Tunnelling Co. Ltd*
[1981] IRLR 477
Employment Appeal Tribunal

The respondent firm were contractors. For many years, part of their work consisted of doing specialist tunnelling and bunkering work at National Coal Board collieries. Mr Jones was first employed by the respondents in December 1964 to work on a contract at Chatterley Whitfield Colliery, which was about two miles from his home. He was sent a statement of the terms and conditions of employment. The only reference to his place of employment was the word 'Chatterley'. In 1969, Mr Jones ceased working at Chatterley and started to work at Hem Heath Colliery, some 12 to 13 miles from his home. In October 1973, he was issued with a fresh statement of terms and conditions. This stated that he was to work 'at Hem Heath Colliery or such place or places in the UK the employers may decide from time to time'. A further statement was issued in April 1976. This stipulated: 'You may be required to transfer from one site to another on the instruction of the Employer.'

In March 1980, the respondents' contract with the National Coal Board at Hem Heath Colliery came to an end. The employers told Mr Jones that they had work available for him on the construction of a bunker at Florence Colliery. This colliery was very close to Hem Heath Colliery and equally accessible to Mr Jones's home. Mr Jones, however, did not accept this work. Instead he obtained employment with the NCB and claimed a redundancy payment from the respondents.

An industrial tribunal held that the employers were entitled under the contract to require Mr Jones to work at the Florence Colliery and to do bunkering work. Accordingly, there had been no breach of contract by the employers and Mr Jones had not been dismissed in law.

Jones's appeal to the EAT was unsuccessful, although the EAT's grounds for rejection were not the same as the tribunal's.

BROWNE-WILKINSON J: The starting point must be that a contract of employment cannot simply be silent on the place of work: if there is no express term, there must be either some rule of law that in *all* contracts of employment the employer is (or alternatively is not) entitled to transfer the employee from his original place of work or some term regulating the matter must be implied into each contract. We know of no rule of law laying down the position in relation to all contracts of employment, nor do we think it either desirable or possible to lay down a single rule. It is impossible to conceive of any fixed rule which will be equally appropriate to the case of, say, an employee of a touring repertory theatre and the librarian of the British Museum. Therefore, the position must be regulated by the express or implied agreement of the parties in each case. In order to give the contract business efficacy, it is necessary to imply *some* term into each contract of employment.

The term to be implied must depend on the circumstances of each case. The authorities show that it may be relevant to consider the nature of the employer's business, whether or not the employee has in fact been moved during the employment, what the employee was told when he was employed, and whether there is any provision made to cover the employee's expenses when working away from daily reach of his home. These are only examples; all the circumstances of each case have to be considered: see *O'Brien* v *Associated Fire Alarms Ltd* [1969] 1 All ER 93; *Stevenson* v *Teesside Bridge and Engineering Ltd* [1971] 1 All ER 296; *Times Newspapers* v *Bartlett* (1976) 11 ITR 106.

Looking at the circumstances of this case, what would the parties have said had an officious bystander asked them 'At what sites can Mr Jones be asked to work?'. The employers might have replied 'Anywhere in the United Kingdom'. But the industrial tribunal's findings indicate that Mr Jones, as one would expect, would have objected to being transferred anywhere outside daily reach of his home. The employers were in business as contractors working at different sites; so the parties must have envisaged a degree of mobility. In 1969, Mr Jones himself was moved from his original place of work to Hem Heath Colliery without objection. All the statements of terms and conditions subsequently issued contain mobility clauses, albeit in varying terms. From these factors we think that the plain inference is that the employers were to have *some* power to move Mr Jones's place of work and that the reasonable term to imply (as the lowest common denominator of what the parties would have agreed if asked) is a power to direct Mr Jones to work at any place within reasonable daily reach of Mr Jones's home. Such a term would permit Mr Jones to be required to work at Florence Colliery . . .

... [I]t is essential to imply *some* term into the contract in order to give the contract business efficacy: there must be some term laying down the place of work. In such a case, it seems to us that there is no alternative but for the tribunal or court to imply a term which the parties, if reasonable, would probably have agreed if they had directed their minds to the problem. Such a term will not vary the express contractual terms. This view is supported by the very many cases in which the courts have decided what terms as to mobility ought to be included in a contract of employment ...

Note

The EAT had reservations regarding the industrial tribunal's alternative conclusion that, by failing to object to the new statement of terms and conditions in 1973 and 1976 (which both provided for mobility between sites), Jones had assented to a variation in the terms of his employment. (For further reference to this aspect of the case, see p. 87 note 2.)

Courtaulds Northern Spinning Ltd v *Sibson*
[1988] IRLR 276
Court of Appeal

There was no express term in the contract as to the employee's place of work or the employer's right of transfer. The employee, an HGV driver, resigned and claimed constructive dismissal after he was required to move to another depot following a union membership dispute. An industrial tribunal held that any right to require the employee to move was subject to the limitations that the transfer was reasonable and made for operational reasons. The Court of Appeal, however, allowed the employer's appeal.

SLADE LJ: The most salient factors seem to me to be these. Mr Sibson was employed as a heavy goods vehicle driver. The very nature of his employment, therefore, meant that he would spend by far the greater part of his working hours *on the road*. Though constant reference has been made in the course of argument to Greengate as Mr Sibson's 'place of work', it was in truth no more than a starting and finishing place for his work shifts – just as the bus depot will ordinarily be no more than a starting and finishing place for the work shifts of a bus driver. (The present case is quite different, for example, from that of a shop assistant whose place of work will ordinarily be a particular shop in a particular locality throughout the working day.) Mr Sibson was initially asked to report to the Greengate depot and to work with that as his base, and had in fact worked from that base since the start of his employment. The employer had other depots at Bolton, Mansfield, Worksop and Chaderton, which was only about a mile away. There was no union membership agreement.

Against this background, in asking myself the question 'What term with regard to mobility would the parties, if reasonable, have agreed (in 1973) if they had directed their minds to the problem?' I find little difficulty in supplying the answer.

Mr Philipson based his argument on the modest submission that parties, if reasonable, would have at least agreed that Courtaulds should have the right to transfer Mr Sibson to Chadderton if it saw fit. I do not disagree with this submission, so far as it goes, but would go further. If reasonable, the parties would, in my judgment, have been likely to agree the term which Browne-Wilkinson J in *Jones* (at p. 480, para. 16) described as the 'lowest common denominator', namely a power in the employer to direct the employee to work at any place within reasonable daily reach of Mr Jones' home – and I would add *for any reason*. I cannot see how Mr Sibson could reasonably have objected to a term giving the contract this limited degree of flexibility when he entered the employment in 1973. If the evidence had disclosed any special circumstances which, as at that time, made it a matter of importance to him that he should continue to be based at Courtaulds' Greengate depot rather than at (say) Chadderton, the Industrial Tribunal would no doubt have said so.

Lord Denning MR was prepared to imply essentially the same term in the *O'Brien* case [1969] 1 All ER 93 at p. 96, where he expressed it as a term that 'they should be employed within daily travelling distance of their homes or if you please within a reasonable distance of their homes.'

In my judgment there was no need or justification for the Industrial Tribunal to import into the implied term a requirement that the employer's request to the employee to work at another place must itself be 'reasonable' – still less that a request could only be reasonable if made 'for genuine operational reasons'. Any such fetter on the employer's right to request the employee to move would have been potentially uncertain and difficult in operation and the employer could, I think, reasonably have objected to it. On the other hand, so far as I can see, all the protection which the employee could reasonably have demanded would have been conferred by the requirement of reasonable daily travelling distance.

Notes

1. Holland and Chandler ((1988) 17 ILJ 253) expose the strange logic employed in this judgment:

. . . Slade LJ (delivering the only judgment) argued that post-contractual conduct provided evidence of the *reasonable* intentions of the parties at the time of the contract's formation. His conclusion was that the parties would have been likely to agree that the employer had the power to direct the employee to work at any place within reasonable daily commuting distance; and that that requirement need not be reasonable, nor result from any genuine operational reasons, but *could be for any reason*. This assumes that the parties, as reasonable men, would have accepted the inclusion of a term which allowed one party absolute discretion over its operation; a discretion that need bear no relation to reasonableness or even managerial necessity. Indeed, Slade LJ felt that the employer could reasonably object to any such fetter on his rights. But what of Sibson's reasonable objections to the exercise of any unrestricted managerial prerogative?

2. Following *Sibson's* case, it would appear that in the absence of an express mobility clause in the contract, there is a strong presumption that the courts will be prepared to imply a term to the effect that the employee's place of work covers all sites within reasonable daily travelling distance of his home (see also *O'Brien* v *Associated Fire Alarms Ltd* [1969] 1 All ER 93 and *Jones* v *Associated Tunnelling Co. Ltd* [1981] IRLR 477).

VI Constructing the Contract of Employment: Characteristic or Imposed Terms

I. Smith, 'The Creation of the Contract of Employment' in *Butterworths Employment Law Guide* (1996) 2nd edn, p. 15

One important aspect of the wide, reasonableness test for implied terms is that it can be used by a court or tribunal for a purpose other than that of giving effect to what may (or may not) have been the basis of the agreement between that particular employer and that particular employee. It may be used instead as a device to *regulate* contracts of employment by the imposition of implied terms based on the nature of the employment itself. Such terms might be considered to be characteristic or 'imposed' terms which will normally be implied into employment contracts (either generally, or into contracts of a particular type) unless there is clear evidence that the parties did not intend them to apply. Such terms have little or nothing to do with any supposed intention of the parties themselves. The implied term is here simply used as a device with which to apply what are really just free-standing rules and concepts of the law of employment.

The scope and content of these characteristic or imposed terms is illustrated below in Part X of this Chapter.

VII Constructing the Contract of Employment: Work Rules

Secretary of State for Employment v *ASLEF (No. 2)*
[1972] 2 QB 455
Court of Appeal

The Court of Appeal had to determine whether the respondent union's 'work to rule' was in breach of contract. In disputing this, the union claimed that it was merely following the employer's rule book to the letter. (For other aspects of this case see p. 168.)

LORD DENNING MR: Each man signs a form saying that he will abide by the rules, but these rules are in no way terms of the contract of employment. They are only instructions to the man as to how he is to do the work.

Question
What are the implications of this approach for the scope of managerial prerogative unilaterally to alter rules?

Note
It is probable, however, that those sections of rule books which cover matters of which written notice must be given by statute will provide strong prima facie evidence of contractual terms.

VIII Constructing the Contract of Employment: Custom and Practice

Sagar v *Ridehalgh & Son Ltd*
[1931] 1 Ch 310
Court of Appeal

The plaintiff, a weaver, was employed by the defendant under an oral contract of employment. His wages were determined by reference to a collective agreement between the employers and the workers' unions.

Evidence showed a custom observed by most mills in Lancashire for deductions to be made for work which was not done with reasonable care and skill. Sagar challenged the lawfulness of this practice but was unsuccessful.

LAWRENCE LJ: . . . [T]he practice of making reasonable deductions for bad work has continually prevailed at the defendant's mill for upwards of thirty years, and during the whole of that time all weavers employed by the defendants have been treated alike in that respect. The practice was therefore firmly established at the defendant's mill when the plaintiff entered upon his employment there. Further, I think it is clear that the plaintiff accepted employment in the defendant's mill on the same terms as others employed at that mill . . . Although I entirely agree with the learned judge in finding it difficult to believe that the plaintiff did not know of the existence of the practice at the mill, I think it is immaterial whether he knew it or not, as I am satisfied that he accepted his employment on the same terms as to deductions for bad work as other workers at the mill.

Notes
1.   If a custom is to have legal effect, it must be 'reasonable, certain and notorious'. There is some confusion as to whether there is an additional requirement that the individual worker must be aware of the practice. This was not required in *Sagar* but in *Meek* v *Port of London* [1918] 1 Ch 415, the long-established deduction of income tax was not incorporated into the employee's contract because employees were unaware of it.
2.   For an example of a recent, unsuccessful attempt to imply a term via custom and practice, see *Quinn* v *Calder Industrial Materials Ltd* [1996] IRLR 126, EAT.

IX   Constructing the Contract of Employment: Statutory Implied Terms

A: Some examples

Equal Pay Act 1970

1.   Requirement of equal treatment for men and women in same employment
(1)   If the terms of a contract under which a woman is employed at an establishment in Great Britain do not include (directly or by reference to a collective agreement or otherwise) an equality clause they shall be deemed to include one.

Employment Rights Act 1996

PART III   GUARANTEE PAYMENTS

28.   Right to guarantee payment
(1)   Where throughout a day during any part of which an employee would normally be required to work in accordance with his contract of employment the employee is not provided with work by his employer by reason of—

(a)   a diminution in the requirements of the employer's business for work of the kind which the employee is employed to do, or

(b)   any other occurrence affecting the normal working of the employer's business in relation to work of the kind which the employee is employed to do,

the employee is entitled to be paid by his employer an amount in respect of that day.

(2)   In this Act a payment to which an employee is entitled under subsection (1) is referred to as a guarantee payment.

(3)   In this Part—

(a)   a day falling within subsection (1) is referred to as a 'workless day', and

(b)   'workless period' has a corresponding meaning.

B: *National Minimum Wage Act 1998*

National Minimum Wage Act 1998

1.   Workers to be paid at least the minimum wage

(1)   A person who qualifies for the national minimum wage shall be remunerated by his employer in respect of his work in any pay reference period at a rate which is not less than the national minimum wage.

(2)   A person qualifies for the national minimum wage if he is an individual who—

(a)   is a worker;

(b)   is working, or ordinarily works, in the United Kingdom under his contract; and

(c)   has ceased to be of compulsory school age.

(3)   The national minimum wage shall be such single hourly rate as the Secretary of State may from time to time prescribe.

(4)   For the purposes of this Act 'a pay reference period' is such period as the Secretary of State may prescribe for the purpose.

Notes

1.   With effect from 1 April 1999, all relevant workers became entitled to the national minimum wage. The statutory provisions relating to the national minimum wage are contained in the National Minimum Wage Act (NMWA) 1998 as augmented by the National Minimum Wage Regulations (NMWR) 1999 (SI 1999/584). The NMWA 1998 contains the basic framework of the statutory scheme, and the NMWR contain the detail on the applicable rate and the methods of calculation to be applied in order to assess whether the rate has been complied with in any particular case.

2.   The introduction of a national minimum wage was one of the first measures announced by the new Labour Government when it came into office. The adoption of this measure does clearly represent an important step back to intervention and the re-establishment of a framework of minimum workplace standards. In the wages field it also marks a return to compulsory wage-setting as a feature of the employment scene which has been missing since the abolition of the Wages Councils in 1993. The new provisions do, however, go further than that legislation given that they establish a *national* minimum wage applicable to most eligible workers aged 26 or above. In contrast, the Wages Councils were limited to specific areas of the labour market in which low pay was particularly prevalent, and where collective

bargaining as a means of negotiating wage minima and other wage-related entitlements, and of maintaining pay levels by periodic revision, did not operate effectively.

In dealing with wages, the Act represents a significant extension of the 'floor of rights' concept. Until the arrival of the 1998 Act, matters of pay had largely remained unregulated other than by statutory restrictions on pay rises during periods of wage controls and by protective legislation (now mostly in Pts I and II of the ERA 1996 dealing with such matters as the provision of pay particulars in the written statement, deductions of wages, itemised pay statements, and so forth).

3.   The involvement of the State, and State agencies, in measures for raising low wages does, in fact, go back a long way. In 1797, for example, the Speenhamland system in Berkshire entailed a system of poor relief which included wages 'top-ups' for labourers at times when wage levels fell. By 1909, and following the Fair Wages Resolutions system, Winston Churchill's Trade Boards Act 1909 laid the foundations for minimum wage schemes in some industries. Part of the rationale for the Act was that the 'sweated trades', in which employers paid abnormally low wages, placed a burden on the rest of society and were seen as 'subsidised' by the poor relief system and the charities. They were also, to some extent, regarded as engaging in unfair competition by other employers who paid higher wages to their workers. The Act was primarily designed to improve the protection given by the Fair Wages Resolution of 1891. Other precedents for the 1998 statute can be found in legislation like the Holidays with Pay Act 1938 and the Wages Councils Act 1945.

In introducing the 1998 Act, the Government has also had some regard to the position in other EC Member States. In all cases these countries have some form of minimum wage system, although they vary considerably in form and operation. In adopting the new measures a similar approach has been taken to that in countries like France and The Netherlands where minimum wage levels are generally set by reference to a minimum hourly rate (and in some instances a monthly minimum level of income for groups working above a set level of weekly hours).

4.   The Government's policy on the minimum wage has been driven by a number of policy objectives. First and foremost has been its concern, since its Commission on Social Justice reported, about the problems generated by low wages. But a separate, and perhaps equally important agenda, has resulted from the Government's declared objective of reducing the 'burden' placed on the State benefits system by low pay. The link between falling average pay, particularly in sectors formerly covered by the Wages Councils and in public sector pay (aggravated by a number of factors, including compulsory competitive tendering), and the on-costs to the State (in the form of State benefits expenditure and increased NHS costs), has convinced the Government that it was right to proceed with its minimum wage proposal. By putting responsibility back onto employers (at least in *part*, given the on-going importance of benefits support) it believes that there will, in time, be a

slow-down in the escalating demands placed on the welfare system. (For further discussion of the policies behind the Act, see Bob Simpson, 'A Milestone in the Legal Regulation of Pay: The National Minimum Wage Act 1988' (1999) 28 ILJ 1; and George Sayers Bain, 'The National Minimum Wage: Further Reflections' (1999) 21 *Employee Relations*, Nos 1 and 2, pp. 15–25.)

National Minimum Wage Act 1998

3. Exclusion of, and modifications for, certain classes of person

(1) This section applies to persons who have not attained the age of 26.

(1A) This section also applies to persons who have attained the age of 26 who are—

(a) within the first six months after the commencement of their employment with an employer by whom they have not been previously employed;

(b) participating in a scheme under which shelter is provided in return for work;

(c) participating in a scheme designed to provide training, work experience or temporary work;

(d) participating in a scheme to assist in the seeking or obtaining of work; or

(e) attending a course of higher education requiring attendance for a period of work experience.

(2) The Secretary of State may by regulations make provision in relation to any of the persons to whom this section applies—

(a) preventing them being persons who qualify for the national minimum wage; or

(b) prescribing an hourly rate for the national minimum wage other than the single hourly rate for the time being prescribed under section 1(3) above.

(3) No provision shall be made under subsection (2) above which treats person differently in relation to—

(a) different areas;

(b) different sectors of employment;

(c) undertakings of different sizes; or

(d) different occupations.

(4) If any description of persons who have attained the age of 26 is added by the regulations under section 4 below to the descriptions of persons to whom this section applies, no provision shall be made under subsection (2) above which treats persons of that description differently in relation to different ages over 26.

4. Power to add to the persons to whom section 3 applies

(1) The Secretary of State may by regulations amend section 3 above by adding descriptions of persons who have attained the age of 26 to the descriptions of persons to whom the section applies.

(2) No amendment shall be made under subsection (1) above which treats persons differently in relation to—

(a) different areas;

(b) different sectors of employment;

(c) undertakings of different sizes;

(d) different ages over 26; or

(e) different occupations.

Notes

1. The Act provides for the establishment of a minimum basic hourly rate of pay for workers over the age of 26. Provision exists (in s. 3) for preventing those under 26 qualifying for the national minimum wage at all, or for prescribing differentiated rates within that group according to age. There is also power to extend those restrictions to people who are aged 26 or over; but this does not explain on what basis this can be done, or provide limitations on the power (s. 4). Both those sections do, however, make it clear that the Secretary of State may not, when setting lower rates, differentiate between different areas, sectors of employment, undertakings of different sizes, or different occupations.

2. The provisions relating to the rate of the national minimum wage are contained in Pt II of NMWR 1999, regs 11 to 13. The Government decided that the standard minimum rate for those aged 22 or more would £3.60 per hour from 1 April 1999 except for those undertaking 'accredited training' (and subject to the possibility of regulations excluding specified groups up to the age of 26 from this). The rate for those aged 18–21 is £3.00 per hour, with an increase to £3.20 expected from June 2000. The accredited training rate is £3.20 an hour for those aged 22 or over who are starting a new job with a new employer. But it should be noted that this reduced rate is possible only for the first six months of a new job — thereafter the £3.60 rate is payable. The rates apply to both existing and new workers from 1 April 1999, and this extends to all workers irrespective of whether they are paid hourly, weekly, monthly, by the 'session' or whatever other system.

Before making the first regulations under s. 1(3) setting the initial rate, or under s. 1(4) fixing the 'pay reference period', the Secretary of State was required to refer a number of key matters to the Low Pay Commission for their consideration. These included the level of the single hourly rate; the method or methods for determining the hourly rate at which a person is to be treated as remunerated; and the question of possible exclusions of those under 26 (s. 5). Following receipt of the Low Pay Commission's recommendations (by the Prime Minister and the Employment Secretary), if the Secretary of State decided to make regulations differing from those recommendations (or adding to them) then a report was required to be laid before Parliament explaining the reasons for the decision.

After the 'first' regulations were made (the NMWR 1999), which followed the procedures required for involving the Low Pay Commission and informing Parliament of the actions taken, the Secretary of State was thereafter no longer obliged to refer matters to the Low Pay Commission for its views before making revising regulations, for example when changing the minimum wage or related regulations setting out entitlements. Basically, he will at that time have a discretion whether or not to refer proposed changes; and he will also have a general power to refer 'such matters' as he 'thinks fit' to them for their consideration (s. 6).

3. In contrast with social security benefits, which are uprated at the start of each tax and benefits year by an uprating order, there is no requirement stipulating that there *must* be an annual uprating or even a 'review'. Nor is there any indexation procedure (as there will be under the Employment Relations Act 1999 for awards and payments made under the ERA 1996).

4.   As well as paying the required wage (from 1 April 1999), employers are required to keep adequate records to show that the wage has been paid, and to produce such records on request (by workers, the enforcement agency, tribunals, and courts). In proceedings the onus is generally on the employer to show that the wage has been paid correctly. It is a criminal offence to refuse to pay the minimum wage, or to fail to keep proper records. There is no provision for agreements between an employer and workers to 'opt out' of the requirements.

(i) Individuals Qualifying for the Minimum Wage

As we have seen, s. 1(2) of the NMWA 1998 states that a person qualifies for the national minimum wage if he or she is an individual who is a worker; is working, or ordinarily works, in the United Kingdom under his contract; and has ceased to be of compulsory school age. 'Worker' for the purposes of the 1998 Act is widely defined.

National Minimum Wage Act 1998

54. Meaning of 'worker', 'employee' etc.

(1)   In this Act 'worker' (except in the phrases 'agency worker' and 'home worker') means an individual who has entered into or works under (or, where the employment has ceased, worked under)—

(a)   a contract of employment; or

(b)   any other contract, whether express or implied and (if it is express) whether oral or in writing, whereby the individual undertakes to do or perform personally any work or services for another party to the contract whose status is not by virtue of the contract that of a client or customer of any profession or business undertaking carried on by the individual;

and any reference to a worker's contract shall be construed accordingly.

Note

This wide definition is intended as an anti-avoidance measure. It seeks to exclude only the genuinely self-employed from its ambit and makes it extremely difficult for any employer to restructure its working relationships in order to avoid paying the national minimum wage and gaining an unfair competitive advantage in relation to market rivals. Moreover, the definition of 'worker' in the 1998 Act is effectively widened to include agency workers (s. 34) and home workers (s. 35).

National Minimum Wage Act 1998

Special classes of persons

34. Agency workers who are not otherwise 'workers'

(1)   This section applies in any case where an individual ('the agency worker')—

(a)   is supplied by a person ('the agent') to do work for another ('the principal') under a contract or other arrangements made between the agent and the principal; but

(b)   is not, as respects that work, a worker, because of the absence of a worker's contract between the individual and the agent or the principal; and

(c)   is not a party to the contract under which he undertakes to do the work for another party to the contract whose status is, by virtue of the contract, that of a client or customer of any profession or business undertaking carried on by the individual.

(2)   In a case where this section applies, the other provisions of this Act shall have effect as if there were a worker's contract for the doing of the work by the agency worker made between the agency worker and—

(a)   whichever of the agent and the principal is responsible for paying the agency worker in respect of the work; or

(b)   if neither the agent nor the principal is responsible, whichever of them pays the agency worker in respect of the work.

35.   Home workers who are not otherwise 'workers'

(1)   In determining for the purposes of this Act whether a home worker is or is not a worker, section 54(3)(b) . . . shall have effect as if for the word 'personally' were substituted '(whether personally or otherwise)'.

(2)   In this section 'home worker' means an individual who contracts with a person, for the purposes of that person's business, for the execution of work to be done in a place not under the control or management of that person.

Notes

1.   By virtue of s. 35(1), home workers are covered even where they sub-contract work to family or friends. The minimum wage also applies to workers from outside the UK working in the UK (however long their stay is). British workers who normally work in the UK, and who are temporarily working abroad, are also subject to the minimum wage requirement.

It may be noted that the Secretary of State may by regulations made under s. 41 apply the Act, with or without modifications, to any *other* individuals of a prescribed description who would not otherwise be classed as a 'worker'. By s. 42, the Act can also be applied to 'offshore employment'. In the latter case, an Order in Council made under s. 42 can apply the Act (or some of it) to individuals who are not necessarily British subjects, and to bodies corporate whether or not they are incorporated under UK law. In doing so, the Order could confer jurisdiction on courts or tribunals outside the UK.

2.   The national minimum wage will not extend, however, to 16- and 17-year-olds; apprentices who start their apprenticeship before they are 18; or those starting an apprenticeship at 18 (at least until they attain the age of 19 whereupon they will qualify for the £3.00 rate). Trainees on government-funded training schemes are outside the minimum wage scheme unless they are employed by the employer. In this case they will normally have to be 18 and above, and paid their wages by the employer, to qualify. The following groups are also excluded:

(a)   *share fishermen* (including fishing vessels' master and crew who are remunerated in respect of that employment only by a share in the profits or gross earnings of the vessel) (s. 43);

(b)   certain *voluntary workers*, including those employed by charities, voluntary organisations, associated fund-raising bodies, or statutory bodies, who in respect of their employment do not receive, and are not entitled to receive, monetary payments of any description or payments for expenses, and have no benefits in kind other than for subsistence or accommodation which is 'reasonable in the circumstances of the employment' (s. 44, and the detailed provisions which amplify these points in s. 44(2)–(4));

(c) *prisoners* (including those detained or on temporary release) in respect of work done in pursuance of prison rules (s. 45).

Also excluded from the minimum wage requirements are friends and neighbours working under informal arrangements, and people living and working within the family (au pairs, nannies, companions, etc.). Nor do they apply to family members who live at home and work in the family business (NMWR 1999, reg. 2(2)).

3. There are provisions in the Act for 'harmonising' it with requirements in the Agricultural Wages Act 1948 (and equivalent legislation in Scotland and Northern Ireland) and the other legislation on remuneration which will still apply (with modifications) to agricultural workers. Accordingly, wages set by the Agricultural Wages Boards can continue to apply to such workers. There are mechanisms for ensuring that wage minima set by that legislation are consistent with the Act (and for amending the agricultural workers legislation): see s. 47 and sch. 2 to the 1998 Act. As well as ensuring that agricultural workers get the national minimum wage (and in some cases more than the minimum wage) there is also provision in s. 46 for ensuring that underpaying employers are not prosecuted twice. It is also made clear (by s. 46(2)) that workers cannot recover unpaid amounts under both sets of legislation in respect of the same work.

4. To deal with potential problems in determining who is a worker's immediate 'employer', the Act says in s. 48 that where the immediate employer of a worker is himself in the employment of some other person, and the worker is employed on the premises of that other person, that other 'person' will be 'deemed for the purposes of this Act to be the employer of the worker jointly with the immediate employer'. In practical terms this means that if the immediate employer defaulted in meeting the requirements to pay the minimum wage then the other employer could be responsible in default.

(ii) Operation of the Wage Provisions

Section 1(3) of the NMWA 1998 requires the national minimum wage to be expressed as a single hourly rate. However, the variety and complexity of payment systems necessitated regulatory guidance in order to determine whether any particular worker is being paid at the national minimum wage rate. Three questions must be answered: the period over which a worker's pay is calculated (the 'pay reference period'); the payments which count for calculating a worker's pay; and the hours during which the worker is deemed to be working for the purposes of the national minimum wage.

The pay reference period A worker does not have to be paid the national minimum wage for each and every hour worked, but he or she must be paid the national minimum wage *on average* in each 'pay reference period' (PRP).

This is defined as a calendar month or, where the worker is paid by reference to a shorter period, that period (NMWR 1999, reg. 10(1)).

Payments made by an employer to a worker in any PRP include:

(a)   all payments received by the worker in that period(reg. 30(a));

(b)   any payments earned by the worker in that period but not received by him or her until the following PRP (reg. 30(b));

(c)   if the worker does not get paid until he or she submits a completed timesheet or other similar record to the employer, and he or she submits that less than four working days before the end of the PRP following the one in which the work was done, payments made in either the PRP in which the completed record was submitted or the one after that.

Where payments are 'transferred' from the PRP in which they were received to the period when they were earned, they cannot also be allocated to the former period. In other words, double-counting is not permitted.

What is 'pay' for minimum wage purposes?   In determining whether the national minimum wage is being complied with, it is necessary to exclude certain items from gross pay and to include others. It goes without saying that the inclusion of items that should be excluded is likely to be a major cause of 'underpayment' for minimum wage purposes. Particular care will therefore be needed with this aspect of the scheme.

National minimum wage pay is gross pay less any items that should be excluded. The following do *not* count towards national minimum wage pay:

- any loans or advances of wages made to workers (reg. 8(a));
- pension payments, lump sums paid at retirement and compensation for losing a job (reg. 8(b));
- court or tribunal awards, or payments to settle actual or potential court or tribunal proceedings, other than payment of an amount due under the workers' contract (reg. 8(c));
- redundancy payments (reg. 8(d));
- awards under suggestion schemes (reg. 8(e));
- payments during absences from work (such as sick pay, holiday pay, maternity pay and guarantee payments) and payments for rest breaks or during industrial action (reg. 31(1)(b));
- the actual or notional monetary value of all benefits in kind, whether or not they are taxable, other than living accommodation (reg. 9(a)), for which there is a maximum permitted off-set of £19.95 per week;
- the monetary value of vouchers, stamps or similar documents that are exchangeable for money, goods and/or services (reg. 9(b));
- premium payments for overtime and shiftworking to the extent that they exceed the lowest hourly rate payable for that work (reg. 31(1)(c)(i));
- premium payments for output work so far as they exceed the rate normally applicable to that work (reg. 31(1)(c)(ii));

- allowances attributable to a particular aspect of a worker's working arrangements or to his or her working or personal circumstances that are not consolidated into his or her basic pay, e.g., unsocial hours payments, on-call or standby payments, payments for performing additional duties, payments for working in unpleasant or dangerous conditions or in a particular area (e.g., London weighting) and being available for work when no work is provided) (regs 2(1) and 31(1)(d));
- service charges, tips, gratuities or cover charges that are not paid through the payroll (reg. 31(1)(e));
- deductions made by the employer from the workers' pay, or payments made by the worker to the employer, in respect of the worker's expenditure in connection with his or her job (regs 32(1)(a) and 34(1)(a)), e.g., cost of a uniform, tools or other equipment;
- payments made by a worker to a third party on account of such expenditure, or refunds of such payments made by the employer (regs 34(1)(b) and 31(1)(f)), e.g., travelling expenses, overnight accommodation;
- deductions made by the employer from the worker's pay, or payments made by the worker to the employer, for the employer's 'own use and benefit' (regs 32(1)(b) and 34(1)(c)) with the exception of those made: (i) in respect of the worker's conduct or any other event for which he or she, either alone or with other workers, is contractually liable (e.g. disciplinary deductions or fines); (ii) to repay a loan or an advance of wages made to the worker; (iii) to recover or refund an accidental overpayment of wages made to the worker; or (iv) in respect of a worker's purchase of shares (regs 33 and 35(a)–(d)).

Hours: calculating the hours for which the national minimum wage must be paid   Broadly, the rules of the scheme may depend on the type of work being done. The four main types of working dealt with are time working; salaried hours working; 'output' work; and unmeasured work:

(a) Timeworking   For the purposes of the scheme this refers to systems where a worker is paid according to the number of hours he or she is at work, even if this may vary. The majority of workers in the UK work under this type of arrangement. In addition, for the purposes of the scheme, people paid on piecework systems (i.e., according to how much they produce) are treated as timeworkers to the extent that they work within identifiable hours of work. For example, a worker who is paid according to the number of toys he or she produces, but who works a six-hour day, will need to be paid at a level of at least the national minimum wage for each hour he or she works in his or her pay period.

A 'timeworker' for the scheme's purposes excludes those paid an annual salary, but includes someone who works to agreed hours or time periods. Those undertaking piecework within set hours are also treated in accordance with timeworking rules.

The times when the worker is expected to be working, and is at the workplace and working, must be within the national minimum wage calculation. The times spent during meal or rest breaks are, however, excluded (reg. 15(7)). If the worker is at work, and *available* for work, that time must be included, even if work is not provided (reg. 15(1)). Being 'on call' at home does not count, however.

Although travel time between home and work is not to be included for national minimum wage purposes, travel in connection with the worker's job *is* included. This includes travel between work assignments, and any time in which travel during a work period and for work purposes is required (reg. 15(2)(a)). This extends to travel for training purposes (other than travel from home to a training centre). Absences from work, and pay during those absences, are ignored. The time spent on holidays, maternity leave, and sick leave does not count for national minimum wage purposes. Time during which a worker is engaged in industrial action does not count as time when the national minimum wage is payable, and any pay actually received during such periods is disregarded when calculating minimum wage payments (reg. 15(6)).

(b)   *Salaried workers*   This includes people who are paid an annual salary; paid under their contract of employment for a set number of hours, or minimum hours each year; or paid for set periods referable to a year (e.g., for 52 weeks, at 52 equal instalments). It extends to people whose work may vary, either in terms of pay following increases, or because of additional payments over and above their basic pay. The basic rules are similar to those described for timeworkers. The key difference is that most time during the salary period is counted, so that rest periods and other periods when the person is not working are not taken away from the time that counts for pay purposes. For some workers this can, of course, make a significant difference for national minimum wage purposes. That said, there may be periods when under the contract pay is not paid, or it is paid at reduced amounts, e.g., during a period of sickness or recovery from injury. Such periods must be taken away from the total hourage for which the national minimum wage is payable in the PRP. Unpaid leave, industrial action, and other periods in which pay does not have to continue under the contract do not count towards the time when the national minimum wage is payable.

It is, of course, helpful if the basic hours which the worker is expected to work have been agreed (and this can be done on an annualised basis, or by reference to a weekly or monthly norm). This will facilitate calculation of the salaried hours worked in the worker's PRP. Once it is clear what the hours are, and the salary is known, calculation of an hourly rate is usually straightforward.

(c)   *'Output' Work*   Output work can be defined for the purposes of the scheme as work which is remunerated according to work performance, whether measured by reference to 'pieces' produced, business transacted, work results achieved, etc. As discussed above, piecework is one form of output work. If such work is done within set hours then it comes within the timeworking arrangements already explained. If it is not then there are two options available under the scheme. The worker's hours can be assessed according to:

(i)   a 'fair estimate agreement'; or
(ii)   paying on the basis of the hours *actually worked.*

Fair estimate agreements must be agreed between the employer and the worker concerned before the PRP commences. Such an agreement must be in writing and identify the hours likely to be worked during the PRP. In addition, it must be fair to the extent that the number of hours mutually agreed must be at least four-fifths of the number of hours which an average worker would take to do the same job and in the same working conditions (reg. 25(2)). The worker must record the actual hours of output work undertaken in the PRP, and then give that record to the employer to form part of the employer's records. Finally, there must be a contract giving the worker the right to be paid an agreed rate for each 'piece', sale, etc., in the PRP. A single agreement can be used for more than just the initial PRP as long as the worker undertakes the same work in each of the later periods. In the absence of a valid fair estimate agreement the worker must be paid at or above the national minimum wage for each hour actually worked.

   (d)   'Unmeasured' work   This is work which is not within one of the types already discussed, and in which employment or tasks are undertaken but there are no agreed hours or times within which work is completed. It would apply, for example, in situations in which staff are 'on call' or work 'when required'. To calculate the hours worked, and at which the national minimum wage is payable, there are two options available:

   (i)   the worker and employer agree a 'daily average agreement' which records the average hours that the worker is likely to be working on jobs, tasks, etc.;
   (ii)   the employer pays the hours actually worked at or above the national minimum wage.

If the first method is adopted, daily average hours must be a realistic average in terms of the work that is likely (the onus of showing this being on the employer for enforcement purposes). As with fair estimate arrangements (see above), a single agreement can be used for later pay reference periods if there is no change in the average number of hours.

(iii)   Record-keeping, Minimum Wage 'Statements', and Enforcement
Record-keeping   Employers are required by ss. 9–12 of the NMWA 1998 to keep and preserve records in accordance with the regulations made under s. 9. As well as facilitating enforcement, these records may, of course, be important in the event of proceedings in tribunals and the courts.

National Minimum Wage Act 1998

10. Worker's right of access to records
   (1)   A worker may, in accordance with the following provisions of this section—

    (a)   require his employer to produce any relevant records; and

    (b)   inspect and examine those records and copy any part of them.

(2)   The rights conferred by subsection (1) above are exercisable only if the worker believes on reasonable grounds that he is or may be being, or has or may have been, remunerated for any pay reference period by his employer at a rate which is less than the national minimum wage.

Notes

1.   There is no formal requirement on employers to specify national minimum wage entitlements on pay slips. But as the government has advised, it is prudent for employers to try to ensure that workers know how their pay has been calculated, and how the national minimum wage scheme operates in relation to their pay. This will assist in avoiding complaints and time spent on answering inquiries from employees who think their pay may be incorrect.

2.   The inspection must be for the *purpose* of establishing that the worker has been underpaid in that way (s. 10(3)). In other words, inspections cannot be carried out for any *other* or *wider* purposes. An employer who is given a 'production notice' by the worker (which must request production and identify the period the worker is concerned about) could at that stage object, particularly if he thinks that these requirements are *not* satisfied. There is nothing in the legislation to that effect, however, so an employer would need to be cautious in rejecting requests for access, and be sure that he has good grounds for objection. An employer's right to object seems to be implicit given that s. 11 sets up an appeal mechanism by which a complaint can be made to an employment tribunal that there has been a failure to produce records or allow the worker to exercise the other rights associated with a production notice (such as the right to be 'accompanied by such other person as the worker may think fit': s. 10(4)(b)).

Following receipt of a production notice, the employer is required:

    (a)   to give the worker reasonable notice of the place and time at which the relevant records will be produced (namely the worker's place of work, or other place at which it is reasonable for him to attend, or which may be agreed);

    (b)   to produce the records before the end of 14 days following the date of receipt of the notice (or a later time if this is agreed during that 14-day period).

3.   Complaints to the tribunal that the employer has failed to produce some or all of the records required, or otherwise failed to allow the rights referred to above to be exercised, can be made under s. 11(1). If the tribunal finds the complaint to be well-founded it shall:

    (a)   make a declaration to that effect;

    (b)   make an award that the employer pay to the worker a sum equal to 80 times the hourly amount of the national minimum wage in force when the award is made.

Minimum wage statements   Regulations may make provision for the details of the minimum wage statement which is to be given to workers 'at or before the time at which any payment of remuneration is made to the worker'. Basically this would be an extension of existing requirements as to itemised pay statements; and for this purpose the jurisdiction of tribunals to deal with references under the ERA 1996, ss. 11 and 12 would be extended. It would enable tribunals to hear complaints and thereupon determine what workers should be receiving, and what should be included in pay statements regarding entitlements under the 1998 Act.

It is interesting to note that no regulations have been made under NMWA s. 12 as a result of consultations on the draft regulations. A number of employer respondents saw the costs involved in providing such a statement as disproportionate given the numbers involved. Simpson has observed:

Workers who are employees still will have the right to an itemised pay statement under section 8 of the Employment Rights Act 1996. If they are aware of the NMW rate applicable to them, and the government said that it intended to spend some £2 million on publicising the introduction of the NMW, they may be able to calculate whether or not they are being paid less than their NMW entitlement. Many workers who do not have employee status will have nothing to go on. The desire to be seen to respond to pressure from business not to impose what employers perceive to be unacceptable and unnecessary cost would appear to have blinded the government to what was earlier seen to be the desirability if not the necessity of putting in place a range of linked enforcement mechanisms. (Simpson, R., 'Implementing the National Minimum Wage – The 1999 Regulations' (1999) 28 ILJ 171, at p.180)

Enforcement   Sections 13–16 and 19–22 of the 1998 Act contain a variety of important enforcement measures. Officers can be appointed for the purposes of monitoring the operation of the Act – initially these will be drawn from the Inland Revenue. Those provisions give these officers powers, including the ability to inspect records and enter premises 'at all reasonable times'; and to require 'relevant persons' to 'attend before an officer at such time and place' as may be specified in written notices to furnish explanations in response to questions about records. A 'relevant person' can include employers, agents, workers, servants of an employer, or people who qualify for the national minimum wage.

National Minimum Wage Act 1998

19.   Power of officer to issue enforcement notices

(1)   If an officer acting for the purposes of this Act is of the opinion that a worker who qualifies for the national minimum wage has not been remunerated for any pay reference period by his employer at a rate at least equal to the national minimum wage, the officer may serve a notice (an 'enforcement notice') on the employer requiring the employer to remunerate the worker for the pay reference periods ending on or after the date of the notice at a rate equal to the national minimum wage.

(2)   An enforcement notice may also require the employer to pay the worker within such time as may be specified in the notice the sum due to the worker under section

17 . . . in respect of the employer's previous failure to remunerate the worker at a rate at least equal to the national minimum wage.

(3)   An enforcement notice may relate to more than one worker (and, where it does so, may be so framed as to relate to workers specified in the notice or to workers of a description so specified).

Notes

1.   The power contained in s. 19(3) may be particularly relevant where, for example, a trade union has contacted the officers and asks them to investigate alleged underpayment of wages by a particular employer, or even by employers of a specific group of workers in an industry.

2.   Appeal to an employment tribunal against an enforcement notice is provided for by s. 19(4)–(9), but the appeal will need to be made promptly and within the time limit of four weeks following date of service of the notice. As well as being able to rescind notices if it allows an appeal, the tribunal is given power to rectify enforcement notices. In some circumstances the notice may contain errors, but s. 19(10) is wide enough to enable the notice to be treated as if it had been rectified at the time it was served. This is obviously intended to prevent undue delays occurring following service of an inaccurate notice.

(iv)   Non-compliance: Tribunal and Civil Proceedings

National Minimum Wage Act 1998

17.   Non-compliance: worker entitled to additional remuneration
(1)   If a worker who qualifies for the national minimum wage is remunerated for any pay reference period by his employer at a rate which is less than the national minimum wage, the worker shall be taken to be entitled under his contract to be paid, as additional remuneration in respect of that period, the amount described in subsection(2) below.

(2)   That amount is the difference between—
(a)   the relevant remuneration received by the worker for the pay reference period; and
(b)   the relevant remuneration which the worker would have received for that period had he been remunerated by the employer at a rate equal to the national minimum wage.

(3)   In sub-section (2) above, 'relevant remuneration' means the remuneration which falls to be brought into account for the purposes of regulations under section 2.

Tribunal and court proceedings regarding 'additional remuneration'   Having identified what the worker's legal entitlement is, the Act provides several ways in which it may be *secured*. Section 18 makes it clear that for the purposes of s. 17 the worker and the employer will be regarded as having that relationship for the purposes of the application of Pt II of the ERA 1996. This contains the 'protection of wages' provisions which enable workers to make complaints to an employment tribunal in respect of unauthorised 'deductions'. To facilitate proceedings, either before a tribunal under Pt II or a court in a claim in contract, in relation to any 'additional remuneration' due, s. 18 *deems* a worker to have a contract in relation to that amount. This may, of course, not be necessary in many cases. But in cases where this might prove to be a procedural obstacle, s. 18 supplies the necessary contractual relationship.

Non-compliance notices and penalties   As well as assisting workers in tribunal and court proceedings, the Act sets out in ss. 20–22 a system for dealing with non-compliance with enforcement notices. This can involve either a complaint under s. 23(1)(a) of the ERA 1996 (deductions from wages in contravention of s. 13 of the 1996 Act) by an officer on behalf of the worker to an employment tribunal, or commencement of other civil proceedings for recovery of sums due under s.17, based on a claim in contract.

Officers may in accordance with s. 21 serve a 'penalty notice' if they are satisfied that a person on whom an enforcement notice has been served has failed, in whole or in part, to comply with the notice. The notice must stipulate, among other things:

(a)   the time within which the penalty must be paid (which cannot be less than four weeks from date of service);

(b)   the period to which the penalty relates;

(c)   the respects in which the officer is of the opinion that the enforcement notice has not been complied with;

(d)   the calculation of the amount of the penalty.

The penalty is calculated at a rate equal to twice the hourly amount of the national minimum wage (as in force at the time of the date of the penalty notice) in respect of each worker to whom the failure to comply relates for each day during which the failure to comply has continued. Section 22 gives recipients an appeal right. Appeals must be brought within four weeks following the date of service of the notice.

(v)   Criminal Penalties
In addition to the civil remedies referred to, the 1998 Act contains a number of criminal penalties in respect of default.

National Minimum Wage Act 1998

31.   Offences
(1)   If the employer of a worker who qualifies for the national minimum wage refuses or wilfully neglects to remunerate the worker for any pay reference period at a rate which is at least equal to the national minimum wage that employer is guilty of an offence.

Notes
1.   The section's other offences relate to such matters as failing to keep records; making false entries in records; intentionally delaying or obstructing officers; and refusing to answer questions or furnish information.

2.   A defence is available under s. 31(8) that the person charged exercised all due diligence and took all reasonable precautions to secure that the provisions of the Act, and regulations made under it, were complied with by him and by any person under his control.

(vi)   Unfair Dismissal and Right Not To Suffer 'Detriment'
Linked to the enforcement measures described, the NMWA 1998 gives workers several important rights in relation the minimum wage.

National Minimum Wage Act 1998

23.   The right not to suffer detriment
(1)   A worker has the right not to be subjected to any detriment by any act, or any deliberate failure to act, by his employer, done on the ground that—
        (a)   any action was taken, or was proposed to be taken, by or on behalf of the worker with a view to enforcing, or otherwise securing the benefit of, a right of the worker's to which this section applies; or
        (b)   the employer was prosecuted for an offence under section 31 . . . as a result of action taken by or on behalf of the worker for the purpose of enforcing, or otherwise securing the benefit of, a right of the worker's to which this section applies; or
        (c)   the worker qualifies, or will or might qualify, for the national minimum wage or for a particular rate of national minimum wage.

Notes
1.   Section 23(2) makes it clear that it is immaterial for the purposes of s. 23(1)(a) or (b) whether or not the worker actually *has* the right concerned, or whether it has been infringed or not. It will, however, be necessary to show that the claim to the right and, if applicable, the claim that it has been infringed is made in good faith. The section applies to rights to bring complaints before the tribunals, and rights to additional remuneration.
2.   Complaints may be made to an employment tribunal by a worker that he has been subjected to a detriment in contravention of s. 23. Limits are placed on the compensation that may be made; details are as set out in s. 24(3)–(5).
3.   A new s. 104A is inserted in the ERA 1996 providing for dismissal to be treated as unfair if it was for any of the reasons specified in that section. The grounds mirror the provisions referred to above in relation to detrimental action.

X   The Characteristic Rights and Obligations of the Employer and Employee

Duties of employer:

(a)   To pay wages.
(b)   To provide work (?).
(c)   To exercise care.
(d)   To cooperate.
(e)   To provide access to a grievance procedure.

Duties of employee:

(a)   To obey reasonable orders.
(b)   To exercise reasonable care and competence.
(c)   To maintain fidelity (which may be broken down into the following sub-headings):

    (i)   honesty;
    (ii)   not to compete;
    (iii) not to misuse confidential information;
    (iv)   not to impede the employers' business;
    (v)   the duty to account.

(i)   The Obligation to Pay Wages

What effect does sickness absence have on the obligation to pay wages?

Mears v Safecar Security Ltd
[1982] IRLR 183
Court of Appeal

For other aspects of this case, see p. 96.

Mr Mears, a security guard, received a s. 1 statement which did not indicate whether or not he was entitled to sick pay. He applied to an industrial tribunal for a declaration as to what particulars should have been included. The tribunal – applying *Orman v Saville Sportswear Ltd* [1960] 3 All ER 105 – held that a term that wages would be paid during sickness must be implied, unless the employers could show otherwise, which they had failed to do. The tribunal also concluded that the implied sick pay term would provide for the deduction of social security benefits received by Mr Mears.

STEPHENSON LJ: In *Orman's* case Mr Justice Pilcher said that the authorities which had been cited to him

> establish the following proposition. Where the written terms of the contract of service are silent as to what is to happen in regard to the employee's right to be paid whilst he is absent from work due to sickness, the employer remains liable to continue paying so long as the contract is not determined by proper notice, except where a condition to the contrary can properly be inferred from all the facts and the evidence in the case. If the employer seeks to establish an implied condition that no wages are payable, it is for him to make it out, and the court, in construing the written contract, will not accept any implied term which will not pass the test laid down by Lord Justice Scrutton in *Reigate v Union Manufacturing Co.* [[1916] 1 KB 592].

Mr Clark has submitted that that proposition correctly stated the law and the effect of the earlier authorities Alternatively he preferred to adopt the somewhat narrower submission made by Mr Bridge in *Orman's* case (at page 1060 of the report) that

> When the contract contains no express term and no unexpressed term can properly be implied as to the remuneration during periods of illness, the presumption is that

the contractual remuneration remains payable until the contract of service is determined.

As, however, that presumption must prevail unless rebutted and the employer is the party who will want to rebut it, it appears in fact to place the onus of rebutting it on the employer, as Mr Justice Pilcher said.

In the Employment Appeal Tribunal's judgment, now reported in [1981] IRLR 99, Mr Justice Slynn reviewed those authorities, which were the decisions of this court in *Marrison v Bell* [1939] 2 KB 187, *Petrie v MacFisheries Ltd* [1940] 1 KB 265, and *O'Grady v M. Saper Ltd* [1940] 2 KB, 469 to which he added *Hancock v BSA Tools Ltd* [1939] 4 All ER 538, a decision of Mr Justice Atkinson given between the decision of the Court of Appeal, of which he had been a member, in *Petrie's* case, and the decision in *O'Grady's* case. Mr Justice Slynn ended his review of those cases with the following citation from the judgment of Lord Justice MacKinnon in *O'Grady's* case, at page 529

> The whole question in such a case as this is what the terms of the contract between the employer and the servant were and what those terms provided in regard to payment of wages to him during his absence from the service by reason of illness . . . Was it agreed that the man should be paid when he was ready and willing to work, or that he should be paid only when he was actually working? . . . In this case, as it seems to me, there was abundant evidence that the terms, not expressed but no doubt implied, upon which this man was employed were that he should not be paid wages whilst he was sick. Conclusive evidence of that is furnished by the fact that on at least three occasions during the time he had been employed he was not paid wages when he was away sick, and he acquiesced in that position.
> . . .

[THE EAT's] decision disapproves the conclusion of Mr Justice Pilcher as expressed in the proposition cited from *Orman's* case and substitutes an approach to the facts and evidence in each case with an open mind unprejudiced by any preconception, presumption or assumption. With this I respectfully agree.

. . . For this court to affirm the Employment Appeal Tribunal's decision involves preferring, or as I think being bound by the latest of conflicting decisions of this court at least when that decision has considered earlier conflicting decisions and resolved the conflict. *Barrington v Lee* [1972] 1 QB 326. If *Marrison v Bell* had stood alone I think I would have felt bound by it to follow *Orman* case in justice to the reporter of *Marrison* case I have to say that I regard his headnote as correctly stating the main point there argued and decided, in spite of the criticism diverted in *Petrie* case from the decision to the report of it. But we are bound to follow *O'Grady's* case . . .

Here the facts and circumstances all pointed, as I have said against the term of which Mr Mears wanted the Tribunal to include particulars and in favour of a term that there was to be no sick pay. If there had been no factors pointing either way, nothing for or against sick pay, then the statutory duty to determine particulars of a term or condition to comply with [ERA 1996, s. 1(4)(d)(ii)] could have been discharged only by resorting to the presumption that the wage is to be paid till the employment is ended, whether the employee works or is absent from work. That was, I think, rightly recognised by the Employment Appeal Tribunal in the conclusion of the passage which I have already referred to in the judgment of Mr Justice Slynn. Those sentences reflect and follow what Lord Justice du Parcq who had been a party to the decision in *Marrison's* case said in *Petrie's* [1940] 1 KB at page 265, echoed by Mr Justice Atkinson in the same case at page 270.

That is what is left of the presumption attributed to *Marrison* v *Bell* and it does not apply to this case. To apply it, as if there were 'nothing more', would be manifestly unjust for it would require the Industrial Tribunal to compel an employer, who though in breach of his statutory duty to give the required particulars would never have agreed to pay any employee wages when absent sick, to pay them to an employee who never expected to get them. The Employment Appeal Tribunal was right in holding that they were not driven by law to uphold a conclusion so repugnant to common sense and the justice of the case.

To sum up the guidance which I would give to Industrial Tribunals in every reference under s. 11 in which an employee asks the Industrial Tribunal to determine the particulars required by s. 1 of a term (or terms) of which no written particulars have been given by his employer, the Tribunal must act under [s. 12(1)], and their first duty is to determine whether that term has been agreed expressly by word of mouth or by necessary implication. If it has, the Tribunal determines that particulars of it ought to be included in the employee's statement of terms. If it has not, the Tribunal has to find and imply the term which all the facts and circumstances, including the subsequent actions of the employer and employee, show were agreed or must have been agreed and to determine that particulars of that term ought to be included. Where, as here, the Tribunal is searching for the right term to imply relating to the payment of wages during absence through sickness and are left by lack of material in doubt about that particular term, the doubt will be resolved in favour of the employee by *Marrison* v *Bell* as interpreted in the authorities ending with this case. When the missing term relates to payment of wages during periods of absence through sickness, the Tribunal must approach the search for the missing term by considering all the facts and circumstances, including the subsequent conduct of the parties, and only if they do not indicate what that term is or must be, should the Tribunal assume that it is a term that wages should be paid during those periods and determine that that is the term of which particulars ought to be included.

In most cases the Tribunal will have enough material, as had this Tribunal, to determine what has, or would have been agreed between employer and employee and so ought to have been particularised by the employer. By the end of the 13 weeks [now 2 months] allowed by s. 1 of the Act, or by the time the employee's complaint is heard by the Tribunal the problem of what was agreed generally 'solvitur ambulando', and the way in which the employment has worked in practice will supply the missing term on one or other of the common law principles of necessary implication. But there may be cases in which the Tribunal are left in doubt as to what has been agreed and what particulars ought to have been included. What then? Is the Tribunal to decide what term should have been agreed? Is the statutory duty to determine particulars as being those which ought to have been given in a statement, a duty to decide what the Tribunal think the parties ought to have agreed? Can the employer shelter behind s. 2(1) by stating that there are no particulars to be entered under the statutory head on which the employee relies?

If the employer has stated that there are no particulars to be entered thereunder, but the Tribunal find that there are because the term has been agreed, then they can act probably by amendment or substitution under [s. 12(2)] rather than under [s. 12(1)]. But what if no particulars have been entered because the relevant term has not been agreed? Is the Tribunal stopped by s. 2(1) from going behind the employer's negative statement and inserting particulars which he shall be deemed to have given?

It may be that we are here considering cases which Parliament never considered and questions to which only Parliament can supply answers. But I am inclined to think that when any of the terms specified in the statute has not been agreed, the Tribunal have nevertheless to state it for them. This they can only do by deciding which term fits in best with all the circumstances of the case, which may be getting near to deciding what is a reasonable term, or a term which, to quote the Industrial Tribunal's decision, would be sensible if the parties had in fact agreed it.

S[ection]. 11 would seem to impose on the Tribunal the statutory duty to find the specified terms, and in the last resort invent them for the purpose of literally writing them into the contract. In discharging that duty, the Tribunal can and must go into all the facts and circumstances of the case and, when those fail to provide a basis for implying a specified term, to justice, and the implication of a reasonable term. If the Tribunal have not enough material in the facts and circumstance to determine what *would* have been agreed, they must determine what *should* have been agreed, bearing in mind that it is the employer's breach of *his* statutory duty which has made the employee's application for a reference necessary and that in consequence they would generally be right to resolve any doubt about what particulars ought to be included in favour of the employee.

But this is not a case of that kind, and we have not been asked to consider it on the basis that there was insufficient material for the implication of the relevant term without resorting to considering what would be reasonable or just. Not having heard argument on that aspect of the statutory duty. I express no concluded opinion upon it. No authoritative guidance can be given on it until Tribunals are faced with a decision which requires it. But I have ventured to raise questions which the sections we have had to consider, including in particular s. 2(1), inevitably raise, in the hope that Parliament may find time to consider whether some amendment of those sections might not clarify the statutory duty thereby intended to be imposed on Industrial Tribunals . . .

If the first issue is decided in the company's favour, it is unnecessary to consider the second issue. I would only comment that on the facts of this case two Tribunals widely experienced in such matters, have unanimously concluded that if Mr Mears was entitled to sick pay it would be paid nett after deduction of Social Security benefits, and it would have taken cogent argument, possibly exceeding even Mr Clark's powers of persuasion to convince me that there was any error of law in the decision of either Tribunal on the point.

Note

In the course of his judgment, Stephenson LJ suggested (*obiter*) that where the parties have failed to agree on a relevant term specified in what is now ERA 1996, Part I, 's. 12 would seem to impose on the tribunal the statutory duty to find the specified terms, and in the last resort invent them for the purpose of literally writing them into the contract'. This view has received considerable criticism and has now been rejected by the Court of Appeal in *Eagland* v *British Telecommunications plc* [1992] IRLR 323. Lord Justice Parker thought it 'undesirable' that the guidance given in *Mears* 'should remain in the authorities'. Lord Justice Leggatt stated:

For my part I too am unable to envisage circumstances in which it might become appropriate for an Industrial Tribunal to invent a term. I use the word 'invent' as it was used by Lord Justice Stephenson . . . in the sense of determining either what term should have been agreed or what term would have been reasonable. If an essential term, such as a written statement must contain, has not been agreed, there will be no agreement. If it has, it is the duty of the Industrial Tribunal, where necessary, to identify the term as having been agreed, whether expressly, by necessary implication, or by inference from all the circumstances, including in particular the conduct of the parties, without recourse to invention.

Question
Is there likely to be a difference in outcome depending on whether the approach is 'identification' or 'invention' of the missing term?

Note
The following cases consider the question of lay-offs and the obligation to pay.

Hanley v *Pease & Partners Ltd*
[1915] 1 KB 698
King's Bench Division

Mr Hanley, a cokeman, was required to work on Sundays. On one Sunday, he overslept and failed to turn up for work. The following day he arrived for work but was suspended without pay for one day. He claimed damages for the loss of one day's pay on the Monday. At first instance his claim was rejected, but was successful on appeal.

LUSH J: Whether the right of a master to dismiss a servant for misconduct or breach of duty or anything else of the kind is treated as a right arising out of the ordinary right of a contracting party to put an end to the contract when there has been a repudiation by the other party, or whether it is treated as a right which the master has on the ground that obedience to lawful orders must be treated as a condition of the contract, is wholly immaterial. I do not think it is necessary to say which is the proper way to regard it, because in either view the right of the master is merely an option. The contract has become a voidable contract. The master can determine it if he pleases. Assuming that there has been a breach on the part of the servant entitling the master to dismiss him, he may if he pleases terminate the contract, but he is not bound to do it, and if he chooses not to exercise that right but to treat the contract as a continuing contract not withstanding the misconduct or breach of duty of the servant, then the contract is for all purposes a continuing contract subject to the master's right in that case to claim damages against the servant for his breach of contract. But in the present case after declining to dismiss the workman – after electing to treat the contract as a continuous one – the employers took upon themselves to suspend him for one day; in other words to deprive the workman of his wages for one day, thereby assessing their own damages for the servant's misconduct at the sum which would be represented by one day's wages. They have no possible right to do that. Having elected to treat the contract as continuing it was continuing. They might have had a right to claim damages against the servant, but they could not justify their act in suspending the workman for the one day and refusing to let him work and earn wages.

Note
As a result of this decision, it is clear that employers cannot suspend without pay where there is no express or contractual right to do so – see *Marshall* v *Midland Electric* [1945] 1 All ER 653.

Devonald v *Rosser & Sons*
[1906] 2 KB 728
Court of Appeal

Devonald was a pieceworker employed at a tinplate works. His contract of employment gave him an entitlement to one month's notice of termination of employment. Devonald's employers found they could not run at a profit because of depressed market conditions. They gave Devonald a month's notice but closed down the works immediately. Devonald claimed damages for the wages he lost during this period, arguing that there was an implied term that he would be provided with work during the notice period.

LORD ALVERSTONE CJ: . . . In my opinion the necessary implication to be drawn from this contract is at least that the master will find a reasonable amount of work up to the expiration of a notice given in accordance with the contract. I am not prepared to say that that obligation is an absolute one to find work at all events, for the evidence showed that it was subject to certain contingencies, such as breakdown of machinery and want of water and materials. But I am clearly of opinion that it would be no excuse to the master, for non-performance of his implied obligation to provide the workman with work, that he could no longer make his plates at a profit either for orders or for stock . . .

Browning v *Crumlin Valley Collieries Ltd*
[1926] 1 KB 522
King's Bench Division

Browning and others were miners who refused to work in the defendant's mine because it had become unsafe. It was found as a fact that this was not due to the fault of the employer, but was caused by natural forces. The miners sought to recover compensation for the wages they lost during the period when the mine was closed to allow the essential repair work to be done.

GREER J: The consideration for work is wages, and the consideration for wages is work. Is it to be implied in the engagement that the wages are to be paid when through no fault of the employer the work cannot be done? The principle that ought to guide the Court when asked to say whether any term should be read by implication into a written contract was stated by Bowen LJ, in *The Moorcock* [(1889) 16 Probate Division 64], and his words have ever since been accepted as the guiding principle. In any case in which it is necessary to ascertain whether any and what term should be implied in a written contract the correct application of this guiding principle has to be determined. Bowen LJ, said: 'Now, an implied warranty, or, as it is called, a covenant in law, as distinguished from an express contract or express warranty, really is in all cases founded on the presumed intention of the parties, and upon reason. The implication which the law draws from what must obviously have been the intention of the parties, the law draws with the object of giving efficacy to the transaction and preventing such a failure of consideration as cannot have been within the contemplation of either side' . . .

It seems to me that there must in the circumstances of the present case be some implied term. The men did not work, they were not ready and willing to work in the state the mine was in, and the agreement is silent on the question whether they are in these circumstances entitled to be paid wages. Were the mineowners to bear 'all the chances of failure' due to the operation of natural forces without any fault on their part? Were the perils of the transaction in that event to be all on one side, or must the consequences be divided between the two parties, the employers losing the advantages of continuing to have their coal gotten and being compelled to undertake expensive repairs, and the men on their part losing their wages for such time as was reasonably required to put the mine into a safe condition? The latter, I think, must be presumed to have been the intention of both parties. I am satisfied that no employer would have consented to agree that the workmen should be free to withhold their work if the mine became dangerous through no fault on his part and yet should be entitled to be paid their wages. I think the employer would only have agreed to the workmen's right to withhold their labour under these circumstances, subject to the condition that they should not be entitled to their wages. Further, it seems to me clear from the way in which the present case was conducted, and from the evidence given by several witnesses, that this was the usual understanding of the effect of the men's contract of employment. . . .

Great reliance was placed by Mr Matthews on the decision in *Devonald* v *Rosser & Son*, but in that case the defendant's failure to provide work for the plaintiff so as to enable him to earn his piecework pay was due to the employer deciding that owing to bad trade it would pay him better to close down. It was not due to a cause over which he had no control, it was neither illegal nor impossible for him to continue to find work for the plaintiff, and the Court expressly left open the question whether the plaintiff could have succeeded if the stoppage had been due to such a cause, indicating, I think, that they inclined to the opinion that he could not: see per Lord Alverstone CJ, and per Sir Gorell Barnes, President, where the learned President uses these words: 'I can quite understand that, having regard to a certain set of circumstances, such as breakage of machinery, it may be reasonable to hold that it was the intention of the parties that those risks should be shared, that risks of that character which are known to both parties, and which prevent both from doing what was contemplated, should excuse from the obligation to maintain the continuance of the work.' I think these observations apply *a fortiori* to contracts between mineowners and their workpeople.

Note
Freedland has criticised the *Browning* decision as comparable 'to a hypothetical finding that the owner of a factory was not responsible to his employees for the shut-down of a building where the roof collapsed as a result of the gradual and perceptible erosion of the fabric by wind and rain' (*The Contract of Employment*, p. 59). Wedderburn wonders, given that the judges were saying the intention of the parties must have been to share the loss of this natural event, 'would they have said the same if a crop of diamonds had appeared?' (*The Worker and The Law*, 3rd ed. (Harmondsworth: Penguin, 1986), p. 231).

Question
Do you think that the decision in *Browning* accords with contemporary views as to the extent of an employer's responsibilities?

Notes
1. An express term or custom may permit lay-off without pay. From the Second World War there have developed many collectively bargained provisions for guaranteed minimum weekly wages in the event of lay-off or

short-term working, though these payments are generally subject to suspension in the event of industrial action. In the absence of collectively agreed arrangements there is a restricted right to guarantee payments in every contract of employment (see now ERA 1996, ss. 28–35).

2. Part I of the Wages Act 1986 came into force at the beginning of 1987. It replaced the protection, formerly provided by the Truck Acts, from arbitrary deductions from wages. The relevant provisions are now contained in Pt II of ERA 1996. Section 13 of the 1996 Act allows deductions to be made only if they are authorised or required by a written term of the contract of employment or of some other agreement, or by a term (whether oral or written) whose existence has been explained in writing. The meaning of 'wages' is given in s. 27.

Employment Rights Act 1996

27.   Meaning of 'wages' etc.

(1)   In this Part 'wages', in relation to a worker, means any sums payable to the worker in connection with his employment, including—

(a)   any fee, bonus, commission, holiday pay or other emolument referable to his employment, whether payable under his contract or otherwise,

(b)   statutory sick pay under Part XI of the Social Security Contributions and Benefits Act 1992,

(c)   statutory maternity pay under Part XII of that Act,

(d)   a guarantee payment (under section 28 of this Act),

(e)   any payment for time off under Part VI of this Act or section 169 of the Trade Union and Labour Relations (Consolidation) Act 1992 (payment for time off for carrying out trade union duties etc.),

(f)   remuneration on suspension on medical grounds under section 64 of this Act and remuneration on suspension on maternity grounds under section 68 of this Act,

(g)   any sum payable in pursuance of an order for reinstatement or re-engagement under section 113 of this Act,

(h)   any sum payable in pursuance of an order for the continuation of a contract of employment under section 130 of this Act or section 164 of the Trade Union and Labour Relations (Consolidation) Act 1992, and

(j)   remuneration under a protective award under section 189 of that Act, but excluding any payments within subsection (2).

(2)   Those payments are—

(a)   any payment by way of an advance under an agreement for a loan or by way of an advance of wages (but without prejudice to the application of section 13 to any deduction made from the worker's wages in respect of any such advance),

(b)   any payment in respect of expenses incurred by the worker in carrying out his employment,

(c)   any payment by way of a pension, allowance or gratuity in connection with the worker's retirement or as compensation for loss of office,

(d)   any payment referable to the worker's redundancy, and

(e)   any payment to the worker otherwise than in his capacity as a worker.

(3)   Where any payment in the nature of a non-contractual bonus is (for any reason) made to a worker by his employer, the amount of the payment shall for the purposes of this Part—

(a)   be treated as wages of the worker, and

(b)   be treated as payable to him as such on the day on which the payment is made.

(4)   In this Part 'gross amount', in relation to any wages payable to a worker, means the total amount of those wages before deductions of whatever nature.

(5)   For the purposes of this Part any monetary value attaching to any payment or benefit in kind furnished to a worker by his employer shall not be treated as wages of the worker except in the case of any voucher, stamp or similar document which is—

(a)   of a fixed value expressed in monetary terms, and

(b)   capable of being exchanged (whether on its own or together with other vouchers, stamps or documents, and whether immediately or only after a time) for money, goods or services (or for any combination of two or more of those things).

13.   Right not to suffer unauthorised deductions

(3)   Where the total amount of wages paid on any occasion by an employer to a worker employed by him is less than the total amount of the wages properly payable by him to the worker on that occasion (after deductions), the amount of the deficiency shall be treated for the purposes of this Part as a deduction made by the employer from the worker's wages on that occasion.

Delaney v *Staples (t/a De Montfort Recruitment)*
[1992] IRLR 191
House of Lords

Miss Delaney was summarily dismissed by her employer and given a cheque for £82 as payment in lieu of notice. Subsequently, the employer stopped the cheque, alleging that Delaney had taken away confidential information and that, therefore, he was entitled to dismiss her without notice.

Miss Delaney complained to an industrial tribunal under the Wages Act 1986 with regard to a number of matters, including the failure to pay her the £82 in lieu of notice. The tribunal rejected this aspect of her claim, holding that payment in lieu did not fall within the definition of 'wages' as set out in what is now ERA 1996, s. 27. Her appeal on this issue was rejected by the EAT, the Court of Appeal and the House of Lords.

LORD BROWNE-WILKINSON: . . . The proper answer to this case turns on the special definition of 'wages' in [s. 27] of the Act. But it is important to approach such definition bearing in mind the normal meaning of that word. I agree with the Court of Appeal that the essential characteristic of wages is that they are consideration for work done or to be done under a contract of employment. If a payment is not referable to an obligation on the employee under a subsisting contract of employment to render his services it does not in my judgment fall within the ordinary meaning of the word 'wages'. It follows that if an employer terminates the employment (whether lawfully or not), any payment in respect of the period after the date of such termination is not a payment of wages (in the ordinary meaning of that word) since the employee is not under obligation to render services during that period.

The phrase 'payment in lieu of notice' is not a term of art. It is commonly used to describe many types of payment, the legal analysis of which differs. Without attempting to give an exhaustive list, the following are the principal categories:

1.   An employer gives proper notice of termination to his employee, tells the employee that he need not work until the termination date and gives him the wages attributable to the notice period in a lump sum. In this case (commonly called 'garden leave') there is no breach of contract by the employer. The employment continues until the expiry of notice: the lump sum payment is simply advance payment of wages.

2.   The contract of employment provides expressly that the employment may be terminated either by notice or, on payment of a sum in lieu of notice, summarily. In such a case if the employer summarily dismisses the employee he is not in breach of contract provided that he makes the payment in lieu. But the payment in lieu is not a payment of wages in the ordinary sense since it is not a payment for work to be done under the contract of employment.

3.   At the end of the employment, the employer and the employee agree that the employment is to terminate forthwith on payment of a sum in lieu of notice. Again, the employer is not in breach of contract by dismissing summarily and the payment in lieu is not strictly wages since it is not remuneration for work done during the continuance of the employment.

4.   Without the agreement of the employee, the employer summarily dismisses the employee and tenders a payment in lieu of proper notice. This is by far the most common type of payment in lieu and the present case falls into this category. The employer is in breach of contract by dismissing the employee without proper notice. However, the summary dismissal is effective to put an end to the employment relationship, whether or not it unilaterally discharges the contract of employment. Since the employment relationship has ended, no further services are to be rendered by the employee under the contract. It follows that the payment in lieu is not a payment of wages in the ordinary sense since it is not a payment for work done under the contract of employment.

The nature of a payment in lieu falling within the fourth category has been analysed as a payment by the employer on account of the employee's claim for damages for breach of contract. In *Gothard* v *Mirror Group Newspapers Ltd* [1988] IRLR 396, 14, Lord Donaldson Lymington MR stated the position to be as follows:

> If a man is dismissed without notice, but with money in lieu, what he receives is, as a matter of law, payment which falls to be set against, and will usually be designed by the employer to extinguish, any claim for damages for breach of contract, i.e. wrongful dismissal. During the period to which the money in lieu relates he is not employed by his employer.

In my view that statement is the only possible legal analysis of a payment in lieu of the fourth category. But it is not, and was not meant to be, an analysis of a payment in lieu of the first three categories, in none of which is the dismissal a breach of contract by the employer. In the first three categories, the employee is entitled to the payment in lieu not as damages for breach of contract but under a contractual obligation on the employer to make the payment.

Against that background. I turn to the relevant provisions of the Act. Section 1(1) prohibits an employer from making 'any deduction from any wages of any worker employed by him' unless such deduction is of a kind authorised by s. 1 of the Act. Therefore, to fall within the prohibition contained in s. 1 two things have to be demonstrated: first, that there has been a 'deduction': second that the deduction was made from 'wages'.

[His Lordship then proceeded to set out what is now ERA 1996, s. 13(3)] . . .].

The Court of Appeal in this case held that a total failure to make any payment of a sum due could be a 'deduction' within this definition. There is no appeal against

that decision, nor has there been any submission that it was wrong. I must therefore proceed on the basis that it is correct, without expressing any view of my own one way or the other.
[His Lordship then proceeded to set out the definition of 'wages' now found in ERA 1996, s. 27] . . .]
The critical question is whether a payment in lieu falls within this wide definition as being a sum payable to an employee 'in connection with his employment'.
. . .
. . . The first inquiry must be whether the language of the Act throws any light on the problem. The words 'in connection with his employment' are very wide, in my judgment quite wide enough to include a payment in lieu. I do not agree with the Court of Appeal that prima facie the words are not wide enough to include a payment in lieu because such payments are payments of damages for breach of contract. First, not all payments in lieu (other than garden leave) are payments of damages. Even in the fourth category of case where payments in lieu are properly analysed as being payment of damages, that does not in my judgment mean that they are not payments 'in connection with' the employment. Apart from a context indicating the contrary view, payments connected with the termination of employment (whether or not characterised as damages) are quite capable of being described as being made 'in connection with that employment.'
Nor do I get any help from the items expressly included and excluded by [ERA 1996, s. 27(1) and (2)]. Given the presence of express inclusions as well as express exclusions, there is no room for an argument that by expressly excluding certain items that draftsman was indicating that such items would otherwise be payments 'in connection with' the employment. Nor can I detect a rough division between the express inclusions as being payments arising from services rendered under the contract and the express exclusions as payments arising from events on or after the termination of the employment. For example, the advances of wages and expenses incurred in carrying out the employment (both of which are excluded items under [ERA 1996, s. 27(2)(a) and (b)] both relate to acts occurring during the subsistence of the contract of employment.
. . .
Therefore on the language of the Act, I find neither anything which cuts down the wide meaning of the words 'in connection with his employment' nor anything which demonstrates that Parliament intended payments in lieu to fall within the definition of 'wages'. I turn therefore to the way in which the Act would operate if payments in lieu were included in the word 'wages'. Like the Court of Appeal. I find that the provisions of the Act cannot be made to work if payments in lieu are included in the meaning of wages. I will demonstrate the difficulties by reference to the fourth and most common category of payment in lieu, i.e. where the worker is summarily dismissed in breach of contract and the employer makes no payment in lieu or a payment in lieu of a sum less than the full amount of the wages for the notice period.
First, in order to demonstrate that such payment in lieu is a 'deduction' the worker will have to satisfy the requirements of [ERA 1996, s. 13(3)]. He will have to show that there was an occasion on which 'wages' were payable to him and the amount of the wages which should properly have been paid to him on that occasion. These requirements cannot be satisfied in relation to a payment in lieu. There is no 'occasion' on which the payment in lieu was 'properly' payable. The worker has no contractual or other right to the lump sum of liquidated damages at any time prior to the judgment. Even assuming that the occasion for such payment in lieu was the date of summary dismissal, what was the sum 'properly' then payable? If the worker obtains

alternative employment during the notice period, the damages for wrongful dismissal on account of loss of wages which would be payable by the employer falls to be reduced by the wages received by the worker from the alternative employment during the notice period. It is therefore impossible at the time of dismissal to quantify the correct amount of the payment in lieu. Accordingly there is no way in which the amount of the 'deduction' can be calculated under [s. 13(3)].

Next, under [ERA 1996, s. 23(2)(a)] a complaint to an Industrial Tribunal in relation to an improper deduction has to be made within three months of 'the date of payment of the wages from which the deduction was made'. As I have said, it is impossible to identify the date on which the payment in lieu should have been made. Therefore the time limit in [s. 23(2)] cannot be calculated.

Next, under the general law an employer, in paying damages for wrongful dismissal or a payment in lieu by way of liquidated damages, is entitled to set off any cross-claim he may have against his employee. For example, in the present case the employer, Mr Staples, was asserting a cross-claim against Miss Delaney for an alleged breach of her duty of confidentiality. If a payment in lieu constitutes 'wages' for the purposes of the Act, no such deduction of cross-claims is permissible since it would not be authorised by [s. 13]. Moreover, if the employer were to exercise his right of set-off under the general law by deducting the amount of his cross-claim from a payment in lieu, if the payment in lieu is 'wages' the worker could apply to the Industrial Tribunal for an order that the employer repay the unauthorised deduction even if it was a legitimate cross-claim. The Industrial Tribunal would be bound to order such repayment [s. 24] and in consequence the employer would lose his right to enforce his cross-claim in any proceedings to the extent of the sum wrongly deducted: [s. 25(4)]. I find it impossible to believe that Parliament in passing this legislation intended, by a side wind, to alter the common law rights of employers and workers on the termination of employment.

For these reasons, I am forced to the conclusion that payments in lieu of the fourth category do not fall within the statutory definition of 'wages'. Where then is the dividing line to be drawn? In my judgment one is thrown back to the basic concept of wages as being payments in respect of the rendering of services during the employment, so as to exclude all payments in respect of the termination of the contract, save to the extent that such latter payments are expressly included in the definition in [s. 27(1)]. It follows that payments in respect of 'garden leave' (my category 1) are 'wages' within the meaning of the Act since they are advance payments of wages falling due under a subsisting contract of employment. But all other payments in lieu, whether or not contractually payable (my categories 2, 3 and 4), are not wages within the meaning of the Act since they are payments relating to the termination of the employment, not to the provision of services under the employment. To draw a distinction between those cases where the payment in lieu is contractually based and the normal payment in lieu which consists of liquidated damages would be to invite numerous disputes as to the jurisdiction of the Industrial Tribunal, which cannot have been Parliament's intention. For these reasons, I agree with the decision of the Court of Appeal.

This conclusion produces an untidy and unsatisfactory result. On any dismissal, the summary procedure of the Industrial Tribunal under the Act will be exercisable in relation to unpaid wages (in the ordinary sense), holiday pay, commission, maternity leave etc, but claims relating to the failure to give proper notice will continue to have to be brought in the County Court. The employee is therefore forced either to bring two sets of proceedings or to proceed wholly in the County Court on a claim for damages. To be forced to bring two sets of proceedings for small sums of money in relation to one dismissal is wasteful of time and money. It brings the law into disrepute and is not calculated to ensure that employees recover their full legal entitlement when wrongfully dismissed. The position is capable of remedy by an order under s. 131 of the Employment Protection (Consolidation) Act 1978 [now ETA 1996, s. 3(1)] which enables the Minister to confer jurisdiction on Industrial Tribunals to deal with claims for breach of contract. As the judgment of Lord Donaldson of Lymington MR in the present case shows, the courts have been suggesting that this power be exercised for nearly 20 years, so far without success [1991] IRLR 112, 31–8. I believe that all your Lordships are of the view that the present unsatisfactory position calls for fresh consideration by the Minister.

My Lords, for these reasons I would dismiss the appeal.

Note

In *Delaney* v *Staples (t/a De Montfort Recruitment)* [1991] IRLR 112, the Court of Appeal held that the Act can apply to a simple non-payment. This conclusion was not the subject of an appeal to the House of Lords. One division of the EAT had consistently held that the Act only applied to a 'deduction', not a failure to pay altogether (which therefore remained a matter for the county court). However, the Court of Appeal approved the view of other EAT decisions, that the statutory definition of a deduction in what is now ERA 1996, s. 13(3) has to be applied literally, thus ignoring any common law distinction between non-payment and deduction.

The Act was concerned with unauthorised deduction. But [s. 13(3)] made it plain that, leaving aside errors of computation, any shortfall in the amount of wages properly payable was to be treated as a deduction. That being so, a dispute on whatever grounds as to the amount of wages properly payable could not have the effect of taking the case outside [s. 13(3)]. (per Nicholls LJ)

Thus, Miss Delaney could bring industrial tribunal proceedings to recover £55.50 unpaid commission and holiday pay outstanding on her dismissal, as an unauthorised deduction. From a policy standpoint this must be correct. The distinction made by Wood J in *Alsop* v *Star Vehicle Contracts Ltd* [1990] ICR 378 and *Barlow* v *Whittle* [1990] ICR 270 would have had the result that an underpaid employee would be able to go to the industrial tribunal, whereas an employee not paid at all would be forced to go to the ordinary courts. As Mr Justice Nicholls put it, 'This hardly seems sensible'.

Question

The House of Lords conclusion in *Delaney* is recognised by Lord Browne-Wilkinson as producing 'an untidy and unsatisfactory result'. What prompts this conclusion, and how far will the orders made under EPCA 1978, s. 131 (now ETA 1996, s. 3(1)) – set out at p. 21 – help matters?

Notes

1. The assumption behind the legislation is that freedom of contract is a sufficient general protection against the level and purpose of deductions. However, there is a degree of recognition of the need to give an additional

element of protection to workers in retail employment, where the deduction from wages for cash shortages or stock deficiencies is a relatively common practice.

The workers covered are those whose employment involves them in the sale or supply of goods or services (including financial services) directly to members of the public, fellow workers or other individuals in their personal capacities (ERA 1996, s. 17). This definition would encompass those employed as petrol station cashiers, shop assistants, waiters and bank cashiers, but would leave other equally vulnerable groups without special protection, e.g. warehouse and stockroom staff, kitchen staff, etc. For those who do fall within the protected category, s. 18 limits the amount that may be deducted in respect of cash and stock shortages on any one pay day to one-tenth of the gross wages due on that day.

The limitations on the amount deducted or demanded at any one time are not aimed at limiting the overall size of the worker's liability to the employer; the provisions merely serve to allow liability to be discharged by 'easy payments'. There seems no reason why an employer cannot recover for cash shortages or stock deficiencies far in excess of the 10 per cent figure by spreading the deductions or payments over several pay days.

Section 22 makes it clear that the 10 per cent limit does not apply to the 'final payment of wages', i.e. wages for the last period the worker is employed before termination or, if paid later, wages in lieu of notice. Therefore, an employer who has not been able to recover the total liability during the currency of the contract may do so without limit at its termination. Indeed, it may be argued that some employers will be tempted to dismiss workers responsible for cash shortages and stock deficiencies in order to avoid the 10 per cent deduction/payment threshold and to recover their losses immediately. This would result in an onerous double indemnity for workers in retail employment, particularly those who lack the requisite length of employment to qualify for unfair dismissal rights.

2.   Section 23 of the Act allows the worker the right to complain to an employment tribunal, within three months, of any alleged infringement of the restrictions imposed by ss. 13, 15 and 18.

Where the tribunal finds the complaint well founded, it must make a declaration to that effect and either:

(a)   order the employer to repay to the worker the amount of deduction or payment if made in contravention of general restrictions under s. 1; or

(b)   in the case of breach of the 10 per cent deduction/payment threshold for retail workers, order repayment of the amount which exceeded the limit.

It appears the tribunal order can relate to all such deductions/payments which have been made in breach of the provisions. In this regard the remedy is more effective than the one offered by statute for unnotified deductions under ERA 1996, s. 12(4), the latter allowing only for the recoupment of deductions which have taken place in the preceding 13 weeks.

3. Section 11 of the Wages Act 1986 repealed the Truck Acts 1831–1940 and any other statutes connected with the payment of wages, including the Payment of Wages Act 1960. The last statute allowed an employer to arrange for wages to be paid into an individual's bank account, by money order, postal order or by cheque, where that individual consented in writing. Either party could terminate such an agreement by giving four weeks' notice. The effect of these repeals is to remove the manual worker's right to be paid in the 'coin of the realm'.

4. Deductions from the wages of those taking industrial action are exempted from the requirement of the ERA 1996 by s. 14(5). The subsection does not provide any positive authority to the employer to make deductions from salary. Whether such a right exists remains a question governed by the common law.

Miles v *Wakefield Metropolitan District Council*
[1987] IRLR 193
House of Lords

Mr Miles was a superintendent registrar of births, marriages and deaths. He normally worked 37 hours per week, three of which were on Saturday mornings.

Between August 1981 and October 1982, as part of industrial action, Mr Miles refused to carry out marriages on Saturday mornings. The council made it clear that if he was not prepared to undertake the full range of his duties on Saturdays, he would not be required to attend for work and would not be paid. Accordingly, although Mr Miles performed other work on Saturday mornings, the council withheld 3/37ths of his pay for the relevant period, effectively not paying him for Saturday mornings.

Mr Miles brought an action claiming the sums withheld, but his claim was ultimately dismissed by the House of Lords.

LORD TEMPLEMAN: . . . In a contract of employment wages and work go together. The employer pays for work and the worker works for his wages. If the employer declines to pay, the worker need not work. If the worker declines to work, the employer need not pay. In an action by a worker to recover his pay he must allege and be ready to prove that he worked or was willing to work. Different considerations apply to a failure to work by sickness or other circumstances which may be governed by express or implied terms or by custom. In the present case the plaintiff disentitled himself for his salary for Saturday morning because he declined to work on Saturday morning in accordance with his duty.

Where industrial action takes the form of working inefficiently, the employer may decline to accept any work and the worker will not then be entitled to wages.

I agree with my noble and learned friend Lord Bridge of Harwich that industrial action can take many forms and that the legal consequences of industrial action will depend on the rights and obligations of the worker, the effect of the industrial action on the employer and the response of the employer. For my part, however, I take the provisional view that on principle a worker who, in conjunction with his fellow workers, declines to work efficiently with the object of harming his employer, is no more entitled to his wages under the contract than if he declined to work at all. The worker whose industrial action takes the form of 'going slow' inflicts intended damage which may be incalculable and non-apportionable but the employer, in order to avoid greater damage, is obliged to accept the reduced work the worker is willing to perform. In those circumstances, the worker cannot claim that he is entitled to his wages under the contract because he is deliberately working in a manner designed to harm the employer. But the worker will be entitled to be paid on a quantum meruit basis for the amount and value of the reduced work performed and accepted. In the present case, the council, by their letter dated 18.10.81, refused to accept any work from the plaintiff unless he worked normally and discharged all his duties. The plaintiff offered to work inefficiently on Saturday but could not compel the council to accept that offer, and upon their refusal to accept that offer, he ceased to be entitled to be paid for Saturday. My present view is that a worker who embarks on any form of industrial action designed to harm his employer gives up his right to wages under his contract of employment, in the hope that the industrial action will be successful in procuring higher wages in the future, and possibly in the hope that negotiations which end the industrial dispute will provide for some payment for the period of the industrial action.

LORD BRIGHTMAN: If an employee offers partial performance, as he does in some types of industrial conflict falling short of a strike, the employer has a choice. He may decline to accept the partial performance that is offered, in which case the employee is entitled to no remuneration for his unwanted services, even if they are performed. That is the instant case. Or the employer may accept the partial performance. If he accepts the partial performance as if it were performance which satisfied the terms of the contract, the employer must pay the full wage for the period of the partial performance because he will have precluded or estopped himself from asserting that the performance was not that which the contract required. But what is the position if the employee offers partial performance and the employer, usually of necessity, accepts such partial performance, the deficient work being understood by the employer and intended by the employee to fall short of the contractual requirements and being accepted by the employer as such? There are, as it seems to me, two possible answers. One possible answer is that the employer must pay the full wage but may recover by action or counterclaim or set-off damages for breach of contract. The other possible answer is that the employee is only entitled to so much remuneration as represents the value of the work he has done, i.e. quantum meruit. My noble and learned friend, Lord Templeman, prefers the latter solution, and so do I. My reason is this. One has to start with the assumption that the employee sues for his pay; the employer is only bound to pay the employee that which the employee can recover by action. The employee cannot recover his contractual wages because he cannot prove that he has performed or ever intended to perform his contractual obligations. If wages and work are interdependent, it is difficult to suppose that an employee who has voluntarily declined to perform his contractual work can claim his contractual wages. The employee offers partial performance with the object of inflicting the maximum damage on the employer at the minimum inconvenience to himself. If, in breach of his contract, an employee works with the object of harming his employer, he can hardly claim that he is working under his contract and is therefore entitled to his contractual wages. But nevertheless in the case supposed the employee has provided *some* services, albeit less than the contract required, and the employer has received those (non-contractual) services; therefore the employer must clearly pay something – not the contractual wages because the contractual work has deliberately not been performed. What can he recover? Surely the value of the services which he gave and which the employer received, i.e. quantum meruit.

LORD BRIDGE OF HARWICH: . . . Industrial action can take many different forms and there are a variety of options open to an employer confronted by such action. In particular I should, for my part, have preferred to express no opinion on questions arising in the case of an employee who deliberately 'goes slow' or otherwise does his work in a less than satisfactory way, when the employer nevertheless acquiesces in his continuing to work the full number of hours required under his contract. There may be no single, simple principle which can be applied in such cases irrespective of differences in circumstances. But I find it difficult to understand the basis on which, in such a case, the employee in place of remuneration at the contractual rate would become entitled to a quantum meruit. This would presuppose that the original contract of employment had in some way been superseded by a new agreement by which the employee undertook to work as requested by the employer for remuneration in a reasonable sum. This seems to me to be contrary to the realities of the situation.

Note

The House of Lords do not definitely answer the question of what the position would be where the employee goes slow or works to rule in breach of contract and the employer accepts (albeit reluctantly) the reduced work as partial performance of the contract (this was not a problem on the facts of the *Miles* case because his employers had refused his offer to attend on Saturday mornings to perform other duties). As will be seen from the extract above, this is a difference of judicial view.

Question

Can you explain the competing views?

Wiluszynski v *Tower Hamlets London Borough Council*
[1989] IRLR 259
Court of Appeal

On the facts, the employee was informed that he should not attend work if he was not prepared to carry out his full duties and that if he carried out work it would be regarded as unauthorised and undertaken in a voluntary capacity. However, throughout the month-long industrial dispute, Mr W. (an estate officer in the housing department) continued to report for work and carried out his duties normally and conscientiously – except for a limited form of industrial action which involved refusing to deal with enquiries from councillors about their constituents' housing problems. Estate officers normally received only a handful of such queries per week. Indeed, once the dispute was over, Mr W. dealt with all the outstanding councillor enquiries in less than three hours. Nevertheless, the Council saw the answering of councillor queries as a significant part of officers' duties and refused to pay W. and the other officers any salary for the whole month of the dispute. The Court of Appeal upheld the employer's right to take that course of action.

NICHOLLS LJ: The defendant did not wish to take any steps, and it did not take any steps, physically to prevent the plaintiff and the other estate officers concerned from remaining at their desks. For instance, the defendant did not attempt to call in the police or security staff, or apply to the court for an injunction. For its part, the union did not wish to call its members out on strike, with all the ensuing dislocation to the defendant's numerous tenants, and it did not do so. Accordingly, the plaintiff and his colleagues insisted on continuing to work. The upshot was that, although the defendant had said it would not accept services which amounted to no more than partial performance of the employees' duties, in fact it did accept such services.

On analysis, the plaintiff's case is that the defendant thereby resiled from its attitude as stated in the letter of 14 August. By accepting the services proffered, it waived its rights not to pay for those services. The defendant must therefore pay the plaintiff his salary, less a deduction for his failure to carry out one part of his duties: answering Members' Enquiries.

I cannot accept this argument. Implicit in this argument, with its reliance on the defendant's 'acceptance' of the plaintiff's services is the notion that in the event the defendant acted inconsistently with the attitude expressed in its warning letter, and that having chosen or elected so to act, it could not subsequently rely on the terms of the letter. But a person is not treated by the law as having chosen to accept that which is forced down his throat despite his objections. The rationale underlying the principle of waiver is that a person cannot have it both ways: he cannot blow hot and cold; he cannot eat his cake and have it; he cannot approbate and reprobate. But this does not mean that an employer of a large workforce is required physically to eject a defaulting employee from his office, or prevent him from going round the estate of houses for which he is responsible, on penalty that if he, the employer, does not do so he must pay the employee for the work which the employee insists on carrying out contrary to the employer's known wishes.

Question

The interesting feature of this case was the rather narrow view of what constitutes 'acceptance' of the part performance. Indeed, would you agree that Lord Justice Nicholls does appear to be allowing the employer to 'have his cake and eat it'?

Note

See also *British Telecommunications plc* v *Ticehurst* [1992] IRLR 219, CA, set out at p. 727.

(ii)   An Obligation to Provide Work?

Turner v *Sawdon & Co.*
[1901] 2 KB 653
Court of Appeal

Turner was a salesman who was paid a fixed salary and was not entitled to commission. He brought an action for breach of contract because, although his salary continued to be paid, he was given no work to do.

A.L. SMITH MR: The real question which the plaintiff thought to raise, and which was raised, was whether beyond the question of remuneration there was a further obligation on the masters that, during the period over which the contract was to extend, they should find continuous, or at least some, employment for the plaintiff. In my opinion such an action is unique – that is an action in which it is shown that the master is willing to pay the wages of his servant, but is sued for damages because the servant is not given employment. In *Turner* v *Goldsmith* [1891] 1 QB 544 the wages were to be paid in the form of commission, and that impliedly created a contract to find employment for the servant. This contract is different, being to employ for wages which are to be paid at a certain rate per year. I do not think this can be read otherwise than as a contract by the master to retain the servant, and during the time covered by the retainer to pay him wages under such a contract. It is within the province of the master to say that he will go on paying the wages, but that he is under no obligation to provide work. The obligation suggested is said to arise out of the undertaking to engage and employ the plaintiff as their representative salesman. It is said that if the salesman is not given employment which allows him to go on the market his hand is not kept in practice, and he will not be so efficient a salesman at the end of the term. To read in an obligation of that sort would be to convert the retainer at fixed wages into a contract to keep the servant in the service of his employer in such a manner as to enable the former to become *au fait* at his work. In my opinion, no such obligation arose under this contract, and it is a mistake to stretch the words of the contract so as to include in what is a mere retainer an obligation to employ the plaintiff continuously for the term of his service.

Collier v *Sunday Referee Publishing Co. Ltd*
[1940] 2 KB 647
King's Bench Division

Collier was employed as the chief sub-editor of the *Sunday Referee* news-paper. His employers sold the newspaper and the new owners did not wish to employ Collier, and so his employers retained him. They continued to pay his wages but gave him no work to do. He claimed damages arising from his employer's breach of contract in not providing him with work. The High Court upheld his claim.

ASQUITH J: It is true that a contract of employment does not necessarily, or perhaps normally, oblige the master to provide the servant with work. Provided I pay my cook her wages regularly she cannot complain if I choose to take any or all of my meals out. In some exceptional cases there is an obligation to provide work. For instance, where the servant is remunerated by commission, or where (as in the case of an actor or singer) the servant bargains, among other things, for publicity, and the master, by withholding work, also withholds the stipulated publicity: *Marbe* v *George Edwardes (Daly's Theatre) Ltd* [1928] 1 KB 269; but such cases are anomalous, and the normal rule is illustrated by authorities such as *Lagerwall* v *Wilkinson, Henderson & Clarke Ltd* [80 LT 55] and *Turner* v *Sawdon & Co.* [1901 2 KB 653] where the plaintiffs (a commercial traveller and a salesman respectively, retained for a fixed period and remunerated by salary) were held to have no legal complaint so long as the salary continued to be paid, notwithstanding that owing to their employers' action they were left with nothing to do. The employers were not bound to supply work to enable the employee, as the phrase goes, to 'keep his hand in', or to avoid the reproach of idleness, or even to make a profit out of a travelling allowance. In such a case there is no breach of contract, but the result is much the same as if there had been, because in either event the plaintiff is entitled to a sum or sums which are measured prima facie by the amount of salary in respect of the unexpired period of service.

I do not hold that in the present case there was in the contract of employment an implied stipulation for publicity and an obligation to provide work for the purpose of providing publicity. But I do hold that the very foundation of the contract was the appointment of the plaintiff, during the contract period to a specific office. The defendants engaged the plaintiff, not to perform at large the sort of work commonly performed by any chief sub-editor. They engaged him to fill the office of chief sub-editor of a specific Sunday newspaper. By selling that newspaper they destroyed the office to which they had appointed him. That this is a breach of contract, I cannot doubt.

Breach v Epsylon Industries Ltd
[1976] IRLR 180
Employment Appeal Tribunal

Breach worked as the employer's chief engineer. The contracts on which he was employed were transferred to an overseas office and he was left with no work to do. He claimed that the failure to provide him with work amounted to a constructive dismissal and that he was entitled to a redundancy payment. The industrial tribunal rejected his claim and he appealed to the EAT.

PHILLIPS J: The difficulty that we find in the case is this: *Turner v Sawdon & Co* [1901] 2 KB 653 is a decision in the Court of Appeal. It is binding upon us as it was binding upon the industrial tribunal. However, it appears from the judgments in that case, and in particular from the observations of Stirling LJ, that there may well be cases which are exceptions to the general rule and where it can be said that from the nature of the employment, the circumstances in which it has to be served, and so on, there is indeed an obligation on the part of the employer to provide work. The line is a difficult one to draw. It may be said that the underlying thought in *Turner v Sawdon* is somewhat out of date and old fashioned now; that fact, if it be a fact, cannot invalidate the binding effect of that decision, but it may within limits lead to the consequence that a consideration of the facts will more easily lead to the conclusion that the case is one where there is such an obligation to provide work.

. . . It seems to us at least possible that the tribunal was saying to themselves that *Turner v Sawdon & Co* lays down a principle of law of the effect that employers are under no obligation to provide their employees with work to do. If that is so, then, with respect, there was a misdirection because it was necessary to look at the background to the contract to see how it should be construed, and whether a term ought not to be implied that in the circumstances of this case there was an obligation on the employers to provide work suitable for a chief engineer. If the tribunal did consider that, and if in fact, after considering all the material factors, they reached the view that there was no such implied term in the present case, then again with respect the decision is faulty, because it does not set out as it should do the reasoning by which that conclusion was reached.

Note
The EAT concluded that the industrial tribunal had made an error of law and remitted the case for rehearing.

Langston v *Amalgamated Union of Engineering Workers*
[1974] IRLR 182
National Industrial Relations Court

Langston objected on principle to the 'closed shop' and had refused to join the union. Following industrial action in protest against Langston's continued employment, the employers suspended him from work on full pay. In the course of legal action taken against the union under the now repealed Industrial Relations Act 1971, it was contended that, by inducing Langston's employers to suspend him, the union had induced a breach of contract.

SIR JOHN DONALDSON: The crucial question to be asked is, 'What is the consideration moving from the employers under the contract of employment?' In the case of theatrical performers it is a salary plus the opportunity of becoming better known. Thus a failure to pay the salary produces a partial failure of the consideration, and thus a breach of contract. But so does the cancellation of the performance even if the salary is paid: see *Herbert Clayton and Jack Waller Ltd* v *Oliver* ([1930] AC 209). Similarly the consideration in a commission or piece work contract of employment is the express obligation to pay an agreed rate for work done plus the implied obligation to provide a reasonable amount of work: see *Devonald* v *Rosser & Son* ([1906] 2 KB 728). In a contract for the employment of one who needs practice to maintain or develop his skills, the consideration will include an obligation to pay the salary or wage, but it may also extend to an obligation to provide a reasonable amount of work. The complainant's work as a spot welder may have been in the 'skilled' category, but we do not think that he needs practice in order to maintain his skills. There are, however, other cases in which the sole consideration moving from the employer is the obligation to pay a wage. An example is provided by *Turner* v *Sawdon & Co.* ([1901] 2 KB 653).

The complainant told us: 'I have always worked for my money. I have my pride. I would not be content to get my money for nothing.' We entirely accept what he says, but it does not follow that this was known to his employers when he was engaged. Still less does it follow that his contract of employment was made on the basis that his employers agreed to provide sufficient work to give the complainant a measure of job satisfaction. However, on the facts of this case we think that he comes into the piece worker category. The consideration moving from the employers was to pay him his basic wage for the normal working week, plus premium payments for hours actually worked on night shift or on overtime. The complainant, in common with other employees, was obliged to work days or nights and in such shop as the employers might require. But this right to require him to work a particular shift or in a particular place was not unfettered. Both night shifts and overtime had advantages and disadvantages. It was not only the employers' right but also their duty, forming part of the consideration, to allocate days, nights, overtime and place of work in such a way as to give all a fair opportunity of enjoying the rough as well as the smooth and, in particular, of earning premium payments. Once the employers suspended the complainant, they deprived him of his opportunity of earning premium payments. This was a breach of his contract of employment.

It is perfectly true, and greatly to the employers' credit, that they have sought to calculate what he would have earned if he had not been suspended. They paid him his basic wage week by week and later paid him a further sum in respect of lost premium payments. The calculation was long and difficult and during the hearing they agreed that an error had been made. They then agreed to pay him a further sum. No one can be quite sure that the sums are right now, but they have done their best. But this does not matter. These additional sums are not wages or premium payments. They are damages for breach of contract by failing to allow him the opportunity of earning a like amount.

Note

In *Langston* v *AUEW (No. 1)* [1974] 1 All ER 980, Lord Denning had attempted to completely sweep away the 'no right to work' rule. Commenting on the rule as set in the dictum of Asquith J in *Collier*, Lord Denning stated:

That was said 33 years ago. Things have altered much since then. We have repeatedly said in this court that a man has a right to work, which the courts will protect . . . I would not wish to express any decided view, but simply state the argument which could be put forward for Mr Langston. In these days an employer, when employing a skilled man, is bound to provide him with work. By which I mean that the man should be given the opportunity of doing his work when it is available and when he is ready and willing to do it.

As we have seen, when the *Langston* case came up for full consideration by the NIRC, Sir John Donaldson was not so expansive in approaching the right to work and preferred to fit the case within one of the established exceptions. Nevertheless after the *Breach* case, the exceptions are very wide, allowing plenty of room for judicial discretion in what is perceived to be a deserving case.

(iii)   Care

Lister v Romford Ice and Cold Storage Co. Ltd
[1957] AC 555
House of Lords

L was a lorry-driver employed by R Ltd, who negligently injured a fellow-employee, L's father, while packing his lorry in the course of his employment. L's father sued the company and obtained damages in respect of their vicarious liability. The company's insurers, exercising their rights of subrogation, then brought an action against L in the company's name. They claimed: (1) contribution from L as a joint tortfeasor under the provisions of the Law Reform (Married Women and Tortfeasors) Act 1935, s. 6; and (2) damages for breach of an implied term in his employment contract that he would use reasonable skill and care in his driving.

In the High Court, Ormerod J gave judgment for the company, holding that they were entitled under the 1935 Act to a contribution that would amount to a complete indemnity. L's appeal was dismissed by the Court of Appeal, Denning LJ dissenting; and L unsuccessfully appealed to the House of Lords.

VISCOUNT SIMONDS: . . . It is, in my opinion, clear that it was an implied term of the contract that the appellant would perform his duties with proper care. The proposition of law stated by Willes J in *Harmer* v *Cornelius* [(1858) 5 CBNS 236 at 246] has never been questioned: 'When a skilled labourer,' he said, 'artizan, or artist is employed, there is on his part an implied warranty that he is of skill reasonably competent to the task he undertakes, – Spondes peritiam artis. Thus, if an apothecary, a watch-maker, or an attorney be employed for reward, they each impliedly undertake to possess and exercise reasonable skill in their several arts. . . . An express promise or express representation in the particular case is not necessary.' I see no ground for excluding from, and every ground for including in, this category a servant who is employed to drive a lorry which, driven without care, may become an engine of destruction and involve his master in very grave liability. Nor can I see any valid reason for saying that a distinction is to be made between possessing skill and exercising it. No such distinction is made in the cited case: on the contrary, 'possess' and 'exercise' are there conjoined. Of what advantage to the employer is his servant's undertaking that he possesses skill unless he undertakes also to use it? I have spoken of using skill rather than using care, for 'skill' is the word used in the cited case, but this embraces care. For even in so-called unskilled operations an exercise of care is necessary to the proper performance of duty.

I have already said that it does not appear to me to make any difference to the determination of any substantive issue in this case whether the respondents' cause of action lay in tort or breach of contract. But, in deference to Denning LJ, I think it right to say that I concur in what I understand to be the unanimous opinion of your Lordships that the servant owes a contractual duty of care to his master, and that the breach of that duty founds an action for damages for breach of contract, and that this (apart from any defence) is such a case. It is trite law that a single act of negligence may give rise to a claim either in tort or for breach of a term express or implied in a contract. Of this the negligence of a servant in performance of his duty is a clear example.

I conclude, then, the first stage of the argument by saying that the appellant was under a contractual obligation of care in the performance of his duty, that he committed a breach of it, that the respondents thereby suffered damage and they are entitled to recover that damage from him, unless it is shown either that the damage is too remote or that there is some other intervening factor which precludes the recovery.

[His Lordship turned to the question of indemnity, and discussed the various ways in which the alleged term had been formulated. In the course of concluding that no such term could be implied into the contract, his Lordship said: '[It was not] suggested that in the present case there were any features which distinguished the relation of the appellant and the respondents from that of any other driver and his employer. That is why at the outset of this opinion I said that this appeal raises a question of general importance. For the real question becomes, not what terms can be implied in a contract between two individuals who are assumed to be making a bargain in regard to a particular transaction or course of business; we have to take a wider view, for we are concerned with a general question, which, if not correctly described as a question of status, yet can only be answered by considering the relation in which the drivers of motor-vehicles and their employers generally stand to each other. Just as the duty of care, rightly regarded as a contractual obligation, is imposed on the servant, or the duty not to disclose confidential information (see *Robb* v *Green* [1895] 2 QB 315), or the duty not to betray secret processes (see *Amber Size and Chemical Co Ltd* v *Menzel* [1913] 2 Ch 239), just as the duty is imposed on the master not to require his servant to do any illegal act, just so the question must be asked and answered whether in the world in which we live today it is a necessary condition of the relation of master and man that the master should, to use a broad colloquialism, look after the whole matter of insurance. If I were to try to apply the familiar tests where the question is whether a term should be implied in a particular contract in order to give it what is called business efficacy, I should lose myself in the attempt to formulate it with the necessary precision. The necessarily vague evidence given by the parties and the fact that the action is brought without the assent of the employers shows at least ex post facto how they regarded the position. But this is not conclusive; for, as I have said, the solution of the problem does not rest on the implication of a term in a particular contract of service but upon more general considerations.

LORD RADCLIFFE [dissenting]: . . . On the first point [i.e. what liability did the appellant incur as a result of his negligent driving?] I think it plain that the law does impute to an employee a duty to exercise reasonable care in his handling of his employer's property. It is the fact of such employment that places the property within his control; and if, as must be the case, he owes a general duty to all concerned not to be negligent in his exercise of that control, it would be a surprising anomaly that, merely because there was also a contractual relationship between himself and his employer, the standard of his obligation to his employer were to be somehow lower than the standard of his obligation to the outside world.

I cannot see any good reason why we should uphold the existence of such an anomaly. If the contract of employment is viewed as a general legal relationship in which the law imputes certain rights and responsibilities to each side, it would assign a very undignified position to the employee to suppose that the employer takes him 'with all faults' and that the employee does not by virtue of his engagement impliedly undertake to use all reasonable care in the conduct of his employer's affairs. To say this is to say nothing new in the law. I am satisfied that from early times the law has consistently recognised the existence of this duty. I need not lengthen my opinion by reciting the authorities, some of which are noticed by others of your Lordships.

It was much canvassed in argument before your Lordships whether, if there was some such duty on the appellant, it was anything more than the general duty he owed the world to avoid the tort of negligence. . . .

It is perhaps sufficient if I say that, in my view, this question is a somewhat artificial one. The existence of the duty arising out of the relationship between employer and employed was recognised by the law without the institution of an analytical inquiry whether the duty was in essence contractual or tortious. What mattered was that the duty was there. A duty may exist by contract, express or implied. Since, in any event, the duty in question is one which exists by imputation or implication of law and not by virtue of any express negotiation between the parties, I should be inclined to say that there is no real distinction between the two possible sources of obligation. But it is certainly, I think, as much contractual as tortious. Since in modern times the relationship between master and servant, between employer and employed, is inherently one of contract, it seems to me entirely correct to attribute the duties which arise from that relationship to implied contract. It is a familiar position in our law that the same wrongful act may be made the subject of an action either in contract or in tort at the election of the claimant, and, although the course chosen may produce certain incidental consequences which would not have followed had the other course been adopted, it is a mistake to regard the two kinds of liability as themselves necessarily exclusive of each other.

[His Lordship went on to hold, contrary to Viscount Simonds, that there was also an implied term in the contract to the effect that the employer would not seek to be indemnified by the employee in the event of third party liability.]

[Lord Morton and Lord Tucker delivered judgments concurring with Viscount Simonds; Lord Somervell agreed with Lord Radcliffe.]

Appeal dismissed

Notes

1. Since 1957, there has been a 'gentlemen's agreement' among insurance companies not to bring such actions against workers.

2. For a discussion of the scope of the employer's duty to take reasonable care for an employee's safety, see *Johnstone* v *Bloomsbury Health Authority* [1991] IRLR 118 Court of Appeal (an extract from the case is included at p. 825).

Spring* v *Guardian Assurance plc
[1994] IRLR 460
House of Lords

Mr Spring claimed damages for economic loss from his former employers. He claimed that, in supplying a reference containing allegedly inaccurate information to a prospective employer, they had broken a duty of care to Mr Spring and were liable in the tort of negligent misstatement. In the High Court, the judge allowed the claim. The Court of Appeal allowed the appeal of Mr Spring's former employers and set aside the judgment in the plaintiff's favour. The House of Lords, by a majority of 4 to 1, allowed Mr Spring's appeal.

LORD SLYNN OF HADLEY: . . . two questions therefore arise. The first is whether the nature of the tort of defamation and the tort of injurious falsehood is such that it would be wrong to recognise the possibility of a duty of care in negligence for a false statement. The second question is whether, independently of the existence of the other two torts, and taking the tests adopted by Lord Bridge of Harwich in *Caparo Industries plc* v *Dickman* [1990] 2 AC 605, a duty of care can in any event arise in relation to the giving of a reference. If the answer to the first is no, and to the second yes, then it remains to consider whether in all the circumstances such a duty of care was owed in this case by an employer to an ex-employee.

As to the first question, the starting point in my view is that the suggested claim in negligence and the torts of defamation and injurious and malicious falsehood do not cover the same ground, as Mr Tony Weir shows in his note in (1993) CLJ 376. They are separate torts, defamation not requiring a proof by the plaintiff that the statement was untrue (though justification may be a defence) or that he suffered economic damage, but being subject to defences quite different from those in negligence, such as the defence of qualified privilege which makes it necessary to prove malice. Malicious falsehood requires proof that the statement is false, that harm has resulted and that there was express malice. Neither of these involves the concept of a duty of care. The essence of a claim in defamation is that a person's reputation has been damaged; it may or not involve the loss of a job or economic loss. A claim that a reference has been given negligently is essentially based on the fact, not so much that reputation has been damaged, as that a job, or an opportunity, has been lost. A statement carelessly made may not be defamatory — a statement that a labourer is 'lame', a secretary 'very arthritic', when neither statement is true, though they were true of some other employee mistakenly confused with the person named.

I do not consider that the existence of either of these two heads of claim, defamation and injurious falsehood, a priori prevents the recognition of a duty of care where, but for the existence of the other two torts, it would be fair, just and reasonable to recognise it in a situation where the giver of a reference has said or written what is untrue and where he has acted unreasonably and carelessly in what he has said.

The policy reasons underlying the requirement that the defence of qualified privilege is only dislodged if express malice is established do not necessarily apply in regard to a claim in negligence. There may be other policy reasons in particular situations which should prevail. Thus, in relation to a reference given by an employer in respect of a former employee or a departing employee (and assuming no contractual obligation to take care in giving a reference) it is relevant to consider the changes which have taken place in the employer/employee relationship, with far greater duties imposed on the employer than in the past, whether by statute or by judicial decision, to care for the physical, financial and even psychological welfare of the employee.

As to the second question, it is a relevant circumstance that in many cases an employee will stand no chance of getting another job, let alone a better job, unless he is given a reference. There is at least a moral obligation on the employer to give it. This is not necessarily true when the claim is laid in defamation, even if on an occasion of qualified privilege. In the case of an employee or ex-employee the damage is clearly foreseeable if a careless reference is given; there is as obvious a proximity of relationship in this context as can be imagined. The sole question therefore, in my view, is whether balancing all the factors (Lord Bridge in *Caparo*) as to whether 'the situation should be one in which the court considers it fair, just and reasonable that the law should impose a duty of a given scope upon the one party for the benefit of the other'.

Hedley Byrne & Co. Ltd. v *Heller & Partners Ltd.* [1964] AC 465 does not decide the present case, but I find it unacceptable that the person to whom a reference is given about an employee X should be able to sue for negligence if he relies on the statement (and, for example, employs X who proves to be inadequate for the job) as it appears to be assumed that he can; but that X who is refused employment because the recipient relies on a reference negligently given should have no recourse unless he can prove express malice as defined by Lord Diplock in *Horrocks* v *Lowe* [1975] AC 135 at pp. 149–151.

I do not accept the in terrorem arguments that to allow a claim in negligence will constitute a restriction on freedom of speech or that in the employment sphere employers will refuse to give references or will only give such bland or adulatory ones as is forecast. They should be and are capable of being sufficiently robust as to express frank and honest views after taking reasonable care both as to the factual content and as to the opinion expressed. They will not shrink from the duty of taking reasonable care when they realise the importance of the reference both to the recipient (to whom it is assumed that a duty of care exists) and to the employee (to whom it is contended on existing authority there is no such duty). They are not being asked to warrant absolutely the accuracy of the facts or the incontrovertible validity of the opinions expressed, but to take reasonable care in compiling or giving the reference and in verifying the information on which it is based. The courts can be trusted to set a standard which is not higher than the law of negligence demands. Even if it is right that the number of references given will be reduced, the quality and value will be greater and it is by no means certain that to have more references is more in the public interest than to have more careful references.

Those giving such references can make it clear what are the parameters within which the reference is given, such as stating their limited acquaintance with the individual either as to time or as to situation. This issue does not arise in the present case but it may be that employers can make it clear to the subject of the reference that they will only give one if he accepts that there will be a disclaimer of liability to him and to the recipient of the reference.

Nor does it follow that if a duty of care is recognised in some situations it must exist in all situations. It seems to me that for the purposes of deciding whether the law recognises the duty as being fair, just and reasonable, there may be a difference between the situation where it is an employer or ex-employer who gives a reference and the situation where a reference is given by someone who has only a social acquaintance with the person who is the subject of the reference. There may be difficult situations in between but these will, as is the common practice, have to be worked out in particular situations.

I do not for my part consider that to recognise the existence of a duty of care in some situations when a reference is given necessarily means that the law of defamation has to be changed or that a substantial section of the law relating to defamation and malicious falsehood is 'emasculated' (Court of Appeal [1993] IRLR 122 at p. 131, 100). They remain distinct torts. It may be that there will be less resort to these torts because a more realistic approach on the basis of a duty of care is adopted. If to recognise that such a duty of care exists means that there have to be such changes — either by excluding the defence of qualified privilege from the master/servant situation or by withdrawing the privilege where negligence as opposed to express malice is shown — then I would in the interests of recognising a fair, just and reasonable result in the master/servant situation accept such change.

Note:

1. Lords Goff, Slynn and Woolf held that there was also an implied term in the contract of employment which places a duty on the employer to take due care and skill in preparation of references.

2. According to Lord Slynn and Lord Woolf, there are circumstances in which it is necessary to imply a term into the contract of employment that the employer will provide the employee with a reference at the request of a prospective employer. Such circumstances might arise where the contract relates to an engagement of a class where it is normal practice to require a reference from a previous employer and that the employee cannot be expected to enter that class unless and until a reference is supplied.

(iv)   The Duty to Cooperate

Isle of Wight Tourist Board v *Coombes*
[1976] IRLR 413
Employment Appeal Tribunal

Mrs Coombes was personal secretary to the Director of the Board. She resigned when, in her hearing and after an altercation, the Director said to a fellow employee, 'she is an intolerable bitch on a Monday morning'. Her unfair dismissal claim was upheld by an industrial tribunal and the EAT rejected the employer's appeal.

BRISTOW J: . . . [T]he relationship between somebody in the position of the director of this board and his personal secretary must be one of complete confidence. They must trust each other; they must respect each other. I suspect one should go further and say that, if the work is to be done properly, they must like each other.

Malik v BCCI SA (in liq)
[1997] IRLR 462
House of Lords

In litigation arising out of the collapse of BCCI, the House of Lords decided that the employee's contracts contained an implied term that the bank would not, without reasonable and proper cause, conduct itself in a manner likely to destroy or seriously damage the relationship of confidence and trust between employer and employee.

LORD STEYN: . . .

The implied term of mutual trust and confidence

The employees do not rely on a term implied in fact. They do not therefore rely on an individualised term to be implied from the particular provisions of their employment contracts considered against their specific contextual setting. Instead they rely on a standardised term implied by law, that is, on a term which is said to be an incident of all contracts of employment: *Scally* v *Southern Health and Social Services Board* [1991] IRLR 522, at 525, 12. Such implied terms operate as default rules. The parties are free to exclude or modify them. But it is common ground that in the present case the particular terms of the contracts of employment of the two employees could not affect an implied obligation of mutual trust and confidence.

The employees' primary case is based on a formulation of the implied term that has been applied at first instance and in the Court of Appeal. It imposes reciprocal duties on the employer and employee. Given that this case is concerned with alleged obligations of an employer I will concentrate on its effect on the position of employers. For convenience I will set out the term again. It is expressed to impose an obligation that the employer shall not:

. . . without reasonable and proper cause, conduct itself in a manner calculated and likely to destroy or seriously damage the relationship of confidence and trust between employer and employee.

See *Woods* v *WM Car Services (Peterborough Ltd* [1981] IRLR 347 (Browne-Wilkinson J), approved in *Lewis* v *Motorworld Garages Ltd* [1985] IRLR 465 and *Imperial Group Pension Trust Ltd* v *Imperial Tobacco Ltd* [1991] IRLR 66. A useful anthology of the cases applying this term, or something like it, is given in Sweet and Maxwell's *Encyclopedia of Employment Law* (loose leaf edn), vol. 1, paragraph 1.507, pp. 1467–1470. The evolution of the term is a comparatively recent development. The obligation probably has its origin in the general duty of cooperation between contracting parties: B.A. Hepple, *Employment Law*, 4th edn (1981), paragraphs 291–292, pp. 134–135. The reason for this development is part of the history of the development of employment law in this century. The notion of a 'master and servant' relationship became obsolete. Lord Slynn of Hadley recently noted 'the changes which have taken place in the employer and employee relationship, with far greater duties imposed on the employer than in the past, whether by statute or judicial decision, to care for the physical, financial and even psychological welfare of the employee': *Spring* v *Guardian Assurance plc* [1994] IRLR 460 at 474, 86. A striking illustration of this change is *Scally*, to which I have already referred, where the House of Lords implied a term that all employees in a certain category had to be notified by an employer of their entitlement to certain benefits. It was the change in legal culture which made possible the evolution of the implied term of trust and confidence.

There was some debate at the hearing about the possible interaction of the implied obligation of confidence and trust with other more specific terms implied by law. It is true that the implied term adds little to the employee's implied obligations to serve his employer loyally and not to act contrary to his employer's interests. The major importance of the implied duty of trust and confidence lies in its impact on the obligations of the employer: Douglas Brodie, 'Recent Cases, Commentary, The Heart of the Matter: Mutual Trust and Confidence' (1996) 25 ILJ 121. And the implied obligation as formulated is apt to cover the great diversity of situations in which a balance has to be struck between an employer's interest in managing his business as he sees fit and the employee's interest in not being unfairly and improperly exploited.

The evolution of the implied term of trust and confidence is a fact. It has not yet been endorsed by your Lordships' House. It has proved a workable principle in practice. It has not been the subject of adverse criticism in any decided cases and it has been welcomed in academic writings. I regard the emergence of the implied obligation of mutual trust and confidence as a sound development.

Given the shape of the appeal, my preceding observations may appear unnecessary. But I have felt it necessary to deal briefly with the existence of the implied term for two reasons. First, the implied obligation involves a question of pure law and your Lordships' House is not bound by any agreement of the parties on it or by the acceptance of the obligation by the judge or the Court of Appeal. Secondly, in response to a question, counsel for the bank said that his acceptance of the implied obligation is subject to three limitations:

(1)   That the conduct complained of must be conduct involving the treatment of the employee in question;

(2)   That the employee must be aware of such conduct while he is an employee;

(3)   That such conduct must be calculated to destroy or seriously damage the trust between the employer and employee.

In order to place these suggested limitations in context it seemed necessary to explain briefly the origin, nature and scope of the implied obligation. But subject to examining the merits of the suggested limitations, I am content to accept the implied obligation of trust and confidences as established.

Breach of the implied obligation

Two preliminary observations must be made. First, the sustainability of the employees' claims must be approached as if an application to strike out was under consideration. That is how the judge and the Court of Appeal approached the matter. And the same approach must now govern. Secondly, given the existence of an obligation of trust and confidence, it is important to approach the question of a breach of that obligation correctly. Mr Douglas Brodie of Edinburgh University, in his helpful article to which I have already referred, put the matter succinctly (pp. 121–122):

In assessing whether there has been a breach, it seems clear that what is significant is the impact of the employer's behaviour on the employee rather than what the employer intended. Moreover, the impact will be assessed objectively.

Both limbs of Mr Brodie's observations seem to me to reflect classic contract law principles and I would gratefully adopt his statement.

Notes

1.   The impact of the decision in *Malik v BBCI* on the scope of damages for wrongful dismissal is considered following a further extract from the case at p. 403.

2.   We shall see in Chapter 7 on termination of employment that, in the context of unfair dismissal, the courts have been prepared to make expansive use of the implied term that the employer must not seriously damage the relationship of trust and confidence between employer and employee.

3.   Failure to investigate grievances in certain specific instances has in the past been regarded as a breach of the obligation of trust and confidence on the part of the employer. More recently, the EAT has held that there is a *general* implied term that an employer will reasonably and promptly afford a reasonable opportunity to its employee to obtain redress of any grievance he or she may have (*W. A. Goold (Pearmak) Ltd v McConnell and another* [1995] IRLR 516, an extract appears at p. 397).

4.   The duty of cooperation is not merely one way and, as we shall see, is placed equally on the employee.

(v)   Obedience to Reasonable Orders

Ottoman Bank v *Chakarian*
[1930] AC 277
Privy Council

Chakarian worked for the bank in Turkish Asia Minor. In 1919 he had narrowly escaped execution at the hands of the Turkish forces. He requested a transfer outside Turkey but this was refused by his employer. Chakarian fled from Constantinople to Athens and was summarily dismissed by the bank. The Privy Council upheld his claim for wrongful dismissal.

LORD THANKERTON: . . . [T]he risk of personal danger which caused the respondent's flight from Constantinople, in disregard of the appellants' repeated refusals to allow him to leave, was real and justified from the point of view of his personal safety. . . . It was not seriously maintained by the appellants that their order to the respondent to remain in Constantinople was a lawful order which the respondent was bound to obey at the grave risk to his person. In their Lordships' opinion, the risk to the respondent was such that he was not bound to obey the order, which was therefore not a lawful one.

Note

In a case heard by the same court on the same day, *Bouzouru v Ottoman Bank* [1930] AC 271, PC, the appellant refused to accept a transfer to a branch in Turkey on the grounds of his lack of knowledge of Turkish and the hostile attitude of the civil authorities he would have to deal with. His claim was dismissed, there being no evidence that the transfer would have put him in personal danger.

Morrish v Henlys (Folkestone) Ltd
[1973] 2 All ER 137
National Industrial Relations Court

SIR HUGH GRIFFITHS: This is an appeal from an industrial tribunal which, on 26 October 1972, awarded the appellant the sum of £100 on the ground that he had been unfairly dismissed by the respondents on 3 August 1972. The appellant appeals against the amount of the award. The respondents cross-appeal on the ground that he was not unfairly dismissed.

The facts are in a small compass and are not in dispute. For nearly four years the appellant had been employed by the respondents as a stores driver, and he drove one vehicle all the time. It was his duty to draw diesel oil for the vehicle as and when it was required. On the morning of 2 August 1972 he drew five gallons of diesel oil from one of his employers' forecourt pumps and recorded this on a document called a monthly fuel invoice. He entered in this document the date, the number of the vehicle, the amount and grade of fuel, and he signed it. Next day he drew another five gallons, but when he went to record it on the invoice he discovered that the figure of five gallons he had entered on the previous day had been altered to seven. He changed it back to five. Later that day he found that the entry had again been altered to seven, and again he changed it to five. Still later, he saw that a further entry had been made which showed that on 2nd August two gallons of diesel had been drawn by the vehicle he was driving on that day, and this entry was signed by the manager, Mr Wilkes. The appellant had by this time learned that the manager had made the previous alterations to his figure of five, and so, after crossing out the number of his vehicle against the entry of two gallons, he went to see the manager. A heated interview ensued. Mr Wilkes explained that there was no suggestion that the appellant had in fact drawn seven gallons and not five gallons, but that there was a deficiency of two gallons in the forecourt pumps and the alteration was merely to cover this deficiency and the forecourt staff. The appellant was not willing to have an entry recorded which showed that two gallons of diesel had been put into the vehicle which he was driving, when this was not in fact the case, even if it was against the signature of the manager. The manager told the appellant that as he would not accept his instructions to leave the record showing two gallons attributed to that vehicle, he had no alternative but to give him notice; and this he did. On these facts the tribunal held that the appellant had been unfairly dismissed.

The respondents contended that as there was evidence before the tribunal that it was a common practice to alter the records in this way to cover deficiencies, it was unreasonable of the appellant to object, and he should have accepted the manager's instructions. Accordingly his refusal to do so was an unreasonable refusal to obey an order, which justified dismissal. We cannot accept this submission. It involves the proposition that it is an implied term of an employee's contract of service that he should accept an order to connive at the falsification of one of his employers' records. The proposition only has to be stated to be seen to be untenable. In our view, the appellant was fully entitled to refuse to be in any way party to a falsification of this record and the tribunal was manifestly right in holding that he had been unfairly dismissed. The cross-appeal therefore fails.

. . .

Appeal allowed on other grounds.

Cresswell v Board of Inland Revenue
[1984] ICR 508
Chancery Division

The Inland Revenue Board introduced a new computerised system (COP 1) which replaced the traditional manual method of tax coding. The employees unsuccessfully sought a declaration that the employers were acting in breach of contract in requiring them to operate the computerised system.

WALTON J: The description of the job of a Tax Officer is like the description of the job of any other grade, namely 'the general duties appropriate to the grade concerned.' Bearing this in mind, it will be convenient, as a form of shorthand, to refer to the jobs as those of Clerical Assistant [CA], [Tax Officer] TO or [Tax Officer Higher Grade] TOHG as the case may be.

Granted that down to the present the work of each of these three grades has been done manually, with pen, paper and pocket calculator, if the employer changes this so as largely to remove the necessity to use pen and paper but requires the person concerned to use a computer instead, or in some cases in addition, is the nature of the job thereby fundamentally changed? I do not think that the drawing of parallels with other situations really assists because, at the end of the day, it is the precise impact which is made by the computerisation programme on the day-to-day work of these three grades which is in question. . . .

. . . there can really be no doubt as to the fact that an employee is expected to adapt himself to new methods and techniques introduced in the course of his employment (*cf. North Riding Garages Ltd* v *Butterwick* [1967] 2 QB 56). Of course, in a proper case the employer must provide any necessary training or re-training . . . it will, in all cases, be a question of pure fact as to whether the re-training involved the acquisition of such esoteric skills that it would not be reasonable to expect the employee to acquire them. In an age when the computer has forced its way into the school room and where electronic games are played by schoolchildren in their own homes as a matter of everyday occurrence, it can hardly be considered that to ask an employee to acquire basic skills as to retrieving information from a computer or feeding such information into a computer is something in the slightest esoteric or, even nowadays, unusual. . . .

Of course the changes in working methods and practices which COP brings in its train are great – although I think that the evidence has tended to exaggerate them. But that, as it seems to me, is not the point. COP merely introduces up to date modern methods for dealing with bulk problems: it leaves the jobs-done by those who operate the new methodology precisely the same as before, although the content of some of the jobs, most notably that of the grade CA, will have been considerably altered, but in no case altered anything like sufficiently to fall outside the original description of the proper functions of the grade concerned.

Moreover, the contrary conclusion would fly in the face of common sense. Although doubtless, all of us, being conservative (with a small 'c') by nature desire nothing better than to be left to deepen out accustomed ruts, and hate change, a TO has no right to remain in perpetuity doing one defined type of work in one particular way.

(vi)   The Duty of Fidelity

A variety of employee obligations fall within this broad heading. The common thread is that a breach of each of the obligations will destroy the employer's trust and confidence in the employee.

(vii)   The Obligation to Account

Reading v Attorney-General
[1951] AC 507
House of Lords

The appellant was a sergeant in the Royal Army Medical Corps stationed in Egypt. While wearing uniform, he accompanied a number of civilian lorries carrying illicit brandy and whisky in and about Cairo. He earned £20,000 in this way. Having been court martialled and sent to prison for two years, he claimed the return of the money. The House of Lords rejected his claim.

LORD PORTER: . . . . [I]t is a principle of law that if a servant, in violation of his duty of honesty and good faith, takes advantage of his service to make a profit for himself, in this sense, that the assets of which he has control, or the facilities which he enjoys, or the position which he occupies, are the real cause of his obtaining the money . . . i.e. if they play a predominant part in his obtaining the money, then he is accountable for it to the master. It matters not that the master has not lost any profit, nor suffered any damage.

(viii)   A Duty to Disclose Misdeeds?

Bell v Lever Brothers Ltd
[1932] AC 161
House of Lords

Bell was employed as chairman of a subsidiary of Lever Brothers Ltd. Bell's fixed-term contract was terminated and he received £30,000 in compensation. Subsequently, the company discovered that Bell had committed breaches of contract for which he could have been dismissed without compensation. The company's claim for repayment was rejected by the House of Lords.

LORD ATKIN: It is said that there is a contractual duty of the servant to disclose his past faults. I agree that the duty in the servant to protect his master's property may involve the duty to report a fellow servant whom he knows to be wrongfully dealing with that property. The servant owes a duty not to steal, but having stolen, is there a superadded duty to confess that he has stolen? I am satisfied that to imply such a duty would be a departure from the well established usage of mankind and would be to create obligations entirely outside the normal contemplation of the parties concerned.

Sybron Corporation v Rochem
[1983] IRLR 253
Court of Appeal

Mr Wilfred Roques was the Director of Operations, European Zone, for Gamblen UK, a company owned by the Sybron Corporation. During his employment, payments were made on his behalf by the company into a pension scheme. When he retired in 1973 he was given a lump sum payment.

Subsequently, it was discovered that Roques, together with his main subordinates, had been conspiring to set up in direct competition with Gamblen. The company sought restitution of the pension payments, claiming that, under the rules of the pension scheme, Roques could have been dismissed for gross misconduct and the payments would not have been made. The Court of Appeal held that the company was entitled to recover the payments it had made.

STEPHENSON LJ: In *Bell* v *Lever Bros* nothing was said about a duty to disclose the misconduct of fellow servants, except by Lord Justice Scrutton in the Court of Appeal and Lord Atkin in the House of Lords. Beginning at the bottom of p. 586 of the report in the Court of Appeal, Lord Justice Scrutton said:

I do not propose to lay down any general rule for disclosure by servants: I only desire to say that I notice that Wright J held himself bound by the remark of Avory J. in *Healey* v *Société Anonyme Française Rubastic* [1917] 1 KB 946: 'I cannot accept the view that an omission to confess or disclose his own misdoing was, in itself a breach of the contract on the part of the plaintiff'. This statement was also accepted, though I think it was not material to his decision, by Lord Warrington in *Ramsden* v *David Sharratt & Sons Ltd* 30 CC 314, (1930) 35 CC 314. I must reserve myself liberty to reconsider this as a general rule if it becomes relevant in any subsequent case. I cannot think that a servant who knows his fellow servant is stealing the goods of his employer is under no obligation to disclose this to his employer. If the servant himself has stolen goods, and his employer, finding out the theft, accuses an innocent fellow servant of having committed it, is not the real thief bound to inform his employer of his delinquency? His theft is a vital breach of his contract of employment; is he not bound by his contract of service to inform his employer of acts detrimental to his employer? However, it is not in the present case necessary to lay down any general rule: it is enough to deal with the present case.

There, as Mr Munby rightly pointed out, Lord Justice Scrutton is, as it were, talking on what he says about a duty, which he plainly accepted, to disclose a theft by a fellow servant to his duty to disclose his own theft, which was also accepted by Lord Justice Scrutton and the other Lords Justices but has been negatived by the House of Lords. At p. 228 of the report in the House of Lords, Lord Atkin said this:

It is said that there is a contractual duty of the servant to disclose his past faults. I agree that the duty in the servant to protect his master's property may involve the duty to report a fellow servant whom he knows to be wrongfully dealing with that property. The servant owes a duty not to steal, but, having stolen, is there superadded a duty to confess that he has stolen? I am satisfied that to imply such a duty would be a departure from the well established usage of mankind and would be to create obligations entirely outside the normal contemplation of the parties concerned.

So there again, what that judge is saying about the duty to report a fellow servant is linked to the question of a duty to report his own wrongdoing, but it is I think significant that Lord Atkin is agreeing that the duty of a servant to protect his master's property 'may involve the duty to report a fellow servant whom he knows to be wrongfully dealing with that property', although the learned Lord was of the firm view that he had no such duty to report his own wrongful conduct. It is, as I have already indicated, puzzling that it never seems to have occurred to counsel or to any of the many judges who dealt with the case of *Bell* v *Lever Bros*, that they might have to consider the duty of Bell to report Snelling's misconduct, or Snelling's duty to report Bell's.

But the question was not there considered, let alone decided, and there is the direct authority of a decision of this court, in a case in which *Bell* v *Lever Bros* was considered, that there is in certain circumstances a duty to report the misconduct of fellow servants. That case is *Swain* v *West (Butchers) Ltd*, reported at first instance in [1936] 1 AER 224 and in this court in [1936] 3 All ER 261. There the plaintiff was employed for a term of five years as a general manager of the defendant company. His contract of service provided, *inter alia*, that he would do all in his power to promote, extend and develop the interests of the company. The managing director gave the plaintiff certain unlawful orders, which orders the plantiff carried out. The matter came to the notice of the chairman of the board of directors who, in an interview with the plaintiff, told the plaintiff that if he gave conclusive proof of the managing director's dishonesty he would not be dismissed. The plaintiff duly supplied the information required and was then dismissed, the defendants alleging fraud and dishonesty. The plaintiff did not deny the allegations, but he brought an action for breach of contract and wrongful dismissal on the grounds that under the terms of a verbal agreement between the plaintiff and the chairman it was not open to the defendants to rely upon information given by the plaintiff relating to his own fraud and dishonesty. It was held that it was the plaintiff's duty, as part of his contract of service, to report to the board of directors any acts which were not in the interests of the company; that there was therefore no consideration for the alleged verbal agreement and the defendant company was not prevented from relying upon the information received from the plaintiff.

. . .

It follows from that decision, which is consistent with *Bell's* case and is binding upon us, that there is no general duty to report a fellow-servant's misconduct or breach of contract; whether there is such a duty depends on the contract and on the terms of employment of the particular servant. He may be so placed in the hierarchy as to have a duty to report either the misconduct of his superior, as in *Swain's* case, or the misconduct of his inferiors, as in this case. Mr Munby will not have it that Mr Roques' No. 2 was subordinate to Mr Roques, or that the other managers involved in the conspiracy were his subordinates or inferiors; but on this point I agree with the judge and I refer, again without apology and with approval, to the way in which he put the matter, this time at p. 234 of the transcript of his judgment:

> I do not think [said the judge] that there is any general duty resting upon an employee to inform his master of the breaches of duty of other employees; the law would do industrial relations generally no great service if it held that such a duty did in fact exist in all cases. The duty must, in my view, depend upon all the circumstances of the case, and the relationship of the parties to their employer and *inter se*. I think it would be very difficult to have submitted, with any hope of success, that Messrs Bell and Snelling, having been appointed to rescue the affairs of their employers' African subsidiary in effect jointly, ought to have denounced each other

that is a reference to the finding that Messrs Bell and Snelling were, according to the report of the case in the House of Lords, in joint management and therefore one was not subordinate to the other.

The learned judge goes on:

However, where there is an hierarchical system, particularly where the person in the hierarchy whose conduct is called into question is a person near the top who is responsible to his employers for the whole of the operation of a complete sector of the employers' business – here the European Zone – then in my view entirely different considerations apply.

That the principle of disclosure extends at least as far as I think it extends (and perhaps further, but that is of no consequence for present purposes) has been decided once for all, so far as this court is concerned, by the case of *Swain* v *West (Butchers) Limited*, a decision of the Court of Appeal. The case of *Bell* v *Lever Bros* was very much in the forefront of everybody's mind in that case, but none of the Lords Justices thought it had any bearing on the case before them.

(ix) Competition While in Employment

The courts are very reluctant to accept that what workers do in their spare time should be of any concern of the employer (see *Nova Plastics Ltd* v *Froggett* [1982] IRLR 146). However, sometimes they are bound to do so. An employer's interests would clearly be harmed by an employee's spare-time work if this involved direct competition with the employer's business.

Hivac Ltd v Park Royal Scientific Instruments Ltd
[1946] 1 Ch 169
Court of Appeal

Hivac manufactured midget valves for hearing aids. Two of its employees worked in their spare time for Park Royal, a competitor, and also encouraged certain of their fellow employees to do the same. There was, however, no evidence that the employees had passed on confidential information to Park Royal. Hivac applied for an injunction to restrain Park Royal from employing or procuring to be employed certain of Hivac's employees in such a way as to cause a breach of such employees' contracts. The Court of Appeal granted the injunction.

LORD GREENE MR: It has been said on many occasions that an employee owes a duty of fidelity to his employer. As a general proposition that is indisputable. The practical difficulty in any given case is to find exactly how far that rather vague duty of fidelity extends. Prima facie it seems to me on considering the authorities and the arguments that it must be a question on the facts of each particular case. I can very well understand that the obligation of fidelity, which is an implied term of the contract, may extend very much further in the case of one class of employee than it does in others. For instance, when you are dealing, as we are dealing here, with mere manual workers whose job is to work five and a half days for their employer at a specific type of work and stop their work when the hour strikes, the obligation of fidelity may be one the operation of which will have a comparatively limited scope. The law would, I think, be jealous of attempting to impose on a manual worker restrictions, the real effect of which would be to prevent him utilising his spare time. He is paid for five and a half days in the week. The rest of the week is his own, and to impose upon a man, in relation to the rest of the week, some kind of obligation which really would unreasonably tie his hands and prevent him adding to his weekly money during that time would, I think, be very undesirable. On the other hand, if one has employees of a different character, one may very well find that the obligation is of a different nature. A manual worker might say: 'You pay me for five and a half days work. I do five and a half days work for you. What greater obligation have I taken upon myself? If you want in some way to limit my activities during the other day and a half of the week, you must pay me for it.' In many cases that may be a very good answer. In other cases it may not be a good answer because the very nature of the work may be such as to make it quite clear that the duties of the employee to his employer cannot properly be performed if in his spare time the employee engages in certain classes of activity. One example was discussed in argument, that of a solicitor's clerk who on Sundays it was assumed went and worked for another firm in the same town. He might find himself embarrassed because the very client for whom he had done work while working for the other firm on the Sunday might be a client against whom clients of his main employer were conducting litigation, or something of that kind. Obviously in a case of that kind, by working for another firm he is in effect, or may be, disabling himself from performing his duties to his real employer and placing himself in an embarrassing position. I can well understand it being said: 'That is a breach of the duty of fidelity to your employer because as a result of what you have done you have disabled yourself from giving to your employer that undivided attention to his business which it is your duty to give.' I merely put that forward, not for the purpose of laying down the law or expressing any concluded opinion, but merely as illustrating the danger of laying down any general proposition and the necessity of considering each case on its facts.

The authorities which have been cited are few, and the facts with which they were concerned differed from the facts of this particular case. For instance, the authority on which reliance was principally placed was *Wessex Dairies Ltd* v *Smith* [1935] 2 KB 80 in this court. There the defendant, who was a dairy roundsman, in his master's time proceeded to solicit customers of his master for the purpose of obtaining their custom in a business which he was shortly about to set up for himself. That is, I should have thought, a clear case, because he was doing it first of all in his master's time; and in his master's time he was making use of the information which his master had placed at his disposal, namely, the identity of the various customers and their particular requirements. Greer LJ, in the course of his judgment, placed some emphasis on the fact that the case was one in which the servant was using his master's time for the purpose of furthering his own interest. . . .

Maugham LJ started his judgment with the following words: 'The claim in this case raises a question of some interest in relation to the duty of a servant to his master during the period of his employment.' He goes on and examines the earlier case of *Nichol* v *Martyn* [(1799), 2 Esp 732], which is not satisfactorily reported, and *Robb* v *Green* [1895] 2 QB 315, and he then said this, after looking at Hawkins J's judgment in that case: 'That appears to show that Hawkins J did not take the view, which the other passage I read seems to indicate, that a servant can properly canvass his master's customers for himself as from a near approaching day. The question to be determined essentially depends upon the term to be implied in the ordinary case of a contract of employment in the absence of express agreement.' Then he refers to the fact that there was a reference to the duty of fidelity in the contract, but he said that he wished to decide the case on a wider ground. He quotes a passage from A. L. Smith LJ in *Robb* v *Green*, where he said: '"I think that it is a necessary implication which must be engrafted on such a contract that the servant undertakes to serve his master with good faith and fidelity".' Then he says: 'On the other hand, it has been held that while the servant is in the employment of the master he is not justified in making a list of the master's customers.' That is what had been done in *Robb v Green* and that immediately introduces a quite different set of ideas because if a servant took copies of his master's list of customers; he would be quite obviously committing a breach of duty in making use of something which is the master's property, namely, the list of customers, for an improper purpose, other than that for which he was employed. . . .

Talbot J appears to have agreed with both the judgments pronounced, and we have to consider to what extent the judgments assist us in deciding on an interlocutory application the proper course for this court to pursue.

Anything that I say on this matter stands, of course, to be varied and corrected when the full facts are known, but prima facie it appears to me the question we have to consider resolves itself into these elements. First of all, what was done here was done in the spare time of the employees. That leads to this: we have to consider what implication, if any, needs to be read into the contract of service with regard to the employee's use of his spare time. Does that implication in any way restrict him, or, rather (which is the practical question here) did that implication make it a breach of duty on his part to do what he did, with the consequential result that the defendants, in persuading the employees to do what they did, procured a breach of contract? I think the judgment of Maugham LJ in *Wessex Dairies Ltd v Smith*, which is quite deliberately placed by him on a broad ground, does lead to this. Although the case before him was concerned with an employee who had done certain things in his employer's time, I cannot find that in his reasoning that was regarded as an essential part of the offence. I cannot read the judgment as meaning that if the roundsman had on a Saturday afternoon, when his work was over, gone round to all these customers and canvassed them, he would have been doing something he was entitled to do. It would be a curious result if, quite apart from making use of the list of customers or his special knowledge or anything of that kind, he could set himself during his spare time deliberately to injure the goodwill of his master's business by trying to get his customers to leave him. Then again the question here is not a question of getting the customers to leave the business but a question of building up a rival in business to the prejudice of the goodwill of the employer's business.

I am not ashamed to confess that in the course of the argument my mind has fluctuated considerably on this question. As I see it, the court stands in a sense between Scylla and Charybdis, because it would be most unfortunate if anything we said, or any other court said, should place an undue restriction on the right of the workman, particularly a manual workman, to make use of his leisure for his profit. On the other hand, it would be deplorable if it were laid down that a workman could, consistently with his duty to his employer, knowingly, deliberately and secretly set himself to do in his spare time something which would inflict great harm on his employer's business. I have endeavoured to raise the questions in the way that they appeal to me and, on the best consideration I can give to the matter, I think that the plaintiffs are prima facie right in this case.

Notes

1. Working in competition or disclosing confidential information may provide a fair reason for dismissal. In *Smith v Du Pont (UK) Ltd* [1976] IRLR 107, Mrs Smith worked as a secretary and on two previous occasions had been warned about dealing with a former employee of the company who now worked for a rival concern. She was dismissed when the company learned that she had given information of a contact – 'the name of the buyer at

Sainsbury's' – to the former employee. The industrial tribunal took the view that, although the information was of no great weight which would in fact damage the company, in view of the earlier warnings, Mrs Smith 'seemed to be setting up her judgement against that of the company'. In the circumstances, there was no obligation on the company to wait 'until she passed on information of significance'. The dismissal was held to be fair.

2. One exception to the duty not to misuse confidential information arises where disclosure by the employee or ex-employee is in the public interest. In *Initial Services Ltd v Putterill* [1968] 1 QB 396, Lord Denning stated that the exception against disclosure went beyond disclosure of crime or fraud on the part of the employer, 'it extends to any misconduct of such a nature that it ought in the public interest to be disclosed to others'. Moreover, disclosure in the public interest may be particularly justified where the disclosure is to the proper authorities, e.g. a regulatory body, as in *Re a Company's Application* [1989] ICR 449, ChD. For a detailed discussion of this area see Vickers, L., *Protecting Whistleblowers at Work*, London: Institute of Employment Rights, 1995.

3. In 1998, the Government supported Richard Shepherd's Private Member's Bill on public interest disclosure or 'whistle-blowing'. The Public Interest Disclosure Act 1998 came into force on 1 January 1999 and its aim is to protect individuals against dismissal or victimisation where they make disclosures to their employer, to another responsible person or a 'person prescribed' about criminal offences, failure to meet legal obligations, miscarriages of justice, health, safety and environmental dangers and deliberate concealment of information relating to these matters (For a more detailed discussion of the Act and its impact on the law of unfair dismissal, see Chapter 6 at pp. 441–445; see also the note by Lewis, D., (1998) 27 ILJ 325.)

(x)   Competition by Ex-employees

As a general rule, ex-employees are free to go into competition with their former employer. However, in certain restricted circumstances, the duty of fidelity survives the termination of the employment relationship.

Wessex Dairies Ltd v Smith
[1935] 2 KB 80
Court of Appeal

MAUGHAN LJ: In this case the question is whether the defendant acted with fidelity when, on the Saturday in question and perhaps on previous day of the week, in going his round he informed the customers that he would cease on Saturday to be in the employment of the plaintiffs, that he was going to set up business for himself, and would be in a position to supply them with milk. He was plainly soliciting their custom as from Saturday evening. In my opinion that was deliberate as it was a successful canvassing at a time when the defendant was under an obligation to serve the plaintiff with fidelity. I am of opinion therefore that he committed a breach of his implied contract . . .

Robb v *Green*
[1895] 2 QB 315
Court of Appeal

The defendant, an employee of the plaintiff who was a tradesman, left his service and set up a similar business on his own. Before he left, he copied out lists of the plaintiff's customers and tried to persuade them to transfer their custom to himself.

LORD ESHER MR: The question arises whether such conduct is a breach of contract. That depends upon the question whether in a contract of service the Court can imply a stipulation that the servant will act in good faith towards his master. I think that in a contract of service the Court must imply such a stipulation as I have mentioned, because it is a thing which must necessarily have been in the view of both parties when they entered into the contract. It is impossible to suppose that a master would have put a servant into a confidential position of this kind, unless he thought that the servant would be bound to use good faith towards him; or that the servant would not know, when he entered into that position, that the master would rely on his observance of good faith in the confidential relation between them.

Note
The above cases show that an employee may not do anything while still employed which is breach of the duty of fidelity (see also *Sanders* v *Parry* [1967] 2 All ER 803; *Roger Bullivant Ltd* v *Ellis* [1987] IRLR 491; *Johnson & Bloy (Holdings) Ltd* v *Wolstenholme* [1987] IRLR 499; *Adamson* v *B & L Cleaning Services Ltd* [1995] IRLR 193, EAT). However, in the absence of an express covenant, there is no general restriction on ex-employees canvassing or doing business with customers of their former employers. This rule applies to solicitors as much as to any other trade or profession (see *Wallace Brogan & Co.* v *Cove and others* [1997] IRLR 453, CA).

Nevertheless, as the next case extract clearly indicates, ex-employees are entitled to make use of their knowledge and skill acquired while in their employer's business and, in this sense, the implied duty of fidelity is narrower than in the case of existing employees.

Faccenda Chicken Ltd v *Fowler*
[1986] IRLR 69
Court of Appeal

Fowler had been employed as a sales manager of Faccenda Chicken Ltd's chicken marketing business until he resigned, along with eight other employees, in order to establish a rival operation selling fresh chickens from refrigerated vehicles. Neither Fowler nor any of the other former employees were subject to any express agreement restricting activities after leaving Faccenda's employ. Faccenda claimed that Fowler and his colleagues had broken their contracts by using confidential sales information, relating to the requirements of their customers and the prices they paid, to the detriment of the company. The High Court, Chancery Division (Goulding J) dismissed the claims for damages. Faccenda appealed to the Court of Appeal.

NEILL LJ: . . . Having considered the cases to which we were referred, we would venture to state these principles as follows:

(1)   Where the parties are, or have been, linked by a contract of employment, the obligations of the employee are to be determined by the contract between him and his employer: cf *Vokes Ltd* v *Heather* [1945] 62 RPC 131, 141.

(2)   In the absence of any express term, the obligations of the employee in respect of the use and disclosure of information are the subject of implied terms.

(3)   While the employee remains in the employment of the employer the obligations are included in the implied term which imposes a duty of good faith or fidelity on the employee. For the purpose of the present appeal it is not necessary to consider the precise limits of this implied term, but it may be noted:

(a)   that the extent of the duty of good faith will vary according to the nature of the contract (see *Vokes Ltd* v *Heather* (ibid));

(b)   that the duty of good faith will be broken if an employee makes or copies a list of the customers of the employer for use after his employment ends or deliberately memorises such a list, even though, except in special circumstances, there is no general restriction on an ex-employee canvassing or doing business with customers of his former employer (see *Robb* v *Green* [1895] 2 QB 315 and *Wessex Dairies Ltd* v *Smith* [1935] 2 KB 80).

(4)   The implied term which imposes an obligation on the employee as to his conduct after the determination of the employment is more restricted in its scope than that which imposes a general duty of good faith. It is clear that the obligation not to use or disclose information may cover secret processes of manufacture such as chemical formulae (*Amber Size & Chemical Co.* v *Menzel* [1913] 2 Ch 239)), or designs or special methods of construction (*Reid and Sigrist Ltd* v *Moss and Mechanism Ltd* [1932] 49 RPC 461), and other information which is of a sufficiently high degree of confidentiality as to amount to a trade secret.

The obligation does not extend, however, to cover all information which is given to or acquired by the employee while in his employment, and in particular may not cover information which is only 'confidential' in the sense that an unauthorised disclosure of such information to a third party while the employment subsisted would be a clear breach of the duty of good faith.

This distinction is clearly set out in the judgment of Mr Justice Cross (as he then was) in *Printers & Finishers Ltd* v *Holloway* [1965] RPC 239, where he had to consider whether an ex-employee should be restrained by injunction from making use of his recollection of the contents of certain written printing instructions which had been made available to him when he was working in his former employers' flock printing factory. In his judgment, delivered on 29.4.64 (not reported on this point in [1965] 1 WLR 1, 3), he said this ([1965] RPC 253):

In this connection one must bear in mind that not all information which is given to a servant in confidence and which it would be a breach of his duty for him to disclose to another person during his employment is a trade secret which he can be prevented from using for his own advantage after the employment is over, even though he has entered into no express convenant with regard to the matter in hand.

For example, the printing instructions were handed to Holloway to be used by him during his employment exclusively for the plaintiffs' benefit. It would have been a breach of duty on his part to divulge any of the contents to a stranger while he was employed, but many of these instructions are not really 'trade secrets' at all. Holloway was not, indeed, entitled to take a copy of the instructions away with him; but in so far as the instructions cannot be called 'trade secrets' and he carried them in his head, he is entitled to use them for his own benefit or the benefit of any future employer.

The same distinction is to be found in *E Worsley & Co. Ltd* v *Cooper* [1939] 1 All ER 290 where it was held that the defendant was entitled, after he had ceased to be employed, to make use of his knowledge of the source of the paper supplied to his previous employer. In our view it is quite plain that this knowledge was nevertheless 'confidential' in the same sense that it would have been a breach of the duty of good faith for the employee, while the employment subsisted, to have used it for his own purposes or to have disclosed it to a competitor of his employer.

(5) In order to determine whether any particular item of information falls within the implied term so as to prevent its use or disclosure by an employee after his employment has ceased, it is necessary to consider all the circumstances of the case. We are satisfied that the following matters are among those to which attention must be paid:

(a) The nature of the employment. Thus employment in a capacity where 'confidential' material is habitually handled may impose a high obligation of confidentiality because the employee can be expected to realise its sensitive nature to a greater extent than if he were employed in a capacity where such material reaches him only occasionally or incidentally.

(b) The nature of the information itself. In our judgment the information will only be protected if it can properly be classed as a trade secret or as material which, while not properly to be described as a trade secret, is in all the circumstances of such a highly confidential nature as to require the same protection as a trade secret *eo nomine*. The restrictive covenant cases demonstrate that a covenant will not be upheld on the basis of the status of the information which might be disclosed by the former employee if he is not restrained, unless it can be regarded as a trade secret or the equivalent of a trade secret: see, for example, *Herbert Morris Ltd* v *Saxelby* [1916] 1 AC 688, 710 by Lord Parker of Waddington; *Littlewoods Organisation Ltd* v *Harris* [1977] 1 WLR 1472, 1484 per Megaw LJ.

We must therefore express our respectful disagreement with the passage in Goulding J's judgment where he suggested that an employer can protect the use of information in his second category, even though it does not include either a trade secret or its equivalent by means of a restrictive covenant. As Lord Parker of Waddington made clear in *Herbert Morris Ltd* v *Saxelby* [1916] 1 AC 688, 709, in a passage to which Mr Dehn drew our attention, a restrictive covenant will not be enforced unless the protection sought is reasonably necessary to protect a trade secret or to prevent some personal influence over customers being abused in order to entice them away.

In our view the circumstances in which a restrictive covenant would be appropriate and could be successfully invoked emerge very clearly from the words used by Cross J in *Printers & Finishers Ltd* v *Holloway* . . . (in a passage quoted later in his judgment by Goulding J [1984] IRLR 61, 66):

If [the managing director] is right in thinking that there are features in his process which can fairly be regarded as trade secrets and which his employers will inevitably carry away with them in their heads, then the proper way for the plaintiffs to protect themselves would be by exacting covenants from their employees restricting their field of activity after they have left their employment, not by asking the court to extend the general equitable doctrine to prevent breaking confidence beyond all reasonable bounds.

It is clearly impossible to provide a list of matters which will qualify as trade secrets or their equivalent. Secret processes of manufacture provide obvious examples, but innumerable other pieces of information are *capable* of being trade secrets, though the secrecy of some information may be only short-lived. In addition, the fact that the circulation of certain information is restricted to a limited number of individuals may throw light on the status of the information and its degree of confidentiality.

(c) Whether the employer impressed on the employee the confidentiality of the information. Thus, though an employer cannot prevent the use or disclosure *merely* by telling the employee that certain information is confidential, the attitude of the employer towards the information provides evidence which may assist in determining whether or not the information can properly be regarded as a trade secret. It is to be observed that in *E. Worsley & Co. Ltd* v *Cooper* [1939] 1 All ER 290 Morton J at page 307 attached significance to the fact that no warning had been given to the defendant that 'the source from which the paper came was to be treated as confidential'.

(d) Whether the relevant information can be easily isolated from other information which the employee is free to use or disclose. In *Printers & Finishers Ltd* v *Holloway* [1965] RPC 239, Cross J at page 256 considered the protection which might be afforded to information which had been memorised by an ex-employee. He put on one side the memorising of a formula or a list of customers or what had been said (obviously in confidence) at a particular meeting, and continued:

> The employee might well not realise that the feature or expedient in question was in fact peculiar to his late employer's process and factory; but even if he did, such knowledge is not readily separable from his general knowledge of the flock printing process and his acquired skill in manipulating a flock printing plant, and I do not think that any man of average intelligence and honesty would think that there was anything improper in his putting his memory of particular features of his late employer's plant at the disposal of his new employer.

For our part we would not regard the separability of the information in question as being conclusive, but the fact that the alleged 'confidential' information is part of a package and that the remainder of the package is not confidential is likely to throw light on whether the information in question is really a trade secret.
. . .

Information about the price to be charged for a new model of a car or some other product or about the prices negotiated, for example, for various grades of oil in a highly competitive market in which it is known that prices are to be kept secret from competitors occur to us as providing possible further instances of information which is entitled to protection as having the requisite degree of confidentiality.

But in the present case the following factors appear to us to lead to the clear conclusion that neither the information about prices nor the sales information as a whole had the degree of confidentiality necessary to support Faccenda's case. We would list these factors as follows:

(1) The sales information contained some material which Faccenda conceded was not confidential if looked at in isolation.

(2)   The information about the prices was not clearly severable from the rest of the sales information.

(3)   Neither the sales information in general, nor the information about the prices in particular, though of some value to a competitor, could reasonably be regarded as plainly secret or sensitive.

(4)   The sales information, including the information about prices, was necessarily acquired by the respondents in order that they could do their work. Moreover, as the judge observed in the course of his judgment, each salesman could quickly commit the whole of the sales information relating to his own area to memory.

(5)   The sales information was generally known among the van drivers who were employees, as were the secretaries, at quite a junior level. This was not a case where the relevant information was restricted to senior management or to confidential staff.

(6)   There was no evidence that Faccenda had ever given any express instructions that the sales information or the information about prices was to be treated as confidential.

We are satisfied that, in the light of all the matters set out by the judge in his judgment, neither the sales information as a whole nor the information about prices looked at by itself fell within the class of confidential information which an employee is bound by an implied term of his contract of employment or otherwise not to use or disclose after his employment has come to an end.

Accordingly these appeals must be dismissed.

Note
This is an important decision and, indeed, Professor R.W. Rideout has stated 'that there is no question but that this decision rewrites the duty of confidentiality contained in the law of employment' (15 ILJ 183, at p. 187).

Question
What prompted Professor Rideout to make such a statement?

(xi)   Restraint of Trade Clauses
The second exception to ex-employees' freedom to go into competition with their former employer may be a restraint of trade clause in the contract of employment. Given the weakness of the implied term of confidentiality once employment has ended, many employers would be well advised to protect themselves against the divulgence of trade secrets or loss of customers by the insertion of such clauses in the contract. Note, however, that in *Faccenda*, (above) the Court of Appeal expressly disagreed with the statement of Goulding J, at first instance, that confidential information which became part of the employee's skill and knowledge could be protected by an express restraint of trade clause. Therefore, only trade secrets (as defined in *Faccenda*) or customer connections may be protected by such a clause. Furthermore, the restrictive covenant must be shown to go no further, in terms of time and area of restraint, than is reasonable for the protection of the employer's proprietary interests and must be generally in the public interest.

Littlewoods Organisation Ltd v *Harris*
[1977] 1 WLR 1472
Court of Appeal

The plaintiff ran a retail chainstore business and mail order business in the UK. The main rival in the field was Great Universal Stores Ltd (GUS) which had some 200 subsidiary companies carrying on business throughout the world. Between them the plaintiff and GUS conducted two-thirds of all mail order business in the UK. The defendant was executive director of the plaintiff's mail order business.

Clause 8 of his service agreement provided:

In the event of the determination of this agreement . . . the [defendant] shall not at any time within 12 months after such determination: — (i) Enter into a Contract of Service or other Agreement of a like nature with Great Universal Stores Ltd or any company subsidiary thereto or be directly or indirectly engaged concerned or interested in the trading or business of the said Great Universal Stores Ltd or any such company aforesaid.

On 4 January 1977, the defendant resigned and refused to give an assurance that he would not work with GUS within the 12-month period as set out in the clause. The plaintiff sought an injunction restraining entry into employment with GUS. At first instance, Caulfield J refused to grant the injunction on the ground that the plaintiff had not demonstrated that it had confidential information or trade secrets which could be properly protected by the restraint. The plaintiff's appeal to the Court of Appeal was successful.

MEGAW LJ: Counsel for the defendant in this context of construction has relied strongly on the decision of this court in *Commercial Plastics Ltd* v *Vincent* [1965] 1 QB 623. That was a case in which the court, having held that there were confidential matters which could have been protected by a properly drawn covenant, refused, though with obvious regret, to uphold the covenant on the ground that it was too widely drawn. There were two respects in which it was held that it was too widely drawn. First, the business, including the secrets which it was sought to protect, was limited to trading in the United Kingdom, whereas the words in the letter in which the restrictive provision was contained did not express such a limitation. The words of the letter were:

In view of the highly technical and confidential nature of this appointment you have agreed not to seek employment with any of our competitors in the PVC calendering field, for at least one year after leaving our employ.

The second respect in which the covenant was held to be too wide was that it was not restricted to the particular, rather specialised, type of technological information with which the defendant had been concerned while he was in the plaintiff's employment.

Counsel for the defendant submits that that case is an authority binding on this court showing that it is not permissible to construe the clause in this case in any way which is limited beyond the terms which it actually contains. I have felt very much impressed by that submission; and if, in the end, I had thought that the ratio decidendi of that case was relevant to the present case, I should without hesitation have followed it. Counsel for the defendant says that one of the elements in respect of which the present covenant is too wide is that it is expressed perfectly generally so far as geography is concerned, it is not limited to the UK, and the plaintiffs cannot properly claim any protection in respect of any operations which may be conducted outside the UK by any company to which the defendant hereafter may be employed in the Great Universal Stores group.

It seems to me on full consideration of *Commercial Plastics Ltd* v *Vincent* that it was there accepted and assumed that the agreement there in question was properly to be construed as being universal in its operation and was properly to be construed as applying over the whole area of the business concerned. It was not argued, on the basis of the authorities such as those which I have recently cited, that the court could and should as a matter of construction treat the covenant as being less wide than its literal words appeared to make it, having regard to all the surrounding circumstances which existed at the time when the covenant was entered into. For that reason I have reached the conclusion that *Commercial Plastics Ltd* v *Vincent* is not an authority which precludes us from putting on cl.8 of the agreement a construction which in my judgment is, on the basis of the authorities which I have cited, and on the circumstances appearing in the evidence, the proper construction.

Counsel for the defendant was disposed to stress the point that the covenant does not purport to relate in any way to confidential information, much less to indicate what the sphere of that confidential information is. I do not regard that as being a fatal objection to it. The difficulty which I regard as most serious as against the enforceability of the covenant is the width of the phrase 'any companies subsidiary thereto'. Let me just read the subclause again:

> . . . the Divisional Director shall not . . . (i) Enter into a Contract of Service or other Agreement of a like nature with Great Universal Stores Limited or any company subsidiary thereto or be directly or indirectly engaged concerned or interested in the trading or business of the said Great Universal Stores Limited or any such company aforesaid.

Great Universal Stores Ltd have many such companies. Many of them on the evidence which was accepted by Caulfield J have no connection with mail order trade. Many of them, I think, are concerned with business outside the UK. So far as they are concerned, if they are on the true construction to be included in this clause then it would be too wide and, regrettable though it might be, it would be the duty of this court to hold that the covenant could not stand and it would not be enforceable. But, applying the principles of construction which I derive from the cases which I have cited, in my judgment the words 'any company subsidiary thereto' are properly to be read by reference to the circumstances existing at the time when the contract was made. Just as in *Moenich* v *Fenestre* (1892) 67 LT 602, CA when Lindley LJ and the other members of the court were able to interpret the phrase in that case as meaning something different from its literal words because of the nature of the business with reference to which it was made, so here I think that 'any company subsidiary thereto' ought to be treated in this way. 'Any company subsidiary thereto' means any subsidiary which at any relevant moment of time during the period covered by the covenant is concerned wholly or partly in the mail order business carried on in the UK. That would include, for example, a subsidiary which was concerned with the buying of goods which were going to be used by some other company in the group in the mail order business in the UK. It would include any subsidiary in which it was sought to employ the defendant, whatever the function of that subsidiary and whether or not there might be any reference thereto in his contract of service, to deal in any way with, or advise in any way, or give anyone information relating to the mail order business in the UK. It will, I hope, be clear from what I have said that I am not suggesting that the covenant requires to be rewritten. I am interpreting the covenant as I understand it ought to be interpreted in the circumstances which exist in this case, as I conceive to have been done in the cases which I have cited.

Greer v *Sketchley Ltd*
[1979] IRLR 445
Court of Appeal

Mr Greer was employed by Sketchleys for some 20 years. In 1974 he was made director of their dry cleaning business, with special responsibility for the Midlands area. The activities of the company covered all the Midlands and London area but they did not include the North of England, Scotland, Devon and Cornwall, N. Ireland and the greater part of Wales.

Mr Greer's contract stated:

In view of the access to trade secrets and secret processes which the Employee may have during the course of his employment hereunder he shall not within a period of 12 months from the termination thereof either directly or indirectly and either alone or in association with any other person firm or company engage in any part of the United Kingdom in any business which is similar to any business involving such trade secrets and/or secret processes carried on by the Company or any of its subsidiaries during the course of his employment hereunder.

In 1977, Mr Greer decided to leave and was offered a job with another firm in the dry cleaning business. Mr Greer sought a declaration that the restraint clause was invalid. The High Court declared it to be invalid and this finding was upheld by the Court of Appeal.

LORD DENNING MR: In a way, as the *Littlewoods* case illustrated, it is often difficult to sort out what is confidential and what is not. Sometimes it is permissible to make an agreement, as in that particular case, saying that the man is not to go to a rival concern for 12 months. That is what happened in the *Littlewoods* case. The Great Universal Stores in effect approached Mr Harris and offered him all sorts of better terms and induced him to go to them. That was a breach of the restrictive covenant which Littlewoods had expressly made saying that Mr Harris was not to go to their rival the Great Universal Stores for 12 months. That clause was held valid because it was the one way of protecting the position. But in this particular case it seems to me, for all Mr Buckley's admirable arguments, this is a much wider clause which says that he shall not engage in any part of the United Kingdom in any similar business. If Sketchleys operated all over England, Scotland and Wales, it might be reasonable to have such a covenant, but Sketchleys do not operate as widely. In 1974 their operations were confined to the Midlands and the South of England, excluding Wales, Cornwall and Devon and Lancashire right up to the north. Sketchleys did not cover any of that area. Was it reasonable for them to have a covenant restraining Mr Greer from going to any of these other parts of England, Scotland and Wales? Suppose for instance, there had been a group of dry cleaning shops in the Tyne and Wear conurbation or in the Lancashire conurbation or Glasgow and Edinburgh or down in Devon, Sketchleys had not any kind of operation in those areas then. Was it reasonable to restrain him from engaging in any of those businesses or with any of those groups which were in those areas in which Sketchleys did not operate at all? It is said by Mr Buckley that they might expand into those areas in the future. Now over three years later they have not expanded into Devon and Cornwall or into Yorkshire or Lancashire or into the North of England or into Scotland. It seems to me that that problematical and possible expansion into all these other areas is much too vague and much too wide to justify restraint over every part of the United Kingdom.

Notes

1.   Even if the restraint is reasonable as between the parties, it may still be struck down as unlawful and void if it is regarded by the court as being contrary to public policy. In *Bull* v *Pitney-Bowes* [1966] 3 All ER 384, the plaintiff had been employed by the defendants for 25 years. It was a condition of his employment that he should become a member of a non-contributory pension scheme. Rule 16 of this scheme provided that a retired member should be liable to forfeit his pension rights if he was 'engaged or employed in any activity or occupation which is in competition with or detrimental to the interests of [the defendants]'. On his retirement, the plaintiff entered the employment of a competing company. On being warned that he might lose his pension rights unless he left his new employment, he sued for a declaration that rule 16 was an unreasonable restraint of trade and therefore void. Thesiger J held that rule 16 was a restraint of trade, and further that it was unenforceable because it was against public policy. It was contrary to public policy that the community should be deprived of the services of a man skilled in a particular trade or technique. (See also *Greig* v *Insole* [1978] 1 WLR 302.)

2.   The employer's main remedy for breach of a restraint of trade clause is an injunction although it is also possible to seek damages. It has been held that an injunction to restrain the use of trade secrets should not last longer than is necessary to prevent the defendant from taking unfair advantage of the springboard gained by use of the information obtained (see *Roger Bullivant Ltd* v *Ellis* [1987] IRLR 491).

(xii)   Inventions by Employees

Prior to the passing of the Patents Act 1977, the common law implied a term into every contract of employment that inventions produced in the course of employment became the property of the employer (see *British Syphon Co. Ltd* v *Homewood* [1956] 1 WLR 1190). This position prompted one commentator to remark that: '. . . in few areas of British law can the effect of the imbalance of bargaining power between employer and employee have led so clearly to injustice as in the distribution of the fruits of inventions made by an employee while in his employer's services'. (Phillips, 'Employee Inventions and the New Patents Act' (1978) 7 ILJ 30.)

The Patents Act 1977 replaces the earlier law in respect of the ownership of inventions; the right of the employee to be rewarded; the amount of the reward and the exclusion of statutory rights.

(xiii)   Right to Employees' Inventions

Patents Act 1977

39.   Right to employees' inventions

(1)   Notwithstanding anything in any rule of law, an invention made by an employee shall, as between him and his employer, be taken to belong to his employer for the purposes of this Act and all other purposes if—

(a)   it was made in the course of the normal duties of the employee or in the course of duties falling outside his normal duties, but specifically assigned to him, and the circumstances in either case were such that an invention might reasonably be expected to result from the carrying out of his duties; or

(b)   the invention was made in the course of the duties of the employee and, at the time of making the invention, because of the nature of his duties and the particular responsibilities arising from the nature of his duties he had a special obligation to further the interests of the employer's undertaking.

(2)   Any other invention made by an employee shall, as between him and his employer, be taken for those purposes to belong to the employee.

. . .

40.   Compensation of employees for certain inventions

(1)   Where it appears to the court or the comptroller on an application made by an employee within the prescribed period that the employee has made an invention belonging to the employer for which a patent has been granted, that the patent is (having regard among other things to the size and nature of the employer's undertaking) of outstanding benefit to the employer and that by reason of those facts it is just that the employee should be awarded compensation to be paid by the employer, the court or the comptroller may award him such compensation of an amount determined under section 41 below.

(2)   Where it appears to the court or the comptroller on an application made by an employee within the prescribed period that—

(a)   a patent has been granted for an invention made by and belonging to the employee;

(b)   his rights in the invention, or in any patent or application for a patent for the invention, have since the appointed day been assigned to the employer or an exclusive licence under the patent or application has since the appointed day been granted to the employer;

(c)   the benefit derived by the employee from the contract of assignment, assignation or grant or any ancillary contract ('the relevant contract') is inadequate in relation to the benefit derived by the employer from the patent; and

(d)   by reason of those facts it is just that the employee should be awarded compensation to be paid by the employer in addition to the benefit derived from the relevant contract;

the court or the comptroller may award him such compensation of an amount determined under section 41 below.

(3)   Subsections (1) and (2) above shall not apply to the invention of an employee where a relevant collective agreement provides for the payment of compensation in respect of inventions of the same description as that invention to employees of the same description as that employee.

(4)   Subsection (2) above shall have effect notwithstanding anything in the relevant contract or any agreement applicable to the invention (other than any such collective agreement).

(5)   If it appears to the comptroller on an application under this section that the application involves matters which would more properly be determined by the court, he may decline to deal with it.

(6)   In this section—

'the prescribed period', in relation to proceedings before the court, means the period prescribed by rules of court, and

'relevant collective agreement' means a collective agreement within the meaning of the Trade Union and Labour Relations Act 1974, made by or on behalf of a trade union to which the employee belongs, and by the employer or an employers' association to which the employer belongs which is in force at the time of the making of the invention.

(7)   References in this section to an invention belonging to an employer or employee are references to it so belonging as between the employer and the employee.

41.   Amount of compensation

(1)   An award of compensation to an employee under section 40(1) or (2) above in relation to a patent for an invention shall be such as will secure for the employee a fair share (having regard to all the circumstances) of the benefit which the employer has derived, or may reasonably be expected to derive, from the patent or from the assignment, assignation or grant to a person connected with the employer of the property or any right in the invention or the property in, or any right in or under, an application for that patent.

(2)   For the purposes of subsection (1) above the amount of any benefit derived or expected to be derived by an employer from the assignment, assignation or grant of—

(a)   the property in, or any right in or under, a patent for the invention or an application for such a patent; or

(b)   the property or any right in the invention;

to a person connected with him shall be taken to be the amount which could reasonably be expected to be so derived by the employer if that person had not been connected with him.

(3)   Where the Crown or a Research Council in its capacity as employer assigns or grants the property in, or any right in or under, an invention, patent or application for a patent to a body having among its functions that of developing or exploiting inventions resulting from public research and does so for no consideration or only a nominal consideration, any benefit derived from the invention, patent or application by that body shall be treated for the purposes of the foregoing provisions of this section as so derived by the Crown or, as the case may be, Research Council.

In this subsection 'Research Council' means a body which is a Research Council for the purposes of the Science and Technology Act 1965.

(4)   In determining the fair share of the benefit to be secured for an employee in respect of a patent for an invention which has always belonged to an employer, the court or the comptroller shall, among other things, take the following matters into account, that is to say—

(a) the nature of the employee's duties, his remuneration and the other advantages he derives or has derived from his employment or has derived in relation to the invention under this Act;

(b) the effort and skill which the employee has devoted to making the invention;

(c) the effort and skill which any other person has devoted to making the invention jointly with the employee concerned, and the advice and other assistance contributed by any other employee who is not a joint inventor of the invention; and

(d) the contribution made by the employer to the making, developing and working of the invention by the provision of advice, facilities and other assistance, by the provision of opportunities and by his managerial and commercial skill and activities.

(5) In determining the fair share of the benefit to be secured for an employee in respect of a patent for an invention which originally belonged to him, the court or the comptroller shall, among other things, take the following matters into account, that is to say—

(a) any conditions in a licence or licences granted under this Act or otherwise in respect of the invention or the patent;

(b) the extent to which the invention was made jointly by the employee with any other person; and

(c) the contribution made by the employer to the making, developing and working of the invention as mentioned in subsection (4)(d) above.

(6) Any order for the payment of compensation under section 40 above may be an order for the payment of a lump sum or for periodical payment, or both.

. . .

42. Enforceability of contracts relating to employees' inventions

(1) This section applies to any contract (whenever made) relating to inventions made by an employee, being a contract entered into by him—

(a) with the employer (alone or with another); or

(b) with some other person at the request of the employer or in pursuance of the employee's contract of employment.

(2) Any term in a contract to which this section applies which diminishes the employee's rights in inventions of any description made by him after the appointed day and the date of the contract, or in or under patents for those inventions or applications for such patents, shall be unenforceable against him to the extent that it diminishes his rights in an invention of that description so made, or in or under a patent for such an invention or an application for any such patent.

(3) Subsection (2) above shall not be construed as derogating from any duty of confidentiality owed to his employer by an employee by virtue of any rule of law or otherwise.

. . .

(xiv) The Duty of Fidelity: Impeding the Employer's Business

Secretary of State for Employment v Associated Society of Railway Engineers & Firemen (No. 2)
[1972] 2 QB 455
Court of Appeal

This case concerned an application by the Secretary of State for a ballot of railwaymen under the provisions of the Industrial Relations Act 1971.

The railwaymen were engaged in industrial action in support of a pay claim. The action consisted of an overtime ban and a work to rule. In order to gain a ballot order, the Secretary of State had to establish, *inter alia*, that the railwaymen were in breach of their contracts of employment. The Court of Appeal held that the work to rule was a breach of contract and overturned previous assumptions that a strict work to rule did not amount to a breach.

LORD DENNING MR: . . . Now I quite agree that a man is not bound positively to do more for the employer than his contract requires. He can withdraw his goodwill if he pleases. But what he must not do is wilfully to obstruct his employer as he goes about his business. . . . If he, with the others takes steps wilfully to disrupt the undertaking, to produce chaos so that it will not run as it should, then each one who is a party to those steps is guilty of a breach of contract. It is no answer for any of them to say 'I am only obeying the rule book or that I am not bound to do more than a 40 hour week'. That would be all very well if done in good faith without any wilful disruption of services; but what makes it wrong is the object with which it is done.

BUCKLEY LJ: . . . [I]n my judgment, in the case of a contract of a commercial character the wilful act of one party which, although not, maybe, departing from the literal letter of the agreement, nevertheless defeats the commercial intention of the parties in entering into the contract, constitutes a breach of an implied term of the contract to perform the contract in such a way as not to frustrate that commercial objective.

(xv) A 'New' Implied Term: the Employer's Obligation to Bring Contingent Rights to the Attention of Employees

Scally and others v Southern Health & Social Services Board
[1991] IRLR 522
House of Lords

The plaintiffs were medical practitioners employed in the Northern Ireland health service. They sought to sue their employers for loss sustained by them by reason of their employers' failure to bring to their notice their right to purchase added years of pension entitlement before that right lapsed.

LORD BRIDGE OF HARWICH: . . . Will the law then imply a term in the contract of employment imposing such an obligation on the employer? The implication cannot, of course, be justified as necessary to give business efficacy to the contract of employment as a whole. I think there is force in the submission that, since the employee's entitlement to enhance his pension rights by the purchase of added years is of no effect unless he is aware of it, and since he cannot be expected to become aware of it unless it is drawn to his attention, it is necessary to imply an obligation on the employer to bring it to his attention to render efficacious the very benefit which the contractual right to purchase added years was intended to confer. But this may be stretching the doctrine of implication for the sake of business efficacy beyond its proper reach. A clear distinction is drawn in the speeches of Viscount Simonds in *Lister* v *Romford Ice and Cold Storage Co Ltd* [1957] AC 555, 576 and Lord Wilberforce in *Liverpool City Council* v *Irwin* [1977] AC 239, 255 between the search for an implied term necessary to give business efficacy to a particular contract and the search, based on wider considerations, for a term which the law will imply as a necessary incident of a definable category of contractual relationship. If any implication is appropriate here, it is, I think, of this latter type. Carswell J accepted the submission that any formulation of an implied term of this kind which would be effective to sustain the plaintiffs' claims in this case must necessarily be too wide in its ambit to be acceptable as of general application. I believe, however, that this difficulty is surmounted if the category of contractual relationship in which the implication will arise is defined with sufficient precision. I would define it as the relationship of employer and employee where the following circumstances obtain: (1) the terms of the contract of employment have not been negotiated with the individual employee but result from negotiation with a representative body or are otherwise incorporated by reference; (2) a particular term of the contract makes available to the employee a valuable right contingent upon action being taken by him to avail himself of its benefit; (3) the employee cannot, in all the circumstances, reasonably be expected to be aware of the term unless it is drawn to his attention. I fully appreciate that the criterion to justify an implication of this kind is necessity, not reasonableness. But I take the view that it is not merely reasonable, but necessary, in the circumstances postulated, to imply an obligation on the employer to take reasonable steps to bring the term of the contract in question to the employee's attention, so that he may be in a position to enjoy its benefit. Accordingly I would hold that there was an implied term in each of the plaintiff's contracts of employment of which the Boards were in each case in breach.

Note

In *University of Nottingham* v *(1) Eyett (2) The Pensions Ombudsman* [1999] IRLR 87, the High Court held that the implied duty of trust and confidence does not include a positive obligation on the employer to warn an employee who is proposing to exercise important rights in connection with the contract of employment that the way he is proposing to exercise them may not be the most financially advantageous. Thus, the pensions ombudsman erred in holding that the employers were in breach of their implied duty in failing to alert the employee that, in view of the way his pension was calculated, he was making a financial mistake by not delaying his proposed date of retirement for a few days. *Scally* was distinguished on the basis that Mr Eyett:

... undoubtedly knew of the existence of his early retirement rights. He was also able, *pace* the ombudsman, to have worked out for himself how best to avail himself of those rights by carefully studying the information set out in the explanatory booklet. There is no suggestion that he ever asked for advice as to whether the choice he was making was a suitable one, nor, as I have already indicated, was there any finding that the university knew that he was making a decision under the influence of a mistake. (*per* Hart J)

3 EQUAL PAY

I Introduction

The Equal Pay Act (EPA) 1970 requires the equal treatment of men and women in the same employment. The Act was passed with the intention of bringing about equality in respect of pay and other terms and conditions within a person's existing contract of employment. To this extent an equality clause is implied into every contract of employment.

Equal Pay Act 1970

1. Requirement of equal treatment for men and women in same employment

(1) If the terms of a contract under which a woman is employed at an establishment in Great Britain do not include (directly or by reference to a collective agreement or otherwise) an equality clause they shall be deemed to include one.

Note

Whilst the Act uses the word 'woman' throughout, men obviously have exactly the same rights under the Act; realistically, however, equality is a woman's problem. This is borne out by the number of female applicants, particularly in respect of the equal value provisions.

The annual employment tribunal and EAT statistics reproduced in *Labour Market Trends* continue to show that the success rate in equal pay claims is low, with a high percentage of cases being withdrawn. This would suggest that the Equal Pay Act itself may be a significant obstacle to a successful outcome.

The 1999 New Earnings Survey shows that the pay gap between men and women has closed slightly. However, in real terms the gap is still significant with men earning an average of 19 per cent more than women – a reduction of 1 per cent from 1998. The average weekly wage for women is £326.50 and for men, £442.40.

Table 1 Outcomes of employment tribunal cases; Great Britain; 1997–1999

	Total number of registered cases disposed of		ACAS conciliated settlements		Withdrawal		Successful at tribunal	
	1997–98	1998–99	1997–98	1998–99	1997–98	1998–99	1997–98	1998–99
Equal pay	1,483	1,530	253	517	1,069	650	18	7
Race discretion	2,194	2,694	661	813	727	871	119	131
Sex discrimination	2,839	4,025	1,005	1,791	1,070	1,334	224	270

. . .

Source: Labour Market Trends, September 1999.

Notes
1. While the trade unions have been distinctly laggardly in this field, the support of a strong union cannot be under-estimated. This can be seen from the successful equal value claims of cashiers at Marks & Spencer and Sainsburys' who, with the support of USDAW, their trade union, were able to attain the same rates of pay as male warehouse man without recourse to a full tribunal hearing. This is clearly the best way to proceed if the complainant is in the fortunate position of being one of a number of women pursuing a claim against a large employer, as they are then more likely to obtain the support of their trade union. Unfortunately this does not help those women who do not have a male comparator and as a result have no remedy under the Act. These are the women who are caught in the low pay trap. Nor does the Act offer much support to the lone woman working for the non-unionised small employer in the private sector, who may have a male comparator but may find that the struggle is not worthwhile. In an ideal world employers would implement the equality clause automatically, but in reality they do not without any risk of harsh penalties being imposed on them.

2. The National Minimum Wage Act 1998 introduced for the first time in the UK a statutory national minimum wage. There is a two-tier system which sets the minimum rate of hourly pay at £3.60 for those over 26 years and £3.00 for those below that age. This Act will have an impact on equality and pay as it effectively moves women or men out of the low pay trap, i.e. those women who are in low paid jobs with no male comparator. See Bob Simpson, 'A Milestone in the Legal Regulation of Pay: The National Minimum Wage Act 1998' (1999) 28 ILJ 1.

S. Sachdev and F. Wilkinson, *Low Pay, the Working of the Labour Market and the Role of the Minimum Wage* (1998) p. 54 Institute of Employment Rights

The case for a high legal minimum wage consists of arguments of both economic efficiency and social justice. In the interests of fairness and a civilised society there should be a minimum acceptable reward for effort expended in wage labour. The problem of a shortage of jobs productive enough to provide this minimum reward cannot be solved by low wages but should instead be sought by effective aggregate demand, and industrial and labour market policy designed to generate economic growth. Minimum wage protection can contribute to this by exerting economic pressure on employers to improve management, technology and products and by encouraging them to make better use of their workers by improved training and personnel policy. It also raises the level of demand and hence employment by redistributing income to the poor who consume a high proportion of their income. But a minimum wage needs to be both set at a higher level than that which is often canvassed and be part of a broader package of labour market reforms to make a significant impact. To be effective, a framework of minimum rights needs to be integrated into a broader bargaining agenda to encourage innovation and investment. Unless it is married to proposals to underpin collective bargaining and restore fairness to the labour market the impact of a minimum wage will be limited.

The purpose of a minimum wage is to insert a floor into an increasingly segmented labour market with growing inequality. To be credible the minimum wage has to be sufficiently high to guarantee a living wage for a reasonable number of hours worked and to be effective there should be as few exemptions as possible. The role of the minimum wage is to improve the workings of the labour market. Any exemptions which mean that workers can be employed at wages below the legal minimum risks undermining its integrity by providing the opportunities for substituting cheaper labour for those legally protected. . . .

3.   A successful challenge to the two-year limitation on arrears of renumeration in s. 2(5) EPA was made in *Levez* v *TH Jennings (Harlow Pools) Ltd (No. 2)* [1999] IRLR 764. The conclusion of the EAT being that such a limitation was in breach of EC law; the most appropriate limit being the six year time limit to be found in the Limitation Act 1980.

4.   See Gabrielle Cox, *Working Women, A Study of Pay and Hours* (Greater Manchester Low Pay Unit 1989), for research into the position of women in the labour market, in particular an analysis of New Earnings Survey, hours of work, holidays etc.

5.   Peggy Kahn, 'Unequal Opportunities: Woman, Employment and the Law', in S. Edwards (ed.) *Gender, Sex and the Law* (Croom Helm, 1986) analyses women's earnings, the position of women as part-time employees and the inadequacies of the EPA 1970 in bringing about equality.

6.   While the EPA 1970 has its deficiencies, the impact of Article 141 (ex 119) of the Treaty of Rome continues to help make our domestic law more flexible. The fact that the article is directly applicable and that domestic law must be applied and interpreted subject to it, is an essential ingredient in the continuing promotion of equal pay for men and women; this can be seen in the case of *Pickstone* v *Freemans plc* [1988] IRLR 357. Obviously the Equal Pay Directive No. 75/117 also has had an important role to play, in that it requires Member States to amend their own laws so that they comply with the Directive.

II European Community Law

Article 141 (ex 119) establishes the principle of equal pay for equal work. The article is directly enforceable in the Member States and takes precedence over domestic law. It has to be read subject to Directive 75/117, the Equal Pay Directive. While the directive is not directly enforceable against individual employers, Article 141 (ex 119) must be interpreted in accordance with the directive; consequently, in effect it is applied directly.

Treaty of Rome

Article 141 (ex Article 119)
1.   Each Member State shall ensure that the principle of equal pay for male and female workers for equal work or work of equal value is applied.

2. For the purpose of this Article, 'pay' means the ordinary basic or minimum wage or salary and any other consideration, whether in cash or in kind, which the worker receives directly or indirectly, in respect of his employment, from his employer.

Equal pay without discrimination based on sex means:

(a) that pay for the same work at piece rates shall be calculated on the basis of the same unit of measurement;

(b) that pay for work at time rates shall be the same for the same job.

3. The Council, acting in accordance with the procedure referred to in Article 251, and after consulting the Economic and Social Committee, shall adopt measures to ensure the application of the principle of equal opportunities and equal treatment of men and women in matters of employment and occupation, including the principle of equal pay for equal work or work of equal value.

4. With a view to ensuring full equality in practice between men and women in working life, the principle of equal treatment shall not prevent any Member State from maintaining or adopting measures providing for specific advantages in order to make it easier for the under-represented sex to pursue a vocational activity or to prevent or compensate for disadvantages in professional careers.

Council Directive No. 75/117
(OJ 1975, L45/19)

Article 1
The principle of equal pay for men and women outlined in Article 119 [now 141] of the Treaty, hereinafter called 'principle of equal pay', means, for the same work or for work to which equal value is attributed, the elimination of all discrimination on grounds of sex with regard to all aspects and conditions of remuneration.

In particular, where a job classification system is used for determining pay, it must be based on the same criteria for both men and women and so drawn up as to exclude any discrimination on grounds of sex.

Article 2
Member States shall introduce into their national legal system such measures as are necessary to enable all employees who consider themselves wronged by failure to apply the principle of equal pay to pursue their claims by judicial process after possible recourse to other competent authorities.

Article 3
Member States shall abolish all discrimination between men and women arising from laws, regulations or administrative provisions which is contrary to the principle of equal pay.

Article 4
Member States shall take the necessary measures to ensure that provisions appearing in collective agreements, wage scales, wage agreements or individual contracts of employment which are contrary to the principle of equal pay shall be, or may be declared, null and void or may be amended.

Article 5
Member States shall take the necessary measures to protect employees against dismissal by the employer as a reaction to a complaint within the undertaking or to any legal proceedings aimed at enforcing compliance with the principle of equal pay.

Article 6
Member States shall, in accordance with their national circumstances and legal systems, take the measures necessary to ensure that the principle of equal pay is applied. They shall see that effective means are available to take care that this principle is observed.

Jenkins v Kingsgate (Clothing Productions) Ltd
[1981] IRLR 228
European Court of Justice

Mrs Jenkins was employed as a machinist by a manufacturer of ladies' clothing. She worked on a part-time basis of 30 hours per week. All male machinists except one were employed on a full-time basis. The hourly rate for full-time workers was 9½ pence higher than that paid to part-time employees. Mrs Jenkins based her claim under the EPA 1970 on the fact that she was doing 'like work' to that of a full-time male employee. The industrial tribunal dismissed her claim on the basis that there was a valid general material difference defence (EPA 1970, s. 1(3)). The EAT accepted that she could not succeed under the EPA 1970 but agreed to refer the matter to the European Court of Justice (ECJ) to determine whether the employer's practice contravened Article 119 (now 141).

It was held that Article 119 (now 141) is directly applicable in the national courts to a situation where the payment of lower hourly rates of remuneration for part-time work than for full-time work represents discrimination based on the difference of sex.

DECISION: In the fourth and last question, the national court asks whether the provisions of Article 119 [now 141] of the Treaty are directly applicable in the circumstances of this case.

As the Court has stated in previous decisions (judgment of 8.4.76 in Case 43/75, *Defrenne* [1976] ECR 455; judgment of 27.3.80 in Case 129/79, *Wendy Smith* [1980] ECR 1275 ([1980] IRLR 210) and judgment of 11.3.81 in Case 69/80, *Worringham* ([1981] IRLR 178)), Article 119 [now 141] of the Treaty applies directly to all forms of discrimination which may be identified solely with the aid of criteria of equal work and equal pay referred to by the article in question, without national or Community measures being required to define them with greater precision in order to permit of their application. Among the forms of discrimination which may be thus judicially identified, the Court mentioned in particular cases where men and women receive unequal pay for equal work carried out in the same establishment or service, public or private.

Where the national court is able, using the criteria of equal work and equal pay, without the operation of Community or national measures, to establish that the payment of lower hourly rates of remuneration for part-time work than for full-time work represents discrimination based on difference of sex the provisions of Article 119 [now 141] of the Treaty apply directly to such a situation.

Article 1 of Council Directive No. 75/117 of 10.2.75.

The national court also raises with regard to Article 1 of Council Directive No. 75/117 of 10.2.75 the same questions of interpretation as those examined above in relation to Article 119 [now 141] of the Treaty.

As may be seen from the first recital in the preamble the primary objective of the above-mentioned Directive is to implement the principle that men and women should receive equal pay which is 'contained in Article 119 [now 141] of the Treaty'. For that purpose the fourth recital states that 'it is desirable to reinforce the basic laws by standards aimed at facilitating the practical application of the principle of equality'.

The provisions of Article 1 of that Directive are confined, in the first paragraph, to re-stating the principle of equal pay set out in Article 119 [now 141] of the Treaty and specify, in the second paragraph, the conditions for applying that principle where a job classification system is used for determining pay.

It follows, therefore, that Article 1 of Council Directive No. 75/117 which is principally designed to facilitate the practical application of the principle of equal pay outlined in Article 119 [now 141] of the Treaty in no way alters the content or scope of that principle as defined in the Treaty.

Barry v *Midland Bank plc*
[1999] IRLR 581
House of Lords

Mrs Barry was employed as a full-time clerk for 11 years from 1979, working 35 hours per week, until she took maternity leave. She was permitted to return from maternity leave in October 1990 on a part-time basis under the bank's 'key time' scheme, working the equivalent of 17½ hours per week. About one-sixth of the bank's staff are key-time workers, and 96 per cent of these are women.

In 1993, her employment was terminated after her application for voluntary severance was accepted and she received a payment of £5,806 under the security of employment agreement negotiated between the bank and her union, Bifu (now Unifi). Severance pay under this scheme is based on years of service, whether part-time or full-time, but only on the final pay the employee was earning at the date of termination. In accordance with this, Mrs Barry received a payment of 42 weeks' pay based on her final part-time salary.

Mrs Barry brought a complaint that this aspect of the scheme discriminated against her contrary to the Equal Pay Act and to Article 119 of the EC Treaty (now Article 141 EC). Her complaint was that this method of calculation failed to recognise that she had worked full time for 11 years. Instead, she was treated the same as an employee who had worked part time throughout. Therefore, Mrs Barry argued that the scheme disadvantaged part-time workers, and thus indirectly discriminated against women on grounds of sex, in that by applying a condition that she had to be working full time at the date of termination in order to avoid having her years of full-time service being counted as years of part-time service, it did not take into account any full-time service a part-time worker may have had.

It was held that a security of employment agreement, whereby severance pay was calculated on the basis of the employee's current pay at the date of termination, was not indirectly discriminatory against women contrary to Article 119 (now 141) of the EC Treaty, even though the scheme made no allowance for employees whose hours of work fluctuated, thereby disadvantaging part-time workers by not taking into account any full-time service they may have had.

LORD SLYNN OF HADLEY: . . . The question is thus whether Mrs Barry can establish indirect discrimination by showing (a) that she belongs to a group of employees which is differently and less well-treated than others, and (b) whether that difference affects considerably more women than men and, if she can, (c) whether the bank can show that the difference in treatment is objectively justified (*Stadt Lengerich v Helmig* [1995] IRLR 216, *Kowalska v Freie und Hansestadt Hamburg* [1990] IRLR 447 and *Bilka-Kaufhaus GmbH v Weber von Hartz* [1986] IRLR 317).

All employees receive a payment based on their final salary and the number of years' service. Prima facie, there is no discrimination, but Mrs Barry says that her group consists of employees who have changed from full-time to part-time treatment and they are less well-treated than those who have changed from part time to full time or those who have always been full time.

There is no doubt on the basis of a long line of authority that this severance payment is pay within the meaning of Article 119 [now 141] of the Treaty and that different treatment of part-time workers may constitute indirect discrimination where the great majority of part-time workers are women.

The first question which arises is whether there is a difference in treatment at all between full-time and part-time workers for the purposes of the Act and the Treaty. In that regard, it is not sufficient merely to ask whether one gets more or less money than the other. It is necessary to consider whether, taking account of the purpose of the payment, there is a difference in treatment. The purpose of the payment here is to provide support for lost income during the period immediately following redundancy. As the industrial tribunal put it, it is 'to cushion employees against unemployment and job loss' (decision 15 June 1995). It is not to remunerate for past service (when it would be necessary to have regard to actual service at different periods) even if the payment takes into account years of service to reflect loyalty to the employer. See *Kowalska v Freie und Hansestadt Hamburg* [1990] IRLR 447 and *Barber v Guardian Royal Exchange Assurance Group* [1990] IRLR 240. In the latter case, at 257, 13, the European Court of Justice said that a redundancy payment 'makes it possible to facilitate his adjustment to the new circumstances resulting from the loss of his employment and . . . provides him with a source of income during the period in which he is seeking new employment.'

The weekly amount lost during the redundancy period is thus the amount of salary being paid at the end of the employment; it is not, therefore, a relevant difference in treatment to base all employees' severance payments on their final salary. In principle, the position is the same here as under the statutory scheme for redundancy pay and the statutory scheme for payment in lieu of notice when payment is related to years of service but is based on final salary. The payment reflects the actual salary the employee would have received during the notice period and not some notional amount calculated on types and hours of service over the whole period of employment. In the present case, there is no relevant difference in treatment because all employees, men and women, full-time and part-time, of all ages, receive a payment based on final salary. To relate severance pay to the number of hours proportionately worked at redundancy is, as I see it, consistent with the judgment of the European Court in the *Kowalska* case, supra.

This approach seems to me also to be consistent with the approach of the European Court in *Helmig*, supra, at paragraphs 21–25, where it was held that there was no difference in treatment where part-time workers received the standard rate for basic hours of work but an extra rate was paid for hours above 38 per week. The full-time workers got the increase over the normal contractual hours whereas the part-time workers did not get the increase until they did more than 38 hours a week and so did not get it when they had completed their normal contractual hours. The crucial factor, however, was that they got the same rate for the first 38 hours.

Notes

1. With respect to the difference in pay between full-time and part-time workers in *Jenkins'* case, the ECJ concluded that this did not amount to discrimination prohibited by 'Article 119 [now 141] unless it is in reality merely an indirect way of reducing the level of pay of part-time workers on the ground that the group of workers is composed exclusively or predominantly of women'.

The issue of qualifying periods denying part-time employees access to employment rights and therefore discriminating against females was considered in *R v Secretary of State for Employment, ex parte EOC* [1994] 2 WLR 409 and *R v Secretary of State for Employment, ex parte Seymour-Smith and Perez* [1999] IRLR 253 (see Chapter 2). The potential impact of these decisions has been somewhat diminished by the Employment Protection (Part-time Employees) Regulations 1995 (SI 1995/31) and the Employment Relations Act 1999, the latter reducing the qualifying period for unfair dismissal claims from two years to one year (1 June 1999).

2. Following *Jenkins'* case it was thought that Article 119 (now 141) was not applicable in cases of unintentional indirect discrimination, i.e it would apply only to overt intentional acts, although it could be implied into the EPA 1970. This point was clarified in *Bilka-Kaufhaus v Weber von Hartz* [1986] IRLR 317, where the ECJ ruled that such discrimination was within Article 119 (now 141).

3. Where part-time female employees claim that a difference in pay impacts on part-time staff, it is still a requirement that the claimant produce statistical evidence concerning the disadvantaged group. This is particularly the case where not all of the part-time staff are treated less favourably. In *Barry v Midland Bank plc* a female part-time employee claimed that the severance pay awarded to part-time staff was less favourable than for full-time staff but could not produce statistics for her disadvantaged group. In any event, the severance scheme was objectively justifiable in this case, as its primary aim was to cushion the effects of unemployment and to compensate employees for the loss of their jobs – legitimate non-discriminatory aims *per* Peter Gibson LJ, at p.145.

The decision in *Barry v Midland Bank plc* suggests that indirect discrimination cannot be established under Article 141 (ex 119) where there is no relevant difference in treatment, even though there is a disparate impact.

4. The ECJ found in *Angestelltenbetriebstrat der Wiener Gebietskrankenkasse v Wiener Gebietskrankenkasse* [1999] IRLR 804 that psychotherapists with a

degree in Psychology, most of whom were women, did not do 'the same work within the meaning of Article 141 (ex 119) as higher paid and predominantly male doctors employed as psychotherapists'. Whilst the two groups performed for the most part identical work, they had received different professional training and, because of the different scope of the qualifications resulting from that training, were called upon to perform different tasks. It transpired that in treating patients, the two groups drew upon knowledge and skills acquired from their different disciplines. Whilst one may conclude that this is a questionable decision, particularly as they were carrying out identical tasks, it may have been more appropriate for the female psychologists to claim work of equal value.

5. Directive 75/117 is binding in so far as the EPA 1970 should be interpreted so as to avoid conflict with EC law. Directives require the Member State to amend their domestic legislation accordingly. This posed a problem for the UK which was challenged by the European Commission for failing to implement in its own legislation the principle of equal pay for work of equal value as laid down in Directive 75/117.

Commission of the European Communities v United Kingdom of Great Britain and Northern Ireland
[1982] IRLR 333
European Court of Justice

This case arose out of allegations made by the European Commission that the UK equal pay legislation did not comply with the requirements of European Community law.

Article 119 (now 141) of the Treaty of Rome required that 'Each Member State shall during the first stage ensure and subsequently maintain the application of the principle that men and women should receive equal pay for equal work.' This principle of equal pay for equal work was defined in EEC Directive No. 75/117 (the 'equal pay directive') as meaning 'for the same work or for work to which equal value is attributed, the elimination of all discrimination on grounds of sex with regard to all aspects and conditions of remuneration. In particular, where a job classification system is used for determining pay, it must be based on the same criteria for both men and women and so drawn up so as to exclude any discrimination on grounds of sex.'

The UK Equal Pay Act provides for equal treatment for men and women as regards remuneration in two sets of circumstances: 1. Where a woman is employed on 'like work' with a man, like work being defined in s. 1(4) as work of the same or broadly similar nature where the differences if any between what the woman does and what the man does are not of practical importance in relation to terms and conditions. 2. Where a woman is employed on work rated as equivalent with that of a man. Section 1(5) provides that 'A woman is to be regarded as employed on work rated as equivalent with that of any man if, but only if, her job and their job have been given an equal value, in terms of the demand made on a worker under various headings (for instance, effort, skill, decision-making), on a study undertaken with a view to evaluating in those terms the jobs to be done by all or any of the employees in an undertaking or group of undertakings . . .'.

According to the European Commission, the UK legislation was not in accordance with Community law because a woman cannot obtain equal pay in respect of work which, although not the same as, nevertheless has a value equal to that of her male counterpart unless a job evaluation scheme or study is applied in the establishment in which they are employed.

It was held by the ECJ that the EPA 1970 did not comply with Directive 75/117. Where there is a disagreement as to the application of the concept of equal pay for work of equal value a worker should be entitled to pursue a claim before an appropriate authority. Any method which excludes this prevents the aims of the directive from being achieved. Under the EPA 1970 there is no means whereby a worker may pursue an equal value claim if the employer refuses to introduce a job classification system.

DECISION: The first article of the Directive, which the Commission considers has not been applied by the United Kingdom, provides that:

The principle of equal pay for men and women outlined in Article 119 (now 141) of the Treaty, hereinafter called 'principle of equal pay', means, for the same work or for work to which equal value is attributed, the elimination of all discrimination on grounds of sex with regard to all aspects and conditions of remuneration.

In particular, where a job classification system is used for determining pay, it must be based on the same criteria for both men and women and so drawn up as to exclude any discrimination on grounds of sex.

The reference to 'work to which equal value is attributed' is used in the United Kingdom in the Equal Pay Act 1970, as amended by the Sex Discrimination Act 1975. S. 1(5) of the Act provides that:

A woman is to be regarded as employed on work rated as equivalent with that of any men if, but only if, her job and their job have been given an equal value, in terms of the demand made on the worker under various headings (for instance effort, skill, decision), on a study undertaken with a view to evaluating in those terms the jobs to be done by all or any of the employees in an undertaking or group of undertakings, or would have been given an equal value but for the evaluation being made on a system setting different values for men and women on the same demand under any heading.

Comparison of those provisions reveals that the job classification system is, under the Directive, merely one of several methods for determining pay for work to which equal value is attributed, whereas under the provision in the Equal Pay Act quoted above the introduction of such a system is the sole method of achieving such a result.

It is also noteworthy that, as the United Kingdom concedes, British legislation does not permit the introduction of a job classification system without the employer's consent. Workers in the United Kingdom are therefore unable to have their work rated as being of equal value with comparable work if their employer refuses to introduce a classification system.

The United Kingdom attempts to justify that state of affairs by pointing out that Article 1 of the Directive says nothing about the right of an employee to insist on having pay determined by a job classification system. On that basis it concludes that the worker may not insist on a comparative evaluation of different work by the job classification method, the introduction of which is at the employer's discretion.

The United Kingdom's interpretation amounts to a denial of the very existence of a right to equal pay for work of equal value where no classification has been made. Such a position is not consonant with the general scheme and provisions of Directive No. 75/117. The recitals in the preamble to that Directive indicate that its essential purpose is to implement the principle that men and women should receive equal pay contained in Article 119 (now 141) of the Treaty and that it is primarily the responsibility of the Member States to ensure the application of this principle by means of appropriate laws, regulations and administrative provisions in such a way that all employees in the Community can be protected in these matters.

To achieve that end the principle is defined in the first paragraph of Article 1 so as to include under the term 'the same work', the case of 'work to which equal value is attributed', and the second paragraph emphasises merely that where a job classification system is used for determining pay it is necessary to ensure that it is based on the same criteria for both men and women and so drawn up as to exclude any discrimination on grounds of sex.

It follows that where there is disagreement as to the application of that concept a worker must be entitled to claim before an appropriate authority that his work has the same value as other work and, if that is found to be the case, to have his rights under the Treaty and the Directive acknowledged by a binding decision. Any method which excludes that option prevents the aims of the Directive from being achieved.

That is borne out by the terms of Article 6 of the Directive which provides that Member States are, in accordance with their national circumstances and legal systems, to take the measures necessary to ensure that the principle of equal pay is applied. They are to see that effective means are available to take care that this principle is observed.

In this instance, however, the United Kingdom has not adopted the necessary measures and there is at present no means whereby a worker who considers that his post is of equal value to another may pursue his claims if the employer refuses to introduce a job classification system.

Pickstone & others (respondents) v *Freemans Plc (appellants)*
[1988] IRLR 357
House of Lords

In the present case the respondent, Mrs Pickstone, who is employed by the appellant employers as a 'warehouse operative', claims that her work as such is of equal value with that of a man, Mr Phillips, who is employed in the same establishment as a 'checker warehouse operative', and who is paid £4.22 per week more than she is paid. However, it happens to be the fact that one man is employed in the establishment as a warehouse operative doing the same work as Mrs Pickstone. The employers maintain that the existence of this fact precludes Mrs Pickstone from claiming equal pay with Mr Phillips under s. 1(2)(c) of the Act of 1970 as amended, notwithstanding that she may be performing work of equal value with his and notwithstanding that the difference in pay may be the result of discrimination on grounds of sex.

This argument is based on the words in para. (c) 'not being work in relation to which para. (a) or (b) above applies'. The employers say that the work on which Mrs Pickstone is employed is work to which para. (a) applies because it is like work with a man in the same employment, namely the one male warehouse operative. So Mrs Pickstone's work does not qualify under para. (c).

The EAT [1986] IRLR 335 dismissed the appeal against this decision. The EAT concluded that the 'words in para. (c) mean what they appear to say – namely, that "equal value" only falls to be considered where the work of the comparator is neither "like work" nor "equivalent work" to which paras. (a) and (b) apply'. The EAT did not purport to construe EEC law, because it held that the issue could be determined under domestic law.

The Court of Appeal [1987] IRLR 218 held that the words of s. 1(2)(c) were unambiguous and had the effect that a woman employed on work which is the same as that of one man but which is also of equal value with the work of another man could not claim equal pay with that other man where she was already being paid as much as the man engaged on the same work as herself.

However it concluded her claim was not barred under Article 119 [now 141] which must prevail. The employers appealed to the House of Lords.

It was held dismissing the appeal, that EPA 1970, s. 1(2)(c) should be construed in such a way that it is consistent with the objects of the EC Treaty, the provisions of the Equal Pay Directive and the rulings of the European Court.

LORD KEITH OF KINKEL: The question is whether the exclusionary words in para. (c) are intended to have effect whenever the employers are able to point to some man who is employed by them on like work with the woman claimant within the meaning of para. (a) or work rated as equivalent with hers within the meaning of para. (b), or whether they are intended to have effect only where the particular man with whom she seeks comparison is employed on such work. In my opinion the latter is the correct answer. The opposite result would leave a large gap in the equal work provision, enabling an employer to evade it by employing one token man on the same work as a group of potential women claimants who were deliberately paid less than a group of men employed on work of equal value with that of the women. This would mean that the United Kingdom had failed yet again fully to implement its obligations under Article 119 (now 141) of the Treaty and the Equal Pay Directive, and had not given full effect to the decision of the European Court in *Commission of the European Communities* v *United Kingdom* [1982] IRLR 333. It is plain that Parliament cannot possibly have intended such a failure. The draft Regulations of 1983 were presented to Parliament as giving full effect to the decision in question. The draft Regulations were not subject to the Parliamentary process of consideration and amendment in Committee, as a Bill would have been. In these circumstances and in the context of s. 2 of the European Communities Act 1972 I consider it to be entirely legitimate for the purpose of ascertaining the intention of Parliament to take into account the terms in which the draft was presented by the responsible Minister and which formed the basis of its acceptance. The terms in which it was presented to the House of Commons are set out in the speech of my noble and learned friend, Lord Templeman.

Much the same was said before the House of Lords. There was no suggestion that the exclusionary works in para. (c) were intended to apply in any other situation than where the man selected by a woman complainant for comparison was one in relation to whose work para. (a) or para. (b) applied. It may be that, in order to confine the words in question to that situation, some necessary implication falls to be made into their literal meaning. The precise terms of that implication do not seem to me to matter. It is sufficient to say that the words must be construed purposively in order to give effect to the manifest broad intention of the maker of the Regulations and of Parliament. I would therefore reject the appellant's argument.

LORD TEMPLEMAN: According to the employers in the present appeal, the Regulations of 1983 had the additional effect of depriving some women of the right to pursue their claims by judicial process or otherwise although they considered themselves wronged by failure to apply the principle of equal pay. The respondents may have a valid complaint in that they are not receiving equal pay with Mr Phillips for work of equal value. But if the respondents seek to remedy that discrimination under s. 1(2)(c) of the act of 1970 as amended by the Regulations, they will be debarred because they are employed on 'work in relation to which para. (a) or (b) above applies'. It is said that para. (a) operates, not because the respondents are employed on like work with Mr Phillips but because the respondents are employed on like work with some other man. Since para. (c) is expressed to apply only when a woman is employed on work which is not 'work in relation to which para. (a) or (b) above applies,' it follows, so it is said, that where a woman is employed on like work with any man or where a woman is employed on work rated as equivalent with any man, no claim can be made under para. (c) in respect of some other man who is engaged on work of equal value. In my opinion para. (a) or (b) only debars a claim under para. (c) where para. (a) or (b) applies to the man who is the subject of the complaint made by the woman. If the Tribunal decide that the respondents are engaged 'on like work' with Mr Phillips then para. (a) applies and the respondents are not entitled to proceed under para. (c) and to obtain the report of an ACAS expert. If there is a job evaluation study which covers the work of the respondents and the work of Mr Phillips then the respondents are debarred from proceeding under para. (c) unless the job evaluation study itself was discriminatory.

Whenever there is a claim for equal pay, the complainant, or the complainant's trade union representative supporting the claimant, may wish to obtain a report from an ACAS expert under para. (c) to use for the purpose of general pay bargaining and in the hope of finding ammunition which will lead to a general increase in wage levels irrespective of discrimination. For this purpose the more ACAS reports there are the better. It may be significant that in the present case a claim is made under para. (c) and not under para. (a) as well, or, in the alternative, although it is obvious that work of equal value in terms of the demands made on a woman under such headings as effort, skill and decision which may amount to discrimination under para. (c) may also be work of a broadly similar nature with differences of no practical importance which found a complaint under para. (a). If there is discrimination in pay the Industrial Tribunal must be able to grant a remedy. But the remedy available under para. (c) is not to be applied if the complainant has a remedy in respect of the male employee with whom she demands parity under para. (a) or if para. (b) applies to the woman and to that male employee. To prevent exploitation of para. (c) the Tribunal must decide in the first instance whether the complainant and the man with whom she seeks parity are engaged on 'like work' under para. (a). If para. (a) applies, no ACAS report is required. If para. (a) does not apply, then the Tribunal considers whether para. (b) applies to the complainant and the man with whom she seeks parity; if so, the Tribunal can only proceed under para. (c) if the job evaluation study obtained for the purposes of para. (b) is itself discriminatory. If para. (b) applies then, again, no ACAS report is necessary. If paras. (a) and (b) do not apply, the Tribunal must next consider whether there are reasonable grounds for determining that the work of the complainant and the work of the man with whom she seeks parity is of equal value. If the Tribunal are not so satisfied, then no ACAS report is required. The words in para. (c) on which the employers rely were not intended to create a new form of permitted discrimination. Para. (c) enables a claim to equal pay as against a specified man to be made without injustice to an employer. When a woman claims equal pay for work of equal value, she specifies the man with whom she demands parity. If the work of the woman is work in relation to which para. (a) or (b) applies in relation to that man, then the woman cannot proceed under para. (c) and cannot obtain a report from an ACAS expert. In my opinion there must be implied in para. (c) after the word 'applies' the words 'as between the woman and the man with whom she claims equality.' This construction is consistent with Community law. The employers' construction is inconsistent with Community law and creates a permitted form of discrimination without rhyme or reason.

Macarthys Ltd v *Smith*
[1980] ICR 672
European Court of Justice

M, a man, was employed as the manager of one of the stockrooms of the employers' warehouses, at a remuneration of about £60 a week. On 20 October 1975, he left. For four months the post was not filled and then the employee was appointed, her duties differing slightly from M's. She was paid £50 a week. On 9 March 1977, she left her employment. She brought proceedings before an industrial tribunal claiming that, by virtue of s. 1(1) and (2)(a) of the Equal Pay Act 1970, her contract of employment should be treated as modified with regard to her remuneration so as to entitle her to pay equal to M's pay at the termination of his employment. The tribunal upheld her claim and decided that the employee was entitled to compare the work done by her with M's work and that her services and those of M were broadly comparable so as to justify calculating her remuneration on the same basis as his.

The EAT dismissed the employers' appeal. The Court of Appeal (Lord Denning MR dissenting) held that the words in s. 1(2) of the Act of 1970, as amended, by the use of the present tense looked to the present and the future and thus, giving them the grammatical construction, they were consistent with a comparison between a man and a woman contemporaneously in the same employment, but, bearing in mind that construction of the section, the application of Article 119 (now 141) of the EEC Treaty to the circumstances of the section was not easy to discern and that a reference should be made to the European Court of Justice.

On the reference to the European Court of the questions, *inter alia*, whether the principle of equal pay for equal work, contained in Article 119 (now 141) of the Treaty and Article 1 of the EEC Council Directive of

February 10, 1975 (75/117/EEC), was confined to situations in which men and women were contemporaneously doing equal work for their employer it was held that the principle in Article 119 (now 141) of the EEC Treaty that men and women should receive equal pay for equal work was not confined to situations in which men and women were contemporaneously doing equal work for the same employer; and that the principle applied to a case where, having regard to the nature of her services, a woman had received less pay than a man who was employed prior to the woman and did equal work for the employer.

DECISION: . . . The employers contended that, according to its natural and ordinary meaning, the Equal Pay Act 1970 makes it impermissible for a woman to compare her situation with that of a man formerly in the employment of the same employer. In their submission, such an interpretation would not be inconsistent with the principle of equal pay for men and women laid down in Article 119 [now 141] of the EEC Treaty.

6. For her part, the employee contended that the employers' interpretation was contrary to Article 119 [now 141] and to article 1 of Directive No. 75/117/EEC in that the principle of equal pay for equal work is not confined to situations in which men and women are contemporaneously doing equal work for their employer but that, on the contrary, that principle also applies where a worker can show that she receives less pay in respect of her employment than she would have received if she were a man doing equal work for the employer or than had been received by a male worker who had been employed prior to her period of employment and had been doing equal work for her employer.

7. In order to decide the dispute the Court of Appeal formulated four questions worded as follows:

1. Is the principle of equal pay for equal work, contained in Article 119 [now 141] of the EEC Treaty and Article 1 of the EEC Council Directive of February 10, 1975 (75/117/EEC), confined to situations in which men and women are contemporaneously doing equal work for their employer?

2. If the answer to question (1) is in the negative, does the said principle apply where a worker can show that she receives less pay in respect of her employment from her employer: (a) than she would have received if she were a man doing equal work for the employer; or (b) than had been received by a male worker who had been employed prior to her period of employment and who had been doing equal work for the employer?

3. If the answer to question (2)(a) or (b) is in the affirmative, is that answer dependent upon the provisions of Article 1 of the Directive?

4. If the answer to question (3) is in the affirmative, is Article 1 of the Directive directly applicable in member States?

8. It follows from the wording of these questions, as much as from the reasons given in the order making the reference, that the questions relating to the effect of the Directive and to the interpretation of Article 1 thereof only arise if the application of Article 119 [now 141] of the Treaty should not permit the issue raised in the proceedings to be resolved. It is therefore appropriate to consider first how Article 119 [now 141] is to be interpreted having regard to the legal situation in which the dispute has its origin.

The interpretation of Article 119 [now 141] of the EEC Treaty

9.   According to the first paragraph of Article 119 [now 141] the member states are obliged to ensure and maintain 'the application of the principle that men and women should receive equal pay for equal work.'

10.   As the court indicated in *Defrenne* v *Sabena* [1976] ICR 547, that provision applies directly, and without the need for more detailed implementing measures on the part of the Community or the member states, to all forms of direct and overt discrimination which may be identified solely with the aid of the criteria of equal work and equal pay referred to by the article in question. Among the forms of discrimination which may be thus judicially identified, the court mentioned in particular cases where men and women receive unequal pay for equal work carried out in the same establishment or service.

11.   In such a situation the decisive test lies in establishing whether there is a difference in treatment between a man and a woman performing 'equal work' within the meaning of Article 119 [now 141]. The scope of that concept, which is entirely qualitative in character in that it is exclusively concerned with the nature of the services in question, may not be restricted by the introduction of a requirement of contemporaneity.

12.   It must be acknowledged, however, that, as the Employment Appeal Tribunal properly recognised, it cannot be ruled out that a difference in pay between two workers occupying the same post but at different periods in time may be explained by the operation of factors which are unconnected with any discrimination on grounds of sex. That is a question of fact which it is for the court or tribunal to decide.

13.   Thus the answer to the first question should be that the principle that men and women should receive equal pay for equal work, enshrined in Article 119 [now 141] of the EEC Treaty, is not confined to situations in which men and women are contemporaneously doing equal work for the same employer.

14.   The second question put by the Court of Appeal and expressed in terms of alternatives concerns the framework within which the existence of possible discrimination in pay may be established. This question is intended to enable the court to rule upon a submission made by the employee and developed by her before the European Court of Justice to the effect that a woman may claim not only the salary received by a man who previously did the same work for her employer but also, more generally, the salary to which she would be entitled were she a man, even in the absence of any man who was concurrently performing, or had previously performed, similar work. The employee defined this term of comparison by reference to the concept of what she described as 'a hypothetical male worker.'

15.   It is clear that the latter proposition, which is the subject of question 2(a), is to be classed as indirect and disguised discrimination, the identification of which, as the court explained in *Defrenne* v *Sabena* [1976] ICR 547, implies comparative studies of entire branches of industry and therefore requires, as a prerequisite, the elaboration by the Community and national legislative bodies of criteria of assessment. From that it follows that, in cases of actual discrimination falling within the scope of the direct application of Article 119 [now 141], comparisons are confined to parallels which may be drawn on the basis of concrete appraisals of the work actually performed by employees of different sex within the same establishment or service.

16.   The answer to the second question should therefore be that the principle of equal pay enshrined in Article 119 [now 141] applies to the case where it is established that, having regard to the nature of her services, a woman has received less pay than a man who was employed prior to the woman's period of employment and who did equal work for the employer.

17.   From the foregoing it appears that the dispute brought before the national court may be decided within the framework of an interpretation of Article 119 [now 141] of the Treaty alone. In those circumstances it is unnecessary to answer the questions submitted in so far as they relate to the effect and to the interpretation of EEC Council Directive (75/117/EEC).

Notes

1.   The decision in *Pickstone* does not provide an automatic right to claim work of equal value; it is subject to an assessment by the industrial tribunal of whether this is the correct head of claim, first after considering 'like work' and secondly 'work rated equivalent'. However, the decision is important not only for showing the effect of EC law on domestic law, but also for ensuring that employers do not avoid their obligations under the EPA 1970 by employing a token man to work alongside women.

2.   The impact of Article 141 (ex 119) and Directive 75/117 can be seen in *Macarthys Ltd* v *Smith*. The EPA 1970 must be interpreted in the light of this decision, thereby allowing any applicant the right of comparison with a predecessor. Furthermore, in *Murphy* v *Bord Telecom Eireann* [1988] IRLR 267, where a female employee was doing work of a higher value than her male comparator, the ECJ held that the words 'equal value' should include higher or greater value. In fact, to conclude otherwise would have created an anomaly, allowing an employer to assign additional or more onerous duties to workers of a particular sex, who could then be paid at a lower wage.

3.   An analysis of the decisions in *Pickstone, Murphy* and *Hayward* v *Cammell Laird Shipbuilders Ltd* [1988] IRLR 257, in respect of the permitted comparisons which can be made by a complainant, was undertaken by Peter Schofield, (1988) 17 ILJ, at pp. 241–4.

4.   For a discussion of the impact of EC law, see C. McCrudden (ed.), *Women, Employment and European Equality Law* (Eclipse Publications, 1987) and E. Ellis, *European Community Sex Equality Law* (Oxford University Press, 1991).

5.   The importance of Article 141 (ex 119) is well illustrated by case law interpreting the word 'pay'.

Barber v *Guardian Royal Exchange Assurance Group*
[1990] IRLR 240
European Court of Justice

Mr Barber was a member of the Guardian Royal Exchange pension fund. The pension scheme was non-contributory and a 'contracted-out' scheme.

Under the Guardian's pension scheme, the normal pensionable age was fixed for the category of employees to which Mr Barber belonged at 62 for men and at 57 for women. That difference was equivalent to that which exists under the State social security scheme, where the normal pensionable age is 65 for men and 60 for women. Members of the Guardian's pension fund were entitled to an immediate pension on attaining the normal pensionable age provided for by that scheme. Entitlement to a deferred pension payable at the normal pensionable age was also conferred on members of the fund who were at least 40 years old and had completed 10 years' service with the Guardian when the employment relationship was terminated.

The Guardian Royal Exchange Assurance Guide to Severance Terms, which formed part of Mr Barber's contract of employment, provided that, in the event of redundancy, members of the pension fund were entitled to an immediate pension subject to having attained the age of 55 for men or 50 for women. Staff who did not fulfil those conditions received certain cash benefits calculated on the basis of their years of service and a deferred pension payable at the normal pensionable age.

Mr Barber was made redundant with effect from 31 December 1980 when he was aged 52. The Guardian paid him the cash benefits provided for in the Severance Terms, the statutory redundancy payment and an *ex gratia* payment. He would have been entitled to a retirement pension as from the date of his 62nd birthday. It is undisputed that a woman in the same position as Mr Barber would have received an immediate retirement pension as well as the statutory redundancy payment and that the total value of those benefits would have been greater than the amount paid to Mr Barber.

Mr Barber initially based his claim a breach of the SDA 1975. This claim was rejected by the industrial tribunal and the EAT on the ground that it related to retirement which was excluded by SDA 1975, s. 6(4). The EAT also held that there was no claim under EC law as questions relating to entitlement to benefit fell within the terms of the Equal Treatment Directive which is not directly applicable between individuals.

Mr Barber appealed to the Court of Appeal, which stayed the proceedings and asked the Court of Justice to give a preliminary ruling on the following questions:

1. When a group of employees are made compulsorily redundant by their employer in circumstances similar to those of this case and receive benefits in connection with that redundancy, are all those benefits 'pay' within the meaning of Article 119 (now 141) of the EEC Treaty and the Equal Pay Directive (75/117/EEC), or do they fall within the Equal Treatment Directive (76/207/EEC), or neither?

2. Is it material to the answer to question 1 that one of the benefits in question is a pension paid in connection with a private occupational pension scheme operated by the employer ('a private pension')?

3. Is the principle of equal pay referred to in Article 119 (now 141) and the Equal Pay Directive infringed in the circumstances of the present case if:

(a) a man and a woman of the same age are made compulsorily redundant in the same circumstances, and in connection with that redundancy, the woman receives an immediate private pension but the man receives only a deferred private pension; or

(b) the total value of the benefits received by the woman is greater than the total value of the benefits received by the man?

4.   Are Article 119 (now 141) and the Equal Pay Directive of direct effect in the circumstances of this case?

5.   Is it material to the answer to question 3 that the woman's right to access to an immediate pension provided for by the severance terms could only be satisfied if she qualified for an immediate pension under the provisions of the private occupational scheme in that she was being treated as retired by the Guardian because she was made redundant within seven years of her normal pension date under the pension scheme?

The ECJ held that benefits paid on redundancy amounted to 'pay' and fell within the scope of Article 119 (now 141). This includes redundancy payments made under a statutory scheme and *ex gratia* payments. A pension paid under a contracted-out private occupational pension scheme also fell within the scope of Article 119 (now 141).

The first question

In its first question the Court of Appeal seeks to ascertain, in substance, whether the benefits paid by an employer to a worker in connection with the latter's compulsory redundancy fall within the scope of Article 119 [now 141] of the Treaty and the Directive on equal pay or within the scope of the Directive on equal treatment.

The Court has consistently held (see, in particular, its judgment of 31 March 1981 in Case 96/80, *Jenkins* v *Kingsgate* [1981] IRLR 228 at para.22) that the first of those two Directives, which is designed principally to facilitate the application of the principle of equal pay outlined in Article 119 [now 141] of the Treaty, in no way alters the content or scope of that principle as defined in the latter provision. It is therefore appropriate to consider, in the first place, whether Article 119 [now 141] applies in circumstances such as those of this case.

As the Court has held, the concept of pay, within the meaning of the second paragraph of Article 119 [now 141], comprises any other consideration, whether in cash or in kind, whether immediate or future, provided that the worker receives it, albeit indirectly, in respect of his employment from his employer (see, in particular, the judgment of 9 February 1982 in Case 12/81 *Garland* v *British Rail Engineering* [1982] IRLR 111 at para. 5). Accordingly, the fact that certain benefits are paid after the termination of the employment relationship does not prevent them from being in the nature of pay, within the meaning of Article 119 [now 141] of the Treaty.

The second question

The schemes in question are the result either of an agreement between workers and employers or of a unilateral decision taken by the employer. They are wholly financed by the employer or by both the employer and the workers without any contribution being made by the public authorities. Accordingly such schemes form part of the consideration offered to workers by their employer.

Thirdly, it must be pointed out that, even if the contributions paid to those schemes and the benefits which they provide are in part a substitute for those of the general statutory scheme, that fact cannot preclude the application of Article 119[now 141]. It is apparent from the documents before the Court that occupational schemes such as that referred to in this case may grant to their members benefits greater than those which would be paid by the statutory scheme, with the result that their economic function is similar to that of the supplementary schemes which exist in certain

Member States, where affiliation and contribution to the statutory scheme is compulsory and no derogation is allowed. In its judgment of 13 May 1986 in Case 170/84 (*Bilka-Kaufhaus* v *Weber von Hartz* [1986] IRLR 317) the Court held that the benefits awarded under a supplementary pension scheme fell within the concept of pay, within the meaning of Article 119 (now 141).

It must therefore be concluded that, unlike the benefits awarded by national statutory social security schemes, a pension paid under a contracted-out scheme constitutes consideration paid by the employer to the worker in respect of his employment and consequently falls within the scope of Article 119 [now 141] of the Treaty.

The third and fifth questions
In the case of the first of those two questions thus formulated, it is sufficient to point out that Article 119 [now 141] prohibits any discrimination with regard to pay as between men and women, whatever they system which gives rise to such inequality. Accordingly, it is contrary to Article 119 [now 141] to impose an age condition which differs according to sex in respect of pensions paid under a contracted-out scheme, even if the difference between the pensionable age for men and that for women is based on the one provided for by the national statutory scheme.

As regards the second of those questions, it is appropriate to refer to the judgments of 30 June 1988 in Case 318/85 (*Commission of the European Communities* v *France* [1988] ECR 3559 at para. 27) and of 17 October 1989 in Case 109/88 (*Handels og Kontorfunktionaerernes Forbund i Danmark* v *Dansk Arbeidsgiverforening acting on behalf of Danfoss* [1989] IRLR 532 at para. 12), in which the Court emphasised the fundamental importance of transparency and, in particular, of the possibility of a review by the national courts, in order to prevent and, if necessary, eliminate any discrimination based on sex.

With regard to the means of verifying compliance with the principle of equal pay, it must be stated that if the national courts were under an obligation to make an assessment and a comparison of all the various types of consideration granted, according to the circumstances, to men and women, judicial review would be difficult and the effectiveness of Article 119 [now 141] would be diminished as a result. It follows that genuine transparency, permitting an effective review, is assured only if the principle of equal pay applies to each of the elements of remuneration granted to men or women.

The fourth question
In view of the answer given to the first question, it is unnecessary to discuss the effects of the Directive on equal pay. As for Article 119 [now 141], it is appropriate to refer to the established caselaw, which was reviewed by the Court in particular in its judgment of 31 March 1981 in Case 96/80 (*Jenkins*, cited above, at para. 17) and according to which that provision applies directly to all forms of discrimination which may be identified solely with the aid of the criteria of equal work and equal pay referred to by the Article in question, without national or Community measures being required to define them with greater precision in order to permit their application.

If a woman is entitled to an immediate retirement pension when she is made compulsorily redundant, but a man of the same age is entitled in similar circumstances only to a deferred pension, then the result is unequal pay as between those two categories of workers which the national court can itself establish by considering the components of the remuneration in question and the criteria laid down in Article 119 [now 141].

The answer to the fourth question must therefore be that Article 119 [now 141] of the Treaty may be relied upon before the national courts and it is for those courts to safeguard the rights which that provision confers on individuals, in particular where a contracted-out pension scheme does not pay to a man on redundancy an immediate pension such as would be granted in a similar case to a woman.

Specialarbejderforbundet i Danmark v *Dansk Industri, acting for Royal Copenhagen A/S*
[1995] IRLR 648
European Court of Justice

This case concerned an equal pay claim brought on behalf of 'blue-pattern painters' employed by the Danish ceramics producer, Royal Copenhagen. They compared their work with male automatic-machine operators. The 26 automatic-machine operators, all men, are part of the 200-worker turners' group. The blue-pattern painters comprise 155 women and one man. They form part of the 453-worker painters' group. This group also included 51 ornamental-plate painters, all women.

All the employees are covered by the same collective agreement, under which they are paid in part on a piecework basis (i.e. the level of their pay is wholly or partly dependent on their output) although they could opt to be paid a fixed hourly rate which was the same for all groups. In practice, about 70 per cent of the turners and 70 per cent of the painters are paid by the piece, with their pay consisting of a fixed element, paid as a basic hourly wage, and a variable element, paid by reference to the number of items produced.

In April 1990, the average hourly pay of the automatic-machine operators paid by the piece was Danish Krone (DKR) 103.93, including a fixed element of DKR 71.69. During the same period the average hourly pay of the blue-pattern painters paid by the piece was DKR 91, including a fixed element of DKR 57. The average hourly pay of the ornamental-plate painters paid by the piece was DKR 116.20, including a fixed element of DKR 35.85.

The Specialarbejderforbundet, the Danish union for semi-skilled workers, brought an equal pay claim on grounds that the work of the blue-pattern painters was of equal value to that of the automatic-machine operators, but the average hourly piecework pay for the predominantly female group was less than that of the men's group. It sought a ruling that Royal Copenhagen should be required to bring the average hourly rate of the blue-pattern painters up to the level of the automatic-machine operators.

The national court's first question asks whether Article 119 [now 141] of the Treaty and the Directive apply to piecework pay schemes in which pay depends entirely or in large measure on the individual output of each worker.

Article 119 [now 141], by stating expressly in subparagraph (a) of its third paragraph that equal pay without discrimination based on sex means that pay for the same work at piece rates is to be calculated on the basis of the same unit of measurement, itself provides that the principle of equal pay applies to piecework pay schemes.

Moreover the Court has already held that Article 119 [now 141] prohibits any discrimination with regard to pay as between men and women, whatever the system which gives rise to such inequality (case 262/88 *Barber* v *Guardian Royal Exchange Assurance Group* IRLR 240 [1990], paragraph 32).

That conclusion is borne out by the first paragraph of Article 1 of the Directive, which provides that the prindple of equal pay for men and women means the elimination of all discrimination on grounds of sex 'with regard to all aspects and conditions of remuneration'.

The reply to the first question should accordingly be that Article 119 [now 141] of the Treaty and the Directive apply to piecework pay schemes in which pay depends entirely or in large measure on the individual output of each worker.

. . .

It follows from paragraph 12 of this judgment that in a piecework pay scheme the principle of equal pay requires that the pay of two groups of workers, one consisting predominantly of men and the other predominantly of women, is to be calculated on the basis of the same unit of measurement.

Where the unit of measurement is the same for two groups of workers carrying out the same work or is objectively capable of ensuring that the total individual pay of workers in the two groups is the same for work which, although different, is considered to be of equal value, the principle of equal pay does not prohibit workers belonging to one or the other group from receiving different total pay if that is due to their different individual output.

It follows that in a piecework pay scheme the mere finding that there is a difference in the average pay of two groups of workers, calculated on the basis of the total individual pay of all the workers belonging to one or the other group, does not suffice to establish that there is discrimination with regard to pay.

It is for the national court, which alone is competent to assess the facts, to decide whether the unit of measurement applicable to the work carried out by the two groups of workers is the same or, if the two groups carry out work which is different but considered to be of equal value, whether the unit of measurement is objectively capable of ensuring that their total pay is the same. It is also for that court to ascertain whether a pay differential relied on by a worker belonging to a group consisting predominantly of women as evidence of sex discrimination against that worker compared with a worker belonging to a group consisting predominantly of men is due to a difference between the units of measurement applicable to the two groups or to a difference in individual output.

The Court has, however, held (case C-127/92 *Enderby* v *Frenchay Health Authority* [1993] IRLR 591, paragraphs 13 and 14) that the burden of proof, which is normally on the worker bringing legal proceedings against his employer with a view to removing the discrimination of which he believes himself to be the victim, may be shifted when that is necessary to avoid depriving workers who appear to be the victims of discrimination of any effective means of enforcing the principle of equal pay. Thus in particular where an undertaking applies a system of pay which is wholly lacking in transparency, it is for the employer to prove that his practice in the matter of wages is not discriminatory if a female worker establishes, in relation to a relatively large number of employees, that the average pay for women is less than that for men (case 109/88 *Handels- og Kontorfunktionaerernes Forbund i Danmark* v *Dansk Arbejdsgiverforening* ('*Danfoss*') [1989] IRLR 532, paragraph 16). Similarly, where significant statistics disclose an appreciable difference in pay between two jobs of equal value, one of which is carried out almost exclusively by women and the other predominantly by men, so that there is a prima facie case of sex discrimination, Article 119 [now 141] of the Treaty requires the employer to show that that difference is based on objectively justified factors unrelated to any discrimination on grounds of sex (*Enderby*, cited above, paragraphs 16 and 19).

Admittedly, in a piecework pay scheme such a prima facie case of discrimination does not arise solely because significant statistics disclose appreciable differences between the average pay of two groups of workers, since those differences may be due to differences in individual output of the workers constituting the two groups.

If, however, in a system such as that in the main proceedings where the individual pay taken into account in calculating the average pay of the two groups of workers consists of a variable element depending on each worker's output and a fixed element differing according to the group of workers concerned (fourth question, paragraph (e)), it is not possible to identify the factors which determined the rates or units of measurement used to calculate the variable element in the pay (fourth question, paragraph (g)), the objective of not depriving workers of any effective means of enforcing the principle of equal pay may require the employer to bear the burden of proving that the differences found are not due to sex discrimination.

It is for the national court to ascertain whether, in the light in particular of those factors and the extent of the differences between the average pay of the two groups of workers, the conditions for so shifting the burden of proof are satisfied in the main proceedings. If so, it will be open to the employer for example to demonstrate that the pay differentials are due to differences in the choice by the workers concerned of their rate of work (fourth question paragraph (c)) and to rely on major differences between total individual pay within each of those groups (fourth question, paragraph (d)).

The reply to the second question in conjunction with paragraphs (c), (d), (e) and (g) of the fourth question should accordingly be that the principle of equal pay set out in Article 119 [now 141] of the Treaty and Article 1 of the Directive means that the mere finding that in a piecework pay scheme the average pay of a group of workers consisting predominantly of women carrying out one type of work is appreciably lower than the average pay of a group of workers consisting predominantly of men carrying out another type of work to which equal value is attributed does not suffice to establish that there is discrimination with regard to pay. However, where in a piecework pay scheme in which individual pay consists of a variable element depending on each worker's output and a fixed element differing according to the group of workers concerned it is not possible to identify the factors which determined the rates or units of measurement used to calculate the variable element in the pay, the employer may have to bear the burden of proving that the differences found are not due to sex discrimination.

. . .

There can be sex discrimination between two groups of workers only if the two groups carry out, if not the same work, at least work to which equal value is attributed.

A pay differential between two groups of workers does not constitute discrimination contrary to Article 119 [now 141] of the Treaty and to the Directive if it may be explained by objectively justified factors unrelated to any discrimination on grounds of sex (see in particular case 170/84 *Bilka-Kaufhaus GmbH* v *Weber von Hartz* [1986] IRLR 317, paragraph 30).

The national court, which is alone competent to assess the facts, must consequently ascertain whether, in the light of the facts relating to the nature of the work carried out and the conditions in which it is carried out, equal value may be attributed to it, or whether those facts may be considered to be objective factors unrelated to any discrimination on grounds of sex which are such as to justify any pay differentials.

The reply to the fourth question, paragraphs (a), (f), (h) and (i), should accordingly be that, when ascertaining whether the principle of equal pay has been observed, it is for the national court to decide whether, in the light of circumstances such as, first, the fact that the work done by one of the groups of workers in question involves machinery and requires in particular muscular strength whereas that done by the other group is manual work requiring in particular dexterity and, secondly, the fact that there are differences between the work of the two groups with regard to paid breaks, freedom to organise one's own work and work-related inconveniences, the two types of work are of equal value or whether those circumstances may be considered to be objective factors unrelated to any discrimination on grounds of sex which are such as to justify any pay differentials.

Notes

1.   The judgment of the ECJ in *Barber* placed a limitation on the retrospective impact of their decision by restricting claims for equality in pensions under Article 119 (now 141) to claims made after the date of the judgment, except for those who have before that date initiated legal proceedings or raised an equivalent claim under the applicable national law. This restriction was placed to reduce the financial consequences of the decision. The decision in *Ten Oever* v *Stichting Bedrijfspensioenfonds voor het Glazenwassers-en Schoon-maakbedrijf* [1992] IRLR 601 confirms that there cannot be retrospective claims.

2.   See Sue Ward, 'The *Barber* judgment: implications for employers', *Equal Opportunities Review*, 1990, vol. 32, at p. 40 for an analysis of the impact of the *Barber* decision.

3.   The issue of what is included in the word 'pay' in Article 141 (ex 119) has been considered in cases other than *Barber* but not with the same legal and financial implications. In *Rinner-Kuhn* v *FWW Spezial-Gebaudereinigung GmbH* [1989] IRLR 493, wages continued to be paid to employees who fell ill. To qualify for this continuing payment an employee's normal working hours had to exceed 10 hours a week or 45 hours a month. German national legislation permitted employers to operate such an exclusion. The ECJ held that such payments amounted to 'pay' within the meaning of Article 141 (ex 119) and that Article 141 (ex 119) prevails over national legislation where the provision affects a considerably greater number of women than men, unless the Member State can show that the legislation is justified by objective factors unrelated to any discrimination on grounds of sex. This decision throws considerable doubt on the legality of excluding employees from the receipt of or access to pay-related benefits based on hours or even length of service where it has a disparate impact on one particular sex. See also *Arbeiterwohl-fahrt der Stadt Berlin ev* v *Botel* [1992] IRLR 423, in which the ECJ held that paid leave, in this particular case to attend training courses, amounted to 'pay' within the meaning of Article 119 (now 141) and Directive 75/117. To fail to pay part-time employees 'who were generally women' the same as

full-time employees in these circumstances amounted to indirect discrimination contrary to Article 119 (now 141). Furthermore, whilst bridging pensions amount to 'pay', it is not contrary to Article 141 (ex 119) for an employer to reduce the amount of bridging pension to take into account the State pension which the employee will receive, even though in the case of men and women aged between 60 and 65 the result is that the female ex-employee receives a smaller bridging pension (*Roberts* v *Birds Eye Walls Ltd* [1994] IRLR 29). Interestingly the ECJ, in *Stadt Lengerich* v *Angelika Helming* [1995] IRLR 216, held that payment of overtime rates only where normal working hours for full-time workers were exceeded did not discriminate against part-time female employees, as in effect full-time and part-time employees were being treated equally. However, it could be argued that this ignores the fact that part-time employees are predominantly female and as a result subject to indirect discrimination, as the rule clearly disadvantaged them since part-time employees would in this case have had to work 38 hours per week to obtain overtime pay.

In *Gillespie* v *Northern Health and Social Services Board* [1996] IRLR 214, the ECJ ruled that women on maternity leave are not entitled to full pay. This ruling was based on the special position of such women who are not therefore in a comparable position to men or other women. Reference should also be made to *Webb* v *EMO Air Cargo (UK) (No. 2)* [1995] IRLR 645 as a clear distinction has developed between the treatment of the pregnant woman and the woman on maternity leave. Furthermore, the 'sick man' remains a legitimate comparison.

In *Todd* v *Eastern Health and Social Services Board* [1997] IRLR 410, in which maternity pay provisions were less generous than sick pay provisions, it was held by NICA that maternity pay and sick pay could not be treated the same, i.e. as a 'disability' in that a healthy pregnancy could not be treated as either a disability or equivalent to an illness (see J. Conaghan, 'Pregnancy, Equality and the ECJ: Interrogating Colette Gillespie' (1998) 3 *International Journal on Discrimination Law*, pp. 115–33). However, the decision in *Todd* must now be read in the light of the decision of the ECJ in *Handells-Og Kontorfunktionaererernes Vorbund I Danmark Acting on behalf of Pedersen* v *Faellsforeningen vor Danmarks Brugsforeninger Acting on behalf of Kvickly Skive* [1999] IRLR 55 (see below). Ruling on Danish employment law, which provided that pregnant employees who are ill before the beginning of the maternity leave period are entitled to pay only if the illness is unconnected with pregnancy, the ECJ concluded that it was contrary to Article 119 (now 141) and the Equal Pay Directive to deprive a woman of her full pay when she is unfit for work before the beginning of her maternity leave as a result of a pregnancy-related condition, when a worker is in principle entitled to receive full pay in the event of incapacity for work on grounds of illness. Such treatment was based essentially on pregnancy and thus was discriminatory. However, Article 119 (now 141) and the Equal Pay Directive do not preclude national legislation, which provides that a pregnant woman is not entitled to be paid where, before the beginning of maternity leave, she is absent from work not because of any incapacity for work but by reason either of routine pregnancy-related inconveniences or because of a medical recommendation intended to protect the unborn child. Loss of pay in such circumstances is not treatment based essentially on the pregnancy, but rather is based on the choice made by the employee not to work.

The distinction between these two scenarios in *Pedersen* is, it is suggested, extremely subtle. Both appear to be pregnancy-related; however, the former is an incapacity to work by reason of the pregnancy and the latter is apparently not!

4. Lastly, in *Garland* v *British Rail Engineering Ltd* [1982] IRLR 111, the ECJ held that concessionary rail travel given to employees after retirement amounted to 'pay' and thereby fell within the scope of Article 119 (now 141). As a result the provision of such facilities which had only been accorded to former male employees discriminated against former female employees.

Questions

1. Following the decision in *Barry* v *Midland Bank plc*, when is the most appropriate time to consider 'justification'?

2. How can the effect of the decision in *Pickstone* be by-passed?

3. What is the current position on the relationship between the three heads of claim under the EPA 1970? Is this affected by EC law?

4. What is the impact of the *Barber* decision on the Social Security Act 1989? Is there any effect on the UK State pension scheme?

5. Would there still be inequality in piecework payments if the women carried out particularly dextrous work, or the men used greater physical strength?

III Equal Pay Act 1970

Equal Pay Act 1970

1. Requirement of equal treatment for men and women in same employment

(1) If the terms of a contract under which a woman is employed at an establishment in Great Britain do not include (directly or by reference to a collective agreement or otherwise) an equality clause they shall be deemed to include one.

(2) An equality clause is a provision which relates to terms (whether concerned with pay or not) of a contract under which a woman is employed (the 'woman's contract'), and has the effect that—

(a) where the woman is employed on like work with a man in the same employment—

(i) if (apart from the equality clause) any term of the woman's contract is or becomes less favourable to the woman than a term of a similar kind in the contract under which that man is employed, that term of the woman's contract shall be treated as so modified as not to be less favourable, and

(ii) if (apart from the equality clause) at any time the woman's contract does not include a term corresponding to a term benefiting that man included in the contract under which he is employed, the woman's contract shall be treated as including such a term;

(b)   where the woman is employed on work rated as equivalent with that of a man in the same employment—

(i)   if (apart from the equality clause) any term of the woman's contract determined by the rating of the work is or becomes less favourable to the woman than a term of a similar kind in the contract under which that man is employed, that term of the woman's contract shall be treated as so modified as not to be less favourable, and

(ii)   if (apart from the equality clause) at any time the woman's contract does not include a term corresponding to a term benefiting that man included in the contract under which he is employed and determined by the rating of the work, the woman's contract shall be treated as including such a term.

(c)   where a woman is employed on work which, not being work in relation to which paragraph (a) or (b) above applies, is, in terms of the demands made on her (for instance under such headings as effort, skill and decision), of equal value to that of a man in the same employment—

(i)   if (apart from the equality clause) any term of the woman's contract is or becomes less favourable to the woman than a term of a similar kind in the contract under which that man is employed, that term of the woman's contract shall be treated as so modified as not to be less favourable, and

(ii)   if (apart from the equality clause) at any time the woman's contract does not include a term corresponding to a term benefiting that man included in the contract under which he is employed, the woman's contract shall be treated as including such a term.

(3)   An equality clause shall not operate in relation to a variation between the woman's contract and the man's contract if the employer proves that the variation is genuinely due to a material factor which is not the difference of sex and that factor—

(a)   in the case of an equality clause falling within subsection (2)(a) or (b) above, must be a material difference between the woman's case and the man's; and

(b)   in the case of an equality clause falling within subsection (2)(c) above, may be such a material difference.

(4)   A woman is to be regarded as employed on like work with men if, but only if, her work and theirs is of the same or a broadly similar nature, and the differences (if any) between the things she does and the things they do are not of practical importance in relation to terms and conditions of employment; and accordingly in comparing her work with theirs regard shall be had to the frequency or otherwise with which any such differences occur in practice as well as to the nature and extent of the differences.

(5)   A woman is to be regarded as employed on work rated as equivalent with that of any men if, but only if, her job and their job have been given an equal value, in terms of the demand made on a worker under various headings (for instance effort, skill, decision), on a study undertaken with a view to evaluating in those terms the jobs to be done by all or any of the employees in an undertaking or group of undertakings, or would have been given an equal value but for the evaluation being made on a system setting different values for men and women on the same demand under any heading.

(6)   Subject to the following subsections, for purposes of this section—

(a)   'employed' means employed under a contract of service or of apprenticeship or a contract personally to execute any work or labour, and related expressions shall be construed accordingly;

. . .

(c)   Two employers are to be treated as associated if one is a company of which the other (directly or indirectly) has control or if both are companies of which a third person (directly or indirectly) has control,
and men shall be treated as in the same employment with a woman if they are men employed by her employer or any associated employer at the same establishment or at establishments in Great Britain which include that one and at which common terms and conditions of employment are observed either generally or for employees of the relevant classes.

2A.   Procedure before tribunal in certain cases

(1)   Where on a complaint or reference made to an employment tribunal under section 2 above, a dispute arises as to whether any work is of equal value as mentioned in section 1(2)(c) above the tribunal may either—

(a)   proceed to determine that question; or

(b)   unless it is satisfied that there are no reasonable grounds for determining that the work is of equal value as so mentioned, require a member of the panel of independent experts to prepare a report with respect to that question;
and, if it requires the preparation of a report under paragraph (b) of this subsection, it shall not determine that question unless it has received the report.

(2)   Without prejudice to the generality of subsection (1) above, there shall be taken, for the purposes of that paragraph, to be no reasonable grounds for determining that the work of a woman is of equal value as mentioned in section 1(2)(c) above if—

(a)   that work and the work of the man in question have been given different values on a study such as is mentioned in section 1(5) above; and

(b)   there are no reasonable grounds for determining that the evaluation contained in the study was (within the meaning of subsection (3) below) made on a system which discriminates on grounds of sex.

(3)   An evaluation contained in a study such as is mentioned in section 1(5) above is made on a system which discriminates on grounds of sex where a difference, or coincidence, between values set by that system on different demands under the same or different headings is not justifiable irrespective of the sex of the person on whom those demands are made.

(4)   In paragraph (b) of subsection (1) above the reference to a member of the panel of independent experts is a reference to a person who is for the time being designated by the Advisory, Conciliation and Arbitration Service for the purposes of that paragraph as such a member, being neither a member of the Council of that Service nor one of its officers or servants.

As noted in the introduction to this chapter, the EPA 1970 introduces an equality clause into all contracts of employment. This clause operates automatically to bring about equality between a male's and female's terms of employment. In reality most claims relate to rate of pay. Where the employer fails to put the equality clause into effect, the EPA 1970 as amended provides three heads of claim for an applicant; these are known as 'like work', 'work rated as equivalent' and 'work of equal value'. Any applicant must have a comparator of the opposite sex with whom a comparison can be made. The comparator may be employed by the same or an associated employer, at the same establishment or at an establishment where common terms and conditions are observed. Most of the contentious issues relate to the interpretation of the wording of the Act.

A: What Amounts to 'Pay'?

Hayward v Cammell Laird Shipbuilders Ltd
[1988] IRLR 257
House of Lords

Hayward was employed as a canteen cook. She claimed equal pay for work of equal value with the tradesmen in the shipyard who were paid a higher basic and overtime rate. The industrial tribunal referred the case to the independent expert who found that her work was of equal value to that of her male comparators. The employer did not raise a s. 1(3) defence and the industrial tribunal found in her favour.

At a further hearing, the employers contended that they did not have to pay Miss Hayward the same basic wage and overtime rates as her male comparators because, considered as a whole, her terms and conditions were not less favourable. Although Miss Hayward received lower basic pay and overtime rates, she had a paid meal break, additional holidays and better sickness benefits. On the employers' valuation of these benefits, when they were taken into account, she was better off on the whole than her comparators.

The industrial tribunal and subsequently the EAT ruled that EPA 1970, s. 1(2)(c) should be interpreted as meaning that, when implementing an equal value award, equal pay means terms relating to pay which, considered as a whole, are not less favourable. The EAT also emphasised that if each term relating to pay had to be looked at individually, it would produce 'leap-frogging' which would result in widespread chaos. The Court of Appeal also dismissed Hayward's appeal, stating it was artificial to look merely at one part of the overall remuneration package.

The House of Lords held, allowing her appeal, that a woman who can point to a term of her contract which is less favourable than a term of a similar kind in the man's contract is entitled to have that term made not less favourable irrespective of whether she is treated as favourably as the man when the whole of her contract and the whole of his contract are considered.

LORD GOFF OF CHIEVELEY: Section (2) is subdivided into three subsubsections – the first, (a), being concerned with like work, the second, (b), with work rated as equivalent, and the third, (c), with work of equal value. Each of these subsubsections makes provisions for two alternative situations – (i) where any term of the woman's contract is (or becomes) less favourable to her than a term of a similar kind in the male comparator's contract, and (ii) where the woman's contract does not include a term corresponding to a term benefitting the male comparator included in his contract. I will call the first situation the case of the less favourable term, and the second situation the case of the absent term.

In considering the question of construction, it is plain that we have to consider it in relation both to the case of the less favourable term, and the case of the absent term, for the same policy considerations must underlie each. Furthermore, I find it easier to approach the problem by considering first the case of the absent term, because the provisions of subsubsection (ii) of each subsection are in simpler terms than those of subsubsection (i), and are therefore easier to construe.

What does subsubsection (ii) in each case provide? It provides that if the woman's contract does not include a term corresponding to a term benefitting the male comparator included in his contract, her contract shall be treated as including such a term. Next, what does such a provision mean? If I look at the words used, and give them their natural and ordinary meaning, they mean quite simply that one looks at the man's contract and at the woman's contract, and if one finds in the man's contract a term benefitting him which is not included in the woman's contract, then that term is treated as included in hers. On this simple and literal approach, the words 'benefitting that man' mean precisely what they say – that the term must be one which is beneficial to him, as opposed to being burdensome. So if, for example, the man's contract contains a term that he is to be provided with the use of a car, and the woman's contract does not include such a term, then her contract is to be treated as including such a term.

It is obvious that this approach cannot be reconciled with the approach favoured by the Court of Appeal, because it does not require, or indeed permit, the court to look at the overall contractual position of each party, or even to look at their overall position as regards one particular matter, for example, 'pay' in the wide sense adopted by the Court of Appeal. To achieve that result, it would be necessary, in subsubsection (ii), to construe the word 'term' as referring to the totality of the relevant contractual provisions relating to a particular subject matter, for example 'pay' or alternatively to construe the words 'benefitting that man' as importing the necessity of a comparison in relation to the totality of the relevant contractual provisions concerning a particular subject matter and then for a conclusion to be reached that, on balance, the man has thereby benefitted. The latter construction I find impossible to derive from the words of the statute; and, to be fair, I do not think that there is any evidence that it would have found favour with the Court of Appeal. But what of the former, which is consistent with the judgment of the Court of Appeal? Again, I find myself unable to accept it. First, it would mean that the situation of the absent term must be confined only to those cases where there was *no* provision relating, for example, to pay – or, I suppose, to overtime, or to some other wholly distinct topic. I cannot think that that was the intention of the legislature. In commonsense terms, it means that subsubsection (ii) would hardly ever be relevant at all; certainly, since every contract of employment makes some provision for 'pay' in the broad sense adopted by the Court of Appeal, subsubsection (ii) would never be relevant in relation to pay or any other form of remuneration in cash or in kind or in the form of other benefits. I find this proposition to be startling. Second, it imposes upon the word 'term' a meaning which I myself do not regard as its natural or ordinary meaning. If a contract contains provisions relating to (1) basic pay, (2) benefits in kind such as the use of a car, (3) cash bonuses, and (4) sickness benefits, it would never occur to me to lump all these together as one 'term' of the contract, simply because they can all together be considered as providing for the total 'remuneration' for the services to be performed under the contract. In truth, these would include a number of different terms; and in my opinion it does unacceptable violence to the words of the statute to construe the word 'term' in subsubsection (ii) as embracing collectively all these different terms.

It is against the background of this reasoning in relation to the case of the absent term, that I turn to subsubsection (i) and the case of the less favourable term. Here the Court of Appeal was able to build their construction upon the basis of a reference, in the subsubsection, to 'a term of a similar kind' in the male comparator's contract. They considered that these words referred necessarily to a term relating to the same overall subject matter, in particular pay; and that the question whether the relevant term in the woman's contract was less favourable than that in the man's contract could only sensibly be considered by comparing all the provisions relating to this subject matter in the contracts of each. From this they derived the broad meaning of the word 'term' which I have described.

For my part, I cannot accept this reasoning. Suppose that there is a term in a woman's contract which provides that she is to be paid £x per hour, and that there is a term in the male comparator's contract that he is to be paid £y per hour, y being greater than x. On the natural and ordinary meaning of the words in the statute, there is, in my opinion, in such a case, a term of the woman's contract which is less favourable to her than a term of a similar kind in the male comparator's contract; and that would be so even if there was some other provision in her contract which conferred upon her a benefit (which fell within her overall 'remuneration') which the man was not entitled to receive under his contract, such as, for example, the use of a car. I do not consider that the words 'a term of a similar kind' are capable of constituting a basis for building the construction of the word 'term' favoured by the Court of Appeal. Again, in my opinion, the words mean precisely what they say. You look at the two contracts: you ask yourself the commonsense question – is there in each contract a term of a similar kind, i.e. a term making a comparable provision for the same subject matter; if there is, then you compare the two, and if, on that comparison, the term of the woman's contract proves to be less favourable than the term of the man's contract, then the term in the woman's contract is to be treated as modified so as to make it not less favourable. I am, of course, much fortified in this approach in that it appears to me to be consistent with the only construction of subsubsection (ii), concerned with the case of the absent term, which I find to be acceptable. But, in addition, I feel that the Court of Appeal's attempt to introduce the element of overall comparison placed them firmly, or rather infirmly, upon a slippery slope; because, once they departed from the natural and ordinary meaning of the word 'term,' they in reality found it impossible to control the ambit of the comparison which they considered to be required. For almost any, indeed perhaps any, benefit will fall within 'pay' in the very wide sense favoured by them, in which event it is difficult to segregate any sensible meaning of the word 'term'.

Notes

1. There is little doubt that had the Court of Appeal's approach been adopted regarding the meaning of 'pay', i.e. the whole remuneration package, a woman whose contract lacked a particular term would have been prevented from bringing an action because all contracts of employment contain a term relating to or equivalent to remuneration.

2. The ECJ 's interpretation of the word 'pay' is extremely wide and has had a significant impact on the EPA 1970 – see the *Barber* case and *McKechnie* v *UBM Building Supplies (Southern) Ltd* [1991] IRLR 283, in which it was decided that a scheme which made *ex gratia* redundancy payments to women up to the age of 60 years and men up to the age of 65 years was covered by Article 119 (now 141) of the Treaty of Rome.

3. The genuine material factor defence (EPA 1970, s. 1(3)) was not pleaded in *Hayward's* case, although Lord Mackay stated *obiter* at p. 261:

. . . s. 1(3) would not provide a defence to an employer against whom it was shown that a term in the woman's contract was less favourable to her than a corresponding term in the man's contract on the basis that there was another term in the woman's contract which was more favourable to her than the corresponding term in the man's contract. At the very least for s. 1(3) to operate it would have to be shown that the unfavourable character of the term in the woman's contract was in fact due to the difference in the opposite sense in the other term and that the difference was not due to the reason of sex. I consider that counsel for the appellant succeeds on the natural reading of the words of s. 1(2) which are in issue and that your Lordships do not require to reach any final conclusion in this case on the meaning and effect of s. 1(3).

Question
Is the issue of mutual enhancement/leap-frogging a problem?

B: *What is Meant by 'Same Employment'?*

Leverton v Clwyd County Council
[1989] IRLR 28
House of Lords

Mrs Leverton was employed by the council as a nursery nurse in infants' school. She brought an equal value claim comparing herself with male clerical staff employed in different establishments. At the time of the industrial tribunal hearing, Mrs Leverton's annual salary was £5,058 and that of her comparators ranged from £6,081 to £8,532. Both Mrs Leverton and her comparators were employed pursuant to the Scheme of Conditions of Service of the NJC for Local Authorities' Administrative, Professional, Technical and Clerical Services. Under the terms of that agreement, nursery nurses are paid under scale 1. The comparators were at different points on scales 3 and 4.

The right to equal pay is restricted to men and women 'in the same employment'. Section (6) of the Equal Pay Act stipulates that 'men shall be treated as in the same employment with a woman if they are men employed by her employer . . . at the same establishment or at establishments in Great Britain which include that one and at which common terms and conditions of employment are observed either generally or for employees of the relevant classes.'

The employers contended that common terms and conditions were not observed for the relevant employees, notwithstanding that they were covered by the same collective agreement and there were many common terms of employment, because the nurses worked 32½ hours per week and had 70 days' annual holiday as against the comparators' 37-hour week and 20 days' basic annual holiday entitlement.

The Court of Appeal dismissed Leverton's appeal in respect of EPA 1970, s. 1(6) and supported the view of the industrial tribunal that a s. 1(3) defence was applicable.

On appeal, the House of Lords held that s. 1(6) calls for a comparison between the terms and conditions of employment observed at the establishment at which the woman is employed and the establishment at which the men are employed, and applicable either generally, i.e. to all the employees at the relevant establishments, or to a particular class or classes of employees to which both the woman and the men belong.

LORD BRIDGE: On the question of whether the appellant was in the same employment as the comparators working at different establishments, the view which prevailed with the majority of the Industrial Tribunal, the Employment Appeal Tribunal, and the majority of the Court of Appeal was that the comparison called for by s. 1(6) was between the terms and conditions of employment of the appellant on the one hand and of the comparators on the other and that it was only if this comparison showed their terms and conditions of employment to be 'broadly similar' that the test applied by the phrase 'common terms and conditions of employment' in s. 1(6) was satisfied. The majority of the Industrial Tribunal affirmed by the Employment Appeal Tribunal and the majority of the Court of Appeal, held that the difference in this case in working hours and holidays was a radical difference in the 'core terms' of the respective contracts of employment which prevented the comparison from satisfying the statutory test. The contrary view embraced by the dissenting member of the Industrial Tribunal and by May LJ in the Court of Appeal was that the comparison called for was much broader, viz a comparison between the terms and conditions of employment observed at two or more establishments, embracing both the establishment at which the woman is employed and the establishment at which the men are employed, and applicable either generally, i.e. to all the employees at the relevant establishments, or to a particular class or classes of employees to which both the woman and the men belong. Basing himself implicitly on this view, the dissenting member of the Industrial Tribunal expressed his conclusion in the matter tersely. Having referred to the purple book, he said:

3. Within that agreement there are nine sections and numerous clauses. They do not apply, with few exceptions, to any particular grade. It is clearly a general agreement and not specific to any particular group or class of employee. 4. It is, in my opinion, beyond doubt that the applicant and the comparators are employed on common terms and conditions, i.e. the APT & C agreement, and clearly it is within the provisions of s. 1(6).

My Lords, this is an important difference in principle which depends on the true construction of s. 1(6). I have no hesitation in preferring the minority to the majority view expressed in the courts below. It seems to me, first, that the language of the subsection is clear and unambiguous. It poses the question whether the terms and conditions of employment 'observed' at two or more establishments (at which the relevant woman and the relevant men are employed) are 'common', being terms and conditions of employment observed 'either generally or for employees of the relevant classes.' The concept of common terms and conditions of employment observed generally at different establishments necessarily contemplates terms and conditions applicable to a wide range of employees whose individual terms will vary greatly inter se. On the construction of the subsection adopted by the majority below the phrase 'observed either generally or for employees of the relevant classes' is given no content. Terms and conditions of employment governed by the same collective agreement seem to me to represent the paradigm, though not necessarily the only example, of the common terms and conditions of employment contemplated by the subsection.

But if, contrary to my view, there is any such ambiguity in the language of s. 1(6) as to permit the question whether a woman and men employed by the same employer in different establishments are in the same employment to depend on a direct comparison establishing a 'broad similarity' between the woman's terms and conditions of employment and those of her claimed comparators, I should reject a construction of the subsection in this sense on the ground that it frustrates rather than serves the manifest purpose of the legislation. That purpose is to enable a woman to eliminate discriminatory differences between the terms of her contract and those of any male fellow employee doing like work, work rated as equivalent or work of equal value, whether he works in the same establishment as her or in another establishment where terms and conditions of employment common to both establishments are observed. With all respect to the majority view which prevailed below, it cannot, in my opinion, possibly have been the intention of Parliament to require a woman claiming equality with a man in another establishment to prove an undefined substratum of similarity between the particular terms of her contract and his as the basis of her entitlement to eliminate any discriminatory differences between those terms.

On the construction of s. 1(6) which I would adopt there is a sensible and rational explanation for the limitation of equality claims as between men and women employed at different establishments to establishments at which common terms and conditions of employment are observed. There may be perfectly good geographical or historical reasons why a single employer should operate essentially different employment regimes at different establishments. In such cases the limitation imposed by s. 1(6) will operate to defeat claims under s. 1 as between men and women at the different establishments. I take two examples by way of illustration. A single employer has two establishments, one in London and one in Newcastle. The rates of pay earned by persons of both sexes for the same work are substantially higher in London than in Newcastle. Looking at either the London establishment or the Newcastle establishment in isolation there is no sex discrimination. If the women in Newcastle could invoke s. 1 of the Act of 1970 to achieve equality with the men in London this would eliminate a differential in earnings which is due not to sex but to geography. Section. 1(6) prevents them from doing so. An employer operates factory A where he has a long standing collective agreement with the ABC union. The same employer takes over a company operating factory X and becomes an 'associated employer' of the persons working there. The previous owner of factory X had a long standing collective agreement with the XYZ union which the new employer continues to operate. The two collective agreements have produced quite different structures governing pay and other terms and conditions of employment at the two factories. Here again s. 1(6) will operate to prevent women in factory A claiming equality with men in factory X and vice versa. These examples are not, of course, intended to be exhaustive. So long as Industrial Tribunals direct themselves correctly in law to make the appropriate broad comparison, it will always be a question of fact for them, in any particular case, to decide whether, as between two different establishments, 'common terms and conditions of employment are observed either generally or for employees of the relevant classes.' Here the majority of the Industrial Tribunal misdirected themselves in law and their conclusion on this point cannot be supported.

Note

While the difference in hours and holiday entitlement did not prevent there being common terms and conditions in *Leverton's* case, the House of Lords concluded that the industrial tribunal had not erred in finding that there was a genuine material factor defence provided by this difference in hours and holidays which justified the difference in pay (EPA 1970, s. 1(3)). Basically the men had to work much longer hours and had shorter holidays to earn their salaries.

British Coal Corporation v Smith
[1996] IRLR 404
House of Lords

Some 1,286 women employed by British Coal as canteen workers or cleaners submitted applications between December 1986 and April 1988 claiming equal pay for work of equal value and comparing their work with that of 150 comparators employed either as surface mineworkers or clerical workers. Canteen workers employed by British Coal were predominantly women, cleaners were mainly women, clerical workers were approximately half men and half women, and surface mineworkers were men. The claimants were employed at 47 different establishments, and the comparators were employed at 14 different establishments.

. . . In the Court of Appeal [1994] IRLR 342, the case was heard consecutively with *North Yorkshire County Council v Ratcliffe* The Court of Appeal allowed the employers' appeal in respect of s. 1(6) and the appeal by canteen workers and cleaners in respect of s. 1(3). The Court of Appeal held that 'common terms and conditions' within the meaning of s. 1(6) of the Equal Pay Act are 'the same' terms and conditions rather than terms and conditions which are 'broadly similar' or 'to the same overall effect'. Accordingly, s. 1(6) permits the choice of a male comparator from a separate establishment, if the terms and conditions of employment for men of the relevant class at his establishment are common with meaning the same as, those of men of the relevant class employed at the woman's establishment, or which would be available for male employees for that work at her establishment. In this case, the Court of Appeal held the terms and conditions on which the male comparator class of surface mineworkers were employed were not the same, regardless of the establishments at which they worked, since the terms entitling them to an incentive bonus and to concessionary coal were agreed and implemented at local level with widely varying results. Therefore, the claimants were limited in their choice of male comparators who were surface workers to the district or other area in respect of which the same terms of employment as regards the payment of an incentive bonus and the concessionary coal allowance were agreed. Thus, the industrial tribunal had erred in finding that all the comparators named by every applicant, other than those employed at the same establishment as the applicant, were in 'the same employment' as the applicant for the purposes of s. 1(6).

It was held that the applicant canteen workers and cleaners were in the 'same employment' (within the meaning of s. 1(6) EPA 1970) as their male comparators in different establishments employed as surface mineworkers because there were 'common terms and conditions of employment' observed as between the establishments.

LORD SLYNN: . . . It is plain that from the beginning, although the woman had to show that her comparator or comparators ('men') was or were employed by her employer or by an associated employer of her employer, and that she could not point to higher wages being paid by other employers, yet she was not limited to selecting male workers from the place where she herself worked. The reason for this is obvious, since otherwise an employer could so arrange things as to ensure that only women worked at a particular establishment or that no man who could reasonably be considered as a possible comparator should work there. A woman can thus point to men employed in her own establishment or in other establishments of her employer in Great Britain. But the other establishments which include her establishment must be ones at which common terms and conditions of employment are observed generally or for employees of the relevant classes. The words 'which include that one' may at first sight be puzzling since she can under the earlier words point to men employed at the same establishment as hers. The words are, however, to be read with the following words: 'at which common terms . . . are observed'. Those common terms must thus be observed not only at other establishments but also at the establishment at which the woman works if employees of the relevant classes are employed there.

Common terms and conditions of employment must be observed either generally (i.e. for all or perhaps for most workers) or for employees of the relevant classes. Subject to a misdirection in law, it is for the industrial tribunal to decide on the evidence what is or are the relevant class or relevant classes. It has been said by the corporation that the relevant class here is 'ancillary workers' so that all the claimants must be treated as one relevant class. The effect of that would be that not all ancillary workers in the relevant class would be women, even though a majority might still be. In my view, having regard to the nature of the work and the different ways in which their pay structures were established, the industrial tribunal was perfectly entitled to take the various categories of worker separately. Thus canteen workers and cleaners are separate groups largely composed of women.

The real question, however, is what is meant by 'common terms of conditions of employment' and between whom do such terms and conditions have to be common?

It is plain and it is agreed between the parties that the woman does not have to show that she shares common terms and conditions with her comparator, either in the sense that all the terms are the same, since necessarily his terms must be different in some respect if she is to show a breach of the equality clause, or in regard to terms other than that said to constitute the discrimination.

It is accepted by the corporation that for the purposes of this appeal as between the different establishments common terms and conditions do in any event apply to the two classes of applicants, canteen workers and cleaners. What therefore has to be shown is that the male comparators at other establishments and at her establishment share common terms and conditions. If there are no such men at the applicant's place of work then it has to be shown that like terms and conditions would apply if men were employed there in the particular jobs concerned.

The corporation contends that the applicants can only succeed if they can show that common terms and conditions were observed at the two establishments for the relevant classes in the sense that they apply 'across the board'; in other words the terms and conditions of the comparators (e.g. surface mineworkers) are 'common in substantially all respects' for such workers at her pit and at the places of employment of the comparators. This in effect means that all the terms and conditions must be common, i.e. the same, subject only to de minimis differences.

The applicants reject this and contend that it is sufficient if there is a broad similarity of terms rather than that they are strictly coterminous.

Your Lordships have been referred to a number of dictionary definitions of 'common', but I do not think that they help. The real question is what the legislation was seeking to achieve. Was it seeking to exclude a woman's claim unless, subject to de minimis exceptions, there was complete identity of terms and conditions for the comparator at his establishment and those which applied or would apply to a similar male worker at her establishment? Or was the legislation seeking to establish that the terms and conditions of the relevant class were sufficiently similar for a fair comparison to be made, subject always to the employer's right to establish a 'material difference' defence under s. 1(3) of the Act?

If it was the former then the woman would fail at the first hurdle if there was any difference (other than a de minimis one) between the terms and conditions of the men at the various establishments, since she could not then show that the men were in the same employment as she was. The issue as to whether the differences were material so as to justify different treatment would then never arise.

I do not consider that this can have been intended. The purpose of requiring common terms and conditions was to avoid it being said simply: 'a gardener does work of equal value to mine and my comparator at another establishment is a gardener.' It was necessary for the applicant to go further and to show that gardeners at other establishments and at her establishment were or would be employed on broadly similar terms. It was necessary but it was also sufficient.

Whether any differences between the woman and the man selected as the comparator were justified would depend on the next stage of the examination under s. 1(3). I do not consider that the s. 1(3) enquiry, where the onus is on the employer, was intended to be excluded unless the terms and conditions of the men at the relevant establishments were common in the sense of identical. This seems to me to be far too restrictive a test.

Notes

1.   In *Lawson v Britfish Ltd* [1988] IRLR 53, the EAT, in considering the application of s. 1(6)(c) and the words 'common terms and conditions', concluded that these words do not relate to employment at the same establishment. Once it is established that the applicant and her comparator are employed at the same establishment the issue of whether there are common terms and conditions does not arise. The decision of the EAT in *Scullard v Knowles* [1996] IRLR 344 moves away from the more restrictive aspects of the interpretation of s. 1(6) which confine comparison to associated companies. It is suggested that s. 1(6) should be displaced by the wider interpretation to be found in Article 141 (ex 119) which encompasses comparators employed 'in the same establishment or service', thereby increasing the scope for public sector employees to make equal pay claims.

2.   However, in *Lawrence v Regent Office Care Limited* [1999] IRLR 148, the EAT were not prepared to widen the interpretation of Article 119 (now 141) to allow former employees of a County Council, who were now employed by private contractors, which had successfully tendered to provide the school meal service, to bring an equal pay claim comparing themselves with current employees of the Council whose work had been rated as of equal value to their own. The EAT concluded that to bring an equal pay claim 'the applicant and comparator must be in a loose and non-technical sense in the same establishment or service, even though it is not necessary for the same entity

to be employer of both applicant and comparator, or for the employers to be associated'.

3. The word 'employed' in EPA 1970, s. 1(6) has a wider meaning than is ordinarily provided by employment protection legislation. It includes not only persons in the master-servant relationship but also those who are self-employed yet are engaged in an activity to execute personally work or labour – see *Quinnen v Hovells* [1984] IRLR 227, a sex discrimination case, the SDA 1975 providing a similar definition of the word 'employment'. In *Mirror Group Newspapers Ltd v Gunning* [1986] IRLR 27 (another sex discrimination case), the Court of Appeal considered the words 'a contract personally to execute any work or labour'. It held that it includes any contract where the dominant purpose is that the person contracting to provide services under it performs personally the work which forms the subject matter of the contract. It is a qualitative rather than a quantitative test and requires consideration of the type of work or labour to be performed.

As the right to protection is given to those 'employed', it will not necessarily be defeated even where the contract of employment is tainted by illegality (*Leighton v Michael & Charalambous* [1996] IRLR 67).

Questions

1. Did Mrs Leverton 'cast her net too widely' in respect of her comparators (*obiter* Lord Bridge)?
2. Following *Leverton's* case, would Miss Hayward's claim have been defeated?
3. What is there to prevent a female employee based at the employer's Cardiff factory comparing herself with a male employee at his London factory?
4. Following the decision in *Scullard*, what options are available for the applicant in selecting s. 1(6) comparators?

C: 'Like Work'

To succeed in a claim based on 'like work' under the EPA 1970, s. 1(2)(a), it must be shown that the applicant is employed on the same work or work of a broadly similar nature to the comparator. As a result of s. 1(4) of the Act, any differences between their jobs which are not of practical importance can be disregarded, but regard should be had to the frequency with which such differences occur in practice and the nature and extent of the differences.

E. Coomes (Holdings) Ltd v Shields
[1978] IRLR 263
Court of Appeal

Miss Shields was employed as a counterhand in the appellants' book-makers' shop in Sussex Street, London, on an hourly rate of 92p. A male counterhand, Mr Rolls, was also employed at this shop on the higher rate of £1.06 an hour. The shop was one of nine operated by the company that it considered to be vulnerable to trouble, both from risk of attack on the premises by robbers, particularly when the shop was opened in the morning, and from the risk of disturbance from customers in the shop.

To guard against these potential dangers, it was the policy of the company to employ male counterhands at these nine shops. The main work of these men was the same as that of the women counterhands but, in addition, they were required to be around when the manager opened up in the morning, as a reinforcement in case of trouble; they were required, simply by their presence, to act as a deterrent to potential rowdy or violent customers and to deal with these if the need arose; and they were also used in the transporting of cash between branches.

The industrial tribunal held that Miss Shields was not employed on 'like work' her male comparator because his duties of deterring trouble amounted to differences of practical importance for the purposes of EPA 1970, s. 1(4). The EAT allowed Miss Shields appeal.

The Court of Appeal's, dismissing the employer's appeal, held that s. 1(4) requires a comparison to be made not between the contractual obligations of the man on the one hand and the woman on the other, but between the things that each actually does and the frequency with which they are done. The industrial tribunal had erred in paying too much attention to the contractual obligations and too little to the fact that the man had never, on the evidence, had to deal with any disturbance or attempted violence.

LORD DENNING MR: The only thing that is clear to me is that, when men and women are engaged on like work in the same establishment, the women are to be paid the same 'rate for the job' as the men. That is, usually an hourly rate. But an exception can be made where a man deserves more than the woman because he has special personal claims to a higher rate because of his superior skill or responsibility or merit, so long as it is not based on the difference in sex. I turn to the sections which bear this out.

S. 1(4) – 'LIKE WORK'

When a woman claims equal pay with a man in the same employment, she has first to show that she is employed on 'like work' with him. This is defined in s. 1(4), which proceeds in this fashion:

First, her work and that of the men must be 'of the same or a broadly similar nature'. Instances of the 'same nature' are men and women bank cashiers at the same counter; or men and women serving meals in the same restaurant. Instances of a 'broadly similar nature' are men and women shop assistants in different sections of the same department store; or a woman cook who prepares lunches for the directors and the men chefs who cook breakfast, lunch and teas for the employees in the canteen – see *Capper Pass Ltd* v *Lawton* [1976] IRLR 366.

Second, there must be an inquiry into (i) the 'differences between the things that the woman does and the things that the men do'; and (ii) a comparison of them so as to see 'the nature and extent of the differences' and the 'frequency or otherwise with which such differences occur in practice': and (iii) a decision as to whether those differences are, or are not 'of practical importance in regard to terms and conditions of employment'.

This involves a comparison of the two jobs – the woman's job and the man's job – and making an evaluation of each job as a job irrespective of the sex of the worker and of any special personal skill or merit that he or she may have. This evaluation should be made in terms of the 'rate for the job' usually a payment of so much per hour. The rate should represent the value of each job in terms of the demand made on a worker under such headings as effort, skill, responsibility, or decision. If the value of the man's job is worth more than the value of the woman's job, it is legitimate that the man should receive a higher 'rate for the job' than the woman. For instance, a man who is dealing with production schedules may deal with far more important items than the woman – entailing far more serious consequences from a wrong decision. So his job should be rated higher than hers, see *Eaton* v *Nuttall* [1977] IRLR 71. But, if the value of the woman's job is equal to the man's job, each should receive the same rate for the job. This principle of 'equal value' is so important that you should ignore differences between the two jobs which are 'not of practical importance'. The employer should not be able to avoid the principle by introducing comparatively small differences in 'job content' between men and women: nor by giving the work a different 'job description'. Thus where a woman driver in a catering department drives vans within the factory premises to and from the kitchens and a man driver in a transport section drives vans on the public highway, it could properly be held that the differences were 'not of practical importance' and she should receive the same 'rate for the job' an hour rate as he, see *British Leyland* v *Powell* [1978] IRLR 57. Again in a hospital, the attendance on patients may be done by women called 'nurses' and men called 'orderlies': and there may be differences in 'job content' in that, while both do many similar things, the men 'orderlies' deal with the special needs of men patients, but these differences are not such as to warrant a 'wage differential' between the nurses and the orderlies – see *Brennan* v *Prince William Hospital* (1974) 503 Fed Rep 2nd, page 282.

Nor should the employer be able to avoid the principle of 'equal value' by having the work (at the same job) done by night or for longer hours. The only legitimate way of dealing with might work or for longer hours is by paying a night shift premium or overtime rate assessed at a reasonable figure. Article 119 of the Treaty says specifically that the 'pay for work at time rates shall be the same for the same job'. The decided cases are to the same effect – see *Schulz* v *American Can Company* (1970) 424 Fed Rep 2nd 358; *Dugdale* v *Kraft Foods* [1976] IRLR 204; *Electrolux Ltd* v *Hutchinson* [1977] IRLR 410.

If it is found that the differences are 'not of practical importance' then the woman is employed on 'like work' with the men: and her contract is deemed to include an equality clause giving her the same 'rate for the job' as the men, see s. 1(2).

S. 1(3) PERSONAL DIFFERENCES
Section 1(3) says that a variation in pay is justifiable 'if the employer proves that the variation is genuinely due to a material difference (other than the difference of sex) between her case and his'.

This sub-section deals with cases where the woman and the man are doing 'like work', but the personal equation of the man is such that he deserves to be paid at a higher rate than the woman. Even though the two jobs, viewed as jobs, are evaluated equally, nevertheless there may quite genuinely, be 'material differences' between the two people who are doing them – which merit a variation in pay – irrespective of whether it is a man or woman doing the job. One instance is length of service. In many occupations, a worker, be he man or woman, gets an increment from time to time, according to his seniority or length of service. Another instance is special personal skill or qualifications. In many occupations a degree or diploma is a qualification for higher pay, irrespective of sex. So is a higher grading for skill or capacity within the firm itself, see *National Vulcan Insurance* v *Wade* [1978] IRLR 225. Likewise, a bigger output or productivity may warrant a 'wage differential' so long as it is not based on sex. So may the place of work, see *NAAFI* v *Varley* [1976] IRLR 408. In all these cases the two jobs are evaluated equally as jobs, but, nevertheless, there are material differences (other than sex) which warrant a 'wage differential' between the two persons doing them.

But the escape route offered by s. 1(3) is so open to abuse that the section requires that the variation should be 'genuinely due' to the difference and that the employer should 'prove' it – not by an excessively high standard of proof, but by the ordinary standard of the balance of probabilities – 'see *National Vulcan Insurance* v *Wade*'.

Notes

1.   Lord Denning spent some time in *Shields's* case considering the applicability of EC law, and while he was content to conclude that Miss Shields and her comparator were employed on 'like work', he had wondered whether her comparator deserved a higher rate of pay for his 'protective role'. However, in considering the supremacy of EC law he stated:

. . . Under that law it is imperative that 'pay for work at time rates shall be the same for the same job'; and that 'all discrimination on the ground of sex shall be eliminated with regard to all aspects and conditions of remuneration'. The differences found by the majority of the Industrial Tribunal are all based on sex. They are because he is a man. He only gets the higher hourly rate because he is a man. In order to eliminate all discrimination, there should be an equality clause written into the woman's contract.

2.   The issue of what amounts to 'like work' within EPA 1970, s. 1(4) has arisen in numerous cases. What the student must not forget is that although 'like work' may be established the employer may yet be able to justify the difference in pay under s. 1(3) of the Act.

Notes

1.   The decision in *Capper Pass* v *Lawton* [1976] IRLR 366 proposed a two-stage test for establishing 'like work' within EPA 1970, s. 1(4). First, is the work which the woman does and the work which the man does of the same or a broadly similar nature? Secondly, if it is work of a broadly similar nature, are the differences in the work of practical importance in relation to terms and conditions of employment?

2.   Other cases have concluded in respect of EPA 1970, s. 1(4) that the time at which work is done is irrelevant – *Dugdale* v *Kraft Foods Ltd* [1976] IRLR 368 and *Sherwin* v *National Coal Board* [1978] IRLR 122; although if, for example, night work brings with it additional responsibilities, then this may amount to a difference of practical importance in relation to terms and conditions; at the very least this may allow the payment of shift premiums (*Calder & Cizakowsky* v *Rowntree Mackintosh Confectionery Ltd* [1993] IRLR 212).

Thomas v National Coal Board
[1987] IRLR 451
Employment Appeal Tribunal

This consolidated equal pay case involved claims by over 1,500 women canteen assistants employed at collieries throughout the country comparing their work to that of a named comparator, a Mr Tilstone, employed until his retirement in 1985 as a canteen assistant at the Hem Heath colliery in North Staffordshire on permanent night work at a higher rate.

In 1966, because of recruitment difficulties, it was decided to treat night work in canteens in North Staffordshire as surface work and pay a higher rate. Mr Tilstone was recruited on this rate in 1973. From 1975, however, all canteen workers, both men and women, were recruited at the lower canteen workers' rate.

. . . [I]t was argued by the employers that there is an implicit requirement under equal pay law that the male comparator selected should be representative of the men performing like work and that he should not be an anomalous man. The industrial tribunal rejected this contention as a question of law, holding that the statute referred to 'a man' and not 'a representative man'.

Thirdly, whether the applicants were employed on 'like work' with their male comparator? The industrial tribunal concluded by a majority that there was a difference of practical importance between the things that Mr Tilstone did as a canteen assistant on permanent night work and the things that the applicants did. That difference was that Mr Tilstone was required to work permanently at night alone. According to the majority, this was not a difference in the 'mere time' at which the work was performed which could be recognised by the separate allowance of time and one-fifth for working unsocial hours; it was a difference in the personal risk and responsibility forming part of the conditions under which the work was performed.

The EAT held that the appellant's were not employed on 'like work' with their comparator within the meaning of EPA 1970, s. 1(4) on the ground that the additional responsibility entailed in work permanently at night alone and without supervision was a 'difference of practical importance in relation to terms and conditions of employment'.

SIR RALPH KILNER-BROWN: Counsel for the National Coal Board recognised that there is an arguable point of law on this issue and also that it would not be sufficient to avoid the problem merely by saying that it was a question of fact and that it was open to the majority to find as they did. If necessary he would fall back on that, but his primary argument was that the majority had not misdirected themselves in law. His submission was that the Act itself refers to what is done 'in practice' and it is therefore not right to argue, as both counsel for the applicants did, that an industrial tribunal has to look at theoretical possibilities arising out of the terms of the contract. This was not a situation in which there was an apparent similarity in the work and in which the only difference related to the time at which it was done. The tribunal had to look, as they did, at the circumstances in which the apparently similar work was done. The circumstances of permanent night duty produced added responsibility which was a difference of practical importance. In so far as there is a question of law to be decided we prefer the argument on behalf of the National Coal Board. This was an issue as to which, provided the approach in law was correct, an industrial tribunal could on the evidence have found either way, as the division of opinion properly discloses. Neither conclusion can be said to be wholly unreasonable. Consequently the majority decision prevails and the women fail at the second hurdle.

Note

It is clear that the work done in practice is the nub of the comparison and cannot be ignored. Where, therefore, the comparator is paid more for some aspect of the job which he personally does, this aspect cannot be disregarded in deciding whether he and the applicant are employed on 'like work' (*Maidment* v *Cooper & Co. (Birmingham) Ltd* [1978] IRLR 462). A key factor may be the degree of responsibility between the man's job and woman's job (*Eaton Ltd* v *Nuttall* [1977] IRLR 71).

Question

How can an employer pay employees on night work more pay than those doing the same work during the day without contravening the EPA 1970? See *Calder & Cizakowsky* v *Rowntree Mackintosh Confectionery Ltd* [1993] IRLR 212.

D: Work Rated as Equivalent

This head of claim under EPA 1970, s. 1(2)(b), is dependent upon the existence of a valid job evaluation scheme, i.e. analytical and non-discriminatory. There is no obligation on employers to carry out such schemes. However, where a job evaluation scheme has been carried out the applicant may claim that his or her work has been rated as equivalent under such a scheme. Where the job evaluation scheme does not meet the requirements of s. 1(5), in that it is not analytical or is discriminatory, the applicant may challenge the scheme using the equal value provisions.

Bromley and Others v *H. & J. Quick Ltd*
[1988] IRLR 249
Court of Appeal

The respondents employed the 11 appellant women as clerical workers. The women brought an equal value claim comparing their work to that of male managers. The employer challenged this claim on the basis that a job evaluation study within s. 1(5) of the Act had been carried out and this had given different values to the women's jobs and those of their comparators. The job evaluation scheme carried out by consultants on the part of the employer involved job ranking and paired comparisons. Some representative jobs produced descriptions based on selected factors, skill/training/experiences, mental demand, responsibility, physical environment, external contacts. Benchmark jobs were selected from the representative jobs and the necessary paired comparisons and ranking made. The jobs of the appellants and three out of the four comparators were not assessed by using factor values but were merely slotted into the job ranking order by management.

The Court of Appeal (allowing the appeal) held that s. 1(5) requires an evaluation to be made of the demands of the job under various heading (for example effort, skill, decision making. If s. 2A(2)(a) of the Act is to be successfully pleaded the employer must show that both the work of the woman and the work of the man has been valued in terms of the demands made on them under the various headings.

DILLON LJ: It may be noted that s. 1(5) serves two different functions under the Act. On the one hand, if a woman wants to claim that she is within subheading (b) of s. 1(2) as a woman employed on work rated as equivalent with that of a man she has to point to a job evaluation study such as is mentioned in s. 1(5) which has so rated the work of her job. On the other hand, if an application is made by the woman employee to an industrial tribunal and the employer wishes to avoid a reference to a member of the panel of independent experts for report, it is for the employer to show if he can, under s. 2A(2),

(a)   that the work of the woman and the work of the man in question have been given different values on a job evaluation study such as is mentioned in s. 1(5), and

(b)   that there are no reasonable grounds for determining that the evaluation contained in that study was, within the meaning of s. 2A(3), made on a system which discriminated on grounds of sex.

It is in this latter context that the questions have arisen in the present case, since the respondent company sought to have the appellants' claims dismissed by the industrial tribunal under s. 2A(1) because of the job evaluation study that there had been. The onus was therefore initially, in my judgment, on the respondent company to show, to put it briefly.

(a)   that there had been a job evaluation study which satisfied the requirements of s. 1(5) and thus was 'a study such as is mentioned in s. 1(5)', and

(b)   that there are no reasonable grounds for determining that the evaluation contained in that study was tainted by sex discrimination.

. . .

What s. 1(5) does require is, however, a study undertaken with a view to evaluating jobs in terms of the demand made on a worker under various headings (for instance effort, skill, decision). To apply that to s. 2A(2)(a) it is necessary, in my judgment, that both the work of the woman who has made application to the industrial tribunal and the work of the man who is her chosen comparator should have been valued in such terms of demand made on the worker under various headings. Mr Lester submitted that the method used on undertaking a study within s. 1(5) must necessarily be 'analytical', a word he used in the sense of describing the process of dividing a physical or abstract whole into its constituent parts to determine their relationship or value. Sir Ralph Kilner-Brown criticised the use of the word 'analytical' as a gloss on the section. In my judgment, the word is not a gloss, but indicates conveniently the general nature of what is required by the section, viz that the jobs of each worker covered by the study must have been valued in terms of the demand made on the worker under various headings. The original application of s. 1(5) to women within subheading (b) in s. 1(2) of the Act (women employed on work rated equivalent to that of a man) necessarily required that the woman's work and the man's should each have been valued in terms of the demand made on the worker under appropriate headings; the wording of s. 2A(2)(a), read with that of s. 1(5), necessarily shows that the same applies to the present appellants who claim to be within subheading (c), and their male comparators. It is not enough, in my judgment, that the 23 benchmark jobs were valued – if indeed they were (and on this I do not go so far as Woolf LJ as I do not find it necessary to do so) – on the factor demand basis required by s. 1(5), if the jobs of the appellants and their comparators were not.

But on the facts it is clear that none of the comparators' jobs and none of the appellants' jobs, save those of Mrs Bromley and Mrs Owen at the appeal stage, were ever valued according to the demands made on the worker under the five or six selected headings. The relative weightings of the selected factors had indeed been worked out by reference to the 23 benchmark jobs as I have indicated. But short of the appeal stage those weightings were not used in evaluating any of the other jobs, nor were those other jobs, including those of the appellants and their comparators, broken down under the factor headings. What happened at the appeal stage in relation to Mrs Bromley and Mrs Owen makes no difference to the outcome in their cases, since there was never any appeal by their comparator.

Notes

1.   If a woman's job is ranked as equal to that of a man under a valid scheme, she may use s. 1(2)(b) to pursue her claim, even if the scheme has not been implemented, as long as it is complete and the parties have accepted its validity (*Arnold* v *Beecham Group Ltd* [1982] IRLR 307). A person will be deemed to be on 'work rated as equivalent' even though the same points may not have been awarded under the job evaluation scheme where conversion from points to grades puts the respective jobs on the same grade (*Springboard Sunderland Trust* v *Robson* [1992] IRLR 261).

2.   In *Eaton* v *Nuttall Ltd*, the EAT concluded that a valid job evaluation scheme required an objective assessment of the nature of the work. In an appendix to the case the principal methods of job evaluation are reproduced from the ACAS Guide No. 1.

Eaton v Nuttall Ltd
[1977] IRLR 71
Employment Appeal Tribunal

APPENDIX
As not all concerned are familiar with Job Evaluation, we set out below a note on the principal methods (*see*: ACAS Guide No. 1).

Job ranking
This is commonly thought to be the simplest method. Each job is considered as a whole and is then given a ranking in relation to all other jobs. A ranking table is then drawn up and the ranked jobs grouped into grades. Pay levels can then be fixed for each grade.

Paired comparisons

This is also a simple method. Each job is compared as a whole with each other job in turn and points (0, 1 or 2) awarded according to whether its overall importance is judged to be less than, equal to or more than the other. Points awarded for each job are then totalled and a ranking order produced.

Job classification

This is similar to ranking except that it starts from the opposite end; the grading structure is established first and individual jobs fitted into it.

A broad description of each grade is drawn up and individual jobs considered typical of each grade are selected as 'benchmarks'. The other jobs are then compared with these benchmarks and the general description are placed in their appropriate grade.

Points assessment

This is the most common system in use. It is an analytical method, which, instead of comparing whole jobs, breaks down each job into a number of factors – for example, skills, responsibility, physical and mental requirements and working conditions. Each of these factors may be analysed further.

Points are awarded for each factor according to a predetermined scale and the total points decide a job's place in the ranking order. Usually, the factors are weighted so that, for example, more or less weight may be given to hard physical conditions or to a high degree of skill.

Factor comparison

This is also an analytical method, employing the same principles as points assessment but using only a limited number of factors, such as skill, responsibility and working conditions.

A number of 'key' jobs are selected because their wage rates are generally agreed to be 'fair'. The proportion of the total wage attributable to each factor is then decided and a scale produced showing the rate for each factor of each key job. The other jobs are then compared with this scale, factor by factor, so that a rate is finally obtained for each factor of each job. The total pay for each job is reached by adding together the rates for its individual factors

Note

Discriminatory job evaluation schemes can be challenged not only under the EPA 1970 and the SDA 1975, but also under Article 1(2) of the Equal Pay Directive, which provides that a 'job classification system must be based on the same criteria for both men and women and so drawn up as to exclude any discrimination on grounds of sex'.

Rummler v *Dato-Druck GmbH*
[1987] IRLR 32
European Court of Justice

This case concerned whether the job grading system adopted by a German printing firm contravened the EEC Equal Pay Directive, Article 1(2) of which stipulates that a job classification system 'must be based on the same criterion for both men and women and so drawn up as to exclude any discrimination on the grounds of sex'.

The scheme in question provided for seven pay grades, with jobs classified according to previous knowledge required, concentration, effort and exertion, and responsibility. Mrs Rummler's job was classified in pay grade III. In terms of effort and exertion, this grade covered tasks requiring medium and sometimes high muscular effort. Grade II covered jobs requiring muscular effort ranging from slight to medium. Grade IV jobs required medium or, on occasion, high levels of exertion of various kinds, especially of the kind entailed by machine-dependent work.

Mrs Rummler took the view that she should have been placed in grade IV. Her job required her to pack parcels weighing in excess of 20 kg. She argued that for *her*, that was heavy physical work. The employers argued that by the effort criterion, Mrs Rummler's work should be placed in grade II as requiring a low level of muscular effort.

The Oldenburg Labour Court sought guidance on whether the Equal Pay Directive permits the use of physical effort as a job evaluation factor and, if so, whether this should be measured according to the extent to which the work requires effort or exertion or is physically heavy for women?

The ECJ held that a job classification system is not discriminatory solely because one of its criteria is based on characteristics more commonly found in men. However, to avoid being discriminatory overall, if the nature of the work permits, the system should take into account other criteria for which female employees may show a particular aptitude.

DECISION: . . . *Question 1*
This question from the referring Court is directed fundamentally at ascertaining whether a job classification system which is based on criteria of muscular effort or exertion and the degree to which work is physically heavy is compatible with the principle of equal pay for men and women.
. . .
This principle is effected through Article 1(2) which stipulates that a job classification system 'must be based on the same criteria for both men and women and so drawn up as to exclude any discrimination on the grounds of sex'.

The principle of equal pay therefore requires fundamentally that the nature of the work to be done must be considered objectively. Equal work or work to which equal value is attributed must be remunerated equally regardless of whether it is done by a man or by a woman. If a job classification system is used in determining pay, then on the one hand it must be based on the same criteria regardless of whether the work is to be done by a man or by a woman while on the other it may not be so designed overall as to lead in fact to general discrimination against employees of one sex with regard to those of the other sex.

Thus criteria which correspond to the work to be performed are in accordance with the provisions of Article 1 of the Directive if the work by its nature requires particular physical exertion or is physically heavy. It is compatible with the prohibition of discrimination to apply a criterion in setting differentiated pay grades which takes account of the objectively measurable level of physical strength needed to do the job or the objective degree to which the work is physically heavy.

Even if a particular criterion, such as that of the muscular exertion needed, may in fact favour male employees on the grounds that it may be assumed that they generally have greater physical strength than female employees, then that particular criterion should be considered along with the others which play a part in determining pay within the overall job classification system when assessing whether that criterion is discriminatory. A system is not discriminatory solely because one of its criteria is based on characteristics more commonly found among men. If a job classification system is not to be discriminatory overall and is to be in accordance with the principles of the Directive, it must, however, be so designed that, if the nature of the work under discussion so permits, it includes as 'work to which equal value is attributed' work in which other criteria are taken into account for which female employees may show particular aptitude.

It is the task of the national courts to decide in individual cases whether the job classification system in its entirety permits fair account to be taken of all the criteria on the basis of which pay is determined according to the requirements of the performance of individual tasks throughout the company.

Therefore, in answer to question 1, Council Directive 75/117 of 10.2.75 on the approximation of the laws of the Member States to implement the principle of equal pay for men and women does not preclude the use of the criterion of muscular effort or exertion or the criterion of the degree to which work is physically heavy in a job classification system for the purposes of determining pay if the work to be done, with respect to the tasks involved, does in fact require a certain level of physical strength provided that the system as a whole precludes all discrimination on grounds of sex by taking account also of other criteria.

. . .

The answers to the questions as interpreted above arise out of the conclusions drawn in connection with question 1, that is, that there is no provision in the Directive which prohibits account being taken in determining a pay grade of criteria based on the level of intensity of muscular effort objectively required for a certain job or on the level of physical difficulty of the work connected with the job.

The Directive sets out the principle that equal work must be remunerated with equal pay. It follows from this that work performed must be remunerated according to its nature. Criteria based solely on values relating to employees of only one sex bring with them a threat of discrimination; this could jeopardise achievement of the Directive's primary goal, equal treatment for equal work. This is true even where the criterion is based on values which correspond to the average performance of employees of the sex of which it is assumed that it has less natural aptitude in relation to the criterion, for this produces another form of discrimination in pay – work which objectively requires use of greater physical strength is paid in the same way as work requiring use of less physical strength.

Failure to take into account values which correspond to the average capability of female employees when laying down a stepped pay scale based on amount of muscular effort and exertion can certainly lead to female employees being unable to take on jobs which would over-tax their physical strength and so lead to them being disadvantaged. This difference in treatment may, however, be justified objectively by the nature of the job if it is necessary to guarantee payment appropriate to the effort required to perform the work and this meets a genuine need on the part of the company (judgment of 13.5.86 in case 170/84, *Bilka-Kaufhaus*, not yet published [sic]). As already indicated, the job classification system must, however, insofar as the tasks involved allow it, include other criteria which ensure that the system in its entirety is not discriminatory.

Therefore, in answer to questions 2 and 3, it follows from Directive 75/117 that:

- the criteria used to put employees into pay grades must ensure equal pay for work objectively demonstrated to be equal, regardless of whether the work is done by a male or a female employee;

- that a form of discrimination on the grounds of sex as prohibited by the Directive is in fact in operation if, in assessing the level of effort or exertion needed, values are used which represent the average capabilities of employees of only one sex;
- that if, however, a job classification system is not to be discriminatory overall, then, insofar as the nature of the tasks to be done allow this, criteria should be used which can measure particular aptitude on the part of employees of both sexes.

Question

Would s. 1(5) have been satisfied had the jobs of the appellants in *Bromley's* case been given factor values under a job evaluation scheme?

E: 'Equal Value'

The provisions under EPA 1970, s. 1(2)(c) relating to equal value were introduced in 1983. The applicant may claim the same pay as a man if she is doing work of the same value in terms of the demands made on her. An equal value claim may be pursued even though there is a man employed in the same job as the woman (see *Pickstone* v *Freemans Plc* [1988] IRLR 357). The procedure for equal value claims is important as the industrial tribunal must be satisfied that there is prima facie evidence to support the applicant's claim before appointing an independent expert to evaluate the jobs. However, it is clear from the decision in *Wood* v *William Ball Ltd* [1999] IRLR 773 that the parties must be given the opportunity to adduce such evidence.

The Sex Discrimination and Equal Pay (Miscellaneous Amendments) Regulations 1996 (SI 1996/438), reg. 3 provides the employment tribunal with the power to determine the claim for itself without reference to an independent expert. A genuine material factor defence may be raised at the preliminary hearing. If the defence succeeds, obviously no reference will be made to the independent expert. If the defence fails, the employer will generally not be permitted to raise the defence at the reconvened hearing in response to the independent expert's report (reg. 9(2E)). The employment tribunal may determine that the findings of the independent expert are not binding on the parties.

Tennants Textile Colours Ltd v *Todd*
[1989] IRLR 3
Northern Ireland Court of Appeal

The applicant was employed as a laboratory assistant. She claimed that she was employed on work of equal value to that of two male comparators employed as laboratory technicians. A Northern Ireland industrial tribunal referred the complaint to an independent expert, Mrs Olive Lundy. The independent expert concluded that the applicant was employed on work of equal value to that of one of her comparators.

On 28 May 1986 the industrial tribunal decided to admit the report in evidence. The employers then sought an adjournment in order to obtain a report from their own expert witness. The tribunal granted the adjournment but ruled that the findings of fact contained in the report of the independent expert would be binding on both parties 'in circumstances where the report had already been admitted in evidence'.

When the hearing was resumed, the employers' expert witness submitted evidence. The industrial tribunal found the facts relating to the work of the applicant and her comparators to be as set out in the independent expert's report. The tribunal went on to hold that:

(1)   once the report of an independent expert has been admitted in evidence, the conclusions contained therein should only be rejected if it were shown that they were so plainly wrong that they could not be accepted;

(2)   the independent expert's report was very comprehensive and there was no intrinsic reason to reject the conclusions contained therein;

(3)   the evidence of the employers' expert witness was insufficient to persuade the tribunal to reject the conclusions arrived at by the independent expert; and

(4)   on the basis of the report of the independent expert, the applicant's claim that her work was of equal value to that done by one of her comparators had been sustained.

The employers appealed to the Northern Ireland Court of Appeal by way of case stated. The questions referred for the court's determination were:

(1)   whether the tribunal erred in law in ruling that, the independent expert's report having been admitted, the findings of fact contained therein were binding on both parties;

(2)   whether the tribunal erred in law in finding that the burden of proof was on the appellant to persuade the tribunal that the independent expert's report should be rejected;

(3)   whether the tribunal erred in law in finding that it could only reject the independent expert's report if the evidence were such as to show that it was so plainly wrong that it could not be accepted.

The Court held, allowing the appeal, that the independent expert's report is not binding on the parties. Its admission as evidence does not prevent the parties producing evidence to contradict its conclusions; nor does it prevent the tribunal from rejecting it.

LOWRY LCJ: The court, allowing this appeal, has answered the questions in the affirmative and remitted the case to a differently constituted tribunal, but, in view of the novelty of the point in issue, we undertook to set out the reasons for our decision.

Miss Beale, for the appellants, described the appeal as a landmark case and stated that we were concerned only with the status of the independent expert's report and with the tribunal's approach to it, submitting that the tribunal had abdicated in favour of the expert its judicial function of deciding the case: in this instance that error told unfairly in favour of the applicant, but in different circumstances it could equally unfairly benefit the employer and prejudice an applicant.

Rule of Procedure 8(1), said Miss Beale, was intended to give freedom and flexibility to the tribunal, but it now found itself strictly bound by paras. (2A) to (2E). Para. (2C), subject to the exceptions there mentioned, restricted the rights of the parties but did not prevent a party from making submissions to contradict the conclusions of the expert or inhibit the tribunal itself from asking questions. On any interpretation rule 8(2C) did not make the findings of fact in the independent expert's report 'binding on both parties'. To illustrate the standing and authority of an expert's testimony she cited *Davie* v *Edinburgh Magistrates* (1953) SC 34, 39, *R* v *Lanfear* [1968] 1 All ER 683 and Phipson on Evidence 13th ed. (1982) paragraphs 27-10, 12 and 34. She also referred to *Hayward* v *Cammell Laird* [1984] IRLR 463, where paragraph 10 of the industrial tribunal's decision reads as follows:

10. Procedure at the hearing is governed by rule 8 of the Regulations, and of particular significance is para. (2C) of that rule which provides:

'Except as provided in rule 7A(9) or by para. (2D) of this rule, no party to a case involving an equal value claim may give evidence upon, or question any witness upon, any matter of fact upon which a conclusion in the report of the expert is based.'

Such a rule does, of course, cut across what is taken for granted in other types of case as being normal procedure, and imposes a severe constraint upon the manner in which the content of the report can be tested. That that must prove difficult, and indeed irksome, to a respondent is entirely understandable but, nevertheless, it is a part of the scheme of things which the legislature has, in its wisdom, thought proper to adopt, as is the effective removal from the tribunal of its own primary fact-finding role. Clearly, or so it seems to us, the most effective (although, of course, not the only) way of mounting any attack upon the independent expert's report must be to commission and present an expert's report of one's own. Then, the tribunal may well be faced with a divergence of findings between which it will have to choose, and give its reasons for so doing. However, that course of action was not taken by the respondents on this occasion and, apart from the independent expert's report, no other report was available to the tribunal. Mr James sought to call evidence the object of which was to controvert the findings of fact of the independent expert as to, for example, the working conditions of the applicant and the comparators. The tribunal declined to allow this, having regard to the provisions of rule 8(2C), and rule 7A(9) was not invoked.
2. Did the tribunal err in law in finding that the burden of proof was on the appellant to persuade the tribunal that the independent expert's report should be rejected?

While the scheme of the legislation was to obviate the need for recourse by the tribunal to an independent expert if it was perfectly clear that the claimant could not win (see ss. 1(3) and 2A(1)(a)), to obtain a report from one of a selected panel of experts was mandatory in all other cases (s. 2A(1)(b)) and was by the Rules of Procedure given a status of unusual authority and importance, as Mr Kerr has pointed out. According to rule 7A(7) and (8), the expert's report *must* be admitted as evidence unless, for one of three specific reasons, the tribunal forms the view that it ought not to be received; in that event the procedure for obtaining the report from an independent expert must start all over again.
We surmise that whoever conceived the idea of a reference to an independent expert intended that expert's report to be conclusive but then drew back. And therefore we

suspect that the proponents (and also the amenders) of this legislation might have incurred the censure of Lady Macbeth for 'Letting "I dare not" wait upon "I would", Like the poor cat i' the adage.'

Reports obtained in the circumstances created by the present Act and Rules must obviously carry considerable weight, as was clearly intended, but there is no provision or principle that the party challenging an independent expert's report has to 'persuade the tribunal that the independent expert's report should be rejected' or that the tribunal 'could only reject the independent expert's report if the evidence were such as to show that it was so plainly wrong that it could not be accepted', as stated in paragraph 23 of the tribunal's decision. The burden of proving a claim under the Act of 1970 is on the applicant. The burden does not *in point of law* become heavier if the independent expert's report is against the applicant. Nor, if that report is in favour of the applicant, is the burden of proof transferred to the employer.

Notes

1. The procedure and role of the independent expert in equal value claims has become a dominant issue because of the burden on the employment tribunal to avoid unnecessary expense and delay which may be incurred if a referral is made to the independent expert. An independent expert must now estimate how long it will take to prepare his report, and in the event of a delay he must inform the employment tribunal. However, the issue of what amounts to equal value has yet to be considered at the highest level. The tribunals arrived at conflicting conclusions in *Wells* v *F. Smales & Son (Fish Merchants)* (1985) COIT 1643/113 and *Brown & Royle* v *Cearns & Brown* (1985) COIT 1614/215. In the former, whilst some of the applicants scored a higher score than their comparator in the independent expert's report and were therefore found to be on work of equal value, some of the applicants scored between 79 per cent and 95 per cent of the comparator's score. These too were found to be on work of equal value by the tribunal, although not by the expert, on the grounds that the scores were so close and the differences between them and the comparator were not relevant or real material differences. However, in the latter case, the applicant's score was 95 per cent of her comparator's, yet the tribunal found that her work was not of equal value as precise equality or greater value was required. The application of a 'broad brush' approach was confirmed in *Pickstone* v *Freemans plc* (1993) COIT 28811/84.

2. See Szyszczak, E., 'Pay Inequalities and Equal Value Claims' (1985) 48 *Modern Law Review*, pp. 139–55, which considers the impact of the 1983 amendment and suggests that the equal value amendment will have a very limited effect on the earnings differential between men and women. At the same time, however, the scope and potential of EC law as a means of challenging the EPA 1970 is recognised.

F: *Genuine Material Difference/Factor*

The EPA 1970, s. 1(3) provides a defence for the employer. Although the wording of s. 1(3)(a) and (b) is slightly different, in practical terms the test for establishing the defence is the same. In respect of equal value claims, at present a s. 1(3) defence may be raised at the preliminary hearing. However, changes to the rules of procedure preclude the employment tribunal from considering the defence at the full hearing other than in exceptional circumstances where it has been considered at the preliminary hearing (Industrial Tribunals (Constitution and Rules of Procedure) Regulations 1993 and the Amendment Regulations 1994). The burden of proof is on the employer to show not only that the variation in pay is genuinely due to a material difference/factor, but also to prove that this is not due to a difference of sex (*The Financial Times Ltd* v *Byrne & Others (No. 2)* [1992] IRLR 163.

Bilka-Kaufhaus v *Weber von Hartz*
[1986] IRLR 317
European Court of Justice

Bilka-Kaufhaus is a department store in the Federal Republic of Germany. It has an occupational pension scheme for its employees which supplements the state pension scheme. Under the rules of the occupational scheme, part-time employees are eligible for pensions only if they have worked full time for at least 15 years over a total period of 20 years.

Mrs Weber von Hartz was employed as a sales assistant for 15 years, but over the last few years of her employment she chose to work part-time. Since she had not worked full-time for the minimum period of 15 years, the employers refused to pay her an occupational pension under the scheme.

In proceedings before the German labour courts, Mrs Weber argued that the occupational pension scheme was contrary to the principle of equal pay for men and women laid down in Article 119 (now 141) of the EEC Treaty. She contended that the requirement of a minimum period of full-time employment placed women at a disadvantage, since they were more likely than their male colleagues to take part-time work so as to be able to care for their family and children. The employers argued that there were objectively justified economic grounds for the exclusion of part-time workers, emphasising that the employment of full-time workers entails lower ancillary costs and permits the use of staff throughout opening hours.

The ECJ held that an occupational scheme which excludes part-time employees infringed Article 119 (now 141), where that exclusion affected a far greater number of women than men, unless the undertaking could show that the exclusion was based on objectively justified factors unrelated to any discrimination on the grounds of sex; this may include economic grounds.

LORD MACKENZIE STUART: . . . In the first of its questions the national court asks whether a staff policy pursued by a department store company excluding part-time employees from an occupational pension scheme constitutes discrimination contrary to Article 119 [now 141] where that exclusion affects a far greater number of women than men.

In order to reply to that question reference must be made to the judgment of 31.3.81 (Case 96/80, *Jenkins* v *Kingsgate*, [1981] IRLR 228).

In that judgment the Court considered the question whether the payment of a lower hourly rate for part-time work than for full-time work was compatible with Article 119 [now 141].

Such a practice is comparable to that at issue before the national court in this case: Bilka does not pay different hourly rates to part-time and full-time workers, but it grants only full-time workers an occupational pension. Since, as was stated above, such a pension falls within the concept of pay for the purposes of the second paragraph of Article 119 [now 141] it follows that, hour for hour, the total remuneration paid by Bilka to full-time workers is higher than that paid to part-time workers.

The conclusion reached by the Court in its judgment of 31.3.81 is therefore equally valid in the context of this case.

If, therefore, it should be found that a much lower proportion of women than of men work full time, the exclusion of part-time workers from the occupational pension scheme would be contrary to Article 119 [now 141] of the Treaty where, taking into account the difficulties encountered by women workers in working full time, that measure could not be explained by factors which exclude any discrimination on grounds of sex.

However, if the undertaking is able to show that its pay practice may be explained by objectively justified factors unrelated to any discrimination on grounds of sex there is no breach of Article 119 [now 141].

The answer to the first question referred by the national court must therefore be that Article 119 [now 141] of the EEC Treaty is infringed by a department store company which excludes part-time employees from its occupational pension scheme, where that exclusion affects a far greater number of women than men, unless the undertaking shows that the exclusion is based on objectively justified factors unrelated to any discrimination on grounds of sex.

Question 2(a)

In its second question the national court seeks in essence to know whether the reasons put forward by Bilka to explain its pay policy may be regarded as 'objectively justified economic grounds', as referred to in the judgment of 31.3.81, where the interests of undertakings in the department store sector do not require such a policy.

In its observations Bilka argues that the exclusion of part-time workers from the occupational pension scheme is intended solely to discourage part-time work, since in general part-time workers refuse to work in the late afternoon and on Saturdays. In order to ensure the presence of an adequate workforce during those periods it was therefore necessary to make full-time work more attractive than part-time work, by making the occupational pension scheme open only to full-time workers. Bilka concludes that on the basis of the judgment of 31.3.81 it cannot be accused of having infringed Article 119 [now 141].

In reply to the reasons put forward to justify the exclusion of part-time workers Mrs Weber von Hartz points out that Bilka is in no way obliged to employ part-time workers and that if it decides to do so it may not subsequently restrict the pension rights of such workers, which are already reduced by reason of the fact that they work fewer hours.

According to the Commission, in order to establish that there has been no breach of Article 119 [now 141] it is not sufficient to show that in adopting a pay practice which in fact discriminates against women workers the employer sought to achieve objectives other than discrimination against women. The Commission considers that in order to justify such a pay practice from the point of view of Article 119 [now 141] the employer must, as the Court held in its judgment of 31.3.81, put forward objective economic grounds relating to the management of the undertaking. It is also necessary to ascertain whether the pay practice in question is necessary and in proportion to the objectives pursued by the employer.

It is for the national court, which has sole jurisdiction to make findings of fact, to determine whether and to what extent the grounds put forward by an employer to explain the adoption of a pay practice which applies independently of a worker's sex but in fact affects more women than men may be regarded as objectively justified economic grounds. If the national court finds that the measures chosen by Bilka correspond to a real need on the part of the undertaking, are appropriate with a view to achieving the objectives pursued and are necessary to that end, the fact that the measures affect a far greater number of women than men is not sufficient to show that they constitute an infringement of Article 119 [now 141].

The answer to question 2(a) must therefore be that under Article 119 [now 141] a department store company may justify the adoption of a pay policy excluding part-time workers, irrespective of their sex, from its occupational pension scheme on the ground that it seeks to employ as few part-time workers as possible, where it is found that the means chosen for achieving that objective correspond to a real need on the part of the undertaking, are appropriate with a view to achieving the objective in question and are necessary to that end.

Question
Bilka is noted for introducing the concept of indirect discrimination into Article 141 (ex 119). How far has this concept been imported into the EPA 1970? See *Enderby* v *Frenchay Area Health Authority* [1993] IRLR 591; *Staffordshire County Council* v *Black* [1995] IRLR 234 and *Ratcliffe* v *North Yorkshire County Council* [1995] IRLR 439.

Rainey v *Greater Glasgow Health Board*
[1987] IRLR 26
House of Lords

Mrs Rainey and her male comparator, Mr Crumlin, were employed at Belvidere Hospital, Glasgow as prosthetists. At the time of the industrial tribunal hearing, Mrs Rainey earned £7,295 pa and Mr Crumlin was paid £10,085. It was conceded that they were employed on like work, but the employers contended that the variation in pay was 'genuinely due to a material difference other than the difference of sex' between the two cases.

In 1980, it had been decided to set up a prosthetic fitting service within the National Health Service in Scotland. Until then, all qualified pros-thetists were employed by private contractors. It was decided that the remuneration of employees in the new prosthetic service should be related to the NHS Whitley Council scale and that the appropriate pay scale for them would be that for medical physics technicians. However, in order to attract a sufficient number of experienced prosthetists, it was regarded as advantageous to obtain the transfer of prosthetists employed by private contractors into the NHS and it was considered that it would be necessary to offer them the same level of pay as they enjoyed in the private sector. It was therefore agreed that all employees who were willing to transfer from private contractors would have the option of remaining on their existing rates of pay and conditions of service, subject to future changes as negotiated by their trade union, ASTMS, for the prosthetists employed by contractors.

Mr Crumlin transferred to the NHS on these terms. He commenced employment on 1 July 1980 at a salary of £6,680. Mrs Rainey went straight into the NHS after her training was completed. She commenced employment on 1 October 1980 at a starting salary of £4,773.

After the block transfer in 1980, no transfers on special terms were permitted, and all new entrants were engaged on the NHS scale of remuneration.

The House of Lords held, dismissing Mrs Rainey's appeal, the difference in pay was due to a genuine material difference within EPA 1970, s. 1(3). The onus is on the employer to establish objectively justified grounds for the difference in pay between the woman and the man. Such grounds may be economic or for administrative efficiency in a concern not engaged in commerce or business.

LORD KEITH OF KINKEL: The facts found by the industrial tribunal make it clear that the Secretary of State for Scotland decided, as a matter of general policy, that the Whitley Council scale of remuneration and negotiating machinery, which applied throughout the National Health Service in Scotland, was appropriate for employees in the prosthetic service. It was also decided that the appropriate part of the scale for such employees was that applicable to medical physics technicians, presumably because the nature of their work was considered comparable to that of the prosthetists. So all direct entrants to the service, whether male or female, were to be placed on that part of the scale and made subject to Whitley Council negotiations. But it was apparent that the new service would not get off the ground unless a sufficient number of the prosthetists in the employment of the private contractors could be attracted into it. So the further policy decision was taken to offer these prosthetists the option of entering the service at their existing salaries and subject to the ASTMS negotiating machinery. As it happened, all the prosthetists privately employed were male. In the result, Mr Crumlin had the benefit of the offer and so emerged with a higher salary and better prospects for an increase than did the appellant, who did not have that benefit.

The main question at issue in the appeal is whether those circumstances are capable in law of constituting, within the meaning of s.1(3) of the Act of 1970, 'a material difference (other than the difference of sex) between her case and his'.

. . .

In my opinion these statements (per Lord Denning and Lawton LJ in *Clay Cross (Quarry Services) Ltd* v *Fletcher* [1978] FRLR 361 at pp. 363 and 364 respectively) are unduly restrictive of the proper interpretation of s.1(3). The difference must be 'material', which I would construe as meaning 'significant and relevant', and it must be between 'her case and his'. Consideration of a person's case must necessarily involve consideration of all the circumstances of that case. These may well go beyond what is not very happily described as 'the personal equation', i.e. the personal qualities by way of skill, experience or training which the individual brings to the job. Some circumstances may on examination prove to be not significant or not relevant, but others may do so, though not relating to the personal qualities of the employer. In particular, where there is no question of intentional sex discrimination whether direct or indirect (and there is none here) a difference which is connected with economic factors affecting the efficient carrying on of the employer's business or other activity may well be relevant.

The European Court had occasion to consider the question afresh in *Bilka-Kaufhaus GmbH* v *Weber von Hartz* (Case 170/84) [1986] IRLR 317. A German department store operated an occupational pension scheme for its employees, under which part-time employees were eligible for pensions only if they had worked full time for at least 15 years over a total period of 20 years. That provision affected disproportionately more women than men. A female part-time employee claimed that the provision contravened Article 119 [now 141] of the Treaty. The employers contended that it was based upon objectively justified economic grounds, in that it encouraged full-time work which resulted in lower ancillary costs and the utilisation of staff throughout opening hours. The European Court by its decision made it clear that it was not sufficient for the employers merely to show absence of any intention to discriminate, saying, at pp. 320–321:

> It is for the national court, which has sole jurisdiction to make findings of fact, to determine whether and to what extent the grounds put forward by an employer to explain the adoption of a pay practice which applies independently of a worker's sex but in fact affects more women than men may be regarded as objectively justified economic grounds. If the national court finds that the measures chosen by Bilka correspond to a real need on the part of the undertaking, are appropriate with a view to achieving the objectives pursued and are necessary to that end, the fact that the measures affect a far greater number of women than men is not sufficient to show that they constitute an infringement of Article 119 [now 141]. The answer to question 2(a) must therefore be that under Article 119 [now 141] a department store company may justify the adoption of a pay policy excluding part-time workers, irrespective of their sex, from its occupational pension scheme on the ground that it seeks to employ as few part-time workers as possible, where it is found that the means chosen for achieving that objective correspond to a real need on the part of the undertaking, are appropriate with a view to achieving the objective in question and are necessary to that end.

It therefore appears that the European Court has resolved the doubts expressed by Browne-Wilkinson J in *Jenkins* v *Kingsgate (Clothing Productions) Ltd* [1981] IRLR 228 and established that the true meaning and effect of Article 119 [now 141] in this particular context is the same as that there attributed to s. 1(3) of the Act of 1970 by the Employment Appeal Tribunal. Although the European Court at one point refers to 'economic' grounds objectively justified, whereas Browne-Wilkinson J speaks of 'economic or other reasons', I consider that read as a whole the ruling of the European Court would not exclude objectively justified grounds which are other than economic, such as administrative efficiency in a concern not engaged in commerce or business.

The decision of the European Court on Article 119 [now 141] must be accepted as authoritative and the judgment of the Employment Appeal Tribunal on s. 1(3) of the Act of 1970, which in my opinion is correct, is in harmony with it. There is now no reason to construe s. 1(3) as conferring greater rights on a worker in this context than does Article 119 [now 141] of the Treaty. It follows that a relevant difference for purposes of s. 1(3) may relate to circumstances other than the personal qualifications or merits of the male and female workers who are the subject of comparison.

In the present case the difference between the case of the appellant and that of Mr Crumlin is that the former is a person who entered the National Health Service at Belvidere Hospital directly while the latter is a person who entered it from employment with a private contractor. The fact that one is a woman and the other a man is an accident. The findings of the industrial tribunal make it clear that the new prosthetic service could never have been established within a reasonable time if Mr

Crumlin and others like him had not been offered a scale of remuneration no less favourable than that which they were then enjoying. That was undoubtedly a good and objectively justified ground for offering him that scale of remuneration. But it was argued for the appellant that it did not constitute a good and objectively justified reason for paying the appellant and other direct entrants a lower scale of remuneration. This aspect does not appear to have been specifically considered by either of the tribunals or by their Lordships of the First Division, apart from Lord Grieve who said [1985] IRLR 414, 425:

> I accept that the facts which provided the evidence before both tribunals were sufficient to explain why Mr Crumlin (and his colleagues) were paid on a scale equivalent to that which they had been receiving while employed in the private sector, but in my opinion that evidence is not sufficient to explain why, when the National [Health] Service door was opened to the appellant (and other prosthetists not previously employed in the private sector) the appellant (and her fellow prosthetists) were paid on a lower scale. In the absence of a reasonable explanation as to why the appellant was paid on a lower scale than Mr Crumlin I am of opinion that the respondents have not discharged the onus placed upon them by s. 1(3) of the Act of 1970, and that the majority of the Employment Appeal Tribunal were not entitled on the facts before them to conclude that they had.

The position in 1980 was that all National Health Service employees were paid on the Whitley Council scale, and that the Whitley Council negotiating machinery applied to them. The prosthetic service was intended to be a branch of the National Health Service. It is therefore easy to see that from the administrative point of view it would have been highly anomalous and inconvenient if prosthetists alone, over the whole tract of future time for which the prosthetic service would endure, were to have been subject to a different salary scale and different negotiating machinery. It is significant that a large part of the difference which has opened up between the appellant's salary and Mr Crumlin's is due to the different negotiating machinery. Accordingly, there were sound objectively justified administrative reasons, in my view, for placing prosthetists in general, men and women alike, on the Whitley Council scale and subjecting them to its negotiating machinery. There is no suggestion that it was unreasonable to place them on the particular point on the Whitley Council scale which was in fact selected, ascertained by reference to the position of medical physics technicians and entirely regardless of sex. It is in any event the fact that the general scale of remuneration for prosthetists was laid down accordingly by the Secretary of State. It was not a question of the appellant being paid less than the norm but of Mr Crumlin being paid more. He was paid more because of the necessity to attract him and other privately employed prosthetists into forming the nucleus of the new service.

I am therefore of the opinion that the grounds founded on by the board as constituting the material difference between the appellant's case and that of Mr Crumlin were capable in law of constituting a relevant difference for purposes of s. 1(3) of the Act of 1970, and that on the facts found by the industrial tribunal they were objectively justified.

Enderby v Frenchay Health Authority
[1993] IRLR 591
European Court of Justice

Dr Pamela Enderby, a senior speech therapist, claimed that she was employed on work of equal value with male principal grade pharmacists and clinical psychologists employed in the National Health Service. At the relevant time, her annual pay as a chief III grade speech therapist was £10,106, while that of a principal clinical psychologist was £12,527 and that of a Grade III principal pharmacist was £14,106. The pay of speech therapists generally was up to 60 per cent less than that of pharmacists.

The industrial tribunal dismissed the complaints. It held that the employers had established a material factor defence within the meaning of s. 1(3) by showing that the variation in pay 'arose because of the bargaining structure and its history which was non-discriminatory, and from the structures within their own professions which were also non-discriminatory'.

The industrial tribunal found in the alternative, however, that the employers had not shown that the difference in pay with respect to pharmacists was due to market forces because market forces could not explain the whole of the difference.

Dr Enderby did not appeal against the finding that there was no direct discrimination in the wage-setting process. Her appeal was based on the contention that under EEC law she had established a prima facie case of indirect sex discrimination in pay by showing that she was a member of a predominantly female group doing work of presumed equal value with her male comparator employed in a group which is predominantly male and that she was paid less than him. The employers cross-appealed against the industrial tribunal's failure to find that the difference in pay between the speech therapists and pharmacists was due to market forces and was permissible under s. 1(3) of the Equal Pay Act.

The EAT [1991] IRLR 44 dismissed Dr Enderby's appeal. It held that the mere fact of a difference in pay is not sufficient to found an allegation of unintentional indirect discrimination, without the identification of a barrier, requirement or condition causing disparate impact. The EAT took the view that if the factor causing the disparate impact has no taint of gender, there is nothing which requires justification. It is the cause which requires justification, not simply the result. It is only if a woman is paid less because she is a woman that she has suffered discrimination and without such discrimination a woman is not entitled to equal pay for work of equal value.

The EAT also allowed the cross-appeal against the industrial tribunal's decision, holding that once it had been found by the tribunal that market forces played *a* part in the difference of pay between speech therapists and pharmacists, that was sufficient. It was not necessary for the employers to establish that the factor of market forces justified the whole of the difference.

The Court of Appeal [1992] IRLR 15 referred the following questions for consideration by European Court of Justice:

Question 1
Does the principle of equal pay enshrined in Article 119 (now 141) of the Treaty of Rome require the employer to justify objectively the difference in pay between job A and job B?

Question 2
If the answer to question 1 is in the affirmative can the employer rely as sufficient justification for the difference in pay upon the fact that the pay of jobs A and B respectively have been determined by different collective bargaining processes which (considered separately) do not discriminate on grounds of sex and do not operate so as to disadvantage women because of their sex?

Question 3
If the employer is able to establish that at times there are serious shortages of suitable candidates for job B and that he pays the higher remuneration to holders of job B so as to attract them to job B but it can also be established that only part of the difference in pay between job B and job A is due to the need to attract suitable candidates to job B:

(a)   is the whole of the difference of pay objectively justified; or

(b)   that part but only that part of the difference which is due to the need to attract suitable candidates to job B objectively justified; or

(c)   must the employer equalise the pay of jobs A and B on the ground that he has failed to show that the whole of the difference is objectively justified?

The first question . . .
It is normally for the person alleging facts in support of a claim to adduce proof of such facts. Thus, in principle, the burden of proving the existence of sex discrimination as to pay lies with the worker who, believing himself to be the victim of such discrimination, brings legal proceedings against his employer with a view to removing the discrimination.

However, it is clear from the case law of the Court that the onus may shift when that is necessary to avoid depriving workers who appear to be the victims of discrimination of any effective means of enforcing the principle of equal pay. Accordingly, when a measure distinguishing between employees on the basis of their hours of work has in practice an adverse impact on substantially more members of one or other sex, that measure must be regarded as contrary to the objective pursued by Article 119 [now 141] of the Treaty, unless the employer shows that it is based on objectively justified factors unrelated to any discrimination on grounds of sex (judgments in Case 170/84 *Bilka-Kaufhaus* [1986] IRLR 317; Case C-33/89 *Kowalska* [1990] IRLR 447, at paragraph 16; and Case C-184/89 *Nimz* [1991] IRLR 222). . . .

However, if the pay of speech therapists is significantly lower than that of pharmacists and if the former are almost exclusively women while the latter are predominantly men, there is a prima facie case of sex discrimination, at least where the two jobs in question are of equal value and the statistics describing that situation are valid.

It is for the national court to assess whether it may take into account those statistics, that is to say, whether they cover enough individuals, whether they illustrate purely fortuitous or short-term phenomena, and whether, in general, they appear to be significant.

Where there is a prima facie case of discrimination, it is for the employer to show that there are objective reasons for the difference in pay. Workers would be unable to enforce the principle of equal pay before national courts if evidence of a prima facie case of discrimination did not shift to the employer the onus of showing that the pay differential is not in fact discriminatory (see, by analogy, the judgment in *Danfoss* [1989] IRLR 532).

In these circumstances, the answer to the first question is that, where significant statistics disclose an appreciable difference in pay between two jobs of equal value, one of which is carried out almost exclusively by women and the other predominantly by men, Article 119 [now 141] of the Treaty requires the employer to show that that difference is based on objectively justified factors unrelated to any discrimination on grounds of sex.

The second question . . .

. . . As is clear from Article 4 of Council Directive 75/117/EEC of 10 February 1975 on the approximation of the laws of the Member States relating to the application of the principle of equal pay for men and women (Official Journal 1975 L.45, p. 19), collective agreements, like laws, regulations or administrative provisions, must observe the principle enshrined in Article 119 [now 141] of the Treaty.

The fact that the rates of pay at issue are decided by collective bargaining processes conducted separately for each of the two professional groups concerned, without any discriminatory effect within each group, does not preclude a finding of prima facie discrimination where the results of those processes show that two groups with the same employer and the same trade union are treated differently. If the employer could rely on the absence of discrimination within each of the collective bargaining processes taken separately as sufficient justification for the difference in pay, he could, as the German Government pointed out, easily circumvent the principle of equal pay by using separate bargaining processes.

Accordingly, the answer to the second question is that the fact that the respective rates of pay of two jobs of equal value, one carried out almost exclusively by women and the other predominantly by men, were arrived at by collective bargaining processes which, although carried out by the same parties, are distinct, and, taken separately, have in themselves no discriminatory effect, is not sufficient objective justification for the difference in pay between those two jobs.

The third question

The Court has consistently held that it is for the national court, which has sole jurisdiction to make findings of fact, to determine whether and to what extent the grounds put forward by an employer to explain the adoption of a pay practice which applies independently of a worker's sex but in fact affects more women than men may be regarded as objectively justified economic grounds (judgments in Case 170/84 *Bilka-Kaufhaus*, cited above, at paragraph 36 and Case C-184/89 *Nimz* . . .). Those grounds may include, if they can be attributed to the needs and objectives of the undertaking, different criteria such as the worker's flexibility or adaptability to hours and places of work, his training or his length of service (judgment in Case 109/88 *Danfoss* . . .).

The state of the employment market, which may lead an employer to increase the pay of a particular job in order to attract candidates, may constitute an objectively justified economic ground within the meaning of the case law cited above. How it is to be applied in the circumstances of each case depends on the facts and so falls within the jurisdiction of the national court.

If, as the question referred seems to suggest, the national court has been able to determine precisely what proportion of the increase in pay is attributable to market forces, it must necessarily accept that the pay differential is objectively justified to the extent of that proportion. When national authorities have to apply Community law, they must apply the principle of proportionality.

If that is not the case, it is for the national court to assess whether the role of market forces in determining the rate of pay was sufficiently significant to provide objective justification for part or all of the difference.

The answer to the third question, therefore, is that it is for the national court to determine, if necessary by applying the principle of proportionality, whether and to what extent the shortage of candidates for a job and the need to attract them by higher pay constitutes an objectively justified economic ground for the difference in pay between the jobs in question.

Ratcliffe v *North Yorkshire County Council*
[1995] IRLR 439
House of Lords

Following a job evaluation scheme, the jobs of catering assistants were rated as being of equal value to those of refuse collectors and leisure attendants employed by the council. The same rate of pay was duly awarded. However, the school meals service was put out to competitive tendering and as a result it was decided that the catering staff could no longer be paid on the basis of local government terms and conditions. The catering staff were duly dismissed and re-employed at lower hourly rates. The catering staff then claimed equal pay.

LORD SLYNN: . . . There has been much argument in this case as to the relationship between s. 1 of the Act of 1970 and s. 1 of the Sex Discrimination Act 1975. The latter distinguishes between (a) a case where an employer on the ground of her sex treats a woman less favourably than he treats or would treat a man, and (b) a case where the employer applies to a woman a requirement or condition which he applies or would apply equally to a man, but which is such that the proportion of women who can comply with it is considerably smaller than the proportion of men who can comply with it and which the employer cannot show to be justifiable irrespective of the sex of the person to whom it is applied and which is to the detriment of a woman because she cannot comply with it. The first '(a)' is commonly referred to as 'direct' discrimination, the latter ('b') as 'indirect' discrimination. It is submitted that this distinction must be introduced equally into the Act of 1970. For my part I do not accept that this is so. There is no provision in the Act of 1975 which expressly incorporates the distinction into the Act of 1970 even though Schedule 1 to the Act of 1975 incorporated a number of amendments into the Act of 1970 and even though Part II of that Schedule set out the Act of 1970 in full in its amended form.

In my opinion the Act of 1970 must be interpreted in its amended form without bringing in the distinction between so-called 'direct' and 'indirect' discrimination. The relevant question under the Act of 1970 is whether equal treatment has been accorded for men and women employed on like work or for men and women employed on work rated as equivalent. Whether they are employed on work rated as equivalent depends on whether the woman's job and the man's job had been given an equal value in terms of the demand made on a worker under various headings on a study undertaken with a view to evaluating in those terms the jobs to be done by all or any of the employees in an undertaking.

In the present case it is plain that such evaluation was made and the women were found to be engaged on work rated as equivalent to work done by men. That is sufficient for the women to be entitled to a declaration by the industrial tribunal in their favour unless s. 1(3) of the Act of 1970 as set out previously is satisfied.

This was the question for the industrial tribunal to consider. By a majority they were satisfied that the employers had failed to show that the variation between the applicants' contracts and those of their male comparators was due to a material factor which was not the difference of sex.

In my opinion it is impossible to say that they were not entitled on the evidence to come to that conclusion. It is obvious that the employers reduced the applicants wages in order to obtain the area contracts and that to obtain the area contracts they had to compete with Commercial Catering Group who, the tribunal found, employed only women and 'because of that, employed them on less favourable terms than the council did previously under the NJC agreement' (majority conclusion paragraph 2). The fact, if it be a fact, that CCG discriminated against women in respect of pay and that the DSO had to pay no more than CCG in order to be competitive does not however conclude the issue. The basic question is whether the DSO paid women less than men for work rated as equivalent. The reason they did so is certainly that they had to compete with CCG. The fact, however, is that they did pay women less than men engaged on work rated as equivalent. The industrial tribunal found and was entitled to find that the employers had not shown that this was genuinely due to a material difference other than the difference of sex.

The women could not have found other suitable work and were obliged to take the wages offered if they were to continue with this work. The fact that two men were employed on the same work at the same rate of pay does not detract from the conclusion that there was discrimination between the women involved and their male comparators. It means no more than that the two men were underpaid compared with other men doing jobs rated as equivalent.

Questions
1. Is there a difference between objectively justified administrative reasons and administrative convenience? What has *Rainey's* case done to the 'personal equation' test, and does the difference in the wording of s. 1(3)(a) and (b) continue to be of significance?
2. What impact has the decision in *Enderby* had on the criteria for justifying inequalities as propounded in *Rainey*?
3. Can an 'understandable error' amount to a genuine material difference/factor?

Notes
1. The hurdles raised by the EAT in *Enderby* have been removed by the decision of the ECJ. The applicant need not identify a requirement or condition, or show gender-based disparate impact in alleging indirect discrimination relating to pay. Indirect discrimination will be presumed whenever there is significant statistical evidence to show that a predominantly female group of workers is doing work of equal value but is being paid less than a male group of workers. The onus then moves to the employer to show that the difference is objectively justified. This should have a considerable impact on equal value claims based on job segregation. It should also impact upon the interpretation of the SDA 1975 and RRA 1976.

2. Enderby also makes inroads into the market forces defence. This is no longer a blanket defence to a claim of indirect discrimination. The ECJ felt that, where market forces is pleaded, the tribunals must assess what proportion of the pay differential can be attributed to market forces as objectively justified by the employer. This may, indeed, result in applicants being awarded proportional equal pay rather than nothing where the market forces defence is successful.

3. Non-discriminatory collective bargaining will no longer objectively justify an act of discrimination. The employer must now, in establishing a defence under s. 1(3), justify the discriminatory result not just the cause. In *British Road Services* v *Loughran* [1997] IRLR 1992, the Northern Ireland Court of Appeal considered how far separate pay structures based on different collective agreements amounted to an objective justification for the purposes of s. 1(3). The Northern Ireland Court of Appeal decided that 'where a significant number of the claimant's group are women, an employer cannot rely merely on the existence of a separate collective agreement. Nor does the decision in *Enderby* require the group to be exclusively women before the s. 1(3) defence is to be used'.

Handels-og Kontorfunktionaererernes Forbund i Danmark v *Dansk Arbejdsgiverforening (acting for Danfoss)*
[1989] IRLR 532
European Court of Justice

In accordance with a collective agreement between HK, the Danish Union of Commercial and Clerical Staff (hereafter the staff union) and DA, the Danish Association of Employers (hereafter the employers' association), Danfoss pays the same basic minimum pay to workers in the same pay grade. Grading is determined by job classification. Article 9 of the collective agreement, however, allows the company to make additional payments to individuals within a grade on the basis of the employee's 'flexibility', defined as including an assessment of their capacity, quality of work, autonomy, and responsibilities. In addition, pay is increased on the basis of the employee's vocational training and seniority.

The union pointed out that within a pay grade the average pay of women was less than that of men and it contended that the employer's pay system discriminated on the grounds of sex contrary to the provisions of Danish law implementing the EEC Equal Pay Directive.

Under Danish law, when two parties to a collective agreement are in dispute on whether pay in an undertaking is discriminatory, in the event of a failure to agree, the case is referred to an industrial arbitration tribunal. Before the arbitration tribunal, the staff union submitted the results of a statistical survey covering the pay of 157 Danfoss employees which showed a difference of 6.85 per cent between the average pay of male and female workers within the relevant pay grades. The union contended that this difference in itself showed pay discrimination. It argued that because of the way in which pay is determined in Denmark, a woman would not be able to avail herself of the right to equal pay if she could not base her claim on statistical data.

The industrial arbitration tribunal decided to stay the proceedings and submitted a number of questions to the European Court of Justice for a preliminary ruling on the interpretation of the Equal Pay Directive.

The ECJ held that the effect of Directive 75/117 is that where the employer operates a pay structure which lacks transparency in respect of the criteria used for the payment of employees, the burden of proof is on the employer to show that his pay practice is not discriminatory where a female worker establishes by comparison with a relatively large number of employees, that the average pay of female employees is lower than that of male employees.

Concerning the burden of proof (questions 1(A) and 3(A))
The file shows that the main dispute between the parties originates in the fact that the mechanism of individual increases applied to the basic wage is operated in such a way that a female worker is incapable of identifying the causes of a difference in pay between her and a male worker carrying out the same work. The workers do not actually know which are the criteria for the increases which are applied to them and how they are applied. They are only informed of the amount of their increased wages, without being able to establish the effect each of the criteria for the increases has had. Those who fall into a particular pay grade are, therefore, unable to compare the different components of their pay with those of the pay of their fellow workers who are part of the same grade.

In those circumstances the questions submitted by the national court must be understood as seeking to establish whether the Equal Pay Directive must be interpreted as meaning that, where an undertaking applies a pay system which is characterised by a total lack of transparency, the burden of proof is on the employer to show that his pay practice is not discriminatory, if a female worker establishes that, by comparison with a relatively high number of employees, the average pay of female workers is lower that that of male workers.

In this respect it should be recalled, first of all, that in its decision of 30 June 1988 (*Commission of the European Communities* v *France*, 318/86, not yet published, point 27) the Court condemned a system of recruitment characterised by a lack of transparency as being contrary to the principle of equality of access to employment, on the grounds that such lack of transparency prevented any form of control on the part of the national courts.

It should be emphasised, moreover, that in a situation where a mechanism of individual pay increases characterised by a total lack of transparency is involved, female workers can only establish a difference between average pay. They would be deprived of any effective means of ensuring the respect of the principle of equal pay before the national court if the effect of furnishing such proof was not to impose the burden of proof on the employer to show that his pay practice is, in fact, not discriminatory.

In those conditions, the answer to questions 1(A) and 3(A) must be that the Equal Pay Directive must be interpreted as meaning that when an undertaking applies a system of pay which is characterised by a total lack of transparency, the burden of proof is on the employer to show that his pay practice is not discriminatory, where a female worker establishes, by comparison with a relatively large number of employees, that the average pay of female workers is lower than that of male workers.

Concerning the lawfulness of the incremental criteria concerned (questions 1(B) and 2(A) and (C))

These questions seek essentially to ascertain whether the Directive must be interpreted as meaning that, when it appears that the application of incremental criteria such as flexibility, vocational training or the seniority of the worker works systematically to the disadvantage of female workers, the employer may nevertheless justify their use, and, if so, under what conditions. In order to answer this question, each of the criteria must be examined separately.

First of all, concerning the criterion of flexibility the file does not show clearly the scope to be given to it. At the hearing the Employers' Association stated that the fact of being willing to work at different hours does not in itself justify a wage increase. In order to apply the criterion of flexibility the employer would make an overall assessment of the quality of the work carried out by his employees. For this purpose, he would take into account in particular their zeal at work, their sense of initiative and the amount of work done.

In those circumstances a distinction is to be made according to whether the criterion of flexibility is used in order to reward the quality of the work carried out by the employee or whether it is used to reward the adaptability of the employee to variable work schedules and places of work.

In the first case, the criterion of flexibility is indisputably totally neutral from the point of view of sex. Where it results in systematic unfairness to female workers that can only be because the employer has applied it in an abusive manner. It is inconceivable that the work carried out by female workers would be generally of a lower quality. The employer may not therefore justify the use of the criterion of flexibility so defined where its application shows itself to be systematically unfavourable to women.

It would be different in the second case. If it were understood as referring to the adaptability of the worker to variable work schedules and places of work, the criterion of flexibility may also operate to the disadvantage of female workers who, as a result of household and family duties for which they are often responsible may have greater difficulty than male workers in organising their working time in a flexible manner.

In its judgment of 13 May 1986 (*Bilka-Kaufhaus GmbH* v *Weber von Hartz* [1986] IRLR 317), the Court took the view that the policy of an undertaking which results in workers, who are excluded from an occupational pension scheme, might affect a much higher number of women than men, taking into account the difficulties encountered by female workers in working full-time. The Court nevertheless held that the undertaking might establish that its pay practice was determined by objectively justified factors unrelated to any discrimination based on sex and that, if the undertaking succeeded, there was no infringement of Article 119 [now 141] of the Treaty. Those considerations also apply in the case of a pay practice which gives special rewards for the adaptability of workers to variable work schedules and places of work. The employer may, therefore, justify payment for such adaptability by showing that it is of importance in the performance of the specific duties entrusted to the worker concerned.

Second, as regards the criterion of vocational training, it cannot be ruled out that it may act to the detriment of female workers insofar as they have fewer opportunities to obtain vocational training which is as advanced as that of male workers, or that they use those opportunities to a lesser extent. However, having regard to the considerations laid down in the aforementioned judgment of 13 May 1986, the employer may justify rewarding specific vocational training by demonstrating that that training is of importance for the performance of the specific duties entrusted to the worker.

Third, as regards the criterion of seniority, it cannot be ruled out either that, like that of vocational training, it may result in less favourable treatment of female workers than for male workers, insofar as women have entered the labour market more recently than men or are subject to more frequent interruptions of their careers. However, since seniority goes hand in hand with experience which generally places a worker in a better position to carry out his duties, it is permissible for the employer to reward it without the need to establish the importance which it takes on for the performance of the specific duties to be entrusted to the worker.

Strathclyde Regional Council v *Wallace*
[1998] IRLR 146
House of Lords

Each of the nine respondent women teachers performed the duties of a principal teacher. However, none of them was appointed to the position of a principal teacher and none of them received the salary appropriate for the holder of an appointment as a principal teacher. They were among a group of 134 unpromoted teachers who claimed to be carrying out principal teachers' duties, 81 of whom were men and 53 women.

The nine women brought equal pay claims, identifying at least one male comparator who had been appointed as a principal teacher and was receiving a salary appropriate to that responsibility The industrial tribunal found that the applicants had been performing like work.

Given the gender composition of the unpromoted teachers, it was an agreed fact that the disparity in pay was not based on sex. The employers argued that the variation in pay between the applicants and their male comparators was due to a combination of material factors. These included that the promotion structure for teachers was established by statute and posts were filled only on merit after competition, and that financial constraints prevented the applicants from being appointed principal teachers when it might have been appropriate.

It was held that the industrial tribunal had erred in law in finding that the employers had failed to prove that the variation in pay between the applicants, who had acted as principal teachers but had not been paid the salary for that post, and their male comparators appointed as principal teachers, was genuinely due to a material factor other than sex within the meaning of s. 1(3) of the Equal Pay Act, in circumstances in which it was agreed that the disparity in pay had nothing to do with gender. The industrial tribunal erred in holding that in order for the employers to succeed in a s. 1(3) defence, they had to establish that the reasons for the difference in pay justified the disparity.

LORD BROWNE-WILKINSON: [Section 1(3)] provides a defence if the employer shows that the variation between the woman's contract and the man's contract is 'genuinely' due to a factor which is (a) material and (b) not the difference of sex. The requirement of genuineness would be satisfied if the industrial tribunal came to the conclusion that the reason put forward was not a sham or a pretence. For the matters relied upon by the employer to constitute 'material factors' it would have to be shown that the matters relied upon were in fact causally relevant to the difference in pay, i.e. that they were significant factors. Finally, the employer had to show that the difference of sex was not a factor relied upon. This final point is capable of presenting problems in other cases. But in the present case it presents none: there is no suggestion that the matters relied on were in any way linked to differences in sex.

If that approach had been adopted by the industrial tribunal, this case would have been straightforward. The five factors summarised by the industrial tribunal were undoubtedly genuine reasons for there being a difference between the pay of the appellants and that of principal teachers. They were also significant and causally relevant factors leading to that disparity. They did not relate to sex in any way. Therefore, on the straight forward application of the section the respondents have established a subsection (3) defence. There is nothing in the words of the subsection which requires the employer to 'justify' the factors giving rise to this disparity by showing that there was no way in which the employer could have avoided such disparity if he had adopted other measures.

How then did the industrial tribunal come to mislead itself by introducing into the case the concept of 'justification'?

The answer is that they wrongly thought that the authorities demanded such justification in every case where an employer seeks to establish a subsection (3) defence whereas, on a proper reading, the question of justification only arises where a factor relied upon is gender discriminatory. Although in the present case there is no question of gender discrimination, the authorities are in such a state of confusion that it is desirable for your Lordships to seek to establish the law on a clear and sound basis.

. . .

In my judgment, the law was correctly stated by Mummery J giving the judgment of the Employment Appeal Tribunal in *Tyldesley* v *TML Plastics Ltd* [1996] IRLR 395, in which he followed and applied the earlier EAT decisions in *Calder* v *Roundtree Mackintosh Confectionery Ltd* [1993] IRLR 212 and *Yorkshire Blood Transfusion Service* v *Plaskitt* [1994] ICR 74. The purpose of s. 1 of the Equal Pay Act 1970 is to eliminate sex discrimination in pay not to achieve fair wages. Therefore, if a difference in pay is explained by genuine factors not tainted by discrimination that is sufficient to raise a valid defence under subsection (3); in such a case there is no further burden on the employer to 'justify' anything. However, if the factor explaining the disparity in pay is tainted by sex discrimination (whether direct or indirect) that will be fatal to a defence under subsection (3) unless such discrimination can be objectively justified in accordance with the tests laid down in the *Bilka* and *Rainey* cases.

Snoxell v *Vauxhall Motors*
[1977] IRLR 123
Employment Appeal Tribunal

Miss Snoxell and Mrs Davis had been employed by the company for many years as inspectors of motor machine parts. They worked alongside male inspectors, including a group of men designated OX – the red circle group. The men in this group were paid at a higher rate than the two women although it was common ground that they were all employed on the same work. The red-circle group was formed in 1970 as a result of a revision of the existing pay structure and arose as a result of the fact that at this revision, it was realised that male inspector jobs previously graded X2 should be regraded into a lower category under the new structure (H3). It was these former X2 male inspectors who were red-circled and ultimately received the special designation OX. Because the former grade X2 was a male grade, there were no women in it and thus no women fell to receive the protections accorded to the employees in this grade when the new structure was introduced. Thus there were no women in the red circle. In June 1975, Miss Snoxell and Mrs Davies took advantage of the company's offer to transfer women employed on like work with men to the appropriate male rate and were then regraded H3. Grade H3 thus currently consists of men who entered employment after 1970 to do quality control stores inspection work and women who were performing that work prior to 1970 and those who have joined the company since. The continuation of the OX category is not subject to a fixed time limit or any phasing out provisions.

It was held, allowing Miss Snoxell's and Mrs Davies's appeal, that the correct approach for an industrial tribunal, confronted with a claim by an employer under s. 1(3) of the Equal Pay Act that a variation resulting from red-circling was genuinely due to a material difference other than the difference of sex, is to elicit and analyse *all* the circumstances of the particular case, including the situation prior to the formation of the red circle. It is necessary to examine the origin of the red-circling, to see whether in other respects the arrangements are unisex and non-discriminatory, and generally to look at all the facts in order to see whether the employers, upon whom lies a heavy burden of proof, have satisfied the requirements of s. 1(3). In this context, that there was no discriminatory motive or intent is irrelevant.

PHILLIPS J: Mr Lester submitted that s. 1(3) is not a general escape clause designed to enable employers to phase in equal pay gradually; that was provided for in the Equal Pay Act 1970 itself which did not come into operation until 29 December 1975, five years after it was enacted. Nor, he submitted, could reliance be placed on s. 1(3) where the facts said to constitute the difference other than sex could be shown to have their origin in sex discrimination. Thus in the present case, although the immediate cause of the discrimination lay in the fact that the male inspectors were 'red-circled' whereas Miss Snoxell and Mrs Davies were not, and although they were 'red-circled' in order to preserve their status for reasons unconnected with sex, it was necessary to look to see why Miss Snoxell and Mrs Davies were not also within the red circle. The answer was that, because they were women, they were not able to enter Grade X2, and so did not qualify. Thus at the root of the difference relied upon lay sex discrimination, and it would be contrary to the purpose and intent of the Equal Pay Act 1970 to allow such an answer to the claim.

Mr Grabiner submitted that the reason for the red-circling of the male inspectors had nothing to do with sex discrimination, but was intended merely to preserve their status, and that it was not brought into existence to discriminate against women. If there had been no circle, he submitted, all the men and women would have been paid the same. The difference for the purpose of s. 1(3) was the formation of the red circle. The substantive cause of the discrimination, he submitted, was the formation of the red circle, and it was the effective cause. Thus there was no discrimination, and a good answer to the claim was available to Vauxhall Motors Ltd under s. 1(3).

Putting these arguments side by side it can be seen that the solution depends upon whether, in analysing the history of the difference in treatment of Miss Snoxell and Mrs Davies on the one hand and the red circle male inspectors on the other, one stops at the moment of the formation of the circle or looks further back to see why Miss Snoxell and Mrs Davies were not within it. The arguments presented to us have, not surprisingly, considered questions of causation, and it has been said that the inability of Miss Snoxell and Mrs Davies to join the red circle was, or was not, the effective cause of the current variation in the terms of their contracts of employment. It seems to us that this earlier discrimination can be said to be an effective cause of the current variation. But we would put the matter more broadly. The onus of proof under s. 1(3) is on the employer and it is a heavy one. Intention, and motive, are irrelevant; and we would say that an employer can never establish in the terms of s. 1(3) that the variation between the woman's contract and the man's contract is genuinely due to a material difference (other than the difference of sex) between her case and his when it can be seen that past sex discrimination has contributed to the variation. To allow such an answer would, we think, be contrary to the spirit and intent of the Equal Pay Act 1970, construed and interpreted in the manner we have already explained. It is true that the original discrimination occurred before 29 December 1975 and accordingly was not then unlawful; nonetheless it cannot have been the intention of the Act to permit the perpetuation of the effects of earlier discrimination . . .

Notes

1. The onus is on the employer to establish a s. 1(3) defence. The current criteria for deciding whether a genuine material factor defence has been established is to be found from the decisions in *Bilka-Kaufhaus* and *Rainey*, i.e. that any difference is based on objectively justified factors unrelated to sex. It must be shown that there is a real need on the part of the undertaking and that the difference was an appropriate way of achieving the objective necessary to that end. This test acknowledges that there may be numerous grounds such as market forces, administrative efficiency, economics, merit, service, red-circling etc. which can justify the difference in the terms of a woman's contract compared with a male.

The issue of the time at which work is done has generally been irrelevant to any decision regarding equality of pay. However, *Calder & Cizakowsky* v *Rowntree Mackintosh Confectionery Ltd* [1993] IRLR 212 adds further documented evidence that the courts are prepared to adopt a flexible approach to this issue when it arises as a genuine material defence. The application of *Danfoss* is also of interest, in that the Court took the view that 'transparency' does not require a precise explanation of how the premium was achieved.

Furthermore, as the EPA 1970 and SDA 1975 are to be regarded as a single code, the criteria used to establish the justification defence under s. (1) (b) of the SDA 1975 should be the same as the criteria used for EPA 1970, s. 1(3); it follows that this must be the case in respect of justification under s. 1(1)(b) of the Race Relations Act 1976 (see *Hampson* v *Department of Education and Science* [1989] IRLR 69).

2. Following *Strathclyde*, in justifying a difference in pay it need only be causally relevant to the difference in pay. The reason for the difference must be explained by the employer; arguably this is now a subjective rather than an objective test. The case goes on to reinforce the point that the right to equal pay is not the same as a right to fair pay.

3. See Gill, T., 'Making equal pay defences transparent' (1990) 33 *Equal Opportunities Review* 48, for an analysis of the impact of the *Danfoss* case and its relationship to the decision in *Bilka-Kaufhaus* and *Reed Packaging Ltd* v *Boozer*. See also Gay, V. (1989) 18 *Industrial Law Journal*, No. 1, pp. 63–6, for a discussion of the impact of *Reed's* case in respect of collective bargaining as a material factor defence; and Kilpatrick, C. (1994) 23 *Industrial Law Journal*, No. 4, for a critical evaluation of s. 1(3).

Questions
1.   Can a job evaluation scheme ever be 'objectively justified'?
2.   If a variation in pay is not based on sex, does the employer have to justify the difference under s. 1(3)?

Notes
1.   There have been a number of works highlighting deficiencies in the current equal pay legislation. For example, note the recommendations of the EOC in *Equal Pay for Men and Women, Strengthening the Acts* (EOC, 1990). See also Scorer, C. and Sedley, A., *Amending the Equality Laws* (NCCL, 1983).
2.   For a critical review of the problems faced by complainants, see Gregory, J., *Trial by Ordeal* (EOC, 1989), in which a study was made of those complainants who lost their tribunal hearings. This research highlights the problems of stress, lack of representation (only about 50 per cent were represented in some way) and victimisation (few of the applicants interviewed in the research remained with the same employer). Leonard, A., *Pyrrhic Victories: Winning Sex Discrimination and Equal Pay Cases in the Industrial Tribunals* (EOC 1987) examines whether those complainants who succeeded in their application before the employment tribunal were in the real sense victors. Again, the problems of victimisation and stress were highlighted.

Equal Opportunities Commission, *Equality in the 21st Century: A New Approach* (1998)

SUMMARY OF RECOMMENDATIONS AND QUESTIONS

The following is a summary of the EOC's recommendations and questions, with paragraph numbers to enable you to identify them in the text. Your views on any of the recommendations and questions would be welcome.

I   A SINGLE STATUTE (11)
• The SDA, EqPA and other relevant laws should be replaced by a new statute.
• The new statute should incorporate European Community law.
• The new statute should be based on the principle of a fundamental right to equal treatment between men and women.

- The new statute should guarantee freedom from discrimination on grounds, for example, of sex, pregnancy, marital or family status, gender reassignment and sexual orientation. The grounds should not be exhaustive.

. . .

II TYPES OF DISCRIMINATION (19)
- The new statute should provide for the burden of proof to shift to the respondent once the complainant proves less favourable treatment in circumstances consistent with grounds of sex.
- The new statute should contain the terms 'direct' and 'indirect' discrimination, as well as their definitions.
- The new statute should incorporate the definition of indirect discrimination contained in the Council Directive on the Burden of Proof as adopted by the EC Council on 24th July 1997.
- The definition of indirect discrimination should also extend to 'policy' as well as 'provision, criterion or practice'.

Victimisation (21)
- The provisions on victimisation should be strengthened to make clear that any person suffering detriment as a result of anything done under or by reference to the new statute can seek full protection and remedies from the tribunals.
- A fast track procedure should be introduced to deal with alleged victimisation.
- Tribunals should be given powers to impose financial penalties and make orders to deter further victimisation, in addition to granting appropriate remedies to the victim.

Sexual Harassment (22)
- The new statute should expressly prohibit sexual harassment and should incorporate the definition of sexual harassment contained in the European Commission Recommendation.
- It should be made clear that the prohibition of sexual harassment should apply across the areas of education and training and the provision of goods, facilities or services as well as in employment.

III RIGHTS IN EMPLOYMENT
Maternity Rights (29-30)
- The provisions concerning the treatment of pregnant women and new mothers should be simplified and consolidated into a single statutory framework.
- The provisions should be incorporated into the new statute.

. . .

Parental Leave (31)
. . .

Equal Pay (41 and 45)
- Employers should be placed under a statutory duty to review their pay systems and pay structures, in line with the EOC's Code of Practice on Equal Pay to identify areas of potential and actual pay inequality between men and women which cannot be objectively justified.
- Employers should be required to publish the results of their reviews to their employees with a programme for dealing with any pay inequalities.

- In the absence of a review or if it appears inadequate or unfair, the EOC should be empowered to intervene and set objectives and programmes for employers by means of directions.
- In the event of any non-compliance by an employer with his/her statutory duties or of any failure to comply in whole or in part with any directions given by the EOC, the EOC should be empowered to bring proceedings against an employer in respect of any non-compliance or failure.˙ (See also recommendations at paragraph 48 below.)
- Any contractor seeking contracts or financial aid from central or local government or from any publicly funded organisation should be required to demonstrate full compliance with the obligations described above and in paragraphs 47 and 48 below as a condition of eligibility.
- The industrial tribunals should have a power not only to grant an individual remedy in an individual case but to make a general finding and to make changes to a collective agreement or pay structure consistent with its findings in the case.
- The industrial tribunal or a similarly constituted body should have jurisdiction to determine allegations of discrimination in the terms of collective agreements and pay structures on the application of any interested party including the EOC.

IV STATUTORY MONITORING (49)
- Employers (with the exception of private households) should be placed under a statutory duty to monitor their workforce in such terms and at such intervals as may be prescribed.
- Employers should be required to produce for inspection by the EOC on demand their monitoring records.
- If the records are inadequate or suggestive of inadequacies in the employer's equal opportunities practices, the EOC should be empowered to investigate the employer's policies and practices with a view to prescribing a remedial programme to be completed by the employer within a specified period.
- The EOC should be empowered to bring proceedings against an employer in respect of any breach of these statutory obligations.
- Tribunals should be empowered to impose a financial penalty on an employer as well as awarding remedies where appropriate to individuals or ordering collective remedial action.

V THE PUBLIC DOMAIN (52)
- A statutory duty should be placed on all bodies carrying out a service or undertaking of a public nature, to work towards the elimination of unlawful discrimination and to promote equality of opportunity.
- Such bodies should also be required to publish summaries of their equality programmes and progress in their annual reports so as to enable the public to evaluate their work in this area.

. . .

State Activities (54)
- The new statute should be drafted to remove the restrictive interpretation in the *Amin* decision and to impose equality obligations in the full range of Government activities.

Public Appointments (56)
- The new statute should make clear that it extends to all public appointments (paid or unpaid), including judicial appointments.

VI   KEY EXCEPTIONS AND OTHER MATTERS

Private Clubs (63)
- The new statute should include within its scope all private members' clubs which have in the previous two year period admitted both sexes to some membership category and/or where some club facilities and services have been available to both men and women.

Privacy and Decency (65)
- The new statute should contain a clear definition of the term 'serious embarrassment' and the circumstances in which the exception in s. 35(1)(c) might apply.

. . .

Safety (67)
- In respect of safety there should be no changes to the current law.
- Transport organisations should treat public safety as a priority for men and women.

. . .

Insurance (81)
- The exception for insurance and related matters should be repealed.

Sport (85)
- The exception in S. 44 of the SDA should no longer permit the exclusion of young people of school age from competing in any sport, game or other competitive activity.

Armed Forces (87)
- The exception based on 'combat effectiveness' should be repealed.
- The exception in respect of cadet training corps should be repealed.

. . .

VII   EDUCATION (90)
- School Organisation Committees and Adjudicators as provided for in the School Standards and Framework Bill should be brought within the scope of Sections 23 and 25 of the SDA.

VIII   ENFORCEMENT PROCEEDINGS

Individual Proceedings

. . .

Tribunals and Courts (96)
- A discrimination division should be established within the industrial tribunals to hear both employment and non-employment cases of discrimination.

The Value of Litigation (99)
- The industrial tribunal should be empowered to make general findings of discrimination where appropriate.
- The industrial tribunal should be empowered to make the EOC a party to the proceedings where it appears likely that a general finding may be appropriate.

Representative Proceedings (101)
- The EOC should be given a general power to bring legal proceedings in its own name where it believes a discriminatory act has taken place or a discriminatory practice exists.

Formal Investigations (102)
- Formal investigations should be subject to strict time limits set out in statute.
- The scope of non-discrimination notices should be extended to require, where appropriate, the cessation of specific practices which have led to the discrimination identified.
- In lieu of a non-discrimination notice the EOC should be enabled to accept legally binding and enforceable undertakings from persons and organisations which have agreed to make the necessary changes.

IX   REMEDIES (104)

The following additional powers should be available to the tribunals:
- In employment cases, interim relief should be available to preserve a complainant's position pending a hearing.
- In addition to the remedies now available, a full range of mandatory orders should be available to the tribunal.
- An industrial tribunal should be able to order appointment, promotion, reinstatement or re-engagement, where it appears appropriate to do so.
- The tribunal should be able to award continuing payments of compensation until a stipulated event such as promotion or engagement occurs.
- An industrial tribunal should be able to order that a respondent take such action as is reasonably necessary to negate the effect of the discrimination not only on the applicant but on any other person in his or her employment similarly affected.
- The time limit for issuing an Originating Application in sex discrimination cases should be extended from three months to six months. The time for issuing a Questionnaire under Section 74 should be extended to four weeks after lodging the IT1.
- Respondents should be obliged to furnish replies to the Section 74 Questionnaire within eight weeks of its date of issue. Where they do not do so, the tribunal should be under a duty to draw an inference that the respondents are refusing to reply, or any other inference it considers appropriate.
- The special procedure for notification in education cases under Section 66(5) should be repealed.

Note

The Code of Practice on Equal Pay provides guidelines for eliminating discrimination from pay systems.

Equal Opportunities Commission, *Code of Practice on Equal Pay (1997)*

Review of pay systems for sex bias

25.a) Pay arrangements are frequently complicated and the features which can give rise to sex discrimination are not always obvious. Although pay systems reviews are not required by law, they are recommended as the most appropriate method of ensuring that a pay system delivers equal pay free from sex bias.

b) A pay systems review also provides an opportunity to investigate the amount of information employees receive about their pay. Pay systems should be clear and easy to understand. Where they are not and where pay differentials exist, these may be inferred to be due to sex discrimination (see page 5). It is therefore in an employer's interest to have transparent pay systems to prevent unnecessary equal pay claims.

c) The Equal Opportunities Commission recommends that a pay systems review should involve the following stages:

Stage One
Undertake a thorough analysis of the pay system to produce a breakdown of all employees, which covers for example, sex, job title, grade, whether part-time or full-time, with basic pay, performance ratings and all other elements of remuneration.

Stage Two
Examine each element of the pay system against the data obtained in stage one (see paragraph 27).

Stage Three
Identify any elements of the pay system which the review indicates may be the source of any discrimination.

Stage Four
Change any rules or practices, including those in collective agreements, which stages 1 to 3 have identified as likely to give rise to discrimination in pay. It is recommended that this should be done in consultation with employees, trade unions or staff representatives where appropriate. Stages 1 to 3 may reveal that practices and procedures in relation to recruitment, selection and access to training have contributed to discrimination in pay; in that event, these matters should also be addressed.

Stage Five
Analyse the likely effects of any proposed changes in practice to the pay system before implementation, to identify and rectify any discrimination which could be caused.

Stage Six
Give equal pay to current employees. Where the review shows that some employees are not receiving equal pay for equal work and the reasons cannot be shown to be free of sex bias, then a plan must be developed for dealing with this.

Stage Seven
Set up a system of regular monitoring to allow checks to be made to pay practices.

Stage Eight
Draw up and publish an equal pay policy with provision for assessing the new pay system or modification to a system in terms of sex discrimination. Also, in the interests of transparency, provide pay information as described on page 5 where this is not already usual practice.

4 DISCRIMINATION IN THE WORKPLACE

I Introduction

The Sex Discrimination Act (SDA) 1975 and the Race Relations Act (RRA) 1976 make certain types of discrimination unlawful. This is not, however, the sole purpose of this legislation as both statutes are intended to bring about the elimination of discrimination and promote equality of opportunity for men and women and racial groups. The RRA 1976 has as its model the SDA 1975, accordingly the wording of the RRA 1976 corresponds for the most part with that of the SDA 1975. To these measures the Disability Discrimination Act 1995 (DDA) may be added.

While this chapter concentrates on discrimination in employment, it should be noted that the statutes are much wider in scope, covering discrimination in education, housing, the provision of goods, facilities and services etc. The statutes are also responsible for the setting up of the Equal Opportunities Commission (EOC), the Commission for Racial Equality (CRE) and the National Disability Council, respectively, whose duties involve promoting equality and reviewing the legislation. The Commissions are required to produce an annual report; and all three have published a code of practice. The EOC and CRE may also lend their support to complainants, although there is no obligation to do so (SDA 1975, s. 75 and RRA 1976, s. 66); the Secretary of State may provide this support under the DDA 1995, s. 56. The Commissions have the power to carry out formal investigations (RRA 1976, ss. 48–49 and SDA 1975, ss. 57–60). The CRE in particular has carried out investigations into racial policy and practice by Government departments and at a number of large establishments – see *Immigration Control & Procedures: Report of a Formal Investigation* (1985); *Massey Ferguson Perkins Ltd – Report of a Formal Investigation* (1982); *Rank Leisure Ltd – Report of a Formal Investigation* (1983).

The 1998 statistics continue to show a steady increase in the number of sex, race and disability discrimination cases referred to ACAS (see Chapter 3). In total, 16,260 discrimination complaints were received. The breakdown is as follows: sex discrimination 6,882; equal pay 3,447; race 3,173; disability 2,758. This increase not only reflects a continued awareness of the potential scope of the legislation, but also, in respect of the SDA 1975, the impact of EC law. The statistics also reveal that there is a long way to go before discrimination is eliminated; it is open to debate whether the legislation, either existing or amended, can actually do this. (See *Equality in the 21st Century: A New Approach* (EOC, 1998); *Second Review of the Race Relations Act* (CRE, 1991).)

Stereotyping of people by sex, race and disability is one of the principal causes of discrimination, although clearly there are other factors, such as ignorance and self-interest, which play a part. A study of the impact of gender and the family in the recruitment process was undertaken by M. Curran, *Stereotypes and Selection* (EOC, 1985). While the research was confined to clerical and retail posts, it revealed inherent discrimination in the selection process, from advertisements to selection criteria, based on explicit gender preferences; many employers believing they had a legitimate right to base selection for employment on gender and take into account family commitments. The research also highlighted the fact that discrimination founded in stereotyping is not necessarily against women but can work against men. Nevertheless, it should be recognised that the stereotyping of women has far-reaching consequences, in that it can lead to job segregation, which in turn may prevent women obtaining equality in respect of their terms and conditions of employment due to a lack of comparator.

M. Curran, *Stereotypes and Selection* (1985), pp. 51, 52

Direct sex discrimination in recruitment is not confined to preferences for appointing a woman, or for appointing a man, and the survey also revealed substantial, *prima facie* unlawful, direct sex discrimination in employers' considerations of the family commitments of job applicants. Almost three-quarters of the employers in the survey said that they preferred not to employ the mothers of young children, but did not express any preference about the parental status of male job applicants. If these preferences were reflected in the actual selection decisions made by employers (and all the evidence suggests that they were), they would constitute unlawful direct sex discrimination since mothers were, on grounds of sex, treated less favourably than fathers.

The survey thus revealed a widespread intention, on the part of employers, to adopt selection criteria which would result in *prima facie* unlawful direct discrimination. In addition there was considerable potential for unlawful indirect discrimination in the adoption of arbitrary age requirements and the use of internal and informal methods of recruitment, which might inhibit applications from members of one sex. More generally, employers gave considerable emphasis to subjective factors such as 'personality', manner and appearance, assessments of which are both susceptible to gender stereotyping and sufficiently indeterminate to obscure the operation of more direct discrimination.

Most of the vacancies (86 per cent) yielded applications from women and from men and employers rarely made reference to gender as a factor in shortlisting applicants for interview, or in their selection decisions. However, these decision processes resulted in almost half of the employers interviewing one gender only, and in a clear tendency to select an employee of the 'preferred' or customary gender. The jobs which offered better pay and prospects tended to be offered to men. Family commitments were also rarely mentioned as shortlisting or selection criteria, but only one of the 82 women appointed to the jobs in the survey was known by her employer to have a child under school age.

In general there was a widespread acceptance, among the recruitment decision makers who participated in the survey, that gender and family commitments were attributes of job applicants on which it was legitimate for them to 'take a view'. This acceptance was reinforced by the routine collection of personal information on the application forms used by their own and other organisations. Although some employers clearly took account of the personal circumstances of individual job applicants, most interpreted information about applicants' gender, marital status and parenthood in terms of their generalised 'commonsense' stereotypes of male and female roles in society. The precedents in the Industrial Tribunal cases cited in this report suggest that interview questions and selection decisions based on these stereotypes are likely to constitute unlawful direct sex discrimination.

The picture of the recruitment process which emerges from the survey is one of complex, implicit and often subjective criteria being weighed in the balance by an employer who is often 'spoilt for choice'. In this context it is difficult for an 'outsider', be they researcher, job applicant or Industrial Tribunal, to identify the ultimate rationale for a particular selection decision.

In the recruitment exercises studied in the survey it seems unlikely that *any* of the job applicants would be aware of the preferences regarding gender and family which employers expressed in the survey interviews, since interviewers and recruiters did not feel any need to justify or explain their selection decisions to successful or to unsuccessful applicants. Indeed past tribunal cases suggest that job applicants are unlikely to challenge the actions of employers under the Sex Discrimination Act unless either a clear intention to discriminate has been revealed, or the unsuccessful applicant has some access to information about the person who was selected. Neither of these conditions would apply to the majority of the cases in the survey in which an intention to adopt *prima facie* unlawful discriminatory criteria was revealed. Since the legal remedy for unlawful discrimination in recruitment is dependent on an individual job applicant taking a case to an Industrial Tribunal, the opaque and complex nature of the processes of recruitment and selection thus serves to inhibit any challenge to unlawful direct discrimination. In the case of indirect discrimination these difficulties of enforcement are compounded both by the fact that certain issues, e.g., the discriminatory impact of internal and informal recruitment, have not yet been fully tested in law, and by the imprecise notion of the 'justifiability' of indirectly discriminatory criteria and recruitment practices.

Note

The EOC recognises that one way of eradicating stereotyping is through education. Practical guidance can be found in *Fair and Efficient Selection* (EOC, 1993), which highlights the following assumptions which may result in discrimination in the recruitment of staff.

Equal Opportunities Commission, *Fair and Efficient Selection* (1993), pp. 2–6

There are two basic attitudes and beliefs which can, and do, influence decision and actions at every one of the steps involved in the recruitment and selection process. These merit consideration at the outset.

1   SEX DIFFERENCES IN ABILITIES, PHYSICAL AND TEMPERAMENTAL CHARACTERISTICS

There are many commonly-held beliefs about sex differences in abilities, physical characteristics and temperament. Some of these, such as alleged differences in intelligence, are not true. There are however some abilities, physical and temperamental characteristics, in which there are differences. But usually these are of little or no importance in selection. The differences which do exist are differences on the average and tell us nothing about individuals. The most obvious example is perhaps height. It is true that the average height of men is greater than the average height of women. But the range of heights of women and of men is far greater than the difference between the two averages. The ranges therefore overlap greatly. The fact is that there are a lot of women who are taller than many men. In making a selection decision for any job for which there is a justifiable minimum height, it would therefore be wrong to exclude all women. The only fair and efficient procedure is to assess each candidate, man or woman, as an individual and not to make any generalised assumptions. This particularly applies in respect of physical or mental abilities. It may well be true that one sex is better than the other on average in, say, verbal, mathematical or spatial ability. This may change with time but even now does not, and should not, mean that we exclude one sex entirely from consideration. To do so would amount to a breach of the Sex Discrimination Act.

To achieve fair assessment, selectors should forget all that they have ever believed or been told about sex differences in abilities, etc. and try to make assessments, as objectively as possible, about each person. The main exceptions arise when we select for one of the few jobs which fall within the Sex Discrimination Act's definition of a 'genuine occupational qualification' . . .

A special word is necessary regarding sex differences in temperamental characteristics because this is an area which is richest in generalisations, inaccuracies and myths. Research has revealed some differences, for example that men tend to be more aggressive than women. But this again is a difference between averages and tells us nothing about any individual. As can easily be observed, there are some women who are high up the scale for aggressiveness and some men near the bottom end. So general assumptions about men or women should not cause selectors to prejudge any individual because 'men are like this' or 'women are like that'.

This kind of generalisation (often called 'stereotyping') is not easy to overcome and anyone carrying out selection needs consciously to be aware of the danger and resist it at all times. This effort will not easily succeed because of the widespread, pervasive and continuous expression of uninformed and exaggerated beliefs, in everyday life, in the media and in literature. But the methods suggested below, for systematic selection procedures, should do much to help selectors avoid 'stereotyping'.

2   'MEN'S WORK' AND 'WOMEN'S WORK'

It is common to hear jobs referred to as 'men's work' or 'women's work'. Such distinctions are no more than acceptance of the existing conventions which are based upon nothing more than the customs of a bygone age. Women now do work which would have been regarded as utterly unsuitable for them before the first world war. No-one then would have accepted that women could do many of the jobs they are now doing, such as bus-driving or welding. Nor would they have accepted that men could be nurses and midwives, as they now are.

The convention that only women should use typewriters has no foundation in genuine sex differences in the abilities required. The irrational nature of the convention is shown by the fact that it is acceptable for journalists and authors to type. And it has been accepted for many years that men can operate keyboards (and be highly paid for it) provided they are setting type rather than typing on paper.

One other perspective in this matter comes from comparisons with other countries. In some eastern European countries women have, for many years, done engineering and other work which, with few exceptions, is regarded here as unusual for women. And there is no reason to believe that the physical and psychological characteristics of women in these other countries differ from those of women here.

In general, then, there is little or no rationale behind the idea of 'men's work' and 'women's work'. Whenever recruiting or promoting into any job which has in the past been done only by men or only by women, the selector should stop and question why this has been so and whether there are any rational reasons for it. Further he/she should question whether the existing practice is even lawful under the Sex Discrimination Act. Unless the previous single-sex recruitment proves to be both rational and lawful, it should cease.

There will quite often be difficulties to be overcome. There may, for example, be effects upon the wage structure and differentials, especially where only women have been employed on wages less than those paid to men for work of equal value – a situation which is still common but which should be changed as a result of the amendment to the Equal Pay Act introduced on January 1st 1984.

There may be industrial relations difficulties, but these should not be exaggerated. Most unions now have definite policies on securing equal opportunities for their members. In any case, such difficulties should not, and indeed must not, be allowed to prevent the ending of unfair, inefficient and unlawful practices.

A further difficulty may arise from the attitudes of women themselves. As both recent research and experience have shown, there are situations in which some women are unwilling to undertake jobs previously done only by men. The reasons can be complex. If, however, employers act in ways which are sensitive to the feelings of those concerned, but are nevertheless firm in their policies, the hesitation can be overcome. Usually, one or two individuals will be prepared to 'have a go', demonstrate that the fears were unjustified and so encourage movement towards a fairer and more efficient selection or promotion procedure.

Finally, it should not be assumed that people working part-time will be uninterested in full-time vacancies. Failure to consider part-timers (who are likely to be women) for full-time jobs may give rise to unlawful sex and/or marriage discrimination. Conversely, it should not be assumed that no men will be interested in obtaining part-time work.

. . .

Notes
1. The codes of practice, where they are adopted by employers, are probably the most effective way of promoting equality and eliminating discrimination. The alternatives include closing loopholes in the existing legislation, giving greater powers to the Commissions, increased penalties and such things as

quotas, positive discrimination (see McCrudden, C., 'Rethinking Positive Action' (1986) 15 ILJ 219). Some concession to this may be found in Article 141(4) (ex 119, see Chapter 3) following the amendment of Article 119 by the Treaty of Amsterdam, which recognises that Member States may adopt measures provided for specific advantages in order to make it easier for the under-represented sex to pursue a vocational activity, or to prevent or compensate for disadvantages in professional careers.

2. For a discussion of discrimination based on social prejudices, such as sexuality, dress, criminal records, politics and disability, see Lord Wedderburn, *The Worker and The Law* (Penguin, 1986), pp. 447–57. See also 'Facial Discrimination; Extending Handicap Law to Employment Discrimination on the Basis of Physical Appearance' (1987) 100 HLR 2035.

II European Community Law

European Community law is particularly relevant to sex discrimination and has had significant impact in this field through Directive 76/207 – the Equal Treatment Directive – which can be enforced directly in the UK national courts against the State or an organ of the State but not against a private employer. Unfortunately the EC has not made the same stand on race discrimination, there being nothing in EC law which correlates with Article 141 (ex 119) of the Treaty of Rome and its directives in this area. However, Article 39 (ex 48) of the Treaty provides some protection in relation to a person's right to work in other countries within the Community (see below).

Council Directive No. 76/207 (OJ 1976, L 39/40)

Article 1

1. The purpose of this Directive is to put into effect in the Member States the principle of equal treatment for men and women as regards access to employment, including promotion, and to vocational training and as regards working conditions and, on the conditions referred to in paragraph 2, social security. This principle is hereinafter referred to as 'the principle of equal treatment.'

2. With a view to ensuring the progressive implementation of the principle of equal treatment in matters of social security, the Council, acting on a proposal from the Commission, will adopt provisions defining its substance, its scope and the arrangements for its application.

Article 2

1. For the purposes of the following provisions, the principle of equal treatment shall mean that there shall be no discrimination whatsoever on grounds of sex either directly or indirectly by reference in particular to marital or family status.

2. This Directive shall be without prejudice to the right of Member States to exclude from its field of application those occupational activities and, where appropriate, the training leading thereto, for which, by reason of their nature or the context in which they are carried out, the sex of the worker constitutes a determining factor.

3. This Directive shall be without prejudice to provisions concerning the protection of women, particularly as regards pregnancy and maternity.

4. This Directive shall be without prejudice to measures to promote equal opportunity for men and women, in particular by removing existing inequalities which affect women's opportunities in the areas referred to in Article 1(1).

Article 3

1. Application of the principle of equal treatment means that there shall be no discrimination whatsoever on grounds of sex in the conditions, including selection criteria, for access to all jobs or posts, whatever the sector or branch of activity, and to all levels of the occupational hierarchy.

2. To this end, Member States shall take the measures necessary to ensure that:

(a) any laws, regulations and administrative provisions contrary to the principle of equal treatment shall be abolished;

(b) any provisions contrary to the principle of equal treatment which are included in collective agreements, individual contracts of employment, internal rules of undertakings or in rules governing the independent occupations and professions shall be, or may be declared, null and void or may be amended;

(c) subject eligibility for employment to conditions of registration with employment offices or impede recruitment of individual workers where persons who do not reside in the territory of that State are concerned . . .

Marshall v Southampton and South-West Hampshire Area Health Authority (Teaching)
[1986] IRLR 140
European Court of Justice

The retirement policy of the respondent health authority was that 'the normal retirement age will be the age at which social security pensions become payable', i.e. 60 for women and 65 for men. In certain circumstances retirement at the State pension age could be postponed by mutual agreement. Accordingly, Miss Marshall continued to work after age 60. When she was dismissed at age 62, the sole reason given for her dismissal was that she had passed the normal retirement age applied by the respondents to women. She would not have been dismissed when she was if she had been a man.

Miss Marshall complained to an industrial tribunal that her dismissal amounted to unlawful discrimination contrary to the Sex Discrimination Act and the EEC Equal Treatment Directive. The Tribunal dismissed her complaint under the Sex Discrimination Act on the ground that the case fell within s. 6(4) which permits discrimination on the ground of sex arising from a provision in relation to retirement. Her claim under Community law was upheld. On appeal, however, the EAT held that although Miss Marshall's dismissal violated the principle of equal treatment laid down in EEC Directive 76/207, such violation could not be relied upon in proceedings before a UK court or tribunal ([1983] IRLR 237).

Miss Marshall appealed to the Court of Appeal which applied to the European Court of Justice for a ruling on the following questions:

1. Whether the respondents' dismissal of the appellant after she had passed her 60th birthday pursuant to their retirement age policy and on the

grounds only that she was a woman who had passed the normal retiring age applicable to women, was an act of discrimination prohibited by Directive 76/207.

2. If the answer to (1) above is in the affirmative, whether or not Directive 76/207 can be relied upon by the appellant in the circumstances of the present case in national courts or tribunals, notwithstanding the inconsistency (if any) between the Directive and s. 6(4) of the Sex Discrimination Act 1975.

The ECJ held that the dismissal of a woman solely because she has attained the State pension age which is different for men and women contravenes Article 5(1) of Directive 76/207. This matter did not fall within the exclusion provided by Article 7(1) of Directive 79/7 – the Social Security Directive – which applies only to the determination of pensionable age for the purposes of granting old-age and retirement pensions. Article 5(1) may be relied upon against a State authority as employer in order to avoid the application of any national provision which does not conform with that article.

DECISION: . . . By the first question the Court of Appeal seeks to ascertain whether or not Article 5(1) of Directive no. 76/207 must be interpreted as meaning that a general policy concerning dismissal, followed by a State authority, involving the dismissal of a woman solely because she has attained or passed the qualifying age for a State pension, which age is different under national legislation for men and for women, constitutes discrimination on grounds of sex, contrary to that directive.

The appellant and the Commission consider that the first question must be answered in the affirmative.

According to the appellant, the said age limit falls within the term 'working conditions' within the meaning of Articles 1(1) and 5(1) of Directive no. 76/207. A wide interpretation of that term is, in her opinion, justified in view of the objective of the EEC Treaty to provide for 'the constant improving of the living and working conditions of [the Member States'] peoples' and in view of the wording of the prohibition of discrimination laid down in the above-mentioned articles of Directive no. 76/206 and in Article 7(1) of Regulation no. 1612/68 of the Council of 15.10.68 on freedom of movement of workers within the Community (Official Journal, English Special Edition 1968 (II), p. 475).

The appellant argues furthermore, that the elimination of discrimination on grounds of sex forms part of the *corpus* of fundamental human rights and therefore of the general principles of Community law. In accordance with the case law of the European Court of Human Rights, those fundamental principles must be given a wide interpretation and, conversely, any exception thereto, such as the reservation provided for in Article 1(2) of Directive no. 76/207 with regard to social security, must be interpreted strictly.

In addition, the appellant considers that the exception provided for in Article 7(1) of Directive no. 79/7 with regard to the determination of pensionable age for the purposes of granting old-age and retirement pensions, is not relevant since, unlike Case 19/81 (*Burton* v *British Railways Board* [1982] IRLR 116), this case does not relate to the determination of pensionable age. Moreover, in this case there is no link between the contractual retirement age and the qualifying age for a social security pension.

The Commission emphasises that neither the respondent's employment policy nor the State social security scheme makes retirement compulsory upon a person's reaching pensionable age. On the contrary, the provisions of national legislation take into account the case of continued employment beyond the normal pensionable age. In those circumstances, it would be difficult to justify the dismissal of a woman for reasons based on her sex and age.

The Commission also refers to the fact that the Court has recognised that equality of treatment for men and women constitutes a fundamental principle of Community law.

The respondent maintains, in contrast, that account must be taken, in accordance with the *Burton* case, of the link which it claims exists between the retirement ages imposed by it in the context of its dismissal policy, on the one hand, and the ages at which retirement and old-age pensions become payable under the State social security scheme in the United Kingdom, on the other. The laying down of different ages for the compulsory termination of a contract of employment merely reflects the minimum ages fixed by that scheme, since a male employee is permitted to continue in employment until the age of 65 precisely because he is not protected by the provision of a State pension before that age, whereas a female employee benefits from such protection from the age of 60.

The respondent considers that the provision of a State pension constitutes an aspect of social security and therefore falls within the scope not of Directive no. 76/207 but of Directive no. 79/7, which reserves to the Member States the right to impose different ages for the purpose of determining entitlement to State pensions. Since the situation is therefore the same as that in the *Burton* case, the fixing by the contract of employment of different retirement ages linked to the different minimum pensionable ages for men and women under national legislation does not constitute unlawful discrimination contrary to Community law.

The United Kingdom, which also takes that view, maintains, however, that treatment is capable of being discriminatory even in respect of a period after retirement in so far as the treatment in question arises out of employment or employment continues after the normal contractual retirement age.

The United Kingdom maintains, however, that in the circumstances of this case there is no discrimination in working conditions since the difference of treatment derives from the normal retirement age, which in turn is linked to the different minimum ages at which a State pension is payable.

The Court observes in the first place that the question of interpretation which has been referred to it does not concern access to a statutory or occupational retirement scheme, that is to say the conditions for payment of an old-age or retirement pension, but the fixing of an age limit with regard to the termination of employment pursuant to a general policy concerning dismissal. The question therefore relates to the conditions governing dismissal and falls to be considered under Directive no. 76/207.

Article 5(1) of Directive no. 76/207 provides that application of the principle of equal treatment with regard to working conditions, including the conditions governing dismissal, means that men and women are to be guaranteed the same conditions without discrimination on grounds of sex.

In its judgment in the *Burton* case the Court has already stated that the term 'dismissal' contained in that provision must be given a wide meaning. Consequently, an age limit for the compulsory dismissal of workers pursuant to an employer's general policy concerning retirement falls within the term 'dismissal' construed in that manner, even if the dismissal involves the grant of a retirement pension.

As the Court emphasised in its judgment in the *Burton* case, Article 7 of Directive no. 79/7 expressly provides that the Directive does not prejudice the right of Member

States to exclude from its scope the determination of pensionable age for the purposes of granting old-age and retirement pensions and the possible consequences thereof for other benefits falling within the statutory social security schemes. The Court thus acknowledged that benefits tied to a national scheme which lays down a different minimum pensionable age for men and women may lie outside the ambit of the aforementioned obligation.

However, in view of the fundamental importance of the principle of equality of treatment, which the Court has reaffirmed on numerous occasions, Article 1(2) of Directive no. 76/207, which excludes social security matters from the scope of that Directive, must be interpreted strictly. Consequently, the exception to the prohibition of discrimination on grounds of sex provided for in Article 7(1)(a) of Directive no. 79/7 applies only to the determination of pensionable age for the purposes of granting old-age and retirement pensions and the possible consequences thereof for other benefits.

In that respect it must be emphasised that, whereas the exception contained in Article 7 of Directive no. 79/7 concerns the consequences which pensionable age has for social security benefits, this case is concerned with dismissal within the meaning of Article 5 of Directive no. 76/207.

Consequently, the answer to the first question referred to the Court by the Court of Appeal must be that Article 5(1) of Directive no. 76/207 must be interpreted as meaning that a general policy concerning dismissal involving the dismissal of a woman solely because she has attained the qualifying age for a State pension, which age is different under national legislation for men and for women, constitutes discrimination on grounds of sex, contrary to that Directive.

The second question
Since the first question has been answered in the affirmative, it is necessary to consider whether Article 5(1) of Directive no. 76/207 may be relied upon by an individual before national courts and tribunals.

The appellant and the Commission consider that that question must be answered in the affirmative. They contend in particular, with regard to Articles 2(1) and 5(1) of Directive no. 76/207, that those provisions are sufficiently clear to enable national courts to apply them without legislative intervention by the Member States, at least so far as overt discrimination is concerned.

In support of that view, the appellant points out that directives are capable of conferring rights on individuals which may be relied upon directly before the courts of the Member States; national courts are obliged by virtue of the binding nature of a directive, in conjunction with Article 5 [now 10] of the EEC Treaty, to give effect to the provisions of directives where possible, in particular when construing or applying relevant provisions of national law (judgment of 10.4.84 in Case 14/83, *Von Colson and Kamann* v *Land Nordrhein-Westfalen* [1984] ECR 1891). Where there is any inconsistency between national law and Community law which cannot be removed by means of such a construction, the appellant submits that a national court is obliged to declare that the provision of national law which is inconsistent with the directive is inapplicable.

The Commission is of the opinion that the provisions of Article 5(1) of Directive no. 76/207 are sufficiently clear and unconditional to be relied upon before a national court. They may therefore be set up against s. 6(4) of the Sex Discrimination Act, which, according to the decisions of the Court of Appeal, has been extended to the question of compulsory retirement and has therefore become ineffective to prevent dismissals based upon the difference in retirement ages for men and for women.

The respondent and the United Kingdom propose, conversely, that the second question should be answered in the negative. They admit that a directive may, in certain specific circumstances, have direct effect as against a Member State in so far as the latter may not rely on its failure to perform its obligations under the directive. However, they maintain that a directive can never impose obligations directly on individuals and that it can only have direct effect against a Member State *qua* public authority and not against a Member State *qua* employer. As an employer a State is no different from a private employer. It would not therefore be proper to put persons employed by the State in a better position than those who are employed by a private employer.

With regard to the legal position of the respondent's employees the United Kingdom states that they are in the same position as the employees of a private employer. Although according to United Kingdom constitutional law the health authorities, created by the National Health Service Act 1977, as amended by the Health Services Act 1980 and other legislation, are Crown bodies and their employees are Crown servants, nevertheless the administration of the National Health Service by the health authorities is regarded as being separate from the Government's central administration and its employees are not regarded as civil servants.

Finally, both the respondent and the United Kingdom take the view that the provisions of Directive no. 76/207 are neither unconditional nor sufficiently clear and precise to give rise to direct effect. The Directive provides for a number of possible exceptions, the details of which are to be laid down by the Member States. Furthermore, the wording of Article 5 is quite imprecise and requires the adoption of measures for its implementation.

It is necessary to recall that, according to a long line of decisions of the Court (in particular its judgment of 19.1.82 in Case 8/81, *Becker* v *Finanzamt Münster-Innenstadt* [1982] ECR 53), wherever the provisions of a directive appear, as far as their subject-matter is concerned, to be unconditional and sufficiently precise, those provisions may be relied upon by an individual against the State where that State fails to implement the Directive in national law by the end of the period prescribed or where it fails to implement the Directive correctly.

That view is based on the consideration that it would be incompatible with the binding nature which Article 189 [now 249] confers on the Directive to hold as a matter of principle that the obligation imposed thereby cannot be relied on by those concerned. From that the Court deduced that a Member State which has not adopted the implementing measures required by the Directive within the prescribed period may not plead, as against individuals, its own failure to perform the obligations which the Directive entails.

With regard to the argument that a directive may not be relied upon against an individual, it must be emphasised that according to Article 189 [now 249] of the EEC Treaty the binding nature of a directive, which constitutes the basis for the possibility of relying on the directive before a national court, exists only in relation to 'each Member State to which it is addressed'. It follows that a directive may not of itself impose obligations on an individual and that a provision of a directive may not be relied upon as such against such a person. It must therefore be examined whether, in this case, the respondent must be regarded as having acted as an individual.

In that respect it must be pointed out that where a person involved in legal proceedings is able to rely on a directive as against the State he may do so regardless of the capacity in which the latter is acting, whether employer or public authority. In either case it is necessary to prevent the State from taking advantage of its own failure to comply with Community law.

It is for the national court to apply those considerations to the circumstances of each case; the Court of Appeal has, however, stated in the order for reference that the respondent, Southampton and South-West Hampshire Area Health Authority (Teaching), is a public authority.

The argument submitted by the United Kingdom that the possibility of relying on provisions of the Directive against the respondent *qua* organ of the State would give rise to an arbitrary and unfair distinction between the rights of State employees and those of private employees does not justify any other conclusion. Such a distinction may easily be avoided if the Member State concerned has correctly implemented the Directive in national law.

Finally, with regard to the question whether the provision contained in Article 5(1) of Directive no. 76/207, which implements the principle of equality of treatment set out in Article 2(1) of the Directive, may be considered, as far as its contents are concerned, to be unconditional and sufficiently precise to be relied upon by an individual as against the State, it must be stated that the provision, taken by itself, prohibits any discrimination on grounds of sex with regard to working conditions, including the conditions governing dismissal, in a general manner and in unequivocal terms. The provision is therefore sufficiently precise to be relied on by an individual and to be applied by the national courts.

Coote v *Granada Hospitality Ltd*
[1998] IRLR 656
European Court of Justice

Belinda Coote was employed by Granada from December 1992 to September 1993. She brought a sex discrimination complaint against them, alleging that she had been dismissed because of pregnancy. This complaint was settled.

In July 1994, Ms Coote had difficulties in finding employment and alleged that Granada had failed to provide an employment agency with a reference. She brought proceedings claiming that this was a reaction to her previous complaint and amounted to unlawful victimisation contrary to s. 4 of the Sex Discrimination Act. Section 4(1) provides that it is discrimination if a person is treated less favourably than others because that person has brought proceedings under the Sex Discrimination Act. However, the victimisation is unlawful only in any of the circumstances set out in the Act.

The European Court of Justice held: Article 6 of the EC Equal Treatment Directive, which provides that Member States are to introduce into their national legal systems such measures as are necessary to enable all persons who consider themselves the victims of discrimination 'to pursue their claims by judicial process', requires Member States to ensure judicial protection for workers whose employer, after the employment relationship has ended, refuses to provide references as a reaction to legal proceedings brought to enforce compliance with the principle of equal treatment.

By virtue of Article 6, all persons have the right to obtain an effective remedy in a competent court against measures which they consider interfere with the equal treatment for men and women laid down in the

Directive. It is for the Member States to ensure effective judicial control of compliance with the applicable provisions of Community law and of national legislation intended to give effect to the rights for which the Directive provides.

DECISION: . . . the questions put by the national court must be understood as seeking to ascertain, for the purpose of interpreting national provisions transposing the Directive, whether the Directive requires Member States to introduce into their national legal systems such measures as are necessary to ensure judicial protection for workers whose employer, after the end of the employment relationship, refuses to provide references as a reaction to proceedings brought to enforce compliance with the principle of equal treatment within the meaning of the Directive.

On this point, it should be noted that Article 6 of the Directive requires Member States to introduce into their national legal systems such measures as are necessary to enable all persons who consider themselves the victims of discrimination 'to pursue their claims by judicial process'. It follows from that provision that the Member States must take measures which are sufficiently effective to achieve the aim of the Directive and that they must ensure that the rights thus conferred can be effectively relied upon before the national courts by the persons concerned (see, in particular, *Von Colson and Kamann*, paragraph 18; case 222/84 *Johnston* v *Chief Constable of the Royal Ulster Constabulary* [1986] IRLR 263, paragraph 17; and case *C-271/91 Marshall* v *Southampton and South-West Hampshire Area Health Authority* [1993] IRLR 445, paragraph 22).

The requirement laid down by that article that recourse be available to the courts reflects a general principle of law which underlies the constitutional traditions common to the Member States and which is also enshrined in Article 6 of the European Convention for the Protection of Human Rights and Fundamental Freedoms of 4 November 1950 (see, in particular, *Johnston,* paragraph 18).

By virtue of Article 6 of the Directive, interpreted in the light of the general principle stated above, all persons have the right to obtain an effective remedy in a competent court against measures which they consider to interfere with the equal treatment for men and women laid down in the Directive. It is for the Member States to ensure effective judicial control of compliance with the applicable provisions of Community law and of national legislation intended to give effect to the rights for which the Directive provides (*Johnston,* paragraph 19).

As the Court has also held (case C-271/91. *Marshall,* paragraph 34), Article 6 of the Directive is an essential factor for attaining the fundamental objective of equal treatment for men and women, which, as the Court has repeatedly held (see, inter alia, case *C-13/94 P* v *S and Cornwall County Council* [1996] IRLR 347, paragraph 19), is one of the fundamental human rights whose observance the Court has a duty to ensure.

The principle of effective judicial control laid down in Article 6 of the Directive would be deprived of an essential part of its effectiveness if the protection which it provides did not cover measures which, as in the main proceedings in this case, an employer might take as a reaction to legal proceedings brought by an employee with the aim of enforcing compliance with the principle of equal treatment. Fear of such measures, where no legal remedy is available against them, might deter workers who considered themselves the victims of discrimination from pursuing their claims by judicial process, and would consequently be liable seriously to jeopardise implementation of the aim pursued by the Directive.

In those circumstances, it is not possible to accept the United Kingdom Government's argument that measures taken by an employer against an employee as a reaction to legal proceedings brought to enforce compliance with the principle of equal treatment do not fall within the scope of the Directive if they are taken after the employment relationship has ended.

Notes

1. It is now firmly established that national law should be interpreted in accordance with the Directives. Failure to do so may result in a challenge such as Marshall's. The decision in *Marshall's* case led to the SDA 1986, which made unlawful discrimination in retirement ages for all employees.

2. The issue of whether an employer is an organ or emanation of the State, thereby allowing an action based on Directive 76/207, was raised in *Doughty* v *Rolls Royce plc* [1992] IRLR 126 and *Foster* v *British Gas plc* [1990] IRLR 354. In the former the Court of Appeal held that Rolls Royce was not an 'organ or emanation of the State' as there was a lack of sufficient State control. In the latter, being a reference by the House of Lords, the ECJ attempted to give meaning to the words 'organ or emanation of the State' as follows:

Unconditional and sufficiently precise provisions of a Directive can be relied on against an organisation, whatever its legal form, which is subject to the authority or control of the State or which has been made responsible, pursuant to a measure adopted by the State, for providing a public service under the control of the State and has for that purpose special powers beyond those which result from the normal rules applicable between individuals.

The House of Lords, in applying this principle, concluded that British Gas was an organ or emanation of the State (see *Foster* v *British Gas* [1991] IRLR 268).

3. The SDA 1986 also puts into effect the decision in *Commission of the European Communities* v *United Kingdom* [1984] ICR 192, in which the ECJ concluded that the SDA 1975 did not comply with Directive 76/207 as it specifically exempted small businesses and partnerships from the provisions of the Act nor did it have within its remit non-contractual collective agreements and practices (ss.1 and 6).

4. The relationship between EC law and domestic law has been reaffirmed in *Blaik* v *The Post Office* [1994] IRLR 280 in which the EAT held that 'if there is sufficient remedy given by domestic law, it is unnecessary and impermissible to explore the same complaint under the equivalent provisions in a Directive. It is only if there is a disparity between the two that it becomes necessary to consider whether the provisions in EC law are directly enforceable by the complainant . . .'.

5. Rather controversially the ECJ ruled in *Kalanke* v *Freie Hansestadt Bremen* [1995] IRLR 660 that preferential treatment for women who are equally qualified with men is contrary to Directive 76/207, even where women are under-represented in the grade concerned.

As a result the EC has issued a proposed amendment to Article 2(4) which makes it clear that in certain circumstances, preferential treatment of a particular sex at the point of selection is not contrary to EC law. Such an amendment would allow positive action measures to promote equal opportunities for women and men, in particular by removing existing factors of inequality which affect women's opportunities in the employment area. While positive action would encourage the appointment of women or men to posts where they are currently under-represented, such preferential treatment does not preclude assessment of the particular circumstances of an individual case (see 68 EOR p. 39). Such positive action would still be contrary to the SDA 1975 (see *Jepson & Dyas-Elliot* v *The Labour Party* [1996] IRLR 116).

6.   The Burden of Proof Directive 97/307 (below) will have the effect of shifting the burden of proof from the complainant once the facts establishing discrimination have been determined. If the employer then fails to prove that there is no discrimination, discrimination must be inferred.

Article 4

1.   Member States shall take such measures as are necessary . . . to ensure that, when persons who consider themselves wronged because the principle of equal treatment has not been applied to them establish . . . facts from which it may be presumed that there has been direct of indirect discrimination, it shall be for the respondent to prove that there has been no breach of the principle of equal treatment.

2.   This Directive shall not prevent Member States from introducing rules of evidence which are more favourable to plaintiffs.

7.   The decision in *Coote* makes it clear that the remedies for victimisation must be effective and therefore appropriate to the nature of the complaint.

8.   See Usher, J., 'European Community Equality Law: Legal Instruments and Judicial Remedies', in C. McCrudden (ed.), *Women Employment and European Equality Law* (Eclipse, 1987), at pp. 171–4, for a discussion of the direct effect of directives.

9.   For further consideration of the effect of *Marshall* on cases such as *Burton* v *British Railways Board* [1982] QB 1080 and *Roberts* v *Tate and Lyle Industries Ltd* [1986] ICR 371, see Townshend-Smith, R., *Sex Discrimination in Employment: Law, Practice and Policy* (Sweet & Maxwell, 1989), pp. 194–5.

Treaty Establishing the European Economic Community

Article 39 (ex 48)

1.   Freedom of movement for workers shall be secured within the Community by the end of the transitional period at the latest.

2.   Such freedom of movement shall entail the abolition of any discrimination based on nationality between workers of the Member States as regards employment, emuneration and other conditions of work and employment.

3.   It shall entail the right, subject to limitations justified on grounds of public policy, public security or public health:

   (a)   to accept offers of employment actually made;

   (b)   to move freely within the territory of Member States for this purpose;

   (c)   to stay in a Member State for the purpose of employment in accordance with the provisions governing the employment of nationals of that State laid down by law, regulation or administrative action;

(d)   to remain in the territory of a Member State after having been employed in that State, subject to conditions which shall be embodied in implementing regulations to be drawn up by the Commission.

4.   The provisions of this Article shall not apply to employment in the public service.

Groener v *Minister for Education*
[1990] 1 CMLR 401
European Court of Justice

Mrs Groener, the applicant in the main proceedings, who was a Dutch national, had, since September 1982, been working as a part-time teacher of art at the College of Marketing and Design, Dublin. That establishment came under the authority of the City of Dublin Vocational and Educational Committee, which is a public body responsible for the administration of vocational education subsidised by the State in the Dublin area. In July 1984, Mrs Groener entered a competition with a view to obtaining a permanent teaching post. She was successful in the competition but failed the special examination in Irish. Circular Letter no. 28/79 of the Irish Minister of Education requires candidates for permanent posts as assistant lecturer, lecturer or senior lecturer in the City of Dublin or any post subject to any other Vocational Educational Committee to demonstrate their knowledge of the Irish language. Such proof may be supplied either by production of a certificate ('*An Ceard Teastas Gaeilge*') or by passing a special examination in the Irish language. It was not disputed that the post in question fell within the scope of that circular letter.

Mrs Groener challenged the refusal to appoint her before the Irish courts. She argued that Circular Letter 28/79 was incompatible with Article 48 (now 39) EEC and Article 3 of Council Regulation 1612/68 on freedom of movement for workers within the Community (hereinafter referred to as 'the Regulation'), which prohibit discrimination against Community nationals.

On referral to the ECJ, it was held that a permanent full-time post of lecturer in public vocational education institutions is a post of such a nature as to justify the requirement of linguistic knowledge, within the meaning of the last subparagraph of Article 3(1) of Council Regulation 1612/68, provided that the linguistic requirement in question is imposed as part of a policy for the promotion of the national language which is, at the same time, the first official language and provided that that requirement is applied in a proportionate and non-discriminatory manner.

DECISION: . . . [10]   Considering that the application raised certain questions of interpretation of those provisions of Community law, the High Court, Dublin, referred the following question to the Court for a preliminary ruling:

1.   Where provisions laid down by law, regulation or administrative action make employment in a particular post in a member-State conditional upon the Applicant having a competent knowledge of one of the two official languages of that

member-State, being a language which nationals of other member-States would not normally know but would have to learn for the sole purpose of complying with the condition, should Article 3 of Council Regulation 1612/68 be construed as applying to such provisions on the ground that their exclusive or principal effect is to keep nationals of other member-States away from the employment offered?

2.   In considering the meaning of the phrase 'the nature of the post to be filled' in Article 3 of Regulation 1612/68, is regard to be had to a policy of the Irish State that persons holding the post should have a competent knowledge of the Irish language, where such knowledge is not required to discharge the duties attached to the post?

3.(1)   Is the term 'public policy' in Article 48(3) [now 39(3)] of the EEC Treaty to be construed as applying to the policy of the Irish State to support and foster the position of the Irish language as the first official language?

(2)   If it is, is the requirement that persons seeking appointment to posts as lecturer in vocational education institutions in Ireland, who do not possess '*An Ceard-Teastas Gaeilge*', shall undergo a special examination in Irish with the view to satisfying the Department of Education of their competency in Irish, a limitation justified on the grounds of such policy?

. . .

[12]   It should be borne in mind first of all that the second indent of Article 3(1) of Regulation 1612/68 provides that national provisions or administrative practices of a member-State are not to 'apply where, though applicable irrespective of nationality, their exclusive or principal aim or effect is to keep nationals of other member-States away from the employment offered'. The last subparagraph of Article 3(1) provides that that provision is not to 'apply to conditions relating to linguistic knowledge required by reason of the nature of the post to be filled'.

[13]   It is apparent from the documents before the Court that the obligation to prove a knowledge of the Irish language imposed by the national provisions in question applies without distinction to Irish and other Community nationals, except as regards the exemptions which may be allowed for nationals of other member-States.

[14]   Since the second indent of Article 3(1) is not applicable where linguistic requirements are justified by the nature of the post, it is appropriate to consider first the second question submitted by the national court, which is essentially whether the nature of a permanent full-time post of lecturer in art in public vocational education institutions is such as to justify the requirement of a knowledge of the Irish language.

[15]   According to the documents before the Court, the teaching of art, like that of most other subjects taught in public vocational education schools, is conducted essentially or indeed exclusively in the English language. It follows that, as indicated by the terms of the second question submitted, knowledge of the Irish language is not required for the performance of the duties which teaching of the kind at issue specifically entails.

[16]   However, that finding is not in itself sufficient to enable the national court to decide whether the linguistic requirement in question is justified 'by reason of the nature of the post to be filled', within the meaning of the last subparagraph of Article 3(1) of Regulation 1612/68.

[17]   To apprehend the full scope of the second question, regard must be had to the special linguistic situation in Ireland, as it appears from the documents before the Court. By virtue of Article 8 of the Bunreacht na hEireann (Irish Constitution)

1.   The Irish language as the national language is the first official language.

2. The English language is recognised as a second official language.

3. Provision may, however, be made by law for the exclusive use of either of the said languages for any one or more official purposes, either throughout the State or in any part thereof.

[18] As is apparent from the documents before the Court, although Irish is not spoken by the whole Irish population, the policy followed by Irish Governments for many years has been designed not only to maintain but also to promote the use of Irish as a means of expressing national identity and culture. It is for that reason that Irish courses are compulsory for children receiving primary education and optional for those receiving secondary education. The obligation imposed on lecturers in public vocational education schools to have a certain knowledge of the Irish language is one of the measures adopted by the Irish Government in furtherance of that policy.

[19] The EEC Treaty does not prohibit the adoption of a policy for the protection and promotion of a language of a member-State which is both the national language and the first official language. However, the implementation of such a policy must not encroach upon a fundamental freedom such as that of the free movement of workers. Therefore, the requirements deriving from measures intended to implement such a policy must not in any circumstances be disproportionate in relation to the aim pursued and the manner in which they are applied must not bring about discrimination against nationals of other member-States.

[20] The importance of education for the implementation of such a policy must be recognised. Teachers have an essential rôle to play, not only through the teaching which they provide but also by their participation in the daily life of the school and the privileged relationship which they have with their pupils. In those circumstances, it is not unreasonable to require them to have some knowledge of the first national language.

[21] It follows that the requirement imposed on teachers to have an adequate knowledge of such a language must, provided that the level of knowledge required is not disproportionate in relation to the objective pursued, be regarded as a condition corresponding to the knowledge required by reason of the nature of the post to be filled within the meaning of the last subparagraph of Article 3(1) of Regulation 1612/68.

[22] It must also be pointed out that where the national provisions provide for the possibility of exemption from that linguistic requirement where no other fully qualified candidate has applied for the post to be filled, Community law requires that power to grant exemptions to be exercised by the Minister in a non-discriminatory manner.

[23] Moreover, the principle of non-discrimination precludes the imposition of any requirement that the linguistic knowledge in question must have been acquired within the national territory. It also implies that the nationals of other member-States should have an opportunity to re-take the oral examination, in the event of their having previously failed it, when they again apply for a post of assistant lecturer of lecturer.

[26] Accordingly, the reply to the second question must be that a permanent full-time post of lecturer in public vocational education institutions is a post of such a nature as to justify the requirement of linguistic knowledge, within the meaning of the last subparagraph of Article 3(1) of Council Regulation 1612/68, provided that the linguistic requirement in question is imposed as part of a policy for the promotion of the national language which is, at the same time, the first official language and provided that that requirement is applied in a proportionate and non-discriminatory manner.

Questions
1.   Can the decision in *Burton* v *British Railways Board* [1982] QB 1080 still be justified?
2.   Does the language justification defeat the purpose of Article 39 (ex 48) of the Treaty of Rome?
3.   How far are EC resolutions and recommendations enforceable within a Member State; what is the effect on the resolution on sexual harassment? See *Grimaldi* v *Fonds des Maladies Professionelles* [1990] IRLR 400.
4.   Is there a remedy for post-employment victimisation? See *Coote* v *Granada Hospitality Ltd* [1998] IRLR 656 (above).

III   Sex and Race Discrimination

The SDA 1975 and the RRA 1976 make discrimination on the grounds of sex, marital status and race unlawful. Both statutes recognise two main types of discrimination – direct and indirect, although these words are not actually used. Additionally there is victimisation and, under the RRA 1976, segregation. The SDA 1975 offers protection from discrimination to men and women alike; while the RRA 1976 protects members of a racial group against discrimination on racial grounds, the latter terms being subject to interpretation. Although the SDA 1975 offers protection against discrimination on the grounds of marital status, i.e. because a person is married, it does not offer the same protection to single people.

Specific protection is now afforded to part-time employees by virtue of s. 19 of the Employment Relations Act 1999. Section 19 provides that the Secretary of State shall make regulations for ensuring that part-time employees are treated no less favourably than persons in full-time employment. In addition, s. 20 provides that the Secretary of State may issue a Code of Practice containing guidance for the purpose of, *inter alia*, eliminating discrimination against part-time workers in the field of employment as well as facilitating the development of opportunities for part-time work. The Government has launched a public consultation on the proposed regulations. While we await them, it is clear that there is likely to be some protection from direct discrimination, and one would hope that it would extend to indirect discrimination.

The SDA 1975 and the EPA 1970 are to be regarded as a single code and are mutually exclusive in their remit; the EPA 1970 covering pay and terms regulated by the contract of employment and the SDA 1975 covering all other matters.

As the wording of the SDA 1975 and RRA 1976 are virtually the same the precedents are relevant to both areas of discrimination.

A: Direct Discrimination

Sex Discrimination Act 1975

1.   Sex discrimination against women
(1)   A person discriminates against a woman in any circumstances relevant for the purposes of any provision of this Act if—

(a) on the ground of her sex he treats her less favourably than he treats or would treat a man . . .

Race Relations Act 1976

1. Racial discrimination
(1) A person discriminates against another in any circumstances relevant for the purposes of any provision of this Act if—
(a) on racial grounds he treats that other less favourably than he treats or would treat other persons . . .

(i) 'Racial Grounds'
While the meanings of 'sex' and 'marital status' do not pose any problems of interpretation, the meaning of 'racial grounds' as defined by RRA 1976, s. 3(1) does.

Race Relations Act 1976

3. Meaning of 'racial grounds', 'racial group' etc.
(1) In this Act, unless the context otherwise requires—
'racial grounds' means any of the following grounds, namely colour, race, nationality or ethnic or national origins;
'racial group' means a group of persons defined by reference to colour, race, nationality or ethnic or national origins, and references to a person's racial group refer to any racial group into which he falls.

Mandla v Dowell Lee
[1983] IRLR 209
House of Lords

The plaintiffs, father and son, were Sikhs. They alleged that the defendant school and its headmaster had committed an act of unlawful discrimination contrary to the RRA 1976 by refusing to offer the son a place in the school unless he removed his turban and cut his hair in conformity with the school rules so as to be able to wear the school uniform.

It was held that Sikhs were a racial group within the meaning of RRA 1976, s. 3(1), as such a group can be defined by reference to its ethnic origins if it constitutes a separate and distinct community associated with common racial origin.

LORD FRASER OF TULLYBELTON: It is not suggested that Sikhs are a group defined by reference to colour, race, nationality or *national* origins. In none of these respects are they distinguishable from many other groups, especially those living, like most Sikhs, in the Punjab. The argument turns entirely upon whether they are a group defined by *'ethnic* origins'. It is therefore necessary to ascertain the sense in which the word 'ethnic' is used in the Act of 1976. We were referred to various dictionary definitions. The Oxford English Dictionary (1897 edition) gives two meanings of 'ethnic'. The first is 'pertaining to nations not Christian or Jewish; gentile, heathen, pagan'. That clearly cannot be its meaning in the 1976 Act, because it is inconceivable that Parliament would have legislated against racial discrimination intending that the protection should not apply either to Christians or (above all) to Jews. Neither party contended that that was the relevant meaning for the present purpose. The second meaning given in the Oxford English Dictionary (1897 edition) was 'pertaining to race; peculiar to a race or nation; ethnological'. A slighter shorter form of that meaning (omitting 'peculiar to a race or nation') was given by the Concise Oxford Dictionary in 1934 and was expressly accepted by Lord Denning MR as the correct meaning for the present purpose. Oliver and Kerr LJJ also accepted that meaning as being substantially correct, and Oliver LJ at [1983] IRLR 17 said that the word 'ethnic' in its popular meaning involved essentially a racial concept – the concept of something with which the members of the group are born; some fixed or inherited characteristic. The respondent, who appeared on his own behalf, submitted that that was the relevant meaning of 'ethnic' in the 1976 Act, and that it did not apply to Sikhs because they were essentially a religious group, and they shared their racial character-istics with other religious groups, including Hindus and Muslims, living in the Punjab.

My Lords, I recognise that 'ethnic' conveys a flavour of race but it cannot, in my opinion, have been used in the 1976 Act in a strictly racial or biological sense. For one thing, it would be absurd to suppose that Parliament can have intended that membership of a particular racial group should depend upon scientific proof that a person possessed the relevant distinctive biological characteristics (assuming that such characteristics exist). The practical difficulties of such proof would be prohibitive, and it is clear that Parliament must have used the word in some more popular sense. For another thing, the briefest glance at the evidence in this case is enough to show that, within the human race, there are very few, if any, distinctions which are scientifically recognised as racial. I respectfully agree with the view of Lord Simon of Glaisdale in *Ealing LBC* v *Race Relations Board* [1972] AC 342, 362, referring to the long title of the Race Relations Act 1968 (which was in terms identical with part of the long title of the 1976 Act) when he said:

Moreover 'racial' is not a term of art, either legal or, I surmise, scientific. I apprehend that anthropologists would dispute how far the word 'race' is biologically at all relevant to the species amusingly called homo sapiens.

A few lines lower down, after quoting part of s. 1(1) of the Act, the noble and learned Lord said this:

This is rubbery and elusive language – understandably when the draftsman is dealing with so unprecise a concept as 'race' in its popular sense and endeavouring to leave no loophole for evasion.

I turn, therefore, to the third and wider meaning which is given in the 1972 Supplement to the Oxford English Dictionary. It is as follows: 'pertaining to or having common racial, cultural, religious, or linguistic characteristics, esp. designating a racial or other group within a larger system'. Mr Irvine, for the appellant, while not accepting the third (1972) meaning as directly applicable for the present purpose, relied on it to this extent, that it introduces a reference to cultural and other characteristics, and is not limited to racial characteristics. The 1972 meaning is, in my opinion, too loose and vague to be accepted as it stands. It is capable of being read as implying that any one of the adjectives, 'racial, cultural, religious *or* linguistic' would be enough to constitute an ethnic group. That cannot be the sense in which 'ethnic' is used in the 1976 Act, as the Act is not concerned at all with discrimination on religious grounds. Similarly, it cannot have been used to mean simply any 'racial *or other* group'. If that were the meaning of 'ethnic', it would add nothing to the word group, and would lead to a result which would be unacceptably wide. But in seeking for the true meaning of 'ethnic' in the statute, we are not tied to the precise definition in any dictionary. The value of the 1972 definition is, in my view, that it shows that ethnic has come to be commonly used in a sense appreciably wider than the strictly racial or biological. That appears to me to be consistent with the ordinary experience of those who read newspapers at the present day. In my opinion, the word 'ethnic' still retains a racial flavour but it is used nowadays in an extended sense to include other characteristics which may be commonly thought of as being associated with common racial origin.

For a group to constitute an ethnic group in the sense of the 1976 Act, it must, in my opinion, regard itself, and be regarded by others, as a distinct community by virtue of certain characteristics. Some of these characteristics are essential; others are not essential but one or more of them will commonly be found and will help to distinguish the group from the surrounding community. The conditions which appear to me to be essential are these: — (1) a long shared history, of which the group is conscious as distinguishing it from other groups, and the memory of which it keeps alive; (2) a cultural tradition of its own, including family and social customs and manners, often but not necessarily associated with religious observance. In addition to those two essential characteristics the following characteristics are, in my opinion, relevant; (3) either a common geographical origin, or descent from a small number of common ancestors; (4) a common language, not necessarily peculiar to the group; (5) a common literature peculiar to the group; (6) a common religion different from that of neighbouring groups or from the general community surrounding it; (7) being a minority or being an oppressed or a dominant group within a larger community, for example a conquered people (say, the inhabitants of England shortly after the Norman conquest) and their conquerors might both be ethnic groups.

A group defined by reference to enough of these characteristics would be capable of including converts, for example, persons who marry into the group, and of excluding apostates. Provided a person who joins the group feels himself or herself to be a member of it, and is accepted by other members, then he is, for the purposes, of the Act, a member. That appears to be consistent with the words at the end of subsection (1) of s. 3:

References to a person's racial group refer to any group into which he falls.

In my opinion, it is possible for a person to fall into a particular racial group either by birth or by adherence, and it makes no difference, so far as the 1976 Act is concerned, by which route he finds his way into the group. This view does not involve creating any inconsistency between direct discrimination under para. (a) and indirect discrimination under para. (b). A person may treat another relatively unfavourably 'on racial grounds' because he regards that other as being of a particular race, or belonging to a particular racial group, even if his belief is, from a scientific point of view, completely erroneous.

Notes

1. The criteria laid down in *Mandla's* case have been used successfully in *Commission for Racial Equality* v *Dutton* [1989] IRLR 8, to establish that gypsies are an ethnic group. However, in *Dawkins* v *Crown Suppliers* [1993] IRLR 284, the Court of Appeal concluded that Rastafarians did not fulfil the

criteria because there was no group history, descent or language; they were in effect a religious sect and therefore outside the scope of the Act.

Muslims are not protected by the direct discrimination provisions in the RRA 1976, s. 1(1)(a) but may be able to show indirect discrimination (see p. 273) on the basis of ethnic group (see *Malik v Bertram Personnel Group* (1990) No: 4343/90).

2.   Jews have posed something of a problem for the courts because religious discrimination is outside the scope of the RRA 1976. It has been concluded that Jews are a racial group as well as a religious group (see *Seide v Gillette Industries Ltd* [1980] IRLR 427 and *Simon v Brimham Associates* [1987] IRLR 307). It would appear that whether the act of discrimination falls within the statute is dependent upon the reasons for the discrimination.

3.   The meaning of 'national origins' was considered in *Tejani v The Superintendent Registrar for the District of Peterborough* [1986] IRLR 502, CA, which concluded that 'national' must be equated with race not 'citizenship'; but see *Ealing London Borough Council v Race Relations Board* [1972] AC 342, where it was concluded that unless the context otherwise requires, 'nationality' includes 'citizenship'.

'National origins' was further defined in *Northern Joint Police Board v Power* [1997] IRLR 610 as having identifiable elements, both historically and geographically, which, at least at some point in time, reveal the existence of a nation. It was concluded that as England and Scotland were once separate nations, the complainant could base his claim that he was discriminated against because he was English on national origins.

4.   Discrimination on grounds of marital status is also covered by the SDA 1975. In *Hayle and Clunie v Wiltshire Healthcare NHS Trust* (1999) Case No. 140 1250/98, a requirement to work rotating shifts was found indirectly to discriminate against married people with childcare responsibilities.

5.   The Human Rights Act 1998 will, when it comes into force in 2001, provide some protection from discrimination on the grounds of *inter alia* 'religion, politics or other opinion, national or social origin, association with national minority, property, birth and other status'. Discrimination is prohibited under the Human Rights Act 1998 only insofar as it relates to other articles of the Human Rights Convention, such as freedom of association, privacy etc. All primary legislation must be read subject to the European Convention on Human Rights and such legislation must be interpreted in the light of Human Rights decisions of the European Convention on Human Rights. An individual may challenge existing legislation on the basis of incompatibility; such a challenge will be heard by the High Court. The Secretary of State has the power to amend legislation deemed to be incompatible by an Order in Council. For a detailed analysis of the application of the 1998 Act to employment law, see Keith Ewing, 'The Human Rights Act and Labour Law' (1998) 27 ILJ, No. 4, pp. 275–92.

Questions
1.   Must the alleged discriminator know of the ethnic origins of the complainant to be guilty of discrimination?

2.   Can language alone establish ethnic origin? See *Gwynedd County Council* v *Jones* [1986] ICR 833.

3.   Would a black citizen of the USA be protected by the RRA 1976?

(ii)   What is Direct Discrimination?

This type of discrimination involves treating someone less favourably on racial grounds or because of their sex. It covers acts of overt discrimination. Comparison can be made with the hypothetical man or person. As discrimination has become more covert and subtle, direct discrimination has proved to be difficult to establish. However, recent developments in the case law have improved the position for the complainant.

Although the following case is not an employment case it lays down the test for establishing direct discrimination.

R v Birmingham City Council, ex parte Equal Opportunities Commission
[1989] IRLR 173
House of Lords

Birmingham City Council makes provision for some 600 children to enter voluntary-aided grammar schools at age 11 each year. As a result of the selection policies of the schools, 390 places are allocated for boys and 210 for girls.

The EOC brought a suit seeking a declaration that the council was in breach of s. 23(1) of the Sex Discrimination Act. This provides that: 'It is unlawful for a local education authority, in carrying out such of its functions under the Education Acts 1944 to 1981 as do not fall under section 22, to do any act which constitutes sex discrimination.'

On behalf of the EOC, it was argued that in providing selective secondary education, the council was carrying out a function under s. 8(1) of the Education Act 1944; that s. 23(1) of the SDA obliged the council not to discriminate on grounds of sex in carrying out that function; and that the council was discriminating against girls in the provision of grammar school education by treating girls less favourably on the ground of their sex.

It was held that girls had been treated less favourably 'on the ground of their sex' by the council's provision of fewer places in selective schools for girls, notwithstanding the fact that there was no intention or motive on the part of the council to discriminate. Such an intention is not a necessary condition of liability.

LORD GOFF OF CHIEVELEY: The first argument advanced by the council before your Lordships' House was that there had not been, in the present case, less favourable treatment of the girls on grounds of sex. Here two points were taken. It was submitted (1) that it could not be established that there was less favourable treatment of the girls by reason of their having been denied the same opportunities as the boys for selective education unless it was shown that selective education was better than non-selective education, and that no evidence to that effect was called before McCullough J; and (2) that, if that burden had been discharged, it still had to be shown that there was less favourable treatment on grounds of sex, and that involved establishing an intention or motive on the part of the council to discriminate against the girls. In my opinion, neither of these submissions is well founded.

As to the first it is not, in my opinion, necessary for the commission to show that selective education is 'better' than non-selective education. It is enough that, by denying the girls the same opportunity as the boys, the council is depriving them of a choice which (as the facts show) is valued by them, or at least by their parents, and which (even though others may take a different view) is a choice obviously valued, on reasonable grounds, by many others. This conclusion has been reached by all the judges involved in the present case; and it is consistent with previous authority (see, in particular, *Gill v El Vino Co. Ltd* [1983] IRLR 206 and *R v Secretary of State for Education and Science ex parte Keating* (1985) 84 LGR 469). I have no doubt that it is right. As to the second point, it is, in my opinion, contrary to the terms of the statute. There is discrimination under the statute if there is less favourable treatment on the ground of sex, in other words if the relevant girl or girls would have received the same treatment as the boys but for their sex. The intention or motive of the defendant to discriminate, though it may be relevant so far as remedies are concerned (see s. 66(3) of the Act of 1975), is not a necessary condition to liability; it is perfectly possible to envisage cases where the defendant had no such motive, and yet did in fact discriminate on the ground of sex. Indeed, as Mr Lester pointed out in the course of his argument, if the council's submission were correct it would be a good defence for an employer to show that he discriminated against women not because he intended to do so but, for example, because of customer preference, or to save money, or even to avoid controversy. In the present case, whatever may have been the intention or motive of the council, nevertheless it is because of their sex that the girls in question receive less favourable treatment than the boys, and so are the subject of discrimination under the Act of 1975. This is well established in a long line of authority: see, in particular, *Jenkins v Kingsgate (Clothing Productions) Ltd (No. 2)* [1981] IRLR 388, pp. 393, 394 per Browne-Wilkinson J and *ex parte Keating* per Taylor J at p. 475; see also *Ministry of Defence v Jeremiah* [1979] IRLR 436 per Lord Denning MR. I can see no reason to depart from this established view.

Noone v North West Thames Regional Health Authority
[1988] IRLR 195
Court of Appeal

Dr Noone was born and obtained her initial qualifications in Sri Lanka. She applied for a vacancy as a consultant microbiologist with the respondents. She was one of three candidates interviewed by the Advisory Appointments Committee, whose function is to select a candidate on the basis of 'suitability'. The qualities considered by the committee were training, qualifications, experience and personality. Despite superior qualifications, experience and publications than the successful candidate, Dr Noone was not appointed. She complained that she had been discriminated against on grounds of her race.

On the facts and having regard to the appellant's superior qualifications, experience and publications, it was held there was sufficient material to infer discrimination on racial grounds.

MAY LJ: . . . The first step is to decide whether or not there has been an act of discrimination at all; the next is to decide whether or not there was a difference in race; then one must consider whether there is any positive evidence which supports an allegation of discrimination on racial grounds. The Appeal Tribunal correctly commented that this is notoriously difficult to find. They referred to *Khanna* v *Ministry of Defence* [1981] IRLR 331, holding that that case was authority for the proposition that, where the primary facts indicate a discrimination and a difference of race, then the employer is called upon to give an explanation. If this is inadequate or, still more, is patently unsatisfactory or untrue, then it is open to the Tribunal to draw the inference that the discrimination was on racial grounds. *Khanna's* case was referred to in the course of the argument before us, although not ultimately relied on by counsel for the appellant. Thus it is unnecessary for me to say more about the decision than that, with respect, I do not find it altogether satisfactory. See *Morris* v *London Iron and Steel Co. Ltd* [1987] IRLR 182. In these cases of alleged racial discrimination it is always for the complainant to make out his or her case. It is not often that there is direct evidence of racial discrimination, and these complaints more often than not have to be dealt with on the basis of what are the proper inferences to be drawn from the primary facts. For myself I would have thought that it was almost common sense that, if there is a finding of discrimination and of difference of race and then an inadequate or unsatisfactory explanation by the employer for the discrimination, usually the legitimate inference will be that the discrimination was on racial grounds.

. . . As I have said earlier in this judgment, these racial discrimination claims are never easy, and so much depends on the inferences which the industrial tribunal think it right to draw from the evidence and material put before it. If there is no evidence or material from which an Industrial Tribunal can draw the inference of racial discrimination then, of course, they should not do so. On the other hand, one must not forget that it is the industrial tribunal who see and hear the persons actually involved. Perhaps more than in most cases the assessment by the industrial tribunal of the thinking of the person or persons against whom the allegation of racial discrimination is made is most important. As is well known, appeals lie from an industrial tribunal to the Employment Appeal Tribunal only on a point of law, and it is only when the latter is satisfied that there was no material upon which the former could reach the conclusion that they did that the Appeal Tribunal should entertain the appeal. As I have already indicated, I do not find the Employment Appeal Tribunal's reasoning on this aspect of the case convincing. If in the circumstances of the instant case the discrimination is held to have been based on a personal bias or personal prejudice, it seems to me to be only a very small step to go on and conclude that the discrimination was racial.

In my opinion there was material upon which the industrial tribunal was entitled to reach the conclusion that there had been racial discrimination in this case. In the first place, although I appreciate that the argument is potentially circular, there was the fact that of the three short-listed candidates the appellant was Sri Lankan and the other two were English. Secondly, it is, I think, remarkable that despite the appellant's superior qualifications, experience and publications, she was placed third by all the members of the AAC; this even by Dr McSwiggan, notwithstanding the view that he took of the appellant's qualifications and abilities.

Next I cannot think that this industrial tribunal erred in the description that it gave in paragraph 20 of its reasons of how the health authority's case before it vacillated. There was a legally qualified chairman, and I am by no means satisfied from a careful study of the notes of evidence that the comments in paragraph 20 were unjustified.

Then the industrial tribunal had before it the evidence of the appellant's husband, about which they directed themselves very carefully that he might well be partial. However, he himself was a consultant microbiologist, and he had sat on a number of similar committees to the AAC in the instant case. He spoke of his wife's qualifications and experience, but he also went on in the course of his evidence to say: 'There are often strong vested interests in the appointments. I am giving evidence because I feel generally about the discrimination that takes place in medical appointments', and in re-examination he said: 'I think Dr Kirk was chosen because doctors choose to appoint people like themselves – their values, their culture, one you tend to go for – tend to overlook objective factors – you have to discipline yourself hard not to – it doesn't come naturally.'

Finally, the industrial tribunal had Drs Wilson and Webster giving evidence before them. They will have been able to assess what in truth their approach to this particular selection had been. There is no doubt that Dr Webster was looking for a candidate who would 'fit in' with the existing establishment, and I think that the industrial tribunal was entitled to conclude that she felt that the appellant would not fit in because of her Sri Lankan background. All this, having regard to the appellant's superior qualifications, experience and publications, was in my opinion at least sufficient material upon which the industrial tribunal could conclude that there had been racial discrimination in this case. Accordingly, I would allow this appeal and reinstate the finding of the industrial tribunal.

BALCOMBE LJ: The evidential difficulty of a person who alleges, and therefore has to prove, racial discrimination has been recognised by the courts. In *Khanna v Ministry of Defence* [1981] IRLR 331, an Employment Appeal Tribunal, presided over by Browne-Wilkinson J (as he then was), said, at p. 333, para. 16:

> The right course in this case was for the industrial tribunal to take into account the fact that direct evidence of discrimination is seldom going to be available and that, accordingly, in these cases the affirmative evidence of discrimination will normally consist of inferences to be drawn from the primary facts. If the primary facts indicate that there has been discrimination of some kind, the employer is called on to give an explanation and, failing clear and specific explanation being given by the employer to the satisfaction of the industrial tribunal, an inference of unlawful discrimination from the primary facts will mean the complaint succeeds.

A fuller exposition of the same problem was given by another Employment Appeal Tribunal, under the same President, in *Chattopadhyay v Headmaster of Holloway School* [1982] IRLR 487 at p. 490, para. 18.

> As has been pointed out many times, a person complaining that he has been unlawfully discriminated against faces great difficulties. There is normally not available to him any evidence of overtly racial discriminatory words or actions used by the respondent. All that the applicant can do is to point to certain facts which, if unexplained, are consistent with his having been treated less favourably than others on racial grounds. In the majority of cases it is only the respondents and their witnesses who are able to say whether in fact the allegedly discriminatory act was motivated by racial discrimination or by other, perfectly innocent, motivations. It is for this reason that the law has been established that if the applicant shows that he has been treated less favourably than others in circumstances which are consistent with that treatment being based on racial grounds, the Industrial Tribunal should draw an inference that such treatment was on racial grounds, unless the respondent

can satisfy the Industrial Tribunal that there is an innocent explanation: see, e.g. *Oxford v Department of Health and Social Security* [1977] IRLR 225; *Wallace v South Eastern Education and Library Board* [1980] IRLR 193 and *Khanna v Ministry of Defence* [1981] IRLR 331.

A further difficulty arises from the fact that the suitability of candidates can rarely be measured objectively. Often subjective judgments will be made. That is why it is important that there should be clear criteria for the selection of candidates for employment or promotion: see paragraph 1.13 of the Race Relations Code of Practice, which came into effect on 1.4.84, under the Race Relations Code of Practice Order 1983 (SI 1983 No. 1081), and which has statutory effect under s. 47 of the Race Relations Act 1971.

In the present case it was clear that there was no direct evidence of racial discrimination against Dr Noone. The industrial tribunal found that, although all three candidates who were interviewed were suitably qualified for the post, the experience, training and academic output of Dr Noone exceeded that of the other applicants. (This was conceded by Dr Wilson.) Notwithstanding this, the authority's pleaded answer to Dr Noone's case was based on her lack of training and experience. The industrial tribunal also found:

> Initially the cross-examination was conducted upon the basis that the applicant lacked the training and experience to undertake responsibility for running the microbiology department at consultant level. The ground then shifted and suggestions were made that the applicant was really rather more of an academic who wanted to be tucked away in intellectual pursuits. When Dr Wilson was taken through her publications he admitted that they were in the main clinically orientated.

In the light of these facts it seems to me that the industrial tribunal was justified in approaching this case on the basis that Dr Noone was treated less favourably than the other applicants, and that the authority had to show that there was a non-racial explanation for her failure to be appointed to the vacant post . . .

Notes

1. The burden is on the applicant to show less favourable treatment, as opposed to merely different treatment, compared with that of the opposite sex or a person of a different race. Note the impact of the Burden of Proof Directive 97/307.

The case of *Qureshi v London Borough of Newham* [1991] IRLR 264 considered when an inference of discrimination can be made by the industrial tribunal. The Court of Appeal determined, applying *Noone*, that such an inference can be made only after an act of discrimination has been established. In this particular case the equal opportunities policy was so bad that every race was a victim. There was therefore no discrimination with regard to Mr Qureshi. The Court went on to conclude that the Acts did not impose a duty to be a good employer.

While discrimination may be inferred, the decision in *Zafar v Glasgow City Council* [1998] IRLR 37 concludes that the guidance in *King* (see below) should be followed if an inference is to take place and that *Chattopadhyay v Headmaster of Holloway School* [1981] IRLR 487 should not be followed.

2.   A summary of the current law on proving direct discrimination has been provided by Neil LJ in *King* v *The Great Britain-China Centre* [1991] IRLR 513, at p. 518:

(1)   It is for the applicant who complains of racial discrimination to make out his or her case. Thus if the applicant does not prove the case on the balance of probabilities he or she will fail.

(2)   It is important to bear in mind that it is unusual to find direct evidence of racial discrimination. Few employers will be prepared to admit such discrimination even to themselves. In some cases the discrimination will not be ill-intentioned but merely based on an assumption 'he or she would not have fitted in'.

(3)   The outcome of the case will therefore usually depend on what inferences it is proper to draw from the primary facts found by the Tribunal. These inferences can include, in appropriate cases, any inferences that it is just and equitable to draw in accordance with s. 65(2)(b) of the 1976 Act from an evasive or equivocal reply to a questionnaire.

(4)   Though there will be some cases where, for example, the non-selection of the applicant for a post or for promotion is clearly not on racial grounds, a finding of discrimination and a finding of a difference in race will often point to the possibility of racial discrimination. In such circumstances the Tribunal will look to the employer for an explanation. If no explanation is then put forward or if the Tribunal considers the explanation to be inadequate or unsatisfactory it will be legitimate for the Tribunal to infer that the discrimination was on racial grounds. This is not a matter of law but, as May LJ put it in *Noone*, 'almost common sense'.

(5)   It is unnecessary and unhelpful to introduce the concept of a shifting evidential burden of proof. At the conclusion of all the evidence the Tribunal should make findings as to the primary facts and draw such inferences as they consider proper from those facts. They should then reach a conclusion on the balance of probabilities, bearing in mind both the difficulties which face a person who complains of unlawful discrimination and the fact that it is for the complainant to prove his or her case.

3.   It was thought that the test for establishing less favourable treatment on grounds of sex or race had been clarified by the decision in the *Birmingham City Council* case (above) which confirmed that motive and intention were irrelevant, no matter how good and genuine (see *Greig* v *Community Industry* [1979] ICR 356). Furthermore, the House of Lords upheld the use of a simple 'but for' test to establish that the treatment was gender- or race-based. This was supported by the decision of the House of Lords in *James* v *Eastleigh Borough Council* [1990] IRLR 298, overruling the decision of the Court of Appeal ([1989] IRLR 318) that the reason for the act of discrimination was relevant – in this particular case the reason given was 'to aid the needy'. However, the dissenting judgment of Lord Lowry is of interest as it highlights succinctly the debate between a 'causative construction' as opposed to a 'subjective construction' of the words 'on the ground of his sex'; Lord Lowry preferring the latter interpretation which would allow consideration of reason, intention or motive. Interestingly the decision in *Zafar* (above) moves towards the dissenting judgment of Lord Lowry, although it is still true to say that a benign motive cannot justify an act of discrimination. It has been suggested that the approach in *Zafar* is further supported by the decision in *Martins* v

Marks and Spencer plc [1998] IRLR 326. If this approach is correct then the test for establishing direct discrimination has become harder for the complainant. See Bob Watt '*Goodbye*' '*but – for*' '*hello*' '*but – why*'? (1998) 27 ILJ No. 2, pp. 121–32 for a detailed analysis of the possible impact of *Zafar*.

James v Eastleigh Borough Council
[1990] IRLR 298
House of Lords

LORD LOWRY (dissenting): My Lords, the facts of this appeal are simple, but I confess to having had some difficulty in deciding it. I can discern in your Lordships' speeches, which I have had the advantage of reading in draft, two logical and persuasive trains of thought which lead to opposite conclusion, and the question is how to choose between them.

The case has been presented by the plaintiff as an example of direct discrimination, an apt and by now customary description of a breach of s. 1(1)(a) of the Sex Discrimination Act 1975 which, as applied to men, provides:

A person discriminates against a [man] in any circumstances relevant for the purposes of any provision of this Act if— (a) on the ground of [his] sex he treats [him] less favourably than he treats or would treat a [woman].

There are two questions for decision: (1) What, on its true construction, does this provision mean? (2) When the provision, properly construed, is applied to the facts, did the Council discriminate against the appellant contrary to s. 1(1)(a)?

With a view to construction, the crucial words are 'on the ground of his sex'. Mr Lester for the appellant, submits that this phrase means 'due to his sex' and does not involve any consideration of the reason which has led the alleged discriminator to treat the man less favourably than he treats or would treat a woman. I shall call this the causative construction and will presently advert to it. Mr Beloff, for the Council, contends for what I shall call the subjective construction, which involves considering the reason why the discriminator has treated the man unfavourably. He submits that this construction accords with the plain meaning of the words and the grammatical structure of the sentence in which they occur. I accept Mr Beloff's construction and I proceed to explain why I do so.

On reading s. 1(1)(a), it can be seen that the discriminator does something to the victim, that is, he treats him in a certain fashion, to wit, less favourably than he treats or would treat a woman. And he treats him in that fashion on a certain *ground*, namely, *on the ground of his sex*. These words, it is scarcely necessary for me to point out, constitute an adverbial phrase modifying the transitive verb 'treats' in a clause of which the discriminator is the subject and the victim is the object. While anxious not to weary your Lordships with a grammatical excursus, the point I wish to make is that the *ground* on which the alleged discriminator treats the victim less favourably is inescapably linked to the subject and the verb; it is the reason which has caused him to act. The meaning of the vital words, in the sentence where they occur, cannot be expressed by saying that the victim receives treatment which on the ground of (his) sex is less favourable to him than to a person of the opposite sex. The structure of that sentence makes the words 'on the ground of his sex' easily capable of meaning 'due to his sex' if the context so requires or permits.

. . .

I feel that I would have no difficulty in dealing with this argument, but for the fact that it has commended itself to the majority of your Lordships, including the author of the passage in question. It is therefore with even more than the usual measure of respect that I make the observations which follow. In their context both of the statements which I have extracted are perfectly correct statements of fact, but that does not mean that they are a guide to the proper construction of s. 1(1)(a), which I have considered above. The defence was not that the less favourable treatment was a purely undesigned and adventitious consequence of the Council's policy. It would have had to be admitted that the Council, however regretfully, knew it was treating the girls less favourably than the boys and that owing to the shortage of school places it had deliberately decided so to treat them because they were girls. The defence, based on absence of intention and motive, was rightly rejected and no other defence was made or could have been made. Whichever construction of s. 1(1)(a) had been applied, the Council would have lost, and no rival constructions of that provision were discussed. It is, I consider, worth noting that the examples and the cases which my noble and learned friend mentions are consistent with the subjective construction. If a men's hairdresser dismisses the only woman on his staff because the customers prefer to have their hair cut by a man, he may regret losing her but he treats her less favourably because she is a woman, that is, on the ground of her sex, having made a deliberate decision to do so. If the foreman dismisses an efficient and co-operative black road sweeper in order to avoid industrial action by the remaining (white) members of the squad, he treats him less favourably on racial grounds. If a decision is taken, for reasons which may seem in other respects valid and sensible, not to employ a girl in a group otherwise consisting entirely of men, the employer has treated that girl less favourably than he would treat a man and he has done so consciously on the ground (which *he considers* to be a proper ground) that she is a woman. In none of these cases is a defence provided by an excusable or even by a worthy motive.

It can thus be seen that the causative construction not only gets rid of unessential and often irrelevant mental ingredients, such as malice, prejudice, desire and motive, but also dispenses with an essential ingredient, namely, the ground on which the discriminator acts. The appellant's construction relieves the complainant of the need to prove anything except that A has done an act which results in less favourable treatment for B by reason of B's sex, which reduces to insignificance the words 'on the ground of'. Thus the causative test is too wide and is grammatically unsound, because it necessarily disregards the fact that the less favourable treatment is meted out to the victim *on the ground of* the victim's sex.

Notes

1.   For a discussion of the impact of the decisions in *R v Birmingham City Council, ex parte EOC* and *James v Eastleigh Borough Council*, see Holmes, A., and Migdal, S., '*James v Eastleigh Borough Council* Revisited' (1990) 11 *Business Law Review*, No. 12, p. 293.

2.   Note the decision of the Court of Appeal in *Dhatt v McDonalds Hamburgers Ltd* [1991] IRLR 130 where, in applying RRA 1976, s. 3(4), which requires comparison with persons whose circumstances are the same as or not materially different from those of the complainant, it was held that an Indian national who was requested by his employer to produce evidence of his right to work in the UK could not compare himself with British and EC nationals who were not requested to produce such evidence. As all other nationalities

with whom he should have compared himself are required either to have a work permit or indefinite leave to enter (as the complainant had), he had not been treated less favourably. Such a restrictive interpretation of s. 3(4) in allowing nationality to be treated as a relevant ground, will have the effect of preventing comparison with the indigenous nationality. For a critique of this case, see Anon, 'Nationality discrimination protection limited' (1991) *Equal Opportunities Review*, No. 36, pp. 35–6. Also Ross, J., 'Race Discrimination and the Importance of Asking the Right Question' (1991) 20 ILJ No. 3, p. 208.

3.   The wording of the RRA 1976, s. 1(1)(a) is slightly different from that of the SDA 1975, s. 1(1)(a), and is therefore wider in scope, allowing a complaint of direct discrimination where a person is treated less favourably because of another person's race. See *Zarczynska* v *Levy* [1979] 1 WLR 125 and *Weathershield Ltd (t/a Van and Truck Rentals)* v *Sargent* [1999] IRLR 94.

4.   The SDA 1975, s. 5(3) and the RRA 1976, s. 3, require a 'like with like' comparison for the purposes of determining whether there has been an act of discrimination (see *Bain* v *Bowles* [1991] IRLR 356).

5.   Whether an act of discrimination has taken place is a finding in fact; the jurisdiction of the emloyment tribunal on this matter being limited to acts which are the subject of the complaint in the originating application. It is not open to the emloyment tribunal to find another act of discrimination of which complaint has not been made (*Chapman* v *Simon* [1994] IRLR 124).

6.   The contentious issues of dress codes and direct discrimination was raised again in *Smith* v *Safeway plc* [1996] IRLR 456. The Court of Appeal overturned the decision of the EAT, ruling that different dress codes for men and women are to be judged on what is 'conventional'. Such an approach, if even-handed, is not discriminatory, even if its content is different for men and women. In this case to dismiss a male employee because the length of his hair was unconventional, but to allow a female employee with long hair to continue in employment in a similar post did not amount to less favourable treatment.

Questions
1.   Would the decision in *R* v *Birmingham City Council, ex parte EOC* be the same had the subjective construction proposed by Lord Lowry been adopted?
2.   How far does the decision in *Noone* overcome the problem of the burden of proof raised in *Khanna* v *Ministry of Defence* [1981] ICR 653? (See *King* v *The Great Britain-China centre* (above).)
3.   If all employees and prospective employees are asked the same question, can there be a complaint of discrimination?
4.   Does the fact that an employer's policy results in potential discrimination against all races allow him to escape the provisions of the RRA 1976? (See *Qureshi* v *London Borough of Newham* [1991] IRLR 264.)
5.   Is it discrimination to refuse a man entry to premises because he is wearing an earring when females wearing earrings are allowed to enter?

6. How far has the decision in *Noone* been marginalised by the decision in *Zafar?*

(iii)   Sexual and Racial Harassment

Sexual and racial harassment are not catered for by separate provisions in the respective Acts. To establish harassment the complainant must establish direct discrimination. The watershed for claims of harassment as an act of discrimination was the case of *Strathclyde Regional Council* v *Porcelli* [1986] IRLR 134 (below). Since then there has been a rapid increase in the number of claims both of sexual and racial harassment, even though there is no clear concept of what type of conduct amounts to harassment. Nor have recent complainants been deterred by the difficulties faced in bringing themselves within the wording of s. 1(1)(a) of the Acts and having then to show 'detriment' under SDA 1975, s. 6(2)(b) and RRA 1976, s. 4(2)(c) (see *De Souza* v *Automobile Association* [1986] IRLR 103).

Strathclyde Regional Council v *Porcelli*
[1986] IRLR 134
Court of Session

Mrs Porcelli was employed as a science laboratory technician at Bellahouston Academy. At the end of 1982, two male technicians, Coles and Reid, were appointed. According to Mrs Porcelli, the two men sexually harassed her as part of a campaign to try to persuade her to leave the school. For example, she alleged that one of the men repeatedly made suggestive remarks to her and deliberately brushed against her. The industrial tribunal found that Coles deliberately withheld information from Mrs Porcelli emanating from the principal teacher of chemistry; some of Mrs Porcelli's personal belongings were deliberately thrown out; Coles and Reid stored heavy apparatus and large storage jars in a cupboard at such a height that a ladder was required to enable Mrs Porcelli to gain access to them. Life became so unpleasant for Mrs Porcelli that she ceased to use the technician's room for breaks. She eventually applied for a transfer to another school which subsequently took place.

It was held that the respondent had been treated less favourably on the ground of her sex within the meaning of SDA 1975, s. 1(1)(a), as the unfavourable treatment meted out included a significant element of a sexual character to which a man would not be vulnerable. In this case the nature of sexual harassment was adopted because she was a woman. Since this form of treatment would not have been used against an equally disliked man, the treatment of the respondent was different in a material respect from that which would have been inflicted on a male colleague.

LORD EMSLIE: After some initial hesitation which I freely confess I have come to be of opinion that for the reasons advanced by the learned Dean of Faculty for the respondent the submissions for the appellants fall to be rejected. Section 1(1)(a) is concerned with 'treatment' and not with the motive or objective of the person responsible for it. Although in some cases it will be obvious that there is a sex related purpose in the mind of a person who indulges in unwanted and objectionable sexual overtures to a woman or exposes her to offensive sexual jokes or observations that is not this case. But it does not follow that because the campaign pursued against Mrs Porcelli as a whole had no sex related motive or objective, the treatment of Mrs Porcelli by Coles, which was of the nature of 'sexual harassment' is not to be regarded as having been 'on the ground of her sex' within the meaning of s. 1(1)(a). In my opinion this particular part of the campaign was plainly adopted against Mrs Porcelli because she was a woman. It was a particular kind of weapon, based upon the sex of the victim, which, as the industrial tribunal recognised would not have been used against an equally disliked man. Indeed, I do not understand from the reasons of the industrial tribunal that they were not entirely satisfied upon that matter, and they were in my opinion well entitled to be so satisfied upon a proper interpretation of s. 1(1)(a). As I read their reasons the decision against Mrs Porcelli, which they reached with evident regret, proceeded only upon their view that Coles and Reid would have treated an equally disliked male colleague just as unfavourably as they had treated Mrs Porcelli. It is at this point, in my opinion, that their decision is vulnerable.

The industrial tribunal reached their decision by finding that Coles' and Reid's treatment of an equally disliked male colleague would have been just as unpleasant. Where they went wrong, however, was in failing to notice that a material part of the campaign against Mrs Porcelli consisted of 'sexual harassment', a particularly degrading and unacceptable form of treatment which it must be taken to have been the intention of Parliament to restrain. From their reasons it is to be understood that they were satisfied that this form of treatment – sexual harassment in any form – would not have figured in a campaign by Coles and Reid directed against a man. In this situation the treatment of Mrs Porcelli fell to be seen as very different in a material respect from that which would have been inflicted on a male colleague, regardless of equality of overall unpleasantness, and that being so it appears to me that upon a proper application of s. 1(1)(a) the industrial tribunal ought to have asked themselves whether in that respect Mrs Porcelli had been treated by Coles (on the ground of her sex) 'less favourably' than he would have treated a man with whom her position fell to be compared. Had they asked themselves that question it is impossible to believe that they would not have answered it in the affirmative. In the result it has not been shown that the Employment Appeal Tribunal were not entitled to substitute their own decision in Mrs Porcelli's favour for that of the industrial tribunal and I am of opinion that the appeal by Strathclyde Regional Council should be refused.

Jones v *Tower Boot Co. Ltd*
[1997] IRLR 168
Court of Appeal

Raymondo Jones, whose mother was white and father black, worked for the employers as a machine operative from 16 April 1992, until he resigned a month later. During that time he was subjected to a number of incidents of racial harassment from work colleagues. One employee burnt his arm with a hot screwdriver, metal bolts were thrown at his head, his legs were whipped with a piece of welt, someone stuck a notice on his back bearing the words 'Chipmonks are go', and he was repeatedly called names such as 'chimp', 'monkey' and 'baboon'.

WAITE LJ: . . . **The governing principles of statutory construction**
Two principles are in my view involved. The first is that a its statute is to be construed according to its legislative purpose, with due regard to the result which it is the stated or presumed intention of Parliament to achieve and the means provided for achieving it ('the purposive construction'); and the second is that words in a statute are to be given their normal meaning according to general use in the English language unless the context indicates that such words have to be given a special or technical meaning as a term of art ('the linguistic construction'). It will be convenient to deal with those separately.

The purposive construction
The legislation now represented by the Race and Sex Discrimination Act currently in force broke new ground in seeking to work upon the minds of men and women and thus affect their attitude to the social consequences of difference between the sexes or distinction of skin colour. Its general thrust was educative, persuasive, and (where necessary) coercive. The relief accorded to the victims (or potential victims) of discrimination went beyond the ordinary remedies of damages and an injunction – introducing, through declaratory powers in the court or tribunal and recommendatory powers in the relevant Commission, provisions with a proactive function, designed as much to eliminate the occasions for discrimination as to compensate its victims or punish its perpetrators. These were linked to a code of practice of which courts and tribunals were to take cognisance. Consistently with the broad front on which it operates, the legislation has traditionally been given a wide interpretation — see for example *Savjani* v *IRC* [1981] 1 QB 458 at p. 466 where Templeman LJ said of the Race Relations Act:

> . . . the Act was brought in to remedy a very great evil. It is expressed in very wide terms, and I should be slow to find that the effect of something which is humiliatingly discriminatory in racial matters falls outside the ambit of the Act.

Since the getting and losing of work, and the daily functioning of the workplace, are prime areas for potential discrimination on grounds of race or sex, it is not surprising that both Acts contain specific provisions to govern the field of employment. Those provisions are themselves wide-ranging – as is evidenced, for example, by the inclusion of contract workers without employee status within the scheme of the legislation. There is no indication in the Act that by dealing specifically with the employment field Parliament intended in any way to limit the general thrust of the legislation.

A purposive construction accordingly requires s. 32 of the Race Relations Act (and the corresponding s. 41 of the Sex Discrimination Act) to be given a broad interpretation. It would be inconsistent with that requirement to allow the notion of the 'course of employment' to be construed in any sense more limited than the natural meaning of those everyday words would allow.

The linguistic construction
Mr Buckhaven's argument is attractively simple. Vicarious liability is a doctrine of tortious liability which has been applied by the common law to the employment context. Part Three of the Race Relations Act applies expressly to discrimination in the employment field. The two fields are the same. Words and phrases that have acquired a familiar and particular meaning through case law applied to employers' liability in the former context must therefore have been intended by Parliament to have the same meaning when applied to employers' liability in the latter context.

Mr Allen QC, while acknowledging that there is a broad conceptual similarity between the employers' responsibility that applies in both contexts, submits that substantial differences emerge when vicarious liability in tort is analysed and contrasted with the statutory scheme of which s. 32 forms part. The employer's authority, for example is a crucial element in vicarious liability in tort – as evidenced by the statement in *Salmond* (20th edition) in paragraph 21.5 that:

> A master is not responsible for a wrongful act done by his servant unless it is done in the course of his employment. It is deemed to be so done if it is either (1) a wrongful act authorised by the master, or (2) a wrongful and unauthorised way of doing some act authorised by the master.

That is to be contrasted with the position under s. 32(1) of the Race Relations Act, where all actions by a person in the course of employment are attributed to the employer 'whether or not . . . done with the employer's knowledge or approval'. Mr Allen points to other distinctions, such as the greater range of remedies available under the statute (including damages for injury to feelings) than those available in tort against an employer at common law, and the total absence from the concept of vicarious liability in tort of any provision corresponding to the reasonable steps defence under s. 32(3).

I am persuaded that Mr Allen's submission is to be preferred, and that there is here no sufficient similarity between the two contexts to justify, on a linguistic construction, the reading of the phrase 'course of employment' as subject to the gloss imposed on it in the common law context of vicarious liability.

The position apart from authority
Both approaches to statutory construction therefore lead to the same interpretation. But even more compelling, in my view, is the anomaly which would result (as the minority member Mr Blyghton pointed out) from adopting any other interpretation. Mr Buckhaven accepts (indeed in his written argument he relies upon) the fact that an inevitable result of construing 'course of employment' in the sense for which he contends will be that the more heinous the act of discrimination, the less likely it will be that the employer would be liable. That, he argues, is all to the good. Parliament must have intended the liability of employers to be kept within reasonable bounds.

I would reject that submission entirely. It cuts across the whole legislative scheme and underlying policy of s. 32 (and its counterpart in sex discrimination), which is to deter racial and sexual harassment in the workplace through a widening of the net of responsibility beyond the guilty employees themselves, by making all employers additionally liable for such harassment, and then supplying them with the reasonable steps defence under s. 32(3) which will exonerate the conscientious employer who has used his best endeavours to prevent such harassment, and will encourage all employers who have not yet undertaken such endeavours to take the steps necessary to make the same defence available in their own workplace. . . .

Notes
1. It is clear that harassment does not have to involve physical contact; neither does it have to be a course of conduct (see *Bracebridge Engineering Ltd v Darby* [1990] IRLR 3, where it was concluded that a single serious incident will suffice). More controversially, it would appear that any lewd behaviour, even though not initially directed at the complainant, will amount to harassment, in circumstances where, despite the complainant's objections, the behaviour continues. The industrial tribunal in *Johnstone* v *Fenton Barns (Scotland) Ltd* (1990) Case No. S/1688/89 concluded that this was evidence

that the treatment had been 'meted out' to the complainant in accordance with the *ratio* of *Strathclyde Regional Council* v *Porcelli*.

The employer is vicariously liable for *all* acts of discrimination carried out by his employees while acting within the course of their employment (SDA 1975, s. 41 and RRA 1976, s. 32). Harassment does not automatically take an employee outside the course of his employment. This is certainly the case with respect to supervisors, line managers, etc., but not always so with respect to employees on the same level or grade (compare *Strathclyde Regional Council* v *Porcelli* with *Irving* v *Post Office* [1987] IRLR 289 and *Bracebridge Engineering Ltd* v *Darby* (see Chapter 5)). Furthermore, if the employer is not found to be vicariously liable for the alleged act of discrimination, an action based on victimisation is almost bound to fail; so ruled the CA in *Waters* v *Commissioner of Police of the Metropolis* [1997] IRLR 589.

The test for establishing vicarious liability in discrimination cases has finally been clarified by the Court of Appeal in *Jones* v *Tower Boot Company Ltd* [1997] IRLR 168. In adopting a purposive approach to interpreting s. 32 of the RRA, it clearly distinguishes between the common law test for vicarious liability and that which had generally been applied to statutory vicarious liability. See also *Sidhu* v *Aerospace Composite Technology Ltd* [1999] IRLR 683. See P. Roberts and L. Vickers, 'Harassment at work as discrimination: the current debate in England and Wales' (1998) 3 IJDL 91.

2.   It is worth noting that liability for an act of discrimination passes to the transferee following the transfer of the undertaking under the Transfer of Undertakings (Protection of Employment) Regulations 1981, reg. 5(2)(b) (see *DJM International Ltd* v *Nicholas* [1996] IRLR 76).

3.   Some clarification has been given to the term 'unwanted conduct' in the EC Code of Practice on sexual harassment. To amount to 'unwanted' it is not dependent upon rejection of the act by the complainant. This allows a single act to amount to harassment and prevents a situation arising whereby the harasser can argue that as this was the first time, he or she could not have known that the conduct was unwanted until it was actually rejected. In practical terms 'unwanted' is essentially the same as unwelcome or uninvited (*Institu Cleaning Co. Ltd* v *Heads* [1995] IRLR 4).

4.   Following *De Souza* v *Automobile Association* (below), it is firmly established that racial insults may amount to racial harassment; although the complainant will have to show that they were directed at him or her and that he or she has suffered a detriment.

De Souza v *Automobile Association*
[1986] IRLR 103
Court of Appeal

MAY LJ: Racially to insult a coloured employee is not enough by itself, even if that insult caused him or her distress; before the employee can be said to have been subjected to some 'other detriment' the court or Tribunal must find that by reason of the act or acts complained of a reasonable worker would or might take the view that he had thereby been disadvantaged in the circumstances in which he had thereafter to work.

. . .

  If in the passage from his judgment Lord McDonald must be read as holding that an employee could only be said to have been subjected to a detriment within the true construction of s. 6(2)(b) of the 1975 Act, or s. 4(2)(c) of the 1976 Act, if the result of the sexual or racial discrimination complained of was either dismissal or other disciplinary action by the employer, or some action by the employee such as leaving the employment on the basis of constructive dismissal, or seeking transfer to another plant, then with respect I think that this was too limited an approach. Thus if in another case the discrimination was such that the putative reasonable employee could justifiably complain about his or her working conditions or environment, then whether or not these were so bad as to be able to amount to constructive dismissal, or even if the employee was prepared to work on and put up with the harassment, I think this too could contravene the subsections. For my part I cannot accept Mr Tabachnik's submission that the word 'detriment' is to be looked at only from the viewpoint of the employer: the whole of the facts of the case have to be considered in the light of the proper construction of s. 4(2)(c) of the 1976 Act or s. 6(2)(b) of the 1975 Act which I have sought to indicate.

  What then is the result when these principles are applied to the instant case? First, even though the use of the insulting word in respect of the appellant may have meant that she was being considered less favourably, whether generally or in an employment context, than others, I for my part do not think that she can properly be said to have been 'treated' less favourably by whomsoever used the word, unless he intended her to overhear the conversation in which it was used, or knew or ought reasonably to have anticipated that the person he was talking to would pass the insult on or that the appellant would become aware of it in some other way. I do not find any sufficient findings of fact to this effect by the Industrial Tribunal.

  Secondly, and as I have said earlier, in my opinion the appellant could only be held to have been subject to some detriment within s. 4(2)(c) of the 1976 Act if not only the same conditions to which I have just referred obtained – for instance that she was intended to overhear it said – but also that both she was and the reasonable coloured secretary in like situation would or might be disadvantaged, that is placed at a disadvantage in the circumstances and conditions in which they were working in the way I have indicated. Although the Industrial Tribunal said that the use of the insult showed that all was not well in the appellant's department at the time of the remark and that there was an element of racial prejudice there, I do not read this as a finding of fact at all, but in any event certainly not one that the appellant was disadvantaged in the sense and context to which I have referred. Further, if this was intended to be a finding of fact to this effect within the principles I have outlined, I respectfully do not think that there was any evidence to support it.

Notes

1.   The employment tribunals have taken a pragmatic approach to the issue of racial abuse and have proved willing to find that the victim of racial abuse has suffered a detriment (see *Straker* v *McDonald's Hamburgers Ltd* (1989) 18273/88; *Eribenne* v *Grand Metropolitan Retailing Ltd* (1990) 2537/90).

2.   Establishing 'detriment' within SDA 1975, s. 6(2)(b) was clarified by the decision in *Wileman* v *Minilec Engineering Ltd* [1988] IRLR 144, where it was stated (*obiter*) by Popplewell J, at p. 147: '"Sexual Harassment" is legal shorthand for activity which is easily recognisable as "subjecting her to any other detriment".'

Whilst this may ease the burden on the complainant, compensation for harassment relates to the degree of detriment. Evidence as to the complainant's attitude to sexual matters is therefore admissible in assessing injury to feelings (see *Snowball* v *Gardner Merchant Ltd* [1987] IRLR 397 and *Wileman* v *Minilec Engineering Ltd* (above), the former confirming that evidence of sexual 'activities' was admissible for the purpose of assessing detriment; the latter justifying the award of a paltry sum as compensation on the ground that as the complainant had been scantily clad in posing for photographs she had suffered little injury to her feelings). Such decisions must deter the victim of harassment from bringing a claim.

3. An employer may avoid liability if he can show that he acted as a reasonable employer in taking all reasonable steps to prevent the discrimination (SDA 1975, s. 41 and RRA 1976, s. 32). Following *Balgobin* v *Tower Hamlets London Borough Council* [1987] IRLR 401, these sections can be satisfied by the existence of an equal opportunities policy and evidence that complaints of discrimination are investigated, even though, as in this particular case, the employer takes no action against the alleged harasser because of the 'lack of evidence'. Townshend-Smith, R., *Sex Discrimination in Employment: Law, Practice and Policy* (Sweet & Maxwell, 1989), at p. 54, quite rightly takes the view that the EAT, in declaring that it was difficult to see what additional steps could have been taken by the employer, misinterpreted SDA 1975, s. 41(3):

Apart from showing unawareness of employer policies in respect of sexual harassment, this misinterprets s. 41(3) which places on the employer the burden of showing that all reasonable steps were taken. Employers should be required to show both that the policy was effectively implemented and made known to the employees, and that under it sexual harassment was a specific disciplinary offence. The danger is that tribunals may make decisions on the basis of how important *they* think it is to have effective anti-discrimination policies. It is certain that merely telling employees that they should not discriminate cannot be enough.

4. See Holmes, A., and Migdal, S., 'Harassment at Work: Guidelines for Employers' (1991) 12 *Business Law Review*, No. 4, p. 112, for a review of the case law on sexual harassment. Also Rubenstein, M., *Dignity of Women at Work* (Commission of the European Communities, 1988) for a comprehensive comparative study of national laws relating to sexual harassment in Member States of the EC.

5. The report by Rubenstein has led to the declaration and adoption of Recommendation 92/C 27/04 on the protection of the dignity of men and women at work, and the publication of a code of practice to combat sexual harassment (see below). For a discussion of the legal impact of this development, see Rubenstein, M., 'Sexual Harassment: European Commission Recommendation and Code of Practice' (1992) 21 ILJ No. 1, p. 70. For a discussion of the inadequacies of the provisions relating to sexual harassment, see K. Bakirci, 'Sexual harassment in the workplace in relation to EC legislation' (1998) 3 IJDL 3.

6. The Criminal Justice and Public Order Act 1994 makes intentional harassment a criminal offence; it is suggested that the Act applies to the workplace. The Employment Rights Act 1996 ensures the restriction of publicity in cases involving sexual harassment. The Protection from Harassment Act 1997 creates a criminal offence of harassment (s. 2) as well as providing civil remedies (s. 3) in the form of damages and an injunction. It is unclear how far the Act covers harassment in the workplace; however, the Act refers to harassing a person including alarming the person or causing the person distress. It is clear that an act of harassment must have occurred on more than one occasion for there to be liability under the 1997 Act. There is no provision, however, for vicarious liability so many complainants may wish to rely first and foremost on the SDA 1975 and RRA 1976.

7. According to the EAT in *Burton* v *DeVere Hotels* [1996] IRLR 596, an employer can be liable for subjecting the employee to the detriment of harrassment even where the conduct is outside the scope of the harasser's employment, or where the harasser is a third party, provided the employer could have prevented the harrassment from taking place by applying the standards of good practice. In *Burton*, the hotel employers were held to have 'subjected' two black waitresses to the detriment of racial abuse when they exposed them to racist remarks and other offensive conduct by Bernard Manning, the guest speaker at a Round Table dinner, and from some of the other diners.

Recommendation 92/C 27/04 on the Protection of the Dignity of Men and Women at Work

Article 1
It is recommended that the Member States take action to promote awareness that conduct of a sexual nature, or other conduct based on sex affecting the dignity of women and men at work, including conduct of superiors and colleagues, is unacceptable if:

(a)   such conduct is unwanted, unreasonable and offensive to the recipient;

(b)   a person's rejection of, or submission to, such conduct on the part of employers or workers (including superiors or colleagues) is used explicitly or implicitly as a basis for a decision which affects that person's access to vocational training, access to employment, continued employment, promotion, salary or any other employment decisions; and/or

(c)   such conduct creates an intimidating, hostile or humiliating work environment for the recipient;

and that such conduct may, in certain circumstances, be contrary to the principle of equal treatment within the meaning of Articles 3, 4 and 5 of Directive 76/207/EEC.

Article 2
It is recommended that Member States take action, in the public sector, to implement the Commission's Code of Practice on the protection of the dignity of women and men at work, annexed hereto. The action of the Member States, in thus initiating and pursuing positive measures designed to create a climate at work in which women and men respect one another's human integrity, should serve as an example to the private sector.

Article 3
It is recommended that Member States encourage employers and employee representatives to develop measures to implement the Commission's Code of Practice on the
protection of the dignity of women and men at work.

Article 4
Member States shall inform the Commission within three years of the date of this
recommendation of the measures taken to give effect to it, in order to allow the
Commission to draw up a report on all such measures. The Commission shall, within
this period, ensure the widest possible circulation of the Code of Practice. The report
should examine the degree of awareness of the Code, its perceived effectiveness, its
degree of application and the extent of its use in collective bargaining between the
social partners.

Article 5
This recommendation is addressed to the Member States.

Questions
1. In what circumstances would an employer be vicariously liable for
pornographic material being posted up on the walls of a factory workshop?
2.   Would a homosexual be afforded protection from harassment by the SDA
1975? See *Smith* v *Gardner Merchant Ltd* [1998] IRLR 510.

(iv)   Segregation
Segregation of employees is a type of direct discrimination. It is unlawful only
under the RRA 1976, s. 1(2).

Race Relations Act 1976

1.   Racial discrimination
(1) . . .
(2)   It is hereby declared that, for the purposes of this Act, segregating a person
from other persons on racial grounds is treating him less favourably than they are
treated.

Note
To establish segregation the complainant must show that his employer had a
policy to segregate workers of different races, or that it was a deliberate act
on the part of the employer; this may be difficult to prove hence the small
number of cases pursued using s. 1(2).

Pel Ltd v *Modgill*
[1980] IRLR 142
Employment Appeal Tribunal

Mr Modgill and 15 other African Asians employed by Pel Ltd in their paint
shop complained that they had been discriminated against contrary to the
Race Relations Act by the company and by their union, the Furniture,
Timber and Allied Trades Union (FTATU).

The company, it was claimed, discriminated in their acts and attitudes in relation to the appointment of a separate shop steward, in wage negotiations and transfers. There was also said to be a breakdown of communications. In addition, the complainants alleged that the company had segregated them from other persons on racial grounds within the meaning of s. 1(2) of the Act.

The EAT held that the tribunal had erred in concluding that segregation had taken place merely from the fact that only Asians were employed in the paint shop. This situation had arisen not from any intention on the part of the employer but from the acts of the Asian employees who worked in the paint shop.

SLYNN J: Apart from this question of communication, what really troubled the Tribunal most, in the case of the company, was the allegation that there had been segregation. It is this point which Mr Michael Howard has put in the forefront of his argument on behalf of the company. There is no doubt that if an employer does keep apart one person from others on the grounds of his race, that amounts to discrimination on the part of the employer. If it can be shown that it is the policy of the company to keep a man of one colour apart from others, and that it does in fact happen, then a Tribunal clearly is entitled to find that there has been discrimination contrary to the provisions of the Act . . .

Then it is said that if one turns to the facts it is plain that only Asians are employed in the paint spray shop; that they are sent there because it is a dirty job which others did not want. We have been told that at the time of the applications only Asian workers were employed in that shop . . .

The Tribunal had evidence which they appear to have accepted, in the body of their decision, that when vacancies arose in the paint shop they were filled by persons introduced by those who were already working there or those who were leaving. The Tribunal recite evidence that relatives had been introduced into this shop by those already working there. Indeed, the evidence was that, in a significant number of cases, people had applied for employment even before the company knew that there was either a vacancy or was about to be a vacancy because one of the Asian workers was to leave. The evidence even went further than that. Mr Barron, who was in charge of this shop, gave evidence, which the Tribunal appear to have accepted, that over the past 12 months or more, when a vacancy occurred in the department, someone came to him and asked about the job – on one occasion it was one of the existing personnel who came to ask; sometimes before he knew that a particular man was going to leave. Mr Barron agreed, so the Tribunal recite in their decision, that he had not had from the personnel department any applicants during the past two years, except in one instance when white persons were sent to him but they were persons who were not interested in the job. And so the facts appear to be that here, for a period of something like two years, the personnel department of the company had not had to select or interview persons for employment in this particular area. Those who worked there had produced candidates for appointment to Mr Barron and he had found men who were able and willing to take on the job. It seems to us that the Tribunal accepted that there arose a situation, really by the acts of those working in the paint shop itself, that all the workers were in fact Asian. This had not always been the position. A few years ago there had been a number of white men working there, and there had been some coloured, non-Asian workers there as well. But over a period the position had changed and, by the introduction of cousins and friends, Asians alone worked there.

The Tribunal, as we read their decision, really decided the case on the basis that there had been what they called 'indirect' or 'secondary' discrimination because the company had not had a more positive employment policy which would have removed any element of factual segregation, or suspicion of it, arising in the paint shop. This appears to suggest that it was the opinion of the Industrial Tribunal, not so much that the company had by its own acts segregated these men in this particular area away from others, but that it had not prevented the men themselves from coming together in this way. What appears to be suggested is that the company ought to have taken steps to ensure that for some of these jobs, white or non-Asian or coloured men were put in, and that Asians were not allowed to take on these jobs on the grounds of their colour, in order to prevent this segregation in fact arising. We repeat that had there been here evidence of a policy to segregate, and of the fact of segregation arising as a result of the company's acts, that might well have constituted a breach of the legislation; but it does not seem to us that there was evidence to support that position. We do not consider that the failure of the company to intervene and to insist on white or non-Asian workers going into the shop, contrary to the wishes of the men to introduce their friends, itself constituted the act of segregating persons on racial grounds within the meaning of s. 1(2) of the Act. A refusal to appoint other applicants because of their colour, or because they were Asians, might in itself indeed have amounted to discrimination within the meaning of the Act. Because of the view of the Tribunal in this case, in particular in regard to the company, we have considered this matter with some anxiety; but we are quite satisfied that what was relied upon by the Tribunal, namely the lack of communication, can only go to a question of efficiency and does not establish that there has been less favourable treatment of these applicants than others. Nor do we consider that, in law, the failure to have the policy referred to, on the facts of this case, is capable of constituting segregation of a person from others on racial grounds within the meaning of the Act.

B: Indirect Discrimination

Indirect discrimination is a practice which has a disparate or an adverse impact on a particular gender or race. There does not have to be evidence of overt prejudice. Indeed, the practice will at least superficially appear to be gender and race neutral, in that it will apply equally to men and women and to all races. In effect the issue is whether the practice in question adversely affects an individual who is a member of a minority group within the meaning of the respective Acts.

Sex Discrimination Act 1975

1. Sex discrimination against women

(1) A person discriminates against a woman in any circumstances relevant for the purposes of any provision of this Act if—

(a) . . .

(b) he applies to her a requirement or condition which applies or would apply equally to a man but—

(i)   which is such that the proportion of women who can comply with it is considerably smaller than the proportion of men who can comply with it, and

(ii) which he cannot show to be justifiable irrespective of the sex of the person to whom it is applied, and

(iii) which is to her detriment because she cannot comply with it.

Race Relations Act 1976

1. Racial discrimination

(1) A person discriminates against another in any circumstances relevant for the purposes of any provision of this Act if—

(a) . . .

(b) he applies to that other a requirement or condition which he applies or would apply equally to persons not of the same racial group as that other but—

(i) which is such that the proportion of persons of the same racial group as that other who can comply with it is considerably smaller than the proportion of persons not of that racial group who can comply with it; and

(ii) which he cannot show to be justifiable irrespective of the colour, race, nationality or ethnic or national origins of the person to whom it is applied; and

(iii) which is to the detriment of that other because he cannot comply with it.

(i) What Amounts to a Requirement or Condition?

The complainant must isolate a requirement or condition which the employer applies equally to persons of a different gender, marital status and race. While it can be difficult to find a specified requirement or condition, in practice having to comply with a particular practice or procedure will probably suffice. In addition, a complainant under the RRA 1976 would have to show membership of a racial group.

Perera v The Civil Service Commission and the Department of Customs and Excise
[1983] IRLR 166
Court of Appeal

Mr Perera, who was born in Sri Lanka, claimed that he had been rejected on a number of occasions for jobs in the Civil Service on grounds of his colour or national origin. This appeal was in respect of his claim that he had been indirectly discriminated against in respect of his applications to be a legal assistant. His claim that he had been indirectly discriminated against in relation to his application for the post of an administrative trainee as a result of the employers' imposition of an upper age limit was upheld by the EAT.

Dismissing his appeal, the Court of Appeal held that the appellant had failed to establish that the factors taken into account by the interviewing board in not appointing the appellant, amounted to a requirement or condition within the meaning of s. 1(1)(b). A requirement or condition is a 'must'; something which has to be complied with; the lack of compliance with it on the part of the applicant must operate as an absolute bar.

STEPHENSON LJ: The matters which have to be established by an applicant who claims that he has been discriminated against indirectly are, first of all, that there has been a requirement or condition, as Mr Perera put it, a 'must'; something which has to be complied with. Here there was a requirement or condition for candidates for the post of legal assistant in the Civil Service; it was that the candidate should be either a qualified member of the English Bar or a qualified Solicitor of the Supreme Court of this country – an admitted man or a barrister; and those conditions or requirements – those 'musts' – were fulfilled by Mr Perera. But, as he admitted in his argument before the Appeal Tribunal and before this court, there is no other express require-ment or condition, and he has to find a requirement or condition in the general combination of factors which he says the Interviewing Board took into account. He cannot formulate, as in my judgment he has to, what the particular requirement or condition is which he says has been applied to him and to his attempt to obtain a post of legal assistant. That is the hurdle which, as it seems to me, he is unable to get over. If he were able to prove a particular requirement or condition, he would then have to prove that it had been applied by the Commission's Interviewing Board. Then he would have to prove one further thing, namely, that a substantially smaller proportion of persons of his racial group would be able to comply with that requirement than the proportion of similarly qualified persons in a different racial group – similarly qualified because, as Miss Caws has pointed out, like must be compared with like.

That is made clearer still by a provision in the statute which I had intended to read but failed to read; it is s. 3(4), which provides:

A comparison of the case of a person of a particular racial group with that of a person not of that group under s. 1(1) must be such that the relevant circumstances in the one case are the same, or not materially different, in the other.

That has been vividly described by Mr Justice Phillips in another judgment of the Appeal Tribunal reported in the same volume, *Price v Civil Service Commission* [1977] IRLR 291, at 294, as a 'pool' of qualified persons; you do not compare all the population of, in this case, Sri Lanka with all the population of England or any other racial group; you compare the persons in those two groups similarly qualified, and if you do that it is quite plain that in this case there was no evidence to prove that a substantially smaller proportion of persons from Sri Lanka who had got over the hurdle of Bar examinations or solicitor's final examinations than the proportion of barristers or solicitors from other racial groups could comply with anything that might be called a requirement or condition which would satisfy these examiners, as it were, of their suitability for the post of legal assistant.

Mr Perera referred us to two unreported decisions of the Appeal Tribunal, one a judgment of Mr Justice Slynn in *Bains v Avon County Council*, No. 143 of 1978 and the other a decision of Mr Justice Waterhouse in *Watches of Switzerland v Savell*, decided on 17.11.82. In the first of those cases there were arguments as to whether the provision of an age bracket was a requirement or not. Miss Caws has satisfied me that that matter was left open by the Appeal Tribunal, who decided that there had been no indirect discrimination on the applicant's failure to prove the third matter, namely that relating to a substantial proportion of the applicant's own racial group.

In the *Savell* case Mr Justice Waterhouse stressed that there should be a liberal approach to indirect discrimination. It was apparently a case in which all applications for promotion had to be channeled through a particular person, and it was in relation to that circumstance that Mr Justice Waterhouse, in giving the judgment of the Appeal Tribunal, said what he did; and I appreciate the importance of looking at the way in which what is alleged to be a discriminatory requirement or condition operates, as is clear when one looks at the origin of this provision in the United States and decisions there, on which this statutory provision in s. 1(1)(b) is based. I do not find that the Industrial Tribunal singled out the four factors which are singled out by the Employment Appeal Tribunal and on which Mr Perera so strongly relies. But in my opinion none of those factors could possibly be regarded as a requirement or a condition in the sense that the lack of it, whether of British nationality or even of the ability to communicate well in English, would be an absolute bar. The whole of the evidence indicates that a brilliant man whose personal qualities made him suitable as a legal assistant might well have been sent forward on a short list by the Interviewing Board in spite of being, perhaps, below standard on his knowledge of English and his ability to communicate in that language.

That is only an illustration, but once it appears clear from the evidence that the Industrial Tribunal were entitled to conclude that it was personal qualities for which the Interviewing Board were mainly looking, and it was personal qualities, as stated in the chairman's report and as was made clear by the markings of all the members of the Tribunal, which, in the opinion of the Board, Mr Perera lacked, and that that was the reason for not sending him forward on the short list, the case of indirect discrimination which Mr Perera seeks to make in my opinion falls to the ground.

As I have said, I think the Appeal Tribunal correctly stated the law as to indirect discrimination. I agree with them that there was no application here of any requirement or condition, and no evidence of it. In my judgment Mr Perera has failed to prove what he has to prove in order to show a case of indirect discrimination.

Raval v Department of Health and Social Security
[1985] IRLR 370
Employment Appeal Tribunal

WAITE J (*obiter*): There appear to us to be as many as ten questions to which an answer has to be found by the Industrial Tribunal (although of course the scheme of the legislation is such that a particular answer to one question may conclude the whole issue and make it unnecessary to ask the remainder). In stating what in our judgment those questions are, we shall be adopting a formulation which was approved (indeed largely inspired) by Mr Sedley who appeared for the appellant applicant on the instructions of the Commission for Racial Equality, and which has not been criticised by Miss Cotton for the respondents. The questions are the following:

(1)   Does the applicant belong to the racial group or groups to which he/she claims to belong?

(2)   Has the respondent applied to the applicant any and if so what requirement or condition in the arrangements made by him for the purposes of determining who should be offered the relevant employment?

If so, (3) When was such requirement or condition applied to the applicant? (The answer to such question being hereinafter referred to as 'the material time'.)

(4)   Did such requirement or condition apply to other persons not of the same racial group as the applicant?

If so, (5) What are the relevant circumstances necessary to ensure that the proportionate comparison to be made under s.1(1)(b)(i) complies with the 'like with like' requirement in s.3(4)?

(6)   Within what section of the community does the proportionate comparison fall to be made?

(7)   Does the application of the proportionate comparison within such community section result in a finding that the proportion of persons in the same racial group as the applicant who could comply with the condition or requirement at the material time is considerably smaller than the proportion of persons *not* of that racial group who could comply with it?

(8)   Can the requirement or condition be shown by the respondent to be justifiable, irrespective of any racial factor? If not,

(9)   Could the applicant at the material time comply with the requirement or condition? If not,

(10)   Was it to his/her detriment that he/she could not do so?

Price v Civil Service Commission
[1978] 1 All ER 1228
Employment Appeal Tribunal

The appellant, a woman, was born in 1940. She joined the Civil Service as a clerical officer at the age of 17 and served for two years. At the age of 20 she married and had two children. As well as looking after the children she did some work, mostly part-time. In 1975 she saw an advertisement in a newspaper inviting applications for appointment in the Civil Service as an executive officer. No mention was made then of any age limits. She applied and was sent a booklet setting out in detail the conditions of the appointment; in particular it was stated that candidates 'should be at least 17½ years and under 28 years of age on the 31st December 1976', a condition with which she was unable to comply. She complained to an industrial tribunal that, under s. 1(1)(b) of the Sex Discrimination Act 1975 the age range was discriminatory because the proportion of women who could comply with it, particularly the upper age limit of 28, was considerably smaller than the proportion of men who could do so since many women in their twenties were engaged in bringing up and looking after young children and were thus prevented from applying.

It was held, allowing Price's appeal, that 'can comply' meant can comply in practice; this did not involve consideration of what was 'theoretically possible'. (See further, (iii) below.)

PHILLIPS J: Experience shows that when considering s. 1(1)(b) it is necessary to define with some precision the requirement or condition which is called in question. Even when the facts are not in dispute it is possible to formulate the requirement or condition, usually at all events, in more than one way; the precise formulation is important when considering sub-paras (i), (ii) and (iii). A fair way of putting it in the present case seems to be that candidates for the post of executive officer must not be over 28 years of age. We do not accept the submission of counsel for the commission that the words 'can comply' must be construed narrowly, and we think that the industrial tribunal were wrong to accept this submission. In one sense it can be said that any female applicant can comply with the condition. She is not obliged to marry, or to have children, or to mind children; she may find somebody to look after them, and as a last resort she may put them into care. In this sense no doubt counsel for the commission is right in saying that any female applicant can comply with the condition. Such a construction appears to us to be wholly out of sympathy with the spirit and intent of the 1975 Act. Further, it should be repeated that compliance with sub-para. (i) is only a preliminary step, which does not lead to a finding that an act is one of discrimination unless the person acting fails to show that it is justifiable. 'Can' is defined (Shorter Oxford English Dictionary) as 'to be able: to have the power or capacity.' It is a word with many shades of meaning, and we are satisfied that it should not be too narrowly, or too broadly, construed in its context in s.1(1)(b)(i). It should not be said that a person 'can' do something merely because it is theoretically possible for him to do so: it is necessary to see whether he can do so in practice. Applying this approach to the circumstances of this case, it is relevant in determining whether women can comply with the condition to take into account the current usual behaviour of women in this respect, as observed in practice, putting on one side behaviour and responses which are unusual or extreme.

Knowledge and experience suggest that a considerable number of women between the mid-twenties and the mid-thirties are engaged in bearing children and in minding children, and that while many find it possible to take up employment many others, while desiring to do so, find it impossible, and that many of the latter as their children get older find that they can follow their wish and seek employment. This knowledge and experience is confirmed by some of the statistical evidence produced to the industrial tribunal (and by certain additional statistical evidence put in by consent of the parties on the hearing of the appeal). This demonstrates clearly that the economic activity of women with at least one A level falls off markedly about the age of 23, reaching a bottom at about the age of 33 when it climbs gradually to a plateau at about 45.

Basing ourselves on this and other evidence, we should have no hesitation in concluding that our own knowledge and experience is confirmed, and that it is safe to say that the condition is one which it is in practice harder for women to comply with than it is for men. We should be inclined to go further and say that there are undoubtedly women of whom it may be properly said in the terms of s. 1(1)(b)(i) that they 'cannot' comply with the condition, because they are women; that is to say because of their involvement with their children. But this is not enough to enable Miss Price to satisfy the requirements of sub-para. (i). The difficulty we have is in saying whether the proportion of women who can comply with the condition is *considerably smaller* than the proportion of men who can comply with it . . .

Notes

1.   The decision in *Perera* has in effect been challenged by the EAT in *Falkirk Council* v *Whyte* [1997] IRLR 560. The EAT confirmed that a 'desirable' qualification could amount to a requirement or condition where 'it was clear that the qualification operated as the decisive factor in the selection process'. The EAT not only chose not to follow *Perera,* but also welcomed a more liberal approach to determining 'requirement or condition' and not having to establish an absolute bar. This is not the first time the decision in *Perera* has been questioned.

2.   There has been a series of cases considering the issue whether an obligation to work full-time amounts to a requirement or condition for the purposes of s. 1(1)(b). As this affects many women who wish to return to work after maternity leave or while they have children at primary school, it has become an important issue. Initially, in *The Home Office* v *Holmes* [1984] IRLR 299, it was held that such a requirement fell within the meaning of s. 1(1)(b) in that it was an essential part of the employee's contract as, unless she went on working full-time, she would not be allowed to continue her job. However, in *Clymo* v *London Borough of Wandsworth* [1989] IRLR 241, it was held (at p. 247) that where full-time working had been offered and accepted by the applicant and was part of the nature of the job, it could not be said that a requirement or condition had been applied to the applicant. The main

problem with this case is that the EAT distinguished between jobs at management/ supervisory level and lower grade jobs; in the former, full-time working would be part of the nature of the job, whereas in the latter it would amount to a requirement or condition. The matter has to some extent been settled by the decision in *Briggs* v *North Eastern Education and Library Board* [1990] IRLR 181, where it was held (per Hutton LCJ at p. 186) that the decision in *Holmes* was to be preferred to that in *Clymo*, and accordingly even though the nature of the job required full-time working this did not prevent there being a requirement or condition being applied to the applicant. Lastly, where a person returns to part-time work having worked full-time, the employer does not discriminate in dictating the days and hours worked in respect of the part-time employment (see *Greater Glasgow Health Board* v *Carey* [1987] IRLR 484), as this can be justified on the terms of administrative efficiency.

A contractual term which imposes an obligation on a party to the contract amounts to the application of a requirement or condition within s. 1(1)(b) SDA 1975, notwithstanding that the term has not been invoked. A mobility clause in the present case was such a requirement/condition which had a disparate impact on women as the number of women who could comply with the clause was considerably smaller than the number of men (*Meade-Hill & National Union of Civil Servants* v *British Council* [1995] IRLR 478, CA). Naturally the employer has every right at the time of applying the clause to justify it objectively.

3. In the light of the decision in *Enderby* v *Frenchay Health Authority* [1993] IRLR 591, it was argued that it was no longer necessary to establish a requirement or condition under domestic law. This argument was, however, rejected in *Bhudi & Others* v *IMI Refiners Ltd* [1994] IRLR 204 in which it was held that *Enderby* was solely concerned with the interpretation of Article 119 (now 141) of the EC Treaty and that there was no obligation to construe s. 1(1)(b) in such a way as to disregard the express provision relating to proof of a 'requirement or condition'.

(ii)   What Amounts to a Considerably Smaller Proportion?
Once the complainant has established that a requirement or condition has been applied to him which is also applied equally to other persons, he must then show adverse impact. There is little doubt that this can be the most contentious part of his claim. The appropriate pool for comparison must be selected, preferably supported by statistical evidence. It is then a matter for the industrial tribunal whether it will accept the pool selected by the complainant, for whom this area is full of pitfalls.

Pearse* v *Bradford Metropolitan Council
[1988] IRLR 379
Employment Appeal Tribunal

Miss Pearse was employed as a part-time lecturer in the department of applied and community services at Ilkley College. The employers had a vacancy for a full-time post as senior lecturer/coordinator of the student counselling service. However, under a 'ring-fence' agreement with the union, any vacancy was to be advertised first within the college in which it arose and the only persons eligible to apply for the post in the first instance were full-time employees of the authority. If that advertisement did not result in an appointment being made, the post was re-advertised within the authority as a whole, but the same limitations were placed on who could apply. Only if there were still no suitable applicants, was the vacancy to be generally advertised.

Miss Pearse claimed that the selection arrangements were indirectly discriminatory on grounds of sex. She argued that the employers' requirement that only full-time employees could apply for the post was such that the proportion of women who could comply with it was considerably smaller than the proportion of men who could comply with it within the meaning of s. 1(1)(b)(i) of the Sex Discrimination Act.

At the industrial tribunal hearing, Miss Pearse submitted statistics showing that only 21.8 per cent of the female academic staff employed in the college were employed full-time compared with 46.7 per cent of male academic staff who could comply with the full-time working requirement. The employers argued, however, that the correct comparison was between women and men who had appropriate qualifications for the vacant post, either within the existing academic staff of the college or in the community at large.

The EAT held, dismissing Pearse's appeal, the industrial tribunal was entitled to find that the correct pool for comparison was from those with appropriate qualifications for the vacant post, rather than those eligible for the job.

HUTCHINSON J: Before the Tribunal the contentions that were advanced on each side in relation to the selection of a pool were as follows. The appellant contended that regard should be had to the whole of the academic staff at the college. If she was right, then the results in terms of figures and proportions which we have already mentioned followed. The respondents disputed this approach, and advanced alternative contentions: first that it was appropriate for purposes of comparison to have regard to those in the community at large who had appropriate qualifications for the vacant post. Alternatively, they argued, regard should be had to those within the existing academic staff of the college who had appropriate qualifications for the vacant post. Dealing with those rival contentions the Tribunal directed themselves in accordance with the authority of *Kidd* v *DRG (UK) Ltd* [1985] IRLR 190 – an authority to which we shall return – and continued:

> On this basis the Tribunal accept the respondents' submission that the correct pool is from those with the appropriate qualifications for the vacant post. Accepting that as the appropriate pool, we find no evidence by the applicant that from that group the proportion of men who could apply was greater than the proportion of women. The Tribunal are fully entitled to refuse to draw an inference without evidential support regarding the proportionate capacity of persons of a particular sex status within the pool which they are required to consider to comply with a condition of full-time employment.

As was pointed out in the course of the hearing, it is not entirely clear from this language whether the Tribunal was accepting the first or the second of the respondents' alternatives – all that is clear is that they were accepting one or other of them and rejecting the argument advanced by the appellant . . .

Mr Cottle, recognising that unless he can successfully attack the Tribunal's resolution of this question the appeal must fail, argues that their selection of such a pool – that is to say a pool determined by those within whatever proportion of the community they were considering who were possessed of the requisite qualifications – was wrong in law because it conflicted with the statutory provisions. As we understood his argument it amounted to this: that the pool must bear relation to those eligible to apply and those not eligible, rather than to the capacity to carry out the job. The latter, he submitted, involved the introduction of an extra element uncalled for by the statutory provisions, because the requirement in question bites on eligibility to apply and not on capacity to carry out the job. In effect, he was submitting that the nature of the requirement necessarily determines the pool. It is an error of law he contended for the Tribunal to select a pool which is not as close as possible to the requirement.

In approaching the primary submissions made on this topic by Mr Cottle and Mrs Sutcliffe we have regard to what was said by this Tribunal in the case to which the Industrial Tribunal referred – namely the case of *Kidd*:

> We reject the argument that the choice of section of the population required to give effect to s. 5(3) of the Act is a question of law; nor do we think that the decision in *Price's* case [1977] IRLR 291 (which at paragraph 12 took care to disavow any intention of laying down a binding proposition) gives the argument any support. The choice of an appropriate section of the population is in our judgment an issue of fact (or perhaps strictly a matter for discretion to be exercised in the course of discharging an exclusively fact-finding function) entrusted by Parliament to the good sense of the Tribunals, whose selection will be influenced by the need to fit it as closely as possible to the varying circumstances of each case. Of course in those exceptional cases where it can be shown that good sense has not prevailed, and the Tribunal has chosen to make the proportionate comparison within an area of society so irrationally inappropriate as to put it outside the range of selection for any reasonable Tribunal, then the Tribunal would have fallen into an error of law which could be corrected in the appellate jurisdiction.

> We confess that we are unable to see how, given this approach, it can possibly be contended that a Tribunal which introduces a concept which has to do with ability to perform the job can be said, as Mr Cottle submits, to be disregarding the relevant statutory provisions. On the contrary, it seems to us that not only does such an approach not infringe the statutory requirements, but it has a great deal to commend it. What could be more sensible, when considering what selection to make for purposes of comparison in relation to a requirement or condition biting upon an application for a post requiring particular qualifications, to look to those qualified to apply? The irrationality of looking elsewhere, and the startling results that might follow if one were to do so, need no elaboration.

Notes

1. The problems faced by the complainant in selecting the correct pool originate from the case of *Kidd v DRG (UK) Ltd* [1985] IRLR 190, which upheld the virtually unchallengeable right of the tribunal to decide the proper

section of the community for the purposes of making a comparison; the pool being a question of fact in each case. The tribunal's selection of the pool can only be challenged as an error of law where 'it is so irrationally inappropriate as to put it outside the range of selection for any reasonable tribunal' (at p. 195). In addition, a tribunal which refuses to make assumptions such as fewer married women being able to work full-time because they are likely to be involved in caring for children, without the support of statistical evidence, is not acting unreasonably. Furthermore, in *R* v *Secretary of State for Education, ex parte Schaffter* [1987] IRLR 53, the court expressed concern about the potential risk of incorporating discrimination into the pool for comparison, emphasising that this should be avoided at all costs.

2. The selection of the correct pool and the proof of disparate impact are critical stages in establishing indirect discrimination. The decision of the Court of Appeal in *Jones* v *University of Manchester* [1993] IRLR 193 illustrates that any attempt by the applicant to manipulate the size of the pool for his or her own benefit will not be upheld. Following *Pearse*, the pool should comprise those qualified for the job in question, excluding the requirement complained of. In Mrs Jones's case this should have been all those graduates with the required experience. However, Mrs Jones as a mature graduate attempted to limit the pool to mature graduates. The Court would not accept this further subdivision of the pool.

3. Once the appropriate and (it is hoped) correct pool has been selected, supported by the necessary statistical evidence, a calculation is needed to show disparate impact. This is expressed in terms of proportion not numbers, and therefore an absolute comparison is not required. Palmer, C., *Discrimination in Employment* (LAG, 1992), at p. 41, provides the following calculation:

(a) take the number of women in the pool;
(b) take the number of women in the pool who can meet the challenged requirement or condition;
(c) divide (b) by (a) to give the proportion of women in the pool who can satisfy the challenged requirement or condition.

The same calculation is done for men and the comparison is then between the fraction or percentage arrived for the women and men.

A similar calculation can be done in respect of racial groups.

Guidance is also given in *Jones* v *Chief Adjudication Officer* [1990] IRLR 533 (alleged discrimination regarding the receipt of social security benefits), where Mustill LJ, at p. 537, laid down the criteria for establishing disparate impact:

What we must consider is whether, if one looks not at individuals but at the population of claimants as a whole, it can be seen that there is indirect discrimination. The parties agree that for this purpose it is the effect, not the intent, of the legislation which counts. They also agree that what was called the 'demographic' argument represents one way in which indirect discrimination can be established. As I understand it, the process for establishing discrimination on this basis takes the following shape. (For ease of illustration, I will assume that the complaint stems from the failure of a woman to satisfy a relevant positive qualification for selection, and that only one such qualification is in issue.)

1.   Identify the criterion for selection;
2.   Identify the relevant population, comprising all those who satisfy all the other criteria for selection. (I do not know to what extent this step in the process is articulated in the cases. To my mind it is vital to the intellectual soundness of the demographic argument);
3.   Divide the relevant population into groups representing those who satisfy the criterion and those who do not;
4.   Predict statistically what proportion of each group should consist of women;
5.   Ascertain what are the actual male/female balances in the two groups;
6.   Compare the actual with the predicted balances;
7.   If women are found to be under-represented in the first group and over-represented in the second, it is proved that the criterion is discriminatory.

This is a more complicated scheme which appears to work only where there is more than one requirement or condition. Also it ignores the fact that each individual has the right not to be discriminated against, not just the group to which he or she belongs.

4.   Further guidance on establishing 'a considerably smaller proportion of a particular sex' can be found in *London Underground Ltd* v *Edwards (No. 2)* [1998] IRLR 364, per Potter LJ at p. 369. In the *Edwards* case, whilst 100 per cent (2,023) of male train operators could comply with the requirement or condition compared to 95.2 per cent of female train operators (20 out of 21), it was found to have a disproportionate effect on the women when the actual numbers involved were considered, i.e. not a single man was affected by the requirement or condition:

. . . In my view, there is a dual statutory purpose underlying the provisions of s. 1(1)(b) and in particular the necessity under subparagraph (i) to show that the proportion of women who can comply with a given requirement or condition is 'considerably smaller' than the proportion of men who can comply with it. The first is to prescribe as the threshold for intervention a situation in which there exists a substantial and not merely marginal discriminatory effect (disparate impact) as between men and women, so that it can be clearly demonstrated that a prima facie case of (indirect) discrimination exists, sufficient to require the employer to justify the application of the condition or requirement in question: see subparagraph (ii). The second is to ensure that a tribunal charged with deciding whether or not the requirement is discriminatory may be confident that its disparate impact is inherent in the application of the requirement or condition and is not simply the product of unreliable statistics or fortuitous circumstance. Since the disparate impact question will require to be resolved in an infinite number of different employment situations, well but by no means comprehensively exemplified in the arguments of Mr Allen, an area of flexibility (or margin of appreciation), is necessarily applicable to the question f whether a particular percentage is to be regarded as 'substantially smaller' in any given case.

5.   For a discussion of the American approach, which adopts a 'four-fifths rule' for determining disparate impact, see Townshend-Smith, R., *Sex*

Discrimination in Employment: Law, Practice and Policy (Sweet & Maxwell, 1989), at p. 76.

6. For a critical examination of indirect discrimination, see the research paper undertaken by Byre, A., *Indirect Discrimination* (EOC, 1987).

7. 'Nil' has been held to be 'a considerably smaller proportion' (*Greencroft Social Club & Institute* v *Mullen* [1985] ICR 796).

(iii) What is Meant by 'Can Comply'?

The complainant must show that a considerably smaller proportion of women/his racial group 'can comply' with the requirement or condition compared to men or other persons. The interpretation of these words was determined in the next case.

Clarke v *Eley (IMI) Kynoch Ltd*
[1982] IRLR 482
Employment Appeal Tribunal

Mrs Clarke and Miss Powell were both employed part-time at the company's munitions factory in Birmingham. They were among 60 part-time women to be made redundant on 23 October 1981. At the same time, 20 full-time men and 26 full-time women were also dismissed for reasons of redundancy. The dismissal of the part-timers was in accordance with the company's redundancy selection procedure of dismissing part-timers first before applying the last in first out criterion to full-timers on a unit basis. That procedure was ratified by the union, the TGWU, after a mass meeting of employees had voted in its favour.

The circumstances of the two applicants are different. Miss Powell started work in 1975. She had a child in 1978. The industrial tribunal found that at no time did her domestic circumstances permit her to be a full-time worker. Mrs Clarke, on the other hand, started work in 1967. She has two adult children who had left school by 1975 or 1976. The tribunal found that once both her children had left school there was thereafter no domestic reason why she should not have worked full time. The importance of the distinction between the domestic circumstances of the two ladies is that down to early 1980 there was nothing to prevent a part-time worker transferring so as to become a full time worker. However, as from the middle of 1980 such transfer was not possible.

The EAT held, allowing Clarke's appeal, for the purposes of s. 1(1)(b), the relevant point of time at which the ability or inability of an applicant to comply with a requirement or condition has to be shown is the date on which she alleges she has suffered detriment. This is the same point in time as that at which the requirement or condition has to be fulfilled. Therefore, the words 'can comply' in s. 1(1)(b)(i) and 'cannot comply' in s. 1(1)(b)(iii) do not include past opportunities to comply.

Consequently, the applicant Mrs Clarke had discharged the burden imposed on her since she had shown that she personally suffered the detriment of dismissal, the reason being that at the time she was dismissed she could not comply with the requirement that she should be a full-time worker. It was irrelevant that at some earlier date she could have avoided that detriment by becoming a full-time worker.

BROWNE-WILKINSON J: . . . *Do the words 'can comply' in para. (1) and 'cannot comply' in para. (iii) include past opportunities to comply?*

The question is whether the applicant's inability to comply with a requirement or condition has to be judged as at the date of selection for redundancy or dismissal or as at some earlier date. The point has a dual importance in this case. First, if it is legitimate to have regard to the ability of part-time workers to become full-time workers before 1980, then for the purposes of para. (i) the proportion of women who 'can comply' at that earlier date will be different from the proportion who 'can comply' in 1981 when transfer from part-time to full-time workers had become impossible. Secondly, the Industrial Tribunal held that Mrs Clarke failed to satisfy the requirement of para. (iii) because at some earlier date she could have transferred to full-time work and if she had done so she would not have suffered the detriment.

On this issue we are unable to agree with the Industrial Tribunal. Counsel are agreed that the relevant point in time at which the ability to comply has to be assessed must be the same under both para. (i) and para. (iii). We will consider the case under para. (iii) first. The Industrial Tribunal, although accepting that both ladies had suffered a detriment, said that they had to show that they could not comply as individuals with the requirement to be full-time workers. No doubt this was a paraphrase of the statutory words, but we think that the paraphrase may have led the Industrial Tribunal astray. Para. (iii) does not in terms impose on the complainant the burden of showing that she cannot comply with the requirement: she has to show that the requirement 'is to her detriment *because* she cannot comply with it'. The paragraph imposes the burden of showing detriment to the individual applicant by reason of inability to comply. If one asked the question 'At what date is the detriment to be demonstrated?' there can only be one answer: namely, at the date the discriminatory conduct has operated so as to create the alleged detriment. In this case the detriment relied upon is the dismissal for redundancy. Therefore the relevant question under para. (iii) is 'did the applicant suffer the detriment of dismissal for redundancy because she could not comply with the requirement to be a full-time worker'? So analysed, it seems to us that under para. (iii) the only material question is whether *at the date of the detriment* she can or cannot comply with the requirement. If she can, para. (iii) is not satisfied; if she cannot, it is satisfied. The use of the present tense – 'is' to her detriment because she 'cannot' comply – shows that only one point in time is being looked at.

If we are right in thinking that the date of detriment is the only relevant date under para. (iii), we think that counsel are right in conceding that the same date is the only relevant date under para. (i). If that is not the relevant date for the purposes of para. (i) what other date is to be taken? The proportion of men and women who can comply with any given requirement may well vary from time to time. In this case for example the company is arguing that the requirements of para. (i) have not been satisfied because there was no evidence before the Industrial Tribunal as to what proportion of women part-time workers could, like Mrs Clarke, in the past have become full time workers. If that line of inquiry is open, then the proportion of part-time workers whose domestic circumstances permitted them to take full time work will vary from time to time. At what point in time is the comparison between women and men to be made?

For these reasons we think that for all the purposes of s. 1(1)(b) the relevant point of time at which the ability or inability to comply has to be shown is the date on which the applicant alleges she has suffered detriment. This is in fact the same point in time as 'that at which the requirement or condition has to be fulfilled': see *Steel* v *Union of Post Office Workers* [[1977] IRLR 288].

Note

The date on which compliance with the requirement or condition is to be judged is the date on which it is applied, not at some future date (*Raval* v *DHSS* [1985] IRLR 370).

(iv) 'Detriment'

The complainant must show that the requirement or condition is to his or her detriment because he or she *cannot* comply with it, i.e. there must be *locus standi*. As can be seen from *Clarke's* case (above), the inability to comply must be judged at the date the requirement has to be fulfilled, which is also the same point in time at which the detriment is suffered.

The 'detriment' referred to in SDA 1975, s. 6(2)(b) does not have to be a detriment of a different kind to that which must be shown under s. 1(1)(b)(iii). It is entirely consistent with the scheme and language of the Act that the same disadvantage to the complainant may be relied on in both sections (see *Holmes* v *Home Office* (above)).

Lord Wedderburn, '*The Worker and the Law*' (Penguin Books, 1986), 3rd edn, at pp. 466–8, considers the meaning of 'detriment' and criticises the attitude of, in particular, the appeal courts to such matters.

Questions

1. Can comparison with the population as a whole ever be 'appropriate'?
2. How does one decide what percentage is 'considerably smaller'? Is there any solution to this?
3. Can it be argued that because a person is a victim of discrimination this is in itself a 'detriment' within RRA 1976, s. 1 and s. 4 and SDA 1975, s. 6, respectively?
4. Where an employer has alternative criteria for a job or position, does the fact that only one has a disparate impact contravene the legislation? See *Meer* v *London Borough of Tower Hamlets* [1988] IRLR 399.

(v) Justification

Section 1(1)(b) provides a defence for the employer in that he is given the opportunity to justify the requirement or condition. The test for establishing justification is the same as the test for establishing a genuine material difference/factor under EPA 1970, s. 1(3) (see *Rainey* v *Greater Glasgow Health Board* [1987] IRLR 26 and *Bilka-Kaufhaus GmbH* v *Weber von Hartz* [1986] IRLR 317). This was confirmed in the following case.

Hampson v Department of Education and Science
[1989] IRLR 69
Court of Appeal

This case was concerned with RRA 1976, s. 41.

Mrs Hampson is a Hong Kong Chinese woman who was refused qualified teacher status in England. She claimed that this was the result of the application of indirectly discriminatory criteria by the Secretary of State for Education.

Mrs Hampson had taken a two years' initial teacher training course in Hong Kong, qualifying her to teach there. Eight years' later, she took a third year full-time teaching course in Hong Kong. Subsequently, she came to England and sought qualified teacher status.

Section 27 of the Education Act 1980 provides that: 'The Secretary of State may by regulations make provision . . . for requiring teachers at schools . . . to possess such qualification as may be determined by or under the regulations . . .' Regulation 13(1) of the Education (Teachers) Regulations 1982 provides that 'no person shall be employed as a teacher at a school unless he is qualified . . . as mentioned in Schedule 5'. Schedule 5 provides for the Secretary of State to determine who is a 'qualified teacher' and stipulates that the Secretary of State will approve as a qualified teacher a person who has completed an approved UK course for initial teacher training or a person who has successfully completed a course 'approved as comparable' to such a course.

Mrs Hampson's application was turned down on grounds that her training was not 'comparable' to that provided in the UK, as required by the 1982 Regulations. This was said to be because, unlike courses in the UK, her initial training was two rather than three years and because the content of courses in Hong Kong did not meet the Department of Education's standards.

It was held, on the meaning of 'justifiable' within s. 1(1)(b), that it requires an objective balance to be struck between the discriminatory effect of the requirement or condition and the reasonable needs of the person who applies it. The tests of justifiability in related fields should be consistent with each other.

BALCOMBE LJ: [Commenting on the meaning put forward in *Ojutiku* v *Manpower Services Commission* [1982] IRLR 418, *Steel* v *Union of Post Office Workers* [1977] IRLR 288 and *Singh* v *Rowntree Mackintosh Ltd* [1979] IRLR 199.]

However, I do derive considerable assistance from the judgment of Lord Justice Stephenson [in *Ojutiku*]. At p. 423 he referred to:

> . . . the comments, which I regard as sound, made by Lord McDonald, giving the judgment of the Employment Appeal Tribunal in Scotland in the cases of *Singh* v *Rowntree Mackintosh Ltd* [1979] IRLR 199 upon the judgment of the Appeal Tribunal given by Phillips J in *Steel* v *Union of Post Office Workers* to which my Lords have referred.

> What Phillips J there said is valuable as rejecting justification by convenience and requiring the party applying the discriminatory condition to prove it to be justifiable in all the circumstances on balancing its discriminatory effect against the discriminator's need for it. But that need is what is reasonably needed by the party who applies the condition; . . .

In my judgment 'justifiable' requires an objective balance between the discriminatory effect of the condition and the reasonable needs of the party who applies the condition.

This construction is supported by the recent decision of the House of Lords in *Rainey* v *Greater Glasgow Health Board* [1987] IRLR 26, a case under the Equal Pay Act 1970, and turning on the provisions of s. 1(3) of that Act which at the material time was in the following terms:

> An equality clause shall not operate in relation to a variation between the woman's contract and the man's contract if the employer proves that the variation is genuinely due to a material difference (other than the difference of sex) between her case and his.

The House of Lords held, applying the decision of the European Court in *Bilka-Kaufhaus GmbH* v *Weber von Hartz* [1986] IRLR 317, that to justify a material difference under s. 1(3) of the 1970 Act, the employer had to show a real need on the part of the undertaking, objectively justified, although that need was not confined to economic grounds; it might, for instance, include administrative efficiency in a concern not engaged in commerce or business. Clearly it may, as in the present case, be possible to justify by reference to grounds other than economic or administrative efficiency.

At p. 31 Lord Keith of Kinkel (who gave the leading speech, with which all the other law lords agreed) said, in reference to an argument based on s. 1(1)(b)(ii) of the Sex Discrimination Act 1975, which is identical, mutatis mutandis, to s. 1(1)(b)(ii) of the 1976 Act:

> This provision has the effect of prohibiting indirect discrimination between women and men. In my opinion it does not, for present purposes, add anything to s. 1(3) of the Act of 1970, since, upon the view which I have taken as to the proper construction of the latter, a difference which demonstrated unjustified indirect discrimination would not discharge the onus placed on the employer. Further, there would not appear to be any material distinction in principle between the need to demonstrate objectively justified grounds of difference for purposes of s. 1(3) and the need to justify a requirement or condition under s. 1(1)(b)(ii) of the Act of 1975.

Mr Sedley constructed an elaborate argument designed to show that *Ojutiku* had been overruled by *Rainey*. (This argument will be found set out in detail in the judgment of the EAT in [1988] IRLR at pp. 93–95. However, I do not find it necessary to consider this argument further here. For my part I can find no significant difference between the test adopted by Lord Justice Stephenson in *Ojutiku* and that adopted by the House of Lords in *Rainey*. Since neither Lords Justices Eveleigh nor Kerr in *Ojutiku* indicated what they considered the test to be – although Lord Justice Kerr said what it was not – I am content to adopt Lord Justice Stephenson's test as I have expressed it above, which I consider to be consistent with *Rainey*. It is obviously desirable that the tests of justifiability applied in all these closely related fields should be consistent with each other.

NOURSE LJ: I agree with Lord Justice Balcombe that the best interpretation which can be put on the authorities, in particular on the decisions of this court in *Ojutiku* v *Manpower Services Commission* [1982] IRLR 418 and of the House of Lords in *Rainey* v *Greater Glasgow Health Board* [1987] IRLR 26, is that the correct test is one which requires an objective balance to be struck between the discriminatory effect of the requirement or condition and the reasonable needs of the person who applies it. If, and only if, its discriminatory effect can be objectively justified by those needs will the requirement or condition be 'justifiable' within s. 1(1)(b)(ii) of the Race Relations Act.

Notes
1. *Hampson* went on appeal to the House of Lords ([1990] IRLR 302) where the argument was directed solely on the interpretation of RRA 1976, s. 41.
2. There has been much criticism of the *Ojutiku* case, and although the decision in *Hampson* appears to confirm that it is not inconsistent with *Rainey* and *Bilka-Kaufhaus*, it has been considered that *Rainey* in fact supersedes it (see Townshend-Smith, R., *Sex Discrimination in Employment: Law, Practice and Policy* (Sweet & Maxwell, 1989), pp. 79–83).
3. Whether a requirement or condition can be justified is a question of fact for the tribunal applying the test in *Rainey*. In the past a wide range of practices have been justified on the following grounds: safety (*Singh* v *Rowntree Mackintosh* [1979] IRLR 199; *Panesar* v *Nestlé Co.* [1980] ICR 144); qualifications (*Raval* v *DHSS* [1985] IRLR 370); part-time employment (*Greater Glasgow Health Board* v *Carey* [1987] IRLR 494; *Kidd* v *DRG (UK) Ltd* [1985] IRLR 190).

Questions
1. Should the issue of justification be a question left to the discretion of the tribunal (see *Clarke* v *Eley (IMI) Kynoch Ltd* [1982] IRLR 482) bearing in mind that there is no appeal on a question of fact?
2. How far has the decision in *Ojutiku* been eroded? (See *Greater Manchester Police Authority* v *Lea* [1990] IRLR 372.)
3. How far is the test of 'objectively justified' being judged through the eyes of a subjective tribunal?
4. How far is the test laid down in *Bilka-Kaufhaus* appropriate for judging health and safety issues?

C: Pregnancy

Discrimination on grounds of pregnancy or maternity is not automatically unlawful; whereas dismissals on grounds of or in connection with pregnancy are automatically unfair (Employment Rights Act 1996, s. 99). The only mention of pregnancy or childbirth in the SDA 1975 is to be found in s. 2(2), which prevents a man claiming discrimination on the basis of the special treatment received by women in connection with pregnancy and childbirth.

The appeal courts originally took a strong line on discrimination in respect of pregnancy by concluding that it was outside the SDA 1975, as a pregnant female complainant was not able to show that the less favourable treatment was on grounds of her sex as she had no one with whom she could compare herself since men could not become pregnant (see *Turley* v *Allders Department Stores Ltd* [1980] ICR 66). This position was remedied to some extent by the decision in *Hayes* v *Malleable Working Men's Club* [1985] IRLR 367, which drew on the comparison between a pregnant woman and a sick man. While this analogy was originally followed in our national courts (see *Webb* v *Emo Air Cargo (UK) Ltd* [1993] IRLR 27, it has been superseded by the ruling of the ECJ.

Webb v *EMO Air Cargo (UK) Ltd (No. 2)*
[1995] IRLR 645
House of Lords

The respondent firm had 16 employees. It had an import department of four staff, including an import operations clerk, Mrs Stewart. In June 1987, it became known that Mrs Stewart was pregnant and would be taking maternity leave at the end of the year. Mrs Webb was taken on as an import operations clerk on 1 July. It was recognised that she would need six months' training from Mrs Stewart and would then be able to act as her temporary replacement. It was anticipated that Mrs Webb would probably stay in employment when Mrs Stewart returned.

Several weeks after starting work, however, Mrs Webb discovered that she was pregnant and so informed the employers. The employers took the view that they had no alternative but to dismiss her. She complained that she had been discriminated against on grounds of sex.

The House of Lords held that the appellant's dismissal did not constitute unlawful direct discrimination since a hypothetical man required for the same purpose who would also be unavailable at the material time would have been treated similarly. The case was remitted to the ECJ for them to determine whether a dismissal in these circumstances was discriminatory under EC law. The ECJ ([1994] IRLR 482) ruled that Directive 76/207 precluded dismissal of an employee who is recruited for an unlimited term with a view, initially, to replacing another employee during the latter's maternity leave and who cannot do so because, shortly after her recruitment, she is herself found to be pregnant. The case returned to the House of Lords.

LORD KEITH: . . . The ruling of the European Court of Justice was given on 14 July 1994 ([1994] IRLR 482). The paragraphs of the ruling principally relevant are these (p. 494):

24. First, in response to the House of Lords' inquiry, there can be no question of comparing the situation of a woman who finds herself incapable, by reason of pregnancy discovered very shortly after the conclusion of the employment contract, of performing the task for which she was recruited with that of a man similarly incapable for medical or other reasons.

25. As the applicant rightly argues, pregnancy is not in any way comparable with a pathological condition, and even less so with unavailability for work on non-medical grounds, both of which are situations that may justify the dismissal of a woman without discriminating on grounds of sex. Moreover, in *Handels- og Kontorfunktionaererernes Forbund i Danmark* v *Dansk Arbejdsgiverforening*, C-179/88 [1991] IRLR 31, the Court drew a clear distinction between pregnancy and illness, even where the illness is attributable to pregnancy but manifests itself after the maternity leave. As the Court pointed out, at paragraph 16, there is no reason to distinguish such an illness from any other illness.

26. Furthermore, contrary to the submission of the United Kingdom, dismissal of a pregnant woman recruited for an indefinite period cannot be justified on grounds relating to her inability to fulfil a ' fundamental condition of her employment contract. The availability of an employee is necessarily, for the employer, a

precondition for the proper performance of the employment contract. However, the protection afforded by Community law to a woman during pregnancy and after childbirth cannot be dependent on whether her presence at work during maternity is essential to the proper functioning of the undertaking in which she is employed. Any contrary interpretation would render ineffective the provisions of the Directive.
27.   In circumstances such as those of the applicant, termination of a contract for an indefinite period on grounds of the woman's pregnancy cannot be justified by the fact that she is prevented, on a purely temporary basis, from performing the work for which she has been engaged: see *Habermann-Beltermann* v *Arbeiterwohlfahrt, Bezirksverband Ndb /Opf e V*, C-421/92 [1994] IRLR 364 at p. 367, 25; and paragraphs 10 and 11 of the Advocate-General's Opinion in this case, ante, at [1994] IRLR 491.
28.   The fact that the main proceedings concern a woman who was initially recruited to replace another employee during the latter's maternity leave but who was herself found to be pregnant shortly after her recruitment cannot affect the answer to be given to the national court.
29.   Accordingly, the answer to the question submitted must be that Article 2(1) read with Article 5(1) of Directive (76/207/EEC) precludes dismissal of an employee who is recruited for an unlimited term with a view, initially, to replacing another employee during the latter's maternity leave and who cannot do so because, shortly after recruitment, she is herself found to be pregnant.

It is apparent from the ruling of the Court, and also from the Opinion of the Advocate-General, that it was considered to be a relevant circumstance that the appellant had been engaged for an indefinite or unlimited period.
. . . The ruling of the European Court proceeds on an interpretation of the broad principles dealt with in Articles 2(1) and 5(1) of the Directive 76/207/EEC. Sections 1(1)(a) and 5(3) of the Act of 1975 set out a more precise test of unlawful discrimination and the problem is how to fit the terms of that test into the ruling. It seems to me that the only way of doing so is to hold that, in a case where a woman is engaged for an indefinite period, the fact that the reason why she will be temporarily unavailable for work at a time when to her knowledge her services will be particularly required is pregnancy is a circumstance relevant to her case, being a circumstance which could not be present in the case of the hypothetical man. It does not necessarily follow that pregnancy would be a relevant circumstance in the situation where the woman is denied employment for a fixed period in the future during the whole of which her pregnancy would make her unavailable for work, nor in the situation where after engagement for such a period the discovery of her pregnancy leads to cancellation of the engagement.

Note
The impact of Directive 76/207, in particular Article 2(3), can be seen in the following cases.

Dekker v *Stichting Vormingscentrum Voor Jonge Volwassenen (VJV-Centrum) Plus*
[1991] IRLR 27
European Court of Justice

Elizabeth Dekker applied for a post of training instructor in a youth centre run by VJV. She was pregnant when she applied and so informed the selection committee. The committee recommended Mrs Dekker as the most suitable candidate, but the VJV Board decided that they could not take her on. The reason given to Mrs Dekker was that VJV were advised that their insurer, the Risk Fund for Special Education, would not reimburse the sickness benefits which VJV would have to pay to Mrs Dekker during her maternity leave because she was pregnant at the time of her application.

Under Dutch law covering the public sector, an employee who is unable to perform his or her duties as a result of illness is entitled to 100 per cent of most recent monthly salary for the first year and 80 per cent for the next year. The relevant Royal decree provides that inability to work due to illness shall be treated in the same way as 'incapacity as a result of pregnancy and confinement'.

However, under the rules of the Risk Fund for Special Education, the fund's managers were entitled to refuse reimbursement of sickness benefit to the employer in the event of an insured person becoming unable to perform his or her duties within six months of the date on which the insurance cover was taken out, if the inability to work was foreseeable at the time when the cover commenced. In Mrs Dekker's case, the employers were concerned that pregnancy would be regarded as a foreseeable incapacity when the employment began. Accordingly, VJV contended that if they were not reimbursed, they would not be able to employ a replacement for Mrs Dekker during her absence, which would mean that they would lose some of their training places.

Mrs Dekker claimed damages, arguing that the refusal of employment was contrary to the provisions of the Dutch equal treatment law of 1 March 1980 implementing EEC Equal Treatment Directive 76/207. The Dutch courts held that the equal treatment law had been violated, but rejected the complaint on grounds that the employer had raised an acceptable ground for justification under Dutch law, which resulted in the violation of the law losing its unlawful character.

The ECJ held that refusing to employ a suitable female applicant on the ground of the possible adverse consequences arising from employing a woman who is pregnant at the time of the application is in contravention of Directive 76/207, Articles 2(1) and 3(1). If the principal reason for the act of discrimination is pregnancy then direct discrimination has occurred.

DECISION: As employment can only be refused because of pregnancy to woman, such a refusal is direct discrimination on grounds of sex. A refusal to employ because of the financial consequences of absence connected with pregnancy must be deemed to be based principally on the fact of the pregnancy. Such discrimination cannot be justified by the financial detriment in the case of recruitment of a pregnant woman suffered by the employer during her maternity leave.

The fact that pregnancy is treated in the same way as illness and that the provisions of the Sick Act and the Sickness Benefit Regulations concerning payments of sickness benefit in connection with pregnancy are not identical, cannot be considered to result in discrimination on grounds of sex within the meaning of the Directive. Finally, where refusal to recruit by an employer because of the financial consequences of absence connected with pregnancy results in direct discrimination, there is no need to investigate whether national provisions like those referred to above are such that the employer is more or less compelled not to recruit pregnant women, which would result in discrimination within the meaning of the Directive.

It follows from the above considerations that the answer to the first question submitted for a preliminary ruling must be that an employer is acting in direct contravention of the principle of equal treatment referred to in Articles 2(1) and 3(1) of Council Directive 76/207 of 9 February 1976 on the implementation of the principle of equal treatment for men and women as regards access to employment, vocational training and promotion, and working conditions if he refuses to enter into a contract of employment with a female applicant found suitable by him for the post in question, where such refusal is on the ground of the possible adverse consequences for him arising from employing a woman who is pregnant at the time of the application, because of a Government Regulation concerning incapacity to work which treats inability to work because of pregnancy and confinement in the same way as inability to work because of illness.

Handels-og Kontorfunktionaerernes Forbund I Danmark v *Dansk Arbejdsgiverforening (acting for Aldi Marked KIS)*
[1991] IRLR 31
European Court of Justice

Mrs Hertz was employed by Aldi Marked in July 1982 as a part-time cashier and saleswoman. She gave birth to a child in June 1983 after a complicated pregnancy during which she was mainly on sick leave. After the expiry of her statutory entitlement to 24 weeks' maternity leave from the date of birth, she resumed work at the end of 1983 and had no health problems until June 1984. However, between June 1984 and June 1985, as a result of an illness arising out of her pregnancy and confinement, she was off work for 100 days. In June 1985, the employers dismissed Mrs Hertz on grounds of her repeated absences due to illness.

It was held that Directive 76/207, Articles 2 and 5 do not preclude dismissals resulting from absences due to an illness which originated in pregnancy or confinement. The dismissal of a female worker because of her pregnancy constitutes direct discrimination on grounds of her sex, in the same way as does the refusal to recruit a pregnant woman. However, in considering the treatment of a woman where an illness occurs after maternity leave, even though it is connected to the pregnancy or confinement, comparison must be made with the treatment of a sick man. If sickness absence would lead to dismissal of a male worker under the same conditions there is no direct discrimination on grounds of sex.

DECISION: Article 2(1) of the Directive provides that 'the principle of equal treatment shall mean that there shall be no discrimination whatsoever on grounds of sex, either directly or indirectly by reference in particular to marital or family status.' In the words of Article 5(1) 'the application of the principle of equal treatment with regard to working conditions, including the conditions governing dismissal, means that men and women shall be guaranteed the same conditions without discrimination on grounds of sex.'

Article 2(3) of the Directive provides that 'this Directive shall be without prejudice to provisions concerning the protection of women, particularly as regards pregnancy and maternity.'

It follows from the aforementioned provisions of the Directive that the dismissal of a female worker because of her pregnancy constitutes direct discrimination on grounds of sex, as does also the refusal to recruit a pregnant woman (see [Dekker] case 177/88, [1991] IRLR 27).

On the other hand, the dismissal of a female worker because of repeated sickness absence which does not have its origin in pregnancy or confinement does not constitute direct discrimination on grounds of sex, insofar as such sickness absence would lead to the dismissal of a male worker under the same conditions.

It should be pointed out that the Directive does not deal with the case of an illness which has its origin in pregnancy or confinement. It does, however, allow for national provisions which ensure specific rights for women in respect of pregnancy and maternity, such as maternity leave. It follows that during the maternity leave from which she benefits under national law, a woman is protected from dismissal because of her absence. It is a matter for each Member State to fix the period for maternity leave in such a way as to allow female workers to be absent during the period during which problems due to pregnancy and confinement may arise.

In regard to an illness which appears after maternity leave, there is not reason to distinguish an illness which has its origin in pregnancy or confinement from any other illness. Such a pathological condition therefore falls under the general scheme applicable to an illness.

Female and male workers are in fact equally exposed to illness. Although it is true that certain problems are specifically linked to one sex or another, the only question is whether a woman is dismissed for absence due to illness on the same conditions as a man: if that is the case, there is no direct discrimination on grounds of sex.

Handels-og Kontorfunktionaerernes Forbund i Danmark, acting on behalf of Høj Pedersen v Faellesforeningen for Danmarks Brugsforeringer, acting on behalf of Kvickly Skive
[1999] IRLR 55
European Court of Justice

Under the Danish employment law relating to non-manual workers, employees who are absent from work due to illness are entitled to full pay. Special provision is made, however, in respect of pregnant workers. Where an employee is pregnant, she is entitled to only half pay from her employer for a maximum of five months over a period beginning not earlier than three months before the confinement and ending not later than three months after the confinement. A pregnant employee who contracts an illness before the beginning of maternity leave is entitled to pay only if the illness is unconnected with pregnancy. If the illness is pregnancy-related, the employee has no right to pay and is only entitled to social security benefits. Even if a pregnant worker is not unfit, Danish law allows an employer to suspend the employee on half pay if it considers that she cannot be provided with work.

The four applicants all had abnormal pregnancies before the three months preceding the expected date of confinement. They brought proceedings challenging the rule that women who are unfit for work for a reason connected with the pregnancy before the three-month period preceding their confinement are not entitled to full pay.

The European Court held that it is contrary to the Equal Treatment Directive and to the Pregnant Workers Directive for national legislation to provide that an employer may send home a woman who is pregnant, although not unfit for work, without paying her salary in full when he considers that he cannot provide work for her.

DECISION: . . . It is true that, by reserving to Member States the right to retain or introduce provisions which are intended to protect women in connection with 'pregnancy and maternity', Article 2(3) of Directive 76/207 recognises the legitimacy, in terms of the principle of equal treatment, of protecting a woman's biological condition during and after pregnancy (Webb, cited above, paragraph 20).

However, legislation such as that at issue in the main proceedings cannot fall within the scope of that provision.

It appears from the order for reference that the Danish legislation is aimed not so much at protecting the pregnant woman's biological condition as at preserving the interests of her employer. The national court states that such legislation is based on the idea that, given the nature of the employment, the employer may impose requirements with regard to the employee's working capacity which justify her ceasing work at a date prior to the three-month period preceding the confinement.

Turning to Directive 92/85, it must be noted that Articles 4 and 5 set up an assessment and information procedure in respect of activities liable to involve a risk to safety or health or an effect on workers who are pregnant or breastfeeding. That procedure can lead to the employer making a temporary adjustment in working conditions and/or working hours or, if such an adjustment is not feasible, a move to another job. It is only when such a move is also not feasible that the worker is granted leave in accordance with national legislation or national practice for the whole of the period necessary to protect her safety or health.

It is clear from the order for reference that legislation such as that at issue in the main proceedings does not satisfy the substantive and formal conditions laid down in Directive 92/85 for granting the worker leave from her duties since, first, the reason for giving leave to the employee is based on the interest of the employer and, secondly, that decision can be taken by the employer without first examining the possibility of adjusting the employee's working conditions and/or working hours or even the possibility of moving her to another job.

Brown v Rentokil Ltd
[1998] IRLR 445
European Court of Justice

Mary Brown was employed as a service driver, transporting and changing Sanitact units in shops and other centres. In August 1990, she found out she was pregnant. From 16 August, she was absent continuously for a variety of pregnancy-related causes and never worked again. The employers operated a working rule under which an employee who exceeded 26 weeks' continuous sick leave was dismissed. In accordance with this rule, Mrs Brown was dismissed in February 1991. She then had 18 months' service, which was insufficient to bring an unfair dismissal complaint under the law as it then stood. She claimed that she had been discriminated against on grounds of sex.

DECISION: . . . According to settled case law of the Court of Justice, the dismissal of a female worker on account of pregnancy, or essentially on account of pregnancy, can affect only women and therefore constitutes direct discrimination on grounds of sex (see *case 177/88 Dekker* v *Stichting Vormingscentrum voor Jong Volwassenen (VJV-Centrum) Plus* [1991] IRLR 27, paragraph 12; *Hertz*, cited above, paragraph 13; case *C-421/92 Habermann-Beltermann* v *Arbeiterwohlfahrt Bezirksverbank Ndb/Opf eV* [1994] IRLR 364, paragraph 15; and case *C-32/93 Webb* v *EMO Air Cargo* [1994] IRLR 482, paragraph 19).

. . .

At the outset, it is clear from the documents before the Court that the question concerns the dismissal of a female worker during her pregnancy as a result of absences through incapacity for work arising from her pregnant condition. As Rentokil points out, the cause of Mrs Brown's dismissal lies in the fact that she was ill during her pregnancy to such an extent that she was unfit for work for 26 weeks. It is common ground that her illness was attributable to her pregnancy.

However, dismissal of a woman during pregnancy cannot be based on her inability, as a result of her condition, to perform the duties which she is contractually bound to carry out. If such an interpretation were adopted, the protection afforded by Community law to a woman during pregnancy would be available only to pregnant women who were able to comply with the conditions of their employment contracts, with the result that the provisions of Directive 76/207 would be rendered ineffective (see *Webb*, cited above, paragraph 26).

Although pregnancy is not in any way comparable to a pathological condition (*Webb*, cited above, paragraph 25), the fact remains, as the Advocate-General stresses in point 56 of his Opinion, that pregnancy is a period during which disorders and complications may arise compelling a woman to undergo strict medical supervision and, in some cases, to rest absolutely for all or part of her pregnancy. Those disorders and complications, which may cause incapacity for work, form part of the risks inherent in the condition of pregnancy and are thus a specific feature of that condition.

. . .

The second part of the first question

The second part of the first question concerns a contractual term providing that an employer may dismiss workers of either sex after a stipulated number of weeks of continuous absence.

It is well settled that discrimination involves the application of different rules to comparable situations or the application of the same rule to different situations (see, in particular, case *C-342/93 Gillespie and others* v *Northern Health and Social Services Board and others* [1996] IRLR 214, paragraph 16).

Where it is relied on to dismiss a pregnant worker because of absences due to incapacity for work resulting from her pregnancy, such a contractual term, applying both to men and to women, is applied in the same way to different situations since, as is clear from the answer given to the first part of the first question, the situation of a pregnant worker who is unfit for work as a result of disorders associated with her pregnancy cannot be considered to be the same as that of a male worker who is ill and absent through incapacity for work for the same length of time.

Consequently, application of that contractual term in circumstances such as the present constitutes direct discrimination on grounds of sex.

The answer to the second part of the first question must therefore be that the fact that a female worker has been dismissed during her pregnancy on the basis of a contractual term providing that the employer may dismiss employees of either sex after a stipulated number of weeks of continuous absence cannot affect the answer given to the first part of the first question.

Notes

1. The impact of the decision in *Dekker* is reflected in the ECJ ruling in *Webb*. The latter case reaffirms the principle that discriminatory treatment on grounds of pregnancy or maternity amounts to sex discrimination as such treatment is gender-specific: the comparative approach is no longer necessary. However, see M Rubenstein (Highlights, IRLR vol. 23, no. 9, September 1994) for further debate on the use of the comparative approach.
2. The restriction of the decision in *Webb* to contracts for an indefinite period has been qualified by the ruling of the EAT in *Caruana v Manchester Airport plc* [1996] IRLR 378. In this case it was held that protection should be afforded to women on fixed-term contracts, but this would be confined to situations where the woman was available for work.
3. The decisions in *Brown* and *Pedersen* highlight the difference in EC law between pregnant workers and those on maternity leave. Pregnancy is protected *per se* from discrimination under Article 141 (ex 119) and the Equal Treatment Directive. Those on maternity leave are provided with specific protection in the Pregnant Workers Directive but cannot claim discrimination in comparing themselves with the sick man.
4. For a critique of the legal position on pregnancy and discrimination, see Morris, A., and Nott, S., 'The Legal Response to Pregnancy' (1992) *Journal of the Society of Public Teachers of Law*, vol. 12, No. 1, p. 54.
5. There is no automatic right for women returning from maternity leave to job share (*British Telecommunications plc v Roberts and Longstaff* [1996] IRLR 60). The EAT concluded that where the employer turned down this request, it did not amount to direct discrimination. However, there is still a possibility that it amounts to indirect discrimination.

Also, in *Handels Og Kontorfunktionaerenes Vorbund i Danmark (Acting on behalf of Larson) v Dansk Handel and Service (Acting oh behalf of Fotex Supermarket)* [1997] IRLR 643, the ECJ confirmed that a woman is not automatically protected from dismissal due to an illness originating from her pregnancy where it occurs outside the maternity leave period. Dismissals occurring after the maternity leave period has ended should be compared to the treatment of the sick man.
6. The Trade Union Reform and Employment Rights Act (TURERA) 1993 implemented the EC Pregnant Workers Directive (92/85/EEC), and as a result there were extensive amendments to the EPCA 1978. These provisions can now be found in the Employment Rights Act 1996 as amended by the Employment Relations Act 1999.

The new maternity leave and parental leave provisions can be found in Part I of Sch. 4 of the Employment Relations Act 1999 which is substituted for Part VIII of the Employment Rights Act 1996. These become Part 8 of the

ERA 1996. The main changes are an extended maternity leave period to no less than 18 weeks; a compulsory maternity leave period of at least two weeks within the 18-week period; and the maintenance of terms and conditions of employment as if the employee had not been absent including, on returning to work, seniority pension rights and similar rights. Such rights are also maintained following the return from the additional maternity leave period.

Part I of Schedule 4 of the Employment Relations Act 1999 also makes provision for parental leave. However, the details regarding the entitlement to parental leave are to be found in separate regulations. The regulations will detail who is entitled to parental leave, the duration of the leave and the circumstances in which it may be taken. It is also expected that the regulations will cover the transfer of parental leave between persons with responsibility for the care of the child.

The draft regulations propose that parents will have a statutory right to a total of 13 weeks' unpaid leave for each child who meets the conditions; in this case, under five years old or adopted after 15 December 1999 and under the age of 18 years. Employers may set up distinct parental leave schemes in agreement with trade unions. A model parental leave scheme is to be found in the regulations – see The Maternity and Parental Leave Regulations 1999.

Part II of Sch. 4 of the Employment Relations Act 1999 makes provision for time off for domestic incidents, and has restricted this to time off for dependants. This is clearly a narrower provision than that originally provided for in the Employment Relations Bill. The essence of s. 57A is that an employee is entitled to take a reasonable amount of time off during his working hours in order to deal with the 'unexpected incidents relating to a dependant', for example, a dependant being injured. A dependant is clearly defined in s. 57A(3). An employee may complain to an employment tribunal if an employer unreasonably refuses a request to take time off.

These new 'family friendly' policies are further supported by s. 47C of the 1996 Act, which provides that an employee has the right not to be subjected to any detriment by any act or any deliberate failure to act by his employer done for a prescribed reason, i.e. relating to pregnancy, childbirth or maternity; ordinary, compulsory or additional maternity leave; parental leave or time off under s. 57A. If an employee was subjected to a detriment, e.g. dismissal, this would allow a complaint to an employment tribunal.

The DTI have produced an assessment of the regulatory impact on employment of the Act (February 1999).

Questions
1.   Is the dismissal on moral grounds of an unmarried pregnant woman direct discrimination? See *Berrisford* v *Woodard Schools (Midland Division) Ltd* [1991] IRLR 247; *O'Neill* v *Governors of St Thomas More RCVA Upper School;* and *Bedfordshire County Council* [1996] IRLR 372.
2.   Does the dismissal of a woman who has had an hysterectomy amount to discrimination on the basis that it equates with pregnancy as being something only a woman can undergo?

3.   Can pregnancy discrimination amount to indirect discrimination? See Robert Wintemute, 'When is Pregnancy Discrimination Indirect Discrimination?' (1998) 27 ILJ No. 1, pp. 23–36.

D: Sexual Orientation

A contentious issue which is now being given serious consideration by the courts is whether discrimination on grounds of sexual orientation falls within EC law and the SDA 1975.

In *R* v *Ministry of Defence ex parte Smith* [1996] IRLR 100, a challenge was made against dismissal from the armed forces of four people on grounds that they were homosexual and that this amounted to discrimination. The Court of Appeal ruled that in judging the Ministry of Defence's policy at the time of the dismissals in 1994, it was not irrational as it was supported by both Houses of Parliament: 'Furthermore there was nothing in the Equal Treatment Directive which suggests that the drafters were addressing their minds in any way whatever to problems of discrimination on grounds of sexual orientation. Indeed, *obiter*, it was concluded that a specific Directive was needed, not an extended construction of the Directive.'

This approach was further supported by the CA in *Smith* v *Gardner Merchant Ltd* [1998] IRLR 510, in which it was held that discrimination on the grounds of sexual orientation was not discrimination on grounds of sex and was therefore outside the Act. However, the following case provided some protection for transsexuals.

P v *S & Cornwall County Council*
[1996] IRLR 347
European Court of Justice

The applicant was employed from 1 April 1991 as the general manager of a unit of an educational establishment, operated by the County Council. The respondent S was the head of the establishment. The applicant was taken on as a male employee, but in April 1992 she informed S that she proposed to have a gender reassignment. She explained the background of her medical condition. She later wrote to S explaining that she was to embark on a 'life test', a one-year period during which a patient planning to undergo an operation for gender reassignment lives in the mode of the proposed gender.

The governors of the establishment were informed, and during the summer P took sick leave for initial surgical treatment. However, at the beginning of September 1992, she was given three months' notice of dismissal. She was not permitted to return from sick leave in her female gender role. The final surgical operation took place before the notice of dismissal expired.

P complained that she had been discriminated against on grounds of sex.

DECISION: The principle of equal treatment 'for men and women' to which the Directive refers in its title, preamble and provisions means, as Articles 2(1) and 3(1) in particular indicate, that there should be 'no discrimination whatsoever on grounds of sex'.

Thus, the Directive is simply the expression, in the relevant field, of the principle of equality, which is one of the fundamental principles of Community law.

Moreover, as the Court has repeatedly held, the right not to be discriminated against on grounds of sex is one of the fundamental human rights whose observance the Court has a duty to ensure (see, to that effect, case 149/77 *Defrenne* v *Sabena (No. 3)* [1978] ECR 1365, paragraphs 26 and 27, and joined cases 75/82 and 117/82 *Razzouk and Beydoun* v *Commission* [1984] ECR 1509, paragraph 16).

Accordingly, the scope of the Directive cannot be confined simply to discrimination based on the fact that a person is of one or other sex. In view of its purpose and the nature of the rights which it seeks to safeguard, the scope of the Directive is also such as to apply to discrimination arising, as in this case, from the gender reassignment of the person concerned.

Such discrimination is based, essentially if not exclusively, on the sex of the person concerned. Where a person is dismissed on the ground that he or she intends to undergo, or has undergone, gender reassignment, he or she is treated unfavourably by comparison with persons of the sex to which he or she was deemed to belong before undergoing gender reassignment.

To tolerate such discrimination would be tantamount as regards such a person, to a failure to respect the dignity and freedom to which he or she is entitled, and which the Court has a duty to safeguard.

Dismissal of such a person must therefore be regarded as contrary to Article 5(1) of the Directive, unless the dismissal could be justified under Article 2(2). There is, however, no material before the Court to suggest that this was so here.

It follows from the foregoing that the reply to the questions referred by the industrial tribunal must be that, in view of the objective pursued by the Directive, Article 5(1) of the Directive precludes dismissal of a transsexual for a reason related to a gender reassignment.

Smith v Gardner Merchant Ltd
[1998] IRLR 510
Court of Appeal

Paul Smith was employed as a barman in August 1992. He is a homosexual. He was dismissed in April 1994 following a complaint by another employee, Barbara Touhy, that he had treated her in a threatening and aggressive manner. He claimed that he was sexually harassed by Ms Touhy by reason of his sexual orientation. He alleged that she had made offensive remarks about his sexuality. It was argued that such treatment was contrary to the Sex Discrimination Act in that Ms Touhy's allegations would not have been made against a gay woman. He also alleged that he suffered less favourable treatment by reason of his sexual orientation when the employers decided to dismiss him rather than Ms Touhy.

An employment tribunal regarded the claim as one of discrimination on grounds of sexual orientation. It accepted the hypothesis that Mr Smith was sexually harassed by reason of his sexual orientation and that he suffered less favourable treatment by reason of his sexual orientation when he was dismissed, but it held as a preliminary point of law that a claim of discrimination on grounds of sexual orientation was not within the tribunal's jurisdiction under the Sex Discrimination Act.

The Court of Appeal held that the employment tribunal and the EAT had not erred in finding that discrimination on grounds of sexual orientation is not discrimination on the ground of sex within the meaning of the Sex Discrimination Act. A person's sexual orientation is not an aspect of his or her sex. The employment tribunal had erred, however, in failing to find whether the appellant had been less favourably treated on grounds of sex than a homosexual woman when he was harassed by a female work colleague and dismissed by the respondent employers.

SIR CHRISTOPHER SLADE: . . . The preliminary point of law identified by the industrial tribunal was whether or not the appellant's claim of discrimination 'on grounds of his sexual orientation' was within the tribunal's jurisdiction under the provisions of the Sex Discrimination Act 1975 ('the Act'). Having attached this label to the claim, the tribunal decided that it did not fall within its jurisdiction and accordingly dismissed it. The Employment Appeal Tribunal decided that the industrial tribunal had reached the correct decision on this point and that there was no reason to remit the case to the industrial tribunal for further consideration.

At the time when these two tribunals gave their decisions, the judgment of the European Court of Justice in *Grant v South-West Trains Ltd* (case C-249/96 [[1998] IRLR 206 had not yet been handed down. In that case the Court held in terms (at p. 8) that 'Community law as it stands at present does not cover discrimination based on sexual orientation, such as that in issue in the main proceedings.' Superficially, therefore, that judgment lends strong support to the decisions of the tribunals below.

In my judgment, however, things have gone wrong in this case for three reasons. First, for the reasons given by my Lords, as a matter of principle, it would have been far better if the industrial tribunal had proceeded to hear the case in full, instead of attempting to isolate a preliminary question of law.

Secondly, having made the attempt, it formulated a question which in my judgment was not an appropriate one, because it overlooked the possibility that, on the particular facts of some cases, discrimination which is motivated by considerations relating to the claimant's sexual orientation may be capable of constituting 'discrimination' falling within s. 1(1)(a) of the Act. Simon Brown LJ gave a simple example of such a case in a sentence in his judgment in *R v Ministry of Defence ex parte Smith* [1995] IRLR 585, at 594, 82, saying. 'If of course, an employer were willing to employ lesbians but not male homosexuals, that would be discrimination on grounds of sex.' The correctness of that proposition, which Simon Brown LJ regarded as self-evident, was not challenged in this court. True it is that in many cases where the discrimination is motivated by considerations relating to the claimant's sexual orientation, this will not be capable of falling within s. 1(1)(a), because it will be based *solely* on such considerations and cannot properly be described as being 'on the ground of [his] [her] sex'. Simon Brown LJ gave an example of such a case in the same judgment where he said (ibid): 'Where, as here, an employer refuses to accept homosexuals of either sex, that is discrimination on grounds of orientation.' In such circumstances the discrimination cannot properly be described as being on the ground of the complainant's sex, because it is applied equally to persons of both sexes. Similarly, in the *Grant* case the condition regarding travel concessions, imposed by the undertaking's regulations, applied in the same way to both male and female workers, so that it could not be said to be based on the sex of the worker. In my judgment, however, the two tribunals below, by failing to recognise the possibility that in some circumstances discrimination stemming from the victim's sexual orientation may at the same time constitute discrimination 'on the ground of [his] [her] sex', erred in law.

The third reason why in my judgment things have gone wrong in this case is that the tribunals below failed to take adequate account of the fact that the appellant's complaints are made under two distinct heads, namely (a) those based on the conduct of Ms Touhy and (b) those based on the conduct by his employers of the disciplinary process and their decision to dismiss him rather than Ms Touhy, and that different considerations may apply to these two heads. Though this is not entirely clear, one possible reading of the appellant's second head of complaint is that the reason why his employers treated him as he alleges was simply because he was a man and Ms Touhy was a woman, and not because he was homosexual. The question formulated by the industrial tribunal for its decision was in my judgment an inappropriate one for the further reason that it failed to take account of the matters referred to in this paragraph.

For these reasons I agree that this appeal must be allowed and that the matter must be remitted to the industrial tribunal.

It remains to consider the guidance which should be given to that tribunal. Plainly, its first task will be to find the facts, throughout bearing in mind the two separate heads under which the appellant's complaints are made. It will then be necessary to consider each of these complaints in turn, in the light of the relevant statutory provisions.

As to the first head of complaint, for the reasons given by Ward LJ, I agree that the proper comparator must be a homosexual woman. If I have correctly understood Beldam LJ's judgment, he is of the opinion that, if sexual harassment by Ms Touhy is proved, the simple question for the tribunal will be whether the harassment occurred because the appellant was a man rather than a woman, and that, in posing the question, his sexual orientation will be irrelevant. With great respect, I find myself unable to agree with his conclusion on this point for the reasons given by Ward LJ in his judgment, with which reasons I am in full agreement. I would like to add the following observations in this context.

Sexual harassment is not as such specifically provided for in the Act and in my judgment gives rise to no points of legal principle different from any other claim made in reliance on s. 6(2)(b) of the Act. If it is to give rise to a claim in the present case at all, it will not be enough for the appellant to show that, by reason of such harassment, he has been subjected to 'detriment' within the meaning of s. 6(2)(b). He will also have to show that the subjection to such detriment constituted discrimination within the meaning of s. 1(1)(a). While s. 1(1)(a) will oblige him to satisfy the tribunal that Ms Touhy treated him less favourably on the ground of his sex than she would have treated a woman, s. 5(3) will require that in effecting such comparison the tribunal shall compare like with like: (see *Bain* v *Bowles* [1991] IRLR 356 at p. 358, per Dillon LJ).

In my judgment, the only proper way for the tribunal to compare like with like will be to compare the treatment which Ms Touhy directed to the appellant with the treatment she would have directed to a female homosexual. If the facts were to show that she had a rooted aversion to homosexuals of either sex and that she would have subjected a female homosexual to the like harassment, the appellant's claim under this head would inevitably fail because no discrimination under s. 1(1)(a) would have been established. In my judgment, the appellant's only hope of success under this head will lie in satisfying the tribunal that the harassment occurred because he was a man with a particular relevant personal characteristic rather than a woman with the same relevant characteristic. The relevant characteristic in the present case happens to be homosexuality It might have been some form of physical disability (e.g. blindness) or lack of an educational qualification (e.g. a university degree), in which case similar principles would in my judgment have fallen to be applied. I do not for my part see how the industrial tribunal can be expected to reach the right answer in regard to the first head of complaint unless the question which it asks itself includes a reference to such highly relevant characteristic of the appellant.

I should add that neither the decision in *Grant* nor any other authority cited to us in my judgment precludes the possibility of a valid claim under s. 1(1)(a) of the Act arising from discrimination against homosexuals of one sex in circumstances when it would not have been directed against homosexuals of the other sex. This possibility was specifically envisaged by Simon Brown LJ in the passage from his judgment in the *Ministry of Defence* case quoted above.

Grant v South-West Trains Ltd
[1998] IRLR 206
European Court of Justice

Lisa Grant was a clerical worker employed by South-West Trains (SWT). She was refused a travel pass for her female partner, with whom she had lived in a stable relationship. Her contract of employment with SWT provided that: 'You will be granted such free and reduced rate travel concessions as are applicable to a member of your grade. Your spouse and dependants will also be granted travel concessions.' SWT's staff travel facilities privilege ticket regulations provide that: 'Privilege tickets are granted to a married member of staff . . . for one legal spouse . . . Privilege tickets are granted for one common law spouse (of the opposite sex) subject to a statutory declaration being made that a meaningful relationship has existed for a period of two or more years.' Ms Grant's request for travel concessions for her partner was turned down because her partner was not of the opposite sex. She claimed that this was contrary to EC law. She pointed out that her male predecessor in her post, who cohabited with a woman, had received the benefit in respect of his partner.

The European Court of Justice held: A refusal by an employer to grant travel concessions to a person of the same sex with whom a worker has a stable relationship does not constitute discrimination based directly on the sex of the worker prohibited by Article 119 (now 141) of the EC Treaty or the Equal Pay Directive, even where such concessions are allowed to the person of the opposite sex with whom a worker has a stable relationship outside marriage.

DECISION: In the light of all the material in the case, the first question to answer is whether a condition in the regulations of an undertaking such as that in issue in the main proceedings constitutes discrimination based directly on the sex of the worker. If it does not, the next point to examine will be whether Community law requires that stable relationships between two persons of the same sex should be regarded by all employers as equivalent to marriages or stable relationships outside marriage between two persons of opposite sex. Finally, it will have to be considered whether discrimination based on sexual orientation constitutes discrimination based on the sex of the worker.

First, it should be observed that the regulations of the undertaking in which Ms Grant works provide for travel concessions for the worker, for the worker's 'spouse', that is, the person to whom he or she is married and from whom he or she is not legally separated, or the person of the opposite sex with whom he or she has had a 'meaningful' relationship for at least two years, and for the children, dependent members of the family, and surviving spouse of the worker.

The refusal to allow Ms Grant the concessions is based on the fact that she does not satisfy the conditions prescribed in those regulations, more particularly on the fact that she does not live with a 'spouse' or a person of the opposite sex with whom she has had a 'meaningful' relationship for at least two years.

That condition, the effect of which is that the worker must live in a stable relationship with a person of the opposite sex in order to benefit from the travel concessions, is, like the other alternative conditions prescribed in the undertaking's regulations, applied regardless of the sex of the worker concerned. Thus travel concessions are refused to a male worker if he is living with a person of the same sex, just as they are to a female worker if she is living with a person of the same sex.

Since the condition imposed by the undertaking's regulations applies in the same way to female and male workers, it cannot be regarded as constituting discrimination directly based on sex.

Second, the Court must consider whether, with respect to the application of a condition such as that in issue in the main proceedings, persons who have a stable relationship with a partner of the same sex are in the same situation as those who are married or have a stable relationship outside marriage with a partner of the opposite sex.

Ms Grant submits in particular that the laws of the Member States, as well as those of the Community and other international organisations, increasingly treat the two situations as equivalent.

While the European Parliament, as Ms Grant observes, has indeed declared that it deplores all forms of discrimination based on an individual's sexual orientation, it is nevertheless the case that the Community has not as yet adopted rules providing for such equivalence.

As for the laws of the Member States, while in some of them cohabitation by two persons of the same sex is treated as equivalent to marriage, although not completely, in most of them it is treated as equivalent to a stable heterosexual relationship outside marriage only with respect to a limited number of rights, or else is not recognised in any particular way.

The European Commission of Human rights for its part considers that despite the modern evolution towards homosexuality, stable homosexual relationships do not fall within the scope of the right to respect for family life under Article 8 of the Convention (see in particular the decisions in application No. 9369/81, *X and Y* v *the United Kingdom*, 3 May 1983, Decisions and Reports 32, p. 220; application No. 11716/85, *S* v *the United Kingdom*, 14 May 1986, DR 47 p. 274, paragraph 2; and application No. 15666/89, *Kerkhoven and Hinke* v *the Netherlands*, 19 May 1992, unpublished, paragraph 1), and that national provisions which, for the purpose of protecting the family, accord more favourable treatment to married persons and person of opposite sex living together as man and wife than to persons of the same sex in a stable relationship are not contrary to Article 14 of the Convention, which prohibits inter alia discrimination on the ground of sex (see the decisions in *S* v *the United Kingdom*, paragraph 7; application No. 14753/89, *C and L M* v *the United*

Kingdom 9 October 1989, unpublished, paragraph 2; and application No. 16106/90, *B* v *the United Kingdom*, 10 February 1990, DR 64, p. 278, paragraph 2).

In another context, the European Court of Human Rights has interpreted Article 12 of the Convention as applying only to the traditional marriage between two persons of opposite biological sex (see the *Rees* judgment of 17 October 1986, Series A No. 106, p. 19, §49, and the *Cossey* judgment of 27 September 1990, Series A No. 184, p. 17, §43).

It follows that, in the present state of the law within the Community, stable relationships between two persons of the same sex are not regarded as equivalent to marriages or stable relationships outside marriage between persons of opposite sex. Consequently, an employer is not required by Community law to treat the situation of a person who has a stable relationship with a partner of the same sex as equivalent to that of a person who is married to or has a stable relationship outside marriage with a partner of the opposite sex.

In those circumstances, it is for the legislature alone to adopt, if appropriate, measures which may affect that position.

Notes

1. The issue of discrimination of transsexuals, i.e. those who are undergoing or have undergone gender reassignment, has been resolved not only through the case law — see *Chessington World of Adventures Ltd* v *Reed* [1997] IRLR 556 which followed the decision in *P* v *S* – but also in the recent amendment to the SDA 1975 by the Sex Discrimination (Gender Reassignment) Regulations 1999 (SI 1999/1102) which brings this type of discrimination within the SDA 1975. See also *Mills and the CPS* v *Marshall* [1998] IRLR 494.

2. The question of protection from discrimination for homosexuals is still open to debate. The decision in *Smith* v *Gardner Merchant* provides a potential cause of action, particularly where there has been homophobic abuse. However, it seems fairly clear that discrimination on the grounds of sexual orientation is not, *per se*, unlawful as it is not covered by Article 141 (ex 119) of the EC Treaty or the SDA 1975. This has been further confirmed in *R* v *Secretary of State for Defence, ex parte Perkins (No. 2)* [1998] IRLR 508 which applied the judgment of the ECJ in *Grant*. Notwithstanding this, there may be some redress under the Human Rights Act 1998. Indeed, the European Court of Human Rights has recently held that the MoD are in breach of Article 8 of the European Convention on Human Rights in banning homosexuals from the armed forces (see *Smith & Grady* v *UK* [1999] IRLR 734).

Question

In determining whether harassment of a homosexual amounts to sex discrimination, who is the comparator?

IV Victimisation

Both the SDA 1975, s. 4 and the RRA 1976, s. 2, make unlawful victimisation by employers against those employees who have either brought proceedings under the respective statutes, or have given evidence in proceedings taken against the employer. Whether these provisions deter victimisation is open to question. There is evidence that action taken under the Acts has an adverse impact on the relationship between the employer and employee – see Leonard, A., *Pyrrhic Victories* (EOC, 1986).

Sex Discrimination Act 1975

4. Discrimination by way of victimisation
(1) A person ('the discriminator') discriminates against another person ('the person victimised') in any circumstances relevant for the purposes of any provision of this Act if he treats the person victimised less favourably than in those circumstances he treats or would treat other persons, and does so by reason that the person victimised has—

(a) brought proceedings against the discriminator or any other person under this Act or the Equal Pay Act 1970 or Part I of Schedule 5 to the Social Security Act 1989, or

(b) given evidence or information in connection with proceedings brought by any person against the discriminator or any other person under this Act or the Equal Pay Act 1970 or Part I of Schedule 5 to the Social Security Act 1989, or

(c) otherwise done anything under or by reference to this Act or the Equal Pay Act 1970 or Part I of Schedule 5 to the Social Security Act 1989, in relation to the discriminator or any other person, or

(d) alleged that the discriminator or any other person has committed an act which (whether or not the allegation so states) would amount to a contravention of this Act or give rise to a claim under the Equal Pay Act 1970 or proceedings under Part I of Schedule 5 to the Social Security Act 1989,

or by reason that the discriminator knows the person victimised intends to do any of those things, or suspects the person victimised has done, or intends to do, any of them.

(2) Subsection (1) does not apply to treatment of a person by reason of any allegation made by him if the allegation was false and not made in good faith.

(3) For the purposes of subsection (1), a provision of Part II or III framed with reference to discrimination against women shall be treated as applying equally to the treatment of men and for that purpose shall have effect with such modifications as are requisite.

Race Relations Act 1976

2. Discrimination by way of victimisation
(1) A person ('the discriminator') discriminates against another person ('the person victimised') in any circumstances relevant for the purposes of any provision of this Act if he treats the person victimised less favourably than in those circumstances he treats or would treat other persons, and does so by reason that the person victimised has—

(a) brought proceedings against the discriminator or any other person under this Act; or

(b) given evidence or information in connection with proceedings brought by any person against the discriminator or any other person under this Act; or

(c)   otherwise done anything under or by reference to this Act in relation to the discriminator or any other person; or

(d)   alleged that the discriminator or any other person has committed an act which (whether or not the allegation so states) would amount to a contravention of this Act,

or by reason that the discriminator knows that the person victimised intends to do any of those things, or suspects that the person victimised has done, or intends to do, any of them.

(2)   Subsection (1) does not apply to treatment of a person by reason of any allegation made by him if the allegation was false and not made in good faith.

Nagarajan v *London Regional Transport*
[1999] IRLR 572
House of Lords

Gregory Nagarajan, who is of Indian racial origin, was employed by London Underground Ltd (LUL) as a station foreman between June 1979 and December 1988, from January 1988 for four months as a travel information assistant with London Regional Transport (LRT), the holding company for LUL, and from May 1989 until October 1989 as duty train manager with LUL.

Over the years, Mr Nagarajan brought a number of complaints of race discrimination and victimisation against LRT, LUL and some of their employees. Some of these were settled on payment of compensation, some were successful before the industrial tribunal, and some were unsuccessful.

In 1989, Mr Nagarajan issued three originating applications alleging race discrimination by LUL. One of these was settled in September 1989 by payment to him of £20,000. After a period of unemployment, in September 1990, at the suggestion of his former manager, Mr Nagarajan again applied for a travel information post with LRT. (That application was rejected and led to the victimisation proceedings reported at ([1994] IRLR 61 EAT.)

In December 1992, he made another application for a travel information post. He was interviewed for this post in 1993 but was unsuccessful. He brought fresh proceedings alleging that LRT's central personnel manager, Mr Swiggs, and LRT discriminated against him by victimisation.

Their Lordships held that the Court of Appeal had erred in holding that on a true construction of s. 2(1) of the Race Relations Act, a person alleged to have been victimised must establish that in treating him less favourably than he treats or would treat another, the alleged discriminator had a motive which was consciously connected with the race relations legislation. The decision of the employment tribunal, that the appellant had been victimised in respect of an unsuccessful application for a vacancy because the interviewers were 'consciously or subconsciously' influenced by the fact that he had brought proceedings against the employers, would be restored.

LORD STEYN: . . . The focus of s. 1(1)(a) of the Act of 1976 is broad: it deals with the entire spectrum of direct discrimination. Section 2(1) is narrower in scope and targets cases where a specific protected act is the reason for the less favourable treatment. Nevertheless, there is no obvious explanation for not requiring proof of motive in s. 1(1)(a) but requiring a conscious motivation by the discriminator to treat the employee less favourably in s. 2(1). Counsel for LRT sought with the aid of the *Oxford English Dictionary* to argue that the difference in wording between 'on the ground of' ('on racial grounds') in s. 1(1)(a) and 'by reason that' in s. 2(1) indicate a legislative intention to make clear that in the latter provision a conscious motivation is required. It can readily be accepted that depending on the context the two expressions are capable of yielding different shades of meaning. But counsel put a weight on the difference of wording which it will not bear in the setting of the Act. The expressions appear in parallel provisions and are readily capable of parallel meanings. Counsel for LRT also relied on the marginal note to s. 2(1), viz 'Discrimination by way of victimisation'. At best this is a makeweight argument. In any event, s. 2(1) does not as counsel suggested define 'victimisation'. It uses the phraseology of 'the person victimised,' which carries no overtones of conscious motivation, as a useful shorthand expression in a provision containing language reminiscent of s. 1(1)(a). That is the origin of the marginal note. The fact that the words 'Discrimination by way of victimisation', divorced from the present context, would in ordinary speech usually import a conscious motive is of little weight. After all, it could be said that the marginal note to s. 1 ('Racial discrimination') conveys the idea of conscious discrimination. Yet it is settled that s. 1(1)(a) does not require proof of conscious motivation. The linguistic arguments put forward by LRT are transparently weak.

The question is whether there is any policy justification for the interpretation upheld by the Court of Appeal. The purpose of s. 2(1) is clear. Its primary purpose is to give to persons victimised on account of their reliance on rights under the Act effective civil remedies, thereby also creating a culture which may deter individuals from penalising those who seek to enforce their rights under the Act. Despite valiant efforts counsel for LRT was unable to point to any plausible policy reason for requiring conscious motivation under s. 2(1) but not under s. 1(1)(a). On the contrary, counsel for LRT accepted that victimisation is as serious a mischief as direct discrimination. In these circumstances policy considerations point towards similar interpretations.

For my part, it is not the logic of symmetry that requires the two provisions to be given parallel interpretations. It is rather a pragmatic consideration. Quite sensibly in s. 1(1)(a) cases the tribunal simply has to pose the question: why did the defendant treat the employee less favourably? They do not have to consider whether a defendant was consciously motivated in his unequal treatment of an employee. That is a straightforward way of carrying out its task in a s. 1(1)(a) case. Common sense suggests that the tribunal should also perform its functions in a s. 2(1) case by asking the equally straightforward question: did the defendant treat the employee less favourably because of his knowledge of a protected act? Given that it is unnecessary in s. 1(1)(a) cases to distinguish between conscious and subconscious motivation, there is no sensible reason for requiring it in s. 2(1) cases. Moreover, the threshold requirement laid down by the Court of Appeal in respect of s. 2(1) cases would tend to complicate the task of the tribunal. It would render the protection of the rights guaranteed by s. 2(1) less effective: see *Coote* v *Granada Hospitality Ltd* [1998] IRLR 656 ECJ at p. 666, paragraphs 22–24.

The Court of Appeal relied strongly on an observation by Slade LJ in *Aziz* [v *Trinity Street Taxis Ltd* [1988] IRLR 204] (at 211, 59). The passage in *Aziz* is in conclusionary form: it is to the effect that s. 2(1) contemplates 'a motive which is consciously connected with the race relations legislation'. But as the headnote of *Aziz* makes clear, the case was decided on a causative approach. In any event, the case pre-dates the decisions of the House of Lords in the *Equal Opportunites Commission* and *Jones* cases. A contemporary reviewer of *Aziz* argued convincingly that in the light of the decision in the House of Lords in the *Equal Opportunities Commission* case the observation of Slade LJ cannot stand: Jennifer Ross, *Reason, Ground, Intention, Motive and Purpose* (1990) 53 MLR 391. She said that the obiter dictum of Slade LJ 'wrongly emphasises the underlying motivation of the alleged discriminator rather than the immediate cause of the unfavourable treatment.' I agree.

Note

The decision in *Nagarajan* finally overturns the restrictive approach adopted in *Aziz* v *Trinity Street Taxis Ltd* [1988] IRLR 204. The test for establishing direct discrimination and victimisation is now the same.

The decision in *Coote* v *Granada Hospitality Limited* (see p. 259) may allow a complainant to challenge the potential inadequacy of the SDA 1975 as it relates to victimisation using Article 6 of Directive 76/207. Additional redress is also provided by the public in the Public Interest Disclosure Act 1998.

V Discrimination in Employment

Sex Discrimination Act 1975

6. Discrimination against applicants and employees

(1)   It is unlawful for a person, in relation to employment by him at an establishment in Great Britain, to discriminate against a woman—

(a)   in the arrangements he makes for the purpose of determining who should be offered that employment, or

(b)   in the terms on which he offers her that employment, or

(c)   by refusing or deliberately omitting to offer her that employment.

(2)   It is unlawful for a person, in the case of a woman employed by him at an establishment in Great Britain, to discriminate against her—

(a)   in the way he affords her access to opportunities for promotion, transfer or training, or to any other benefits, facilities or services, or by refusing or deliberately omitting to afford her access to them, or

(b)   by dismissing her, or subjecting her to any other detriment.

(3)   [repealed]

(4)   Subsections (1)(b) and (2) do not apply to provision in relation to death or retirement except as provided in subsections (4A) and (4B) below.

(4A)   Subsection (4) does not prevent the application of subsections (1)(b) and (2) to provision in relation to retirement in so far as those subsections render it unlawful for a person to discriminate against a woman—

(a)   in such of the terms on which he offers her employment as make provision in relation to the way in which he will afford her access to opportunities for promotion, transfer or training or as provide for her dismissal or demotion; or

(b)   in the way he affords her access to opportunities for promotion transfer or training or by refusing or deliberately omitting to afford her access to any such opportunities; or

(c) by dismissing her or subjecting her to any detriment which results in her dismissal or consists in or involves her demotion.

(4B) Subsection (4) does not prevent the application of subsections (1)(b) and (2) to provision in relation to death or retirement in so far as those subsections render it unlawful for a person to discriminate against a woman—

(a) in such of the terms on which he offers her employment as make provision in relation to the way in which he will afford her access to any benefits, facilities or services under an occupational pension scheme; or

(b) in the way he affords her access to any such benefits, facilities or services; or

(c) by refusing or deliberately omitting to afford her access to any such benefits, facilities or services; or

(d) by subjecting her to any detriment in connection with any such scheme; but an act of discrimination is rendered unlawful by virtue of this subsection only to the extent that the act relates to a matter in respect of which an occupational pension scheme has to comply with the principle of equal treatment in accordance with Part I of Schedule 5 to the Social Security Act 1989.

(4C) In the application of subsection (4B) to discrimination against married persons of either sex, Part I of Schedule 5 to the Social Security Act 1989 shall be taken to apply to less favourable treatment of married persons on the basis of their marital status as it applies in relation to less favourable treatment of persons on the basis of sex, and references to persons of either sex shall be construed accordingly.

(5)–(8) [*omitted*]

Race Relations Act 1976

4. Discrimination against applicants and employees

(1) It is unlawful for a person, in relation to employment by him at an establishment in Great Britain, to discriminate against another—

(a) in the arrangements he makes for the purpose of determining who should be offered that employment; or

(b) in the terms on which he offers him that employment; or

(c) by refusing or deliberately omitting to offer him that employment.

(2) It is unlawful for a person, in the case of a person employed by him at an establishment in Great Britain, to discriminate against that employee—

(a) in the terms of employment which he affords him; or

(b) in the way he affords him access to opportunities for promotion, transfer or training, or to any other benefits, facilities or services, or by refusing or deliberately omitting to afford him access to them; or

(c) by dismissing him, or subjecting him to any other detriment.

(3) Except in relation to discrimination falling within section 2, subsections (1) and (2) do not apply to employment for the purposes of a private household.

Saunders v *Richmond-upon-Thames LBC*
[1977] IRLR 362
Employment Appeal Tribunal

Miss Saunders applied for a job with Richmond BC as a golf professional. She was one of seven candidates short-listed and interviewed. However, she was not asked to attend for a second interview. She alleged that certain questions had been asked during her interview which were discriminatory.

It was held, dismissing Saunder's appeal, that the questions asked did not amount to discrimination within SDA 1975, s. 1(1)(1)(a) and s. 6. The SDA 1975 did not make it automatically unlawful to ask a woman any questions which would not be asked of a man.

PHILLIPS J: During her interview Miss Saunders was asked about 19 questions, of which she claimed that seven were discriminatory in the sense summarised in the first contention. They were these (Reasons, para. 18):

(1)   Are there any women golf professionals in clubs?

(2)   So you'd be blazing the trail would you?

(4)   Do you think men respond as well to a woman golf professional as to a man?

(8)   If all this is true, you are obviously a lady of great experience, but don't you think this type of job is rather unglamorous?

(9)   Don't you think this is a job with rather long hours?

(10)   I can see that you could probably cope with the playing and teaching side of the job, but I am rather concerned as to whether you could cope with the management side.

(12)   If some of the men were causing trouble over the starting times on the tee, do you think you would be able to control this?'

Mr Beloff's submission was that it was, as a matter of law, discriminatory within s. 1(1)(a) and 6(1)(a) to ask these questions. We do not agree. Assuming that the asking of questions may constitute 'arrangements' within s. 6(1)(a) the question whether they do must be one of fact in each case. The issue would be whether by asking the question she was, on the ground of her sex, treated less favourably than a man would be treated (s. 1(1)(a)). This would involve a consideration of the circumstances in which, and the purpose for which, the question was asked. In our judgment the Industrial Tribunal approached the matter correctly in this way in para. 18 of the Reasons for their Decision. They, having considered the matter, found as a fact that the questions of which complaint was made were not discriminatory. That is not a finding with which it is open to us to interfere.

Accordingly we reject the first contention.

However, it may be helpful to add a few words on the subject. Mr Beloff stressed the fact that since the enactment of the Sex Discrimination Act 1975 it is necessary for everyone, and in particular employers, to reconsider their approach to such matters and to rid themselves of (what are now) out-of-date ideas and prejudices. It is thus essential for an appointing committee to realise that (unless in exceptional cases) the sex of the applicant is totally irrelevant considered as a qualification or disqualification for a particular employment. If strength is a necessary qualification for appointment it is permissible to reject a woman because she is weak, but not because she is a woman. No doubt, this approach requires a difficult re-adjustment of mental attitudes among many people, and it is now entirely improper to regard a particular job as being 'suitable' or 'unsuitable' for a man or for a woman as the case may be. There is probably not much doubt that such questions as (1) 'Are there any women golf professionals in clubs?' or (4) 'Do you think men respond as well to a woman golf professional as to a man?' reflect, in part at least, what is now an out-of-date and proscribed attitude of mind. That such questions were asked may be very relevant when it comes to be determined (the second contention) whether there has been discrimination in not appointing a woman, and that is why we said earlier that the facts underlying the first contention are relevant upon a consideration of the second contention. But we do not think that it is unlawful to ask such questions, or that Mr Beloff is right when he says that it is now unlawful to ask a woman (or a man) any question which would not be asked of a man (or a woman). Indeed it may be desirable to do so. To take the example cited in the course of argument: suppose a man be considered as an applicant for the headship of a single sex girls' boarding school. If appointed it is obvious that in practice he might have problems with the girls which would be different from those which a female head would have. An appointing committee might well think it proper to enquire whether he had insight into this problem, and was prepared, and was the sort of man who would be able, to deal with it. For that reason they might well wish to enquire whether he had given consideration to his ability as a man to deal with pupils all of whom were girls. It would be absurd to regard such a question as in itself and by itself discriminatory. Indeed, so to rule would scarcely assist the cause of those who are active in the promotion of sex equality. If such questions were to be forbidden, they would not be asked; but not to ask them would not change the mental attitudes of those who would have asked them had they been allowed to do so. All that would be achieved would be that those of that cast of mind would continue to act in the same way as they would have acted had they been allowed to ask the question, but it will never be known, by examining the type of questions they do ask, the way in which they approached the problem. Assuming an employer who is in fact biased and prejudiced, this fact is much more likely to be revealed, and redress to be obtained, if he is free to ask what questions he likes, and thereby to show his true colours.

Notes
1. While it may not be unlawful at present to ask questions about family or domestic circumstances if it is relevant to do so, employers should consider the answers objectively. The danger is that many employers have stereotyped assumptions about, for example, women with young children, and as a result such things are in effect considered subjectively. However, should the employer be challenged in the tribunals he will have to defend his reason for not employing the complainant as being the genuine reason as opposed to the existence of a covert reason (*Owen* v *Briggs & Jones* [1982] IRLR 502).
2. Any complaint of 'subjecting to a detriment' must now relate to treatment of the employee by the employer during the existence of the contract of employment. As the provisions of s. 4 and s. 6 respectively are in the present tense, it must be presumed that the discrimination must take place during the subsistence of the employment relationship (*Nagarajan* v *Agnew et. al.* [1994] IRLR 61).

Question
If the same question is asked of all applicants for a job, can there be a complaint of discrimination? (See *Dhatt* v *McDonalds Hamburgers Ltd* [1991] IRLR 130.)

VI Genuine Occupational Qualifications

Both the SDA 1975 and the RRA 1976 provide specific defences for an employer against a claim of discrimination in the form of 'genuine occupational qualifications' (GOQs). Note the reduced number of GOQs under the

RRA 1976. In relation to the SDA 1975, the majority of GOQs relate to decency and privacy where this is a necessity.

Sex Discrimination Act 1975

7. Exception where sex is a genuine occupational qualification
    (1)   In relation to sex discrimination—
    (a)   section 6(1)(a) or (c) does not apply to any employment where being a man is a genuine occupational qualification for the job, and
    (b)   section 6(2)(a) does not apply to opportunities for promotion or transfer to, or training for, such employment.
    (2)   Being a man is a genuine occupational qualification for a job only where—
    (a)   the essential nature of the job calls for a man for reasons of physiology (excluding physical strength or stamina) or, in a dramatic performance or other entertainment, for reasons of authenticity, so that the essential nature of the job would be materially different if carried out by a woman; or
    (b)   the job needs to be held by a man to preserve decency or privacy because—
    (i)   it is likely to involve physical contact with men in circumstances where they might reasonably object to its being carried out by a woman, or
    (ii)   the holder of the job is likely to do his work in circumstances where men might reasonably object to the presence of a woman because they are in a state of undress or are using sanitary facilities; or
    (ba)   the job is likely to involve the holder of the job doing his work, or living, in a private home and needs to be held by a man because objection might reasonably be taken to allowing to a woman—
    (i)   the degree of physical or social contact with a person living in the home, or
    (ii)   the knowledge of intimate details of such a person's life, which is likely, because of the nature or circumstances of the job or of the home, to be allowed to, or available to, the holder of the job; or
    (c)   the nature or location of the establishment makes it impracticable for the holder of the job to live elsewhere than in premises provided by the employer, and—
    (i)   the only such premises which are available for persons holding that kind of job are lived in, or normally lived in, by men and are not equipped with separate sleeping accommodation for women and sanitary facilities which could be used by women in privacy from men, and
    (ii)   it is not reasonable to expect the employer either to equip those premises with such accommodation and facilities or to provide other premises for women; or
    (d)   the nature of the establishment, or of the part of it within which the work is done, requires the job to be held by a man because—
    (i)   it is, or is part of, a hospital, prison or other establishment for persons requiring special care, supervision or attention, and
    (ii)   those persons are all men (disregarding any woman whose presence is exceptional), and
    (iii)   it is reasonable, having regard to the essential character of the establishment or that part, that the job should not be held by a woman; or
    (e)   the holder of the job provides individuals with personal services promoting their welfare or education, or similar personal services, and those services can most effectively be provided by a man, or
    (g)   the job needs to be held by a man because it is likely to involve the performance of duties outside the United Kingdom in a country whose laws or

customs are such that the duties could not, or could not effectively, be performed by a woman, or

(h)   the job is one of two to be held by a married couple.

(3)   Subsection (2) applies where some only of the duties of the job fall within paragraphs (a) to (g) as well as where all of them do.

(4)   Paragraph (a), (b), (c), (d), (e), or (g) of subsection (2) does not apply in relation to the filling of a vacancy at a time when the employer already has male employees—

(a)   who are capable of carrying out the duties falling within that paragraph, and

(b)   whom it would be reasonable to employ on those duties and

(c)   whose numbers are sufficient to meet the employer's likely requirements in respect of those duties without undue inconvenience.

Race Relations Act 1976

5.   Exceptions for genuine occupational qualifications

(1)   In relation to racial discrimination—

(a)   section 4(1)(a) or (c) does not apply to any employment where being of a particular racial group is a genuine occupational qualification for the job; and

(b)   section 4(2)(b) does not apply to opportunities for promotion or transfer to, or training for, such employment.

(2)   Being of a particular racial group is a genuine occupational qualification for a job only where—

(a)   the job involves participation in a dramatic performance or other entertainment in a capacity for which a person of that racial group is required for reasons of authenticity; or

(b)   the job involves participation as an artist's or photographic model in the production of a work of art, visual image or sequence of visual images for which a person of that racial group is required for reasons of authenticity; or

(c)   the job involves working in a place where food or drink is (for payment or not) provided to and consumed by members of the public or a section of the public in a particular setting for which, in that job, a person of that racial group is required for reasons of authenticity; or

(d)   the holder of the job provides persons of that racial group with personal services promoting their welfare, and those services can most effectively be provided by a person of that racial group.

(3)   Subsection (2) applies where only some of the duties of the job fall within paragraph (a), (b), (c) or (d) as well as where all of them do.

(4)   Paragraph (a), (b), (c) or (d) of subsection (2) does not apply in relation to the filling of a vacancy at a time when the employer already has employees of the racial group in question—

(a)   who are capable of carrying out the duties falling within that paragraph; and

(b)   whom it would be reasonable to employ on those duties; and

(c)   whose numbers are sufficient to meet the employer's likely requirements in respect of those duties without undue inconvenience.

Etam Plc v *Rowan*
[1989] IRLR 150
Employment Appeal Tribunal

Mr Rowan applied for a vacancy as a sales assistant at the employers' shop in Glasgow selling women's and girl's clothing. He was not considered for the post because of his sex. He complained that he had been unlawfully discriminated against. The employers contended that being a woman was a genuine occupational qualification for the post within the meaning of s. 7(2)(b) of the Sex Discrimination Act because personal contact with customers when they were in a state of undress was an essential part of the job. The employers submitted that it was a major part of the job to work in the fitting rooms and to measure customers uncertain about their size.

It was held, dismissing the employer's appeal, that being a woman was not a genuine occupational qualification for a job of sales assistant in a women's clothing shop so as to entitle the employer to refuse to consider a man for the post.

MAYFIELD LJ: The Industrial Tribunal heard evidence from the manageress, Mrs Murphy, and Miss Douglas, who had been employed by the appellants for four and a half years as a sales assistant but latterly as a cashier. Mrs Murphy, in her evidence, explained that there were a variety of tasks to be covered including receiving deliveries, working on the cash desk, working in the fitting room, working on security at the fitting room door and working on the sales floor. She made up a rota each day which involved the staff in changing duty every hour or so. She emphasised the importance of the fitting room contact with the customers and felt that it would not be possible to be a sales assistant without being able to go into the fitting room. Her evidence was that there was always an assistant on duty at the door of the fitting room, and it was a duty of that assistant to check into the fitting room the number of garments which a customer took in to try on, and to check that the same number of garments came out again. Sometimes a further assistant would be placed inside the fitting room to keep an eye on stock which was going into the fitting room and going out again.

Shop assistants on shop floor duty would go in and out of the fitting room providing service to customers who were trying clothes on. Her view was that it would be impossible for a man to carry out the functions within the fitting room because that would not be acceptable to female customers. The Industrial Tribunal accepted that view. Even if a man did not go into the fitting room, he would from time to time be required to carry out work which involved passing the entrance to the fitting room. There was a curtain which screened the fitting room from the main part of the shop, but she maintained that curtain was frequently left open. Her estimate of the time spent by a sales assistant in the fitting room was that it would occupy a considerable amount of the time of a sales assistant's duties. She gave a tentative view that perhaps 25% of a sales assistant's time might be spent either on security duty at the door of the fitting room, or inside the fitting room. She did not think it would be possible to reorganise the allocation of duties within the shop so that a male sales assistant could be employed in such a manner that he would not have to go into the fitting room. She accepted that there were other companies with a lay-out similar to that of the respondents which employed male sales assistants.

Another difficulty arose when measuring customers who were unsure of their size. Head office circulars, however, suggested to the Industrial Tribunal that that would occur only occasionally. Mrs Murphy, however, said it happened very frequently. In any event, she did not consider that the respondent's appearance was smart enough to consider him as a likely candidate.

The Industrial Tribunal held on the consideration of the evidence of Miss Douglas that there were considerable discrepancies between the evidence of Mrs Murphy and

Miss Douglas. The rota system, according to Miss Douglas, was very much less strictly adhered to than that indicated by Mrs Murphy. She accepted that while a man might have to pass by the entrance to the fitting area, if there was a door or the curtain was kept closed, that would not be a problem. Miss Douglas also stated that the sales assistants selling on the shop floor did not normally accompany a customer into the fitting room, but normally only took her as far as the security curtain at the door of the fitting room and then left the customer, unless a message was sent back out to her requiring her to give some further service to the customer in the fitting room. Sometimes the customer in the fitting room simply asked the security person at the door to send in an assistant and an assistant would go in. Miss Douglas's view was that the need for customers to be measured occurred less frequently than had been indicated by Mrs Murphy.

The Industrial Tribunal also recorded that the respondent was given a card by the job centre to go to the shop at Argyle Street and speak to Mrs Murphy. He was told by an assistant, whom he first saw, that a man would not be considered for the post. When he did see Mrs Murphy she told him that she would not consider employing a male assistant.

The Industrial Tribunal held that his appearance at the Tribunal was particularly clean and smart, contrary to what Mrs Murphy had stated, although the respondent had accepted that as he had been unemployed for a period he was not as smart as he was at the hearing.

The Industrial Tribunal came to the conclusion that the appellants had failed to establish that being female was a genuine occupational qualification for employment as a sales assistant in the appellants' establishment. They held that the work carried out in the fitting room, while important, did not lead them to the conclusion that the amount of time spent in the fitting room was as great as had been suggested by Mrs Murphy, or that the rota system of carrying out the duties was as incontrovertible as Mrs Murphy had suggested.

They came to the conclusion that the respondent would have been able to adequately carry out the bulk of the job of sales assistant, and such parts as he could not carry out could easily have been done by other sales assistants without causing any inconvenience or difficulty for the appellants.

. . .

The conclusion of the Industrial Tribunal was that the respondent would have been able to adequately carry out the bulk of the job of sales assistant, and that the parts that were not appropriate to a man could easily have been done by other sales assistants without causing real inconvenience or difficulty for the appellants.

In our view the Industrial Tribunal considered the relevant factors and it was not our understanding of the submissions that any real criticism was made of the Industrial Tribunal's approach. What did seem to be suggested was that they were not entitled to reach the conclusion they did on the facts found by them. We do not agree with that submission. In our view this is not a case where what was being asked of the appellants was the need to carry out a considerable reorganisation. Nor is it, of course, open to an Industrial Tribunal to tell employers how to manage their business (*Timex Corporation* v *Hodgson* [1981] IRLR 530).

In our view the Industrial Tribunal, however, were not doing that. What they considered was the application of s. 7(4) of the Act. In our view, the Industrial Tribunal on the evidence were entitled to conclude that the respondent would have been able to adequately carry out the bulk of the job of sales assistant, and such parts as he could not carry out could easily have been done by other sales assistants without causing any inconvenience or difficulty for the appellants.

Tottenham Green under Fives Centre v *Marshall (No. 2)*
[1991] IRLR 162
Employment Appeal Tribunal

The appellants run a day care centre in Tottenham. They are managed by a committee of parents and funded by the London Borough of Haringey. The Centre has a policy of maintaining a balance between those of different ethnic background both among the children taken and the staff.

When an Afro-Caribbean nursery worker left, it was decided to replace her with another person of Afro-Caribbean origin. At the relevant time, 84 per cent of the children were of Afro-Caribbean origin and the Centre had four white staff, one Greek Cypriot and one other Afro-Caribbean. Accordingly, the advertisement stipulated that the post was for an 'Afro-Caribbean worker' and said that the applicant would need 'a personal awareness of Afro-Caribbean culture' and 'an understanding of the importance of anti-racist and anti-sexist child care'.

Mr Marshall, a white, did not see the advertisement, but heard about the vacancy and telephoned for an application form. He did not answer the question on the form about his ethnic origin. When this was drawn to his attention and he said that he was white, he was told that he would not be suitable for the job. He complained that he had been unlawfully discriminated against on grounds of race.

It was held, allowing the employer's appeal, the tribunal had erred in concluding that the applicants had failed to show that being Afro-Caribbean was a genuine occupational qualification within RRA 1976, s. 5(2)(d). The exception in s. 5(2)(d) applied where the duty was genuine and not so trivial that it could be disregarded. Therefore the requirement that the post holder should be Afro-Caribbean because such a person was more likely to be able to speak and read in dialect fell within this GOQ.

KNOX J: . . . We are, however, bound by findings of fact unless there is no evidence upon which that finding could be based, or we come to the conclusion that the finding is a perverse one. We are not satisfied that from a factual point of view that particular finding is perverse. That, of course, does not conclude the question because there remains the issue whether, given that this particular service was in the nature of a desirable extra, it is something which can legitimately fall out of view in deciding whether or not the exception in s. 5(2)(d) applies.

Two other passages are to be found in the Industrial Tribunal's decision, which is under review, regarding the ability to speak a West Indian dialect. One is in paragraph 13 where they refer to the passage that I have alluded to about an African person qualifying and the Industrial Tribunal remarks that that confirms their view that the dialect-speaking requirement could be dispensed with and finally we find this in paragraph 17:

As stated above, we do not consider that this was a requirement which was rated as fundamental to the post or an integral requirement with the other three.

That was appended to the general finding that the requirements listed by the respondents could most effectively be provided by any trained nursery assistant with the sole exception of the knowledge of West Indian dialect. In three different ways, therefore, the Industrial Tribunal has stated the way in which the ability to read and talk where necessary in dialect was viewed in contra-distinction to the other personal services. There is a perfectly clear finding that the other three could most effectively be provided by any trained nursery assistant, and no question therefore arises of our finding any error of law in that respect. With regard to the ability to read and talk where necessary in dialect, we have as we have explained above, a finding of fact which is binding upon us, that it is variously described, as a desirable extra; a requirement that could be dispensed with; and not a requirement that was rated as fundamental to the post; or an integral requirement with the other three.

The issue before us is within a small compass but nonetheless not entirely straightforward, and that is: whether it is open to an Industrial Tribunal to disregard a duty in coming to the conclusion that it does not figure for the purposes of deciding whether s. 5(2)(d) applies. One can set on one side two particular categories which it was common ground between the parties did not apply in this case but undoubtedly would be properly disregarded by an Industrial Tribunal which was looking at duties that had to be taken into account for the purposes of this exception. The first of those two categories is what lawyers call matters which are de minimis, that is to say, of such trivial nature as properly to be disregarded. Mr Meeran, who appeared for the applicant, Mr Gary Marshall, very properly disclaimed any reliance on the ability to read and talk when necessary in dialect as being something that was so trivial that it ought to be wholly disregarded.

The other category which would clearly very properly be disregarded in any case, is one where the duty in question is included as a sham or smokescreen to avoid the requirement that there should be no racial discrimination or indeed for any other purposes. It is common ground that this is not relevant in this particular case where as Mr Meeran was at pains to make clear to us, there is no suggestion at all that there was any desire to act otherwise than in a proper manner and there is no question of a sham duty being invented for the purpose of qualifying for the exception in s. 5(2)(d).

What remains is a relatively unimportant but not trivial duty and we have reached the conclusion that it is not the correct view of the meaning of this paragraph that the Industrial Tribunal can make an evaluation of the importance of the duty in question and disregard it although it is satisfied that it is something that is not so trivial that it can properly be disregarded altogether. It seems to us that subsection (3) indicates clearly that one of the duties of the job if it falls within any of the relevant paragraphs, in our case paragraph (d) of the preceding subsection, will operate to make the exception available. That is what one can discern that Parliament intended to provide.

There is no suggestion at all that one has to look to see whether some duties are more important than others, and once one reaches that conclusion, it seems to us, that as a matter of law it is not an answer to a reliance on s. 5(2)(d) that relevant duty is either only a desirable extra, or something that could be dispensed with, or something which is not fundamental to the post. It is still one of the duties of the job and in those circumstances, it not being trivial and it being genuine, it seems to us that the exception necessarily did apply.

Notes
1. The meaning of 'personal services' in RRA 1976, s. 5(2)(d), was also raised in *London Borough of Lambeth* v *Commission for Racial Equality* [1990] IRLR 231, where it was held that 'personal' involved direct contact between the service provider and the recipient.

2.   Where an employer has yet to employ 'other employees' (s. 7(4)) he can rely on a GOQ even though, once he has hired staff, he may not be able to establish a GOQ (*Lazertop Ltd* v *Webster* [1997] IRLR 498).
3.   Positive discrimination is not permitted under the SDA 1975 or the RRA 1976, although s. 48 and s. 38 respectively permit an employer to encourage applications from black or female/male applicants in certain circumstances.

VII   Compensation

The upper limits on awards of compensation made under the SDA 1975 and RRA 1976 have been removed. It is also clear that an award may include compensation for injury to feelings as well as aggravated damages, although exemplary damages cannot be awarded (see *Deane* v *London Borough of Ealing* [1993] IRLR 209 and *Ministry of Defence* v *Meredith* [1995] IRLR 539).

Marshall v *Southampton & South-West Hampshire Area Health Authority (No. 2)*
[1993] IRLR 445
European Court of Justice

Miss Marshall worked from July 1966 to March 1980 as a senior dietician for the Health Authority. At that time, the retirement policy of the Health Authority was that, in accordance with the State pension age, women should retire at age 60 and men at 65, but that retirement at those ages could be postponed by mutual agreement. Miss Marshall continued to work until she was dismissed with effect from 31 March 1980 upon reaching age 62. The sole reason given for her dismissal was that she had passed the employers' normal retirement age for women. She would not have been dismissed at that age if she had been a man.

Miss Marshall complained to an Industrial Tribunal that her dismissal amounted to unlawful discrimination contrary to the Sex Discrimination Act and the EEC Equal Treatment Directive 76/207. The Tribunal dismissed her complaint under the Sex Discrimination Act on the ground that the case fell within s. 6(4), which at that time excluded complaints arising from a provision in relation to retirement. Her claim under Community law was upheld.

The EAT [1983] IRLR 237 held that although Miss Marshall's dismissal violated the principle of equal treatment laid down in the Directive, such violation could not be relied upon in proceedings before a UK court or tribunal. Miss Marshall appealed to the Court of Appeal. It referred the matter to the European Court of Justice.

The European Court [1986] IRLR 140 ruled that Article 5(1) of the Equal Treatment Directive must be interpreted as meaning that a general policy concerning dismissal involving the dismissal of a woman solely because she has attained or passed the qualifying age for a State pension, in which age is different under national legislation for men and women, constitutes discrimination on grounds of sex contrary to the Directive. The European Court went on to rule that Article 5(1) may be relied upon as against a State authority acting in its capacity as employer, in order to avoid the application of any national provision which does not conform to Article 5(1).

Upon receiving the European Court's decision, the Court of Appeal allowed Miss Marshall's appeal and remitted the application to the industrial tribunal to consider the question of remedy.

The industrial tribunal [1988] IRLR 325 assessed Miss Marshall's financial loss at £18,405, including £7,710 by way of interest calculated as from the date of dismissal to the date of the award. It awarded Miss Marshall £19,405 compensation (adding £1,000 compensation for injury to feelings), less £6,250 she had already received from the employers. The Tribunal held that the statutory limit on compensation set by s. 65(2) of the Sex Discrimination Act – then £6,250 – did not provide an adequate remedy as required by Article 6 of the EEC Equal Treatment Directive, as interpreted by the European Court in *Von Colson* v *Land Nordrhein-Westfalen*, for somebody who is wronged by unlawful sex discrimination in the employment field. Accordingly, said the Tribunal, the UK Government was in breach of Article 6 of the Equal Treatment Directive, which requires all Member States to introduce into their national legal systems 'such measures as are necessary to enable all persons who consider themselves wronged . . . to pursue their claims by judicial process'. As construed in *Von Colson*, that judicial process must include an adequate remedy. Therefore, Miss Marshall, as an employee of an emanation of the State, was entitled to rely upon Article 6 in a complaint before the Industrial Tribunal. The Tribunal consequently ignored the limit on compensation under the Sex Discrimination Act.

The employers appealed only against the award of interest. The EAT [1989] IRLR 459 allowed the appeal. The EAT held that Miss Marshall was not entitled to rely upon Article 6 of the Equal Treatment Directive. It took the view that EEC law established that where a State has provided access to the courts, the remedies are for the State, subject only to the principle of de minimis, and Article 6 has no direct effect.

The Court of Appeal [1990] IRLR 481, by a majority, dismissed Miss Marshall's appeal. The Court of Appeal also took the view that a sex discrimination complainant cannot rely on Article 6 of the Directive to override the limit on compensation in the Sex Discrimination Act. According to the majority of the Court of Appeal, the *Von Colson* decision was clear authority that the provisions as to compensation which the European Court held to be implicit in Article 6 are not 'unconditional and sufficiently precise' so as to have direct effect.

The House of Lords referred the following questions to the European Court of Justice for a preliminary ruling:

1.   Where the national legislation of a Member State provides for the payment of compensation as one remedy available by judicial process to

a person who has been subjected to unlawful discrimination of a kind prohibited by Council Directive 76/207/EEC of 9 February 1976 ('the Directive'), is the Member State guilty of a failure to implement Article 6 of the Directive by reason of the imposition by the national legislation of an upper limit of £6,250 on the amount of compensation recoverable by such a person?

2.   Where the national legislation provides for the payment of compensation as aforesaid, is it essential to the due implementation of Article 6 of the Directive that the compensation to be awarded—

(a)   should not be less than the amount of the loss found to have been sustained by reason of the unlawful discrimination, and

(b)   should include an award of interest on the principal amount of the loss so found from the date of the unlawful discrimination to the date when the compensation is paid?

3.   If the national legislation of a Member State has failed to implement Article 6 of the Directive in any of the respects referred to in questions 1 and 2, is a person who has been subjected to unlawful discrimination as aforesaid entitled as against an authority which is an emanation of the Member State to rely on the provisions of Article 6 as overriding the limits imposed by the national legislation on the amount of compensation recoverable?

The ECJ held that it is contrary to Article 6 of EEC Equal Treatment Directive 76/207 for national provisions to lay down an upper limit on the amount of compensation recoverable by a victim of discrimination in respect of the loss and damage sustained.

Real equality of opportunity cannot be attained in the absence of measures appropriate to restore such equality when it has not been observed. In the event of a discriminatory dismissal, where financial compensation is the measure adopted in order to restore equality, it must be adequate, in that it must enable the loss and damage actually sustained as a result of the discriminatory dismissal to be made good in full in accordance with the applicable national rules. An upper limit, of the kind in the present case, on the amount of compensation recoverable by a victim of discrimination cannot, by definition, constitute proper implementation of article 6, since it limits the amount of compensation a priori to a level which is not necessarily consistent with the requirement of ensuring real equality of opportunity through adequate reparation for the loss and damage sustained as a result of discriminatory dismissal.

Similarly, an award of interest, in accordance with applicable national rules, must be regarded as an essential component of compensation for the purposes of restoring full equality of treatment, since full compensation for the loss and damage sustained as a result of discriminatory dismissal cannot leave out of account factors, such as the effluxion of time, which may in fact reduce its value. Therefore, reparation of such loss and damage may not be limited by excluding an award of interest to compensate for the loss sustained by the recipient of the compensation as a result of the effluxion of time until the capital sum awarded is actually paid.

DECISION: Article 6 of the Directive puts Member States under a duty to take the necessary measures to enable all persons who consider themselves wronged by discrimination to pursue their claims by judicial process. Such obligation implies that the measures in question should be sufficiently effective to achieve the objective of the Directive and should be capable of being effectively relied upon by the persons concerned before national courts.

As the Court held in the judgment in Case 14/83 *Von Colson and Kamann* v *Land Nordrhein-Westfalen* [1984] ECR 1891, at paragraph 18, Article 6 does not prescribe a specific measure to be taken in the event of a breach of the prohibition of discrimination, but leaves Member States free to choose between the different solutions suitable for achieving the objective of the Directive, depending on the different situations which may arise.

However, the objective is to arrive at real equality of opportunity and cannot therefore be attained in the absence of measures appropriate to restore such equality when it has not been observed. As the Court stated in paragraph 23 of the judgment in *Von Colson and Kamann*, cited above, those measures must be such as to guarantee real and effective judicial protection and have a real deterrent effect on the employer.

Such requirements necessarily entail that the particular circumstances of each breach of the principle of equal treatment should be taken into account. In the event of discriminatory dismissal contrary to Article 5(1) of the Directive, a situation of equality could not be restored without either reinstating the victim of discrimination or, in the alternative, granting financial compensation for the loss and damage sustained.

Where financial compensation is the measure adopted in order to achieve the objective indicated above, it must be adequate, in that it must enable the loss and damage actually sustained as a result of the discriminatory dismissal to be made good in full in accordance with the applicable national rules.

The first and second questions

In its first question, the House of Lords seeks to establish whether it is contrary to Article 6 of the Directive for national provisions to lay down an upper limit on the amount of compensation recoverable by a victim of discrimination.

In its second question, the House of Lords asks whether Article 6 requires (a) that the compensation for the damage sustained as a result of the illegal discrimination should be full and (b) that it should include an award of interest on the principal amount from the date of the unlawful discrimination to the date when compensation is paid.

The Court's interpretation of Article 6 as set out above provides a direct reply to the first part of the second question relating to the level of compensation required by that provision.

It also follows from that interpretation that the fixing of an upper limit of the kind at issue in the main proceedings cannot, by definition, constitute proper implementation of Article 6 of the Directive, since it limits the amount of compensation a priori to a level which is not necessarily consistent with the requirement of ensuring real equality of opportunity through adequate reparation for the loss and damage sustained as a result of discriminatory dismissal.

With regard to the second part of the second question relating to the award of interest, suffice it to say that full compensation for the loss and damage sustained as a result of discriminatory dismissal cannot leave out of account factors, such as the effluxion of time, which may in fact reduce its value. The award of interest, in accordance with the applicable national rules, must therefore be regarded as an essential component of compensation for the purposes of restoring real equality of treatment.

Accordingly, the reply to be given to the first and second questions is that the interpretation of Article 6 of the Directive must be that reparation of the loss and damage sustained by a person injured as a result of discriminatory dismissal may not be limited to an upper limit fixed a priori or by excluding an award of interest to compensate for the loss sustained by the recipient of the compensation as a result of the effluxion of time until the capital sum awarded is actually paid.

The third question
In its third question, the House of Lords seeks to establish whether a person who has been injured as a result of discriminatory dismissal may rely, as against an authority of the State acting in its capacity as employer, on Article 6 of the Directive in order to contest the application of national rules which impose limits on the amount of compensation recoverable by way of reparation.

It follows from the considerations set out above as to the meaning and scope of Article 6 of the Directive, that that provision is an essential factor for attaining the fundamental objective of equal treatment for men and women, in particular as regards working conditions, including the conditions governing dismissal, referred to in Article 5(1) of the Directive, and that, where, in the event of discriminatory dismissal, financial compensation is the measure adopted in order to restore that equality, such compensation must be full and may not be limited a priori in terms of its amount.

Accordingly, the combined provisions of Article 6 and Article 5 of the Directive give rise, on the part of a person who has been injured as a result of discriminatory dismissal, to rights which that person must be able to rely upon before the national courts as against the State and authorities which are an emanation of the State.

The fact that Member States may choose among different solutions in order to achieve the objective pursued by the Directive depending on the situations which may arise, cannot result in an individual's being prevented from relying on Article 6 in a situation such as that in the main proceedings where the national authorities have no degree of discretion in applying the chosen solution.

It should be pointed out in that connection that, as appears in particular from the judgment in Joined Cases C-6/90 and C-9/90 *Francovich and others* v *Italian Republic* [1992] IRLR 84, at paragraph 17, the right of a State to choose among several possible means of achieving the objectives of a Directive does not exclude the possibility for individuals of enforcing before national courts rights whose content can be determined sufficiently precisely on the basis of the provisions of the Directive alone.

Accordingly, the reply to be given to the third question is that a person who has been injured as a result of discriminatory dismissal may rely on the provisions of Article 6 of the Directive as against an authority of the State acting in its capacity as an employer in order to set aside a national provision which imposes limits on the amount of compensation recoverable by way of reparation.

Notes
1. In *Marshall's* case it was made quite clear by the ECJ, in applying *Von Colson and Kamann* v *Land Nordrhein Westfalan* (Case 14/83) [1984] ECR 1891, that UK domestic law and the interpretation by the national courts of both EC law and domestic law continued to contravene the Equal Treatment

Directive. See the Sex Discrimination and Equal Pay (Remedies) Regulations 1993.

2. It is well established that injury to feelings is to be regarded as a fundamental element in awarding compensation (*Murray* v *Powertech* [1992] IRLR 257) and accordingly should be incorporated into the award (see *Sharifi* v *Strathclyde Regional Council* [1992] IRLR 259, where an award of £500 was deemed to be inadequate as being the minimum amount which should be awarded in any case).

3. The decision of the CA in *Sheriff* v *Klyne Tugs (Lowestoft) Ltd* [1999] IRLR 481 provides a potential new head of damages for personal injury in discrimination cases. Where an applicant can show that the act of discrimination resulted in personal injury the employment tribunal must award compensation for it.

4. Although compensation is the main remedy there are other remedies such as declaration of rights and recommendations, but these have limited effect.

5. For a study of the effect of successful complaints, see Leonard, A., *Pyrrhic Victories: Winning Sex Discrimination and Equal Pay Cases in the Industrial Tribunals* (EOC, 1987).

VIII   Disability Discrimination Act 1995

This Act is intended to prevent discrimination on grounds of disability in employment, in relation to the provision of goods, facilities and services, premises, further and higher education and public transport, including taxis, public service vehicles and railways. It further requires employers to accommodate the needs of disabled persons to enable them to carry out their jobs.

Many aspects of the DDA will be familiar to those with knowledge of the SDA, although the DDA is not a mirror image of the existing legislation.

Disability Discrimination Act 1995

1. Meaning of 'disability' and 'disabled person'
    (1) Subject to the provisions of Schedule 1, a person has a disability for the purposes of this Act if he has a physical or mental impairment which has a substantial and long-term adverse effect on his ability to carry out normal day-to-day activities.
    (2) In this Act 'disabled person' means a person who has a disability.

3. Guidance
    (1) Secretary of State may issue guidance about the matters to be taken into account in determining—
        (a) whether an impairment has a substantial adverse effect on a person's ability to carry out normal day-to-day activities; or
        (b) whether such an impairment has a long-term effect.
    . . .

PART II   EMPLOYMENT

Discrimination by employers

4. Discrimination against applicants and employees
    (1) It is unlawful for an employer to discriminate against a disabled person—

(a)   in the arrangements which he makes for the purpose of determining to whom he should offer employment;

(b)   In the terms on which he offers that person employment; or

(c)   by refusing to offer, or deliberately not offering, him employment.

(2)   It is unlawful for an employer to discriminate against a disabled person whom he employs—

(a)   in the terms of employment which he affords him;

(b)   in the opportunities which he affords him for promotion, a transfer, training or receiving any other benefit;

(c)   by refusing to afford him, or deliberately not affording him, any such opportunity; or

(d)   by dismissing him, or subjecting him to any other detriment.

(3)   Subsection (2) does not apply to benefits of any description if the employer is concerned with the provision (whether or not for payment) of benefits of that description to the public, or to a section of the public which includes the employee in question, unless—

(a)   that provision differs in a material respect from the provision of the benefits by the employer to his employees; or

(b)   the provision of the benefits to the employee in question is regulated by his contract of employment; or

(c)   the benefits relate to training.

(4)   In this Part 'benefits' includes facilities and services.

(5)   In the case of an act which constitutes discrimination by virtue of section 55, this section also applies to discrimination against a person who is not disabled.

(6)   This section applies only in relation to employment at an establishment in Great Britain.

5. Meaning of 'discrimination'

(1)   For the purposes of this Part, an employer discriminates against a disabled person if—

(a)   for a reason which relates to the disabled person's disability, he treats him less favourably than he treats or would treat others to whom that reason does not or would not apply; and

(b)   he cannot show that the treatment in question is justified.

(2)   For the purposes of this Part, an employer also discriminates against a disabled person if—

(a)   he fails to comply with a section 6 duty imposed on him in relation to the disabled person; and

(b)   he cannot show that his failure to comply with that duty is justified.

(3)   Subject to subsection (5), for the purposes of subsection (1) treatment is justified if, but only if, the reason for it is both material to the circumstances of the particular case and substantial.

(4)   For the purposes of subsection (2), failure to comply with a section 6 duty is justified if, but only if, the reason for the failure is both material to the circumstances of the particular case and substantial.

(5)   If, in a case falling within subsection (1), the employer is under a section 6 duty in relation to the disabled person but fails without justification to comply with that duty, his treatment of that person cannot be justified under subsection (3) unless it would have been justified even if he had complied with the section 6 duty.

(6)   Regulations may make provision, for purposes of this section, as to circumstances in which—

   (a)   treatment is to be taken to be justified;

   (b)   failure to comply with a section 6 duty is to be taken to be justified;

   (c)   treatment is to be taken not to be justified;

   (d)   failure to comply with a section 6 duty is to be taken not to be justified.

   (7)   Regulations under subsection (6) may, in particular—

     (a)   make provision by reference to the cost of affording any benefit; and

     (b)   in relation to benefits under occupational pension schemes, make provision with a view to enabling uniform rates of contributions to be maintained.

6. Duty of employer to make adjustments

   (1)   Where—

     (a)   any arrangements made by or on behalf of an employer, or

     (b)   any physical feature of premises occupied by the employer, place the disabled person concerned at a substantial disadvantage in comparison with persons who are not disabled, it is the duty of the employer to take such steps as it is reasonable, in all the circumstances of the case, for him to have to take in order to prevent the arrangements or feature having that effect.

   (2)   Subsection (1)(a) applies only in relation to—

     (a)   arrangements for determining to whom employment should be offered;

     (b)   any term, condition or arrangements on which employment, promotion, a transfer, training or any other benefit is offered or afforded.

   (3)   The following are examples of steps which an employer may have to take in relation to a disabled person in order to comply with subsection (1)—

     (a)   making adjustments to premises;

     (b)   allocating some of the disabled person's duties to another person;

     (c)   transferring him to fill an existing vacancy;

     (d)   altering his working hours;

     (e)   assigning him to a different place of work;

     (f)   allowing him to be absent during working hours for rehabilitation, assessment or treatment;

     (g)   giving him, or arranging for him to be given, training;

     (h)   acquiring or modifying equipment;

     (i)   modifying instructions or reference manuals;

     (j)   modifying procedures for testing or assessment;

     (k)   providing a reader or interpreter;

     (l)   providing supervision.

   (4)   In determining whether it is reasonable for an employer to have to take a particular step in order to comply with subsection (1), regard shall be had, in particular, to—

     (a)   the extent to which taking the step would prevent the effect in question;

     (b)   the extent to which it is practicable for the employer to take the step;

     (c)   the financial and other costs which would be incurred by the employer in taking the step and the extent to which taking it would disrupt any of his activities;

     (d)   the extent of the employer's financial and other resources;

     (e)   the availability to the employer of financial or other assistance with respect to taking the step.

This subsection is subject to any provision of regulations made under sub-section (8).

   (5)   In this section, 'the disabled person concerned' means—

     (a)   in the case of arrangements for determining to whom employment should be offered, any disabled person who is, or has notified the employer that he may be, an applicant for that employment;

(b)   in any other case, a disabled person who is—
    (i)   an applicant for the employment concerned; or
    (ii) an employee of the employer concerned.
(6)   Nothing in this section imposes any duty on an employer in relation to a disabled person if the employer does not know, and could not reasonably be expected to know—
    (a)   in the case of an applicant or potential applicant, that the disabled person concerned is, or may be, an applicant for the employment; or
    (b)   in any case, that that person has a disability and is likely to be affected in the way mentioned in subsection (1).
(7)   Subject to the provisions of this section, nothing in this Part is to be taken to require an employer to treat a disabled person more favourably than he treats or would treat others.
(8)   Regulations may make provision, for the purposes of subsection (1)—
    (a)   as to circumstances in which arrangements are, or a physical feature is, to be taken to have the effect mentioned in that subsection;
    (b)   as to circumstances in which arrangements are not, or a physical feature is not, to be taken to have that effect;
    (c)   as to circumstances in which it is reasonable for an employer to have to take steps of a prescribed description;
    (d)   as to steps which it is always reasonable for an employer to have to take;
    (e)   as to circumstances in which it is not reasonable for an employer to have to take steps of a prescribed description;
    (f)   as to steps which it is never reasonable for an employer to have to take;
    (g)   as to things which are to be treated as physical features;
    (h)   as to things which are not to be treated as such features.
(9)   Regulations made under subsection (8)(c), (d), (e) or (f) may, in particular, make provision by reference to the cost of taking the steps concerned.
(10) Regulations may make provision adding to the duty imposed on employers by this section, including provision of a kind which may be made under subsection (8).
(11) This section does not apply in relation to any benefit under an occupational pension scheme or any other benefit payable in money or money's worth under a scheme or arrangement for the benefit of employees in respect of—
    (a)   termination of service;
    (b)   retirement, old age or death;
    (c)   accident, injury, sickness or invalidity; or
    (d)   any other prescribed matter.
(12) This section imposes duties only for the purpose of determining whether an employer has discriminated against a disabled person; and accordingly a breach of any such duty is not actionable as such.

Clark v *TDG Ltd t/a Novacold*
[1999] IRLR 318
Court of Appeal

Darren Clark was employed by TDG Ltd, who trade as Novacold, as a process operator in manual and physically-demanding jobs from July 1995 to January 1997. In August 1996, he suffered a back injury at work and was diagnosed as having soft tissue injuries around the spine. He was absent from work from September 1996 and was paid full sick pay for 16 weeks.

The company obtained a medical report from Mr Clark's general practitioner an 6 December, indicating that it was extremely difficult to anticipate his return to work in the near future. He was unable to walk short distances and could not lift any heavy weights. A second medical report at the end of December, this time from Mr Clark's orthopaedic consultant, predicted that the injury should improve over a period of 12 months from the time of injury. However, the consultant was unable to give an exact time when it would be possible for Mr Clark to return to work. On that basis, the company dismissed Mr Clark in January 1997. He complained that he had been discriminated against contrary to the Disability Discrimination Act.

The Court of Appeal held: the employment tribunal and the EAT erred in holding that the applicant had not been treated less favourably for a reason which related to his disability than others to whom that reason did not apply within the meaning of s. 5(1)(a) of the Disability Discrimination Act, when he was dismissed on grounds of his absence due to disability. The tribunal and the EAT erred in reaching that conclusion on the reasoning that the applicant was treated no differently than a person who was off work for the same amount of time, but for a reason other than disability, would have been treated.

MUMMERY LJ: . . . [T]he 1995 Act adopts a significantly different approach to the protection of disabled persons against less favourable treatment in employment. The definition of discrimination in the 1995 Act does not contain an express provision requiring a comparison of the cases of different persons in the same, or not materially different, circumstances. The statutory focus is narrower: it is on the 'reason' for the treatment of the disabled employee and the comparison to be made is with the treatment of 'others to whom that reason does not or would not apply'. The 'others' with whom comparison is to be made are not specifically required to be in the same, or not materially different, circumstances: they only have to be persons 'to whom that reason does not or would not apply'.

This is to be contrasted not only with the different approach in the 1975 and the 1976 Acts, but also with the express requirement of comparison with the treatment of other persons 'whose circumstances are the same' stipulated in victimisation cases by s. 55(1)(a) of the 1995 Act.

The result of this approach is that the reason would not apply to others even if their circumstances are different from those of the disabled person. The persons who are performing the main functions of their jobs are 'others' to whom the reason for dismissal of the disabled person (i.e. inability to perform those functions) would not apply.

In the context of the special sense in which 'discrimination' is defined in s. 5 of the 1995 Act it is more probable that Parliament meant 'that reason' to refer only to the facts constituting the reason for the treatment, and not to include within that reason the added requirement of a causal link with disability: that is more properly regarded as the cause of the reason for the treatment than as in itself a reason for the treatment This interpretation avoids the difficulties which would be encountered in many cases in seeking to identify what the appeal tribunal referred as 'the characteristics of the hypothetical comparator'. . . .

Summary
In brief, the legal position is that:

(1) Less favourable treatment of a disabled person is only discriminatory under s. 5(1) if it is unjustified.

(2) Treatment is less favourable if the reason for it does not or would not apply to others.

(3) In deciding whether that reason does not or would not apply to others, it is not appropriate to make a comparison of the cases in the same way as in the 1975 and the 1976 Acts. It is simply a case of identifying others to whom the reason for the treatment does not or would not apply The test of less favourable treatment is based on the reason for the treatment of the disabled person and not on the fact of his disability. It does not turn on a like-for-like comparison of the treatment of the disabled person and of others in similar circumstances.

(4) The act of dismissal from employment falls within s. 5(1), but not within s. 5(2) and s. 6; but an employee who has been dismissed may bring a case under s. 5(2) for pre-dismissal discrimination involving a breach of a s. 6 duty.

(5) A s. 5(2) claim for a breach of a s.6 duty is not dependent on successfully establishing a claim under s. 5(1). They are different causes of action, even though, as recognised by s. 5(3), they may overlap.

(6) The question whether treatment has been shown to be justified is a question of fact to be determined on a proper self-direction on the relevant law. Such a self-direction includes taking into account those parts of the Code of Practice which a reasonable tribunal would regard as relevant to the determination of that question.

Notes

1. Further clarification is provided by the Disability Discrimination (Meaning of Disability) Regulations 1996. Guidance has also been issued for determining questions relating to the definition of disability.

Early case law from the EAT suggests that determining whether there is a 'disability' may be an issue. The EAT appears to be focusing on 'what the employer knows'. For example, in *O'Neill* v *Symm & Co. Ltd* [1998] IRLR 225, the EAT concluded that the employer must have knowledge of the disability. In this particular case, an employer who dismissed an employee for repeated absences due to ME, was found not to have discriminated against her as they were aware only that she had a viral illness and did not know that ME had been diagnosed.

The EAT has encouraged employment tribunals to adopt a purposive approach to the construction of the DDA 1995 with explicit reference being made to guidance issued by the Secretary of State and the Codes of Practice (see *Goodwin* v *The Patent Office* [1999] IRLR 4).

2. The statute requires the tribunal to look at the evidence by reference to four different conditions:

(a) Does the applicant have an impairment which is either mental or physical? Mental impairment includes an impairment which results from or consists of a mental illness provided that the mental illness is 'clinically well-recognised'. If there is doubt as to whether a mental illness falls within the definition, it would be advisable to ascertain whether the illness is mentioned in the World Health Organisation's International Classification of Diseases.

(b) Does the impairment affect the applicant's ability to carry out normal day-to-day activities in one of the respects set out in Sch. 1, para. 4(1), and does it have an adverse effect? The Act is concerned with a person's ability to carry out activities. The fact that a person can carry out such activities does not mean that his ability to carry them out has not been impaired. The focus of the Act is on the things that the applicant either cannot do or can do only with difficulty, rather than on the things that the person can do.

(c) Is the adverse effect substantial? 'Substantial' means 'more than minor or trivial' rather than 'very large'. The tribunal may take into account how the applicant appears to the tribunal to 'manage', although it should be slow to regard a person's capabilities in the relatively strange adversarial environment as an entirely reliable guide to the level of ability to perform normal day-to-day activities. The tribunal should examine how an applicant's abilities have actually been affected whilst on medication and then consider the 'deduced effects' — the effects which it thinks there would have been but for the medication — and whether the actual and deduced effects on ability to carry out normal day-to-day activities are clearly more than trivial.

(d) Is the adverse effect long-term? The case of *Greenwood* v *British Airways plc* [1999] IRLR 600 considers the appropriate time for determining whether a disability has a long-term effect. Whilst the EAT concluded that the relevant date was up to and including the employment tribunal hearing, interestingly Rubenstein (IRLR Highlights October 1999) suggests that this is incorrect and that the correct date is at the time of the alleged act of discrimination. Certainly, the latter is in line with other aspects of discrimination law.

3. Section 4 makes it unlawful for an employer to discriminate against a disabled person, and this extends to the same aspects of employment as can be found in the SDA 1975 and the RRA 1976, i.e. recruitment, promotion, dismissal, etc.

There is, however, a limitation to be found in s. 5 which restricts discrimination falling within the Act to direct discrimination. Further contravention may arise if the employer fails to comply with the s. 6 duty to make adjustments to premises etc. without justification.

In establishing direct discrimination within the DDA 1995 (s. 5), it has become clear that a 'like with like' comparison is not required. Indeed, there is no reference to such a comparison in the DDA 1995. The applicant merely needs to show less favourable treatment than other employees relating to his disability, i.e. 'But for his disability, would he have been treated more favourably?' (*British Sugar Ltd* v *Kirker* [1998] IRLR 624). This has removed one hurdle for the applicant in disability discrimination cases. The second issue in *Clark* was the recognition that even where there had been a dismissal, the applicant could still claim that the employer had failed to make reasonable adjustments to avoid the dismissal (see 4. below).

Guidance has been provided in *Baynton* v *Sauras General Engineers Ltd* [1999] IRLR 604 for establishing justification under s. 5(1)(a) and s. 5(3).

The employer must show that 'the reason for the act of discrimination was material to the circumstances of the case and substantial and that he has not, without justification, failed to comply with any duty under s. 6'.

4.   The issue of 'reasonable adjustments' is also proving to be contentious.

In *Morse* v *Wiltshire County Council* [1998] IRLR 352, the EAT held that a duty to make reasonable adjustments (s. 6) applies in a dismissal situation, even though dismissal is not expressly referred to in s. 6. In adopting a purposive approach, the EAT concluded that under s. 6 an employer should see if he can take steps reasonably to avoid dismissing a disabled employee. The test for determining whether there was a duty to make an adjustment, and whether the employer's failure to make an adjustment is justified, is an objective one.

In *Rideout* v *TC Group* [1998] IRLR 628, the EAT concluded that there was no duty to make reasonable adjustments if the employer did not know or could not have reasonably been expected to know that the person had a disability and was likely to be placed at a substantial disadvantage in comparison with persons who were not disabled. The extent of the duty must therefore be measured against the actual or assumed knowledge of the employer, both as to the disability and its likelihood of causing the individual a substantial disadvantage in comparison with persons who are not disabled.

The duty under s. 6 does not extend to the provision of a personal carer and is restricted to job related matters (*Kenny* v *Hampshire Constabulary* [1999] IRLR 76).

5.   The Act applies only to employers of 20 or more employees. A complaint made under the Act may be heard by an employment tribunal.

6.   The Act is further supplemented by the Disability Discrimination (Employment) Regulations 1996 which allow employers to justify on grounds of cost less favourable treatment of a disabled employee for pension and sick pay purposes relating to the definition of disability etc. (see 68 EOR 1996).

7.   For a critique of the DDA 1995, see Doyle, B. 'Disabled Workers' Rights, The Disability Discrimination Act and the UN Standard Rules' (1996) 25 ILJ, No. 1, p. 1, in which Doyle criticises the failure of the DDA 1995 to meet UN Standard Rules on disability and which, he feels, reflects the lack of commitment to the elimination of disability discrimination.

5 TERMINATING THE CONTRACT

A variety of common law and statutory employment rights are dependent upon a dismissal taking place. But, as will be seen below, there are a number of instances where termination may take place without dismissal as such. In certain cases, statute seeks to ameliorate the harshness of the common law position by deeming a dismissal to have taken place, thus enhancing employment protection, e.g. ERA 1996, s. 136 (redundancy), s. 95 (unfair dismissal) (referred to below). In other areas, however, the old common law rules remain unqualified by statute and it then becomes a question of judicial policy as to how far the common law doctrines, such as frustration, should be allowed to operate in a modern system of employment protection.

I Termination Involving Dismissal at Common Law

A: Dismissal with Notice

The general principle is that either party to the contract of employment can bring it to an end by giving notice to the other. Once notice is given, it cannot be withdrawn unilaterally.

If the contract is for a fixed period, then the employment cannot lawfully be terminated before the end of that period unless, of course, the employee is in breach of contract or unless the contract provides for prior termination by notice.

The length of notice required to bring a contract to an end should be expressly agreed by the parties. If no notice is expressly agreed then the law requires that 'reasonable notice' should be given, with the length depending on such factors as the seniority and status of the employee. Apart from any contractual provision for notice, an employee is entitled to a statutory minimum period of notice, which statutory period takes precedence over any lesser contractual notice entitlement (ERA 1996, s. 86(3)).

Employment Rights Act 1996

86. Rights of employer and employee to minimum notice

(1) The notice required to be given by an employer to terminate the contract of employment of a person who has been continuously employed for one month or more—

(a) is not less than one week's notice if his period of continuous employment is less than two years,

(b) is not less than one week's notice for each year of continuous employment if his period of continuous employment is two years or more but less than twelve years, and

(c) is not less than twelve weeks' notice if his period of continuous employment is twelve years or more.

(2) The notice required to be given by an employee who has been continuously employed for one month or more to terminate his contract of employment is not less than one week.

. . .

Notes

1. The minimum notice provision does not prevent either party from waiving the right to notice, affect the right of either party to terminate the contract without notice in response to a serious breach of contract by the other (see below), or prevent the employee accepting a payment *in lieu of notice* (ERA 1996, s. 86(3) and (6)).

2. Employers will often decide that it is in their interests not to require dismissed employees to work out their notice. At best such workers will lack motivation and at worst they may try to find a way of getting their own back! When such workers are given pay in lieu of notice, the law regards this as the payment of damages for wrongful dismissal (see p. 401).

B: Summary Dismissal for Fundamental Breach

(i) What Conduct is Sufficient to Warrant Termination?

The conduct of the employee may be viewed as sufficiently serious to justify immediate termination of employment without notice. In this event, the employee will lose entitlement to both contractual and statutory minimum notice.

Theft of or wilful damage to the employer's property, violence at work, dishonesty and other criminal offences will normally justify instant dismissal. Disobedience to lawful and reasonable orders may justify instant dismissal, but not in every case – all the circumstances must be considered. Ordinarily, lesser misdemeanours would require the employer to give a warning as to future behaviour before dismissing. But a combination of lesser offences may justify instant termination.

Pepper v *Webb*
[1969] 2 All ER 216
Court of Appeal

HARMAN LJ: . . . [T]he employee began (as they said) to lose interest; he did not give satisfaction. There were complaints of inefficiency and an insolent manner – what the judge described as 'dumb insolence' – at times. Things went on very uncomfortably during April, May and June. During part of that time he was very short of help; the promised second gardener did not turn up until May, though there was a third – jobbing – gardener from Monday to Friday.

The matter came to a head on Saturday 10th June, when the employer's wife went out between 9.0 a.m. and 10.0 a.m. and found that there were some fuchsia plants and geranium plants that had not yet been planted. She told the employee to put them in at once or they would die. There had been a good many plants – sweet peas in particular, and dahlias – that had died, according to her, from neglect previously, though it is fair to say that the employee denies it. Anyway on the morning of 10th June she said 'Put in these plants'. There were fuchsias, geraniums and some heath plants. The employee said: 'I am leaving at 12 o'clock; you can do what you like about them. If you don't like it you can give me notice'; and he walked off. The employer's wife was upset and went in and complained to the employer. He says that he went out to speak to the employee. The employee says he was ordered into the house but that is not accepted by the judge. I think that probably the critical interview occurred in the garden. Anyhow according to the employer, he went out, not with the idea of sacking the employee – because he could ill afford to do that in June – but in order to remonstrate with him, and he apparently said 'This job will only take you half an hour: why make all this trouble and fuss about it?' It was then fairly near 12 noon, which was shutting-up time for the employee. The employee, I think, must have lost his temper, for he said: 'I couldn't care less about your bloody greenhouse and your sodding garden'; and he walked off. The employer felt that he could not abide that degree of insolence and he gave him notice forthwith; and this action is for seven weeks' wages on the footing that that dismissal was not justified.

Now what will justify an instant dismissal? – something done by the employee which impliedly or expressly is a repudiation of the fundamental terms of the contract; and in my judgment if ever there was such a repudiation this is it. What is the gardener to do? He is to look after the garden and he is to look after the greenhouse. If he does not care a jot about either then he is repudiating his contract. That is what it seems to me the employee did, and I do not see, having done that, that he can complain if he is summarily dismissed. It is said on his behalf that one act of temper, one insolent outburst, does not merit so condign a punishment; but this, according to his employer, and I think rightly on the evidence, was the last straw. The employee had been acting in a very unsatisfactory way ever since April. He had that morning refused to obey the employer's wife's quite reasonable instructions, and when he in addition behaved in this way to the remonstrances of his employer I think he brought his dismissal upon himself and cannot complain of it. In my judgment, therefore, the appeal should be allowed and the claim dismissed.

KARMINSKI LJ: I agree that this appeal must be allowed. In my view the essential question here is whether the employer was justified in his summary dismissal of the employee on the ground of wilful disobedience of a lawful and reasonable order. Harman LJ, has set out the facts and I do not propose to add anything to what he has said. It has long been a part of our law that a servant repudiates the contract of service if he wilfully disobeys the lawful and reasonable orders of his master. There is no suggestion here that the order initiated by the employer's wife, and repeated by the employer a couple of hours later, was other than lawful. I see nothing on the facts before the learned deputy county court judge to suggest that that order was unreasonable; and there is ample evidence to show that the refusal by the employee was wilful. That being so, I have come to the conclusion that the employer was fully justified in dismissing the employee summarily.

Wilson v *Racher*
[1974] IRLR 114
Court of Appeal

Philip Wilson was the head gardener on Mr Racher's estate. He was dismissed following an incident in which Racher accused Wilson of shirking his work and in the course of the ensuing argument Wilson used obscene language.

EDMUND-DAVIES LJ: On Sunday 11.6.72, the defendant sacked the plaintiff. The plaintiff asserts that this constituted a wrongful dismissal and entitled him to the damages awarded by the learned judge. As to the quantum of those damages, no question arises. The sole issue here is whether the circumstances were such that the defendant acted wrongfully in prematurely terminating the plaintiff's employment.

There is no rule of thumb to determine what misconduct on the part of a servant justifies summary termination of his contract. For the purpose of the present case, the test is whether the plaintiff's conduct was insulting and insubordinate to such a degree as to be incompatible with the continuance of the relation of master and servant (per Hill, J, in *Edwards* v *Levy* (1860) 2F and F p. 94, at p. 95). The application of such test will, of course, lead to varying results according to the nature of the employment and all the circumstances of the case. Reported decisions provide useful, but only general guides, each case turning upon its own facts. Many of the decisions which are customarily cited in these cases date from the last century and may be wholly out of accord with the current social conditions. What would today be regarded as almost an attitude of Czar-serf, which is to be found in some of the older cases where a dismissed employee failed to recover damages, would, I venture to think, be decided differently to-day. We have by now come to realise that a contract of service imposes upon the parties a duty of mutual respect.

What happened on Sunday the 11th June emerges from the learned judge's clear and helpful judgment, in which he reviews all the facts and sets out his findings. This Court lacks the advantage of seeing and hearing the witnesses which was enjoyed by the trial judge. It needs to be stressed that the appellant now challenges none of his findings of fact. The story began on the preceding Friday afternoon when the plaintiff had been trimming a new yew hedge with an electric cutter. It was a damp afternoon, but the plaintiff carried on, taking shelter when the rain became heavy and then resuming his work when conditions improved. But at about quarter to four the rain was so heavy that the plaintiff could not continue because there was danger of his being electrocuted by the cutter. He then proceeded to oil and clean his tools until his day's work was over. But he did make one mistake. He left a ladder leaning against a young yew hedge, which was an unfortunate thing to do. To that extent, the plaintiff was guilty of some dereliction of duty. But on the Sunday afternoon that was by no means the only topic discussed between the parties. It was after luncheon that the defendant and his wife and three young children were in the garden when the plaintiff passed and greeted them. The defendant asked where he was going, and the plaintiff replied that he was going to the garden shed to get his boots. Thereafter the defendant showered the plaintiff with questions. He shouted at him, and he was very aggressive. He accused the plaintiff of leaving his work prematurely on the Friday afternoon. The plaintiff explained that he had stopped cutting the hedge only because it would have been dangerous to continue, whereupon the defendant said, 'I am not bothered about you, Wilson, that's your lookout'. Though there was some reference to the ladder, the defendant did not make clear what his complaint was. But when the defendant accused the plaintiff of shirking his work on the Friday afternoon, there is no doubt that the plaintiff used most regrettable language, and it is part of my unpleasant duty to repeat it so as to make clear what happened. The plaintiff said: 'If you remember it was pissing with rain on Friday. Do you expect me to get fucking wet?' The learned judge, who found that Mrs Racher and the children did not hear those words, said: 'The plaintiff had a clear conscience, and he did reply somewhat robustly when he expressed the state of the weather. I think he felt under a certain amount of grievance at that remark.'

According to the learned judge, 'The defendant then moved to what he thought was stronger ground', thereby obviously referring to the defendant's determination to get rid of the plaintiff. The judge dealt with an allegation about a line of string having been left in the garden by the plaintiff, and commented: 'A more trivial complaint it would be difficult to imagine. It was an extremely trivial complaint, if indeed justified at all. I think it is clear from this and other evidence that Mr Racher sets very high standards and this seems to me to be an absurdly high standard of tidiness.' The learned judge continued: 'The defendant's second barrel is very odd and illustrates that the defendant was determined to get the plaintiff on something.' There was a dispute as to whether the string belonged to the plaintiff or to the defendant, and there was a complaint about leaving other things lying about. The judge accepted that the plaintiff moved away in an attempt to avoid any further altercation. But he was called back, and was then showered with questions. Mr Racher was pressing him and going on at him, and this was, indeed, confirmed to some extent by the evidence of the defendant himself. Finally, the plaintiff told the defendant, 'Get stuffed', and, 'Go and shit yourself'.

These last two expressions were used by the plaintiff immediately he was dismissed. He later apologised to Mrs Racher for using such language, as to which the learned judge said, 'One cannot condone them or commend them, but he said that when subjected to a number of petty criticisms and was not being allowed to go.' Despite the use of such language, the judge held that the plaintiff was entitled to say that he had been wrongly dismissed.

[His Lordship then examined and distinguished *Pepper* v *Webb* (above) on the grounds it concerned a history of uncooperative behaviour on the part of employee rather than one isolated outburst of bad temper. He continued . . .]

The present case, too, has to be looked at against the whole background. On the judge's findings, here was a competent, diligent and efficient gardener who, apart from one complaint of leaving a ladder against a yew tree, had done nothing which could be regarded as blameworthy by any reasonable employer, applying proper standards. Here, too, was an employer who was resolved to get rid of him; an employer who would use every barrel in the gun that he could find, or thought available; and an employer who was provocative from the outset and dealt with the plaintiff in an unseemly manner. The plaintiff lost his temper. He used obscene and deplorable language. He was therefore deserving of the severest reproof. But this was a solitary occasion. Unlike *Pepper* v *Webb*, there was no background either of inefficiency or of insolence. The plaintiff tried to avert the situation by walking away, but he was summoned back and the defendant continued his gadfly activity of goading him into intemperate language. Such are the findings of the county court judge.

In those circumstances, would it be just to say that the plaintiff's use of this extremely bad language on a solitary occasion made impossible the continuance of the master and servant relationship, and showed that the plaintiff was indeed resolved to follow a line of conduct which made the continuation of that relationship impossible? The learned judge thought the answer to that question was clear, and I cannot say that he was manifestly wrong. On the contrary, it seems to me that the parties could have made up their differences. The plaintiff apologised to Mrs Racher. There are no grounds for thinking that if the defendant had given him a warning that such language would not be tolerated, and further, if he had manifested recognition that he himself had acted provocatively, the damage done might well have been repaired and some degree of harmony restored. Perhaps there was such instinctive antipathy between the two men that the defendant would, nevertheless, have been glad to get rid of the plaintiff when 23.10.72 arrived.

In my judgment, in the light of the findings of fact the learned judge arrived at a just decision. That is not to say that language such as that employed by the plaintiff is to be tolerated. On the contrary, it requires very special circumstances to entitle a servant who expresses his feelings in such a grossly improper way to succeed in an action for wrongful dismissal. But there were special circumstances here, and they were of the defendant's own creation. The plaintiff, probably lacking the educational advantages of the defendant, and finding himself in a frustrating situation despite his efforts to escape from it, fell into the error of explosively using this language. To say that he ought to be kicked out because on this solitary occasion he fell into such grave error would, in my judgment, be wrong. . . .

CAIRNS LJ: I agree that this appeal should be dismissed for the reasons which my Lord has given, and I only add, out of respect for the argument addressed to the Court by Mr Connell on behalf of the appellant, a few words about the other authority which he cited, namely, *Laws* v *London Chronicle (Indicator Newspapers) Ltd* ([1959] 1 WLR 698). That was a case where the plaintiff had been dismissed for disobedience. Lord Evershed, Master of the Rolls, in the course of a judgment with which the other members of the Court, Lords Justice Jenkins and Willmer, agreed, said at page 701: '. . . one act of disobedience or misconduct can justify dismissal only if it is of a nature which goes to show (in effect) that the servant is repudiating the contract, or one of its essential conditions; and for that reason, therefore, I think that you find in the passages I have read that the disobedience must at least have the quality that it is "wilful": it does (in other words) connote a deliberate flouting of the essential contractual conditions.'

There is certainly nothing more essential to the contractual relation between master and servant than the duty of obedience. Another duty on the part of the servant, particularly in the case of a man in such employment as this plaintiff had, a gardener in a domestic situation, is the duty of courtesy and respect towards the employer and his family. That is an important part of his obligations. But I would apply to that duty the same considerations as Lord Evershed applied in relation to the duty of obedience. In my view, this was not a case where it can be said with any justice to the plaintiff that the way in which he behaved, regrettable though it was, was such as to show 'deliberate flouting of the essential contractual conditions', having regard to the unjust accusation which had been made against him.

Denco Limited v *Joinson*
[1991] IRLR 63
Employment Appeal Tribunal

The applicant was instantly dismissed for unauthorised access to computer information which the employer considered was done to assist the employee in his capacity as a union representative. The tribunal refused to accept that such conduct could justify dismissal without prior warning. The EAT allowed the employer's appeal.

WOOD J: The industrial members are clear in their view that in this modern industrial world if an employee deliberately uses an unauthorised password in order to enter or to attempt to enter a computer known to contain information to which he is not entitled, then that of itself is gross misconduct which prima facie will attract summary dismissal, although there may be some exceptional circumstances in which such a response might be held unreasonable. Basically, this is a question of 'absolutes' and can be compared with dishonesty. However, because of the importance of preserving the integrity of a computer with its information it is important that management should make it abundantly clear to its workforce that interfering with it will carry severe penalties.

Although it is not necessary to decide the practice in this case, cases may yet arise where evidence will show that the very tampering itself could produce malfunction with consequent damage and loss of information.

An analogy may be drawn with a situation where an employee enters the management offices of a company where he has no right to be, goes into an office, sees a key on the desk which he knows is the key to the filing cabinet which contains information to which he is not entitled and thereafter opens the filing cabinet and takes out a file.

If in the present case it had been material to consider whether there was evidence which in all the circumstances entitled management reasonably to have suspicion about the applicant's motive or purpose, then the present industrial members take the view that there was abundant such evidence. I agree with them.

When considering the issue of motive the Tribunal at one point say:

> . . . Nor can we see on the menu anything to indicate that there was information which would have been the slightest use to Mr Joinson in his capacity as union negotiator.

With respect that does not seem to us to be the point. The issue is what did the applicant contemplate he might obtain by way of information by using the password of the wages department at Intek – a company by which he was not employed and the only connection with which would have been as a negotiator of pay.

(ii) Elective v Automatic Theories of Termination

There has been a long-running judicial debate as to whether the breach automatically ends the contract, or whether it is only so effective once the innocent party elects to accept the breach. The view that 'an unaccepted repudiation is a thing writ in water and no value to anybody' (per Asquith LJ in *Howard* v *Pickford Tool Co. Ltd* [1951] 1 KB 417, at p. 421) has now been accepted by the House of Lords as applicable to contracts of employment just as it applies to the law of contract generally (see *Rigby* v *Ferodo Ltd* [1988] ICR 29, at p. 363 below). If it were otherwise the guilty party could, by his default, 'call the tune'. Note, however, the recent judicial support for the 'automatic theory' by Ralph Gibson LJ in *Boyo* v *London Borough of Lambeth* [1995] IRLR 50, considered below at p. 365.

Thomas Marshall (Exports) Limited v *Guinle and Others*
[1979] Ch 227
Chancery Division

In 1972, the defendant had been appointed to a 10-year fixed-term contract as managing director with the plaintiff company. There were various usual restrictions on competition and use of confidential information in his contract effective both during and for five years after the end of the contract. During his employment, the defendant used, without his employer's knowledge, confidential information for use in his own private companies and solicited the plaintiff's customers. The defendant resigned in 1977 with over four years of his contract to run. The plaintiff successfully sought injunctions against the defendant and his private companies, preventing solicitation of the plaintiff's customers and/or use of confidential information. Amongst other things, the defendant sought to argue that because he had broken the contract he was no longer bound by its terms.

MEGARRY V-C: I shall take first Mr Hutchison's submission that the defendant's service agreement was terminated by his unilateral repudiation of it on December 5, 1977, even though the company never accepted it as ending the agreement. This is a striking contention. It means that although the defendant and the company contractually bound themselves together for ten years from September 2, 1972, so that the agreement still has over 4½ years to run, the defendant, and also the company, was able at any time, without the consent of the other, to bring the contract to an end simply by saying so; and that is just what the defendant has done. Mr Hutchison accepted that the general rule was that a contract was not determined merely by the wrongful repudiation of it by one party, and that it was for the innocent party to decide whether to treat the contract as having determined or as continuing in existence. That rule, however, did not apply to contracts of employment, for they were subject to a special exception. Under the exception, any contract of employment could at any time be brought to an end by either party repudiating it. This exception, however, was itself subject to an exception, and that was where despite the repudiation the mutual confidence between the parties remained unimpaired. In that exceptional case the normal rule for contracts still applied, and the contract remained in being unless the innocent party elected to treat the repudiation as terminating it.
. . .

At least one thing is plain, and that is that the authorities on the point are in a far from satisfactory state. Let me say at the outset that I have great difficulty in accepting the view that contracts of employment are an exception to the general rule for repudiation, and that they are terminated forthwith by the repudiation, whether or not the innocent party elects to accept it as doing this. Indeed, Mr Hutchison was unable to contend that such a doctrine was right, and in order to make his proposition viable he had to narrow it to a substantial degree. Let me attempt to summarise the matter.

First, there will usually be a wide range of acts and omissions which will constitute a repudiation of a contract, whether for service or otherwise. In addition to an outright refusal to perform the contract, there are many other acts and omissions which can amount to a repudiation which will entitle the innocent party to treat the contract as being at an end. Such acts or omissions may consist either of a fundamental breach of the contract or the breach of a fundamental term of it: I adopt the distinction made by Lord Upjohn in *Suisse Atlantique Société d'Armement Maritime SA* v *NV Rotterdamsche Kolen Centrale* [1967] 1 AC 361, 421, 422. If cases of master and servant are an exception from the rule that an unaccepted repudiation works no determination of the contract, and instead are subject to what I have called the doctrine of automatic determination, the result would be that many a contract of employment would be determined forthwith upon the commission of a fundamental breach, or a breach of a fundamental term, even though the commission of this breach was unknown to the innocent party, and even if, had he known, he would have elected to keep the contract in being.

That would indeed be a remarkable result. I may take as an example a case that was not cited during argument, *Boston Deep Sea Fishing and Ice Co. v Ansell* (1888) 39 Ch D 339. That case, like this, concerned a managing director who was faithless to his company. He took a secret commission, but before he was discovered the company dismissed him: and this was before his five years' contract had run very long. It was held that when the company discovered his fraudulent conduct the company could sustain his dismissal on that ground. Bowen LJ pointed out, at p. 365, that the determination of the contract by the company could be looked at in two ways. One way was to regard it as the exercise by the company of its contractual right to dismiss a servant guilty of a breach of his implied condition to render faithful service. The other way was to treat the act as being a wrongful repudiation of the contract by the managing director which, being accepted by the company, determined the contract. This determination, it will be observed, occurs not on the date when the repudiatory act is done, but 'from the time the party who is sinned against elects to treat the wrongful act of the other as a breach of the contract.' It will be obvious how ill the views of Bowen LJ accord with the idea that 'the repudiation of a contract of employment . . . terminates the contract without the necessity for acceptance by the injured party.'

In order to avoid difficulties such as these, Mr Hutchison reformulated the doctrine of automatic determination. He said that in master and servant cases a breach of contract amounting to a repudiation did not forthwith determine the contract unless the party breaking the contract intended to bring the contract to an end. This, of course, is a very substantial narrowing of the doctrine as stated in the cases. It also emphasises the shift in intention. Whereas for contracts in general it is the innocent party who decides whether the contract continues or is at an end, for master and servant it is the guilty party who has the choice, or at least the initial choice; for presumably if the wrongdoer sought to keep the contract alive, the innocent party would then be able to elect nevertheless to treat it as having come to an end.

It is plain that some such narrowing and reformulation of the doctrine is necessary if absurd results are to be avoided. It is also plain that nothing in the cases which have been put before me point to such a reformulation. It also produces a result which seems to me to be far from just. Why should a person who makes a contract of service have the right at any moment to put an end to his contractual obligations? No doubt the court will not decree specific performance of the contract, nor will it grant an injunction which will have the effect of an order for specific performance: but why should the limitation of the range of remedies for the breach invade the substance of the contract? Why should it deprive the innocent party of any right to elect how to treat the breach, except, perhaps, in remainder and subject to the wrongdoer's prior right of election?

Second, it is difficult, if not impossible, to reconcile the doctrine of automatic determination with a number of authorities which, for the most part, do not appear to have been cited in any of the cases that I have mentioned. I need say no more about the *Boston* case, but I must refer to some others. Johanna Wagner contracted to sing for a period for Benjamin Lumley, and not to sing for anyone else. She then agreed to sing for someone else for a larger sum, but Lord St Leonards LC granted an injunction to restrain her from doing so: *Lumley v Wagner* (1852) 1 De GM & G 604. A company engaged a confidential clerk named Heuer for five years, the clerk agreeing to devote his whole time to the company's service and not during his engagement to engage as principal or servant in any business relating to goods of any description sold or made by the company. After some three years Heuer left and became employed by other manufacturers in the same line of business as the company. The Court of Appeal held that the company was entitled to an interlocutory injunction restraining Heuer from carrying on or being engaged in a business relating to goods of a description sold or made by the company: *William Robinson & Co. Ltd* v *Heuer* [1898] 2 Ch 451. Bette Davis, the film actress, entered into a contract with a film company for a period, agreeing to render her exclusive services as an actress to that company, and not during that period to render any services for any other stage or motion picture production or business. During the period of the contract the actress refused to be bound by it, and contracted with a third person to appear as a film artist. At the trial of the action Branson J granted an injunction which restrained the actress from rendering services in any motion picture or stage production for anyone save the film company: *Warner Brothers Pictures Incorporated* v *Nelson* [1937] 1 KB 209. Not surprisingly, Mr Hutchison was obliged to contend that the last two cases were both wrongly decided; and the same would seem to apply to the first of the three.

To these three cases I may add one where the injunction was refused: *Ehrman* v *Bartholomew* [1898] 1 Ch 671. That was a case of a traveller for a firm of wine merchants who was employed for 10 years under a contract to devote the whole of his time during usual business hours to the business of the firm, and not to employ himself in any other business or transact any business with or for any other person. Within a year the traveller had left the firm and had entered the service of other wine merchants. On motion, Romer J refused the firm an injunction which would restrain the traveller from engaging or employing himself in any other business. This was on the ground that the restriction was too wide, since it extended to all businesses and not merely to special services as in *Lumley* v *Wagner*, 1 De GM & G 604.

Apart from the citation of *Lumley* v *Wagner* in *Hill* v *C.A. Parsons & Co. Ltd* [1972] Ch 305 (see pp. 323, 324), none of these authorities seem to have been considered in any of the recent cases on automatic determination that I have mentioned. Yet if the doctrine of automatic determination is good law, all that Johanna Wagner, Heuer and Bette Davis had to do was to say that their contracts were at an end, and so they were free from the restrictions that they imposed while their employment continued. The claims to an injunction would thus have failed instead of succeeding. Sir William Jowitt KC and Mr J.D. Cassels KC, who appeared for Bette Davis, ought to have won instead of losing. Nor need the wine traveller have had to base his contentions on the width of the restrictions. I realise, of course, that in his dissenting judgment in *Hill* v *C.A. Parsons & Co. Ltd* at pp. 322, 323, 325, Stamp LJ referred to *Lumley* v *Wagner* as being 'a much criticised decision,' and spoke of the 'sure and safe guide' propounded by Lindley LJ in *Whitwood Chemical Co.* v *Hardman* [1891] 2 Ch 416, 426–428. At the same time I have to remember that at p. 427 Lindley LJ accepted *Lumley* v *Wagner* as having 'more or less definitely' laid down that where there was an express negative prohibition (which was lacking in the case before him) the court could enforce it by injunction. That, of course, was exactly what Sir Nathaniel Lindley – by then Master of the Rolls – did some seven years later in *William Robinson & Co. Ltd* v *Heuer* [1898] 2 Ch 451. As I have mentioned, Stamp LJ was considering a very different type of injunction; to restrain an employer from acting on a notice dismissing a servant is far removed from restraining the servant from acting in breach of his obligations to the employer.

There is one other case that I should refer to, although it was not mentioned in argument. That is *Howard* v *Pickford Tool Co. Ltd* [1951] 1 KB 417. This was cited in *Hill* v *C.A. Parsons & Co. Ltd* [1972] Ch 305 (though only in argument), but was not cited in any of the other automatic determination cases. There, a company contracted to employ the plaintiff as managing director for six years. Within six months the plaintiff, while continuing to act as managing director, brought proceedings against the company. In these, he claimed that the conduct of the chairman was such as to show that the company no longer intended to be bound by the contract; and he sought a declaration that the company had repudiated the contract, and that it no longer bound him. On the full doctrine of automatic determination, the chairman's conduct, if established, determined the contract. On the watered-down version, it determined the contract if the company intended it to do this. What happened in fact was that the Court of Appeal struck out the statement of claim. At p. 421 Sir Raymond Evershed MR said that as the plaintiff had not accepted the repudiation but had gone on performing his part of the contract, 'the alleged act of repudiation is wholly nugatory and ineffective in law.' On the same page Asquith LJ said that 'an unaccepted repudiation is a thing writ in water and of no value to anybody: it confers no legal rights of any sort or kind.' It seems to me to be quite impossible to add the gloss 'except in master and servant cases, where an unaccepted repudiation is etched in granite and is beautiful to the repudiator'; for the case was itself a master and servant case. Yet some gloss of this sort seems to be required if any doctrine of automatic determination is good law.

Quite apart from that case, there is the question whether I am required to treat the *Lumley* v *Wagner* line of authorities, which include a decision of the Court of Appeal, as having been overturned sub silentio in the automatic determination cases. I do not think that I can be. Those cases speak in a voice which is far from clear; and of the conflicting dicta, there seems to me to be great force in what was said in the *Decro-Wall* case, and by Sachs LJ in *Hill* v *C.A. Parsons & Co. Ltd.* I can see no ratio decidendi in any of the automatic determination cases which is necessarily inconsistent with the ratio decidendi in any of the *Lumley* v *Wagner* line of cases. Further, none of the automatic determination cases have had to deal with the question whether, by unilaterally refusing to serve, the servant can thereby release himself not merely from any further obligation to serve but also from any restrictions, whether imposed by his contract or implied by law, which apply only while the contract of service exists. Furthermore, I think the courts must beware of allowing a restriction of the range of remedies which it is proper to grant to destroy or unduly impair the rights of the parties.

Above all, I think the courts must be astute to prevent a wrongdoer from profiting too greatly from his wrong. If without just cause a servant who has contracted to serve for a term of years refuses to do so, it is easy to see that the court is powerless to make him do what he has contracted to do: neither by decreeing specific performance nor by granting an injunction can the court make the servant perform loyally what he is refusing to do, however wrongfully. If such an order were to be made, the ultimate sanction for disobedience is committal to prison; and this, far from forcing the servant to work for his master, would effectively stop him from doing this. But why should the court's inability to make a servant work for his employer mean that as soon as the servant refuses to do so the court is forthwith disabled from restraining him from committing any breach, however flagrant, of his other obligations during the period of his contract? I would wholly reject the doctrine of automatic determination, whether in its wide form or in its narrowed version.

I accept, of course, that there are difficulties in almost any view that one takes. To say that a contract of service remains in existence despite the servant's resolute refusal to do any work under it produces odd results. Here, however, I am concerned only with the issue whether the servant's wrongful refusal to serve has set him free of the obligations which bound him while his contract of service continued. Furthermore, since what is before me is a mere motion for an interlocutory injunction, strictly speaking all that I have to do before I turn to consider the balance of convenience is to see whether there is a serious question to be tried, and whether the company has any real prospect of succeeding at the trial: see *In re Lord Cable, decd.* [1977] 1 WLR 7, 19. To these questions I would answer with an unhesitating Yes. But, as I have mentioned, the interlocutory stage is so important to both parties that I have examined the authorities in some detail, and I think it right, for their assistance, to express my views more fully. I may summarise them as follows. First, in my judgment the service agreement between the parties has not been determined but remains still in force. Second, the defendant is subject to all the obligations that flow from his being bound by the service agreement. Third, as the service agreement is still in force, clause J2, which provides for the defendant to be free from restrictions when he ceases to be managing director, has not come into operation, and that is so whether or not the two provisos are satisfied. Fourth, there is ample jurisdiction in the court to grant an injunction to restrain the defendant from doing acts contrary to his obligations under the service agreement, subject always to the exercise of the court's discretion whether to grant an injunction at all, and, if so, in what width.

London Transport Executive v *Clarke*
[1981] ICR 355
Court of Appeal

LORD DENNING MR (dissenting): [The facts] give rise to this question: when and by whom was this contract of employment 'terminated?' Was it terminated by the employee himself when he went off on February, 28, 1979, without leave for a holiday in Jamaica? Or was it terminated by London Transport when they wrote the letter of March 26, 1979, taking his name off the books?

The common law
It is over 50 years ago now that I studied in depth the common law relating to the discharge of contract by breach or by incapacity or by repudiation. The result is to be found in *Smith's Leading Cases*, 13th ed. (1929), vol. II, pp. 46–56. I adhere to what I then said. All I would say is that nowadays some people seem to think that a contract is never discharged by a breach – no matter how fundamental – unless it is accepted by the other side. That is a great mistake. It is the result of the modern phraseology about 'repudiatory breach.' A repudiation by words only, saying that he will not perform a future obligation – an anticipatory breach – is, of course, a thing 'writ in water.' It is as nothing unless and until it is accepted. But a repudiatory breach is better described as a 'fundamental breach' or a 'breach going to the root of the contract.' Such a breach may well lead to the discharge of a contract without any need for acceptance. The classic instance is where a singer genuinely fell ill and could not attend the rehearsals. Her incapacity discharged the theatre from further performance, without any talk of acceptance. It would be just the same if she had not really been ill but had pretended to be ill and thus been guilty of a breach going to the root of the contract. Again the contract would be discharged without any talk of acceptance. That is clear from the illuminating judgment of Blackburn J in *Poussard* v *Spiers & Pond* [1876] 1 QBD 410, 414–415, which I have often quoted.

If we put anticipatory breach on one side, these actual breaches can be divided at common law into three categories. I will illustrate the position from some modern cases. First, in *Laws* v *London Chronicle (Indicator Newspapers) Ltd* [1959] 1 WLR 698, the managing director at a business meeting said to the lady representative: 'You stay where you are.' She did not do so but walked out of the room. Till then she had been a good employee. She was dismissed. Her conduct was a breach of her contract of employment, but it did not go to the root of the contract such as to justify her dismissal. The company were liable in damages for wrongful dismissal. Second, in *Pepper* v *Webb* [1969] 1 WLR 514, the lady of the house asked the head gardener to put some plants in the greenhouse. He said he was not going to do it. The master of the house went out and said to him: 'The job will only take half-an-hour. Why make all this fuss about it?' The head gardener said: 'I couldn't care less about your bloody greenhouse and your sodding garden.' It was a breach going to the root of the contract. It gave the master an option whether to dismiss him or not. He elected to dismiss him. It was justifiable. The master was not liable for wrongful dismissal. Third, but if the head gardener had just walked off and got another job, it would be a breach which discharged the contract of employment without any need for acceptance. If the head gardener had disliked his new job and came back after a fortnight, the master would have been entitled to say: 'You gave up your job here. I cannot have you back now.'

The statute

Under our modern legislation a new question arises. It arises under [ERA 1996, s. 94], re-enacting earlier sections going back to 1971. When an employee is dismissed for misconduct, we have to ask – and to answer – the question: who 'terminates' the contract? If the employer terminates it, it is taken to be unfair unless the employer proves that it was fair. But, if the employee terminates it by his own misconduct, he gets nothing.

Much difference of opinion has been evoked amongst the judges on that question under the Act. So much so that I feel it is desirable for this court to afford some guidance. I think it is best done by applying the common law principles which I have just stated. The cases fall into two groups.

The employee terminates it

The first group is when the misconduct of the employee is such that it is completely inconsistent with the continuance of the contract of employment. So much so that the ordinary member of the tribunal would say of him: 'He sacked himself.' In these cases it is the employee himself who terminates the contract. His misconduct itself is such as to evince an intention himself to bring the contract to an end. Such as when an employee leaves and gets another job, or when he absconds with money from the till, or goes off indefinitely without a word to his employer. If he comes back and asks for his job back, the employer can properly reply: 'I cannot have you back now.' There is no election in that case. The man dismisses himself. In the words of Shaw LJ in *Gunton* v *Richmond-upon-Thames London Borough Council* [1980] ICR 755, 763, there is a 'complete and intended withdrawal of his service by the employee.'

The employer terminates it

The second group is where the misconduct of the employee is bad enough to justify the employer at common law in dismissing him, but leaves it open to the employer whether to dismiss him for it or not. His misconduct is such as to show that he is not going to fulfil his duties as he ought to do: but nevertheless it is not such as to be entirely disruptive of the contract. He does not sack himself, but he is guilty of a breach which entitles the employer at common law to dismiss him. If the employer does elect to dismiss him, it is the employer who terminates the contract.

. . .

TEMPLEMAN LJ: I can see no reason why a contract of employment or services should be determined by repudiation and not by the acceptance of repudiation. The argument has little practical importance at common law. The only difference which would exist at common law between self-dismissal and accepted repudiation is that self-dismissal would determine the contract when the worker walked out or otherwise committed a repudiatory breach of the contract whereas accepted repudiation determines the contract when the employer expressly or impliedly gives notice to the worker that the employer accepts the repudiation and does not wish to affirm the contract. But, in practice, at common law self-dismissal and acceptance of repudiation in contracts of service are usually simultaneous both being implied rather than express where affirmation of the contract would be meaningless; in any event, they involve similar consequences in almost all cases. A difficulty, however, arises under the Act of 1978 if Mr Scrivener's argument of a special category of determination of a contract by self-dismissal is correct. When a worker commits a breach of contract, neither he nor the employer nor in the final analysis the industrial tribunal may be entirely clear whether the breach is repudiatory or not. Whatever the nature of the breach, the worker may seek expressly or impliedly to persuade the employer to affirm the contract and to allow the worker to continue in or resume his employment. If the employer does not allow the worker to continue or resume his employment, then if Mr Scrivener is right an industrial tribunal must first decide whether the worker's breach of contract is repudiatory or not. If the breach of contract is so fundamental as to be repudiatory of the contract, then the tribunal must decide whether the repudiatory act is of a special kind which amounts to self-dismissal. If these matters are decided in favour of the employer, then the tribunal is not authorised to consider whether in the circumstances the refusal of the employer to affirm the contract and to allow the worker to continue or resume employment is fair or unfair unless, despite the finding of self-dismissal, the worker is able to establish conduct on the part of the employer which converts self-dismissal into constructive dismissal. If the tribunal decide that the breach of contract by the worker was not repudiatory or if the tribunal decide that the repudiatory breach was not of the special kind which amounts to self-dismissal, then they must conclude that the contract was terminated by the employer and they must then consider whether the employer satisfies the onus of proving that the termination of the contract which amounts to dismissal was in fact fair dismissal.

These complications arise, and only arise, if there is grafted on to the old common law rule that a repudiated contract is only terminated by acceptance, an exception in the case of contracts of employment. In my view any such exception is contrary to principle, unsupported by authority binding on this court and undesirable in practice. If a worker walks out of his job and does not thereafter claim to be entitled to resume work, then he repudiates his contract and the employer accepts that repudiation by taking no action to affirm the contract. No question of unfair dismissal can arise unless the worker claims that he was constructively dismissed. If a worker walks out of his job or commits any other breach of contract, repudiatory or otherwise, but at any time claims that he is entitled to resume or to continue his work, then his contract of employment is only determined if the employer expressly or impliedly asserts and accepts repudiation on the part of the worker. Acceptance can take the form of formal writing or can take the form of refusing to allow the worker to resume or continue his work. Where the contract of employment is determined by the employer purporting to accept repudiation on the part of the worker, the tribunal must decide whether the worker has been unfairly dismissed.

In my judgment, the acceptance by an employer of repudiation by a worker who wishes to continue his employment notwithstanding his repudiatory conduct constitutes the determination of the contract of employment by the employer; the employer relying on the repudiatory conduct of the worker must satisfy the tribunal in the words of section 57(3) [now ERA 1996, s. 98(4)] that in the circumstances, having regard to equity and the substantial merits of the case, the employer acted reasonably in treating the repudiatory conduct as sufficient reason for accepting repudiation and thus determining the contract.

Rigby v *Ferodo Ltd*
[1988] ICR 29
House of Lords

The employee, a lathe operator with a 12-week notice entitlement, had a 5 per cent wage reduction imposed by his employers who were in financial difficulties. The trade union was approached but no decision was taken as to whether to accept the reduction; the only vote was against industrial action if the reduction was imposed. The pay cut was imposed on 18 September 1982. The employee continued to work and, in 1984, success-fully sued for the return of the money he had lost since the imposition of the pay cut. The House of Lords upheld his claim. The employer had been guilty of a fundamental breach in reducing the wage and, since that breach had not been accepted by the employee, he was entitled to recover a sum representing his lost wages.

LORD OLIVER: The principal argument advanced on the appellant's behalf was to the following effect. It was not contended and could not, in the light of the trial judge's findings of fact, be contended that the appellant's repudiation of its contractual obligation to pay the agreed wages in full was ever expressly accepted by Mr Rigby. Equally it is accepted that, as a general rule, an unaccepted repudiation leaves the contractual obligations of the parties unaffected. It is, however, argued that contracts of employment form a special category of their own, constituting an exception to the general rule. The wrongful repudiation of the fundamental obligations of either party under such a contract, it is said, not only brings to an end the relationship of employer and employee (which, as a practical matter, cannot continue in the face of a refusal to perform or accept the services which the employee has agreed to perform) but also, of itself and by itself, terminates the contract of service forthwith without the necessity of any acceptance, express or implied, by the party not in default. Thus, it is argued, when the appellant's management implemented the reduction of Mr Rigby's wages without his agreement and against his will, his contract of employment with the appellant was terminated – wrongfully terminated, no doubt, but terminated – and could no longer be claimed by him to be subsisting. His sole remedy, therefore, was to sue for damages and the only damage suffered was the amount of the shortfall from the original contractual wage over the period of 12 weeks on the expiration of which the contract could have been lawfully terminated.

Mr Wingate-Saul QC, on behalf of the appellant, accepts that this argument is inconsistent with the number of reported decisions of the Court of Appeal – in particular *Gunton* v *Richmond-upon-Thames London Borough Council* [1980] ICR 755; *London Transport Executive* v *Clarke* [1981] ICR 355 and *Norwest Holst Group Administration Ltd* v *Harrison* [1985] ICR 668 – but submits that those cases, in so far as they rested upon the proposition that an acceptance of a wrongful repudiation of a contract of employment is necessary to bring the contract to an end, were wrongly decided and that your Lordships should prefer the dissenting views of Shaw LJ in *Gunton's* case [1980] ICR 755 and of Lord Denning MR in *London Transport Executive* v *Clarke* [1981] ICR 355. In his dissenting judgment in *Gunton's* case, Shaw LJ expressed the view that the practical basis for according an election to the injured party has no reality in relation to a contract of service where the repudiation takes the form of an express and direct termination of the contract in contravention of its terms. The contrary (and majority) view is that, whilst from a practical point of view a wrongful dismissal puts an end to the status of the dismissed employee as an employee and confines him to a remedy in damages for breach of contract (so that there will normally be little difficulty in inferring an acceptance of the repudiation), there is no reason in principle why, if the employee clearly indicates that he does not accept the employer's breach as a termination of the contract, it should not remain on foot and enforceable so far as concerns obligations which do not of necessity depend on the existence of the relationship of master and servant. My Lords, there is much to be said for both views and the majority opinion in *Gunton's* case [1980] ICR 755 has not been without its critics. But although it seems that one reason at least why the Court of Appeal here thought it right to grant leave to appeal to your Lordships' House was to afford an opportunity for a consideration of the correctness or otherwise of that majority opinion, the instant case is not on any analysis one of wrongful dismissal but is concerned with a very different state of facts, including the actual and intended continuation of the relationship of employer and employee without interruption. Having regard to the fact that your Lordships have not found it necessary to call upon counsel for the respondent, it would not, in my view, be appropriate that your Lordships should decide a not unimportant point of law which, on the facts before your Lordships, is of academic interest only.

Whatever may be the position under a contract of service where the repudiation takes the form either of a walk-out by the employee or of a refusal by the employer any longer to regard the employee as his servant, I know of no principle of law that any breach which the innocent party is entitled to treat as repudiatory of the other party's obligations brings the contract to an end automatically. No authority has been cited for so broad a proposition and indeed Mr Wingate-Saul has not contended for it. What he has submitted is that where there is a combination of three factors, that is to say, (a) a breach of contract going to an essential term, (b) a desire in the party in breach either not to continue the contract or to continue it in a different form and (c) no practical option in the other party but to accept the breach, then the contract is automatically brought to an end. My Lords, for my part, I have found myself unable either to accept this formulation as a matter of law or to see why it should be so. I entirely fail to see how the continuance of the primary contractual obligation can be made to depend upon the subjective desire of the contract-breaker and I do not understand what is meant by the injured party having no alternative but to accept the breach. If this means that, if the contract-breaker persists, the injured party may have to put up with the fact that he will not be able to enforce the primary obligation of performance, that is, of course, true of every contract which is not susceptible of a decree of specific performance. If it means that he has no alternative to accepting the breach as a repudiation and thus terminating the contract, it begs the question. For my part, I can see no reason in law or logic why, leaving aside for the moment the extreme case of outright dismissal or walk-out, a contract of employment should be on any different footing from any other contract as regards the principle that 'an unaccepted repudiation is a thing writ in water and of no value to anybody': *per* Asquith LJ in *Howard* v *Pickford Tool Co. Ltd* [1951] 1 KB 417, 421.

Notes

1. In *MacRuary* v *Washington Irvine Ltd* IDS Brief 518 June 1994 (noted by Miller, 'Unilateral Variation of Terms: Rights and Remedies' [1995] ILJ 162), the employer sought to withdraw a guaranteed entitlement to two hours' overtime per week. MacRuary continued working under protest at the change and claimed, successfully, that the change was an unlawful deduction of wages within the meaning of s. 7 of the Wages Act 1986 (now ERA 1996, s. 27). Miller argues that cases like *Rigby* v *Ferodo* can be dealt with, as an alternative course of action, under the protection of wages provisions now contained in ERA 1996, Part II.

2. What action is necessary to amount to an acceptance of a repudiatory breach of contract? In *Gunton* v *London Borough of Richmond-upon-Thames* [1980] ICR 755, the Court of Appeal not only approved the elective theory of termination but also held (per Buckley LJ) that acceptance of a repudiatory breach will be 'readily inferred'. However, to infer acceptance 'readily' is to blur the distinction between the elective and automatic theories of termination. Both aspects of *Gunton* were doubted by all three members of the Court of Appeal in the recent decision of *Boyo* v *London Borough of Lambeth*.

Boyo v London Borough of Lambeth
[1995] IRLR 50
Court of Appeal

Boyo was employed by Lambeth as an accountant. His contract entitled him to four weeks' notice of termination unless he was guilty of gross misconduct, in which case he could be dismissed summarily. He was accused of offences of fraud (of which he was ultimately acquitted) and in August 1991 he was suspended on full pay. His bail conditions prevented him having any contact with his employers, and on 28 October he was charged with the separate offence of conspiracy to pervert the course of justice. On 29 October, Lambeth purported to terminate his contract of employment on the ground that it had been frustrated. Boyo rejected that termination and turned up for work on 3 November but was barred. He continued to insist that he was available for work. He issued unfair dismissal proceedings in late November 1991 and County Court proceedings for wrongful dismissal in May 1992 after his acquittal of all criminal charges. At the county court hearing in December 1992, the employers conceded that the contract had not been frustrated; neither had Boyo been guilty of gross misconduct to warrant summary dismissal. The issue for the court, therefore, was when did the contract end so as to be able to calculate the amount of damages. The County Court judge held:

(a) The letter of 29 October 1991 was an effective termination of the contract of employment.

(b) Boyo's refusal to accept such termination was 'contrary to reality' (i.e. supporting the automatic theory of termination).

(c)   In any event, Boyo could not obtain salary for periods during which he did not work.

(d)   He was entitled to damages covering one month's loss of notice plus five months, being the period he assessed for the employer to carry out proper disciplinary procedures.

Both parties appealed. The Court of Appeal held:

(a)   But for *Gunton* it would have held that an unaccepted wrongful dismissal did bring the contract to an end.

(b)   It could not accept that acceptance should readily be inferred.

(c)   It would not interfere with the damages awarded by the County Court judge.

RALPH GIBSON LJ: There has long been an unresolved controversy, as is pointed out in vol. 16 of the fourth edition of *Halsbury's Laws*, 1992, at paragraph 303, as to whether (i) the contract of employment is an exception to normal contract law so that an employee wrongfully dismissed by his employer must accept that repudiation because, according to the 'unilateral' theory, the employee's only remedy in law becomes one of damages, and a repudiation of a contract of employment automatically terminates it; or (ii) contracts of employment are not formally exceptions to the normal rule that a repudiation of a contract is not effective unless and until the innocent party accepts that repudiation: see the cases there cited. The arguments and authorities have been considered in various cases including *Gunton* and *Dietman* v *London Borough of Brent* [1988] IRLR 299.

The matter was argued in *Rigby* v *Ferodo Ltd* [1987] IRLR 516, but it was held by the House of Lords that it was not, for the decision of that appeal, necessary to decide the question. Lord Oliver at paragraph 11 said:

In his dissenting judgment in *Gunton's* case, Shaw LJ expressed the view that the practical basis for according an election to the injured party has no reality in relation to a contract of service where the repudiation takes the form of an express and direct termination of the contract in contravention of its terms. The contrary (and majority) view is that, whilst from a practical point of view a wrongful dismissal puts an end to the status of the dismissed employee as an employee and confines him to a remedy in damages for breach of contract (so that there will normally be little difficulty in inferring an acceptance of the repudiation), there is no reason in principle why, if the employee clearly indicates that he does not accept the employer's breach as a termination of the contract, it should not remain on foot and enforceable so far as concerns obligations which do not of necessity depend on the existence of the relationship of master and servant . . . there is much to be said for both views . . .

The decision of this Court in *Gunton's* case, however, was binding upon Judge James and is binding upon this Court in respect of matters of decision there set out. The facts of this case, as it seems to me, raise the question as to which of the two theories is correct. . . .

It is next, therefore, necessary to determine what was decided by this court in *Gunton's* case. The facts were that Mr Gunton was employed as a college registrar under a contract terminable by one month's notice. Regulations which prescribed a procedure for the dismissal of employees on disciplinary grounds formed part of his contract. On 14 January 1976 the defendant gave notice to terminate Mr Gunton's contract on 14 February and he was told he was not required to attend work. The reason for the dismissal was disciplinary but the procedure had not been fully followed. Mr Gunton brought in 1976 an action for a declaration that the purported termination of his contract was void and that he remained registrar. The judge at the trial in October 1978 declared that the notice was ineffective lawfully to determine the contract of employment and on Mr Gunton at trial electing to claim damages at common law, ordered an enquiry as to damages on the basis that Mr Gunton was entitled to remain in his employment until retirement, unless in the meantime liable to redundancy or dismissal under the procedure, and subject to the obligation of the plaintiff to mitigate his loss.

As I understand the effect of that order, Mr Gunton would have been entitled to recover either his salary, since he was willing to perform his obligations, or damages in the amount of his salary, subject to reduction for failure to mitigate if any, from the date of the notice on 14 January 1976, giving credit for any payment, down to the date of assessment of damages and, thereafter, such sum as represented his probable earnings, having regard to the assessed risks of redundancy, discharge on disciplinary grounds and, pursuant to the duty to mitigate, the amount of probable future earnings. That, in substance, is what the plaintiff claims in this action should have been awarded by the judge.

In *Gunton's* case Shaw LJ held that Mr Gunton could not remain idle and demand his salary, because he had not earned it. If he claimed damages he must, by implication treat his contract as at an end because the court would not reinstate him by an order for specific performance. Mr Gunton had, since his dismissal, had other employments for short terms. That would constitute acceptance of the repudiation but that was not necessary: the wrongful dismissal in January 1976 brought the contract to a summary end. It did not matter for calculation of damages because, if the contract was brought to an end, as Shaw LJ held that it was, and if Mr Gunton suffered damage as a result of the disciplinary procedure not being followed, he would be entitled to recover that damage. He therefore concurred with the order proposed by Buckley LJ.

Buckley LJ approached the issue of damages as follows. The council's dismissal of Mr Gunton was wrongful but it was nevertheless a dismissal and de facto it brought his employment to an end. Having considered the previous decisions on the effect of a wrongful repudiation upon a contract of employment, Buckley LJ (p. 771) held that the doctrine of the need for acceptance of a repudiating act operated in the case of a contract for personal services as in the generality of contracts. Cases of wrongful dismissal, however, in breach of a contract of personal services have certain special features: they include the fact that a servant cannot sue in debt under the contract of remuneration in respect of any period after the wrongful dismissal because the right to receive remuneration and the obligation to render services are mutually interdependent. A wrongfully dismissed servant had, in the absence of special circumstances, no option but to accept the master's repudiation of the contract. Therefore, in the absence of special circumstances, the court should easily infer that the innocent party has accepted the guilty party's repudiation of the contract. Mr Gunton accepted repudiation at the trial if not earlier.

Lord Justice Buckley dealt with the damages in *Gunton's* case as follows:

(a) If the master, who is entitled to dismiss on not less than three months' notice, purports to dismiss summarily, the dismissal is a nullity and the servant can recover as damages for breach of contract three months' remuneration and no more, subject to mitigation: i.e. for the three months following dismissal.

(b)   But if the master were to dismiss the servant summarily and the servant did not accept the master's repudiation of the contract until the end of 10 weeks from the exclusion of the servant from his employment, then, if acceptance of repudiation is required in master and servant cases, the master is guilty of a breach of contract continuing from day to day for refusing to offer employment from the date of exclusion down to the date of acceptance and thereafter on the basis of wrongful repudiation.

(c)   The servant could not claim damages under the second head in relation to a period of three months from the date of acceptance, as well as damages under the first head in relation to the 10-week period, because his cause of action would have arisen when wrongfully excluded from his employment. Subsequent acceptance of the repudiation would not create a new cause of action although it might affect the remedy. The question must be for how long the servant could have insisted at the date of commencement of the cause of action upon being continued in his employment.

(d)   Therefore, Mr Gunton was entitled at 14 January 1976 when he was excluded from his employment, to insist upon a right not to be dismissed on disciplinary grounds until the disciplinary procedures were recommenced and carried out in due order but with reasonable expedition. He was thus entitled at 14 January to damages assessed upon the basis of a reasonable period from 14 January 1976 plus one month.

For my part, I have difficulty in accepting in full the validity of this reasoning. In *Sanders* v *Ernest Neale Ltd* [1974] IRLR 236, in one of the cases cited by Lord Justice Buckley in *Gunton*, Sir John Donaldson, president of the NIRC, referred to the reasoning of Sachs LJ and of Salmon LJ in the *Decro-Wall* case [1971] 1 WLR 361. He continued:

In essence it proceeds by the following stages.

(i)   A servant cannot sue for wages if he has not rendered services, and the wrongful dismissal prevents him from rendering services.

(ii)   This leaves him with a claiim for damages as his only remedy.

(iii)   Any claim for damages is subject to a duty to mitigate the loss and the only way to perform this duty is to accept the repudiation as terminating the contract of employment and seek other employment.

If there is any fault in this line of reasoning, it lies in point (i). Why should not the servant sue for wages if it is the act of the employer which has prevented his performing the condition precedent of rendering services? And if he can sue in debt for his wages, no duty to mitigate would arise and there would be no practical necessity to accept a wrongful dismissal as terminating the contract of employment, provided that the employer is solvent and the servant is sure that the dismissal was wrongful.

Further, if there is a requirement of law for acceptance by the servant of the repudiation by the master, I am unable to see why it is not a requirement for a real acceptance, that is to say a conscious acceptance intending to bring the contract to an end or the doing of some act which is inconsistent with continuation of the contract. If that is right, I do not understand how the courts would apply the notion of 'easily inferring that the innocent party has accepted . . . the repudiation'. Further, I do not understand why the taking of employment should automatically constitute accept-ance. If I tell my employer, who has in breach of contract refused to let me do my work, that I do not accept his repudiation – and that I shall get another job but remain willing and able to do my work when sent for by him – why should I be treated as having accepted what I have not accepted? And should it make any difference that I know enough of the law to give such a notice to my repudiating employer?

To the majority of the court in *Gunton's* case, however, it was clear that it would be contrary to the basic concepts of the law of contract, in the absence of special circumstances in which the court may prevent an employer from implementing a decision to dismiss, to require an employer who has de facto dismissed a servant in breach of contract, to pay damages on the basis that the employer's obligation to the servant continues after the end of that period of time by which under the terms of the contract the employer could lawfully have brought it to an end as from the date of the dismissal. That was also the opinion of Shaw LJ who agreed with that of Sir John Donaldson expressed in the case of *Sanders v Neale*. I agree with it also.

I also accept that principle must permit the continued existence, after a wrongful dismissal which brings the de facto relationship of master and servant to an end, of obligations contained in the contract which, in Lord Oliver's words in *Ferodo*, 'do not of necessity depend on the existence of the relationship of master and servant', such as the provision for disciplinary proceedings when held to be relevant to the assessment of damages, or to a term restricting the actions of the servant after termination of the contract such as was considered by Sir Robert Megarry VC in *Thomas Marshall (Exports) Ltd v Guinle* [1978] IRLR 174.

Subject to that qualification, if it were open to this Court to depart from the conclusion of the majority in *Gunton*, I would prefer the view expressed by Sir John Donaldson in *Sanders*'s case. It seems to me, however, that this Court is not free to depart from that decision with reference to any matter which was in that case a ground of decision. The grounds of decision include the reasoning stated by Buckley LJ which, as set out above, limited recovery by Mr Gunton to the reasonable time for disciplinary procedures plus one month from the date of wrongful exclusion.

STAUNTON AND PURCHAS LLJ: *Gave concurring judgments.*

Question
What choices does an employee have when faced with a repudiatory breach by his or her employer? See generally McColgan, 'Remedies for Breach of Employment Contracts' [1992] ILJ 58.

(iii)   An Employee who accepts a Breach of Contract by his Employer can nevertheless include that Breach as part of Conduct Justifying Later Resignation

Lewis v Motorworld
[1986] ICR 157
Court of Appeal

In December 1981, the employer, in breach of the employment contract, demoted the applicant and reduced his pay. The employee accepted the breach and affirmed the contract but over the following eight months his employer persistently criticised him until finally, in August 1982, the applicant resigned and complained of unfair dismissal, relying on both the demotion and the constant criticism. The tribunal dismissed the claim holding that the applicant could not rely upon the demotion to justify his resignation because that breach had been accepted, and that the criticism thereafter was not so fundamental a breach as to entitle the applicant to claim that he had been constructively dismissed. The Court of Appeal allowed the employee's appeal, holding that a breach that had been affirmed by an employee could nevertheless form part of a course of conduct justifying resignation.

GLIDEWELL LJ: The principles to be found in the relevant authorities can, I believe, be summarised as follows.

(1) In order to prove that he has suffered constructive dismissal, an employee who leaves his employment must prove that he did so as the result of a breach of contract by his employer, which shows that the employer no longer intends to be bound by an essential term of the contract: see *Western Excavating (ECC) Ltd* v *Sharp* [1978] ICR 221.

(2) However, there are normally implied in a contract of employment mutual rights and obligations of trust and confidence. A breach of this implied term may justify the employee in leaving and claiming he has been constructively dismissed: see *Post Office* v *Roberts* [1980] IRLR 347 and *Woods* v *W.M. Car Services (Peterborough) Ltd* [1981] ICR 666, 670, *per* Browne-Wilkinson J.

(3) The breach of this implied obligation of trust and confidence may consist of a series of actions on the part of the employer which cumulatively amount to a breach of the term, though each individual incident may not do so. In particular in such a case the last action of the employer which leads to the employee leaving need not itself be a breach of contract; the question is, does the cumulative series of acts taken together amount to a breach of the implied term? (See *Woods* v *W.M. Car Services (Peterborough) Ltd* [1981] ICR 666.) This is the 'last straw' situation.

(4) The decision whether there has been a breach of contract by the employer so as to constitute constructive dismissal of the employee is one of mixed law and fact for the industrial tribunal. An appellate court, whether the Employment Appeal Tribunal or the Court of Appeal, may only overrule that decision if the industrial tribunal have misdirected themselves as to the relevant law or have made a finding of fact for which there is no supporting evidence or which no reasonable tribunal could make: see *Pedersen* v *Camden London Borough Council (Note)* [1981] ICR 674 and *Woods* v *W.M. Car Services (Peterborough) Ltd* [1982] ICR 693 both in the Court of Appeal, applying the test laid down in *Edwards* v *Bairstow* [1956] AC 14.

This case raises another issue of principle which, so far as I can ascertain, has not yet been considered by this court. If the employer is in breach of an express term of a contract of employment, of such seriousness that the employee would be justified in leaving and claiming constructive dismissal, but the employee does not leave and accepts the altered terms of employment; and if subsequently a series of actions by the employer might constitute together a breach of the implied obligation of trust and confidence; is the employee then entitled to treat the original action by the employer which was a breach of the express terms of the contract as a part – the start – of the series of actions which, taken together with the employer's other actions, might cumulatively amount to a breach of the implied terms? In my judgment the answer to this question is clearly 'yes.' . . .

Questions

1. After *Rigby* v *Ferodo*, to what extent, if at all, can an unaccepted termination by breach be effective? Does there remain a difference, for example, between an out-and-out dismissal in breach of contract and an

employer's breach of contract in circumstances where the contractual relationship persists despite the disagreement between the parties? Compare the speeches of Lord Denning in *London Transport Executive* v *Clarke* and Lord Oliver in *Rigby* v *Ferodo*.

2. Should employment law now be *sui generis*, i.e. prepared to develop its own principles independent of the general law of contract? Consider, in this regard, the judgment of Ralph Gibson LJ in *Boyo* v *London Borough of Lambeth* (above).

Note

For a detailed discussion of this area, see Ewing, K.D., 'Remedies for Breach of the Contract of Employment', *Cambridge Law Journal*, vol. 52, no. 3, November 1993, pp. 437–69.

II Terminations Which may not Amount to Dismissal

A: Frustration

Morgan v Manser
[1947] 2 All ER 666
King's Bench Division

STREATFIELD J: If there is an event or change of circumstances which is so fundamental as to be regarded by the law as striking at the root of the contract as a whole, and as going beyond what was contemplated by the parties and such that to hold the parties to the contract would be to bind them to terms which they would not have made had they contemplated that event or those circumstances, then the contract is frustrated by that event immediately and irrespective of the volition or the intention of the parties, or their knowledge as to that particular event, and this even though they have continued for a time to treat the contract as still subsisting.

Note

Frustration automatically terminates a contract without the need for affirmation or acceptance by the innocent party. If frustration is established, there will be no dismissal and therefore, no right to claim unfair dismissal or redundancy payments. For this reason the courts have shown a degree of reluctance about applying the doctrine of frustration fully to contracts of employment.

The usual frustrating events in this area are sickness and imprisonment.

(i) Sickness

Notcutt v Universal Equipment Co. (London) Limited
[1986] ICR 414
Court of Appeal

The applicant had begun working for the employer in 1957 under a contract which permitted termination on one week's notice and provided for no remuneration during periods of sickness. In 1983, he suffered a coronary attack, and by July 1984 it was clear that he would not be able to work again. Accordingly, he was given 12 weeks' notice of termination. He brought an action in the county court claiming 12 weeks' sick pay on the basis that he was absent from work during the period of notice. The Court of Appeal agreed his contract had ended due to frustration prior to the notice period by reason of his illness.

DILLON LJ: The arguments of Mr Allen for the employee were first, and generally, that the doctrine of frustration can have no application to a periodic contract of employment because there is no need for it – the contract can always be terminated by short or relatively short notice. And secondly that in the circumstances of the present case there was no frustration as absence for sickness, injury or incapacity was envisaged by the contract and also by paragraph 3 of Schedule 3 to the Act.

In *Harman* v *Flexible Lamps Ltd* [1980] IRLR 418 Bristow J commented, at p. 419:

In the employment field the concept of discharge by operation of law, that is frustration, is normally only in play where the contract of employment is for a long term which cannot be determined by notice. Where the contract is terminable by notice, there is really no need to consider the question of frustration and if it were the law that in circumstances such as are before us in this case an employer was in a position to say 'this contract has been frustrated', then that would be a very convenient way in which to avoid the provisions of the Employment Protection (Consolidation) Act. In our judgment, that is not the law in these sort of circumstances.

In the present case, the argument of frustration is of course unashamedly put forward to avoid the provisions of the Act; in that it has succeeded in the court below. Notwithstanding the views expressed by Bristow J however there have been several cases in the National Industrial Relations Court and the Employment Appeal Tribunal in which those courts have considered that a contract of employment which is terminable by relatively short notice is in law capable of being terminated, without notice, by frustration as a result of the illness of the employee, and those courts have endeavoured to list by way of guideline the factors of which account should be taken in considering whether a particular such contract has been so frustrated: see *Marshall* v *Harland & Wolff Ltd* [1972] ICR 101; *Egg Stores (Stamford Hill) Ltd* v *Leibovici* [1977] ICR 260 and *Hart* v *A.R. Marshall & Sons (Bulwell) Ltd* [1977] ICR 539. The judge in the present case was in his judgment endeavouring to apply the guidelines laid down in those cases to the facts of the present case.

In this court in *Hare* v *Murphy Brothers Ltd* [1974] ICR 603, 607, Lord Denning MR held that a contract of employment of a workman was frustrated when the man was sentenced to imprisonment for 12 months. In reaching that conclusion Lord Denning MR considered by way of analogy that if the man had been grievously injured in a road accident and incapacitated for eight months his contract of employment would be frustrated. However, though the man's contract was presumably determinable on short notice, no argument was founded on this; the discussion seems to have been over whether the contract was terminated by frustration or by repudiatory breach on the part of the man in committing the offence for which he was imprisoned.

For my part, as a periodic contract of employment determinable by short, or relatively short, notice may none the less be intended in many cases by both parties to last for many years and as the power of the employer to terminate the contract by notice is subject to the provisions for the protection of employees against unfair dismissal now in the Act of 1978 [now the ERA 1996], I can see no reason in principle why such a periodic contract of employment should not, in appropriate circumstances, be held to have been terminated without notice by frustration according to the accepted and long established doctrine of frustration in our law of contract. The mere fact that the contract can be terminated by the employer by relatively short notice cannot of itself render the doctrine of frustration inevitably inapplicable. Accordingly the words of Bristow J in *Harman v Flexible Lamps Ltd* [1980] IRLR 418, 419, cited earlier in this judgment, must be taken as no more than a warning that the court must look carefully at any submission that a periodic contract of employment has been discharged by frustration if that submission is put forward to avoid the provisions of the Act. If Bristow J intended to go further than that I cannot agree with him.

Williams v Watsons Luxury Coaches Limited
[1990] IRLR 164
Employment Appeal Tribunal

WOOD J: A modern statement of the principles involved is to be found in *Paal Wilson & Co. A/S v Partenreederei Hannah Blumenthal* [1983] 1 AC 854, 909, where Lord Brandon of Oakbrook says:

> there are two essential factors which must be present in order to frustrate a contract. The first essential factor is that there must be some outside event or extraneous change of situation, not foreseen or provided for by the parties at the time of contracting, which either makes it impossible for the contract to be performed at all, or at least renders its performance something radically different from what the parties contemplated when they entered into it. The second essential factor is that the outside event or extraneous change of situation concerned, and the consequences of either in relation to the performance of the contract, must have occurred without either the fault or the default of either party to the contract.

In the field of employment law the doctrine has found its expression in respect of two types of events – imprisonment and illness. It is only the latter which is relevant for our present purposes. The four leading cases are *Marshall v Harland & Wolff Ltd* [1972] ICR 101; *Egg Stores (Stamford Hill) Ltd v Leibovici* [1977] ICR 260; *Hart v A.R. Marshall & Sons (Bulwell) Ltd* [1977] ICR 539 and *Notcutt v Universal Equipment Co. (London) Ltd* [1986] ICR 414.

A number of principles relevant to the application of the doctrine to contracts of employment can be derived from these decisions which, in any event, are rare occurrences in the realm of employment law.

First, that the court must guard against too easy an application of the doctrine, more especially when redundancy occurs and also when the true situation may be a dismissal by reason of disability. Secondly, that although it is not necessary to decide that frustration occurred on a particular date, nevertheless an attempt to decide the relevant date is far from a useless exercise as it may help to determine in the mind of the court whether it really is a true frustration situation. Thirdly, that there are a number of factors which may help to decide the issue as they may each point in one or other direction. These we take from the judgment of Phillips J in *Egg Stores (Stamford Hill) Ltd v Leibovici* [1977] ICR 260, 265:

> Among the matters to be taken into account in such a case in reaching a decision are these: (1) the length of the previous employment; (2) how long it had been

expected that the employment would continue; (3) the nature of the job; (4) the nature, length and effect of the illness or disabling event; (5) the need of the employer for the work to be done, and the need for a replacement to do it; (6) the risk to the employer of acquiring obligations in respect of redundancy payments or compensation for unfair dismissal to the replacement employee; (7) whether wages have continued to be paid; (8) the acts and the statements of the employer in relation to the employment, including the dismissal of, or failure to dismiss, the employee; and (9) whether in all the circumstances a reasonable employer could be expected to wait any longer.

To these we would add the terms of the contract as to the provisions for sickness pay, if any, and also, a consideration of the prospects of recovery. Fourthly – see *F.C. Shepherd & Co. Ltd v Jerrom* [1986] ICR 802 – the party alleging frustration should not be allowed to rely upon the frustrating event if that event was caused by that party – at least where it was caused by its fault.

(ii)   Imprisonment

Shepherd & Co. Limited v *Jerrom*
[1986] IRLR 358
Court of Appeal

The applicant had entered into a four-year apprenticeship when, after 21 months, he was sentenced to a minimum of six months in Borstal. On his release, his employers refused to take him back and he complained of unfair dismissal. The tribunal rejected the employer's argument that the contract had been frustrated by reason of the custodial sentence, but the Court of Appeal allowed the employer's appeal.

BALCOMBE LJ: The only case in the Court of Appeal in which the question has been considered is *Hare* v *Murphy Brothers* [1974] IRLR 342. That is not a very satisfactory decision: one side was not represented and did not appear, so the court heard argument from one side only. Lord Denning MR, held that a sentence of imprisonment did frustrate the contract of employment; Lord Justice Stephenson held that the sentence of imprisonment did terminate the employment, and it mattered not whether the termination was labelled a frustrating event, repudiatory conduct, a breach going to the root of the contract of employment, or impossibility of performance. Lord Justice Lawton did not deal with this question. In my judgment *Hare* v *Murphy Brothers* is not a decision which binds this Court to hold that a sentence of imprisonment is capable of frustrating a contract of employment. Nevertheless I find the reasoning of Lord Denning MR, highly persuasive. There are decisions of lower courts that a sentence of imprisonment is capable of frustrating a contract of employment – see *Harrington* v *Kent County Council* [1980] IRLR 353; *Chakki* v *United Yeast Co. Limited* [1982] ICR 140; to the contrary effect is *Norris* v *Southampton City Council* [1982] IRLR 141 – but none of these decisions is binding upon us.

In *Universal Cargo Carriers Corporation* v *Citati* [1957] 2 QB 401, 436–8 Mr Justice Devlin (as he then was) considered the law relating to anticipatory breach of contract.

The law on the right to rescind is succinctly stated by Lord Porter in *Heyman* v *Darwins Ltd* [1942] AC 356, 397 . . . as follows:
'The three sets of circumstances giving rise to a discharge of contract are tabulated by Anson as: (1) renunciation by a party of his liabilities under it; (2) impossibility

created by his own act . . . In the case of the first two, the renunciation may occur or impossibility be created either before or at the time for performance' . . . the first two state the two modes of anticipatory breach . . . A renunciation can be made either by words or by conduct, provided it is clearly made. It is often put that the party renunciating must 'evince an intention' not to go on with the contract. The intention can be evinced either by words or by conduct. The test of whether an intention is sufficiently evinced by conduct is whether the party renunciating has acted in such a way as to lead a reasonable person to the conclusion that he does not intend to fulfil his part of the contract . . . Since a man must be both ready and willing to perform, a profession by words or conduct of inability is by itself enough to constitute renunciation. But unwillingness and inability are often difficult to disentangle, and is rarely necessary to make the attempt. Inability often lies at the root of unwillingness to perform. Willingness in this context does not mean cheerfulness; it means simply an intent to perform. To say: 'I would like to but I cannot' negatives intent just as much as 'I will not' . . . If a man says 'I cannot perform,' he renounces his contract by that statement, and the cause of the inability is immaterial.

Mr Clark, appearing for the apprentice before us, submits that this principle enunciated by Mr Justice Devlin that impossibility of performance of contractual obligation created by the act of a party to the contract amounts to the renunciation (or repudiation) of the contract by that party is but the obverse of the coin, where the reverse is Lord Brandon's second factor in *Paal Wilson & Co. Partenreederei*. Accordingly he submits that . . . this cannot be a case of frustration: it must be a case of repudiation by the apprentice.

While I can see the logical attraction of that submission, and whatever may be the rule in the case of a commercial contract, I find difficulty in applying it to the case of a contract of employment and the imprisonment of the employee. What is the conduct of the employee by which he 'evinces an intention' not to go on with the contract? It cannot be the commission of the criminal offence, since in most cases it will not follow that he will necessarily suffer a sentence of imprisonment. What is the position between the commission of the offence and trial, while it remains uncertain whether the employee will be imprisoned, or will suffer some other punishment which will not necessarily prevent him from fulfilling his obligations under his contract of employment? What is the position of an employee who is remanded in custody pending trial: does this 'evince an intention' not to go on with the contract? For myself, I find it impossible to give a sensible answer to these questions. Further, I agree with Lord Denning's analysis of the position in *Hare v Murphy Brothers* (supra). In that case the National Industrial Relations Court had held that Mr Hare's sentence of imprisonment was not a frustrating event because it was brought about by his own act in committing the offence for which he was sentenced to imprisonment. It was, however, a breach by him of his contract of so serious a nature, bearing in mind the length of time during which he would be away from work and the importance of his position as foreman, that it went to the root and constituted a repudiation of his contract of employment. In criticising that decision Lord Denning MR, said:

I cannot agree with that reasoning. In the first place, I do not think that Mr Hare was guilty of any breach of contract. Take the brawl in March 1971 when Mr Hare struck a blow by which he unlawfully wounded someone or other. That was quite unconnected with his employment. It was no breach by him of his contract of employment.

Take next the sentence of imprisonment for 12 months in June 1971. That, too, was not a breach by him. If he had been given a suspended sentence or put on probation he would not be guilty of any breach of his contract of employment. Nor is it when he is sentenced to 12 months. That was the act of the court which sentenced him. It was no breach by him. But nevertheless – contrary to the Industrial Court – I think there was a frustrating event. The sentence of 12 months' imprisonment frustrated the contract of employment. I know that it was brought about by his own act, namely, the unlawful wounding. In that way it may be said to be 'self-induced'; but still it was a frustrating event.

In my judgment that analysis is entirely consistent with the realities of the situation.

I appreciate that mine may be a simplistic approach to a difficult jurisprudential problem, but I am conscious that employment law is today largely administered by industrial tribunals, often without the benefit of legal representation of some or all of the parties before them. In my view it is important that, if possible, the legal concepts relating to the existence and termination of a contract of employment should be readily comprehensible. If that approach involves a degree of inconsistency between contracts of employment and commercial contracts, then that is a price I am prepared to pay.

Accordingly, I answer question 2 above in the affirmative: a custodial sentence imposed upon an employee is capable of frustrating a contract of employment.

Note

While frustration arguments may well succeed in exceptional cases, the courts are generally reluctant to apply the doctrine. In *Williams* v *Watsons Luxury Coaches Ltd* (above), the EAT attributed this judicial caution to the view that the doctrine can do harm to good industrial relations, as it provides an easy escape from the obligations of investigation which should be carried out by a reasonable employer. It is therefore better for the employer to take dismissal action.

Question

Should 'frustration' arguments have any part to play in the supposedly 'user-friendly' remedies of unfair dismissal or redundancy? (See Hepple, R., 'Restructuring Employment Rights' (1986) 15 ILJ 69; Collins, H., *Justice in Dismissal* (Oxford: Clarendon Press), 1992, pp. 44–5.)

B: Termination by Mutual Agreement

(i)   Genuine Mutual Agreement

Birch and Humber v The University of Liverpool
[1985] IRLR 165
Court of Appeal

The applicants were members of the University's technical staff. In 1981, a Premature Retirement Compensation Scheme was introduced. It was made clear that the scheme was not a redundancy scheme and that any retirement pursuant to the scheme could only take place with the agreement of both the University and the employee. In 1982, the University announced that there was a need to cut back staff but expressed the hope that such could take place by way of early retirement rather than redundancy. The applicants applied for early retirement under the scheme and, having been granted it, thereafter applied to the tribunal on the grounds that they had been dismissed by reason of redundancy. The Court of Appeal agreed with the EAT finding that the applicants' employment ended not by a dismissal but by mutual agreement.

ACKNER LJ: The decision whether or not there has been a dismissal within the meaning of s. 83 [now ERA 1996, s. 136] has to be decided before one considers whether the result of that dismissal is to entitle the employee to make a claim for redundancy payments. The two are disassociated. Miss Cotton has shown us no authority for the proposition, which I find a strange one, that the mere fact that the requirement of the business for employees is expected to diminish, should make it in law not possible to have a determination of the contract by mutual consent. I put to her the simple example of an employer who envisages some time in the future, e.g. because of new technology, the need to slim down his workforce and makes an offer to those who are prepared to resign rather than to wait to volunteer for redundancy and supports that offer with a financial inducement which is far in excess of what is likely to be obtained under the redundancy legislation. It seems to me clear that in such a situation, assuming no question of any coercion of any kind, that if that offer is accepted there can be no question of there having been a dismissal . . .

Since the appellants' case is based on s. 83(2)(a) of the 1978 Act [now ERA 1996, s. 136(1)(a)], it may perhaps be worth making one observation as to the construction of the relevant wording of that subsection, which reads as follows:

83(2)   An employee shall be treated as dismissed by his employer if, but only if—
    (a)   the contract under which he is employed by the employer is terminated by the employer, whether it is so terminated by notice or without notice . . .

In my opinion this subsection, on its true construction, is directed to the case where, on a proper analysis of the facts, the contract of employment is terminated by the employer alone. It is not apt to cover the case where, on such an analysis, the contract of employment has been terminated by the employee, or by the mutual, freely given, consent of the employer and the employee. In a case where it has been terminated by such mutual agreement, it may properly be said that the contract has been terminated by both the employer and the employee jointly, but it cannot, in my view, be said that it has been terminated by the employer alone.

(ii)   The Employer Cannot Impose the Agreement

Igbo v Johnson Matthey Chemical Limited
[1986] IRLR 215
Court of Appeal

Mrs Igbo wanted to take extended leave to visit her husband and children in Nigeria. The employers were prepared to grant such leave but only on the basis of Mrs Igbo agreeing that, should she not return by 28 September 1983, her contract would be automatically terminated. Mrs Igbo returned to the UK on 26 September but did not report for work on 28 September due to sickness. The employer treated her contract as ended in accordance with a letter signed by Mrs Igbo. The Court of Appeal held that she had been dismissed and, in so doing, overruled the decision on virtually identical facts, in *British Leyland (UK) Limited* v *Ashraf* [1978] IRLR 330 (EAT).

PARKER LJ: Before proceeding to a consideration of the merits of the contention we should mention three matters. First there is no question of the respondents' seeking to behave improperly in granting leave on the terms here agreed. It is a common practice and designed to ensure that employees, particularly perhaps those going overseas, do not overstay their leave, a situation which occurs all too frequently. The respondents, in common with many employers, use the method here adopted to protect themselves from such occurrences. Secondly, there is no doubt that Mrs Igbo had the terms explained to her before she signed the copy of the letter of 18 August.

Thirdly, however, despite the above it must be recognised that the effect of the terms, if *Ashraf's* case is right, can be very harsh. An employee who had been employed for many years with an impeccable record might, for example, be knocked down by a car when within mere feet of the factory gate, which he was about to enter at the proper time. If he managed to crawl to the gate and was then promptly sent home by the employers in an ambulance his contract would not terminate. If, however, he could not move and was taken away by an ambulance without getting inside the gate, his contract would terminate. If he was able to report for work the next day and was turned away he would then be left without remedy either at common law or under the 1978 Act [now the ERA 1996]. No doubt it would be said that in such circumstances no employer would dream of turning him away, but this only serves to show that in substance he would, if turned away, be being dismissed. Furthermore, to say of an employee who failed to return to work in such circumstances that there was a consensual termination of the contract offends against common sense. There would be nothing consensual about it. The employee's desire throughout would clearly have been that the contract should continue.

With this preliminary we turn to s. 140 of the 1978 Act [now the ERA 1996, s. 203]. It provides:

(1) Except as provided by the following provisions of this section, any provision in an agreement (whether a contract of employment or not) shall be void in so far as it purports—

(a) to exclude or *limit* the operation of any provision of this Act; or

(b) to preclude any person from presenting a complaint to, or bringing any proceedings under this Act before, an industrial tribunal.

It is common ground, and was established in *Joseph* v *Joseph* [1967] 1 Ch 78, that the words 'in so far as it purports to exclude or limit', mean 'in so far as it has the effect of excluding or limiting'. The appellant relies on subsection (1)(a) only. The question is, therefore, whether any provision in the Holiday Agreement has the effect of excluding or limiting the operation of any provision of the Act. It is indisputable that the Holiday Agreement (so far as it was valid) had the effect of varying the conditions of the appellant's contract of employment. She contends that the provision for automatic termination of the contract on failure to return to work has the effect of excluding or limiting the operation of ss. 54 and 55 of the Act [now the ERA 1996, ss. 94 and 95] . . .

It is clear that both before and after 18 August Mrs Igbo had the right conferred by s. 54(1) and thus that neither s. 54 nor s. 55 was 'excluded' by the Holiday

Agreement. It is however equally clear that but for the provision for automatic termination she would had the respondents turned her off on 28 September have been dismissed within the meaning of s. 55. The termination provision therefore, it is said, had the effect of 'limiting the operation' of ss. 54 and 55. To this the respondents answer that it did nothing of the sort. Its effect was only to bring the contract to an end otherwise than in one of the four ways which, by subsections (2) and (3) of s. 55, alone constitute dismissal for the purposes of s. 54, namely by consensual agreement.

It is, we think, important to dispose at the outset of any idea that the termination of a contract of employment by agreement by itself prevents an employee being dismissed for the purposes of the 1978 Act. Every fixed term contract is terminated by consensual agreement on its expiry date, yet non-renewal constitutes dismissal under s. 55(2)(b). Every contract which is subject to termination on notice terminates by agreement if the employer gives proper notice, yet such termination constitutes dismissal under s. 55(2)(a). Hence, if on 18 August Mrs Igbo and the respondents had agreed that her contract should end on 28 September without more, she would have had a contract for a fixed term and non-renewal on that date would have constituted dismissal. Furthermore it is to be noted that, by virtue of s. 55(3), an employee under a valid notice, who gives notice to leave before the expiry of the notice is nevertheless taken to have been dismissed. This can, as it seems to us, only be due to the fact that the employee is in such circumstances treated by the Act as being not genuinely willing to leave. He will have departed voluntarily before he need have done but he will only have done so because he was under notice.

If the respondents' contention is correct, it must follow that the whole object of the Act can be easily defeated by the inclusion of a term in a contract of employment that if the employee is late for work on the first Monday in any month, or indeed on any day, no matter for what reason, the contract shall automatically terminate. Could it be said that such a provision did not limit the operation of ss. 54 and 55? In our judgment it could not. Such a provision would vitally limit the operation of s. 54(1), for the right not to be unfairly dismissed would become subject to the condition that the employee was on time for work on the first Monday in each month, or every day, as the case might be.

Hellyer Bros Limited v *Atkinson and Dickinson*
[1994] IRLR 88
Court of Appeal

The applicants were crew members on fishing boats owned by their employers. It was customary to sign a crew agreement which lasted for several voyages, after which the employee would be asked to 'sign off' and sign a new agreement to cover the next series of fishing trips. Both applicants 'signed off' their previous voyages, Atkinson before and Dickinson after, having been told that their employers were decommissioning their ships. They both sought redundancy payments. The employer argued unsuccessfully that they had terminated their employment by mutual consent and, accordingly, had not been dismissed.

HENRY LJ: [The] findings by the Tribunal were of mixed law and fact, in this case predominantly fact. An appeal only lies from the Industrial Tribunal on questions of law. And here there was ample evidence to support the factual findings. So the employer's task in upsetting those findings is formidable.

They sought before the EAT and in this Court to do it in this way. First, they rely on the terms of the crew agreement:

The form and provisions of this agreement are approved by the Department of Trade & Industry under s. 1(3) of the Merchant Shipping Act 1970.

If the form and provisions of this agreement are amended or clauses are added without the prior approval of the Department it will not be regarded as approved under the said section of the Act.

. . .

Contractual clauses
    (ii)   It is agreed that: . . .
    (iii)   After one voyage has been completed by a seaman under this agreement, either the seaman or the employer may give to the other notice (in writing or orally before a witness) to terminate the seaman's employment under this agreement, such notice to take effect at a port in the United Kingdom and to be given not less than 29 hours either before the vessel is due to arrive at that port, or before it is due to sail, if the employment is to terminate at the port where the vessel is when the notice is given . . .
    (v)   In relation to an individual seaman this agreement may be terminated:
        (a)   by mutual consent;
        (b)   by appropriate notice in accordance with the terms of this agreement;
        (c)   by loss or total unseaworthiness of the vessel.

Next, they point out that it is common ground between the parties that the Industrial Tribunal must have based their decision on subsection (a) of s. 83(2) of the 1978 Act [now the ERA 1996, s. 136(1)(a)]; namely, that the contracts of employment were terminated by the employer, whether by notice or without notice.

Here the employers did not give 24 hours' written notice in terminating the contract to the employees; and nor was any such notice given orally in the presence of a witness. So the employers refer to clause (v) (see above) and say that, of the three ways of terminating an agreement with an individual seaman there set out, this contract could only have been determined on grounds (a) or (b). It was not determined on ground (b) (the giving of appropriate notice in accordance with the terms of this agreement), as the employers had not given appropriate notice. Therefore, by a process of elimination, the termination of the agreement must in law have been under ground (a), by mutual consent (despite the Tribunal's emphatic finding that it was not). And if it was by mutual consent, then of course the employees were not dismissed by reason of redundancy.

That submission, advanced by Mr Pardoe QC on behalf of the employers, is in my view hopeless.

First, clause (v) does not list all the ways of terminating the contract; it only lists those 'clean break' terminations of the contract which leave neither party with any common law cause of action arising out of the contract. The Industrial Tribunal on the evidence inevitably and rightly found that the service agreements were not determined by mutual consent. There is nothing in this contract which could require that truth to be ignored or reversed.

In these cases the effective notice of termination was the information that the vessel would not be sailing for a bit in Mr Atkinson's case, and not sailing at all in Mr Dickinson's case. Each such notice was given more than 24 hours before the vessels were to sail – as they were to be decommissioned. So the imperfection in each notice was simply as to form: it was not given in writing, and was not given in the presence of a witness. Had any seaman been pedantic enough to have objected to these formalities being ignored, doubtless the employers' representatives would immediately have put it in writing or repeated it once a witness had been found. But the normal seaman would act just as these men did – waive the formalities and accept the inevitable.

And that is what the EAT found: an implicit finding of waiver by the Industrial Tribunal. So it clearly was. But Mr Pardoe submits that as these crew agreements and as any variation of them required the approval of the DTI, so any waiver by an individual of formalities inserted for his protection in all cases requires the same approval before acquiring force in law; and absent that approval, any such waiver must be ignored. Such, he submits, is the proper construction of s. 1(3), and represents the intention of Parliament.

On the facts of this case such a submission is legalism gone mad. There are certain statutory protections which the law does not permit parties to contract out of, such protections usually being inserted to remedy the weak bargaining power of the protected party. But that is not this case. These seamen were faced with the inevitable. They sensibly and realistically did not insist on being told the bad news again, albeit more formally. The contractual requirements as to the formalities attendant on the giving of notice offered them no useful protection in the circumstances. This was a classic waiver in the sense of a voluntary forbearance to insist on pedantic performance of – in this case – a now irrelevant contractual formality. The suggestion that by some malign legal alchemy that forbearance turned the plain fact that they had been dismissed by their employer into a termination of their longstanding employment by mutual consent, depriving them of their redundancy payments, is in my view without any merit and fails.

 . . .

Appeal dismissed with costs. Leave to appeal to the House of Lords refused.

Note

As a result of the Court of Appeal's decision, the Government has announced that it would set up a fund to compensate trawlermen made redundant in the late 1970s and early 1980s, who were misled by local officials of the Department of Employment into believing that they failed to qualify for a redundancy payment. This is long overdue. It had been agreed, as long ago as 1983, that *ex gratia* payments should be made in cases where there was evidence of misdirection leading to a claim not being submitted in time and where the claim, had it been submitted in time, would have been valid. However, in *McLeod and others* v *Hellyer Bros Ltd* [1987] IRLR 232, the Court of Appeal held that most of the claims by trawlermen would fail because of lack of continuity of employment. The *Atkinson* decision changes that position and the Government will make payments, including interest for the whole period since the men were dismissed.

At common law, termination without dismissal also occurs on the death of an employee or on the death of an individual employer (ERA 1996, s. 136(5) allows a redundancy claim by an employee in such circumstances).

The contract may also be terminated by expiry of time if a fixed-term contract. This is discussed below at pp. 398–401.

A contract will also be deemed terminated on dissolution of a partnership or on appointment of a receiver save that such events in the context of a transfer may, of course, be covered by the Transfer of Undertakings Regulations (see Chapter 7).

III   Constructive Dismissal

Employment Rights Act 1996

95.   Circumstances in which an employee is dismissed
(1)   For the purposes of this Part an employee is dismissed by his employer if (and, subject to subsection (2) and section 96, only if)—
. . .
(c)   the employee terminates the contract under which he is employed (with or without notice) in circumstances in which he is entitled to terminate it without notice by reason of the employer's conduct.

A: Dismissal or Resignation?

(i)   Are the Words or Actions of Resignation Unambiguous?

Sovereign House Security Services Limited v *Savage*
[1989] IRLR 115
Court of Appeal

Savage, a security officer, was told that he was to be suspended pending police investigations into the theft of money from the employer's offices. Savage told his immediate superior to pass on the fact that he was 'jacking it in'. The Court of Appeal agreed that the employer was entitled to treat these words as amounting to a resignation.

MAY LJ: In my opinion, generally speaking, where unambiguous words of resignation are used by an employee to the employer direct or by an intermediary, and are so understood by the employer, the proper conclusion of fact is that the employee has in truth resigned. In my view tribunals should not be astute to find otherwise. However, in some cases there may be something in the context of the exchange between the employer and the employee or, in the circumstances of the employee him or herself, to entitle the Tribunal of fact to conclude that notwithstanding the appearances there was no real resignation despite what it might appear to be at first sight.

We were referred in this connection to the earlier decision in this court of *Sothern* v *Franks Charlesly & Co* [1981] IRLR 278. In that case a partnership secretary to a firm of solicitors had in circumstances into which it is wholly unnecessary to go, said, 'I am resigning'. Both the Industrial Tribunal and the Employment Appeal Tribunal held that those words were ambiguous and that in consequence the employee had been dismissed. When the matter reached this court, it took a different view, concluded that that words were wholly unambiguous and that in the circumstances there had been a resignation and not a dismissal. Nevertheless in his judgment Fox LJ at para. 19 in the report said this:

As regards Mrs Sothern's intentions when she said, 'I am resigning', it seems to me that when the words used by a person are unambiguous words of resignation and so understood by her employers, the question of what a reasonable employer might have understood does not arise. The natural meaning of the words and the fact that the employer understood them to mean that the employee was resigning cannot be overridden by appeals to what a reasonable employer might have assumed. The non-disclosed intention of a person using language as to his intended meaning is not properly to be taken into account in determining what the true meaning is.

I turn to para. 21:

Secondly, this is not a case of an immature employee, or of a decision taken in the heat of the moment, or of an employee being jostled into a decision by the employers.

The learned Lord Justice was there contemplating the possibility to which I have referred, that if one is concerned with an immature employee or decisions taken in the heat of the moment, then what might otherwise appear to be a clear resignation, should not be so construed.

Dame Elizabeth Lane, in giving the second judgment of the court, agreed with the decision that there had been a resignation, but in the course of her judgment, referring to the words used, she said this:

Those were not idle words or words spoken under emotional stress which the employers knew or ought to have known were not meant to be taken seriously. Nor was it a case of employers anxious to be rid of an employee who seized upon her words and gave them a meaning which she did not intend. They were sorry to receive the resignation and said so.

So Dame Elizabeth Lane was again taking the same approach as Fox LJ: generally speaking a resignation is to be imputed, but there may be circumstances in which, notwithstanding what would appear at first sight, the circumstances are such that what occurred was a dismissal rather than a resignation.

(ii)   Allowance for 'Heat of the Moment' Utterances

Tanner v *Kean*
[1978] IRLR 160
Employment Appeal Tribunal

The employee had been loaned £275 so that he could buy his own vehicle, thereby making it unnecessary to use the employer's van outside work hours. Nevertheless Tanner continued to use the van for his own purposes. On discovering this the employer said 'What's my fucking van doing outside; you're a tight bastard. I've just lent you £275 to buy a car and you're too tight to put juice in it. That's it; you're finished with me.' The EAT agreed that these words should not have been treated by the employee as a dismissal.

PHILLIPS J: Turning to the appeal, the first thing to note is that there is only an appeal to us on a question of law. No doubt there are some words and acts which as a matter of law could be said only to constitute dismissal or resignation, or of which it could be said that they could not constitute dismissal or resignation. But in many cases they are in the middle territory where it is uncertain whether they do or not, and there it is necessary to look at all the circumstances of the case, in particular to see what was the intention with which the words were spoken.

In the present case the words are those set out in paragraph 1 of the Reasons: 'What's my fucking van doing outside; you're a tight bastard. I've just lent you £275 to buy a car and you are too tight to put juice in it. That's it; you're finished with me.' Part of the circumstances were that that was said in a country club to which Mr Tanner had taken the firm's van, and where he acted as a part-time doorman and had met Mr Kean, his employer. It seems to us – and although they do not say so, no doubt it seemed to the Tribunal – that those words, in all the circumstances of the case, were not as a matter of law in one category or the other; in other words, whether what was said constituted a dismissal depended on all the circumstances of the case. In our judgment the test which has to be applied in cases of this kind is along these lines. Were the words spoken those of dismissal, that is to say, were they intended to bring the contract of employment to an end? What was the employer's intention? In answering that a relevant, and perhaps the most important, question is how would a reasonable employee, in all circumstances, have understood what the employer intended by what he said and did? Then in most of these cases, and in this case, it becomes relevant to look at the later events following the utterance of the words and preceding the actual departure of the employee. Some care, it seems to us, is necessary in regard to later events, and it might be put, we think, like this: that later events, unless relied on as themselves constituting a dismissal, are only relevant to the extent that they throw light on the employer's intention; that is to say, we would stress, his intention at the time of the alleged dismissal. A word of caution is necessary because in considering later events it is necessary to remember that a dismissal or resignation, once it has taken effect, cannot be unilaterally withdrawn. Accordingly, as it seems to us, later events need to be scrutinised with some care in order to see whether they are genuinely explanatory of the acts alleged to constitute dismissal, or whether they reflect a change of mind. If they are in the former category they may be valuable as showing what was really intended.

Note

See also *Kwik-fit (GB) Limited* v *Lineham* [1992] ICR 183.

B: *The Concept of Constructive Dismissal*

Western Excavating (ECC) Limited v *Sharp*
[1978] QB 761
Court of Appeal

An employee was suspended without pay for having taken time off without permission. He was, therefore, short of money and sought an advance against accrued holiday pay from his employer, which request was refused. He then asked for a loan which was also refused. Accordingly, he resigned in order to obtain his accrued holiday pay. The industrial tribunal held he was justified in terminating his contract because of the employer's behaviour. The Court of Appeal overturned the decision, Lord Denning giving the seminal judgment on the proper test to be applied in considering an averment of constructive dismissal.

LORD DENNING MR: [Lord Denning was referring to the definition of 'constructive dismissal' set out in TULRA 1974. That same definition is now contained in ERA 1996, s. 95(1)(c) . . .] The rival tests are as follows.

The contract test

On the one hand, it is said that the words of paragraph 5(2)(c) express a legal concept which is already well settled in the books on contract under the rubric 'discharge by breach.' If the employer is guilty of conduct which is a significant breach going to the root of the contract of employment, or which shows that the employer no longer intends to be bound by one or more of the essential terms of the contract, then the employee is entitled to treat himself as discharged from any further performance. If he does so, then he terminates the contract by reason of the employer's conduct. He is constructively dismissed. The employee is entitled in those circumstances to leave at the instant without giving any notice at all or, alternatively, he may give notice and say he is leaving at the end of the notice. But the conduct must in either case be sufficiently serious to entitle him to leave at once. Moreover, he must make up his mind soon after the conduct of which he complains: for, if he continues for any length of time without leaving, he will lose his right to treat himself as discharged. He will be regarded as having elected to affirm the contract.

The unreasonableness test

On the other hand, it is said that the words of paragraph 5(2)(c) do not express any settled legal concept. They introduce a new concept into contracts of employment. It is that the employer must act reasonably in his treatment of his employees. If he conducts himself or his affairs so unreasonably that the employee cannot fairly be expected to put up with it any longer, the employee is justified in leaving. He can go, with or without giving notice, and claim compensation for unfair dismissal.

The result

In my opinion, the contract test is the right test. My reasons are as follows. (i) The statute itself draws a distinction between 'dismissal' in paragraph 5(2)(c) and 'unfairness' in paragraph 6(8). If Parliament intended that same test to apply, it would have said so. (ii) 'Dismissal' in paragraph 5(2) goes back to 'dismissal' in the Redundancy Payments Act 1965. Its interpretation should not be influenced by paragraph 6(8) which was introduced first in 1971 in the Industrial Relations Act 1971. (iii) Paragraph 5(2)(c) uses words which have a legal connotation, especially the words 'entitled' and 'without notice.' If a non-legal connotation were intended, it would have added 'justified in leaving at once' or some such non-legal phrase. (iv) Paragraph 5(2)(a) and (c) deal with different situations. Paragraph 5(2)(a) deals with cases where the employer himself terminates the contract by dismissing the man with or without notice. That is, when the employer says to the man: 'You must go.' Paragraph 5(2)(c) deals with the cases where the employee himself terminates the contract by saying: 'I can't stand it any longer. I want my cards.' (v) The new test of 'unreasonable conduct' of the employer is too indefinite by far. It has led to acute difference of opinion between the members of tribunals. Often there are majority opinions. It has led to findings of 'constructive dismissal' on the most whimsical grounds. The Employment Appeal Tribunal tells us so. It is better to have the contract test of the common law. It is more certain: as it can well be understood by intelligent laymen under the direction of a legal chairman. (vi) I would adopt the reasoning of the considered judgment of the Employment Appeal Tribunal in *Wetherall (Bond St. W1) Ltd* v *Lynn* [1978] 1CR 205, 211:

> Parliament might well have said, in relation to whether the employer's conduct had been reasonable having regard to equity and the substantial merits of the case, but

it neither laid down that special statutory criterion or any other. So, in our judgment, the answer can only be, entitled according to law, and it is to the law of contract that you have to look.

(vii)   The test of unreasonableness gives no effect to the words 'without notice.' They impose a legal test which no test of 'unreasonableness' can do.

Conclusion

The present case is a good illustration of a 'whimsical decision.' Applying the test of 'unreasonable conduct,' the industrial tribunal decided by a majority of two to one in favour of the employee. All three members of the Employment Appeal Tribunal would have decided in favour of the employers, but felt that it was a matter of fact on which they could not reverse the industrial tribunal. So counting heads, it was four to two in favour of the employers, but yet the case was decided against them – because of the test of 'unreasonable conduct.'

If the contract test had been applied, the result would have been plain. There was no dismissal, constructive or otherwise, by the employers. The employers were not in breach at all. Nor had they repudiated the contract at all. The employee left of his own accord without anything wrong done by the employers. His claim should have been rejected. The decision against the employers was most unjust to them. I would allow the appeal, accordingly.

LAWTON LJ: For the purpose of this judgment, I do not find it either necessary or advisable to express any opinion as to what principles of law operate to bring a contract of employment to an end by reason of an employer's conduct. Sensible persons have no difficulty in recognising such conduct when they hear about it. Persistent and unwanted amorous advances by an employer to a female member of his staff would, for example, clearly be such conduct; and for a chairman of an industrial tribunal in such a case to discuss with his lay members whether there had been a repudiation or a breach of a fundamental term by the employer would be for most lay members a waste of legal learning. There may occasionally be border-line cases which would require a chairman to analyse the legal principles applicable for the benefit of the lay members; but when such cases do occur he should try to do so in the kind of language which 19th century judges used when directing juries about the law applicable to contracts of employment, rather than the language which nowadays would be understood and appreciated by academic lawyers. I appreciate that the principles of law applicable to the termination by an employee of a contract of employment because of his employer's conduct are difficult to put concisely in the language judges use in court. Lay members of industrial tribunals, however, do not spend all their time in court and when out of court they may use, and certainly will hear, short words and terse phrases which describe clearly the kind of employer of whom an employee is entitled without notice to rid himself . . .

Notes

1. At the time of this decision, many commentators took the view that the contractual test would unduly limit the scope of constructive dismissal. However, this has not occurred because of the development of an implied duty to maintain trust and confidence (see p. 144 and below) and a willingness, on occasion, to circumvent the strict contractual approach (see *Greenaway Harrison* v *Wiles* [1994] IRLR 380, EAT). As a result the distinction between the *Western Excavating (ECC) Ltd* v *Sharp* approach and the discredited 'reasonableness' test looks slim indeed as is illustrated by looking at just some of the situations where the implied obligation has been held to be broken:

(a)   Failing to respond to an employee's complaint about the lack of adequate safety equipment (*British Aircraft Corporation Ltd* v *Austin* [1978] IRLR 332).

(b)   Undermining the authority of senior staff over subordinates (*Courtaulds Northern Textiles Ltd* v *Andrew* [1979] IRLR 84).

(c)   Failing to protect an employee from harassment from fellow employees (*Wigan Borough Council* v *Davies* [1979] IRLR 127).

(d)   Failing properly to investigate allegations of sexual harassment or treating the complaint with sufficient seriousness (*Bracebridge Engineering Ltd* v *Derby* [1990] IRLR 3, see below).

(e)   Foul language by employer (*Palmanor Ltd* v *Cedron* [1978] IRLR 303, see below).

(f)   Imposing a disciplinary penalty grossly out of proportion to the offence (*British Broadcasting Corporation* v *Beckett* [1983] IRLR 43.

(g)   A series of minor incidents of harassment over a period of time which cumulatively amount to repudiation: the so-called 'last straw' doctrine (*Woods* v *WM Car Services (Peterborough) Ltd* [1982] ICR 693, see below).

2.   Whether the employer's behaviour is sufficient to justify the resignation is a question of fact for the tribunal; accordingly the appeal court should not lightly interfere with the decision of the tribunal on this question. This point was emphasised in the following case. This case also provides useful guidance on the scope of constructive dismissal.

Woods v *WM Car Services (Peterborough) Limited*
[1981] ICR 666
Employment Appeal Tribunal

New owners of a business, having agreed to continue employment of employees on no less favourable terms than previously, asked the applicant to accept a lower wage and work longer hours. The applicant, having been told that if she did not accept the new terms she would be dismissed, left. The EAT refused to interfere with the tribunal's finding that she had not been constructively dismissed.

BROWNE-WILKINSON J: . . . In our view it is clearly established that there is implied in a contract of employment a term that the employers will not, without reasonable and proper cause, conduct themselves in a manner calculated or likely to destroy or seriously damage the relationship of trust and confidence between employer and employee . . . To constitute a breach of this implied term it is not necessary to show that the employer intended any repudiation of the contract: the tribunal's function is to look at the employer's conduct as a whole and determine whether it is such that its effect, judged reasonably and sensibly, is such that the employee cannot be expected to put up with it . . . The conduct of the parties has to be looked at as a whole and its cumulative impact assessed . . .

Note

Subsequently, the Court of Appeal dismissed the employee's appeal ([1982] ICR 693).

C: *Examples of Conduct Justifying Resignation*

(i) *Assault*

Bracebridge Engineering Limited v Darby
[1990] IRLR 3
Employment Appeal Tribunal

Mrs Darby was physically manhandled into the works manager's office and indecently assaulted by the chargehand and the works manager. The next morning she complained to the general manager but because the offenders denied everything no action was taken. Mrs Darby resigned and complained of both sex discrimination and of unfair dismissal. Both applications succeeded and the EAT rejected the employer's appeal.

WOODS J: . . . The second limb is the issue of constructive dismissal. The Tribunal dealt with it late in their decision after the findings of the fact about the enquiry. The enquiry was carried out by Miss Reynolds who has some 10 years' experience as the general manager. She saw the applicant, Mrs Darby, on two occasions. First of all on her own and later with the men involved. The Tribunal find that the enquiry was rather superficial. Their summary is to be found in paragraphs 27–29 of the decision. They deal with it in this way. They said:

> The applicant goes on to complain of constructive dismissal and that that dismissal was unfair. What she is in effect saying is that following these incidents she made a complaint, but her allegations were not treated seriously and she felt compelled to terminate her employment. This brings us to the interview with Miss Reynolds. The first point is the extent of the applicant's complaint at the time. She complained of being carried by Mr Smith and Mr Daly to Mr Daly's office, and Miss Reynolds was told of the assault there by Mr Daly. The applicant believes that she also mentioned the further assault by Mr Smith in the office. We take the view that even if that were not so, Miss Reynolds did receive complaints of serious misconduct involving both men.
>
> According to the company's own disciplinary procedure (which has been produced) Miss Reynolds ought to have been aware that such an allegation could have led to her suspending Mr Smith and Mr Daly and should in any event have led to a full investigation. The complaints were of assaults with sexual overtones which made them extremely serious. The view that we take is that the enquiry by Miss Reynolds was not an indepth enquiry following serious allegations. It may be that at the end of the day Miss Reynolds felt that in the circumstances she had done her best. We feel that she was too easily persuaded that there was insufficient evidence to substantiate the claims. Had there been a full investigation enquiries might have been made of Mrs Merritt and Tina to whom the applicant immediately complained. It would have been necessary to enquire whether the applicant had been guilty of misconduct in attempting to leave early. As it was Miss Reynolds accepted this to be so without any investigation and that Mr Smith was correct in speaking to the applicant.

We feel at the end of the day the applicant was entitled to say her allegations had not been treated as seriously as they ought. That on the other hand she was being reprimanded without the complaint against her being enquired into. She was entitled to take the view her allegations were being brushed aside.

Then they accept her evidence that at the end of the incident she was disgusted. They felt that she was entitled to be disgruntled and then they go on:

We feel taking into account the particular circumstances including the nature of the events, her long service to the respondents and the inadequacy of the enquiry she was justified in terminating her contract of employment. We find she left because of the conduct of the respondents within s. 55(2)(c) of the Act [now ERA 1996, s. 95(1)(c)]. For these reasons we find the applicant was constructively dismissed and that dismissal was unfair. We uphold her complaint.

They then assessed compensation.

Mr de Mello criticises the directions which the Tribunal gave itself on the issue of constructive dismissal. He points to the phrase referring to the conduct of the respondents and to s. 55(2)(c) of the 1978 Act [now ERA 1996, s. 95(1)(c)]. We hope we sufficiently summarise his argument in this way. He submits that the Tribunal have fallen into the trap which existed before the decision in the Court of Appeal in *Western Excavating* v *Sharp* [1978] IRLR 27 where the Court of Appeal dealt with the two arguments of constructive dismissal: one whether it was based on the reasonable attitude of the employer and the other where it was based on strictly contractual basis. It was resolved in that case that the proper basis was the contractual basis; one therefore needs to look to see what were the terms of the contract and what was the fundamental serious or important term of which there was a breach and which was of sufficient severity that the employee was entitled to say 'that indicates that I cannot properly continue under the terms of the contract', and to accept that repudiation which acceptance needed to be made within a reasonable time. We repeat that principle without looking in detail at the wording of Lord Denning in that case. The submission here is that the Tribunal failed to make the proper approach.

We were told that in fact *Western Excavating* was cited to the Tribunal and in any event it is well known that the learned chairman of this Tribunal is extremely experienced. It may be because in their Reasons they dealt at great length and necessary length with all the factual background and the details of the case that when they came to deal with constructive dismissal they dealt with it in paragraph 30 quite shortly right at the end of the judgment. Had the matter not been preceded by the sexual discrimination problems and the findings of fact, the reasoning might have been set out at greater length. Therefore, looking at these decisions as a whole, although the wording is capable of criticism we feel that the learned chairman, especially as *Western Excavating* was cited to him, in fact was well aware of the principles involved and did apply them. But lest there be any feeling that the matter has not been sufficiently investigated here on behalf of the company, it is right to say this: that the findings of fact were perfectly clear. If the Tribunal had directed itself *in extenso* in law then it would have asked itself whether on the facts as found by the Tribunal the term whereby the mutual obligation, trust, confidence and support and the obligation not to undermine the confidence of the female staff had been breached. In a case of this nature where sexual discrimination and investigation are concerned it is an extremely important one for the female staff.

The findings of fact were that this lady, Mrs Darby, had clearly been greatly upset and suffered shock and trauma as a result of this extremely unpleasant incident in the

office of the chargehand. She made her complaint that it had not been treated with
the seriousness and the gravity which it should. The Tribunal found on the facts that
there had been a breach of that term. Thereafter the question would have been 'had
it been accepted as repudiation?' and that followed a week later when Mrs Darby left.
Thirdly, they decided it was a reasonable period of time in which she had to make up
her mind. It seems again to those sitting with me with experience of situations such
as this, that it was evidently reasonable that she should be allowed a week in which to
decide about it, the more especially as she might have been waiting for the chairman,
Mr Reynolds, to return and he did not return until just after she had left. In the
circumstances, therefore, if properly directed we have no doubt that the only
conclusion to which the Tribunal could have come on its finding of fact was that there
had been a constructive dismissal.

(ii) Abuse

Palmanor Limited v *Cedron*
[1978] IRLR 303
Employment Appeal Tribunal

The applicant was employed at a night club and, one night, after he had
previously arranged to attend later than normal, he was wrongly accused
by the night club manager of being late. The manager then became abusive
saying 'You are a big bastard, a big cunt, you are pig-headed, you think you
are always right'. When Cedron objected the manager responded, 'I can
talk to you any way I like, you big cunt' and 'If you leave me now, don't
bother to collect your money, papers or anything else. I'll make sure you
don't get a job anywhere in London'. Cedron resigned and his claim that
he had been constructively dismissed by reason of this abuse was upheld
by the EAT.

SLYNN J: We have considered anxiously the words used in the Decision of this
Tribunal, because the Decision of the Court of Appeal in *Western Excavating (ECC)
Ltd* v *Sharp* was not given until after the Tribunal had come to their determination.
The Tribunal's words which to us appear to be important are that the various matters
to which they referred 'rendered this conduct which entitled the applicant to treat
himself as dismissed' under the paragraph of the Schedule. It can be said, as Mr Jarvis
in his attractive and persuasive argument has said, that this is doing no more than
asking the question, was this reasonable conduct? Mr Jarvis points to another
reference in the Decision of the Industrial Tribunal where Mr Owide is said to have
acted unreasonably. On the other hand it is clear from the judgment of Lord Denning
MR that there may be cases where conduct is sufficiently serious to entitle an
employee to leave at once. Certainly Lawton LJ gave instances of this kind of
behaviour on the part of an employer which would be regarded as so intolerable that
an employee could not be expected to put up with it. It seems to us that in a case of
this kind the Tribunal is required to ask itself the question whether the conduct was
so unreasonable, that it really went beyond the limits of the contract. We observe that
in the course of the argument on behalf of the applicant, Mr Cedron, it was submitted
that the treatment that the employee was accorded was a repudiation of the contract.
    We consider here that the Tribunal has not been shown to have failed to ask itself
the right question – that they have, reading their Decision as a whole, approached the

matter in the right way and have considered whether the behaviour of Mr Owide was really so intolerable that Mr Cedron could not be expected to stay. It is to be observed that this is not simply a case, like some of the cases which have been cited to us, where merely abusive language was used. Mr Jarvis has cited a number of cases where foul language was used and yet that was held not to justify dismissal. We attach importance to the fact that what Mr Owide said, after Mr Cedron had sought to argue with him that he had no right to speak like that, was 'If you don't like it, you can go', and 'I can talk to you any way I like'; and then he added further abusive language. Moreover Mr Cedron, whose evidence was clearly accepted by the Tribunal, also contends that he was told by Mr Owide 'I'll make sure you don't get another job anywhere in London'. Before the Tribunal it was suggested that the words 'if you leave me now, don't bother to collect your money' indicated that Mr Owide did not intend there to be a dismissal or did not consider that Mr Cedron was in any way no longer part of his staff. But we think, taking the position as a whole, that the Tribunal here cannot be said to have erred in law. Moreover it seems to us that although it is quite right that in these cases Tribunals have to be careful not to attach too great importance to words used in the heat of the moment or in anger, as was stressed in the case of *Chesham Shipping Ltd v C.A. Rowe* [1977] IRLR 391, nonetheless there comes a time when the language is such that even if the person using it is in a state of anger, an employee cannot be expected to tolerate it. Accordingly we are of the view that the attack on the Decision that there had been an unfair dismissal, fails.

(iii)   Enforcement of Mobility Clause

United Bank Limited v Akhtar
[1989] IRLR 507
Employment Appeal Tribunal

The applicant had been employed at the employer's branch in Leeds since 1978. In 1987 he was asked, in accordance with a mobility clause in the contract, to move to its branch in Birmingham. He was given very short notice and offered no financial assistance with the move. He refused and claimed constructive dismissal. His claim succeeded before the tribunal which held that there was an implied term that the mobility clause would be exercised by the employer in such a way as to make it feasible for the employee to comply with the requirement to move branches, i.e. by giving reasonable notice and offering financial assistance. The EAT dismissed the employer's appeal.

KNOX J: As regards the giving of relocation allowance or other allowances, it is of course plain that the bank has a discretion. It seems to us that there is a fallacy in the argument that an employee, by accepting employment on terms which include the grant of such a discretion to an employer, was thereby accepting that he would be under an obligation to move without any financial assistance at all, if the bank thought fit to require such a move.

What Mr Akhtar, by signing the contract, accepted was that there was conferred upon the bank a discretion. What Mr Akhtar did not, in our view, accept, was that the bank, in any particular circumstances, would not necessarily be under an obligation to exercise that discretion. It seems to us that there is a clear distinction between implying a term which negatives a provision which is expressly stated in the contract and implying a term which controls the exercise of a discretion which is expressly conferred in a contract. The first is, of course, impermissible. We were referred to authority for that proposition but authority is hardly needed for it. The second, in our judgment, is not impermissible because there may well be circumstances where discretions are conferred but, nevertheless, they are not unfettered discretions, which can be exercised in a capricious way.

The same acceptance of an implied obligation to cooperate and not to frustrate another party's attempt to perform a contract, would appear to point in the same direction because the facts, as found by the Industrial Tribunal, in our judgment, clearly indicate that the bank was acting or, rather, failing to act, in a manner which frustrated Mr Akhtar's attempts to perform the obligation which he accepted of removing his seat of activities on behalf of the bank from Leeds to Birmingham.

It, therefore, follows that the contract does, in our view, include as a necessary implication, first the requirement to give reasonable notice and, secondly, the requirement so to exercise the discretion to give relocation or other allowances in such a way as not to make performance of the employee's duties impossible.

We see no conflict between that conclusion and the well-established principles to which Mr Lynch drew our attention that terms can only be implied in contract at common law in clearly defined circumstances and according to well-established rules. The first to which we were referred was that no term can be implied which is contrary to or inconsistent with an express term and, upon this aspect of the matter, we have already expressed our view. There is no conflict between a limit on the way in which a discretion can be exercised, on the one hand, and the existence of the discretion on the other.

Secondly, we accept that it is now well-established that implications of a term in a contract, which the parties have reduced to writing, can only be made first to give business efficacy to their contracts; secondly, where the implication is to give effect to an obvious combined intention of the parties; and, thirdly, where it is a necessary addition to the expression of the particular relationship between the parties and an implication which completes their contractual arrangements. Reference was made to *Chitty on Contracts*, paragraph 847, which sums up this branch of the law by saying: 'The touchstone is always necessity and not merely reasonableness'.

Those arguments are aimed at the construction of the contract and the question whether or not an implication can be made in it.

The third principle, which is enunciated by Mr Justice Browne-Wilkinson's judgment, from which I read an extract, is of much wider import and is capable of applying to a series of actions by an employer, which individually can be justified as being within the four corners of the contract because we take it as inherent in what fell from Mr Justice Browne-Wilkinson that there may well be conduct which is either calculated or likely to destroy or seriously damage the relationship of confidence and trust between employer and employee, which a literal interpretation of the written words of the contract might appear to justify, and it is in this sense that we consider that in the field of employment law it is proper to imply an over-riding obligation in the terms used by Mr Justice Browne-Wilkinson, which is independent of, and in addition to, the literal interpretation of the actions which are permitted to the employer under the terms of the contract. On that aspect of the matter, we have the Industrial Tribunal's finding that the situation here was that the bank's conduct, in which we include inactivity rather than activity, was such that if one looks at it reasonably and sensibly, it was such that the employee could not be expected to put up with it.

White v Reflecting Roadstuds Limited
[1991] IRLR 331
Employment Appeal Tribunal

Mr White had for four years worked in the despatch department. He was then moved to the highly paid but more onerous mixing department, which move White disliked and asked to be changed. This request was refused and White's attendance at work declined to such extent that he was given a written warning; but the situation did not improve and others in the mixing department resented White's attitude. Accordingly, in October 1988 he was moved to the pressing department which carried with it a dramatic drop in pay. White resigned a few months later and claimed constructive dismissal. White's contract included the right of the employer to move employees to different departments. The tribunal upheld the claim; following the decision in *United Bank* v *Akhtar* it held that the mobility use was subject to implied terms that it would be exercised in a reasonable manner and not in such a way as would result in a reduction in pay. The EAT allowed the employer's appeal and, in so doing, limited the application of the *Akhtar* principle.

WOOD J (referring to *United Bank Ltd* v *Akhtar*): This case must be examined with care. It is too broad an understanding of the words of Mr Justice Knox to say that the implied term was that the employer should act reasonably. We do not so understand him and indeed, so to find would fly in the face of authority of *Western Excavating* (supra) itself. It would be to reintroduce the reasonable test by the back door. The term found to be implied by Mr Justice Knox and those sitting with him was that an employer when dealing with a mobility clause in a contract of employment should not exercise his discretion in such a way as to prevent his employee from being able to carry out his part of the contract. That is a very different consideration.

Question
Is the distinction between *United Bank* v *Akhtar* and *White* v *Reflecting Roadstuds Ltd* one of substance or merely one of semantics?

Notes
1. A mobility clause may be unlawfully discriminatory within the meaning of SDA 1975, s. 77. See *Meade-Hill and National Union of Civil Servants* v *British Council* [1995] IRLR 478, referred to at p. 296.
2. The tribunal will be slow to imply employee acceptance of a unilaterally imposed mobility clause.

Aparau v Iceland Frozen Foods
[1996] IRLR 119
Employment Appeal Tribunal

Following a takeover Aparau, who was employed as a cashier, was given new terms and conditions including a requirement that she may be required 'to move to a different location at any time'. She did not return the form indicating her consent to the change of terms but continued to work for a further 12 months before resigning when asked to work elsewhere. The EAT agreed that she had been constructively dismissed.

HICKS J: . . . We deal then with those three ways in which the tribunal reached its conclusion.

As to the first, whether Mrs Aparau accepted the new terms which the respondents, Iceland Frozen Foods, sought to incorporate in the contract, we start from the position that Iceland Foods were not entitled unilaterally to alter the contract, nor indeed do they put their case on that basis. The question is whether there was a fresh contract, whether by way of the old or substitution for it. Clearly, in the traditional analysis of contract formation, the circulation by Iceland Frozen Foods of those terms was an offer Mrs Aparau could accept or reject. The mode of acceptance was in fact specified by Iceland Frozen Foods, the person making the offer, because, as I have said, the form contained in Clause 20 an express acceptance which the employee was invited to sign and return.

We therefore start from the position which is helpfully summarised in *Chitty on Contracts* 27th Edition, paragraph 2–042:

An offer which requires the acceptance to be expressed or communicated in a certain way can generally be accepted only in that way.

Then at paragraph 2–045:

Even if the prescribed method of acceptance is not complied with, the offeror would no doubt be bound if he had acquiesced in a different mode of acceptance and had so waived the stipulated mode.
At 2–047:

An offeree who does nothing in response to an offer is not bound by its terms. This is so even though the offer provides that it can be accepted by silence.
At 2–050:

The general rule that there can be no acceptance by silence does not mean that an acceptance always has to be given in so many words. An offer can be accepted by conduct; and this is never thought to give rise to any difficulty where the conduct takes the form of a positive act.

So much by way of background and really uncontroversial general principles.

The difficulty in the present case was of course that there was no positive act of acceptance, neither the prescribed act of signing and returning the duplicate form nor any other positive act in the sense of a change, because all that happened was that Mrs Aparau went on working at the same place and being paid exactly as before. The question is whether her doing so, and specifically in the terms of the industrial tribunal's judgment doing so for as long as 12 months, could of itself amount to an acceptance.

There is, in our view, a helpful passage on the application of the general principles to the particular circumstances of an employment contract in the case in this Appeal Tribunal of *Jones* v *Associated Tunnelling Co. Ltd* [1981] IRLR 477, and the relevant passage begins in paragraph 21 of the judgment, where the tribunal was dealing again, with a case where there had been varied terms issued by the employers but not signed by the employee who had simply continued working without outward change of circumstance. Dealing with the situation where an employer issues a statutory statement of terms of conditions of employment, the tribunal say this:

> . . . the first of such statements to be issued is often compelling evidence of what terms have in fact been agreed.

That, I interpose, is not strictly applicable here, because it seems from the Industrial Tribunal's findings that the Bejam contract was not simply a statutory statement, but was in fact the contract. However, that does not affect what follows in the judgment in the *Jones* case, which continues:

> But where there are two or more statements which are not in identical terms, the later statement can only be evidence of an agreed variation of the original terms. Such variation may be either express or implied. If, as in the present case, there is no evidence of any oral discussion varying the original terms, the fact that a statement of terms and conditions containing different terms has been issued cannot be compelling evidence of an express oral variation. The most that can be said is that by continuing to work without objection after receiving such further statement, the employee may have impliedly agreed to the variation recorded in the second statement or be estopped from denying it.
>
> In our view, to imply an agreement to vary or to raise an estoppel against the employee on the grounds that he has not objected to a false record by the employers of the terms actually agreed is a course which should be adopted with great caution. If the variation related to a matter which has immediate practical application (e.g. the rate of pay) and the employee continues to work without objection after effect has been given to the variation (e.g. his pay packet has been reduced) then obviously he may well be taken to have impliedly agreed. But where, as in the present case, the variation has no immediate practical effect the position is not the same. It is the view of both members of this tribunal with experience in industrial relations (with which the chairman, without such experience, agrees) that it is asking too much of the ordinary employee to require him either to object to an erroneous statement of his terms of employment having no immediate practical impact on him or to be taken to have assented to the variation. So to hold would involve an unrealistic view of the inclination and ability of the ordinary employee to read and fully understand such statements.
>
> Even if he does read the statement and can understand it, it would be unrealistic of the law to require him to risk a confrontation with his employer on a matter which has no immediate practical impact on the employee. For those reasons, as at present advised, we would not be inclined to imply any assent to a variation from a mere failure by the employee to object to the unilateral alteration by the employer of the terms of employment contained in a statutory statement.

(iv)   Removal of Privileges

Dryden v *Greater Glasgow Health Board*
[1992] IRLR 469
Employment Appeal Tribunal

The applicant smoked 30 cigarettes a day and her job was such that she could not leave the premises during the day in order to partake of a cigarette. Until 1991, the employer set aside smoking places. These were withdrawn, and Dryden resigned and claimed constructive dismissal. The EAT agreed that the introduction of a 'no smoking' policy by the employer did not justify the resignation.

LORD COULSFIELD: . . . We are not aware of any case concerned with the present situation, in which what is sought is to treat a change in the rules governing behaviour in the place of work which affects all employees as a repudiatory breach of an implied term in relation to one employee. There can, in our view, be no doubt that an employer is entitled to make rules for the conduct of employees in their place of work, as he is entitled to give lawful orders, within the scope of the contract; nor can there be any doubt, in our view, that once it has been held that there is no implied term in the contract which entitled the employee to facilities for smoking, a rule against smoking is, in itself, a lawful rule. The appellant's argument in the present case can only succeed if it is shown that the Industrial Tribunal erred in law. The suggested error is that the Industrial Tribunal failed to approach the question from the point of view of the specific circumstances of the appellant. The Industrial Tribunal did, however, have regard to the circumstances of the appellant, along with all the other circumstances of the case. What the appellant's argument really involves, therefore, is the submission that if an employer introduces a rule which applies to all employees generally, but one with which one employee is unable to comply, the employer must be held to repudiate the contract in relation to that employee. We do not think that any of the terms implied in *United Bank* v *Akhtar* supra or *Woods* supra, or the principles underlying them, go so far as to justify restricting the employer's ability to make and alter working rules to that extent. It may not be difficult to envisage an implied term to the effect that the employer will not change the rules of the workplace in a way which adversely affects an employee or group of employees without reasonable notice or without consultation or, perhaps, without some substantial reason. It is very much more difficult to envisage that, in the absence of a relevant particular term in the contract, it might be held that there was an implied term restricting the employer's right to change the working rules by reference to the views, or even the requirements, of each particular employee. In *Woods* [1982] IRLR 413 in the Court of Appeal Watkins LJ said at p. 416:

> Employers must not, in my opinion, be put in a position where, through the wrongful refusal of their employees to accept change, they are prevented from introducing improved business methods in furtherance of seeking success for their enterprise.

The context of that observation was rather different from that of the present case, and Watkins LJ was concerned with a refusal to accept change rather than an inability to do so. Nevertheless, in our view, the same point does apply here, and it is necessary to exercise caution before holding that there are implied contract terms which restrict the employer's power to control what happens in the workplace by making, and altering from time to time, rules for the conduct of the work and the employees. It must also be borne in mind that the term held to be implied in *Woods* [1981] IRLR 347 at p. 349 was that:

> . . . the employers will not, *without reasonable and proper cause*, conduct themselves in a manner calculated to destroy or seriously damage the relationship of confidence and trust . . .

Where a rule is introduced for a legitimate purpose, the fact that it bears hardly on a particular employee does not, in our view, in itself justify an inference that the employer has acted in such a way as to repudiate the contract with that employee. There may well be rules which are unwelcome to some employees but welcome to others, and a rule banning smoking might be an example of the kind. That being so, we cannot see that there is any justification for the appellant's argument that where the employer introduces a rule which is to apply generally but with which a particular employee cannot comply, it follows that there is repudiatory conduct on the part of the employer.

It has repeatedly been held that the question whether or not there has been repudiatory conduct is one of the particular facts. In the present case, the Industrial Tribunal has considered the whole facts and circumstances very fully, and, in our view, there is no reason to think that they have erred in their assessment of them or fallen into any error of law. It seems to us, indeed, that once the suggestion that there might be an implied term in the appellant's contract, to the effect that she would continue to enjoy some facilities for smoking during working hours, is out of the picture, the result at which the Industrial Tribunal arrived must be the correct one, in the circumstances of this case. The appeal must, therefore, be refused.

(v) Failure to Provide or Implement Proper Grievance Procedures

W. A. Goold (Pearmak) Ltd v McConnell and Another
[1995] IRLR 516
Employment Appeal Tribunal

McConnell was employed by Goold as a jewellery salesman and was paid both a salary and commission. In 1992, changes in selling methods resulted in a significant drop in his salary. There was no established procedure for dealing with McConnell's concerns and he had not been given a written statement of terms and conditions indicating how a grievance should be pursued. McConnell raised his concerns with the manager, an incoming new managing director, and attempted to see the chairman. Nothing was done and he resigned. The EAT agreed that his resignation was justified by the failure to implement a grievance procedure.

MORRISON J: . . . It seems to us quite clear that the breach of contract identified by the industrial tribunal related to the way the employees' grievances were dealt with. Their process of reasoning was that Parliament requires employers to provide their employees with written particulars of their employment in compliance with the statutory requirements. Section 3(1) of the Employment Protection (Consolidation) Act 1978 (as amended) [now ERA 1996, s. 3(1)] provides that the written statement required under s.1 of the Act shall include a note specifying, by description or otherwise, to whom and in what manner the employee may apply if he is either dissatisfied with any disciplinary decision or has any other grievance, and an explanation of any further steps in the grievance procedure. It is clear therefore, that Parliament considered that good industrial relations requires employers to provide their employees with a method of dealing with grievances in a proper and timeous fashion. This is also consistent, of course, with the codes of practice. That being so, the industrial tribunal was entitled, in our judgment, to conclude that there was an implied term in the contract of employment that the employers would reasonably and promptly afford a reasonable opportunity to their employees to obtain redress of any grievance they may have. It was in our judgment rightly conceded at the industrial tribunal that such could be a breach of contract.

Further, it seems to us that the right to obtain redress against a grievance is fundamental for very obvious reasons. The working environment may well lead to employees experiencing difficulties, whether because of the physical conditions under which they are required to work, or because of a breakdown in human relationships, which can readily occur when people of different backgrounds and sensitivities are required to work together, often under pressure.

There may well be difficulties arising out of the way that authority and control is exercised – sometimes by people who themselves have insufficient experience and training to exercise such power wisely.

It is of course regrettable, in this case, that the employers have failed to comply with their statutory obligations, or to appreciate the need to provide a specific mechanism whereby a genuine sense of grievance can be ventilated and redressed. Instead, the employees in this case were fobbed off, and Mr Maloney plainly felt his authority was threatened by the employees' wish to speak to the chairman. The provision of a sensible grievance procedure would cost nothing and may well have avoided this litigation.

IV   Fixed-term, 'Task' and Contingent Contracts

Employment Rights Act 1996

95.   Circumstances in which an employee is dismissed
(1)   For the purposes of this Part an employee is dismissed by his employer if (and, subject to subsection (2) and section 96, only if)—

. . .

(b)   he is employed under a contract for a fixed term and that term expires without being renewed under the same contract, . . .

Wiltshire County Council v *NATFHE and Guy*
[1980] IRLR 198
Court of Appeal

Mrs Guy had been employed as a part-time teacher at Swindon College from 1969 to 1977. At the beginning of each academic year, she signed a new contract requiring her to teach certain classes at an hourly rate of pay, although there was no guarantee that the classes would run and she was entitled to be paid only for those classes she actually taught. She ceased working in any year whenever her particular courses came to an end, which may have been prior to the actual end of the academic year. Her contract was not renewed for the 1977/78 session and she claimed unfair dismissal or redundancy. On the preliminary point of law as to whether the industrial tribunal had jurisdiction, the Court of Appeal agreed that Mrs Guy had been employed on a fixed-term contract.

LORD DENNING MR: If I may seek to draw the matter together, it seems to me that if there is a contract by which a man is to do a particular task or to carry out a particular purpose, then when that task or purpose comes to an end the contract is discharged by performance. Instances may be taken of a seaman who is employed for the duration of a voyage – and it is completely uncertain how long the voyage will last. His engagement comes to an end on its completion. Also of a man who is engaged to cut down trees, and, when all the trees have been cut down, his contract is discharged by performance. In neither of those instances is there a contract for a fixed term. It is a contract which is discharged by performance. There is no 'dismissal'. A contract for a particular purpose, which is fulfilled, is discharged by performance and does not amount to a dismissal.

Mr Justice Phillips mentioned contracts which are terminable on a completely uncertain event such as the duration of the government or the life of the sovereign, or something like that. It seems to me that such a contract is not employment for a fixed term at all. It does not come within the provision. It is not the subject of 'dismissal' unless it is terminated by the employer under [ERA 1996, s. 95(1)(a)] or the employee under [ERA 1996, s. 95(1)(c).

So we come back to the facts of this particular case. Looking at it, it seems to me that this contract is capable of one or other of two alternative interpretations:—

On the one hand, it can be said that this is a contract for a fixed term, namely for the session 1976/1977, starting from the beginning of the autumn term and ending on the last day of the summer term: and during that session Mrs Guy is to teach such courses in such circumstances as may be required of her and be paid for such time as she has taught during that stated period. On that interpretation of the contract, it seems to me that it is a contract for a 'fixed term'. Even though her work may end early in June because there is no more work for her to do, nevertheless it is still a contract for a fixed term. That is one alternative interpretation.

On the other hand, it can be said that it is not for a fixed term at all. It is a contract whereby she is to do specific work – teaching the students on these courses. She is to do it during the academic session, but nevertheless the contract is only for those particular purposes. When those come to an end, then it is not a contract for a fixed term, but a contract which is discharged by performance.

On which side is the court to come down on those alternative solutions? The Industrial Tribunal and the Employment Appeal Tribunal thought that this was a contract for a 'fixed term' from the beginning of the autumn term to the last day of the summer term. During that time she had to do such work as she was required to do. That seems to me to be an intelligible and sensible view. This court should not interfere with their decision. I would therefore dismiss the appeal.

Brown and others v *Knowsley Borough Council*
[1986] IRLR 102
Employment Appeal Tribunal

This was a representative action by a Mrs Hoste on behalf of a number of temporary teachers employed on similar bases. Mrs Hoste had been employed on a series of fixed-term contracts from 1979 to 1984. The employment was subsidised by the Manpower Services Commission and the contract provided that her appointment would 'only last as long as sufficient funds are provided either by the Manpower Services Commission or by other firms/sponsors to fund it'. In August 1984, her contract was terminated because MSC sponsorship had ended. She claimed a redundancy payment. The tribunal held that she had not been 'dismissed' because her contract was not for a fixed term but for a particular purpose. Before the EAT, the employer also argued that the contract was automatically determinable on the non-happening of a future event, i.e. the ending of MSC sponsorship. The EAT dismissed the employees' appeal.

POPPLEWELL J: The argument which has been put foward by the respondents is this: that the Industrial Tribunal were right to conclude that she was employed for a specific purpose; that that specific purpose having ceased, the contract was discharged by performance; alternatively, that it was terminable on the happening or non-happening of a future event and it was terminable in the sense that it automatically terminated when the non-payment by the Manpower Services Commission occurred – it required no action by the employer; it simply terminated.

. . . The argument that she was employed for a specific purpose comes from the decision of *Wiltshire County Council* and, more particularly, in the judgment of Ackner LJ at paragraph 31 where he said:

Like the Industrial Tribunal, I after some hesitation, have also accepted that Mrs Guy was employed on a fixed term contract starting at the beginning of the autumn term and ending on the last day of the summer term. Had Mr Irvine been right in his submission that the contract was to perform a particular task, namely to teach certain courses the length of which was not known when the contract was made, she would not in my judgment have been employed for a fixed term. When the courses ended, her contract would have come to an end because she would have completed the task and the contract would have been discharged by performance.

Speaking for myself, I do not find it particularly easy to see that this was a contract for a particular purpose. However, the dicta of Ackner LJ supported that and we would not interfere with the Industrial Tribunal's finding on that matter. I would prefer to put it on the basis that this contract was terminable on the happening or non-happening of a future event. Looking at the wording of the letter, it is clear to us that it does not require any action by anybody. The contract comes to an end automatically when there are insufficient funds provided by the Manpower Services Commission.

Questions
1. Is the distinction between a contract for a fixed term and a contract for a particular purpose one of easy application?
2. Does Popplewell J's introduction of automatic termination on the happening or non-happening of a future event clarify or muddy the waters in this area?

Dixon v BBC
[1979] ICR 281
Court of Appeal

Dixon and another were employed by the BBC under fixed-term contracts due to expire on 1 May 1976 'unless previously determined by one week's prior notice in writing on either side'.

The BBC wrote, stating that the contracts would not be renewed and the employees claimed unfair dismissal. The tribunal held that since the contracts were determinable by one week's notice they were not fixed-term contracts within the meaning of the Act so that the employees had not been 'dismissed'. The EAT allowed the employees' appeal and the Court of Appeal concurred with the view of the EAT.

LORD DENNING MR: Take this present case of Mr Dixon. His last two contracts were for two months and another for four weeks, each containing a provision for a week's notice. Were those contracts for a 'fixed term'? Looking at the general purpose and intention of the statute, each contract must have been employment for a 'fixed term' within the meaning of the statute. Otherwise you get an absurd position. If a man was employed for four weeks (and there was no clause in his contract making it determinable by a week's notice) he can claim for dismissal when the four weeks come to an end. But by inserting in the contract a clause for a week's notice, the employer can get rid of any employee under the statute when the period of four weeks comes to an end. On the other hand, if the employer, within the four weeks, determines it by one week's notice, then he will be liable to answer a complaint of unfair dismissal. It would mean that an employer could always evade the Act by inserting a simple clause 'determinable by one week's notice.' That can never have been the intention of the legislature at all. The words 'a fixed term' must include a specified stated term even though the contract is determinable by notice within its term.

V   Remedies

A: Damages

As stated earlier, as long as reasonable notice is given, the common law permits termination of a contract of employment. Accordingly, it is only when the employer fails to give the required notice or wages in lieu of notice that the common law action of wrongful dismissal will lie. Even then, the damages will be limited to the monies properly due during the period of notice that should have been given together with monies to cover the period which, in the opinion of the court, would have elapsed for the employer to carry out proper dismissal procedures. See *Dietman* v *London Borough of Brent* [1987] IRLR 146 and *Boyo* v *London Borough of Lambeth* [1995] IRLR 50 (above).

The limited nature of damages for wrongful dismissal was determined by the House of Lords in *Addis* v *Gramophone Co. Ltd* [1909] AC 488. For almost 90 years, this judgment has been accepted as authority for the proposition that damages for wrongful dismissal cannot include compensation (i) for the manner of dismissal, i.e. for injured feelings; or (ii) for loss an employee might sustain from the fact that the dismissal itself makes it more difficult for him or her to obtain future employment. The rationale for this approach is that since the employer could, at any time, terminate the contract lawfully by giving notice or pay in lieu of notice, this is all that the employee has lost through being wrongfully dismissed.

As a result, the dismissed employee will find the remedies offered by an application to the tribunal under ERA 1996 based on unfair dismissal more attractive than a wrongful dismissal claim. However, the common law action remains attractive to the fixed-term employee and, as we shall see, the employee who is seeking a remedy other than damages.

McMullen has argued ((1997) 26 ILR 246, at p. 246) that

the twin rules [established in *Addis*] are clearly inconsistent with the modern view of the duties owed by employers to employees. As Lord Slynn observed in *Spring* v *Guardian Assurance* [1994] 3 All ER 129, the law today imposes 'far greater duties' on employers than in the past 'to care for the physical, financial and even psychological welfare of the employee'. But while courts in other jurisdictions have, from time to time, circumvented or even ignored *Addis* (see *Brown* v *Waterloo Regional Board of Commissioners of Police* (1982) 136 DLR (3d) 49; *Pilon* v *Peugeot Canada Ltd* (1980) 114 DLR (3d) 378; *Ogilvy and Mather (New Zealand)* v *Turner* [1996] 1 NZLR 641), UK courts have been bound by this antiquated House of Lords authority (see *Shove* v *Downs Surgical plc* [1984] ICR 532, 542; *Bliss* v *South East Thames Regional Health Authority* [1987] ICR 700).

Bliss v *South East Thames Regional Health Authority*
[1987] ICR 700
Court of Appeal

The plaintiff was employed as a consultant orthopaedic surgeon and had written a number of angry and offensive letters to a colleague with whom he was in dispute. The tone and content of these letters raised some doubt in the employer's mind about the plaintiff's ability to do his job.

The employer asked the plaintiff to undergo a psychiatric examination but this request was refused. The employer suspended the plaintiff in May 1980 and disciplinary proceedings were brought against him but these were discontinued in July 1981. Subsequently, the employer gave the plaintiff until August 1981 to return to work.

By solicitor's letter dated 25 September 1981, the plaintiff claimed that, by its conduct, the employer had repudiated the contract and that the plaintiff accepted the repudiation. The plaintiff brought an action for breach of contract, seeking damages for frustration and mental distress. The judge allowed the plaintiff the sum of £2,000 under this head. The employer's appeal against this award was allowed by the Court of Appeal.

DILLON LJ: It remains to consider the final point on the cross-appeal, viz. the validity of the judge's award of £2,000 with interest by way of general damages for frustration and mental distress. In making such an award, the judge considered that he was justified by the decision of Lawson J in *Cox* v *Philips Industries Ltd* [1976] ICR 138. With every respect to them, however, the views of Lawson J in that case and of the judge in the present case are on this point, in my judgment, wrong.

The general rule laid down by the House of Lords in *Addis* v *Gramophone Co. Ltd* [1909] AC 488 is that where damages fall to be assessed for breach of contract rather than in tort it is not permissible to award general damages for frustration, mental distress, injured feelings or annoyance occasioned by the breach. Modern thinking tends to be that the amount of damages recoverable for a wrong should be the same whether the cause of action is laid in contract or in tort. But in the *Addis* case Lord Loreburn regarded the rule that damages for injured feelings cannot be recovered in contract for wrongful dismissal as too inveterate to be altered, and Lord James of Hereford supported his concurrence in the speech of Lord Loreburn by reference to his own experience at the Bar.

There are exceptions now recognised where the contract which has been broken was itself a contract to provide peace of mind or freedom from distress: see *Jarvis* v *Swans Tours Ltd* [1973] QB 233 and *Heywood* v *Wellers* [1976] QP 446. Those decisions, do not however cover this present case.

In *Cox* v *Philips Industries Ltd* [1976] ICR 138 Lawson J took the view that damages for distress, vexation and frustration, including consequent ill-health, could be recovered for breach of a contract of employment if it could be said to have been in the contemplation of the parties that the breach would cause such distress etc. For my part, I do not think that that general approach is open to this court unless and until the House of Lords has reconsidered its decision in the *Addis* case.

Note
In the next case, we see the House of Lords side-stepping the antiquated precedent of *Addis* on the basis that it was decided before the development of the implied term of trust and confidence. In doing so, the House of Lords established the general principle that damages are available where breach of the duty of trust and confidence makes it more difficult for an employee to obtain further employment.

Malik v BCCI SA (in liq.)
[1997] IRLR 462
House of Lords

Mr Malik and Mr Mahmud were formerly employed by the Bank of Credit and Commerce International (BCCI) for periods of 16 and 12 years respectively. Both were dismissed on grounds of redundancy by the provisional liquidators following the bank's collapse. Neither had since been able to obtain employment in the financial services sector.

Mr Malik and Mr Mahmud claimed 'stigma' damages for pecuniary loss allegedly caused by the bank's breach of an implied contractual obligation of trust and confidence. They maintained that their mere association with the bank at the moment of its liquidation and the alleged fraudulent practices which subsequently came to light put them at a disadvantage in the employment market, even though they were personally innocent of any wrongdoing. The liquidators rejected the claims.

The employees appealed against that decision. Mr Justice Evans-Lombe decided as a preliminary issue that the evidence failed to disclose a reasonable cause of action or a sustainable claim for damages. The Court of Appeal affirmed that decision, holding that, in reality, the damages claimed were for injury to the employees' previously existing reputations and therefore, in accordance with the general principles established in *Addis* v *Gramophone Co. Ltd* [1995] IRLR 375, they were not legally recoverable. Mr Malik and Mr Mahmud had their appeals allowed by the House of Lords.

LORD NICHOLLS OF BIRKENHEAD: . . . In the Court of Appeal and in your Lordships' House the parties were agreed that the contracts of employment of these two former employees each contained an implied term to the effect that the bank would not, without reasonable and proper cause, conduct itself in a manner likely to destroy or seriously damage the relationship of confidence and trust between employer and employee. Argument proceeded on this footing, and ranged round the type of conduct and other circumstances which could or could not constitute a breach of this implied term. The submissions embraced questions such as the following: whether the trust-destroying conduct must be directed at the employee, either individually or as part of a group; whether an employee must know of the employer's trust-destroying conduct while still employed; and whether the employee's trust must actually be undermined. Furthermore, and at the heart of this case, the submissions raised an important question on the damages recoverable for breach of the implied term, with particular reference to the decisions in *Addis* v *Gramophone Co. Ltd* [1909] AC 488 and *Withers* v *General Theatre Corporation Ltd* [1933] 2 KB 536.

A dishonest and corrupt business

These questions are best approached by focusing first on the particular conduct of which complaint is made. The bank operated its business dishonestly and corruptly. On the assumed facts, this was not a case where one or two individuals, however senior, were behaving dishonestly. Matters had gone beyond this. They had reached the point where the bank itself could properly be identified with the dishonesty. This was a dishonest business, a corrupt business.

It is against this background that the position of an innocent employee has to be considered. In my view, when an innocent employee of the bank learned the true nature of the bank's business, from whatever source, he was entitled to say: 'I wish to have nothing more to do with this organisation. I am not prepared to help this business, by working for it. I am leaving at once.' This is my intuitive response in the case of all innocent employees of the business, from the most senior to the most junior, from the most long-serving to the most recently joined. No one could be expected to have to continue to work with and for such a company against his wish.

This intuitive response is no more than a reflection of what goes without saying in any ordinary contract of employment, namely, that in agreeing to work for an employer the employee, whatever his status, cannot be taken to have agreed to work in furtherance of a dishonest business. This is as much true of a doorkeeper or cleaner as a senior executive or branch manager.

An implied obligation

Two points can be noted here. First, as a matter of legal analysis, the innocent employee's entitlement to leave at once must derive from the bank being in breach of a term of the contract of employment which the employee is entitled to treat as a repudiation by the bank of its contractual obligations. That is the source of his right to step away from the contract forthwith.

In other words, and this is the necessary corollary of the employee's right to leave at once, the bank was under an implied obligation to its employees not to conduct a dishonest or corrupt business. This implied obligation is no more than one particular aspect of the portmanteau, general obligation not to engage in conduct likely to undermine the trust and confidence required if the employment relationship is to continue in the manner the employment contract implicitly envisages.

Second, I do not accept the liquidators' submission that the conduct of which complaint is made must be targeted in some way at the employee or a group of employees. No doubt that will often be the position, perhaps usually so. But there is no reason in principle why this must always be so. The trust and confidence required in the employment relationship can be undermined by an employer, or indeed an employee, in many different ways. I can see no justification for the law giving the employee a remedy if the unjustified trust-destroying conduct occurs in some ways but refusing a remedy if it occurs in others. The conduct must, of course, impinge on the relationship in the sense that, looked at objectively, it is likely to destroy or seriously damage the degree of trust and confidence the employee is reasonably entitled to have in his employer. That requires one to look at all the circumstances.

Breach

The objective standard just mentioned provides the answer to the liquidators' submission that unless the employee's confidence is actually undermined there is no breach. A breach occurs when the proscribed conduct takes place: here, operating a dishonest and corrupt business. Proof of a subjective loss of confidence in the employer is not an essential element of the breach, although the time when the employee learns of the misconduct and his response to it may affect his remedy.

Remedies: (1) acceptance of breach as repudiation

The next step is to consider the consequences which flow from the bank being in breach of its obligation to its innocent employees by operating a corrupt banking business. The first remedy of an employee has already been noted. The employee may treat the bank's conduct as a repudiatory breach, entitling him to leave. He is not compelled to leave. He may choose to stay. The extent to which staying would be more than an election to remain, and would be a waiver of the breach for all purposes, depends on the circumstances.

I need say no more about waiver in the present case. The assumed facts do not state whether the appellants first learned of the corrupt nature of BCCI after their dismissal on 3 October 1991, or whether they acquired this knowledge earlier, in the interval of three months between the appointment of the provisional liquidators on 5 July 1991 and 3 October 1991. If anything should turn on this, the matter can be investigated further in due course.

In the nature of things, the remedy of treating the conduct as a repudiatory breach, entitling the employee to leave, can only avail an employee who learns of the facts while still employed. If he does not discover the facts while his employment is still continuing, perforce this remedy is not open to him. But this does not mean he has no remedy. In the ordinary course breach of a contractual term entitles the innocent party to damages.

Remedies: (2) damages

Can an employee recover damages for breach of the trust and confidence term when he first learns of the breach after he has left the employment? The answer to this question is inextricably bound up with the further question of what damages are recoverable for a breach of this term. In turn, the answer to this further question is inextricably linked with one aspect of the decision in *Addis* v *Gramophone Co. Ltd* [1909] AC 488.

At first sight, it seems almost a contradiction in terms that an employee can suffer recoverable loss if he first learns of the trust-destroying conduct after the employment contract has already ended for other reasons. But of the many forms which trust-destroying conduct may take, some may have continuing adverse financial effects on an employee even after his employment has ceased. In such a case, the fact that the employee only learned of the employer's conduct after the employment had ended ought not, in principle, to be a bar to recovery. If it were otherwise, an employer who conceals a breach would be better placed than an employer who does not.

Premature termination losses

This proposition calls for elaboration. The starting point is to note that the purpose of the trust and confidence implied term is to facilitate the proper functioning of the contract. If the employer commits a breach of the term, and in consequence the contract comes to an end prematurely, the employee loses the benefits he should have received had the contract run its course until it expired or was duly terminated. In addition to financial benefits such as salary and commission and pension rights, the losses caused by the premature termination of the contract ('the premature termination losses') may include other promised benefits, for instance, a course of training, or publicity for an actor or pop star. Prima facie, and subject always to established principles of mitigation and so forth, the dismissed employee can recover damages to compensate him for these promised benefits lost to him in consequence of the premature termination of the contract.

It follows that premature termination losses cannot be attributable to a breach of the trust and confidence term if the contract is terminated for other reasons, for instance, for redundancy or if the employee leaves of his own volition. Since the trust-destroying conduct did not bring about the premature termination of the contract, ex hypothesi the employee did not sustain any loss of pay and so forth by reason of the breach of the trust and confidence term. That is the position in the present case.

Continuing financial losses

Exceptionally, however, the losses suffered by an employee as a result of a breach of the trust and confidence term may not consist of, or be confined to, loss of pay and other premature termination losses. Leaving aside injured feelings and anxiety, which are not the basis of the claim in the present case, an employee may find himself worse off financially than when he entered into the contract. The most obvious example is conduct, in breach of the trust and confidence term, which prejudicially affects an employee's future employment prospects. The conduct may diminish the employee's attractiveness to future employers.

The loss in the present case is of this character. BCCI promised, in an implied term, not to conduct a dishonest or corrupt business. The promised benefit was employment by an honest employer. This benefit did not materialise. Proof that Mr Mahmud and Mr Malik were handicapped in the labour market in consequence of BCCI's corruption may not be easy, but that is an assumed fact for the purpose of this preliminary issue.

There is here an important point of principle. Are financial losses of this character, which I shall call 'continuing financial losses', recoverable for breach of the trust and confidence term? This is the crucial point in the present appeals. In my view, if it was reasonably foreseeable that a particular type of loss of this character was a serious possibility, and loss of this type is sustained in consequence of a breach, then in principle damages in respect of the loss should be recoverable.

In the present case the agreed facts make no assumption, either way, about whether the appellants' handicap in the labour market was reasonably foreseeable by the bank. On this there must be scope for argument. I would not regard the absence of this necessary ingredient from the assumed facts as a sufficient reason for refusing to permit the former employees' claims to proceed further.

The contrary argument of principle is that since the purpose of the trust and confidence term is to preserve the employment relationship and to enable that relationship to prosper and continue, the losses recoverable for breach should be confined to those flowing from the premature termination of the relationship. Thus, a breach of the term should not be regarded as giving rise to recoverable losses beyond those I have described as premature termination losses. In this way, the measure of damages would be commensurate with, and not go beyond, the scope of the protection the trust and confidence term is intended to provide for the employee.

This is an unacceptably narrow evaluation of the trust and confidence term. Employers may be under no common law obligation, through the medium of an implied contractual term of general application, to take steps to improve their employees' future job prospects. But failure to improve is one thing, positively to damage is another. Employment, and job prospects, are matters of vital concern to most people. Jobs of all descriptions are less secure than formerly, people change jobs more frequently, and the job market is not always buoyant. Everyone knows this. An employment contract creates a close personal relationship, where there is often a disparity of power between the parties. Frequently the employee is vulnerable. Although the underlying purpose of the trust and confidence term is to protect the employment relationship, there can be nothing unfairly onerous or unreasonable in requiring an employer who breaches the trust and confidence term to be liable if he thereby causes continuing financial loss of a nature that was reasonably foreseeable. Employers must take care not to damage their employees' future employment prospects, by harsh and oppressive behaviour or by any other form of conduct which is unacceptable today as falling below the standards set by the implied trust and confidence term.

This approach brings one face to face with the decision in the wrongful dismissal case of *Addis* v *Gramophone Co. Ltd* [1909] AC 488. It does so, because the measure of damages recoverable for breach of the trust and confidence term cannot be decided without having some regard to a comparable question which arises regarding the measure of damages recoverable for wrongful dismissal. An employee may elect to treat a sufficiently serious breach of the trust and confidence term as discharging him from the contract and, hence, as a constructive dismissal. The damages in such a case ought, in principle, to be the same as they would be if the employer had expressly dismissed the employee. The employee should be no better off, or worse off, in the two situations. In principle, so far as the recoverability of continuing financial losses are concerned, there is no basis for distinguishing (a) wrongful dismissal following a breach of the trust and confidence term, (b) constructive dismissal following a breach of the trust and confidence term, and (c) a breach of the trust and confidence term which only becomes known after the contract has ended for other reasons. The present case is in the last category, but a principled answer cannot be given for cases in this category without considering the other two categories from which it is indistinguishable.

Addis v Gramophone Co.

Against this background I turn to the much-discussed case of *Addis* v *Gramophone Co. Ltd* [1909] AC 488, Mr Addis, it will be recalled, was wrongfully and contumeliously dismissed from his post as the defendant's manager in Calcutta. At trial he was awarded damages exceeding the amount of his salary for the period of notice to which he was entitled. The case is generally regarded as having decided, echoing the words of Lord Loreburn LC, at p. 491, that an employee cannot recover damages for the manner in which the wrongful dismissal took place, for injured feelings or for any loss he may sustain from the fact that his having been dismissed of itself makes it more difficult for him to obtain fresh employment. In particular, *Addis* is generally understood to have decided that any loss suffered by the adverse impact on the employee's chances of obtaining alternative employment is to be excluded from an assessment of damages for wrongful dismissal: see, for instance, *O'Laoire* v *Jackel International Ltd (No. 2)* [1991] IRLR 170, following earlier authorities; in Canada, the decision of the Supreme Court in *Vorvis* v *Insurance Corporation of British Columbia* [1989] 58 DLR (4th) 193, 205; and, in New Zealand, *Vivian* v *Coca-Cola Export Corporation* [1984] 2 NZLR 289, 292; *Whelan* v *Waitaki Meats Ltd* [1991] 2 NZLR 74, where Gallen J disagreed with the decision in *Addis*; and *Brandt* v *Nixdorf Computer Ltd* [1991] 3 NZLR 750.

For present purposes, I am not concerned with the exclusion of damages for injured feelings. The present case is concerned only with financial loss. The report of the facts in *Addis* is sketchy. Whether Mr Addis sought to prove that the manner of his dismissal caused him financial loss over and above his premature termination losses is not clear beyond a peradventure. If he did, it is surprising that their Lordships did not address this important feature more specifically. Instead there are references to injured feelings, the fact of dismissal of itself, aggravated damages, exemplary damages amounting to damages for defamation, damages being compensatory and not punitive, and the irrelevance of motive. The dissenting speech of Lord Collins was based on competence to award exemplary or vindictive damages.

However, Lord Loreburn's observations were framed in quite general terms, and he expressly disagreed with the suggestion of Lord Coleridge CJ in *Maw* v *Jones* [1890] 25 QBD 107, 108, to the effect that an assessment of damages might take into account the greater difficulty which an apprentice dismissed with a slur on his character might have in obtaining other employment. Similarly general observations were made by Lord James of Hereford, Lord Atkinson, Lord Gorell and Lord Shaw of Dunfermline.

In my view, these observations cannot be read as precluding the recovery of damages where the manner of dismissal involved a breach of the trust and confidence term and this caused financial loss. *Addis* v *Gramophone Co. Ltd* was decided in the days before this implied term was adumbrated. Now that this term exists and is normally implied in every contract of employment, damages for its breach should be assessed in accordance with ordinary contractual principles. This is as much true if the breach occurs before or in connection with dismissal as at any other time.

This approach would accord, in its result, with the approach adopted by courts and tribunals in unfair dismissal cases when exercising the statutory jurisdiction . . . to award an amount of compensation which the court or tribunal considers 'just and reasonable' in all the circumstances. Writing on a clean slate, the courts have interpreted this as enabling awards to include compensation in respect of the manner and circumstances of dismissal if these would give rise to a risk of financial loss by, for instance, making the employee less acceptable to potential employers see ss. 123 and 124 of the Employment Rights Act 1966 and *Norton Tool Co. Ltd* v *Tewson* [1972] IRLR 86.

I do not believe this approach gives rise to artificiality. On the contrary, the trust and confidence term is a useful tool, well established now in employment law. At common law damages are awarded to compensate for *wrongful* dismissal. Thus, loss which an employee would have suffered even if the dismissal had been after due notice is irrecoverable, because such loss does not derive from the wrongful element in the dismissal. Further, it is difficult to see how the mere fact of wrongful dismissal, rather than dismissal after due notice, could of itself handicap an employee in the labour market. All this is in line with *Addis*. But the manner and circumstances of the dismissal, as measured by the standards of conduct now identified in the implied trust and confidence term, may give rise to such a handicap. The law would be blemished if this were not recognised today. There now exists the separate cause of action whose absence Lord Shaw of Dunfermline noted with 'a certain regret': see *Addis* v

Gramophone Co. Ltd [1909] AC 488, 504. The trust and confidence term has removed the cause for his regret.

. . .

Furthermore, the fact that the breach of contract injures the plaintiff's reputation in circumstances where no claim for defamation would lie is not, by itself, a reason for excluding from the damages recoverable for breach of contract compensation for financial loss which on ordinary principles would be recoverable. An award of damages for breach of contract has a different objective: compensation for financial loss suffered by a breach of contract, not compensation for injury to reputation.

Sometimes, in practice, the distinction between damage to reputation and financial loss can become blurred. Damage to the reputation of professional persons, or persons carrying on a business, frequently causes financial loss. Nonetheless, the distinction is fundamentally sound, and when awarding damages for breach of contract courts take care to confine the damages to their proper ambit: making good financial loss. In *Herbert Clayton and Jack Waller Ltd* v *Oliver* [1930] AC 209, 220, when considering an award of damages to an actor who should have been billed to appear at the London Hippodrome, Lord Buckmaster regarded loss of publicity rather than loss of reputation as the preferable expression. In *Aerial Advertising Co.* v *Batchelor's Peas Ltd (Manchester)* [1938] 2 All ER 788, 796–797, where aerial advertising ('Eat Batchelor's Peas') took place during Armistice Day services, Atkinson J was careful to confine damages to the financial loss flowing from public boycotting of the defendant's goods and to exclude damages for loss of reputation. Lord Denning MR drew the same distinction in *GKN Centrax Gears Ltd* v *Matbro Ltd* [1976] 2 Lloyd's Rep 555, 573.

Breach of contract and existing reputation
The second submission concerning reputation was that the appellants' claims for damages to their existing reputations is barred by the decision of the Court of Appeal in *Withers* v *General Theatre Corporation Ltd* [1933] 2 KB 536.

There is an acute conflict between this decision and the earlier decision, also of the Court of Appeal, in *Marbe* v *George Edwardes (Daly's Theatre) Ltd* [1928] 1 KB 269. In *Marbe*, clear views were expressed that when assessing damages for loss flowing from a failure to provide promised publicity, the loss may include loss to existing reputation: see Bankes LJ at p. 281 and Atkin LJ at p. 288. In Withers, equally clear views were firmly stated to the contrary by all three members of the court: see Scrutton LJ at p. 547, Greer LJ at p. 554 and Romer LJ at p. 556. I have to say that, faced with the embarrassing necessity to choose, I prefer the views expressed in *Marbe*. They accord better with principle. Loss of promised publicity might cause an actor financial loss, for two reasons: first, through loss of opportunity to enhance his professional reputation and, secondly, his absence from the theatre scene might actually damage his existing professional reputation. If as a matter of fact an actor does suffer financial loss under both heads, and that is a question of evidence, I can see no reason why the law should deny recovery of damages in respect of the second head of loss.

Conclusion
For these reasons I would allow these appeals. The agreed set of assumed facts discloses a good cause of action. Unlike the courts below, this House is not bound by the observations in *Addis* v *Gramophone Co. Ltd* [1909] AC 488 regarding irrecoverability of loss flowing from the manner of dismissal, or by the decision in *Withers* v *General Theatre Corporation Ltd* [1933] 2 KB 536.

I add some cautionary footnotes, having in mind the assumed facts in the present case. First, when considering these appeals I have been particularly conscious of the potential difficulties which claims of this sort may present for liquidators. I am conscious that the outcome of the present appeals may be seen by some as opening the door to speculative claims, to the detriment of admitted creditors. Claims of handicap in the labour market, and the other ingredients of the cause of action now under consideration, may give rise to lengthy and costly investigations and, ultimately, litigation. If the claims eventually fail, liquidators may well be unable to recover their costs from the former employees. The expense of liquidations, and the time they often take, are matters already giving rise to concern. I am aware of the dangers here, but it could not be right to allow 'floodgates' arguments of this nature to stand in the way of claims which, as a matter of ordinary legal principle, are well founded. After all, if the former employee's claim is well founded in fact as well as in law, he himself is a creditor and ought to be admitted as such.

Secondly, one of the assumed facts in the present case is that the employer was conducting a dishonest and corrupt business. I would like to think this will rarely happen in practice. Thirdly, there are many circumstances in which an employee's reputation may suffer from his having been associated with an unsuccessful business, or an unsuccessful department within a business. In the ordinary way this will not found a claim of the nature made in the present case, even if the business or department was run with gross incompetence. A key feature in the present case is the assumed fact that the business was dishonest or corrupt. Finally, although the implied term that the business will not be conducted dishonestly is a term which avails all employees, proof of consequential handicap in the labour market may well be much more difficult for some classes of employees than others. An employer seeking to employ a messenger, for instance, might be wholly unconcerned by an applicant's former employment in a dishonest business, whereas he might take a different view if he were seeking a senior executive.

Note

1.   The decision of their Lordships now brings the position with regard to damages at common law into line with that of statutory compensation for unfair dismissal (see *Norton Tool Co. Ltd* v *Tewson* [1972] ICR 501, an extract appears at p. 492. However, *Malik* does not affect the first limb of *Addis* – damages for distress caused by dismissal. An arbitrary or oppressive dismissal may cause distress but it will not always make it more difficult for the employee to secure future alternative employment. It is arguable that the implied duty of trust and confidence is just as relevant to a claim for damages for distress as for the inability to find new employment. The facts in *Malik* did not allow their Lordships to take this further step and we await further developments in the case law.

2.   In the subsequent case of *Johnson* v *Unisys Ltd* [1999] IRLR 91 the Court of Appeal attempted to limit *Malik*. The plaintiff was summarily dismissed on the grounds of gross misconduct. He relied on *Malik* to claim damages for wrongful dismissal, alleging that, because of the manner in which he was dismissed, he had suffered a mental breakdown and had been unable to work. His claim was struck out and this was upheld by the Court of Appeal on the basis that *Malik* does not apply where there is an express dismissal. In the view of Lord Woolf MR, where there is an express dismissal, *Addis* continues to be the binding authority for the principle that damages for wrongful dismissal cannot include compensation for the manner of the dismissal, for

the employee's distressed feelings, or for the fact that the manner of dismissal of itself hampers the employee's prospects of obtaining new employment. As Rubenstein argues:

> This is extremely difficult to reconcile with the general view that *Malik* overruled *Addis*, a view based on Lord Nicholls' explicit statement in *Malik* that 'this House is not bound by the observations in *Addis v Gramophone Co. Ltd* regarding irrecoverability of loss flowing from the manner of dismissal'. Lord Woolf says: 'I am far from certain what Lord Nicholls meant by this statement. However, I do not accept that by his comment he was intending to overrule *Addis*'. With respect to the Master of the Rolls, this is a curious conclusion indeed. Even if Lord Nicholls cannot be regarded as conclusively intending to overrule the limitation on damages imposed by *Addis* in wrongful dismissal cases by the particular statement quoted in *Johnson*, the matter is surely put beyond doubt by his further statements (unquoted by the Court of Appeal) that *Addis* 'cannot be read as precluding the recovery of damages where the manner of dismissal involved a breach of the trust and confidence term and this caused financial loss'; that 'the manner of dismissal and circumstances of the dismissal, as measured by the standards of conduct now identified in the implied trust and confidence term, may give rise to' a handicap in the labour market, which must be recognised; and that damages for breach of the implied obligation 'should be assessed in accordance with ordinary contractual principles. This is as much true if the breach occurs before or in connection with dismissal as at any other time.' ('Highlights' [1999] IRLR 74)

3. Subsequently, five former employees of BCCI brought test cases on the claim for stigma damages (*Bank of Credit and Commerce International SA (in compulsory liquidation) v Ali and Others (No. 3)* [1999] IRLR 508). The claims were unsuccessful because none of the test case employees was able to adduce evidence to establish that the publicity given to the bank's wrongdoing blighted their prospects of obtaining fresh employment so as to cause them financial loss entitling them to stigma damages. Lightman J sets out rigorous criteria in this respect. The stigma must be the effective cause of the loss alleged. It is not sufficient that it was the occasion for the loss, and no presumption will be made that stigma played a part in unsuccessful job applications: 'The burden of proof is upon the employees to establish as a matter of fact on the balance of probabilities a causal link between the breach of the T&C term by the bank and the loss to them, and accordingly that the breach created a stigma affecting them which was a cause of a job application not succeeding or the loss of the opportunity of obtaining a job or of the loss of a job or a particular level of remuneration'.

B: When Will Remedies Other than Damages be Granted?

(i) Equitable Remedies

The common law has been most reluctant to enforce contracts of employment by remedies which require the contract to continue, i.e. injunction and specific performance. There are a number of reasons for this. First, damages are often adequate as a remedy, and it is general rule of contract that where this is the case then the equitable remedies of injunction and specific

performance should not be considered. Secondly, and perhaps most importantly, contracts of employment require mutual trust and confidence. This
element would be missing if employer and employee were to continue a
relationship of service against the will of one or the other. As Fry LJ said in
De Francesco v *Barnum* (1890) 45 Ch D 430, the courts 'are very unwilling
to extend decisions the effect of which is to compel persons who are not
desirous of maintaining personal relations with one another to continue those
personal relations . . . I think the courts are bound to be jealous lest they
should turn contracts of service into contracts of slavery'.

However, in recent years, the courts, prompted by the decision of the
Court of Appeal in *Hill* v *C.A. Parsons & Co. Ltd* [1972] 1 Ch 305, have
shown a greater willingness to grant these equitable remedies:

(a)   where proper contractual procedures have not been complied with
prior to dismissal; and

(b)   where mutual trust and confidence remains between the parties.

Irani v *Southampton and South-West Hampshire Health Authority*
[1985] IRLR 203
Queen's Bench Division

A part-time ophthalmologist was dismissed after having quarrelled with his
consultant, his employers considering after an *ad hoc* inquiry that the
differences were irreconcilable and that they could not, therefore, continue
to work together. However, the employers failed to carry out the disputes
procedure laid down by the Whitley Council for the Health Services (the
'blue book', procedure), the conditions of which were incorporated into the
contract of employment. Irani successfully sought an injunction preventing
his dismissal until the proper disputes procedure had been adhered to.

WARNER J: I mentioned that Mr Clifford seeks to distinguish *Hill* v *C.A. Parsons &
Co. Ltd* on the ground that it was a very exceptional case indeed. I find it helpful in
that respect to refer to the judgment of Mr Justice Megarry (as he then was) in *Chappel*
v *Times Newspapers Ltd* [1975] IRLR 90 where, he deals with the reasons why *Hill* v
Parsons was such an exceptional case. He says this:

There were three main grounds for this decision. First, there was still complete
confidence between employer and employee. The defendant did not want to
terminate the plaintiff's employment but he had been coerced by the union.
Second, the Industrial Relations Act 1971 was expected to come into force shortly.
It had been passed but the relevant parts had not been brought into operation. As
soon as the Act was in force, one probable result would be that the closed shop
would no longer be enforceable and that the plaintiff would be free to remain a
member of the union of his choice. He would also obtain the rights conferred by
the Act to compensation for unfair dismissal if he was then dismissed. Third, in the
circumstances of the case, damages would not be an adequate remedy.

I will take those three reasons seriatim and, in relation to each, compare the
situation here. First:

complete confidence between employer and employee. The defendant did not want
to terminate the plaintiff's employment but had been coerced by the union.

I have already mentioned the fact that the defendant authority here makes no complaint as to or criticism of Mr Irani's conduct or professional competence. Mr Clifford submitted at one time that the real distinction between this case and *Hill* v *C.A. Parsons & Co. Ltd* was that in *Hill* v *C.A. Parsons & Co. Ltd* the employers positively wanted their employee back. There are passages in the report of *Hill* v *C.A. Parsons & Co. Ltd* which show, it seems to me, that that was not so. Lord Denning, at page 316 said:

If ever there was a case where an injunction should be granted against the employers, this is the case. It is quite plain that the employers have done wrong. I know that the employers have been under pressure from a powerful trade union. That makes plain their conduct, but it does not excuse it. They have purported to terminate Mr Hill's employment by notice which is too short by far. They seek to take advantage of their own wrong by asserting that his services were terminated by their own 'say-so' at the date selected by them – to the grave prejudice of Mr Hill. They cannot be allowed to break the law in this way. It is, to my mind, a clear case for an injunction.

Lord Justice Sachs, at pages 320/321 said:

For the defendants it was suggested that an order of the court, if made as claimed, would endanger industrial peace as between the defendant company and its employees.

Lord Justice Stamp, at page 323 said:

On behalf of the defendant it is pointed out, and I think this is a more realistic approach, that it is not correct to say that the defendants are willing to employ the plaintiff but that the true position is that they would be willing to do so but for the fact that they have under pressure entered into an agreement with DATA requiring them to dismiss him and that this agreement cannot be broken without dire consequences. Unless therefore the court is prepared to infer, as I do not think it ought to do, that the defendants' opposition to the making of an order for specific performance is not genuine, it appears to me that the existence of the fears which dictated the dismissal is a strong ground for not making an exception to the general rule that the court will not order specific performance of a contract of employment.

I think the true position here is that the defendant authority would be willing to continue employing Mr Irani were it not for the fact that they are convinced that his and Mr Walker's continued employment are incompatible.

Mr Clifford more happily, I think, expressed the distinction between this case and the *Parsons* case in this way. He said that in the *Parsons* case the defendant fought the case because it was in fear of what the trade union might do if it did not, whereas here the defendant is fighting the case because it genuinely wants to be rid of Mr Irani. But, to revert to what I said earlier when I quoted from the judgment of Lord Justice Geoffrey Lane in the *Chappell* case, it remains the fact that the defendant authority has perfect faith in the honesty, integrity and loyalty of Mr Irani.

Turning to Mr Justice Megarry's second reason for the decision in the *Parsons* case, it seems to me that there is a comparable reason here. In the *Parsons* case, Mr Hill was seeking the protection of the Industrial Relations Act. Here Mr Irani is seeking the protection of section 33 of the blue book to which he is entitled if the circumstances are appropriate.

Thirdly, as Mr Harwood-Stevenson has pointed out, this is a case – and I anticipate now on what I shall have to say in a moment about some subsidiary submissions of Mr Clifford – where damages would not be an adequate remedy.

If I were to decline to grant the injunction sought by Mr Harwood-Stevenson, I would in effect be holding that, without doubt, an authority in the position of the defendant is entitled to snap its fingers at the rights of its employees under the blue book. Indeed, that is what Mr Clifford invites me to hold. He invites me to hold that, despite the existence in the blue book of sections 33 and 40, a health authority is entitled to dismiss a medical practitioner summarily and to say that, if and in so far as his rights under those sections are infringed, his remedy lies in damages only. If that is correct, it means that the same applies to clause 190 in the red book, as indeed in 1958 Mr Justice Barry held that it did. It means that for the price of damages – and the authorities show that damages at common law for wrongful dismissal are not generous – a health authority may, among other things, ignore the requirement at the end of clause 190 that:

> where the Secretary of State's decision cannot be given before the expiry of the notice given, such notice shall be extended for a month or longer period by the authority until the Secretary of State's decision is given.

The development of the law since the decision in [*Barber* v *Manchester Regional Hospital Board* [1958] 1 WLR 181] leads me to the conclusion that it is open to question whether that is right. If it is not right, nor can it be right, in my view, that, in the case of a more junior practitioner, the employing authority can ignore the rules in the blue book. For those reasons I reject Mr Clifford's primary submission.

In his subsidiary submissions, he took issue with Mr Harwood-Stevenson on the latter's grounds for saying that in this case damages would not be an adequate remedy. As to the point made by Mr Harwood-Stevenson on the basis of Mr Coley's evidence that, if dismissed by the defendant, Mr Irani will never again be able to secure employment in the National Health Service, Mr Clifford said that if, at the trial, Mr Irani could show that he was entitled to the benefit of section 33 and that, as a result of the action of the defendant authority, he never could again obtain employment within the National Health Service, damages could be assessed. Similarly, he said that if Mr Irani could show at the trial that he was indeed entitled to treat private patients in the Lymington Hospital and that, because of the action of the defendant authority, he had been deprived of that right, again damages could be assessed.

I do not myself find those submissions very convincing, any more than I find convincing Mr Clifford's further submission that Mr Irani ought to put to the test his ability to obtain employment elsewhere in the National Health Service. (Mr Clifford pointed out in that connection that Mr Irani also works in London.) Mr Clifford conceded however that, whatever might be the answers to those points, he had no answer, if he was wrong – as I have held – in his primary submission, to the point made by Mr Harwood-Stevenson that, if no injunction issued now, it was very possible that at the trial it would be too late for Mr Irani to rely on section 33 because he would by then have ceased to be an employee of the defendant authority.

I accordingly propose to grant the injunction sought by Mr Harwood-Stevenson.

Powell v *Brent London Borough Council*
[1988] ICR 176
Court of Appeal

The plaintiff had been 'promoted' from Senior Benefits Officer to Principal Benefits Officer after a competitive promotion procedure. However, one of the unsuccessful candidates complained of breaches of the Council's equal opportunities policy in the selection procedures and it was decided to re-advertise the post. The plaintiff sought an injunction preventing the re-advertising of the post. Pending that application, she had been allowed to continue doing the work of a Principal Benefits Officer. The question arose as to whether an interlocutory injunction should be granted pending the hearing of the main action. The Court of Appeal held that it should.

NICHOLLS LJ: . . . [I]f at the trial the court should decide, contrary to the council's contention, that the plaintiff was validly and effectually appointed as Principal Benefits Officer (Policy and Training), it seems to me that, as the evidence stands, this might be a case in which the court might decide that, if it were otherwise appropriate to grant an injunction, an injunction should be granted, there being no sufficient evidence of any lack of the necessary degree of confidence of the council in the plaintiff. I therefore think that, on the evidence now before the court, this is a case in which, exceptionally, if the plaintiff succeeded at the trial she might be confirmed in her post in the defendant council's organisation by grant of a suitably worded injunction.

If the plaintiff should so succeed but an interlocutory injunction is refused, an award of damages would not wholly recompense her. Making up the loss of salary would leave her uncompensated for her distress and embarrassment in having to resume her former job meanwhile and not having the opportunity to take up the more senior post at once. I do not find this uncompensatable loss weighty, but I find the equivalent loss in the case of the council even less compelling. The council offered to this court an undertaking, pending the trial or further order, not to re-advertise or fill the post of Principal Benefits Officer. So pending the trial the only 'loss' suffered by the council if an injunction is now granted but is discharged at the trial will be having to accept the plaintiff as Principal Benefits Officer against their will pending the trial. But, looking at the matter practically, the up to date position is that it is now some five months since the plaintiff assumed the role of Principal Benefits Officer, and there is no evidence from the council that it has become apparent, over this period, that, through lack of the particular abilities required for this post or clash of personalities or otherwise, the plaintiff is not able satisfactorily to discharge the office of Principal Benefits Officer in the council's organisation or that unsatisfactory consequences may ensue if, pending the trial, she continues to discharge the functions of her new post. This is so despite the absence of such evidence and the inferences that might be drawn from this having been mentioned specifically to Mr Newman on the first day of the hearing of this appeal.

Notes

1.   Most recently, in *Anderson v Pringle of Scotland Ltd* [1998] LRLR 64, the Scottish Court of Session granted an issue to restrain an employer from dismissing an employee in breach of the terms of a redundancy selection procedure. The important issue in the case was whether the trust and confidence requirement applied to redundancy selection. In the earlier ease of *Alexander v Standard Telephones and Cables* [1990] ICR 291, the view was taken that it was axiomatic that an employer had less confidence in the employees it proposed to make redundant than in those it proposed to retain. In Anderson, Lord Prosser took a different approach and stated:

If there were any question of mistrust, the position would no doubt be very different; but at least on the material before me, I am not persuaded that there is a true analogy between the respondents' preference for other employees and the need for confidence which is inherent in the employer/employee relationship.

This must surely be correct. Trust and confidence in an employee is not destroyed purely because of an economic downturn. The question for the court is whether the necessary trust and confidence to continue the employment relationship exists, so as to grant the injunction, not whether the employer has even more confidence in the workers it has not selected for redundancy.

2.   In exceptional circumstances, equitable remedies may be granted even where mutual trust and confidence have been lost, so long as the court is satisfied that 'a workable situation' can prevail.

Wadcock v London Borough of Brent
[1990] IRLR 223
Queen's Bench Division

The plaintiff had been employed as a social worker since 1975. The employer re-organised the work so that social workers were appointed to one of three specialist teams. Wadcock refused to indicate his preference and was placed, against his wishes, in the special needs division. The plaintiff refused to work in the new team from the due date of 21 November, but on 7 December he did attach himself to the special needs team although he remained uncooperative. On 8 December, he was dismissed with 12 weeks' notice. He sought an injunction preventing the dismissal pending trial of his application for a declaration that the council's demand that he work in the special needs division was unlawful. Despite Wadcock being prepared to work in that division until trial the council rejected the proposal on the basis of the 'breakdown of confidence between the plaintiff and defendant'. The High Court granted the interlocutory injunction.

MERVYN DAVIES J: . . . [I]t seems to me quite impossible to conclude that if an injunction is made in the terms sought in paragraph (2) in the notice of motion there will arise between the parties a 'workable situation' as that phrase is used above. On the other hand, there is no doubt that Mr Wadcock is a competent social worker and would be well able to work in special needs if he were minded to obey the orders of his team leader and other superiors. That he may have discussed his own position with some of his 'clients' is lamentable but perhaps understandable. As a separate point, I have in mind that Mr Wadcock may have been deprived of the protection of the disciplinary procedure.

In these circumstances I propose to make an Order embracing these provisions:

(a) On Mr Wadcock undertaking henceforth to work in accordance with the orders, instructions and wishes expressed orally or in writing by his team leader for the time being or by any other member of the Social Services Department having authority over him, Brent are to allow Mr Wadcock, pending trial, to work for them in special needs at the usual rate of pay;

(b) I will retain this matter pending trial and give leave to Brent to apply on two days' notice to revoke this Order should Mr Wadcock's undertaking be breached in any respect. If Mr Wadcock is not willing to give that undertaking unreservedly, there will be no order on the motion.

Robb v *London Borough of Hammersmith and Fulham*
[1991] IRLR 72
Queen's Bench Division

The plaintiff was employed by the defendant as its Director of Finance. The council had been involved in financial dealings which, in May 1990, had been declared illegal by the High Court. Accordingly, disciplinary procedures were invoked against Robb. Robb was asked to take leave with pay while preliminary investigations were undertaken. Negotiations then took place to achieve a mutually agreed termination of Robb's contract of employment and, as a result, the disciplinary procedures were discontinued. However, the negotiations broke down, and on 26 July 1990 Robb was summarily dismissed. He sought an injunction restraining the employers from dismissing him until all the proper contractual disciplinary procedures had been carried out. He did not wish to be reinstated but sought continuation of his suspension with pay until those procedures had been completed. The High Court granted his application.

MORLAND J: I now conclude as to why in my judgment, the plaintiff has established that he is entitled to the injunctive relief sought:

(1)   The defendants are in admitted breach of contract in ending the paragraph 41 procedure and dismissing the plaintiff summarily without notice.

(2)   Although damages would be an adequate remedy for the defendants' breach of contract in summarily dismissing the plaintiff and he would be entitled to damages representing not only loss of salary during the three-month notice and a time extended for the probable length of the paragraph 41 procedure to completion, damages would not be an adequate remedy for the manner of his unlawful dismissal and his deprivation of the paragraph 41 procedure.

(3)   Without the injunction sought, the plaintiff has lost the opportunity of ventilating his case and justifying himself at the hearings and enquiries under the paragraph 41 procedure. The Industrial Tribunal is not a suitable alternative Tribunal for adjudicating on the capabilities of the plaintiff in such complex matters as interest swaps.

(4)   The paragraph 41 procedure is workable now but could well become impracticable if delayed until the conclusion of the trial.

(5)   Injunctive relief now restores the plaintiff to his position and entitlement to paragraph 41 procedure which the defendants unlawfully deprived him of in the last week of July.

In my judgment the balance of convenience requires me to give the relief sought, otherwise, to echo the words of Warner J in *Irani* v *Southampton and South-West Hampshire Health Authority* [1985] IRLR 203, the defendants would be 'snapping their fingers' at the legal rights of the plaintiff.

(ii)   Public Law Remedies
Order 53 of the Rules of the Supreme Court 1981 (CPR sch. 1) sets out a judicial review procedure for dealing with complaints in the public law

domain. It is a procedure designed to limit complaints about actions by administrative bodies. For example, complaints generally have to be brought within three months of the matter complained of and there is a two-stage procedure. An applicant first needs to apply for leave to seek judicial review and, having overcome that hurdle, to show at the full hearing that the administrative body has, in some way, acted in breach of the various rules of administrative law. While the leave procedure was designed as a hurdle intended to filter out unmeritorious claims, it has been seen and used as a cheap and speedy way of obtaining the views of a High Court judge on the merits of a claim. Many applications for 'leave' are paper applications made only in writing, i.e. application and affidavit in support showing grounds. Frequently the granting of leave is seen as sufficient support for the merits of a claim so as to persuade the respondent to seek to settle the matter without the need for, and avoiding the publicity of, a full hearing.

As regards contracts of employment, the most important administrative law principle is the requirement to act according to the rules of natural justice and fairness. Because of the import of this principle and the relatively inexpensive nature of the application for leave, those employed in the public domain have been tempted to seek judicial review of the termination of their contracts of employment. The courts, however, have attempted to close the door to such applications by reference to what is called the 'public law/private law divide' (see *O'Reilly* v *Mackman* [1983] 2 AC 237). Just because one is employed in the public domain has been held not to be a sufficient reason to justify a public law remedy. In most cases the complaint will be of breach of the employee's private contractual rights and the complainant is restricted to a private law action for breach of contract.

R v *East Berkshire Health Authority, ex parte Walsh*
[1984] IRLR 278
Court of Appeal

Mr Walsh was a senior nursing officer employed under a contract of service by the health authority. He was dismissed by a district nursing officer and applied for judicial review to quash the dismissal on the grounds that the district nursing officer had no power to dismiss him and there had been a breach of natural justice in the procedure which led up to his dismissal. The health authority, however, contended that judicial review was not the appropriate procedure by which to remedy his alleged grievance. The judge rejected the health authority's argument, but the Court of Appeal accepted it.

SIR JOHN DONALDSON MR: The ordinary employer is free to act in breach of his contracts of employment and if he does so his employee will acquire certain private law rights and remedies in damages for wrongful dismissal, an order for reinstatement or re-engagement and so on. Parliament can underpin the position of public authority employees by directly restricting the freedom of the public authority to dismiss, thus giving the employee 'public law' rights and at least making him a potential candidate for administrative law remedies. Alternatively, it can require the authority to contract with its employees on specified terms with a view to the employee acquiring 'private law' rights under the contract of employment. If the authority fails or refuses thus to create 'private law' rights for the employee, the employee will have 'public law' rights to compel compliance, the remedy being mandamus requiring the authority so to contract or a declaration that the employee had those rights. If, however, the authority gives the employee the required protection, a breach of that contract is not a matter of 'public law' and gives rise to no administrative law remedies.

Notes

1.   For a detailed review of the principles and authorities in this area, see *Roy v Kensington and Chelsea and Westminster Family Practitioner Committee* [1992] IRLR 233, HL; and *McLaren v Home Office* [1990] IRLR 338, CA.

2.   A call for a re-consideration of the public law/private law divide has been made by Lord Lowry in *R v Secretary of State for Employment, ex parte EOC* [1994] IRLR 176 at p. 183:

. . . I have never been entirely happy with the wide procedural restriction for which *O'Reilly v Mackman* [1983] 2 AC 237 is an authority, and I hope that that case will one day be the subject of your Lordships' further consideration.

6 UNFAIR DISMISSAL

I Introduction

Royal Commission on Trade Unions and Employers' Associations (Cmnd 3623, 1968)

521. In the eye of the law employer and employee are free and equal parties to the contract of employment. Hence, either employer or employee has the right to bring the contract to an end in accordance with its terms. Thus, an employer is legally entitled to dismiss an employee whenever he wishes and for whatever reasons, provided only that he gives due notice. At common law he does not even have to reveal his reason, much less to justify it.

. . .

526. We share in full the belief that the present situation is unsatisfactory. In practice there is usually no comparison between the consequences for an employer if an employee terminates the contract of employment and those which will ensue for an employee if he is dismissed. In reality people build much of their lives around their jobs. Their incomes and prospects for the future are inevitably founded in the expectation that their jobs will continue. For workers in many situations dismissal is a disaster. For some workers it may make inevitable the breaking up of a community and the uprooting of homes and families. Others, and particularly older workers, may be faced with the greatest difficulty in getting work at all. The statutory provision for redundancy goes some way to recognise what is really at stake for an employee when his job is involved, but it is no less at stake if he is being dismissed for alleged incompetence or for misconduct than if he is being dismissed for redundancy. To this it is no answer that good employers will dismiss employees only if they have no alternative. Not all employers are good employers. Even if the employer's intentions are good, is it certain that his subordinate's intentions are always also good? And even when all concerned in management act in good faith, are they always necessarily right? Should their view of the case automatically prevail over the employee's.

. . .

528. From the point of view of industrial peace, it is also plain that the present situation leaves much to be desired. In 1964–66 some 276 unofficial strikes took place

each year on average as a result of disputes about whether individuals should or should not be employed, suspended or dismissed. The committee on dismissals analysed stoppages – whether official or unofficial – arising out of dismissals *other than redundancies* over this period and found that there were on average 203 a year. It can be argued that the right to secure a speedy and impartial decision on the justification for a dismissal might have averted many of these stoppages, though some cases would no doubt still have occurred where workers were taking spontaneous action to try to prevent a dismissal being given effect.

529.   For all these reasons we believe it urgently necessary for workers to be given better protection against unfair dismissal.

Notes

1.   In 1964, the Government announced its acceptance of ILO Recommendation No. 119 (1963) on the termination of employment, which provides that an employer should not dismiss an employee without a valid reason and without the dismissed employee having a right to complain to an independent tribunal. This, together with the Royal Commission's proposals, led to the enactment of the first statutory provisions in the Industrial Relations Act 1971, which came into force on 28 February 1972. For a detailed analysis of the aims and origins of the legislation, see Collins, C., *Justice in Dismissal: The Law of Termination of Employment* (Oxford: Clarendon Press, 1992), ch. 1.

2.   The Royal Commission's argument that the introduction of the right to claim unfair dismissal would reduce the industrial action over matters of discipline has not been sustained. Strikes over non-redundancy dismissals, accounting on average for 10 per cent of stoppages in 1964–66, still made up 9 per cent of stoppages in 1982 (see Dickens et al., *Dismissed: A Study of Unfair Dismissal and the Industrial Tribunal System* (Oxford: Blackwell), 1985, pp. 224–7).

3.   Until relatively recently, the legislation governing unfair dismissal remained largely unaltered, the major amendments being concerned with the introduction of protection for those employees dismissed for non-union membership. The other significant change concerned the qualification period necessary to claim, which was raised from 26 weeks in 1979 to two years in 1985. Following the proposal contained in the Government's *Fairness at Work* White Paper (Cm 3968, May 1998), the qualifying period was reduced to one year with effect from 1 June 1999 (Unfair Dismissal and Statement of Reasons for Dismissal (Variation of Qualifying Period) Order 1999) (SI 1999/1436).

In 1978, an attempt was made to consolidate the legislation in the Employment Protection (Consolidation) Act. After 1978, a number of amendments were made via a succession of Employment Acts, the Sex Discrimination Act 1986, the Trade Union Reform and Employment Rights Act 1993 and a number of pieces of subordinate legislation. As a result, a further consolidation statute was necessary in the form of the Employment Rights Act 1996.

With the election of the Labour Government, further and more far-reaching changes to the unfair dismissal regime have been introduced. The

Employment Rights (Dispute Resolution) Act 1998 contains provisions to implement those aspects of the Green Paper, *Resolving Employment Rights Disputes: Options for Reform* (CM 2707, 1994), which attracted wide support and required primary legislation. The most significant change under the Act is to grant ACAS powers to fund and provide an arbitration scheme for unfair dismissal claims. This will be available as an alternative to an employment tribunal hearing and will be voluntary on both sides. It is ACAS's intention that the scheme will be phased in during 1999.

In *Fairness at Work*, the Government put forward a number of proposals aimed at strengthening the unfair dismissal remedy. These included:

(a)   abolishing the maximum limit on the compensatory award;
(b)   index-linking limits on the basic award, subject to a maximum rate;
(c)   prohibiting the use of waivers for unfair dismissal claims but continuing to allow them for redundancy payments;
(d)   creating a legal right for individuals to be accompanied by a fellow employee or trade union representative of their choice during grievance and disciplinary hearings; and
(e)   reducing the qualifying period for claimants to one year.

The Employment Relations Act 1999 and a ministerial order have implemented these proposals with one exception. The ceiling on the compensation award has not been completely removed but the maximum limit has been raised from £12k to £50k.

The following cases offer two judicial perspectives on the legislation.

W. Devis & Sons Ltd v Atkins
[1976] IRLR 16
Employment Appeal Tribunal

PHILLIPS J, President: The expression unfair dismissal is in no sense a common sense expression capable of being understood by the man in the street.

Cook v Thomas Linnell & Sons Ltd
[1977] ICR 770
Employment Appeal Tribunal

PHILLIPS J, President: It is important that the operation of the legislation in relation to unfair dismissal should not impede employers unreasonably in the efficient management of their business, which must be in the interests of all.

Question
What impression do the above extracts convey regarding the operation of the law of unfair dismissal? Compare your view with the critique offered at the end of this chapter.

II   Establishing Unfair Dismissal

We can analyse the law of unfair dismissal in four stages (see the Flowchart below).

STAGE ONE – Has a dismissal taken place?
STAGE TWO – Is the applicant qualified to make a claim?
STAGE THREE – Is the dismissal fair or unfair?
STAGE FOUR – What remedies are available?

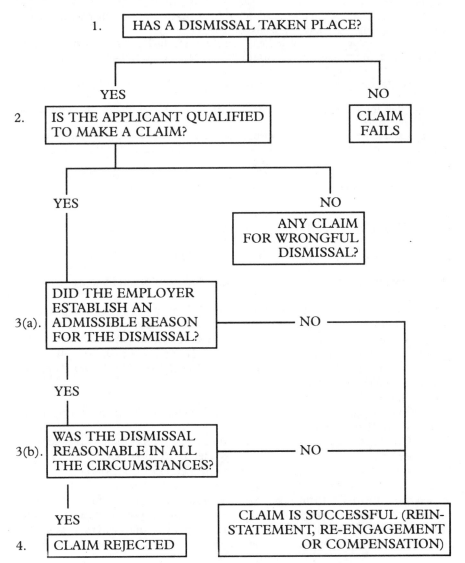

A: Stage One – Has a Dismissal Taken Place?

Employment Rights Act 1996

95.   Circumstances in which an employee is dismissed
(1)   For the purposes of this Part an employee is dismissed by his employer if (and, subject to subsection (2) and section 96, only if)—
(a)   the contract under which he is employed is terminated by the employer (whether with or without notice),
(b)   he is employed under a contract for a fixed term and that term expires without being renewed under the same contract, or
(c)   the employee terminates the contract under which he is employed (with or without notice) in circumstances in which he is entitled to terminate it without notice by reason of the employer's conduct.
(2)   An employee shall be taken to be dismissed by his employer for the purposes of this Part if—
(a)   the employer gives notice to the employee to terminate his contract of employment, and
(b)   at a time within the period of that notice the employee gives notice to the employer to terminate the contract of employment on a date earlier than the date on which the employer's notice is due to expire;
and the reason for the dismissal is to be taken to be the reason for which the employer's notice is given.

Note
See Chapter 5 for a full discussion of the concept of dismissal.

B: Stage Two — Is the Applicant Qualified to Make a Claim?

The following employees generally are excluded from the right to claim unfair dismissal:
(a)   Workers who fail to satisfy the status of 'employee' (see Chapter 2).
(b)   Employees who have not worked for a continuous period of one year.
(c)   Those who ordinarily work outside Great Britain (ERA 1996, s. 196). This depends on whether the worker's 'base' is outside the UK (see *Wilson* v *Maynard Shipbuilding Consultants AB* [1977] IRLR 491, CA; *Janata Bank Ltd* v *Ahmed* [1981] IRLR 457, CA).
(d)   Share fishermen (ERA 1996, s. 199).
(e)   The police and prison officers (ERA 1996, s. 200); members of the armed forces (ERA 1996, s. 192).
(f)   Crown employees where the relevant Minister has issued an excepting certificate on grounds of national security (see ERA 1996, s. 193); *Council of Civil Service Unions* v *Minister for the Civil Service* [1985] ICR 14).
(g)   Employees reaching retirement age: to claim employees must not have passed the 'normal retiring age' for employees in that position; or, where there is no normal retirement age, must not have passed their sixty-fifth birthday (ERA 1996, s. 109(1)). It has been held that where a contract specifies a retirement age then it can be presumed to be the 'normal retiring

age' (see *Nothman* v *Barnet London Borough Council* [1979] IRLR 35, HL.) But this presumption can be rebutted by evidence that the contractual age has been abandoned in practice. The test of whether this has happened is to ascertain what would be the reasonable expectation or understanding of employees holding that position at the relevant time (*Waite* v *Government Communications Headquarters* [1983] ICR 653, HL). *Hughes* v *Department of Health & Social Security* [1985] AC 776, concerned the question whether employers can effectively alter a normal retirement age established by practice by a simple announcement to that effect. The House of Lords held that this was possible, since an announcement would vary the expectations of the employees affected. (See also *Brooks* v *British Telecommunications plc* [1992] IRLR 66, CA).

(h) Workers who, at the time of their dismissal, are taking industrial action which has lasted more than eight weeks, and there has been no selective dismissal or re-engagement of those taking the action. Unofficial strikers may be selectively dismissed or re-engaged (TULR(C)A 1992, ss. 237, 238, 238A; see Chapter 9).

(i) Those employees covered by a disciplinary procedure, voluntarily agreed between employers and an independent trade union, where the Secretary of State has designated it to apply instead of the statutory scheme. The designation will be granted only if the voluntary scheme is at least as beneficial to employees as statutory protection (ERA 1996, s. 110).

(j) Illegal contracts: a contract of employment to do an act which is unlawful is unenforceable. The position is different, however, if the contract is capable of being performed lawfully, and was initially intended to be so performed, but has in fact been performed by unlawful means. In this situation, the contract will be unenforceable only if the employee was a knowing and willing party to the illegality and stood to benefit (see *Hewcastle Catering Ltd* v *Ahmed and Elkamah* [1991] IRLR 473, CA).

(k) Where a settlement of the claim has been agreed with the involvement of an ACAS Conciliation Officer and the employee has agreed to withdraw his/her complaint (ERA 1996, s. 203(2)(e)). Where the employee enters into a valid compromise contract satisfying the conditions set out in s. 203(3). These include that the employee should have taken independent legal advice.

(i)   Claim in Time

Employment Rights Act 1996

111.   Complaints to industrial tribunal

(2) Subject to subsection (3), an industrial tribunal shall not consider a complaint under this section unless it is presented to the tribunal—

(a) before the end of the period of three months beginning with the effective date of termination, or

(b) within such further period as the tribunal considers reasonable in a case where it is satisfied that it was not reasonably practicable for the complaint to be presented before the end of that period of three months.

Palmer v *Southend-on-Sea Borough Council*
[1984] IRLR 119
Court of Appeal

Mr Palmer and Mr Saunders, both employed by the Council for nearly 25 years, were charged with theft in the summer of 1980 and were suspended on half pay. In April 1981, the two men were convicted of theft in the Crown Court and were summarily dismissed by their employer on 8 April. The employees' appeal against dismissal was dismissed on 22 April and, on the following day, the Council's Chief Executive wrote to the employees' trade union representative in the following terms:

> . . . in the event of an appeal to a higher court against the Crown Court's decision being decided in favour of your members, [the Appeal's Committee] would (without any promise as to the outcome of such consideration) be prepared to look at the matter again.

On 19 February 1982, the Court of Appeal, Criminal Division, quashed the convictions and, on the same day, the employees' union official wrote to the Council seeking their reinstatement. This request was refused on 1 April 1982 and, on 28 April 1982, Mr Palmer and Mr Saunders filed applications for unfair dismissal.

A preliminary hearing was held to determine whether or not it had been reasonably practicable for the complaints to have been presented within the three-month time limit set out in what is now ERA 1996, s. 111(2). On behalf of the employees, it was argued that on a proper construction of the Chief Executive's letter of 23 April 1981, the Council's domestic procedure had not been exhausted; that in the event of a successful appeal against conviction, they would have the right to ask for a review, and that it was a reasonable course of action not to make a complaint to an industrial tribunal and thus prejudice their domestic appeals before the Court of Appeal had announced its decision. This argument was rejected by the industrial tribunal and the employees' appeals were rejected by both the EAT and the Court of Appeal.

MAY LJ: . . . In an obiter dictum in the judgment of the Employment Appeal Tribunal in *Crown Agents* v *Lancal* [1978] IRLR 512 to which we have already referred, Kilner Brown, J said:

> Merely as a statement of general principle, it would seem to us that in cases where a person is going through a conciliation process, or is taking up a domestic appeal procedure, whether it be on discipline, or whether it be for medical reasons, that common sense would indicate that while he is going through something which involves him and his employer directly he should be able to say 'It is not reasonably three months.' This is the view not only of this particular division of the Appeal Tribunal but we have taken steps to canvass the views of other members, including other judicial members. The view of the Appeal Tribunal as a whole is that normally though by no means always. It would be open to say in the case of a person who is

going through an appeal process and loses, that not only does the date go back to the original date of dismissal but that the applicant so caught by the effluxion of time should be able to satisfy an Industrial Tribunal that he is entitled to the benefit of what is usually called the 'escape' clause.

However in *Bodha v Hants Area Health Authority* [1982] ICR 200 another division of the Appeal Tribunal presided over by Browne-Wilkinson J as he was them disagreed in these terms:

Despite the reference to there having been consultation with other members of this Appeal Tribunal, the fact that both the argument and the judgment were concluded on the same date shows that such consultation was obviously not very widespread. For the reasons we have given, we do not think we should follow that dictum having had the matter fully argued before us. There may be cases where the special facts (additional to the bare fact that there is an internal appeal pending) may persuade an Industrial Tribunal, as a question of fact, that it was not reasonably practicable to complain to the Industrial Tribunal within the time limit. But we do not think that the mere fact of a pending internal appeal, by itself, is sufficient to justify a finding of fact that it was not 'reasonably practicable' to present a complaint to the industrial tribunal.

In the light of the passages from earlier judgments of this court which we have quoted in this judgment, we respectfully prefer the views on the effect of a pending internal appeal on the question whether it has been reasonably practicable to present a complaint within the time limit expressed by the Employment Appeal Tribunal in *Bodha's* case to those expressed in the *Crown Agents* decision.

However, in *Bodha's* case the Employment Appeal Tribunal also said:

The statutory test remains one of practicability. The statutory words still require the Industrial Tribunal to have regard to what *could* be done albeit what is practicable in a common-sense way. The statutory test is not satisfied just because it was reasonable not to do what could be done . . . Reasonably practicable means 'reasonably capable of being done' not 'reasonable'.

If, in this dictum, the learned President was intending to limit the meaning of the phrase 'reasonably practicable' to that which is reasonably capable *physically* of being done, then on the authorities to which we have referred this we think would be too restrictive a construction.

In the end, most of the decided cases have been decisions on their own particular facts and must be regarded as such. However we think that one can say that to construe the words 'reasonably practicable' as the equivalent of 'reasonable' is to take a view too favourable to the employee. On the other hand 'reasonably practicable' means more than merely what is reasonably capable physically of being done different, for instance, from its construction in the context of the legislation relating to factories: compare *Marshal v Gotham* [1954] AC 360. In the context in which the words are used in the 1978 Consolidation Act, however ineptly as we think, they mean something between these two. Perhaps to read the word 'practicable' as the equivalent of 'feasible' as Sir John Brightman did in *Singh's* case and to ask colloquially and untrammelled by too much legal logic 'was it reasonably feasible to present the complaint to the Industrial Tribunal within the relevant three months?' – is the best approach to correct application of the relevant subsection.

What, however, is abundantly clear on all the authorities is that the answer to the relevant question is pre-eminently an issue of fact for the Industrial Tribunal and that it is seldom that an appeal from its decision will be. Dependent upon the circumstances of the particular case, an Industrial Tribunal may wish to consider the manner in which and reason for which the employee was dismissed, including the extent to which, if at all, the employer's conciliator appeals machinery has been used. It will no doubt investigate what was the substantial cause of the employee's failure to comply with the statutory time limit: whether he had been physically prevented from complying with the limitation period, for instance by illness or a postal strike or something similar. It may be relevant for the Industrial Tribunal to investigate whether at the time when he was dismissed, and if not then when thereafter, he knew that he had the right to complain that he had been unfairly dismissed, in some cases the Tribunal may have to consider whether there has been any misrepresentation about any relevant matter by the employer to the employee. It will frequently be necessary for it to know whether the employee was being advised at any material time and, if so, by whom of the extent of the advisors' knowledge of the facts of the employee's case; and of the nature of any advice which they may have given to him. In any event it will probably be relevant in most cases for the Industrial Tribunal to ask itself whether there has been any substantial fault on the part of the employee or his advisor which has led to the failure to comply with the statutory time limit. Any list of possible relevant considerations, however, cannot be exhaustive and, as we have stressed, at the end of the day the matter is one of fact for the Industrial Tribunal taking all the circumstances of the given case into account.

Question
Do you agree with the approach adopted in this case?

Note
In *Biggs* v *Somerset County Council* [1996] IRLR 203, Neill LJ said that while the phrase 'not reasonably practicable' might apply to a mistake of fact, it did not cover a mistake of law.

Machine Tool Industry Research Association v *Simpson*
[1988] IRLR 212
Court of Appeal

Ms Simpson was told and accepted that she was being dismissed for redundancy. Subsequently, however, she heard that another employee had been re-engaged, and that caused her to form the belief that the real reason for her dismissal may not have been redundancy.

She made a complaint of unfair dismissal but this was received by the industrial tribunal some three days outside the statutory three-month time limit. The industrial tribunal held that in the circumstances it had not been reasonably practicable for Mrs Simpson to present her claim in time, that it was presented within a reasonable time thereafter and that they had jurisdiction to consider her complaint. The EAT and the Court of Appeal dismissed the employers' appeal against that decision.

PURCHAS LJ: Taken in the context of the whole of [s. 111] and applying the plain reading to the words of the section, for my part I see little difficulty in the view that fundamentally the exercise to be performed is a study of the subjective state of mind of the employee when, at a late stage, he or she decides that after all there is a case to bring before the industrial tribunal. There is no indication in the wording of the section that it is necessary for an applicant to be relieved of the strict time limit to establish, as facts, those facts which have caused a genuine frame of mind, and reasonably so caused it, to form a decision to present a complaint to the tribunal out of time.

So one turns to look to see how the subjective state of mind must be approached.

In my judgement, the submissions made by Mr Ouseley (amicus curiae) are correct. They not only reflect the ordinary meaning of the section, to which I have just referred, but are supported by such authority as is available to this court. Mr Ouseley submitted that the expression 'reasonably practicable' imports three stages, the proof of which rests on the applicant. The first proposition relevant to this case is that it was reasonable for the applicant not to be aware of the factual basis upon which she could bring an application to the tribunal during the currency of the three-month limitation period. Mr Ouseley argues with some force that if that is established it cannot be reasonably practicable to expect an applicant to bring a case based upon facts of which she is ignorant. Secondly, the applicant must establish that the knowledge which she gains has, in the circumstances, been reasonably been gained by her, and that knowledge is either crucial, fundamental or important – it matters not which particular epithet, if any, is applied – to her change of belief from one which she does not believe that she has grounds for an application, to a belief which she reasonably and genuinely holds, that she has a ground for making such an application. I am grateful to adopt the summary of that concept in the words that Mr Ouseley used, that it is an objective qualification of reasonableness, in the circumstances, to a subjective test of the applicant's state of mind.

The third ground, which Mr Ouseley accepts is really a restatement of the first two, is that the acquisition of this knowledge had to be crucial to the decision to bring the claim in any event.

Note

The above cases show that the time limit is rigorously applied. Such is the stringency of the approach that it has been held that an applicant may not use the excuse that his or her failure to claim was due to a mistake of a 'skilled adviser' such as a lawyer, trade union official or Citizens' Advice Bureau worker (*Riley* v *Tesco Stores Ltd* [1980] IRLR 103).

However, in *Jean Sorelle Ltd* v *Rybak* [1991] IRLR 153, the EAT held that there is a clear factual difference between, on the one hand, advice obtained from someone who is asked, whether for a fee or not, to advise the applicant in the presentation of a claim against the employer and, on the other hand, advice obtained from an industrial tribunal employee. Therefore, the fact that Ms Rybak was given erroneous advice concerning the final date for presentation of her claim by an industrial tribunal clerk provided grounds to excuse her late claim.

In the next extract, we see the 'skilled adviser' test under even stronger attack.

London International College v Sen
[1993] IRLR 333
Court of Appeal

Dr Sen was given erroneous advice regarding the time limit from a solicitor, and then received the same advice from a member of staff of the Central

Office of the Industrial Tribunals when he telephoned to check. As a result, he presented his claim one day late. Upholding a tribunal finding in favour of Dr Sen, the EAT held that there is no rule that taking the advice of a solicitor makes it reasonably practicable to comply with the time limit. The Court of Appeal dismissed the employer's appeal.

SIR THOMAS BINGHAM MR: Mr Pitt-Payne [Counsel for the appellant employer] drew our attention to two authorities in particular, the first of them *Dedman v British Building & Engineering Appliances Ltd* [1973] IRLR 379 and the second *Riley and another v Tesco Stores Ltd* [1980] IRLR 103 (CA). Those authorities, Mr Pitt-Payne contended, gave support to the principle for which he contended.

I would for my part accept that those authorities, and in particular the passages referred to, do lend support to the proposition for which Mr Pitt-Payne contended. When a prospective complainant consults a solicitor or a trade union official or similar adviser, the authorities do suggest that he can no longer say that it was not reasonably practicable for him to comply with the time limit even if the adviser advised wrongly.

I must, however, say that, for my part, I find the rationale of that principle very hard to understand. If the test is whether it was reasonably practicable or practically possible or reasonably feasible to present the complaint in time, it would seem to me irrelevant whether or not the complainant had consulted a solicitor. That would seem to me to be a possible approach to the language of the section but it is one which previous authority has firmly rejected and such authority has concentrated on the state of mind of the prospective complainant and the extent to which he understood his position. If, however, it is his state of mind and his understanding of his position which matters, it seems strange to me that a complainant who is misled by incorrect advice into misapprehending his rights is unable to rely on the escape clause provided in [s. 111(2)]. If the rationale is that he cannot rely on the escape clause because in such circumstances it is his adviser and not the employer who should compensate him, then there would appear, as the authorities suggest, to be a distinction between a solicitor who is prima facie liable for misleading advice and other sources of advice which are not, or may not be, liable for giving incorrect advice. In the second category I would put an employee of an Industrial Tribunal whose liability for incorrect advice is at best far from clear.

I do not for my part find it easy to apply these principles because, as I have indicated, I do not find it easy to understand them. I question, however, whether the earlier cases were really purporting to lay down a rule of law to govern what is essentially a question of fact, and I am not persuaded that the prospective complainant loses for all time his rights to rely on the escape clause in [s. 111(2)] absolutely once he consults a solicitor potentially liable for wrong advice if, as in the present case, he distrusts that advice and immediately proceeds to obtain further advice from a body such as an Industrial Tribunal which may not be so liable. That, in effect, was the decision both of the Industrial Tribunal and of the Employment Appeal Tribunal and I do not, for my part, feel able to say that they were wrong in law to reach the conclusion that they did.

Note

Where the applicant discovers new facts surrounding his or her dismissal, the relevant date for assessing the reasonableness of the applicant's belief in the existence of a cause of action is the date when he or she was considering making the complaint. Indeed, where *two* grounds of challenge subsequently come to light, the correct approach is to apply the 'reasonably practicable' test to each individually (see *Marley (UK) Ltd and another v Anderson* [1996] IRLR 163, CA).

(ii) 'The Effective Date of Termination'
Establishing the date of termination will determine whether a claim is made in time, whether the applicant possessed the requisite continuity of employment at the date of dismissal, whether the retirement age exclusion is to operate in any particular case and, if the claim is successful, when to calculate compensation.

Employment Rights Act 1996

97. Effective date of termination
   (1)   Subject to the following provisions of this section, in this Part 'the effective date of termination'—
      (a)   in relation to an employee whose contract of employment is terminated by notice, whether given by his employer or by the employee, means the date on which the notice expires,
      (b)   in relation to an employee whose contract of employment is terminated without notice, means the date on which the termination takes effect, and
      (c)   in relation to an employee who is employed under a contract for a fixed term which expires without being renewed under the same contract, means the date on which the term expires.

Notes
1.   Two useful cases in this area are *Robert Cort & Sons v Charman* [1981] IRLR 437 and *Stapp v The Shaftesbury Society* [1982] IRLR 326, which both uphold the view that the effective date of termination (EDT) is the actual date of termination regardless of whether the employment was lawfully or unlawfully terminated. So where, as in *Robert Cort & Sons v Charman*, an employee is immediately dismissed with wages in lieu of notice, the 'effective date of termination' is the actual date on which the employee is told of the dismissal and not the date on which notice would expire (see also *Batchelor v British Railways Board* [1987] IRLR 136).
2.   Where the dismissed employee exercises a right of appeal, the question may arise as to the EDT, does the EDT become the date of the determination of the appeal, or does the original date of dismissal still stand as the EDT?
   The leading case on this question is the Court of Appeal's decision in *J. Sainsbury Ltd v Savage* [1981] ICR 1, where it was held that if the dismissed employee invokes an internal appeal which is subsequently rejected, the EDT is the date of the original dismissal, unless the contract provides to the contrary. This approach was expressly approved by the House of Lords in the important case of *West Midlands Cooperative Society Ltd v Tipton* [1986] IRLR 112, which is discussed in more detail at p. 461.
3.   Section 97(2) artificially extends the EDT, either where summary dismissal has occurred despite a period of statutory minimum notice under s. 86, or where the statutory notice required to be given is longer than the actual notice given. In either case, the ending of the s. 86 notice period is treated as the EDT.

A question arises as to whether the s. 97(2) extension of the EDT will apply in the event of a dismissal for 'gross misconduct'. This is because s. 86(6) declares that the minimum notice entitlement under the section 'does not affect any right of either party . . . to treat the contract as terminable without notice by reason of the conduct of the other party'.

The only authority on this point is *Lanton Leisure Ltd* v *White & Gibson* [1987] IRLR 119. In this case, the EAT ruled that an employer cannot avoid the effect of what is now s. 97(2) merely by dismissing summarily and labelling his reason for dismissal as gross misconduct. The EAT decided that, in such a case, 'it is first necessary to find out by means of an enquiry on the merits whether there was in fact such conduct which would enable an employer to terminate without notice'. Since the tribunal's decision on whether there has been conduct meriting summary dismissal will be virtually the same as whether the dismissal was fair or unfair, it would appear that in practice s. 86(6) does not prevent the operation of s. 97(2).

C: Stage Three: Is the Dismissal Fair or Unfair?

(i)   Potentially Fair Dismissals

Employment Rights Act 1996

98.   General

(1)   In determining for the purposes of this Part whether the dismissal of an employee is fair or unfair, it is for the employer to show—

(a)   the reason (or, if more than one, the principal reason) for the dismissal, and

(b)   that it is either a reason falling within subsection (2) or some other substantial reason of a kind such as to justify the dismissal of an employee holding the position which the employee held.

(2)   A reason falls within this subsection if it—

(a)   relates to the capability or qualifications of the employee for performing work of the kind which he was employed by the employer to do,

(b)   relates to the conduct of the employee,

(c)   is that the employee was redundant, or

(d)   is that the employee could not continue to work in the position which he held without contravention (either on his part or on that of his employer) of a duty or restriction imposed by or under an enactment.

(3)   In subsection (2)(a)—

(a)   'capability', in relation to an employee, means his capability assessed by reference to skill, aptitude, health or any other physical or mental quality, and

(b)   'qualifications', in relation to an employee, means any degree, diploma or other academic, technical or professional qualification relevant to the position which he held.

W. Devis & Sons Ltd v *Atkins*
[1977] AC 931
House of Lords

The employee was dismissed because of his refusal to comply with his employers' wishes. The employers subsequently discovered that the employee had been guilty of serious misconduct. At the hearing of the employee's unfair dismissal claim, the employers sought to adduce evidence of his misconduct to show that they had acted reasonably in the circumstances in dismissing the employee. Permission was refused. The House of Lords upheld the industrial tribunal's decision.

VISCOUNT DILHORNE: [The statutory provision to which Viscount Dilhorne refers is TULRA 1974, Sch. 1, para. 6(8). The corresponding provision is now ERA 1996, s. 98(4)]. . . . Reverting now to paragraph 6(8) it is to be observed that the paragraph does not require the tribunal to consider whether the complainant in fact suffered any injustice by being dismissed. If it had, then I see no reason to suppose that evidence subsequently discovered of the complainant's misconduct would not have been relevant to that question and admissible. The onus is on the employer to show what the reason was (paragraph 6(1)) and that it was a reason falling within paragraph 6(2) or some other substantial reason of a kind such as to justify the dismissal of an employee holding the position which that employee held. In this case the employer's reason fell within paragraph 6(2) as it related to the conduct of the respondent.

Then paragraph 6(8) requires the determination of the question whether the dismissal was unfair 'having regard to the reason shown by the employer' to depend on whether in the circumstances the employer had acted 'reasonably in treating it as a sufficient reason for dismissing the employee.'

'It' must refer to the reason shown by the employer and to the reason for which the employee was dismissed. Without doing very great violence to the language I cannot construe this paragraph as enabling the tribunal to have regard to matters of which the employer was unaware at the time of dismissal and which therefore cannot have formed part of his reason or reasons for dismissing an employee.

Paragraph 6(8) appears to me to direct the tribunal to focus its attention on the conduct of the employer and not on whether the employee in fact suffered any injustice. If in the tribunal's view the employer has failed to satisfy it that he acted reasonably in treating the reason shown to be the reason for the dismissal as a sufficient reason for that dismissal, the conclusion will be that the dismissal was unfair . . .

In my opinion it is not the case that an employer can establish that a dismissal was fair by relying on matters of which he did not know at the time but which he ought reasonably to have known. The Schedule does not so provide. If, however, the reasons shown appear to have been a sufficient reason, it cannot, in my opinion, be said that the employer acted reasonably in treating it as such if he only did so in consequence of ignoring matters which he ought reasonably to have known and which would have shown that the reason was insufficient. . . .

Notes

1. The ERA 1996, s. 92, provides that an employee who is under notice or who been dismissed has the right, on request to the employer, to be provided within 14 days with a written statement of reasons for the dismissal. The period of continuous employment necessary for ex-employees to exercise this right was reduced from two years to one year with effect from 1 June 1999 (see the Unfair Dismissal and Statement of Reasons for Dismissal (Variation of Qualifying Period) Order 1999). The significance of s. 92 is that a written statement provided under the section is expressly made admissible in subsequent proceedings. Any basic inconsistency between the contents of the statement and the reason actually put forward before the tribunal could seriously undermine the employer's case.

If an employer unreasonably refuses to comply with the request or provides particulars which are 'inadequate or untrue', the employee may present a complaint to an industrial tribunal, who may declare what it finds the reasons for dismissal are and also make an award of two weeks' wages to the employee.

The statement provided by the employer must at least contain a simple statement of the essential reasons for the dismissal but no particular form is required. Indeed, it has been held that it is acceptable for a written statement to refer the employee to earlier correspondence which contain the reasons for dismissal, attaching a copy of that correspondence (*Kent County Council* v *Gilham & Others* [1985] IRLR 16).

It does not matter whether the reason put forward by the employer is 'intrinsically a good, bad or indifferent one'; at this stage the tribunal is only concerned with identifying the genuine reason for the dismissal. So, in *Harvard Securities plc* v *Younghusband* [1990] IRLR 17, where the employers stated that they had dismissed the employee for divulging confidential information to a third party, whether the employers were correct in describing that information as 'confidential' was irrelevant to the identification of their reason for dismissal.

2.   The ERA 1996, s. 107, sets out the position where there is pressure on an employer to dismiss.

Employment Rights Act 1996

107.   Pressure on employer to dismiss unfairly
   (1)   This section applies where there falls to be determined for the purposes of this Part a question—
      (a)   as to the reason, or principal reason, for which an employee was dismissed,
      (b)   whether the reason or principal reason for which an employee was dismissed was a reason fulfilling the requirement of section 98(1)(b), or
      (c)   whether an employer acted reasonably in treating the reason or principal reason for which an employee was dismissed as a sufficient reason for dismissing him.
   (2)   In determining the question no account shall be taken of any pressure which by calling, organising, procuring or financing a strike or other industrial action, or threatening to do so, was exercised on the employer to dismiss the employee; and the question shall be determined as if no such pressure had been exercised.

Nevertheless, a trade union or union official who has exerted pressure to force the employer to dismiss a non-union member, may be joined in subsequent unfair dismissal proceedings and be ordered to pay all or part of any compensation awarded (TULR(C)A 1992, s. 160).

(ii)   Dismissals Which are Deemed to be Unfair
Certain reasons for dismissal are regarded as automatically unfair. These are as follows:

(a) *Dismissal for trade union membership and activity, or because of refusal to join a trade union or particular trade union; selection for redundancy on grounds related to union membership or activities* (TULR(C)A 1992, ss. 152 and 153; see Chapter 8).

(b) *Dismissal on the grounds of pregnancy or childbirth*

Employment Rights Act 1996

99. Pregnancy and childbirth

(1) An employee who is dismissed shall be regarded for the purposes of this Part as unfairly dismissed if—

(a) the reason (or, if more than one, the principal reason) for the dismissal is that she is pregnant or any other reason connected with her pregnancy,

(b) her maternity leave period is ended by the dismissal and the reason (or, if more than one, the principal reason) for the dismissal is that she has given birth to a child or any other reason connected with her having given birth to a child,

(c) her contract of employment is terminated after the end of her maternity leave period and the reason (or, if more than one, the principal reason) for the dismissal is that she took, or availed herself of the benefits of, maternity leave,

(d) the reason (or, if more than one, the principal reason) for the dismissal is a relevant requirement, or a relevant recommendation, as defined by section 66(2), or

(e) her maternity leave period is ended by the dismissal, the reason (or, if more than one, the principal reason) for the dismissal is that she is redundant and section 77 has not been complied with.

(2) For the purposes of subsection (1)(c)—

(a) a woman takes maternity leave if she is absent from work during her maternity leave period, and

(b) a woman avails herself of the benefits of maternity leave if, during her maternity leave period, she avails herself of the benefit of any of the terms and conditions of her employment preserved by section 71 during that period.

(3) An employee who is dismissed shall also be regarded for the purposes of this Part as unfairly dismissed if—

(a) before the end of her maternity leave period she gave to her employer a certificate from a registered medical practitioner stating that by reason of disease or bodily or mental disablement she would be incapable of work after the end of that period,

(b) her contract of employment was terminated within the period of four weeks beginning immediately after the end of her maternity leave period in circumstances in which she continued to be incapable of work and the certificate remained current, and

(c) the reason (or, if more than one, the principal reason) for the dismissal is that she has given birth to a child or any other reason connected with her having given birth to a child.

(4) Where—

(a) an employee has the right conferred by section 79,

(b) it is not practicable by reason of redundancy for the employer to permit her to return in accordance with that right, and

(c) no offer is made of such alternative employment as is referred to in section 81,

the dismissal of the employee which is treated as taking place by virtue of section 96 is to be regarded for the purposes of this Part as unfair.

Brown v *Stockton-On-Tees Borough Council*
[1988] IRLR 263
House of Lords

Mrs Brown was employed by the respondents as a care supervisor on a Youth Training Scheme funded by the Manpower Services Commission. The Commission withdrew their support from that scheme and decided to fund instead a revised one-year scheme employing fewer staff. All existing staff were invited to apply for appointments under the new scheme. If their applications were not successful, then their employment would terminate on grounds of redundancy. Mrs Brown was not selected for one of the posts because she was pregnant and would require six to eight weeks' maternity leave during the currency of the one-year scheme.

Although an industrial tribunal upheld her claim for unfair dismissal on grounds of pregnancy contrary to what is now ERA 1996, s. 99(1)(a), this decision was overturned by the EAT. According to the EAT, the reason for her dismissal was redundancy; she had been selected for redundancy in accordance with the employers' selection criteria and the dismissal was reasonable in all the circumstances within the meaning of what is now ERA 1996, s. 98(4). The Court of Appeal upheld that view on the grounds that where an employee is selected for redundancy on grounds of pregnancy, the principal reason for the dismissal is redundancy and fairness of the dismissal is tested under what is now ERA 1996, s. 98(4) and not s. 99. The House of Lords allowed Mrs Brown's appeal.

LORD GRIFFITHS: [Section 99] must be seen as part of social legislation passed for the specific protection of women and to put them on an equal footing with men. I have no doubt that it is often a considerable inconvenience to an employer to have to make the necessary arrangements to keep a woman's job open for her whilst she is absent from work in order to have a baby, but this is a price that has to be paid as a part of the social and legal recognition of the equal status of women in the workplace. If an employer dismisses a woman because she is pregnant and is not prepared to make the arrangements to cover her temporary absence from work he is deemed to have dismissed her unfairly. I can see no reason why the same principle should not apply if in a redundancy situation an employer selects the pregnant woman as the victim of redundancy in order to avoid the inconvenience of covering her absence from work in the new employment he is able to offer to others who are threatened with redundancy. It surely cannot have been intended that an employer should be entitled to take advantage of a redundancy situation to weed out his pregnant employees.

Notes

1. The reasoning in *Brown* was applied by the EAT in *Clayton* v *Vigers* [1990] IRLR 177. Mrs Vigers was employed as a dental assistant to Mr Clayton. She was dismissed by her employer during her maternity leave because he was unable to make temporary arrangements to cover her absence from work. In upholding the tribunal's finding of unfair dismissal, the EAT stated that the words 'any other reason connected with her pregnancy' in what is now s. 99(1)(a) should be 'read widely so as to give full effect to the mischief at which the statute was aimed'. Therefore, it is sufficient if the

reason for the dismissal is 'associated with pregnancy' or the after-effects of pregnancy.

2. Prior to the passage of TURERA 1993, this additional legislative protection for pregnant women was available only to those with two years' continuous service. If a woman did not have the necessary qualifying service, however, she could still challenge a pregnancy dismissal by way of the sex discrimination legislation (see our discussion of these issues in Chapter 4). Doubts as to whether the two-year barrier complied with the Equal Treatment Directive persuaded the Government to extend protection to all pregnant employees irrespective of their length of service (see now ERA 1996, s. 108(3)(b)).

(c) *Dismissal because of a conviction which is 'spent' under the terms of the Rehabilitation of Offenders Act 1974* (see s. 4(3)(b), p. 479).

(d) *Dismissal connected with the transfer of an undertaking unless there are 'economic, technical or organisational' reasons entailing changes in the workforce* (see the Transfer of Undertakings Regulations 1981, reg. 8, and Chapter 7).

(e) *Dismissal on the ground of redundancy if the circumstances constituting the redundancy also applied equally to one or more employees in the same undertaking who held posts similar to that held by the dismissed employee and they have not been dismissed and:*

(i)   the reason (or, if more than one, the principal reason) for selecting the employee was union-related (TULR(C)A 1992, s. 153); or

(ii)   the reason for the dismissal was because of pregnancy or childbirth, or because the employee had been involved in raising or taking action on health and safety issues (see (f) below); asserted certain statutory rights (see (g) below); performed (or proposed to perform) any functions as a trustee of an occupational pension scheme (see (h) below); performed (or proposed to perform) the functions or activities of an employee representative for the purpose of consultation over redundancies or the transfer of an undertaking; or, as a 'protected' or 'opted out' shop or betting worker, refused to work on a Sunday (see (i) below) (ERA 1996, s. 105).

(f) *Dismissal of employees in health and safety cases* (ERA 1996, s. 100).

Employment Rights Act 1996

100. Health and safety cases

(1)   An employee who is dismissed shall be regarded for the purposes of this Part as unfairly dismissed if the reason (or, if more than one, the principal reason) for the dismissal is that—

(a)   having been designated by the employer to carry out activities in connection with preventing or reducing risks to health and safety at work, the employee carried out (or proposed to carry out) any such activities,

(b)   being a representative of workers on matters of health and safety at work or member of a safety committee—

(i)   in accordance with arrangements established under or by virtue of any enactment, or

(ii)   by reason of being acknowledged as such by the employer, the employee performed (or proposed to perform) any functions as such a representative or a member of such a committee,

    (c) being an employee at a place where—

        (i)   there was no such representative or safety comrnittee, or

        (ii) there was such a representative or safety committee but it was not reasonably practicable for the employee to raise the matter by those means,

he brought to his employer's attention, by reasonable means, circumstances connected with his work which he reasonably believed were harmful or potentially harmful to health or safety,

    (d) in circumstances of danger which the employee reasonably believed to be serious and imminent and which he could not reasonably have been expected to avert, he left (or proposed to leave) or (while the danger persisted) refused to return to his place of work or any dangerous part of his place of work, or

    (e) in circumstances of danger which the employee reasonably believed to be serious and imminent, he took (or proposed to take) appropriate steps to protect himself or other persons from the danger.

    (2) For the purposes of subsection (1)(e) whether steps which an employee took (or proposed to take) were appropriate is to be judged by reference to all the circumstances including, in particular, his knowledge and the facilities and advice available to him at the time.

    (3) Where the reason (or, if more than one, the principal reason) for the dismissal of an employee is that specified in subsection (1)(e), he shall not be regarded as unfairly dismissed if the employer shows that it was (or would have been) so negligent for the employee to take the steps which he took (or proposed to take) that a reasonable employer might have dismissed him for taking (or proposing to take) them.

Note

This is part of an new set of employment protection rights introduced by TURERA 1993 in order to implement the EC Framework Directive on measures to encourage improvements in the safety and health of workers at work (89/391). A dismissal in any of the above situations will be automatically unfair, except where the employer is able to establish a defence of 'negligence' by the employee. Selection for redundancy in any of the above situations will be for an 'inadmissible' reason, and therefore automatically unfair (ERA 1996, s. 105(3)). There are no qualifying hours of work or periods of service in order to enforce either of the dismissal protection rights.

By virtue of ERA 1996, s. 44, such workers also have the right not to suffer any detriment short of dismissal.

The remedies are akin to those available in the case of victimisation relating to trade union membership (see Chapter 8). In the case of dismissal, employees will also be able to apply for 'interim relief' pending the full hearing of an industrial tribunal complaint (see p. 645, note 4).

    (g) *Dismissal following disputes over working time.*

Employment Rights Act 1996

101A. Working time cases

An employee who is dismissed shall be regarded for the purposes of this Part as unfairly dismissed if the reason (or, if more than one, the principal reason) for the dismissal is that the employee—

(a) refused (or proposed to refuse) to comply with a requirement which the employer imposed (or proposed to impose) in contravention of the Working Time Regulations 1998,

(b) refused (or proposed to refuse) to forgo a right conferred on him by those Regulations,

(c) failed to sign a workforce agreement for the purposes of those Regulations, or to enter into, or agree to vary or extend, any other agreement with his employer which is provided for in those Regulations, or

(d) being—

(i) a representative of members of the workforce for the purposes of Schedule 1 to those Regulations, or

(ii) a candidate in an election in which any person elected will, on being elected, be such a representative,

performed (or proposed to perform) any functions or activities as such a representative or candidate.

Note

Although protection in the Working Time Regulations is given broadly to 'workers', the protection of this section is given to 'employees' in line with the remainder of unfair dismissal law.

Exercise of statutory rights under the Regulations is also covered by s. 104(4)(d), as added, and protection is given against redundancy selection on those grounds (s. 105(4A)). The qualifying period does not apply, nor the upper age limit (ss. 108(3), 109(2)), and interim relief and a special award of compensation are available (ss. 118(3), 128(1)).

For further discussion of the Working Time Regulations, see p. 876.

(h) *Dismissal on the grounds of the assertion of a statutory right* (ERA 1996, s. 104).

Employment Rights Act 1996

104. Assertion of statutory right

(1) An employee who is dismissed shall be regarded for the purposes of this Part as unfairly dismissed if the reason (or, if more than one, the principal reason) for the dismissal is that the employee—

(a) brought proceedings against the employer to enforce a right of his which is a relevant statutory right, or

(b) alleged that the employer had infringed a right of his which is a relevant statutory right.

(2) It is immaterial for the purposes of subsection (1)—

(a) whether or not the employee has the right, or

(b) whether or not the right has been infringed;

but, for that subsection to apply, the claim to the right and that it has been infringed must be made in good faith.

(3) It is sufficient for subsection (1) to apply that the employee, without specifying the right, made it reasonably clear to the employer what the right claimed to have been infringed was.

(4) The following are relevant statutory rights for the purposes of this section—

(a)   any right conferred by this Act for which the remedy for its infringement is by way of a complaint or reference to an industrial tribunal,

(b)   the right conferred by section 86 of this Act, and

(c)   the rights conferred by sections 68, 86, 146, 168, 169 and 170 of the Trade Union and Labour Relations (Consolidation) Act 1992 (deductions from pay, union activities and time off)[, and

(d)   the rights conferred by the Working Time Regulations 1998.]

Notes

1.   A welcome and long overdue amendment to the legislation achieved by TURERA 1993. Previously, only those who were involved in asserting rights against sex and race discrimination were offered any measure of protection against victimisation. The amendments introduced by TURERA 1993 also render selection for redundancy on the ground that the employee has asserted a relevant statutory right an inadmissible reason (see ERA 1996, s. 105(7)). There is no qualifying period of employment for those victimised in the manner described by s. 104 (see ERA 1996, s. 108(3)(g)).

2.   *Mennell v Newell & Wright (Transport Contractors) Ltd* (1997) IRLR 519 was the first case to be considered by the Court of Appeal under this jurisdiction. The applicant was dismissed after having refused to accept new contractual arrangements, which included a clause permitting the employers to recover certain training costs by way of deduction from final salary on termination of employment. As he lacked the then normal requirement of two years' service for unfair dismissal, Mr Mennell claimed that there was a contravention of s. 104 because the deduction of wages without consent would be unlawful. The industrial tribunal held that there was no actual infringement of any right relating to wages which could form the basis of a claim, and therefore no infringement of a relevant statutory right. The Court of Appeal, however, confirmed that there *can* be a claim based on dismissal for asserting a statutory right even where there was no showing that the relevant statutory right had been infringed by the employers.

It is sufficient if the employee has alleged that his employer infringed his statutory right and that the making of that allegation was the reason or the principal reason for his dismissal. The allegation need not be specific, provided that it has been made reasonably clear to the employer what right was claimed to have been infringed. The allegation need not be correct, either as to entitlement to the right or as to its infringement, provided that the claim was made in good faith. (per Mummery LJ).

However, in the instant case, as the employee was unable to show that he had ever made an allegation that the employers were in breach of a statutory right, such an allegation could not have been the reason for his dismissal and his claim failed.

Question

In practice, will it be easy to distinguish between a dismissal for refusing to accept a contractual change (as in Mennell) and dismissal for protesting that the proposed contractual change breaches a statutory right?

3. Section 25 of the National Minimum Wage Act 1998 inserts a new s. 104A and a new s. 105(7A) into the ERA 1996. They provide that employees who are dismissed or selected for redundancy will be regarded as unfairly dismissed if the sole or main reason for the dismissal or selection was that:

(a) they asserted in good faith their right to the national minimum wage, their right of access to records or their right to recover the difference between what (if anything) they have been paid and the national minimum wage; or

(b) as a result of such an assertion, their employer was prosecuted for an offence under the Act; or

(c) they qualify, or will or might qualify for the national minimum wage or for a particular national minimum wage rate.

The normal qualifying period for unfair dismissal does not apply (s. 108(3) (gg)), nor does the upper age limit (s. 109(2)(gg)).

(i) *An employee who is a trustee of an occupational pension scheme established under a trust will be regarded as unfairly dismissed if the reason (or, if more than one, the principal reason) for the dismissal is that the employee performed (or proposed to perform) any of the functions of a trustee* (ERA 1996, s. 102).

(j) *A 'protected' or 'opted-out' shop or betting worker who is dismissed for refusing to work on a Sunday shall be regarded as unfairly dismissed. Similarly, it will be unfair to dismiss a shop or betting worker because he or she gave (or proposed to give) an opting-out notice to the employer* (ERA 1996, s. 101).

Broadly, a shop or betting worker is 'protected' if, before the commencement dates of the legislation which liberalised Sunday trading and betting, he or she was not required under the contract of employment to work on Sunday. A shop or betting worker who is contractually required to work on a Sunday may give three months' written notice of his or her intention to 'opt out' of Sunday working at the end of the notice period but not before (ERA 1996, Pt IV).

(k) *Dismissal for making a protected disclosure.*

Employment Rights Act 1996

103A. Protected disclosure
An employee who is dismissed shall be regarded for the purposes of this Part as unfairly dismissed if the reason (or, if more than one, the principal reason) for the dismissal is that the employee made a protected disclosure.

Part IVA of the 1996 Act defines protected disclosures:

Employment Rights Act 1996

PART IVA
PROTECTED DISCLOSURES

43A. Meaning of 'protected disclosure'
In this Act a 'protected disclosure' means a qualifying disclosure (as defined by section 43B) which is made by a worker in accordance with any of sections 43C to 43H.

43B.   Disclosures qualifying for protection

(1)   In this Part a 'qualifying disclosure' means any disclosure of information which, in the reasonable belief of the worker making the disclosure, tends to show one or more of the following—

    (a)   that a criminal offence has been committed, is being committed or is likely to be committed,

    (b)   that a person has failed, is failing or is likely to fail to comply with any legal obligation to which he is subject,

    (c)   that a miscarriage of justice has occurred, is occurring or is likely to occur,

    (d)   that the health or safety of any individual has been, is being or is likely to be endangered,

    (e)   that the environment has been, is being or is likely to be damaged, or

    (f)   that information tending to show any matter falling within any one of the preceding paragraphs has been, or is likely to be deliberately concealed.

(2)   For the purposes of subsection (1), it is immaterial whether the relevant failure occurred, occurs or would occur in the United Kingdom or elsewhere, and whether the law applying to it is that of the United Kingdom or of any other country or territory.

(3)   A disclosure of information is not a qualifying disclosure if the person making the disclosure commits an offence by making it.

(4)   A disclosure of information in respect of which a claim to legal professional privilege (or, in Scotland, to confidentiality as between client and professional legal adviser) could be maintained in legal proceedings is not a qualifying disclosure if it is made by a person to whom the information had been disclosed in the course of obtaining legal advice.

(5)   In this Part 'the relevant failure', in relation to a qualifying disclosure, means the matter falling within paragraphs (a) to (f) of subsection (1).

43C.   Disclosure to employer or other responsible person

(1)   A qualifying disclosure is made in accordance with this section if the worker makes the disclosure in good faith—

    (a)   to his employer, or

    (b)   where the worker reasonably believes that the relevant failure relates solely or mainly to—

        (i)   the conduct of a person other than his employer, or

        (ii)   any other matter for which a person other than his employer has legal responsibility,

to that other person.

(2)   A worker who, in accordance with a procedure whose use by him is authorised by his employer, makes a qualifying disclosure to a person other than his employer, is to be treated for the purposes of this Part as making the qualifying disclosure to his employer.

43D.   Disclosure to legal adviser

A qualifying disclosure is made in accordance with this section if it is made in the course of obtaining legal advice.

43E.   Disclosure to Minister of the Crown

A qualifying disclosure is made in accordance with this section if—

    (a)   the worker's employer is—

        (i)   an individual appointed under any enactment by a Minister of the Crown, or

    (ii)   a body any of whose members are so appointed, and

(b)   the disclosure is made in good faith to a Minister of the Crown.

43F. Disclosure to prescribed person

(1) A qualifying disclosure is made in accordance with this section if the worker—

    (a)   makes the disclosure in good faith to a person prescribed by an order made by the Secretary of State for the purposes of this section, and

    (b)   reasonably believes—

        (i)   that the relevant failure falls within any description of matters in respect of which that person is so prescribed, and

        (ii)   that the information disclosed, and any allegation contained in it, are substantially true.

(2) An order prescribing persons for the purposes of this section may specify persons or descriptions of persons, and shall specify the descriptions of matters in respect of which each person, or persons of each description, is or are prescribed.

43G. Disclosure in other cases

(1) A qualifying disclosure is made in accordance with this section if—

    (a)   the worker makes the disclosure in good faith,

    (b)   he reasonably believes that the information disclosed, and any allegation contained in it, are substantially true,

    (c)   he does not make the disclosure for purposes of personal gain,

    (d)   any of the conditions in subsection (2) is met, and

    (e)   in all the circumstances of the case, it is reasonable for him to make the disclosure.

(2) The conditions referred to in subsection (1)(d) are—

    (a)   that, at the time he makes the disclosure, the worker reasonably believes that he will be subjected to a detriment by his employer if he makes a disclosure to his employer or in accordance with section 43F,

    (b)   that, in a case where no person is prescribed for the purposes of section 43F in relation to the relevant failure, the worker reasonably believes that it is likely that evidence relating to the relevant failure will be concealed or destroyed if he makes a disclosure to his employer, or

    (c)   that the worker has previously made a disclosure of substantially the same information—

        (i)   to his employer, or

        (ii)   in accordance with section 43F.

(3) In determining for the purposes of subsection (1)(e) whether it is reasonable for the worker to make the disclosure, regard shall be had, in particular, to—

    (a)   the identity of the person to whom the disclosure is made,

    (b)   the seriousness of the relevant failure,

    (c)   whether the relevant failure is continuing or is likely to occur in the future,

    (d)   whether the disclosure is made in breach of a duty of confidentiality owed by the employer to any other person,

    (e)   in a case falling within subsection (2)(c)(i) or (ii), any action which the employer or the person to whom the previous disclosure in accordance with section 43F was made has taken or might reasonably be expected to have taken as a result of the previous disclosure, and

    (f)   in a case falling within subsection (2)(c)(i), whether in making the disclosure to the employer the worker complied with any procedure whose use by him was authorised by the employer.

(4)   For the purposes of this section a subsequent disclosure may be regarded as a disclosure of substantially the same information as that disclosed by a previous disclosure as mentioned in subsection (2)(c) even though the subsequent disclosure extends to information about action taken or not taken by any person as a result of the previous disclosure.

43H.   Disclosure of exceptionally serious failure
(1)   A qualifying disclosure is made in accordance with this section if—
(a)   the worker makes the disclosure in good faith,
(b)   he reasonably believes that the information disclosed, and any allegation contained in it, are substantially true,
(c)   he does not make the disclosure for purposes of personal gain,
(d)   the relevant failure is of an exceptionally serious nature, and
(e)   in all the circumstances of the case, it is reasonable for him to make the disclosure.
(2)   In determining for the purposes of subsection (1)(e) whether it is reasonable for the worker to make the disclosure, regard shall be had, in particular, to the identity of the person to whom the disclosure is made.

43J.   Contractual duties of confidentiality
(1)   Any provision in an agreement to which this section applies is void in so far as it purports to preclude the worker from making a protected disclosure.
(2)   This section applies to any agreement between a worker and his employer (whether a worker's contract or not), including an agreement to refrain from instituting or continuing any proceedings under this Act or any proceedings for breach of contract.

Notes
1.   As noted in Chapter 2, the Public Interest Disclosure Act 1998 began life as a Private Member's Bill. Its aims are 'to protect individuals who make certain disclosures of information in the public interest; to allow such individuals to bring action in respect of victimisation; and for connected purposes. Section 103A was incorporated within the ERA 1996 by s.5 of the 1998 Act. No qualifying period of service is required and the normal age restrictions on claimants are lifted. Section 105(6A) of the ERA 1996 also makes it unfair to select employees for redundancy if the reason (or, if more than one, the principal reason) for which the employee was selected for dismissal was that he or she made a protected disclosure.
2.   Section 127B of the ERA 1996 empowers the Secretary of State to make regulations determining how compensation for dismissal in breach of s. 103A or s. 105(6A) is to be calculated. By virtue of amendments to s. 128(1)(b) and s. 129(1), the interim relief remedy is extended to protected disclosure dismissals.
3.   While only *employees* can claim unfair dismissal as a result of making a protected disclosure, the Act protects a much wider category of workers from suffering a detriment where such disclosures are made. Indeed, s. 43K(1) of ERA 1996 seeks to include individuals who would not normally fit within the statutory definition of 'worker' set out in s. 230(3). The extended definition encompasses agency workers; certain workers who would not otherwise be covered because they are not obliged to carry out all of their duties personally;

NHS practitioners such as GPs, dentists, opticians and pharmacists; and certain work experience trainees.

4.   The definition of 'detriment' makes it clear that it covers both actions and deliberate failures to act (ERA 1996, s. 47B(1)). Examples of detriment might include dismissal, pay cuts, or failure to offer a pay rise or training opportunities.

5.   Compensation for suffering a detriment is normally unlimited. However, a limit is imposed on those workers who have suffered a detriment by having their employment terminated. In such a case, compensation must not exceed that which could be awarded to an employee making a claim for unfair dismissal under s. 103A (see ERA 1996, s. 49(6)). The aim of this provision is to ensure that those who are not employees do not receive higher compensation than employees claiming unfair dismissal for making a protected disclosure. In any case, such an eventuality is much less likely with the increase in the compensatory award for unfair dismissal brought about by the Employment Relations Act 1999.

6.   For a detailed discussion of the Public Interest Disclosure Act 1998, see Lewis, D., (1998) 27 ILJ 325, who concludes:

Whilst this legislation is to be welcomed for extending individual rights, its limitations in promoting a culture of openness must also be acknowledged First, it does not *oblige* employers either to have a policy on the reporting of concerns about impropriety, or a procedure for making disclosures. Secondly, there is nothing to prevent employers refusing to hire workers on the basis that they are known to have made a protected disclosure. Thirdly, the sheer complexity of the amendments to the ERA 1996 means that potential disclosers will need proper advice if they are to discharge the burdens that are imposed upon them. Unfortunately, advisers will also have to point out that !f a reasonable belief turns out to be incorrect, defamation proceedings could be commenced against a worker who has made a protected disclosure! Where there has been sufficient publication, a discloser who failed to establish the truth of the allegations would have to rely on the defence of qualified privilege. In the author's opinion, it would have been useful if the Act had expressly provided that those who make a protected disclosure are entitled to rely on this defence. Indeed, since disclosures are only protected if they are made 'in good faith', it might be argued that the defence of absolute privilege should be available.

(l)   *Dismissal for exercising the right to be accompanied or to accompany at a disciplinary or grievance hearing* (Employment Relations Act 1999, s. 12). For further details see pp. 456–459.

(iii)   *Did the Employer Act Reasonably?*

Employment Rights Act 1996

98.   General

. . .

(4)   Where the employer has fulfilled the requirements of subsection (1), the determination of the question whether the dismissal is fair or unfair (having regard to the reason shown by the employer)—

(a)   depends on whether in the circumstances (including the size and administrative resources of the employer's undertaking) the employer acted reasonably or
unreasonably in treating it as a sufficient reason for dismissing the employee, and

(b)   shall be determined in accordance with equity and the substantial merits of
the case.

Note

Prior to 1980, the burden of proof in unfair dismissal claims at this stage was
on the employer. The EA 1980 amended the test, primarily by removing the
requirement that the employer *shall* satisfy the industrial tribunal as to the
reasonableness of his action, and so rendered the burden of proof 'neutral'.
A further amendment required tribunals to have regard to the size and
administrative resources of the employer's undertaking in assessing the
reasonableness of the dismissal. The specific reference to size and administrative resources is an encouragement to tribunals to be less exacting in their
examination of the disciplinary standards and procedures of small employers.

Iceland Frozen Foods v *Jones*
[1982] IRLR 439
Employment Appeal Tribunal

BROWNE-WILKINSON J: Since the state of the present law can only be found by
going through a number of different authorities, it may be convenient if we should
summarise the present law. We consider that the authorities establish that in law the
correct approach for the industrial tribunal to adopt in answering the question posed
by [ERA 1996, s. 98(4)] is as follows:

(1)   the starting point should always be the words of [s. 98(4)] themselves;

(2)   in applying the section an industrial tribunal must consider the reasonableness
of the employer's conduct, not simply whether they (the members of the industrial
tribunal) consider the dismissal to be fair;

(3)   in judging the reasonableness of the employer's conduct an industrial tribunal
must not substitute its decision as to what was the right course to adopt for that of
the employer;

(4)   in many (though not all) cases where there is a band of reasonable responses
to the employee's conduct within which one employer might reasonably take one view,
another might quite reasonably take another;

(5)   the function of the industrial tribunal, as an industrial jury, is to determine
whether in the particular circumstances of each case the decision to dismiss the
employee fell within the band of reasonable responses which a reasonable employer
might have adopted. If the dismissal falls within the band, the dismissal is fair; if the
dismissal falls outside the band it is unfair.

Note
See also *British Leyland (UK) Ltd* v *Swift* [1981] IRLR 91, CA.

Question
To what extent does the 'band of reasonable responses' test restrict managerial prerogative in the area of dismissal?

Notes

1. 1. More recently, in *Haddon v Van Den Bergh Foods Ltd* [1999] IRLR 672, the EAT has held that the 'range of reasonable responses' test is an unhelpful gloss on the statute and should no longer be applied by employment tribunals. Instead, the test of fairness should be applied 'without embellishment, and without using mantras so favoured by lawyers in this field' (per Morrison J). In place of the authorities favouring the band of reasonableness test, the EAT advocates the approach adopted in *Gilham v Kent County Council (No. 2)* [1985] IRLR 18, CA. This latter decision emphasised that whether a dismissal was fair or unfair is a pure question of fact for the tribunal. We await guidance from the Court of Appeal on what is the correct test for reasonableness.

2. The following case examines the substantive merits of the decision to dismiss.

Proctor v British Gypsum Ltd
[1992] IRLR 7
Employment Appeal Tribunal

Mr Proctor, an acting foreman, was dismissed for assaulting a fellow employee who was under his supervision. Fighting was specified in the employer's disciplinary rules as gross misconduct which 'may result in dismissal'. Mr Proctor claimed unfair dismissal arguing that his dismissal was inconsistent with the penalty imposed in the past and that, therefore, the normal disciplinary result for fighting was not dismissal. The majority of the tribunal concluded that the employers had considered each incident on its merits and that the decision to dismiss was reasonable in all the circumstances of the case. Mr Proctor's appeal was dismissed by the EAT.

WOOD J (President): There are three cases to which we were referred and which are the three principal cases relevant to this issue. The first is *The Post Office v Fennell* [1981] IRLR 221. This case establishes that it is open to an Industrial Tribunal to classify as unfair a dismissal which demonstrates inconsistency on the part of the employer even though in any and every respect the employer's actions have been reasonable. It also stresses as indicated in the judgment of Lord Justice Brandon that it was for the Industrial Tribunal to say what weight they attach to the evidence and that inconsistency was essentially a question of fact for the Industrial Tribunal.

The second case is *Hadjioannou v Coral Casinos Ltd* [1981] IRLR 352. The facts of that case are not particularly material but its importance is in the guidance given by this Court presided over by Mr Justice Waterhouse in paras. 24, 25 and 26:

24. In resisting the appeal, counsel for the respondents, Mr Tabachnik, has submitted that an argument by a dismissed employee based upon disparity can only be relevant in limited circumstances. He suggests that, in broad terms, there are only three sets of circumstances in which such an argument may be relevant to a decision by an Industrial Tribunal under [s. 98 of the Act of 1996]. Firstly, it may be relevant if there is evidence that certain categories of conduct will be either overlooked, or at least will not be dealt with by the sanction of dismissal. Secondly, there may be cases in which evidence about decisions made in relation to other cases

supports an inference that the purported reason stated by the employers is not the real or genuine reason for a dismissal. Mr Tabachnik illustrates that situation by the argument advanced in the present case on behalf of the appellant, that the general manager was determined to get rid of him and merely used the evidence about the incidents with customers as an occasion or excuse for dismissing him. If that had been the case, the Industrial Tribunal would have reached a different conclusion on the appellant's complaint but they considered the submissions about it and rejected them. Thirdly, Mr Tabachnik concedes that evidence as to decisions made by an employer in truly parallel circumstances may be sufficient to support an argument, in a particular case, that it was not reasonable on the part of the employer to visit the employee's conduct with the penalty of dismissal and that some lesser penalty would have been appropriate in the circumstances.

25.   We accept that analysis by counsel for the respondents of the potential relevance of arguments based on disparity. We should add, however, as counsel has urged upon us, that Industrial Tribunals would be wise to scrutinise arguments based on upon disparity with particular care. It is only in the limited circumstances that we have indicated that the argument is likely to be relevant and there will not be many cases in which the evidence supports the proposition that there are other cases which are truly similar, or sufficiently similar, to afford an adequate basis for the argument. The danger of the argument is that a Tribunal may be led away from a proper consideration of the issues raised by [s. 98(4) of the Act of 1996]. The emphasis in that section is upon the particular circumstances of the individual employee's case. It would be most regrettable if Tribunals or employers were to be encouraged to adopt rules of thumb, or codes, for dealing with industrial relations problems and, in particular, issues arising when dismissal is being considered. It is of the highest importance that flexibility should be retained, and we hope that nothing that we say in the course of our judgment will encourage employers or Tribunals to think that a tariff approach to industrial misconduct is appropriate. One has only to consider for a moment the dangers of the tariff approach in other spheres of the law to realise how inappropriate it would be to import it into this particular legislation.

26.   At the end of the argument, we have not been persuaded that the evidence in this case established any inconsistency of treatment by the respondents of employees in relation to breaches of the socialising rule. It was open to the Industrial Tribunal to take the view that inconsistency had not been established and this part of the appeal is based on an issue of fact rather than one involving a question of law. For that reason we are unable to uphold the appeal on the ground of disparity.

Finally, we would refer to the recent decision in this Court of *Cain* v *Leeds Western Health Authority* [1990] IRLR 168 (Sir David Croom-Johnson, T.S. Batho and R.J. Lewis). Mr Batho is a member of the present Court. In that case Mr Cain was a hospital laundry worker and was summarily dismissed by the health authority on the ground of gross misconduct for fighting with a fellow employee. He complained to an Industrial Tribunal of unfair dismissal. The Tribunal considered the cases of two other employees which had not resulted in dismissal for gross misconduct put forward as comparable, but rejected consideration of those two further cases on the ground that they had occurred seven years earlier at different hospitals. The reason for rejecting those comparables was that the other cases had been dealt with by different personnel on behalf of the authority and could not necessarily be said to be therefore comparable with the present case in assessing inconsistency. This Court held that an employer must act consistently between all employees and it was no answer that the decision in the other cases had been taken by different servants or agents of the employer. This was held to amount to material misdirection.

As in so many aspects of industrial relations a reasoned and reasonable balance must be sought. This is emphasised in *Hadjioannou*. Before reaching a decision to dismiss an employer should consider truly comparable cases of which he knew or ought reasonably to have known. The information may be forthcoming at the initial stage or on appeal. If the employee or those representing him know of other such incidents it will no doubt be in his best interests that they should be identified or at least drawn to the attention of the employer. If necessary an adjournment can be taken for further investigation. A small concern may not keep any records of dismissal; a large employer may do so as a matter of sound administration. We do not suggest any obligation so to do. Unless the personnel manager has been in post for a substantial period it may be reasonable to make enquiry of others, as did Mr Scott in the present case.

Industrial situations within a unit or on a site may change from time to time as may physical conditions. There may be an increase in dishonesty, fighting or absenteeism. Thus, it may not be reasonable to look back more than a few years.

These may be some but by no means all the factors which may be relevant to the approach of this employer in these circumstances. The question will always be one of fairness.

Whatever the relevant factors, the overriding principles must be that each case must be considered on its own facts and with freedom to consider mitigating aspects. The dangers of a tariff and of untrue comparability are only too obvious. Not every case of leniency should be considered to be a deviation from declared policy.

For the reasons we have given, this appeal is dismissed. Leave to appeal.

Notes
1. See also *London Borough of Harrow* v *Cunningham* [1996] IRLR 356, EAT.
2. With regard to disciplinary matters, employers should practise procedural fairness.

Trade Union and Labour Relations (Consolidation) Act 1992

207. Effect of failure to comply with Code
(1) A failure on the part of any person to observe any provision of a Code of Practice issued under this Chapter shall not of itself render him liable to any proceedings.
(2) In any proceedings before an industrial tribunal or the Central Arbitration Committee any Code of Practice issued under this Chapter by ACAS shall be admissible in evidence, and any provision of the Code which appears to the tribunal or Committee to be relevant to any question arising in the proceedings shall be taken into account in determining that question.

Note
The concept of procedural fairness is not expressly articulated in the legislation, but its development was influenced by the Code of Practice which was introduced to accompany the legislation. The Code was originally issued by

ACAS under the EPA 1975, s. 6, and was brought into effect on 20 June 1977 (by SI 1977/867). The revised Code was issued under TULR(C)A 1992, s. 201, and came into effect on 5 February 1998 (SI 1998/44).

ACAS Code of Practice 1
Disciplinary Practices and Procedures in Employment

Essential features of disciplinary procedures
9. Disciplinary procedures should not be viewed primarily as a means of imposing sanctions. They should also be designed to emphasise and encourage improvements in individual conduct.

10. Disciplinary procedures should:
(a) Be in writing.
(b) Specify to whom they apply.
(c) Provide for matters to be dealt with quickly.
(d) Indicate the disciplinary actions which may be taken.
(e) Specify the levels of management which have the authority to take the various forms of disciplinary action, ensuring that immediate superiors do not normally have the power to dismiss without reference to senior management.
(f) Provide for individuals to be informed of the complaints against them and to be given an opportunity to state their case before decisions are reached.
(g) Give individuals the right to be accompanied by a trade union representative or by a fellow employee of their choice.
(h) Ensure that, except for gross misconduct, no employees are dismissed for a first breach of discipline.
(i) Ensure that disciplinary action is not taken until the case has been carefully investigated.
(j) Ensure that individuals are given an explanation for any penalty imposed.
(k) Provide a right of appeal and specify the procedure to be followed.

The procedure in operation
11. When a disciplinary matter arises, the supervisor or manager should first establish the facts promptly before recollections fade, taking into account the statements of any available witnesses. In serious cases consideration should be given to a brief period of suspension while the case is investigated and this suspension should be with pay. Before a decision is made or penalty imposed the individual should be interviewed and given the opportunity to state his or her case and should be advised of any rights under the procedure, including the right to be accompanied.

12. Often supervisors will give informal oral warnings for the purpose of improving conduct when employees commit minor infringements of the established standards of conduct. However, where the facts of the case appear to call for disciplinary action, other than summary dismissal, the following procedure should normally be observed:
(a) In the case of minor offences the individual should be given a formal oral warning or if the issue is more serious, there should be a written warning setting out the nature of the offence and the likely consequences of further offences. In either case the individual should be advised that the warning constitutes the first formal stage of the procedure.
(b) Further misconduct might warrant a final written warning which should contain a statement that any recurrence would lead to suspension or dismissal or some other penalty, as the case may be.

(c) The final step might be disciplinary transfer, or disciplinary suspension without pay (but only if these are allowed for by an express or implied condition of the contract of employment), or dismissal, according to the nature of the misconduct. Special consideration should be given before imposing disciplinary suspension without pay and it should not normally be for a prolonged period.

13. Except in the event of an oral warning, details of any disciplinary action should be given in writing to the employee and if desired, to his or her representative. At the same time the employee should be told of any right to appeal, how to make it and to whom.

14. When determining the disciplinary action to be taken the supervisor or manager should bear in mind the need to satisfy the test of reasonableness in all the circumstances. So far as possible, account should be taken of the employee's record and any other relevant factors.

15. . . .

16. . . .

17. . . .

Records
18. Records should be kept, detailing the nature of any breach of disciplinary rules, the action taken and the reasons for it, whether an appeal was lodged, its outcome and any subsequent developments. These records should be carefully safeguarded and kept confidential.

19. Except in agreed special circumstances breaches of disciplinary rules should be disregarded after a specified period of satisfactory conduct.

Note
In 1987, ACAS produced an updated and enlarged draft code of practice for the consideration of Lord Young, the then Secretary of State for Employment. The draft code offered advice on the handling of dismissals in general, together with more detailed consideration of common types of disciplinary problems such as absenteeism, sub-standard work and dishonesty. This guidance was based on the principles which had emerged from 15 years of unfair dismissal case law. Unfortunately, the draft code was rejected by Lord Young because he thought it over-lengthy and too detailed, 'aimed primarily at lawyers and personnel managers in larger firms', and incapable of application by a small employer. Following rejection of the draft code, ACAS published much of the material it contained in the form of an advisory handbook entitled *Discipline at Work*. Though the handbook has no statutory force, given that it concisely summarises the views of the leading cases on what constitutes good disciplinary practice, it is well worthy of careful study and may well be influential in employment tribunal adjudications.

Auguste Noel Ltd v *Curtis*
[1990] IRLR 326
Employment Appeal Tribunal

Mr Curtis, a 'multi-drop' driver, was dismissed on 18 March 1988 for an act of misconduct involving mishandling company property. In deciding to dismiss him for that offence, the employer took into account two previous written warnings; one dated 16 October 1987 concerning his relationship with other employees and the other, dated 25 February 1988, which referred to unsatisfactory documentation and absenteeism. The EAT held that the tribunal had been wrong to find that the dismissal for mishandling company property was unfair because, in deciding to dismiss for that reason, the employer had taken into account two final written warnings for different offences.

WOOD J: . . . [I]t can very rarely be said, if ever, that warnings are irrelevant to the consideration of an employer who is considering dismissal. The mere fact that the conduct was of a different kind on those occasions when warnings were given does not seem to us to render them irrelevant. It is essentially a matter of balance, of doing what is fair and reasonable in the circumstances and the employer is entitled to consider the existence of warnings. He is entitled to look at the substance of the complaint on each of those occasions, how many warnings there have been, the dates and the periods of time between those warnings and indeed all the circumstances of the case.

Notes
1. Given the relative lack of authority on the point and the fact that the advice in ACAS Code No. 1 and the advisory handbook seems to affirm the basis that warnings are being given for the same reason, it may be that employers are still best advised to keep warnings for different offences separate. Of course, there may come a point when the cumulative effect of a number of warnings on different matters provides reasonable grounds to dismiss on the ground of generally unacceptable behaviour (see Smith, I. T., and Thomas, G. H., and Wood's *Industrial Law* (6th edn) (London: Butterworths, 1996), p. 371).
2. The advisory handbook produced by ACAS also covers cases of gross misconduct.

Discipline at Work, The ACAS Advisory Handbook, 1987

Dismissal without notice
Employers should give all employees a clear indication of the type of misconduct which in the light of the requirements of the employer's business, will warrant dismissal without the normal period of notice or pay in lieu of notice. So far as possible the types of offence which fall into this category (gross misconduct) should be clearly specified in the rules.

A dismissal for gross misconduct should only take place after the normal investigation to establish all the facts. The employee should be told of the complaint and given an opportunity to state his or her case and be represented.

Gross misconduct is generally seen as misconduct serious enough to destroy the employment contract between the employer and employee and make any further working relationship and trust impossible. It is normally restricted to very serious offences – for example physical violence, theft or fraud – but may be determined by the nature of the business and other circumstances.

Note

The ERA 1996, s. 3(1)(a), requires that the written statement of terms of employment must include 'any disciplinary rules applicable to the employee'. However, the EA 1989 removed the statutory requirement to provide a note of disciplinary rules and appeals procedure where the number of employees of the employer and any associated employer is fewer than 20 (see now ERA 1996, s. 3(3)). This amendment is yet a further example of the previous Government's policy of deregulation in the name of encouraging the growth of small businesses. However, given that a factor which will be influential in many dismissal cases is whether the employer adequately brought the existence of a particular disciplinary rule to the attention of an employee, small employers might be well-advised not to take advantage of this exemption.

Ladbroke Racing v *Arnott*
[1983] IRLR 154
Court of Session

The applicants were employed in a betting shop. The employer's disciplinary rules specifically provided that employees were not permitted to place bets or to allow other staff to do so. Two of the applicants had placed such bets, one for her brother on one occasion, and the other occasionally for old-age pensioners, and the third, the office manager, had condoned these actions. All three employees were dismissed and an industrial tribunal found the dismissals to be unfair. This decision was upheld by the EAT and the Court of Session.

LORD DUNPARK: It was the appellants who failed to appreciate that paragraph 6(8) [see now ERA 1996, s. 98(4)] required them to have regard to all the circumstances of the case against each employee if they were to satisfy the industrial tribunal that their dismissals were fair. If the appellants' attitude is that any breach, however minor, of the rule, which carries the penalty of immediate dismissal, warrants immediate dismissal, then they cannot meet the standard set by paragraph 6(8). As there was no positive evidence in this case that the appellants' reason for dismissal was based upon factors other than breach of the rule *per se*, they could not comply with the provisions of paragraph 6(8), which the Appeal Tribunal correctly describes as 'over-riding provisions'. That means that they are superimposed on the rule which carries the penalty of instant dismissal, so that the appellants could not satisfy these provisions by imposing that penalty without regard to any facts or circumstances other than the breach *per se*.

Ulsterbus v *Henderson*
[1989] IRLR 253
Northern Ireland Court of Appeal

Mr Henderson was dismissed from his job as a bus conductor following a complaint that he had failed to give tickets in return for payment of fares. An industrial tribunal upheld his complaint of unfair dismissal. One of the grounds for this finding was the fact that it had not been made clear in the company's disciplinary procedure that offences of this nature would attract the sanction of dismissal.

The Northern Ireland Court of Appeal allowed the employer's appeal and quashed the industrial tribunal's decision.

O'DONNELL LJ: There may be circumstances in which it would be unreasonable for an employer to dismiss an employee for a minor misdemeanour without warning that dismissal might result from such an act. The failure to give tickets in return for payment was a most serious offence and was likely to lead to dismissal; such a result would be obvious to any employee.

Dairy Produce Packers Ltd v *Beverstock*
[1981] IRLR 265
Employment Appeal Tribunal

Mr Beverstock worked as a delivery man. He was dismissed for drinking at a public house in working time. Mr Beverstock claimed unfair dismissal and adduced evidence of three other employees who had been found drunk at work or had arrived late smelling of drink: all had been warned but none dismissed. The employer argued that Mr Beverstock's offence was more serious because he worked away from factory and how he conducted himself had to be based on trust.

LORD MACDONALD: . . . [A] reasonable employer may require to impose different standards with regard to the question of alcohol dependent upon a number of factors, such as the nature of his business, the extent to which other personnel may be put at risk and the effect which conduct of this nature may have on public opinion. Where it is considered necessary to have specific penalties attached to the use of alcohol in a particular enterprise then it is proper, as the industrial tribunal have pointed out, that this should be clearly laid down and made a term of the contract of employment.

In the present case there is no such clear term contained in the contract of employment: it was argued on behalf of the appellants that the view which a reasonable employer would take would be that in the circumstances of the present case the offence of drinking during working hours outside the factory was more serious than similar drinking within the factory premises.

. . . In our opinion this is an argument which seeks to add yet another category of offence relating to alcohol and certainly if it had been the intention of the appellants that such a distinction fell to be made they should have had this clearly spelt out in the contracts of employment which they entered into with the employers.

Question
Is it possible to rationalise the approaches adopted in the *Henderson* and *Beverstock* cases?

Notes
1. While it is clear that the employer does not need to list every offence which could lead to dismissal, the offences which are listed will be taken as an indication of the character and class of offence which the employer views

as gross misconduct. Therefore, a dismissal for an offence of a less serious class or of an entirely different character than those set out in the disciplinary rules is likely to be regarded as unfair (see *Dietman* v *London Borough of Brent* [1988] IRLR 299, CA).

2. For an interesting application of the rules relating to gross misconduct, see *Denco* v *Joinson* [1991] IRLR 63, where an employee's unauthorised access to a computer warranted summary dismissal. The employee's motive was held to be irrelevant (an extract from the judgment in this case is included at p. 354).

(iv) Hearings

ACAS Code of Practice 1
Disciplinary Practices and Procedures in Employment

11. . . . Before a decision is made or a penalty imposed the individual should be interviewed and given the opportunity to state his or her case and should be advised of any rights under the procedure, including the right to be accompanied.

Notes
1. In *Ulsterbus* v *Henderson* (above), an industrial tribunal upheld Mr Henderson's complaint of unfair dismissal. One of the grounds for this finding was that, at the formal disciplinary proceedings which led to his dismissal, Mr Henderson was not provided with the opportunity to question the passengers who had made the complaint. The Northern Ireland Court of Appeal allowed the employer's appeal and quashed the industrial tribunal's decision. O'Donnell LJ said:

What the tribunal appears to be suggesting is that in certain circumstances it is incumbent on a reasonable employer to carry out a quasi-judicial investigation with a confrontation of witnesses, and cross-examination of witnesses. While some employers might consider this to be necessary or desirable, to suggest as the tribunal did, that an employer who failed to do it in a case such as this was acting unreasonably. . . . is in my view unsupportable.

2. It is a general principle that a person who holds an inquiry must be seen to be impartial, that justice must not only be done but be seen to be done, and that if a reasonable observer with full knowledge of the facts would conclude that the hearing might not be impartial that is enough.

An illustration of an application of these principles is to be found in the decision of the EAT in *Moyes* v *Hylton Castle Working Men's Social Club and Institute* [1986] IRLR 483, where two witnesses to an alleged act of sexual harassment by a club steward towards a barmaid also were members of the committee which dismissed the steward. The EAT held the dismissal to be unfair on the ground that it was a breach of natural justice for an apparently biased committee to decide the disciplinary matter. While the general rule is that if a person has been a witness or she should not conduct the inquiry, the EAT did identify certain exceptions, e.g. the one-man firm.

Employment Relations Act 1999

Disciplinary and grievance hearings

10. Right to be accompanied

(1) This section applies where a worker—

(a) is required or invited by his employer to attend a disciplinary or grievance hearing, and

(b) reasonably requests to be accompanied at the hearing.

(2) Where this section applies the employer must permit the worker to be accompanied at the hearing by a single companion who—

(a) is chosen by the worker and is within subsection (3),

(b) is to be permitted to address the hearing (but not to answer questions on behalf of the worker), and

(c) is to be permitted to confer with the worker during the hearing.

(3) A person is within this subsection if he is—

(a) employed by a trade union of which he is an official within the meaning of sections 1 and 119 of the Trade Union and Labour Relations (Consolidation) Act 1992,

(b) an official of a trade union (within that meaning) whom the union has reasonably certified in writing as having experience of, or as having received training in, acting as a worker's companion at disciplinary or grievance hearings, or

(c) another of the employer's workers.

(4) If—

(a) a worker has a right under this section to be accompanied at a hearing,

(b) his chosen companion will not be available at the time proposed for the hearing by the employer, and

(c) the worker proposes an alternative time which satisfies subsection (5), the employer must postpone the hearing to the time proposed by the worker.

(5) An alternative time must—

(a) be reasonable, and

(b) fall before the end of the period of five working days beginning with the first working day after the day proposed by the employer.

(6) An employer shall permit a worker to take time off during working hours for the purpose of accompanying another of the employer's workers in accordance with a request under subsection (1)(b).

(7) Sections 168(3) and (4), 169 and 171 to 173 of the Trade Union and Labour Relations (Consolidation) Act 1992 (time off for carrying out trade union duties) shall apply in relation to subsection (6) above as they apply in relation to section 168(1) of that Act.

11. Complaint to employment tribunal

(1) A worker may present a complaint to an employment tribunal that his employer has failed, or threatened to fail, to comply with section 10(2) or (4).

(2) A tribunal shall not consider a complaint under this section in relation to a failure or threat unless the complaint is presented—

(a) before the end of the period of three months beginning with the date of the failure or threat, or

(b) within such further period as the tribunal considers reasonable in a case where it is satisfied that it was not reasonably practicable for the complaint to be presented before the end of that period of three months.

(3) Where a tribunal finds that a complaint under this section is well-founded it shall order the employer to pay compensation to the worker of an amount not exceeding two weeks' pay.

(4) Chapter II of Part XIV of the Employment Rights Act 1996 (calculation of a week's pay) shall apply for the purposes of subsection (3); and in applying that Chapter the calculation date shall be taken to be—

(a) in the case of a claim which is made in the course of a claim for unfair dismissal, the date on which the employer's notice of dismissal was given or, if there was no notice, the effective date of termination, and

(b) in any other case, the date on which the relevant hearing took place (or was to have taken place).

(5) The limit in section 227(1) of the Employment Rights Act 1996 (maximum amount of week's pay) shall apply for the purposes of subsection (3) above.

(6) No award shall be made under subsection (3) in respect of a claim which is made in the course of a claim for unfair dismissal if the tribunal makes a supplementary award under section 127A(2) of the Employment Rights Act 1996 (internal appeal procedures).

12. Detriment and dismissal

(1) A worker has the right not to be subjected to any detriment by any act, or any deliberate failure to act, by his employer done on the ground that he—

(a) exercised or sought to exercise the right under section 10(2) or (4), or

(b) accompanied or sought to accompany another worker (whether of the same employer or not) pursuant to a request under that section.

(2) Section 48 of the Employment Rights Act 1996 shall apply in relation to contraventions of subsection (1) above as it applies in relation to contraventions of certain sections of that Act.

(3) A worker who is dismissed shall be regarded for the purposes of Part X of the Employment Rights Act 1996 as unfairly dismissed if the reason (or, if more than one, the principal reason) for the dismissal is that he—

(a) exercised or sought to exercise the right under section 10(2) or (4), or

(b) accompanied or sought to accompany another worker (whether of the same employer or not) pursuant to a request under that section.

(4) Sections 108 and 109 of that Act (qualifying period of employment and upper age limit) shall not apply in relation to subsection (3) above.

(5) Sections 128 to 132 of that Act (interim relief) shall apply in relation to dismissal for the reason specified in subsection (3)(a) or (b) above as they apply in relation to dismissal for a reason specified in section 128(1)(b) of that Act.

(6) In the application of Chapter II of Part X of that Act in relation to subsection (3) above, a reference to an employee shall be taken as a reference to a worker.

13. Interpretation

(1) In sections 10 to 12 and this section 'worker' means an individual who is—

(a) a worker within the meaning of section 230(3) of the Employment Rights Act 1996,

(b) an agency worker,

(c) a home worker,

(d) a person in Crown employment within the meaning of section 191 of that Act, other than a member of the naval, military, air or reserve forces of the Crown, or

(e) employed as a relevant member of the House of Lords staff or the House of Commons staff within the meaning of section 194(6) or 195(5) of that Act.

(2)   In subsection (1) 'agency worker' means an individual who—

(a)   is supplied by a person ('the agent') to do work for another ('the principal') by arrangement between the agent and the principal,

(b)   is not a party to a worker's contract, within the meaning of section 230(3) of that Act, relating to that work, and

(c)   is not a party to a contract relating to that work under which he undertakes to do the work for another party to the contract whose status is, by virtue of the contract, that of a client or customer of any professional or business undertaking carried on by the individual;

and, for the purposes of sections 10 to 12, both the agent and the principal are employers of an agency worker.

(3)   In subsection (1) 'home worker' means an individual who—

(a)   contracts with a person, for the purposes of the person's business, for the execution of work to be done in a place not under the person's control or management, and

(b)   is not a party to a contract relating to that work under which the work is to be executed for another party to the contract whose status is, by virtue of the contract, that of a client or customer of any professional or business undertaking carried on by the individual;

and, for the purposes of sections 10 to 12, the person mentioned in paragraph (a) is the home worker's employer.

(4)   For the purposes of section 10 a disciplinary hearing is a hearing which could result in—

(a)   the administration of a formal warning to a worker by his employer,

(b)   the taking of some other action in respect of a worker by his employer, or

(c)   the confirmation of a warning issued or some other action taken.

(5)   For the purposes of section 10 a grievance hearing is a hearing which concerns the performance of a duty by an employer in relation to a worker.

(6)   For the purposes of section 10(5)(b) in its application to a part of Great Britain a working day is a day other than—

(a)   a Saturday or a Sunday,

(b)   Christmas Day or Good Friday, or

(c)   a day which is a bank holiday under the Banking and Financial Dealings Act 1971 in that part of Great Britain.

Notes

1.   The purpose of s. 10 is to create a statutory right for a worker to be accompanied by a fellow employee or trade union official of his or her choice. The 1999 Act does not place a duty on trade union officials or fellow employees to perform the role as the accompanying individual.

2.   Section 13(4) and (5) define 'disciplinary' and 'grievance' hearings for the purposes of s. 10. A grievance hearing is defined as a hearing which 'concerns the performance of a duty by the employer in relation to a worker'. According to the explanatory notes produced by the Department of Trade and Industry to accompany the legislation, this means a legal duty, i.e. statutory, contractual or common law. The purpose of the subsection is to seek to ensure that workers do not have the right to be accompanied at hearings where trivial or minor complaints are dealt with.

3.   The provisions are silent regarding the situations in which the worker may ask to be legally represented. At present, the case law on this indicates that an employer is not obliged to afford legal representation, and s. 10's silence on the matter would appear to give this unsatisfactory position implicit statutory support. *Sharma v British Gas Corporation*, EAT 495/82, 27 July 1983, is one example of where it was held that there is no requirement to afford legal representation. However, there are a number of possible situations where this might well be essential, particularly where the worker is due to be involved in criminal and civil proceedings, and where he or she may have wider concerns (commercial, intellectual property, etc.) to protect in addition to his or her job.

4.   Section 10(2) states that the companion is permitted to address the hearing and to confer with the worker during the hearing, but he or she is not permitted to answer questions on behalf of the worker.

5.   Section 11 provides that a complaint may be made to a tribunal that an employer has failed, or has *threatened* to fail, to comply with the right to accompaniment. An award not exceeding two weeks' pay may be ordered. If the issue arises in the context of unfair dismissal proceedings, no award under this head may be made if the tribunal makes a supplementary award under ERA 1996, s. 127A(2) where the employer provided a procedure for appealing against the dismissal but has prevented the employee from using it.

6.   Section 12 provides that the worker has the right not to be subject to any detriment by any act, or failure to act by his employer, on the grounds that he or she sought to exercise the right to be accompanied or sought to accompany a worker in accordance with s. 10. It expressly provides that accompanying workers have these rights whether or not they share the same employer as the worker seeking accompaniment. An employer will not, however, be required to pay his employee for time taken off to accompany another employer's worker.

By virtue of s. 12(3), where the reason for a dismissal is the exercising of rights under s. 10, or the fact that a person has accompanied another in accordance with that section, the dismissal will be automatically unfair. Subsection (4) provides that rights under the section are not subject to any age limit or qualifying period. Subsection (5) extends the availability of interim relief, provided for by ss. 128–132 of ERA 1996, to dismissals for seeking the right to be accompanied.

7.   For the purposes of these new rights, a 'worker' is defined in s. 13 in wider terms than just an 'employee'. It extends to 'worker' as already defined in ERA 1996, s. 230(3) (contracts of employment and other contracts whereby the person undertakes personal services or work), and also to agency and homeworkers (as defined by s. 13(2), (3)) and Crown servants, among others.

(v)   Appeals

Discipline at Work, The ACAS Advisory Handbook, 1987

What should an appeals procedure contain?
It should:
• Specify any time-limit within which the appeal should be lodged.

- Provide for appeals to be dealt with speedily, particularly those involving suspension without pay or dismissal.
- Wherever possible, provide for the appeal to be heard by an authority higher than that taking the disciplinary action.
- Spell out the action which may be taken by those hearing the appeal.
- Provide that the employee, or a representative if the employee so wishes, has an opportunity to comment on any new evidence arising during the appeal before any decision is taken.

Small firms
In small firms there may be no authority higher than the manager who decided disciplinary action. If this is the case the same person who took the disciplinary action should hear the appeal and act as impartially as possible. The occasion should be seen as an opportunity to review the original decision in an objective manner and at a quieter time. This can more readily be achieved if some time is allowed to lapse before the appeal hearing.

Employment Rights Act 1996

127A. Internal appeal procedures
(1)   Where in a case in which an award of compensation for unfair dismissal falls to be made under section 112(4) or 117(3)(a) the tribunal finds that—
(a)   the employer provided a procedure for appealing against dismissal, and
(b)   the complainant was, at the time of the dismissal or within a reasonable period afterwards, given written notice stating that the employer provided the procedure and including details of it, but
(c)   the complainant did not appeal against the dismissal under the procedure (otherwise than because the employer prevented him from doing so),
the tribunal shall reduce the compensatory award included in the award of compensation for unfair dismissal by such amount (if any) as it considers just and equitable.
(2)   Where in a case in which an award of compensation for unfair dismissal falls to be made under section 112(4) or 117(3)(a) the tribunal finds that—
(a)   the employer provided a procedure for appealing against dismissal, but
(b)   the employer prevented the complainant from appealing against the dismissal under the procedure,
the award of compensation for unfair dismissal shall include a supplementary award of such amount (if any) as the tribunal considers just and equitable.
(3)   In determining the amount of a reduction under subsection (1) or a supplementary award under subsection (2) the tribunal shall have regard to all the circumstances of the case, including in particular the chances that an appeal under the procedure provided by the employer would have been successful.
(4)   The amount of such a reduction or supplementary award shall not exceed the amount of two weeks' pay.

Note
This section was added by the Employment Rights (Dispute Resolution) Act 1998 s. 13, as from 1 January 1999. Its aim is to encourage recourse to internal appeals against dismissal.

West Midlands Cooperative Society v Tipton
[1986] IRLR 112
House of Lords

Mr Tipton was summarily dismissed by his employers on the grounds of his poor attendance record. He was not permitted to exercise his contractual right to appeal against the dismissal.

An industrial tribunal found the dismissal to be unfair. On appeal to the EAT, the employers argued that in determining the fairness of the dismissal the industrial tribunal should not have taken into account their refusal to permit an appeal. This argument was based on an interpretation of the decision of the House of Lords in *W. Devis & Sons Ltd* v *Atkins* [1977] IRLR 314, where it was held that in assessing fairness a tribunal cannot have regard to matters of which the employer was unaware at the time of the dismissal. This argument was rejected by the EAT but succeeded before the Court of Appeal. The House of Lords restored the decision of the EAT that the dismissal was unfair.

LORD BRIDGE OF HARWICH: The lynchpin of the argument for the respondents is the decision of this House in *W Devis & Sons Ltd* v *Atkins* [1977] IRLR 314. . . .

Under [s. 98 of the 1996 Act] there are three questions which must be answered in determining whether a dismissal was fair or unfair:

(1)   What was the reason (or principal reason) for the dismissal?

(2)   Was *that* reason a reason falling within subsection (2) of [s. 98] or some other substantial reason of a kind such as to justify the dismissal of an employee holding the position which that employee held?

(3)   Did the employer act reasonably or unreasonably in treating *that* reason as a sufficient reason for dismissing the employee?

As to question (1), Cairns LJ said in *Abernethy* v *Mott. Hay & Anderson* [1974] IRLR 213 at p. 215, in a passage approved by Viscount Dilhorne in the case of *Devis:*

A reason for the dismissal of an employee is a set of facts known to the employer, or it may be of beliefs held by him, which cause him to dismiss the employee. If at the time of his dismissal the employer gives a reason for it, that is no doubt evidence, at any rate as against him, as to the real reason, but it does not necessarily constitute the real reason. He may knowingly give a reason different from the real reason out of kindness . . .

. . .

The reason shown by the employer in answer to question (1) may, therefore, be aptly termed the real reason. Once the real reason is established the answer to question (2) will depend on the application of the statutory criteria to that reason. Then comes the crucial question (3): did the employer act reasonably or unreasonably in treating the real reason as a sufficient reason for dismissing the employee? Conduct of the employee unrelated to the real reason for dismissal obviously cannot affect the answer to this question. This, and no more than this, is what the case of *Devis* decided. But I can see nothing in the language of the statute to exclude from consideration in answering question (3) 'in accordance with equity and the substantial merits of the case' evidence relevant to show the strength or weakness of the real reason for dismissal which the employer had the opportunity to consider in the course of an appeal heard pursuant to a disciplinary procedure which complies with the statutory code of practice. The apparent injustice of excluding, in relation to this question, misconduct of the employee which is irrelevant to the real reason for dismissal is mitigated, as I have earlier pointed out, by the provisions relating to compensation in such a case. But there is nothing to mitigate the injustice to an employee which would result if he were unable to complain that his employer, though acting reasonably on the facts known to him when he summarily dismissed the employee, acted quite unreasonably in maintaining his decision to dismiss in the face of mitigating circumstances established in the course of the domestic appeal procedure which a reasonable employer would have treated as sufficient to excuse the employee's offence on which the employer's real reason for the dismissal depended. Adopting the analysis which found favour in *J Sainsbury Ltd v Savage* [1980] IRLR 109, if the domestic appeal succeeds the employee is reinstated with retrospective effect; if it fails the summary dismissal takes effect from the original date. Thus, in so far as the original dismissal and the decision on the domestic appeal are governed by the same consideration, so, the real reason for dismissal, there is no reason to treat the effective date of termination as a watershed which separates the one process from the other. Both the original and the appellate decision by the employer, in any case where the contract of employment provides for an appeal, and the right of appeal is invoked by the employee, are necessary elements in the overall process of terminating the contract of employment. To separate them and to consider only one half of the process in determining whether the employer acted reasonably or unreasonably in treating his real reason for dismissal as sufficient is to introduce an unnecessary artificiality into proceedings on a claim of unfair dismissal calculated to defeat, rather than accord, with the 'equity and substantial merits of case' and for which the language of the statute affords no warrant.

This is the conclusion I should reach as a matter of construction, taking due account of the decision in the case of *Devis*, if there were no other authority to guide me. But the conclusion is powerfully reinforced by the series of decisions of the Employment Appeal Tribunal, to which I have earlier referred, with which it is in full accord. The relevant cases are *Rank Xerox (UK) Ltd v Goodchild* [1979] IRLR 185; *Quantrill v Eastern Counties Omnibus Co. Ltd* (unreported), 30.6.80; *National Heart and Chest Hospitals Board of Governors v Nambiar* [1981] IRLR 196; *Sillifant v Powell Duffryn Timber Ltd* [1983] IRLR 91; and *Greenall Whitley plc v Carr* [1985] IRLR 289. . . .

. . . A dismissal is unfair if the employer unreasonably treats his real reason as a sufficient reason to dismiss the employee, either when he makes his original decision to dismiss or when he maintains that decision at the conclusion of an internal appeal. By the same token, a dismissal may be held to be unfair when the employer has refused to entertain an appeal to which the employee was contractually entitled and thereby denied to the employee the opportunity of showing that, in all the circumstances, the employer's real reason for dismissing him could not reasonably be treated as sufficient. There may, of course, be cases where, on the undisputed facts, the dismissal was inevitable, as for example where a trusted employee, before dismissal, was charged with, and pleaded guilty to, a serious offence of dishonesty committed in the course of his employment. In such a case the employer could reasonably refuse to entertain a domestic appeal on the ground that it could not affect the outcome. It has never been suggested, however, that this was such a case.

Note

In *Parkinson v March Consulting Ltd* [1997] IRLR 308, CA, it was held that where dismissal is with notice it may be necessary for a tribunal to consider fairness in the circumstances at the time of giving notice *and* when the notice expires. This could result in factors or evidence arising during the notice period becoming relevant to the eventual decision. This approach was subsequently endorsed by the Court of Appeal's decision in *Alboni v Ind Coope Retail Ltd* [1998] IRLR 131.

Ms Alboni and her former partner were employed under a joint contract of employment as manager and manageress of a public house. The contract contained an express term that, 'your employment is inextricably bound to that of your partner, therefore if the employment of either of you terminates, [that of] the other person will terminate automatically.' When Ms Alboni's partner resigned, she was given eight weeks' notice. The vacancy was advertised, and she put a proposal to the respondents that she should remain as sole manager which they promised to consider. Although this proposal eventually came to nothing, the tribunal took into account the employers' readiness to consider any application from Ms Alboni to manage the pub single-handed in their finding that her dismissal was fair. This approach was found to be an error of law by the EAT because a tribunal is not allowed to consider 'events which had post-dated the dismissal'. However, the Court of Appeal restored the decision of the industrial tribunal. After referring to the decision in Parkinson, Simon Brown LJ stated:

I do not find the majority decision in that case altogether easy to follow, and it occurs to me it may in future give rise to difficulties of application. For present purposes, however, it seems to make it entirely clear that the industrial tribunal in the present case were not merely entitled, but were bound to have regard to events between notice and dismissal, both for s. 98(1) purposes and also, indeed to my mind *a fortiori*, for s. 98(4) purposes.

Question
The principle established by the Court of Appeal in *Alboni* and *Parkinson* has been criticised by Michael Rubenstein, editor of the IRLR, on the basis that 'it will serve as an incentive to employers to dismiss first and ask questions later' ('Highlights' [1998] LRLR 107). Do you share his concern?

Sartor v P&O European Ferries (Felixstowe) Ltd
[1992] IRLR 273
Court of Appeal

Miss Sartor was employed as a stewardess on one of the respondent's ships. Her employers decided to institute disciplinary proceedings against her following reports from customs officers that a catering-size pack of tea bags had been seen in her car when leaving the docks.

At that time, Miss Sartor was on a week's leave and she was telephoned and told not to report for duty at the end of leave period but to attend a disciplinary hearing. She was given no information about the reason for the hearing.

At the disciplinary hearing before the ship's master it was decided to dismiss Miss Sartor and she appealed against that decision. Her appeal was heard by the deputy personnel manager and the catering and purchasing manager who, after rehearing all the evidence and giving Miss Sartor an opportunity to state her case, decided to affirm the appeal. Her claim for unfair dismissal was dismissed by the industrial tribunal, the EAT and the Court of Appeal.

RALPH GIBSON LJ: . . . [T]he appellant ought to have been told the terms of the charge against her before the hearing before the captain. Nevertheless, the appeal was by way of rehearing and there was on that occasion no significant defect in the proceedings. Any defects in what had gone on before were cured by the opportunity to appeal.

Note
The following cases demonstrate the courts' renewed emphasis on procedural rectitude.

Polkey v *A.E. Dayton Services*
[1987] IRLR 503
House of Lords

Polkey was one of four van drivers employed by the respondent company. As part of a reorganisation, it was decided to replace the four van drivers with two van salesmen and a sales representative. Only one of the four van drivers was considered suitable for transfer to the new duties and accordingly the other three were made redundant.

The first that Mr Polkey knew of the position was when he was called into the office of the branch manager and told that he was being made redundant. He was immediately driven home by one of the drivers, who was himself dismissed on his return.

Mr Polkey's claim of unfair dismissal was rejected by the industrial tribunal and his appeals were dismissed by the EAT and the Court of Appeal. The Court of Appeal endorsed the principles set out in *British Labour Pump Co. Ltd* v *Byrne* [1979] IRLR 94, and approved by the Court of Appeal in *Wass* v *Binns* [1982] ICR 347, and held that Mr Polkey's dismissal was not unfair, despite the employer's failure to consult with him, because such consultation would not have made any difference to the result. The House of Lords allowed Mr Polkey's appeal and remitted the case to a new industrial tribunal.

LORD MACKAY OF CLASHFERN: This appeal raises an important question in the law of unfair dismissal. Where an industrial tribunal has found that the reason for an applicant's dismissal was a reason of a kind such as could justify the dismissal and has found that there has been a failure to consult or warn the applicant in accordance with the code of practice, should the tribunal consider whether, if the employee had been consulted or warned before dismissal was decided upon, he would nevertheless have been dismissed? The answer depends upon the application to this situation of [what is now ERA 1996 s. 98(4)].

. . . [T]he subject matter for the tribunal's consideration is the employer's action in treating the reason as a sufficient reason for dismissing the employee. It is that action and that action only that the tribunal is required to characterise as reasonable or unreasonable. That leaves no scope for the tribunal considering whether, if the employer had acted differently, he might have dismissed the employee. It is what the employer did that is to be judged, not what he might have done. On the other hand, in judging whether what the employer did was reasonable it is right to consider what a reasonable employer would have had in mind at the time he decided to dismiss as the consequence of not consulting or not warning.

If the employer could reasonably have concluded in the light of the circumstances known to him at the time of dismissal that consultation or warning would be utterly useless he might well act reasonably even if he did not observe the provisions of the code. Failure to observe the requirement of the code relating to consultation or warning will not necessarily render a dismissal unfair. Whether in any particular case it did so is a matter for the industrial tribunal to consider in the light of the circumstances known to the employer at the time he dismissed the employee.

I turn to consider how these views accord with the decided cases. Very early in the history of this legislation and its statutory predecessors Sir John Donaldson in *Earl* v *Slater & Wheeler (Airlyne) Ltd* [1972] IRLR 115 said:

> With respect to the tribunal, we think that it erred in holding that an unfair procedure which led to no injustice is incapable of rendering unfair a dismissal which would otherwise be fair. The question in every case is whether the employer acted reasonably or unreasonably in treating the reason as sufficient for dismissing the employee and it has to be answered with reference to the circumstances known to the employer at the moment of dismissal. If an employer thinks that his accountant may be taking the firm's money, but has no real grounds for so thinking and dismisses him for this reason, he acts wholly unreasonably and commits the unfair industrial practice of unfair dismissal, notwithstanding that it is later proved that the accountant had in fact been guilty of embezzlement. Proof of the embezzlement affects the amount of the compensation, but not the issue of fair or unfair dismissal.

. . .

This approach to the legislation was endorsed in this House in *W. Devis & Sons Ltd* v *Atkins* [1977] IRLR 314. Viscount Dilhorne, in a speech with which the other members of the House sitting in the appeal agreed, said of the statutory predecessor of s. 57(3) [see now ERA 1996, s. 98(4)], at p. 317:

> It [para. 6(8) of Schedule 1 to the Trade Union and Labour Relations Act 1971] appears to me to direct the Tribunal to focus its attention on the conduct of the employer and not on whether the employee in fact suffered any injustice.

After quoting, with approval, the principal part of the passage I have already cited from Sir John Donaldson in *Earl* v *Slater & Wheeler (Airlyne) Ltd* and after referring to the statutory provision then entitling the Tribunal to take the code into account Viscount Dilhorne said, at p. 318:

> It does not follow that non-compliance with the code necessarily renders a dismissal unfair, but I agree with the view expressed by Sir John Donaldson in *Earl* v *Slater & Wheeler (Airlyne) Ltd* [1972] IRLR 115 that a failure to follow a procedure prescribed in the code may lead to the conclusion that a dismissal was unfair, which, if that procedure had been followed, would have been held to have been fair.

So far, the current of decision is entirely in accordance with the views I have expressed, but the Tribunal in the present case were bound by a stream of authority applying the so-called *British Labour Pump* principle *(British Labour Pump Co. Ltd* v *Byrne* [1979] IRLR 94).

Browne-Wilkinson J in *Sillifant* v *Powell Duffryn Timber Ltd* [1983] IRLR 91 thus described the principle, at p. 92:

> Even if, judged in the light of the circumstances known at the time of dismissal, the employer's decision was not reasonable because of some failure to follow a fair procedure yet the dismissal can be held fair if, on the facts proved before the Industrial Tribunal, the Industrial Tribunal comes to the conclusion that the employer could reasonably have decided to dismiss if he had followed a fair procedure.

It is because one of its statements is contained in *British Labour Pump Co. Ltd* v *Byrne* that it has been called the *British Labour Pump* principle although it did not originate in that decision. In *Sillifant's case* the Employment Appeal Tribunal were urged to hold that the principle was unsound and not to give effect to it. After referring to the cases which introduced this principle, namely *Charles Letts & Co. Ltd* v *Howard* [1976] IRLR 248, a decision relating only to compensation, *Lowndes* v *Specialist Heavy Engineering Ltd* [1976] IRLR 246, *British United Shoe Machinery Co. Ltd* v *Clarke* [1977] IRLR 297 and the *British Labour Pump* case itself, Browne-Wilkinson J continued at p. 97:

> Apart therefore from recent Court of Appeal authority and the *Lowndes* case, the *British Labour Pump* principle appears to have become established in practice without it being appreciated that it represented a fundamental departure from both basic principle and the earlier decisions. If we felt able to do so we would hold that it is wrong in principle and undesirable in its practical effect. It introduces just that confusion which *Devis* v *Atkins* was concerned to avoid between the fairness of the dismissal (which depends solely upon the reasonableness of the employer's conduct) and the compensation payable to the employee (which takes into account the conduct of the employee whether known to the employer or not). In our judgment, apart from the authority to which we are about to refer, the correct approach to such a case would be as follows. The only test of the fairness of a dismissal is the reasonableness of the employer's decision to dismiss judged at the time at which the dismissal takes effect. An Industrial Tribunal is not bound to hold that *any* procedural failure by the employer renders the dismissal unfair: it is one of the factors to be weighed by the Industrial Tribunal in deciding whether or not the dismissal was reasonable within s. 57(3) [see now ERA 1996, s. 98(4)]. The weight to be attached to such procedural failure should depend upon the circumstances known to the employer at the time of dismissal, not on the actual consequence of such failure. Thus in the case of a failure to give an opportunity to explain, except in the rare case where a reasonable employer could properly take the view on the facts known to him at the time of dismissal that no explanation or mitigation could alter his decision to dismiss, an Industrial Tribunal would be likely to hold that the lack of 'equity' inherent in the failure would render the dismissal unfair. But there may be cases where the offence is so heinous and the facts so manifestly clear that a reasonable employer could, on the facts known to him at the time of dismissal, take the view that whatever explanation the employee advanced it would make no difference: see the example referred to by Lawton LJ in *Bailey* v *BP Oil (Kent Refinery) Ltd* [1980] IRLR 287. Where, in the circumstances known at the time of

dismissal, it was not reasonable for the employer to dismiss without giving an opportunity to explain the facts subsequently discovered or proved before the Industrial Tribunal show that the dismissal was in fact merited, compensation would be reduced to nil. Such an approach ensures that an employee who could have been fairly dismissed does not get compensation but would prevent the suggestion of 'double standards' inherent in the *British Labour Pump* principle. An employee dismissed for suspected dishonesty who is in fact innocent has no redress: if the employer acted fairly in dismissing him on the facts and in the circumstances known to him at the time of dismissal the employee's innocence is irrelevant. Why should an employer be entitled to a finding that he acted fairly when, on the facts known and in the circumstances existing at the time of dismissal, his actions were unfair but which facts subsequently coming to light show did not cause any injustice? The choice in dealing with [s. 98(4)] is between looking at the reasonableness of the employer or justice to the employee. *Devis* v *Atkins* shows that the correct test is the reasonableness of the employer; the *British Labour Pump* principle confuses the two approaches.'

I gratefully adopt that analysis. The Employment Appeal Tribunal, however, went on to hold that they were bound by the decision of the Court of Appeal in *W & J Wass* v *Binns* [1982] IRLR 283 which held that the *British Labour Pump* principle is good law . . .

[The] reasons given by the Court of Appeal in the present case for supporting the *British Labour Pump* principle involve an impermissible reliance upon matters not known to the employers before the dismissal and a confusion between unreasonable conduct in reaching the conclusion to dismiss, which is a necessary ingredient of an unfair dismissal, and injustice to the employee which is not a necessary ingredient of an unfair dismissal, although its absence will be important in relation to a compensatory award.

It follows that I do not agree with the decision of the Court of Appeal in the present case and this appeal should be allowed, the *British Labour Pump* principle and all decisions supporting it are inconsistent with the relevant statutory provision and should be overruled, and, in particular, the decision of the Court of Appeal in *W & J Wass Ltd* v *Binns* [1982] IRLR 283 should be overruled.

LORD BRIDGE OF HARWICH: Employers contesting a claim of unfair dismissal will commonly advance as their reason for dismissal one of the reasons specifically recognised as valid by s. 57(2)(a), (b) and (c) of the Employment Protection (Consolidation) Act 1978 [see now ERA 1996, s. 98(2)(a), (b) and (c)]. These, put shortly, are: (a) that the employee could not do his job properly; (b) that he had been guilty of misconduct; (c) that he was redundant. But an employer having prima facie grounds to dismiss for one of these reasons will in the great majority of cases not act reasonably in treating the reason as a sufficient reason for dismissal unless and until he has taken the steps, conveniently classified in most of the authorities as 'procedural', which are necessary in the circumstances of the case to justify that course of action. Thus, in the case of incapacity, the employer will normally not act reasonably unless he gives the employee fair warning and an opportunity to mend his ways and show that he can do the job; in the case of misconduct, the employer will normally not act reasonably unless he investigates the complaint of misconduct fully and fairly and hears whatever the employee wishes to say in his defence or in explanation or mitigation; in the case of redundancy, the employer will normally not act reasonably unless he warns and consults any employees affected or their representative, adopts a fair basis on which to select for redundancy and takes such steps as may be reasonable to avoid or minimise redundancy by redeployment within his own organisation. If an employer has failed to take the appropriate procedural steps in any particular case, the one question the Industrial Tribunal is *not* permitted to ask in applying the test of reasonableness posed by [s. 98(4)] is the hypothetical question whether it would have made any difference to the outcome if the appropriate procedural steps had been taken. On the true construction of [s. 98(4)] this question is simply irrelevant. It is quite a different matter if the Tribunal is able to conclude that the employer himself, at the time of the dismissal, acted reasonably in taking the view that, in the exceptional circumstances of the particular case, the procedural steps normally appropriate would have been futile, could not have altered the decision to dismiss and therefore could be dispensed with. In such a case the test of reasonableness under [s. 98(4)] may be satisfied.

My Lords, I think these conclusions are fully justified by the cogent reasoning of Browne-Wilkinson J in *Sillifant* v *Powell Duffryn Timber Ltd* [1983] IRLR 91 to which my noble and learned friend the Lord Chancellor has already drawn attention.

If it is held that taking the appropriate steps which the employer failed to take before dismissing the employee would not have affected the outcome, this will often lead to the result that the employee, though unfairly dismissed, will recover no compensation, or, in the case of redundancy, no compensation in excess of his redundancy payment. Thus in *Earl* v *Slater & Wheeler (Airlyne) Ltd* [1972] IRLR 115 the employee was held to have been unfairly dismissed, but nevertheless lost his appeal to the Industrial Relations Court because his misconduct disentitled him to any award of compensation, which was at that time the only effective remedy. But in spite of this the application of the so-called *British Labour Pump* principle (*British Labour Pump Co. Ltd* v *Byrne* [1979] IRLR 94) tends to distort the operation of the employment protection legislation in two important ways. First, as was pointed out by Browne-Wilkinson J in *Sillifant's case*, if the Industrial Tribunal, in considering whether the employer who has omitted to take the appropriate procedural steps acted reasonably or unreasonably in treating his reason as a sufficient reason for dismissal, poses for itself the hypothetical question whether the result would have been any different if the appropriate procedural steps had been taken, it can only answer that question on a balance of probabilities. Accordingly, applying the *British Labour Pump* principle, if the answer is that it probably would have made no difference, the employee's unfair dismissal claim fails. But if the likely effect of taking the appropriate procedural steps is only considered, as it should be, at the stage of assessing compensation, the position is quite different. In that situation, as Browne-Wilkinson J puts it in *Sillifant's* case, at p. 96:

> There is no need for an 'all or nothing' decision. If the Industrial Tribunal thinks there is a doubt whether or not the employee would have been dismissed, this element can be reflected by reducing the normal amount of compensation by a percentage representing the chance that the employee would still have lost his employment.

The second consideration is perhaps of particular importance in redundancy cases. As Industrial Tribunal may conclude, as in the instant case, that the appropriate procedural steps would not have avoided the employee's dismissal as redundant. But if, as your Lordships now hold, that conclusion does not defeat his claim of unfair dismissal, the Industrial Tribunal, apart from any question of compensation, will also have to consider whether to make any order under s. 69 of the Act of 1978 [see now

ERA 1996, s. 113]. It is noteworthy that an Industrial Tribunal may, if it thinks fit, make an order for re-engagement under that section and in so doing exercise a very wide discretion as to the terms of the order. In a case where an Industrial Tribunal held that dismissal on the ground of redundancy would have been inevitable at the time when it took place, even if the appropriate procedural steps had been taken, I do not, as at present advised, think this would necessarily preclude a discretionary order for re-engagement on suitable terms, if the altered circumstances considered by the Tribunal at the date of the hearing were thought to justify it.

For these reasons and for those given by my noble and learned friend the Lord Chancellor I would allow the appeal and remit the case to be heard by another Industrial Tribunal.

Notes

1. It has been argued that there is a significant practical difference between asking whether at the time of the dismissal the employer had reasonable grounds for believing that a fair procedure would have been 'utterly useless' (the new test) and asking whether, in retrospect, it would have made any difference to the outcome (the old test). As a result it is likely that failure to follow a fair procedure may well lead to a finding of unfair dismissal in a much increased proportion of cases.

In *Duffy* v *Yeomans and Partners Ltd* [1994] IRLR 642, CA, it was held that *Polkey* does not require that the employer must have consciously taken a decision not to consult with the employee. According to Balcombe LJ, it is sufficient that, judged objectively, the employer does what a reasonable employer might do. The dangers inherent in this objective text is that it resembles the 'did it make any difference?' test that *Polkey* rejected.

2. Even post-*Polkey*, the courts and tribunals have still shown a propensity to forgive minor procedural lapses, provided that in the overall context of the case they did not result in unfairness: see *Eclipse Blinds Ltd* v *Wright* [1992] IRLR 133 (set out at p. 475), *Westminster City Council* v *Cabaj* [1996] IRLR 399, CA, and the next case.

Fuller v *Lloyds Bank plc*
[1991] IRLR 337
Employment Appeal Tribunal

Mr Fuller was dismissed following an incident which occurred in a public house on Christmas Eve, when a fellow employee received severe facial injuries from a glass held by Mr Fuller. During the course of the employer's disciplinary proceedings, statements were taken from a number of witnesses. Those statements formed the basis of the employer's decision to dismiss Mr Fuller. However, they were never disclosed to Mr Fuller or his union representative.

Mr Fuller's complaint of unfair dismissal was rejected by the industrial tribunal and his appeal against that decision was dismissed by the EAT.

KNOX J: That it is desirable in the normal state of affairs for the material upon which a disciplinary investigation is founded and on which any penalties may be based on the person who is being disciplined, to be available to that person is something with which we heartily agree. It has frequently been emphasised, in this Tribunal and elsewhere, that this is a matter which should, in the normal course of events, be shown to a person in Mr Fuller's shoes.

We were referred specifically to two recent decisions in the EAT, *Linfood Cash & Carry Ltd* v *Thomson* [1989] IRLR 235 and *Louies* v *Coventry Hood & Seating Co. Ltd* [1990] IRLR 324 in both of which sentiments in that regard were uttered by Mr Justice Wood.

In the former, the *Linfood Cash & Carry Ltd* case at p. 237, 20 there are set out 10 paragraphs of general guidance prefaced by a statement that: 'Every case must depend upon its own facts, and circumstances may vary widely.' They are prefaced also with the hope that what are described as 'comments' may prove to be of assistance. The first of those 'comments' reads as follows:

The information given by the informant should be reduced into writing in one or more statements. Initially these statements should be taken without regard to the fact that in those cases where anonymity is to be preserved, it may subsequently prove to be necessary to omit or erase certain parts of the statements before submission to others, in order to prevent identification and paragraph 7:

The written statement of the informant – if necessary with omissions to avoid identification – should be made available to the employee and his representatives.

. . .

The other decision of late, the *Louies* case, contains a passage at p. 326, 11, where Mr Justice Wood said this:

It does seem to me that it must be a very rare case indeed for the procedures to be fair where statements which have been given in writing by witnesses and upon which in essence the employer is going to rely almost entirely – and that is this case – that an employee should not have a sight of them or that he should not be told very clearly exactly what is in them or possibly have them read to him.

. . .

The appeal before us is based on two alternative grounds.

The first is that there is an error of law involved in the Industrial Tribunal's approach in this matter. That approach was that whereas the Industrial Tribunal identified, in the passages which I have already read, the failure by the bank to provide material to Mr Fuller and his representatives, which should properly have been provided, that nevertheless was not conclusive and the dismissal was not, in the circumstances, unfair.

Having set out the well-known passage which originally derives from *Byrne* v *Kinematograph Renters Society Ltd* [1958] 1 WLR 762, a decision of Mr Justice Harman, and which was adopted by the Privy Council in the *University of Ceylon* v *Fernando* [1960] 1 WLR 225, the Industrial Tribunal considered that the three requirements identified in that citation of authority had in fact been supplied in this case.

Those requirements are, and I quote the passage in question:

What then are the requirements of natural justice in a case of this kind? First, I think that the person accused should know the nature of the accusation made; second, that he should be given an opportunity to state his case; and, third, of course, that the Tribunal should act in good faith.

Mr Justice Harman said: 'I do not myself think that there really is anything more.' In that context the Industrial Tribunal said this:

> There is no dispute that the respondents did tell the applicant the nature of the case which was made against him and indeed they set out a charge in formal terms. What they did not set out was the evidence, the material on which they were proposing to reach their decision.

They then set out certain reasons why, in this case, the material was not supplied, to which I will return later on the second branch of the appellant's argument.

They went on to express their conclusion on this aspect of the matter in the following terms:

> We have come to the conclusion that in the particular circumstances of this case failure to provide the witness statements did not go outside the band of reasonable procedures which should have been carried out. The allegation in essence was a simple one and the applicant knew exactly what was being alleged. Indeed he knew the identity of many of the witnesses and had received witness statements produced by the police for the criminal prosecution. The police witness statements produced before us maintain the same essential allegations as are contained in the witness statements.

It was submitted to us in answer to the predictable claim on behalf of the bank, that that was a finding of fact, that Mr Fuller knew exactly what was being alleged against him, that there was a fundamental error in principle in the Industrial Tribunal's approach in this sense, that the Industrial Tribunal had found that there was a certain policy of not disclosing witness statements and that it had been in pursuance of that policy that the non-disclosure of those statements had ensued.

It argued that the process of reasoning of the Industrial Tribunal in finding that that failure did not go outside the band of reasonable procedures which should have been carried out, carried in it the same fatal flaw as was identified in the well-known decision of the House of Lords in *Polkey* v *A.E. Dayton Services* [1987] IRLR 503 and that on analysis the Industrial Tribunal was saying that although the procedure was defective, Mr Fuller would, in any event, have been properly found guilty of the conduct with which he was charged and that in those circumstances the dismissal was not unfair.

If that analysis was correct we would certainly accept that the dismissal would have been shown to be unfair. But we are not satisfied that the analysis is an accurate one.

In our judgment where one has a procedural defect, which we entirely accept there was in this case, and whether that procedural defect is based on a policy adopted for good, bad or indifferent reasons, the question for investigation by an Industrial Tribunal does not alter simply because the defect was a matter of policy. There remain essentially the requirements that have been, over the years, many times identified and were stated in *British Home Stores Ltd* v *Burchell* [1978] IRLR 379 to which the Industrial Tribunal had regard.

The third essential element for present purposes in that investigation is, did the employer 'operate a reasonable procedure which entitles them to say they acted reasonably in dismissing the applicant.' I quote what the Industrial Tribunal said on this score. It could be translated into terms of unfairness, did the employer's procedure constitute a fair process.

That will always remain an essential matter for investigation and this case is no exception to that.

The actual defect has, however, to be analysed in the context of what has occurred, and it may be that that analysis will produce the conclusion that there was a defect of such seriousness that the procedure was not fair. In that event there will have been necessarily an unfair dismissal, although there may well be a conclusion that the compensation has to be severely limited because of the potential justification for the decision that the employer took albeit in an unfair way.

What will not be a relevant subject of enquiry, in our view, is the motivation of the employer in adopting the policy which led to the procedural defect. That has to be judged by its fruits rather than by the reason for its adoption.

The other possibility is that the procedural defect does not produce a procedure which is in itself unfair, but it may nevertheless be that the results taken overall are unfair, and there again, the conclusion that the Industrial Tribunal will reach will be that the dismissal cannot in those circumstances be upheld as anything other than unfair.

But here again, the motivation of the employer in adopting the original defective procedure is in our view nothing to do with that conclusion, which is an objective one in all the circumstances of the case.

In this case the Industrial Tribunal has undoubtedly seen the defect and has identified it quite accurately. It has nevertheless come to what we regard as a dual conclusion.

First of all, it concluded that the defect was not such as to render the procedure intrinsically unfair so as to require the dismissal not to stand as fair.

Secondly, the Industrial Tribunal came, as we see it, to the conclusion that overall the process whereby Mr Fuller was dismissed was not unfair.

(iv)   Some Common Disciplinary Issues

(a)   Sub-standard Work

Alidair Ltd v *Taylor*
[1978] IRLR 82
Court of Appeal

A summary of the facts appears at p. 474.

LORD DENNING MR: Wherever a man is dismissed for incapacity or incompetence it is sufficient that the employer honestly believes on reasonable grounds that the man is incapable or incompetent. It is not necessary for the employer to prove that he is in fact incapable or incompetent.

Cook v *Thomas Linnell & Sons Ltd*
[1977] IRLR 132
Employment Appeal Tribunal

Mr Cook was employed as manager of one of the respondents' 'non-food' depots from 1966 to 1974. He was then promoted to manager of a food depot in Norwich although he had no previous experience of that side of the business. In May 1976 he was dismissed on grounds of poor performance. The industrial tribunal and EAT found the dismissal to be fair.

PHILLIPS J: A central theme in Mr Tabachnik's submission [on behalf of Mr Cook] was that although there was plenty of contemporary evidence to show that the employers had lost confidence in the ability of Mr Cook as a manager there was no hard factual evidence of a particular kind to support that judgment. Criticism and exhortation, he submitted, however strong, do not by themselves provide evidence of incapacity. It amounts to no more than an assertion of an opinion. It seems to us that this goes too far, although we accept that there is something in the point. When responsible employers have genuinely come to the conclusion over a reasonable period of time that a manager is incompetent we think that it is some evidence that he is incompetent. When one is dealing with routine operations which may be more precisely assessed there is no real problem. It is more difficult when one is dealing with such imponderables as the quality of management, which in the last resort can only be judged by those competent in the field. In such cases as this there may be two extremes. At one extreme is the case where it can be demonstrated, perhaps by some calamitous performance, that the manager is incompetent. The other extreme is the case where no more can be said that in the opinion of the employer the manager is incompetent, that opinion being expressed for the first time before his dismissal. In between will be cases such as the present where it can be established that throughout the period of employment concerned the employers had progressively growing doubts about the ability of the manager to perform his tasks satisfactorily. If that can be shown, it is in our judgment some evidence of his incapacity. It will then be necessary to look to see whether there is any other supporting evidence.

Notes

1. The ACAS Advisory Handbook offers the following guidance on how alleged poor performance cases should be approached:

* The employee should be asked for an explanation and the explanation checked
* Where the reason is the lack of the required skills, the employee should, wherever practicable, be assisted through training and given reasonable time to reach the required standard of performance
* Where despite encouragement and assistance the employee is unable to reach the required standard of performance, consideration should be given to finding suitable alternative work
* Where alternative work is not available, the position should be explained to the employee before dismissal action is taken
* An employee should not normally be dismissed because of poor performance unless warnings and a chance to improve have been given
* If the main cause of poor performance is the changing nature of the job, employers should consider whether the situation may properly be treated as redundancy rather than a capability issue.

2. While in most cases of poor performance a system of warnings should be operated, there are rare occasions where the employee commits a single mistake and the actual or potential consequences of that mistake are so serious that to warn would not be appropriate. This circumstance was discussed by the Court of Appeal in the next case.

Alidair Ltd v *Taylor*
[1978] IRLR 82
Court of Appeal

A commercial pilot made a faulty landing while flying 77 passengers in reasonable weather conditions. No one was hurt but the aircraft sustained considerable damage. He was dismissed following an inquiry into the incident. His claim of unfair dismissal was rejected by the industrial tribunal, EAT and Court of Appeal.

LORD DENNING MR: There are activities in which the degree of professional skill which must be required is so high, and the potential consequences of the smallest departure from that high standard are so serious, that one failure to perform in accordance with those standards is enough to justify the dismissal. The passenger carrying airline pilot, the scientist operating the nuclear reactor, the chemist in charge of research into the possible effects of, for example, thalidomide, the driver of the Manchester to London express, the driver of an articulated lorry full of sulphuric acid, are all in situations in which one failure to maintain the proper standard of professional skill can bring about a major disaster.

(b)   Long-term Sickness Absence   In cases of exceptionally severe and incapacitating illness where it is highly unlikely that the employee will ever be fit to return to work, the contract may be regarded as frustrated and therefore terminated by operation of law other than dismissal. The rules governing the doctrine of frustration and its relationship to long-term sickness absence and imprisonment were discussed at pp. 371–376.

Given that the frustration doctrine offers employers a convenient way in which to avoid the unfair dismissal provisions, the courts are generally reluctant to apply it to contracts which are terminable by notice. Therefore, in less drastic cases of long-term sickness absence, a body of case law has developed on the question of the fairness of a dismissal in such circumstances.

Spencer v *Paragon Wallpapers Ltd*
[1976] IRLR 373
Employment Appeal Tribunal

PHILLIPS J: There is no doubt that the industrial tribunal directed their minds to the correct question in this case. . . . They took into account the nature of the illness, the likely length of the continuing absence, the need for the employers to have done the work which the employee was engaged to do . . . The basic question which has to be determined in every case is whether, in all the circumstances, the employer can be expected to wait any longer and, if so, how much longer? Every case will be different, depending on the circumstances.

East Lindsey District Council v *Daubney*
[1977] IRLR 181
Employment Appeal Tribunal

PHILLIPS J: Unless there are wholly exceptional circumstances before an employee is dismissed on the grounds of ill-health it is necessary that he should be consulted and the matter discussed with him, and that in one way or another steps should be taken by the employer to discover the true medical position. We do not propose to lay down detailed principles to be applied in such cases, for what will be necessary in one case may not be appropriate in another. But if in every case employers take such steps as are sensible according to the circumstances to consult the employee and to discuss the matter with him, and to inform themselves upon the true medical position, it will be found in practice that all that is necessary has been done. Discussions and consultation will often bring to light facts and circumstances of which the employers were unaware, and which will throw new light on the problem. Or the employee may wish to seek medical advice on his own account, which, brought to the notice of the employers' medical advisers, will cause them to change their opinion. There are many possibilities. Only one thing is certain, and that is that if the employee is not consulted, and given an opportunity to state his case, an injustice may be done.

Note

The need for consultation with the employee was stressed in *Spencer* and strongly affirmed by the EAT's decision in *Daubney*. On the other hand, consultation has not always been required by industrial tribunals. In *Taylor-plan Catering (Scotland) Ltd v McInally* [1980] IRLR 53, it was suggested that where a tribunal finds that the circumstances were such that a consultation would have made no difference to the result, lack of consultation could be justified. In this case, the EAT was of the view that the guidelines in *British Labour Pump* could be applied in cases involving ill health. With the rejection of those guidelines by the House of Lords in *Polkey* it is likely that consultation will be required in the vast majority of cases. However, minor or understandable breaches of procedure in ill-health dismissals may be excused: see *A. Links & Co. Ltd v Rose* [1991] IRLR 353 and the next case.

Eclipse Blinds v Wright
[1992] IRLR 133
Court of Session, Inner House

Mrs Wright, a registered disabled person, had been employed by the appellant company since 1978. She was regarded as an excellent employee but, from 1985, her health deteriorated and her rate of sickness absence increased. At the end of 1987, she became a part-time worker and her attendance showed some improvement.

However, in March 1989, Mrs Wright became ill and was off work for some time. In May, she submitted a sick note for a further 13 weeks. She told the personnel officer that she thought her health was improving. She gave permission for her GP to be contacted in order to obtain his view as to her ability to return to work after 13 weeks. The GP's prognosis was not good and he could not see any possibility of her returning to work in the near future.

In the light of the GP's report, the company reluctantly decided that they would have to dismiss Mrs Wright and employ a permanent replacement. The director who took the decision decided against interviewing Mrs Wright. He was concerned that she did not appear to appreciate the seriousness of her condition and thought that her health was improving. He therefore decided to write to her, rather than running the risk of an interview where it might be difficult to avoid disclosing information about Mrs Wright's health of which she was unaware.

An industrial tribunal held that, in the circumstances, Mrs Wright's dismissal was not rendered unfair by the employer's failure to consult. The EAT, in allowing an appeal against that decision, considered that a sensitive consultation should have been carried out and a failure to consult was not justified. The Court of Session, Inner House, allowed the employer's appeal.

LORD ALLANBRIDGE: It is true that Lord McDonald in *Taylorplan Catering (Scotland) Ltd* v *McInally* [1980] IRLR 53 referred to what is expected in the normal case as regards the necessity for consultation, whereas Mr Justice Phillips referred to 'wholly exceptional circumstances' in several of the English cases in 1977. However, in our opinion these two approaches to the question of whether or not a consultation should have been held are not inconsistent with each other. One is the converse of the other, as if a case is wholly exceptional it is not normal. This was the view reached by this Court in the case of *A Links & Company Ltd* v *Rose* [1991] IRLR 353, but it is fair to note that, as stated at p. 12, there was no dispute in that case as to the duty of an employer who is considering dismissing an employee on the grounds of ill health, so the alleged inconsistency was not argued. In that case this Court held that it would require to go to a fresh Industrial Tribunal to decide inter alia whether consultation was appropriate in the circumstances because there had been no consideration given to that matter at the original hearing.

However, in the case of *A Links & Company Ltd*, it was also held by this Court, at p. 355, 6, that an Industrial Tribunal in approaching the question as to whether the employer acted fairly or unfairly must determine, as a matter of fact and judgment, what consultation, if any, was necessary or desirable in the known circumstances of the particular case. We are quite satisfied that that is the correct approach. We stress that it is a matter of fact to be determined by the Industrial Tribunal. This is also the approach suggested by Lord President Emslie at p. 238, para. 14 in *Leonard* v *Fergus & Haynes Civil Engineering Ltd* [1979] IRLR 235, CS. Furthermore, the Lord Chancellor in a somewhat different ease did stress that the matters of consultation or warning were matters for an Industrial Tribunal to consider in the light of the circumstances known to the employer at the time he dismissed the employee (see *Polkey* v *A.E. Dayton Services* [1987] IRLR 503] at p. 504. para. 5).

In this case it was quite clear from the agreed facts that the Industrial Tribunal did consider all the necessary and relevant facts. This was a case that the Industrial Tribunal decided was not normal and was exceptional as regards the question of consulting with the applicant. They accepted in terms, at p. 4H of their decision, that in normal circumstances the employers would have been expected to consult with the applicant before telling her she was to be dismissed. However, they decided, as stated at p. 5A-B, that Mr McNeil had a genuine concern to avoid giving the applicant information with regard to her health of which she did not appear to be aware and therefore concluded that his decision could not be said, in all the circumstances, to be so unreasonable as to render the dismissal unfair. This was a judgment which the Industrial Tribunal was entitled to make on the facts and it was therefore not open to the Employment Appeal Tribunal to displace that judgment on fact by its own view or judgment. No error in law by the Industrial Tribunal had occurred.

In this situation we allow the appeal, reverse the Appeal Tribunal and restore the decision of the Industrial Tribunal.

Notes

1. An employer will be expected to make a reasonable effort to inform himself of the true medical position, and this will normally entail consulting the employee and seeking, with the employee's consent, a medical opinion. A model letter of enquiry to an employee's general practitioner, approved by the BMA, is included as Appendix 4(vii) to the ACAS Advisory Handbook.

2. The Access to Medical Reports Act 1988 now regulates the supply of medical reports on employees to employers. The Act obliges an employer to inform an employee of its intention to ask the employee's doctor for a medical report and to obtain the employee's consent. There is also a requirement that the employee be informed of the following rights under the Act: the right to refuse consent for the employer to approach the GP; the right of access to the report both before and after it is supplied to the employer; the right to refuse consent to the report being supplied to the employer; the right to amend the report where it is considered by the employee to be 'incorrect and misleading'. The right to amend is qualified by the fact that the Act allows the doctor to accept or reject the amendments. However, where the doctor does not accept the patient's amendments, he or she must attach a statement of the patient's views to the report (s. 5(2)(b)).

If an employee does refuse to give consent to allow the employer to approach his or her GP, it may be taken by the tribunal to confirm the employer's doubts that he or she is fit to carry out his or her duties (see *Leeves v Edward Hope Ltd,* COIT 19464/77 July 1977).

Many employers now make it a term of employment that the employee must agree, if and when requested, to undergo a medical examination by the organisation's own occupational health practitioner or by an independent doctor to be nominated by the employer. The provisions of the Access to Medical Reports Act 1988 apply only to reports requested from the employee's *own* doctor.

3. For a checklist on handling long-term sickness absence, see the ACAS Advisory Handbook, *Discipline at Work,* 1987, p. 42.

(c) Persistent Absenteeism While long-term absence is treated as a matter of incapability, it is clear that persistent absenteeism should be regarded as a matter of misconduct and can be dealt with under the ordinary disciplinary procedure (see *International Sports Ltd* v *Thomson* [1980] IRLR 340; *Rolls Royce* v *Walpole* [1980] IRLR 343).

The following extract from the ACAS handbook provides a checklist of what the courts and tribunals expect from employers in handling cases of frequent and persistent short-term absence:

Discipline at Work, ACAS Advisory Handbook, 1987

- Absences should be investigated promptly and the employee asked to give an explanation
- Where there is no medical advice to support frequent self-certificated medical absences, the employee should be asked to consult a doctor to establish whether

medical treatment is necessary and whether the underlying reasons for absence is work-related

- If after investigation it appears that there were no good reasons for the absences, the matter should be dealt with under the disciplinary procedure
- Where absences arise from temporary domestic problems, the employer in deciding appropriate action should consider whether an improvement in attendance is likely
- In all cases the employee should be told what improvement in attendance is expected and warned of the likely consequence if this does not happen
- If there is no improvement, the employee's age, length of service, performance, the likelihood of a change in attendance, the availability of suitable alternative work and the effect of past and future absences on the business should all be taken into account in deciding appropriate action.

(d) *Dishonesty and other Criminal Offences*

ACAS Code of Practice 1
Disciplinary Practice and Procedures in Employment

15.(c) **Criminal offences outside employment**. These should not be treated as automatic reasons for dismissal regardless of whether the offence has any relevance to the duties of the individual as an employee. The main considerations should be whether the offence is one that makes the individual unsuitable for his or her type of work or unacceptable to other employees. Employees should not be dismissed solely because a charge against them is pending or because they are absent through having been remanded in custody.

Notes

1. Nevertheless, there may be cases where the period of absence on remand is lengthy and the employer may be held to be justified, in the interests of the business, in seeking a permanent replacement (see *Kingston v British Railways Board* [1984] IRLR 146, CA). Indeed, a lengthy period in custody on remand or a sentence of imprisonment on conviction may result in a finding that the employment contract has been 'frustrated'.

2. An employee may be fairly dismissed where he or she conceals from his or her employer a criminal conviction imposed before the employment began and which is not a 'spent' conviction under the Rehabilitation of Offenders Act 1974. Whether or not a conviction is spent and the individual is a 'rehabilitated person' under the Act depends upon the severity of the sentence and the time which has elapsed since it was imposed. A sentence of life imprisonment or a sentence exceeding 30 months are never spent. There is a sliding scale for the periods of time for the conviction to become spent, from six months for an absolute discharge, five years for a fine, seven years for a period of imprisonment under six months and up to 10 years where there is a sentence of six months to two and a half years.

3. In *Securicor Guarding Ltd v R* [1994] IRLR 633, the EAT gave its explicit support to the principles set out in para. 15(c) of the Code. The applicant, who worked as a security guard on the premises of an important customer, was charged with sex offences against children. He was dismissed even though he denied the charges to the employers; a collective agreement provided for suspension on full pay where investigations into misconduct could not be completed; and the employers never contacted the customer concerned to discuss the matter. Upholding the finding of unfair dismissal, the EAT stated: 'It does appear to us that it would be a very remarkable thing if it could be said that wherever an employee is in a sensitive position the mere fact that he has been charged with an offence will justify an employer not in suspending him; not in taking him away from a sensitive position; but in dismissing him.'

Rehabilitation of Offenders Act 1974

4. Effect of rehabilitation

(3) Subject to the provisions of any order made under subsection (4) below—

. . .

(b) a conviction which has become spent or any circumstances ancillary thereto, or any failure to disclose a spent conviction or any such circumstances, shall not be a proper ground for dismissing or excluding a person from any office, profession, occupation or employment, or for prejudicing him in any way in any occupation or employment.

Notes

1. See *Property Guards Ltd* v *Taylor and Kershaw* [1982] IRLR 175.

2. The scope of this provision is limited by subsequent regulations made under s. 4(4) which exclude certain professions and employments from the Act. Exempted groups include: medical practitioners, lawyers, accountants, veterinary surgeons, dentists, nurses, opticians, pharmaceutical chemists, judicial appointments, justices' clerks, probation officers, those employed by local authorities in connection with the provision of social services, and those offices and employments concerned with the provisions of services, schooling, training etc. to persons under the age of 18 where the holder will have access to young persons (or employment on premises used for providing such services) (see the Rehabilitation of Offenders Act 1974 (Exceptions) Order 1975 (SI 1975/1023) as amended by the Rehabilitation of Offenders Act 1974 (Exceptions) (Amendment) Orders 1986 (SI 1986/1249 and SI 1986/2268).

An employer, when recruiting to an exempted occupation, should inform candidates in writing that spent convictions must be disclosed. If a person is then employed having failed to disclose a conviction, the employer may be held to have acted fairly if it dismisses on subsequent discovery of the conviction (see *Torr* v *British Railways Board* [1977] ICR 785).

(e) *Suspected Dishonesty Within Employment*

BHS v *Burchell*
[1978] IRLR 379
Employment Appeal Tribunal

The employee successfully appealed to the EAT against a finding by an industrial tribunal that her dismissal for suspected dishonesty was fair.

ARNOLD J: What the tribunal have to decide every time is, broadly expressed, whether the employer who discharged the employee on the ground of the misconduct in question (usually, though not necessarily, dishonest conduct) entertained a reasonable suspicion amounting to a belief in the guilt of the employee of that misconduct at that time. That is really stating shortly and compendiously what is in fact more than one element. First of all, there must be established by the employer the fact of that belief; that the employer did believe it. Secondly, that the employer had in his mind reasonable grounds upon which to sustain that belief. And thirdly, we think, that the employer, at the stage at which he formed that belief on those grounds, at any rate at the final stage at which he formed that belief on those grounds, had carried out as much investigation into the matter as was reasonable in all the circumstances of the case. It is the employer who manages to discharge the onus of demonstrating those three matters, we think, who must not be examined further. It is not relevant, as we think, that the tribunal would themselves have shared that view in those circumstances. It is not relevant, as we think, for the tribunal to examine the quality of the material which the employer had before him, for instance to see whether it was the sort of material, objectively considered, which would lead to a certain conclusion on the balance of probabilities, or whether it was the sort of material which would to the same conclusion only upon the basis of being 'sure' as it is now said more normally in a criminal context, or, to use the more old-fashioned term, such as to put the matter 'beyond reasonable doubt'. The test, and the test all the way through, is reasonableness; and certainly, as it seems to us, a conclusion on the balance of probabilities will in any surmisable circumstance be a reasonable conclusion.

Notes
1. The *BHS* v *Burchell* approach was subsequently approved by the Court of Appeal in *W. Weddel & Co. Ltd* v *Tepper* [1980] IRLR 96, CA.
2. In *Boys and Girls Welfare Society* v *McDonald* [1996] IRLR 129, the EAT warned industrial tribunals against an unduly mechanistic application of the *Burchell* guidelines. The EAT stated that *Burchell* was decided before the amendment to EPCA 1978, s. 57(3), which established a neutral burden of proof. Therefore, a simplistic application of the *Burchell* test in each and every case involving dismissal on grounds of conduct raises a danger of the tribunal falling into error by placing the onus on the employer to satisfy it as to reasonableness. Nor is *Burchell* to be understood as saying that an employer who fails one or more of the three tests is, without more, guilty of unfair dismissal. The tribunal must ask itself whether dismissal fell within the range of reasonable responses.

Question
What if the criminal court subsequently acquits a person dismissed for suspected dishonesty?

Monie v *Coral Racing Ltd*
[1980] IRLR 96
Court of Appeal

The appellant worked for the respondent company as an area manager with control over 19 betting shops, and only he and his assistant knew the combination for the safe in the area headquarters. While Mr Monie was on holiday, his assistant discovered that £1,750 was missing from the safe. There were no indications that either the premises or the safe had been forcibly entered, and the respondents' security officer concluded that one or other or both were guilty. Both were dismissed. Monie appealed to the managing director, who accepted that the Monie had not been dishonest but that his admitted laxity in security matters justified dismissal in any event.

A tribunal found the dismissal fair on the basis of the employers' reasonable suspicion of dishonesty. The EAT held that suspicion was not sufficient to establish a sufficient reason for dismissal and that there were no grounds in this case for a reasonable belief in dishonesty; but that the dismissal was fair on the basis on Monie's laxity. Monie's appeal to the Court of Appeal was rejected. One of the issues for the Court of Appeal was whether it was fair to dismiss for suspected dishonesty in the particular circumstances of the case.

STEPHENSON LJ: To treat belief in the guilt of the particular employee as applicable to a situation in which an employer finds himself reasonably believing in the guilt of one or more of two employees but unable in fairness to decide which of them is guilty is to pervert a valuable guideline to interpreting and applying the statute in a way which turns justice into an inflexible rule which constrains tribunals to decide cases contrary to justice and equity and to the letter and spirit of the statute.

SIR DAVID CAIRNS: There has been much discussion as to whether a man can be fairly dismissed by reason of a reasonable suspicion of dishonesty or whether actual belief that he had been dishonest is necessary . . . This court has . . . given its approval to a type of test which requires something more than reasonable suspicion. This derived from a passage in the judgment of Arnold J in *British Home Stores* v *Burchell*. . . .

While guidelines such as those provided by Arnold J are helpful each case must in the end depend on its own facts. There is a great deal of difference between a case where only one man is under suspicion on the ground of some evidence of greater or less weight and a case where it is virtually certain that a serious theft has been committed by one or both of two men and it is impossible to tell which.

DUNN LJ: I agree with my Lords that in a situation of this kind, where there is a reasonable suspicion that one of two or possibly both employees must have acted dishonestly it is not necessary for the employer to believe that either of them acted dishonestly.

Note

This principle concerning 'blanket' dismissals has subsequently been extended by the EAT to cases of conduct or capability not involving dishonesty: see *Whitbread & Co.* v *Thomas* [1988] IRLR 43. According to this case, an employer who cannot identify which member of a group was responsible for an act can fairly dismiss the whole group, even where it is probable that not all were guilty of the act, *provided three conditions are satisfied*:

(a) the act in question must be such that, if committed by an identified individual, it would justify dismissal of that individual;

(b)   the tribunal must be satisfied that the act was committed by one or more of the group, all of whom can be shown to be individually capable of having committed the act complained of;

(c)   the tribunal must be satisfied that there has been a proper investigation by the employer to identify the person or persons responsible for the act.

(See also *Parr* v *Whitbread plc* [1990] IRLR 39, EAT.)

Frames Snooker Centre v *Boyce*
[1992] IRLR 472
Employment Appeal Tribunal

Burglaries at the employers' premises led to the view that they must have been an 'inside job'. Police suspicions focused on the three managers, but they could not narrow their suspicions further and made no arrests. After a further burglary, the employers decided on dismissal, but only dismissed two of the three, the third manager being the daughter of the owners, in whose honesty the employers had confidence. One of the two dismissed claimed unfair dismissal, on the ground that it was unfair to dismiss only two of the three. The industrial tribunal found the dismissal unfair, but this view was overturned on appeal.

HAGUE J: As a general rule, if the circumstances of the members of the group in relation to the relevant offences are similar, it is likely to be unreasonable for the employer to dismiss one or more members of the group and not others, and those dismissed will thus succeed in a claim for unfair dismissal. But if the employer is able to show that he had solid and sensible grounds (which do not have to be related to the relevant offence) for differentiating between members of the group and not dismissing one or more of them, that will not of itself render the dismissal of the remainder unfair.

D: Stage Four: What Remedies are Available?

Employment Rights Act 1996

112.   The remedies: orders and compensation
(1)   This section applies where, on a complaint under section 111, an industrial tribunal finds that the grounds of the complaint are well-founded.
(2)   The tribunal shall—
   (a)   explain to the complainant what orders may be made under section 113 and in what circumstances they may be made, and
   (b)   ask him whether he wishes the tribunal to make such an order.
(3)   If the complainant expresses such a wish, the tribunal may make an order under section 113.
(4)   If no order is made under section 113, the tribunal shall make an award of compensation for unfair dismissal (calculated in accordance with sections 118 to 127) to be paid by the employer to the employee.

Note

Although reinstatement and re-engagement orders are regarded as primary remedies by the statute, in practice compensation is the normal remedy for unfair dismissal, such orders being made by tribunals in 0.3 per cent only of successful cases. As a result, the re-employment of dismissed workers has been described as 'the lost remedy' (see Dickens et. al., *Dismissed* (Oxford: Basil Blackwell, 1985)).

There may be many reasons for the level of re-engagement/reinstatement orders. By the time the tribunal hearing is held – normally three to four months after the dismissal – the applicant may have found another job. Even if this is not the case, the passage of time and the adversarial nature of the proceedings may result in the relationship between the parties breaking down so severely that it would be unrealistic to expect them to resume a normal working relationship (see Lewis P., 'An analysis of why legislation has failed to provide employment protection for unfairly dismissed employees', *British Journal of Industrial Relations*, vol. XIX no. 3, November 1981, pp. 316–26).

(i)   Reinstatement and Re-engagement

Employment Rights Act 1996

113.   The orders

An order under this section may be—

(a)   an order for reinstatement (in accordance with section 114), or

(b)   an order for re-engagement (in accordance with section 115), as the tribunal may decide.

114.   Order for reinstatement

(1)   An order for reinstatement is an order that the employer shall treat the complainant in all respects as if he had not been dismissed.

(2)   On making an order for reinstatement the tribunal shall specify—

(a)   any amount payable by the employer in respect of any benefit which the complainant might reasonably be expected to have had but for the dismissal (including arrears of pay) for the period between the date of termination of employment and the date of reinstatement,

(b)   any rights and privileges (including seniority and pension rights) which must be restored to the employee, and

(c)   the date by which the order must be complied with.

(3)   If the complainant would have benefited from an improvement in his terms and conditions of employment had he not been dismissed, an order for reinstatement shall require him to be treated as if he had benefited from that improvement from the date on which he would have done so but for being dismissed.

(4)   In calculating for the purposes of subsection (2)(a) any amount payable by the employer, the tribunal shall take into account, so as to reduce the employer's liability, any sums received by the complainant in respect of the period between the date of termination of employment and the date of reinstatement by way of—

(a)   wages in lieu of notice or ex gratia payments paid by the employer, or

(b)   remuneration paid in respect of employment with another employer,

and such other benefits as the tribunal thinks appropriate in the circumstances.

(5)   Where a dismissal is treated as taking place by virtue of section 96, references in this section to the date of termination of employment are to the notified date of return.

115. Order for re-engagement

(1)   An order for re-engagement is an order, on such terms as the tribunal may decide, that the complainant be engaged by the employer, or by a successor of the employer or by an associated employer, in employment comparable to that from which he was dismissed or other suitable employment.

(2)   On making an order for re-engagement the tribunal shall specify the terms on which re-engagement is to take place, including—

(a)   the identity of the employer,

(b)   the nature of the employment,

(c)   the remuneration for the employment,

(d)   any amount payable by the employer in respect of any benefit which the complainant might reasonably be expected to have had but for the dismissal (including arrears of pay) for the period between the date of termination of employment and the date of re-engagement,

(e)   any rights and privileges (including seniority and pension rights) which must be restored to the employee, and

(f)   the date by which the order must be complied with.

(3)   In calculating for the purposes of subsection (2)(d) any amount payable by the employer, the tribunal shall take into account, so as to reduce the employer's liability, any sums received by the complainant in respect of the period between the date of termination of employment and the date of re-engagement by way of—

(a)   wages in lieu of notice or ex gratia payments paid by the employer, or

(b)   remuneration paid in respect of employment with another employer, and such other benefits as the tribunal thinks appropriate in the circumstances.

(4)   Where a dismissal is treated as taking place by virtue of section 96, references in this section to the date of termination of employment are to the notified date of return.

116. Choice of order and its terms

(1)   In exercising its discretion under section 113 the tribunal shall first consider whether to make an order for reinstatement and in so doing shall take into account—

(a)   whether the complainant wishes to be reinstated,

(b)   whether it is practicable for the employer to comply with an order for reinstatement, and

(c)   where the complainant caused or contributed to some extent to the dismissal, whether it would be just to order his reinstatement.

(2)   If the tribunal decides not to make an order for reinstatement it shall then consider whether to make an order for re-engagement and, if so, on what terms.

(3)   In so doing the tribunal shall take into account—

(a)   any wish expressed by the complainant as to the nature of the order to be made,

(b)   whether it is practicable for the employer (or a successor or an associated employer) to comply with an order for re-engagement, and

(c)   where the complainant caused or contributed to some extent to the dismissal, whether it would be just to order his re-engagement and (if so) on what terms.

(4)   Except in a case where the tribunal takes into account contributory fault under subsection (3)(c) it shall, if it orders re-engagement, do so on terms which are, so far as is reasonably practicable, as favourable as an order for reinstatement.

(5)   Where in any case an employer has engaged a permanent replacement for a dismissed employee, the tribunal shall not take that fact into account in determining, for the purposes of subsection (1)(b) or (3)(b), whether it is practicable to comply with an order for reinstatement or re-engagement.

(6)   Subsection (5) does not apply where the employer shows—

(a)   that it was not practicable for him to arrange for the dismissed employee's work to be done without engaging a permanent replacement, or

(b)   that—

(i)   he engaged the replacement after the lapse of a reasonable period, without having heard from the dismissed employee that he wished to be reinstated or re-engaged, and

(ii)   when the employer engaged the replacement it was no longer reasonable for him to arrange for the dismissed employee's work to be done except by a permanent replacement.

117.   Enforcement of order and compensation

(1)   An industrial tribunal shall make an award of compensation, to be paid by the employer to the employee, if—

(a)   an order under section 113 is made and the complainant is reinstated or re-engaged, but

(b)   the terms of the order are not fully complied with.

(2)   Subject to section 124, the amount of the compensation shall be such as the tribunal thinks fit having regard to the loss sustained by the complainant in consequence of the failure to comply fully with the terms of the order.

(3)   Subject to subsections (1) and (2), if an order under section 113 is made but the complainant is not reinstated or re-engaged in accordance with the order, the tribunal shall make—

(a)   an award of compensation for unfair dismissal (calculated in accordance with sections 118 to 127), and

(b)   except where this paragraph does not apply, an additional award of compensation of an amount not less than twenty-six nor more than fifty-two weeks' pay, to be paid by the employer to the employee.

(4)   Subsection (3)(b) does not apply where—

(a)   the employer satisfies the tribunal that it was not practicable to comply with the order,

(b)   [deleted by Employment Relations Act 1999, s. 33]

(7)   Where in any case an employer has engaged a permanent replacement for a dismissed employee, the tribunal shall not take that fact into account in determining for the purposes of subsection (4)(a) whether it was practicable to comply with the order for reinstatement or re-engagement unless the employer shows that it was not practicable for him to arrange for the dismissed employee's work to be done without engaging a permanent replacement.

(8)   Where in any case an industrial tribunal finds that the complainant has unreasonably prevented an order under section 113 from being complied with, in making an award of compensation for unfair dismissal (in accordance with sections 118 to 127) it shall take that conduct into account as a failure on the part of the complainant to mitigate his loss.

124.   Limit of compensatory award etc.

(1)   The amount of—

(a)   any compensation awarded to a person under section 117(1) and (2), or

(b)   a compensatory award to a person calculated in accordance with section 123,

shall not exceed £50,000.

(1A)   Subsection (1) shall not apply to compensation awarded, or a compensatory award made, to a person in case where he is regarded as unfairly dismissed by virtue of section 100, 103A, 105(3) or 105(6A).

(2)   [Deleted by ERA 1999, s. 36]

(3)   In the case of compensation awarded to a person under section 117(1) and (2), the limit imposed by this section may be exceeded to the extent necessary to enable the award fully to reflect the amount specified as payable under section 114(2)(a) or section 115(2)(d).

(4)   Where—

(a)   a compensatory award is an award under paragraph (a) of subsection (3) of section 117, and

(b)   an additional award falls to be made under paragraph (b) of that subsection, the limit imposed by this section on the compensatory award may be exceeded to the extent necessary to enable the aggregate of the compensatory and additional awards fully to reflect the amount specified as payable under section 114(2)(a) or section 115(2)(d).

Notes

1.   The provisions which now appear as ERA 1996, s. 124(3) and (4) were originally inserted by TURERA 1993, s. 30. These changes and other changes made in the compensation provisions (see below) are designed to tackle the weaknesses graphically illustrated in *O'Laoire* v *Jackel International Ltd* [1990] IRLR 70. An industrial tribunal, as part of an order for reinstatement, specified that the complainant should receive a sum totalling £27,833 gross representing back-pay between the date of the dismissal and the date of reinstatement. The employers refused to comply with the order and the complainant was awarded compensation of £12,185 (including an additional award) which was maximum which at that time could be awarded given the statutory limit on unfair dismissal compensation awards. His actual losses, as found by the tribunal, exceeded £100,000. The complainant then sought to enforce in the county court the provisions relating to back-pay set out in the reinstatement order. The Court of Appeal held that such an action was not available to the complainant. A reinstatement order is wholly unenforceable. If such an order is not complied with, whether wholly or in part, the complainant's only remedy is to apply to the employment tribunal for compensation. The monetary provisions of a reinstatement order do not create a cause of action enforceable through the county courts.

Noting the injustice of the position in the case of higher-paid employees, the Master of the Rolls expressed the view that the present maximum level of compensation for unfair dismissal could positively discourage employers from complying with an order for reinstatement. He felt the time had arrived for a fundamental review of the compensation limits.

2.   In the more frequent situation of a total failure to comply with the order, the tribunal will award compensation using the normal rules of computation plus an 'additional award' (see ERA 1996, s. 117).

3. It is a defence to the granting of the additional award if the employer can show that it was not practicable to comply with the order. Impracticability is therefore a possible defence at two stages in the process of tribunal decision making. The following circumstances have been held to render a reinstatement/re-engagement impracticable.

(a) Where it would inevitably lead to industrial unrest (*Coleman* v *Magnet Joinery Ltd* [1974] IRLR 343).

(b) Where there is no suitable vacancy. A re-engagement order does not place a duty on the employer to search for and find work for the dismissed employee irrespective of existing vacancies (*Freemans plc* v *Flynn* [1984] IRLR 486).

(c) Where the employee believes himself or herself to be a victim of conspiracy by the employers, or he or she is not likely to be a satisfactory employee in any circumstances if reinstated or re-engaged (*Nothman* v *Barnet London Borough Council (No. 2)* [1980] IRLR 65).

(d) Where there must exist a close personal relationship, reinstatement can only be appropriate in exceptional circumstances, and to enforce it upon a reluctant employer is not a course which an employment tribunal should pursue unless persuaded by powerful evidence that it would succeed (*obiter* from *Enessy Co. SA t/a The Tulchan Estate* v *Minoprio and Minoprio* [1978] IRLR 489).

(ii)   Compensation

Employment Rights Act 1996

118.   General
(1) Where a tribunal makes an award of compensation for unfair dismissal under section 112(4) or 117(3)(a) the award shall consist of—
(a) a basic award (calculated in accordance with sections 119 to 122 and 126), and
(b) a compensatory award (calculated in accordance with sections 123, 124, 126 and 127).
(2) [Deleted by the Employment Rights Act 1999, s. 33]
(3) Subsection (2) applies where the reason (or, if more than one, the principal reason)—
(a) in a redundancy case, for selecting the employee for dismissal, or
(b) otherwise, for the dismissal,
is one of those specified in section 100(1)(a) and (b), 102(1) or 103.

119.   Basic award
(1) Subject to the provisions of this section, sections 120 to 122 and section 126, the amount of the basic award shall be calculated by—
(a) determining the period, ending with the effective date of termination, during which the employee has been continuously employed,
(b) reckoning backwards from the end of that period the number of years of employment falling within that period, and
(c) allowing the appropriate amount for each of those years of employment.

(2)   In subsection (1)(c) 'the appropriate amount' means—

(a)   one and a half weeks' pay for a year of employment in which the employee was not below the age of forty-one,

(b)   one week's pay for a year of employment (not within paragraph (a)) in which he was not below the age of twenty-two, and

(c)   half a week's pay for a year of employment not within paragraph (a) or (b).

Notes

1.   The number of years' service that can be taken into account is subject to a maximum of 20 years (s. 119(3)). A week's pay is calculated in accordance with ERA 1996, ss. 220–229 and is based on gross pay. The maximum allowable for a week's pay is currently £220 (1999/2000). Therefore, in general, the maximum payment under this head of calculation in the year 1999/2000 is £220 × 20 × 1½ = £6,600.

Various payments and employment tribunal awards under TULR(C)A 1992 and ERA 1996 are subject to minimum and/or maximum limits. Prior to the passage of Employment Relations Act 1999, some of these limits were required to be reviewed each calendar year (for example, the limit on a week's pay used in calculating statutory redundancy payments and the basic and additional awards which may be made on a finding of unfair dismissal). Other awards and payments were not required to be reviewed annually but could be increased at the Secretary of State's discretion (for example, the compensatory award in unfair dismissal cases). Section 34 of the Employment Relations Act 1999 now provides that limits on these payments and awards will instead be index-linked.

Section 34(1) sets out the awards and payments to be index-linked. Section 34(2) provides that the limits on these payments and awards will be linked to percentage changes in the retail prices index, using the September index in each year as the reference point.

2.   The basic award used to be subject to a minimum award of two weeks' pay but this was abolished by the EA 1980. Therefore, given the operation of the deduction provisions set out below, it is possible for a tribunal to reduce the basic award to nil. However, there are two situations where a minimum award is still maintained:

(a)   Where the industrial tribunal finds that the reason or principal reason for the dismissal was redundancy but—

(i)   the employee refused or left suitable alternative employment, or

(ii)   the employee's contract was renewed or he or she was re-engaged within four weeks,

the employee will be entitled to a basic award of two weeks' pay (ERA 1996, s. 121). This is despite the fact that he or she would not be considered to be dismissed for the purposes of claiming statutory redundancy payments.

(b)   Where the dismissal is regarded as 'automatically unfair' because it is related to membership/non-membership of a trade union or union activity under TULR(C)A 1992, s. 152 or s. 153, the basic award (before any reduction for reasons set out below) will be a minimum of £2,900 in 1999/2000 and is subject to annual review (ERA 1996, s. 120).

3. If the complainant is 64 years of age, entitlement goes down one-twelfth for each whole month which has elapsed between the complainant's 64th birthday and the effective date of termination. For example, an employee aged 64 years and six months would have his or her basic award reduced by $\frac{6}{12}$ (half) (ERA 1996, s. 119(4), (5)).

4. Where the applicant has received a redundancy payment, whether under the statutory or a private scheme, the basic award will be reduced by the amount of that payment (ERA 1996, s. 122(4)(a)).

5. Where the employee has unreasonably refused an offer of reinstatement by the employer, the basic award will be reduced by an amount which the tribunal considers just and equitable (ERA 1996, s. 122(1)).

6. Where the employer makes an *ex gratia* payment which is specifically intended to cover any liability to compensation, if large enough this may also be set off against any entitlement to a compensatory award (see *Chelsea Football & Athletic Club* v *Heath* [1981] IRLR 73).

7. Where the tribunal considers that any conduct of the complainant before the dismissal (or, where the dismissal was with notice, before the notice was given), was such that it would be just and equitable to do so, it may reduce the basic award (ERA 1996, s. 122(2)).

8. The ERA 1996, s. 123, provides for the calculation of any compensatory award made under s. 118 of the Act.

Employment Rights Act 1996

123. Compensatory award

(1) Subject to the provisions of this section and sections 124 and 126, the amount of the compensatory award shall be such amount as the tribunal considers just and equitable in all the circumstances having regard to the loss sustained by the complainant in consequence of the dismissal in so far as that loss is attributable to action taken by the employer.

(2) The loss referred to in subsection (1) shall be taken to include—

(a) any expenses reasonably incurred by the complainant in consequence of the dismissal, and

(b) subject to subsection (3), loss of any benefit which he might reasonably be expected to have had but for the dismissal.

(3) The loss referred to in subsection (1) shall be taken to include in respect of any loss of—

(a) any entitlement or potential entitlement to a payment on account of dismissal by reason of redundancy (whether in pursuance of Part XI or otherwise), or

(b) any expectation of such a payment,

only the loss referable to the amount (if any) by which the amount of that payment would have exceeded the amount of a basic award (apart from any reduction under section 122) in respect of the same dismissal.

Note

The aim of the compensatory award is to reimburse the employee for any financial loss experienced; it is not to punish the employer for poor personnel practices (see *Clarkson International Tools Ltd* v *Short* [1973] IRLR 90). It follows, therefore, that if the employee has in fact suffered no loss then he or she should not receive a compensatory award. We have already discussed the decision of the House of Lords in *Polkey* v *A.E. Dayton Services Ltd* [1987] IRLR 503, where it was held that a dismissal could not be held to be substantively fair merely because with hindsight a procedural lapse would not have made any difference to the outcome. However, the reasoning of their Lordships in that case fully accepts the position that if failures in procedure would not have prevented the dismissal taking place then this should be reflected in the level of the compensatory award.

Rao v *Civil Aviation Authority*
[1994] IRLR 240
Court of Appeal

Mr Rao had a long record of poor attendance, for which he received a warning. After a medical showed no definite cause, he was dismissed. This was held to be procedurally unfair by the industrial tribunal. It decided against reinstatement and awarded compensation based on the following considerations:

(a) both basic and compensatory awards were to be reduced for contributory fault;
(b) to the reduced figure for the compensatory award there should then be a further reduction of 80 per cent on account of their finding that had the employers followed a fair procedure, there was only a 20 per cent chance of Mr Rao's employment continuing.

Mr Rao appealed against this decision arguing that the tribunal had adopted too strict a test in deciding whether re-employment was practicable. In addition, he alleged that by reducing the compensatory award because of the employee's conduct and then reducing it further on account that he would still have been dismissed even if the correct procedure had been followed, the tribunal had imposed a double penalty. Both the EAT and the Court of Appeal dismissed Mr Rao's appeal.

SIR THOMAS BINGHAM MR: It is argued by Mr Rao, who appears in this appeal in person, that a further deduction is not justified and that any appropriate deduction is to be made under [what is now ERA 1996 s. 123(1)]. Against that Mr McManus, representing the Authority, argues that a further deduction is permissible if warranted in the judgment of the Tribunal on the facts. In support of that he points both to the practice of the Employment Appeal Tribunal and more significantly to the fact that there are these two subsections in [what is now s. 123], one of which, subsection (1), is clearly directed primarily to the issue of loss and the second to the question of a reduction of the compensatory award to the extent considered just and equitable having regard to the employee's conduct and the extent to which it caused or contributed to any action of the employer.

For my part I consider that it is permissible in principle for a deduction to be made under both [s. 123(1)] and [s. 123(6)], and I would think the section curiously drafted if indeed both those subsections were directed to the same thing. It would, however, seem to me appropriate that those making this calculation should first of all assess what is the amount of the loss which the employee has sustained under subsection (1), and thereafter, and in the light of that finding, make their decision as to the extent to which the employee caused or contributed to the dismissal and on the question of what reduction it would be fair and equitable to make having regard to that finding. It does therefore seem to me that the 80% deduction should be considered first, and the contributory just and equitable finding should follow.

One asks, therefore, whether the Tribunal said anything different. To my mind it is extremely doubtful whether the Tribunal had anything different in mind, in particular because they did in fact specify the 80% deduction as one that they thought appropriate but did not specify any percentage in relation to the [s. 123(6)] deduction. It therefore seems to me that, whether as a result of science or the way that they set about it, they did exactly what the section indicates. Insofar as their statement of principle may suggest anything different, I think that may very well be because they were addressing themselves to the calculation of the basic award under [what is now ERA 1996 s. 122(2)] as well, and in that case there is no equivalent of [s. 123(1)]. Be that as it may, it seems to me plain that the next task of the Tribunal, when the matter eventually returns, is for them to consider what percentage deduction should be made from the basic award under [s. 122(2)] and what deduction, if any, should be made from the compensatory award under [s. 123(6)]. I say 'if any' because the fact that an 80% deduction has been made may very well in many cases, if not in this case, have a very significant bearing on what further deduction may fall to be made. That is, however, a question for the Tribunal, and to my mind there is no real room for doubt as to the manner in which they should or indeed propose to set about it. I therefore would dismiss the appeal and the matter will then go back to the Tribunal for the final assessment of the compensation. Mr Rao, who has argued his own case with skill and moderation, has pleaded that in view of the lapse of time that there has already been, it is desirable that the final decision before the Industrial Tribunal should be as early as possible. I am for my part extremely sympathetic to that desire on his part, and I would content myself with observing that the delay does not in any sense appear to be one that could be laid at the door of the Tribunal. Nonetheless, I hope the matter can be finally resolved as soon as possible.

Red Bank Manufacturing Co. Ltd v *Meadows*
[1992] IRLR 209
Employment Appeal Tribunal

Mr Meadows was made redundant after 32 years' employment with the company. An industrial tribunal found the dismissal unfair because the employers had failed to consult with the employee before dismissing him. In assessing the amount of compensation to be awarded, the tribunal based its calculation on the difference between Mr Meadows's actual earnings since dismissal and what he would have received in the job from which he was dismissed.

The employers appealed against the sum awarded on the following grounds. First, even if a fair procedure had been followed, no job would have been offered to Mr Meadows and that, therefore, compensation should be nil or, at the very least, reduced by a percentage. Secondly, since Mr Meadows's old job had been extinguished by redundancy, his loss of earnings could at best have been the difference between his actual earnings in his new job and what he would have earned in any job he might have been offered by the appellants. The EAT accepted this as the correct approach and remitted the case to the industrial tribunal for further consideration as to the appropriate award.

TUCKER J: . . . [I]t seems to us that since the decision in *Polkey* it is necessary for a tribunal when calculating the amount to be awarded for compensation to ask itself this two-stage question: If the proper procedure had been followed, and if consultation had taken place, would it have resulted in an offer of employment? This was the question to which the tribunal did address themselves in the earlier hearing, and to which they gave the answer that it might have done so. What the tribunal failed to do, and what in our view they should have done, was to go on to consider first what that employment would have been, and second what wage would have been paid in respect of it.

Norton Tool Co. v *Tewson*
[1972] IRLR 86
National Industrial Relations Court

(One of the earliest unfair dismissal cases but a case which still provides valuable guidance to industrial tribunals in approaching the compensatory award).

SIR JOHN DONALDSON P: . . . [T]he passage in the tribunal's reasons dealing with compensation is short:

With regard to the [employee's] loss of wages, he was paid 64p per hour for a 40 hour week, which works out at a weekly wage of £25.60. He was out of work for four weeks, so that he has lost four weeks' wages. In addition, we are entitled to take into account the circumstances of his dismissal; the fact that it was abrupt, that a sacking without notice involves a degree of stigma and that furthermore the [employee] had 11 years' service with the employers and he had lost the benefit of that.

. . . the amount to be awarded is that which is just and equitable in all the circumstances, having regard to the loss sustained by the complainant. 'Loss' in the context of section 116 [of the Industrial Relations Act 1971, and the precursor of ERA 1996, s. 123(1)] does not include injury to pride or feelings. In its natural meaning the word is not to be so construed, and that this meaning is intended seems to us to be clear from the elaboration contained in s. 116(2) [see now ERA 1996, s. 123(2)]. The discretionary element is introduced by the words 'having regard to the loss'. This does not mean that the court or tribunal can have regard to other matters, but rather that the amount of compensation is not precisely and arithmetically related to the proved loss . . .

But it is a corollary of the discretion conferred upon the tribunals that it is their duty to set out their reasoning in sufficient detail to show the principles upon which they have proceeded. . . . Were it otherwise, the parties would in effect be deprived of their right of appeal on questions of law. No great elaboration is required and the task should not constitute a burden. Indeed, the need to give reasons may well assist in the process of properly making the discretionary assessment of damages.

In the present case the tribunal has not made entirely clear the principles upon which it has acted and to that extent it has erred in law. . . .

In these circumstances, and in the light of the request of the parties to which we have already referred, we shall substitute our own award. In our judgement the employee is entitled to compensation in the sum of £375. This sum we regard just and equitable in all the circumstances having regard to the loss sustained by him. That loss falls to be considered under the following heads.

(a) Immediate loss of wages

The Contracts of Employment Act 1963, as amended by the Act of 1971, entitles a worker with more than ten years' continuous employment to not less than six weeks' notice to terminate his employment. [NB: an employee who had Mr Tewson's length of service would now be entitled to at least 12 weeks' notice (ERA 1996, s. 86).] Good industrial relations practice requires the employer either to give this notice or pay six weeks' wages in lieu. The employee was given neither. In an action for damages for wrongful, as opposed to unfair, dismissal he could have claimed that six weeks' wages, but would have had to give credit for anything which he earned or could have earned during the notice period. In the event he would have had to give credit for what he earned in the last two weeks, thus reducing his claim to about four weeks' wages. But if he had been paid the wages in lieu of notice at the time of his dismissal, he would not have to make any repayment upon obtaining further employment during the notice period. In the context of compensation for unfair dismissal we think that it is appropriate and in accordance with the intentions of Parliament that we should treat the employee as having suffered a loss in so far as he receives less than he would have received in accordance with good industrial practice. Accordingly, no deduction has been made for his earnings during the notice period.

We have no information as to whether the £25.60 per week is a gross or a take-home figure. The relevant figure is the take-home pay since this and not the gross pay is what he should have received from his employer.

(b) Manner of dismissal

As the employee secured employment within four weeks of his dismissal and we have taken full account of his loss during this period, we need only consider whether the manner and circumstances of his dismissal could give rise to any financial loss at a later stage by, for example, making him less acceptable to potential employers or exceptionally liable to selection for dismissal. There is no evidence of any such disability and accordingly our assessment of the compensation takes no account of the manner of his dismissal. This took place during a heated exchange of words between him and one of the directors.

(c) Future loss of wages

There is no evidence to suggest that the employee's present employment is any less secure than his former employment, and we have therefore taken no account of possible future losses due to short-time working, lay-off or unemployment, apart from loss of his rights in respect of redundancy and unfair dismissal which are considered separately below.

(d)   Loss of protection in respect of unfair dismissal or dismissal by reason of redundancy
These losses may be more serious. So long as the employee remained in the employ
of the employers he was entitled to protection in respect of unfair dismissal. He will
acquire no such rights against his new employers until he has worked for them for at
least two years . . . Accordingly, if he is unfairly dismissed during this period, his
remedy will be limited to claiming damages for wrongful dismissal, which are unlikely
to exceed six weeks' wages and may be less. Furthermore, upon obtaining further
employment he will be faced with starting a fresh two-year period. This process could
be repeated indefinitely, so that he was never again protected in respect of unfair
dismissal. Whilst it is impossible for us to quantify this loss, which must be much
affected by local conditions, we think that we shall do the employee no injustice if we
include £20 in our assessment on account of it.

Notes
1.   Immediate loss of wages represents loss of net earnings from the date of
dismissal until the date of the hearing. It may include sums covering overtime
payments and tips which may not be counted under the narrower rules
governing a 'week's pay' for the purpose of the basic award. Furthermore, for
the purpose of calculating immediate loss of wages, there is no limit on the
amount of the weekly wage as there is when the basic award is calculated.
    The tribunal will take account of wages paid in lieu of notice and earnings
in other employments and set these payments off against the compensation
otherwise payable under this head. The one exception to this principle of
deduction is where the employee receives earnings from a new employment
during what should have been his/her notice period with the former employer:
in this case the amount earned will not normally be deducted from compensation (see *Babcock FATA Ltd* v *Addison* [1987] IRLR 173, CA).
2.   Loss of fringe benefits such as company car, private health care, low
interest loan or subsidised accommodation will also be taken into account
in assessing compensation for both past and future loss. The ERA 1996,
s. 123(2)(a), makes specific reference to the inclusion of 'any expenses
reasonably incurred by the complainant in consequence of the dismissal'.
This might include the expenses incurred in looking for alternative employment but does not include the legal costs involved in bringing the unfair
dismissal action.
3.   Where the complainant is still without a job at the date of the hearing,
or has taken a job which is at a lower wage, the tribunal will have to embark
on a highly speculative exercise of forecasting the future losses which or she
is likely to sustain, including wages, pensions and other fringe benefits. Given
that assessment of future loss can only be an approximation, and the fact that
the statute gives a wide discretion to the tribunal, an award will not be
overturned on appeal unless clearly misguided.
4.   Loss of non-transferable pension rights on dismissal can be substantial.
In *Copson* v *Eversure Accessories Ltd* [1974] IRLR 247, two types of loss were
identified: (a) loss of the pension earned up to the date of dismissal, e.g. 15
years' service towards a pension of £X in 20 years' time at the age of 65; and
(b) the individual's loss of future opportunity to improve on his or her

pension position, i.e. the opportunity of improving his or her position until the time at which the pension becomes payable. Given the complexities and uncertainties surrounding loss of pension rights, a document was drawn up in 1980 by the Government Actuary's Department for the guidance of industrial tribunals. In 1991, this document was replaced by a new set of guidelines prepared by a committee of industrial tribunal chairs in consultation with the Actuary's Department: *Industrial Tribunals: Compensation for Loss of Pension Rights* (HMSO, 1991). The booklet gives general guidance on several aspects of pension loss with specific advice on the three main heads of loss: loss of pension rights from the date of the dismissal to the date of hearing; loss of future rights; and loss of enhancement of accrued rights. The authors emphasise that they are only offering guidelines and that it is always open to the parties to present their own actuarial assessments. Nevertheless, in this area of uncertainty the booklet will undoubtedly be very influential.

5. As is the case with the common law action for wrongful dismissal, no account will be taken of injury to feelings in assessing the compensatory award. However, there may be the exceptional case where the manner of the dismissal has had a tangible effect on the complainant's future employment prospects (e.g. by damaging his or her reputation in the trade or industry) and in such a case compensation may be claimed under this head (see *Vaughan* v *Weighpack Ltd* [1974] IRLR 105).

6. Where the employee is dismissed, he or she will have 'to start from scratch' in terms of building the necessary periods of continuous employment required to claim unfair dismissal and redundancy payment rights in the future. As a result, the tribunal will normally award a nominal sum as compensation for the loss of this protection. In *S. H. Muffett Ltd* v *Head* [1986] IRLR 488, the appropriate figure was assessed to be normally £100.

7. Deductions may be made from the compensatory award under ERA 1996, s. 123.

Employment Rights Act 1996

123. Compensatory award

(6) Where the tribunal finds that the dismissal was to any extent caused or contributed to by any action of the complainant, it shall reduce the amount of the compensatory award by such proportion as it considers just and equitable having regard to that finding.

Notes

1. Normally, the same percentage deduction will apply to both basic and compensatory awards (*RSPCA* v *Cruden* [1986] IRLR 83).

2. If the employee is found to have contributed to the dismissal, the award of compensation may be reduced by as much as 100 per cent (*W. Devis & Sons Ltd* v *Atkins* [1977] IRLR 314, HL).

3. In *Nelson* v *British Broadcasting Corporation (No. 2)* [1979] IRLR 346, the Court of Appeal emphasised that while there must be a finding that there was

conduct on the part of the employee in connection with the dismissal which was culpable or blameworthy, it

> does not necessarily have to involve conduct amounting to a breach of contract or a tort. It . . . also includes conduct which while not amounting to a breach of contract or a tort is nevertheless perverse or foolish or bloody minded. It may also include conduct which though not meriting any of those more pejorative epithets, is nevertheless unacceptable in the circumstances.

4.   It is easy to envisage the rules on contributory fault operating in cases of misconduct, but can they also apply in cases of dismissal for incapability? Conflicting answers have been given to this question. In *Kraft Foods Ltd* v *Fox* [1977] IRLR 431, it was held that where employees are doing their best and their best is not good enough, it would be wrong to reduce compensation on the basis of contributory fault. However, in *Moncur* v *International Paint Co. Ltd* [1978] IRLR 223, it was doubted whether an act or failing which is attributable to a defect of character or personality of the claimant, and which is not within his or her control to alter, can never be material when deciding the contributory fault. This approach has now received the approval of the EAT in *Finnie* v *Top Hat Frozen Foods Ltd* [1985] IRLR 365. While there is some doubt, therefore, about whether contributory fault is applicable in every type of incapability dismissal, it is clear that the principle of contribution *will* apply where the so-called incapability was due to the employee's laziness, negligence or idleness (see *Sutton & Gates (Luton) Ltd* v *Boxall* [1978] IRLR 486).

In *Slaughter* v *C. Brewer & Sons Ltd* [1990] IRLR 426, the EAT stated that, while ill-health will rarely justify a deduction for contributory fault, it may justify a reduction under the general just and equitable ground in ERA 1996, s. 123(1), where it is clear that the employee is incapable of doing the job.

5.   Section 123(4) of the 1996 Act further requires the claimant to mitigate his or her loss.

Employment Rights Act 1996

123.   Compensatory award
   (4)   In ascertaining the loss referred to in subsection (1) the tribunal shall apply the same rule concerning the duty of a person to mitigate his loss as applies to damages recoverable under the common law of England and Wales or (as the case may be) Scotland.

Notes
1.   A complainant must make reasonable attempts to obtain alternative employment. Unreasonable refusal of an offer of reinstatement by the same employer may amount to a failure to mitigate (*Sweetlove* v *Redbridge & Waltham Forest Area Health Authority* [1979] IRLR 195).
2.   There is an unresolved conflict as to whether a failure to invoke a right of appeal amounts to a failure to take reasonable steps to mitigate loss

allowing the employment tribunal to reduce compensation accordingly. See *Hoover Ltd* v *Forde* [1980] ICR 239 which favours this approach and the decision of the Scottish EAT in *William Muir (Bond 9) Ltd* v *Lamb* [1985] IRLR 95 which came out strongly against it. More recently, *Lamb* was followed by the EAT in *Lock* v *Connell Estate Agents* [1994] IRLR 444. See now ERA 1996 s. 127A (discused at p. 460).

3. Where the employer is able to establish that the complainant has failed to mitigate loss, this can result in reduction of the compensatory reward.

4. Any *ex gratia* payment made by the employer will be deducted from the compensatory award. The ERA 1996, s. 124(5)(a), makes it clear that the amount of the *ex gratia* payment must be taken into account *before* the statutory maximum is applied (see *McCarthy* v *British Insulated Callendars Cables* [1985] IRLR 94).

Similarly, the statutory maximum will only be imposed after the deduction of the percentage determined for contributory fault. On this basis, it is still possible for complainants to receive a maximum compensatory award despite being held to have contributed their own dismissal. There is a conflict of authority as to whether payments made by the employer to the complainant should be deducted before or after deductions for contributory fault (*Clement-Clarke International Ltd* v *Manley* [1979] ICR 74; cf. *UBAF Bank Ltd* v *Davis* [1978] IRLR 442).

5. In calculating compensation for unfair dismissal industrial tribunals no longer deduct sums – as they did prior to 1977 – in respect of unemployment benefit or income support which the complainant may have received from the Department of Employment or the DSS. Under the Employment Protection (Recoupment of Unemployment Benefit and Supplementary Benefit) Regulations 1977, the tribunal, when making an award of compensation, must identify the 'prescribed element' of the award. This element represents the amount of the compensatory award which is attributable to the loss of earnings between date of termination and the end of the tribunal proceedings. This part of the award must then be withheld from the complainant by the former employer. The Department of Employment will then serve on the employer a recoupment notice which requires the employer to pay back to them from the 'prescribed element' an amount representing any social security benefits which have been paid to the employee. Once this has been done, the balance of the 'prescribed element' must be paid by the employer to the successful complainant. The Recoupment Regulations only apply where unemployment benefit or income support was actually claimed during the period.

In assessing future loss, the tribunal also does not have to take into account the possibility of the receipt of future benefits by the complainant. Where compensation is based on unemployment for X weeks, for example, then the complainant is disqualified from receipt of benefit during this period (see Social security (Unemployment, Sickness and Invalidity Benefit) Regulations 1983 (SI 1983 No. 1598), reg. 7(1)(K) and Income Support (General) Regulations 1987 (SI 1987 No. 1967), reg. 35(1)(b)).

E: Unfair Dismissal Statistics

Compensation awarded to people by tribunals – unfair dismissal cases, 1997–1999

Compensation (£)	1997–98		1998–99	
	Numbers	*Per cent*	**Numbers**	*Per cent*
Less than 100	23	1	25	1.1
100–149	18	0.8	22	1.0
150–199	21	0.9	35	1.5
200–299	71	3.2	81	3.5
300–399	49	2.2	54	2.3
400–499	51	2.3	76	3.3
500–749	161	7.2	137	5.9
750–999	116	5.2	121	5.2
1,000–1,499	260	11.7	246	10.7
1,500–1,999	198	8.9	173	7.5
2,000–2,499	151	6.8	156	6.8
2,500–2,999	141	6.3	107	4.6
3,000–3,999	191	8.6	183	7.9
4,000–4,999	153	6.9	152	6.6
5,000–5,999	102	4.6	135	5.9
6,000–6,999	92	4.1	118	5.1
7,000–7,999	67	3	82	3.6
8,000–8,999	60	2.7	66	2.9
9,000 and over	303	13.6	341	14.8
All	**2,228**	*100*	**2,310**	*100*
Median	£2,422		£2,388	

Source: Labour Market Trends, September 1999, p. 495.

All unfair dismissal cases proceeding to a tribunal hearing; Great Britain; 1997–1999

	Number		Percentage of unfair dismissal cases proceeding to a hearing		Percentage of all unfair dismissal applications	
	1997–98	1998–99	1997–98	1998–99	1997–98	1998–99
Cases dismissed						
Out of scope	1,322	814	14.0	8.0	3.8	2.5
Other reasons	4,745	6,079	50.4	60.0	13.5	18.6
All cases dismissed	**6,067**	**6,893**	**64.4**	**68.0**	**17.2**	**21.1**
Cases upheld						
Reinstatement or re-engagement	26	28	0.3	0.3	0.1	0.1
Remedy left to parties	689	627	7.3	6.2	2.0	1.9
Compensation	2,228	2,310	23.7	22.8	6.3	7.1
No award made	407	281	4.3	2.7	1.2	0.9
All cases upheld	**3,350**	**3,246**	**35.6**	**32.0**	**9.5**	**9.9**
All cases proceeding to a hearing	**9,417**	**10,139**	**100.0**	**100.0**	**26.8**	**31.1**

Source: Employment Tribunals Service

Source: Labour Market Trends, September 1999, p. 494.

Question
What do the statistics set out tell us about:

(a)   success rates?
(b)   frequency of reinstatement or re-engagement?
(c)   typical compensation levels?

III   The Law Of Unfair Dismissal: A Critique

Critics of this legislation (see Collins, H., 'Capitalist Discipline and Corporatist Law' (1982) 11 ILJ 78, at p. 170; see also Denham, D.J., 'Unfair Dismissal Law and the Legitimation of Managerial Control', *Capital & Class*, 41, Summer 1990, p. 83) argue that the law has been unsuccessful as an effective control upon managerial prerogative in relation to dismissals and that, far from acting as a constraint on power, the law actually legitimates managerial control. An explanation for the weakness of the law lies in the attitude of the appeal court judges to the legislation. The judges are not happy with the unfair dismissal provisions because they are perceived to be 'corporatist' in that they overstep the boundary between matters which are suitable for State intervention and those which are not. The judges feel unhappy about meddling in affairs they have always thought should be left to individuals to resolve. Consequently, the courts and tribunals are unwilling to substitute their own standards of fairness for management opinion and instead have the tendency to endorse the ordinary practices of employers. Once this occurs it is inevitable that the concept of fairness will tend to favour managerial control. Evidence of this approach can be seen in the following areas:

(i)   The Concept of the Reasonable Employer
Earlier in the chapter we saw that in assessing reasonableness, the question is what the reasonable employer would have done in the circumstances and not what the employment tribunal would have thought. In this sense, the courts do not set the norms of behaviour but merely reflect existing managerial standards. A notorious example of this approach can be seen in the next case.

Saunders v *Scottish National Camps Association Ltd*
[1980] IRLR 174
Employment Appeal Tribunal

The employee was a maintenance handyman at a children's camp. He was dismissed on the ground of being a homosexual. A psychiatrist gave evidence before the tribunal that, having examined Saunders, he considered that he represented no danger to young people; and further, that heterosexuals were as likely as homosexuals to represent such a danger. The dismissal was held to be fair because a considerable proportion of employers would take the view that the employment of a homosexual should be restricted, particularly when required to work in close proximity to children. Mr Saunders' appeal was rejected by the EAT.

LORD McDONALD: It was argued on behalf of the appellant that the tribunal had made illegitimate and misinformed use of their knowledge and experience of how a reasonable employer would react. They had assumed, it was argued, in the teeth of the evidence that homosexuals created a special risk to the young. This does less than justice to their finding which is that a considerable proportion of employers would take the view that the employment of a homosexual should be restricted, particularly when required to work in proximity and contact with children. Whether that view is scientifically sound may be open to question but there was clear evidence from the psychiatrist that it exists as a fact. That evidence the tribunal were entitled to accept and it appears to have coincided with their own knowledge and experience.

(ii)   Overriding Contractual Rights
One of the most controversial areas of unfair dismissal has concerned the correct approach to the situation where the employer wishes to reorganise the business in such a way that changes result in the employees' terms and conditions of employment. These changes may not fall within the legal concept of redundancy because the work that the employee does is not diminished (see *Johnson* v *Nottinghamshire Combined Police Authority* [1974] IRLR 20; *Lesney Products Ltd* v *Nolan* [1977] IRLR 77). The test of fairness is not inevitably controlled by the content of the contract of employment. As a result, the courts and tribunals have been prepared to hold as fair dismissals where the employee has refused to agree to a change in terms and conditions of employment in line with the employer's perception of business efficacy. Dismissals for refusal to agree to unilateral changes in job content, pay, location and hours of work have been held to be for 'some other substantial reason' and fair (see, for example, *Ellis* v *Brighton Cooperative Society* [1976] IRLR 419).

Hollister v *National Union of Farmers*
[1979] IRLR 238
Court of Appeal

Hollister was employed by the National Union of Farmers as a group secretary in Cornwall. In 1976, the union decided to reorganise its insurance business in Cornwall, and this resulted in radical changes in the terms and conditions of the Cornish group secretaries. These changes were negotiated at head office level without consultation with the group secretaries affected. Mr Hollister refused to accept the new contract and was dismissed.

An industrial tribunal found that there was 'some other substantial reason' for the dismissal and that the employers had acted reasonably. The EAT allowed Mr Hollister's appeal on the ground that there had been insufficient consultation. The Court of Appeal restored the decision of the tribunal.

LORD DENNING MR: The question which is being discussed in this case is whether the reorganisation of the business, which the National Farmer's Union felt they had to undertake in 1976, coupled with Mr Hollister's refusal to accept the new agreement, was a substantial reason of such a kind as to justify the dismissal of the employee. Upon that there have only been one or two cases. One we were particularly referred to was the case of *Ellis* v *Brighton Cooperative Society Ltd* [1976] IRLR 419, where it was recognised by the Court that reorganisation of business may on occasion be a sufficient reason justifying the dismissal of an employee. They went on to say:

> Where there has been a properly consulted-upon reorganisation which, if it is not done, is going to bring the whole business to a standstill, a failure to go along with the new arrangements may well – it is not bound to but it may well – constitute 'some other substantial reason'.

Certainly, I think, everybody would agree with that. But in the present case Mr Justice Arnold expanded it a little where there was some sound, good business reason for the reorganisation. I must say I see no reason to differ from Mr Justice Arnold's view on that. It must depend on all the circumstances whether the reorganisation was such that the only sensible thing to do was to terminate the employee's contract unless he would agree to a new arrangement. It seems to me that paragraph may well be satisfied, and indeed was satisfied in this case, having regard to the commercial necessity of the arrangements being made and the termination of the relationship with the Cornish Mutual, and the setting up of a new relationship via the National Farmers' Union Mutual Insurance Ltd. On that rearrangement being made, it was absolutely essential for new contracts to be made with the existing group secretaries: and the only way to deal with it was to terminate the agreements and offer them reasonable new ones. It seems to me that would be, and was, a substantial reason of a kind sufficient to justify this kind of dismissal.

Notes
1. The tribunal will expect the employer to lead evidence to show why it was felt to be necessary to impose the changes (*Banerjee* v *City and East London AHA* [1979] IRLR 147), and it is also material for the tribunal to know whether the company was making profits or losses (*Ladbroke Courage Holidays Ltd* v *Asten* [1981] IRLR 59).
   On the other hand, the courts and tribunals have not imposed particularly strict criteria when judging the 'substantiality' of the decision to reorganise. In *Ellis* (above) it was suggested that the test was whether, if the changes were not implemented, the whole business would be brought to a standstill. A much less stringent test was formulated by Lord Denning in *Hollister* where he felt that the principle should extend to situations 'where there was some sound, good business reason for the reorganisation'. In subsequent cases, the EAT has been prepared to dilute the test even further; in one case requiring only that the changes were considered as 'matters of importance' or to have 'discernible advantages to the organisation' (*Banerjee* (above)) and in another demanding that the reorganisation be 'beneficial' (*Bowater Containers Ltd* v *McCormack* [1980] IRLR 50).
2. Surveys of the case law on reorganisation or 'business efficacy' tend to show the adoption of a strong conception of managerial prerogative by the courts and tribunals (see Painter, 'Any Other Substantial Reason: A Managerial Prerogative?' (1981) *New Law Journal* 131; Bowers and Clark, 'Unfair

Dismissal and Managerial Prerogative: A Study of "Other Substantial Reason"' (1981) 10 ILJ 34).

In *Evans* v *Elementa Holdings Ltd* [1982] IRLR 143, a case involving the imposition of an obligation to work overtime, the EAT moved some way to redressing this imbalance in favour of managerial prerogative in holding that, if it was unreasonable to expect an employee to accept the changes, it was unfair for the employer to dismiss. This view, however, was not accepted by a differently constituted EAT in *Chubb Fire Security Ltd* v *Harper* [1983] IRLR 311. In their view the correct approach, in accordance with the decision of the Court of Appeal in *Hollister* (above), was for the industrial tribunal to concentrate on whether it was reasonable for the employer to implement the reorganisation by terminating existing contracts and offering new ones. 'It may be perfectly reasonable for an employee to decline to work extra overtime, having regard to his family commitments. Yet from the employer's point of view, having regard to his business commitments, it may be perfectly reasonable to require an employee to work overtime.'

3. Some form of consultation over the reorganisation has been expected in the past in order to maintain the fairness of the dismissal. The dilution of the importance of consultation in *Hollister* – where the Court of Appeal held that consultation is only one of the factors to be taken into account when judging reasonableness and lack of it would not necessarily render a dismissal unfair – should be reassessed following the decision of the House of Lords in *Polkey* v *A.E. Dayton Services Ltd*. Having said that, there is no clear guidance on the form the consultation should take. In *Ellis* v *Brighton Cooperative Society Ltd*, the EAT were satisfied that the requirement of consultation had been fulfilled by union agreement to the scheme even though Ellis, as a non-union member, had little chance in participating in the scheme. In *Martin* v *Automobile Proprietary Ltd* [1979] IRLR 64, on the other hand, there are suggestions that non-union members should expect to be individually consulted.

(iii)   The Dilution of Procedural Fairness

An additional criticism of the approach of the judges was their increasing willingness to put less emphasis on the need to follow a fair procedure. Since, the *Polkey* decision, however, it may well be that flouting procedures will result in a finding of unfair dismissal in a much larger number of cases. But employees in such cases may find that they have achieved a Pyrrhic victory, because the tribunal may reduce their compensation to nil if it is found that they were in any way at fault for their dismissal (see *Rao* v *Civil Aviation Authority* [1992] IRLR 203 and *Red Bank Manufacturing Co. Ltd* v *Meadows* [1992] IRLR 209 at pp. 491–92).

(iv)   Conclusion

These illustrations tend to confirm the view that the judges are most reluctant to trespass too far into the area of managerial prerogative. If they do intervene it has been to regulate the procedure by which the decision to dismiss is effected rather than to question the substance of the decision.

Bob Hepple, 'The Fall and Rise of Unfair Dismissal', in William McCarthy (ed.), *Legal Intervention in Industrial Relations: Gains and Losses* (1992) p. 95

The question therefore becomes: how can one create *universalized* security of employment, at a reasonable level, for individuals while retaining economic flexibility? In my view, the key lies in the development of democratic participation. The first principle is universality, that is, the coverage of the *whole* employed workforce within the scope of unfair dismissal law. The second principle is that of representative institutions to control dismissals. In the British context, this might be achieved by building trade unions into the procedures for handling all types of dismissal, and by facilitating a speedy non-legalistic system of enforcement through an inspectorate with powers to reinstate workers subject to an appeal to a tribunal. The present two-stage approach to the determination of unfairness could be replaced by a broad concept of 'just cause' under which the substantive interests of management and the employee would be equally considered. But unfair dismissal law itself cannot operate in a vacuum. There is little point in developing this particular human rights guarantee in the employment relationship unless there are also macro-economic policies directed towards the growth of employment and welfare.

7 REDUNDANCY

I Introduction

Professor Grunfeld, *Law of Redundancy* 3rd ed. (1989), pp 2–3

The original Act's purpose was to mitigate the resistance of individual employees (and their unions) to the extensive changes which have accompanied and will continue to accompany the response of British industry, commerce and finance to the searching demands of world trade and competition. . . . In pursuing the 'policy that unnecessary workmen should not be retained in any industry but should be released so as to be free to take employment elsewhere' (*Hawkins* v *Thomas Foreman and Sons Ltd* [1967] ITR 59, at p. 61), the new legislation tempered the wind of industrial and commercial change to the redundant employee by providing an additional pecuniary cushion against the ancient hardship of loss of employment. The principal end of the Act was the national economic one of facilitating higher standards of efficiency and effectiveness in industry and commerce; the means used are of a social character, an extension on a selective basis of the social security system dealing with employment.

By the early 1960s, industrial innovation highlighted overmanning in almost all industries. The Government's response was the introduction, in 1965, of the Redundancy Payments Act (now repealed but the main provisions of which are now to be found in the ERA 1996). The 1965 Act is regarded as the first attempt to set up a specific and discrete body of employment law. Hitherto, employment legislation sought to do nothing more than tinker with existing common law principles of contract law which were of general application. For the first time, the Act gave positive rights to employees by recognising the concept of a proprietary right in a job, the loss of which merited compensation.

The sum awardable pursuant to the statutory scheme is calculated in exactly the same way as for a basic award for unfair dismissal (see Chapter

6), although many employers have, in conjunction with the unions, negotiated and agreed upon their own more generous schemes. The entitlement to a redundancy payment arises irrespective of whether or not the employee gains immediate alternative employment with another employer. Generally, it is to be hoped that the employer will make the payment voluntarily, thereby avoiding the necessity for an application to the employment tribunal for enforcement. If the employer is unable to make the payment, e.g. by reason of insolvency, then a government fund is available to satisfy a claim to a redundancy payment. This was originally known as the Redundancy Fund but is now encompassed in the National Insurance Fund. Until the Employment Act 1989, some employers were also able to apply to this Fund for a rebate against redundancy payments made. When this allowance ended, in 1989, it had been restricted to a 35 per cent rebate for those employing fewer than 10.

The Redundancy Payment Act 1965 was passed some six years before the introduction of the right not to be unfairly dismissed. Prior to 1971, dismissed employees sought to bring themselves within the provisions of the 1965 Act in order to claim their redundancy payment. Today, however, it is the employer who is rather more anxious to argue that the dismissal was due to redundancy. The affected employee would rather claim that he or she was unfairly dismissed simply because of the greater financial award available, having regard to the fact that with unfair dismissal a compensatory award may be made in addition to the basic award.

Lloyd v *Brassey*
[1969] 2 QB 98
Court of Appeal

LORD DENNING MR: . . . As this is one of our first cases on the Redundancy Payments Act 1965, it is as well to remind ourselves of the policy of this legislation. As I read the Act, a worker of long standing is now recognised as having an accrued right in his job; and his rights gain in value with the years. So much so that if the job is shut down he is entitled to compensation for loss of the job – just as a director gets compensation for loss of office. The director gets a golden handshake. The worker gets a redundancy payment. It is not unemployment pay. I repeat 'not'. Even if he gets another job straightaway, he nevertheless is entitled to a full redundancy payment. It is, in a real sense, compensation for long service. No man gets it unless he has been employed for at least two years by the employer; and then the amount of it depends solely upon his age and length of service . . .

Notes
1. For a discussion of the policy objectives underlying the Redundancy Payments Act 1965, see Davies, P. and Freedland, M., *Labour Law Text and Materials*, 2nd ed. (1984), pp. 394–6; Fryer, 'The Myths of the Redundancy Payments Act' (1973) 2 ILJ 1. The latter takes a more critical perspective on the policy objectives of the legislation than that adopted by Professor Grunfeld in the extract which introduced this chapter.

2. See p. 598 *et seq* for discussion of the law relating to unfair selection for redundancy.

Question
In times of high unemployment, can the award of a sum equal to the basic award be regarded as adequate compensation for the loss of the right to keep a job?

II Who Qualifies for a Redundancy Payment?

In order to qualify for a redundancy payment the applicant must show that:

(a) he or she is a qualifying employee; and
(b) he or she has been dismissed; and
(c) redundancy was the reason for the dismissal (ERA 1996, s. 135).

A: Employees Who do Not Qualify

In order to be entitled to a redundancy payment, an applicant must first ensure that he or she does not fall foul of the list of excluded persons contained in the ERA 1996, the main ones being:

(a) those who are under 18 years of age (s. 211(2) and s. 155), or who have reached retirement age (s. 156).

(b) those with less than two years' continuous employment (s. 155). At the time of writing we await a determination by the House of Lords of the question whether the two-year qualifying period for unfair dismissal and redundancy amounts to indirect discrimination against women contrary to European law (see *R v Secretary of State for Employment ex parte Seymour-Smith and Perez* [1999] IRLR 253, ECJ, discussed at p. 65).

(c) share fishermen, NHS employees, Crown servants and persons ordinarily working abroad (unless at the time they were made redundant they were working within Great Britain on their employer's instructions) (see ss. 159, 191 and 196);

(d) those refusing suitable alternative employment with the same or an associated employer (s. 141(2)) (see III below);

(e) those employed on a fixed-term contract for two years or more who, before the term expires, agree in writing to exclude their right to make a redundancy claim (s. 197(3)).

(f) those subject to an agreement made between an employers organisation and a trade union pursuant to which an application for exemption from the Act has been granted by ministerial order (s. 157);

(g) those dismissed for misconduct (see s. 140 below);

(h) prima facie, those who have failed to make a claim for payment in writing to their employers or to an employment tribunal within six months of the 'relevant date' of termination. However, if an employee submits a claim within a further six-month period, the tribunal has a discretion to make an award (ss. 164(1) and (2)).

Note

The EPCA 1978, like its predecessors, barred the right of part-time workers to claim statutory employment rights. Schedule 13 of the 1978 Act prohibited those working fewer than 16 hours per week from claiming redundancy payments. However, the House of Lords, in *R v Secretary of State for Employment ex parte EOC* [1995] 1 AC 1, held that such a bar was unlawfully discriminatory and breached the EC Equal Treatment Directive (see p. 61). Following the *EOC* case there was some uncertainty as to whether a lesser 'hour' qualification (e.g. eight hours) might be valid. This uncertainty has been removed by the Employment Protection (Part-time Employees) Regulations 1995, which make the number of hours worked totally irrelevant.

B: Dismissal

The definition of dismissal for redundancy purposes (s. 136) is the same as that for unfair dismissal (s. 95, see p. 424).

(i)   Dismissal for Misconduct

Employment Rights Act 1996

140.   Summary dismissal

(1)   Subject to subsections (2) and (3), an employee is not entitled to a redundancy payment by reason of dismissal where his employer, being entitled to terminate his contract of employment without notice by reason of the employee's conduct, terminates it either—

(a)   without notice,

(b)   by giving shorter notice than that which, in the absence of conduct entitling the employer to terminate the contract without notice, the employer would be required to give to terminate the contract, or

(c)   by giving notice which includes, or is accompanied by, a statement in writing that the employer would, by reason of the employee's conduct, be entitled to terminate the contract without notice.

Notes

1. This is a somewhat puzzling provision. After all, if an employee is dismissed for misconduct then that would be the principal reason for the dismissal and not redundancy. There is no clear decision on what this provision is intended to achieve. In *Sanders v Ernest A. Neale Ltd* [1974] ICR 565 (below), however, it was suggested that what is now s. 140 will exclude a claim where the employee is dismissed for redundancy but in circumstances where the employer could have dismissed for cause.

2. Because most forms of industrial action are viewed as breaches of contract, workers engaged in this form of activity may fall foul of this provision.

3. The exceptions to the operation of s. 140(1), i.e. s. 140(2) and (3), are referred to in the note at p. 509.

Sanders v Ernest Neale
[1974] 3 All ER 327
National Industrial Relations Court

Two employees were dismissed by reason of redundancy and other members of the workforce went on strike in protest. They were dismissed and the factory eventually closed down. The dismissed strikers then claimed redundancy payments but their claims were rejected since their dismissal was by reason of misconduct (i.e. the strike) and not redundancy.

DONALDSON P: . . . We should like to take this opportunity of exorcising the ghost of 'self-induced redundancy'. It can certainly occur, but as such it has no legal significance. Interruption of service due to industrial action can cause customers to look to competitors or to turn to substitute materials or services. This can lead to a diminution in the requirements of the business for employees to carry out work of a particular kind and to workers being dismissed. But the mere fact that the employees' action created the redundancy situation does not disentitle them to a redundancy payment. The entitlement depends on the words of the statute and there is no room for any general consideration of whether it is equitable that the employee should receive a payment.

The first issue in a redundancy claim is whether the applicant was dismissed by the employer. What constitutes such a dismissal is set out in s. 3 of the Redundancy Payments Act 1965 and it is for the employee to prove the dismissal if it is not admitted. The second issue is whether the employee has been dismissed by reason of redundancy. Here it is for the employer to prove either that there was no redundancy situation or that the dismissal was neither wholly nor mainly attributable to that situation (see the presumption set out in s. 9(2) of the 1965 Act). He may, of course, prove both. What is a redundancy situation is defined by s. 1(2) of the 1965 Act, but it should be remembered that the mere fact that the employer proposes a change in the terms and conditions of employment and is unable to carry on his business on the existing terms does not of itself prove that a redundancy situation exists (see *Chapman* v *Goonvean* [1973] ICR 310 and *Johnson* v *Nottinghamshire Combined Police Authority* [1974] ICR 170). If the employer fails or does not attempt to prove the absence of a redundancy situation, he can still try to show that the dismissal was wholly or mainly attributable to some other cause.

In the present appeals there was indeed a redundancy situation, but the tribunal found that it in no way caused the dismissals. The converse was true. It was the dismissals which caused the redundancy. The appellants were dismissed because they persistently refused to work normally. Their claim fails not because the redundancy was self-induced, but because it did not cause their dismissal.

Note
The disentitlement imposed by ERA 1996, s. 140(1), is subject to two significant exceptions:

(a) If the dismissal for gross misconduct takes place when the employee is already under the 'obligatory period' of notice for redundancy, the employee may apply to the employment tribunal which can award all or part of the redundancy payment (s. 140(3)). (The obligatory period is defined by s. 136(4) and is the period of notice which by statute or the contract the employer is obliged to give in order lawfully to terminate the contract.) In

Lignacite Products Limited v *Krollman* [1979] IRLR 22, an employee, having been given notice of redundancy, was thereafter caught stealing and summarily dismissed. The EAT agreed that it was right to reduce his redundancy award by 40 per cent.

(b)   If the misconduct takes the form of participation in a strike during the 'obligatory period' of notice, then any dismissal for that form of 'misconduct' will not operate to disqualify the payment claim (s. 140(2)). Protection will be lost, however, where an employee who is already on strike is then dismissed for reasons which might amount to redundancy. (See *Simmons* v *Hoover Limited* [1977] QB 284.)

(ii)   Dismissal – the Onus of Proof
The onus of proof is upon the applicant to show that he or she was dismissed.

Morton Sundour Fabrics Limited v Shaw
[1966] ITR 327
Queen's Bench Division

A foreman was warned he would be made redundant in the near future. The foreman immediately secured alternative employment, gave his employer one month's notice and claimed redundancy. It was held that he was not entitled to a redundancy payment because the warning did not amount to a dismissal.

WIDGERY J: As a matter of law an employer cannot dismiss his employee by saying: 'I intend to dispense with your services at some time in the coming months'. In order to terminate the contract of employment the notice must either specify the date or contain material from which that date is positively ascertainable. It is, I think, evident from what the tribunal has found that nothing which the employers in this case said to Mr Shaw in the early days of March could possibly be interpreted as specifying a date upon which he was to go, or as giving material upon which such a date might be ascertained. It was on its face not inappropriately described by Mr Henry in his argument to us as a warning of what was to come. If that is the true position, then nothing done by the employers at the beginning of March operated to terminate the contract of employment, and it would follow that the actual terminating event was the notice given by Mr Shaw later that month and not any action taken by the employers. That is a result achieved by applying the strict principles of law to this case, as in my judgment they clearly must be applied.

Question
To what extent does the approach evidenced in this case advance the policies supposedly underlying the redundancy payments scheme?

Burton Allton & Johnson v Peck
[1975] ICR 193
Queen's Bench Division

An employee was told by his employer that it would be in his own interests to accept redundancy. He thereupon volunteered for redundancy. It was held, nevertheless, that he had been dismissed.

GRIFFITHS J: It must be appreciated that it is to be hoped that in the large majority of cases where a man is made redundant, it will be effected after discussions and where both parties are in agreement that that is the best course to take. In any large organisation one expects to find that there are consultations between management and unions to thrash out the whole redundancy situation, that the employees are then brought into the discussions and that the first to be made redundant are those who volunteer for it. One also hopes that before they are made redundant very serious attempts will have been made to have other employment ready for them. But the fact that all that is done does not prevent the dismissal, when it comes, being a dismissal within the terms of section 3(1)(a) of the Act of 1965 [now ERA 1996, s. 136]. . . .

Mr Brown also relied on a decision of the Divisional Court in *Hempel* v *Parrish* (1968) 3 ITR 240, but the facts there were very different. Mr Parrish ran a small one man business as a painter and decorator, Mr Hempel was a friend of his, and the two men had worked together, although in law with the relationship of master and servant, for many years. Times became difficult and they both decided that they would temporarily go and work for another firm until, it was hoped, business would pick up and Mr Parrish would be able to resume again his own business. In that case the Divisional Court refused to reverse the decision of the industrial tribunal, which had held that there had been no dismissal under those circumstances. That is a very different case from the present one, and it is interesting to observe that even in that case Lord Parker CJ only agreed with some reluctance but did so, recognising that it was a question of fact and that it was impossible to say there was no evidence upon which the tribunal could have come to its finding.

The fact that the employee agreed to this redundancy is no ground for holding that it was not a dismissal within the meaning of section 3(1)(a) of the Act of 1965.

Note

Compare this case to *Birch* v *University of Liverpool* [1985] IRLR 165, CA (an extract appears at p. 376).

C: When is the Dismissal by Reason of Redundancy?

(i) The Statutory Presumption

Employment Rights Act 1996

163. References to industrial tribunals
(1) Any question arising under this Part as to—
   (a) the right of an employee to a redundancy payment, or
   (b) the amount of a redundancy payment,
shall be referred to and determined by an industrial tribunal.
(2) For the purposes of any such reference, an employee who has been dismissed by his employer shall, unless the contrary is proved, be presumed to have been so dismissed by reason of redundancy.

Willcox v *Hastings*
[1987] IRLR 298
Court of Appeal

Willcox and Lane were the sole full-time employees of a business owned and run by Willcox's father. The father sold the business to a married couple who intended running the business themselves, employing their son as further assistance. Both Lane and Willcox were dismissed and claimed redundancy payments. Since the new employer could not prove which of them had been made redundant, the Court of Appeal held that both were presumed to have been dismissed 'by reason of redundancy' so that both were entitled to redundancy payments.

LORD DONALDSON MR: What is said . . . is that there is no trace whatsoever of the Tribunal having taken account of s. 91(1) of the Employment Protection (Consolidation) Act 1978 [now ERA 1996, s. 163], which provides as follows:

> Any question arising under this Part as to the right of an employee to a redundancy payment, or as to the amount of a redundancy payment, shall be referred to and determined by an Industrial Tribunal.

Then subsection (2), which is the important subsection:

> For the purposes of any such reference, an employee who has been dismissed by his employer shall, unless the contrary is proved, be presumed to have been so dismissed by reason of redundancy.

The Employment Appeal Tribunal on appeal from the Industrial Tribunal thought that . . . the contrary had been proved. For my part I do not think that that is right.

The reasons given by an Industrial Tribunal, like the reasons given by a judge in his judgment, are not to be construed with the exactitude of a statute. The question is what is the message which is being conveyed by the judgment or, in this case, by the reasons of the Tribunal. The message that I get from paragraph 7 is quite simply this. Two people were dismissed. Two people had to be dismissed because there was a reduction in the requirements of the business to the extent of one employee, and another employee had to make way for the proprietor's son. That is uncontroverted. They then go on to say, 'There is no way in which we can decide which reason operated in respect of which employee. We are simply left with two employees leaving the service of the employer and two reasons, each of which could have been the cause of the departure of one such employee. In those circumstances, we just do not know. Maybe both operated on each. We just do not know'. Had they then added in the presumption, they must, as I think, have reached the conclusion that the employer had failed to rebut it. As is accepted by Mr Marr-Johnson, appearing for the employers, each case has to be looked at individually. This is not a bulk application. Mr Lane is entitled to say on the findings of the Industrial Tribunal, 'They do not know whether I was dismissed wholly or mainly on account of redundancy. Therefore I am entitled to rely on the presumption'. Mr Willcox junior is similarly able to say, 'They do not know. I can rely on the presumption'.

It is an unsatisfactory feature of this particular case that the Solomonic answer is without doubt that there should be one redundancy payment to be divided between the two applicants. It is an injustice if neither applicant can claim a redundancy payment. It is an injustice to the employers if they have to pay two redundancy payments. But we have to administer the law as it is, and, in my judgment, if the presumption in s. 91(2) is brought into account, as it does not appear to have been brought into account by the Industrial Tribunal, then these two applicants succeed.

Note

The Hastings were horrified to find that Lane and Willcox turned up for work the day the Hastings took over the running of the business, but they were, nevertheless, deemed the 'employer' because of the Transfer of Undertakings (Protection of Employment) Regulations 1981. See below, p. 547.

(ii)   The Statutory Definition
The ERA 1996, s. 139(1) defines a dismissal due to redundancy:

Employment Rights Act 1996

139. Redundancy
(1)   For the purposes of this Act an employee who is dismissed shall be taken to be dismissed by reason of redundancy if the dismissal is wholly or mainly attributable to—
    (a)   the fact that his employer has ceased, or intends to cease—
        (i)   to carry on the business for the purposes of which the employee was employed by him, or
        (ii)   to carry on that business in the place where the employee was so employed, or
    (b)   the fact that the requirements of that business—
        (i)   for employees to carry out work of a particular kind, or
        (ii)   for employees to carry out work of a particular kind in the place where the employee was so employed by the employer,
have ceased or diminished or are expected to cease or diminish.
(2)   For the purposes of subsection (1), the business of the employer together with the business or businesses of his associated employers shall be treated as one (unless either of the conditions specified in paragraphs (a) and (b) of that subsection would be satisfied without so treating them).

Note
In the following case the court was asked to investigate an allegation by the applicant employees that the closure of the business was motivated by malice rather than economics, the employer being fed up with alleged bad industrial relations at the plant.

Moon v Homeworthy Furniture (Northern) Ltd
[1977] ICR 177
Employment Appeal Tribunal

KILNER BROWN J: After the evidence of Mr Bullard was given, the chairman of the industrial tribunal with acute cogency asked Mr Stephenson whether or not he accepted that there was a cessation of work and therefore a closure. With integrity and common sense Mr Stephenson conceded the point. Technically, therefore, a redundancy situation was proved up to the hilt. But Mr Stephenson hung on to his proposition that if the reason of redundancy was relied on it ought to be open to challenge the declaration of redundancy on its merits. In the view of this appeal tribunal the argument then rails. There was a long discussion as to the meaning of paragraph 6(8) of Schedule [now ERA 1996, s. 95] and whether or not in the circumstances a reasonable exercise of judgment or assessment of the situation required to make a dismissal fair extended also to the decision to close down the factory. In other words, did the guidelines as to fairness of dismissal entitle the employees to challenge the creation of a redundancy? This brought the industrial tribunal back to realities and Mr Stephenson was asked what evidence he had other than evidence which sought to challenge the validity of the decision to close down. As he had none the tribunal ruled that as this was evidence he could not call he was bereft of any ammunition and his case must go by default.

Notwithstanding the care and the ability with which Mr Stephenson put his case, we are unable to criticise the way in which the chairman handled the matter or to find fault with his reasoning. However we would prefer to put the matter on a much broader and, in our view, more important basis.

The employees were and are seeking to use the industrial tribunal and the Employment Appeal Tribunal as a platform for the ventilation of an industrial dispute. This appeal tribunal is unanimously of the opinion that if that is what this matter is all about then it must be stifled at birth, for it was this imaginary ogre which brought about the demise of the National Industrial Relations Court. The Act of 1974 has taken away all powers of the courts to investigate the rights and wrongs of industrial disputes and we cannot tolerate any attempt by anybody to go behind the limits imposed on industrial tribunals.

Notes
1. This unwillingness to question the need for the redundancies is a further example of a general reluctance on the part of the courts and tribunals to restrain managerial prerogative. For other examples of this reluctance see Chapter 6.
2. The question of the dismissal being made because of the employer ceasing to carry on the business in 'the place' where the employee was employed was considered in the next case.

United Kingdom Atomic Energy Authority v Claydon
[1974] ICR 128
National Industrial Relations Court

Claydon was employed as a draughtsman under a contract which expressly permitted the employer to require its employees to work at any of its establishments in Great Britain or overseas. Claydon had worked since 1964 at the employer's Suffolk plant. In 1971, he was asked to move to its Aldermaston premises. He refused and was dismissed. He claimed, unsuccessfully, that the dismissal was for redundancy.

DONALDSON J: The problems which arose in this case would have been avoided if the employers had exercised their right to require the employee to transfer to Aldermaston. We appreciate that they refrained from doing so with the best of intentions. They were satisfied that the employee was unwilling to transfer and did not wish to be or appear oppressive or abrasive. We think that they made a mistake. If the contract of employment enables an employer to transfer an employee from a place where there is no work to some other place where there is work, the employer should first seek to persuade the employee to transfer voluntarily. If this is unsuccessful, he should require the employee to transfer. This should be clear and may have to be formal, but need not be in the least abrasive. It should spell out the consequences of failing to comply in order that the employee shall be in a position to make up his mind with full knowledge of all the relevant factors.

In the present case, for example, the employers could have written to the employee saying, 'We appreciate that you are reluctant to transfer from Orfordness to Aldermaston. Nevertheless we are faced with the problem that we need your services at Aldermaston and will have no work for you to do at Orfordness. As you will no doubt remember, your appointment in the service of the employers was on terms that the employers reserved the right to require any member of their staff to work at any of their establishments. A copy of the relevant conditions is enclosed. In the circumstances the employers find themselves obliged to require you to work at Aldermaston on and from September 1, 1971. It is for you to decide and let us know whether you are willing to comply with this formal requirement, but it is only fair that we should make it clear that if you are unwilling to do so the employers will be forced to terminate your employment upon the grounds that you have thereby broken your contract. In such an event you would not be entitled to a redundancy payment.'

Many men and women are employed under contracts of employment which provide for transfers over a wide area. If work is short in one place but available elsewhere within the area, there will be no redundancy situation and the employer can dismiss without being liable to make any redundancy payment. If, however, he does so without offering to transfer the employee to a place where work is available, he will risk being liable to pay compensation for unfair dismissal. That does not, of course, arise on the facts of this case, but employers should heed this warning.

Notes

1. As was seen in Chapter 2, even if the contract is silent as to mobility, such a clause may be implied (see *Jones* v *Associated Tunnelling Co. Ltd* [1981] IRLR 477; p. 87, note 2). In *O'Brien* v *Associated Fire Alarms Ltd* [1968] 1 WLR 1916, an expectation that employees should move from Liverpool to Barrow-in-Furness some 120 miles away was held to be something that could not be implied into the contract and amounted, therefore, to a dismissal for redundancy.

2. More recently, this conventional approach evidenced by *Claydon* was challenged by the EAT in *Bass Leisure Ltd* v *Thomas* [1994] IRLR 104. In this decision, the EAT ruled that 'the place' where an employee was employed for redundancy payment purposes does not extend to any place where he or she could be contractually required to work. According to the EAT, 'the place where an employee was employed for the purposes of [what is now ERA 1996, s. 139(1)(a) and (b)] is to be established by a factual inquiry, taking into account the employee's fixed or changing places of work and any contractual terms which go to evidence or define the place of employment and its extent, but not those (if any) which make provision for the employee to be transferred to another'.

The EAT's reasoning in *Bass Leisure* has now received the approval of the Court of Appeal in the following case.

High Table Ltd v *Horst*
[1997] IRLR 513
Court of Appeal

Mrs Horst was employed as a silver-service waitress by the appellant company, which provided catering services for companies and firms in the

City of London and elsewhere. Her letter of appointment specified that she was appointed as waitress to one particular client, Hill Samuel, and she worked there from July 1988 until her dismissal.

The appellants' staff handbook, which formed part of the employees' terms of employment, provided that, 'Your place of work is as stated in your letter of appointment, which acts as part of your terms and conditions. However, given the nature of our business, it is sometimes necessary to transfer staff on a temporary or permanent basis to another location. Whenever possible, this will be within reasonable travelling distance of your existing place of work'.

At the beginning of 1993, cuts in Hill Samuel's catering budget necessitated a reorganisation of services provided by the appellants which resulted in the need for fewer waitresses working longer hours. Consequently, Mrs Horst and the two other applicants were dismissed as redundant. The employees presented complaints for unfair dismissal. The industrial tribunal rejected the claims, holding that the employees had been dismissed for redundancy and that, in all the circumstances, the dismissals were fair. On appeal, the EAT decided that the industrial tribunal had facts before it which raised the question as to whether there was any redundancy at all but had failed to consider the matter. The EAT allowed the appeal on that ground and remitted the case for re-hearing.

The main issue on appeal to the Court of Appeal was whether what is now ERA 1996, s. 139(1)(a) and (b) impose a contractual test or a primary factual test in order to determine 'the place where the employee was so employed'.

PETER GIBSON LJ: [Referring to the EAT's reasoning in *Bass Leisure Ltd* v *Thomas* . . .] I am in broad agreement with this interpretation of the statutory language. The question it poses – where was the employee employed by the employer for the purposes of the business? – is one to be answered primarily by a consideration of the factual circumstances which obtained until the dismissal. If an employee has worked in only one location under his contract of employment for the purposes of the employer's business, it defies common sense to widen the extent of the place where he was so employed, merely because of the existence of a mobility clause. Of course, the refusal by the employee to obey a lawful requirement under the contract of employment for the employee to move may constitute a valid reason for dismissal, but the issues of dismissal, redundancy and reasonableness in the actions of an employer should be kept distinct. It would be unfortunate if the law were to encourage the inclusion of mobility clauses in contracts of employment to defeat genuine redundancy claims. Parliament has recognised the importance of the employee's right to a redundancy payment. If the work of the employee for his employer has involved a change of location, as would be the case where the nature of the work required the employee to go from place to place, then the contract of employment may be helpful to determine the extent of the place where the employee was employed. But it cannot be right to let the contract be the sole determinant, regardless of where the employee actually worked for the employer. The question what was the place of employment is one that can safely be left to the good sense of the industrial tribunal.

In my judgment, a remission on the first issue is not justified. It is plain that for all of the employees the place where they were employed by the employers was Hill

Samuel and that there was a redundancy situation there which caused the employees to be dismissed.

Notes

1. 'One point about the reasoning in the judgment is worth special mention, as it emphasises indirectly the often topsy-turvy nature of a redundancy claim. The Court argues that the factual test is necessary to protect Parliament's intention that the importance of an employee's redundancy rights should be recognised, and to ensure that those rights are not to be negated by unscrupulous use by employers of mobility clauses. Put in those terms, the judgment sounds pro-employee. However, the reverse may be the case. On the facts here (waitresses being made redundant by their service company employer when the client no longer wanted their work, with the employer then making no attempt to redeploy them), as is so often the case it was the *employers* who wanted it to be redundancy (as the simplest and cheapest option); the employees wanted it *not* to be redundancy in order to open up the prospect of a finding of unfair dismissal. This can be seen from the actual outcome of the case – the court upheld the employer's appeal and restored the original tribunal's decision that the employees *had* been dismissed for redundancy.

This decision in effect will often make it easier to establish a redundancy, and allow the employer the best of both worlds with a mobility clause – if there is one in the contract and the employee refuses an order to move pursuant to it, there could well be a fair dismissal; if, however, the employer does *not* activate it when work ceases or diminishes in the existing locality, the employer can still rely on a redundancy in spite of the clause. The Court in fact recognised this paradox, but said that 'issues of dismissal, redundancy and reasonableness in the actions of an employer should be kept distinct'. (*Harvey on Industrial Relations and Employment Law*, Bulletin No. 229, August 1997, p. 3.)

2. The emphasis in ERA 1996, s. 139(1)(b), is on the cessation of or diminution in the need for employees to do work of a particular kind, thereby creating a surplus of labour. It is important to appreciate that the crucial element is the excess of labour rather than the diminution in work – the amount of work may remain the same but re-organisation may lead to the need for fewer employees to do it.

McCrea v *Cullen & Davison Ltd*
[1988] IRLR 30
Northern Ireland Court of Appeal

Mr McCrea was employed as manager of the appellant company, which was experiencing financial difficulties. When Mr McCrea had to go into hospital, his work was taken over by Mr Bailey, the company's managing director. Mr Bailey realised that carrying out Mr McCrea's work in addition to his own was both practical and efficient. Accordingly, Mr McCrea was dismissed and given a redundancy payment.

His complaint of unfair dismissal was upheld by an industrial tribunal. According to the tribunal, Mr McCrea was not redundant because the amount of management work had not diminished. Rather, he had been dismissed for 'some other substantial reason' and in the circumstances his dismissal was unfair. The Northern Ireland Court of Appeal allowed the employer's appeal.

(NB: The definition of redundancy set out in s. 11(2)(b) of the Contracts of Employment and Redundancy Payments Act (Northern Ireland) is identical to that contained in ERA 1996, s. 139(1)(b).)

GIBSON LJ: [Referring to s. 11(2)(b)] The most obvious situation for the application of this provision is where the volume of work of a particular employer or in some department of the work of an employer has fallen off or been totally lost. In such a case some or all of the employees engaged in that work are surplus to the requirements of the business and so are redundant. It has been expressly found by the Tribunal that 'there was no evidence of any diminution either in the amount of work or in the type of work carried on' by the company. In this case the separate job of manager has disappeared, but that is not a determining consideration. If a manager is dismissed and another person employed to do his work whether he is given a lesser title such as supervisor, or given a lesser salary, or the converse, there has been no redundancy. The question to be considered is not does the business require a manager but does the business require the work of management carried out by the applicant to be performed by him or another doing the same work and only that work?

The Act was passed at a time when it was generally recognised that if British industry was to recover its competitive position in world markets the widespread practice of overmanning had to be reduced, and the provision of redundancy payments for those who were to lose their jobs in consequence was designed to make the implementation of the policy more acceptable to the trade unions. So it was immediately recognised that the Act applied to a second class of case where there has been no reduction in the volume of work of any particular kind but the requirement of the employer for as many persons to do the work has been reduced because of improved mechanisation, automation or other technical advance. The present case does not fall into that category.

A further situation in which the requirement of a business for fewer employees to do a particular kind of work may arise although there has been no reduction in the volume of work or production is where there has been a reorganisation of the workforce or a reallocation of functions between them disclosing a position of overmanning. It is this situation which at one time appeared to cause a divergence of opinion as to whether any employee dismissed in consequence of such a reorganisation could be said to be redundant within the meaning of the section. Certain portions of the judgments, and particularly those of Lord Denning MR, in *Johnson* v *Nottinghamshire Combined Police Authority* [1974] IRLR 20 and *Lesney Products & Co. Ltd* v *Nolan* [1977] IRLR 77 were by other judges regarded as indicating that if as a result of more efficient organisation or disposition of employees one who was dismissed in consequence could not be said to have been redundant. However, reconsideration of the context in which the observations were made clearly indicates that no such general proposition was intended. As Phillips J pointed out in *Robinson* v *British Island Airways Ltd* [1977] IRLR 477 at p. 478.7:

Reorganisation may or may not end in redundancy: it all depends on the nature and effect of the reorganisation.

The point is well made in the following quotation from the judgment of Cumming-Bruce J in *Delanair Ltd* v *Mead* [1976] IRLR 340 at p. 342.9:

> It is submitted by Mr Irvine on behalf of the employers that the Industrial Tribunal have applied the wrong test and have confused the diminution of work of a particular kind with the diminution of the requirement of the business for employees to carry out such work. It is clear that those two concepts differ in important respects, because the volume of work may remain the same though the requirement of the business for employees to carry it out has diminished. There are two obvious examples: (1) when a new machine is introduced which enables the same volume of work to be carried out by fewer men; (2) where there is overmanning such that on reorganisation of duties or terms and conditions of work the same volume of work is carried out by a slimmed down workforce. Mr Irvine submits that this case illustrates a third example, namely where for reasons of economy the employers introduce a new structure of management and supervision, and so reallocate duties that the same volume of work is carried out without the requirement of a foreman supervisor to organise and oversee its performance. That such reallocation of duties may give rise to dismissal by reason of redundancy is illustrated by *Sutton* v *Revlon Ltd* [1973] IRLR 173 and *Scarth* v *Economic Forestry Ltd* [1973] ICR 322. As Griffiths J said at p. 325 of the latter case: 'The fallacy is to equate the requirement to achieve an end with the requirement of the business to have employees in order to achieve the end'.

Sir Denys Buckley also emphasised the point in *Murphy* v *Epsom College* [1984] IRLR 271 at p. 276.37 as follows:

> Every case of reorganisation must, I think, depend intimately on its particular facts. In each case it must be for the Industrial Tribunal to decide whether the reorganisation and reallocation of functions within the staff is such as to change the particular kind of work which a particular employee, or successive employees, is or are required to carry out, and whether such change has had any, and if so what, effect on the employer's requirement for employees to carry out a particular kind of work.

> S. 11(2)(b) when applied to the facts of this case may be reduced to the proposition that an employee is dismissed by reason of redundancy if the dismissal is attributed to the fact that the requirements of the business for employees to carry out the work of management has diminished. It will be seen that what the section is directed towards is not a diminution in the work of management but a diminution in the requirement of the company for employees to do the work of management. Though the work of management remains to be done the applicant will be redundant if the company has so organised its affairs that the work is done by fewer employees. So the question resolves itself into one of fact, namely, is Mr Bailey merely doing the work formerly done by the applicant, in which case there is no redundancy but the replacement of one employee by another to do the work of the other, or has he undertaken the work of the applicant additionally to his own, in which case there has been a reduction in the number of employees required to do the work and the applicant's dismissal is attributable to redundancy.

Question

In s. 139(1)(b) of the 1996 Act, is 'work of a particular kind' the work which the employee actually performs, or is it the work which the employee could be obliged to perform under the contract of employment?

Nelson v *British Broadcasting Corporation*
[1977] ICR 649
Court of Appeal

Mr Nelson was employed as a producer with the BBC and his contract required him to work 'when how and where' the corporation required. Nelson had been working in the BBC's Caribbean service, but in 1974 that service was cut back and Nelson took the view that he should be transferred to another section of the corporation's overseas service. The BBC was only prepared to move him to a home service and told him that unless he accepted he would be treated as having refused the new post and his contract would be terminated on the ground of redundancy. The BBC claimed, unsuccessfully, that, by reason of the cutbacks in its Caribbean service, Nelson was 'redundant'. By his contract Nelson was required to work anywhere; accordingly the requirements of his job had not ceased or diminished.

ROSKILL LJ: The corporation's case before the industrial tribunal was simplicity itself: 'This man was employed for the purpose of the Caribbean Service. The Caribbean Service was being shut down as a result of Treasury demands for economy. Therefore we could no longer keep him there; his services were not required; and therefore he became redundant; and because he became redundant he cannot claim to have been unfairly dismissed.'

The industrial tribunal, as I said at the beginning of this judgment, accepted that argument and rejected the claim. They went into the matter with very great care. They held that Mr Nelson had become redundant. They reached that conclusion because of an argument that was apparently put forward that it was a term of Mr Nelson's employment that he should be employed for, and for all practical purposes only for, programmes for the Caribbean. That emerges very clearly from the industrial tribunal's reasons. It was said that, notwithstanding the very wide words of clause 8 of the agreement none the less:

> We think it was a term of Mr Nelson's contract of employment, arising by necessary implication or inference from the primary facts, that he was employed for the purposes of broadcasts to the Caribbean.

With great respect to the tribunal, that seems to me to be an impossible conclusion as a matter of law, for this reason: it is a basic principle of contract law that if a contract makes express provision (as clause 8 did) in almost unrestricted language, it is impossible in the same breath to imply into that contract a restriction of the kind that the industrial tribunal sought to do. . . .

Note
Nelson v *BBC* offers employers considerable scope for avoiding successful redundancy claims if they include a flexibility clause in the contract of employment. This issue was considered, and to some extent mitigated, in the next case.

Cowen v *Haden Limited*
[1983] ICR 1
Court of Appeal

The applicant was employed as a divisional contracts surveyor, but his contract enabled the employer to require him to do 'any and all duties which reasonably fall within the scope of his capabilities'. His post disappeared as a result of re-organisation and he argued that he could not be 'redundant' because of the wide scope of his job description and, therefore, he should be treated instead as having been unfairly dismissed. The Court of Appeal (while at the same time endorsing the contractual approach in *Nelson v BBC*) rejected his argument, holding that the requirement only related to jobs reasonably coming within the function of a divisional contracts surveyor.

CUMMING-BRUCE LJ: The first question to be answered is: What particular work was the employee employed to do under his contract of employment? In the first period of employment from June 1977 to August 1978 the answer is to be given by reference to paragraph 1 of the written document entitled 'Terms and conditions of salaried staff.'

The particular work which he was originally employed to do was not simply the work of a quantity surveyor but qualified quantity surveyor work of a particular kind, namely the duties of a regional surveyor, southern region, in the employers' business which was organised with the divisional office beneath which work was divided into a number of territorial regions. So he became responsible for carrying out the functions of the regional surveyor for his region, a job quite different from the jobs of individual surveyors within the region that he supervised.

The effect of the words: 'He will be required to undertake, at the direction of the company, any and all duties which reasonably fall within the scope of his capabilities' was not to give the employers the right to transfer him from his job as regional surveyor to any job as a quantity surveyor in their organisation, but only to require him to perform any duties reasonably within the scope of his capabilities as regional surveyor.

After the employee's heart attack in October, it was desirable in the interests of the employee for the employers to relieve him, if it was practicable, of the heavy burden of travelling imposed upon him by his responsibilities as regional surveyor. They reorganised their business in order to achieve this and created a new job on the establishment of their divisional office, called divisional contracts surveyor. It is clear that this job was created and tailored to fit the employee's individual qualifications with the intention of relieving him of the physically demanding travelling burden that he had had in his previous job as regional surveyor. So he was offered and accepted the new job as assistant to Mr O'Donnell, the divisional surveyor, and the employers replaced him in his original job by appointing Mr Richmond as regional surveyor, southern region. As explained in paragraph 4 of the reasons given by the industrial tribunal, in his new job he had to continue to deal with southern regional work at first because there was an interval before Mr Richmond took up his post as the employee's successor, and then because there were crises in the southern region at Bridgend and in Nigeria, so that Mr O'Donnell and the employee at the divisional office had to step into the breach and help Mr Richmond with his southern regional work.

It is quite clear that the transfer of the employee from his job as regional surveyor, southern region, to his new job as divisional contracts surveyor was a variation of his original contract of employment. He was replaced in his old job, and was offered and accepted a job with new and different responsibilities with a different and increased salary. No formal variation in the job title in his document giving the terms and conditions of salaried staff was made, nor was any formal revision made under paragraph 3 of that document. But the particular work which he was employed to do became the work of divisional contracts surveyor. In that job he was subject to the same term as before, that is, he was 'required to undertake, at the direction of the company, any and all duties which reasonably fall within the scope of his capabilities.'

Such duties were thereafter duties reasonably within the scope of his capabilities as divisional contracts surveyor. Up to his dismissal, those duties included helping out a hard pressed regional surveyor such as Mr Richmond in the southern region, as Mr O'Donnell and the employee in fact did. But after the employee had accepted the job of divisional contracts surveyor, the employers had not the right to require him to transfer from that work to assume the job of any one of their 90 quantity surveyors. There was no suggestion that the employers could or should have done so until he had been dismissed. So upon his contract of employment after the employee had accepted his new job, the particular work upon which he was employed by his contract of employment was the work of divisional contracts surveyor, a job which described the post of assisting Mr O'Donnell at the divisional office, sharing many of his duties including the duty to relieve regional surveyors as and when the need arose.

On the facts found by the industrial tribunal in December 1980 there was no longer a need for a divisional contracts surveyor. There was no longer a requirement of the business for an employee to carry out the particular kind of work of the divisional contracts surveyor because that work had ceased or at least diminished. A redundancy situation existed within the meaning of section 81(2)(b) of the Employment Protection (Consolidation) Act 1978 [now ERA 1996, s. 139(1)(b)].

. . .

On the facts the question and decision in *Nelson's* case is clearly distinguishable from the question that arose for decision by the industrial tribunal in the employee's case. The appeal tribunal took the view that there was a relevant analogy between the employee's rights and duties under the terms and conditions of his employment as divisional contracts surveyor and the rights and duties of Mr Nelson under his contract of employment as a producer and editor grade 3 for the B.B.C. With respect, the appeal tribunal was therein in error. Mr Nelson was employed simply as a producer and editor grade 3. So to establish redundancy within the meaning of section 81(2)(b) of the Act of 1978, the employer had to prove a cessation or diminution of the work of producers and editors grade 3. This the B.B.C. had not sought to do. By his contract the employee was employed to carry out a particular kind of work as a quantity surveyor, that is, the work of the divisional contracts surveyor, and on the finding of the industrial tribunal the employers proved at least diminution in that particular kind of work. It follows that there is nothing in the *Nelson v British Broadcasting Corporation* cases which bound the appeal tribunal to reach the decision which they thought they were bound, though with reluctance, to reach. . . .

Note
A commonsense approach to 'flexibility clauses' was taken by Smith J in the following case:

Johnson v Peabody Trust
[1996] IRLR 387
Employment Appeal Tribunal

Johnson had been employed by the Respondent housing association since 1977. By 1985 he had been promoted to the position of roofer. In 1988, because of the reduction in the amount of repair work, a 'flexibility clause' was introduced whereby, although Johnson was still employed and paid as a roofer, he was expected to undertake general building work. By 1993 Johnson was doing more general work than roofing and the Respondent laid off nine employees including Johnson. Was he dismissed by reason of redundancy within the meaning of what is now ERA 1996, s. 139(1)(b)? The EAT agreed that he was.

SMITH J: . . . In our judgment, in applying the 'contract' test in order to determine whether a redundancy situation exists, the contract should not be read in an over-technical or legalistic way but should be looked at in a common-sense manner in order to ascertain the basic task which the employee is contracted to perform. Where, as here, an employee is employed to perform a particular, well recognised and well defined category of skilled trade, namely roofing work, in our judgment it is that basic contractual obligation which has to be looked at when deciding whether the employer's requirements for work of a particular kind have or have not ceased or diminished. Were it otherwise, an employer could in practice never establish that any skilled tradesman, employed as such, who had accepted a flexibility clause of the kind in this case, had become redundant without establishing that a redundancy situation existed in every single other trade encompassed within the ambit of such a flexibility clause. In our judgment so to construe s. 81(2)(b) of the 1978 Act [now ERA 1996, s. 139(1)(b)] would be to subject the wording to an artificial and overly legalistic construction and would impose an unreasonable burden upon employers.

Notes
1.   See also *Pink* v *White & Co. Limited* [1985] IRLR 489.
2.   In the next case, the EAT declares that the 'contract' versus 'function' debate is based on a misreading both of the statute and of the authorities. In so doing, the EAT seeks to return to first principles in answering the question: what is redundancy?

Safeway Stores plc v *Burrell*
[1997] IRLR 200
Employment Appeal Tribunal

Mr Burrell, a petrol station manager, was told that there would be a re-organisation of the management structure and that the post of 'petrol station manager' would disappear. It would be replaced by a new post of petrol filling station controller (at a lower salary). Existing post-holders could apply for the posts, although as there were fewer posts than managers there would be redundancies. Mr Burrell declined the invitation to apply and brought a complaint of unfair dismissal. He argued that the new job was essentially the same as the old one so that there was no 'redundancy' situation. The employer contended that it was a genuine redundancy, or, alternatively, that there was justification for the dismissal on the basis of 'some other substantial reason', namely, a re-organisation. The majority of the industrial tribunal upheld his claim. Many of the jobs he had actually done (the 'function' test) were still required, albeit by someone with a different job title. The tribunal Chairman (in the minority) looked at what Mr Burrell's contract required (the 'contract' test) and concluded that the job he was *employed* to do 'no longer existed'. The EAT allowed the appeal and remitted the case for reconsideration by another industrial tribunal.

JUDGE PETER CLARK: . . . Free of authority, we understand the statutory framework of s. 81(2)(b) to involve a three-stage process:

(1)   was the employee dismissed? If so,
(2)   had the requirements of the employer's business for employees to carry out work of a particular kind ceased or diminished, or were they expected to cease or diminish? If so,
(3)   was the dismissal of the employee (the applicant before the industrial tribunal) caused wholly or mainly by the state of affairs identified at stage 2 above?

The position is, however, not free of authority Far from it. It is therefore to those authorities, with the assistance of counsel, which we must now turn.
. . .

The correct approach
Like the appeal tribunal in *Cowen* v *Haden Carrier*, we started by looking at the statute and construing the words free of authority. Similarly, we have looked at the authorities. Unlike that tribunal, we return to our original approach and conclude first that it was correct, and secondly that no binding authority causes us to abandon that position. We would summarise it as follows:

(1)   There may be a number of underlying causes leading to a true redundancy situation; our stage 2. There may be a need for economies; a reorganisation in the interests of efficiency; a reduction in production requirements; unilateral changes in the employees' terms and conditions of employment. None of these factors are themselves determinative of the stage 2 question. The only question to be asked is: was there a diminution/cessation in the employer's requirement for *employees* to carry out work of a particular kind, or an expectation of such cessation/diminution in the future [redundancy]? At this stage it is irrelevant to consider the terms of the applicant employee's contract of employment. That will only be relevant, if at all, at stage 3 (assuming that there is a dismissal).
(2)   At stage 3 the tribunal is concerned with causation. Was the dismissal attributable wholly or mainly to the redundancy? Thus–
(a)   Even if a redundancy situation arises, as in *Nelson*, if that does not cause the dismissal, the employee has not been dismissed by reason of redundancy. In *Nelson* the employee was directed to transfer to another job as provided for in his contract. He refused to do so. That was why he was dismissed.
(b)   If the requirement for employees to perform the work of a transport clerk and transport manager diminishes, so that one employee can do both jobs, the dismissed employee is dismissed by reason of redundancy. See [*Carry All Motors Ltd* v *Pennington* [1980] IRLR 455, EAT. The same explanation applies, on the facts, to the eventual decision in [*Robinson* v *British Island Airways* [1977] IRLR 477, EAT. In *Cowen* v *Haden Carrier* the requirement for employees to do the work of a divisional contracts surveyor ceased. The postholder was dismissed. That was a dismissal by reason of redundancy.
(c)   Conversely, if the requirement for employees to do work of a particular kind remains the same, there can be no dismissal by reason of redundancy, notwithstanding

any unilateral variation to their contracts of employment. See *Chapman, Lesney* and [*Johnson* v *Nottinghamshire Combined Police Authority* [1974] ICR 170.

(d)   The contract versus function test debate is predicated on a misreading of both the statute and the cases of *Nelson* and *Cowen* v *Haden Carrier*. Save for the limited circumstances arising from *Nelson* where an employee is redeployed under the terms of his contract of employment and refuses to move, and this causes his dismissal, the applicant/employee's terms and conditions of employment are irrelevant to the questions raised by the statute.

(e)   This explains the concept of 'bumped redundancies'. Take this example: an employee is employed to work as a fork-lift truck driver, delivering materials to six production machines on the shop floor. Each machine has its own operator. The employer decides that it needs to run only five machines and that one machine operator must go. That is a stage 2 redundancy situation. Selection for dismissal is done on the LIFO principle within the department. The fork-lift truck driver has the least service. Accordingly, one machine operator is transferred to driving the truck; the short-service truck driver is dismissed. Is he dismissed by reason of redundancy? The answer is yes. Although under both the contract and function tests he is employed as a fork-lift driver, and there is no diminution in the requirement for fork-lift drivers, nevertheless there is a diminution in the requirement for employees to carry out the operators' work and that has caused the employee's dismissal. See, for example, *W Gimbert & Sons Ltd* v *Spurett* [1967] 2 ITR 308; *Elliott Turbomachinery* v *Bates* [1981] ICR 218. In our judgment, the principle of 'bumped' redundancies is statutorily correct, and further demonstrates the flaw in the 'contract test' adumbrated in *Pink*.

(f)   Our approach is also consistent with the decision of the Court of Appeal in *Murphy* v *Epsom College* [1984] IRLR 271. There, the applicant was one of two plumbers employed by a school. His work consisted mainly of general plumbing work. The employers decided to employ a heating technician to maintain their improved heating system. They then decided to dismiss one of the two plumbers and selected the employee for dismissal. The Court of Appeal upheld the majority view of the industrial tribunal that the reason for dismissal was redundancy. The employer originally had two plumbers; now it only required one. The employee was dismissed by reason of redundancy.

The instant case
In our judgment, the tribunal fell into error in the following respects:

(1)   The majority failed to apply the correct statutory test in finding that the applicant's dismissal was not by reason of redundancy. It failed to ask itself whether there was a stage 2 redundancy situation, looking at the overall requirement of the employer for employees to carry out work of a particular kind, and then to consider whether that redundancy situation caused the applicant's admitted dismissal.

(2)   The majority failed to consider whether Safeway had, in the alternative, established some other substantial reason for dismissal.

(3)   It follows that the tribunal made no finding as to whether or not the employer acted reasonably in treating the true reason for dismissal as a sufficient reason.

The appeal is allowed.

Notes

1.   The reasoning in *Safeway* was not followed by the EAT in *Church* v *West Lancashire NHS Trust* [1998] IRLR 4, EAT. The employer decided to restructure the department in which Mr Church worked. One post was

abolished and all the employees were invited to apply for the remaining posts on a competitive basis. A 'bumping' situation was thereby created which meant that displaced employees replaced those whose jobs were not directly affected by the re-organisation. On that basis, Mr Church was 'bumped' and selected for redundancy, even though his job remained the same and was filled by another employee who otherwise would have been dismissed. Mr Church alleged that, in the circumstances, his dismissal was not by reason of redundancy and was unfair.

The industrial tribunal, relying on a line of authority endorsing the notion of 'bumped' redundancies, in particular the decision of the Divisional Court in *W Gimbert & Sons Ltd* v *Spurrett* [1967] 2 ITR 308, HC, and that of the EAT in *Elliott Turbo Machinery Ltd* v *Bates* [1981] ICR 218, concluded that the reason for Mr. Church's dismissal was redundancy, that he had been fairly selected and properly consulted and that his dismissal was fair.

Subsequent to the tribunal's decision in Church, the EAT concluded in *Safeway Stores Ltd* v *Burrell* that the work of a particular kind referred to in s. 139 did not need to be the work of the dismissed employee. Thus, if the requirements for employees to do A's work had diminished, and A replaced B, whose work was different and for which the requirements for employees had not diminished, then B was dismissed by reason of redundancy. The EAT allowed the employer's appeal.

2.   *Church* makes two main criticisms of *Safeway*. First is that *Safeway* is wrong if and so far as it maintains that the contract of employment is irrelevant in determining whether the business needed fewer employees to early out work of a particular kind. *Church* states that 'the proper test is neither contractual nor functional but a sensible blend of the two'. This view was shared by the EAT in the more recent case of *Shawkat* v *Nottingham City Hospital* [1999] IRLR 340. The second criticism is that the proper meaning of 'work of a particular kind' is that it is 'work of a particular kind which the *relevant employee* was employed to do'. It follows from *Church* that a 'bumped' dismissal is not within the statutory definition of redundancy. If the reasoning in *Church* is correct:

the practical consequence will be to undermine many redundancy selection procedures, especially the more sophisticated seniority-based systems. It will also bring an extra element of uncertainty into redundancy situations. Before deciding to dismiss one employee rather than another for an economic reason, a judgment will have to be made as to whether the work of two employees is sufficiently similar so as to amount to the same 'work of a particular kind'. If it is not, even though the employees may have transferable skills and be subject to a flexibility agreement, the ensuing dismissal would not be on grounds of redundancy, the employee would not be entitled to a statutory redundancy payment, and the employer might have to defend an unfair dismissal claim. Thus, this decision enhances the value of contractual severance terms which will apply to regardless of whether the statutory definition of redundancy is satisfied. (Michael Rubenstein, 'Highlights' [1998] IRLR 1)

3.   The *Safeway/Church* controversy has now been resolved by the House of Lords in the next case.

Murray and another v *Foyle Meats*
[1999] IRLR 56
House of Lords

The applicants were employed as meat plant operatives. They normally worked in the slaughter hall, but under their contracts of employment they could be required to work elsewhere in the factory and occasionally had done so. Employees who worked in other parts of the factory, such as the boning hall or the loading bay, were also engaged as meat plant operatives on similar terms.

In 1995, a decline in the business prompted a re-organisation in the slaughter hall which resulted in the the need to reduce the number of skilled slaughterers. Following consultation with the trade union on the criteria for selection, the applicants were dismissed as redundant. They complained that their dismissals were unfair.

The employers submitted that the applicants' dismissals were wholly attributable to the fact that that the requirements of the business for employees to carry out work of a particular kind, namely, on the slaughtering line, had diminished and therefore fell within the statutory definition of redundancy.

A Northern Ireland employment tribunal accepted the employers' submission and dismissed the applicants' claims. On appeal to the House of Lords, it was submitted for the applicants that 'requirements for employees to carry out work of a particular kind' means 'requirements for employees contractually engaged to carry out work of a particular kind'. Since the employers chose to engage all their employees on similar terms, no distinction could be made between those who worked in the slaughter hall and those who worked elsewhere in the factory, and it was wrong to select for redundancy solely from those who normally worked in the slaughter hall.

The House of Lords dismissed time appeal.

LORD IRVINE OF LAIRG LC: My Lords, the language of para. (b) is in my view simplicity itself. It asks two questions of fact. The first is whether one or other of various states of economic affairs exists. In this case, the relevant one is whether the requirements of the business for employees to carry out work of a particular kind have diminished. The second question is whether the dismissal is attributable, wholly or mainly, to that state of affairs. This is a question of causation. In the present case, the tribunal found as a fact that the requirements of the business for employees to work in the slaughter hall had diminished. Secondly, they found that that state of affairs had led to the appellants being dismissed. That, in my opinion, is the end of the matter.

This conclusion is in accordance with the analysis of the statutory provisions by Judge Peter Clark in *Safeway Stores plc* v *Burrell* IRLR 200 and I need to say no more than that I entirely agree with his admirably clear reasoning and conclusions. But I should, out of respect for the submissions of Mr Declan Morgan QC for the appellants, say something about the earlier cases which may have encouraged a belief that the statute had a different meaning.

In *Nelson* v *British Broadcasting Corporation* [1977] IRLR 148, Mr Nelson was employed by the BBC under a contract which required him to perform any duties to which he might be assigned. In fact he worked for the General Overseas Service broadcasting to the Caribbean. In 1974 the BBC reduced its services to the Caribbean, as a result of which Mr Nelson's services in that capacity were no longer required. When he refused alternative employment, he was dismissed on grounds of redundancy. The industrial tribunal concluded that he had been dismissed for redundancy, apparently on the grounds that a term could be implied into Mr Nelson's contract of employment that he should carry out work on Caribbean programmes. The Court of Appeal rightly rejected the implication of such a term. But they went on to hold that Mr Nelson was therefore not redundant. This was wrong. Whatever the terms of Mr Nelson's contract, it was open to the tribunal to find that he had been dismissed because the BBC's requirements for work on Caribbean programmes had diminished. This was a question of fact.

The basis for the fallacy is to be found in the judgment of Brandon LJ in *Nelson* v *British Broadcasting Corporation (No. 2)* [1979] IRLR 346, when Mr Nelson's case came again before the Court of Appeal. He said (at p. 353) that Mr Nelson had been right in law in maintaining that 'because the work which he was employed to do continued to exist, he was not redundant.' In saying this Brandon LJ appears to have meant that because Mr Nelson was employed to do any work to which he might be assigned with the BBC and because the BBC was still carrying on business, he could not be redundant. In my opinion this cannot be right. The fact was that the BBC's requirements for employees in the General Overseas Service in general and for Caribbean broadcasts in particular had diminished. It must therefore have been open to the tribunal to decide that Mr Nelson's dismissal was attributable to that state of affairs. Of course, the BBC did not necessarily have to respond in that way. They could, for example, have transferred Mr Nelson to broadcasts which were still being maintained at full strength (say, to West Africa) in the place of a less experienced employee and made the latter redundant instead. In that case, it would have been open to the tribunal to find that the other employee had been dismissed on account of redundancy. (Compare *Safeway Stores plc* v *Burrell* [1997] IRLR 200 at p. 207.) In each case, the factual question of whether the dismissal was 'attributable' to the statutory state of affairs is one for the tribunal.

The judgments in the two *Nelson* cases have caused understandable difficulty for industrial tribunals. They have been treated as authority for what has been called the 'contract test', which requires consideration of whether there was a diminution in the kind of work for which, according to the terms of his contract the employee had been engaged. I give one example. In *Pink* v *White* [1985] IRLR 489, Mr Pink was engaged to work in a shoe factory as a 'making and finishing room operative.' In practice, he did more specialised work as sole layer/pre-sole fitter. Because of a reduction in demand, the employer's requirements for making and finishing room operatives in general diminished, but their need for sole layers and pre-sole fitters remained the same. Nevertheless, they selected Mr Pink for redundancy, apparently because he had been absent for lengthy periods and the employer had had to train someone else to do his work while he was away. The argument before the Employment Appeal Tribunal turned on whether the 'contract test' ought to be applied (i.e., did the company need less employees of the kind specified in Mr Pink's contract), in which case he was redundant, or the 'function test' (did it need less employees to do the kind of work he was actually doing), in which case he was not. It held that it was bound by *Nelson* v *British Broadcasting Corporation* [1977] IRLR 148 to apply the contract test and held that Mr Pink was redundant. I have no doubt that on its facts the case was rightly decided, but both the contract test and the function test miss the point. The key word in the statute is 'attributable' and there is no reason in law why the dismissal of an employee should not be attributable to a diminution in the employer's need for employees irrespective of the terms of his contract or the function which he performed. Of course the dismissal of an employee who could perfectly well have been redeployed or who was doing work unaffected by the fall in demand may require some explanation to establish the necessary causal connection. But this is a question of fact, not law.

For these reasons, I would dismiss the appeal.

Note

This decision, it is hoped, has laid to rest the debate as to whether the 'function' or 'contract' test should be applied in redundancy cases. According to the Lord Chancellor, both tests 'miss the point' and a broad-brush approach should be adopted which focuses on causation. As a result a dismissal must now be regarded as by reason of redundancy wherever it is attributable to redundancy. This approach would also appear to encompass 'bumping' within the statutory definition of redundancy.

Questions

1.   If the Lord Chancellor's reasoning in *Murray* is correct, why did Parliament include the phrase 'work of a particular kind' in the statutory definition of redundancy?

2.   If in the process of re-organisation, an employer substantially changes the contractual terms and conditions relating to the existing job, has there been a cessation of the 'particular kind of work'? The following two cases provide the answer.

Lesney Products Limited v *Nolan*
[1977] ICR 235
Court of Appeal

The employees were machine maintenance setters who worked in a toy factory where a three-shift system of day, evening, and night work was in operation. To cut operating costs the night shift was ended for both the direct workers and the setters. The latter, instead of working a day shift with long overtime and a night shift, were asked to work a double-day shift on alternate weeks. Among other things this reduced their opportunities to earn overtime pay, which was not fully recompensed despite payment of a shift premium. Some of the setters were sacked for refusing to accept the changes, and a number of them argued that the changes amounted to a 'redundancy'. The claims were dismissed by the Court of Appeal.

LORD DENNING MR: Now the matter comes before this court. It must say that it is a difficult case. The relevant principles were stated by this court in *Johnson* v *Nottinghamshire Combined Police Authority* [1974] ICR 170, 176:

> It is settled by those cases that an employer is entitled to reorganise his business so as to improve its efficiency and, in so doing, to propose to his staff a change in the terms and conditions of their employment: and to dispense with their services if they

do not agree. Such a change does not automatically give the staff a right to redundancy payments. It only does so if the change in the terms and conditions is due to a redundancy situation.

While I adhere to what I there said, I think the phrase 'a redundancy situation' may be misleading. It is shorthand: and it is better always to check it by the statutory words. The dismissal must be attributable to 'the fact that the requirements of that business for employees to carry out work of a particular kind . . . have ceased or diminished,' etc.

In applying that principle, it is important that nothing should be done to impair the ability of employers to reorganise their work force and their times and conditions of work so as to improve efficiency. They may reorganise it so as to reduce overtime and thus to save themselves money, but that does not give the man a right to redundancy payment. Overtime might be reduced, for instance, by taking on more men: but that would not give the existing staff a right to redundancy payments. Also when overtime is reduced by a reorganisation of working hours, that does not give rise to a right to redundancy payment, so long as the work to be done is the same.

Chapman v Coonvean and Rostowrack China Clay Co. Limited
[1973] ICR 310
Court of Appeal

The employers provided free transport for their employees who lived 30 miles away. This concession was withdrawn on economic grounds. Some employees resigned and claimed redundancy. It was argued for the employees (following *Dutton v C.H. Bailey Ltd* [1968] 2 Lloyd's Rep 122) that the proper approach to their claim was to determine whether in all the circumstances the requirements of the business would have ceased or diminished if the employees had been retained by the company on the old terms. The Court of Appeal, overruling *Dutton's* case, rejected this argument.

LORD DENNING MR: Although the seven men were 'dismissed,' the question is whether they were dismissed 'by reason of redundancy.' This depends on section 1(2) of the Act [now ERA 1996, s. 139(1)(b)] . . . Taking those words as they stand, this case is not one of dismissal for redundancy. The requirements of the business – for the work of these seven men – continued just the same as before. After they stopped work, the firm had to take on seven other men to replace them and to do the work that they had been doing. The requirements for work of that kind in that place had not ceased or diminished, nor were they expected to do so. So it would seem that the case does not come within the statute.

Vaux and Associated Breweries Limited v Ward
[1969] 7 KIR 308
Queen's Bench Division

A traditional hotel and public house was modernised and the employer wanted to introduce younger and more glamorous barstaff. Accordingly, Ward, an employee of some 17 years, was dismissed. It was held that the dismissal was not for redundancy.

LORD PARKER CJ: When the matter came before the Divisional Court, the court took the view that the mere fact that an employee was dismissed because a younger employee was preferred was not of itself a dismissal by reason of redundancy, but that something more would be necessary; the further question had to be answered, namely, whether the particular kind of work on which the barmaid had been engaged had ceased or was likely to cease or diminish or, put more shortly, as I said in giving judgment, 'Was the work that the barmaid in the altered premises was going to do work of a different kind to what a barmaid in the unaltered premises had been doing?'

When the matter went back to the tribunal, further evidence was called, in particular the evidence of a Mr Embleton as to the exact nature of the work expected of the barmaid, both before and after certain alterations had been effected to the premises. In the latest decision, the tribunal unhesitatingly said that the work was in no way different. In paragraph 4 of their reasons it was stated:

> The tribunal were of opinion that the work to be carried out by a barmaid after Mrs Ward was dismissed was not different from that which she had carried out. She was engaged in serving behind the bar, either directly to customers or to waitresses to take to customers. Occasionally, if the waitress was not present, Mrs Ward would carry drinks to customers in the buffet. 70 per cent of the drinks dispensed were beer . . . The present barmaid serves behind the bar, only occasionally going in front of the bar to serve customers.

That finding was followed by this:

> The tribunal reaffirms the findings of fact contained in paragraphs 10 and 11 of the previous reasons. In particular, it reaffirms the opinion expressed in the last sentence of paragraph 11. Its opinion is (and was at the first hearing) that the manager wanted younger staff because they would be physically more attractive than the existing staff, and more likely to attract new customers. The reason was not that the work had changed and could be done more efficiently by younger staff.

I confess that having regard to the history of this matter, and in view of that finding, I should have thought there could only be one answer, namely that the present appellants had discharged the burden upon them, and it had been shown that the dismissal of Mrs Ward was not by reason of redundancy.

North Riding Garages Ltd v *Butterwick*
[1967] 2 QB 56
Queen's Bench Division

The applicant had been employed at a garage in Whitby for some 30 years, rising to the position of workshop manager in charge of the repairs shop. In view of the comparitive smallness of the staff he was expected to spend part of his time performing the mechanics' work on the vehicles. New owners required him to undertake more of a managerial role including the paperwork. He was not able to undertake this new role particularly well and eight months later was dismissed. He claimed that a new sort of employee was now needed to do his job so that the requirements for the work that he had done for some 30 years had diminished. The Court of Appeal rejected this argument.

WIDGERY J: It is we think, important to observe that a claim under [s. 139(1)(b)] is conditional upon a change in the requirements of the business. If the requirement of the business for employees to carry out work of a particular kind increases or remains constant no redundancy payment can be claimed by an employee, in work of that kind, whose dismissal is attributable to personal deficiencies which prevent him from satisfying his employer. The very fact of dismissal shows that the employee's services are no longer required by his employer and that he may, in a popular sense, be said to have become redundant, but if the dismissal was attributable to age, physical disability or inability to meet his employer's standards he was not dismissed on account of redundancy within the meaning of the Act. For the purpose of this Act an employee who remains in the same kind of work is expected to adapt himself to new methods and techniques and cannot complain if his employer insists on higher standards of efficiency than those previously required; but if new methods alter the nature of the work required to be done it may follow that no requirement remains for employees to do work of the particular kind which has been superseded and that they are truly redundant. Thus, if a motor manufacturer decides to use plastics instead of wood in the bodywork of his cars and dismisses his woodworkers, they may well be entitled to redundancy payments on the footing that their dismissal is attributable to a cessation of the requirement of the business for employees to carry out work of a particular kind, namely, woodworking.

If one looks at the primary facts disclosed by the evidence in this case it is difficult to see what is the particular kind of work in which a requirement for employees has ceased or diminished. The vehicle workshop remained, as did the requirement for a workshop manager, and we do not understand the tribunal to have found that the volume of repair work had diminished to such an extent as to make the respondent's dismissal wholly or mainly attributable to that fact. The only possible conclusion which appears to us to have been open to the tribunal on the evidence was that the respondent was dismissed because he could not do his job in accordance with the new methods and new standards required by the appellants.

Note

The court in this case largely ignored the question of when demands for greater efficiency reach the point when the nature of the job changes. Critics of this decision have argued that there is not one single class of workshop manager and that the applicant, who had done nothing but manage a small workshop, had strong grounds to claim that that he was engaged in an entirely different job rather than being inefficient in the old one.

Hindle v *Percival Boats Ltd*
[1969] 1 WLR 174
Court of Appeal

The applicant's forte was in building traditional wooden boats, but increasingly the modern demand was for fibre glass constructed vessels. Hindle was too slow when it came to fibre glass models and he was dismissed for being 'too good and too slow'. He was not replaced but his work was carried on by other members of the workforce. His claim for a redundancy payment was rejected.

SACHS LJ: I would add that provided the requirements of the business referred to in [s. 139(1)(b)] remain constant it does not matter whether the slowness of employee which leads to the failure to 'pay for his keep' stems from the onset of years, from some physical cause, or from over-great addiction to what is sometimes termed perfectionism. Unfortunately for such addicts, perfectionism can produce a form of inefficiency in many walks of life – not merely in a workshop – however much one may praise the look of the product.

The onus placed on the employer by section [163(2)] of the Act is simply to show (using the standard test of balance of probabilities applicable where the facts are largely within the knowledge of a party against whom a claim is made) that the dismissal of the employee was not attributable to redundancy. There are cases, as where the tribunal find in favour of the employer on the first condition precedent, when it is not necessary to inquire further into the precise ground on which the employee was dismissed. But in any event once the tribunal is satisfied that the ground put forward by the employer is genuine and is the one to which the dismissal is mainly attributable the onus is discharged – and it ceases to be in point that the ground was unwise or based on a mistaken view of facts, though such matters may well be relevant for consideration by the tribunal when assessing the truth of the employer's evidence.

The above conclusions are all consistent with my view, differing unfortunately in some respects from those just stated by my Lord, that compensation is provided by the Act for one, but one only, of life's changes of fortune as between employee and employer: that is, dismissal on account of redundancy within the meaning of the Act. It thus neither purports to nor does provide for other changes of fortune, such as ill-health or a deterioration in the employer's views of the capabilities of the employee. Similarly it does not provide for the case where an employer wishes to see if someone else can do the job better: it could indeed be industrially unfortunate if it puts a brake on employers seeking to get the best man for any given job. Nor does it provide for any case where an employer simply wishes not to continue to employ a particular employee . . . so long as the requirements of the business for employees of a particular kind remain the same the Act does not provide for changes consequential upon a reorganisation: (see *North Riding Garages Ltd* v *Butterwick* [1967] 2 QB 56). In short, it does not provide security of employment in the accepted sense of that phrase.

Questions

1. In the light of the above decisions, to what extent, if at all, do you consider the legal concept of 'redundancy' equates with the public understanding of what constitutes a redundancy situation?

2. Consider the proposition that the law on redundancy favours the employer rather than the employee. The view of one commentator is as follows:

Not only are the courts prepared to enlarge managerial discretion under employment contracts at the expense of reducing the chance for a redundancy payment; they are also prepared to give a strict reading to the nature of 'work' in the statutory definition. (Anderman, S.D., *Labour Law: Management Decisions and Workers' Rights*, 2nd ed. (London: Butterworths, 1993) at p. 162.)

Note

For a decision which adopts a narrower approach to 'kind of work', see *Murphy* v *Epsom College* [1984] IRLR 271, CA. In that case, the college's heating system was modernised, and Mr Murphy, one of the college's two existing plumbers, stated that he was not technically qualified to maintain it.

He was dismissed and replaced by a 'heating engineer'. Mr Murphy was unsuccessful in his claim for unfair dismissal. The Court of Appeal upheld the tribunal's decision that the employee was redundant since the college's requirement for plumbers – as opposed to 'heating engineers' – was reduced from two to one.

III Offers of Suitable Alternative Employment

When we considered employees who were disqualified from applying for a redundancy payment, we included those who had refused offers of suitable alternative employment. This is covered by ERA 1996, s. 141, which reads as follows:

Employment Rights Act 1996

141.   Renewal of contract or re-engagement
   (1)   This section applies where an offer (whether in writing or not) is made to an employee before the end of his employment—
      (a)   to renew his contract of employment, or
      (b)   to re-engage him under a new contract of employment,
with renewal or re-engagement to take effect either immediately on, or after an interval of not more than four weeks after, the end of his employment.
   (2)   Where subsection (3) is satisfied, the employee is not entitled to a redundancy payment if he unreasonably refuses the offer.
   (3)   This subsection is satisfied where—
      (a)   the provisions of the contract as renewed, or of the new contract, as to—
         (i)   the capacity and place in which the employee would be employed, and
         (ii)   the other terms and conditions of his employment,
would not differ from the corresponding provisions of the previous contract, or
      (b)   those provisions of the contract as renewed, or of the new contract, would differ from the corresponding provisions of the previous contract but the offer constitutes an offer of suitable employment in relation to the employee.
   (4)   The employee is not entitled to a redundancy payment if—
      (a)   his contract of employment is renewed, or he is re-engaged under a new contract of employment, in pursuance of the offer,
      (b)   the provisions of the contract as renewed or new contract as to the capacity or place in which he is employed or the other terms and conditions of his employment differ (wholly or in part) from the corresponding provisions of the previous contract,
      (c)   the employment is suitable in relation to him, and
      (d)   during the trial period he unreasonably terminates the contract or unreasonably gives notice to terminate it and it is in consequence terminated.

Note
Two questions therefore fall to be considered: (a) is the offer of alternative employment suitable; and (b) if so, is the refusal by the employee to take it up unreasonable? (These two questions do to differing degrees overlap – see the comments of Bristow J in *Spencer* v *Gloucestershire County Council* [1985] IRLR 393, below at page 540.)

A: Suitable alternative employment?

(i)   The General Duty

Vokes v Bear
[1974] ICR 1
National Industrial Relations Court

The applicant was dismissed without any prior warning, with no time off given to find other work and with no attempt made to find alternative employment for him in any of the 299 other companies forming part of the employer's group of companies. The failure to make any attempt to find alternative employment meant that although there was a redundancy situation the dismissal was unfair.

SIR HUGH GRIFFITHS: Having decided that the employee was dismissed by reason of redundancy the tribunal then turned to consider whether nevertheless his dismissal was unfair by virtue of the provisions of section 24(6) of the Industrial Relations Act 1971 [now ERA 1996, s. 98(4)]. The tribunal held that it was unfair because no attempt whatever had been made to see if the employee could have been fitted into some other position in the group before he was dismissed. The evidence showed that the Tilling Group consisted of some 300 companies and there was evidence that at least one of those companies was advertising for persons to fill senior management positions shortly after the employee's dismissal. The Tilling Group apparently had no centralised machinery for providing services to all the companies in the group and it was argued before the tribunal and before this court that in all the circumstances it would have been impracticable to have made any inquiries within the group to see if there was another position that the employee might fill. The tribunal would have none of this argument. They said:

We do not think that such inquiries were impracticable. We think that some inquiries should have been made to see whether it was possible to help someone like [the employee] whose services had proved satisfactory to his employers in every respect. We think the [employers'] failure to consider the question of finding some other position for the [employee] in the group made the dismissal unfair.

We find ourselves in full agreement with the way in which the tribunal expressed themselves. It would have been the simplest of matters to have circulated an inquiry through the group to see if any assistance could be given to the employee in the very difficult circumstances in which he would shortly find himself.

. . .

These employers made no offer of help to the employee before they dismissed him, nor did they allow him any time off to seek work. As the employee reasonably complained: 'It's more difficult to find employment if you have been summarily dismissed than if you are seeking a new job while still in employment.' In so far as it is argued that this paragraph is not meant to apply to managers, we would answer, how is a company to expect its managers to comply with the provision if it treats them as it did the employee? He was literally put out on the pavement at a moment's notice in circumstances which appear to us to have lacked any humanitarian approach on the part of the employers.

But, with whatever indignation we may regard the behaviour of his employers, the question still remains whether the dismissal was fair or unfair within the meaning of section 24(6) of the Act of 1971 [now ERA 1996, s. 98(4)] . . .

Mr Irvine submits that the only 'circumstances' that the tribunal are entitled to take into account are circumstances which relate to or surround the employer's grounds for dismissal and that, as he put it, the tribunal are not entitled to take into account an employer's failure to mitigate the consequences of an otherwise fair dismissal.

It is not altogether easy to see what particular meaning should attach to the words 'in the circumstances,' for if these words were omitted from the subsection it would hardly seem to alter its meaning. Suppose the subsection read: 'the determination of the question whether the dismissal was fair or unfair, having regard to the reason shown by the employer, shall depend on whether he acted reasonably or unreasonably in treating it as a sufficient reason for dismissing the employee.' How is the tribunal to determine whether the employer's action was reasonable or unreasonable unless it considers 'the circumstances' in which it was taken? It cannot decide this matter in the air.

We are unable to accept the submission that 'the circumstances' are limited to those directly affecting the ground of dismissal, in the sense submitted by Mr Irvine. 'The circumstances' embrace all relevant matters that should weigh with a good employer when deciding at a given moment in time whether or not he should dismiss his employee. The subsection is focusing the tribunal's attention upon 'the dismissal,' that is, the dismissal on March 2. The question they have to ask themselves is whether on March 2 the employers were acting reasonably in treating redundancy as a sufficient reason for dismissing the employee on that date. The tribunal are entitled to take into account all the circumstances affecting both the employers and the employee at the time of the dismissal. In the present case, no doubt the time would have come when the employers would have to dismiss the employee for redundancy for the good of the company as a whole, but the tribunal were fully entitled to take the view that that moment had not yet arrived by March 2. The employers had not yet done that which in all fairness and reason they should do, namely, to make the obvious attempt to see if the employee could be placed somewhere else within this large group.

The position is somewhat analogous to the case of a warning. An employer may have good grounds for thinking that a man is not capable of doing his job properly, but in the general run of cases it will not be reasonable for him to regard that lack of capability as a sufficient reason for dismissing him until he is given a warning so that the man has the chance to show if he can do better. So in this case there was a redundancy situation but there was no compelling reason why the axe should fall until the employers had done their best to help the employee. . . .

(ii)   What is Meant by Suitable?

Taylor v Kent County Council
[1969] 2 QB 560
Queen's Bench Division

The applicant lost his post as headmaster due to amalgamation of two schools. He was offered the post of a mobile teacher (at the same salary as he had received as headmaster), forming one of a pool who would serve for short periods at different schools, during which period of service he would be under the control of that particular school's headmaster. He refused the offer. Did he thereby lose his entitlement to a redundancy payment? The Divisional Court held that the offer of alternative employment was not suitable and Taylor was entitled to refuse it.

LORD PARKER CJ: . . . The tribunal in their decision said:

'The suitability of the alternative offer must be considered in all the surrounding circumstances not just one — to wit: status. Taking into account not only the applicant's age, qualifications, experience, loss of status, but also the protection afforded by his contract', — pausing there, that means that his salary as headmaster is going to continue pursuant to section Q of the Burnham award — 'and not forgetting the unfortunate showing at the interview, we have come to the conclusion that in all the circumstances the offer of appointment to the mobile pool was one of suitable employment in relation to the applicant. Of course another headmaster-ship would have been more suitable, but his employers were not in a position to make a written offer of such a post. However, the fact that the offer that was made was less suitable, does not necessarily make it unsuitable.'

Let me say at once, suitability is almost entirely a matter of degree and fact for the tribunal, and not a matter with which this court would wish to or could interfere, unless it was plain that they had misdirected themselves in some way in law, or had taken into consideration matters which were not relevant for the purpose. It is to be observed that so far as age was concerned, so far as qualifications were concerned, so far as experience was concerned, they negative the suitability of this offer, because he is going to be put into a position where he has to go where he is told at any time for short periods, to any place, and be put under a headmaster and assigned duties by him.

The only matter which can be put against that as making this offer suitable is the guarantee of salary under Scale Q. One would think, speaking for myself, that for a headmaster of this experience, he would think an offer which, while guaranteeing him the same salary, reduced his status, was quite unsuitable, To go to quite a different sphere of activity, a director under a service agreement of a company is offered on dismissal a job as a navvy, and it is said: but we will guarantee you the same salary as you have been getting. I should have thought such an offer was plainly unsuitable. Here one wonders whether one of the matters which affected the tribunal was this reference to the words 'Not forgetting the unfortunate showing at the interview.' That is a reference to when he was interviewed, not by the Kent County Council, but by the governors of the school with a view to taking on the headmastership of the new school. One really wonders what the relevance of that was unless it be that the tribunal felt from what they had heard that he was not up to a headmastership at all. But at once one says to oneself: if that was in their mind, it was not evidence upon which they could properly act, having regard to the fact that this man had given satisfaction for some ten years, and if he was not up to his job he could have been dismissed for that reason, and no question of redundancy would have arisen.

But for my part I feel that the tribunal have here misdirected themselves in law as to the meaning of 'suitable employment.' I accept, of course, that suitable employ-ment is as is said: suitable employment in relation to the employee in question. But it does seem to me here that by the words 'suitable employment,' suitability means employment which is substantially equivalent to the employment which has ceased. Section 2(3) [now ERA 1996, s. 141(3)(a)] which I read at the beginning is dealing with the case where the fundamental terms are the same, and then no offer in writing is needed, but when they differ, then it has to be put in writing and must be suitable. I for my part think that what is meant by 'suitable' in relation to the employee means conditions of employment which are reasonably equivalent to those under the previous employment, not the same, because then subsection (2) [now ERA 1996,

s. 141(3)(b)] would apply, but it does not seem to me that by 'suitable employment' is meant employment of an entirely different nature, but in respect of which the salary is going to be the same. Looked at in that way, it seems to me that there could be only one answer in this case, and that is that this man was being asked to do something utterly different; as I have said, just as if a director under a service agreement with a company was being asked to do a workman's job, albeit at the same salary.

(iii)   The Relevance of a Salary Reduction

The mere fact that the alternative post offers less salary or denies the opportunity to earn overtime (as to the latter see *Sheppard* v *National Coal Board* [1966] 1 KIR 101) does not, by itself, make the offer of alternative employment unsuitable.

Hindes v *Supersine Limited*
[1979] ICR 517
Employment Appeal Tribunal

The employee was offered a post at another factory but at a reduced salary. He agreed to try the new job but left after a few days, stating that the smell of paint made him ill. The industrial tribunal dismissed his redundancy application holding that, since he had indicated that the reduction in salary would have been acceptable had he liked his new job, he had accepted that the alternative employment was suitable. The EAT allowed the employee's appeal.

TALBOT J: Therefore, there is stated there a clear way of looking at this: is the employment offered substantially equivalent to the employment which has ceased? It is plain that so far as pay is concerned the new job offered to the employee was not substantially equivalent to the job that had come to an end. Had the matter rested there, then quite clearly (as, indeed, the industrial tribunal rightly said) that would have been the end of the matter on the question of suitability, because the job offered to the employee would have been unsuitable.

Mrs Gill, as we would understand her, would be seen to be saying that there ought not to have been taken into account the fact that, had he liked the new job, he would not have regarded the drop in pay as of importance. That is certainly a matter personal to him; but it would be our view that had the employee disregarded, without any conditions, the change in pay, then what would otherwise have been an unsuitable job, because of the drop in pay, could have been found to be suitable. But, it is plain from the facts of this case that the employee's preparedness to accept the drop in pay was conditional upon his liking the new job in all other respects. The facts also clearly show (because, from the words we have quoted, it is clear that the industrial tribunal accepted what the employee told them) that he did not like the new job and could not tolerate it for the reasons which he stated. Therefore, in those circumstances, the matter goes back to be considered on the question of suitability, namely, whether the drop in pay rendered the job unsuitable. The employee was only prepared to accept the drop in pay if he tolerated the job, and, as he did not tolerate the job, then he is not prepared to accept the drop in pay. In our view the industrial tribunal failed to look at this question in the way that they should have looked at it. It is not a matter of us expressing our view; we are saying that they have omitted to take into consideration that which should have been very much to the forefront of their consideration, namely, that the employee's acceptance of the job was conditional upon his being able to tolerate and like it in other respects. They therefore omitted to consider the vital matter of evidence and in that respect they are in error.

(iv) Reduction of Level of Skill, etc. required

A reduction in the level of expertise and skill required by the new post being offered may make it unsuitable.

Standard Telephones v Yates
[1981] IRLR 21
Employment Appeal Tribunal

The applicant had been employed for 10 years as a card wirer, a job demanding both skill and experience. She was offered the alternative post of an assembly line operator which she refused. The EAT agreed that the offer of alternative employment was not suitable.

BRISTOW J: Now Mr Moss, who has put the company's case with admirable clarity and persistence, says that [the tribunal] went wrong in law in that they applied the wrong test in deciding whether the offer was suitable or not and, in support of his submission, he relied on the decision of the Queen's Bench Division at Court in the case of *Taylor* v *Kent County Council* [1969] 2 QB 560. Mr Moss submits that there Lord Parker CJ laid down as a matter of law that what suitable employment in the predecessor of s. 5(b) [now ERA, s. 141(3)(b)] means is 'employment which is substantially equivalent to the employment which has ceased'. Now no doubt if an Industrial Tribunal finds that the employment offered is employment substantially equivalent to the employment which has ceased, it will find that the offer is an offer of suitable employment but we point out that the words used in the statute where the law is to be found are not an offer of employment which is substantially equivalent to the employment which has ceased but an offer of suitable employment. Whether it is any easier for an Industrial Tribunal which has put upon it by Parliament the duty to make the value judgment whether the offer is of suitable employment will find it any more difficult to do that than to find whether the employment is substantially equivalent to the employment which has ceased, it is perhaps difficult to say. It is merely putting the same problem in other words. But in our judgment, if the Industrial Tribunal, having considered the evidence, comes to the conclusion, in its wisdom as an industrial jury, that the offer is one of suitable employment, the fact that it does not use the words of any gloss which has been put upon the requirements of the statute by the courts, does not mean that it has gone wrong in law. It will only go wrong in law if, having done what the statute requires it to do and considered whether the offer constitutes an offer of suitable employment, it is found that there was no evidence on which it could have come to the conclusion to which it did come; or that it took into consideration something which it should not have done; or left out of consideration something which it should have considered; or that its conclusion is so wildly out of line that it must have misdirected itself and so gone wrong in law – that being the form of error of law which is usually referred to as a 'perverse decision' in this jurisdiction.

Now in our judgment, there was evidence before this Tribunal on which they could find, as they did find, that the offer made was not an offer of suitable employment and what they said was:

First of all the employment was not suitable work. Certainly it was suitable in that the applicant was quite capable of doing it, but it was not work which employed the skills which she had been using for 10 years. Had it been explained to her as Mr Bridges explained it in evidence, namely that she would very quickly find herself in a wiring occupation, then the assembly work might have been suitable alternative employment as a short term measure.

Their conclusion was, having heard the evidence, that her potential, which she was entitled to expect to have the opportunity to use, was greater than the potential required in the boxing department. As we have said, on the evidence before them, it seems to us that it was open to them to come to such a conclusion – whether or not we would have come to it is neither here nor there and it certainly is not a conclusion which could be stigmatised as perverse.

B: The Reasonableness of a Refusal

In assessing the reasonableness or otherwise of the employee's refusal to take up an offer of alternative employment, subjective considerations are taken into account, e.g. the travelling involved and its effect on domestic life, loss of friends and the effect on children's education if a house move is required.

Spencer v Gloucestershire County Council
[1985] IRLR 393
Court of Appeal

The employees were school cleaners who, as a cost cutting exercise, were asked to accept fewer hours. They refused on the basis that they felt they could not do the job properly in the reduced working time. The EAT considered the refusal unreasonable since the employer took the view that whatever could be done within the shorter hours would be acceptable. The Court of Appeal allowed the appeal and, in so doing, made some observations on the overlap between the two questions of suitability of the offer and reasonableness of the refusal.

NEILL LJ: Speaking for myself, it seems to me that it only leads to confusion if one tries to draw too rigid a distinction between suitability of employment and the circumstances which may lead an employee reasonably or, in some cases, unreasonably to refuse to accept a particular offer. Some factors may be common to both aspects of the case. It may be that a factor may reflect both on the suitability of the work for the particular employee and also be something which the employee can take into account when he comes to judge whether he can properly accept the employer's offer. I would deprecate trying to draw too rigid a distinction and say that some particular factors must fall exclusively under one heading and other factors under the other heading. The Industrial Tribunal clearly must look at the two separate points – in other words, whether the employment is suitable in relation to the employee and, secondly, whether or not the employee has unreasonably refused to accept the offer . . .

Returning to the facts of this case, it seems to me that it cannot be right to say as a general proposition that it is not a good reason for an employee to refuse to do work because he considers that the work he is being asked to do does not come up to a standard which he himself wishes to observe. It all depends on the facts of the case. There may well be cases where an employee wishes to apply a wholly unreasonable standard to the work, and say, 'I am only prepared to work to that standard'. But it seems to me that this is eminently a matter for the Industrial Tribunal to evaluate in the particular circumstances. In paragraph 11 the Industrial Tribunal set out the factors which they had in mind. It is clear from the way they expressed themselves in their reasons that they had a substantial amount of evidence from the applicants as to why they (the applicants) thought that the job could not be done satisfactorily in the way in which the employer suggested. In those circumstances, it seems to me, it was for the Industrial Tribunal to decide on the facts then before them whether or not each individual employee had unreasonably refused the offer of employment. With all respect to the Employment Appeal Tribunal, it does not seem to me to be a case where they were entitled to overturn the decision of the Industrial Tribunal.

Paton Calvert & Co. Ltd v *Westerside*
[1979] IRLR 108
Employment Appeal Tribunal

The employee had been sent a redundancy notice, but the employer wrote again to his employees indicating that because of a recently acquired government grant the company was able to continue trading. As a result the employer was able to offer continuing employment on the same terms. Westerside, who was aged 61 and sceptical about the future viability of the company, refused and claimed redundancy having, in the meantime, secured alternative employment elsewhere. The EAT held that the refusal of the offer was reasonable.

SLYNN J: . . . So, adding these three factors together; his age, the new job and also at least the possibility that the company would not necessarily survive, [the tribunal] held that he had not unreasonably refused the offer.

It is contended before us by Mr Leveson, to whom we are indebted for his research and for a very careful and concise argument, that they were wrong. He submits that here the onus was on Mr Westerside to show that he had not unreasonably refused the offer. He says that in a number of cases the particular matters which are here relied on have been held not to be sufficient for the purposes of deciding that a refusal was reasonable.

In the first place he refers us to the case of *Pilkington* v *Pickstone* [1966] ITR 364. There the [Manchester Industrial Tribunal] stressed that the matters which are relevant for the purposes of reasonableness must either be such matters as can be considered as arising between the employer and the employee or in relation to the special circumstances affecting an employee personally. He says here these are not matters of that kind. They are not matters which go to the employer/employee relationship.

He then goes on to say that in the case of *McNulty* v *T Bridges and Company* [1966] 1 ITR 367 the fact that a man has accepted another job does not necessarily make it reasonable for him to refuse an offer or does not mean that he has not unreasonably accepted the new offer from his company. He also says that the fact that an industry may be contracting and that futures were not assured is not of itself a ground for refusing a new offer reasonably, and he refers us to the case of *James and Jones* v *The National Coal Board* [[1969] ITR 70].

He also stressed that in the case of *Morganite Crucible Limited* v *Street* [[1972] ICR 110], John Donaldson stressed that as long as the new employment which is offered is regular employment then it does not matter that it is of a shorter rather than a longer duration. The Court, further, in that case, did recognise that there can be exceptions to that as a general rule.

Now, it is, of course, as Mr Leveson has stressed to us, important to consider the 1965 Act against the Employment Protection Act of 1975, and we desire to say nothing which would in any way impede the desire of employers and union representatives and the Secretary of State to seek to avoid redundancies which may appear to be likely. It is clearly of great importance that discussions should take place so that if possible redundancy notices should be withdrawn and that employees should continue in their employment. But Parliament has clearly provided that if the employee does not unreasonably refuse an offer of further employment he may still be entitled to a redundancy payment.

We follow what has been said that these individual reasons may not in themselves be sufficient to justify as reasonable a refusal of a further offer of employment. We consider, however, that the various factors which are relied upon here are capable of being special circumstances affecting Mr Westerside personally, and, indeed, that the future viability of the company is something which falls into the alternative category of a matter arising between the employer and the employee as referred to in *Pilkington* v *Pickstone*. Moreover, we consider that it is possible for a man's age and for the apparent viability of the company to be capable of creating exceptional cases within the general rule defined in *Morganite Crucible Limited* v *Street*.

We have been referred to a more recent Industrial Tribunal case, *Thomas Wragg & Sons Limited* v *Wood* [[1976] ICR 313]. There the employee was given notice and he obtained other work only one day before the expiry of the 90-day notice. He was given an offer of alternative employment. He was a man of 56. He was a man who feared for future redundancies in the construction industry and the Tribunal there were prepared to accept that the fears of future redundancy were not in themselves necessarily sufficient to justify a refusal to accept a new offer, nor necessarily in itself was the lateness of the offer of new employment. But they paid regard to the fact that the employee in the case had with diligence obtained another employment, and they said that if all those factors were put together, as it was right to put them together, then the Industrial Tribunal had been entitled to conclude that the employee had not unreasonably refused a further offer of employment.

These cases are not always easy, but we are satisfied in the present case that the combination of Mr Westerside's age with the uncertainty as to the future of his employment with the company, which is indicated in the letter of 15 December, coupled with the fact that he had obtained another job thereby avoiding the possibility of his being unemployed in the future, were sufficient to make it not unreasonable for him to refuse that offer. In our view the factors which exist in this case and which have been relied upon by the Tribunal are sufficient to entitle him to say that he was not unreasonable in refusing the offer.

Note

While the courts have high regard to the motives of the employee, the approach is not entirely subjective as the next case illustrates.

Fuller v *Stephanie Bowman (Sales) Limited*
[1977] IRLR 87
Industrial Tribunal

The applicant refused to move with her employers from a West End address to one in Soho, where the new business premises were above a sex shop. Her refusal was held to be unreasonable by the industrial tribunal.

N.F. STOGDEN (Chairman): The applicant said in evidence that she had the strongest objection to money for sex, and she would not work over a sex shop. That could be a valid objection. Personal factors must be taken into consideration. The test is not the attitude of the reasonable woman but reasonable objections of this applicant: *Universal Fisher Engineering Limited v Stratton* (1971) 7 ITR 66, NIRC. Mere fads and fancies are not enough. Apart from that the test is as stated in such cases as *Kerr v National Coal Board* [1970] ITR 48. Whether the refusal of an offer is reasonable is a question of fact for the Tribunal.

The Tribunal, which included a lady member, therefore, decided to view both premises. The Chairman especially was well aware that working over a sex shop could be a reasonable objection in some circumstances. People have just as much right to hold strong views about sex as they do about politics or religion. Of course, for those who disapprove of modern sexual laxity, Mayfair is nearly as bad as Soho, Piccadilly Circus, Shaftesbury Avenue, the Charing Cross Road and that area generally. For those who are shocked there are as many pictures outside cinemas and some theatres as there are in sex shop windows. The only advantage for Mayfair is that in many parts the activities are not so obvious. The Tribunal found that the entrance to the upper part of Berwick Street premises was at the side of the sex shop and no part of it. No prostitutes used the other floors. These were respectively a company office and a tailor. The work in the premises had been reasonably well done and no exception could be taken to anything except the sex shop. Berwick Street has a large street market at the south end, but that was a good 300 yards away. The street has numerous shops and business premises. Most of them have nothing to do with sex. There are few prostitutes' bells. We saw none very close to the premises. Finally the applicant was 53 at the time. She was not likely to be mistaken for a prostitute. The street in daytime is full of shoppers and those going to and from the market. It is certainly not one of the worst streets in Soho.

On the facts the Tribunal considered that the dislike of the Sex shop was not enough to make the refusal of the offer reasonable, especially as there had been no attempts by the applicant to look into the letter of 18 June. Had the applicant's views on sex been so strong that she refused to work anywhere in the West End that might have been different.

Notes

1. The offer of alternative employment must be made before the existing contract is due to end, and the new contract must start within four weeks of the ending of the old one.

2. The ERA 1996, s. 138, allows the employee and employer a four-week trial period before either finally commits themselves to the new contract. If the employer dismisses within the four-week period the employee will be treated as dismissed for redundancy under the old job. If the employee resigns within the four-week period, he or she will be treated as entitled to a redundancy payment under his or her old job if he or she can show that the new employment was unsuitable, etc.

IV Lay-off and Short-time Working

Employment Rights Act 1996

Lay-off and short-time

147. Meaning of 'lay-off' and 'short-time'

(1) For the purposes of this Part an employee shall be taken to be laid off for a week if—

(a) he is employed under a contract on terms and conditions such that his remuneration under the contract depends on his being provided by the employer with work of the kind which he is employed to do, but

(b) he is not entitled to any remuneration under the contract in respect of the week because the employer does not provide such work for him.

(2) For the purposes of this Part an employee shall be taken to be kept on short-time for a week if by reason of a diminution in the work provided for the employee by his employer (being work of a kind which under his contract the employee is employed to do) the employee's remuneration for the week is less than half a week's pay.

148. Eligibility by reason of lay-off or short-time

(1) Subject to the following provisions of this Part, for the purposes of this Part an employee is eligible for a redundancy payment by reason of being laid off or kept on short-time if—

(a) he gives notice in writing to his employer indicating (in whatever terms) his intention to claim a redundancy payment in respect of lay-off or short-time (referred to in this Part as 'notice of intention to claim'), and

(b) before the service of the notice he has been laid off or kept on short-time in circumstances in which subsection (2) applies.

(2) This subsection applies if the employee has been laid off or kept on short-time—

(a) for four or more consecutive weeks of which the last before the service of the notice ended on, or not more than four weeks before, the date of service of the notice, or

(b) for a series of six or more weeks (of which not more than three were consecutive) within a period of thirteen weeks, where the last week of the series before the service of the notice ended on, or not more than four weeks before, the date of service of the notice.

Exclusions

149. Counter-notices

Where an employee gives to his employer notice of intention to claim but—

(a) the employer gives to the employee, within seven days after the service of that notice, notice in writing (referred to in this Part as a 'counter-notice') that he will contest any liability to pay to the employee a redundancy payment in pursuance of the employee's notice, and

(b) the employer does not withdraw the counter-notice by a subsequent notice in writing,

the employee is not entitled to a redundancy payment in pursuance of his notice of intention to claim except in accordance with a decision of an industrial tribunal.

150. Resignation

(1) An employee is not entitled to a redundancy payment by reason of being laid off or kept on short-time unless he terminates his contract of employment by giving such period of notice as is required for the purposes of this section before the end of the relevant period.

(2) The period of notice required for the purposes of this section—

(a) where the employee is required by his contract of employment to give more than one week's notice to terminate the contract, is the minimum period which he is required to give, and

(b) otherwise, is one week.

(3)   In subsection (1) 'the relevant period'—

(a)   if the employer does not give a counter-notice within seven days after the service of the notice of intention to claim, is three weeks after the end of those seven days,

(b)   if the employer gives a counter-notice within that period of seven days but withdraws it by a subsequent notice in writing, is three weeks after the service of the notice of withdrawal, and

(c)   if—

(i)   the employer gives a counter-notice within that period of seven days, and does not so withdraw it, and

(ii)   a question as to the right of the employee to a redundancy payment in pursuance of the notice of intention to claim is referred to an industrial tribunal,

is three weeks after the tribunal has notified to the employee its decision on that reference.

(4)   For the purposes of subsection (3)(c) no account shall be taken of—

(a)   any appeal against the decision of the tribunal, or

(b)   any proceedings or decision in consequence of any such appeal.

151.   Dismissal

(1)   An employee is not entitled to a redundancy payment by reason of being laid off or kept on short-time if he is dismissed by his employer.

(2)   Subsection (1) does not prejudice any right of the employee to a redundancy payment in respect of the dismissal.

152.   Likelihood of full employment

(1)   An employee is not entitled to a redundancy payment in pursuance of a notice of intention to claim if—

(a)   on the date of service of the notice it was reasonably to be expected that the employee (if he continued to be employed by the same employer) would, not later than four weeks after that date, enter on a period of employment of not less than thirteen weeks during which he would not be laid off or kept on short-time for any week, and

(b)   the employer gives a counter-notice to the employee within seven days after the service of the notice of intention to claim.

(2)   Subsection (1) does not apply where the employee—

(a)   continues or has continued, during the next four weeks after the date of service of the notice of intention to claim, to be employed by the same employer, and

(b)   is or has been laid off or kept on short-time for each of those weeks.

Notes

An employer is not entitled to lay off an employee unless there is an express or implied power to do so in the contract. If the employer does not possess this power, any lay-off will amount to a constructive dismissal (see *Jewell* v *Neptune Concrete Ltd* [1975] IRLR 147). Where the employer does possess the contractual authority to lay off, the above provisions seek to offer employees a degree of protection.

V   Transfer of Undertakings

A: Introduction

What happens when a business is sold and the existing workers are not kept or taken on by the new owner? Is that a redundancy situation and, if so, is it the old employer or the new owner who has to take responsibility for meeting any redundancy claims?

The original common law position was set out in the following case.

Nokes v Doncaster Amalgamated Collieries Limited
[1940] AC 1014
House of Lords

The House of Lords had to decide whether, when an order was made under the then companies legislation for the amalgamation of two companies, the contracts of employment were transferred as well as the assets. By a majority (Lord Romer dissenting) it refused to so hold.

LORD ATKIN: When one regards the remarkable legal consequences of the construction adopted by the courts below one is driven to ask what the reasons may be supposed to be that brought about this revolution in the law, and that led to one class of person, companies under the Companies Act, being able to shake off the restrictions which bind ordinary persons, though only when they are minded to transfer their business to another and probably a larger company. Before 1928 no such privilege existed. Amalgamations, a vague term, were possible: companies could dispose of their undertaking to other companies. But it was necessary to invoke the machinery of a winding up: assets would be transferred by conveyances to which the liquidator was party: assignments had to be negotiated: and dissolution of the company could not take place until after the winding up had been completed. But all such sales of undertaking were subject to the ordinary law, and had of course to respect the rights of third parties. Nothing was transferable by a company that was not transferable by an individual: and in particular no one suggested that contracts of service could be transferred. On the contrary, a winding-up order or resolution operated as a discharge of existing servants, resulting in the right to claim damages for wrongful dismissal. It is true that the transferee company would ordinarily offer to employ the former servants of the transferor company: and an unreasonable refusal to accept such offer would mitigate or perhaps get rid of any damages. But the servant was left with his inalienable right to choose whether he would serve a new master or not.

Notes

1.   The rule in *Nokes* was explicable on the basis of freedom of contract. This 'freedom', however, could work against the employee, because a person to whom the business was transferred was under no obligation to offer to employ existing employees working in the transferred business. If no such offer was forthcoming, the employee's only claim was against his or her former – often insolvent – employer. The EPCA 1978, s. 94, modified the common law position and offered protection to the former employer by barring the right of an employee to claim redundancy if, on the change of ownership, he or she refused an offer of alternative employment with the new employer on the same or similar terms. Where the employee accepted the offer of re-engagement by the transferee employer, statutory continuity was and is now preserved by ERA 1996, s. 218(2) (see below).

2.   The Acquired Rights Directive (EC/77/187) set out to change the position and to offer a greater measure of protection to employees caught up

in business transfers. Under pressure from the European Commission and with great reluctance, the Government purported to implement the Directive through the Transfer of Undertakings (Protection of Employment) Regulations 1981. The history of judicial interpretation of these Regulations since 1981 has been one of increasingly pushing back the frontiers of their application to meet the objectives of the EC Directive. The Government has now been forced on a number of occasions to amend the Regulations accordingly. Would this failure to implement the Directive properly give rise to an action for damages against the Government? See *Brasserie du Pêcheur* v *Germany* [1996] IRLR 267 and *Francovich* v *Italy* [1992] IRLR 84, discussed in Chapter 1.

B: The Transfer of Undertakings (Protection of Employment) Regulations 1981

The main effect of the Regulations is that on a business transfer:

(a)   the contracts of employment together with employment rights are automatically transferred to the new owner, thereby completely changing the common law position (reg. 5) and making EPCA 1978, s. 94 redundant (hence its eventual and long overdue repeal by TURERA 1993);
(b)   dismissal connected with the sale of a business may be automatically unfair (reg. 8);
(c)   duties to inform and, in certain circumstances, consult with with any recognised trade union arise (regs 10 and 11).

The House of Lords has made it clear in a number of cases that the Regulations will be applied having regard to a purposive interpretation of the EC Directive. Any ambiguity in the Regulations will be resolved by recourse to the Directive and European Court interpretations thereof. Indeed, as will be seen, the Regulations have been amended where European Court decisions have thrown up any inconsistency between the Directive and the Regulations.

The European Court of Justice has held that the contract is automatically transferred to the new owner only if the employee so consents (see *Katsikas* v *Konstantinidis* [1993] IRLR 179 at page 576 below).

(i)   The Scope of the Regulations

Transfer of Undertakings (Protection of Employment) Regulations 1981 (SI 1981 No. 1794)

2.   Interpretation
(1)   In these Regulations—
. . .

   'relevant transfer' means a transfer to which these Regulations apply and 'transferor' and 'transferee' shall be construed accordingly; and
   'undertaking' includes any trade or business [but does not include any undertaking or part of an undertaking which is not in the nature of a commercial venture.]
. . .

3. A relevant transfer

(1)   Subject to the provisions of these Regulations, these Regulations apply to a transfer from one person to another of an undertaking situated immediately before the transfer in the United Kingdom or part of one which is so situated.

(2)   Subject as aforesaid, these Regulations so apply whether the transfer is effected by sale or by some other disposition or by operation of law.

(3)   Subject as aforesaid, these Regulations so apply notwithstanding—

(a)   that the transfer is governed or effected by the law of a country or territory outside the United Kingdom;

(b)   that persons employed in the undertaking or part transferred ordinarily work outside the United Kingdom;

(c)   that the employment of any of those persons is governed by any such law.

(4)   It is hereby declared that a transfer of an undertaking or part of one—

(a)   may be effected by a series of two or more transactions; and

(b)   may take place whether or not any property is transferred to the transferee by the transferor.

Notes

1.   It will be noted that the original definition of 'undertaking' in reg. 2 excluded non-commercial undertakings. The words in square brackets were removed by TURERA 1993, s. 33(2), in order to bring the Regulations into line with the Directive as interpreted by the ECJ in the *Redmond* case below.

2.   The force of reg. 3(2) is well illustrated by the decision in *Charlton & Charlton* v *Charlton Thermosystems (Romsey) Ltd* [1995] IRLR 79, EAT, in which the appellants were the sole directors and shareholders of the respondent company. On 30 October 1990, the company was 'struck off', but the Charltons continued to trade and to employ the applicants until 16 November 1990. It was held that the Charltons were *personally* responsible to meet the redundancy claim of the applicants; the business had been transferred to them by virtue of reg. 3(2).

3.   Neither the Regulations nor the Directive apply to transfers by way of share sales. This is because both Regulations and Directive refer specifically to a change of employer. In 1974, the original proposal for the Acquired Rights Directive encompassed share transfer cases, but following negotiations its scope was narrowed. Share transfer was and remains one of the most frequent mechanisms for takeovers in the UK, and although there is no change in legal personality of the employer, it may have as serious consequences for employees as a business transfer carried through by other means. This is underlined by *Brookes* v *Borough Care Services* 1998] IRLR 636, EAT. In this case, a transfer had been arranged of certain care homes, on the basis that there would be a transfer under the Regulations, but that the transferees would renegotiate terms and conditions with the staff concerned. When the legality of the agreed variation of terms and conditions was called into question by *Wilson* v *St Helens BC* (see page 585), it was agreed to seek to avoid the Regulations by rearranging matters so as to effect the transfer by the transferee acquiring shares in the transferor instead. In spite of the fact that this device had been adopted to avoid liability, the EAT refused to lift the corporate veil.

The House of Lords Select Committee on the European Communities, with the support of the trade unions and despite opposition from the CBI, recommended that takeovers by share transfer should be brought within the scope of the Directive (HL 38, Session 1995–96, paras 34–38). However, the Government did not support the Select Committee's proposal and the EU Commission did not propose extending the scope of the law to cover share transfers in any of its draft of the Amending Directive (see p. 569–70).

Dr Sophie Redmond Stichting v *Bartol*
[1992] IRLR 366
European Court of Justice

The applicant ran a foundation in Holland which gave assistance to drug addicts. It was originally funded by grants from the local authority, which also provided premises. As from January 1991, those grants were given instead to the Sigma Foundation. The lease of the Redmond building was transferred to Sigma, and Sigma were content to keep on some of the Redmond employees but not all. If the Directive applied, then Sigma were bound to take on all the Redmond employees. In accordance with Dutch law, Redmond applied for permission to terminate the contracts of those employees not required by Sigma. Whether that could happen was referred by the national court to the ECJ, which held that transactions arising out of subsidies to foundations or associations whose services were not remunerated (i.e. non-commercial undertakings) *were* covered by the Directive.

On the concept of 'legal transfer'
It should be recalled that in its judgment of 7 February 1985, *Abels* (135/83, Rep. p. 469, points 11–13), the Court held that the scope of the provision of the Directive at issue cannot be appraised solely on the basis of a textual interpretation because of the differences between the various language versions of that provision and because of the divergencies between the national legislation defining the concept of a contractual transfer.

In consequence the Court gave a sufficiently broad interpretation to that concept to give effect to the purpose of the Directive, which is to ensure that the rights of employees are protected in the event of a transfer of their undertaking, and held that that Directive was applicable wherever, in the context of contractual relations, there is a change in the legal or natural person who is responsible for carrying on the business and who incurs the obligations of an employer towards employees of the undertaking (see most recently the judgment of 15 June 1988, *Bork International* [1989] IRLR 41, 13.

In particular, the Court has held that the scope of the Directive covers the leasing of an establishment followed by the rescinding of that lease and the taking over of the operation by the owner herself (judgment of 17 December 1987, *Ny Molle Kro*, 287/86, [1989] IRLR 37 ECJ, the leasing of a restaurant followed by the rescinding of that lease and the conclusion of a new lease with a new lessee (judgment of 10 February 1988, *Daddy's Dance Hall*, 324/86, [1988] IRLR 315 ECJ) and finally the transfer of a bar-discotheque by means of a lease-purchase agreement and the restoration of the undertaking to its owner as the result of a judicial decision (judgment of 5 May 1988, *Berg*, 144/87 and 145/87 [1989] IRLR 447 ECJ).

As is stressed in the judgment of 15 June 1988 (*Bork*, cited above, point 14), where a lessee who is also the employer ceases to be the employer and a third party becomes the employer thereafter under a contract of sale concluded with the owner, the resulting transaction may fall within the scope of the Directive as defined in Article 1(1) thereof. The fact that in such a case the transfer is effected in two stages, in as much as the undertaking is first returned from the lessee to the owner and the latter then transfers it to the new owner, does not prevent the Directive from applying.

As described in the Order for reference, the transaction to which the preliminary questions put by the Kantonrechter of Groningen relate is governed by comparable reasoning. This is in fact a situation in which a local authority which finances, by a subsidy, the activities of a foundation engaged in providing assistance to drug dependants, decides to terminate this subsidy, as a result of which the activities of that foundation are terminated, in order to switch the subsidy to another foundation pursuing the same activities.

It is true that the judge making the reference asks, in his sixth question, whether the fact that the decision to make the switch is taken unilaterally by the public body, and does not result from an agreement concluded by it with the body subsidised, prevents the Directive from applying in this case.

This question must be answered in the negative.

On the one hand, there is a unilateral decision just as much where an owner decides to change a new lessee as when a public body alters its policy on subsidies. In this respect, the nature of the subsidy, which is granted by a unilateral act accompanied by certain conditions in some Member States, and by subsidy agreements in others, cannot be taken into account. In all cases, the change of the beneficiary of the subsidy takes place in the context of a contractual relationship within the meaning of the Directive and of the case law (judgments of 5 May 1988, *Berg*, cited above, point 19; and of 15 June 1988, *Bork*, cited above, points 13 and 14). Furthermore, although the Redmond foundation disputes in its observations submitted to the Court that agreements had been concluded, the Kantonrechter expressly states in the grounds of its Order that 'the plaintiff, just as much as the Sigma foundation, has declared itself ready to collaborate actively on the 'transfer' of the clients/patients of the plaintiff to the Sigma foundation, to which end a working group for the 'incorporation of the activities of the Redmond foundation into the Sigma foundation' has, furthermore, been set up.'

On the other hand, as is stressed, moreover, by the Commission in its observations, the fact that, in the present case, the transaction arises out of the grant of subsidies to foundations or associations whose services are not remunerated, does not exclude this transaction from the scope of the Directive. In fact, this Directive, as has been noted, has the object of guaranteeing the rights of employees, and it applies to all employees who are covered by protection against dismissal, even if it be limited, under national law . . .

Notes

There must be a transfer of the 'business'. A distinction has been drawn between a sale of the whole business as opposed to a sale of all or part of its assets. Such a distinction had already been drawn for the purposes of deciding the extent of an applicant's continuity of employment under the 1996 Act generally. Those cases are, therefore, applicable here.

2. Article 3(1) of the Directive stipulates that not only the transferor's rights and obligations 'arising from a contract of employment' shall transfer, but

also those 'from an employment relationship'. In this sense Article 3(1) is wider than reg. 5, which appears to limit the effect of the transfer to rights and duties under or in connection with 'a contract of employment'. This raises the question of whether statutory rights are covered and demonstrates the need to retain the statutory provision set out below.

Employment Rights Act 1996

218. Change of employer

(1) Subject to the provisions of this section, this Chapter relates only to employment by the one employer.

(2) If a trade or business, or an undertaking (whether or not established by or under an Act), is transferred from one person to another—

(a) the period of employment of an employee in the trade or business or undertaking at the time of the transfer counts as a period of employment with the transferee, and

(b) the transfer does not break the continuity of the period of employment.

Melon v *Hector Powe Ltd*
[1981] ICR 43
House of Lords

Hector Powe had factories in both England and Scotland. In 1977, Hector Powe decided to sell the the Scottish factory to Executex. The sale included the assignment of the factory lease, plant and machinery and the taking over of work in progress by the purchaser. There was also a clause requiring the purchaser to take on the employees of the factory on similar terms. The employees were taken on by the purchaser but brought a claim for redundancy payments against Hector Powe, their former employer. The House of Lords held that their claim should succeed.

LORD ELWYN JONES: . . .The following finding by the industrial tribunal seems to me to be of some significance in considering the question before us:

It is fair to say, therefore, that the factory at Blantyre before the take-over by Executex, was employed solely in providing garments for sale by the [appellants] and their associated company [Willerby]. After the take-over, however, a different situation prevailed at Blantyre. Executex made garments of a different quality from those made by Hector Powe Ltd. They are in business to manufacture garments on a CMT ['cut, make and trim] basis for whatever customers they can attract.

My Lords, it is clear from the findings of the industrial tribunal that there were some factors pointing towards this transaction being a change of ownership of part of the appellants' business, and other factors pointing towards it being a mere change of ownership of particular assets. The decision between those two views was one of fact and degree for the industrial tribunal, as it must be in all, or almost all, such cases. The industrial tribunal addressed themselves, in my opinion, to the proper question; they expressed themselves thus:

We must look at the true nature of the transaction and try to make up our minds whether or not it truly represented a transfer of a business, or part of a business, or whether it was a convenient method whereby Hector Powe Ltd could dispose of their assets and commitments at Blantyre.

Counsel for the appellants argued that there were no factors which could have been taken to show that this was a mere sale of assets. I cannot agree. One such factor was the difference between the business of the appellants and that of Executex which I have already mentioned and which the industrial tribunal said had impressed them. Another was the absence of any transfer to Executex of the right to use the appellants' name or of any general transfer of assets and liabilities. There was ample material upon which the industrial tribunal was entitled to take the view they did that the Blantyre factory was not transferred to Executex as a going concern. No doubt it was open to the tribunal to have taken the opposite view, but that is nothing to the point.

The appeal must, therefore, fail, unless it can be shown that the industrial tribunal made some error of law in reaching their decision. They are said to have erred by applying the wrong test in asking themselves whether this was a transfer of a going concern. I do not agree. It seems to me that the essential distinction between the transfer of a business, or part of a business, and a transfer of physical assets, is that in the former case the business is transferred as a going concern 'so that the business remains the same business but in different hands' – if I may quote from Lord Denning MR in *Lloyd* v *Brassey* [1969] 2 QB 98, 103 in a passage quoted by the industrial tribunal – whereas in the latter case the assets are transferred to the new owner to be used in whatever business he chooses. Individual employees may continue to do the same work in the same environment and they may not appreciate that they are working in a different business, but that may be the true position on consideration of the whole circumstances. A change in the ownership of a part of a business will, I think, seldom occur, except when that part is to some extent separate and severable from the rest of the business, either geographically or by reference to the products, or in some other way. In the present case, if the factory at Blantyre had been solely devoted to making suits for Willerby, and if it had been transferred to Executex with a view to their continuing the same work, that might well have been a transfer of part of the appellants' business, especially if the transfer had been accompanied by an undertaking by the appellants not to compete with them for Willerby's work. But that is not what happened. After Executex took over the factory they operated it for a different business, and the appellants' guarantee to order 475 suits per week was merely a temporary expedient to help Executex through the initial stages of starting up their business there.

Woodhouse v *Peter Brotherhood Ltd*
[1972] ICR 186
Court of Appeal

The applicant had worked for some 14 years for his ex-employer (Crossleys) at its Sandiacre plant. That plant was sold to Brotherhood who kept on the staff and utilised the plant and machinery. However, Crossleys did not sell its name or goodwill, it simply carried on its business from its Manchester factory. Six years later the applicant was made redundant. Did he have 20 or six years' service? The Court of Appeal held that the sale was of the physical assets and not the business. Accordingly Woodhouse only had six years' service for the purposes of his redundancy payment calculation.

LORD DENNING MR: Now what is the effect of the transfer from Crossleys to Peter Brotherhood Ltd.? It all depends on whether the 'trade or business or an undertaking' of Crossleys was 'transferred from one person to another' . . . I will not go into those provisions again because I went through them in *Lloyd* v *Brassey* [1969] 2 QB 98. I there stated the effect of them and the previous cases in these words, at p. 103:

> If the new owner *takes over* the business as a going concern – so that the business remains the *same* business but in different hands – and the employee keeps the same job with the new owner, then he is not entitled to redundancy payment. His period of employment is deemed to continue without a break in the same job: so that, if he is afterwards dismissed by the new owner for redundancy, his payment is calculated on the whole period in that job.

To that passage I would now add this: if the new owner does *not* take over the business as a going concern, but only takes over the physical assets – using them in a *different* business – then the workman is entitled to redundancy payment from the outgoing owner. He may be taken on by the new owner straight away and thus loses no wages, but nevertheless he is entitled to redundancy payment from the outgoing owner. It is, in a real sense, compensation for long service with that owner. In due course, if he serves more than two years with the new owner, and is afterwards dismissed by the new owner for redundancy, he will be entitled to redundancy payment from the new owner, calculated on his length of service with him.

So, by and large, the Act works fairly. The employee either gets one redundancy payment in respect of his entire service, or he gets two redundancy payments in respect of the two parts of it. But the trouble in this case is that the transfer took place in August 1965 before the Act came into force. So the men may only be entitled to the second period.

So the question is this: was there a 'transfer' of the 'business' or only a transfer of the 'physical assets.' If there was a 'transfer' of the 'business,' the men get redundancy payments for 20 years' service. If there was no transfer of the 'business' but only of the 'physical assets,' they get it for six years' service only.

. . .

This brings me to the present case. It seems to me that this factory is quite different from the farm in *Lloyd* v *Brassey* [1969] 2 QB 98. In that case there was the same business being carried on both before and after the transfer. Here it was a different business. I would ask a similar question to that asked by Salmon LJ in *Lloyd* v *Brassey* [1969] 2 QB 98, 106: if anyone had been asked prior to August 1965: 'What business is being carried on in the factory at Sandiacre?', his answer would have been 'The manufacture of diesel engines.' And if he had been asked the same question in January 1966, his answer would have been 'The manufacture of spinning machines, compressors and steam turbines.' If he had been asked 'Is it the same business?'; he would have said 'No. The manufacture of diesel engines has now gone to Manchester. All that is being done at Sandiacre is the manufacture of spinning machines etc.' True the same men are employed using the same tools: but the business is different.

That is how the majority of the tribunal looked at it. The Industrial Court looked at it differently. They seem to have asked themselves the question; was there a change in the working environment of the men? It seems to me that that was not the right question. The statute requires the tribunal to see whether there was a transfer of the 'business' of the employer. So you look at the nature of the business of the employer and not at the actual work being done by the men. Looking at it in that way, I am quite satisfied that in 1965 Crossleys did *not* transfer their business at Sandiacre to

Peter Brotherhood Ltd. They took it off to Manchester. They only transferred the physical assets to Peter Brotherhood Ltd. The result is that, as from 1965, the men were employed in a different business, namely, that of Peter Brotherhood Ltd.: and are only entitled from Peter Brotherhood to redundancy payment for the period of their service with Peter Brotherhood. So I think the majority of the tribunal were right. I would therefore allow the appeal and restore their decision.

Note

Considerable uncertainty surrounds the question of the extent to which the contracting-out of services is covered by the Acquired Rights Directive and the Transfer of Undertakings (Protection of Employment) Regulations 1981.

Rask and Christensen v *ISS Kantineservice A/S*
[1993] IRLR 133
European Court of Justice

Rask and Christensen were employed in Philips's factory in Denmark as canteen assistants. Philips decided to contract out the running of the canteen to the defendants, ISS, who agreed to offer employment on the same pay to Philips canteen employees. The plaintiffs complained that the date of their monthly salary payment was altered and also that they no longer received shoe and laundry allowances. On announcing that she would not accept the movement of her payment day, Rask was dismissed and claimed unfair dismissal by ISS. The question for the ECJ was whether the contracting out of a service for employees amounted to a transfer of an undertaking within the meaning of the Directive. The ECJ found that there was a transfer.

The defendant in the main proceedings is of the opinion that, on the contrary, an agreement such as that described by the judge making the reference does not constitute a 'transfer of an undertaking' within the meaning of the Directive, unless one is to give to the Directive an excessively broad scope. It maintains, on the one hand, that an agreement of this type does not effect any transfer within the meaning intended by the Directive since it does not confer on the other contracting party either full and entire responsibility for the provision of the services, particularly insofar as the customers and the fixing of prices is concerned, nor ownership of the assets necessary for the provision of these services. It maintains, on the other hand, that an agreement such as this relates to services which cannot be called 'an undertaking' within the meaning of the Directive, taking into account the fact that they are ancillary to the activity of the transferor.

According to the case law of the Court (see the judgment of 5 May 1988, *Berg*, 144/87 and 145/87 [1989] IRLR 447 paragraph 18), the Directive is applicable in any case where, following a legal transfer or merger, there is a change in the legal or natural person who is responsible for carrying on the business and who by virtue of that fact incurs the obligation of an employer vis à vis the employees of the undertaking, regardless of whether or not ownership of the undertaking is transferred.

Under Article 1(1), the protection provided by the Directive applies, in particular, where the transfer only concerns a business or part of a business, that is to say a part of an undertaking. It therefore concerns the employees assigned to that part of the undertaking since, as the Court held in its judgment of 7 February 1985, *Botzen* (186/83, Rep. p. 519, point 15), the employment relationship is essentially character-ised by the link existing between the employee and the part of the undertaking to which he is assigned to carry out his duties.

Thus, where the owner of an undertaking entrusts, by means of an agreement, the responsibility for providing a service to his undertaking, such as a canteen, to the owner of another undertaking who assumes, by reason of it, the obligations of an employer vis à vis the employees who are engaged in the provisions of that service, the resulting transaction is capable of falling within the scope of the Directive as defined in Article 1(1). The fact that, in such a case, the activity transferred is only an ancillary activity of the transferor undertaking not necessarily related to its objects cannot have the effect of excluding that transaction from the scope of the Directive. Similarly, the fact that the agreement between the transferor and the transferee relates to the provision of services provided exclusively for the benefit of the transferor in return for a fee, the form of which is fixed by the agreement, does not prevent the Directive from applying either.

It is for the national judge to assess whether all the factual circumstances as described in his Order for Reference are characteristic of a 'transfer of an undertaking' within the meaning of the Directive. That is why, as a point of information, he should be reminded that he must take into account the following considerations (see, most recently, the judgment of 19 May 1992, *Redmond*, C-29/91 [1992] IRLR 366 at p. 369 paragraphs 23 and 24).

On the one hand, the decisive criterion for establishing whether there is a transfer within the meaning of the Directive is whether the business retains its identity, as would be indicated, in particular, by the fact that its operation was either continued or resumed.

On the other hand, in order to determine whether those conditions are fulfilled, it is necessary to consider all the factual circumstances characterising the transaction in question, including the type of undertaking or business concerned, whether the business's tangible assets, such as buildings and movable property, are transferred, the value of its intangible assets at the time of the transfer, whether or not the majority of its employees are taken over by the new employer, whether or not its customers are transferred and the degree of similarity between the activities carried on before and after the transfer and the period, if any, for which those activities are suspended. It should be noted, however, that all those circumstances are merely single factors in the overall assessment which must be made and cannot therefore be considered in isolation.

Kenny v *South Manchester College*
[1993] IRLR 265
Queen's Bench Division

Prior to April 1993, the Home Office honoured its obligation to provide education in prisons by using teaching staff supplied by the local education authority. From April 1993, those educational services were to be put out for competitive tender to further education colleges now trading as private corporations. The plaintiff had been employed by Cheshire County Coun-cil as a lecturer at a young offenders institution, but the contract to do such work was won by the defendant, South Manchester College. The plaintiff successfully sought a declaration to the effect that his contract would automatically transfer from the County Council to the South Manchester College by virtue of the Directive.

MICHAEL OGDEN QC (sitting as a deputy High Court Judge): It will have been appreciated as I went through the decisions of the European Court that time and time again the Court is reiterating that what I have to do is to consider all the factual circumstances and to assess whether they are characteristic of 'a transfer of an undertaking' within the meaning of the Directive, while reminding myself when doing so of the considerations mentioned in the judgment in *Rask* [1993] IRLR 133 in paragraphs 18 to 20 inclusive. Having undertaken that operation I am satisfied that there is to be a transfer of an undertaking from Cheshire County Council to the defendant within the meaning of Article 1 of the Directive. As Sir Gordon Slynn said in *Spijkers* [1986] 3 ECR 1119, a realistic and robust view must be taken.

Ignoring any transitional arrangements caused by this dispute which I am considering and, therefore, assuming that the situation is that the defendants would move in and take over next Thursday, the reality is as follows. The prisoners and young offenders who attend, say, a carpentry class next Thursday will, save for those released from the institution, be likely in the main to be those who attended the same class in the same classroom the day before and will doubtless be using exactly the same tools and machinery. In the case of Thorne Cross this is particularly likely because the department operates in a purpose-built two-storey building. Furthermore, if the plaintiffs had chosen to apply for employment by the defendant, the same teachers might well be teaching in the same classrooms. If asked after 1 April the question, 'what has happened to the education department at Thorne Cross?' the answer would surely have to be, it has been transferred from the Cheshire County Council, or possibly it might be said from the North Cheshire College, to South Manchester College. That is an obvious question and in my view an obvious answer, and it is certainly one way of reaching an easy conclusion in this case, but I avoid doing it in that fashion and I do what I have been instructed to do in *Rask's* case. I have looked at all the possible considerations there mentioned and indeed any others mentioned by either party. At the end of the day I have come to the conclusion which I have, and if I may say so, have come to it without any difficulty.

In my view the education department will retain its identity and its operation will continue. It will be a going concern (*Rask's* judgment, paragraph 19). In those circumstances the issue which I have to determine must be determined in favour of the plaintiff.

Note
Kenny was approved and supported by the Court of Appeal when applying the Regulations in the following case.

Dines and Others v Initial Health Care Services and Another
[1994] IRLR 336
Court of Appeal

Twelve cleaners were originally employed by Initial Health Care Services to provide cleaning services at a hospital pursuant to a contract gained by Initial from the Area Health Authority. This contract expired on 30 April 1991 and, with effect from 1 May 1991, was awarded to Pall Mall Services (the second respondent). Having failed to obtain the contract, Initial dismissed their 12 employees on the grounds of redundancy. The employees commenced work with Pall Mall at the same hospital as from 1 May 1991 but at a lower rate of pay. They argued successfully before the Appeal Court that this was a transfer within the Transfer of Undertakings Regulations and, therefore, that Pall Mall were obliged to take over the contract of employment from Initial on exactly the same terms as to salary.

NEILL LJ: . . . I have come to the conclusion that the approach of the Industrial Tribunal indicated by the penultimate sentence in paragraph 10 amounts to a misdirection. I should repeat this passage:

> However, when one company enters into competition with a number of other companies to obtain a contract, as happened in this case, and a different company wins the contract from the company that was previously providing the services, then this is a cessation of the business of the first contractors on the hospital premises and the commencement of a new business by [Pall Mall] when they are awarded the contract.

The European cases demonstrate that the fact that another company takes over the provision of certain services as a result of competitive tendering does not mean that the first business or undertaking necessarily comes to an end. Moreover, as was pointed out in the decision in *Daddy's Dance Hall* [1988] IRLR 315 and elsewhere, a transfer may take place in two phases.

I have given careful consideration to whether this passage in paragraph 10 can be interpreted as merely a decision on the facts and no more. It seems to me, however, that with the words 'when one company enters into competition with a number of other companies to obtain a contract, as happened in this case . . .' the Industrial Tribunal was in effect applying a general proposition to the facts of the case. In my judgment the general proposition does not accord with the approach of the European Court.

In these circumstances, I would be disposed to allow the appeal because this misdirection was of fundamental importance.

In some cases this would mean that the matter would have to go back to be reheard by another Industrial Tribunal to reach a conclusion on the particular facts. In the present case, however, there is the special feature that the facts were not in dispute before the Industrial Tribunal and therefore it seems to me that this Court is in as good a position as was the Industrial Tribunal to reach a conclusion. It is true that we do not know what type of equipment was used for the cleaning of the hospital, and it may be that some changes in cleaning methods were introduced by Pall Mall when they took over. Hospital cleaning, however, though of the utmost importance, is not an operation which lends itself to the employment of many different techniques. The cleaning services were to be carried out by (mainly) the same staff on the same premises and for the same authority.

I consider that on the agreed facts there was a transfer of an undertaking for the purpose of the 1981 Regulations. It took place in two phases — (a) the handing back by Initial to the authority on 30 April of the cleaning services at the hospital; and (b) the grant or handing over by the authority to Pall Mall on 1 May of the cleaning services which were operated as from that date by essentially the same labour force.

Note

Following *Dines*, cases have extended the meaning of a 'relevant transfer'. In *Betts* v *Brintel Helicopters and KLM* [1996] IRLR 45, Brintel had until 1995 exclusive rights to service Shell's helicopter requirements for all their North Sea oil rigs. In 1995, Shell decided to split the contract between Brintel and KLM, and 66 Brintel employees were left without jobs. Betts and six others claimed, successfully, that they were now employed by KLM. The High Court held that there had been a transfer of the 'activity' from Brintel to KLM even though there was no transfer of employees or assets.

In *Porter* v *Queens Medical Centre* [1993] IRLR 486, a transfer of paediatric and neo-natal services from two district health authorities to a NHS trust was held to be a relevant transfer.

Questions
1.   What effect does the decisions in *Rask*, *Redmond*, *Kenny* and *Dines* have on the UK Government's policy of contracting out the provision of public services?

See Napier, B., *CCT, Market Testing and Employment Rights* (London: The Institute of Employment Rights, 1993).
2.   Following *Dines* in what circumstances, if any, will a change of contractor following competitive tendering fall outside the Transfer of Undertakings Regulations?

Notes
1.   In *Schmidt*, Case C-392/92, [1994] IRLR 302, the ECJ held that the contracting-out of cleaning involving one person amounted to a protected transfer under the Directive. This case provides a literal interpretation and suggests that the transfer of an entity which retains its economic identity could be found in circumstances in which no assets, tangible or intangible, were transferred, but simply the performance of an identifiable business function.
2.   A case that appeared possibly to be bucking this trend towards a very wide interpretation of what is a relevant transfer is:

Rygaard v *Strø Mølle Akustik A/S*
[1996] IRLR 51
European Court of Justice

Rygaard had been employed by Pedersen, a firm of carpenters in Denmark. Pedersen had a contract to build a canteen for SAS. SAS agreed to let Pedersen give the responsibility for completing part of the canteen to the respondents. On 1 February 1992, Pedersen told Rygaard that they intended winding up their company and that his employment would end in three months' time. In the meantime Rygaard was told to work with the respondents on the completion of the canteen; which he did until he was dismissed by them in May 1992. Had there been a relevant transfer so that Rygaard could bring wrongful dismissal proceedings against the respondents? The ECJ held that there was *not* a relevant transfer.

DECISION: . . . Is Council Directive 77/187/EEC applicable when contractor B, pursuant to an agreement with contractor A, continues part of building works began by contractor A, and

(i)   an agreement is made between contractor A and contractor B under which some of contractor A's workers are to continue working for contractor B and contractor B is to take over materials on the building site in order to complete the contracted work; and

(ii)   after the taking over, there is a period in which contractor A and contractor B are both working on the building works at the same time?

Does it make any difference that the agreement on the completion of the works is entered into between the awarder of the main building contract and contractor B with contractor A's consent?'

By its question the national court is essentially asking whether the taking over, with a view to completing, with the consent of the awarder of the main building contract, works started by another undertaking, of two apprentices and an employee, together with the materials assigned to those works, constitutes a transfer of an undertaking business or part of a business, within the meaning of Article 1(1) of the Directive.

According to the Court's case law, it is clear from the scheme of the Directive and from the terms of Article 1(1) thereof that the Directive is intended to ensure continuity of employment relationships existing within a business, irrespective of any change of ownership. It follows that the decisive criterion for establishing whether there is a transfer for the purposes of the Directive is whether the business in question retains its identity (see, in particular, the judgment in case 24/85 *Spijkers v Benedik* [1986] ECR 1119, paragraph 11).

According to that same judgment in order to ascertain whether that criterion is satisfied, it is necessary to consider whether the operation of the entity in question is actually continued or resumed by the new employer, with the same or similar economic activities (*Spikers v Benedik*, paragraph 12).

It is then necessary to consider all the facts characterising the transaction in question, including the type of undertaking or business concerned, whether or not tangible assets, such as buildings and moveable property, are transferred, the value of the intangible assets at the time of the transfer, whether or not most of the personnel are taken over by the new employer, whether or not customers are transferred and the degree of similarity between the activities carried on before and after the transfer and the period of any suspension of those activities. All those circumstances are, however, only individual factors in the overall assessment to be made and they cannot therefore be considered in isolation (*Spijkers v Benedik*, paragraph 13).

Mr Rygaard considers that those conditions are satisfied in the present case. He observes that the works taken over by Strø Mølle are the same as those which had been entrusted to Svend Pedersen A/S and that the duration of the works cannot be decisive in determining whether a transfer of an undertaking, within the meaning of the Directive, has taken place, just as the scale of the activity transferred was not held to be decisive in *Schmidt v Spar-und Leihkasse des früheren Ämter Bordesholm, Kiel und Cronshagen*, C-392/92 [1994] IRLR 302.

That argument cannot be accepted.

The authorities cited above presuppose that the transfer relates to a stable economic entity whose activity is not limited to performing one specific works contract.

That is not the case of an undertaking which transfers to another undertaking one of its building works with a view to the completion of that work. Such a transfer could come within the terms of the Directive only if it included the transfer of a body of assets enabling the activities or certain activities of the transferor undertaking to be carried on in a stable way.

That is not so where, as in the case now referred, the transferor undertaking merely makes available to the new contractor certain workers and material for carrying out the works in question.

The reply to the question submitted must therefore be that the taking over – with a view to completing, with the consent of the awarder of the main building contract, works started by another undertaking – of two apprentices and an employee, together with the materials assigned to those works, does not constitute a transfer of an undertaking, business or part of a business, within the meaning of Article 1(1) of the Directive.

Note

That the approach in *Rygaard* was to be limited was made clear in *BSG Services* v *Tuck* [1996] IRLR 134, in which Tuck and 13 others were employed by Mid-Bedfordshire District Council as housing maintenance personnel. On 12 February 1993, the Council terminated Tuck's employment (effective 15 May 1993), and on 14 May 1993 it concluded a contract with BSG whereby the latter was to provide the housing maintenance services. BSG intended to use self-employed contractors and did not employ Tuck or any of the other applicants. The EAT agreed that there had been a transfer to BSG and that they were liable to Tuck for unfair dismissal.

Mummery J held that *Rygaard* did not alter the general approach in *Dines* and that the *Rygaard* principle is limited to 'activities under a short-term one-off contract'.

The following ECJ case endorses the view that *Rygaard* is of limited application:

Merckx and Neuhuys v *Ford Motor Co. Belgium*
[1996] IRLR 467
European Court of Justice

Merckx and Neuhuys were employed as car salesmen by Anfo Motors, a Ford dealership in which Ford was the principal shareholder (and who took over defence of the action when Anfo went into liquidation). In 1987 Anfo decided to end the dealership and Ford transferred it to Novarobel – an independent dealer – as from November 1987. No tangible assets were transferred to Novarobel, but Anfo recommended its services to its old customers. Although three-quarters of Anfo's staff were dismissed, the applicants' jobs were to be transferred to Novarobel. The applicants refused to transfer to Novarobel because they were concerned that their level of remuneration would be reduced. They brought proceedings against Anfo (now Ford) claiming breach of contract. The ECJ held that there was a transfer of the undertaking to Novarobel even though there was no contractual link between the two dealers, no tangible assets passed between them and the dealership was carried on by Novarobel under a different name, from different premises and with different facilities. The applicants' objection to transfer meant that Anfo (Ford) had terminated their contract pursuant to Article 4(2) of the Directive (see *Katsikas'* case, below).

DECISION: . . . In order to determine whether that condition is met, it is necessary to consider all the facts characterising the transaction in question, including the type of undertaking or business, whether or not the business's tangible assets, such as buildings and movable property, are transferred, the value of its intangible assets at the time of the transfer, whether or not the majority of its employees is taken over by the new employer, whether or not its customers are transferred and the degree of similarity between the activities carried on before and after the transfer and the period, if any, for which those activities were suspended. It should be noted, however, that all those circumstances are merely single factors in the overall assessment which must be made and cannot therefore be considered in isolation (judgment in case C-29/91 *Redmond Stichting,* cited above, paragraph 24).

In the light of those principles, the Court notes that in the situation with which the main proceedings are concerned Ford, the main shareholder in Anfo Motors, transferred to Novarobel the dealership for the sale of vehicles in the territory covered by Anfo Motors and so transferred the economic risk associated with that business to an undertaking outside its own group of companies, that Novarobel carried on the activity performed by Anfo Motors, without interruption, in the same sector and subject to similar conditions, that it took on part of its staff and that it was recommended to customers in order to ensure continuity in the operation of the dealership.

All those factors, taken as a whole, support the view that the transfer of the dealership in the circumstances of the main proceedings is capable of falling within the scope of the Directive. It must be ascertained, however, whether certain factors relied on by Mr Merckx and Mr Neuhuys may rebut that finding.

First, Mr Merckx and Mr Neuhuys claimed that in the circumstances at issue in the main proceedings there had been neither a transfer of the company's tangible or intangible assets nor at least partial preservation of the undertaking's structure and organisation. Moreover, the municipalities of the Brussels conurbation in which Novarobel has its principal place of business are different from those in which Anfo Motors carried on its business.

Those circumstances are not such as to prevent the application of the Directive, since, having regard to the nature of the activity pursued, the transfer of tangible assets is not conclusive of whether the entity in question retains its economic identity (see to that effect the judgment in case C-392/92 *Schmidt* v *Spar-und Leihkasse der früheren Ämter Bordesholm, Kiel und Cronshagen* [1994] IRLR 302, paragraph 16). The purpose of an exclusive dealership for the sale of motor vehicles of a particular make in a certain sector remains the same even if it is carried on under a different name, from different premises and with different facilities. It is also irrelevant that the principal place of business is situated in a different area of the same conurbation, provided that the contract territory remains the same.

Secondly, Mr Merckx and Mr Neuhuys claimed that there could not be a transfer for the purposes of the Directive when an undertaking definitively ceased trading and was put into liquidation, as was the case with Anfo Motors. In such circumstances, the economic entity had ceased to exist and could not retain its identity.

In that regard, if the Directive's aim of protecting workers is not to be undermined, its application cannot be excluded merely because the transferor discontinues its activities when the transfer is made and is then put into liquidation. If the business of that undertaking is carried on by another undertaking, those facts tend to confirm, rather, that there has been a transfer for the purposes of the Directive.

Thirdly, Mr Merckx and Mr Neuhuys claimed that the fact that the majority of the staff had been dismissed upon the transfer of the dealership indicated that the Directive did not apply.

Article 4(1) of the Directive provides that the transfer of an undertaking, business or part of the business does not in itself constitute grounds for dismissal. However, that provision is not to stand in the way of dismissals that may take place for economic, technical or organisational reasons entailing changes in the workforce.

Accordingly, the fact that the majority of the staff was dismissed when the transfer took place is not sufficient to preclude the application of the Directive. The dismissals might have taken place for economic, techical or organisational reasons, in compliance with Article 4(1), cited above. In any event, failure to comply with that provision could not affect the existence of a transfer for the purposes of the Directive.

Finally, Mr Merckx and Mr Neuhuys claimed that, even if there had in fact been a transfer for the purposes of the Directive, it was not the result of a legal transfer as required by Article 1 thereof. That concept necessarily required the existence of a contractual link between the transferor and the transferee. There was no such link in the present case.

On account of the differences between the language versions of the Directive and the divergences between the laws of the Member States with regard to the concept of legal transfer, the Court has given that concept a sufficiently flexible interpretation in keeping with the objective of the Directive, which is to safeguard employees in the event of a transfer of their undertaking, and has held that the Directive is applicable wherever, in the context of contractual relations, there is a change in the natural or legal person who is responsible for carrying on the business and who incurs the obligations of an employer towards employees of the undertaking (see, inter alia, the judgment in *Redmond Stichting*, cited above, at paragraphs 10 and 11).

The Court has therefore held that the Directive applies to the termination of a lease of a restaurant followed by the conclusion of a new management contract with another operator (case 324/86 *Foreningen af Arbejdsledere i Danmark* v *Daddy's Dance Hall* [1988] IRLR 315), the termination of a lease followed by a sale by the owner (case 101/87 *Bork P International A/S* v *Foreningen af Arbejdsledere i Danmark* [1989] IRLR 41), and also a situation in which a public authority ceases to grant subsidies to a legal person, thereby bringing about the full and definitive termination of its activities in order to transfer them to another legal person with a similar aim (*Redmond Stichting*, cited above).

It is clear from that case law that, for the Directive to apply, it is not necessary for there to be a direct contractual relationship between the transferor and the transferee. Consequently, where a motor vehicle dealership concluded with one undertaking is terminated and a new dealership is awarded to another undertaking pursuing the same activities, the transfer of undertaking is the result of a legal transfer for the purposes of the Directive, as interpreted by the Court.

Furthermore, it is clear from the documents before the Court that the circumstances of the actions brought before the national court are that Ford, the principal shareholder of Anfo Motors, concluded an 'agreement and guarantee' with Novarobel, by which it undertook, inter alia, to bear the expenses relating to certain payments for breach of contract, unlawful dismissal or redundancy which might be payable by Novarobel to members of the staff previously employed by Anfo Motors. That fact confirms that there was a legal transfer within the meaning of the Directive.

Consequently, the answer to the first part of the question as reformulated above must be that Article 1(1) of the Directive must be interpreted as applying where an undertaking holding a motor vehicle dealership for a particular territory discontinues its activities and the dealership is then transferred to another undertaking which takes on part of the staff and is recommended to customers, without any transfer of assets.

The employee's power to prevent the transfer of his contract or the employment relationship

As regards the second part of the question as reformulated above, the Court held in case 105/84 *Foreningen af Arbejdsledere i Danmark v Danmols Inventar* [1985] ECR 2639, paragraph 16, that the protection which the Directive is intended to guarantee is redundant where the person concerned decides of his own accord not to continue the employment relationship with the new employer after the transfer.

It also follows from the judgment in joined cases C-132/91, C-138/91 and C-139/91 *Katsikas and others v Konstantinidis* [1993] IRLR 179, paragraphs 21 and 32, that, whilst the Directive allows the employee to remain in the employ of his new employer on the same conditions as were agreed with the transferor, it cannot be interpreted as obliging the employee to continue his employment relationship with the transferee. Such an obligation would jeopardise the fundamental rights of the employee who must be free to choose his employer and cannot be obliged to work for an employer whom he has not freely chosen.

It follows that, in the event of the employee deciding of his own accord not to continue with the contract of employment or employment relationship with the transferee, it is for the Member States to determine what the fate of the contract of employment or employment relationship should be. The Member States may provide, in particular, that in such a case the contract of employment or employment relationship must be regarded as terminated either by the employee or by the employer. They may also provide that the contract or employment relationship should be maintained with the transferor (judgment in *Katsikas and others*, cited above, paragraphs 35 and 36).

Mr Merckx and Mr Neuhuys claimed, moreover, that in the case in point Novarobel refused to guarantee to maintain their level of remuneration, which was calculated by reference, in particular, to the turnover achieved.

In the light of that submission, it should be noted that Article 4(2) provides that if the contract of employment or the employment relationship is terminated because the transfer within the meaning of Article 1(1) involves a substantial change in working conditions to the detriment of the employee, the employer is to be regarded as having been responsible for termination.

A change in the level of remuneration awarded to an employee is a substantial change in working conditions within the meaning of that provision, even where the remuneration depends in particular on the turnover achieved. Where the contract of employment or the employment relationship is terminated because the transfer involves such a change, the employer must be regarded as having been responsible for the termination.

Consequently, the answer to the second part of the question as reformulated must be that Article 3(1) of the Directive does not preclude an employee employed by the transferor at the date of the transfer of an undertaking from objecting to the transfer to the transferee of the contract of employment or the employment relationship. In such a case, it is for the Member States to determine what the fate of the contract of employment or employment relationship with the transferor should be. However, where the contract of employment or the employment relationship is terminated on account of a change in the level of remuneration awarded to the employee, Article 4(2) of the Directive requires the Member States to provide that the employer is to be regarded as having been responsible for the termination.

Note

The previous Conservative Government's adoption of compulsory competitive tendering (CCT) in the Local Government Planning and Land Act 1980 was an attempt to extend the operation of market forces to the provision of certain services by local government. Unlike almost anywhere else in the EU, local government in the UK was compelled to put specified services out to competitive tender. Existing in-house providers were forced to compete with private contractors. Many other public bodies, such as hospitals, were required to go through a similar exercise. The introduction of compulsory CCT dramatically increased the potential applicability of the Acquired Rights Directive. Confusion over whether the the Directive was relevant to CCT transfers has been claimed to have significantly distorted competition in the UK market for local authority services. (See, for example, the evidence submitted to the House of Lords Select Committee on the European Communities' investigation of the European Commission's proposed revisions to the Directive (House of Lords, 1996).)

Unless resolved, the uncertainties relating to the scope of the law relating to transfers of undertakings are likely to continue to cause problems when CCT is abolished and replaced by a statutory duty on the part of local authorities to make arrangements for the achievement of best value in the performance of their functions (see the Local Government Act 1999, Part I).

A survey of 68 employers recently involved in transfers, conducted by researchers in the Institute of Industrial and Commercial Law, Staffordshire University, revealed widespread non-compliance with the Acquired Rights Directive (see Hardy, S.T., Adnett, N.J., Painter, R.W., *TUPE and CCT Business Transfer: UK Labour Market Views*, Staffordshire University Press, 1998). (For a review of this research report, see Colling, T., 'Views of TUPE and CCT' (1998) 27 ILJ 152. See also Adnett, N.J., Hardy, S.T. and Painter, R.W., 'Business transfers and contracting out: compulsory competitive tendering in tatters?' (1995) 17 *Employee Relations* No. 8, pp. 21–28; Adnett, N.J., and Hardy, S.T., 'The Impact of TUPE on CCT: Evidence from Employers' (1998) 24 *Local Government Studies*, No. 3, pp. 36–50.) Any post-transfer changes to employment terms and conditions were overwhelmingly to the detriment of employees. Reductions in employment terms and overtime pay occurred in the majority of these transfers, with employees suffering reduced basic hourly and sickness pay in at least 40 per cent of cases. From the details supplied, it appears that the scale of any changes was almost universally modest; only in the case of employment and overtime pay were there more than three organisations reporting reductions larger than 5 per cent. Collective agreements were transferred in only 47 per cent of transfers. Although not within the scope of the 1981 Regulations, occupational pensions were transferred in 11 per cent of cases, with a further 75 per cent of contractors claiming to provide equivalent pensions for transferred workers. In relation to the Regulations consultation requirements, few contractors were in full compliance, since in only around 20 per cent of the transfers surveyed were employees informed of the economic consequences of the transfer, such as new job and salary structures, and even fewer were told about the consequences for existing collective agreements.

Other surveys have provided further evidence that CCT worsened pay and conditions of employees working for private contractors and that it had a disparate impact according to the gender predominance of the workforce. (For a summary of the surveys, see 'Goodbye CCT', *IRS Employment Trends*, 647, January 1998, pp. 5–11; on the disparate gender impact of CCT, see Escott, K., and Whitfield, D., *The Gender Impact of CCT in Local Government* (1995), EOC Report. Research Discussion Series No. 12, Centre for Public Services and the judicial corrective applied in *Radcliffe and others v North Yorkshire County Council* [1995] IRLR 398, HL.)

The Staffordshire University survey also established that 80 per cent of its employer respondents were involved in litigation as a consequence of CCT business transfers. As one interviewee put it: '[It's] a story of doom and gloom about the costs of fighting a TUPE case . . . we are frightened.'

Given the prospect of inheriting a workforce with their pre-transfer terms and conditions intact, there is every incentive for the transferee employer to seek to exploit the legal confusion with a view to avoiding the Regulations. The legislative and case law history of the 1981 Regulations provides a number of examples of possible avoidance strategies which have for the most part ultimately foundered as a result of amendment to the Regulations or, more frequently, purposive judicial interpretation. The following case confirms earlier indications that the ECJ was moving away from its previous liberal approach to what constitutes a relevant transfer. In doing so, it opens up a gap in employment protection which can be exploited by employers seeking to avoid legal obligations under the Acquired Rights Directive and Transfer of Undertakings (Protection of Employment) Regulations 1981.

Süzen v Zehnacker Gebaudereinigung GmbH Krankenhausservice
(Case C-13/95) [1997] IRLR 255
European Court of Justice

Zehnacker had a contract to clean a private church-run secondary school in Bonn-Bad-Godesberg. The school terminated the cleaning contract with effect from 30 June 1994 and contracted-out its cleaning to Lefarth instead. Mrs Süzen was employed by Zehnacker and, together with seven other cleaners at the school, was dismissed when the employers lost the contract. She claimed that this dismissal was invalid, relying upon Directive 77/187/EEC.

The Arbeitsgericht (Labour Court) of Bonn referred the following questions to the European Court of Justice for a preliminary ruling:

1. On the basis of the judgments of the Court of Justice of 14 April 1994 in case C-392/92 *Schmidt* and 19 May 1992 in case C-29/91 *Redmond Stichting*, is Directive 77/187/EEC applicable if an undertaking terminates a contract with an outside undertaking in order then to transfer it to another outside undertaking?

2. Is there a legal transfer within the meaning of the Directive in the case of the operation described in Question 1 even if no tangible or intangible business assets are transferred?

Advocate-General La Pergola, whose Opinion delivered on 15 October 1996 is reproduced below, gave the following suggested reply:

In the absence of other factors which might affect the situation, the termination of a cleaning contract with one undertaking and the subsequent award of the same contract to another does not fall within the scope of Directive 77/187/CEE.

DECISION: . . . In *Schmidt,* cited above, the Court held that that provision must be interpreted as covering a situation, such as that outlined in the order for reference, in which an undertaking entrusts by contract to another undertaking the responsibility for carrying out cleaning operations which it previously performed itself, even though, prior to the transfer, such work was carried out by a single employee. Earlier, in *Redmond Stichting,* cited above, the Court took the view in particular that the term 'legal transfer' covers a situation in which a public authority decides to terminate the subsidy paid to one legal person, as a result of which the activities of that legal person are fully and definitively terminated, and to transfer it to another legal person with a similar aim.

By its two questions, which it is appropriate to consider together, the national court asks whether the Directive also applies to a situation in which a person who had entrusted the cleaning of his premises to a first undertaking terminates his contract with the latter and, for the performance of similar work, enters into a new contract with a second undertaking without any concomitant transfer of tangible or intangible business assets from one undertaking to the other.

The aim of the Directive is to ensure continuity of employment relationships within a business, irrespective of any change of ownership. The decisive criterion for establishing the existence of a transfer within the meaning of the Directive is whether the entity in question retains its identity, as indicated inter alia by the fact that its operation is actually continued or resumed (case 24/85 *Spijkers* [1986] ECR 1119, . . . and, most recently, joined cases C-171/94 and C-172/94 *Merckx and Neuhuys* [1996] IRLR 467 . . . see also the advisory opinion of the Court of the European Free Trade Association of 19 December 1996 in case E-2/96 *Ulstein and Røiseng,* not yet reported . . .).

Whilst the lack of any contractual link between the transferor and the transferee or, as in this case, between the two undertakings successively entrusted with the cleaning of a school, may point to the absence of a transfer within the meaning of the Directive, it is certainly not conclusive.

As has been held – most recently in *Merckx and Neuhuys* . . . – the Directive is applicable wherever, in the context of contractual relations, there is a change in the natural or legal person who is responsible for carrying on the business and who incurs the obligations of an employer towards employees of the undertaking. Thus, there is no need, in order for the Directive to be applicable, for there to be any direct contractual relationship between the transferor and the transferee: the transfer may also take place in two stages, through the intermediary of a third party such as the owner or the person putting up the capital.

For the Directive to be applicable, however, the transfer must relate to a stable economic entity whose activity is not limited to performing one specific works contract (case C-48/94 *Rygaard* [1996] IRLR 51 . . . . The term entity thus refers to an organised grouping of persons and assets facilitating the exercise of an economic activity which pursues a specific objective.

In order to determine whether the conditions for the transfer of an entity are met, it is necessary to consider all the facts characterising the transaction in question, including in particular the type of undertaking or business, whether or not its tangible assets, such as buildings and moveable property, are transferred, the value of its intangible assets at the time of the transfer, whether or not the majority of its employees are taken over by the new employer, whether or not its customers are transferred, the degree of similarity between the activities carried on before and after the transfer, and the period, if any, for which those activities were suspended. However, all those circumstances are merely single factors in the overall assessment which must be made and cannot therefore be considered in isolation (see, in particular, *Spijkers* and *Redmond Stichting* . . .).

As observed by most of the parties who commented on this point, the mere fact that the service provided by the old and the new awardees of a contract is similar does not therefore support the conclusion that an economic entity has been transferred. An entity cannot be reduced to the activity entrusted to it. Its identity also emerges from other factors, such as its workforce, its management staff, the way in which its work is organised, its operating methods or indeed, where appropriate, the operational resources available to it.

The mere loss of a service contract to a competitor cannot therefore by itself indicate the existence of a transfer within the meaning of the Directive. In those circumstances, the service undertaking previously entrusted with the contract does not, on losing a customer, thereby cease fully to exist, and a business or part of a business belonging to it cannot be considered to have been transferred to the new awardee of the contract.

It must also be noted that, although the transfer of assets is one of the criteria to be taken into account by the national court in deciding whether an undertaking has in fact been transferred, the absence of such assets does not necessarily preclude the existence of such a transfer (*Schmidt* and *Merckx*, cited above . . .

As pointed out [above], the national court, in assessing the facts characterising the transaction in question, must take into account among other things the type of undertaking or business concerned. It follows that the degree of importance to be attached to each criterion for determining whether or not there has been a transfer within the meaning of the Directive will necessarily vary according to the activity carried on, or indeed the production or operating methods employed in the relevant undertaking, business or part of a business. Where in particular an economic entity is able, in certain sectors, to function without any significant tangible or intangible assets, the maintenance of its identity following the transaction affecting it cannot, logically, depend on the transfer or such assets.

The United Kingdom Government and the Commission have argued that, for the entity previously entrusted with a service contract to have been the subject of a transfer within the meaning of the Directive, it may be sufficient in certain circumstances for the new awardee of the contract to have voluntarily taken over the majority of the employees specially assigned by his predecessor to the performance of the contract.

In that regard, it should be borne in mind that the factual circumstances to be taken into account in determining whether the conditions for a transfer are met include in particular, in addition to the degree of similarity of the activity carried on before and after the transfer and the type of undertaking or business concerned, the question whether or not the majority of the employees were taken over by the new employer (*Spijkers*, cited above, paragraph 13).

Since in certain labour-intensive sectors a group of workers engaged in a joint activity on a permanent basis may constitute an economic entity, it must be recognised that such an entity is capable of maintaining its identity after it has been transferred where the new employer does not merely pursue the activity in question but also takes over a major part, in terms of their numbers and skills, of the employees specially assigned by his predecessor to that task. In those circumstances, as stated in paragraph 21 of *Rygaard*, cited above, the new employer takes over a body of assets enabling him to carry on the activities or certain activities of the transferor undertaking on a regular basis.

It is for the national court to establish, in the light of the foregoing interpretative guidance, whether a transfer has occurred in this case.

The answer to the questions from the national court must therefore be that Article 1(1) of the Directive is to be interpreted as meaning that the Directive does not apply to a situation in which a person who had entrusted the cleaning of his premises to a first undertaking terminates his contract with the latter and, for the performance of similar work, enters into a new contract with a second undertaking, if there is no concomitant transfer from one undertaking to the other of significant tangible or intangible assets or taking over by the new employer of a major part of the workforce, in terms of their numbers and skills, assigned to his predecessor to the performance of the contract.

. . .

Note

According to the ECJ in *Süzen*, an activity does not, in itself, constitute a stable economic entity. Consequently, the ECJ stated, the mere fact that a similar activity is carried on before and after the change of contractors does not mean that there is a transfer of the undertaking. In the case of a labour-intensive undertaking with no significant assets (e.g., contract cleaning) the *Süzen* approach will mean that there will generally be no transfer unless the new contractor takes on the majority of the old contractor's staff (for an example of the UK courts adopting the *Süzen* approach, see *Betts* v *Brintel Helicopters Ltd and KLM ERA Helicopters (UK) Ltd* [1997] IRLR 361).

Süzen is a decision where the court did not attempt to reconcile its decision with the reasoning in *Schmidt*, failed to have regard to the principle of employment protection which underpins the Acquired Rights Directive and opened up a possible evasion strategy for transferee employers. The decision would appear to leave the contractor with the choice as to whether to be bound by the 1981 Regulations by taking on the majority of the existing staff. Where the existing workforce are unskilled and easily replaceable there is no incentive to assume responsibilities towards them. The workforce are relegated to the status of mere assets. As a result, the weakest members of the labour market – the unskilled – are disenfranchised from the protection of the acquired rights legislation.

More recently, however, in *Francisco Hernandez Vidal SA* v *Gomez Perez and others* [1999] IRLR 132; *Sanchez Hidalgo and others* v *Asociacion De Servicios ASEH and Sociedad Cooperativa Minerva* [1999] IRLR 136, we see a possible softening of the *Süzen* approach, though with no clarity in this regard. The focus in these rulings is on whether 'an economic entity' has been transferred, as opposed to whether a 'major part of the workforce' has been taken over, as in *Süzen*. This approach seems to lay emphasis on what the undertaking looked like pre-transfer rather than post-transfer, and as a result reduces the possibility that a transferee can evade the 1981 Regulations by refusing to engage the employees in the undertaking transferred. In respect of the provision of services, the ECJ holds that 'an organised grouping of wage earners who are specifically and permanently assigned to a common task may, in the absence of other factors of production, amount to an economic entity'.

It is frustrating that these recent rulings do not provide clear guidance. In both decisions, the ECJ adopts word-for-word the tests approved in *Süzen*, an approach cynically characterised by Rubenstein as 'jurisprudence by word processor' ([1999] IRLR 73). Both *Gomez* and *Sanchez* slavishly adopt the *Süzen* test:

In order to determine/consider whether the conditions for a transfer of an entity are met, it is necessary to consider all the facts characterising the transaction in question, including in particular the type of undertaking or business, whether or not its tangible assets, such as buildings and movable property, are transferred, the value of its intangible assets at the time of the transfer, *whether or not the majority of its employees are taken over by the new employer*, whether or not its customers are transferred on before and after the transfer, and the period, if any, for which those activities were suspended. However, all those circumstances are merely single factors in the overall assessment which must be made and therefore cannot be considered in isolation. ([1999] IRLR 139 at para. 29; *cf.* [1997] IRLR 259 at para. 14)

It is suggested that a possible route through this confusion would be to adopt the purposive approach adopted by Morrison J in *ECM (Vehicle Delivery Service v Cox and others* [1998] IRLR 416 where he concluded that it would not be proper for a transferee to be able to control the extent of its obligations by refusing to comply with them in the first place. As Morrison J stated: 'The issue as to whether employees should have been taken on cannot be determined by asking whether they were taken on.' (p. 419, at para. 24) This approach focuses attention on the motive for refusing to take on the existing workforce, so as to decide whether the motivation was the avoidance of the Regulations or some other reason. Even then, there will be difficult questions of proof in establishing the true motive. The Court of Appeal has now endorsed Morrison J's approach (see below).

According to Davies, the reasoning in *Süzen* comes very close to the Commission's original proposal which sought to distinguish the mere transfer of an activity from the transfer of an undertaking. Furthermore, it would appear, as Davies argues, 'that the Council has set its seal of approval on what the Court of Justice has done so far in interpreting the scope of the Directive, and has left further consideration of this "hot potato" in the hands of the court' (Davies (1998) 27 JLJ 365, at p. 366; see also Davies (1996) 25 ILJ 193).

In 1998 a Directive (98/50/EEC) amending the Acquired Rights Directive (77/187/EEEC) was adopted. Unfortunately, its definition of the scope of the amended Directive is of little assistance in clarifying matters. Article 1(b) states that there is a transfer 'where there is an economic entity which retains its identity'. This is merely a repetition of the standard test adopted by the ECJ and which has produced such contradictory outcomes. Article 1(b) goes on to define an entity as 'an organised grouping of resources which has the objective of pursuing an an economic activity, whether or not that activity is central or ancillary'. This part of the definition is very similar to the formula adopted by the ECJ's decision in *Süzen*. (For a commentary on the amended Directive, see Davies (1998) 27 ILJ 365.)

ECM (Vehicle Delivery Service) Ltd v Cox and others
[1999] IRLR 559
Court of Appeal

The applicants were employed by Axial Ltd as drivers and yardmen. Axial had a contract with VAG Ltd to deliver Audi and Volkswagen cars imported into the UK through the port of Grimsby.

VAG decided that the delivery contract should be changed in a number of ways and Axial lost the contract to ECM. When ECM was appointed, the site from which the work was carried out was changed, a different system of delivery was introduced and the arrangements for administering the contract were altered.

ECM did not offer employment to any of the employees who had worked on the contract prior to the change of contractor. The employment tribunal found as a fact that this was because the employees were claiming through their trade union representative that the Transfer of Undertakings Regulations 1981 applied and were threatening an action for unfair dismissal if they were not employed by ECM.

In the event, the employees successfully brought unfair dismissal complaints against ECM. The employment tribunal found that there was a relevant transfer to ECM within the meaning of the 1981 Regulations. Subsequent to the tribunal's decision, the ECJ handed down its decision in the *Süzen* case. It was argued on behalf of the employers on appeal that, in the light of *Süzen*, the tribunal had erred in equating the transfer of a service contract with the transfer of an undertaking, and that all that had been transferred in this particular case was a particular activity. On behalf of the applicants, it was argued that *Süzen* does not deal with a situation in which an employer decides not to take on employees in an attempt to avoid the operation of the Regulations.

The EAT dismissed the employers' appeal. finding that the tribunal's decision that there was a transfer of an economic entity which retained its identity was not inconsistent with *Süzen* or with the decision of the Court of Appeal in *Betts v Brintel Helicopters Ltd* [1997] IRLR 361, CA. According to the EAT, when properly understood, there is no conflict with the decision of the European Court in *Schmidt*. There is an economic entity, as distinct from a mere activity, where the employees concerned are dedicated to a particular contract and their employment is contingent upon the continued existence of the service contract. In contrast, there is no transfer of a business where the loss of a customer does not of itself result in dedicated and identified staff losing their employment. The EAT further held that there is nothing in *Süzen* which requires an interpretation of the Regulations which would allow a transferee to cause the Regulations to be disapplied by refusing to take on the workforce.

On appeal to the Court of Appeal, it was argued that there is no transfer of an undertaking where the only continuing feature is the nature of the activity and all that continues is the service itself. The Court of Appeal dismissed the appeal.

MUMMERY LJ: . . . In my judgment, this appeal fails on the ground that there is no error of law in the decision of the employment tribunal. In reaching its conclusion that the 1981 Regulations applied, the employment tribunal had regard to all those factors which were held by the European Court of Justice in *Spijkers* to be relevant to the determination of the issue whether there was a transfer of an undertaking. The employment tribunal considered the factors on each side. They noted the differences in the way that ECM carried out the VAG contract, but pointed out that the customers were essentially the same and that the work that was going on was essentially the same i.e. cars were unloaded at Grimsby, were put onto transporters and were driven to VAG dealers. The result was the same. The employment tribunal were entitled to conclude that, even though ECM did not take on any Axial staff, the identity of the economic entity in the hands of Axial was still retained in the hands of ECM after the loss of the VAG contract. This justified the finding of a transfer.

The employment tribunal applied the correct test, as laid down by the European court in *Spijkers* and followed in other cases, such as *Schmidt* [1994] IRLR 302. Although the *Süzen* decision has been described as involving a shift of emphasis or a clarification of the law, nothing was said in *Süzen* which casts doubts on the correctness of the interpretation of the Directive in the earlier decisions cited to and applied by the employment tribunal in the extended reasons.

In my judgment, it is clear that, but for the argument about the scope and effect of the later decision in *Süzen*, there would be no possible ground of appeal in this case. ECM's case has to be that *Süzen* makes all the difference. It does not in this case. The importance of *Süzen* had, I think, been overstated. The ruling in *Süzen* should be seen in its proper context.

(1) The Court of Justice has not overruled its previous interpretative rulings in cases such as *Spijkers* and *Schmidt*. This is clear not only from the citation of those cases in the judgment in *Süzen*, but also from their continued prominence in the reasoning of the Court of Justice in its post-*Süzen* decision in *Sánchez Hidalgo* [1999] IRLR 136.

(2) It is still the case that it is for the national court to make the 'necessary factual appraisal' in order to decide whether there is a transfer in the light of the criteria laid down by the Court of Justice.

(3) It is still the case that those criteria involve consideration of 'all the facts characterising the transaction in question', as identified in *Spijkers* at paragraph 13 of the judgment of the Court of Justice, in order to determine whether the undertaking has continued and retained its identity in different hands. The employment tribunal carried out a full factual appraisal, applied the correct criteria and concluded that, despite changes in the organisation of the operation for the delivery of cars under the

VAG contract, there was a continuation in the hands of ECM of the existence of the discrete economic entity previously carried on by Axial.

(4) The importance of *Süzen* is that the Court of Justice identified limits to the application of the Directive. On the one hand, it affirmed that:

(a) 'The decisive criterion for establishing the existence of a transfer within the meaning of the Directive is whether the entity in question retains its identity, as indicated inter alia by the fact that its operation is actually continued. . .' (paragraph 10);

(b) a direct contractual link or relationship between the transferor and the transferee is not conclusive against a transfer (paragraphs 12 and 13);

(c) consideration of all the facts characterising the transaction in question is necessary (paragraph 14).

(5) On the other hand, it set limits by indicating that:

(a) '. . . the mere fact that the service provided by the old and the new awardees of a contract is similar does not therefore support the conclusion that an economic entity has been transferred.'

Other factors are important – the workforce, the management staff, its operating methods and its operational resources (paragraph 15):

(b) 'The mere loss of a service contract to a competitor cannot therefore by itself indicate the existence of a transfer within the meaning of the Directive . . . In those circumstances, the service undertaking previously entrusted with the contract does not, on losing a customer, thereby cease fully to exist, and a business or part of a business belonging to it cannot be considered to have been transferred to the new awardee of the contract' (paragraph 16);

(c) The question whether the majority of the employees are taken over by the new employer to enable him to carry on the activities of the undertaking on a regular basis is a factual circumstance to be taken into account, as well as the similarity of the pre- and post-transfer activities and the type of undertaking concerned e.g. in labour-intensive sectors (paragraphs 20 and 21).

(6) This case is unaffected by the limits indicated in *Süzen*. It is not a case (like *Süzen*) of the loss of a contract with one customer being asserted to amount to a transfer of an undertaking. It is not a case like *Betts* of the loss of a contract for one location being asserted to be a transfer of an undertaking. It is not a case of a transfer depending merely on a comparison of the similarity of the activities of Axial and ECM after the loss of the VAG contract by Axial. The transfer was established by the employment tribunal looking at all the relevant facts and concluding that this undertaking was based on the VAG contract and that it continued in different hands, even though no employees of Axial were appointed by ECM. The tribunal was entitled to have regard, as a relevant circumstance, to the reason why those employees were not appointed by ECM. The Court of Justice has not decided in *Süzen* or in any other case that this is an irrelevant circumstance or that the failure of the transferee to appoint any of the former employees of the transferor points conclusively against a transfer.

I would dismiss this appeal.

Note

'Lord Justice Mummery's interpretation may or may not be an accurate reflection of what the European Court intended, but it will be widely welcomed regardless. The Court of Appeal's decision in *ECM* amounts to a dispensation to employment tribunals to determine whether there has been a transfer of undertaking on the basis of all the facts, using the shopping list set out in *Spijkers* and reiterated most recently in *Sanchez Hidalgo*. From a practical standpoint, *ECM* means that a transferee cannot necessarily avoid a TUPE transfer by refusing to take on an existing workforce.' (Rubenstein, M., 'Highlights' [1999] IRLR 506)

Transfer of Undertakings (Protection of Employment) Regulations 1981 (SI 1981 No. 1794)

4. Transfers by receivers and liquidators

(1)   Where the receiver of the property or part of the property of a company or the administrator of a company appointed under Part II of the Insolvency Act 1986 or, in the case of a creditors' voluntary winding up, the liquidator of a company transfers the company's undertaking, or part of the company's undertaking (the 'relevant undertaking') to a wholly owned subsidiary of the company, the transfer shall for the purposes of these Regulations be deemed not to have been effected until immediately before—

(a)   the transferee company ceases (otherwise than by reason of its being wound up) to be a wholly owned subsidiary of the transferor company; or

(b)   the relevant undertaking is transferred by the transferee company to another person;

whichever first occurs, and, for the purposes of these Regulations, the transfer of the relevant undertakings shall be taken to have been effected immediately before that date by one transaction only.

(2)   In this Regulation—

'creditors' voluntary winding up' has the same meaning as in the Companies Act 1948 and

'wholly owned subsidiary' has the same meaning as it has for the purposes of section 150 of the Companies Act 1948.

5. Effect of relevant transfer on contracts of employment, etc.

(1)   Except where objection is made under paragraph (4A) below a relevant transfer shall not operate so as to terminate the contract of employment of any person employed by the transferor in the undertaking or part transferred but any such contract which would otherwise have been terminated by the transfer shall have effect after the transfer as if originally made between the person so employed and the transferee.

(2)   Without prejudice to paragraph (1) above but subject to paragraph (4A) below on the completion of a relevant transfer—

(a)   all the transferor's rights, powers, duties and liabilities under or in connection with any such contract, shall be transferred by virtue of this Regulation to the transferee; and

(b)   anything done before the transfer is completed by or in relation to the transferor in respect of that contract or a person employed in that undertaking or part shall be deemed to have been done by or in relation to the transferee.

(3)   Any reference in paragraph (1) or (2) above to a person employed in an undertaking or part of one transferred by a relevant transfer is a reference to a person so employed immediately before the transfer, including, where the transfer is effected by a series of two or more transactions, a person so employed immediately before any of those transactions.

(4)   Paragraph (2) above shall not transfer or otherwise affect the liability of any person to be prosecuted for, convicted of and sentenced for any offence.

(4A)   Paragraphs (1) and (2) above shall not operate to transfer his contract of employment and the rights, powers, duties and liabilities under or in connection with it if the employee informs the transferor or the transferee that he objects to becoming employed by the transferee.

(4B)   Where an employee so objects the transfer of the undertaking or part in which he is employed shall operate so as to terminate his contract of employment with the transferor but he shall not be treated, for any purpose, as having been dismissed by the transferor.

(5)   Paragraphs (1) and (4A) above are without prejudice to any right of an employee arising apart from these Regulations to terminate his contract of employment without notice if a substantial change is made in his working conditions to his detriment; but no such right shall arise by reason only that, under that paragraph, the identity of his employer changes unless the employer shows that, in all the circumstances, the change is a significant change and is to his detriment.

Notes

1.   In *DJM International v Nicholas* [1996] ICR 214, it was held that reg. 5(2)(b) had the effect of passing liability to the transferee for an allegation of sex discrimination based on the fact that prior to the transfer the applicant had been moved from full-time to part-time employment.

2.   The principal effect of the Regulations is that the common law position has been abolished.

Premier Motors (Medway) Limited v *Total Oil Great Britain Limited*
[1984] 1 WLR 377
Employment Appeal Tribunal

The employer sold the business but the purchaser had no wish to run the business or employ its former employees. Accordingly, while the sale was completed on 1 June 1982 the vendors continued to run the business as licensees of the purchasers until 30 June when the purchasers appointed a caretaker for the premises and the applicants' employment was terminated. The Court of Appeal held that the effect of the Regulations was that on 1 June 1982 the purchasers became the employers of the applicants and, accordingly, it was they who were obliged to meet their redundancy payments.

BROWNE-WILKINSON LJ: . . . In our judgment in the ordinary case the effect of the Regulations is that, if a business is transferred, the employees are automatically transferred with it irrespective of the wishes of the transferee or of the employees. The contract is automatically continued by operation of the Regulations even if the transferee has no wish to continue the employment. In consequence, the employees' contractual and statutory rights become enforceable against the transferee, not the transferor. When, as in the present case, the transferee makes it clear that he will not continue to employ the employees, in our judgment he repudiates the continuing contract and thereby constructively dismisses the employee. The employee is dismissed because of redundancy and becomes entitled to a redundancy payment from the transferee. A transferee of a business who does not wish to take over the employees of that business will even so be liable to the employees for the redundancy payments. To protect himself, the transferee must agree with the transferor either that the transferor will dismiss the employee before the transfer or will indemnify the transferee against redundancy payments and other employment liabilities.

That being in our judgment the clear effect of the Regulations in a case where the transferee is himself going to carry on the business, does it make any difference that the transferee (the purchasers) are not themselves going to carry on the business but are immediately assigning or licensing to a third party (Mr Lawrence) the right to run the business? In our judgment it is impossible to treat such a case differently from the ordinary case without running contrary to the scheme of the Regulations, i.e. the automatic transfer of employment . . .

Morris Angel Ltd v *Hollande*
[1993] IRLR 169
Court of Appeal

Hollande was employed as group managing director of a company called Altolight and all its subsidiaries. His contract contained a restraint of trade clause (clause 15(1)) barring him for one year after leaving the company's employment from soliciting the customers of the company and its subsidiaries. The company was purchased by the plaintiffs and, following completion of the sale agreement, Mr Hollande was dismissed. The plaintiffs subsequently sought to enforce the restraint of trade clause. The question which arose was whether, in the light of reg. 5(1) of the Regulations, the plaintiffs were entitled to enforce the restriction in relation to those who had done business with Altolight or its subsidiaries during the relevant year, or whether the effect of reg. 5(1) was that, following the transfer of the undertaking, the restriction had to be read as relating to those who had done business with the plaintiffs in that period. Allowing the plaintiffs' appeal, the Court of Appeal adopted the former interpretation.

DILLON LJ: The key words in regulation 5(1) are the words: '[the contract] shall have effect after the transfer as if originally made between the person so employed and the transferee.' It does have in a sense retrospective effect. Turner J considered that the service agreement was therefore to be read ab initio as if made between the plaintiffs rather than the company and Mr Hollande. Clause 15(1) was therefore to be read as an agreement by Mr Hollande not in the relevant year to solicit or undertake business for persons who in the previous year – on the facts of this case the year to 29 April 1992 – had done business with the plaintiffs, not the persons who in that year had done business with the company or its subsidiaries – the group. It followed that, as Mr Hollande was not seeking to do business with persons who in the previous year had done business with the plaintiffs, but only with the persons who had done business with the company, there was no covenant available to the plaintiffs under which injunctive relief could be granted. Turner J said:

> It does not seem to me that the plaintiffs have come within measurable distance of being able to assert a valid right which they can enforce under the provisions of clause 15(1) or (2) of the contract of employment.

The difficulty about that approach to my mind is that it turns the obligation on the employee under clause 15(1) into a quite different and possibly much wider obligation than the obligation which bound him before the transfer, that is to say an obligation not to do business, etc. with the persons who had done business in the relevant year with the plaintiffs, not the company. Such an obligation was not remotely in contemplation when the service agreement was entered into and I can see no reason why the regulation should have sought to change the burden on the employee. As Lord Templeman pointed out, the object was that the benefit and burden should devolve on the new employer. That would mean in the present context that the transferee should be able to enforce the same restriction.

The more reasonable construction is in my judgment that the words '[the contract] shall have effect' are to be read as referring to the transferee as the owner of the undertaking transferred or in respect of the undertaking transferred. The effect therefore is that clause 15(1) can be enforced by the plaintiffs if Mr Hollande within the year after 29 April 1992 does business with persons who in the previous year had done business with the undertaking transferred of which the plaintiffs are deemed as a result of the transfer retrospectively to have been the owner. The plaintiffs are thus given locus standi to enforce the restriction.

I therefore respectfully differ from Turner J on the construction point and I would hold so far as that point is concerned that regulation 5(1) entitles the plaintiffs to enforce clause 15(1) as against Mr Hollande if he solicits or does business with those who have done business with the company in the previous year . . .

Notes

1.   In *Allan and Others* v *Stirling District Council* [1994] IRLR 208 the EAT sitting in Scotland held that reg. 5(2) does not release the transferor from its liabilities, e.g. for unfair dismissal, that it would otherwise have to bear had there been no transfer of an undertaking.

Does this pedantic interpretation of reg. 5(2) accord with the spirit of the Transfer of Undertakings Regulations?

2.   The contract is transferred only if the employee consents.

Katsikas v *Konstantinidis*
[1993] IRLR 179
European Court of Justice

The plaintiff was employed as a cook in the defendant's restaurant in Germany. The restaurant was sold to a Mr Mitossis, but the plaintiff had such a dislike of the purchaser that he refused to work for him and was dismissed by the defendant. The plaintiff brought a claim against his original employer, Konstantinidis, who argued that the responsible person was, by virtue of the Directive, the new owner, Mitossis. The ECJ held that the Directive did not preclude an employee objecting to the automatic transfer of his contract. To oblige the employee to work for the new owner would be a breach of his fundamental rights. However, the ECJ also held that it was for Member States to decide what would be the effect of an employee's objection to the transfer of his contract of employment. The Directive does not oblige Member States to provide that the contract of employment or employment relationship be continued where an employee freely decides not to continue employment with the transferee. The fate of the contract of employment or the employment relationship in such cases is for Member States to determine.

In fact, if the Directive, which is intended to achieve only partial harmonisation of the subject-matter (see judgment of *Daddy's Dance Hall* [1988] IRLR 315), allows an employee to remain in employment with a new employer on the same conditions as those agreed with the transferor it cannot be interpreted as obliging the employee to continue his employment relationship with the transferee.

Such an obligation would undermine the fundamental rights of the employee who must be free to choose his employer and cannot be obliged to work for an employer that he has not freely chosen.

It follows from that that the provisions of Article 3(1) of the Directive do not prevent an employee from objecting to the transfer of his contract of employment or of his employment relationship and, thus, from not benefiting from the protection provided to him by the Directive.

Nevertheless, as the Court has held (in its judgment in *Berg and Busschers* [1989] IRLR 447), the purpose of the Directive is not to ensure that the contract of employment or the employment relationship with the transferor is continued where the undertaking's employees do not wish to remain in the transferee's employ.

It follows from that that the Directive does not oblige Member States to provide that the contract of employment or employment relationship be continued with the transferor in a case where an employee freely decides not to continue the contract of employment or the employment relationship with the transferee. In such cases, it is for the Member States to determine the fate of the contract of employment or of the employment relationship.

The Member States may, in particular, provide that in this case, the contract of employment or the employment relationship may be considered as terminated either on the initiative of the employee or on the initiative of the employer. They may also provide that the contract of employment or the employment relationship be continued with the transferor.

Notes

1. As a result of the decision in *Katsikas*, the Government hurriedly introduced an amendment to the Regulations via s. 33(4) of TURERA 1993. The amendments are to found in regs 5(4A) and 5(4B). Regulation 5(4A) provides that the automatic transfer principle shall not apply 'if the employee informs the transferor or transferee that he objects to becoming employed by the transferee'.

The consequences of such an objection are by reg. 5(4B) stated to be that the transfer operates 'to terminate his contract of employment with the transferor' but he 'shall not be treated for any purpose, as having been dismissed by the transferor'.

The cumulative effect of these strange provisions is that, although the worker has a theoretical right to refuse to transfer, if that right is exercised he or she has no rights against either transferee or transferor.

2. In *Photostation Copiers* v *Okuda* [1995] IRLR 11, the EAT held that an employee cannot consent to a transfer if he does not know about it;

accordingly, in such a situation he continued to be employed by the transferor.

3.   Regulation 5(3) appears to indicate that the purchaser of a business takes on its employees only if they were employed by the transferor 'immediately before' the transfer. This wording was interpreted very strictly in *Secretary of State for Employment* v *Spence* [1987] 1 QB 179, where the Court of Appeal held that reg. 5 applies only to employees employed by the transferor at the very moment of transfer. In other words, a business purchaser could not be made liable for dismissals carried out by the vendor before transfer.

In the light of the decision in *Spence*, it was possible for a transferee to make it a condition of purchase that the vendor should dismiss all or some of its employees prior to the transfer date, i.e. that the vendor takes on the responsibility of meeting any redundancy payments. Indeed, an insolvent or near insolvent vendor may not object too much to such a proposal because the likelihood would be that such payments would be met by the State Fund.

This major gap in the protection offered by the Regulations has now been closed as a result of the following case.

Litster v Forth Dry Dock Engineering Limited
[1989] IRLR 161
House of Lords

The employer went into liquidation in September 1983, and at 3.30 pm on 6 February 1984 the 12 applicant employees were summarily dismissed. Later that day, the assets of the business were purchased and the purchaser engaged some of the former employees but not the applicants. The House of Lords held that in the case of an unfair dismissal the words 'immediately before the transfer' must be read as if there were inserted after the words 'or would have been so employed if he had not been unfairly dismissed within the circumstances described in regulation 8(1).' Accordingly the purchaser of the business was held liable to compensate the applicants.

LORD OLIVER: Two questions then arise. First, was the time which elapsed between the dismissals and the transfer of so short a duration that, on the true construction of regulation 5, the appellants were 'employed immediately before' the transfer, as required by sub-paragraph (3) of that regulation? Secondly, if the answer to that question is in the negative, what difference (if any) does it make that the reason, or the principal reason, for the dismissals was, as it clearly was, the imminent occurrence of the transfer so that the dismissals were, by regulation 8(1), deemed to be unfair dismissals?

The expression 'immediately before' is one which takes its meaning from its context, but in its ordinary signification it involves the notion that there is, between two relevant events, no intervening space, lapse of time or event of any significance. If, for instance, the question is whether a deceased person was seized of property immediately before his death, attention is focused upon the very instant at which the death occurred. In construing the Regulations with which this appeal is concerned, one gets little help from the terms of the Directive to which they were intended to give effect. Article 3, as has been seen already, refers to an employment relationship existing 'on the date of the transfer,' but this expression seems to be used interchangeably with the expression 'at the time of the transfer' – in the French text 'au moment du transfert' – which appears to embrace the notion that what has to be regarded is the status of the employee vis-à-vis his employer at the very instant at which the employer's business is transferred.

As will already have become apparent, there have been a number of decisions in which the provisions of regulation 5 have fallen to be construed and your Lordships' attention has, in addition, been drawn to a number of decisions in which Articles 3 and 4 of the Directive have fallen to be interpreted by the European Court of Justice. Before referring to these, however, it may be helpful to consider the Regulations without the assistance of authority, but bearing in mind their overall purpose of giving effect to the provisions of the Directive. To begin with, it is to be noted that the reference in regulation 5(1) to 'a contract which would otherwise have been terminated by the transfer' is, strictly speaking, a mis-description. The reason why a contract of employment is said to 'terminate' on a transfer of the employer's business is simply that such a transfer operates as a unilateral repudiation by the employer of his obligations under the contract and thus as a dismissal of the employee from his service. Because the relationship between employer and employee is of an essentially personal nature, the repudiation severs the factual relationship resulting from the contract, since the primary obligations on both sides are no longer capable of being performed. The contract itself, however, is not, strictly speaking, terminated but remains in being and undischarged so far as the enforcement of secondary obligations are concerned. This may seem a truism but it has, I believe, an importance in the analysis, in particular in relation to the meaning to be ascribed to the words 'terminated by the transfer' in regulation 5(1) and the words 'immediately before the transfer' in regulation 5(3). The necessary assumption in para. (1) of the regulation is that the contract of employment to which the consequence stated in the paragraph is to attach, is one which, apart from the transfer, would have continued in force and that what 'terminates' it, or would, apart from the regulation, have terminated it, is the repudiatory breach constituted by the transfer. That paragraph can, therefore, operate only upon a subsisting contract. There is nothing in the terms of para. (2), if it stood alone, which necessarily involves the same restriction. It is, however, clearly intended merely to supplement the provisions of para. (1), and para. (3) supplies the connection by expressly limiting the operation of both paras. (1) and (2) to the case where the relevant employee is employed in the undertaking 'immediately before the transfer,' that is to say, to the circumstances envisaged in para. (1) in which, apart from the regulation, the event producing the termination is the transfer. The crucial question, therefore, is what is meant by the reference to a contract being terminated 'by' a transfer.

This could embrace a number of different possibilities. If nothing at all occurs to disturb the relationship of master and servant apart from the simple unannounced fact of the transfer of business by the employer, it is the transfer itself which constitutes the repudiatory breach which, apart from regulation 5(1), 'terminates' the contract. If, however, the employer, contemporaneously with the transfer, announces to his workforce that he is transferring the business and that they are therefore dismissed without notice, it is, strictly, the oral notification which terminates the contract; yet it could not, as a matter of common sense, be denied that the contract has been 'terminated by the transfer' of the business, particularly when reference is made to the supplementary provisions of para. (2) of regulation 5 when read in conjunction with para. (3). Similarly, if the employer, a week, or it may be a day, before the actual transfer, hands to each employee a letter announcing that he is proposing to transfer his undertaking at the close of business on the transfer date, at which time the employees are to consider themselves as forthwith dismissed, it could hardly be contended under the Regulations that their employment had not been terminated by the transfer, even though, at the date of the notice, the dismissal might be capable of taking effect independently, in the event, for instance, of the actual transfer of the business being postponed to a date or time later than the expiry of the notice. In each hypothetical case the employer's repudiation of the contract of service is differently communicated but its essential quality of a repudiation by the transfer of the undertaking remains the same and the contract can quite properly be described as having been terminated by the transfer. If, by contrast, the employer announces to his workforce that he is transferring his business to another person at 5.00pm on the following Friday and that they are to consider themselves dismissed from his employment at 4.59pm on that day, it is difficult to see any reason why the interposition of a one-minute interval between the express repudiation becoming effective and the transfer which would, in any event, have operated as a repudiation if nothing had been said, should invest the breach of contract by the employer with some different quality. In each case the effective cause of the dismissal is the transfer of the business, whether it be announced in advance or contemporaneously, or whether it be unannounced, and it would be no misuse of ordinary language in each case to speak of the termination of the contracts of the workforce as having been effected by the transfer. It is absurd to suggest that there is any distinction in substance between any of the hypothetical cases which I have envisaged. Can it, then, one asks, possibly have been the intention of the Secretary of State in framing legislation expressly directed to safe-guarding the rights of employees when an undertaking is transferred, to make its effectiveness depend upon whether the transferor, as a result perhaps of a collusive bargain with the transferee, allows a scintilla temporis to elapse between the operation of a notice dismissing his workforce and the completion of the legal formalities of the transfer which is the true cause of their dismissal, particularly having regard to the provisions of regulation 8, which were clearly intended to have the same effect as Article 4 of the Directive? My Lords, I should be reluctant so to construe the Regulations, quite apart from any authority. When, however, they are considered in the light of the interpretation placed by the European Court of Justice on the provisions of the Directive, it becomes, I think, clear that your Lordships are not compelled to do so.

In the case of *Wendelboe* v *L J Music ApS* (Case 19/83) [1985] ECR 457, the original employer company was on the brink of insolvency. So far as appears, no transfer of their undertaking was in contemplation when financial stringency compelled closure of the business and the dismissal of the major part of the workforce with immediate effect. That occurred on 28.2.80. On 4.3.80 the company was declared insolvent and a little over three weeks later an agreement was concluded transferring the business to a purchaser with effect from 4 March, the court having conduct of the insolvency having authorised the (then prospective) purchaser to use the company's premises and equipment from 5 March onwards. The three plaintiffs were part of the original workforce and had in fact been engaged by the purchaser on 6 March but on terms that they lost their rights to seniority. They sued the original employer for damages for wrongful dismissal and arrears of holiday pay and were met with the defence that under the Danish legislation, which had been passed to give effect to the Directive, all liabilities in respect of their employment had been transferred to the purchaser. The question submitted by the Danish court to the European Court of Justice, pursuant to Article 177 [now 234] of the EEC Treaty, was whether the Directive required member states to enact provisions under which the transferee of an undertaking became liable in respect of obligations concerning holiday pay and compensation to former employees who were not employed in the undertaking on the date of the transfer. That question was answered in the negative, as might indeed have been surmised purely from a textual interpretation of Article 3(1) of the Directive. The following extract from the judgment of the court, at pp. 466–467 is, however, of interest in relation to the question of the relationship between Articles 3 and 4 of the Directive (which are reflected substantially in Articles 5 and 8 of the Regulations):

> That interpretation of the scope of Article 3(1) is also in conformity with the scheme and the purposes of the Directive, which is intended to ensure, so far as possible, that the employment relationship continues unchanged with the transferee, in particular by obliging the transferee to continue to observe the terms and conditions of any collective agreement (Article 3(2)) and by protecting workers against dismissals motivated solely by the fact of the transfer (Article 4(1)). Those provisions relate only to employees in the service of the undertaking on the date of the transfer, to the exclusion of those who had already left the undertaking on that date.
>
> The existence or otherwise of the contract of employment or an employment relationship on the date of the transfer within the meaning of Article 3(1) of the Directive must be established on the basis of the rules of national law, subject however, to observance of the mandatory provisions of the Directive and, more particularly, Article 4(1) thereof, concerning the protection of employees against dismissal by the transferor or the transferee by reason of the transfer. It is for the national courts to decide, on the basis of those factors, whether or not on the date of the transfer, the employees in question were linked to the undertaking by view of a contract of employment or employment relationship.

What is of particular interest here in relation to the questions raised by this appeal, is the statement that Article 4(1), as well as Article 3(1), 'apply only to employees in the service of the undertaking on the date of the transfer' and the observation that the determination according to the rules of national law is 'subject to observance of the mandatory provisions of Article 4(1).' There is clearly scope here for the view that where the employment has been determined by the transferor solely on the ground of the transfer, which Article 4(1) states is not 'to constitute grounds for dismissal *by the transferor or transferee*' (emphasis added) the employee is to be treated as if he had continued to be employed at the date of the transfer. That was a point which did not in fact arise in the *Wendelboe* case but which is reflected in the following passage from the Opinion of the Advocate General, Sir Gordon Slynn, at p. 460:

> Whether or not a contract of employment or an employment relationship is terminated at the time of transfer is of course for national law to determine. However, the first sentence of Article 4(1) provides that 'the transfer of an undertaking, business or part of a business shall not in itself constitute grounds for dismissal by the transferor or transferee.' . . . Where employees are dismissed, with a view to and before, a transfer falling within the Directive and re-engaged immediately by the transferee thereafter, their dismissal must be regarded as contrary to Article 4(1), subject to the exceptions specified in that paragraph. Whether the remedy for such unlawful dismissal consists in a court Order declaring that dismissal to be a nullity or the award of damages or some other effective remedy is for the member states to determine. In any event the member states are required to provide for a remedy which is effective and not merely symbolic . . . If the remedy consists in treating the dismissal as a nullity, then it would follow that the rights and obligations of the employee concerned are transferred to the transferee.

The proposition that Article 4(1) operates, in effect, to prohibit the exclusion of the rights conferred by Article 3 by dismissal of the employee immediately before the transfer, except for one of the reasons specified in the second sentence of the Article, receives some further support from the Opinion of the Advocate General, Sir Gordon Slynn, in the later case of *Foreningen af Arbejdsledere i Danmark* v *A/S Danmols Inventar* (Case 105/84) [1985] ECR 2639, in which he commented on the *Wendelboe* case and observed, at p. 2641:

> in *Wendelboe* v *LJ Music* . . . it has held that only the persons employed by the transferor at the moment of a transfer fall within the provisions; it was also pointed out that Article 4(1) prohibits an employee from being dismissed by reasons solely of such a transfer, subject however to certain exceptions. The effect of the Directive, in my opinion, is that an employee of the transferor at the time of the transfer, is entitled to insist, as against the transferee, on all the rights under his existing employment relationship. By virtue of Article 3 he can thus claim to continue to be employed by the transferee on the same terms as he was employed with the transferor, or if the transferee refuses or fails to observe those terms, he can bring a claim for breach of contract or the relationship against the transferee. Under Article 4, the transfer does not by itself justify its dismissal by the transferor or the transferee unless such dismissal is for economic, technical or organisational reasons entailing changes in the workforce . . . The employer who dismisses an employee for one of the reasons specified in Article 4(1) can thus justify the dismissal. Otherwise if the dismissal or purported dismissal is based on the transfer of the undertaking or business, the employee can insist on his rights under Article 3.

The prohibitory nature of Article 4 was emphasised again in the case of *Foreningen af Arbejdsledere i Danmark* v *Daddy's Dance Hall A/S* (Case 324/86) [1988] IRLR 315, 317 where the court in the course of its judgment observed:

> . . . Directive [(77/187/EEC)] aims at ensuring for workers affected by a transfer of undertaking the safeguarding of their rights arising from the employment contract or relationship. As this protection is a matter of public policy and, as such, outside the control of the parties to the employment contract, the provisions of the Directive, in particular those relating to the protection of workers against dismissal because of transfer, must be considered as mandatory, meaning that it is not permissible to derogate from them in a manner detrimental to the workers.' (See also *Landsorganisationen i Danmark* v *Ny Molle Kro* (Case 287/86) [1989] IRLR 37.)

In a subsequent case: *P Bork International A/S* v *Foreningen of Arbejdsledere i Danmark* (Case 101/87) [1989] IRLR 41, the question arose whether the Directive applied to a situation where the workforce had been dismissed upon the termination by the employee of the lease of the premises on which the undertaking was carried on, the assets of the business having been purchased shortly afterwards by the new lessee of the premises, which re-engaged over half the original workforce. The court held that the Directive applied and in relation to the question of whether workers dismissed before the transfer could claim the benefit of the Directive as against the transferee, said, at p. 44:

> the only workers who may invoke Directive [(77/187/EEC)] are those who have current employment relations or a contract of employment at the date of transfer. The question whether or not a contract of employment or employment relationship exists at that date must be assessed under national law, subject, however, to the observance of the mandatory rules of the Directive concerning the protection of workers against dismissal by reason of the transfer. It follows that workers employed

by the undertaking whose contract of employment or employment relationship has been terminated with effect on a date before that of the transfer, in breach of Article 4(1) of the Directive, must be considered as still employed by the undertaking on the date of the transfer with the consequence, in particular, that the obligations of an employer towards them are fully transferred from the transferor to the transferee, in accordance with Article 3(1) of the Directive. In order to determine whether the only reason for dismissal was the transfer itself, account must be taken of the objective circumstances in which the dismissal occurred, and, in particular, in a case like the present one, the fact that it took place on a date close to that of the transfer and that the workers concerned were re-engaged by the transferee. The factual assessment needed in order to determine the applicability of the Directive is a matter for the national courts, and *having regard to the interpretative criteria laid down by the court.*' (Emphasis added.)

It does not appear that the impact of Article 4 (and thus of regulation 8) on the construction and effect of Article 3 (or regulation 5) in relation to the employee's rights had previously fallen to be considered in any of the reported cases in the United Kingdom. . . .

. . . [In] England in *Secretary of State for Employment* v *Spence* [1986] IRLR 248 . . . the transferor company was in receivership and the receivers had been negotiating a transfer of the business under a threat by the company's major customer to withdraw its work unless a transfer of the business had been agreed by 24.11.83. No sale had been agreed by that date and although on 28.11.83 the negotiations were continuing, the receivers had to decide whether it was proper in the interests of the debenture holders to continue to employ the workforce and to continue trading. Since there was no guarantee that the negotiations would be successful, the decision was taken to cease trading immediately and, at 11.00am on that morning the employees were notified that they were dismissed with immediate effect. In fact, the negotiations were successful and an agreement for the sale of the undertaking was signed at 2.00pm on that day. The employees were in fact re-employed by the transferee but claimed redundancy payments from the redundancy fund under s. 106 of the Act of 1978. The claim was resisted on the ground that, since the claimants were employed 'immediately before the transfer' their employment was continued with the transferee of the business by regulation 5(1), following the decision in the *Anchor Hotel* case [1985] IRLR 452. It is worth noting that it was found as a fact by the Industrial Tribunal, first, that the sequence of events was the result of independent action by the receivers and the transferees and that there was no collusion between them and, secondly, that the reason why the receivers decided to dismiss the workforce was that, until a contract could be renegotiated with the company's principal customer, there was no prospect of any work for the business. It follows from these findings that the reason for the dismissal was not one connected with the transfer but was due to economic considerations, with the result that regulation 8(1) did not render the dismissals unfair. The only question for decision, therefore, was whether having regard to the very short time which in fact elapsed between the dismissals taking effect and the conclusion of the transfer agreement, the workforce was employed 'immediately before the transfer.' After a careful analysis of the cases, the Court of Appeal rejected the approach of the Employment Appeal Tribunal in *Apex* [1984] IRLR 224 and *Anchor Hotel* [1985] IRLR 452 and held that regulation 5(1) can apply only where, at the very moment of transfer, the contract of employment (in the sense of the existing relationship of employer and employee) is still subsisting. If it is not, then there is nothing upon which the regulation can bite, even though the employment has been determined only a matter of minutes (or it may be seconds) before the transfer. My Lords, for my part, I can detect no flaw in the reasoning by which Balcombe LJ, who delivered the leading judgment in the Court of Appeal, reached the conclusion on the facts of that case that regulation 5(1) did not operate to transfer the obligations of the original employer to the transferee. Where, before the actual transfer takes place, the employment of an employee is terminated for a reason unconnected with the transfer, I agree that the question of whether he was employed 'immediately' before the transfer cannot sensibly be made to depend upon the degree of temporal proximity between the two events, except possibly in a case where they are so closely connected in point of time that it is, for practical purposes, impossible realistically to say that they are not precisely contemporaneous. Either the contract of employment is subsisting at the moment of the transfer or it is not, and if it is not, then, on the pure textual construction of regulation 5, neither para. (1) nor para. (2) (which is clearly subsidiary to and complementary with para. (1)) can have any operation. But *Spence's* case [1986] IRLR 248 was decided – and quite properly decided – entirely without reference to the effect of regulation 8(1) and in the context of the two important findings of fact by the Industrial Tribunal to which I have drawn attention. The Court of Appeal did not consider, and was not called upon to consider, a position where, whether under a collusive bargain or otherwise, an employee is dismissed from his employment solely or principally because of the prospective transfer of the undertaking in which he is employed, so that his dismissal is statutorily deemed to be unfair; and, of course, the case was decided without reference to the important *Bork* case [1989] IRLR 41 already referred to which had not been decided at the date of the Court of Appeal's judgment and which had not been reported at the time when the instant case was argued before the Court of Session.

It is, I think, now clear that under Article 4 of the Directive, as construed by the European Court of Justice, a dismissal effected before the transfer and solely because of the transfer of the business is, in effect, prohibited and is, for the purpose of considering the application of Article 3(1), required to be treated as ineffective. The question is whether the Regulations are so framed as to be capable of being construed in conformity with that interpretation of the Directive.

. . . Having regard to the manifest purpose of the Regulations, I do not, for my part, feel inhibited from making such an implication in the instant case. The provision in regulation 8(1) that a dismissal by reason of a transfer is to be treated as an unfair dismissal, is merely a different way of saying that the transfer is not to 'constitute a ground for dismissal' as contemplated by Article 4 of the Directive and there is no good reason for denying to it the same effect as that attributed to that Article. In effect this involves reading regulation 5(3) as if there were inserted after the words 'immediately before the transfer' the words 'or would have been so employed if he had not been unfairly dismissed in the circumstances described in regulation 8(1).' For my part, I would make such an implication which is entirely consistent with the general scheme of the Regulations and which is necessary if they are effectively to fulfil the purpose for which they were made of giving effect to the provisions of the Directive. This does not involve any disapproval of the reasoning of the Court of Appeal in *Spence's* case [1986] IRLR 248 which, on the facts there found by the Industrial Tribunal, did not involve a dismissal attracting the consequences provided in regulation 8(1).

Note

In addition to arguing that the particular transfer is not covered by the 1981 Regulations, two other possibilities exist where a transferee employer is seeking to avoid inheriting the terms and conditions enjoyed by the transferor's workforce. The first is for the transferee to dismiss and then offer to re-engage on new terms and conditions. This will render the transferee liable to unfair dismissal claims and can hardly be held up as good industrial relations practice. The other possibility is for the transferee to seek to negotiate an agreed variation of terms and conditions with the workforce or their representatives. The legal implications of both approaches were considered by the House of Lords in the following cases.

Wilson and others v St Helens Borough Council; British Fuels Ltd v Meade and Baxendale
[1988] IRLR 706
House of Lords

In the *British Fuels* case, Mr Baxendale was employed from 1977, and Mr Meade from 1978, by National Fuels Distributors, a subsidiary of the British Coal Corporation. On 20 August 1992, they were given notice that they were to be dismissed by reason of redundancy, effective from 28 August. They received wages in lieu of notice, statutory and enhanced redundancy pay.

On the same day that they received notice of dismissal, British Fuels Ltd, another subsidiary of the British Coal Corporation, offered them employment with effect from 1 September 1992 on terms that were less favourable than those they had enjoyed with National Fuels Distributors. They accepted the offers of employment and started work for British Fuels Ltd on 1 September. On the same day National Fuels was merged with British Fuels.

Both men sought a declaration from an employment tribunal under what is now s. 11 of the ERA 1996. It was contended that their dismissals were ineffective as a matter of European law. Therefore, it followed that they had transferred to British Fuels on the terms and conditions they had enjoyed with National Fuels Distributors. The claims were rejected and their appeal was dismissed by the EAT. The Court of Appeal decided in the applicants' favour, but gave leave to appeal to the House of Lords.

In the other case, Wilson and his colleagues were employed by Lancashire County Council at Red Bank Controlled Community Home. In 1990, Lancashire gave notice to the home's trustees that, because of funding problems, it would cease to manage the School after 30 September 1992. St Helens Borough Council agreed to take over the control of the home on 1 October 1992, on condition that the running of the School would involve no charge on its own resources. Prior to the transfer, there were negotiations between the transferor and the recognised union, NASUWT. It was agreed that staff at the home would be reduced from 162 to 72, that those transferring to St Helens would be appointed to new posts with different job descriptions, and that those not transferring would be redeployed by Lancashire. It was assumed that the transfer of the management of the home to St Helens was not covered by the 1981 Regulations.

The 72 employees were offered employment by St Helens on terms which were different from those on which they had previously been employed. They were sent letters by Lancashire terminating their employment. After the transfer, nine of the employees, including Mr Wilson, made complaints under the Wages Act, claiming that they were being paid less than they were contractually entitled to when working for Lancashire County Council, and that the difference was an unlawful deduction from their wages which they should be paid. The industrial tribunal dismissed the applications on the grounds that there had been an effective variation in the employees' terms of employment when they agreed new terms following transfer. The EAT, however, held that if the operative reason for an agreed variation in an employee's terms and conditions is the transfer of an undertaking, the variation is ineffective and the terms of the original contact of employment remain in force. The EAT relied on the decision of the ECJ in *Foreningen af Arbejdskdere i Danmark* v *Daddy's Dance Hall* [1988] IRLR 315, where it was held that:

> An employee cannot waive the rights conferred upon him by the mandatory provisions of Directive 77/187/EEC even if the disadvantages resulting from his waiver are offset by such benefits, that taking the matter as a whole, he is not placed in a worse position.

The Court of Appeal allowed the employer's appeal, holding that a dismissal because of a transfer of an undertaking is prohibited and a legal nullity unless the dismissal is for an economic, technical or organisational reason entailing changes in the workforce. In the *Wilson* case, the industrial tribunal was entitled to find that there was an economic, technical or organisational reason for the variation in the terms and conditions of employment which occurred on the transfer, and that the termination of the employees' contracts was not simply due to the transfer. The employees' appeal was dismissed by the House of Lords.

LORD SLYNN OF HADLEY: . . . Two issues are broadly common to the two appeals. The first is whether, on the transfer the employees were entitled to retain the benefit of their previous terms and conditions. The first issue in effect raises the question as to whether the dismissals or purported dismissals by the previous employers took effect or whether they were nullities. Put another way, the question is whether the dismissed employee can compel the transferee to employ him or whether he is given the right to enforce as against the transferee such remedies under national law as he could have enforced against the transferor. The second is whether, if despite dismissal they were entitled to retain the benefit of their previous terms, the employees either by initially agreeing terms with their new employers, or by continuing to work for the new employers or (in the case of Mr Meade and Mr Baxendale by accepting the statement of terms and conditions subsequently) varied any entitlement to the previous terms and conditions.

. . .
    [His Lordship considered the following European authorities: *Wendelboe* v *LJ Music APS*, C-19/83 [1985] ECR 457; *Arbejdlededere i Danmark* v *A/S Danmols Inventar*

('*Mikkelsen's case*'), C-105/84 [1985] ECR 2639; *Katsikas v Konstantinidis and others,* C-139/91 [1993] IRLR 179; *D'Urso and others v Ercole Marelli Elettromeccanica Generale and others,* C-262/89 [1992] IRLR 136; *Rask v ISS Kantineservice, A/S,* C-209/91 [1983] IRLR 133; *Jules Dethier Equipement SA v Dassy and Sovram,* C-319/94 [1998] IRLR 266. Commenting on the contention that the purported dismissals were a nullity – the first issue – he stated:]

In my opinion, the overriding emphasis in the European Court's judgments is that the existing rights of employees are to be safeguarded if there is a transfer. That means no more and no less than that the employee can look to the transferee to perform those obligations which the employee could have enforced against the transferor. The employer, be he transferor or transferee, cannot use the transfer as a justification for dismissal, but if he does dismiss it is a question for national law as to what those rights are. As I have already said, in English law there would as a general rule be no order for specific performance. The claim would be for damages for wrongful dismissal or for statutory rights including, it is true, reinstatement or re-engagement where applicable. It may be in other countries that an order for specific performance could be obtained under the appropriate domestic law and that on this approach different results would be achieved in different Member States. That I do not find surprising or shocking. The Directive is to 'approximate' the laws of the Member States. Its purpose is to 'safeguard' rights on a transfer. The 'rights' of an employee must depend on national rules of the law of contract or of legislation. There is no Community law of contract common to Member States, nor is there a common system or remedies. The object and purpose of the Directive is to ensure in all Member States that on a transfer an employee has against the transferee the rights and remedies which he would have had against the original employer. To that extent it reduces the differences which may exist in the event of a change of employers as to the enforcement by employees of existing rights. They must all provide for enforcement against the transferee of rights existing against the transferor at the time of transfer. It seems to me that the Court has clearly recognised that the precise rights to be transferred depend on national law. But neither the Regulations nor the Directive nor the jurisprudence of the Court create a Community law right to continue in employment which does not exist under national law.

It is said that this is not an adequate remedy because some employees do not have statutory rights – e.g. those in the United Kingdom who have not been employed for a qualifying period – but that is inherent in the differences which exist in the laws of the Member States and seems to me to derive from the wording and limited purpose of the Directive.

Thus, where there is a transfer of an undertaking and the transferee actually takes on the employee the contract of employment is automatically transferred so that, in the absence of a permissible variation, the terms of the initial contract go with the employee, who, though he may refuse to go, cannot as a matter of public policy waive the rights which the Directive and the Regulations confer on him. Where the transferee does not take on the employees who are dismissed on transfer the dismissal is not a nullity, though the contractual rights formerly available against the transferor remain intact against the transferee. For the latter purpose, an employee dismissed prior to the transfer contrary to Article 4(1), i.e. on the basis of the transfer, is to be treated as still in the employment of the transferor at the date of transfer so as to satisfy the rule in *Wendelboe* as consistently followed, e.g. in *Ny Mølle Kro.*

. . .

Accordingly, it is not strictly necessary to deal with the second issue which has been raised as to whether variation of the terms of employment could lawfully be agreed between the parties. Since the matter has been fully argued, particularly in the case of *Wilson*, I express my opinion on the point.

The second issue

. . .

The question as to whether and in what situations, where there has been a transfer and employees have accepted the dismissal, claimed compensation based on it and worked for a long period after the transfer, there can be a valid variation by conduct is not an easy one. I do not accept the argument that the variation is only invalid if it is agreed on or as a part of the transfer itself. The variation may still be due to the transfer and for no other reason even if it comes later. However, it seems that there must, or at least may, come a time when the link with the transfer is broken or can be treated as no longer effective. If the appeal turned on this question I would find it necessary to refer a question to the European Court under Article 177 of the Treaty both in the case of Mr Meade and in the case of Mr Baxendale. Since in my view the dismissal was effective, so that no question of variation falls to be considered, it is not necessary for your Lordships to decide the matter or to refer a question to the European Court.

. . .

It seems to me clear, as Miss Booth QC contended, that the industrial tribunal in *Wilson*'s case found on the evidence before it, and the Court of Appeal accepted, that the home could not continue unless there were radical organisational changes which would reduce the cost of running the school. LCC could not or would not continue to carry the existing costs. St Helens could not take over the running of the school with those costs and without organisational changes and reduced costs. Those changes were for an economic or organisational reason and entailed a change in the workforce since the number of employees at the school was considerably reduced, whether or not the 'eto' defence can strictly be relied on in the present circumstances. The staff had the option of staying with LCC or going to St Helens on the new terms to give effect to these economic and organisational reasons. In the circumstances, the industrial tribunal and the Court of Appeal were entitled to find that the transfer of the undertaking did not constitute the reason for the variation. It was a variation of the terms of employment 'to the same extent as it could have been with regard to the transferor' (*Daddy's Dance Hall*, paragraph 17). That seems to me to be sufficient on the facts to determine the appeal in *Wilson*'s case. But I add that, although on a transfer, the employees' rights previously existing against the transferor are enforceable against the transferee and cannot be amended by the transfer itself, it does not follow there cannot be a variation of the terms of the contract for reasons which are not due to the transfer either on or after the transfer of the undertaking. It may be difficult to decide whether the variation is due to the transfer or attributable to some separate cause. If, however, the variation is not due to the transfer it can, in my opinion, on the basis of the authorities to which I have referred, validly be made.

Conclusion

In the result, however, I would allow the appeal of British Fuels Ltd in both Mr Baxendale's and Mr Meade's cases and I would dismiss the appeal of Mr Wilson and others against St Helens Borough Council.

Notes

1. Following the judgments in *Wilson* and *Meade*, employers who wish to vary terms and conditions after a transfer through voluntary agreement are still left uncertain whether such a change will be effective. On the other hand, employers involved in a transfer can change terms and conditions of employment by dismissing employees with full contractual notice and offering new contracts on the revised terms. However, such a dismissal will be held to be automatically unfair in most cases. The reason for this is that it was held in *Berriman* v *Delabole Slate Ltd* [1985] IRLR 305 that it is not usually possible to establish an economic, technical or organisational reason where the change does not directly entail a reduction in the workforce.

Nevertheless, an employer might decide, following a cost–benefit analysis, that the cost savings achieved through changes in conditions outweigh the costs of any unfair dismissal compensation. This may be a less frequent conclusion in future now that the Employment Relations Act 1999 raises substantially the upper limit on unfair dismissal compensation from £12,000 to £50,000 (and from then on index–linked to the annual rate of inflation). In any event, it may well be that most good employers eschew this 'fire and rehire' strategy, regarding it as a throwback to 'macho management' approaches that gained currency during the 1980s.

In this context then, it is disappointing that good employers who seek to agree changes in term and conditions of employment with their workforce will find that any agreed variation is invalid if the change is prompted by the transfer. Of course, what underlies the 'no waiver' principle is the difficulties in determining whether or not a particular agreement is truly based on the consent of the workers affected. This certainly may be a legitimate concern where employees do not have recourse to trade union representation, but less so where a trade union is recognised and there are established collective bargaining arrangements. There is a contradiction between the 'no waiver' principle and the consultation requirements laid down by the 1981 Regulations and the Acquired Rights Directive. There is little point in engaging in consultation with employee representatives about the consequences of a transfer if an agreement to vary terms and conditions, which is the outcome of the consultative process, is null and void. Moreover, as Rubenstein, commenting on the EAT stage in *Wilson*, observes: 'The decision also creates the paradox that a transferee needing to reduce costs is protected by TUPE if it dismisses employees on the grounds of redundancy, but is precluded from offering to save jobs if costs can be reduced by varying contractual terms.' ('Highlights' [1996] IRLR 317)

This contradiction is further underlined when certain of the amendments to the Acquired Rights Directive are examined. The Directive, as amended, allows Member States options to limit or restrict its operation in relation to transfers by insolvent transferors. Article 4a(2) permits a transferor which is insolvent to agree with transferees and representatives of its employees alterations to the employees' terms and conditions of employment 'designed to safeguard employment opportunities by ensuring the survival of the undertaking'. This provision represents a modification of the principle of the compulsory transfer of employment on the employees' existing terms and conditions where there is collective agreement: a modification firmly rejected by both the British and European courts (see *Forningen af Arbejdsledere i Danmark* v *Daddy's Dance Hall A/S* (case 324/86 [1988] IRLR 315, ECJ, *Rask* v *ISS Kantineservice A/S* [1993] IRLR 133, ECJ; *Crédit Suisse First Boston (Europe) Ltd* v *Lister* [1998] IRLR 700, CA).

2.   Mutually agreed changes will be held to be legitimate only where the reasons for the changes are not causally related to the transfer. So if the employer could show, for example, that negotiations on revised terms and conditions predated the transfer and that these changes would have been put in place irrespective of the transfer, such changes will be valid. Alternatively, where there is a variation in terms and conditions agreed after the transfer, the employer would have to show that changes in market conditions, wholly unrelated to the transfer, prompted the variation. As will be readily appreciated, to determine the issue will involve difficult questions of fact and, as we bid farewell to compulsory competitive tendering and enter the era of 'best value', introduce yet more complexity and confusion into the law relating to employment rights and business transfers.

Transfer of Undertakings (Protection of Employment) Regulations 1981 (SI 1981 No. 1794)

6.   Effect of relevant transfer on collective agreements

Where at the time of a relevant transfer there exists a collective agreement made by or on behalf of the transferor with a trade union recognised by the transferor in respect of any employee whose contract of employment is preserved by Regulation 5(1) above, then—

(a)   without prejudice to section 18 of the 1974 Act or Article 63 of the 1976 Order (collective agreements presumed to be unenforceable in specified circumstances) that agreement, in its application in relation to the employee, shall, after the transfer, have effect as if made by or on behalf of the transferee with that trade union, and accordingly anything done under or in connection with it, in its application as aforesaid, by or in relation to the transferor before the transfer, shall, after the transfer, be deemed to have been done by or in relation to the transferee; and

(b)   any order made in respect of that agreement, in its application in relation to the employee, shall, after the transfer, have effect as if the transferee were a party to the agreement.

7.   Exclusion of occupational pensions schemes

(1)   Regulations five and six above shall not apply—

(a)   to so much of a contract of employment or collective agreement as relates to an occupational pension scheme within the meaning of the Social Security Pensions Act 1975 or the Social Security Pensions (Northern Ireland) Order 1975; or

(b)   to any rights, powers, duties or liabilities under or in connection with any such contract or subsisting by virtue of any such agreement and relating to such a scheme or otherwise arising in connection with that person's employment and relating to such a scheme.

(2)   For the purposes of paragraph (1) above any provisions of an occupational pension scheme which do not relate to benefits for old age, invalidity or survivors shall be treated as not being part of the scheme.

8. Dismissal of employee because of relevant transfer

(1) Where either before or after a relevant transfer, any employee of the transferor or transferee is dismissed, that employee shall be treated for the purposes of Part V of the 1978 Act [now ERA, Part X] and Articles 20 to 41 of the 1976 Order (unfair dismissal) as unfairly dismissed if the transfer or a reason connected with it is the reason or principal reason for his dismissal.

(2) Where an economic, technical or organisational reason entailing changes in the workforce of either the transferor or the transferee before or after a relevant transfer is the reason or principal reason for dismissing an employee—

    (a) paragraph (1) above shall not apply to his dismissal; but

    (b) without prejudice to the application of section 57(3) of the 1978 Act [now ERA, s. 98(4)] or Article 22(10) of the 1976 Order (test of fair dismissal), the dismissal shall for the purposes of section 57(1)(b) of that Act [now ERA, s. 98(1)] and Article 22(2)(b) of that Order (substantial reason for dismissal) be regarded as having been for a substantial reason of a kind such as to justify the dismissal of an employee holding the position which that employee held.

(3) The provisions of this Regulation apply whether or not the employee in question is employed in the undertaking or part of the undertaking transferred or to be transferred.

(4) Paragraph (1) above shall not apply in relation to the dismissal of any employee which was required by reason of the application of section 5 of the Aliens Restriction (Amendment) Act 1919 to his employment.

(5) Paragraph (1) above shall not apply in relation to a dismissal of an employee if—

    (a) the application of section 54 of the 1978 Act [now ERA, s. 94] to the dismissal of the employee is excluded by or under any provisions of Part V or sections 141 to 149 of the 1978 Act [now ERA, s. 196 onwards] or of section 237 or 238 of the Trade Union and Labour Relations (Consolidation) Act 1992; or

    (b) the application of Article 20 of the 1976 Order to the dismissal of the employee is excluded by or under any provision of Part III or Article 76 of that Order.

Notes

1. Regulation 8(5) was introduced by the Collective Redundancies and Transfer of Undertakings (Protection of Employment) (Amendment) Regulations 1995 to reverse the decision in *Milligan* v *Securicor Cleaning Ltd* [1995] IRLR 288 to the effect that an employee did *not* need to have two years' continuous employment to claim unfair dismissal on a transfer pursuant to reg. 8. The effect of the decision was that someone dismissed after one week's employment because of a transfer could claim unfair dismissal, whereas the employee of 23 months' duration dismissed in a non-transfer situation could not! The decision has been overruled by the High Court in *R* v *Secretary of State for Trade and Industry, ex parte Unison* [1996] IRLR 438 (see below).

2. The fundamental principle of the Regulations is that the existing terms and conditions of employment of the transferring employees automatically transfer with them along with the business. The only exception is reg. 7, i.e. rights and benefits under occupational pension schemes. The EC Business Transfers Directive specifically excludes only 'old age, invalidity or survivor's benefits'. In practice, some pension schemes contain other benefits of employment which are not strictly related to old age. TURERA 1993, s. 33,

introduced reg. 7(2), making clear that only old age, invalidity or survivor's benefits under an occupational pension scheme fall under the reg. 7 exception.

3.   Regulation 8 provides that a dismissal of an employee of the transferor or transferee which is connected with the transfer of the business is automatically unfair unless it is for an 'economic, technical or organisational reason entailing changes in the workforce' (the 'ETO' defence). By virtue of reg. 8(2), such dismissals are deemed to be for a substantial reason for the purpose of ERA 1996, s. 98(1), and are fair provided they pass the statutory test of reasonableness. It is now clear that if the employer does successfully establish the ETO defence, an employee can claim a redundancy payment if redundancy was the reason for the transfer dismissal (*Gorictree Ltd* v *Jenkinson* [1984] IRLR 391).

4.   The scope of the ETO defence was considered by the Court of Appeal in *Berriman* v *Delabole Slate Ltd* [1985] IRLR 305. The Court held that in order to come within reg. 8(2), the employer must show that a change in the workforce is part of the economic, technical or organisational reason for dismissal. It must be an objective of the employer's plan to achieve changes in the workforce, not just a possible consequence of the plan. So where an employee resigned following a transfer because the transferee employer proposed to remove his guaranteed weekly wage so as to bring his pay into line with the transferee's existing workforce, the reason behind the plan was to produce uniform terms and conditions and was not in any way to reduce the numbers in the workforce.

5.   A contrasting case is *Crawford* v *Swinton Insurance Brokers Ltd* [1990] IRLR 42. Prior to transfer of the business, Mrs Crawford was a clerk typist working mainly from home. After the transfer, she was offered other work with the changed function of selling insurance. She refused and claimed she had been constructively and unfairly dismissed. The EAT held that if, as a result of an organisational change on a relevant transfer, a workforce is engaged in a different occupation or function, there is a change of workforce for the purpose reg. 8(2) and any dismissal is potentially fair.

6.   It has been held that where a prospective purchaser insists on the prior dismissal of existing employees, this is not an 'economic reason' within the meaning of reg. 8(2) so that a dismissal in such circumstances will be unfair (*Wheeler* v *Patel* [1987] ICR 631). However, *Wheeler* was distinguished by the Court of Appeal in *Whitehouse* v *Chas A. Blachford & Sons Ltd* [1999] IRLR 492. In this case, the transferees were the successful bidders for a contract, but this was made conditional upon a cost reduction to be achieved by making one of the 13 technicians redundant. The man selected, Mr Whitehouse, complained that his dismissal was in breach of the 1981 Regulations and thus unfair. The Court of Appeal, in dismissing his appeal, held that it was open to the employment tribunal to conclude that the transfer was not the reason for the appellant's dismissal and that the dismissal was for an economic or organisational reason. The Court could not accept the argument on behalf of the appellant that there was no difference between a dismissal to

secure the sale of a business – as in *Wheeler* – and a dismissal which was in order to get a contract. The demand for services under the contract was for one less technician, and the position would have been the same if the previous employers had been awarded the contract. In those circumstances, the transfer of the undertaking was the occasion for the reduction in the requirements for the services of the technicians, but it was not the cause or reason for that reduction. The reduction was directly connected with the provision of the services and with the conduct of any business which provided them. That was in no way analogous to the position of the vendor of a business who dismisses employees solely for the purpose of achieving the best price for the business.

Transfer of Undertakings (Protection of Employment) Regulations 1981 (SI 1981 No. 1794)

9. Effect of relevant transfer of trade union recognition

(1) This regulation applies where after a relevant transfer the undertaking or part of the undertaking transferred maintains an identity distinct from the remainder of the transferee's undertaking.

(2) Where before such a transfer an independent trade union is recognised to any extent by the transferor in respect of employees of any description who in consequence of the transfer became employees of the transferee, then, after the transfer—

(a) the union shall be deemed to have been recognised by the transferee to the same extent in respect of employees of that description so employed; and

(b) any agreement for recognition may be varied or rescinded accordingly.

10. Duty to inform and consult trade union representatives

(1) In this Regulation and Regulation 11 below references to affected employees, in relation to a relevant transfer, are to any employees of the transferor or the transferee (whether or not employed in the undertaking or the part of the undertaking to be transferred) who may be affected by the transfer or may be affected by measures taken in connection with it; and references to the employer shall be construed accordingly.

(2) Long enough before a relevant transfer to enable the employer of any affected employees to consult all the persons who are appropriate representatives of any of those affected employees, the employer shall inform those representatives of—

(a) the fact that the relevant transfer is to take place, when, approximately, it is to take place and the reasons for it; and

(b) the legal, economic and social implications of the transfer for the affected employees; and

(c) the measures which he envisages he will, in connection with the transfer, take in relation to those employees or, if he envisages that no measures will be so taken, that fact; and

(d) if the employer is the transferor, the measures which the transferee envisages he will, in connection with the transfer, take in relation to such of those employees as, by virtue of Regulation 5 above, become employees of the transferee after the transfer or, if he envisages that no measures will be so taken, that fact.

(2A) For the purposes of this Regulation the appropriate representatives of any employees are—

(a)   if the employees are of a description in respect of which an independent trade union is recognised by their employer, representatives of the trade union, or

(b)   in any other case, whichever of the following employee representatives the employer chooses—

(i)   employee representatives appointed or elected by the affected employees otherwise than for the purposes of this Regulation, who (having regard to the purposes for and the method by which they were appointed or elected) have authority from those employees to receive information and to be consulted about the proposed dismissals on their behalf;

(ii)   employee representatives elected by them, for the purposes of this Regulation, in an election satisfying the requirements of Regulation 10A(1).

(3)   The transferee shall give the transferor such information at such a time as will enable the transferor to perform the duty imposed on him by virtue of paragraph (2)(d) above.

(4)   The information which is to be given to the appropriate representatives shall be given to each of them by being delivered to them, or sent by post to an address notified by them to the employer, or (in the case of representatives of a trade union) sent by post to the union at the address of its head or main office.

(5)   Where an employer of any affected employees envisages that he will, in connection with the transfer, be taking measures in relation to any such employees he shall consult all the persons who are appropriate representatives of any of the affected employees in relation to whom he envisages taking measures with a view to seeking their agreement to measures to be taken.

(6)   In the course of those consultations the employer shall—

(a)   consider any representations made by the appropriate representatives; and

(b)   reply to those representations and, if he rejects any of those representations, state his reasons.

(6A)   The employer shall allow the appropriate representatives access to the affected employees and shall afford to those representatives such accommodation and other facilities as may be appropriate.

(7)   If in any case there are special circumstances which render it not reasonably practicable for an employer to perform a duty imposed in him by any of paragraphs (2) to (6), he shall take all such steps towards performing that duty as are reasonably practicable in the circumstances.

(8)   Where—

(a)   the employer has invited any of the affected employees to elect employee representatives, and

(b)   the invitation was issued long enough before the time required to give information under paragraph (2) above to allow them to elect representatives by that time, the employer shall be treated as complying with the requirements of this Regulation in relation to those employees if he complies with those requirements as soon as is reasonably practicable after the election of the representatives.

(8A)   If, after the employer has invited affected employees to elect representatives, they fail to do so after a reasonable time, he shall give to each affected employee the information set out in paragraph (2).

10A.   Election of employee representatives

(1)   The requirements for the election of employee representatives under Regulation 10(2A) are that—

(a)   the employer shall make such arrangements as are reasonably practical to ensure that the election is fair;

(b)   the employer shall determine the number of representatives to be elected so that there are sufficient representatives to represent the interests of all the affected employees having regard to the number and classes of those employees;

(c)   the employer shall determine whether the affected employees should be represented either by representatives of all the affected employees or by representatives of particular classes of those employees;

(d)   before the election the employer shall determine the term of office as employee representatives so that it is of sufficient length to enable information to be given and consultations under Regulation 10 to be completed;

(e)   the candidates for election as employee representatives are affected employees on the date of the election;

(f)   no affected employee is unreasonably excluded from standing for election;

(g)   all affected employees on the date of the election are entitled to vote for employee representatives;

(h)   the employees entitled to vote may vote for as many candidates as there are representatives to be elected to represent them or, if there are to be representatives for particular classes of employees, may vote for as many candidates as there are representatives to be elected to represent their particular class of employee;

(i)   the election is conducted so as to secure that—

(i)   so far as is reasonably practicable, those voting do so in secret, and

(ii)   the votes given at the election are accurately counted.

(2)   Where, after an election of employee representatives satisfying the requirements of paragraph (1) has been held, one of those elected ceases to act as an employee representative and any of those employees are no longer represented, those employees shall elect another representative by an election satisfying the requirements of paragraph (1)(a), (e), (f) and (i).

11.   Failure to inform or consult

(1)   Where an employer has failed to comply with a requirement of Regulation 10 or Regulation 10A, a complaint may be presented to an employment tribunal on that ground—

(a)   in the case of a failure relating to the election of employee representatives, by any of his employees who are affected employees,

(b)   in the case of any other failure relating to employee representatives, by any of the employee representatives to whom the failure related,

(c)   in the case of failure relating to representatives of a trade union, by the trade union, and

(d)   in any other case, by any of his employees who are affected employees.

(2)   If on a complaint under paragraph (1) above a question arises whether or not it was reasonably practicable for an employer to perform a particular duty or what steps he took towards performing it, it shall be for him to show—

(a)   that there were special circumstances which rendered it not reasonably practicable for him to perform the duty; and

(b)   that he took all such steps towards its performance as were reasonably practicable in those circumstances.

(2A)   If on a complaint under paragraph (1) a question arises as to whether or not any employee representative was an appropriate representative for the purposes of Regulation 10, it shall be for the employer to show that the employee representative had the necessary authority to represent the affected employees.

(2B)   On a complaint under sub-paragraph (1)(a) it shall be for the employer to show that the requirements in Regulation 10A have been satisfied.

(3)   On any such complaint against a transferor that he had failed to perform the duty imposed upon him by virtue of paragraph (2)(d) or, so far as relating thereto, paragraph (7) of Regulation 10 above, he may not show that it was not reasonably practicable for him to perform the duty in question for the reason that the transferee had failed to give him the requisite information at the requisite time in accordance with Regulation 10(3) above unless he gives the transferee notice of his intention to show that fact; and the giving of the notice shall make the transferee a party to the proceedings.

(4)   Where the tribunal finds a complaint under paragraph (1) above well-founded it shall make a declaration to that effect and may—

(a)   order the employer to pay appropriate compensation to such descriptions of affected employees as may be specified in the award; or

(b)   if the complaint is that the transferor did not perform the duty mentioned in paragraph (3) above and the transferor (after giving due notice) shows the facts so mentioned, order the transferee to pay appropriate compensation to such descriptions of affected employees as may be specified in the award.

(5)   An employee may present a complaint to an industrial tribunal on the ground that he is an employee of a description to which an order under paragraph (4) above relates and that the transferor or the transferee has failed, wholly or in part, to pay him compensation in pursuance of the order.

(6)   Where the tribunal finds a complaint under paragraph (5) above well-founded it shall order the employer to pay the complainant the amount of compensation which it finds is due him.

(7)   [repealed]

(8)   An industrial tribunal shall not consider a complaint under paragraph (1) or (5) above unless it is presented to the tribunal before the end of the period of three months beginning with—

(a)   the date on which the relevant transfer is completed, in the case of a complaint under paragraph (1);

(b)   the date of the tribunal's order under paragraph (4) above, in the case of a complaint under paragraph (5);

or within such further period as the tribunal considers reasonable in a case where it is satisfied that it was not reasonably practicable for the complaint to be presented before the end of the period of three months.

(9)   Section 133 of the EPCA 1978 (functions of conciliation officer) and Articles 58(2) and 62 of the 1976 Order (which make corresponding provision for Northern Ireland) shall apply to the rights conferred by this Regulation and to proceedings under this Regulation as they apply to the rights conferred by that Act or that Order and the industrial tribunal proceedings mentioned therein.

(10)   An appeal shall lie and shall lie only to the Employment Appeal Tribunal on a question of law arising from any decision of, or arising in any proceedings before, an industrial tribunal under or by virtue of these Regulations; and section 13(1) of the Tribunals and Inquiries Act 1971 (appeal from certain tribunals to the High Court) shall not apply in relation to any such proceedings.

(11)   In this Regulation 'appropriate compensation' means such sum not exceeding 13 weeks' pay for the employee in question as the tribunal considers just and equitable having regard to the seriousness of the failure of the employer to comply with his duty.

(12)   Section 220 of the Employment Rights Act 1996 shall apply for calculating the amount of a week's pay for any employee for the purposes of paragraph (11) above; and, for the purposes of that calculation date shall be—

(a) in the case of an employee who is dismissed by reason of redundancy (within the meaning of section 135 of the 1996 Act the date which is the calculation date for the purposes of any entitlement of his to a redundancy payment (within the meaning of that section) or which would be that calculation date if he were so entitled;

(b) in the case of an employee who is dismissed for any other reason, the effective date of termination (within the meaning of section 95 of the 1996 Act) of his contract of employment;

(c) in any other case, the date of the transfer in question.

11A. Construction of references to employee representatives

For the purposes of Regulations 10 and 11 above persons are employee representatives if—

(a) they have been elected by employees for the specific purpose of being given information and consulted by their employer under Regulation 10 above; or

(b) having been elected or appointed by employees otherwise than for that specific purpose; it is appropriate (having regard to the purposes for which they were elected) for their employer to inform and consult them under that Regulation, and (in either case) they are employed by the employer at the time when they are elected or appointed.

12. Restriction on contracting out

Any provision of any agreement (whether a contract of employment or not) shall be void in so far as it purports to exclude or limit the operation of Regulation 5, 8 or 10 above or to preclude any person from presenting a complaint to an industrial tribunal under Regulation 11 above.

Notes

1. The Regulations originally required the employer to consult with representatives of any independent recognised union recognised by him to any extent for the purposes of collective bargaining in respect of employees who might be affected by the transfer. However, following the ECJ decision in *EC Commission v United Kingdom of Great Britain and Northern Ireland*, C-373/92 [1994] IRLR 142, the duty to consult was extended to cover employee representatives. The ECJ held that the Regulations did not comply with the Acquired Rights Directive because they did not provide for a mechanism for consultation where there was no recognised trade union. As a result the Collective Redundancies and Transfer of Undertakings (Protection of Employment) (Amendment) Regulations 1995 (SI 1995/2587) amended the Regulations.

2. Controversially, those Regulations allowed the employer to elect to consult non-union employee representatives even in situations where there was a recognised union. Early in 1998, the Government launched a consultation exercise on possible further amendments to the legislation governing consultation on collective redundancies and transfers of undertakings. The Collective Redundancies and Transfer of Undertakings (Protection of Employment)(Amendment) Regulations 1999 (SI 1999/1925) are the result of that process. Under the amended Regulations, there is now a requirement for employers to consult and/or inform an independent trade union where it is recognised for collective bargaining purposes in respect of any of the affected

employees. It is irrelevant whether those employees are union members, provided they belong to a class, grade or 'description' of employees in respect of which the union is recognised.

3.   Where no union is recognised in relation to any of the affected employees, *and* in relation to affected employees who are not covered by the scope of union recognition, the employer may choose whether to consult or inform existing employee representatives who have the appropriate authority, or employee representatives elected specifically for the purposes of consultation and receiving information.

4.   The Commission was also critical of the UK's failure to provide effective sanctions in the case of failure to inform and consult. As a result, TURERA 1993 raised the maximum compensation payable for a breach of this requirement from two weeks' pay to four weeks' pay. The 1999 Regulations have further raised the maximum to 13 weeks' pay. Also, reg. 11(7), which allowed protective awards under TULR(C)A 1992, ss. 189 and 190 and wages in lieu payable in respect of the protected period to be offset against compensation for failure to inform or consult, was removed by TURERA, 1993, s. 33(7).

VI   Handling the Redundancy Situation: Procedural Correctness

It is not sufficient for the employer to prove the potentially fair reason for dismissal, i.e the redundancy situation. Such dismissal may become unfair if he or she fails to adopt a fair procedure when deciding upon and putting into effect a redundancy programme. The ERA 1996, s. 105, generally makes a dismissal for redundancy automatically unfair if an agreed redundancy selection procedure is not followed. Further, s. 98(4) of the 1996 Act may well lead to a finding that the employer was wrong to treat redundancy as a sufficient reason for dismissal where he or she has failed, for example, to consult with those affected; and, as will be seen, the duties of consultation extend not only to the affected employees but also to any recognised trade union.

A: Pre-redundancy Procedures

Employment Rights Act 1996

105.   Redundancy

(1)   An employee who is dismissed shall be regarded for the purposes of this Part as unfairly dismissed if—

(a)   the reason (or, if more than one, the principal reason) for the dismissal is that the employee was redundant,

(b)   it is shown that the circumstances constituting the redundancy applied equally to one or more other employees in the same undertaking who held positions similar to that held by the employee and who have not been dismissed by the employer, and

(c)   it is shown that any of subsections (2) to (7) applies.

(2) This subsection applies if the reason (or, if more than one, the principal reason) for which the employee was selected for dismissal was that specified in any of paragraphs (a) to (d) of subsection (1) of section 99 (read with subsection (2) of that section) or subsection (3) of that section (and any requirements of the paragraph, or subsection, not relating to the reason are satisfied).

(3) This subsection applies if the reason (or, if more than one, the principal reason) for which the employee was selected for dismissal was one of those specified in subsection (1) of section 100 (read with subsections (2) and (3) of that section).

(4) This subsection applies if either—

(a) the employee was a protected shop worker or an opted-out shop worker, or a protected betting worker or an opted-out betting worker, and the reason (or, if more than one, the principal reason) for which the employee was selected for dismissal was that specified in subsection (1) of section 101 (read with subsection (2) of that section), or

(b) the employee was a shop worker or a betting worker and the reason (or, if more than one, the principal reason) for which the employee was selected for dismissal was that specified in subsection (3) of that section.

(5) This subsection applies if the reason (or, if more than one, the principal reason) for which the employee was selected for dismissal was that specified in section 102(1).

(6) This subsection applies if the reason (or, if more than one, the principal reason) for which the employee was selected for dismissal was that specified in section 103.

(7) This subsection applies if the reason (or, if more than one, the principal reason) for which the employee was selected for dismissal was one of those specified in subsection (1) of section 104 (read with subsections (2 and (3) of that section).

(8) For the purposes of section 36(2)(b) or 41(1)(b), the appropriate date in relation to this section is the effective date of termination.

(9) In this Part 'redundancy case' means a case where paragraphs (a) and (b) of subsection (1) of this section are satisfied.

Notes

1. The ERA 1996, s. 105 and s. 99, make it automatically unfair to select an employee for redundancy on grounds of pregnancy or childbirth, because he or she has made a health and safety complaint or has asserted a statuory right.

2. EPCA 1978 is amended by TURERA 1993, s. 24(3), so that there will be no qualifying period for complaining of unfair dismissal on the grounds of selection for redundancy for an 'inadmissible reason'.

3. Under what was EPCA 1978, s. 59(1)(b), it was automatically unfair to select an employee for redundancy in contravention of a customary arrangement or agreed procedure relating to redundancy and where there were no special reasons justifying departure. This provision was repealed by the Deregulation and Contracting Out Act 1994. Research has shown that the influence of such agreed procedures has declined in recent years, and recent case law had taken a rather generous approach to the scope of the 'special reasons' defence (see Rolls Royce Motor Cars Ltd v Price [1993] IRLR 203, EAT).

4. For discussion of unfair redundancy selection on trade union grounds, now contained in TULR(C)A 1992, s. 153, see p. 644.

5.   In the next case, with regard to what is now ERA 1996, s. 98(4), the
House of Lords emphasised the importance of carrying out proper pre-
redundancy procedures.

Polkey v *A.E. Dayton Services Ltd*
[1988] AC 344
House of Lords

LORD BRIDGE: . . . [I]n the case of redundancy, the employer will normally not act
reasonably unless he warns and consults any employees affected or their representatives, adopts a fair basis on which to select for redundancy and takes such steps as
may be reasonable to avoid or minimise redundancy by redeployment within his own
organisation.

Note
See the full discussion of *Polkey* at p. 464. *Polkey* approved the guidelines as
regards proper procedures laid down by the EAT in the following case.

Williams v *Compair Maxam Ltd*
[1982] ICR 157
Employment Appeal Tribunal

BROWNE-WILKINSON J: . . . [T]here is a generally accepted view in industrial
relations that, in cases where the employees are represented by an independent union
recognised by the employer, reasonable employers will seek to act in accordance with
the following principles:
   1.   The employer will seek to give as much warning as possible of impending
redundancies so as to enable the union and employees who may be affected to take
early steps to inform themselves of the relevant facts consider possible alternative
solutions and, if necessary, find alternative employment in the undertaking or
elsewhere.
   2.   The employer will consult the union as to the best means by which the desired
management result can be achieved fairly and with as little hardship to the employees
as possible. In particular, the employer will seek to agree with the union the criteria
to be applied in selecting the employee to be made redundant. When a selection has
been made, the employer will consider with the union whether the selection has been
made in accordance with those criteria.
   3.   Whether or not an agreement as to the criteria to be adopted has been agreed
with the union, the employer will seek to establish criteria for selection which so far
as possible do not depend solely upon the opinions of the person making the selection
but can be objectively checked against such things as attendance record, efficiency at
the job, experience, of length of service.
   4.   The employer will seek to ensure that the selection is made fairly in accordance
with these criteria and will consider any representations union may make as to such
selection.
   5.   The employer will seek to see whether instead of dismissing as employee he
could offer him alternative employment.
   The lay members stress that not all these factors are present in every case since
circumstances may prevent one or more of them being given effect to. But the lay

members would expect these principles to be departed from only where some good reason is shown to justify such departure. The basic approach is that, in the unfortunate circumstances that necessarily attend redundancies, as much as is reasonably possible should be done to mitigate the impact on the work force and to satisfy them that the selection has been made fairly and not on the basis of personal whim.

That these are the broad principles currently adopted by reasonable employers is supported both by the practice of the industrial tribunals and to an extent by statute. . . .

Notes

1. In Scotland, it has been suggested that the *Williams* v *Compair Maxam* guidelines are more suitable for the larger concerns, particularly the unionised ones. See *Meikle* v *McPhail (Charleston Arms)* [1983] IRLR 351 and *Simpson* v *Findlater* [1983] IRLR 401.

2. Where the employer failed to consult because on a previous occasion the workforce indicated that they would rather have just been told they were going to be made redundant, the dismissal 'for redundancy' was, nevertheless, held to be unfair. See *Ferguson* v *Prestwick Circuits Limited* [1992] IRLR 266.

3. ACAS has published an advisory booklet entitled *Redundancy Handling* (Advisory Booklet No. 12) which provides a useful checklist for employers when considering pre-redundancy procedures.

B: Consultation with the Trade Union

Consultation requirements with the relevant trade union are contained in EEC Redundancy Consultation Directive 1975/129 and were given statutory effect originally by the Employment Protection Act 1975. The provisions are now contained in TULR(C)A 1992, ss. 188–198, which were amended by TURERA 1993 in order to bring our legislation into line with new requirements introduced by Directive 1992/56. The significant amendment was the addition of s. 188(6), which changed what, previously, was merely an obligation to consult and listen to representations to a requirement that employers negotiate with the union and try, thereby, to reach an agreement about such things as ways of avoiding dismissals, reducing the numbers involved and mitigating the consequences of dismissals.

This moved consultation closer to negotiation. Previously, the question of the decision to make redundancies had generally been non-negotiable and trade unions had been restricted to seeking to limit the numbers of employees who were to lose their jobs. Agreement does not have to be achieved, but the employer will have to show that there was a serious attempt to reach a consensus on the above issues.

The original statutory provision (the Employment Protection Act 1975, ss. 99–107) required the employer to consult with representatives of any independent recognised union recognised by him to any extent for the purposes of collective bargaining in respect of employees who might be affected by the transfer. However, following the ECJ decision in *EC*

Commission v *United Kingdom of Great Britain and Northern Ireland*, C-383/92 [1994] IRLR 142 the duty to consult was extended to cover employee representatives. As a result the Collective Redundancies and Transfer of Undertakings (Protection of Employment) (Amendment) Regulations 1995 (SI 1995/2587) amended the TULR(C)A 1992, s. 188. Controversially, those Regulations allowed the employer to elect to consult non-union employee representatives even in situations where there was a recognised union. Early in 1998, the Government launched a consultation exercise on possible further amendments to the legislation governing consultation on collective redundancies and transfers of undertakings. The Collective Redundancies and Transfer of Undertakings (Protection of Employment)(Amendment) Regulations 1999 (SI 1999/1925) are the result of that process. The main – and most controversial – difference from the original proposals is that the obligation to consult and provide information will continue to apply only where an employer 'is proposing to dismiss as redundant 20 or more employees at one establishment within a period of 90 days or less'. More positively, under the amended Regulations, there is now a requirement for employers to consult and/or inform an independent trade union where it is recognised for collective bargaining purposes in respect of any of the affected employees. It is irrelevant whether those employees are union members, provided they belong to a class, grade or 'description' of employees in respect of which the union is recognised.

Where no union is recognised in relation to any of the affected employees, the employer may choose whether to consult and inform existing employee representatives who have the appropriate authority, or employee representatives elected specifically for the purposes of consultation and receiving information. If the employers opt for the latter, the 1999 Regulations introduce detailed statutory requirements for the election of employee representatives (TULR(C)A 1992, s. 188A). If, after the employer invites affected employees to elect representatives, they fail to do so within a reasonable time, it must give to each affected employee the information set out in s. 188(4).

Employers will now have to consult 'all the persons who are appropriate representatives of any of the employees *who may be affected by the proposed dismissals or may be affected by measures taken in connection with those dismissals*' (emphasis added). Clearly, the employees most directly affected are those whom it is proposed to dismiss. However, the employer will now have to analyse any possible consequential impact (direct or indirect) on the workforce that remains.

Failure to adopt proper consultation procedures may lead to a sum of damages (a 'protective award') being awarded in respect of each dismissed employee. The protective award is within the tribunal's discretion. The maximum duration of the protected period under a protective award that may be ordered by a tribunal in respect of employees who have been dismissed is now 90 days in all cases (TULR(C)A 1992, s. 189(4), as amended by the Collective Redundancies and Transfer of Undertakings (Protection of Employment) Regulations 1999). Consequently, the maximum 30-day period, which previously applied to 20 to 99 redundancies, is abolished.

Previously, express protection against detrimental treatment or dismissal in the context of the redundancy and transfers consultation and information procedures (other than in respect of the protection afforded to those taking part in trade union action activities) was limited to employee representatives and candidates for election as such representatives. Protection is extended by the 1999 Regulations to those who 'participated' in an election of employee representatives (see new s. 47(1A) of ERA 1996) or who 'took part' in such an election (see new s. 103(2) of ERA 1996).

Trade Union and Labour Relations (Consolidation) Act 1992

188. Duty of employer to consult representatives

(1) Where an employer is proposing to dismiss as redundant 20 or more employees at one establishment within a period of 90 days or less, the employer shall consult about the dismissals all the persons who are appropriate representatives of any of the employees who may be affected by the proposed dismissals or may be affected by measures taken in connection with those dismissals.

(1A) The consultation shall begin in good time and in any event—

    (a) where the employer is proposing to dismiss 100 or more employees as mentioned in subsection (1), at least 90 days, and

    (b) otherwise, at least 30 days,

before the first of the dismissals takes effect.

(1B) For the purposes of this section the appropriate representatives of any affected employees are—

    (a) if the employees are of a description in respect of which an independent trade union is recognised by their employer, representatives of the trade union, or

    (b) in any other case, whichever of the following employee representatives the employer chooses—

        (i) employee representatives appointed or elected by the affected employees otherwise than for the purposes of this section, who (having regard to the purposes for and the method by which they were appointed or elected) have authority from those employees to receive information and to be consulted about the proposed dismissals on their behalf;

        (ii) employee representatives elected by the affected employees, for the purposes of this section, in an election satisifying the requirements of section 188A(1).

(2) The consultation shall include consultation about ways of—

    (a) avoiding the dismissals,

    (b) reducing the numbers of employees to be dismissed, and

    (c) mitigating the consequences of the dismissals,

and shall be undertaken by the employer with a view to reaching agreement with the appropriate representatives.

(3) In determining how many employees an employer is proposing to dismiss as redundant no account shall be taken of employees in respect of whose proposed dismissals consultation has already begun.

(4) For the purposes of the consultation the employer shall disclose in writing to the appropriate representatives—

    (a) the reasons for his proposals,

    (b) the numbers and descriptions of employees whom it is proposed to dismiss as redundant,

(c)   the total number of employees of any such description employed by the employer at the establishment in question,

(d)   the proposed method of selecting the employees who may be dismissed,

(e)   the proposed method of carrying out the dismissals, with due regard to any agreed procedure, including the period over which the dismissals are to take effect.

(f)   the proposed method of calculating the amount of any redundancy payments to be made (otherwise than in compliance with an obligation imposed by or by virtue of any enactment) to employees who may be dismissed.

(5)   That information shall be given to each of the appropriate representatives by being delivered to them, or sent by post to an address notified by them to the employer (in the case of representatives of a trade union), or sent by post to the union at the address of its head or main office.

(5A)   The employer shall allow the appropriate representatives access to the affected employees and shall afford to those representatives such accommodation and other facilities as may be appropriate.

. . .

(7)   If in any case there are special circumstances which render it not reasonably practicable for the employer to comply with a requirement of subsection (1A), (2) or (4), the employer shall take all such steps towards compliance with that requirement as are reasonably practicable in those circumstances. Where the decision leading to the proposed dismissals is that of a person controlling the employer (directly or indirectly), a failure on the part of that person to provide information to the employer shall not constitute special circumstances rendering it not reasonably practicable for the employer to comply with such a requirement.

(7A)   Where—

(a)   the employer has invited any of the affected employees to elect employee representatives, and

(b)   the invitation was issued long enough before the time when the consultation is required by subsection (1A)(a) or (b) to begin to allow them to elect representatives by that time,

the employer shall be treated as complying with the requirements of this section in relation to those employees if he complies with those requirements as soon as is reasonably practicable after the election of the representatives.

(7B)   If, after the employer has invited affected employees to elect representatives, the affected employees fail to do so within a reasonable time, he shall give to each affected employee the information set out in subsection (4).

(8)   This section does not confer any rights on a trade union, a representative or an employee except as provided by sections 189 to 192 below.

188A.   Election of employee representatives

(1)   The requirements for the election of employee representatives under section 188(1B)(b)(ii) are that—

(a)   the employer shall make such arrangements as are reasonably practical to ensure that the election is fair;

(b)   the employer shall determine the number of representatives to be elected so that there are sufficient representatives to represent the interests of all the affected employees having regard to the number and classes of those employees;

(c)   the employer shall determine whether the affected employees should be represented either by representatives of all the affected employees or by representatives of particular classes of those employees;

(d) before the election the employer shall determine the term of office as employee representatives so that it is of sufficient length to enable information to be given and consultations under section 188 to be completed;

(e) the candidates for election as employee representatives are affected employees on the date of the election;

(f) no affected employee is unreasonably excluded from standing for election;

(g) all affected employees on the date of the election are entitled to vote for employee representatives;

(h) the employees entitled to vote may vote for as many candidates as there are representatives to be elected to represent them or, if there are to be representatives for particular classes of employees, may vote for as many candidates as there are representatives to be elected to represent their particular class of employee;

(i) the election is conducted so as to secure that—

    (i) so far as is reasonably practicable, those voting do so in secret, and

    (ii) the votes given at the election are accurately counted.

(2) Where, after an election of employee representatives satisfying the requirements of subsection (1) has been held, one of those elected ceases to act as an employee representative and any of those employees are no longer represented, they shall elect another representative by an election satisfying the requirements of subsection (1)(a), (e), (f) and (i).

Note

Under s. 188, the obligation to inform and consult arises where the employer is 'proposing to dismiss'. This phrase suggests that there must be something more definite than the contemplation of the possibility of redundancies: see, for example, *APAC v Kirvin Ltd* [1978] IRLR 318 (company in financial difficulties and looking for a buyer, did not 'propose' any redundancies until last prospective purchaser had disappeared); *Hough and Apex v Leyland Daf Ltd* [1991] IRLR 194 ('matters should have reached a stage where a specific proposal has been formulated and that this is a later stage than the diagnosis of a problem and the appreciation that at least one way of dealing with it would be by declaring redundancies'). Section 188(1) is designed to implement Council Directive 75/129/EEC, and Article 2 of that Directive requires consultation 'where an employer is *contemplating* collective redundancies'. It is arguable that the obligation under Article 2 could arise at an earlier stage than that of a definite *proposal* of redundancies. Indeed, in *R v Coal Corporation, ex parte Vardy* [1993] IRLR 103, CA, Glidewell LJ expressed the view that s. 188 failed fully to implement the Directive:

I say this because in the Directive consultation is to begin as soon as an employer contemplates redundancies, whereas under the Act it only needs to begin when he proposes to dismiss as redundant an employee. The verb 'proposes' in its ordinary usage relates to a state of mind which is much more certain and further along the decision-making process than the verb 'contemplate'; in other words, the Directive envisages consultation at an early stage when the employer is first envisaging the possibility that he may have to make employees redundant. Section 188 applies when he has decided that, whether because he has to close a plant or for some other reason, it is his intention, however reluctant, to make employees redundant.

(Cf. Griffin v South West Water Services Ltd [1995] IRLR 15, HC.)
2. Section 188(7) permits a failure to consult where there are 'special circumstances which render it not reasonably practicable for the employer to comply'.

Clarkes of Hove Limited v Bakers' Union
[1978] ICR 1077
Court of Appeal

The employers had been in financial difficulty for some time. On 24 October 1976, all hope of a financial rescue package disappeared and they dismissed all 368 employees and ceased trading. The union complained about the failure to consult. The Court of Appeal held that insolvency was not a 'special circumstance' (in the absence of any special cause for the insolvency) so that consultation should have taken place.

GEOFFREY LANE LJ: . . . [I]t seems to me that the way in which the phrase was interpreted by the industrial tribunal is correct. What they said, in effect, was this, that insolvency is, on its own, neither here nor there. It may be a special circumstance, it may not be a special circumstance. It will depend entirely on the cause of the insolvency whether the circumstances can be described as special or not. If, for example, sudden disaster strikes a company, making it necessary to close the concern, then plainly that would be a matter which was capable of being a special circumstance; and that is so whether the diaster is physical or financial. If the insolvency, however, were merely due to a gradual run-down of the company, as it was in this case, then those are facts on which the industrial tribunal can come to the condusion that the circumstances were not special. In other words, to be special the event must be something out of the ordinary, something uncommon; and that is the meaning of the words 'special' in the context of this Act.

Notes
1. The EC Commission, when amending the Collective Redundancies Directive, took the view that in cases of multi-national corporations, the decision to make redundancies at a particular plant is often made by the parent company. It was felt that the Directive should be amended in order to stop employers using their foreign parent companies as an excuse for their failure to consult. TURERA 1993 included an amendment to TULR(C)A 1992, s. 188(7), in order to comply with the amended Directive. As a result, the 'special circumstances' defence will not apply where the failure arose because a person controlling the employer did not provide the employer with the necessary information.
2. Failure to adopt proper consultation procedures with the trade union may lead to a sum of damages (a 'protective award') being awarded to the union on behalf of the employee(s). The protective award is within the tribunal's discretion, subject to a maximum of 90 days' pay.
3. Prior to the passage of TURERA 1993, TULR(C)A 1992, s. 190(3), allowed the employer to offset any payment of wages or wages in lieu of notice against the protective award. In *Vosper Thorneycroft (UK) Ltd* v *TGWU* [1988]

ICR 270, the EAT held that this meant that the gross amount of such a payment was to be deducted, not just the net amount (so that where the employer had paid 13 weeks' wages in lieu of notice, this extinguished the 90-day protective award completely). In such cases, the penalty for failure to comply with s. 188 was non-existent. An amendment, introduced by TURERA 1993, s. 34(3), repeals TULR(C)A 1992, s. 190(3) and removes the right to offset pay in lieu of notice against liability for a protective award.

8 TRADE UNIONS AND THEIR MEMBERS

I The Trade Union

A: *The Legal Definition*

Trade Union and Labour Relations (Consolidation) Act 1992

1. Meaning of 'trade union'

In this Act a 'trade union' means an organisation (whether temporary or permanent)—

(a) which consists wholly or mainly of workers of one or more descriptions and whose principal purposes include the regulation of relations between workers of that description or those descriptions and employers or employers' associations; or

(b) which consists wholly or mainly of—

(i) constituent or affiliated organisations which fulfil the conditions in paragraph (a) (or themselves consist wholly or mainly of constituent or affiliated organisations which fulfil those conditions) or,

(ii) representatives of such constituent or affiliated organisations, and whose principal purposes include the regulation of relations between workers and employers' associations, or the regulation of relations between its constituent or affiliated organisations.

Midland Cold Storage Ltd v *Turner*
[1972] ICR 773
National Industrial Relations Court

The plaintiffs sought to prevent a joint shop stewards committee from taking industrial action. The action was brought to restrain the commission of certain 'unfair industrial practices' created by the Industrial Relations

Act 1971. It was necessary to establish that the committee was an 'organisation of workers', a term defined by s. 61 of the Act in substantially the same words as in s. 1 (above).

SIR JOHN DONALDSON: . . . It follows that, if Midland are to obtain an order against the committee, they must satisfy us that (a) it is an organisation; (b) consists wholly or mainly of workers; (c) its principal objects include the regulation of relations between workers of that description and employers.

We have no doubt at all that the committee exists and has great influence in the London docks. We have no evidence as to its composition, other than the fact that it has a chairman and secretary, and that, as we infer from its name and our general knowledge of organisation in the docks, it is composed wholly or mainly of trade union shop stewards. It is not recognised by employers, although they are well aware of its existence and may take account of its activities. Furthermore, there is no evidence that it seeks recognition by employers as a bargaining agent for any bargaining unit or as a representative body for or of any union or unions. It is proved to be an influential pressure group. Our general knowledge of the industry tells us that its activities are to some extent coordinated with those of other shop stewards' committees in other docks by a national shop stewards' committee, but that those other committees may have different compositions and functions. If we have to be able to point to evidence to confirm what as members of an industrial court we ought to know and do know, it was provided at a late stage in the hearing by the production of a printed leaflet, purporting to be issued by the committee, referring to support from the national committee. Its most apparent activity seems to consist of the recommending, the taking or abandonment of industrial action in the London docks and organising any such action which may be decided upon. Thereafter it does not seem to enter into negotiations with the employers, but leaves this task to the established union machinery.

Against this background, we are satisfied that prima facie the committee is an organisation and that it consists wholly or mainly of workers as defined in the Act of 1971. However, we are not satisfied that there is a prima facie case for holding that its principal objects include the regulation of relations between workers of that description (namely registered dock workers) and employers. No body whose principal objects included such regulation could fail at least to seek recognition from employers and of such an attempt we have no evidence. Accordingly, we are unable to make any order against the committee as such.

Notes

1. Before 1971, the Registrar of Friendly Societies had the responsibility of maintaining a register of trade unions and most unions complied because there were tax advantages. The Industrial Relations Act 1971 introduced the office of Registrar of Trade Unions and made registration the precondition to any benefits to be gained under the Act. Since it also involved many interventions in the internal affairs of unions and control of the rule book, only a few registered. Any union that did register was expelled from the TUC.

TULRA 1974 reverted to the substance of the pre-1971 approach and the law is now set out in TULR(C)A 1992, ss. 2, 3 and 4. By s. 2, the Certification Officer is charged with the duty of keeping a voluntary list of trade unions and employers' associations. The Certification Officer grants a listing if he is satisfied that the organisation comes within the appropriate definition.

Inclusion on the list is evidence that the organisation is a trade union. Unions on the list receive tax relief in respect of sums paid as 'provident benefits' (Income and Corporation Taxes Act 1988, s. 467) and listing is a precondition for the grant of a certificate from the Certification Officer that the union is 'independent'. Such status is an important attribute in relation to the following rights of unions, officials and members: to take part in trade union activities; to gain information for collective bargaining; to secure consultation over redundancies; to insist on time off for union duties and activities, and to appoint health and safety representatives.

2. At the end of 1996 there were 245 listed trade unions in Great Britain. 11 fewer than the year earlier and less than 18 per cent of the all-time highest total of 1,384 in 1920. Trade union membership, derived from union sources, was 7.94 million, the lowest since 1945. From 1920, there was a steady fall in the number of unions, while the number of members generally increased, reaching a peak of 13.3 million members in 1979. The 1996 figure represents the seventeenth consecutive fall in membership from its 1979 peak. It is now almost 40 per cent below its peak level. The fall in the number of unions is indicative of the continuing process of union mergers and transfers of membership as well as declining unionisation. The proportion of all employees who were union members (union density), estimated from the Labour Force Survey, has fallen from 39 per cent in 1987 to 30 per cent in 1997 (in 1979, membership density peaked at 55.8 per cent of those in employment). The decline in union density has been particularly marked among male employees, manual employees and those in production industries, all areas where it has traditionally been higher and which once formed the core of union membership. By comparison, union density has fallen less slowly among female employees, those working part-time, and non-manual employees. In 1997, an estimated 36 per cent, or 8.1 million, of all employees were covered by collective bargaining over pay and conditions. Employees working in the public sector and in larger workplaces were much more likely to report that they were covered by a collective agreement. (See Cully, M., and Woodland, S., 'Trade union membership and recognition 1996–97: an analysis of data from the Certification Officer and the LFS', *Labour Market Trends*, July 1988, pp. 353–63.)

B: *Certificate of Independence*

Employers who wish to prevent trade unions recruiting their workforce may engage in two forms of 'peaceful competition'. They may ensure that the terms and conditions of their workforce are better than the negotiated rates, or they can encourage the formation of a staff association, which does not pose an effective challenge to management's power. Such organisations are termed 'sweetheart unions'. The certificate of independence is the means by which the law seeks to ensure that such groupings do not receive the rights accorded to independent trade unions.

Trade Union and Labour Relations (Consolidation) Act 1992

5. Meaning of 'independent trade union'
In this Act an 'independent trade union' means a trade union which—
    (a) is not under the domination or control of an employer or group of employers or of one or more employers' associations, and
    (b) is not liable to interference by an employer or any such group or association (arising out of the provision of financial or material support or by any other means whatsoever) tending towards such control;
. . .

Squibb UK Staff Association v *Certification Officer*
[1980] IRLR 431
Court of Appeal

The staff association was refused a certificate of independence. While accepting that the organisation was not under the domination or control of the employer, the Certification Officer took the view that it was 'liable to interference' because it was dependent on the employer for facilities and in a weak financial position. The association successfully appealed to the EAT which took the view that interference had to be 'likely' or 'not unlikely'. The Court of Appeal upheld the Certification Officer's decision.

LORD DENNING MR: One has to envisage the possibility that there may be a difference of opinion in the future between the employers and the staff association. It does not matter whether it is likely or not – it may be completely unlikely – but one has to envisage the possibility of a difference of opinion . . . But when it arises, the questions have to be asked. What is the strength of the employers? What pressures could they bring to bear against the staff association? What facilities could they withdraw? . . .

The employers could take away the four facilities which the Certification Officer mentioned in his reasons. They could take away the facility of time for meetings. They could take away the facility of free use of office accommodation, and so forth. Those are pressures which the employers could bring to bear on their side. On the other side, this association is rather weak. It has a narrow membership base. It has small financial resources. Weighing the two sides, one against the other, the Certification Officer came to the conclusion that the association was liable to interference in this way: the association was so weak that it was vulnerable, in that it was exposed to the risk of interference tending towards control by the employers.

The Employment Appeal Tribunal reversed the Certification Officer. It seems to me that it misdirected itself. It concentrated too much on the 'likelihood of interference' whereas it should have had regard to the 'vulnerability to interference'. I would therefore allow the appeal and restore the decision of the Certification Officer.

Blue Circle Staff Association v *Certification Officer*
[1977] IRLR 20
Employment Appeal Tribunal

CUMMING-BRUCE J: In response to a question from the tribunal the Certification Officer described his approach. He stated that he had found no nice clear yardstick which could be laid against each case, but that it was a case of looking at the factors and doing a balancing act. He then indicated certain criteria which he found useful. In view of the novelty and importance of the subject matter we set out the criteria as the witness described them, though we do not think it would give a fair impression of his evidence if we suggested that he presented them either as comprehensive, or of similar weight in any two cases.

1. *Finance*: If there is any evidence that a union is getting a direct subsidy from an employer, it is immediately ruled out.

2. *Other Assistance*: The Certification Officer's inspectors see what material support, such as free premises, time off work for officials, or office facilities a union is getting from an employer, and attempt to cost them out.

3. *Employer Interference*: If a union is very small, and weak, and gets a good deal of help, then on the face of it its independence must be in danger and liable to interference.

4. *History*: The recent history of a union, important in the case of the Blue Circle Staff Association which before February 1976 was dominated by the employers, is considered. It was not unusual for a staff association to start as a 'creature of management and grow into something independent'. The staff association had started on this road but still had a way to travel.

5. *Rules*: The applicant union's rule book is scrutinised to see if the employer can interfere with, or control it, and if there are any restrictions on membership. If a union is run by people near the top of a company it could be detrimental to the rank and file members.

6. *Single Company Unions*: While they were not debarred from getting certificates, because such a rule could exclude unions like those of the miners and railwaymen, they were more liable to employer interference. Broadly based multi-company unions were more difficult to influence.

7. *Organisation*: The Certification Officer's inspectors then examine the applicant union in detail, its size and recruiting ability, whether it is run by competent and experienced officers, the state of its finance, and its branch and committee structure. Again, if the union was run by senior men in a company, employer interference was a greater risk.

8. *Attitude*: Once the other factors had been assessed, inspectors looked for a 'robust attitude in negotiation' as a sign of genuine independence, backed up by a good negotiating record . . .

Notes

1.   In coming to his decision, the Certification Officer is free to make such inquiries as he thinks fit and 'shall take into account any relevant information submitted to him by any person'. If an applicant union is refused a certificate, an appeal on fact or law lies to the EAT. The right to appeal in TULR(C)A 1992, s. 9(2), is so worded that no other competing union can appeal against the Certification Officer's decision to grant a certificate (*General and Municipal Workers' Union* v *Certification Officer* [1977] ICR 183).

2.   A recent application of the provisions relating to independence can be seen in *Government Communications Staff Federation* v *Certification Officer* [1992] IRLR 260, EAT. Following the Government's decision to ban trade unions at GCHQ, the GC Staff Association was formed. Its application for a certificate of independence was opposed by the TUC and the Council of Civil

Service Unions, and was rejected by the Certification Officer. Its appeal to the EAT was dismissed. Wood P held that it was 'liable to interference by an employer' because:

(a) it was a condition of service that staff were not allowed to be members of other unions, and any attempt to affiliate with another union would probably result in derecognition;

(b) approval or recognition could be withdrawn at any time by the employer on the ground of national security.

C: The Legal Status of a Trade Union

Trade Union and Labour Relations (Consolidation) Act 1992

10. Quasi-corporate status of trade unions

(1) A trade union is not a body corporate but—

(a) it is capable of making contracts;

(b) it is capable of suing and being sued in its own name, whether in proceedings relating to property or founded on contract or tort or any other cause of action; and

(c) proceedings for an offence alleged to have been committed by it or on its behalf may be brought against it in its own name.

(2)–(3) [omitted]

Note

A trade union has a strange status in law. A trade union is not a body corporate, i.e. a separate legal entity, existing independently of its members. It is an unincorporated association and its property must rest in the hands of trustees. When unions first received recognition under law, they were allowed, but not obliged, to register under the Trade Union Act 1871. Whether they were registered or not, unions remained unincorporated associations, and it was therefore assumed that it was impossible to sue them in their own name.

The notorious House of Lords decision in *Taff Vale Railway Co.* v *Amalgamated Society of Railway Servants* [1901] AC 426, held that a trade union registered under the 1871 Act could be sued in tort, registered unions having a rather peculiar quasi-corporate status. The later House of Lords decision in *Bonsor* v *Musicians Union* [1956] AC 104, confirmed this position.

The Industrial Relations Act 1971 then incorporated registered trade unions.

TULRA 1974 essentially restored the pre-1971 position, except that no distinction is now drawn between listed and non-listed trade unions and their status was put on the more satisfactory legal footing, now set out in TULR(C)A 1992, s. 10.

There are, however, some residual consequences of unincorporated status. For example, a trade union does not have the necessary legal personality to suffer injury to its reputation and cannot sue for libel (*EETPU* v *Times Newspapers* [1980] 1 All ER 1097).

D: Restraint of Trade

Trade Union and Labour Relations (Consolidation) Act 1992

11.   Exclusion of common law rules as to restraint of trade

(1)   The purposes of a trade union are not, by reason only that they are in restraint of trade, unlawful so as—

(a)   to make any member of the trade union liable to criminal proceedings for conspiracy or otherwise, or

(b)   to make any agreement or trust void or voidable.

(2)   No rule of a trade union is unlawful or unenforceable by reason only that it is in restraint of trade.

Note

The immunity contained in s. 11 is fundamental if unions are to operate lawfully. Where a union is empowered to take strike action or to impose various other forms of pressure on an employer, at common law these would be regarded as restraints of trade. Consequently, a union would be perceived to be an organisation pursuing purposes in a manner contrary to public policy, and as such would be unable to enforce its rules or protect its funds.

The vulnerability of the unions to the doctrine of restraint of trade was vividly illustrated in *Hornby* v *Close* (1867) LR 2 QB 153. The United Order of Boilermakers, which had registered under the Friendly Societies Act 1855, wanted the help of the courts to prosecute an official who had embezzled its funds. It was refused. Blackburn J said: 'I do not say the objects of this society are criminal. I do not say they are not. But I am clearly of the opinion that the rules referred to are illegal in the sense that they cannot be enforced.'

Consequently, it was recognised by the framers of the Trade Union Act 1871, that if unions were to be made lawful they would need to be granted immunity from this doctrine. TULR(C)A 1992, s. 11, retains this immunity but expands it slightly to cover rules in addition to purposes.

This extension of the immunity to rules was necessary because of the restrictive interpretation placed on 'purposes' by the Court of Appeal in *Edwards* v *SOGAT* [1971] 3 All ER 689. The plaintiff was expelled from the defendant trade union of which he had been classed a temporary member. His expulsion was carried out under r. 18(4)(h) of the union rules which provided for automatic termination of membership for arrears of subscription. The defendant conceded that expulsion for this reason was unlawful because it was based on a misunderstanding about payment of the plaintiff's dues. However, the union argued that his damages should be nominal, since he could have been validly expelled under another rule, r. 18(4)(j), which it was argued gave the union an unfettered right to terminate the membership of temporary members. Sachs LJ rejected this argument and found such an all-empowering rule an unreasonable restraint of trade on the basis that it could not be said that a rule that enabled such 'capricious and despotic action' was proper to the purposes of any trade union.

This approach is now no longer possible given the extended s. 11. However, the reasoning adopted by another judge in the case, Lord Denning, was based on general public policy and a 'right to work' not tied to the doctrine of restraint of trade: if this approach is correct, then s. 11 would not offer immunity in such circumstances.

E: Political Funds and Objects

The Trade Union Act 1913 was enacted in order to restore the right of unions to spend money on political objects following the decision of the House of Lords in *Amalgamated Society of Railway Servants* v *Osborne* [1910] AC 87, which held that it was unlawful for a union to impose on its members a compulsory levy for the purposes of creating a parliamentary fund to promote Labour MPs. However, while the Act allowed trade unions the right to maintain a political fund, it imposed a series of restrictive conditions on their ability to incur expenditure in respect of certain specified political objects. The union was required to ballot its members in order to approve the adoption of political objects, payments in furtherance of such objects had to be made out of a separate political fund, and individual members were allowed to 'contract out' and were safeguarded against discrimination arising from their failure to contribute to the fund.

The two major changes introduced into this system by the Trade Union Act 1984 related to the introduction of periodic ballots to test continued support for the political objects of the union and a new definition of 'political objects'. The law is now contained in TULR(C)A 1992.

The 1992 Act provides that trade unions which maintain political funds must ballot their members at least every 10 years to determine the continued operation of such funds. The Act stipulates rules regarding the conduct of political fund ballots which have to be approved by the Certification Officer. Most notably, the ballot must be a fully postal ballot, the papers being sent out and returned by post. (The other ballot requirements are listed in the section on 'Union Elections and Ballots' at p. 705 *et seq.*)

The second major change concerns the enlarged definition of those objects of expenditure which must be met out of the political fund.

Trade Union and Labour Relations (Consolidation) Act 1992

72. Political objects to which restriction applies

(1) The political objects to which this Chapter applies are the expenditure of money—

(a) on any contribution to the funds of, or on the payment of expenses incurred directly or indirectly by, a political party;

(b) on the provision of any service or property for use by or on behalf of any political party;

(c) in connection with the registration of electors, the candidature of any person, the selection of any candidate or the holding of any ballot by the union in connection with any election to a political office;

(d) on the maintenance of any holder of a political office;

(e)   on the holding of any conference or meeting by or on behalf of a political party or of any other meeting the main purpose of which is the transaction of business in connection with a political party;

(f)   on the production, publication or distribution of any literature, document, film, sound recording or advertisement the main purpose of which is to persuade people to vote for a political party or candidate or to persuade them not to vote for a political party or candidate.

Paul and Frazer v National and Local Government Officers' Association
[1987] IRLR 413
Chancery Division

Mr Paul and Mr Frazer, both members of NALGO, brought an action against the union in respect of a large-scale publicity campaign which it was conducting during the build-up to the local and general elections. The campaign, 'Make People Matter', focused on government policy in the public sector and was part of a wider TUC initiative which designated 1987 as 'Public Services Year'.

The complaints related to leaflets and posters which, it was alleged, were intended to persuade people to vote against the Conservative Party and, as such, were illegal by reason of s. 3(3) of the Trade Union Act 1913 as amended by the Trade Union Act 1984 (now TULR(C)A 1992, s. 72(1)). The union conceded that if the expenditure on the literature in question did fall within what is now TULR(C)A 1992, s. 72(1), then it was unlawful as being *ultra vires* the union, since the union did not, at that time, have a political fund within the meaning of the Act.

The High Court, Chancery Division, declared that the literature was contrary to the relevant provision, that it was *ultra vires* and granted an injunction in the terms sought.

THE VICE CHANCELLOR: . . . I will now turn to consider the literature which is complained of in this case, the effect of which I have sought to summarise. I have no doubt whatsoever that one purpose of the literature, particularly the leaflets, is to persuade people not to vote for the Conservative Party. The burden of the literature is to criticise the record of the Conservative Government which is said to be the run-down of the public services. That censure on the Conservative Government is confined to the Conservative Government. Though Mr Monks, the Union's Deputy Publicity Officer, said, as I am sure is the case, that NALGO have been complaining of government cut-backs since before 1979, it is notable that in no place in the literature is any reference made to any cut-backs earlier than 1979. Each leaflet refers to the Conservative Government only and each leaflet refers to its policies and the implementation of its policies unfavourably. It does not refer to any other government critically or unfavourably, and it contains nothing critical of any other party. What is more, it takes matters of policy which are known to be Conservative Party policy, such as privatisation, and decries them.

The leaflets then go on, having given that one-sided view of the effect of the Conservative policy and its non-coincidence with NALGO policy, to invite the electorate to think and then to vote. Every one of the leaflets complained of expressly invites the member receiving the leaflet to vote. The inference to my mind from the leaflet itself is really overwhelming. It says that the Government's policies since 1979 are bad, you have to think about it, and having thought about it you have to vote. The only rational message to be drawn from that is, 'If you accept the message of the leaflet vote against the Conservatives'.

Each leaflet contains the disclaimer, saying we are not inviting you to vote this way or that. I think where a message is as clear as this one a disclaimer of that kind is no more effective to avoid liability than is a disclaimer where in a libel case it is said that nobody in this book bears any resemblance to anybody in real life. It is not effective to escape liability once one looks at the purpose of the document as a whole. Therefore I have no doubt that one purpose of the literature was to persuade people to vote against the Conservative Party.

However, I am very far from satisfied that it was the sole reason. The documents that I have seen, quite apart from the evidence of Mr Monks persuade me that this was part of a major campaign to do what, in my judgment, was legitimate, namely to bring before the public NALGO's views on public services, to publicise them and to seek to persuade the public mind about them. It was not exclusively intended to last during the election period. Events were and still are fixed to take place in the future. It was certainly part of the purpose of this campaign, and I think probably at the outset the prime purpose, to persuade the public mind as opposed to persuade people to vote directly in a particular way.

But nothing has shown me how it came to be that the eventual leaflet was inviting the public to vote. I found no satisfactory explanation given by Mr Monks, or indeed anybody else, on that. A leaflet which decries one side and then invites you to vote must in my judgment have as its main reason a desire to influence the vote. I accept that the targeting on marginals is attributable in part to the fact that there were limited funds available, public awareness is greater there and media interest is greater. But the truth of the matter is that so is the chances of producing a political change there greater as well.

I think Mr Monks was well aware of the difficulty and was taking great care in what he did. What I am not satisfied about is that his views were reflecting the views of the National Publicity Committee. I think that this union was trying to get as close to the line with Mr Monks' skilled assistance as possible. In my judgment they have gone well over it. Once you start giving biased views of the issues (they may be right views or wrong views but they are biased) at an election time and invite people to vote, you are going beyond exerting pressure on the public to change its mind and through the public to change the *policy* of the Government. You are seeking to change the public's mind with a direct view to them exercising the vote against the policies you are decrying.

For those reasons I reach the conclusion that the main purpose in issuing the leaflets and posters at this time was to influence the public to vote against the Conservative Party.

If there were any doubt about that from the internal nature of the documents and the way in which they were prepared, the adoption of the solution from the Metropolitan District is damning. Both the NEC and the National Publicity Committee affirm that 'the Thatcher Government' has deliberately done something, that 'the Thatcher Government' must therefore be removed and that the union therefore use Public Services Year, which is the Make People Matter campaign, 'to that end'. It seems to me the clearest indication of a view which Mr Monks was anxious should not be expressed but which has been expressed. It seems to me to be a clear intention to use that campaign for the purpose of changing votes, not just minds, against the Conservative Party.

There is one other factor that I think is of some weight. It is apparent that no leaflets have been prepared for use after the completion of the election campaign. It is hard to tie that in with a campaign which is to run for a full year unallied to any question of influencing the vote. The fact that really nothing has been done to produce leaflets or any other form of publicity for the period after the election seems to me indicative of the main purpose being to influence voting, and the literature itself shows that the influence was against the Conservatives.

To sum up, in my judgment what we have here is literature which gives one side of the political argument. It attributes a bad record to the Conservative Party (admittedly indirectly by calling it the Government). That literature is then timed to be published at the time of an election. The same literature invites people to vote, taking into account that one-sided version of the issues involved. In those circumstances it seems to me impossible to say that the main purpose was not to influence the voting. While I have no explanation as to how the reference to voting crept in the fact is that it did. In those circumstances in my judgment the expenditure was unlawful as being in breach of s. 3 of the 1913 Act [now TULR(C)A 1992, s. 72].

. . .

Finally I would like to say that nothing in this judgment should be taken as suggesting that a publicity campaign organised by a union at times other than an election and therefore at a time when neither directly nor indirectly can the union be inviting anybody to exercise a vote at the time, is unlawful, merely because it expresses disapproval of the Government's policy. Unions, like anybody else, are entitled to disapprove of government policy and to say so. The vice in this case to my mind is that they have linked this disapproval in a biased way with an invitation to vote at the time of an election.

Notes

1. Publicity campaigns against privatisation or trade union legislation, for example, will need a thorough vetting if they are to be financed from the general fund. It is important to bear in mind that these changes affect all unions, whether they possess a political fund or not, since they limit the ways in which general funds can be spent.

2. Sections 89–91 of the 1992 Act deal with the case of a union which has a political fund but which fails to renew its resolution, either by failing to get a majority in favour of renewal or by failing to call a ballot within a 10-year period. In such situations, the trade union must ensure that the collection of contributions to the political fund is discontinued 'as soon as is reasonably practicable'. Any contributions which are received after a political resolution has lapsed may be paid into any of its other funds, subject to the individual member's right to claim a refund.

Where a union has held a ballot but fails to secure a majority for renewal, the union is allowed a period of six months during which it may continue to spend on political objects. Unions which fail to call a ballot within the 10-year period are penalised by not being allowed this 'breathing space'. Trade unions which do not run down their political funds in such situations may transfer the money into their non-political funds. Alternatively, the political fund may be frozen until such time as the union can secure a majority in favour of renewal in a subsequent ballot.

Any member who claims that a union has failed to comply with the political fund ballot rules may apply to the High Court (Court of Session in Scotland) or the Certification Officer for a declaration to that effect. The High Court or Certification Officer may, in addition, make an enforcement order specifying the steps the union must take and the time scale within which they must be taken. The court order may be enforced by any individual who was a member both at the time the original order was made and when enforcement proceedings are commenced. The right of enforcement is, therefore, not confined to the original litigant.

F: Contracting Out of the Political Levy and the Check-off

Trade Union and Labour Relations (Consolidation) Act 1992

Duties of employer who deducts union contributions

86.   Certificate of exemption or objection to contributing to political fund

(1)   If a member of a trade union which has a political fund certifies in writing to his employer that, or to the effect that—

(a)   he is exempt from the obligation to contribute to the fund, or

(b)   he has, in accordance with section 84, notified the union in writing of his objection to contributing to the fund, the employer shall ensure that no amount representing a contribution to the political fund is deducted by him from emoluments payable to the member.

(2)   The employer's duty under subsection (1) applies from the first day, following the giving of the certificate, on which it is reasonably practicable for him to comply with that subsection, until the certificate is withdrawn.

(3)   An employer may not refuse to deduct any union dues from emoluments payable to a person who has given a certificate under this section if he continues to deduct union dues from emoluments payable to other members of the union, unless his refusal is not attributable to the giving of the certificate or otherwise connected with the duty imposed by subsection (1).

87.   Application to court in respect of employer's failure

(1)   A person who claims his employer has failed to comply with section 86 in deducting or refusing to deduct any amount from emoluments payable to him may apply to the county court or, in Scotland, the sheriff court.

(2)   If the court is satisfied that there has been such a failure it shall make a declaration to that effect.

(3)   The court may, if it considers it appropriate to do so in order to prevent a repetition of the failure, make an order requiring the employer to take, within a specified time, the steps specified in the order in relation to emoluments payable by him to the applicant.

(4)   Where in proceedings arising out of section 86(3) (refusal to deduct union dues) the question arises whether the employer's refusal to deduct an amount was attributable to the certificate having been given or was otherwise connected with the duty under section 86(1), it is for the employer to satisfy the court that it was not.

Notes

1.   Despite the fact that the Conservative Government initially had proposed substituting contracting in for contracting out, ultimately it did not change

the present system. Instead, discussions between the Department of Employment and the TUC resulted in the latter's Statement of Guidance to its
affiliates. The Secretary of State for Employment, however, made it clear that
the Government would legislate if it believed that the TUC voluntary code
was not working satisfactorily.

The Statement of Guidance advises unions to draw up an information
sheet containing information, *inter alia*, on how to contract out, on the right
not to be discriminated against for non-contribution and on the amount of
the levy as a proportion of the normal subscription. The information sheet
should be supplied to new members, existing members on request and all
union members after any ballot concerning the establishment or continuation
of the political fund.

In relation to 'contracting out' procedures, the statement advises that no
obstacles should be placed in the way of members wishing to 'contract out'
and, in particular, that forms of exemption should be available through
workplace representatives, union branches and the union's head office; that
receipt of completed notices should be acknowledged; that exemption should
be put into effect speedily and that unions should ensure that members who
do not wish to pay the levy do not do so inadvertently (e.g. under check-off
arrangements, below).

The statement also exhorts unions, where they do not already do so, to
provide a right of access for members to the accounts of the political fund.
Also, unions should, in completing their returns to the Certification Officer,
attach a list showing each payment over £250 made from their general funds
to external bodies not falling within the 'political objects' definition, specify
the source and amount of any investment income to the political fund and
show the administrative costs connected with the political fund. Section 86
(above) is designed as a statutory safeguard against this latter eventuality.

2.   Employers are often unwilling to deduct different amounts from employees'
wages, according to whether or not they pay the political levy. As a result, unions
adopted the practice of periodically refunding to exempt members such amounts
deducted by their employer as represent the political levy. This practice, held to
be lawful by the EAT in *Reeves* v *TGWU* [1980] ICR 728, is now outlawed by s.
86(3) of the 1992 Act. Employers are now faced with the choice between the
administrative burden of operating a check-off system which deducts variable
amounts from pay, depending on whether the employee does or does not
contribute to the political fund, or completely abandoning the check-off system.

G: Deduction of Trade Union Membership Subscriptions

Trade Union and Labour Relations (Consolidation) Act 1992

68.   Right not to suffer deduction of unauthorised or excessive subscriptions
   (1)   Where arrangements ('subscription deduction arrangements') exist between
the employer of a worker and a trade union relating to the making from workers'
wages of deductions representing payments to the union in respect of the workers'
membership of the union ('subscription deductions'), the employer shall ensure—

(a) that no subscription deduction is made from wages payable to the worker on any day ('the relevant day') unless it is an authorised deduction, and

(b) that the amount of any subscription deduction which is so made does not exceed the permitted amount.

(2) For the purposes of subsection (1)(a) a subscription deduction is an authorised deduction in relation to the relevant day if—

(a) a document containing the worker's authorisation of the making from his wages of subscription deductions has been signed and dated by the worker, and

(b) the authorisation is current on that day.

(3) For the purposes of subsection (2)(b) an authorisation is current on the relevant day if that day falls within the period of three years beginning with the day on which the worker signs and dates the document containing the authorisation and subsection (4) does not apply.

(4) This subsection applies if a document containing the worker's withdrawal of the authorisation has been received by the employer in time for it to be reasonably practicable for him to secure that no subscription deduction is made from wages payable to the worker on the relevant day.

(5) For the purposes of subsection (1)(b) the permitted amount in relation to the relevant day is—

(a) the amount of the subscription deduction which falls to be made from wages payable to the worker on that day in accordance with the subscription deduction arrangements, or

(b) if there is a relevant increase in the amount of subscription deductions and appropriate notice has not been given by the employer to the worker at least one month before that day, the amount referred to in paragraph (a) less the amount of the increase.

(6) So much of the increase referred to in subsection (5)(b) is relevant as is not attributable solely to an increase in the wages payable on the relevant day.

(7) In subsection (5)(b) 'appropriate notice' means, subject to subsection (8) below, notice in writing stating—

(a) the amount of the increase and the increased amount of the subscription deductions, and

(b) that the worker may at any time withdraw his authorisation of the making of subscription deductions by giving notice in writing to the employer.

(8) Where the relevant increase is attributable to an increase in any percentage by reference to which the worker's subscription deductions are calculated, subsection (7) above shall have effect with the substitution, in paragraph (a), for the reference to the amount of the increase and the increased amount of the deductions of a reference to the percentage before and the percentage after the increase.

(9) A worker's authorisation of the making of subscription deductions from his wages shall not give rise to any obligation on the part of the employer to the worker to maintain or continue to maintain subscription deduction arrangements.

(10) Where arrangements, whether included in subscription deduction arrangements or not, exist between the parties to subscription deduction arrangements for the making from workers' wages of deductions representing payments to the union which are additional to subscription deductions, the amount of the deductions representing such additional payments shall be treated for the purposes of this section (where they would otherwise not be so treated) as part of the subscription deductions.

(11) In this section and section 68A 'employer', 'wages' and 'worker' have the same meanings as in Part I of the Wages Act 1986.

Notes
1.   Under the unamended TULR(C)A 1992, s. 68, union members already had the right to require their employers to stop deducting union subscriptions if they ceased to be members of the union. But in its Green Paper, *Industrial Relations in the 1990s*, the Government expressed concern that existing union members were having their union subscriptions deducted in pursuance of collective agreements made between employers and trade unions, without the express approval of individual members. This, it said, had led to cases of deductions being made from the pay of employees who might not want this arrangement, but whose only recourse would be to terminate their union membership. Similarly, the Government pointed to an instance where a strike 'levy' had been added to the subscriptions, with employers effectively collecting this 'strike pay' for the union. The amendments made by TURERA 1993 to TULR(C)A 1992, s. 62, were designed to rectify these perceived deficiencies.
2.   If a worker suffers a deduction in breach of the new s. 68, he or she may complain to an employment tribunal. If the complaint is upheld the tribunal will make a declaration and order the employer to refund the amount of the unauthorised deduction.

II   Freedom of Association

A: International Standards

International Labour Organisation Convention No. 87 (1948) Freedom of Association and Protection of the Right to Organise

Part 1   Freedom of Association

Article 1
Each Member of the International Labour Organisation for which this Convention is in force undertakes to give effect to the following provisions.

Article 2
Workers and employers, without distinction whatsoever, shall have the right to establish and, subject only to the rules of the organisation concerned, to join organisations of their own choosing without previous authorisation.

Article 3
1.   Workers' and employers' organisations shall have the right to draw up their constitutions and rules, to elect their representatives in full freedom, to organise their administration and activities and to formulate their programmes.
2.   The public authorities shall refrain from any interference which would restrict this right or impede the lawful exercise thereof.

Article 4
Workers' and employers' organisations shall not be liable to be dissolved or suspended by administrative authority. . . .

International Labour Organisation Convention (No. 98) (1949) Concerning the Application of the Principles of the Right to Organise and Bargain Collectively

Article 1

1. Workers shall enjoy adequate protection against acts of anti-union discrimination in respect of their employment.

2. Such protection shall apply more particularly in respect of acts calculated to:

(a) make the employment of a worker subject to a condition that he shall not join a union or shall relinquish trade union membership;

(b) cause the dismissal of or otherwise prejudice a worker by reason of union membership or because of participation in union activities outside working hours or, with the consent of the employer, within working hours.

Note

Given the free market philosophy of the previous Conservative Government, it is perhaps not surprising that the UK has been found to be in breach of International Labour Organisation (ILD) Conventions which this country had ratified. The banning of union membership at Government Communications Headquarters in 1984 was found by the ILO's Committee on Freedom of Association to be in breach of Convention No. 87 (set out above). The second of the three major complaints to the ILO related to the Teachers' Pay and Conditions Act 1987, which effectively abolished collective bargaining for teachers. This time the Government was held to be in breach of Convention No. 98 which provides, amongst other things, 'that machinery appropriate to national conditions shall be taken, where necessary, to encourage and promote the full development and utilisation of machinery for voluntary negotiation between employers or employer's organisations and workers' organisations with a view to the regulation of terms and conditions of employment by means of collective agreements'.

In 1988 a complaint to the ILO was made by the TUC and the NUM relating to various aspects of the Conservative Government's employment legislation. The Committee of Experts concluded that UK labour law had fallen below the acceptable standards set by Convention No. 87 on no fewer than six different grounds (ILO Committee of Experts, Observation 1989 on Convention No. 87). These were as follows:

(a) The GCHQ dismissals of those who refused to relinquish trade union membership. The Committee of Experts, like the Committee on Freedom of Association before them, found that the Government's action was in breach of Art. 2 of Convention No. 87.

(b) The Committee of Experts were of the view that the EA 1988, s. 3 (now TULR(C)A 1992, s. 64), was in conflict with Art. 3 of Convention No. 87. The particular concern revolved around the fact that s. 3 made it unlawful for trade unions to discipline members who refuse to participate in industrial action. In the view of the Committee, Art. 3 requires that 'union members should be permitted, when drawing up their constitutions and rules, to determine whether or not it should be possible to discipline members who refuse to participate in lawful strikes and other industrial action'. They concluded that s. 3 should be amended accordingly.

(c)   The Committee found that s. 8 of the EA 1988 (now TULR(C)A 1992, s. 15), which made it unlawful for the property of any trade union to be applied so as to indemnify any individual against any criminal sanction or contempt of court, was in breach of Art. 3 of Convention No. 87 and should be amended. The statutory provision was held to be an infringement of the right of unions to draw up their constitutions or rules and to organise their administration and activities free of interference by the public authorities, and a denial of the right to utilise their funds as they wish for normal and lawful trade union purposes.

(d)   The Committee expressed the view that the narrowing of the definition of a trade dispute in 1992 and restrictions on secondary action introduced in s. 17 of the EA 1980 unduly restricted workers' legitimate right to strike in protection of their own economic and social interests, as guaranteed by Arts 3, 8 and 10 of the Convention.

(e)   The Committee considered that it was inconsistent with the right to strike as guaranteed by Arts 3, 8 and 10 of the Convention for an employer to be permitted to refuse to reinstate some or all of its employees at the conclusion of a strike, lock-out or other industrial action without those employees having the right to challenge the fairness of that dismissal before an independent court or tribunal. This was exactly the freedom given to employers under EPCA 1978 (now TULR(C)A 1992, s. 238).

(f)   Lastly, the Committee expressed its concern at the volume and complexity of legislative change since 1980: 'Whilst it is true that most of the legislative measures under consideration are not incompatible with the requirements of the Convention, there is a point at which the cumulative effect of legislative changes which are themselves consistent with the principles of freedom of association may nevertheless by virtue of their complexity and extent, constitute an incursion upon the rights guaranteed by the Convention.' The complexity and uncertainty of the law may inhibit industrial action. Concern was also expressed that by giving so much emphasis to individual 'rights', the Government had demonstrated lesser concern for the 'rights' of individual trade unionists. The Committee considered that a more positive statement of these rights would be 'of advantage'.

The Conservative Government did nothing to meet any of the ILO's concerns. Indeed, as we have seen, since the ILO observation was published in 1989, the Conservative Administration introduced yet more legislation, which further weakened job protection for strikers and almost completely outlawed sympathy action. In terms of the complexity of the legislation, the Government made a very limited response by consolidating collective labour law and all the changes made during the 1980s and 1990s into one statute, the Trade Union and Labour Relations (Consolidation) Act 1992. Even then, the new provisions contained in TURERA 1993 further complicated matters.

The response (or lack of it) by the previus Government to the ILO's findings exposes the lack of effective sanctions to deal with those who violate ILO standards.

European Convention for the Protection of Human Rights and Fundamental Freedoms 1950

Article 11
1. Everyone has the right to freedom of peaceful assembly and to freedom of association with others, including the right to form and join trade unions for the protection of his interests.
2. No restrictions shall be placed on the exercise of these rights other than such as are prescribed by law and are necessary in a democratic society in the interests of national security or public safety, for the prevention of disorder or crime, for the protection of health or morals or for the protection of the rights and freedoms of others. This Article shall not prevent the imposition of lawful restrictions on the exercise of these rights by members of the armed forces, of the police or of the administration of the State.

Notes
1. Sheldon Leader has observed:

like most instruments guaranteeing basic rights, the Convention gives with one hand what it then qualifies with another. It provides certain potential rights to trade unionists, as well as to dissident members of trade unions under Article 11(1), while also allowing the state to limit their exercise under Article 11(2) if doing so can be shown, *inter alia*, to protect other competing rights and if it can also be shown that such a limitation is 'necessary in a democratic society'. ('The European Convention on Human Rights, the Employment Act 1988 and the Right to Refuse to Strike' (1991) 20 ILJ 39)

2. The application to the European Commission by the Council of Civil Service Unions, alleging a breach of Article 11 as a result of the ban on union membership at GCHQ, was rejected. The GCHQ workers were involved in the administration of the State and therefore excluded (App. No. 11603 *Council of Civil Service Unions v United Kingdom* 10 EHRR 269). An early action taken by the Labour Government elected in May 1997 was to restore the right of staff at GCHQ to belong to trade unions.
3. In *Young, James and Webster v UK* [1981] IRLR 408, three non-unionists were dismissed by British Rail in 1976 as a result of the signing of a union membership only (closed shop) agreement with the three rail unions. The European Court of Human Rights held by a majority of 18:3 that Article 11 was contravened by UK law which permitted the closed shop at that time, because employees could be dismissed if they refused to join. Those in the minority dissented on the basis of clear evidence from the *travaux preparatoires* that it was intended by those who drafted the Convention that the closed shop should be unaffected because of lack of consensus between States on the issue. The majority, while refusing to decide whether Article 11

guarantees an implied 'negative right' to dissociate as strong as the positive right set out in its text, held that on the facts there was a breach of the Article. This was because the applicants' choice as regards the unions which they could join of their own volition was restricted. Consequently, '[a]n individual does not enjoy the right to freedom of association if in reality the freedom of action or choice which remains available to him is either non-existent or so reduced as to be of no practical value'. However, six judges who concurred with the majority would have gone further and held that Article 11 contained a correlative 'negative right'. More recently, the European Court of Human Rights, claiming that the Convention is a 'living instrument which must be interpreted in the light of present-day conditions', has determined that Article 11 does include a negative right, at least to a limited extent (*Sigurjohnsson* v *Iceland* (1993) 16 EHRR 462).

4. In the course of an analysis of the implications for labour law of the incorporation of the European Convention of Human Rights into domestic law by the Human Rights Act 1998, Ewing observes:

Although perhaps the most obviously applicable provision for labour law, the contribution of article 11 to date has been disappointing, failing to deliver any meaningful protection for trade union activities, while being used as an instrument for undermining trade union security. (Ewing, K.D., 'The Human Rights Act and Labour Law', (1998) 27 ILJ 275, at p. 279)

B: Refusal of Employment on Grounds of Trade Union Membership

Trade Union and Labour Relations (Consolidation) Act 1992

137. Refusal of employment on grounds related to union membership
(1) It is unlawful to refuse a person employment—
    (a) because he is, or is not, a member of a trade union, or
    (b) because he is unwilling to accept a requirement—
      (i) to take steps to become or cease to be, or to remain or not to become, a member of a trade union, or
      (ii) to make payments or suffer deductions in the event of his not being a member of a trade union.
(2) A person who is thus unlawfully refused employment has a right of complaint to an industrial tribunal.
(3) Where an advertisement is published which indicates, or might reasonably be understood as indicating—
    (a) that employment to which the advertisement relates is open only to a person who is, or is not, a member of a trade union, or
    (b) that any such requirement as is mentioned in subsection (1)(b) will be imposed in relation to employment to which the advertisement relates,
a person who does not satisfy that condition or, as the case may be, is unwilling to accept that requirement, and who seeks and is refused employment to which the advertisement relates, shall be conclusively presumed to have been refused employment for that reason.
(4) Where there is an arrangement or practice under which employment is offered only to persons put forward or approved by a trade union, and the trade union puts forward or approves only persons who are members of the union, a person who is not

a member of the union and who is refused employment in pursuance of the arrangement or practice shall be taken to have been refused employment because he is not a member of the trade union.

(5)   A person shall be taken to be refused employment if he seeks employment of any description with a person and that person—

(a)   refuses or deliberately omits to entertain and process his application or enquiry, or

(b)   causes him to withdraw or cease to pursue his application or enquiry, or

(c)   refuses or deliberately omits to offer him employment of that description, or

(d)   makes him an offer of such employment the terms of which are such as no reasonable employer who wished to fill the post would offer and which is not accepted, or

(e)   makes him an offer of such employment but withdraws it or causes him not to accept it.

(6)   Where a person is offered employment on terms which include a requirement that he is, or is not, a member of a trade union, or any such requirement as is mentioned in subsection (1)(b), and he does not accept the offer because he does not satisfy or, as the case may be, is unwilling to accept that requirement, he shall be treated as having been refused employment for that reason.

(7)   Where a person may not be considered for appointment or election to an office in a trade union unless he is a member of the union, or of a particular branch or section of the union or of one of a number of particular branches or sections of the union, nothing in this section applies to anything done for the purpose of securing compliance with that condition although as holder of the office he would be employed by the union.

For this purpose an 'office' means any position—

(a)   by virtue of which the holder is an official of the union, or

(b)   to which Chapter IV of Part I applies (duty to hold elections).

(8)   The provisions of this section apply in relation to an employment agency acting, or purporting to act, on behalf of an employer as in relation to an employer.

Notes

1.   The EA 1988 finally removed all legal protection accorded to the operation of the post-entry closed shop. These provisions did not affect the pre-entry closed shop, i.e. a requirement to be a union member *before* being considered for the job. This gap was closed by the EA 1990, and the relevant provisions are now contained in ss. 137–143 of TULR(C)A 1992.

2.   Complaints of breach of these provisions may be made to an employment tribunal, which may make a declaration, order the employer to pay compensation (up to the limit of the compensatory award for unfair dimissal) and/or recommend that the respondent take remedial action.

C: Action Short of Dismissal on Grounds Related to Union Membership or Activities

146.   Action short of dismissal on grounds related to union membership or activities

(1)   An employee has the right not to *be subjected to any detriment as an individual by an act, or any deliberate failure to act, by his employer if the act or failure to act takes place* for the purpose of—

(a)   preventing or deterring him from being or seeking to become a member of an independent trade union, or penalising him for doing so,

(b)   preventing or deterring him from taking part in the activities of an independent trade union at an appropriate time, or penalising him for doing so, or

(c)   compelling him to be or become a member of any trade union or of a particular trade union or of one of a number of particular trade unions.

(2)   In subsection (1)(b) 'an appropriate time' means—

(a)   a time outside the employee's working hours, or

(b)   a time within his working hours at which, in accordance with arrangements agreed with or consent given by his employer, it is permissible for him to take part in the activities of a trade union;

and for this purpose 'working hours', in relation to an employee, means any time when, in accordance with his contract of employment, he is required to be at work.

(3)   An employee also has the right not to *be subjected to any detriment as an individual by any act, or any other deliberate failure to act, by his employer if the act or failure to act takes place* for the purpose of enforcing a requirement (whether or not imposed by his contract of employment or in writing) that, in the event of his not being a member of any trade union or of a particular trade union or of one of a number of particular trade unions, he must make one or more payments.

(4)   For the purposes of subsection (3) any deduction made by an employer from the remuneration payable to an employee in respect of his employment shall, if it is attributable to his not being a member of any trade union or of a particular trade union or of one of a number of particular trade unions, be treated *a detriment to which he has been subjected as an individual by an act of his employer taking place* for the purpose of enforcing a requirement of a kind mentioned in that subsection.

(5)   An employee may present a complaint to an employment tribunal on the ground that *he has been subjected to a detriment* by his employer in contravention of this section.

Note

The words in italics represent the amendments to s. 146 introduced by the Employment Relations Act 1999, sch. 2. Prior to this amendment, the law was held to protect employees against *positive* acts to prevent or deter trade union membership but not against *omissions* on the same grounds. So, for example, the giving of 'sweetener payments' to employees who agreed to give up collective bargaining did not constitute 'action' against those who refused through an omission to give them the same payments. This was one of the findings of the House of Lords in the next case.

Associated Newspapers Ltd v Wilson;
Associated British Ports v Palmer
[1995] IRLR 258
House of Lords

Mr Wilson was a journalist on the *Daily Mail*. He was a member of the NUJ and father of the chapel. In 1989, the employers gave notice that they were terminating the current collective agreement, withdrawing recognition from the union, and instituting a system of personal contracts. Only those journalists who entered into the new contracts were given a 4.5 per cent pay increase. Mr Wilson refused to sign and so did not get the increase. His complaint to the industrial tribunal was successful but the EAT upheld the employer's appeal. The EAT found that the employer's purpose in offering the financial incentive was not to deter employees from remaining members of the union but to end collective bargaining. In any event, that could not be said to deter employees from union membership or penalise them because of their membership since those who signed the new contracts were free to remain union members.

Mr Palmer was a manual worker employed by Associated British Ports. Such workers were members of the National Union of Rail, Maritime and Transport Workers which, at the relevant time, was recognised by the employers for collective bargaining purposes. In February 1991, all manual workers were sent a letter setting out the terms on which personal contracts would be offered, including substantially higher basic pay and increased overtime rates. In return, the employees were required to relinquish trade union representation by their union, and collectively agreed terms would no longer apply to them. Mr Palmer was one of a small percentage of workers who refused to accept personal contracts. The company continued to negotiate with the union in respect of this group of workers but the pay settlement agreed for them for 1991 was significantly lower than for those manual workers who had agreed personal contracts and agreed to relinquish union representation.

Mr Palmer and others complained that the employers had taken action against them short of dismissal on grounds of their union membership in contravention of what is now TULR(C)A 1992, s. 146. The employers argued that their purpose in offering preferential terms for those who entered into personal contracts was not to prevent or deter employees from continuing to be members but to achieve greater flexibility. They underlined that there was nothing in the personal contract preventing the employee from remaining a trade union member. The industrial tribunal upheld the employees' complaints. While accepting that the employers honestly believed that their purpose was to create greater flexibility, 'the reality is that their purpose was to penalise those who would not forego union representation by not conferring on them the benefits bestowed upon those who were prepared to do so with the objective of achieving greater flexibility'.

The EAT allowed the employers' appeal. According to Wood P, the industrial tribunal had confused their 'purpose' in conferring benefits on those who entered into personal contracts with the 'means' of achieving that purpose and the intermediate or collateral results which might be caused in achieving it. Flexibility was the purpose and ending union representation was the means of achieving it.

Both employee appeals were upheld by the Court of Appeal. According to the Court of Appeal, the right of an employee under EPCA 1978, s. 23(1)(a) (now TULR(C)A 1992, s. 146(1)(a)) was not only a right to union membership itself. Dillon LJ, giving the leading judgment, approved the decision in *Discount Confectionery Ltd* v *Armitage* [1990] IRLR I5, EAT, that there is no genuine distinction between membership of the union and making use of the essential services of the union.

On appeal to the House of Lords, a new point of law was taken which had not been available to the courts below, namely whether the word 'action' in s. 23(1)(a) (now TULR(C)A 1992, s. 146(1)(a)) might properly be construed as including an 'omission'. Section 153(1) of EPCA 1978 provided that: 'In this Act . . . except so far as the context otherwise requires – "act" and "action" each includes omission and references to doing an act or taking action shall be construed accordingly' (see now TULR(C)A 1992, s. 298).

On the authority of the decision in *National Coal Board* v *Ridgway* [1987] ICR 641, CA, the courts below were bound to accept that the application of s. 23(1)(a) had the effect that, if an employer conferred a benefit on employee A which he withheld from employee B, the omission to confer the benefit on B may amount to 'action (short of dismissal) taken against' B for one of the purposes prohibited by s. 23(1), irrespective of whether B had any reasonable expectation of receiving that benefit.

The House of Lords upheld the employers' appeals.

LORD BRIDGE OF HARWICH: . . . Section 153(1) of the Act of 1978 [now s. 298 of TULR(C)A 1992] provides:

> In this Act . . . except so far as the context otherwise requires – 'act' and 'action' each includes omission and references to doing an act or taking action shall be construed accordingly; . . .

The courts below were bound by authority to accept that the application of this definition to section 23(1) has the effect that, if an employer confers a benefit on employee A which he withholds from employee B, the omission to confer the benefit on B may, if the circumstances warrant such a finding, amount to 'action (short of dismissal) taken against' B for one of the purposes prohibited by section 23(1) irrespective of the question whether B had any reasonable expectation of receiving that benefit. This proposition is established by the decision of the Court of Appeal in *National Coal Board* v *Ridgway* [1987] ICR 641. In that case the board employed miners belonging to rival unions, the National Union of Mineworkers ('NUM') and the Union of Democratic Mineworkers ('UDM'), at the same colliery. The Board agreed to pay increased wages to members of the UDM but not to members of the NUM. On application by members of the NUM, the industrial tribunal held that withholding the increase from the applicants was an 'omission' amounting to 'action (short of dismissal) taken against' them for the purpose of penalising them for being members of the NUM and thus was a contravention of section 23(1)(a). This decision was upheld by the Court of Appeal by a majority (Nicholls and Bingham LJJ, May LJ dissenting). May LJ said, at p. 651:

> There must, at the least, have been some obligation to pay or some expectation of receipt to enable one to categorise the non-payment of UDM rates to these applicants as an 'omission' on the part of the board to make such payments.

The majority view was expressed by Nicholls LJ where he said, at p. 656:

> For an act to constitute 'action' within section 23 there does not need to be any reasonable expectation by the employee that the employer would not so behave.

This being so, I see no justification for adding this requirement as a gloss on the language of the statute in the case of an 'omission.' To be within section 23 the conduct complained of has to have been done 'for the purpose of.' If it is for one of the requisite purposes that an employer omits to do something *vis-à-vis* the complainant employee as an individual then, whatever is the nature of the omission, it is impermissible.

The novel question, raised for the first time before your Lordships, is whether the extended meanings of the word 'action' and of the phrase 'taking action' provided by section 153(1) are properly to be applied to section 23(1) or whether this is a case where 'the context otherwise requires.' The crucial phrase to be construed in section 23(1) is 'the right not to have action . . . taken against him.' If this phrase is to be construed as embodying the extended meaning, one must first expand the language so as to include the verb 'omit' or the noun 'omission' to see how it reads. The attempt to do this grammatically without substantially recasting the phrase and introducing additional words at once exposes the difficulty. If the concept of taking action against some person is to embrace the concept of omitting to act, the omission must be an omission to act in that person's favour. I cannot believe that any competent parliamentary draftsman, intending that an omission by an employer to take action in favour of an employee should have the same consequences as positive action taken against him, would fail to spell out the circumstances in which the obligation to take action in favour of the employee was to arise. Otherwise he creates an obvious ambiguity, as the difference of judicial opinion in *National Coal Board* v *Ridgway* well illustrates. To put it no higher, the question whether section 23(1) should be rewritten in some way so as to spell out expressly the meaning of 'action' as including omission, or whether the context requires that the definition be not applied, gives rise to a 'real and substantial difficulty' in the interpretation of the statute 'which classical methods of construction cannot resolve' and thus entitles us to go behind the consolidating Act of 1978 to derive whatever assistance we can in resolving the difficulty from the legislative history: see *Farrell* v *Alexander* [1977] AC 59, 73, per Lord Wilberforce.

The previous Acts consolidated by the Act of 1978 included the Trade Union and Labour Relations Act 1974 and the Employment Protection Act 1975. The definition of 'act' and 'action' now found in section 153(1) of the Act of 1978 was previously in section 30(1) of the Act of 1974 but did not appear anywhere in the Act of 1975. Section 23 of the Act of 1978, however, re-enacts section 53 of the Act of 1975. Thus, prior to the 1978 consolidation, there was no question of applying any definition giving an extended meaning to the word 'action' in the context in which we now have to construe it.

In *Beswick* v *Beswick* [1968] AC 58 one of the issues to be determined was whether the word 'property' in section 56(1) of the Law of Property Act 1925, which is a consolidation Act, should be read in the extended sense given to it by the definition section 205 which provides:

> (1)   In this Act unless the context otherwise requires, the following expressions have the meanings hereby assigned to them respectively, that is to say . . . (xx)   'Property' includes any thing in action, and any interest in real or personal property; . . .

Lord Reid reminded the House, at p. 73, that:

> it is the invariable practice of Parliament to require from those who have prepared a consolidation Bill an assurance that it will make no substantial change in the law

and to have that checked by a committee. On this assurance the Bill is then passed into law, no amendment being permissible.

Lord Reid pointed out that section 56(1) of the Act of 1925 was obviously intended to replace section 5 of the Real Property Act 1845 (8 & 9 Vict. c. 106) which applied only to real property and he concluded, at p. 77:

> By express provision in the definition section a definition contained in it is not to be applied to the word defined if in the particular case the context otherwise requires. If application of that definition would result in giving to section 56 a meaning going beyond that of the old section, then, in my opinion, the context does require that the definition of 'property' shall not be applied to that word in section 56. The context in which this section occurs is a consolidation Act. If the definition is not applied the section is a proper one to appear in such an Act because it can properly be regarded as not substantially altering the pre-existing law. But if the definition is applied the result is to make section 56 go far beyond the pre-existing law. Holding that the section has such an effect would involve holding that the invariable practice of Parliament has been departed from per incuriam so that something has got into this consolidation Act which neither the draftsman nor Parliament can have intended to be there.

By parity of reasoning, if the definition of 'action' in section 153(1) of the Act of 1978 is applied to section 23(1), not only do we encounter the grammatical difficulty to which I have already referred, but we must also conclude that a consolidation Act has substantially altered the pre-existing law in a way that neither the draftsman nor Parliament can have intended. It seems to me plain that both the draftsman of the consolidation Bill and the committee who approved it must have been satisfied that the definitions of 'act' and 'action' taken from the Act of 1974 were excluded by the context of the phrase 'the right not to have action taken against him' in section 53 of the Act of 1975.

Counsel for the applicants in the *Associated British Ports* v *Palmer* appeal sought to surmount this hurdle by submitting that the policy of the relevant employment legislation has consistently outlawed discrimination in any form against employees on account of their union membership and that the language of section 23(1), even if not extended by definition to apply to omissions, should nevertheless be construed liberally as having the same effect as that attributed to it by the majority in *National Coal Board* v *Ridgway* [1987] ICR 641. So far from supporting this submission it seems to me that a closer examination of the legislative history conclusively refutes it. The original enactment, which did indeed embody just such an anti-discrimination policy as that for which counsel now contends, was section 5 of the Industrial Relations Act 1971 which provided, so far as material:

> (1) Every worker shall, as between himself and his employer, have the following rights, that is to say, – (a) the right to be a member of such trade union as he may choose; (b) subject to sections 6 and 17 of this Act, the right, if he so desires, to be a member of no trade union or other organisation of workers or to refuse to be a member of any particular trade union or other organisation of workers; (c) where he is a member of a trade union, the right, at any appropriate time, to take part in the activities of the trade union (including any activities as, or with a view to becoming, an official of the trade union) and the right to seek or accept appointment or election, and (if appointed or elected) to hold office, as such an official.
>
> (2) It shall accordingly be an unfair industrial practice for any employer, or for any person acting on behalf of an employer—

(a) to prevent or deter a worker from exercising any of the rights conferred on him by subsection (1) of this section, or

(b) to dismiss, penalise or otherwise discriminate against a worker by reason of his exercising any such right, or . . .

(4) Where an employer offers a benefit of any kind to any workers as an inducement to refrain from exercising a right conferred on them by subsection (1) of this section, and the employer—

(a) confers that benefit on one or more of those workers who agree to refrain from exercising that right, and

(b) withholds it from one or more of them who do not agree to do so, the employer shall for the purposes of this section be regarded, in relation to any such worker as is mentioned in paragraph (b) of this subsection, as having thereby *discriminated against him* by reason of his exercising that right. (Emphasis added.)

A remedy for a person discriminated against in a way amounting to an 'unfair industrial practice' under this section was provided on complaint to an industrial tribunal under section 106.

It will be noted, first, that section 5 comprehensively outlaws discrimination against a worker on the ground of his membership of a union, non-membership of a union or participation in union activities, either by way of dismissal or by action short of dismissal; secondly, that discrimination which takes the form of an 'omission,' i.e. of withholding from employee A a benefit conferred on employee B, is the subject of the elaborate, explicit and unambiguous formula which the draftsman has used in subsection (4). The Act of 1974 repealed the Act of 1971 but re-enacted many of its provisions, subject to amendment, in Schedule 1. In so far as section 5 of the Act of 1971 was directed against a particular form of unfair dismissal, its effect was preserved by paragraph 6(4) of Schedule 1 to the Act of 1974 and this in turn was re-enacted by section 58(1) of the Act of 1978 (as amended by section 3 of the Employment Act 1982 and Schedule 4 to the Employment Act 1988), which provides:

The dismissal of an employee by an employer shall be regarded for the purposes of this Part as having been unfair if the reason for it (or, if more than one, the principal reason) was that the employee— (a) was, or proposed to become, a member of an independent trade union, or (b) had taken part, or proposed to take part, in the activities of an independent trade union at an appropriate time, or (c) was not a member of any trade union, or of a particular trade union, or of one of a number of particular trade unions, or had refused or proposed to refuse to become or remain a member.

But the Act of 1974 provided no remedy to employees who were discriminated against in ways falling short of dismissal which would previously have infringed the rights conferred on them by section 5 of the Act of 1971. The crucial question is whether, when section 53 of the Act of 1975 reintroduced a measure of protection against action, short of dismissal, of the kind previously prohibited by section 5 of the Act of 1971, the draftsman intended it to extend to cover discrimination of the kind against which section 5(4) of the Act of 1971 had been expressly directed. The language of this previous provision must clearly have been present to the draftsman's mind and, if his intention had been to achieve the same legislative consequence, it is, to my mind, inconceivable that he should not have used either the same language or language substantially to the like effect. In fact, as we have seen he did not even use the word 'discriminate' or adopt the extended definition of 'action' used in the Act of 1974. Finally, section 24(2) of the Act of 1978 provides a time-limit for presenting a complaint to an industrial tribunal under section 23 and the time is to run from 'the date on which there occurred the action complained of.' But nowhere in the Act do we find any provision analogous to those found, for example, in section 76(6) of the Sex Discrimination Act 1975 and section 68(7) of the Race Relations Act 1976, which make the kind of special provision which is needed, where there is a time-limit for complaining to an industrial tribunal, as to the date from which time is to run when the subject of the complaint is an omission.

The line of reasoning which I have followed in the three foregoing paragraphs was discussed in the course of argument and was criticised as unduly literalistic. It was even submitted that the Labour Government which introduced the Act of 1975 could not have intended to provide less effective protection for trade union members than the Act of 1971. A purposive construction to resolve ambiguities of statutory language is often appropriate and necessary. But this is the first time I have heard it suggested that the policy of an enactment to be presumed from the political complexion of the government which introduced it may prevail over the language of the statute. The courts' traditional approach to construction, giving primacy to the ordinary, grammatical meaning of statutory language, is reflected in the parliamentary draftsman's technique of using language with the utmost precision to express the legislative intent of his political masters and it remains the golden rule of construction that a statute means exactly what it says and does not mean what it does not say.

For all these reasons I find it quite impossible to hold that withholding from the applicants in these two appeals the benefits conferred on some of their fellow employees, whatever its purpose may have been, was capable of amounting to a contravention of section 23(1) of the Act of 1978. It follows that I would also overrule the decision of the Court of Appeal in *National Coal Board* v *Ridgway* [1987] ICR 641.

The membership issue

Much of the argument in the courts below and in both appeals before your Lordships was directed to questions relating to the relevant purpose of the employers. It was less than clear in either case what precisely the industrial tribunal had found the employers' purpose to be, leaving it open to argument whether the tribunal had intended to find as a fact in favour of the applicants that the employers' purpose was to deter them from being '[members] of an independent trade union' or to penalise them for being such members and, if so, whether there was evidence to support such a finding. Having reached a conclusion on the new point which is decisive of both appeals, I do not find it necessary to go into these questions in any detail, but I think it appropriate to add some observations relating to one aspect of the approach of the courts below to the question of purpose in respect of a complaint under section 23(1)(a) of the Act of 1978.

Sections 11 to 16 of the Act of 1975 embodied a complex statutory code, the details of which do not now matter, which enabled a trade union to obtain 'recognition' by an employer for the purpose of collective bargaining with him on behalf of its members. But these provisions were repealed by the Employment Act 1980 and since then an employer has been at liberty to decide for himself whether or not to enter into or to continue in force an agreement with a trade union providing for collective bargaining. Whatever the purpose of AN may have been, having given notice to terminate their house agreement with the NUJ, in offering an inducement to employees to sign individual contracts before the notice expired, the only witness called by the employers before the industrial tribunal gave evidence that the management had no intention of deterring their employees from continuing as members of the NUJ; the industrial tribunal's decision does not indicate that they rejected this evidence and in fact the majority of the employees have continued to be members of the NUJ ever since.

In *Associated British Ports v Palmer* it was plain that the employers were seeking by means of an attractive offer to induce their employees voluntarily to quit the union's collective bargaining umbrella and to deal in future directly with the employers over their terms and conditions of employment, but I can see nothing in the evidence recited in the industrial tribunal's decision to suggest that the employers were seeking to induce the employees to give up their union membership.

The industrial tribunal, in *Associated British Ports v Palmer*, in reaching the conclusion that the employers' relevant purpose contravened section 23(1)(a) of the Act of 1978, relied expressly on *Discount Tobacco & Confectionery Ltd v Armitage* (Note), *post*, p. 431 which, they said:

> · is authority for the proposition that there is no genuine distinction between membership of a union on the one hand and making use of the essential services which that union has to offer such as representation on the other.

This approach was analysed and criticised in the judgment of the Employment Appeal Tribunal [1993] ICR 101, 111E-112F. But in the Court on Appeal [1994] ICR 97 the *Armitage* case provided an important link in the chain of reasoning relied on to affirm the decisions of the industrial tribunals in both cases.

Mrs Armitage had been engaged on 1 February 1988 and was dismissed on 15 July 1988. She applied to an industrial tribunal complaining that she had been dismissed by reason of her union membership in contravention of section 58(1) of the Act of 1978. The evidence showed that she had written to her employers on 23 May asking for a statement of her terms of employment but had received no reply. She had then invoked the assistance of her union representative who wrote on her behalf on 23 June complaining of the failure to answer her letter and of various other matters in regard to her terms of employment. The employers gave evidence before the industrial tribunal that Mrs Armitage was dismissed on the ground of her unsuitability or incapacity, but the industrial tribunal disbelieved this evidence and found in terms that she had been dismissed 'by reasons of membership of an independent trade union:' see *post*, p. 432D. On the employers' appeal the Employment Appeal Tribunal concluded that there was material to support this finding. In reaching this conclusion the following passage appears in the judgment delivered by Knox J, *post*, p. 433:

> The evidence, therefore, in relation to union membership that was before the industrial tribunal, was that [Mrs Armitage] made use of her union membership by getting Mr McFadden to help in elucidating and attempting to negotiate the terms of her employment. He did not get very far in the latter because the dismissal supervened so soon but that, Mr West [the employers' representative] accepted, was what in fact she did and the question for this tribunal is whether on that evidence of union involvement, to use a neutral expression, it was possible for the industrial tribunal to reach the conclusion that her dismissal was for membership of the union. Mr West drew a distinction between membership of the union, on the one hand, and resorting to the services of a union officer to elucidate and negotiate the terms of employment, on the other, and he accepted that there was evidence of the latter but said that it did not or could not amount to evidence of the former, membership of the union. We find ourselves unconvinced of that distinction. In our judgment, the activities of a trade union officer in negotiating and elucidating terms of employment is, to use a prayer book expression, the outward and visible manifestation of trade union membership. It is an incident of union membership which is,

if not the primary one, at any rate, a very important one and we see no genuine distinction between membership of a union on the one hand and making use of the essential services of a union, on the other. Were it not so, the scope of section 58(1)(a) of the Act of 1978 would be reduced almost to vanishing point, since it would only be just the fact that a person was a member of a union, without regard to the consequences of that membership, that would be the subject matter of that statutory provision and, it seems to us, that to construe that paragraph so narrowly would really be to emasculate the provision altogether.

In the Court of Appeal [1994] ICR 97 Dillon LJ, with whose judgment Butler-Sloss and Farquharson LJJ agreed, relied on this passage in relation to both appeals. He said in addressing the appeal in *Associated Newspapers Ltd* v *Wilson*, at p. 110:

But the decision on 'purpose' is for the industrial tribunal and *Discount Tobacco & Confectionery Ltd* v *Armitage* [1990] IRLR 15 is authority that an industrial tribunal is entitled to conclude robustly that an employee who has been dismissed or penalised for invoking the assistance of his or her union in relation to his or her employment has been dismissed or penalised for being a member of the union.

I do not question the correctness of the Employment Appeal Tribunal's decision in the *Armitage* case. Once the industrial tribunal had rejected the employers' evidence as to their reason for Mrs Armitage's dismissal, it was an obvious inference that she had been dismissed because the employers resented the fact that she had invited the union to intervene on her behalf. In this narrow context the reasoning of Knox J may have been a legitimate means of refuting a particular argument advanced by the employers' representative. But if the passage cited is held to establish as a general proposition of law that, in the context of section 23(1)(a) and section 58(1)(a) of the Act of 1978, membership of a union is to be equated with using the 'essential' services of that union, at best it puts an unnecessary and imprecise gloss on the statutory language, at worst it is liable to distort the meaning of these provisions which protect union membership as such.

A union which has a collective bargaining agreement with employers is in a position to offer its members the service of negotiating their terms and conditions of employment. A union which has no such agreement with employers is unable to offer its members that service, but is able to offer them other important and valuable services. Thus, it cannot be said that the service of collective bargaining is an essential union service or that membership of a union unable to offer that service is valueless or insignificant. Accordingly, it seems to me that the reasoning of Knox J in the *Armitage* case could not properly be applied to the circumstances of the two cases with which we are concerned. Even if the construction put on section 23(1)(a) by the majority in *National Coal Board* v *Ridgway* [1987] ICR 641 were correct, I do not think that in either of these cases the withholding by the employers from employees who did not sign individual contracts of the benefits conferred on those who did was by itself capable of supporting a finding that the employers' purpose was to deter those in the latter group from being members of a union or to penalise them for being such members.

Notes

1. This decision has been represented as a major blow to freedom of association in the UK. The decision holds that withholding a benefit from an employee who refuses to sign a personal contract in place of collectively

agreed terms does not infringe the employee's right under what was EPCA 1978, s. 23(1)(a)(now TULR(C)A 1992, s. 146). On the same reasoning, discrimination against trade unionists in respect of opportunities for training and promotion, as well as in other aspects of terms and conditions of employment, appears permissible.

The Law Lords reached this conclusion by a 3:2 majority on the grounds that the employee's right 'not to have action . . . taken against him' cannot possibly be construed as including an 'omission to act'. This is despite the statutory definition of 'act' and 'action' which provides that 'in this Act . . . except so far as the context otherwise requires "act" and "action" each includes omission and references to doing an act and taking action shall be construed accordingly'. On the law as it stood following *Wilson*, it would be difficult to conceive of an action short of dismissal which would be covered by this interpretation of the statutory provision. The amendments to s. 146 by the Employment Relations Act 1999, sch. 2, remove this spurious distinction between 'acts' and 'omissions'.

2. All five Law Lords allowed the employers' appeals on another ground, the 'membership issue'. This concerned whether the reference in s. 146(1)(a) to preventing or deterring 'membership' of a trade union (or penalising for it) can be read as including an attack on the *functions or advantages* of trade union membership, in particular being covered by collective bargaining arrangements. In the instant case, the employer was not *overtly* trying to get employees to give up membership *per se*. Lord Lloyd focused on the 'purpose' to be established under s. 146. His Lordship took the view that s. 146 was not to be stretched to safeguard indirectly a union's interest in being recognised. At least three Law Lords came down against the general principle thought to have been established in *Discount Tobacco Ltd* v *Armitage* [1990] IRLR 15, EAT, that there is no distinction between union membership and making use of union services.

The statutory language of s. 146(1)(a) is very similar to that relating to dismissal for union membership grounds. The result of the decision of the House of Lords, therefore, will make it easier for an employer to discriminate generally against trade union activists, so long as union membership is not prohibited.

As the editors of *Harvey* have observed:

On a broader political canvas it could be argued that the decisions in these appeals show fascinating parallels with certain modern, post-eighties views as to the proper functions and place of trade unions (certainly in Tory thinking and possibly now in that of reformist, all-singing-all-dancing Labour), namely that they should be more akin to service industries for their members (from legal advice and representation to credit cards) and are now not inextricably tied to their traditional collective bargaining context – 'Unions may flourish even though they are not recognised for collective bargaining' (per Lord Lloyd). (*Harvey on Industrial Relations and Employment Law*, Bulletin No. 201, April 1995)

3.   While the reasoning behind the decision provides yet another example of the judiciary's lack of empathy with collective action, its practical impact – at

least in terms of TULR(C)A 1992, s. 146(1)(a) and the use of 'sweeteners' to persuade workers to move to personal contracts in place of collectively agreed terms – is limited as a result of a statutory amendment. Subsequent to the Court of Appeal's decision in *Wilson* and *Palmer*, the Government controversially sought to overturn its effects by introducing an amendment to what was then the Trade Union Reform and Employment Rights Bill when it was in the House of Lords (*Hansard* (HL) 24/5/93, cols 12–67). The amendment is contained in TULR(C)A 1992, s. 148(3) and is set out below.
4.   For an analysis of some of the legal issues in this area, see Auerbach, S., *Derecognition and Personal Contracts: Fighting Tactics and the Law* (London: Institute of Employment Rights, 1993).

Trade Union and Labour Relations (Consolidation) Act 1992

148. Consideration of complaint
    (3)   In determining what was the purpose for which [the employer acted or failed to act] in a case where—
    (a)   there is evidence that the employer's purpose was to further a change in his relationship with all or any class of his employees, and
    (b)   there is also evidence that his purpose was one falling within section 146,
the tribunal shall regard the purpose mentioned in paragraph (a) (and not the purpose mentioned in paragraph (b)) as the purpose for which the employer [acted or failed to act, unless it considers that no reasonable employer would act or fail to act in the way concerned] having regard to the purpose mentioned in paragraph (a).

Notes
1.   The words in square brackets represent the consequential amendments following the amendment of s. 146 by the 1999 Act. But that is as far as the amendments go and it is still lawful for employers to offer inducements to employees to sign personal contracts if the purpose is to dismantle collective bargaining arrangements. This is further underlined by the Employment Relations Act 1999, s. 17, which gives power to the Secretary of State to make regulations (subject to an affirmative procedure) to protect workers from detriment and dismissal where they refuse to enter into an individual contract which would replace a collective agreement. However, this power is con-strained by s. 17(4), which stems from the Conservative 'Miller' amendment proposed in the House of Lords. This states:

(4)   The payment of higher wages or higher rates of pay or overtime or the payment of any signing on or other bonuses or the provision of other benefits having a monetary value to other workers employed by the same employer shall not constitute a detriment to any worker not receiving the same or similar payments or benefits within the meaning of subsection (1)(a) of this section so long as—
    (a)   there is no inhibition in the contract of employment of the worker receiving the same from being a member of a trade union, and
    (b)   the said payments of higher wages or rates of pay or overtime or bonuses or the provision of other benefits are in accordance with the terms of a contract of employment and reasonably relate to the services provided by the worker under that contract.

This would seem to make it absolutely clear that the payment of 'sweeteners' to workers in order to induce them to enter into individual contracts is still lawful.
2. An employee who suffers victimisation on trade union grounds may complain to an employment tribunal within three months of the act of victimisation. Where the alleged victimisation is part of a series of similar actions, the complaint must be presented within three months of the last of those actions (TULR(C)A 1992, s. 147)(2) as amended). the following convoluted wording now determines the time limits in dealing with an omission to act (new s. 147(3), inserted by Employment Relations Act 1999, sch. 2):

. . . in the absence of evidence establishing the contrary an employer shall be taken to decide on a failure to act—
    (a)   when he does an act inconsistent with doing the failed act, or
    (b)   if he has done no such inconsistent act, when the period expires within which he might reasonably have been expected to do the failed act if it was to be done.

If the complaint is well-founded, the tribunal must make a declaration to that effect, and it may make an award of compensation which 'shall be such as the tribunal considers just and equitable in all the circumstances having regard to the infringement complained of and to any loss sustained by the complainant which is attributable to the action which infringed his right' (s. 149(1), (2)).
3. In *Brassington* v *Cauldon Wholesale* [1978] IRLR 479, the EAT stated that 'compensation for the employee, not a fine on the employer, however tactfully wrapped up, is the basis for the award'. The complainants were awarded compensation to cover their expenses in going to tribunal and non-pecuniary losses such as 'the stress engendered by such a situation' and the frustration of a 'deep and sincere wish to join a union'. The availability of compensation for non-pecuniary loss was doubted by May LJ in *Ridgway and Fairbrother* v *National Coal Board* [1987] IRLR 80, though Nicholls and Bingham LJJ expressed no view on the matter.
4. The tribunal may reduce the amount of any compensatory award if the action complained of was to any extent caused or contributed to by the complainant (TULR(C)A 1992, s. 149(6)). In determining compensation, no account is to be taken of any pressure exercised on the employer by the threat or use of industrial action. But the employer or employee may apply to have the union or other third party joined as a party to the proceedings. The compensation award may be made wholly or partly against the party so joined (TULR(C)A 1992, s. 150).

D: Dismissal on Grounds Related to Union Membership or Activities

Trade Union and Labour Relations (Consolidation) Act 1992

152. Dismissal on grounds related to union membership or activities
    (1)   For purposes of Part V of the Employment Protection (Consolidation) Act 1978 (unfair dismissal) the dismissal of an employee shall be regarded as unfair if the reason for it (or, if more than one, the principal reason) was that the employee—

(a)   was, or proposed to become, a member of an independent trade union, or

(b)   had taken part, or proposed to take part, in the activities of an independent trade union at an appropriate time, or

(c)   was not a member of any trade union, or of a particular trade union, or of one of a number of particular trade unions, or had refused, or proposed to refuse, to become or remain a member.

(2)   In subsection (1)(b) 'an appropriate time' means—

(a)   a time outside the employee's working hours, or

(b)   a time within his working hours at which, in accordance with arrangements agreed with or consent given by his employer, it is permissible for him to take part in the activities of a trade union; and for this purpose 'working hours', in relation to an employee, means any time when, in accordance with his contract of employment, he is required to be at work.

(3)   Where the reason, or one of the reasons, for the dismissal was—

(a)   the employee's refusal, or proposed refusal, to comply with a requirement (whether or not imposed by his contract of employment or in writing) that, in the event of his not being a member of any trade union, or of a particular trade union, or of one of a number of particular trade unions, he must make one or more payments, or

(b)   his objection, or proposed objection, (however expressed) to the operation of a provision (whether or not forming part of his contract of employment or in writing) under which, in the event mentioned in paragraph (a), his employer is entitled to deduct one or more sums from the remuneration payable to him in respect of his employment, the reason shall be treated as falling within subsection (1)(c).

(4)   References in this section to being, becoming or ceasing to remain a member of a trade union include references to being, becoming or ceasing to remain a member of a particular branch or section of that union or of one of a number of particular branches or sections of that trade union; and references to taking part in the activities of a trade union shall be similarly construed.

Notes

1.   The following two cases provide contrasting examples of judicial approaches to trade union membership discrimination. In *Therm-a-Stor Ltd* v *Atkins* [1983] IRLR 78, CA, a large majority of the shopfloor workforce applied to join the union. The company's response to the union's claim for recognition was to dismiss 20 employees. The selection was left to chargehands and, although there was no evidence that the selections were made on the basis of union membership, all those selected for dismissal were union members. The Court of Appeal held that the dismissals fell outside the section because they were in response to the union's claim for recognition and *not* because of any of the dismissed individuals' union membership or activities. For a more liberal approach see *Discount Tobacco & Confectionary Ltd* v *Armitage* [1990] IRLR 15 discussed in the extract from Lord Bridge's judgment in *Associated British Ports* v *Palmer* (above). The *Armitage* case held that the protection from dismissal in TULR(C)A 1992, s. 152(1)(a) on the grounds of union membership should extend beyond the mere status of union membership and apply to dismissal for making use of the essential services of the union (in that case, seeking union assistance in obtaining a s. 1 statement from the employer). As has been seen, the majority of the House of Lords in *Palmer* suggested that no general principle could be drawn from the case, although it was accepted that it was correct on its own facts. As a result a number

of commentators have suggested that *Armitage* would not be followed in future. However, more recently, the *Armitage* approach has been supported by the EAT (see *Speciality Care plc* v *Pachela* [1996] IRLR 248, EAT).

2. Most cases arising under s. 152 involve the question of whether the dismissal was for taking part in the activities of a trade union at an appropriate time. The scope of the trade union activities protected by s. 152(1)(b) has been viewed restrictively by the courts. It has been held that the personal activities of a union member are not the activities of a trade union within the meaning of s. 152. For example, in *Chant* v *Aquaboats Ltd* [1978] 1 All ER 102, a union member who organised a petition complaining about safety standards was held not to be engaged in trade union activity, notwithstanding the fact that a union official had vetted the petition before it was presented. The EAT stated that 'The mere fact that one or two of the employees making representations happen to be trade unionists, and the mere fact that the spokesman of the men happens to be a trade unionist does not make such representations a trade union activity'. (Note that Mr Chant would now be able to seek protection under ERA 1996, s. 44 which makes it unlawful to victimise employees for raising concerns about safety.)

The courts and tribunals have tended to require that the activity is connected with the institutional aspects of trade unions, such as taking part in trade union meetings, distributing union material, recruiting a fellow employee or consulting a trade union official.

3. For trade union activity to be protected it must take place at 'an appropriate time'. This is defined as not only occasions 'outside the employee's working hours' but also time 'within working hours at which, in accordance with arrangements agreed with, or consent given by his employer, it is permissible for him to take part in those activities' (TULR(C)A 1992, s. 152(2)). Working hours means hours when, in accordance with his contract, the employee is required to be at work. It has been held that 'periods when in accordance his contract the worker is on his employer's premises but not actually working' are outside 'working hours' (per Lord Reid in *Post Office* v *UPW* [1974] IRLR 22). Consequently, the view has been taken that a paid meal break is not a time within working hours so as to require the employer's consent to take part in trade union activities (*Zucker* v *Astrid Jewels Ltd* [1978] IRLR 385).

Where the activities take place within working hours, there must be consent by the employer. Consent may be express or implied. In *Zucker*, for example, the employee alleged that he had been dismissed for discussing trade union matters while working on a machine, and encouraging union recruitment during meal breaks. The EAT held that such conduct could constitute trade union activities at an appropriate time, for the employees were permitted to converse during working hours, and consequently they had an implied right to discuss trade union matters. However, in *Marley Tile Co. Ltd* v *Shaw* [1980] IRLR 25, the Court of Appeal was not prepared to imply the employer's consent from his silence in response to the announcement of an unaccredited shop steward that he would be calling a meeting during working hours.

In *Bass Taverns* v *Burgess* [1995] IRLR 596, CA, a shop steward was demoted and constructively dismissed for criticising the employers during a presentation on the union at an induction course for new managers. An industrial tribunal found that because the employee had abused the privilege given to him by the employers, the dismissal could not be on the grounds of trade union activities. This finding was overruled by the Court of Appeal who rejected the view that there was an implied limitation on the employers' consent to the meeting being used as a recruitment forum such that the recruiter would say nothing to criticise or undermine the company. There was, therefore, no 'abuse of privilege'. According to Balcombe LJ, 'a consent to recruit must include a consent to underline the services which the union can provide. That may reasonably involve a submission to prospective members that in some respects the union will provide a service which the company does not'. One possible limitation expressed in the case is that the section might cease to apply if the employee conducting the recruitment indulged in malicious, untruthful or irrelevant invective.

4. In *Drew* v *St Edmundsbury BC* [1980] IRLR 88, it was held that taking part in industrial action does not constitute taking part in the activities of an independent trade union within the meaning of s. 152 and, as we shall see in Chapter 9, a dismissal for that reason may not be challenged at all if it comes within TULR(C)A 1992, s. 238.

5. In *Birmingham City District Council* v *Beyer* [1977] IRLR 211, the EAT took the view that s. 152 applies only to trade union activities which take place after employment with a particular employer has commenced and 'could not conceivably refer to activities before the employment began'. Subsequently, the EA 1990 made it unlawful to refuse a person employment because he or she is, or is not, a member of a trade union (see now TULR(C)A 1992, s. 137). However, it may be argued that the provision will still not prevent an employer from excluding a candidate on the grounds of past 'activities', or because he or she is regarded as a 'troublemaker'. This sort of victimisation may now be caught by s. 152 as a result of the decision of the Court of Appeal in the next case.

Fitzpatrick v *British Railways Board*
[1991] IRLR 376
Court of Appeal

When Ms Fitzpatrick obtained a job with British Railways Board, she deliberately failed to provide full details of her previous employment or to disclose her former participation in trade union activities. She joined the National Union of Railwaymen and engaged in some recruiting activity, attended some meetings and intended seeking an official position in the union.

Subsequently, her employers came across a newspaper article in which Ms Fitzpatrick was referred to as a union activist with links with ultra-left groups. After some investigation, they decided to dismiss her.

Ms Fitzpatrick claimed that she had been dismissed on grounds of trade union activities and that her dismissal was therefore unfair under what is now TULR(C)A 1992, s. 152(1)(b). The employers argued that she was dismissed because she had obtained the job by deceit. An industrial tribunal found that the reason for Ms Fitzpatrick's dismissal was her previous union activities and her reputation as a militant. By a majority, however, the tribunal held that she was not dismissed for trade union activities within the meaning of s. 152(1)(b). Following the decision in *Birmingham District Council* v *Beyer* [1977] IRLR 211, the EAT concluded that, as far as proposed trade union activities are concerned, in order to fall within s. 152(1)(b) there must be 'some cogent and identifiable act and not some possible trouble in the future'.

The Court of Appeal allowed Ms Fitzpatrick's appeal and substituted a finding that she had been unfairly dismissed.

WOOLF LJ: In this case British Rail purported to dismiss the appellant on the basis of her deceit in concealing her previous trade union activities. If the Industrial Tribunal had accepted that it was her deceit which caused them to dismiss her, or if that was the primary reason for her dismissal, then the situation is that she would not have been able to bring herself within the language of s. 152(1)(b). However, as already indicated, all three members of the Industrial Tribunal accepted that it was not the deceit which was the operative cause for her dismissal.

What the majority concluded was, and I read here from paragraph 27 of the decision:

It was the [appellant's] previous trade union (and possibly her political) activities, which gave her a reputation for being a disruptive force; and that was the prime reason for her dismissal.

That paragraph, in my judgment, discloses a failure on the part of the Industrial Tribunal to answer the critical question. The fact that the appellant had a reputation with regard to trade union activities was, as Miss Booth in her argument made clear, only relevant to British Rail in so far as it would have an effect on what she did while she was employed by them. Miss Booth submits, clearly with justification, that British Rail did not suggest and would not in fact seek to dismiss the appellant merely in order to punish her for her previous trade union activities. Miss Booth submits that what the Industrial Tribunal failed to do was to identify why it was that because of her previous trade union, and possibly political, activities British Rail decided to dismiss the appellant. If the Tribunal had asked the question the answer would have been obvious. It would be that they would fear a repetition of the same conduct while employed by them.

The reason that the majority of the Industrial Tribunal did not address the critical question is probably because of their understanding of the *Beyer* decision. They say, having examined that decision, that so far as proposed activities are concerned it must, and I quote: 'involve some cogent and identifiable act and not some possible trouble in the future'. In other words the Industrial Tribunal are saying that in order to comply with the provisions of s. 152(1)(b) there must have been some activity on the part of the employee to which they took exception, which was not a mere possibility but something which was sufficiently precise to be identifiable in her present employment.

In my judgment, to adopt this approach is to read into the language of s. 152(1)(b) a restriction which Parliament has not identified. To limit the language, in the way which the Industrial Tribunal did, would prevent the actual reason for the dismissal in a case such as this from being considered by the Industrial Tribunal. As long as the reason which motivated the employer falls within the words 'activities that the employee . . . proposed to take part in', there is no reason to limit the language. The purpose of the subsection, in so far as (b) is concerned, is to protect those who engage in trade union activities and I can see no reason why that should not apply irrespective of whether the precise activities can be identified.

If an employer, having learnt of an employee's previous trade union activities, decides that he wishes to dismiss that employee, that is likely to be a situation where almost inevitably the employer is dismissing the employee because he feels that the employee will indulge in industrial activities of a trade union nature in his current employment. There is no reason for a rational and reasonable employer to object to the previous activities of an employee except in so far as they will impinge upon the employee's current employment.

Question
If British Rail had discovered Ms Fitzpatrick's union activism before she was appointed and refused to employ her, would she have had a remedy?

Note
The answer to the question posed above is that an employee who is refused employment on the grounds of his or her trade union activities does not have a remedy. It was hoped that the Government would remedy this omission. In *Fairness at Work*, the Government had proposed to close this loophole and also to prohibit the blacklisting of trade unionists (para. 4.25). The Employment Relations Act 1999 fails to close the loophole, but does offer the prospect of making trade unionist blacklisting unlawful:

3. Blacklists
  (1)   The Secretary of State may make regulations prohibiting the compilation of lists which—
      (a)   contain details of members of trade unions or persons who have taken part in the activities of trade unions, and
      (b)   are compiled with a view to being used by employers or employment agencies for the purposes of discrimination in relation to recruitment or in relation to the treatment of workers.
  (2)   The Secretary of State may make regulations prohibiting—
      (a)   the use of lists to which subsection (1) applies;
      (b)   the sale or supply of lists to which subsection (1) applies.

The Government intends to consult on draft regulations before they are made.

   E: Selection for Redundancy on Grounds Related to Union Membership or Activities

Trade Union and Labour Relations (Consolidation) Act 1992

153.   Selection for redundancy on grounds related to union membership or activities
Where the reason or principal reason for the dismissal of an employee was that he was redundant, but it is shown—

(a)   that the circumstances constituting the redundancy applied equally to one or more other employees in the same undertaking who held positions similar to that held by him and who have not been dismissed by the employer, and

(b)   that the reason (or, if more than one, the principal reason) why he was selected for dismissal was one of those specified in section 152(1), the dismissal shall be regarded as unfair for the purposes of Part V of the Employment Protection (Consolidation) Act 1978 (unfair dismissal).

Notes

1.   Under TURERA 1993, complaints of unfair redundancy selection on trade union grounds are no longer subject to a qualifying period of service (see Sch. 7, para. 1, which amends TULR(C)A 1992, s. 154). This removes a clear inconsistency in the law, where protection against trade union-related dismissals under s. 152(1) applies to all employees but protection against selection for redundancy for trade union-related reasons previously was limited to those with two years' service.

2.   By virtue of amendments introduced by the EA 1982, the amount of compensation to be awarded to employees who are unfairly dismissed (or selected for redundancy) on grounds of trade union membership and activities or non-membership was much higher than for other types of dismissal because a 'special award' was made in addition to the basic and compensatory elements. Also, unlike other cases, where the dismissal is union-related there is a minimum basic award (£2,900 in 1999/2000).

With the raising of the compensation award limit to £50,000, there is less need for the 'special award' in trade union cases. Consequently, s. 33 of the Employment Relations Act 1999 simplifies arrangements by replacing special awards with additional awards.

3.   Either the employer or the applicant may request that a trade union or other party be joined in the proceedings where they have exerted or threatened to exert industrial pressure on the employer to dismiss. If the tribunal finds the complaint of third party pressure well founded, the tribunal has the power to order the trade union or other party to pay any or all of the compensation awarded.

4.   An employee who alleges that he or she has been dismissed for union/ non-union membership or trade union activities can apply to the tribunal for an order for interim relief (TULR(C)A 1992, s. 161).

The order for interim relief is intended to preserve the *status quo* until full hearing of cases which by their very nature can be extremely damaging to the industrial relations in any organisation. Where relief is granted it will result in either the reinstatement/re-engagement of the employee pending full hearing or, in some cases, a suspension of the employee on continued terms and conditions (TULR(C)A 1992, ss. 161–166).

Recently, these provisions have been extended to dismissals of health and safety representatives, employee trustees of occupational pension schemes, and employee representatives for the purposes of consultation over redundancies and business transfers (see ERA 1996, s. 128).

III   Trade Unions and Collective Bargaining

Trade Union and Labour Relations (Consolidation) Act 1992

179.   Collective agreements and collective bargaining

(1)   In this Act 'collective agreement' means any agreement or arrangement made by or on behalf of one or more trade unions and one or more employers or employers' associations and relating to one or more of the matters specified below; and 'collective bargaining' means negotiations relating to or connected with one or more of those matters.

(2)   The matters referred to above are—

(a)   terms and conditions of employment, or the physical conditions in which any workers are required to work;

(b)   engagement or non-engagement, or termination or suspension of employment or the duties of employment, of one or more workers;

(c)   allocation of work or the duties of employment between workers or groups of workers;

(d)   matters of discipline;

(e)   a worker's membership or non-membership of a trade union;

(f)   facilities for officials of trade unions; and

(g)   machinery for negotiation or consultation, and other procedures, relating to any of the above matters, including the recognition by employers or employers' associations of the right of a trade union to represent workers in such negotiation or consultation or in the carrying out of such procedures.

(3)   In this Act 'recognition', in relation to a trade union, means the recognition of the union by an employer, or two or more associated employers, to any extent, for the purpose of collective bargaining; and 'recognised' and other related expressions shall be construed accordingly.

Note

Recognition of a trade union means that the employer has given the trade union negotiating rights over certain issues. In other words, in these areas changes are made as a result of bilateral agreement rather than unilateral decision-making on the part of the employer. Between 1980 and 1999 there was no legal right to recognition. The Industrial Relations Act 1971 provided such a right but the TUC refused to take advantage of the provisions as part of a campaign of general opposition to the legislation. The Employment Protection Act 1975 also allowed for a statutory recognition procedure, but the machinery was so complex that employers were able to challenge ACAS determinations via a series of legal loopholes (see *Grunwick Processing Laboratories* v *Advisory, Conciliation and Arbitration Service* [1978] AC 655). This provided the new Conservative Government with the rationale to abandon the statutory right altogether by the Employment Act 1980.

A: The New Statutory Recognition Procedure

There has been a substantial decline in union recognition in Britain – from 66 per cent of workplaces of 25 or more employees in 1984, to 53 per cent of workplaces in 1990, and to 45 per cent in 1997/98. In that last year, of the

10.1 million employees in workplaces with union recognition, 8.1 million were covered by collective bargaining. This represents a mere 36 per cent of all employees compared to the peak coverage of 85 per cent recorded in 1979 (see Cully, M., *et al.* (1998), *The 1988 Workplace Employee Relations Survey: First Findings*, London: Department of Trade and Industry).

The most significant collective labour law reform proposed in the *Fairness at Work* White Paper was the reintroduction of a legally backed procedure by which trade unions can seek recognition by employers which refuse to agree to collective bargaining on a voluntary basis. The Employment Relations Act 1999 contains provisions that substantially implement the scheme detailed in the White Paper.

(i) Request for Recognition
Section 1 of the 1999 Act inserts a new Sch. A1 into TULR(C)A 1992. Paragraph 1 provides that a trade union (or trade unions) may make a request for recognition in accordance with Part I of the Schedule. Paragraph 2 sets out the definitions, in particular that of a 'bargaining unit':

Trade Union and Labour Relations (Consolidation) Act 1992

SCHEDULE A1
COLLECTIVE BARGAINING: RECOGNITION
PART I
RECOGNITION

2.—(2)   References to the bargaining unit are to the group of workers concerned (or the groups taken together).

(3)   References to the proposed bargaining unit are to the bargaining unit proposed in the request for recognition.

Paragraph 3 offers a narrower definition of 'collective bargaining' than that employed in other parts of the 1992 Act:

3.—(1)   This paragraph applies for the purpose of this part of this Schedule.

(2)   The meaning of collective bargaining given by section 178(1) shall not apply.

(3)   References to collective bargaining are to negotiations relating to pay, hours and holidays; but this has effect subject to sub-paragraph (4).

(4)   If the parties agree matters as the subject of collective bargaining, references to collective bargaining are to negotiations relating to the agreed matters; and this is the case whether the agreement is made before or after the time when the CAC issues a declaration, or the parties agree, that the union is (or unions are) entitled to conduct collective bargaining on behalf of the bargaining unit.

. . .

Request for recognition

4.—(1)   The union or unions seeking recognition must make a request of recognition to the employer.

. . .

5. The request is not valid unless it is received by the employer.

6. The request is not valid unless the union (or each of the unions) has a certificate under section 6 that it is independent.

7.—(1) The request is not valid unless the employer, taken with any associated employer or employers, employs—

(a) at least 21 workers on the day the employer receives the request, or

(b) an average of at least 21 workers in the 13 weeks ending with that day.

. . .

Note

Associated employers are counted as long as they are registered in the UK. It is worth emphasising that the term 'worker' is used rather than the narrower term, 'employee'. Any request for recognition will also be invalid unless it is in writing, identifies the union or unions and the bargaining unit, and states that it is made under the schedule (Sch. A1, para. 8).

After an application has been received, the employer has only 10 working days ('the first period') in which to respond. There are four possible responses:

(a) *The employer agrees the bargaining unit and the union is recognised* (Sch. A1, para. 10(1)). The effect is that recognition is voluntary and not legally enforceable.

(b) *The employer does not accept the request but is willing to negotiate* (Sch. A1, para. 10(2)). There is then a period of negotiations lasting up to 20 days, starting with the day after that on which the first period ends ('the second period'). If the parties agree, this period may be extended. The employer and the union(s) may request ACAS to assist in conducting the negotiations (Sch. A1, para. 10(5)).

(c) *The employer rejects the application or fails to respond.* The union may apply to the Central Arbitration Committee ('CAC') to decide one or more of the following:

(i)   whether the proposed bargaining unit is appropriate or some other bargaining unit is appropriate;

(ii)   whether the union has (or unions have) the support of a majority of the workers constituting the appropriate bargaining unit (Sch. A1, para. 11(2)).

(d) *The employer negotiates in the second period but no agreement is reached.* The union(s) may apply to the CAC to determine the appropriateness of the proposed bargaining unit and whether the union has (or unions have) the support of the majority of the workers constituting the proposed bargaining unit. However, the CAC will not consider an application if the union has rejected or failed to respond to an employer's proposal to involve ACAS in the negotiations within 10 working days of the employer agreeing to negotiate (Sch. A1, para. 12).

If a union applies to the CAC under paras 11 or 12, before the application may proceed the CAC must be satisfied that it is valid and admissible.

Paragraph 14 applies if two or more applications are received by the CAC and the bargaining units proposed or agreed in respect of the applications overlap, i.e. at least one worker is a member of all the bargaining units. In this situation, each application is subject to the '10 per cent' test to determine whether at least 10 per cent of the bargaining unit are union members. If only one application passes the test, it may proceed; if both pass or neither passes, neither application will be successful.

Paragraph 15 requires any application under paras 11 or 12 to be valid in terms of paras 5–9 (see above) and admissible in terms of paras 33–42. The CAC has 10 working days (or longer, if it notifies the union and the employer of its reason for extending the period) in which to decide whether the application is valid and admissible. In order to be admissible, an application must:

(a) be made in such form and be supported by such documents as the CAC specifies (Sch. A1, para. 33);

(b) be copied to the employer, together with any supporting documents (Sch. A1, para. 34);

(c) not cover any workers in respect of whom the union is already recognised, unless that union has no certificate of independence, was previously recognised in respect of the same (or substantially the same) bargaining unit, and ceased to be recognised within three years prior to the application (Sch. A1, para. 35);

(d) satisfy the CAC that at least 10 per cent of the proposed bargaining unit are members of the union and 'a majority of the workers constituting the bargaining unit would be likely to favour recognition of the union (or unions) as entitled to conduct collective bargaining on behalf of the bargaining unit' (Sch. A1, para. 36);

(e) (in the case of an application made by more than one union) show that the unions 'will co-operate with each other in a manner likely to maintain stable and effective collective bargaining' and, if the employer wishes, conduct single-table collective bargaining (Sch. A1, para. 37);

(f) not cover any workers in respect of whom the CAC has already an application, i.e. the bargaining unit must not overlap with another unit in respect of which the CAC has accepted an application (Sch. A1, para.);

(g) not be substantially the same as an application which the CAC accepted within the previous three years (Sch. A1, para. 39); and

(h) not be made within three years of a declaration by the CAC that the union was (or the same group of unions were) not entitled to be recognised in respect of the same (or substantially the same) bargaining unit as in the current application (Sch. A1, para. 40).

(ii)   Appropriate Bargaining Unit

Trade Union and Labour Relations (Consolidation) Act 1992

SCHEDULE A1
COLLECTIVE BARGAINING: RECOGNITION
PART I
RECOGNITION

Appropriate bargaining unit

18.—(1)   If the CAC accepts an application under paragraph 11(2) or 12(2) it must try to help the parties to reach within the appropriate period an agreement as to what the appropriate bargaining unit is.
. . .

Note
The 'appropriate period' is 20 working days starting with the day after that on which the CAC gives notice of acceptance of the application, or such longer period as the CAC may specify with reason (Sch. A1, para. 18(2)). If negotiations with the CAC's assistance fail, the CAC must decide the appropriate bargaining unit within 10 working days of the end of the appropriate period, or such longer period as the CAC may specify with reasons (Sch. A1, para. 19(1) and (2)).

19.—(3)   In deciding the appropriate bargaining unit the CAC must take these matters into account—
    (a)   the need for the unit to be compatible with effective management;
    (b)   the matters listed in sub-paragraph (4), so far as they do not conflict with that need.
    (4)   The matters are—
    (a)   the views of the employer and of the union (or unions);
    (b)   existing national and local bargaining arrangements;
    (c)   the desirability of avoiding small fragmented bargaining units within an undertaking;
    (d)   the characteristics of the workers falling within the proposed bargaining unit and of any other employees of the employer whom the CAC considers relevant;
    (e)   the location of workers.
    (5)   The CAC must give notice of its decision to the parties.

(iii)   Recognition Ballots

Note
Once the bargaining unit is agreed or determined by the CAC, the CAC must be 'satisfied that a majority of the workers constituting the bargaining unit are members of the union (or unions)' (Sch. A1, para. 22). If this condition is met, then the CAC must issue a declaration that the union is recognised 'as entitled to conduct collective bargaining on behalf of workers constituting the bargaining unit' (para. 22(2)) unless any of the following conditions apply:

(a) the CAC is satisfied that a ballot should be held in the interests of good industrial relations;

(b) a significant number of the union members within the bargaining unit inform the CAC that they do not want the union (or unions) to conduct collective bargaining on their behalf;

(c) membership evidence is produced which leaves the CAC to conclude that there are doubts whether a significant number of union members within the bargaining unit want the union (or unions) to conduct collective bargaining on their behalf (para. 22(4)).

In such cases, the CAC must hold a ballot. This is the only significant amendment to the White Paper proposals and represents a dilution of the principle of 'automacity'. Lord McCarthy has questioned the justification for this dilution:

Where are those workers who join unions, pay subscriptions and do not want representation? Who knows of a firm where recognition can only be expected to be good for future relations if it is preceded by a ballot? Perhaps these last minute caveats are best explained as concessions to the more ignorant sections of employer opinion, by negotiators who took them to be largely irrelevant? (*Fairness at Work and Trade Union Recognition: Past Comparisons and Future Problems*, London: The Institute of Employment Rights, 1999, at p. 38)

If the CAC is not satisfied that a majority of the workers constituting the bargaining unit are members of the union (or unions), it 'must give notice to the parties that it intends to arrange for the holding of a secret ballot in which the workers constituting the bargaining unit are asked whether they want the union (or unions) to conduct collective bargaining on their behalf' (Sch. A1, para. 23(2)).

Paragraph 25 of Sch. A1 sets out the requirements for the conduct of recognition ballots. They must be supervised by a qualified independent person appointed by the CAC. The ballot must be held within 20 working days starting with the day after that on which the qualified independent person is appointed, unless the time limit is extended by the CAC. The ballot may be conducted at the workplace or by post, or by a combination of the two, at the discretion of the CAC. In exercising its discretion, the CAC must take into account the likelihood of the ballot being affected by unfairness and malpractice if it were conducted at the workplace(s); costs and practicality; and any such other matters as the CAC considers appropriate. Paragraph 25(9) requires the CAC to inform the employer and union of the arrangements for the ballot as soon as reasonably practicable. The costs of the ballot are to be shared equally by the employer and the union (Sch. A1, para. 28).

As soon as the employer is informed of the holding of the ballot, it must comply with three duties, which are:

(a) to cooperate generally in connection with the ballot, with the union and the person appointed to conduct it;

(b)   to give the union reasonable access to the workers constituting the bargaining unit to allow them to inform the workers of the object of the ballot and to seek their support and their opinions;

(c)   to do the following:

(i)   to give the CAC within a period of 10 working days the names and home addresses of the workers constituting the bargaining unit,

(ii)   to give the CAC as soon as is reasonably practicable the name and address of any worker who joins the unit thereafter, and

(iii)   to inform the CAC as soon as is reasonably practicable of any worker who ceases to be within the unit (Sch. A1, para. 26(1) to (4)).

The second and third duties are not to prejudice the generality of the first duty to cooperate generally. ACAS is to issue a code of practice on reasonable access. The union also has the right to ask the independent person to distribute materials to workers in the unit at their home addresses. This is to be at the union's expense (Sch. A1, para. 26(6)(7)).

Trade Union and Labour Relations (Consolidation) Act 1992

SCHEDULE A1
COLLECTIVE BARGAINING: RECOGNITION
PART I
RECOGNITION

Union recognition

27.—(1)   If the CAC is satisfied that the employer has failed to fulfil any of the three duties imposed by paragraph 26, and the ballot has not been held, the CAC may order the employer—

(a)   to take such steps to remedy the failure as the CAC considers reasonable and specifies in the order, and

(b)   to do so within such period as the CAC considers reasonable and specifies in the order.

(2)   If the CAC is satisfied that the employer has failed to comply with an order under sub-paragraph (1), and the ballot has not been held, the CAC may issue a declaration that the union is (or unions are) recognised as entitled to conduct collective bargaining on behalf of the bargaining unit.

(3)   If the CAC issues a declaration under sub-paragraph (2) it shall take steps to cancel the holding of the ballot; and if the ballot is held it shall have no effect.

28.   [omitted]

29.—(1)   As soon as is reasonably practicable after the CAC is informed of the result of the ballot by the person conducting it, the CAC must act under this paragraph.

(2)   The CAC must inform the employer and the union (or unions) of the result of the ballot.

(3)   If the result is that the union is (or unions are) supported by—

(a)   a majority of the workers voting, and

(b)   at least 40 per cent of the workers constituting the bargaining unit,
the CAC must issue a declaration that the union is (or unions are) recognised as entitled to conduct collective bargaining on behalf of the bargaining unit.

(4)   If the result is otherwise the CAC must issue a declaration that the union is (or unions are) not entitled to be so recognised.

(5)   The Secretary of State may by order amend sub-paragraph (3) so as to specify a different degree of support; and different provision may be made for different circumstances.

. . .

Notes

1.   In drafting the new statutory redundancy procedure, the Government has attempted to learn from the failure of previous recognition legislation (ss. 11 to 16 of the Employment Protection Act 1975). The earlier legal framework's weaknesses were vividly exposed by the Grunwick dispute in the 1970s. In this case, a strike by a minority of the workers resulted in their dismissal. The sacked strikers joined a union which then made a statutory recognition claim to ACAS. George Ward, the Grunwick proprietor, refused ACAS access to the non-striking employees in the workplace. Consequently, ACAS could survey only those employees they could reach – mainly the strikers. Unsurprisingly, the workers surveyed were overwhelmingly in favour of recognition and ACAS reported accordingly.

The House of Lords held that ACAS had acted *ultra vires*. Their Lordships held that s. 12 of the 1975 Act, which had allowed ACAS to make only 'such inquiries as it thinks fit', must be presumed to involve an interest in the views of all workers affected. Although ACAS was not obliged to ascertain the opinion of each and every worker, it could not make a recommendation while being in ignorance of the views of the majority of the workforce or of conflicting opinions held by any significant group. The House of Lords saw no grounds for it to refuse Grunwick the discretionary remedy of a declaration. In their Lordships' view, the company had done nothing wrong, because an employer was under no legal obligation to cooperate with ACAS in its inquiries and consultation in a recognition issue (*ACAS* v *Grunwick Processing Laboratories Ltd* [1978] IRLR 38, HL).

2.   The three duties on employers to cooperate in the ballot (Sch. A1, para. 26) would have certainly had been more effective in a case such as *Grunwick*.

3.   It remains to be seen when the CAC will be any less vulnerable to legal challenges by way of judicial review than ACAS was. However, Sch. A1 seeks to avoid this by requiring the CAC to operate according to closely defined criteria as opposed to exercising wide discretion.

(iv)   Consequences of Recognition

Paragraph 30 of Sch. A1 sets out the consequences of recognition. There is first a period of 30 days, or longer as agreed between the parties, ('the negotiation period') for the parties to agree 'a method by which they will conduct collective bargaining'. If the employer and union are still unable to agree after the 'negotiation period', either party may request the CAC to assist them and there is then a 20-day period, or longer if all agree, ('the agreement period') when the CAC 'must try to help the parties' reach agreement (Sch. A1, para. 31(2)).

Trade Union and Labour Relations (Consolidation) Act 1992

SCHEDULE A1
COLLECTIVE BARGAINING: RECOGNITION

PART I
RECOGNITION

Consequences of recognition

31.—(3) If at the end of the agreement period the parties have not made such an agreement the CAC must specify to the parties the method by which they are to conduct collective bargaining.

(4) Any method specified under sub-paragraph (3) is to have effect as if it were contained in a legally enforceable contract made by the parties.

(5) But if the parties agree in writing—

(a) that sub-paragraph (4) shall not apply, or shall not apply to particular parts of the method specified by the CAC, or

(b) to vary or replace the method specified by the CAC,

the written agreement shall have effect as a legally enforceable contract made by the parties.

(6) Specific performance shall be the only remedy available for breach of anything which is a legally enforceable contract by virtue of this paragraph.

(7) If at any time before a specification is made under sub-paragraph (3) the parties jointly apply to the CAC requesting it to stop taking steps under this paragraph, the CAC must comply with the request.

. . .

Notes

1. The only remedy available for breach of anything which is a legally enforceable contract is 'specific performance', that is, a positive injunction. Of course, breach of an order for specific performance could be contempt of court. It is this enforcement mechanism which has been the subject of most criticism by commentators on the new statutory recognition procedure. Bob Simpson argues: 'It strains credibility beyond breaking point to suppose that the High Court would readily order specific performance, a discretionary remedy, let alone that a striking reversal of the 1980s experience would turn the tables on employers which refused to comply with a court order to observe a DPA [Default Procedure Agreement] by subjecting them to sanctions for contempt.' ((1998) 27 ILJ 245, at p. 246)

Other critics point to the weakness inherent in an imposed procedure and the absence of substantive sanctions. Drawing on the experience in other countries, particularly that of the United States, Lord McCarthy argues that 'reliance on a procedural model affords a recalcitrant management with considerable opportunities for delay and prevarication. They remain free to accept the form of recognition while denying the substance . . . [T]he remedies need to be supplemented by some form of claims procedure. The simplest way would be to provide for legally binding arbitration to be activated by the CAC on proof of persistent employer prevarication and non-observance' ('*Fairness at Work and Trade Union Recognition: Past Compari-*

sons and Future Problems, London: The Institute of Employment Rights, 1999, at p. 4). Indeed, under the previous statutory recognition regime contained in ss. 11–16 of the Employment Protection Act 1975, a recalcitrant employer could be subject to compulsory arbitration before the CAC and the latter award 'improved terms and conditions' which were incorporated into the individual worker's contract and enforced in the ordinary courts.

2.   Part II of Sch. A1 of the 1992 Act is expressed to be concerned with what would be an obvious loophole in the provisions, where the employer agrees voluntarily to negotiate when the union makes an application under this schedule, but either the parties have not agreed a method to conduct collective bargaining or have agreed a method 'but have failed to carry out the agreement' (Sch. A1, para. 59(1)). The CAC must try to help the parties reach agreement, but in the absence of agreement, the CAC must specify the method which again becomes a legally enforceable contract as if made by the parties.

This part of Sch. A1 is drafted widely enough not only to close the loophole mentioned above, but could also cover all current recognition agreements. Further, applications to the CAC to specify a method can be made by unions or employers.

Question

If a union calls its members out on industrial action in breach of an agreed dispute procedure agreement, does that fall within the criterion that 'the parties have agreed such a method but have failed to carry out the agreement'?

The question will be whether the failure must be *ab initio*, or can it be at any time during the course of the agreement. If the latter analysis is correct, how is the system of the CAC specifying the method for collective bargaining which is legally enforceable, to be reconciled with s. 180 of the 1992 Act which provides strict criteria for anything in a collective agreement which restricts the right of workers to strike or take part in other industrial action?

(v)   Changes Affecting the Bargaining Unit

Trade Union and Labour relations (Consolidation) Act 1992

SCHEDULE A1
COLLECTIVE BARGAINING: RECOGNITION

PART III
CHANGES AFFECTING THE BARGAINING UNIT

. . .

Either party believes unit no longer appropriate

66.—(1)   This paragraph applies if the employer believes or the union believes (or unions believe) that the original unit is no longer an appropriate bargaining unit.

(2)   The employer or union (or unions) may apply to the CAC to make a decision as to what is an appropriate bargaining unit.

67.—(1)   An application under paragraph 66 is not admissible unless the CAC decides that it is likely that the original unit is no longer appropriate by reason of any of the matters specified in sub-paragraph (2).

(2)   The matters are—

(a)   a change in the organisation or structure of the business carried on by the employer;

(b)   a change in the activities pursued by the employer in the course of the business carried on by him;

(c)   a substantial change in the number of workers employed in the original unit.

Note

Paragraph 69 gives 10 working days in which the employer and union may attempt to agree a new bargaining unit. If they do so, the CAC must declare the union recognised for the new unit, and the method of collective bargaining for the original unit shall apply to the new unit, with any modifications the CAC deems it necessary to take. If the union and employer fail to agree, para. 70 gives the CAC 10 working days in which to decide:

(a)   whether the original unit is appropriate, using the same criteria as in para. 67(2) above;

(b)   if the original unit is not appropriate, what other unit (if any) is appropriate.

70.—(4)   In deciding what other bargaining unit is or units are appropriate the CAC must take these matters into account—

(a)   the need for the unit or units to be compatible with effective management;

(b)   the matters listed in sub-paragraph (5), so far as they do not conflict with that need.

(5)   The matters are—

(a)   the views of the employer and of the union (or unions);

(b)   existing national and local bargaining arrangements;

(c)   the desirability of avoiding small fragmented bargaining units within an undertaking;

(d)   the characteristics of workers falling within the original unit and of any other employees of the employer whom the CAC considers relevant;

(e)   the location of the workers.

(6)   If the CAC decides that two or more bargaining units are appropriate its decision must be such that no worker falls within more than one of them.

Notes

1.   It is possible for the CAC to decide that no unit is appropriate, in which case the union will be derecognised.

2.   If the CAC decides a new appropriate bargaining unit, it must also determine whether the difference between the new unit and the original unit is such that support for recognition needs to be reassessed. If support does not have to be reassessed because the changes are relatively minor, the CAC must declare the union recognised for the new unit. If support needs to be assessed then tests mirror those in Part I: the CAC has to decide whether the union has 10 per cent membership in the new unit and whether recognition is likely to have majority support. If these tests are not satisfied, the union ceases to be recognised. If the tests are passed, automatic recognition may be granted to unions with over 50 per cent membership of the bargaining unit, or a ballot may be held (Sch. A1, paras 85–89).

(vi)   Statutory Derecognition
Application for derecognition under the statutory procedure set out in Pt IV of Sch. A1 applies only where a declaration of recognition has been made under Pt I or Pt III, or where the union has had a collective bargaining method specified by the CAC under Pt II. Part IV does not apply if a voluntary recognised union is derecognised, and there is nothing to prevent an employer derecognising a union if it currently voluntarily recognises that union. Applications for derecognition may not take place until three or more years after the CAC's original decision. The procedure is very similar to the procedure for statutory recognition.

Paragraph 99 of Sch. A1 provides that if the employer employs an average of fewer than 21 workers he may, at the end of the period of three years, give notice to the union of the fact and state that the existing bargaining arrangements will not apply from the given date which is to be at least 35 working days starting with the day after the union is notified. The union may appeal to the CAC that the employer's notice is inadmissible and/or on the question whether the employer has fewer than 21 workers. The CAC has 10 working days to reach a decision. It may extend this period by giving notice and reasons to the parties.

Paragraphs 104–111 set out the procedures to be followed in circumstances where the employer still has more than 21 workers but applies for derecognition on the basis that three years have passed and the majority of the workers support derecognition. The CAC must not proceed with the application for derecognition unless it decides that:

(a)   at least 10 per cent of the workers constituting the bargaining unit favour an end of the bargaining arrangements; and
(b)   a majority of the workers constituting the bargaining unit would be likely to favour an end of the bargaining arrangements (Sch. A1, para. 110(1)).

Paragraph 112 of Sch. A1 provides that it is not only the employer but also a worker or workers within the bargaining unit who may make an application, after three years have passed, for the bargaining arrangement to end.

Paragraph 116 requires the CAC to help the employer, union and worker with a view either to the employer and union agreeing to end the bargaining arrangements, or the worker withdrawing the application in the 20 days after the application is accepted. If an agreement is reached or the application is withdrawn, the CAC will take no further action. Otherwise, it must hold a ballot.

Paragraph 117 lays down the procedure for ballots on derecognition. They mirror the procedure on recognition, except that there is no provision for automatic derecognition if over 50 per cent of the workers are no longer union members.

Paragraph 121 sets out that the threshold that must be satisfied in the ballot. It is the same as for recognition, namely that the proposition that bargaining arrangements should be ended is supported by a majority of the workers voting and at least 40 per cent of the workers constituting the bargaining unit.

Part V of Sch. A1 provides for a different procedure for derecognition in circumstances where the CAC has issued a declaration that a union is 'automatically' recognised as entitled to conduct collective bargaining on behalf of the bargaining unit (i.e., without a ballot). Again, applications for derecognition will be accepted only three or more years after recognition. An application 'is not admissible unless the CAC is satisfied that fewer than half of the workers constituting the bargaining unit are members of the union (or unions)' (Sch. A1, para. 131(1)). If the CAC is satisfied, a ballot of the workers in the bargaining unit will conducted.

Part VI of Sch. A1 provides that workers will be able to apply to the CAC for derecognition of a union which does not have a certificate of independence and which has been voluntarily recognised by an employer. This is the only exception to the principle that, if the CAC did not declare recognition or prescribe collective bargaining procedures, the statutory derecognition procedure does not apply. An additional difference is that, in the case of applications to derecognise non-independent unions, there is no three-year time bar. The CAC must not proceed with an application unless it decides that at least 10 per cent of the bargaining unit favour an end to collective bargaining arrangements and the majority of the bargaining unit are likely to do so.

(vii)   Worker Protection

Part VIII of Sch. A1 sets out provisions protecting workers from action short of dismissal on grounds relating to recognition or derecognition of the union. Under Sch. A1, para. 156(2), the grounds are that:

(a)   the worker acted with a view to obtaining or preventing recognition of a union (or unions) by the employer under Sch. A1;

(b)   the worker indicated that he supported or did not support recognition of a union (or unions) by the employer under Sch. A1;

(c)   the worker acted with a view to securing or preventing the ending under Sch. A1 of bargaining arrangements;

(d)   the worker indicated that he supported or did not support the ending under Sch. A1 of bargaining arrangements;

(e)   the worker influenced or sought to influence the way in which votes were to be cast by other workers in a ballot arranged under Sch. A1;

(f)   the worker influenced or sought to influence other workers to vote or to abstain from voting in such a ballot;

(g)   the worker voted in such a ballot;

(h)   the worker proposed to do, failed to do, or proposed to decline to do, any of the things referred to in paragraphs (a) to (g).

Under para. 156(3), a ground does not fall within sub-paragraph (2) if it constitutes an unreasonable act or omission by the worker.

The normal time limit of three months for applications to employment tribunals applies, and compensation is to be assessed in the same way as for other claims of detriment as found in s. 146 of the 1992 Act and Pt V of the 1996 Act.

Paragraph 161 of Sch. A1 provides that an employee's dismissal is unfair if the reason for dismissal relates to recognition or derecognition as listed above. Paragraph 162 makes similar provision in respect of selection for redundancy.

Paragraph 164 provides that dismissal as a result of an employee acting or failing to act for or against recognition or derecognition of the union is unfair even if the employee has not completed the qualifying period for unfair dismissal or has passed the normal upper age limit for dismissal protection (see ss. 108 and 109 of the 1996 Act).

(viii)   Training

Section 5 of the Employment Relations Act 1999 inserts a new s. 70B and s. 70C into Part I of TULR(C)A 1992. If a union is recognised under procedures set out in Sch. A1 and the methods for the conduct of collective bargaining have been specified by the CAC, the employer must invite representatives of the union to consult on the employer's policy on training and to consult on the employer's plan for training in the next six months.

The duty applies only in respect of workers within the bargaining unit and the first meeting must be held within six months of the CAC imposing a method of collective bargaining, with periodic meetings every six months or earlier thereafter. The employers are obliged to give the union information which it is in line with good industrial relations practice to provide and which would impede the union in participating in a meeting if it did not have it. The information must be provided at least two weeks before the meeting, and thereafter the union has four weeks in which to make written representations on training matters discussed at the meeting of which the employer must take account.

New s. 70C allows the union to complain to an employment tribunal that the employer has failed to fulfil its s. 70B obligations. This could, for example, consist of a failure to convene meetings or to provide sufficient information to the union prior to a meeting. If the tribunal upholds the complaint, which must be made within three months of the failure, then it may award compensation to each member of the bargaining unit to a maximum of two weeks' pay.

(ix)   The Significance of Recognition for Statutory Rights

A number of important statutory rights are conferred upon an 'independent' trade union if it has been recognised by the employer. These include:

(a)   the right for its members and officials to take time off work (TULR(C)A 1992, ss. 168 and 170);

(b)   the right to information from the employer for the purposes of collective bargaining (TULR(C)A 1992, s. 181);

(c)   the right to consultation over impending redundancies (TULR(C)A 1992, s. 188);

(d)   the right to information and consultation in connection with a transfer of an undertaking (Transfer of Undertakings (Protection of Employment) Regulations 1981 (SI 1981/1794));

(e)   the right to information and consultation under the Health and Safety at Work etc. Act 1974 (Safety Representatives and Safety Committees Regulations 1977 (SI 1977/500) Management of Health and Safety at Work Regulations 1992 (1992/2051));

(f)   rights to information and consultation on occupational pension schemes (Pension Schemes Act 1993, s. 11(5); the Occupational Pension Schemes (Contracting-out) Regulations 1996 (SI 1996/1172); 1993 Act, s. 113; the Occupational Pension Schemes (Disclosure of Information) Regulations (SI 1996/1655, as amended).

National Union of Gold, Silver & Allied Trades v Albury Brothers Ltd
[1978] IRLR 504
Court of Appeal

Eight of the company's 55 employees joined the union, and two days later the union's district secretary wrote to the company requesting a meeting to discuss rates of pay. A meeting was held at which the wages of one employee were discussed but no agreement was concluded. Soon after, four employees were dismissed on the grounds of redundancy without prior consultation with the union. The union alleged that the lack of consultation constituted a breach of what is now TULR(C)A 1992, s. 181.

LORD DENNING MR: A recognition issue is a most important matter for industry; and therefore an employer is not to be held to have recognised a trade union unless the evidence is clear. Sometimes there is an actual agreement of recognition. Sometimes there is an implied agreement of recognition. But at all events there must be something sufficiently clear and distinct by conduct or otherwise so that one can say, 'They have mutually recognised one another, the trade union and the employers, for the purposes of collective bargaining'.

Then one comes to this particular case. Were those few letters and the one meeting recognition of the trade union? It is agreed by Mr Sedley [counsel for the union] that if the employers had simply banged the door and told the union representative to go off, that would not be recognition. Is it recognition when [he] goes along with the letter in his hand and is ready to discuss wages? It seems to me that that is not sufficient. Nor is it sufficient if he starts discussing the wages of one particular man. . . . There must be something a great deal more than that.

Note

See also *USDAW* v *Sketchley* [1981] IRLR 291, where the EAT re-emphasised that the statutory test for recognition required there to be an express or implicit acceptance of the union's role in negotiation over terms and conditions. An agreement to consult is not an agreement to negotiate and does not amount to recognition for the purposes of collective bargaining.

Compare *Joshua Wilson and Brothers Ltd* v *USDAW* [1978] IRLR 120, where although the employer had at no stage *expressly* agreed to recognise the union, the EAT was prepared to infer it from the facts that the employer allowed a shop steward to put up a notice publicising a pay increase agreed by the Joint Industrial Council whose agreements were observed by the employer; the shop steward had been allowed to collect union dues on the premises; and there had been some consultation over changed allocation of duties with the shop steward and with the union's area organiser over discipline and security.

Question

Do you think that the *Joshua Wilson* case was correctly decided? Was there recognition *for the purpose of collective bargaining?*

B: *Effects of Provisions Restricting the Right to take Industrial Action*

Trade Union and Labour Relations (Consolidation) Act 1992

180. Effects of provisions restricting right to take industrial action
(1)   Any terms of a collective agreement which prohibit or restrict the right of workers to engage in a strike or other industrial action, or have the effect of prohibiting or restricting that right, shall not form part of any contract between a worker and the person for whom he works unless the following conditions are met.
(2)   The conditions are that the collective agreement—
(a)   is in writing,
(b)   contains a provision expressly stating that those terms shall or may be incorporated in such a contract,
(c)   is reasonably accessible at his place of work to the worker to whom it applies and is available for him to consult during working hours, and
(d)   is one where each trade union which is a party to the agreement is an independent trade union; and that the contract with the worker expressly or impliedly incorporates those terms in the contract.
(3)   The above provisions have effect notwithstanding anything in section 179 and notwithstanding any provision to the contrary in any agreement (including a collective agreement or a contract with any worker).

C: *Disclosure of Information for the Purposes of Collective Bargaining*

Trade Union and Labour Relations (Consolidation) Act 1992

181.   General duty of employers to disclose information
(1)   An employer who recognises an independent trade union shall, for the purposes of all stages of collective bargaining about matters, and in relation to

descriptions of workers, in respect of which the union is recognised by him, disclose to representatives of the union, on request, the information required by this section.

In this section and sections 182 to 185 'representative', in relation to a trade union, means an official or other person authorised by the union to carry on such collective bargaining.

(2) The information to be disclosed is all information relating to the employer's undertaking which is in his possession, or that of an associated employer, and is information—

(a) without which the trade union representatives would be to a material extent impeded in carrying on collective bargaining with him, and

(b) which it would be in accordance with good industrial relations practice that he should disclose to them for the purposes of collective bargaining.

(3) A request by trade union representatives for information under this section shall, if the employer so requests, be in writing or be confirmed in writing.

(4) In determining what would be in accordance with good industrial relations practice, regard shall be had to the relevant provisions of any Code of Practice issued by ACAS, but not so as to exclude any other evidence of what that practice is.

(5) Information which an employer is required by virtue of this section to disclose to trade union representatives shall, if they so request, be disclosed or confirmed in writing.

182. Restrictions on general duty

(1) An employer is not required by section 181 to disclose information—

(a) the disclosure of which would be against the interests of national security, or

(b) which he could not disclose without contravening a prohibition imposed by or under an enactment, or

(c) which has been communicated to him in confidence, or which he has otherwise obtained in consequence of the confidence reposed in him by another person, or

(d) which relates specifically to an individual (unless that individual has consented to its being disclosed), or

(e) the disclosure of which would cause substantial injury to his undertaking for reasons other than its effect on collective bargaining, or

(f) obtained by him for the purpose of bringing, prosecuting or defending any legal proceedings.

In formulating the provisions of any Code of Practice relating to the disclosure of information, ACAS shall have regard to the provisions of this subsection.

(2) In the performance of his duty under section 181 an employer is not required—

(a) to produce, or allow inspection of, any document (other than a document prepared for the purpose of conveying or confirming the information) or to make a copy of or extracts from any document, or

(b) to compile or assemble any information where the compilation or assembly would involve an amount of work or expenditure out of reasonable proportion to the value of the information in the conduct of collective bargaining.

Notes

1. This right is one of the few statutory props to collective bargaining to have survived the 1980s. But the right is limited in a number of ways. First, it becomes operative only where the union is 'recognised' by the employer and, secondly, it applies only in relation to those matters for which the union is recognised for collective bargaining. Consequently, a union that has achieved 'partial recognition' will not be able to claim information relating to matters outside the sphere of that partial recognition. So, in *R v CAC, ex parte BTP Tioxide Ltd* [1992] IRLR 60, the trade union had secured recognition to bargain in respect of certain terms and conditions but had no negotiating rights over the operation of a particular job evaluation scheme. As a result, the Divisional Court held that the Central Arbitration Committee (CAC) had exceeded its jurisdiction in requiring the employer to disclose to the union information relating to the scheme.

The provision is unlikely to provide an impetus for the extension of union participation into areas of business decision making traditionally outside the scope of collective bargaining, for example, investment strategy. This is because disclosure can only be for the purposes of collective bargaining and that is restrictively defined by TULR(C)A 1992, s. 178.

2. ACAS has produced a Code of Practice, *Disclosure of Information to Trade Unions for Collective Bargaining Purposes* (ACAS Code No. 2, 1977; revised code brought into effect on 5 February 1998 by SI 1998/45), which seeks to provide guidance on the kind of information which should be disclosed. In addition, the Code recommends that

Employers and trade unions should endeavour to arrive at a joint understanding on how the provisions on the disclosure of information can be implemented most effectively. They should consider what information is likely to be required, what is available, and what could readily be made available. Consideration should also be given to the form in which the information will be presented and to whom. In particular, the parties should endeavour to reach an understanding on what information could most appropriately be provided on a regular basis. (para. 22)

3. If a trade union is of the view that the employer has failed to comply with the disclosure provisions, it may complain to the CAC. The CAC may refer the complaint to ACAS for conciliation. If there is no such referral or conciliation fails, the CAC may proceed to hear and determine the claim. Where the claim is upheld, the CAC will specify the information which should have been disclosed and set a deadline for its disclosure (TULR(C)A 1992, s. 183).

If the employer fails to supply the information within the set timescale, the union may present a further complaint to the CAC and claim changes in those parts of the individual contract in respect of which the union is recognised. The right to present a claim expires if the employer discloses the required information before the CAC has made an award on the claim (TULR(C)A 1992, ss. 184–185).

Bowers and Honeyball offer the following observations on the effectiveness of the disclosure provisions:

The policy appears to be that if the union does not have information to achieve meaningful collective bargaining, the CAC will arbitrate the bargaining for it. The employer may render the whole remedial process meaningless, however, if he complies with the statute even at the last minute. The stages may move like a tortoise and the remedy will be effective only long after collective bargaining for the year has been completed. The CAC itself has commented that this remedy, 'is unlikely to be attractive to either party except in very special cases'. This partly explains why less use has been made of the provisions thus far than was originally anticipated. Another explanation suggests that many employers are volunteering to provide the necessary information. (Bowers, J. and Honeyball, S., *Textbook on Labour Law*, 5th ed., London: Blackstone Press, 1998, p. 381.)

4. Given the widespread dismantlement of the statutory props to collective bargaining since 1979, why have the disclosure provisions been retained? Anderman offers the following rationalisation:

One reason why the legislation was retained since 1979 is that it is not simply an advantage for trade unions in the bargaining process. It is also useful to prompt employers to present information in such a way as to produce more realistic demands by trade unions by convincing them to take into greater account the economic problems of the firm.

Indeed, the Act specifically provides that employers do not have to provide original documents, or even copies of original documents, but are entitled to prepare information in a special form to be disclosed to trade unions. This entitlement is a virtual invitation to the sophisticated presentation. (*Labour Law: Management Decisions and Workers' Rights*, 3rd ed., London: Butterworths, 1998, at p. 321.)

5. As we have seen, between 1980 and the introduction of the statutory recognition procedure by the Employment Relations Act 1999, UK law did not attempt to force an employer to recognise and bargain with a trade union. It does impose a general duty on the employer to *provide information* to a recognised trade union for the purposes of collective bargaining (see above). Moreover, in certain specified situations the law goes further and requires the employer to *consult* with a recognised trade union or other employee representatives, i.e. redundancy, transfer of undertakings, health and safety and some pension schemes. But UK law offers no *general* right to consultation on matters of strategic importance to the future of the undertaking. As Anderman observes:

The characteristic feature of the rights of employee representatives in relation to redundancies is that even when they amount to influence over the employer's decision, their focus is upon the effects of specific investment decisions by employers. They offer little guarantee that such consultations can take place in the context of the ongoing investment decisions taken at higher levels of management. (*Labour Law: Management Decisions and Workers' Rights*, 3rd ed., London: Butterworths, 1998, at p. 330.)

Since the 1970s, there have been several EU social policy initiatives which have aimed to provide employee representatives with information and consultation rights in respect of the wider strategic decisions of management. All failed to attract the requisite unanimous support in the Council of Ministers as a result of vetoes by the then Conservative Government. However, in

September 1994, the other Member States, utilising the Maastricht protocol, adopted the European Works Council Directive, (94/45/EC). It became operative two years later, on 22 September 1996. The Commission felt that the legislation was necessary in order to bridge the gap between increasingly transnational corporate decision-making and domestic information and consultation rights.

The Directive initially covered all EC Member States (with the exception of the UK) plus Norway, Iceland and Liechtenstein. Even though technically the Directive did not apply to the UK,

in practice, right from the start, it affected hundreds of UK companies and thousands of UK employees. UK multinationals which operated in two or more of the other seventeen countries were obliged to observe the directive in respect of their overseas employees at least; and most of those multinationals which were caught by the directive (whether based in the UK or not), being obliged to establish transnational consultative machinery for their overseas employees, decided that it was convenient to incorporate their UK employees in that process too. (*Harvey on Industrial Relations and Employment Law*, Vol. 2, N/932, para. 1253.01)

With the election of the new Labour Government in 1997, the UK agreed to sign up to the Directive. As a result, the Directive was readopted by the unanimous agreement of Member States under Article 94 (ex 100) on 15 December 1997. The UK has to give effect to the Directive by December 1999.

The Directive requires large enterprises operating in the European Economic Area to inform and consult workers either by establishing a European Works Council, or by another appropriate procedure. All organisations with more than 1,000 employees in the participating States and at least 150 workers in each of two or more of these countries are covered by the Directive.

Council Directive No. 94/45/EC

SECTION I
GENERAL

Article 1   Objective

1   The purpose of this Directive is to improve the right to information and to consultation of employees in Community-scale undertakings and Community-scale groups of undertakings.

2   To that end, a European Works Council or a procedure for informing and consulting employees shall be established in every Community-scale undertaking and every Community-scale group of undertakings, where requested in the manner laid down in Article 5(1), with the purpose of informing and consulting employees under the terms, in the manner and with the effects laid down in this Directive.

3   Notwithstanding paragraph 2, where a Community-scale group of undertakings within the meaning of Article 2(1)(c) comprises one or more undertakings or groups of undertakings which are Community-scale undertakings or Community-scale

groups of undertakings within the meaning of Article 2(1)(a) or (c), a European Works Council shall be established at the level of the group unless the agreements referred to in Article 6 provide otherwise.

4 Unless a wider scope is provided for in the agreements referred to in Article 6, the powers and competence of European Works Councils and the scope of information and consultation procedures established to achieve the purpose specified in paragraph 1 shall, in the case of a Community-scale undertaking, cover all the establishments located within the Member States and, in the case of a Community-scale group of undertakings, all group undertakings located within the Member States.

5 Member States may provide that this Directive shall not apply to merchant navy crews.

Article 2 Definitions

1 For the purposes of this Directive:

(a) 'Community-scale undertaking' means any undertaking with at least 1,000 employees within the Member States and at least 150 employees in each of at least two Member States;

(b) 'group of undertakings' means a controlling undertaking and its controlled undertakings;

(c) 'Community-scale group of undertakings' means a group of undertakings with the following characteristics:

— at least 1000 employees within the Member States,
— at least two group undertakings in different Member States, and
— at least one group undertaking with at least 150 employees in one Member State and at least one other group undertaking with at least 150 employees in another Member State;

(d) 'employees' representatives' means the employees' representatives provided for by national law and/or practice;

(e) 'central management' means the central management of the Community-scale undertaking or, in the case of a Community-scale group of undertakings, of the controlling undertaking;

(f) 'consultation' means the exchange of views and establishment of dialogue between employees' representatives and central management or any more appropriate level of management;

(g) 'European Works Council' means the council established in accordance with Article 1(2) or the provisions of the Annex, with the purpose of informing and consulting employees;

(h) 'special negotiating body' means the body established in accordance with Article 5(2) to negotiate with the central management regarding the establishment of a European Works Council or a procedure for informing and consulting employees in accordance with Article 1(2).

2 For the purposes of this Directive, the prescribed thresholds for the size of the workforce shall be based on the average number of employees, including part-time employees, employed during the previous two years calculated according to national legislation and/or practice.

Article 3 Definition of 'controlling undertaking'

1 For the purposes of this Directive, 'controlling undertaking' means an undertaking which can exercise a dominant influence over another undertaking ('the controlled undertaking') by virtue, for example, of ownership, financial participation or the rules which govern it.

2 The ability to exercise a dominant influence shall be presumed, without prejudice to proof to the contrary, when, in relation to another undertaking directly or indirectly:

(a) holds a majority of that undertaking's subscribed capital; or

(b) controls a majority of the votes attached to that undertaking's issued share capital; or

(c) can appoint more than half of the members of that undertaking's adminis-trative, management or supervisory body.

. . .

SECTION II
ESTABLISHMENT OF A EUROPEAN WORKS COUNCIL OR AN EMPLOYEE INFORMATION AND CONSULTATION PROCEDURE

Article 4 Responsibility for the establishment of a European Works Council or an employee information and consultation procedure

1 The central management shall be responsible for creating the conditions and means necessary for the setting up of a European Works Council or an information and consultation procedure, as provided for in Article 1(2), in a Community-scale undertaking and a Community-scale group of undertakings.

2 Where the central management is not situated in a Member State, the central management's representative agent in a Member State, to be designated if necessary, shall take on the responsibility referred to in paragraph 1.

In the absence of such a representative, the management of the establishment or group undertaking employing the greatest number of employees in any one Member State shall take on the responsibility referred to in paragraph 1.

3 For the purposes of this Directive, the representative or representatives or, in the absence of any such representatives, the management referred to in the second subparagraph of paragraph 2, shall be regarded as the central management.

Article 5 Special negotiating body

1 In order to achieve the objective in Article 1(1), the central management shall initiate negotiations for the establishment of a European Works Council or an information and consultation procedure on its own initiative or at the written request of at least 100 employees or their representatives in at least two undertakings or establishments in at least two different Member States.

2 For this purpose, a special negotiating body shall be established in accordance with the following guidelines:

(a) The Member States shall determine the method to be used for the election or appointment of the members of the special negotiating body who are to be elected or appointed in their territories.

Member States shall provide that employees in undertakings and/or establishments in which there are no employees' representatives through no fault of their own, have the right to elect or appoint members of the special negotiating body.

The second subparagraph shall be without prejudice to national legislation and/or practice laying down thresholds for the establishment of employee representation bodies.

(b) The special negotiating body shall have a minimum of three and a maximum of 17 members.

(c) In these elections or appointments, it must be ensured:

— firstly, that each Member State in which the Community-scale undertak-ing has one or more establishments or in which the Community-scale

group of undertakings has the controlling undertaking or one or more controlled undertakings is represented by one member,
— secondly, that there are supplementary members in proportion to the number of employees working in the establishments, the controlling undertaking or the controlled undertakings as laid down by the legislation of the Member State within the territory of which the central management is situated.

(d) The central management and local management shall be informed of the composition of the special negotiating body.

3 The special negotiating body shall have the task of determining, with the central management, by written agreement, the scope, composition, functions, and term of office of the European Works Council(s) or the arrangements for implementing a procedure for the information and consultation of employees.

4 With a view to the conclusion of an agreement in accordance with Article 6, the central management shall convene a meeting with the special negotiating body. It shall inform the local managements accordingly.

For the purpose of the negotiations, the special negotiating body may be assisted by experts of its choice.

5 The special negotiating body may decide, by at least two-thirds of the votes, not to open negotiations in accordance with paragraph 4, or to terminate the negotiations already opened.

Such a decision shall stop the procedure to conclude the agreement referred to in Article 6. Where such a decision has been taken, the provisions in the Annex shall not apply.

A new request to convene the special negotiating body may be made at the earliest two years after the above mentioned decision unless the parties concerned lay down a shorter period.

6 Any expenses relating to the negotiations referred to in paragraphs 3 and 4 shall be borne by the central management so as to enable the special negotiating body to carry out its task in an appropriate manner.

In compliance with this principle, Member States may lay down budgetary rules regarding the operation of the special negotiating body. They may in particular limit the funding to cover one expert only.

Article 6   Content of the agreement

1 The central management and the special negotiating body must negotiate in a spirit of cooperation with a view to reaching an agreement on the detailed arrangements for implementing the information and consultation of employees provided for in Article 1(1).

2 Without prejudice to the autonomy of the parties, the agreement referred to in paragraph 1 between the central management and the special negotiating body shall determine:

(a) the undertakings of the Community-scale group of undertakings or the establishments of the Community-scale undertaking which are covered by the agreement;

(b) the composition of the European Works Council, the number of members, the allocation of seats and the term of office;

(c) the functions and the procedure for information and consultation of the European Works Council;

(d) the venue, frequency and duration of meetings of the European Works Council;

(e) the financial and material resources to be allocated to the European Works Council;

(f) the duration of the agreement and the procedure for its renegotiation.

3 The central management and the special negotiating body may decide, in writing, to establish one or more information and consultation procedures instead of a European Works Council.

The agreement must stipulate by what method the employees' representatives shall have the right to meet to discuss the information conveyed to them.

This information shall relate in particular to transnational questions which significantly affect workers' interests.

4 The agreements referred to in paragraphs 2 and 3 shall not, unless provision is made otherwise therein, be subject to the subsidiary requirements of the Annex.

5 For the purposes of concluding the agreements referred to in paragraphs 2 and 3, the special negotiating body shall act by a majority of its members.

Article 7 Subsidiary requirements

1 In order to achieve the objective in Article 1(1), the subsidiary requirements laid down by the legislation of the Member State in which the central management is situated shall apply:

— where the central management and the special negotiating body so decide, or

— where the central management refuses to commence negotiations within six months of the request referred to in Article 5(1), or

— where, after three years from the date of this request, they are unable to conclude an agreement as laid down in Article 6 and the special negotiating body has not taken the decision provided for in Article 5(5).

2 The subsidiary requirements referred to in paragraph 1 as adopted in the legislation of the Member States must satisfy the provisions set out in the Annex.

SECTION III
MISCELLANEOUS PROVISIONS

Article 8 Confidential information

1 Member States shall provide that members of special negotiating bodies or of European Works Councils and any experts who assist them are not authorised to reveal any information which has expressly been provided to them in confidence.

The same shall apply to employees' representatives in the framework of an information and consultation procedure.

This obligation shall continue to apply, wherever the persons referred to in the first and second subparagraphs are, even after the expiry of their terms of office.

2 Each Member State shall provide, in specific cases and under the conditions and limits laid down by national legislation, that the central management situated in its territory is not obliged to transmit information when its nature is such that, according to objective criteria, it would seriously harm the functioning of the undertakings concerned or would be prejudicial to them.

A Member State may make such dispensation subject to prior administrative or judicial authorisation.

3 Each Member State may lay down particular provisions for the central management of undertakings in its territory which pursue directly and essentially the aim of ideological guidance with respect to information and the expression of opinions, on condition that, at the date of adoption of this Directive such particular provisions already exist in the national legislation.

Article 9   Operation of European Works Council and information and consultation procedure for workers
The central management and the European Works Council shall work in a spirit of cooperation with due regard to their reciprocal rights and obligations.

The same shall apply to cooperation between the central management and employees' representatives in the framework of an information and consultation procedure for workers.

Article 10   Protection of employees' representatives
Members of special negotiating bodies, members of European Works Councils and employees' representatives exercising their functions under the procedure referred to in Article 6(3) shall, in the exercise of their functions, enjoy the same protection and guarantees provided for employees' representatives by the national legislation and/or practice in force in their country of employment.

This shall apply in particular to attendance at meetings of special negotiating bodies or European Works Councils or any other meetings within the framework of the agreement referred to in Article 6(3), and the payment of wages for members who are on the staff of the Community-scale undertaking or the Community-scale group of undertakings for the period of absence necessary for the performance of their duties.

Article 11   Compliance with this Directive
1   Each Member State shall ensure that the management of establishments of a Community-scale undertaking and the management of undertakings which form part of a Community-scale group of undertakings which are situated within its territory and their employees' representatives or, as the case may be, employees abide by the obligations laid down by this Directive, regardless of whether or not the central management is situated within its territory.

2   Member States shall ensure that the information on the number of employees referred to in Article 2(1)(a) and (c) is made available by undertakings at the request of the parties concerned by the application of this Directive.

3   Member States shall provide for appropriate measures in the event of failure to comply with this Directive; in particular, they shall ensure that adequate administrative or judicial procedures are available to enable the obligations deriving from this Directive to be enforced.

4   Where Member States apply Article 8, they shall make provision for administrative or judicial appeal procedures which the employees' representatives may initiate when the central management requires confidentiality or does not give information in accordance with that Article.

Such procedures may include procedures designed to protect the confidentiality of the information in question.

Article 12   Link between this Directive and other provisions
1   This Directive shall apply without prejudice to measures taken pursuant to Council Directive 75/129/EEC of 17 February 1975 on the approximation of the laws of the Member States relating to collective redundancies, and to Council Directive 77/187/EEC of 14 February 1977 on the approximation of the laws of the Member States relating to the safeguarding of employees' rights in the event of transfers of undertakings, business or parts of businesses.

2   This Directive shall be without prejudice to employees' existing rights to information and consultation under national law.

Article 13   Agreements in force
1   Without prejudice to paragraph 2, the obligations arising from this Directive shall not apply to Community-scale undertakings or Community-scale groups of undertakings in which, on the date laid down in Article 14(1) for the implementation of this Directive or the date of its transposition in the Member State in question, where this is earlier than the above mentioned date, there is already an agreement, covering the entire workforce, providing for the transnational information and consultation of employees.
2   When the agreements referred to in paragraph 1 expire, the parties to those agreements may decide jointly to renew them.
Where this is not the case, the provisions of this Directive shall apply.

. . .

ANNEX
SUBSIDIARY REQUIREMENTS
referred to in Article 7 of the Directive

1   In order to achieve the objective in Article 1(1) of the Directive and in the cases provided for in Article 7(1) of the Directive, the establishment, composition and competence of a European Works Council shall be governed by the following rules:
(a)   The competence of the European Works Council shall be limited to information and consultation on the matters which concern the Community-scale undertaking or Community-scale group of undertakings as a whole or at least two of its establishments or group undertakings situated in different Member States.
In the case of undertakings or groups of undertakings referred to in Article 4(2), the competence of the European Works Council shall be limited to those matters concerning all their establishments or group undertakings situated within the Member States or concerning at least two of their establishments or group undertakings situated in different Member States.
(b)   The European Works Council shall be composed of employees of the Community-scale undertaking or Community-scale group of undertakings elected or appointed from their number by the employees' representatives or, in the absence thereof, by the entire body of employees.
The election or appointment of members of the European Works Council shall be carried out in accordance with national legislation and/or practice.
(c)   The European Works Council shall have a minimum of three members and a maximum of 30.
Where its size so warrants, it shall elect a select committee from among its members, comprising at most three members.
It shall adopt its own rules of procedure.
(d)   In the election or appointment of members of the European Works Council, it must be ensured:
—   firstly, that each Member State in which the Community-scale undertaking has one or more establishments or in which the Community-scale group of undertakings has the controlling undertaking or one or more controlled undertakings is represented by one member,
—   secondly, that there are supplementary members in proportion to the number of employees working in the establishments, the controlling undertaking or the controlled undertakings as laid down by the legislation of the Member State within the territory of which the central management is situated.

(e) The central management and any other more appropriate level of management shall be informed of the composition of the European Works Council.

(f) Four years after the European Works Council is established it shall examine whether to open negotiations for the conclusion of the agreement referred to in Article 6 of the Directive or to continue to apply the subsidiary requirements adopted in accordance with this Annex.

Articles 6 and 7 of the Directive shall apply, *mutatis mutandis*, if a decision has been taken to negotiate an agreement according to Article 6 of the Directive, in which case 'special negotiating body' shall be replaced by 'European Works Council'.

2 The European Works Council shall have the right to meet with the central management once a year, to be informed and consulted, on the basis of a report drawn up by the central management, on the progress of the business of the Community-scale undertaking or Community-scale group of undertakings and its prospects. The local managements shall be informed accordingly.

The meeting shall relate in particular to the structure, economic and financial situation, the probable development of the business and of production and sales, the situation and probable trend of employment, investments, and substantial changes concerning organisation, introduction of new working methods or production processes, transfers of production, mergers, cut-backs or closures of undertakings, establishments or important parts thereof, and collective redundancies.

3 Where there are exceptional circumstances affecting the employees' interests to a considerable extent, particularly in the event of relocations, the closure of establishments or undertakings or collective redundancies, the select committee or, where no such committee exists, the European Works Council shall have the right to be informed. It shall have the right to meet, at its request, the central management, or any other more appropriate level of management within the Community-scale undertaking or group of undertakings having its own powers of decision, so as to be informed and consulted on measures significantly affecting employees' interests.

Those members of the European Works Council who have been elected or appointed by the establishments and/or undertakings which are directly concerned by the measures in question shall also have the right to participate in the meeting organised with the select committee.

This information and consultation meeting shall take place as soon as possible on the basis of a report drawn up by the central management or any other appropriate level of management of the Community-scale undertaking or group of undertakings, on which an opinion may be delivered at the end of the meeting or within a reasonable time.

This meeting shall not affect the prerogatives of the central management.

4 The Member States may lay down rules on the chairing of information and consultation meetings.

Before any meeting with the central management, the European Works Council or the select committee, where necessary enlarged in accordance with the second paragraph of point 3, shall be entitled to meet without the management concerned being present.

5 Without prejudice to Article 8 of the Directive, the members of the European Works Council shall inform the representatives of the employees of the establishments or of the undertakings of a Community-scale group of undertakings or, in the absence of representatives, the workforce as a whole, of the content and outcome of the information and consultation procedure carried out in accordance with this Annex.

6 The European Works Council or the select committee may be assisted by experts of its choice, in so far as this is necessary for it to carry out its tasks.

7   The operating expenses of the European Works Council shall be borne by the central management.

The central management concerned shall provide the members of the European Works Council with such financial and material resources as enable them to perform their duties in an appropriate manner.

In particular, the cost of organising meetings and arranging for interpretation facilities and the accommodation and travelling expenses of members of the European Works Council and its select committee shall be met by the central management unless otherwise agreed.

In compliance with these principles, the Member States may lay down budgetary rules regarding the operation of the European Works Council. They may in particular limit funding to cover one expert only.

Notes

1. Article 13 of the Directive states that the Directive shall not apply to groups and undertakings where by 22 September 1996 there is already an agreement covering the entire workforce, providing for transnational information and consultation of employees. This provides an incentive to introduce 'customised' voluntary arrangements. Moreover, the exemption from the Directive will continue if renewed upon expiry. In the UK's case, the extension Directive (Article 3) makes it clear that, if an undertaking is brought within the scope of the Directive by its extension to the UK then the undertaking may establish its own voluntary arrangements rather than those imposed by the Directive, provided it does so before the UK implements the Directive.

Wedderburn offers the following cynical analysis of the 'Article 13' procedure:

A management which has offered small advantages to its workforce for an agreement before September 1996 need rarely be bothered by the Directive, and that in itself may encourage others to be less than welcoming towards trade unions . . . Is the new law on consultation an extra prop for, or an extra bulwark against collective bargaining, or *per contra* has the Commission seen in the process of 'social dialogue' the facility for management and labour to move from consultation to negotiation? It is revealing that central management in many multi-nationals has taken the initiative in offering 'Article 13 agreements' – some 140, the Commission thought in May 1996 – many inserting a clause stating that the agreement is made in conformity with Article 13 . . . especially when the ousted Directive does little more than ask for consultation in the form of a genuine exchange of views. True, the 'parties' can make an agreement particularly suited to the undertaking but in most cases the balance of bargaining power is hugely weighted in management's hands . . . Of course, those who come from pluralist union cultures have understandably taken Article 13 to require not two conditions, but three. The first two conditions are beyond dispute; an agreement for transnational consultation which covers the entire workforce. But some hold there is a third condition, namely, the need for a 'representative' union, 'representing', or even binding, the entire workforce. This could of course still be important if such an EWC agreement were challenged With respect, however, this third condition appears to be a false intrusion of domestic concepts. Article 13 demanded a transnational consultation agreement that extends to the whole workforce, but no more. The other party can be any interlocutor so long as the two conditions are met. True, management cannot make an accord with itself but an agreement already in place qualifies if made with any genuine party. Article 13 might have required an independent or 'representative' trade union to be the other party, but it does not do so. ('Consultation and Collective Bargaining in Europe: Success or Ideology', (1997) 26 ILJ 1, at pp. 22–23)

2. In November 1998, the European Commission published a proposal for a Council Directive 'establishing a general framework for informing and consulting employees in the European Community' (COM (98) 612). In the view of the Commission such a measure is necessary in order to bridge gaps in national legislation and to ensure consistency of practice across the Member States. This proposal is strongly opposed by the European-level employers' organisations UNICE and CEEP, which believe that this a matter for regulation at the level of individual Member States. At this juncture, the chances of adoption of the proposed directive would appear remote.

D: Time off for Trade Union Duties and Activities

Trade Union and Labour Relations (Consolidation) Act 1992

168. Time off for carrying out trade union duties

(1) An employer shall permit an employee of his who is an official of an independent trade union recognised by the employer to take time off during his working hours for the purpose of carrying out any duties of his, as such an official, concerned with—

(a) negotiations with the employer related to or connected with matters falling within section 178(2) (collective bargaining) in relation to which the trade union is recognised by the employer, or

(b) the performance on behalf of employees of the employer of functions related to or connected with matters falling within that provision which the employer has agreed may be so performed by the trade union.

(2) He shall also permit such an employee to take time off during his working hours for the purpose of undergoing training in aspects of industrial relations—

(a) relevant to the carrying out of such duties as are mentioned in subsection (1), and

(b) approved by the Trades Union Congress or by the independent trade union of which he is an official.

(3) The amount of time off which an employee is to be permitted to take under this section and the purposes for which, the occasions on which and any conditions subject to which time off may be so taken are those that are reasonable in all the circumstances having regard to any relevant provisions of a Code of Practice issued by ACAS.

(4) An employee may present a complaint to an industrial tribunal that his employer has failed to permit him to take time off as required by this section.

170. Time off for trade union activities

(1) An employer shall permit an employee of his who is a member of an independent trade union recognised by the employer in respect of that description of employee to take time off during his working hours for the purpose of taking part in—

(a) any activities of the union, and

(b)   any activities in relation to which the employee is acting as a representative of the union.

(2)   The right conferred by subsection (1) does not extent to activities which themselves consist of industrial action, whether or not in contemplation or furtherance of a trade dispute.

(3)   The amount of time off which an employee is to be permitted to take under this section and the purposes for which, the occasions on which and any conditions subject to which time off may be so taken are those that are reasonable in all the circumstances having regard to any relevant provisions of a Code of Practice issued by ACAS.

(4)   An employee may present a complaint to an industrial tribunal that his employer has failed to permit him to take time off as required by this section.

Notes

1.   First introduced during the 1970s as part of a general policy to encourage and extend collective bargaining, the rights to paid time off for trade union duties and training and unpaid time off for union members to participate in union activities, were significantly restricted by the Conservative Government through amendments introduced by the EA 1989. In particular, it restricted the range of issues for which paid time off for trade union duties can be claimed to those covered by recognition agreements between employers and trade unions. Under the old definition, officials could seek time off for any of their duties concerned with industrial relations in general. Additionally, union duties must relate to the official's own employer and cannot extend, as was previously the case, to negotiations with an associated employer.

Paid time off for training is now similarly limited to duties relating to matters in respect of which the union is recognised by the employer.

The statutory provisions are supplemented by the ACAS Code of Practice *Time Off For Trade Union Duties and Activities*, which has been twice revised – in 1991 and 1998 – in order to reflect the amendments to the statutory provisions.

There is no minimum period of continuous employment required in order to qualify for these rights. However, in order to claim, and in common with most other employment protection rights, the employee currently must work 16 hours or more per week, or have worked for five years on a normal working week of at least eight hours.

2.   There is also a right under the Health and Safety at Work etc. Act 1974 for safety representatives to claim paid time off in order to fulfil their functions and a right to unpaid leave from certain kinds of public duties (ERA 1996, s. 50).

ACAS Code of Practice No. 2, *Time Off For Trade Union Duties and Activities* (1977) (as revised and brought into effect on 5 February 1998 by SI 1998/46)

Examples of trade union duties

12.   **Subject to the recognition or other agreement, trade union officials should be allowed to take reasonable time off for duties concerned with**

negotiations or, where their employer has agreed, for duties concerned with other functions related to or connected with:

(a) **terms and conditions of employment, or the physical conditions in which workers are required to work**. Examples could include:
- pay
- hours of work
- holidays and holiday pay
- sick pay arrangements
- pensions
- vocational training
- equal opportunities
- notice periods
- the working environment
- utilisation of machinery and other equipment;

(b) **engagement or non-engagement, or termination or suspension of employment or the duties of employment, of one or more workers**. Examples could include:
- recruitment and selection policies
- human resource planning
- redundancy and dismissal arrangements;

(c) **allocation of work or the duties of employment as between workers or groups of workers**. Examples could include:
- job grading
- job evaluation
- job descriptions
- flexible working practices;

(d) **matters of discipline**. Examples could include:
- disciplinary procedures
- arrangements for representing trade union members at internal interviews
- arrangements for appearing on behalf of trade union members, or as witnesses, before agreed outside appeal bodies or industrial tribunals;

(e) **trade union membership or non-membership**. Examples could include:
- representational arrangements
- any union involvement in the induction of new workers;

(f) **facilities for officials of trade unions**. Examples could include any agreed arrangements for the provision of:
- accommodation
- equipment
- names of new workers to the union;

(g) **machinery for negotiation or consultation and other procedures**. Examples could include arrangements for:
- collective bargaining
- grievance procedures
- joint consultation
- communicating with members
- communicating with other union officials also concerned with collective bargaining with the employer.

13.   The duties of an official of a recognised trade union must be connected with or related to negotiations or the performance of functions both in time and subject matter. Reasonable time off may be sought, for example, to:

- prepare for negotiations
- inform members of progress
- explain outcomes to members
- prepare for meetings with the employer about matters for which the trade union has only representational rights.

What are examples of trade union activities?

21. The activities of a trade union member can be, for example:
    - attending workplace meetings to discuss and vote on the outcome of negotiations with the employer
    - meeting full-time officials to discuss issues relevant to the workplace
    - voting in properly conducted ballots on industrial action
    - voting in union elections.

22. Where the member is acting as a representative of a recognised union activities can be, for example, taking part in:
    - branch, area or regional meetings of the union where the business of the union is under discussion
    - meetings of official policy making bodies such as the executive committee or annual conference
    - meetings with full-time officials to discuss issues relevant to the workplace.

23. **There is no right to time off for trade union activities which themselves consist of industrial action.**

Notes

1. The Code (para. 13 above) suggests that time off may be sought for preparation for negotiations and informing members as to their progress and outcome. This would accord with the approach of the Court of Appeal in interpreting the scope of the unamended provision (see *Adlington v British Bakeries (Northern) Limited* [1989] IRLR 218, CA).

2. In *Luce v London Borough of Bexley* [1990] IRLR 422, the EAT held that whether the trade union activity concerned fell within the scope of the provision was a matter of fact and degree:

Although we do not consider that the phrase should be understood too restrictively, we are satisfied that it cannot have been the intention of Parliament to included any activity of whatever nature.

The whole context of the phrase is within the ambit of the employment relationship between that employee and that employer and that trade union. . . . Thus it seems to us in a broad sense the activity should be one which is linked to that employment relationship, i.e. between that employer, that employee and that trade union.

The EAT went on to hold that an industrial tribunal had been entitled to find that teachers were not entitled to time off to lobby Parliament against the Education Reform Bill.

Hairsine v Kingston-Upon-Hull City Council
[1992] IRLR 211
Employment Appeal Tribunal

Mr Hairsine was a shop steward. In April 1989, he was given permission by his employers to attend a union training course taking place on 12 consecutive Thursdays, beginning on 13 April. He was given day release with pay for attendance at all sessions of the course when he would normally be at work.

Mr Hairsine worked a 39-hour week on a shift basis. On 13 April he was rostered to work the shift between 3 p.m. and 11 p.m. On that day, he attended the first session of his union course between 9 a.m. and 4 p.m. He attended work at 4.40 p.m. and stayed until 7 p.m. He then went home. The employers contended that he was not entitled to be paid for the entire shift because he had not worked between 7 p.m. and 11 p.m.

Mr Hairsine argued that, under what is now TULR(C)A 1992, s. 168, he was entitled to be paid for the hours during which he attended the course, whether or not he attended for work in the evening. An industrial tribunal dismissed his claim.

On appeal to the EAT, Mr Hairsine submitted that hours allowed as time off under s. 168 are in substitution for the equivalent number of hours which the employee was contractually liable to work on that day, i.e. they are in lieu of working hours. Therefore, as his course had lasted for the equivalent of an eight-hour shift, he was entitled to be paid for those hours. His attendance at work in the evening was purely voluntary. The EAT dismissed his appeal.

WOOD J (PRESIDENT): 'Time off' is effectively defined within s. 27(1) [now TULR(C)A 1992, s. 168(1)] as time 'during the employee's working hours for the purpose of enabling him . . .' to attend the course. Two conditions must be satisfied therefore. The first is that it must be part of his 'working hours', and secondly, that it must be permitted by the employer for the purpose of 'enabling him to attend' the course. If it fails either condition it is not 'time off' for which an employee is entitled to be paid. We emphasise again that the reasonableness of the terms of the permission are a matter for the Industrial Tribunal if there is any dispute.

This view of the true meaning of 'time off' in s. 27(1) is in our judgment supported by the wording of s. 32(1) [now TULR(C)A 1992, s. 173(1)]. If 'working hours' were intended only to be those hours which he was contracted to work during any given day, then the phrasing of s. 32(1) could have been quite different. The phrase is that time when 'he is required to be *at work*'. It seems to us clear therefore that 'time off' means 'those hours when he would normally have been *at work* and which it was reasonable that he should be allowed to take off in order *to enable him* to attend a course (trade union activities)'.

Looked at in this way the present practice as it is understood by the industrial members to have existed for many years can be allowed to continue.

Let us apply that to some of the examples given already. In each of the examples given arrangements would be sought to be made by agreement that the trade union activity should take place outside those hours during which the employee should be at work. It may be possible to change the working hours so as to minimise interruption with production or service. It may also be possible to change the shifts. However, it may also be necessary, for instance in the case of night duty, to grant 'time off' for the whole of a nightshift in order that the employee should be allowed some sleep, that is if he were on permanent duty and not merely on shifts. It might also be reasonable to allow some 'time off', perhaps one or two hours, from the end of a day's work if there was a substantial distance to travel. All these are matters for negotiation and for a reasonable approach from both sides. In the event of disagreement on what is reasonable to be permitted, the decision is one for the Industrial Tribunal. If an employee shop steward is going to need 'time off' to enable him to attend, then of course he must be paid for that time off.

Turning to the facts of the present case, it seems to us that it was made abundantly clear in the practice operated by the respondents under their policy on the provision of time off for trade union duties and activities that the applicant, Mr Hairsine, was going to be required to attend the evening shift after he had attended his course. There might possibly have been an argument that he should be allowed to arrive late for the evening shift as travel might have been difficult and he had clearly made special arrangements, but that is a minor detail. The case presented to the Tribunal was not an allegation that the terms of the permission were unreasonable, although Ms Smith takes the view that it should have been so presented, nor was that the way in which it was presented to us. The case presented to us is that all hours of a trade union course for which permission has been given are substituted for an equivalent number of hours for which the employee would have been at work and therefore not only is the employee automatically entitled to take the equivalent hours out of his work time but he is entitled to be paid for so doing. It seems to us in the present case that the Tribunal were entirely correct in reaching the conclusion that the hours between 7 pm and 11 pm on his evening shift were not hours for which permission had been granted for 'time off' in order to 'enable him' to attend the morning course. Those hours were not 'time off' within the meaning of the statute and were not therefore hours for which he was entitled to be paid.

As we have already emphasised, one of our members is of the view that the terms of the permission granted were not reasonable. The majority, however, point out that this was not the issue raised before the Industrial Tribunal, nor indeed before this Court. The tone of the decision of the Industrial Tribunal does not indicate that it would have viewed the permission granted in this way, and indeed if it had thought that the issue should have been argued, there was nothing to prevent the Tribunal amending the application and allowing the issue of reasonableness to be raised. That issue would essentially be one for the Tribunal to decide.

We are therefore unable to discern any error of law in the decision of this Industrial Tribunal and this appeal must be dismissed. Leave to appeal.

Question
Do you think it was 'reasonable' of the employers to have expected Mr Hairsine to attend any part of his evening shift after attending the training course between 9 a.m. to 4 p.m.?

ACAS Code of Practice No. 2 *Time Off for Trade Union Duties and Activities* (1977)
(as revised)

25. **The amount and frequency of time off should be reasonable in all the circumstances**. Although the statutory provisions apply to all employers without exception as to size and type of business or service, trade unions should be aware of the wide variety of difficulties and operational requirements to be taken into account when seeking or agreeing arrangements for time off, for example:
- the size of the organisation and the number of workers
- the production process

- the need to maintain a service to the public
- the need for safety and security at all times.

26. Employers in turn should have in mind the difficulties for trade union officials and members in ensuring representation and communications with, for example:
  - shift workers
  - part-time workers
  - those employed at dispersed locations
  - workers with particular domestic commitments.

27. For time off arrangements to work satisfactorily trade unions should:
  - ensure that officials are aware of their role, responsibilities and functions
  - inform management, in writing, as soon as possible of appointments or resignations of officials
  - ensure that officials receive any appropriate written credentials promptly.

28. Employers should consider making available to officials the facilities necessary for them to perform their duties efficiently and communicate effectively with their members, fellow lay officials and full-time officers. Where resources permit the facilities could include:
  - accommodation for meetings
  - access to a telephone and other office equipment
  - the use of notice boards
  - where the volume of the official's work justifies it, the use of dedicated office space.

Notes

1. In *Wignall* v *British Gas Corporation* [1984] IRLR 493, a NALGO official employed as a meter reader for British Gas, had already been granted 12 weeks' leave for union business when he requested a further 10 days' leave in order to edit a union magazine. The EAT upheld the industrial tribunal's decision that it was reasonable for the employers to refuse the further request.

2. In *Ryford Ltd* v *Drinkwater* [1996] IRLR 16, the EAT held that before an employee can establish a right to compensation under s. 168(4) on the ground that his employer 'has failed to permit him to take time off', he must establish, on the balance of probabilities, that the request for time off was made, that it came to the notice of the employer's appropriate representative, and that they either refused it, ignored it or failed to respond to it. Section 168 plainly requires that the employer should know of the request before he can 'fail to permit' time off. The concept of permission must import knowledge of a request for permission.

3. An employee who claims that his or her employer has either failed to permit time off or has failed to pay the whole or part of any amount due under the statutory provisions, may complain to an employment tribunal. Where a tribunal upholds a complaint that time off has been *refused* by the employer, it must make a declaration to that effect and may make an award of compensation which it 'considers just and equitable in all the circumstances having regard to the employer's default . . . and to any loss sustained by the employee' (TULR(C)A 1992, s. 172(2)). If the complaint is of the failure to pay the employee in whole or in part for time off which has been permitted

under the Act, the tribunal must order the employer to pay the amount which it finds to be due.

IV Trade Unions and Their Members

The last two decades or so have witnessed an increasing tendency to subject internal union affairs to legal regulation. Although the Donovan Commission (1968), para. 622, found 'it unlikely that abuse of power by trade unions is widespread', it still recommended that the Chief Registrar of Trade Unions be given a supervisory role over the content of union rules and that an independent review body should be created to deal with arbitrary exclusion and expulsions. Section 65 of the Industrial Relations Act 1971 laid down a number of 'guiding principles' for trade union rules which forbid, *inter alia*, arbitrary or unreasonable exclusions from membership and unfair or unreasonable disciplinary action. In the 1980s, we witnessed considerable statutory intervention in this field. Moreover, judicial intervention via the common law has also played a major role in the trend towards intervention in internal union affairs.

A: The Residual Importance of The Common Law

Statutory protection for individuals has increased markedly since 1980, with the enactment of the right not to be unreasonably excluded or expelled from union membership where there is a closed shop in operation (EA 1980, s. 4) and the right not to be disciplined for certain listed reasons (EA 1988, s. 3). The Trade Union Reform and Employment Rights Act 1993 introduced yet more restrictions on trade union freedoms within this sphere by enlarging the scope of unjustifiable discipline and enacting a general right not to be excluded and expelled from a trade union unless for a statutory 'permitted reason'. Nevertheless, an examination of the common law on admission, discipline and expulsion is relevant, 'first, because common law actions may still have a considerable impact (as was seen particularly in the miners' strike of 1984/85) and secondly, because the statutory provisions for the most part build upon the common law foundation rather than replacing it' (Smith, I.T., and Thomas, G.H., *Smith and Woods, Industrial Law*, 6th ed., London: Butterworths, 1996, p. 520). Additionally, an analysis of the common law provides context and meaning to the form which has been adopted for statutory intervention.

(i) The Union Rule Book and the Courts

The starting point for judicial involvement has traditionally been the contract of membership. The professed function of the law in this area is to strike a balance between the conflicting notions of union autonomy on the one hand and the rights of the individual member on the other.

In readily intervening to protect the individual, it may be that — as with strike law — the courts have shown little understanding of the needs for collective solidarity within trade unions.

(ii)   Admission to a Union at Common Law

Faramus v *Film Artistes Association*
[1964] 1 All ER 25
House of Lords

Rule 4(2) of the defendant association provided that 'No person who has been convicted in a court of law of a criminal offence (other than a motoring offence not punishable by imprisonment) shall be eligible for, or retain membership of the association'. When he signed the application forms for membership, the appellant denied that he had been convicted of any offence, though he had twice been convicted of minor offences in Jersey several years earlier. After he had been in the union for eight years, his previous convictions were discovered and the union claimed that he was not, and had never been, a member. He sought a declaration that he was a member and an injunction restraining the union from excluding him from membership.

LORD EVERSHED: Like the majority of the Court of Appeal, I am unable to see any ground on which it could be seriously submitted that the rule could be disregarded by the court because of the vagueness of its terms or because its application in certain circumstances might not only be difficult of ascertainment but productive of embarrassment in the conduct of the respondent union's business. Nor can it, as I think, be suggested that to a rule of this kind there can be applied any principle of natural justice. The case is in no sense analogous to the case of rules applicable to someone whose contract of membership is being terminated, where it may well be that for their validity the rules must make provision to enable such a person at any rate to have a proper opportunity to put his case. In the circumstances, therefore, the only ground on which the applicant can, as I think, succeed is if he were able to establish that the terms of this rule operated as unreasonable restraint of trade and that the rule was not saved by s. 3 of the Trade Union Act 1871. . . .

I . . . accept unequivocally the view taken by the majority of the Court of Appeal, and say that if the contract constituted by the rules in this case be or contain (at any rate so far as this sub-rule is concerned) an unreasonable restraint of trade, none the less the rules (and sub-r. (2) of r. 4 in particular) are validated by the section. I add only that it is unreal and impossible, as I think, to sever this particular sub-rule from the rules as a whole and to treat it therefore as something quite distinct not only from the other rules but also from the purposes of the union to which, of course, it is essentially addressed. . . .

Note
The absence of a contractual relationship between the union and the applicant for membership has made it difficult for the courts to find a theoretical basis for review in exclusion cases. The concept of the 'right to work', however, has provided the most radical alternative means of attack for the judges. This was a development carried out almost single-handedly by Lord Denning. Although first discussed in 1952 (*Lee* v *Showmen's Guild* [1952] 2 QB 329, CA), it was used for the first time in the next case.

Nagle v Feilden
[1966] 2 QB 633
Court of Appeal

The stewards of the Jockey Club refused Mrs Nagle a licence to train racehorses in pursuance of their unwritten policy of refusing a licence to a woman. Mrs Nagle sued for an injunction and a declaration that the practice was against public policy, but her statement of claim was struck out as disclosing no cause of action. She appealed against this decision. The Court of Appeal granted an interlocutory injunction on the basis that she had an arguable case.

LORD DENNING: The common law of England has for centuries recognised that a man has a right to work at his trade or profession without being unjustly excluded from it. He is not to be shut out from it at the whim of those having the governance of it. If they make a rule which enables them to reject his application arbitrarily or capriciously, not reasonably, that rule is bad. It is against public policy. The court will not give effect to it.

Note
The interlocutory injunction enabled the parties to reach a settlement. Hence the case did not come to court for final judgment. The case below constituted the most radical application of the 'right to work' doctrine.

Edwards v SOGAT
[1971] Ch 354
Court of Appeal

(The facts of this case are set out at p. 614.)

LORD DENNING MR: I do not think the defendant union, or any other trade union, can give itself by its rules an unfettered discretion to expel a man or to withdraw his membership. The reason lies in the man's right to work. This is now fully recognised by law. It is a right which is of especial importance when a trade union operates a 'closed shop' or '100 per cent membership', for that means that no man can become employed or remain in employment with a firm unless he is a member of the union. If his union card is withdrawn, he has to leave the employment. He is deprived of his livelihood. The courts of this country will not allow so great a power to be exercised arbitrarily or capriciously or with unfair discrimination, neither in the making of rules, nor in the enforcement of them.

Note
Prima facie the *Nagle v Feilden* doctrine would seem equally applicable to those unions operating a closed shop. However, there is a fundamental difficulty. It is not clear that the concept of the 'right to work' is anything more than the doctrine of restraint of trade reinterpreted from the standpoint of the individual. Whenever a union by its rules or policies arbitrarily or unreasonably restrains trade, it necessarily arbitrarily or unreasonably inter-

feres with the right to work. This point is addressed in neither *Nagle* nor *Edwards*.

(iii) Discipline and Expulsion at Common Law

Lee v Showmen's Guild of Great Britain
[1952] 2 QB 329
Court of Appeal

The plaintiff was charged with 'unfair competition' under a union rule. An area committee of the union fined him for breaking the rule. Failure to pay the fine was, under the rules, to result in expulsion. The plaintiff did not pay the fine and was expelled. He sought an injunction to prevent the union from enforcing his expulsion. The Court of Appeal granted the injunction.

DENNING LJ: Although the jurisdiction of a domestic tribunal is founded on contract, express or implied, nevertheless the parties are not free to make any contract they like. There are important limitations imposed by public policy. The tribunal must, for instance, observe the principles of natural justice. They must give the man notice of the charge and a reasonable opportunity of meeting it. Any stipulation to the contrary would be invalid. They cannot stipulate for a power to condemn a man unheard. . . .

Another limitation arises out of the well-known principle that parties cannot by contract oust the ordinary courts of their jurisdiction: see *Scott v Avery* (1865) 5 HL Cas 845 at 846 per Alderson B and Cranworth LC. They can, of course, agree to leave questions of law, as well as questions of fact, to the decision of the domestic tribunal. They can, indeed, make the tribunal the final arbiter on questions of fact, but they cannot make it the final arbiter on questions of law. They cannot prevent its decisions being examined by the courts. If parties should seek, by agreement, to take the law out of the hands of the courts and into the hands of a private tribunal, without any recourse at all to the courts in case of error of law, then the agreement is to that extent contrary to public policy and void . . .

. . . [T]he question whether the committee has acted within its jurisdiction depends, in my opinion, on whether the facts adduced before them were reasonably capable of being held to be a breach of the rules. If they were, then the proper inference is that the committee correctly construed the rules and have acted within their jurisdiction. If, however, the facts were not reasonably capable of being held to be a breach and yet the committee held them to be a breach, then the only inference is that the committee have misconstrued the rules and exceeded their jurisdiction.

Esterman v NALGO
[1974] ICR 625
Chancery Division

The trade union, NALGO, and the local authorities were involved in a pay dispute. NALGO held a ballot on the question of selective strike action but achieved only 49 per cent of the vote in favour. Subsequently the union had instructed its members not to assist in administering local elections.

Esterman defied this instruction and, in consequence, was to be disciplined by the union on the basis that she was guilty of conduct rendering her unfit for membership.

The relevant rule read:

> Any member who disregards any regulation issued by the branch, or is guilty of conduct which, in the opinion of the executive committee, renders him unfit for membership, shall be liable to expulsion.

Esterman sought and obtained an injunction against the union to restrain it from taking disciplinary action against her.

TEMPLEMAN J: In my judgement, when the national executive council take the serious step of interfering with the right of a member to volunteer to take work of any description outside his normal employment, the national executive are only entitled to one hundred per cent and implicit obedience to that order if it is clear that they have been given power to issue the order and if it is clear that they are not abusing that power. If a member disobeys an order of the national executive council which does not satisfy those tests, then it seems to me that he cannot be found guilty on that account of conduct which renders him unfit to be a member of NALGO. . . .

On this application, I have listened to very long and very learned argument on the interesting question of whether, on the true construction of the rules and also on the construction of the procedure for strike action, the national executive council had power to issue the order dated 8 April 1974 [i.e. the instruction to members not to assist in the local elections]. It is sufficient for present purposes that not only am I in some doubt now as to the answer to that question, but also that every member of NALGO who received the order could not have been clear as to whether there was power to issue that particular order. . . .

As at present advised, I emphatically reject the submission that it was the duty of every member blindly to obey the orders of the national executive council in the prevailing circumstances and that he could only disobey the order if he were prepared to take the risk of being expelled from NALGO. I also reject the submission that a member who disobeyed the particular order given by the national executive not to assist returning officers showed prima facie that he was unfit to be a member of NALGO. An Act of Parliament carries penalties for its breach, but it is a fallacy to assume that every democratically elected body is entitled to obedience to every order on pain of being found guilty of being unfit to be a member of an association. It must depend on the order and it must depend on the circumstances and, in my judgement, if implicit obedience is to be exacted, those who issue the order must make quite sure that they have the power, that no reasonable man could be in doubt that they have the power and that they are making a proper exercise of the power, and that no reasonable man could conscientiously say to himself that 'this is an order which I have no duty to obey'. In the present case, it was not so clear.

Notes

1. The *Lee* and *Esterman* cases are important because they emphasise that the courts' jurisdiction between unions and members is based on contract; that questions of interpretation are reserved to the courts; and they indicate the way in which the courts will control general 'blanket' disciplinary provisions. *Esterman's* case shows that the mere fact that the provision is in subjective terms – 'in the opinion of the disciplinary body' – is unlikely to make a difference to the willingness of the courts to intervene.

2.   'The power of a union to discipline a member depends upon the express terms of the rulebook. A power to discipline or expel will not be implied' (*Harvey on Industrial Relations and Employment Law*, volume II, paragraph M 2652). However, in *McVitae* v *Unison* [1996] IRLR 33, ChD, Harrison J felt that this proposition was too broadly stated:

In my view, the court can imply such a disciplinary power, although the court's power to do so is one which should be exercised with care and only where there are compelling circumstances to justify it. The reason why the court should be slow to imply a disciplinary power is that it is penal and could include serious consequences affecting the reputation and livelihood of the union member.

In the instant case, it was held that the circumstances of the case warranted implying such a term. The plaintiffs were former NALGO members against whom disciplinary proceedings had been initiated, but no hearing held, when NALGO merged into Unison and ceased to exist. Charges were brought under the Unison rules but the plaintiffs brought proceedings on the ground that there was no express rule allowing Unison to take disciplinary action in respect of conduct prior to the union's inception. Harrison J rejected this argument and stated:

I cannot conceive that it was intended that there should be a complete amnesty for pre-inception conduct. There is certainly no evidence of such an intention and common sense suggests that it would not have been intended. It offends against common sense that a member who has, for instance, done something dishonest before amalgamation which contravenes both the rules of his former union and the rules of Unison should escape penalty simply because of the amalgamation. As a responsible union, Unison would be just as intent on ensuring that such conduct was disciplined as would have been the former union. It is not in the interests of Unison that they should be unable to regulate their membership or the holding of office in such circumstances. In my judgment, it would have been the expectation of members in such circumstances that the union should be able to take disciplinary action. If they had been asked about it, they would have said that it was so obvious that it must have been intended to form part of the agreement between Unison and its members.

(iv)   Natural Justice

Annamunthodo v *Oilfield Workers' Trade Union*
[1961] 3 All ER 621
Privy Council

The appellant had publicly alleged that the president general of the respondent union had embezzled union funds. The appellant was charged in writing with four specific offences under a named union rule. The maximum penalty for each of the offences was a fine. The initial hearing attended by the appellant was adjourned and he did not attend the remainder of the hearing. He was subsequently informed that he had been convicted on all four charges but had been expelled under a blanket rule with which he had not been charged. The order for expulsion was set aside by the Privy Council.

LORD DENNING: . . . Counsel for the respondent union sought to treat the specific formulation of *charges* as immaterial. The substance of the matter lay, he said, in the *facts* alleged in the letter as to the meetings which the appellant had attended and the allegations he had made. Their Lordships cannot accede to this view. If a domestic tribunal formulates specific charges, which lead only to a fine, it cannot without notice resort to other charges, which lead to far more severe penalties.

White v *Kuzych*
[1951] AC 585
Privy Council

VISCOUNT SIMON: Whatever the correct details may be, their Lordships are bound to conclude that there was, before and after the trial, strong and widespread resentment felt against the respondent by many in the union and that Clark, among others, formed and expressed adverse views about him. If the so-called 'trial' and the general meeting which followed had to be conducted by persons previously free from all bias and prejudice, this condition was certainly not fulfilled. It would, indeed, be an error to demand from those who took part the strict impartiality of mind with which a judge should approach and decide an issue between two litigants – that 'icy impartiality of a Rhadamanthus' which Bowen LJ in *Jackson* v *Barry Rly Co.* [1893] 1 Ch 248 thought could not be expected of an engineer-arbitrator – or to regard as disqualified from acting any member who had held or expressed the view that the 'closed shop' principle was essential to the policy and purpose of the union. What those who considered the charges against the respondent and decided whether he was guilty ought to bring to their task was a will to reach an honest conclusion after hearing what was argued on either side and a resolve not to make their minds up beforehand on his personal guilt, however firmly they held their conviction as to union policy and however strongly they had shared in previous adverse criticism of the respondent's conduct.

Roebuck v *NUM (Yorkshire Area) (No. 2)*
[1978] ICR 676
Chancery Division

The union area president (Arthur Scargill), acting on behalf of the union, had successfully sued a newspaper for libel. In the action two union members had given evidence for the newspaper. At the instigation of Mr Scargill, the area executive resolved to charge those members with conduct detrimental to the interests of the union. The executive found the charges proved and this was confirmed by the area council which had originally referred the matter to the executive. Mr Scargill was president of both bodies and participated in their proceedings, questioning the plaintiffs and taking part in their deliberations. However, he did not vote on the resolution to suspend one of the plaintiffs from office as branch chairman and declare the other ineligible for office in the union for two years. The plaintiffs obtained an injunction to prevent the implementation of the decisions.

TEMPLEMAN J: Mr Roebuck and Mr O'Brien were entitled to be tried by a tribunal whose chairman did not appear to have a special reason for bias, conscious or unconscious, against them. True it is that all members of the executive committee and the area council, in common with all members of a domestic tribunal where the interests of their organisation are at stake, have a general inclination to defend the union and its officers against attack from any source; this fact, every trade unionist and every member of a domestic organisation knows and accepts.

But Mr Scargill had a special position, which clearly disqualified him from taking part in the critical meetings of the executive committee and the area committee which he did take. . . . Whether he recognised the fact or not, Mr Scargill must inevitably have appeared to be biased against Mr Roebuck and Mr O'Brien. The appearance of bias was inevitable; the exercise of bias, conscious or unconscious, was probable. I am content to rest my judgement on the ground that it was manifestly unfair to Mr Roebuck and Mr O'Brien that Mr Scargill should have acted as chairman, and should have played the part which he admits to have played at the relevant meetings of the executive committee and the area council.

(v)   Excluding the Jurisdiction of the Court at Common Law
A union rule which seeks to bar the member from pursuing legal redress is void and unenforceable as against public policy (see *Lee* v *Showmen's Guild* [1952] 2 QB 329, above). Less clear-cut is the validity of a rule that the union's internal disciplinary procedures must be exhausted before a member can apply to the court. The courts recognise that there are many advantages to internal resolution of the dispute.

Leigh v NUR
[1970] Ch 326
Chancery Division

GOFF J: . . . [Wh]ere there is an express provision in the rules that the plaintiff must first exhaust his domestic remedies, the court is not absolutely bound by that because its jurisdiction cannot be ousted, but the plaintiff will have to show cause why it should interfere with the contractual position . . .

. . . [In] the absence of such a provision the court can readily, or at all events more readily, grant relief without prior recourse to the domestic remedies, but may require the plaintiff to resort first to those remedies.

Note
Exhaustion of internal procedures would not be required if the domestic proceedings were irretrievably biased, involved a serious point of law, where fraud is at issue, or where internal procedures would involve excessive delay.

In *Esterman* v *NALGO* (above) the court went further to hold that a plaintiff may bring an action to stop *impending* disciplinary action if he or she can show that there is no lawful basis for them.

The EA 1988, s. 2, provided a new right for union members not to be denied access to the court to pursue a grievance against their union. The relevant provisions are now to be found in TULR(C)A 1992.

Trade Union and Labour Relations (Consolidation) Act 1992

63. Right not to be denied access to the courts

(2) Notwithstanding anything in the rules of the union or in the practice of any court, if a member or former member of the union begins proceedings in a court with respect to a matter to which this section applies, then if—

(a) he has previously made a valid application to the union for the matter to be submitted for determination or conciliation in accordance with the union's rules, and

(b) the court proceedings are begun after the end of the period of six months beginning with the day on which the union received the application,

the rules requiring or allowing the matter to be so submitted, and the fact that any relevant steps remain to be taken under the rules, shall be regarded for all purposes as irrelevant to any question whether the court proceedings should be dismissed, stayed or sisted, or adjourned.

Note

However, TULR(C)A 1992, s. 63(6) states that this six-month rule is without prejudice to any rule of law by which a court could ignore any such union rule already, so the principles discussed in *Leigh* v *NUR* (above) are still relevant.

B: Refusals to Admit and Expulsions in the Interests of Inter-Union Relations

The TUC has drawn up a set of *Principles Governing Relations Between Unions* — the so-called 'Bridlington Principles'. They require every affiliated union to ask all applicants for membership if they are or have recently been a union member. The new union must then ask the old union whether the member has resigned, has any subscription arrears, is 'under discipline or penalty', or if there are any other reasons why he or she should not be accepted. If the old union objects, the dispute may be resolved by the TUC Disputes Committee. Most affiliated unions have a provision in their rule books providing for the automatic termination of membership, following a period of notice, in order to comply with the decision of the Disputes Committee. The courts have upheld the validity of such rules, provided that the power is exercised following a *valid* decision of the Disputes Committee itself (see *Rothwell* v *APEX* [1975] IRLR 375).

In *Cheall* v *APEX* [1983] 2 AC 180, the House of Lords held that an individual trade unionist had no right to be heard by the TUC Disputes Committee before it made its determination. Furthermore, there was 'no existing rule of public policy that would prevent trade unions from entering into arrangements with one another which they consider to be in the interests of their members in promoting order in industrial relations and enhancing their members' bargaining power with their employers'.

In their 1991 Green Paper, *Industrial Relations in the 1990s* (Cm 1602), the Government expressed the view that the law should be amended so as to guarantee freedom of choice where more than one trade union can genuinely claim to be able to represent an employee's interests. In the Government's opinion, a union should not be obliged to accept someone into membership if it does not represent employees of a similar skill or occupation. Nor should it be obliged to accept an applicant who has been an unsatisfactory member of another union because, for example, he has a record of refusing to pay his subscriptions. However, a union should not be at liberty to refuse to accept an individual into membership simply because he was previously a member of another union which claims sole recruitment rights in a particular company or sector. Section 14 of TURERA 1993 was designed to implement these views (see now TULR(C)A 1992, s. 17).

The remedy for an infringement of this right is by way of a complaint to an employment tribunal for a declaration and compensation. The remedies operate in a very similar way to those which apply to unreasonable exclusion or expulsion from a trade union, and to unjustifiable discipline by a trade union (see below).

C: Statutory Controls Over Admissions and Expulsions

(i)   Pre-1980 Law

As we have seen, the Donovan Commission suggested that a review body should be created to hear complaints concerning arbitrary exclusions or expulsions. No such body was ever created by statute, although the Industrial Relations Act 1971, s. 65 did contain provisions prohibiting arbitrary or unreasonable discrimination against applicants as members. A similar provision contained in TULRA 1974, s. 5 was repealed by TULR(A)A 1976. In response, the TUC established its own Independent Review Committee (IRC) in April 1976 to provide a voluntary forum for hearing cases alleging unreasonable exclusion or expulsion from unions operating a closed shop.

The IRC's awards were not legally binding but the affiliates agreed to be bound by them. The remedy was a recommendation that a union admit or re-admit the complainant into membership; the IRC had no authority to award compensation. The major weakness was that an IRC recommendation could not be enforced against employers, i.e. even if the union reinstated a worker there was nothing to force the employer to take an employee back if he or she had been dismissed, though of course there is now the unfair dismissal remedy in such cases.

Once the Government introduced legislation covering the area of admissions and expulsions in unions operating the closed shop, the voluntary machinery, in the words of the TUC, 'faded away'.

(ii)   The Employment Acts 1980–1990

The Conservative Government was not satisfied with the TUC's self-regulation and enacted the EA 1980, s. 4. This reverted the position to broadly that of the period of the Industrial Relations Act 1971, except s. 4 applied *only* where the employer operated a union membership agreement. The EA 1988 introduced more general provisions on unjustifiable discipline by trade unions, which apply in all cases whether inside or outside closed shops (see below). Finally, as we saw earlier in this chapter, closed shops experienced yet a further legal onslaught as a result of the EA 1990, which made it unlawful to refuse a person employment because he or she is or does not wish to become a union member. (See now TULR(C)A 1992, s. 137.)

(iii) Statutory 'Permitted' Reasons

Prior to the passage of TURERA 1993, an individual seeking a job where a 'closed shop' – or 'Union Membership Agreement' – operated had a right (a) not to have his or her membership application unreasonably refused; and (b) not to be unreasonably expelled from the union (TULR(C)A 1992, ss. 174–177). TURERA 1993 replaced these provisions with new ss. 174–177, which provide a general right for workers not to be excluded or expelled from any union unless the exclusion or expulsion is for a statutory 'permitted' reason.

Trade Union and Labour Relations (Consolidation) Act 1992

174. Right not to be excluded or expelled from union

(1) An individual shall not be excluded or expelled from a trade union unless the exclusion or expulsion is permitted by this section.

(2) The exclusion or expulsion of an individual from a trade union is permitted by this section if (and only if)—

(a) he does not satisfy, or no longer satisfies, an enforceable membership requirement contained in the rules of the union,

(b) he does not qualify, or no longer qualifies, for membership of the union by reason of the union operating only in a particular part or particular parts of Great Britain,

(c) in the case of a union whose purpose is the regulation of relations between its members and one particular employer or a number of particular employers who are associated, he is not, or is no longer, employed by that employer or one of those employers, or

(d) the exclusion or expulsion is entirely attributable to his conduct.

(3) A requirement in relation to membership of a union is 'enforceable' for the purposes of subsection (2)(a) if it restricts membership solely by reference to one or more of the following criteria—

(a) employment in a specified trade, industry or profession,

(b) occupational description (including grade, level or category of appointment), and

(c) possession of specified trade, industrial or professional qualifications or work experience.

(4) For the purposes of subsection (2)(d) 'conduct', in relation to an individual, does not include—

(a) his being or ceasing to be, or having been or ceased to be—
    (i)   a member of another trade union,
    (ii) employed by a particular employer or at a particular place, or
    (iii) a member of a political party, or

(b) conduct to which section 65 (conduct for which an individual may not be disciplined by a trade union) applies or would apply if the references in that section to the trade union which is relevant for the purposes of that section were references to any trade union.

(5) An individual who claims that he has been excluded or expelled from a trade union in contravention of this section may present a complaint to an industrial tribunal.

Notes

1. The remedies are complex. A person who has obtained a declaration from a tribunal that he or she was unreasonably excluded or expelled may claim compensation. The applicant must wait for at least four weeks after the date of the declaration (to give the union an opportunity to admit or re-admit), but then has up to six months after the date of the declaration to present a claim for compensation. If he or she has been admitted/re-admitted by the time of the application, complaint lies to an employment tribunal. If the union has refused to abide by the tribunal's initial declaration, complaint lies directly to the EAT. In both cases the amount of compensation will be such as is considered just and equitable in all the circumstances, subject to a maximum. The maximum compensation is 30 times the maximum amount of a week's pay allowable in computing the basic award for unfair dismissal cases, plus the maximum compensatory award for the time being in force in respect of unfair dismissal (TULR(C)A 1992, s. 176(4)(6)). The minimum award before the EAT is £5,000: there is no minimum award before an employment tribunal.

Where the employment tribunal or EAT finds that the exclusion or expulsion complained of was to any extent caused or contributed to by the action of the applicant, it shall reduce the amount of compensation by such proportion as it considers just and equitable in the circumstances (TULR(C)A 1992, s. 176(5); see *Howard* v *NGA* [1985] ICR 101, EAT).

2. In *NACODS* v *Gluchowski* [1996] IRLR 252, EAT, the applicant was suspended from membership of the union as a result of complaints relating to his business activities. He challenged this under TULR(C)A 1992, s. 174, as being an unlawful exclusion or expulsion from the union and his claim was upheld by the industrial tribunal. However, on appeal, the EAT held that the tribunal had erred in holding that the applicant's suspension from the appellant union amounted to 'exclusion'. In reaching that decision, the tribunal had erred in concluding that 'exclusion' must include exclusion from the benefits of membership and the ability to make use of any of its privileges.

According to the EAT, 'exclusion' from a trade union in s. 174(1) refers to a refusal to admit into membership, not to suspension of the privileges of membership. That interpretation was supported by the distinction between trade union membership and enjoyment of the benefits of union membership which was drawn in some of the speeches in the House of Lords in *Associated Newspapers* v *Wilson* and *Associated British Ports* v *Palmer* [1995] IRLR 258, HL. The tribunal's concern that a narrow definition of exclusion would mean that a trade union could impose a permanent suspension and argue that an individual had neither been excluded nor expelled, was misplaced since that kind of situation could lead to a remedy by other routes.

3. Several other statutes are relevant to this area. The RRA 1976, SDA 1975 and Disability Discrimination Act 1995 make it unlawful to discriminate on grounds of sex, race or disability against an applicant for trade union membership. The TULR(C)A, s. 82(c), states that where the union operates a political fund, it must not make contribution to the fund a condition of admission or discriminate against a non-contributor. Union rule books are required to contain a rule to this effect. Lastly, as we see below, the EA 1988 imposed a general prohibition on unjustifiable discipline of trade union members. The law is now set out in TULR(C)A 1992, ss. 64–67, as amended by TURERA 1993, s. 16.

D: *Unjustifiable Discipline*

Trade Union and Labour Relations (Consolidation) Act 1992

64. **Right not to be unjustifiably disciplined**

(1) An individual who is or has been a member of a trade union has the right not to be unjustifiably disciplined by the union.

(2) For this purpose an individual is 'disciplined' by a trade union if a determination is made, or purportedly made, under the rules of the union or by an official of the union or a number of persons including an official that—

    (a) he should be expelled from the union or a branch or section of the union,

    (b) he should pay a sum to the union, to a branch or section of the union or to any other person;

    (c) sums tendered by him in respect of an obligation to pay subscriptions or other sums to the union, or to a branch or section of the union, should be treated as unpaid or paid for a different purpose,

    (d) he should be deprived to any extent of, or of access to, any benefits, services or facilities which would otherwise be provided or made available to him by virtue of his membership of the union, or a branch or section of the union,

    (e) another trade union, or a branch or section of it, should be encouraged or advised not to accept him as a member, or

    (f) he should be subjected to some other detriment;

and whether an individual is 'unjustifiably disciplined' shall be determined in accordance with section 65.

(3) Where a determination made in infringement of an individual's right under this section requires the payment of a sum or the performance of an obligation, no person is entitled in any proceedings to rely on that determination for the purpose of recovering the sum or enforcing the obligation.

(4) Subject to that, the remedies for infringement of the right conferred by this section are as provided by sections 66 and 67, and not otherwise.

(5) The right not to be unjustifiably disciplined is in addition to (and not in substitution for) any right which exists apart from this section; and nothing in this section or sections 65 to 67 affects any remedy for infringement of any such right.

65. **Meaning of 'unjustifiably disciplined'**

(1) An individual is unjustifiably disciplined by a trade union if the actual or supposed conduct which constitutes the reason, or one of the reasons, for disciplining him is—

    (a) conduct to which this section applies, or

(b)   something which is believed by the union to amount to such conduct;
but subject to subsection (6) (cases of bad faith in relation to assertion of wrongdoing).

(2)   This section applies to conduct which consists in—

(a)   failing to participate in or support a strike or other industrial action (whether by members of the union or by others), or indicating opposition to or a lack of support for such action;

(b)   failing to contravene, for a purpose connected with such a strike or other industrial action, a requirement imposed on him by or under a contract of employment;

(c)   asserting (whether by bringing proceedings or otherwise) that the union, any official or representative of it or a trustee of its property has contravened, or is proposing to contravene, a requirement which is, or is thought to be, imposed by or under the rules of the union or any other agreement or by or under any enactment (whenever passed) or any rule of law;

(d)   encouraging or assisting a person—

(i)   to perform an obligation imposed on him by a contract of employment, or

(ii)   to make or attempt to vindicate any such assertion as is mentioned in paragraph (c); or

(e)   contravening a requirement imposed by or in consequence of a determination which infringes the individual's or another individual's right not to be unjustifiably disciplined.

(f)   failing to agree, or withdrawing agreement, to the making from his wages (in accordance with arrangements between his employer and the union) of deductions representing payments to the union in respect of his membership,

(g)   resigning or proposing to resign from the union or from another union, becoming or proposing to become a member of another union, refusing to become a member of another union, or being a member of another union,

(h)   working with, or proposing to work with, individuals who are not members of the union or who are or are not members of another union,

(i)   working for, or proposing to work for, an employer who employs or who has employed individuals who are not members of the union or who are or are not members of another union, or

(j)   requiring the union to do an act which the union is, by any provision of this Act, required to do on the requisition of a member.

(3)   This section applies to conduct which involves the Commissioner for the Rights of Trade Union Members or the Certification Officer being consulted or asked to provide advice or assistance with respect to any matter whatever, or which involves any person being consulted or asked to provide advice or assistance with respect to a matter which forms, or might form, the subject-matter of any such assertion as is mentioned in subsection (2)(c) above.

(4)   This section also applies to conduct which consists in proposing to engage in, or doing anything preparatory or incidental to, conduct falling within subsection (2) or (3).

(5)   This section does not apply to an act, omission or statement comprised in conduct falling within subsection (2), (3) or (4) above if it is shown that the act, omission or statement is one in respect of which individuals would be disciplined by the union irrespective of whether their acts, omissions or statements were in connection with conduct within subsection (2) or (3) above.

(6)   An individual is not unjustifiably disciplined if it is shown—

(a)   that the reason for disciplining him, or one of them, is that he made such an assertion as is mentioned in subsection (2)(c), or encouraged or assisted another person to make or attempt to vindicate such an assertion,

(b)   that the assertion was false, and

(c)   that he made the assertion, or encouraged or assisted another person to make or attempt to vindicate it, in the belief that it was false or otherwise in bad faith, and that there was no other reason for disciplining him or that the only other reasons were reasons in respect of which he does not fall to be treated as unjustifiably disciplined.

(7)   In this section—

'conduct' includes statements, acts and omissions;

'contract of employment', in relation to an individual, includes any agreement between that individual and a person for whom he works or normally works; and

'representative', in relation to a union, means a person acting or purporting to act—

(a)   in his capacity as a member of the union, or

(b)   on the instructions or advice of a person acting or purporting to act in that capacity or in the capacity of an official of the union.

'require' (on the part of an individual) includes request or apply for, and 'requisition' shall be construed accordingly.

'wages' shall be construed in accordance with the definitions of 'contract of employment', 'employer' and related expressions.

(8)   Where a person holds any office or employment under the Crown on terms which do not constitute a contract of employment between him and the Crown, those terms shall nevertheless be deemed to constitute such a contract for the purposes of this section.

Notes

1.   One of the specified grounds where discipline is unjustifiable is where the reason is that a member failed to 'participate in or support a strike or other industrial action' or indicated 'opposition to' such action. The phrase 'other industrial action' is not defined in the Act, but some guidance was offered by the EAT in *Fire Brigades Union* v *Knowles* [1996] IRLR 337. In this case, two full-time fire-fighters were disciplined by their union when, in contravention of union policy, they accepted additional employment as retained (part-time) fire-fighters. The EAT held that the union's policy did not constitute 'other industrial action'. According to Keene LJ:

Not every action which involves pressure on an employer together with some effect on that employer's freedom of action will constitute 'other industrial action'. There must be some action directed against the employer with the object of obtaining some advantage for the employees . . . In the present case, the industrial tribunal appears to have accepted that the ban on combining full-time and retained duties was imposed for safety reasons. There is no suggestion that it was imposed in order to enhance the union's bargaining position when the time came for negotiations on wages or conditions. It seems that there was no ulterior industrial objective to the restriction contained in the union's policy.

Do you agree with this reasoning? Surely, a dispute relating to health and safety issues would fall within the statutory definition of trade dispute for the purpose of establishing tortious liability? (see TULR(C)A 1992, s. 244, discussed at p. 746). The decision in *Knowles* was subsequently upheld by the Court of Appeal (see [1996] IRLR 617).

2.   This is a controversial set of provisions, widely regarded by critics as a 'scab's charter'. A union is prohibited from disciplining a member for not taking part in industrial action notwithstanding that a majority of that member's fellow workers voted in favour of the action in a properly held ballot. As such, TULR(C)A 1992, s. 64 is understandably seen by the union movement as an attack on the fundamental concepts of union solidarity and collectivism.

Ewan McKendrick has argued:

> By prohibiting the exercise of disciplinary sanctions by unions, [section 64] stacks all the disciplinary powers on the side of the employer. In sum [section 64] is an objectionable intervention in union affairs, it is a possible violation of our international obligations and it elevates the individual interest of a union member to a point where it unacceptably undermines the collective strength of the union and represents an unwarranted intrusion into internal union affairs. ('The Rights of Trade Union Members – Part I of the Employment Act 1988' (1988) 17 ILJ No. 3, p. 141, at pp. 149, 150)

3.   TURERA 1993, s. 16, extended the list of conduct for which it is unjustifiable for a trade union to discipline a member (see TULR(C)A 1992, s. 65(2)(f)–(j) above).

4.   A claim must be made to the employment tribunal within three months of the imposition of the disciplinary sanction. There is power to extend the period if the tribunal is satisfied:

(a)   that it was not reasonably practicable for the complaint to have been presented within the three-month limit; and

(b)   that any delay in making the complaint is wholly or partly attributable to any reasonable attempt to appeal internally against the determination to which the complaint relates.

Where the tribunal finds that the complainant has been unjustifiably disciplined, it will make a declaration to that effect. The complainant may then make a further application to the tribunal for compensation, not earlier than four weeks but not later than six months after the date of the initial declaration.

What happens next depends on the trade union's response. If the union has revoked its disciplinary decision and taken all necessary steps to put that decision into effect, the further application is to the employment tribunal. If, on the other hand, the union fails to revoke its decision, the further application is to the EAT.

The amount of compensation to be awarded will be such as is considered to be just and equitable in all the circumstances of the case, subject to the usual rules relating to mitigation of loss and contributory fault.

Where the application is to the employment tribunal, the maximum award is 30 times a week's pay, together with the maximum compensatory award currently available. Where the application is to the EAT, the same maximum figure applies, but there is a fixed minimum award which currently stands at £5,000 (TULR(C)A 1992, s. 67(8)).

E: Trade Union Democracy

(i) Rule Book as Contract and Constitution

At common law, the government and administration of a union must be carried out in accordance with the terms of the contract of membership which are contained primarily in the rule book. A failure to do this will normally constitute a breach of contract, and the courts may well declare it *ultra vires* (beyond the powers of) the union.

The potential for challenging the action taken by a union in breach of its rules was repeatedly illustrated in the cases raised by working miners against various areas of the NUM during the miners' strike of 1984–5. In these cases, the judges relied on a strict construction of the NUM's rule book to establish the requirement for conducting ballots before authorising industrial action. In *Taylor v NUM (Derbyshire Area) (No. 1)* [1984] IRLR 440, it was held that the local area was required by its rules to obtain 55 per cent support in a ballot for strike action before such action could be official, and in *Taylor v NUM (Yorkshire Area)* [1984] IRLR 445, it was held that an area ballot held some two and a half years previously was too remote to be capable of justifying a lawful call for strike action under the rules. In both cases the judges accepted that the strike in reality constituted national action, which was also unlawful in the absence of a national ballot.

Once the strike was declared called in breach of the rules, injunctions were granted preventing the issuing of instructions to the membership not to work, or to cross picket lines (*Taylor v NUM (Derbyshire Area) (No. 1)*). A second consequence of the holding that the action was beyond the rules was that the use of union funds to support the strike could be restrained. In *Taylor v NUM (Derbyshire Area) (No. 3)* [1985] IRLR 99, the judge held that it was *ultra vires* for the union to authorise expenditure on strike action which had been called in breach of the area's rules. Further, the officials who had misapplied union moneys in this way were in breach of the fiduciary duty which they owed to the members, and could be personally liable for such unauthorised expenditure. The miners' cases demonstrated the readiness of the judges to issue interlocutory injunctions to restrain the alleged unlawful behaviour and, as we shall see, the potential for using 'scab' workers to mount legal challenges against a striking union was not lost on the Government when it framed the EA 1988. (For a penetrating analysis of the litigation during the miners' strike, see Ewing, K.D., 'The Strike, the Courts and the Rule-Books', *Industrial Law Journal*, vol. 14, No. 3, pp. 160–75.)

(ii) Union Accounts

Trade Union and Labour Relations (Consolidation) Act 1992

32. Annual return

(1) A trade union shall send to the Certification Officer as respects each calendar year a return relating to its affairs.

(2) The annual return shall be in such form and be signed by such persons as the Certification Officer may require and shall be sent to him before 1st June in the calendar year following that to which it relates.

(3)   The annual return shall contain—
    (a)   the following accounts—
        (i)   revenue accounts indicating the income and expenditure of the trade union for the period to which the return relates,
        (ii)   a balance sheet as at the end of that period, and
        (iii)   such other accounts as the Certification Officer may require,
each of which must give a true and fair view of the matters to which it relates.
    (aa)   details of the salary paid to and other benefits provided to or in respect of—
        (i)   each member of the executive,
        (ii)   the president, and
        (iii)   the general secretary,
by the trade union during the period to which the return relates, and
    (b)   a copy of the report made by the auditor or auditors of the trade union on those accounts and such other documents relating to those accounts and such further particulars as the Certification Officer may require, and
    (c)   a copy of the rules of the trade union as in force at the end of the period to which the return relates;
    (d)   in the case of a trade union required to maintain a register by section 24, a statement of the number of names on the register as at the end of the period to which the return relates and the number of those names which were not accompanied by an address which is a member's address for the purposes of that section;
and shall have attached to it a note of all the changes in the officers of the union and of any change in the address of the head or main office of the union during the period to which the return relates.
(4)   The Certification Officer may, if in any particular case he considers it appropriate to do so—
    (a)   direct that the period for which a return is to be sent to him shall be a period other than the calendar year last preceding the date on which the return is sent;
    (b)   direct that the date before which a return is to be sent to him shall be such date (whether before or after 1st June) as may be specified in the direction.
(5)   A trade union shall at the request of any person supply him with a copy of its most recent return either free of charge or on payment of a reasonable charge.
(6)   The Certification Officer shall at all reasonable hours keep available for public inspection either free of charge or on payment of a reasonable charge, copies of all annual returns sent to him under this section.

Notes

1.   Failure either to submit an annual return or to maintain proper accounts and accounting controls is a criminal offence (TULR(C)A 1992, s. 45(1)). It is also an offence to falsify the accounts (s. 45(4)).

2.   The 1991 Green Paper, *Industrial Relations in the 1990s*, contained a number of proposals for strengthening the law as it affects responsibility of trade union leaders for union finances. In the Government's view, the Lightman Inquiry into allegations of serious misconduct by senior officials of the NUM in the management of the union's finances indicated that the rights of union members in this area need further support (see *The Lightman Report on the NUM*, Penguin, 1990).

Consequently, TURERA 1993 contained amendments:

    (a)   providing the Certification Officer with wider powers to direct a trade union to produce documents relating to its financial affairs and to appoint inspectors to investigate the financial affairs of a trade union where it appears to the Certification Officer that there is impropriety in the conduct of those affairs. It requires reports of investigations to be published. Reports will be admissible in legal proceedings;

(b)   creating new offences in connection with the Certification Officer's proposed powers of inspection and investigation. It would be an offence to contravene any duty or requirement imposed by the Certification Officer or inspectors relating to the production of documents, etc.; to destroy, mutilate or falsify a document relating to the financial affairs of the union (unless there was no intention to conceal information or defeat the law); to fraudulently part with, alter or delete anything in such a document; or to provide or make an explanation or statement, either knowingly or recklessly, which is false;

(c)   increasing the maximum penalty for an offence relating to the duty to keep accounting records or the duties as to annual returns, auditors or members' superannuation schemes, from a fine not exceeding level 3 on the standard scale to a fine not exceeding level 5 (currently £5,000). The new offence of failing to comply with any requirements of the Certification Officers or inspectors relating to the production of financial documents etc. will attract a similar penalty;

(d)   providing that certain offences relating to falsification, destruction, alteration or mutilation of financial documents may result in imprisonment for up to six months, a fine of up to £5,000, or both.

(e)   specifying that instead of a six-month limit, proceedings under the Act should be possible at any time within three years of the relevant offence, provided that the information is laid before the court within six months of the discovery of the offence;

(f)   providing that persons convicted of offences in connection with the financial affairs of trade unions are disqualified from being a member of a union's executive or from being president or general secretary of a union. The disqualification periods are five years or 10 years depending on the gravity of the offence;

(g)   imposing a new statutory duty for a trade union to provide each of its members, on an annual basis, with a written summary of its financial affairs. The statement is to include an indication of what the member may do if he or she suspects an irregularity in the conduct of the union's affairs;

(h)   requiring annual returns to the Certification Officer to identify the salary or other remuneration (including loans and benefits-in-kind) provided out of union funds to each member of the union's principal executive committee, president and general secretary, and to include a statement of the number of names on the union's register of members and how many are not accompanied by an address.

(iii)   Member's Right of Access to Trade Union's Accounts

Trade Union and Labour Relations (Consolidation) Act 1992

28.   Duty to keep accounting records
(1)   A trade union shall—

(a)   cause to be kept proper accounting records with respect to its transactions and its assets and liabilities, and

(b)   establish and maintain a satisfactory system of control of its accounting records, its cash holdings and all its receipts and remittances.

(2)   Proper accounting records shall not be taken to be kept with respect to the matters mentioned in subsection (1)(a) unless there are kept such records as are necessary to give a true and fair view of the state of the affairs of the trade union and to explain its transactions.

29.   Duty to keep records available for inspection

(1)   A trade union shall keep available for inspection from their creation until the end of the period of six years beginning with the 1st January following the end of the period to which they relate such of the records of the union, or of any branch or section of the union, as are, or purport to be, records required to be kept by the union under section 28.

This does not apply to records relating to periods before 1st January 1988.

(2)   In section 30 (right of member to access to accounting records)—

(a)   references to a union's accounting records are to any such records as are mentioned in subsection (1) above, and

(b)   references to records available for inspection are to records which the union is required by that subsection to keep available for inspection.

(3)   The expiry of the period mentioned in subsection (1) above does not affect the duty of a trade union to comply with a request for access made under section 30 before the end of that period.

30.   Right of access to accounting records

(1)   A member of a trade union has a right to request access to any accounting records of the union which are available for inspection and relate to periods including a time when he was a member of the union.

In the case of records relating to a branch or section of the union, it is immaterial whether he was a member of that branch or section.

(2)   Where such access is requested the union shall—

(a)   make arrangements with the member for him to be allowed to inspect the records requested before the end of the period of twenty-eight days beginning with the day the request was made,

(b)   allow him and any accountant accompanying him for the purpose to inspect the records at the time and place arranged, and

(c)   secure that at the time of the inspection he is allowed to take, or is supplied with, any copies of, or of extracts from, records inspected by him which he requires.

(3)   The inspection shall be at a reasonable hour and at the place where the records are normally kept, unless the parties to the arrangements agree otherwise.

(4)   An 'accountant' means a person who is eligible for appointment as a company auditor under section 25 of the Companies Act 1989.

(5)   The union need not allow the member to be accompanied by an accountant if the accountant fails to enter into such agreement as the union may reasonably require for protecting the confidentiality of the records.

(6)   Where a member who makes a request for access to a union's accounting records is informed by the union, before any arrangements are made in pursuance of the request—

(a)   of the union's intention to charge for allowing him to inspect the records to which the request relates, for allowing him to take copies of, or extracts from, those records or for supplying any such copies, and

(b) of the principles in accordance with which its charges will be determined,

then, where the union complies with the request, he is liable to pay the union on demand such amount, not exceeding the reasonable administrative expenses incurred by the union in complying with the request, as is determined in accordance with those principles.

(7) In this section 'member', in relation to a trade union consisting wholly or partly of, or of representatives of, constituent or affiliated organisations, includes a member of any of the constituent or affiliated organisations.

Notes

1. Prior to 1988, an ordinary member did not possess a statutory right to inspect the union's accounts, though he or she might be given that right under the rule book. If there is such a right under a rule, then the member also has the right to be accompanied by an accountant or other agent (see *Norey* v *Keep* [1909] 1 Ch 561 and *Taylor* v *NUM (Derbyshire Area)* [1985] IRLR 65).

The first *statutory* provision giving rights of access to union records, whether or not there is an express rule, was provided by the EA 1988. The relevant provisions are now contained in TULR(C)A 1992, s. 30 (above).

2. Where it is claimed that a union has failed to comply with a request, within 28 days, the member may apply to the court for an order requiring inspection, etc. It is also a criminal offence to fail to keep accounting records available for inspection (TULR(C)A 1992, s. 31).

(iv) Indemnification by Unions of Officials

Trade Union and Labour Relations (Consolidation) Act 1992

15. Prohibition on use of funds to indemnify unlawful conduct

(1) It is unlawful for property of a trade union to be applied in or towards—

(a) the payment for an individual of a penalty which has been or may be imposed on him for an offence or for contempt of court,

(b) the securing of any such payment, or

(c) the provision of anything for indemnifying an individual in respect of such a penalty.

(2) Where any property of a trade union is so applied for the benefit of an individual on whom a penalty has been or may be imposed, then—

(a) in the case of a payment, an amount equal to the payment is recoverable by the union from him, and

(b) in any other case, he is liable to account to the union for the value of the property applied.

(3) If a trade union fails to bring or continue proceedings which it is entitled by bring by virtue of subsection (2), a member of the union who claims that the failure is unreasonable may apply to the court on that ground for an order authorising him to bring or continue the proceedings on the union's behalf and at the union's expense.

(4) In this section 'penalty', in relation to an offence, includes an order to pay compensation and an order for the forfeiture of any property; and references to the imposition of a penalty for an offence shall be construed accordingly.

(5)   The Secretary of State may by order designate offences in relation to which the provisions of this section do not apply.

Any such order shall be made by statutory instrument which shall be subject to annulment in pursuance of a resolution of either House of Parliament.

(6)   This section does not affect—

(a)   any other enactment, any rule of law or any provision of the rules of a trade union which makes it unlawful for the property of a trade union to be applied in a particular way; or

(b)   any other remedy available to a trade union, the trustees of its property or any of its members in respect of an unlawful application of the union's property.

(7)   In this section 'member', in relation to a trade union consisting wholly or partly of, or of representatives of, constituent or affiliated organisations, includes a member of any of the constituent or affiliated organisations.

Notes

1.   Prior to 1988, it was not clear to what extent (if any) a trade union might use its funds to indemnify members for criminal sanctions imposed upon them, e.g. for illegal picketing, or for being held in contempt of court.

The issue was first raised in *Drake* v *Morgan* [1978] ICR 56. During the journalists' strike in 1977, a number of members of the NUJ were charged with offences in connection with picketing and fined. The union's national executive committee passed a resolution that it would indemnify members in respect of these offences, with the exception of four cases involving physical violence. The judge refused the application for an injunction to restrain the union from implementing this resolution, on the basis that the resolution had been passed *after* the offences had been committed, and therefore there was not a general indemnity for members who might commit offences. He thought that different considerations might apply if continued resolutions authorising expenditure from funds might lead to an expectation that a union would indemnify its members against the consequences of future offences (see also *Thomas* v *NUM (South Wales Area)* [1985] IRLR 136).

The Government was of the view that the common law position was unsatisfactory and was anxious to ensure that union officials took the full legal consequences of their unlawful acts, and that they should not rely upon indemnification by their unions. The EA 1988 banned all forms of indemnity, retrospective or prospective. The law is now set out in TULR(C)A 1992, s. 15 (above).

2.   If the property of the union is applied in a manner caught by s. 15, the union may recover its value from the individual indemnified (s. 15(2)).

Any member who claims that the union is *unreasonably* refusing to take steps towards recovery may apply to the court for authority to take such proceedings on behalf of the union, at the union's expense (s. 15(3)). This special provision overcomes the procedural difficulties which might otherwise be created by the rule in *Foss* v *Harbottle* (1843) 2 Hare 461, often applied to unions, which provides that where a wrong has been done to a corporate body, a minority of the members will be bound by a decision of the majority to take no legal action to remedy the wrong, if none of the members in the minority has personally suffered any harm.

Section 15 is without prejudice to any other enactment, trade union rule or provision which would otherwise make it unlawful for trade union property to be used in a particular way (s. 15(6)). Thus, the expenditure of money may be restricted to lawful objects or objects other than industrial action in the union rule book.

McKendrick (op. cit., at p. 152) observes:

As was pointed out in the Green Paper [*Trade Unions and Their Members*], the incorporation of contempt of court opens up considerable 'scope for willing martyrdom' where individual members of the union are named by the plaintiff in the proceedings. In the NUM dispute martyrdom for Mr Scargill was avoided by an anonymous donor paying Mr Scargill's fine but, presumably, were such a fine to be paid in such a way in the future, union members would be able to exercise their right to inspect the union accounts to ensure that the fine was not paid by their union. It is rather surprising that the Government has seen fit to include a provision which increases, rather than decreases, the prospect of martyrdom when they have consistently sought to ensure that remedies are enforceable against union property rather than individual union members.

(v)   Control of Union Trustees

Trade Union and Labour Relations (Consolidation) Act 1992

16.   Remedy against trustees for unlawful use of union property

(1)   A member of a trade union who claims that the trustees of the union's property—

(a)   have so carried out their functions, or are proposing so to carry out their functions, as to cause or permit an unlawful application of the union's property, or

(b)   have complied, or are proposing to comply, with an unlawful direction which has been or may be given, or purportedly given, to them under the rules of the union,

may apply to the court for an order under this section.

(2)   In a case relating to property which has already been unlawfully applied, or to an unlawful direction that has already been complied with, an application under this section may be made only by a person who was a member of the union at the time when the property was applied or, as the case may be, the direction complied with.

(3)   Where the court is satisfied that the claim is well-founded, it shall make such order as it considers appropriate.

The court may in particular—

(a)   require the trustees (if necessary, on behalf of the union) to take all such steps as may be specified in the order for protecting or recovering the property of the union;

(b)   appoint a receiver of, or in Scotland a judicial factor on, the property of the union;

(c)   remove one or more of the trustees.

(4)   Where the court makes an order under this section in a case in which—

(a)   property of the union has been applied in contravention of an order of any court, or in compliance with a direction given in contravention of such an order, or

(b)   the trustees were proposing to apply property in contravention of such an order or to comply with any such direction, the court shall by its order remove all the trustees except any trustee who satisfies the court that there is a good reason for allowing him to remain a trustee.

(5) Without prejudice to any other power of the court, the court may on an application for an order under this section grant such interlocutory relief (in Scotland, such interim order) as it considers appropriate.

(6) This section does not affect any other remedy available in respect of a breach of trust by the trustees of a trade union's property.

(7) In this section 'member', in relation to a trade union consisting wholly or partly of, or of representatives of, constituent or affiliated organisations, includes a member of any of the constituent or affiliated organisations.

Notes

1. It will be remembered that the property of a trade union is vested in trustees on trust for the union (TULR(C)A 1992, s. 12(1)). This arises because a union is an unincorporated association and so, not being a legal person, cannot hold property in its own name.

2. Union officials in general owe a fiduciary duty to their union. In *Taylor* v *NUM (Derbyshire Area) (No. 3)* [1985] IRLR 99, Vinelott J held that union officers who sanctioned payments to unofficial strikers, where such payments were in breach of union rules, were liable to reimburse the trade union.

The role of union trustees came into sharp focus during the miners' strike when there were allegations that the trustees – Scargill, McGahey and Heathfield – were in breach of their fiduciary position through repeatedly being in contempt of court. In November 1984, a receiver was appointed on the ground that the trustees were 'not fit and proper people to be in charge of other people's money'.

3. The EA 1988, s. 9 gave members new powers against trustees of the union's property in respect of the unlawful application of its assets, or in cases where the trustees comply with any unlawful direction given to them under the rules of the union. A claim may be brought where the trustees are proposing to act or have already acted in this way, but to bring a claim in the latter case the claimant must have been a member at the time when the property was applied or the unlawful direction complied with (see now TULR(C)A 1992, s. 16).

4. Commenting on EA 1988, s. 9, Bowers and Auerbach observe that it is:

. . . another measure designed to give members powerful and effective controls over the use of their union's property and funds, thought to be particularly needed in the context of a bitter industrial dispute which a union may be waging in the face of the law and of the courts. Once again, the litigation of the miners' strike has helped both to focus minds on the problem and to suggest a solution. That litigation demonstrated that the courts will not hesitate to respond to individual member actions brought where the union or its officials are thought to be ignoring the rule book or otherwise behaving unlawfully. However, as the Green Paper [*Trade Unions and Their Members*, Paragraph 3.9] pointed out, a right for members to restrain union officials from sponsoring unlawful industrial action, or behaving in an unlawful way, might in practice prove ineffectual, if the situation has been reached where those officials are committed to defying the courts in any event. Section 9 therefore adopts a different strategy which might prove more effective: that of aiming at the union's trustees, who are the legal holders and controllers of its property. The powers to remove trustees and to appoint a receiver can thus be used to take assets completely out of reach and control of officials. (Bowers, J., and Auerbach, S., *The Employment Act 1988*, London: Blackstone Press, 1988, p. 45)

(vi) Union Elections and Ballots
Imposition of balloting requirements was a central feature of the Conservative Government's industrial relations policy, although views on the efficacy of ballots varied over time. The Donovan Commission rejected compulsory *strike* ballots on the ground that the North American experience showed that they are seen as 'tests of solidarity' and nearly always favour industrial action.

The Industrial Relations Act 1971 contained compulsory balloting procedures, but they were employed on only one occasion, during the railwaymen's dispute of 1972, when the subsequent vote resulted 5 to 1 in favour of strike action.

In 1979 the Conservative Government again tried to encourage trade union ballots, providing subsidies from public funds under the EA 1980. The Trade Union Act 1984 went further and required ballots before industrial action, for the principal executive committee and on retaining the political fund. The EA 1988 refined and modified these requirements and also introduced the office of Commissioner for the Rights of Trade Union Members (see below).

Most TUC unions at first refused to accept government funds as part of their overall policy of non-cooperation with the Government's employment legislation. The exceptions were the Electrical, Electronic, Telecommunications, Plumbing Union and the AUEW, who were threatened with TUC discipline for doing so. This policy was subsequently reviewed and the decision whether or not to claim was left to individual unions. By the late 1980s many unions were claiming under the 1980 Act. In 1991, 78 unions made applications in respect of 716 ballots; the Certification Officer made payments during that year of £4 million. This contrasts with applications in respect of 30 ballots and payments amounting to £72,498 in 1984.

At the end of 1992, the then Employment Secretary, Gillian Shepherd, announced plans to phase the scheme out over the next three years. In her view 'the scheme now operates largely as a public subsidy for ballots which unions are required to carry out to meet their obligations under the law' (Hansard (HC) 10.12.92, coll. 797–798). The scheme ceased to operate from 1 April 1996 (see the Funds for Trade Union Ballots (Revocation) Regulations 1993, SI 1993/233).
2. Executive elections are covered by TULR(C)A 1992, Ch. IV.

Trade Union and Labour Relations (Consolidation) Act 1992

CHAPTER IV
ELECTIONS FOR CERTAIN POSITIONS
Duty to hold elections

46. Duty to hold elections for certain positions
  (1) A trade union shall secure—
    (a) that every person who holds a position in the union to which this Chapter applies does so by virtue of having been elected to it at an election satisfying the requirements of this Chapter, and

(b)   that no person continues to hold such a position for more than five years without being re-elected at such an election.

(2)   The positions to which this Chapter applies (subject as mentioned below) are—

(a)   member of the executive,

(b)   any position by virtue of which a person is a member of the executive,

(c)   president, and ·

(d)   general secretary;

and the requirements referred to above are those set out in sections 47 to 52 below.

(3)   In this Chapter 'member of the executive' includes any person who, under the rules or practice of the union, may attend and speak at some or all of the meetings of the executive, otherwise than for the purpose of providing the committee with factual information or with technical or professional advice with respect to matters taken into account by the executive in carrying out its functions.

(4)   This Chapter does not apply to the position of president or general secretary if the holder of that position—

(a)   is not, in respect of that position, either a voting member of the executive or an employee of the union,

(b)   holds that position for a period which under the rules of the union cannot end more than 13 months after he took it up, and

(c)   has not held either position at any time in the period of twelve months ending with the day before he took up that position.

(5)   A 'voting member of the executive' means a person entitled in his own right to attend meetings of the executive and to vote on matters on which votes are taken by the executive (whether or not he is entitled to attend all such meetings or to vote on all such matters or in all circumstances).

(6)   The provisions of this Chapter apply notwithstanding anything in the rules or practice of the union; and the terms and conditions on which a person is employed by the union shall be disregarded in so far as they would prevent the union from complying with the provisions of this Chapter.

Notes

1.   By the Trade Union Act 1984, every *voting* member of the principal executive committee of a trade union had to be elected every five years by all members of the union. The Act overrode anything provided in the rule book of the union, and the union could face an enforcement order in the High Court. The Act also overrode any provision to the contrary in a contract of employment of any executive committee member relating to the tenure.

The 1984 Act related only to a voting member of the executive. But, in certain unions, the president or general secretary do not have a vote. Even if they had a vote, there was nothing to stop the union changing its rules by constitutional means — to remove the right to vote and therefore avoid the application of the Act. Indeed, such a rule change was carried out by the NUM in 1985 to remove their president's vote. This was seen by the Government to be a weakness in its legislative framework and the law was considerably tightened by what Smith and Wood describe as the 'We'll Get Scargill This Time' amendments in the EA 1988. See Smith, I. T., and Thomas, G.H., *Smith and Wood's Industrial Law*, 6th ed. (London: Butterworths, 1996), p. 539.)

2. The Trade Union Act 1984 stipulated a postal ballot as the norm but went on to allow a trade union to opt for a semi or full workplace ballot if the union was satisfied that there were no reasonable grounds to believe that this would not result in a free election as required by the Act. The 1987 Green Paper, however, pointed to 'concern over . . . the non-postal ballot held in 1984 for the election of the Transport and General Workers Union's General Secretary and more recent Civil and Public Services Association elections for General Secretary', as a 'justification for examining this issue more closely'. In the Government's view, postal ballots offered less scope for manipulation in the context of executive elections and political fund ballots. This is despite the fact that the most infamous example of union election malpractice, the ETU case, involved a postal ballot. The EA 1988 ensured that such ballots were to be held by postal voting only. Ballot papers must now both be sent out and returned by post.

Trade Union and Labour Relations (Consolidation) Act 1992

48. Election addresses
(1) The trade union shall—
(a) provide every candidate with an opportunity of preparing an election address in his own words and of submitting it to the union to be distributed to the persons accorded entitlement to vote in the election; and
(b) secure that, so far as reasonably practicable, copies of every election address submitted to it in time are distributed to each of those persons by post along with the voting papers for the election.
(2) The trade union may determine the time by which an election address must be submitted to it for distribution; but the time so determined must not be earlier than the latest time at which a person may become a candidate in the election.
(3) The trade union may provide that election addresses submitted to it for distribution—
(a) must not exceed such length, not being less than one hundred words, as may be determined by the union, and
(b) may, as regards photographs and other matter not in words, incorporate only such matter as the union may determine.
(4) The trade union shall secure that no modification of an election address submitted to it is made by any person in any copy of the address to be distributed except—
(a) at the request or with the consent of the candidate, or
(b) where the modification is necessarily incidental to the method adopted for producing that copy.
(5) The trade union shall secure that the same method of producing copies is applied in the same way to every election address submitted and, so far as reasonably practicable, that no such facility or information as would enable a candidate to gain any benefit from—
(a) the method by which copies of the election addresses are produced, or
(b) the modifications which are necessarily incidental to that method,
is provided to any candidate without being provided equally to all the others.
(6) The trade union shall, so far as reasonably practicable, secure that the same facilities and restrictions with respect to the preparation, submission, length or

modification of an election address, and with respect to the incorporation of photographs or other matter not in words, are provided or applied equally to each of the candidates.

(7)   The arrangements made by the trade union for the production of the copies to be so distributed must be such as to secure that none of the candidates is required to bear any of the expense of producing the copies.

(8)   No-one other than the candidate himself shall incur any civil or criminal liability in respect of the publication of a candidate's election address or of any copy required to be made for the purposes of this section.

49.   Appointment of independent scrutineer

(1)   The trade union shall, before the election is held, appoint a qualified independent person ('the scrutineer') to carry out—

(a)   the functions in relation to the election which are required under this section to be contained in his appointment; and

(b)   such additional functions in relation to the election as may be specified in his appointment.

(2)   A person is a qualified independent person in relation to an election if—

(a)   he satisfies such conditions as may be specified for the purposes of this section by order of the Secretary of State or is himself so specified; and

(b)   the trade union has no grounds for believing either that he will carry out any functions conferred on him in relation to the election otherwise than competently or that his independence in relation to the union, or in relation to the election, might reasonably be called into question.

An order under paragraph (a) shall be made by statutory instrument which shall be subject to annulment in pursuance of a resolution of either House of Parliament.

(3)   The scrutineer's appointment shall require him—

(a)   to be the person who supervises the production and distribution of the voting papers and to whom the voting papers are returned by those voting;

(aa)   to—

(i)   inspect the register of names and addresses of the members of the trade union, or

(ii)   examine the copy of the register as at the relevant date which is supplied to him in accordance with subsection (5A)(a),

whenever it appears to him appropriate to do so and, in particular, when the conditions specified in subsection (3A) are satisfied;

(b)   to take such steps as appear to him to be appropriate for the purpose of enabling him to make his report (see section 52);

(c)   to make his report to the trade union as soon as reasonably practicable after the last date for the return of voting papers; and

(d)   to retain custody of all voting papers returned for the purposes of the election and the copy of the register supplied to him in accordance with subsection (5A)(a)—

(i)   until the end of the period of one year beginning with the announcement by the union of the result of the election; and

(ii)   if within that period an application is made under section 54 (complaint of failure to comply with election requirements), until the Certification Officer or the court authorises him to dispose of the papers or copy.

(3A)   The conditions referred to in subsection (3)(aa) are—

(a)   that a request that the scrutineer inspect the register or examine the copy is made to him during the appropriate period by a member of the trade union or candidate who suspects that the register is not, or at the relevant date was not, accurate and up-to-date, and

(b)   that the scrutineer does not consider that the suspicion of the member or candidate is ill-founded.

(3B)   In subsection (3A) 'the appropriate period' means the period—

(a)   beginning with the first day on which a person may become a candidate in the election or, if later, the day on which the scrutineer is appointed, and

(b)   ending with the day before the day on which the scrutineer makes his report to the trade union.

(3C)   The duty of confidentiality as respects the register is incorporated in the scrutineer's appointment.

(4)   The trade union shall ensure that nothing in the terms of the scrutineer's appointment (including any additional functions specified in the appointment) is such as to make it reasonable for any person to call the scrutineer's independence in relation to the union into question.

(5)   The trade union shall, before the scrutineer begins to carry out his functions, either—

(a)   send a notice stating the name of the scrutineer to every member of the union to whom it is reasonably practicable to send such a notice, or

(b)   take all such other steps for notifying members of the name of the scrutineer as it is the practice of the union to take when matters of general interest to all its members need to be brought to their attention.

(5A)   The trade union shall—

(a)   supply to the scrutineer as soon as is reasonably practicable after the relevant date a copy of the register of names and addresses of its members as at that date, and

(b)   comply with any request made by the scrutineer to inspect the register.

(5B)   Where the register is kept by means of a computer the duty imposed on the trade union by subsection (5A)(a) is either to supply a legible printed copy or (if the scrutineer prefers) to supply a copy of the computer data and allow the scrutineer use of the computer to read it at any time during the period when he is required to retain custody of the copy.

(6)   The trade union shall ensure that the scrutineer duly carries out his functions and that there is no interference with his carrying out of those functions which would make it reasonable for any person to call the scrutineer's independence in relation to the union into question.

(7)   The trade union shall comply with all reasonable requests made by the scrutineer for the purposes of, or in connection with, the carrying out of his functions.

(8)   In this section 'the relevant date' means—

(a)   where the trade union has rules determining who is entitled to vote in the election by reference to membership on a particular date, that date, and

(b)   otherwise, the date, or the last date, on which voting papers are distributed for the purposes of the election.

50.   Entitlement to vote

(1)   Subject to the provisions of this section, entitlement to vote shall be accorded equally to all members of the trade union.

(2)   The rules of the union may exclude entitlement to vote in the case of all members belonging to one of the following classes, or to a class falling within one of the following—

(a)   members who are not in employment;

(b)   members who are in arrears in respect of any subscription or contribution due to the union;

(c)   members who are apprentices, trainees or students or new members of the union.

(3)   The rules of the union may restrict entitlement to vote to members who fall within—

(a)   a class determined by reference to a trade or occupation,

(b)   a class determined by reference to a geographical area, or

(c)   a class which is by virtue of the rules of the union treated as a separate section within the union,

or to members who fall within a class determined by reference to any combination of the factors mentioned in paragraphs (a), (b) and (c).

The reference in paragraph (c) to a section of a trade union includes a part of the union which is itself a trade union.

(4)   Entitlement may not be restricted in accordance with subsection (3) if the effect is that any member of the union is denied entitlement to vote at all elections held for the purposes of this Chapter otherwise than by virtue of belonging to a class excluded in accordance with subsection (2).

51.   Voting

(1)   The method of voting must be by the marking of a voting paper by the person voting.

(2)   Each voting paper must—

(a)   state the name of the independent scrutineer and clearly specify the address to which, and the date by which, it is to be returned,

(b)   be given one of a series of consecutive whole numbers every one of which is used in giving a different number in that series to each voting paper printed or otherwise produced for the purposes of the election, and

(c)   be marked with its number.

(3)   Every person who is entitled to vote at the election must—

(a)   be allowed to vote without interference from, or constraint imposed by, the union or any of its members, officials or employees, and

(b)   so far as is reasonably practicable, be enabled to do so without incurring any direct cost to himself.

(4)   So far as is reasonably practicable, every person who is entitled to vote at the election must—

(a)   have sent to him by post, at his home address or another address which he has requested the trade union in writing to treat as his postal address, a voting paper which either lists the candidates at the election or is accompanied by a separate list of those candidates; and

(b)   be given a convenient opportunity to vote by post.

(5)   The ballot shall be conducted so as to secure that—

(a)   so far as is reasonably practicable, those voting do so in secret, and

(b)   the votes given at the election are fairly and accurately counted.

For the purposes of paragraph (b) an inaccuracy in counting shall be disregarded if it is accidental and on a scale which could not affect the result of the election.

(6)   The ballot shall be so conducted as to secure that the result of the election is determined solely by counting the number of votes cast directly for each candidate.

(7)   Nothing in subsection (6) shall be taken to prevent the system of voting used for the election being the single transferable vote, that is, a vote capable of being given so as to indicate the voter's order of preference for the candidates and of being transferred to the next choice—

(a)   when it is not required to give a prior choice the necessary quota of votes, or

(b) when, owing to the deficiency in the number of votes given for a prior choice, that choice is eliminated from the list of candidates.

Notes

1. Under TULR(C)A 1992, s. 49, both political fund and principal executive committee ballots must be independently scrutinised. TURERA 1993 extended this requirement to industrial action ballots and a failure to subject the ballot to independent scrutiny will render any subsequent industrial action unlawful.

2. The scrutineer must satisfy conditions set down in an order made by the Secretary of State (TULR(C)A 1992, s. 49(2)). Under this order, the following may be scrutineers:

(a) solicitors or accountants qualified to be an auditor;

(b) the Electoral Reform Society, the Industrial Society or Unity Security Services Ltd (Trade Union Ballots and Elections (Independent Scrutineers Qualifications) Order 1988 (SI 1988/2117)).

Trade Union and Labour Relations (Consolidation) Act 1992

52. Scrutineer's report

(1) The scrutineer's report on the election shall state—

(a) the number of voting papers distributed for the purposes of the election,

(b) the number of voting papers returned to the scrutineer,

(c) the number of valid votes cast in the election for each candidate, and

(d) the number of spoiled or otherwise invalid voting papers returned. .

(2) The report shall also state whether the scrutineer is satisfied—

(a) that there are no reasonable grounds for believing that there was any contravention of a requirement imposed by or under any enactment in relation to the election,

(b) that the arrangements made with respect to the production, storage, distribution, return or other handling of the voting papers used in the election, and the arrangements for the counting of the votes, included all such security arrangements as were reasonably practicable for the purpose of minimising the risk that any unfairness or malpractice might occur, and

(c) that he has been able to carry out his functions without such interference as would make it reasonable for any person to call his independence in relation to the union into question;

and if he is not satisfied as to any of those matters, the report shall give particulars of his reasons for not being satisfied as to that matter.

(2A) The report shall also state—

(a) whether the scrutineer—

(i) has inspected the register of names and addresses of the members of the trade union, or

(ii) has examined the copy of the register as at the relevant date which is supplied to him in accordance with section 49(5A)(a),

(b) if he has, whether in the case of each inspection or examination he was acting on a request by a member of the trade union or candidate or at his own instance,

(c)   whether he declined to act on any such request, and

(d)   whether any inspection of the register, or any examination of the copy of the register, has revealed any matter which he considers should be drawn to the attention of the trade union in order to assist it in securing that the register is accurate and up-to-date,

but shall not state the name of any member or candidate who has requested such an inspection or examination.

(3)   The trade union shall not publish the result of the election until it has received the scrutineer's report.

(4)   The trade union shall within the period of three months after it receives the report either—

(a)   send a copy of the report to every member of the union to whom it is reasonably practicable to send such a copy; or

(b)   take all such other steps for notifying the contents of the report to the members of the union (whether by publishing the report or otherwise) as it is the practice of the union to take when matters of general interest to all its members need to be brought to their attention.

(5)   Any such copy or notification shall be accompanied by a statement that the union will, on request, supply any member of the union with a copy of the report, either free of charge or on payment of such reasonable fee as may be specified in the notification.

(6)   The trade union shall so supply any member of the union who makes such a request and pays the fee (if any) notified to him.

Notes

1.   Enforcement of the requirements set out in TULR(C)A 1992, Ch. IV may be sought by way of an application to the Certification Officer or the High Court for a declaration.

In complaints concerning improperly held elections, the complainant must have been a member both at the date of the election *and* when the application is made to the court. If the complaint is that the election has *not* been held, the complainant must be a member on the date of the application. Action must be taken within one year from the default.

The court or the Certification Officer has the power to make an enforcement order. Such an order will require the union to hold an election, to take such other steps to remedy the declared failure within a specified time, or to abstain from certain acts in the future. Failure to comply with the order amounts to a contempt of court (TULR(C)A 1992, ss. 54, 55 and 56).

2.   Part II of the Trade Union Act 1984 withdrew certain of the immunities contained in TULRA 1974, s. 13, in respect of industrial action not approved by a ballot. So, under the original formulation, it was the employers who were seen to be the potential plaintiffs: it did *not* provide a cause of action to trade union members themselves.

At common law the member's rights are very restricted. The member may apply to the High Court for an interim mandatory injunction requiring the union to hold a ballot in accordance with its rules, but such an action requires that there is a positive obligation under union rules to hold a ballot and, even in such a case, an interim injunction may be refused because it is a 'very exceptional form of relief' (see *Taylor* v *NUM (Yorkshire Area)* [1984] IRLR 445). The Green Paper, *Trade Unions and Their Members*, pointed out (para. 2.5) that in the miners' strike (1984/85) there were 19 common law actions brought against the NUM under the rule book for failing to hold a ballot.

The EA 1988 changed the position in line with the proposals contained in the Green Paper and provided a cause of action to members themselves. The complex rules surrounding ballots before industrial action are discussed in detail in Chapter 9.

3. The EA 1988 created the office of the Commissioner of the Rights of Trade Union Members (CRTUM). The Commissioner's main functions were to provide assistance to individuals taking or contemplating certain legal proceedings against unions or union officials. From its inception, CRTUM assisted, on average, 10 applications a year. The Employment Relations Act 1999, s. 28, implements the Government's proposals in Chapter 4 of *Fairness at Work* to abolish the office. The Act gives new powers to the Certification Officer to hear complaints involving most aspects of the law where CRTUM was previously empowered to provide assistance. Section 29 gives effect to Sch. 6, which amends the statutory powers of the Certification Officer as set out in the 1992 Act. The overall effect is to widen the scope for trade union members to make complaints to the CO of alleged breaches of trade union law or trade union rules, thereby enlarging the CO's role as an alternative to the courts as a means to resolve disputes. The Act achieves this by giving the CO order-making powers in areas of trade union law where he previously made only declarations, and by extending his powers to make declarations and orders into areas where previously he had no competence to hear complaints and issue orders.

9 INDUSTRIAL CONFLICT I

I Introduction

Scrutton LJ addressing the University of Cambridge Law Society, 18 November 1920 (1 *Cambridge Law Journal, p. 8*)

The habits you are trained in, the people with whom you mix, lead to your having a certain class of ideas of such a nature that, when you have to deal with other ideas, you do not give as sound and accurate judgements as you would wish. This is one of the great difficulties at present with Labour. Labour says 'Where are your impartial judges? They all move in the same circle as the employers, and they are all educated and nursed in the same ideas as the employers. How can a labour man or a trade unionist get impartial justice?' It is very difficult sometimes to be sure that you have put yourself into a thoroughly impartial position between two disputants, one of your own class and one not of your class.

Lord Wedderburn, 'Industrial Relations and the Courts' (1980) 9 ILJ 65

In strict juridical terms, there does not exist in Britain any 'right' to organise or any 'right' to strike. The law still provides no more than a 'liberty' to associate in trade unions and certain 'liberties' of action by which trade unions can carry on industrial struggle. Statutory provisions protect trade unions or workers' strikes and other industrial action from illegalities which would otherwise be imposed upon them by the law, largely by the common law created by judicial decisions. When he goes into court in 1980 to defend himself, the trade union official believes he is defending his 'rights'; but he finds that judges see his statutory protections as some form of 'privilege'. Such an attitude on the part of the judiciary at once becomes the source of tension, even hostility, between British trade unions and the ordinary courts.

Question
The last extract was written in 1980. In the light of developments over the last decade or so, referred to in Chapter 1, would it not be more relevant to

focus on the tension which now exists between the trade union movement and Parliament?

Notes

1. The perceived problems with the immunities approach as a means of protecting the freedom to strike, have produced calls from a number of quarters for the enactment of a positive right to strike, perhaps adjudicated by a specialised labour court (see Ewing, K.D., 'The Right to Strike', (1986) 15 ILJ 143); Ewing, K.D., *A Bill of Rights for Britain*, (London: Institute of Employment Rights, 1990); Lord Wedderburn, *The Worker and the Law*, 3rd ed. (Harmondsworth: Penguin, 1986), Ch. 10; Welch, R., *The Right to Strike: A Trade Union View* (London: The Institute of Employment Rights, 1991).

The problem with a right to strike, perhaps enshrined in a Bill of Rights along with other protections for workers and their trade unions, is that it will still be up to courts to interpret the scope of such a right. In a number of writings, Lord Wedderburn has advanced the argument that the question of rights *versus* immunities is not of practical relevance, the major issue being the type of forum and procedure for the adjudication of industrial disputes. He advocates the establishment of a system of autonomous labour courts staffed by lay experts in industrial relations and lawyers of both genders and drawn from differing ethnic and class backgrounds (see Wedderburn, Lord, 'The New Politics of Labour Law: Immunities or Positive Rights?' in *Employment Rights in Britain and Europe* (London: Lawrence and Wishart, 1991), Ch. 4); see also Ewing, K. 'Working Life: A new perspective on labour law', (London: The Institute of Employment Rights, Lawrence and Wishart, 1996), Ch. 8.

2. In 1998, 282,000 working days were lost through labour disputes – the third lowest annual figure on record. There were 166 stoppages of work because of labour disputes – the lowest calendar-year total since records began in 1891.

The 1998 total is less than half the average number of working days lost per year in the 1990s to date (706,000) and is considerably lower than the average for both the 1980s (7.2 million) and the 1970s (12.9 million). The number of stoppages has fallen significantly since the 1980s. When the average annual number was 1,129 (the average number to date in the 1990s is 281) ('Labour disputes in 1998', *Labour Market Trends*, June 1999, pp. 299–313).

II Sanctions Against Individual Strikers

Trade Union and Labour Relations (Consolidation) Act 1992

237. Dismissal of those taking part in unofficial industrial action

(1) An employee has no right to complain of unfair dismissal if at the time of dismissal he was taking part in an unofficial strike or other unofficial industrial action.

(1A) Subsection (1) does not apply to the dismissal of the employee if it is shown that the reason (or, if more than one, the principal reason) for the dismissal or, in a redundancy case, for selecting the employee for dismissal was one of those specified in section 99(1) to (3), 100 or 103 of the Employment Rights Act 1996 (dismissal in maternity, health and safety and employee representative cases).

In this subsection 'redundancy case' has the meaning given in section 105(9) of that Act.

(2)   A strike or other industrial action is unofficial in relation to an employee unless—

(a)   he is a member of a trade union and the action is authorised or endorsed by that union, or

(b)   he is not a member of a trade union but there are among those taking part in the industrial action members of a trade union by which the action has been authorised or endorsed.

Provided that, a strike or other industrial action shall not be regarded as unofficial if none of those taking part in it are members of a trade union.

(3)   The provisions of section 20(2) apply for the purpose of determining whether industrial action is to be taken to have been authorised or endorsed by a trade union.

(4)   The question whether industrial action is to be so taken in any case shall be determined by reference to the facts as at the time of dismissal.

Provided that, where an act is repudiated as mentioned in section 21, industrial action shall not thereby be treated as unofficial before the end of the next working day after the day on which the repudiation takes place.

(5)   In this section the 'time of dismissal' means—

(a)   where the employee's contract of employment is terminated by notice, when the notice is given,

(b)   where the employee's contract of employment is terminated without notice, when the termination takes effect, and

(c)   where the employee is employed under a contract for a fixed term which expires without being renewed under the same contract, when that term expires;

and a 'working day' means any day which is not a Saturday or Sunday, Christmas Day, Good Friday or a bank holiday under the Banking and Financial Dealings Act 1971.

(6)   For the purposes of this section membership of a trade union for purposes unconnected with the employment in question shall be disregarded; but an employee who was a member of a trade union when he began to take part in industrial action shall continue to be treated as a member for the purpose of determining whether that action is unofficial in relation to him or another notwithstanding that he may in fact have ceased to be a member.

238.   Dismissals in connection with other industrial action

(1)   This section applies in relation to an employee who has a right to complain of unfair dismissal (the 'complainant') and who claims to have been unfairly dismissed, where at the date of the dismissal—

(a)   the employer was conducting or instituting a lock-out, or

(b)   the complainant was taking part in a strike or other industrial action.

(2)   In such a case an industrial tribunal shall not determine whether the dismissal was fair or unfair unless it is shown—

(a)   that one or more relevant employees of the same employer have not been dismissed, or

(b)   that a relevant employee has before the expiry of the period of three months beginning with the date of his dismissal been offered re-engagement and that the complainant has not been offered re-engagement.

(2A)   Subsection (2) does not apply to the dismissal of the employee if it is shown that the reason (or, if more than one, the principal reason) for the dismissal or, in a redundancy case, for selecting the employee for dismissal was one of those specified in section 99(1) to (3), 100 or 103 of the Employment Rights Act 1996 (dismisaal in maternity, health and safety and employee representative cases).

In this subsection 'redundancy case' has the meaning given in section 105(9) of that Act.

(2B)   Subsection (2) does not apply in relation to an employee who is regarded as unfairly dismissed by virtue of section 238A below.

(3)   For this purpose 'relevant employees' means—

(a)   in relation to a lock-out, employees who were directly interested in the dispute in contemplation or furtherance of which the lock-out occurred, and

(b)   in relation to a strike or other industrial action, those employees at the establishment of the employer at or from which the complainant works who at the date of his dismissal were taking part in the action.

Nothing in section 237 (dismissal of those taking part in unofficial industrial action) affects the question who are relevant employees for the purposes of this section.

(4)   An offer of re-engagement means an offer (made either by the original employer or by a successor of that employer or an associated employer) to re-engage an employee, either in the job which he held immediately before the date of dismissal or in a different job which would be reasonably suitable in his case.

(5)   In this section 'date of dismissal' means—

(a)   where the employee's contract of employment was terminated by notice, the date on which the employer's notice was given, and

(b)   in any other case, the effective date of termination.

238A.   Participation in official industrial action

(1)   For the purposes of this section an employee takes protected industrial action if he commits an act which, or a series of acts each of which, he is induced to commit by an act which by virtue of section 219 is not actionable in tort.

(2)   An employee who is dismissed shall be regarded for the purposes of Part X of the Employment Rights Act 1996 (unfair dismissal) as unfairly dismissed if—

(a)   the reason (or, if more than one, the principal reason) for the dismissal is that the employee took protected industrial action, and

(b)   subsection (3), (4) or (5) applies to the dismissal.

(3)   This subsection applies to a dismissal if it takes place within the period of eight weeks beginning with the day on which the employee started to take protected industrial action.

(4)   This subsection applies to a dismissal if—

(a)   it takes place after the end of that period, and

(b)   the employee had stopped taking protected industrial action before the end of that period.

(5)   This subsection applies to a dismissal if—

(a)   it takes place after the end of that period,

(b)   the employee had not stopped taking protected industrial action before the end of that period, and

(c)   the employer had not taken such procedural steps as would have been reasonable for the purposes of resolving the dispute to which the protected industrial action relates.

(6)   In determining whether an employer has taken those steps regard shall be had, in particular, to—

(a)   whether the employer or a union had complied with procedures established by any applicable collective or other agreement;

(b)   whether the employer or a union offered or agreed to commence or resume negotiations after the start of the protected industrial action;

(c)   whether the employer or a union unreasonably refused, after the start of the protected industrial action, a request that conciliation services be used;

(d)   whether the employer or a union unreasonably refused, after the start of the protected industrial action, a request that mediation services be used in relation to procedures to be adopted for the purposes of resolving the dispute.

(7)   In determining whether an employer has taken those steps no regard shall be had to the merits of the dispute.

(8)   For the purposes of this section no account shall be taken of the repudiation of any act by a trade union as mentioned in section 21 in relation to anything which occurs before the end of the next working day (within the meaning of section 237) after the day on which the repudiation takes place.

239. Supplementary provisions relating to unfair dismissal

(1)   Sections 237 to 238A (loss of unfair dismissal protection in connection with industrial action) shall be construed as one with Part X of the Employment Rights Act 1996 (unfair dismissal); but sections 108 and 109 of that Act (qualifying period and age limit) shall not apply in relation to section 238A of this Act.

(2)   In relation to a complaint to which section 238 or 238A applies, section 111(2) of that Act (time limit for complaint) does not apply, but an industrial tribunal shall not consider the complaint unless it is presented to the tribunal—

(a)   before the end of the period of six months beginning with the date of the complainant's dismissal (as defined by section 238(5)), or

(b)   where the tribunal is satisfied that it was not reasonably practicable for the complaint to be presented before the end of that period, within such further period as the tribunal considers reasonable.

(3)   Where it is shown that the condition referred to in section 238(2)(b) is fulfilled (discriminatory re-engagement), the references in—

(a)   sections 98 to 106 of the Employment Rights Act 1996, and

(b)   sections 152 and 153 of this Act,

to the reason or principal reason for which the complainant was dismissed shall be read as references to the reason or principal reason he has not been offered re-engagement.

(4)   In relation to a complaint under section 111 of the 1996 Act (unfair dismissal: complaint to employment tribunal) that a dismissal was unfair by virtue of section 238A of this Act—

(a)   no order shall be made under section 113 of the 1996 Act (reinstatement or re-engagement) until after the conclusion of protected industrial action by any employee in relation to the relevant dispute,

(b)   regulations under section 7 of the Employment Tribunals Act 1996 may make provision about the adjournment and renewal of applications (including provision requiring adjournment in specified circumstances), and

(c)   regulations under section 9 of that Act may require a pre-hearing review to be carried out in specified circumstances.

Notes

1.   It is interesting to note that what is now TULR(C)A 1992, s. 238, although substantially strengthened by the Conservative Government in 1982 and 1990, owes its origins to the last Labour Government. The policy underlying it is that the courts and tribunals are not appropriate places in which to decide the rights and wrongs of industrial disputes. As such, the provision is very much in line with the earlier abstentionist tradition in British industrial relations.

2. The fact that the employer had until 1999 the legal freedom to sack those taking industrial action, even if the action has been sanctioned by a properly conducted ballot, may have come as a surprise to many trade unionists. Indeed, research conducted by Roger Welch in 1987 established that almost 45 per cent of his sample of active trade unionists believed that employers could not dismiss strikers. This figure increased to 70 per cent if the industrial action involved was short of a strike, such as an overtime ban ('The Right To Strike: A Trade Union View' [1991] IER 25). This misconception is entirely understandable. After all, how can we talk of a right or freedom to strike unless it is possible for workers to withdraw their labour, in whole or in part, without fearing lawful dismissal? Those workers to whom the existence of this legal prop to managerial prerogative will come as no surprise are the News International printers and the P&O seafarers, who during the 1980s fell victim to its use in defeating strikes.

3. The EA 1990 tightened the law even further. No employee can complain of unfair dismissal if at the time of the dismissal he or she was taking part in *unofficial industrial action*. In such a situation the employer may selectively dismiss or re-engage any participating employee without risking unfair dismissal liability (see now TULR(C)A 1992, s. 237, above).

4. In Chapter 4 of *Fairness at Work*, the Government proposed to extend the protection against dismissal to workers taking *official* industrial action in certain circumstances. In proposing the new rights the Government said it believed that 'in general employees dismissed for taking part in lawfully organised official industrial action should have the right to complain of unfair dismissal to a tribunal' (para. 4.22). It then invited views on the tests which should be applied to determine whether dismissals in such circumstances are fair. Subsequently, s. 16 and Sch. 5 of the Employment Relations Act 1999 introduced a new s. 238A into TULR(C)A 1992.

From a trade unionist perspective, the end result is rather disappointing, with only a limited protection against dismissal being extended to those engaged in industrial action. The protection covers only lawfully organised official industrial action and *generally* lasts only for the first eight weeks of the employee's involvement. Given the massive complexity of the law relating to industrial action, it will rarely be the case that workers can be certain that the action they are taking is lawful. If it is found to be unlawful, or their involvement in the dispute extends beyond eight weeks, they risk dismissal without redress unless they can establish selective dismissal/re-engagement within the terms of s. 238. Where the dispute is unofficial, the employee has no protection against dismissal unless it is shown that the reason or principal reason for dismissal or selection for dismissal was one of those specified in ss. 99(1)–(3), 100, 101A(d) or 103 of ERA 1996 (dismissal in maternity, health and safety and employee representative cases) or s. 103A (making a protected disclosure).

The changes introduced by the 1999 Act still fail to guarantee an effective right to strike and are unlikely to satisfy International Labour Organisation Standards.

5. The new rights under s. 238A are not dependent on length of service, so that all employees are covered immediately from the start of their employment. Section 239 is extended to take into account the new provisions and to link them to ERA 1996, Pt X unfair dismissal procedures. Consequential changes are also made to the selective redundancy procedures in s. 105 to take into account the new rights.

Faust v Power Packing Casemakers Ltd
[1983] IRLR 117
Court of Appeal

Three employees refused to work overtime because of a dispute over wages. The industrial tribunal had found their dismissals unfair on the ground that there was no contractual obligation to work overtime.

On appeal to the EAT, the employers argued that the industrial tribunal did not have jurisdiction to consider the complaints since the employees were dismissed for taking part 'in other industrial action' within the meaning of what is now TULR(C)A 1992, s. 238. This argument was accepted by both the EAT and the Court of Appeal.

STEPHENSON LJ: Mr Jones submits that to give these words the extended (and what, contrary to his first submission, I have held to be the natural) meaning which they bear if not confined to breaches of contract, would do injustice and defeat the purpose and object of [s. 238] and its predecessor in the Act of 1975, namely, to deprive an employee of his right to complain to an Industrial Tribunal of unfair dismissal if, and only if, he has been guilty of misconduct or has broken the terms of his contract. If Mr Jones' gloss – for such, contrary to his submission, it clearly is – upon the language of the section is rejected, unscrupulous employers will be allowed, so he submits, to dismiss unfairly and unjustly those who take legitimate industrial action, without any fear of the circumstances being investigated by the statutory Tribunals, or of having to pay compensation or reinstate those unfairly dismissed employees. He calls attention to an obvious misunderstanding by the Appeal Tribunal of the effect of their interpretation of [s. 238]. At p. 6 of the judgment of Mr Justice May he said this:

In our view, the phrase 'other industrial action' in s. 62 of the 1978 Act [now TULR(C)A 1992, s. 238] does not necessarily have to be conduct in breach of contract on the part of the employee and we are, for present purposes, only concerned with the employee. We do not propose to define the phrase 'other industrial action' in s. 62. As we have already said there is no definition in the relevant section in the Act nor in the definition section, and we think that the decision whether or not something was 'other industrial action' within s. 62 can and should be left to the good sense of Industrial Tribunals. They are locally situated. They know the local employment position. They know, for instance, the area's industries. They know what conditions are in the area. They no doubt know, in some cases at any rate, the parties involved. They will be able to ascertain all the relevant facts. They will be able to make findings about what perhaps may be one of the most important aspects of such a case, namely the motives actuating both sides, that is to say, both employer and employee in the dispute concerned. Having considered these and all other matters which they think pertinent and relevant they will be able to decide whether or not the employees were taking 'other industrial action' within [s. 238] and were dismissed in consequence. When one stresses, as we do, that Industrial Tribunals should, in considering this part of the relevant legislation, look at not merely the actions but also the motives of both sides of the dispute, employer and employee, we feel quite happy that this judgment will not provide the licence for many uncompensated dismissals, which Mr Jones suggested would follow our decision.

Now with all that I respectfully agree, except with the statement that Tribunals will be able to ascertain all the relevant facts, including the motives actuating *the employer* and the question whether or not the employees were dismissed in consequence of their industrial action. For once an Industrial Tribunal, in the exercise of its good sense, decides that an employee was, at the date of his dismissal, taking part in industrial action, whether in breach of his contract or not, with the object of applying pressure on his employer or of disrupting his business, the Tribunal must refuse to entertain the complaint or to go into the questions of the employers' motive or reasons for dismissing. And this is a result which requires plain language. If there was any ambiguity in the words of the section, I would reject the Appeal Tribunal's construction of the phrase, their refusal to define it and their leaving its application to the good sense of Industrial Tribunals.

Mr Carr concedes that the criticisms of this part of Mr Justice May's judgment are well founded, but counters the potential injustice relied on by Mr Jones by submitting that the purpose and object of the section is to avoid courts of law and Tribunals being required to investigate the rights and wrongs, or to adjudicate on the merits, of trade disputes in the context of unfair dismissal applications. He referred us to what Lord Scarman said in *NWL Ltd* v *Woods* [1979] IRLR 478 about the policy of the Act of 1974 to exclude trade disputes from judicial review by the courts and to substitute an advisory, conciliation and arbitration process; and he pointed out that such disputes are often complex and to give the determination of them to Industrial Tribunals would defeat the legislative aim of providing cheap and speedy hearings of unfair dismissal complaints by such Tribunals. These considerations must, he submitted, have outweighed with the legislature the potential injustice created by the statutory ban imposed not only on determining complaints by strikers or those engaged in industrial action by [s. 238(1)(b)], but imposed by [s. 238(1)(a)] on determining complaints by employees locked-out by employers at the date of dismissal.

I feel the force of these submissions, but no certainty as to the intention of the legislature in enacting this provision.

In threading my way from sections and subsections to schedules and paragraphs, and from schedule back to section, I may have lost the way, or the thread, or sight of Parliament's aim and object, even if Parliament itself did not. But of this I have no doubt, that as there is no compelling reason why the words of the provision should not be given their natural and ordinary meaning, and good reason why they should not now be defined as once they were, we ought to give them that meaning and apply them, as the Appeal Tribunal did, to the undisputed facts of the case in favour of the respondents.

I would accordingly affirm their decision and dismiss this appeal.

Note

As will be seen later in the chapter, most forms of industrial action involve a breach of contract. A strike, whether or not notice is given, amounts to a fundamental breach of contract entitling the employer to dismiss at common law (see *Simmons* v *Hoover Ltd* [1976] IRLR 266; *Boxfoldia Ltd* v *NGA (1982)* [1988] IRLR 383). Most other forms of industrial action short of a strike also amount to contractual breaches. If workers 'boycott' (refuse to carry out) certain work then they are in breach for refusing to comply with a reasonable order. A 'go-slow' or 'work to rule' probably breaks an implied term not to frustrate the commercial objectives of the business (*Secretary of State for Employment* v *ASLEF (No. 2)* [1972] 2 QB 455, see p. 100). An overtime ban will also certainly amount to breach of contract if the employer is entitled under the contract to demand overtime, but not if overtime is voluntary on the part of the employee. The above case goes even further in the sense that, even on the rare occasion that the industrial action does not amount to a breach of contract, the workers involved will not be protected under the law of unfair dismissal.

The following case is concerned with the question of whether there was a selective dismissal as defined by TULR(C)A 1992, s. 238(2)(a).

P&O European Ferries (Dover) Ltd v *Byrne*
[1989] IRLR 254
Court of Appeal

More than 1,000 P&O employees who were dismissed by the employers while on strike claimed that they had been unfairly dismissed. Mr Byrne's case was the first to come before an industrial tribunal. Mr Byrne alleged that one 'relevant employee' had not been dismissed at the relevant time. The employers applied for an order requiring disclosure of the identity of the employee not dismissed on the ground that it was essential for them to know that information. The industrial tribunal dismissed the employers' application on two grounds: (i) that if the time at which it has to be shown that one or more relevant employees had not been dismissed for the purpose of EPCA 1978, s. 62(2)(a) (now TULR(C)A 1992, s. 238(2)(a)) is the conclusion of the tribunal hearing, disclosure would enable the employers to defeat Mr Byrne's claim by dismissing the employee forthwith; (ii) the order for particulars would enable the employers to defeat the claims of the other 1,024 employees whose complaints had yet to be heard. The EAT upheld the tribunal's view but the employers' appeal to the Court of Appeal was successful.

MAY LJ: . . . The issue which arises on the proper construction of [s. 238] is at what point in time was the Industrial Tribunal required to look, to see whether there had or had not been discrimination, to decide whether or not they had jurisdiction to determine the applications for compensation for unfair dismissal started by Mr Byrne and by his 1,024 fellow employees.

Insofar as the reasons which the Industrial Tribunal gave and in which they were supported by the Employment Appeal Tribunal for not ordering particulars is concerned, I respectfully disagree with both Tribunals. It was, I think, an improper exercise of the discretion of the Tribunals below not to order such particulars on the ground that to do so would enable the employers to put matters right, if one relevant employee had got through the net and was not dismissed at the time when the remaining 1,025 employees were dismissed. It is true that a party to litigation is not entitled to particulars solely for the purpose of ascertaining the names of his opponent's witnesses. But a party is entitled to particulars to enable him to know what case he has to meet, even though giving those particulars will identify one or more of the potential witnesses on behalf of the other party. . . .

The particular parts of [s. 238(2)(a)] which require careful consideration are, first, the word 'determine' in the earlier part of the subsection, and in the next line the words 'unless it is shown'. The use of the word 'determine' is in my judgment arguably ambiguous. One speaks of a determination in the litigious context both of the final decision of the issues in that litigation and also of the actual hearing itself. In one sense a court determines by a trial from the time that the case is called on until the time when the court gives its ultimate decision. But there is no such ambiguity in the words 'unless it is shown'. Those words necessarily direct one's attention to the conclusion of the relevant hearing before the Industrial Tribunal and in my opinion require one to conclude that on its proper construction the material point in time is when the Industrial Tribunal either determines the substantive hearing which involves determining the jurisdiction point as well, or alternatively determines the jurisdiction point on a preliminary hearing prior to going on, or not going on, as the case may be, with the substantive hearing for compensation.

That in my judgment is the clear and plain meaning of the statutory provision and although we were pressed on the one side not to and on the other side to insert words into the subsection and also to adopt what was said to be a purposive construction of [s. 238(2)(a)], to lead us to adopt a construction which looked to the start of the hearing rather than its conclusion as the material time, Mr Supperstone, who has said everything that could be said on behalf of the respondent employee with skill and cogency was in the end, as I think, almost bound to accept that the meaning of the statutory phrase was clear. When pressed to detail the respects in which he suggested that one should give the phrase a narrow rather than a wider construction, as he suggested at one point was the correct approach, he very properly and realistically found himself unable to do so.

I should just mention that Mr Supperstone also pointed to this potential difficulty if the construction for which he contended was not to be accepted and that is that in the circumstances the unknown Mr 'X' is put in an invidious position. If he is called to give evidence to the effect that he was on strike but not dismissed, he would clearly know that the consequence would be that he would in fact immediately be dismissed so as to preclude the continuing existence of any discrimination under the provisions of [s. 238(2)(a)]. But this cannot affect what in my view is the clear and literal meaning of the subsection.

For my part I do not think that much more need be said on this appeal, although that is in no way intended to be disrespectful to the interesting arguments which counsel on both sides have addressed to the court. In my judgment the Industrial Tribunal, and the Employment Appeal Tribunal following them, erred in directing themselves that it was a legitimate reason for refusing to order particulars which the employers had to have in order to meet the case made against them, that to do so might prejudice not only Mr Byrne's claim but also perhaps the claim of the other 1,024 people and indeed might have a deleterious effect on the continued employment prospects of the unknown Mr 'X'. The allegation had been made against the employers that there had been discrimination in that Mr 'X' had not been dismissed and they were entitled to know who he was so that they could meet that case. They were entitled to know that at that stage in the litigation, particularly having regard to the proper construction of [s. 238(2)(a)] which requires one to look to the end of the decision of the relevant determination by the Industrial Tribunal and not the start.

In those circumstances I would allow this appeal and, subject to hearing further from counsel if necessary, make an order directing that the relevant particulars be given by the employee respondent to the employer appellant.

Question
Given the amount of power already ceded to employers by TULR(C)A 1992, s. 239, do you agree with the approach adopted in this case?

Coates and Venables v Modern Methods and Materials Ltd
[1982] IRLR 318
Court of Appeal

In February 1980, weeks of unrest among the employer's workforce came to a head. One of their three factories had been closed and some employees had been transferred. Management called for volunteers for further transfers but none was forthcoming. On Tuesday, 12 February, the workforce met outside the factory gate and nearly all remained there refusing to work.

Mrs Leith, an employee of some seven years' standing, had a history of back trouble. On 11 February she had hurt her back and made an appointment to see her doctor. However, she turned up at the factory on 12 February expecting to work. She did not go in because, she said, those employees who had gone in had been abused by fellow workers and she did not herself wish to suffer that abuse. She stayed at the gate for about one hour and then went home. Mrs Leith then saw her doctor who gave her a note certifying her inability to work. She remained absent until 25 April when she returned to work.

The employers dismissed the applicants when they were taking part in the strike. The applicants contended that Mrs Leith was a 'relevant employee' who had taken part in the strike but had not been dismissed. The industrial tribunal held that Mrs Leith was a 'relevant employee' but this view was rejected by the EAT. The Court of Appeal (Eveleigh LJ dissenting) allowed the appeal of Mrs Coates and Mrs Venables.

STEPHENSON LJ: I have found this a difficult case. It ought to be easy to decide what 'taking part in a strike' means and whether on proved or accepted facts a particular employee was or was not taking part in a strike. The industrial tribunal seem to have found it easy, because they unanimously decided that Mrs Leith was taking part, and on an application for review the chairman thought the weight of the evidence showed that she was taking part and a review had no reasonable prospect of success. I know that the construction of a statute is a question of law; but the meaning of ordinary words is not, and the meaning of 'taking part in a strike' seems to me to be just the sort of question which an industrial jury is best fitted to decide. No member of either tribunal has spelt out its meaning, perhaps because it was thought unwise or impossible to attempt a paraphrase of plain words. But I should be very reluctant to assume that any of them attributed to the words an unnatural meaning which they were incapable of bearing in their context, or to differ from their conclusion that Mrs Leith took part in the strike. Only the plainest error in law would enable me to differ from them on such a finding, particularly when the majority of the appeal tribunal, whose decision convicts them of such error, appear themselves to be influenced by an erroneous conception of their power to interfere with the industrial tribunal's decision.

On the other hand, I think that on the evidence without argument and reflection I should have taken the view which Mrs Leith's employers appear to have taken that she was not on strike or striking or taking part in the strike. That view takes into account her state of mind, her intention, her motive, her wishes. Some support for doing that is to be found in what Talbot J said in giving the judgment of the appeal tribunal in *McCormick v Horsepower Ltd* [1980] ICR 278 at 283 about Mr Brazier not being motivated by fear in refusing to cross the picket line and withdrawing his labour to aid the strikers; and also in what Lawton LJ in the passage I have quoted from his judgment in the Court of Appeal in the same case said obiter about giving help generally and about Mr Brazier not being shown to have had a common purpose with the striking boilermakers. Furthermore, it seems hard on an employer who takes the trouble to investigate an employee's motives and reasons for stopping work to be told, 'You were wrong to accept what she told you; you ought to have dismissed her and so prevented two other strikers from complaining to the industrial tribunal of unfair dismissal.'

On the other side it is said that it would be intolerable to impose on employers the burden, which these employers undertook with one employee, of looking into the mind of every employee withholding his or her labour before deciding whether to dismiss, in order to see if each had some reason for stopping work unconnected with the object of the strike.

I have come to the conclusion that participation in a strike must be judged by what the employee does and not by what he thinks or why he does it. If he stops work when his workmates come out on strike and does not say or do anything to make plain his disagreement, or which could amount to a refusal to join them, he takes part in their strike. The line between unwilling participation and not taking part may be difficult to draw, but those who stay away from work with the strikers without protest for whatever reason are to be regarded as having crossed that line to take part in the strike. In the field of industrial action those who are not openly against it are presumably for it.

This seems to be the thinking behind the industrial tribunal's decision. If the words in question are capable of bearing that meaning, they are capable of being applied to Mrs Leith's actions on the morning of 12 February 1980, though her time outside the factory gates with the strikers was short and her reason for not entering the factory was accepted. In my judgment a reasonable tribunal could give that meaning to the statutory words and could apply them to Mrs Leith. The industrial tribunal did not, therefore, go wrong in law and it was the majority of the appeal tribunal who did.

I would accordingly allow the appeal, set aside the decision of the Employment Appeal Tribunal and restore the decision of the industrial tribunal.

Bigham and Keogh v *GKN Kwikform Ltd*
[1992] IRLR 4
Employment Appeal Tribunal

Mr Keogh was employed as a scaffolder on the employers' site in Greenford, Middlesex. Mr Bigham was a foreman on that site. The site was operated from the employers' Hammersmith depot. Following the employers' proposal to transfer Mr Bigham because of dissatisfaction with his work, the scaffolders went on strike in protest. Those on strike, including Mr Bigham and Mr Keogh, were dismissed as a result.

Less than three months later, Mr Bigham successfully applied for employment at the company's Luton office. On his application form, he stated that he worked for the company previously in Hammersmith, but did not disclose his earlier dismissal from the Greenford site. When Mr Bigham was taken on, the wages clerk at Luton was on holiday. On his return, he realised that Mr Bigham had been previously dismissed and Mr Bigham was immediately dismissed again.

The industrial tribunal accepted that Mr Bigham was not being fraudulent in failing to disclose that he had been dismissed at Greenford but held that

> the re-engagement was effected by a mistake and that it would never have been done had the wages clerk been present and not on holiday. It was not therefore an effective re-engagement for the purpose of permitting these tribunals to assume jurisdiction; if we were to find otherwise it would permit the unscrupulous employee . . . dismissed by a large national organisation simply by some means or other to obtain employment at a distant branch of his company and thereby prevent the operation of the otherwise clear provisions of [s. 238] of the Act.

The EAT allowed Mr Keogh's appeal and remitted the case to the industrial tribunal.

SIR DAVID CROOM-JOHNSON: Large scaffolding firms with decentralised offices and sites and with a large turnover of labour may have difficulties. Taking on Bigham in a hurry, if that is what happened, was a risk and is a risk which employers of that kind who organise their businesses in that way have to run unless they take steps to avoid it.

We have come to the conclusion that on the submissions which have been put before us and the facts as they were established, that GKN must be said to have had constructive knowledge of what went on at Greenford with Bigham. The employer in each case was the same. It was GKN and they had more than one office but they had records relating to them. Mr Bigham, who was acquitted of any intent to defraud, had revealed on the form that he had worked previously for GKN, although he did not say when, and he told them that he had done so at Hammersmith, that is to say through the Hammersmith office including of course the site at Greenford. All that was required on the part of the wages clerk who was engaging him was to pick up the telephone and to telephone through to Hammersmith and ask what they knew about Mr Bigham. If he had done so, he would have been told straight away. 'Oh yes, he is somebody we had to dismiss less than three months ago because he took part in an unofficial strike,' and in those circumstances one can safely assume that the offer of re-engagement which was made at Luton on that day would never have been made. Unfortunately, the enquiry was not made and nothing was done until the full-time wages clerk, who knew all about Mr Bigham's history, returned to work after his holiday.

In the circumstances therefore, on the facts of the present case, and even accepting as we do the construction of [s. 238] as advanced by Mr Moon, we have come to the conclusion that the offer of re-engagement which was made was one which was within the section and accordingly, Mr Bigham having received an offer of re-engagement within the period, Mr Keogh is entitled to say that the Industrial Tribunal had jurisdiction given to it (otherwise than by [s. 238]), which is an excepting section, and accordingly this appeal by Mr Keogh should be allowed.

Notes
1. Those sacked while engaging in industrial action may also find that they have jeopardised any right to claim redundancy payments (see ERA 1996, s. 140).
2. Given that virtually all forms of industrial action constitute a breach of contract, an alternative sanction available to the employer is to make deductions from the wages of those employees engaged in the action (see *Ticehurst and Thompson* v *British Telecommunications* [1992] IRLR 219, CA, below).

III   Legal Action Against the Trade Union and Strike Organisers

In trying to make sense of the law relating to industrial action it is important that a structured approach is adopted. The following three-stage framework of analysis was developed by Brightman LJ in *Marina Shipping Ltd* v *Laughton* [1982] QB 1127, and was subsequently employed by Lord Diplock in *Merkur Island Shipping* v *Laughton* [1983] 2 All ER 189:

STAGE ONE: Does the industrial action give rise to civil liability at common law?

STAGE TWO: If so, is there an immunity from liability provided by what was s. 13 of TULRA 1974 (now TULR(C)A 1992, s. 219)?

STAGE THREE: If so, has that immunity now been removed by virtue of the changes introduced by the Employment Acts 1980–1990, the Trade Union Act 1984 and TURERA 1993?

A: Stage One: Civil Liabilities for Industrial Action

(i)   Industrial Action and the Contract of Employment

Ticehurst and Thompson v *British Telecommunications*
[1992] IRLR 219
Court of Appeal

Mrs Ticehurst, a BT manager, participated in a withdrawal of cooperation organised by her union. The action included working strictly to con-ditioned hours and refusing to undertake new, temporary advancement. Her employers asked her to sign a document undertaking 'to work normally in accordance with the terms of my contract with BT from now on'. When she refused to sign, she was asked to leave the premises and was not paid for the day in question. The same thing occurred on all subsequent working days up to the date when the pay dispute was settled.

At first instance, Mrs Ticehurst's claim for wages due for the relevant period was upheld on the grounds that Mrs Ticehurst was ready and willing to work normally but was not permitted to do so. The Court of Appeal allowed the employer's appeal.

RALPH GIBSON LJ: The implied term upon which BT relies was described in [*Secretary of State for Employment* v *ASLEF (No. 2)* [1972] 2 QB 455]. Although that case arose under the provisions of the Industrial Relations Act 1971, an essential issue was whether the conduct in question constituted a breach of contract according to ordinary common law principles. In April 1972 instructions to union members to work 'strictly to rule' had caused much dislocation of rail services. After resumption of normal working the unions, on the failure of further negotiations, instructed their members to resume 'work to rule'. This Court, dismissing an appeal from the NIRC, held that obedience to instructions to 'work to rule' constituted breach of contract. . . .

The analysis which I respectfully find most apt to define the relevant duties of Mrs Ticehurst under her contract of employment as a manager employed by BT, is that stated by Buckley LJ, namely 'an implied term to serve the employer faithfully within the requirements of the contract'. It is, I think, consistent with the judgments of Lord Denning and Roskill LJ. It was not suggested that there is any express term in the contract of employment of Mrs Ticehurst, or anything else in the general circumstances of this case, which would make it wrong to imply such a term into her contract. It is, in my judgment, necessary to imply such a term in the case of a manager who is given charge of the work of other employees and who therefore must necessarily be trusted to exercise her judgment and discretion in giving instructions to others and in supervising their work. Such a discretion, if the contract is to work properly, must be exercised faithfully in the interests of the employers.

Next, it seems to me clear that participation by Mrs Ticehurst in the concerted action of withdrawal of goodwill, as it was devised and carried out by STE and the members, would constitute a breach of that term if Mrs Ticehurst was intending to continue to participate in it. For example, a manager who intends, when opportunity offers, to consider how much choice she has in performing any task within those listed by STE and then to choose that which would cause the most inconvenience to her employers, is intending, in my judgment, to break her obligation to serve her employers faithfully. Similarly, the doing of the other acts listed in paragraphs 8, 10 and 11 of the statement of the facts above, not from a genuine intention or interest but so as to cause disruption, would be a breach of that obligation. In addition to those acts by Mrs Ticehurst herself, she was intending after 12 April (if she was intending to continue in the action of the withdrawal of goodwill) to continue, as a committee member of the Stone branch of STE, to advise and encourage other members of STE at Stone to carry on that action by herself distributing STE documents and by being available to answer questions of members by telephone. Her name and telephone number were included in documents distributed by the Stone branch committee for that purpose.

I do not accept the submission of Mr Elias that there can be no breach of the implied term for faithful service unless the intended disruption of BT's undertaking was achieved by the action taken, whether to the extent of rendering the business unmanageable or to some other level of disruption. The term is breached, in my judgment, when the employee does an act, or omits to do an act, which it would be within her contract and the discretion allowed to her not to do, or to do, as the case may be, and the employee so acts or omits to do the act, not in honest exercise of choice or discretion for the faithful performance of her work but in order to disrupt the employer's business or to cause the most inconvenience that can be caused. We need not consider the position which would arise if the ill-intentioned course of conduct is shown to have had no significant consequences adverse to the employer and to be incapable of causing any such adverse consequences in future. This action by way of withdrawal of goodwill did have adverse consequences (see paragraph 28 of the facts above) and the fact that STE was asserting that the effect of the action was greater than that in fact achieved does not cause the conduct not to have been a breach of contract.

If on her return to work Mrs Ticehurst was evincing an intention to continue to participate in the action of withdrawal of goodwill, BT was in my judgment entitled on that ground, and without terminating the contract of employment, to refuse to let her remain at work. . . .

Notes
1. See also *Miles* v *Wakefield Metropolitan District Council* [1987] IRLR 193 and *Wiluszynski* v *Tower Hamlets London Borough Council* [1989] IRLR 259: extracts from these cases appear at pp. 132–35.
2. The editors of *Harvey on Industrial Relations and Employment Law* (London: Butterworths) believe that the *Ticehurst* case raises several profoundly important questions (vol. 2, N/1410).

(a)   Is the duty not to be disruptive confined to managerial, supervisory or professional positions, or is it of general application? The editors of *Harvey* take the view that the general tenor of the judgment suggests the latter.

(b)   Does the unlawfulness lie in the intent rather than the effect? The logic of the judgment would suggest that conduct which is intended to disrupt, but which fails to have that effect, is nevertheless a breach of contract.

(c)   If bloody-mindedness on the part of the worker is a breach of contract, is bloody-mindedness on the part of the employer not also a breach of contract? See *Woods* v *WM Car Services (Peterborough) Ltd* [1982] IRLR 413, CA, and *United Bank Ltd* v *Akhtar* [1989] IRLR 507.

(d)   If industrial action is in principle a breach of contract by the workers, are the circumstances relevant in which it takes place? Should we treat workers any differently who are reactively taking industrial action in the face of provocation by their employer as against those who are aggressively pursuing a claim? The editors of *Harvey* think that this is unlikely because the courts would be most reluctant to get involved in the right and wrongs of a particular dispute, but point out an inconsistency with this approach:

The courts cannot say whether industrial action is justified, whatever the circumstances; but they can say that an individual who participates in that very same industrial action is unjustified, whatever the circumstances. Heads the employer wins; tails the worker loses.

(ii)   The Economic Torts: Inducement of Breach of Contract

Lumley v Gye
(1853) 2 E & B 216
Queen's Bench Division

The plaintiff, manager of the Queen's Theatre, had a contract with Joanna Wagner, an opera singer, under which she agreed to perform at his theatre for three months and not to sing anywhere else during that time. The plaintiff sued the defendant for wrongfully inducing the breach of Miss Wagner's contract by persuading her to sing at Her Majesty's Theatre instead.

CROMPTON J: Whatever may have been the origin or foundation of the law as to enticing servants, and whether it be, as contended by the plaintiff, an instance and branch of a wider rule, or whether it be, as contended by the defendant, an anomaly and an exception from the general rule of law on such subjects, it must now be considered clear law that a person who wrongfully and maliciously, or which is the same thing, with notice, interrupts the relation subsisting between master and servant by procuring the servant to depart from the master's service, or by harbouring and keeping him as a servant after he has quitted it and during the time stipulated for as the period of service, whereby the master is injured, commits a wrongful act for which he is responsible at law.

Note
Inducement to breach of contract is the main economic tort and derives from the decision in the above case. Since, as we have seen, virtually all industrial action involves a breach of contract you can readily appreciate that anyone who calls on workers to take industrial action commits the tort. The inducement may take one of two forms: direct (as in *Lumley* v *Gye* itself) and indirect.

Indirect inducement occurs where the unlawful means (e.g., a breach of employment contracts) are used to render performance of the commercial contract by one of the parties impossible.

D.C. Thomson & Co. Ltd v Deakin
[1952] 2 All ER 361
Court of Appeal

D.C. Thomson operated a non-union shop and dismissed a worker who joined the printing union, NATSOPA. A boycott was organised and lorry drivers employed at Bowaters, the company which supplied D.C. Thomson with paper, told Bowaters that they might not be prepared to deliver paper to Thomson. Bowaters never ordered the men to deliver the paper but did inform D.C. Thomson that they would not be able to deliver paper under contract. D.C. Thomson sought an interlocutory injunction against officials of the various unions concerned to restrain them from procuring any breach by Bowaters of their contract with D.C. Thomson.

SIR RAYMOND EVERSHED: It was suggested in the course of argument . . . that the tort must still be properly confined to such direct intervention, that is, to cases where the intervener or persuader uses by personal intervention persuasion on the mind of one of the parties to the contract so as to procure that party to break it.

I am unable to agree that any such limitation is logical, rational or part of law . . . [I]t seems to me that the intervener, assuming in all cases that he knows of the contract and acts with the aim and object of procuring its breach to the damage of B, one of the contracting parties, will be liable not only (1) if he directly intervenes by persuading A to break it, but also (2) if he intervenes by the commission of some act wrongful in itself so as to prevent A from in fact performing his contract; and also (3) if he persuades a third party, for example, a servant of A, to do an act in itself wrongful or not legitimate (as committing a breach of a contract of service with A) so as to render, as was intended, impossible A's performance of his contract with B.

JENKINS LJ: . . . I see no distinction in principle for the present purpose between persuading a man to break his contract with another, preventing him by physical restraint from performing it, making his performance of it impossible by taking away or damaging his tools or machinery, and making his performance of it impossible by depriving him, in breach of their contracts, of the services of his employees. All these are wrongful acts, and if done with knowledge of and intention to bring about a breach of a contract to which the person directly wronged is a party, and, if in fact producing that result, I fail to see why they should not all alike fall within the sphere of actionable interference with contractual relations delimited by Lords MacNaghten and Lindley in *Quinn* v *Leathem* [1901] AC 495.

But, while admitting this form of actionable interference in principle, I would hold it strictly confined to cases where it is clearly shown, first, that the person charged with actionable interference knew of the existence of the contract and intended to procure its breach; secondly, that the person so charged did definitely and unequivocally persuade, induce or procure the employees concerned to break their contracts of employment with the intent I have mentioned; thirdly, that the employees so persuaded, induced or procured did in fact break their contracts of employment; and, fourth, that breach of the contract forming the alleged subject of interference ensued as a necessary consequence of the breaches by the employees concerned of their contracts of employment.

Notes

1. The Court held that the union officials had not directly procured a breach of contract by the suppliers, nor had they intentionally intervened by unlawful means as there had been no breach of contract by the suppliers' employees.

2. The necessary elements of this tort are as follows:

(a) *Knowledge of the contract* ('that the person charged with actionable interference knew of the existence of the contract and intended to procure its breach').

Emerald Construction Co. Ltd v *Lowthian*
[1966] 1 All ER 1013
Court of Appeal

A trade union sought to bring about the termination of a 'labour-only' sub-contract by industrial action. The union officers knew of the existence of the sub-contract but did not know its precise terms until after the industrial action commenced. The action continued after they knew of the precise terms of the sub-contract, under which the main contractor had the right to terminate if the plaintiff sub-contractor did not maintain reasonable progress. The plaintiff sought an interlocutory injunction to stop the defendant union officials from doing anything to procure termination by the main contractors of the sub-contract. The defendants argued unsuccessfully that they had not committed any tort as they did not know the terms of the contract; in particular, they did not know the grounds upon which it could be terminated.

LORD DENNING MR: . . . If the officers of the trade union, knowing of the contract, deliberately sought to procure a breach of it they would do wrong: see *Lumley* v *Gye*. Even if they did not know of the actual terms of the contract, but had the means of knowledge — which they deliberately disregarded — that would be enough. Like the man who turns a blind eye. So here, if the officers deliberately sought to get his contract terminated, heedless of its terms, regardless whether it was terminated by breach or not, they would do wrong. For it is unlawful for a third person to procure a breach of a contract knowingly, or recklessly, indifferent whether it is a breach or not.

(b)   *Intention to cause its breach* ('that the person so charged did definitely and unequivocally persuade, induce or procure the employees concerned to break their contracts of employment with . . . intent'). Compare the following extracts:

D.C. Thomson & Co. Ltd v Deakin
[1952] 2 All ER 361
Court of Appeal

JENKINS LJ: . . . It is now well settled that, apart from conspiracy to injure, no actionable wrong is committed by a person who, by acts not in themselves unlawful prevents another person from obtaining goods or services necessary for the purposes of his business, or who induces others so to prevent that person by any lawful means. It follows in my view, that (again apart from conspiracy to injure) there is nothing unlawful, under the law as enunciated in *Allen* v *Flood* [[1898] AC 1], and subsequent cases, in general appeals to others to prevent a given person from obtaining goods or services, for that is a purpose capable of being lawfully carried out, and there can, therefore, be nothing unlawful in advocating it, unless unlawful means are advocated. The result of such advocacy may well be that unlawful means are adopted by some to achieve the purpose advocated, but that is not to say that a person who advocates the object without advocating the means is to be taken to have advocated recourse to unlawful means. If by reference to the form of actionable interference with contractual rights now propounded, general exhortations issued in the course of a trade dispute, such as 'Stop supplies to X', 'Refuse to handle X's goods', 'Treat X as "black" ', and the like, were regarded as amounting to actionable interference, because persons reached by such exhortations might respond to them by breaking their contracts of employment and thereby causing breaches of contracts between their employers and other persons, and because the person issuing such exhortations must be taken constructively to have known that the employers concerned must have contracts of some kind or other with other persons, and that his exhortations (general as they were) might lead to breaches of those contracts through breaches of contracts of employment committed by persons moved by his exhortations, then the proposition must be accepted that it is an actionable wrong to advocate objects which can be achieved by lawful means because they can also be achieved by unlawful means, and to that proposition I decline to subscribe.

Torquay Hotel Co. Ltd v Cousins
[1969] 2 Ch 106
Court of Appeal

(The facts of this case are set out at p. 734.)

WINN LJ: . . . It was one of [counsel for the defendants'] main submissions that mere advice, warning or information cannot amount to tortious procurement of breach of contract. Whilst granting *arguendi causa* that a communication which went no further would, in general, not, in the absence of circumstances giving a particular significance, amount to a threat or intimidation, I am unable to understand why it may not amount to an inducement. In the ordinary meaning of language it would surely be said that a father who told his daughter that her fiance had been convicted of indecent exposure, had thereby induced her, with or without justification, by truth or by slander, to break her engagement. A man who writes to his mother-in-law telling her that the central heating in his house has broken down may thereby induce her to cancel an intended visit . . .

Notes
1.   The above extracts from *Emerald Construction* and *Torquay Hotel* evidence the ways in which the courts widened the scope of the tort of inducing breach during the 1960s – a decade in which there was a moral panic concerning the British 'strike problem'.
2.   The traditional view is that the defendant must directly intend to injure the claimant. However, in *Falconer* v *ASLEF and NUR* [1986] IRLR 331, the tort of inducement to breach of contract was held to be established where the unions had held a one-day rail strike, thereby inconveniencing the plaintiff's travel arrangements. The unions' argument that it was their intention to harm British Rail, not the plaintiff, was rejected as 'both naive and divorced from reality'. The unions did not appeal against this county court decision because, if it had been upheld, liability under the tort would have been broadened considerably. Subsequently, however, in *Barretts & Baird (Wholesale) Ltd* v *IPCS* [1987] IRLR 3, Henry J stated that to make an individual striker liable in tort to any third party damaged by that strike, the test must be that the striker's *predominant purpose* must be injury to the claimant.

(c)   *Unlawful means* ('that the employees so persuaded, induced or procured did in fact break their contracts of employment').

D.C. Thomson & Co. Ltd v *Deakin*
[1952] 2 All ER 361
Court of Appeal

SIR RAYMOND EVERSHED: I need only add that on the evidence there was no breach of contract by any workman, since Bowaters, for reasons which, I doubt not were prudent, took the line that they would not order any man to load or to deliver paper for the plaintiffs.

(d)   *Causing actual breach* ('that breach of the contract forming the alleged subject of interference ensued as a necessary consequence of the breaches by the employees concerned of their contracts of employment').

D.C. Thomson & Co. Ltd v *Deakin*
[1952] 2 All ER 361
Court of Appeal

JENKINS LJ: Finally, not every breach of a contract of employment with a trading or manufacturing concern by an employee engaged in services required for the performance of a contract between his employer and some other person carries with it as a necessary consequence . . . the breach of the last mentioned contract. For instance, A induces B, C's lorry driver, to refuse, in breach of his contract of employment, to carry goods which C is under contract to deliver to D, and does so with a view to causing the breach of C's contract with D. C could if he chose, engage some other lorry, or arrange alternative means of transport, but does not do so. He fails to deliver the goods, telling D he is prevented from doing so by B's breach of contract. In such circumstances, there has been no direct invasion by A of C's contract with D, and, although A has committed an actionable wrong against C, designed to bring about the breach of C's contract with D, and a breach has in fact occurred, it cannot be said that the breach has in fact been caused by A's wrongful act, and therefore D cannot, in my view, establish as against A an actionable interference with his rights under his contract with C.

Torquay Hotel Co. Ltd v *Cousins*
[1969] 2 Ch 106
Court of Appeal

As a result of picketing of the Imperial Hotel, drivers for the hotel's oil suppliers refused to deliver oil to the hotel. The officials of the union claimed that they had not committed the tort of inducing a breach of the contract to supply as there was in the contract between the hotel and the suppliers an exemption clause exempting the suppliers from liability to deliver.

RUSSELL LJ: It was argued that the exception clause had the effect that Esso could not be in breach of its supply contract if failure to do so was due to labour disputes. In my view, the exception clause means what it says and no more; it *assumes* a failure to fulfil a term of the contract – i.e., a breach of contract – and excludes liability —

i.e., in damages – for that breach in stated circumstances. It is an exception from liability for non-performance rather than an exception for obligation to perform.

WINN LJ: . . . [T]he argument of counsel for the defendants that clause 10 of the written contract between Esso and the Imperial Hotel for a year's supply would have operated to prevent a failure or failures to deliver ordered instalments of fuel thereunder from being a breach does not seem to be sound. As I construe the clause it affords only an immunity against any claim for damages; it could not bar a right to treat the contract as repudiated by continuing breach . . .

DENNING LJ: . . . I have always understood that if one person deliberately interferes with the trade or business of another, and does so by unlawful means, that is, by an act which he is not at liberty to commit, then he is acting unlawfully, even though he does not procure or induce any actual breach of contract.

Question
In what sense is Lord Denning's perception of the scope of liability much wider than that of his fellow Lord Justices?

Note
Justification provides a defence to inducement to breach of contract, but it has been raised successfully in only one case involving industrial action. In *Brimelow* v *Casson* [1924] 1 Ch 302, the defence succeeded where chorus girls were called upon to strike in protest at low wages which in many cases had driven them to prostitution. Apart from this exceptional case, the courts have not been prepared to accept as justification the fact the inducement proceeds from a desire by union officials to protect their members' interests (see *South Wales Miners' Federation* v *Glamorgan Coal Co.* [1905] AC 205).

(iii)   The Economic Torts: Interference with Contract, Trade or Business
In contrast to the well-established tort of inducement to breach of contract, this tort is of more recent vintage. In several cases, Lord Denning MR expressed his view that 'if one party interferes with the trade or business of another, and does so by unlawful means, then he is acting unlawfully, even though he does not procure or induce any actual breach of contract' (*Daily Mirror Newspapers* v *Gardner* [1968] 2 All ER 163; see also the above extract from *Torquay Hotels Co. Ltd* v *Cousins*). Therefore, it will be unlawful to interfere with a contract short of breach, for example by preventing performance in cases where the contract contains a *force majeure* clause, exempting a party in breach from liability to pay damages.

More recently, it would appear that this head of liability is even broader in scope, encompassing any intentional use of unlawful means aimed at interfering with the claimant's trade or business.

Merkur Island Shipping Corporation v *Laughton*
[1983] 2 All ER 189
House of Lords

The plaintiffs were the registered owners of a cargo vessel sailing under a flag of convenience and manned by an Asian crew who were paid below the rates approved by the International Transport Workers Federation (the ITF). The ship was time chartered to charterers, who had in turn sub-chartered it. Both the charter and sub-charter required the captain, acting on behalf of the owners, to 'prosecute his voyages with the utmost despatch' and required the charterers or sub-charterers to provide and pay for towage into and out of berths when the ship docked. Under the terms of the time charter, hire was not payable to the shipowners in the event of time being lost because of a labour dispute.

The ship docked at Liverpool in order to load, and when it was ready to sail the sub-charterers arranged for a tug company, with whom they had a running contract, to move the ship out of dock. The ITF decided to black the ship because of the low rates of pay to the crew and persuaded the tugmen employed by the tug company to refuse to operate tugs assigned to move the ship, with the result that it was prevented from leaving port. The tugmen's refusal to take the vessel out was a breach of their contracts of employment with the tug company.

The plaintiff shipowners applied for, and were granted, an interlocutory injunction requiring the ITF to lift the blacking. The defendants appealed against the injunction, contending, *inter alia*, that the part of the ship-owners' writ relating to unlawful interference with the charter contract disclosed no cause of action at common law. The Court of Appeal dismissed the appeal and the defendants unsuccessfully appealed to the House of Lords.

LORD DIPLOCK: The common law tort relied on by the shipowners under head (1) of the writ is the tort of interfering by unlawful means with the performance of a contract. The contract of which the performance was interfered with was the charter; the form the interference took was by immobilising the ship in Liverpool to prevent the captain from performing the contractual obligation of the shipowners under cl 8 of the charter to 'prosecute his voyages with the utmost despatch'. The unlawful means by which the interference was effected was by procuring the tugmen and the lockmen to break their contracts of employment by refusing to carry out the operations on the part of the tugowners and the port authorities that were necessary to enable the ship to leave the dock.

The reason why the shipowners relied on interference with the performance of the charter rather than procuring a breach of it was the presence in the charter of cll 51 and 60 which were in the following terms:

Clause 51. Blockade/Boycott. In the event of loss of time due to boycott of the vessel in any port or place by shore labour or others, or arising from Government restrictions by reason of the vessel's flag, or arising from the terms and conditions on which the members of the crew are employed, or by reason of the trading of this vessel, payment of hire shall cease for time thereby lost.

Clause 60. Cancellation. Should the vessel be prevented from work for the reasons as outlined in Clauses 49/50/51 and 52 for more than ten days, Charterers shall have the option of cancelling this contract.

My Lords, your Lordships have had the dubious benefit during the course of the argument in this appeal of having been referred once more to many of those cases, spanning more than a century, that were the subject of analysis in the judgment of Jenkins LJ in *D.C. Thomson & Co. Ltd* v *Deakin* [1952] 2 All ER 361, [1952] Ch 646 and led to his statement of the law as to what are the essential elements in the tort of actionable interference with contractual rights by blacking that is cited by Sir John Donaldson MR and, at rather greater length, by O'Connor LJ in their judgments in the instant case. That statement has, for 30 years now, been regarded as authoritative, and for my part, I do not think that any benefit is gained by raking over once again the previous decisions. The elements of the tort as stated by Jenkins LJ were ([1952] 2 All ER 361 at 379–380, [1952] Ch 646 at 697):

> . . . first, that the person charged with actionable interference knew of the existence of the contract and intended to procure its breach; secondly, that the person so charged did definitely and unequivocally persuade, induce or procure the employees concerned to break their contracts of employment with the intent I have mentioned; thirdly, that the employees so persuaded, induced or procured did in fact break their contracts of employment; and, fourthly, that breach of the contract forming the alleged subject of interference ensued as a necessary consequence of the breaches by the employees concerned of their contracts of employment.

D.C. Thomson & Co. Ltd v *Deakin* was a case in which the only interference with contractual rights relied on was procuring a *breach* by a third party of a contract between that third party and the plaintiff. That is why in the passage that I have picked out for citation Jenkins LJ restricts himself to that form of actionable interference with contractual rights which consists of procuring an actual breach of the contract that formed the subject matter of interference; but it is evident from the passages in his judgment which precede the passage I have cited and are themselves set out in the judgment of O'Connor LJ that Jenkins LJ, though using the expression 'breach', was not intending to confine the tort of actionable interference with contractual rights to the procuring of such non-performance of primary obligations under a contract as would necessarily give rise to secondary obligations to make monetary compensation by way of damages. All prevention of due performance of a primary obligation under a contract was intended to be included even though no secondary obligation to make monetary compensation thereupon came into existence, because the secondary obligation was excluded by some force majeure clause.

If there were any doubt about this matter, it was resolved in 1969 by the judgments of the Court of Appeal in *Torquay Hotel Co. Ltd* v *Cousins* [1969] 1 All ER 522, [1969] 2 Ch 106. That was a case in which the contract the performance of which was interfered with was one for the delivery of fuel. It contained a force majeure clause excusing the seller from liability for non-delivery if delayed, hindered or prevented by, inter alia, labour disputes. Lord Denning MR stated the principle thus ([1969] 1 All ER 522 at 530, [1969] 2 Ch 106 at 138):

> . . . there must be *interference* in the execution of a contract. The interference is not confined to the procurement of a *breach* of contract. It extends to a case where a third person *prevents* or *hinders* one party from performing his contract, even though it be not a breach. (Lord Denning's emphasis.)

Parliamentary recognition that the tort of actionable interference with contractual rights is as broad as Lord Denning MR stated in the passage I have just quoted is, in my view, to be found in s. 13(1) of the 1974 Act itself, which refers to inducement not only 'to break a contract', but also 'to interfere with its performance', and treats them as being pari materia [see now TULR(C)A 1992, s. 219(1)].

So I turn to the four elements of the tort of actionable interference with contractual rights as Jenkins LJ stated them, but substituting 'interference with performance' for 'breach', except in relation to the breaking by employees of their own contracts of employment where such breach has as its necessary consequence the interference with the performance of the contract concerned.

The first requirement is actually twofold: (1) knowledge of the existence of the contract concerned and (2) intention to interfere with its performance.

As respect knowledge, the ITF had been given an actual copy of the charter on 19 July 1980, three days after the blacking started but two days before the application to Parker J was made. Quite apart from this, however, there can hardly be anyone better informed than the ITF as to the terms of the sort of contracts under which ships are employed, particularly those flying flags of convenience. I agree with what was said by Sir John Donaldson MR on the question of the ITF's knowledge ([1983] 1 All ER 334 at 349, [1983] 2 WLR 45 at 63):

> Whatever the precise degree of knowledge of the defendants at any particular time, faced with a laden ship which, as they well knew, was about to leave port, the defendants must in my judgment be deemed to have known of the almost certain existence of contracts of carriage to which the shipowners were parties. The wholly exceptional case would be that of a ship carrying the owner's own goods. Whether that contract or those contracts consisted of a time charter, a voyage charter or one or more bill of lading contracts or some or all of such contracts would have been immaterial to the defendants. Prima facie their intention was to immobilise the ship and in so doing to interfere with the performance by the owners of their contract or contracts of carriage; immobilising a laden ship which had no contractual obligation to move would have been a pointless exercise, since it would have brought no pressure to bear on the owners.

The last sentence of this citation deals also with intention. It was the shipowners on whom the ITF wanted to bring pressure to bear, because it was they who were employing seamen at rates of pay lower than those it was the policy of the ITF to enforce. The only way in which income could be derived by the shipowners from the ownership of their ship was by entering into contracts with third parties for the carriage of goods under which a primary obligation of the shipowners would be to prosecute the contract voyages with the utmost dispatch, and their earnings from their ship would be diminished by its immobilisation in port. Diminishing their earnings under the contract of carriage was the only way in which pressure could be brought to bear on the shipowners.

The fulfilment of the second and third requirements, that the ITF successfully procured the tugmen and lock keepers to break their contracts of employment and that the ITF's intention in doing so was to interfere with the performance by the shipowners of their primary obligations to the charterers under the charter, is beyond dispute. So is the fulfilment of the fourth requirement, that the prevention of the performance by the shipowners of their primary obligation under the charter to secure through the captain that the ship, as soon as she had completed loading should proceed from the port of Liverpool on her voyage with the utmost dispatch, was a necessary consequence of the breaches by the tugmen and the lock keepers of their contracts of employment.

On the stage 1 point I accordingly agree with the Court of Appeal that the shipowners, on the evidence that was before Parker J, have made out a strong prima facie case that the ITF committed the common law tort of actionable interference with contractual rights.

Clauses 51 and 60 of the charterparty do not assist the ITF any more than did the force majeure clause in the *Torquay Hotels* case; but cl 51 does show that the ITF's action did in fact succeed in causing damage to the shipowners.

In anticipation of an argument that was addressed to your Lordships on the stage 3 point, I should mention that the evidence also establishes a prima facie case of the common law tort, referred to in s. 13(2) and (3) of the 1974 Act, of interfering with the trade or business of another person by doing unlawful acts. To fall within this genus of torts the unlawful act need not involve procuring another person to break a subsisting contract or to interfere with the performance of a subsisting contract. The immunity granted by s. 13(2) and (3) I will call the 'genus immunity'. Where, however, the procuring of another person to break a subsisting contract *is* the unlawful act involved, as it is in s. 13(1), this is but one species of the wider genus of tort. This I will call the 'species immunity'.

(iv)   Intimidation

The tort of intimidation may take the form of compelling a person by threats of unlawful action to do some act which causes him loss; or of intimidating other persons, by threats of unlawful action, with the intention and effect of causing loss to a third party. Prior to 1964, it was assumed that the tort was confined to threats of physical violence, but in that year the House of Lords held that threats to break a contract were encompassed by the tort.

Rookes v *Barnard*
[1964] AC 1129
House of Lords

BOAC and the draughtsmen's union (AESD) operated an informal closed shop arrangement. The plaintiff was a draughtsman employed by BOAC, and in 1955 he resigned from the union. Officials of the union threatened BOAC that, unless they dismissed the plaintiff, union members would go on strike. Rookes was given notice and his contract of employment was lawfully terminated. He sued the union officials alleging, *inter alia*, intimidation.

LORD DEVLIN: . . . It is not, of course, disputed that if the act threatened is a crime, the threat is unlawful. But otherwise is it enough to say that the act threatened is actionable as a breach of contract or must it be actionable as a tort? My Lords, I see no good grounds for the latter limitation. . . . The essence of the offence is coercion. It cannot be said that every form of coercion is wrong. A dividing line must be drawn and the natural line runs between what is lawful and unlawful as against the party threatened. . . .

I find therefore nothing to differentiate a threat of a breach of contract from a threat of physical violence or any other illegal threat. The nature of the threat is immaterial. . . . All that matters to the plaintiff is that, metaphorically speaking, a club has been used. It does not matter to the plaintiff what the club is made of – whether it is a physical club or an economic club, a tortious club or an otherwise illegal club. If an intermediate party is improperly coerced, it does not matter to the plaintiff how he is coerced.

I think, therefore, that at common law there is a tort of intimidation and that on the facts of this case each of the respondents has committed it, both individually (since the jury has found that each took an overt and active part) and in combination with others.

(v) Conspiracy

This tort may take two forms:

(a)   conspiracy to commit an unlawful act (a conspiracy to commit a crime or tort is clearly included in this category);

(b)   conspiracy to injure by lawful means ('simple conspiracy').

Quinn v Leathem
[1901] AC 495
House of Lords

The plaintiff, a flesher, employed non-union men. The defendants told the plaintiff and one of his best customers, a butcher, that unless he dismissed the non-unionists, they would be subject to industrial action. As a result, the plaintiff lost his customer and the plaintiff sued for conspiracy to injure.

LORD LINDLEY: Black lists are real instruments of coercion, as every man whose name is on one soon discovers to his cost. A combination not to work is one thing, and is lawful. A combination to prevent others from working by annoying them if they do is a very different thing, and is prima facie unlawful. Again, not to work oneself is lawful so long as one keeps off the poor-rates, but to order men not to work when they are willing to work is another thing. A threat to call men out given by a trade union official to an employer of men belonging to the union and willing to work with him is a form of coercion, intimidation and molestation, or annoyance to them and to him very difficult to resist, and, to say the least, requiring justification. None was offered in this case.

Note

This form of conspiracy which was developed in *Quinn v Leathem* is most dangerous, because it makes it unlawful when two or more persons do something which would have been quite lawful if performed by an individual. A conspiracy to injure is simply an agreement to cause deliberate loss to another without justification. The motive or purpose of the defendants is important. If the predominant purpose is to injure the claimant, the conspiracy is actionable. If, on the other hand, the principal aim is to achieve a legitimate goal, the action is not unlawful, even if in so doing the claimant suffers injury. While it took the courts some time to accept trade union objectives as legitimate, later decisions adopted a more liberal stance, as the next extract illustrates.

Crofter Hand-Woven Harris Tweed Co. v Veitch
[1942] AC 435
House of Lords

The millowners on the Island of Lewis refused to enter into a closed shop agreement with the union or grant a pay increase because of competition from the plaintiffs' mills which imported cheap spun yarn from the mainland. The defendant trade union officials instructed their members who were dockers at Stornoway not to handle yarn destined for the plaintiffs. There was no breach of employment contracts by the dockers. The plaintiffs sued the defendants for conspiracy to injure.

LORD WRIGHT: As the claim is for a tort, it is necessary to ascertain what constitutes the tort alleged. It cannot be merely that the appellants' right to freedom in conducting their trade has been interfered with. That right is not an absolute or unconditional right. It is only a particular aspect of the citizen's right to personal freedom, and like other aspects of that right is qualified by various legal limitations, either by statute or common law. Such limitations are inevitable in organised societies where the rights of individuals may clash. In commercial affairs each trader's rights are qualified by the rights of others to compete. Where the rights of labour are concerned, the rights of the employer are conditioned by the rights of the men to give or withhold their services. The right of workmen to strike is an essential element in the principle of collective bargaining. . . .

It is thus clear that employers of workmen or those who like the appellants depend in part on the services of workmen, have in the conduct of their affairs to reckon with this freedom of the men and to realise that the exercise of the men's rights may involve some limitation on their own freedom in the management of their business. Such interference with a person's business, so long as the limitations enforced by law are not contravened, involves no legal wrong against the person. In the present case the respondents are sued for imposing the 'embargo', which corresponds to calling the men out on strike. The dockers were free to obey or not obey the call to refuse to handle the appellants' goods. In refusing to handle the goods they did not commit any breach of contract with anyone; they were merely exercising their own rights. But there might be circumstances which rendered the action wrongful. The men might be called out in breach of their contracts with their employer, and that would be clearly a wrongful act against the employer, an interference with his contractual right, for which damages could be claimed not only as against the contract breaker, but against the person who counselled or procured or advised the breach. . . .

But in *Allen* v *Flood* [1898] AC 1, this House was considering a case of an individual actor, where the element of combination was absent. In that case, it was held, the motive of the defendant is immaterial. Damage done intentionally and even malevolently to another, thus, it was held, gives no cause of action so long as no legal right of the other is infringed. . . . Thus, for the purposes of the present case we reach the position that apart from combination no wrong would have been committed. There was no coercion of the dockers. There were no threats to them. They were legally free to choose the alternative course which they preferred. . . .

. . . The appellants must establish that they have been damnified by a conspiracy to injure, that is, that there was a wilful and concerted intention to injure without just cause, and consequent damage. . . .

I have attempted to state principles so generally accepted as to pass into the realm of what has been called jurisprudence, at least in English law, which has for better or worse adopted the test of self-interest or selfishness as being capable of justifying the deliberate doing of lawful acts which inflict harm, so long as the means employed are not wrongful. The common law in England might have adopted a different criterion and one more consistent with the standpoint of a man who refuses to benefit himself at the cost of harming another. But we live in a competitive and acquisitive society, and the English common law may have felt that it was beyond its power to fix any but the crudest distinctions and metes and bounds which divide the rightful from the wrongful use of the actor's own freedom, leaving the precise application in any particular case to the jury or the judge of fact. If further principles of regulation or control are to be introduced, that is a matter for the legislature . . .

. . . The respondents had no quarrel with the yarn importers. Their sole object, the courts below have held, was to promote their union's interests by promoting the interest of the industry on which the men's wages depended. On these findings, with which I agree, it could not be said that their combination was without sufficient justification. Nor would this conclusion be vitiated, even though their motives may have been mixed, so long as the real or predominant object, if they had more than one object, was not wrongful. Nor is the objection tenable that the respondents' real or predominant object was to secure the employers' help to get 100 per cent membership of the union among the textile workers. Cases of mixed motives or, as I should prefer to say, of the presence of more than one object are not uncommon. If so, it is for the jury or judge of fact to decide which is the predominant object, as it may be assumed the jury did in *Quinn's* case, when they decided on the basis that the object of the combiners was vindictive punishment, not their own practical advantage . . .

Notes

1. The courts have also held combinations to be justified where their purpose was to force an employer to lift a colour bar in a club (*Scala Ballroom (Wolverhampton) Ltd* v *Ratcliffe* [1958] 3 All ER 220, CA) and to enforce a 'closed shop' agreement (*Reynolds* v *Shipping Federation* [1924] 1 Ch 28).

2. Until the decision of the House of Lords in *Lonrho plc* v *Fayed* [1992] 1 AC 1129, it was assumed that both forms of conspiracy required the claimant to show that the predominant purpose of the conspirators was to injure the claimant. In *Fayed*, it was emphasised that, for the purposes of conspiracy to commit an unlawful act, it was merely sufficient to show that the conspirators acted with intent to injure the claimant.

(vi)   Inducement of Breach of Statutory Duty

Meade v Haringey LBC
[1979] 2 All ER 1016
Court of Appeal

School caretakers and ancillary staff threatened to close schools in support of a wage claim. In response, the defendant local authority instructed all headmasters in the area to close the schools and to advise parents not to send their children to school. Parents complained that the local authority was in breach of a statutory duty to make schools available for full-time education. The parents sought a mandatory injunction. By the time the case reached the Court of Appeal, the industrial action had been called off and all the schools were open. While the injunction was refused, the Court held that there had been a prima facie breach of statutory duty.

LORD DENNING MR: Now comes the great question in this case: had the borough council any just cause or excuse for closing the schools as they did? On the evidence as it stands, the borough council were acting under the influence of the trade unions and indeed in combination with them. And the trade unions and their secretaries were, as I see it, acting quite unlawfully. They were calling on the local education authority to break their statutory duty, to close the schools instead of keeping them open as they should have done. Now s. 13 of the Trade Union and Labour Relations Act 1974 as amended gives them immunity if they induce a person to break a contract. But it gives them no immunity if they induce a local authority to break its statutory duty. The law is well-established that a public authority cannot enter into any contract or take any action incompatible with the due exercise of its statutory powers or the discharge of its statutory duties: see *Birkdale District Electric Supply Co. Ltd* v *Southport Corpn* [1926] AC 355 at 364 by Lord Birkenhead. It cannot effectively contract not to exercise its statutory powers or to abdicate its statutory duties: see *Staines Urban District Council's Agreement, Triggs* v *Staines Urban District Council* [1968] 2 All ER 1 at by Cross J. It seems to me that if the local education authority closed the schools, at the behest of the trade unions, or in agreement with them, they were acting unlawfully. The trade unions had no right whatever to ask the borough council to close the schools. The borough council had no business whatever to agree to it. Instead they should have kept the schools open, and risked the consequences of the dispute escalating. Or they should have moved the court for an injunction to restrain the leaders of the trade unions from interfering with the due opening of the schools. I am confident that the people at large would have supported such a move and expect the trade union leaders to obey it, and they would have obeyed it.

(vii)   Economic Duress

Dimskal Shipping Co. SA v International Transport Workers' Federation
[1992] IRLR 78
House of Lords

The plaintiffs, a Panamanian company, owned the 'Evia Luck', a ship registered in Panama, managed from Greece and crewed by Greeks and Filipinos.

When the ship berthed in Sweden, representatives of the Swedish affiliates of the ITF threatened that the ship would be blacked unless ITF employment contracts were entered into with the crew.

As a result of the threats, the plaintiffs orally agreed to pay a sum of US$103,463 to the ITF at its London headquarters, representing all the crew's backdated wages calculated in accordance with ITF wage scales. This sum was paid. In addition, the plaintiffs agreed to pay ITF entrance and membership fees and to make a contribution to the ITF welfare fund. The plaintiffs also agreed to lodge a bank performance guarantee of $200,000 and to provide deeds of undertaking to the effect that they would not institute proceedings against Filipino crew members, that they would enter into an ITF special agreement, that they would provide all crew members with ITF employment contracts, that they would sign a document declaring that they were complying voluntarily with ITF's demands, and that they would provide letters of indemnity for all crew members.

Following a delay in execution of the required documents, the ship was blacked. As a result, the plaintiffs complied with ITF demands and signed the required documents. The plaintiffs also signed a letter of undertaking which included the following clause: 'This undertaking shall be legally enforceable within the meaning of s. 18 of the Trade Union and Labour Relations Act 1974 [now TULR(C)A 1992, s. 179], and be subject to English Law and the jurisdiction of the English courts.' The ship was then allowed to sail.

The plaintiffs sought restitution of the sums totalling US$111, 743 which had been paid to the ITF on the ground that the payments had been made pursuant to contracts void for duress.

The Court of Appeal, overruling the decision of Phillips J, held that whether the economic pressure was legitimate was to be answered by reference to English law. The House of Lords, by a majority, dismissed the ITF's appeal.

LORD GOFF OF CHIEVELEY: The starting-point for the consideration of this question is the decision of your Lordships' House in *The Universe Sentinel* [1982] IRLR 200, and in particular the speech in that case of Lord Diplock, who delivered the leading speech for the majority. For present purposes, the most relevant passage in Lord Diplock's speech is to be found at pp. 205–206, in which he considered the effect upon economic duress, as a basis for obtaining restitution, of the immunity then conferred by the Trade Union and Labour Relations Act 1974 [see now the Trade Union and Labour Relations (Consolidation) Act 1992]. The pressure in that case took the form of blacking the plaintiff's ship, at the instigation of the ITF, while she was lying at Milford Haven. The Act (in this respect no longer in force at the time of the events in the present case) conferred an immunity against an action in tort in respect of pressure of the type there exerted by the ITF. It did not expressly provide for any immunity in respect of an action in restitution. However, Lord Diplock said, at p. 205, 28:

> The use of economic duress to induce another person to part with property or money is not a tort per se; the form that the duress takes may or may not be tortious. The remedy to which economic duress gives rise is not an action for damages but an action for restitution of property or money exacted under such duress and the avoidance of any contract that had been induced by it; but where the particular form taken by the economic duress used is itself a tort, the restitutional remedy for money had and received by the defendant to the plaintiff's use is one which the plaintiff is entitled to pursue as an alternative remedy to an action for damages in tort.
>
> In extending into the field of industrial relations the common law concept of economic duress and the right to a restitutionary remedy for it which is currently in process of development by judicial decisions, this House would not, in my view, be exercising the restraint that is appropriate to such a process if it were so to develop the concept that, by the simple expedient of 'waiving the tort', a restitutionary remedy for money had and received is made enforceable in cases in which Parliament has, over so long a period of years, manifested its preference for a public policy that a particular kind of tortious act should be legitimised in the sense that I am using that expression.
>
> It is only in this indirect way that the provisions of the Trade Union and Labour Relations Act 1974 are relevant to the duress point. The immunities from liability

in tort provided by ss. 13 and 14 [see now TULR(C)A 1992, s. 219] are not directly applicable to the shipowners' cause of action for money had and received. Nevertheless, these sections, together with the definition of trade dispute in s. 29 [now TULR(C)A 1992, s. 244], afford an indication, which your Lordships should respect, of where public policy requires that the line should be drawn between what kind of commercial pressure by a trade union upon an employer in the field of industrial relations ought to be treated as legitimised despite the fact that the will of the employer is thereby coerced, and what kind of commercial pressure in that field does amount to economic duress that entitles the employer victim to restitutionary remedies.

It is not necessary for present purposes to explore the basis of this decision. It appears to bear some affinity to the principle underlying those cases in which the courts have given effect to the inferred purpose of the legislature by holding a person entitled to sue for damages for breach of a statutory duty, though no such right of suit has been expressly created by the statute imposing the duty. It is enough to state that, by parity of reasoning, not only may an action of restitution be rejected as inconsistent with the policy of a statute such as that under consideration in *The Universe Sentinel* [1982] IRLR 200, but in my opinion a claim that a contract is voidable for duress by reason of pressure legitimised by such a statute may likewise be rejected on the same ground.

It is against the background of that decision that the problem in the present case falls to be considered. . . .

Question

Would it be true to say that here is an inverse relationship between the scope of economic duress and the statutory trade dispute immunities?

B: Stage Two: The Immunities

Trade Union and Labour Relations (Consolidation) Act 1992

219. Protection from certain tort liabilities

(1) An act done by a person in contemplation or furtherance of a trade dispute is not actionable in tort on the ground only—

(a) that it induces another person to break a contract or interferes or induces another person to interfere with its performance, or

(b) that it consists in his threatening that a contract (whether one to which he is a party or not) will be broken or its performance interfered with, or that he will induce another person to break a contract or interfere with its performance.

(2) An agreement or combination by two or more persons to do or procure the doing of an act in contemplation or furtherance of a trade dispute is not actionable in tort if the act is one which if done without any such agreement or combination would not be actionable in tort.

Notes

1. Under the Trade Disputes Act 1906, the immunity for inducements to breach in contemplation or furtherance of a trade dispute extended only to contracts of employment. This allowed the courts in the 1960s to find ways of holding trade unionists liable for inducing breaches of commercial contracts (see *J.T. Stratford & Sons Ltd* v *Lindley* [1965] AC 269).

In the mid-1970s immunity was extended to cover the breach of 'any' contract. The relevant provision states that an act done by a person in contemplation or furtherance of a trade dispute shall not be actionable in tort on the ground only 'that it induces another person to break a contract or interferes or induces any other person to interfere with its performance' (now TULR(C)A 1992, s. 219(1)(a)).

As we shall see, however, it is important to view this immunity in the context of subsequent legislative developments. Section 219(1)(a) provides a prima facie immunity, but this immunity may be lost in certain instances, i.e. by taking unlawful secondary action; engaging in secondary picketing; enforcing trade union membership; or taking 'official' industrial action without first having called a secret ballot (s. 219(3), (4)).

2. The TULR(C)A 1992, s. 219(1)(a), provides an immunity against the tort of interference with contract. It does not, however, offer any explicit protection against the wider 'genus' tort of interference with trade or business by unlawful means. As a result it is of crucial importance to discover whether an act which is immune by virtue of s. 219 (inducement to breach of contract, for example) may nonetheless constitute the 'unlawful means' for the tort of interference with trade or business. Before the passage of the EA 1980, TULRA 1974, s. 13(3) (as amended) had stated that 'for the avoidance of doubt' acts already given immunity could not found the unlawful means element of other torts. When the 1980 statute repealed s. 13(3), the legal position became confused. However, it would appear that the correct view is that the repeal of s. 13(3) has not changed the position. According to the House of Lords in *Hadmor Productions Ltd* v *Hamilton* [1982] IRLR 102, s. 13(3) merely confirmed what was obvious anyway from s. 13(1), i.e. inducement is 'not actionable'. So if the unlawful means are immune, then no liability in tort can arise.

3. The TULR(C)A 1992, s. 219(2), now provides the immunity against simple conspiracy originally contained in the Trade Disputes Act 1906.

(i)   The Trade Dispute Immunity

Trade Union and Labour Relations (Consolidation) Act 1992

244.   Meaning of 'trade dispute' in Part V
(1)   In this Part a 'trade dispute' means a dispute between workers and their employer which relates wholly or mainly to one or more of the following—
    (a)   terms and conditions of employment, or the physical conditions in which any workers are required to work;
    (b)   engagement or non-engagement, or termination or suspension of employment or the duties of employment, of one or more workers;
    (c)   allocation of work or the duties of employment between workers or groups of workers;
    (d)   matters of discipline;
    (e)   a worker's membership or non-membership of a trade union;
    (f)   facilities for officials of trade unions; and

(g) machinery for negotiation or consultation, and other procedures, relating to any of the above matters, including recognition by employers or employers' associations of the right of a trade union to represent workers in such negotiation or consultation or in the carrying out of such procedures.

(2) . . .

(3) There is a trade dispute even though it relates to matters occurring outside the United Kingdom, so long as the person or persons whose actions in the United Kingdom are said to be in contemplation or furtherance of a trade dispute relating to matters to matters occurring outside the United Kingdom are likely to be affected in respect of one or more of the matters specified in subsection (1) by the outcome of the dispute.

(4) An act, threat or demand done or made by one person or organisation against another which, if resisted, would have led to a trade dispute with that other, shall be treated as being done or made in contemplation of a trade dispute with that other, notwithstanding that because that other submits to the act or threat or accedes to the demand no dispute arises.

(5) In this section—
'employment' includes any relationship whereby one person personally does work or performs services for another; and
'worker', in relation to a dispute with an employer, means—
(a) a worker employed by that employer; or
(b) a person who has ceased to be so employed if his employment was terminated in connection with the dispute or if the termination of his employment was one of the circumstances giving rise to the dispute.

245. Crown employees and contracts

Where a person holds any office or employment under the Crown on terms which do not constitute a contract of employment between that person and the Crown, those terms shall nevertheless be deemed to constitute such a contract for the purposes of—
(a) the law relating to liability in tort of a person who commits an act which—
(i) induces another person to break a contract, interferes with the performance of that contract or induces another person to interfere with its performance, or
(ii) consists in a threat that a contract will be broken or its performance interfered with, or that any person will be induced to break or interfere with its performance, and
(b) the provisions of this or any other Act which refer (whether in relation to contracts generally or only in relation to contracts of employment) to such an act.

Note

The scope of the 'golden formula' was amended by the EA 1982 and significantly narrowed in the following ways:

(a) A trade dispute must now be 'between workers and *their* employer' (emphasis added), not between 'employers and workers' which was the previous position. Furthermore, in repealing what was s. 29(4) of TULRA 1974, the 1982 Act no longer allowed trade unions and employers' associations to be regarded as parties to a trade dispute in their own right. Under the law as it stood before the 1982 Act, it was possible for there to be a 'trade dispute' between a trade union and an employer, even though none of the employer's workforce was involved in the dispute. In *NWL* v *Woods* [1979]

IRLR 478, for example, the House of Lords held that there was a trade dispute between the owners of a 'flag of convenience' ship and the International Transport Workers' Federation, although there was evidence that the crew did not support the union's action. As a result of the 1982 amendment, the ITF's action would not now be protected within the in contemplation or furtherance of a trade dispute (ICFTD) formula. (See now TULR(C)A 1992, s. 244(1), (5).)

(b) Disputes between 'workers and workers' are now omitted from the 'trade dispute' definition. While this means that disputes not involving an employer are unlawful, in practice it is rare for an employer not to be party to inter-union disputes. A demarcation dispute between unions will usually involve a dispute with an employer regarding terms and conditions of employment.

(c) Since 1982, disputes relating to matters occurring outside the UK have been excluded from the immunity, unless the UK workers taking action in furtherance of the dispute are likely to be affected by its outcome in terms of the matters listed in s. 244 (see TULR(C)A 1992, s. 244(3)). This means that solidarity action taken by British workers in order to advertise the plight of workers in other countries will be unlawful. In any event, this sort of solidarity action would probably be regarded as a political rather than a trade dispute (*BBC* v *Hearn* [1977] IRLR 269).

(d) A trade dispute must now relate 'wholly or mainly' to terms and conditions of employment and the other matters listed as legitimate in TULRA(C)A 1992, s. 244. Under the law existing prior to the 1982 Act, the dispute merely had to be 'connected' with such matters. The amended phrase marked a return to the form of words used under the Industrial Relations Act 1971 and was inserted to overrule another aspect of the decision of the House of Lords in *NWL* v *Nelson* (above). In this case it was argued that the predominant purpose behind the 'blacking' of the 'Nawala' was the ITF's campaign against 'flags of convenience' shipping, and little to do with a trade dispute. The House of Lords did not agree, stating that as long as there was a genuine connection between the dispute and the subjects listed in the 1974 Act, it did not matter that other issues were predominant. The amendment wrought by the 1982 Act means that a mere connection with the matters specified in s. 244 will no longer suffice. So a dispute which is held to be predominantly a trade dispute will fall outside the trade dispute formula. In many instances it will be extremely difficult to decide which is the predominant element in the dispute, and this can be illustrated by the case set out below, the first case to deal with the issue.

Mercury Communications Ltd v *Scott-Garner*
[1983] IRLR 494
Court of Appeal

Mercury had been granted a government licence to run a private telecommunications system. The Post Office Engineers Union (POEU) objected to the government's policy of 'liberalisation' and ultimate 'privatisation' of the industry. The union instructed its members employed by British Telecom (BT) to refuse to connect Mercury's telecommunication system to the BT network. The Court of Appeal reversed the trial judge's finding that there was a trade dispute and granted an injunction to prevent the union continuing its instruction.

MAY LJ: The union saw the attempt to interconnect Mercury as the thin end of the wedge which could ultimately lead to the failure of their campaign against liberalisation and then privatisation. If this campaign failed, there was, it was said, a serious risk of redundancies and, amongst other things, the likelihood that BT would become less profitable, which would also reduce the scope for improvement in the terms and conditions of employment of its employees. In the various affidavits sworn by Mr Stanley [the General Secretary of the union] and filed on the defendants' behalf in these proceedings this is repeated and emphasised – for instance in paragraph 10 of his first affidavit:

> I therefore wish to state unequivocally and with all the emphasis at my command that the purpose and object of the industrial action complained of by the plaintiffs is to prevent the risk of job losses arising from the entry into the market of an unwelcome competitor.

Mercury's claim necessarily involves an attack on the genuineness of these contentions of Mr Stanley. Their case in brief is that the blacking of Mercury and its shareholders was part of the union's relatively long-standing campaign against Mercury and the government and the policies of liberalisation and thereafter privatisation for which they stand. Of course Mr Stanley has to base himself upon an alleged risk of redundancies, because under the relevant legislation as now enacted this is the only defence that the union can have in this action, and in particular against the interlocutory injunctions now sought. . . .

Further, although I fully appreciate that we live in a time of high unemployment with fears of redundancy prevalent throughout industry, the evidence that we presently have leads me to the conclusion that to the knowledge of the union BT clearly anticipated being able to accommodate any job losses that might result either from competition or from technological advance, by natural wastage and retirement.

Finally, in my opinion all these matters have to be considered in the context that there is no doubt that the union is and has for some time been conducting a campaign against liberalisation and privatisation, in which the defence of its members' jobs and conditions of service has only been one of the issues.

I think that from the union's own documents which are before us this has been and is in substantial degree a political and ideological campaign seeking to maintain the concept of public monopoly against private competition. I have no doubt that those who strenuously contend for the continuation of the monopoly in the postal and telecommunication fields honestly and fervently believe that this is in the best interests of the jobs and conditions of service of those working in the industry. It does not however follow that industrial action taken to further that campaign amounts to a dispute which is wholly or mainly about fears of redundancies if that monopoly is not maintained. Doing the best I can, I have come to the conclusion that it is unlikely that the defendants in this case will succeed in satisfying a court at trial that the dispute between BT and its employees over the blacking of Mercury and its shareholders was a trade dispute within the relevant legislation as now enacted. . . . [I]n the present case the real dispute, as I think, is not between BT and the union but between the union and the government. The industrial action is no doubt being used as a bargaining counter in the dispute between the union and the government. . . .

Question
In the light of the reasoning in this case, to what extent do you think that the following questions posed by Otto Kahn-Freund are apposite?

Is not every major industrial problem a problem of governmental economic policy? Is it not true that, not only in publicly owned industries, governmental decisions on wages policies – whether statutory or not – on credits and subsidies, on the distribution of industry and on housing and town planning, and on a thousand other things, affect the terms and conditions of employment as much as the decisions of individual firms? (*Labour and the Law*, 3rd ed, Davies, P., and Freedland, N. (London: Sweet & Maxwell 1983), p. 317.)

London Borough of Wandsworth v National Association of Schoolmasters/Union of Women Teachers
[1983] IRLR 344
Court of Appeal

The Education Reform Act 1988 contains provisions for a national curriculum, defining the core and foundation subjects and the key stages in a pupil's assessment. Under the Act, the Secretary of State could lay down attainment targets, programmes of studies and assessment arrangements. The first statutory assessment tests were planned to take place in June 1993 for pupils in key stage 3.

Under the Schoolteachers Pay and Conditions Act 1991, conditions relating to remuneration, professional duties and working time are prescribed by the Secretary of State. Since 1990, the union had been campaigning for a maximum limit to the working hours of teachers. In February 1993, the union balloted its members on the following question: 'In order to protest against the excessive workload and unreasonable imposition made upon teachers, as a consequence of the national curriculum and testing, are you willing to take action, short of strike action?' An 88 per cent majority voted in favour of industrial action and the union instructed its members to boycott 'all the unreasonable and unnecessary elements of assessment connected with the national curriculum'.

The plaintiffs brought an action to restrain the union from continuing to issue the instruction and to call off the boycott. They contended that the union was inducing breaches of contracts of employment which the teachers had with the plaintiffs and that the union could not rely on TULR(C)A 1992, s. 219, because the dispute was not a 'trade dispute' within the meaning of s. 244.

Mantill J dismissed the application and the plaintiffs' appeal was dismissed by the Court of Appeal.

NEILL LJ: It is for the union to establish that they are protected from liability in tort by the provisions of the 1992 Act. By s. 219 it is provided:

An act done by a person in contemplation or furtherance of a trade dispute is not actionable in tort on the ground only:

(a)   that it induces another person to break a contract or interferes or induces another person to interfere with its performance . . .

It is accepted on behalf of the union that their members who are schoolteachers are contractually obliged to carry out assessments and tests in accordance with the national curriculum. It is further accepted that unless protected by s. 219 the union is liable in tort by inducing its members to break their contracts of employment by the instructions it gave in relation to the boycott of certain parts of the test. The union asserts, however, that a trade dispute exists between the union and a minister of the crown so as to attract immunity in accordance with s. 219 and s. 244. It is necessary to set out the relevant provisions of s. 244 of the 1992 Act. The section provides:

(1)   In this part a 'trade dispute' means a dispute between workers and their employer which relates wholly or mainly to one or more of the following:

(a)   terms and conditions of employment . . .

(2)   A dispute between a minister of the crown and any workers shall notwithstanding that he is not the employer of those workers be treated as a dispute between those workers and their employer if the dispute relates to matters which:

(a)   . . .

(b)   cannot be settled without him exercising the power conferred on him by or under an enactment.

The primary case for the union is that there is a trade dispute within the meaning of s. 244(2)(b) between the union and the Secretary of State because there is a dispute which relates wholly or mainly to the terms and conditions of employment of its members and that the dispute cannot be settled without the Secretary of State exercising the power conferred on him by or under either the 1991 Act or the 1988 Act. It is said that the dispute relates to the statutory conditions of employment defined in s. 1(2) of the 1991 Act and that the principal way in which the Secretary of State could settle the dispute would be by limiting the working time prescribed in the 1992 Document or by modifying the professional duties imposed on schoolteachers in the 1992 Document.

On behalf of the council, on the other hand, it was submitted that on a proper analysis of the dispute and of the evidence relating to it, it was apparent that the dispute was not wholly or mainly a dispute relating to terms and conditions of employment but was primarily or substantially concerned with the objections and reservations which members of the union had about the procedures which were to be used for the assessments and tests associated with the national curriculum. It is not a dispute about working time but a dispute about the content of the work which the national curriculum required schoolteachers to undertake. Mr Naismith put the matter succinctly in paragraph 3 of his affidavit:

The union has never suggested that the terms and conditions of employment of its members ought to be changed. Rather, it was complaining about the content of their jobs.

The arguments before us occupied several hours. In the end, the question to be determined is one of fact which has to be decided on the evidence contained in the affidavits and in the documents.

On behalf of the union, emphasis was placed on the longstanding and increasing concern of the union and its members about workload (which in this context meant working hours). The union also relied heavily on the wording of the question posed in the ballot paper and on the accompanying documents. In addition counsel drew our attention to passages in the affidavit of Mr de Gruchy in which he said (paragraph 20) that the object of the industrial action was to persuade the Secretary of State to reduce the excessive workload of teachers by exercising his powers to amend the conditions document and the statutory instruments governing the national curriculum, and (paragraph 25) where he said that even if the assessment and testing arrangements were substantially redesigned to meet the professional concerns of teachers, the union would still be recommending their members to take action because of the extra workload. Counsel accepted that Mr de Gruchy's view as to the nature of the dispute could not be conclusive but he submitted that the decision of the Court of Appeal in *Mercury Communications Ltd* v *Scott-Garner and Post Office Engineering Union* [1983] IRLR 494 was clearly distinguishable. In the present case the statement by Mr de Gruchy was not merely an *ipse dixit* of one party in interlocutory proceedings which was challenged by other evidence, but was evidence in an action tried by affidavit which remained uncontradicted by the later affidavit of Mr Naismith. Furthermore, an opportunity had been given by the order of Mr Justice Sedley for the cross-examination of witnesses.

On behalf of the council, on the other hand, it was submitted that the documents disclosed that although the workload was a factor which was of importance to the schoolteachers, their real concern was with the content of the work they had to do following the introduction of the national curriculum. The repeated reference to the 'unreasonable imposition made upon teachers' was in the context a reference to content rather than working time. 'Workload' was an ambiguous word which could apply to content as well as to time. In particular, counsel drew our attention to the letter which Mr de Gruchy sent to the Secretary of State on 25 February 1993. In view of the importance which counsel attached to this letter we should read part of it. In the second paragraph it reads:

The NAS/UWT officers have considered your letter and asked me to make the following points. You rightly observe that there is a gulf between us regarding key stage 3 English tests. The gulf extends to many other areas as well . . .

We believe that the system of testing and assessment you are imposing will do great damage to the educational interests of pupils. It will also continue to impose massive and escalating workload burdens upon teachers. Far from harming the children we feel that the boycott, if that materialises, will be of great benefit to pupils. It would halt the alarming and relentless march of the bureaucratic nightmare of testing, form filling and reporting which is making teaching more and more difficult in schools. Furthermore, there is no proposal for strike action. Our members would continue to teach, test and report to parents appropriately.

Far from enlightening parents, the system you are imposing is confusing them . . .

We have also had the opportunity of considering your statement last Friday, 19 February. We noted the marginal change you made in respect of reporting the key stage 3 test. Your statement took no account of the workload concern of teachers. Your statement took no account of the unreasonable impositions which the nature of the test placed upon teachers.

Furthermore, your statement, 19 February, appeared to us to be a totally inadequate response to the concerns the six teacher organisations had jointly made known to you in the letter of 9 February. Four specific areas of concern were raised with you. Your marginal adjustment to the reporting procedures makes no impact whatsoever on any of those four points.

Accordingly, bearing in mind your letter to me, 10 February, your refusal to meet with NAS/UWT and your statement of 19 February, we see no reason why we should not proceed to test our members' views in the ballot we have announced.

It was said that though there had been earlier complaints about working hours and working time, the nature of the dispute was to be gathered from the correspondence between the participants to the dispute — the union and the Secretary of State. The letter of 25 February showed quite clearly that the real concern of the union's members was with the curriculum and the assessment procedures.

We have come to a clear conclusion in this case. We have not set out all the relevant documents but we have had an opportunity to read them and study them. It seems to us to be quite clear that looking at the history since 1990 there has been increasing concern expressed by the union on behalf of its members with regard to working time. This concern came to a head as the date for the key stage 3 testing approached. It is quite clear that members of the union have criticisms to make about the national curriculum on educational grounds. This was recognised by Mr de Gruchy in paragraph 3 of his affidavit, but he added: 'Of most concern to the union in relation to its members is the excessive and unnecessary workload that the national curriculum imposes on teachers.'

That statement, which remains uncontradicted, is to be read in the context as referring primarily to the extra time which teachers have to work. Furthermore, we attach considerable importance to the wording of the question posed in the ballot paper. It is to be remembered that the ballot was authorised by the union Executive at the meeting on 5 February 1993.

In our judgment the dispute does mainly relate to the terms and conditions of employment of the union's members and is a trade dispute within the meaning of s. 244 of the 1992 Act. We consider that the judge reached the correct decision on these facts and we would dismiss the appeal.

Order that the appeal be dismissed with costs. Leave to appeal to the House of Lords refused.

University College London Hospital NHS Trust v *Unison*
[1999] IRLR 31
Court of Appeal

University College London Hospital NHS Trust (UCLH) was, at all material times, in the business of providing hospital services at a group of hospitals, including University College Hospital in London. It employed over 5,000 staff most of whom (particularly the non-clinical and nursing staff) were members of UNISON.

In 1998, UCLH intended and was negotiating to transfer a part or parts of its business to a transferee consortium of private companies under the Private Finance Initiative whereby the private companies would, pursuant to the contracts to be negotiated, first erect and then run for UCLH a new hospital for a period of, in the first instance, 30 years.

UNISON were opposed in principle to this method of financing the new hospital, regarding it as a form of privatisation. The union sought to persuade the trust to enter into a contractual arrangement with the consortium, under which the consortium, and its associates, subcontractors and successors, would agree to guarantee for 30 years that it would observe equivalent terms and conditions to those of the trust, not just for staff transferring over but for new employees as well.

When the trust refused to agree to include this in the contract with the consortium, UNISON gave notice of a ballot in relation to a trade dispute. This was described as relating to: 'The failure of the trust to agree that TUPE protection should be written into the Hospital New Build PFI Project, for the duration of the contract'. As a result of the ballot, there was an overwhelming majority in favour of strike action.

The trust applied to the High Court for an interlocutory injunction restraining the strike. Mr Justice Timothy Walker granted the injunction on grounds that it was unlikely that the union would succeed at trial of the action in establishing immunity for the strike action. He held that the definition of a 'trade dispute' in s. 244 of the Trade Union and Labour Relations (Consolidation) Act 1992 was unlikely to be satisfied.

The judge took the view that the dispute was not about terms and conditions of employment, but about the terms and conditions of contracts yet to be entered into between the plaintiff employer and the new employers who were to take over the provision of services at the hospital. He considered that the reference in the ballot paper to 'future employees' did not fall within the definition of 'worker' in s. 244(5) because 'the Act does not protect a dispute involving workers yet to be engaged'. He also held that the court was likely to find that the dispute related mainly to the union's political objective of opposing the private finance initiative as a matter of policy. The Court of Appeal dismissed the appeal. Leave to appeal to the House of Lords was refused.

LORD WOOLF MR: . . . As I have already indicated, there can be two strands to a policy. A union can have a policy of opposing a particular course of action root and branch which is seeking to achieve a political objective. At the same time it could have a more limited objective, namely to alleviate the adverse consequences which it anticipates could flow from the more general policy. That more limited objective can be the reason for taking strike action. That more limited policy can comply with the requirements of s. 244.

I therefore turn to consider whether the more limited policy and objective of the union in this case falls within the requirements of s. 244. In doing so, I note that the statutory categories of permitted purposes must be the predominant purpose. The dispute must relate wholly or mainly to those purposes. If it relates to them, that is not sufficient to fulfil the statutory requirement.

Together with the objectives of obtaining a guarantee for existing employees, the union is seeking to secure the same guarantee for employees who have never been employed by the trust. As the 30-year period for which the guarantee is at present being sought progresses, there is bound to be a situation which will arise where the great majority of the employees will never have been employed by the trust. I cannot see how it is possible to apply the language of s. 244(1)(a) and (5) in a way which covers the terms and conditions of employment of employers of a third party who have never been employed by the employer who is to be the subject of the strike action. This in itself is fatal to the case which the defendants advance on this appeal.

In addition, so far as existing employees are concerned, the strike seeks to achieve protection for them in relation to employment with the so-far-unidentified future employer. Recognising that this does not readily fall within the language of s. 244, Mr Hendy submits that the obtaining of the future protection does relate wholly or mainly to the existing terms and conditions of the employees of the trust because it will provide those employees with a sense of security which they would not otherwise have. He rightly submits that the terms and conditions of employment referred to can be threatened with change in the future. In addition, he submits that a correct reading of subsection (5) has the effect of creating a distinction between the parties to the dispute and to the subject matter of the dispute. While he accepts that the parties to the dispute must be the existing employees and the existing employer (here the trust), there is no such restriction on the subject matter of the dispute.

In support of that argument he attaches particular importance to that part of the language of subsection (5) which, so far as relevant, states:

(5)   In this section—
. . .

'worker', in relation to a dispute with an employer, means—
(a)   a worker employed by that employer.

Mr Hendy submits that the words 'in relation to a dispute with an employer' are confined to identifying the employer. He submits that the definition does not relate to the categories set out in subsection 1(a) to (g) which are the subject matter of the dispute. He points out that there would be no purpose served by the use of the words 'in relation to a dispute with an employer' in subsection (5) if his submission was not correct. The subsection could read '"worker" means a worker employed by that employer', but it does not; it is confined. As to that argument, I see its force. However, in my judgment, it does not assist Mr Hendy because, on the facts which are before the court, while it is true that a consequence of obtaining a guarantee would be to give the existing employees the additional security to which he refers, and therefore to that extent a matter which relates to their terms and conditions of employment, that is not the dispute which those employees are wholly or mainly concerned about. They are wholly or mainly concerned about the dispute with different employment; the employment with the so-far-unidentified new employer. For that reason, even with regard to the employees who are already employed by the trust, I consider that on the facts which are before the court, it is unlikely that the union could take advantage of the statutory immunity.
. . .

The third matter to which I draw attention is the different strands of the ballot paper. This refers to the subsequent staff. In view of what I have said about staff who have never been employed by the trust, it seems to me that that is an impermissible subject for the ballot. As it is impossible to identify the motives of those who voted in favour of strike action for doing so, it follows that this nullifies the ballot which took place. In addition, the ballot paper is very persuasive evidence as to what is the proposed purpose of the strike. The terms of the ballot paper support that it was for different purposes, one of which is clearly flawed.

The failure to meet the requirements of s. 244, coupled with the defect in the ballot paper, means that this appeal must be dismissed. On the true approach to the statutory provisions to which I have referred, the only conclusion which a court could reach on the evidence which is before us is that the proposed strike is not subject to the protection of the Act. In those circumstances, Mr Hendy does not argue that it would not be appropriate to grant an injunction.

Accordingly, this appeal must be dismissed.

Note

As of result of this decision, industrial action may not be called for by trade unions unless the dispute is with an existing employer and in relation to existing terms and conditions. A strike call over future terms and conditions with an unidentified future employer will be held to be an unlawful inducement to breach of contract. Moreover, any worker who took industrial action in such a situation would risk dismissal without redress.

The decision represents a significant constraint on the ability of trade unions to put pressure on a transferor employer to insert terms in the transfer agreement which provide better protection than employees would have under the Transfer of Undertakings (Protection of Employment) Regulations 1981, for example, ensuring comparable occupational pension rights. Surely, it should be legitimate for workers to attempt to persuade their existing employer to make arrangements in respect of their terms and conditions when working for a new employer. As Rubenstein observes: 'After all, the commercial transfer will be replete with terms protecting the interests of the transferor once the transfer has taken place. Why shouldn't the law allow pressure for these to include terms protecting the interests of the transferor's employees?' (Rubenstein, M., 'Highlights' [1999] IRLR 2)

(ii)   In Contemplation or Furtherance of a Trade Dispute

Express Newspapers Ltd v *McShane*
[1980] AC 672
House of Lords

In the course of a dispute with provincial newspapers, the National Union of Journalists (NUJ) called on journalists employed by the Press Association (who were still supplying vital copy to the newspapers) to strike. When this call was not fully supported, the NUJ called on its members on the National Newspapers to refuse to handle any copy from the Press Association. This action was restrained by the Court of Appeal on the ground that it was not reasonably capable of achieving the objective of the trade dispute. The House of Lords allowed the union's appeal:

LORD DIPLOCK: My Lords, during the past two years there has been a series of judgments in the Court of Appeal given upon applications for interlocutory injunctions against trade union officials. These have the effect of imposing on the expression 'an act done by a person in contemplation or furtherance of a trade dispute' for which immunity from civil actions for specified kinds of torts is conferred by s. 13(1) of the Trade Union and Labour Relations Act, 1974 (as now amended), an interpretation restrictive of what, in common with the majority of your Lordships, I believe to be its plain and unambiguous meaning. The terms in which the limitations upon the ambit of the expression have been stated are not identical in the various judgments, but at the root of all of them there appears to lie an assumption that Parliament cannot really have intended to give so wide an immunity from the common law of tort as the words of ss. 13 and 29 would, on the face of them, appear to grant to everyone who engages in any form of what is popularly known as industrial action.

My Lords, I do not think that this is a legitimate assumption on which to approach the construction of the Act, notwithstanding that the training and traditions of anyone whose life has been spent in the practice of the law and the administration of justice in the courts must make such an assumption instinctively attractive to him. But the manifest policy of the Act was to strengthen the role of recognised trade unions in collective bargaining, so far as possible to confine the bargaining function to them, and, as my noble and learned friend Lord Scarman recently pointed out in *The Nawala (NWL) Ltd* v *Woods and another* [1979] 1 WLR 1294, to exclude trade disputes from judicial review by the courts. Parliament, as it was constituted when the Act and the subsequent amendments to it were passed, may well have felt so confident that trade unions could be relied upon always to act 'responsibly' in trade disputes that any need for legal sanctions against their failure to do so could be obviated.

This being so, it does not seem to me that it is a legitimate approach to the construction of the sections that deal with trade disputes, to assume that Parliament did *not* intend to give to trade unions and their officers a wide discretion to exercise their own judgment as to the steps which should be taken in an endeavour to help the workers' side in any trade dispute to achieve its objectives. And if their plain and ordinary meaning is given to the words 'An act done by a person in contemplation or furtherance of a trade dispute,' this, as it seems to me, is what s. 13 does. In the light of the express reference to the 'person' by whom the act is done and the association of 'furtherance' with 'contemplation' (which cannot refer to anything but the state of mind of the doer of the act) it is, in my view, clear that 'in furtherance' too can only refer to the state of mind of the person who does the act, and means: with the purpose of helping one of the parties to a trade dispute to achieve their objectives in it.

Given the existence of a trade dispute (the test of which, though broad, is nevertheless objective, see *The Nawala*), this makes the test of whether an act was done 'in furtherance of' it a purely subjective one. If the party who does the act honestly thinks at the time he does it that it may help one of the parties to the trade dispute to achieve their objectives and does it for that reason, he is protected by the section. I say 'may' rather than 'will' help, for it is in the nature of industrial action that success in achieving its objectives cannot be confidently predicted. Also there is nothing in the section that requires that there should be any proportionality between on the one hand the extent to which the act is likely to, or be capable of, increasing the 'industrial muscle' of one side to the dispute, and on the other hand the damage caused to the victim of the act which, but for the section, would have been tortious. The doer of the act may know full well that it cannot have more than a minor effect in bringing the trade dispute to the successful outcome that he favours, but nevertheless is bound to cause disastrous loss to the victim, who may be a stranger to the dispute and with no interest in its outcome. The act is none the less entitled to immunity under the section.

It is, I think, these consequences of applying the subjective test that, not surprisingly, have tended to stick in judicial gorges: that so great damage may be caused to innocent and disinterested third parties in order to obtain for one of the parties to a trade dispute tactical advantages which in the court's own view are highly speculative and, if obtained, could be no more than minor. This has led the Court of Appeal to seek to add some objective element to the subjective test of the *bona fide* purpose of the person who did the act.

. . . [a] test, suggested by Lord Denning in the instant case, is that the act done must have some 'practical' effect in bringing pressure to bear upon the opposite side to the dispute; acts done to assist the morale of the party to the dispute whose cause is favoured are not protected. [Alternatively] there is the test favoured by Lawton and Brandon LJJ, in the instant case: the act done must, in the view of the court, be reasonably capable of achieving the objective of the trade dispute.

My Lords, these tests though differently expressed, have the effect of enabling the court to substitute its own opinion for the *bonà fide* opinion held by the trade union or its officers, as to whether action proposed to be taken or continued for the purpose of helping one side or bringing pressure to bear upon the other side to a trade dispute is likely to have the desired effect. Granted *bona fides* on the part of the trade union or its officer this is to convert the test from a purely subjective to a purely objective test and for the reasons I have given I do not think the wording of the section permits of this. The belief of the doer of the act that it will help the side he favours in the dispute must be honest; it need not be wise, nor need it take account of the damage it will cause to innocent and disinterested third parties. Upon an application for an interlocutory injunction the evidence may show positively by admission or by inference from the facts before the court that the act was not done to further an existing trade dispute but for some ulterior purpose such as revenge for previous conduct. Again, the facts in evidence before the court may be such as will justify the conclusion that no reasonable person versed in industrial relations could possibly have thought that the act was capable of helping one side in a trade dispute to achieve its objectives. But too this goes to honesty of purpose alone not to the reasonableness of the act, or its expediency. . . .

. . . The withdrawal of PA copy from the provincial newspapers would be a crucial factor in strengthening the bargaining position of the striking journalists, but in view of PA's attitude this could only be achieved by forcing it to close down or at any rate to reduce its services drastically, by withdrawing journalistic labour from it. PA was not an NUJ closed shop and for economic reasons even the NUJ members on its staff were not likely to be enthusiastic at the prospect of being called out on strike. For my part I see no reason for doubting the honesty of the belief held by Mr MacShane and Mr Dennis [another NUJ official], that the response of their members to the strike-call at PA might well be less numerous and less enduring if they knew that fellow members of their union on the national newspapers were continuing to make use of copy produced by those whom they would regard as 'blacklegs' at PA.

I would allow this appeal.

LORD WILBERFORCE (dissenting): . . . My Lords, the issue which has to be resolved in the present case arises out of the very great extension of industrial action which has occurred in recent years. When trade disputes were confined to disputes between employees in an undertaking and their employers or between employees in an undertaking, it was not difficult to decide whether industrial action was in contemplation or furtherance of a trade dispute. . . .

. . . industrial action has been greatly widened. It may extend to customers or suppliers of a party to the dispute, on the basis that through them pressure upon the party is intensified. In still other cases, of which *Associated Newspapers Group Ltd* v *Wade* [1979] IRLR 201 is one and this is another, it may extend to customers or suppliers of such suppliers or customers. Such second stage customers or suppliers may, and probably will, have no dispute with those calling for the industrial action, and no interest in the first stage dispute though some of their workers may have sympathy with it. Moreover they may, as here, have no means of influencing that dispute or of making concessions which might bring that dispute to an end. The question therefore whether action against such innocent and powerless third parties or parties even more remote from the original trade dispute is in 'furtherance' of that dispute becomes one that is difficult to answer. The answer must depend upon some test other than the possibility of pressure being exercised upon the original party, because none can be so exercised.

The answer given to this question by the appellants is that it is enough if there is a genuine belief that action against the innocent and powerless third party will further the cause of those taking the action. By to 'further' they mean – and this fits the dictionary definition – to help or encourage. So what is asserted is a purely subjective test, such as might be satisfied by [the General Secretary of the NUJ] Mr Ashton's words – 'I believe that this trend (*viz* of PA journalists to join the PA strike) may be damaged or reversed if copy produced by those breaking the strike is handled by our members elsewhere.' My Lords, with all deference to those of your Lordships who are of this opinion, I am unable to accept this. I recognise, of course, that the trend of recent legislation has been to widen, and to widen greatly, the extent of immunity from civil action of trade unions and officials and members of trade unions. The policy no doubt is to substitute for judicial control or review over trade disputes and their consequences, other machinery including conciliation procedures. But it would be wrong, in my opinion, to suppose that judicial review has been excluded altogether.
. . .

. . . It is clear enough that 'in contemplation of' are not words exclusively subjective. It cannot be enough for someone to depose, in general terms, which cannot be probed, that he had a trade dispute in mind. The words, to me, presuppose an actual or emerging trade dispute as well as the mental contemplation of it. Similarly, 'in furtherance' may quite well include, as well as an intention to further, an actual furtherance (help or encouragement) or the capability of furtherance. Secondly, so to construe the phrase is not to impose upon it a limitation. There is much in the cases to the effect that 'the words must be given some limitation' and to this the appellants object. The words, they say, and I agree, must be given their natural meaning and the courts must not approach them with a disposition to cut them down. But it is always open to the courts – indeed their duty – with open-ended expressions such as those involving cause, or effect, or remoteness, or in the context of this very Act, connection with (cf *BBC* v *Hearn* [1977] IRLR 273), to draw a line beyond which the expression ceases to operate. This is simply the common law in action. It does not involve the judges in cutting down what Parliament has given: it does involve them in interpretation in order to ascertain how far Parliament intended to go.

Notes

1.   See also *Duport Steels Ltd* v *Sirs* [1980] 1 All ER 529, HL.

2.   It was, however, the approach of the Court of Appeal, and Lord Denning in particular, which most closely accorded with the newly elected Conservative Government's perspective on industrial relations. As a result, the EA 1980 included provisions which aimed to control, *inter alia*, 'secondary action' and, to use the words of one government spokesman, to 'return the law to Denning'. This legislation commenced the new legislative policy of stripping away the immunities.

C: Stage Three: Removal of the Immunities

The scope of the immunities was restricted by the legislation of the 1980s: the Employment Acts 1980–1990, the Trade Union Act 1984, and the Trade

Union Reform and Employment Rights Act 1993. In this section we examine the restriction of secondary action; the provisions removing immunity in respect of actions aimed at enforcing the closed shop or trade union recognition on an employer; the loss of immunity for unlawful picketing; the requirements for secret ballots before industrial action; and industrial action taken in support of dismissed 'unofficial strikers'.

(i)   Statutory Control of Secondary Action

Trade Union and Labour Relations (Consolidation) Act 1992

224.   Secondary action

(1)   An act is not protected if one of the facts relied on for the purpose of establishing liability is that there has been secondary action which is not lawful picketing.

(2)   There is secondary action in relation to a trade dispute when, and only when, a person—

(a)   induces another to break a contract of employment or interferes or induces another to interfere with its performance, or

(b)   threatens that a contract of employment under which he or another is employed will be broken or its performance interfered with, or that he will induce another to break a contract of employment or interfere with its performance,

and the employer under the contract of employment is not the employer party to the dispute.

(3)   Lawful picketing means acts done in the course of such attendance as is declared lawful by section 220 (peaceful picketing)—

(a)   by a worker employed (or, in the case of a worker not in employment, last employed) by the employer party to the dispute, or

(b)   by a trade union official whose attendance is lawful by virtue of subsection (1)(b) of that section.

(4)   For the purposes of this section an employer shall not be treated as party to a dispute between another employer and workers of that employer; and where more than one employer is in dispute with his workers, the dispute between each employer and his workers shall be treated as a separate dispute.

. . .

Notes

1.   Section 17 of the EA 1980 removed the protection provided by TULRA 1974, s. 13(1) (as amended) against liability for interfering with commercial contracts by secondary action unless the action satisfied conditions which enabled it to pass through one of three 'gateways to legality', the most important of which being the so-called 'first customer/first supplier' gateway. This permitted secondary action to be lawfully organised if it involved employees of persons who were in direct contractual relations with the employer involved in the primary dispute. The second gateway extended the 'first customer/first supplier' rule to cover cases where the supply which was disrupted was between the secondary employer and an employer 'associated' with the primary employer. This gateway applied only where the supplies which were disrupted were in substitution for the goods which but for the dispute would have been supplied by or to the primary employer. The third

gateway maintained immunity where the secondary action was a consequence of lawful picketing.

While the policy behind EA 1980, s. 17 is straightforward, its drafting was massively complex. Lord Denning described it as 'the most tortuous section I have ever come across' (*Hadmor Productions* v *Hamilton* [1981] IRLR 210). Indeed, the complexity of the section was one of the reasons put forward for its repeal by the EA 1990, s. 4. The aim of s. 4 of the 1990 Act was that only direct disputes between an employer and its workers should attract immunity under what is now TULR(C)A 1992, s. 219. The only exception was to be secondary action arising out of lawful picketing – the only 'gateway to legality' to be retained from the repealed s. 17 of the 1980 Act.

2.   The TULR(C)A 1992, s. 224(4) seeks to limit any attempt to extend the notion of the primary employer. The subsection states that an employer is not to be regarded as party to a dispute between another employer and its workers. This would appear to confirm the thinking of the House of Lords in *Dimbleby & Sons Ltd* v *National Union of Journalists* [1984] ICR 386, that an employer, even though associated with the employer involved in the primary dispute, was not to be regarded as party to that dispute.

(ii)   Unlawful Picketing
Actions such as picketing a place other than your own place of work will not attract immunity under s. 219 (see TULR(C)A 1992, s. 219(3) and the following chapter).

(iii)   Enforcing Union Membership

Trade Union and Labour Relations (Consolidation) Act 1992

222.   Action to enforce trade union membership
(1)   An act is not protected if the reason, or one of the reasons, for which it is done is the fact or belief that a particular employer—
   (a)   is employing, has employed or might employ a person who is not a member of a trade union, or
   (b)   is failing, has failed or might fail to discriminate against such a person.
(2)   For the purposes of subsection (1)(b) an employer discriminates against a person if, but only if, he ensures that his conduct in relation to—
   (a)   persons, or persons of any description, employed by him, or who apply to be, or are, considered by him for employment, or
   (b)   the provision of employment for such persons.
is different, in some or all cases, according to whether or not they are members of a trade union, and is more favourable to those who are.
(3)   An act is not protected if it constitutes, or is one of a number of acts which together constitute, an inducement or attempted inducement of a person—
   (a)   to incorporate in a contract to which that person is a party, or a proposed contract to which he intends to be a party, a term or condition which is or would be void by virtue of section 144 (union membership requirement in contract for goods or services), or
   (b)   to contravene section 145 (refusal to deal with person on grounds relating to union membership).

(4)   References in this section to an employer employing a person are to a person acting in the capacity of the person for whom a worker works or normally works.

(5)   References in this section to not being a member of a trade union are to not being a member of any trade union, of a particular trade union or of one of a number of particular trade unions.

Any such reference includes a reference to not being a member of a particular branch or section of a trade union or of one of a number of particular branches or sections of a trade union.

Note

We have already referred to the fact that the EA 1988 put further curbs on the closed shop. Section 10 removed the immunities contained in TULRA 1974, s. 13 (as amended) from primary industrial action where the reason, or one of the reasons, for the action is that the employer is employing, has employed or might employ a person who is not a member of a trade union or that the employer is failing, has failed or might fail to discriminate against such a person. As we saw in our chapter on unfair dismissal, s. 11 made it unfair for an employer to dismiss or to take action short of dismissal against an employee on the ground of the employee's non-membership of a union or a particular union. In both the situations covered by ss. 10 and 11, the fact that the closed shop has been approved in a ballot is an irrelevancy. (See now TULR(C)A 1992, s. 222.)

Section 14 of the EA 1982 withdrew the immunity where the reason for the industrial action is to compel another employer to 'recognise, negotiate or consult' with one or more trade unions, or to force the employer to discriminate in contract or tendering on the ground of union membership or non-membership in the contracting or tendering concern. (See now TULR(C)A 1992, s. 225.)

(iv)   Secret Ballots before Industrial Action
(See TULR(C)A 1992, ss. 226–235.)

Official industrial action will only attract the immunity offered by TULR(C)A 1992, s. 219, if the majority of union members likely to be called upon to take industrial action have supported that action in a properly conducted ballot. As we have already seen, the requirements for a lawful ballot and the ways in which a union can be held to be vicariously responsible for industrial action saw considerable additions and modifications as a result of the Employment Acts 1988 and 1990. Yet further requirements were added by TURERA 1993. To supplement these requirements, the Department of Employment issued a Code of Practice on Trade Union Ballots on Industrial Action. Originally issued in 1990, a revised version was brought into effect on 20 May 1991 by the Employment Code of Practice (Trade Union Ballots on Industrial Action) Order 1991 (SI 1991/989). A new Code of Practice on Industrial Action Ballots and Notice to Employers has now replaced the 1991 version and was brought into force on 17 November 1995. Breach of the Code does not of itself give rise to civil or criminal liability, but any court or tribunal must, where it is relevant, take it into account as evidence of good industrial relations practice (TULR(C)A 1992, s. 207).

The ballot and notice requirements are set out in TULR(C)A 1992, ss. 226–235B. The provisions are complex. The Government invited suggestions in *Fairness at Work* to clarify and simplify the law in this area. A large number of responses were received, especially from trade unions and legal bodies. The Employment Relations Act 1999, s. 4 gives effect to Sch. 3, which, drawing on some of the suggestions, amends the law in certain respects.

Trade Union and Labour Relations (Consolidation) Act 1992

226. Requirement of ballot before action by trade union

(1) An act done by a trade union to induce a person to take part, or continue to take part, in industrial action

(a) is not protected unless the industrial action has the support of a ballot, and

(b) where section 226A falls to be complied with in relation to the person's employer, is not protected as respects the employer unless the trade union has complied with section 226A in relation to him.

In this section 'the relevant time', in relation to an act by a trade union to induce a person to take part, or continue to take part, in industrial action, means the time at which proceedings are commenced in respect of the act.

(2) Industrial action shall be regarded as having the support of a ballot only if—

(a) the union has held a ballot in respect of the action—

(i) in relation to which the requirements of section 226B so far as applicable before and during the holding of the ballot were satisfied,

(ii) in relation to which the requirements of sections 227 to 231 were satisfied, and

(iii) in which the majority voting in the ballot answered 'Yes' to the question applicable in accordance with section 229(2) to industrial action of the kind to which the act of inducement relates;

(b) such of the requirements of the following sections as have fallen to be satisfied at the relevant time have been satisfied, namely—

(i) section 226B so far as applicable after the holding of the ballot, and

(ii) section 231B;

(bb) section 232A does not prevent the industrial action from being regarded as having the support of the ballot; and

(c) the requirements of section 233 (calling of industrial action with support of ballot) are satisfied.

Any reference in this subsection to a requirement of a provision which is disapplied or modified by section 232 has effect subject to that section.

(3) Where separate workplace ballots are held by virtue of section 228(1)—

(a) industrial action shall be regarded as having the support of a ballot if the conditions specified in subsection (2) are satisfied, and

(b) the trade union shall be taken to have complied with the requirements relating to a ballot imposed by section 226A if those requirements are complied with, in relation to the ballot for the place of work of the person induced to take part, or continue to take part, in the industrial action.

(3A) If the requirements of section 231A fall to be satisfied in relation to an employer, as respects that employer industrial action shall not be regarded as having the support of a ballot unless those requirements are satisfied in relation to that employer.

(4) For the purposes of this section an inducement, in relation to a person, includes an inducement which is or would be ineffective, whether because of his unwillingness to be influenced by it or for any other reason.

Note

Section 231A of the 1992 Act requires unions to inform employers about the result of an industrial action ballot which involves their employees. In cases where a union ballots its members employed by different employers, the union must supply the information to each of the employers concerned. Under the previous law, a failure to inform some, but not all, of the employers could make it unlawful for the union to induce any of its balloted members to take action. Paragraph 2(3) of Sch. 3 to the 1999 Act changes the law by making it lawful in these circumstances for a union to call on its members to take action where they are employed by an employer who was informed of the result. It will remain unlawful, however, for a union to induce its members to take action if their employer was not informed of the result.

Trade Union and Labour Relations (Consolidation) Act 1992

226A. Notice of ballot and sample voting paper for employers

(1) The trade union must take such steps as are reasonably necessary to ensure that—

(a) not later than the seventh day before the opening day of the ballot, the notice specified in subsection (2), and

(b) not later than the third day before the opening day of the ballot, the sample voting paper specified in subsection (3),

is received by every person who it is reasonable for the union to believe (at the latest time when steps could be taken to comply with paragraph (a)) will be the employer of persons who will be entitled to vote in the ballot.

(2) The notice referred to in paragraph (a) of subsection (1) is a notice in writing—

(a) stating that the union intends to hold the ballot,

(b) specifying the date which the union reasonably believes will be the opening day of the ballot, and

(c) containing such information in the union's possession as would help the employer to make plans and bring information to the attention of those of his employees who it is reasonable for the union to believe (at the time when the steps to comply with that paragraph are taken) will be entitled to vote in the ballot.

(3) The sample voting paper referred to in paragraph (b) of subsection (1) is—

(a) a sample of the form of voting paper which is to be sent to the employees who it is reasonable for the trade union to believe (at the time when the steps to comply with paragraph (a) of that subsection are taken) will be entitled to vote in the ballot, or

(b) where they are not all to be sent the same form of voting paper, a sample of each form of voting paper which is to be sent to any of them.

(3A) These rules apply for the purposes of paragraph (c) of subsection (2)—

(a) if the union possesses information as to the number, category or work-place of the employees concerned, a notice must contain that information (at least);

(b) if a notice does not name any employees, that fact shall not be a ground for holding that it does not comply with paragraph (c) of subsection (2).

(3B)   In subsection (3) references to employees are to employees of the employer concerned.

(4)   In this section references to the opening day of the ballot are references to the first day when a voting paper is sent to any person entitled to vote in the ballot.

(5)   This section, in its application to a ballot in which merchant seamen to whom section 230(2A) applies are entitled to vote, shall have effect with the substitution in subsection (3), for references to the voting paper which is to be sent to the employees, of references to the voting paper which is to be sent or otherwise provided to them.

Notes

1.   If a trade union decides to call on its members to take or continue industrial action, it has no immunity from legal liability unless it holds a properly conducted secret ballot in advance of the proposed action. Unions are required under the 1992 Act to give to the employers concerned advance notice in writing both of the ballot and of any official industrial action which may result. The ballot notice must describe, so that their employer can readily ascertain them, the employees who it is reasonable for the union to believe will be entitled to vote. Likewise, the notice of official industrial action must describe, so that their employer can readily ascertain them, the employees the union intends should take part in the action. The current law has been interpreted by the courts (most notably, in the case *Blackpool and the Fylde College* v *National Association of Teachers in Further and Higher Education* [1994] ICR 648, CA, and [1994] ICR 982, HL) as requiring the union in certain circumstances to give to the employer the names of those employees which it is balloting or calling upon to take industrial action. The 1999 Act amends the 1992 Act so as to ensure that unions are never required by the law to disclose the names of their members to employers in these circumstances.

Paragraph 3 of Sch. 3 to the 1999 Act deals with the provisions of the 1992 Act which provide for a notice to be issued in advance of the ballot. It amends s. 226A(2) to redefine the purpose for which the notice is required as being to enable the employer to make plans to deal with the consequences of any industrial action and to provide information to those employees who are being balloted. Paragraph 3(3) inserts a new s. 226A(3A), which sets out the type of information which is to be included in the notice in order to satisfy the new s. 226A(2). It has the effect that a union is required to provide only information in its possession and that it is not required to name the employees concerned. Section 234A of the 1992 Act, which provides for a notice to be issued in advance of official industrial action, is amended in similar terms.

2.   Section 226A(1) of the 1992 Act provides that a union proposing to conduct an industrial action ballot must ensure that a sample voting paper is received by every person who it is reasonable for the union to believe will be the employer of a person or persons who will be entitled to vote in the ballot. The sample voting paper must be received not later than the third day before the opening of the ballot. Section 226A(3) has the effect that where more than one employer is involved and different forms of voting paper are used, samples of all the different forms of the voting paper must be sent to every employer.

Paragraph 3(3) of Sch. 3 to the 1999 Act inserts a new s. 226A(3B), which amends the requirement on unions so that they must ensure only that each employer receives the sample voting paper (or papers, where more than one form exists) which is to be sent to persons employed by that employer. In other words, unions are no longer required to ensure that an employer receives sample forms which are to be sent only to the employees of other employers.

Question

Is the amended obligation to supply information any less onerous than its predecessor?

Trade Union and Labour Relations (Consolidation) Act 1992

226B. Appointment of scrutineer

(1) The trade union shall, before the ballot in respect of the industrial action is held, appoint a qualified person ('the scrutineer') whose terms of appointment shall require him to carry out in relation to the ballot the functions of—

(a) taking such steps as appear to him to be appropriate for the purpose of enabling him to make a report to the trade union (see section 231B); and

(b) making the report as soon as reasonably practicable after the date of the ballot and, in any event, not later than the end of the period of four weeks beginning with that date.

(2) A person is a qualified person in relation to a ballot if—

(a) he satisfies such conditions as may be specified for the purposes of this section by order of the Secretary of State or is himself so specified; and

(b) the trade union has no grounds for believing either that he will carry out the functions conferred on him under subsection (1) otherwise than competently or that his independence in relation to the union, or in relation to the ballot, might reasonably be called into question.

An order under paragraph (a) shall be made by statutory instrument which shall be subject to annulment in pursuance of a resolution of either House of Parliament.

(3) The trade union shall ensure that the scrutineer duly carries out the functions conferred on him under subsection (1) and that there is no interference with the carrying out of those functions from the union or any of its members, officials or employees.

(4) The trade union shall comply with all reasonable requests made by the scrutineer for the purposes of, or in connection with, the carrying out of those functions.

226C. Exclusion for small ballots

Nothing in section 226B, section 229(1A)(a) or section 231B shall impose a requirement on a trade union unless—

(a) the number of members entitled to vote in the ballot, or

(b) where separate workplace ballots are held in accordance with section 228(1), the aggregate of the number of members entitled to vote in each of them, exceeds 50.

Notes

1. Provided that those entitled to vote are accorded the opportunity, a simple majority of those voting is all that is required: there is no requirement

for an *absolute* majority of those voting in the ballot (s. 226(2)(a)(iii); see *West Midlands Trowel Ltd* v *TGWU* [1994] IRLR 578, CA). However, it should be noted that the Code of Practice on Industrial Action Ballots and Notice to Employers advises unions that in deciding whether to call industrial action a relevant consideration should be the size of that majority and the number of those voting in the ballot (para. 59(e)). It is also possible that a low turnout may provide evidential support for a claim by the employer or a member that the ballot is invalid because certain members have been denied their entitlement to vote, or that the union has not taken reasonably practicable steps to ensure that those entitled to vote have an opportunity to do so (ss. 227(1) and 230(1) and (2); and see *British Railways Board* v *NUR* [1989] IRLR 349, an extract appears at p. 775).

2.   Section 227(1) of the 1992 Act provides that entitlement to vote in an industrial action ballot must be accorded equally to all union members who it is reasonable at the time of the ballot for the union to believe will be induced to take part in the industrial action. No other members are entitled to vote. As unamended, Section 227(2) provided that these requirements were not satisfied if 'any person' who was a member at the time of the ballot and who was denied an entitlement to vote was subsequently induced by the union to take part in the action.

The effect of these provisions was that unions were free to induce new members who joined the union after the ballot to take industrial action. However, they could not induce any members to take action if they were members at the time of the ballot but were denied an entitlement to vote. This included cases where members changed their job after the ballot and became employed within the group of workers which the union was proposing should take industrial action.

Paragraph 4 of Sch. 3 to the 1999 Act repeals s. 227(2). Paragraph 6 inserts a new s. 232A into the 1992 Act, which defines circumstances where a union which induces a member to take industrial action who was denied an entitlement to vote in the ballot loses its protection from liability in tort. The effect of the new section is to maintain that protection for unions which induce members to take action where they were not balloted unless it was reasonable at the time of the ballot for the union to believe that they would be induced to take part. These provisions should enable unions to induce members who changed job after the ballot to take action. Paragraph 2(2) makes a consequential change to s. 226 of the 1992 Act, which defines the circumstances where industrial action can be regarded as having the support of a ballot.

3.   Under TULR(C)A 1992, s. 228, separate ballots are generally required for each workplace.

Trade Union and Labour Relations (Consolidation) Act 1992

228.   Separate workplace ballots

(1)   Subject to subsection (2), this section applies if the members entitled to vote in a ballot by virtue of section 227 do not all have the same workplace.

(2) This section does not apply if the union reasonably believes that all those members have the same workplace.

(3) Subject to section 228A, a separate ballot shall be held for each workplace; and entitlement to vote in each ballot shall be accorded equally to, and restricted to, members of the union who—

(a) are entitled to vote by virtue of section 227, and

(b) have that workplace.

(4) In this section and section 228A 'workplace' in relation to a person who is employed means—

(a) if the person works at or from a single set of premises, those premises, and

(b) in any other case, the premises with which the person's employment has the closest connection.

228A. Separate workplaces: single and aggregate ballots

(1) Where section 228(3) would require separate ballots to be held for each workplace, a ballot may be held in place of some or all of the separate ballots if one of subsections (2) to (4) is satisfied in relation to it.

(2) This subsection is satisfied in relation to a ballot if the workplace of each member entitled to vote in the ballot is the workplace of at least one member of the union who is affected by the dispute.

(3) This subsection is satisfied in relation to a ballot if entitlement to vote is accorded to, and limited to, all the members of the union who—

(a) according to the union's reasonable belief have an occupation of a particular kind or have any of a number of particular kinds of occupation, and

(b) are employed by a particular employer, or by any of a number of particular employers, with whom the union is in dispute.

(4) This subsection is satisfied in relation to a ballot if entitlement to vote is accorded to, and limited to, all the members of the union who are employed by a particular employer, or by any of a number of particular employers, with whom the union is in dispute.

(5) For the purposes of subsection (2) the following are members of the union affected by a dispute—

(a) if the dispute relates (wholly or partly) to a decision which the union reasonably believes the employer has made or will make concerning a matter specified in subsection (1)(a), (b) or (c) of section 244 (meaning of 'trade dispute'), members whom the decision directly affects,

(b) if the dispute relates (wholly or partly) to a matter specified in subsection (1)(d) of that section, members whom the matter directly affects,

(c) if the dispute relates (wholly or partly) to a matter specified in subsection (1)(e) of that section, persons whose membership or non-membership is in dispute,

(d) if the dispute relates (wholly or partly) to a matter specified in subsection (1)(f) of that section, officials of the union who have used or would use the facilities concerned in the dispute.

Notes

1. As originally enacted, the Trade Union Act 1984 required a single ballot of all those who were expected to take part in the industrial action. This position was, however, changed by the EA 1988 and a union intending to organise industrial action generally must organise separate ballots for each place of work. Industrial action may not be lawfully taken at a particular

workplace unless a majority of members have voted in favour of the action at that workplace.

2. The TULR(C)A 1992, s. 228A, provides certain exceptions to the requirement of separate ballots.

University of Central England v NALGO
[1993] IRLR 81
Queen's Bench Division

LATHAM J: In these two actions applications are made for injunctions on behalf of two of the new universities against the National and Local Government Officers' Association, restraining that association from holding industrial action without the support of a ballot, complying with ss. 10 and 11 of the Trade Union Act 1984. The particular industrial action against which the applications are directed is a one-day strike on 20 August this year, hence the urgency of the application today, although it is right to say that the union intends there to be, according to its present plans, further industrial action thereafter.

The background, very shortly, is this. As I have indicated, the two plaintiffs are now two of the new universities who used to be polytechnics and were members of the employers' association known as the Polytechnic and College Employers' Forum, which has for a number of years now negotiated with the National and Local Government Officers' Association, amongst others, the terms and conditions of their employees. It is said that the arrangements which were made for the collective bargaining were not such as to underpin the bargaining structure with any contractual entitlements as between employees and employers by reason of the parties' membership of the negotiating body. But I do not think that matters for the purposes of today.

The fact is that in practice – it is plain from the evidence before me that this is essentially accepted – the employing authorities complied with the recommendations which were negotiated in that forum, subject only to there being variations on occasions of the time of implementation. I am prepared to accept that it may well be that the plaintiffs to these actions consider that they are not, as I have already indicated, bound to comply with that, but I do not believe for the purposes of this application that the issue depends on whether they were so bound or not. The fact is that the expectation certainly of the defendants would reasonably be that the recommendations would be accepted.

The position today is that negotiations have in fact taken place for the 1992/93 pay year, and those negotiations ended on 3 July 1992. The consequence was that the employers' representatives offered a pay increase of 4.3 per cent, which has been rejected by the unions. The defendants have held a ballot, but that ballot was held of all their members affected by these negotiations in all the former polytechnics and colleges covered by the negotiating forum. The consequence of that ballot was that there was a majority in favour of strike action of 3,630 to 3,004 on a 59 per cent turnout.

The two plaintiffs are aggrieved by that decision for two reasons. One is that they consider that their own employees, who are members of the defendant union, were not themselves in favour of strike action; and that may or may not be factually correct. It certainly of itself has no legal significance. Their second grievance is that the ballot which was carried out was not a lawful ballot for the purposes of justifying, or to be more exact protecting, the defendants in relation to their strike call. The plaintiffs assert that, for the purposes of ss. 10 and 11 of the 1984 Act, the ballot had to be a ballot of each individual employer and it was not open to the defendants to protect their position by way of what one might loosely call the nationwide ballot.

. . .

. . . I am quite satisfied that, provided the defendants can show that it was reasonable for them to believe, and they did believe, that there was some common factor relating to the terms or conditions of employment in respect of which the industrial action is called for, they are entitled to hold a ballot of all their members affected by that factor, whether they are employed by the same employer or not. I am comforted to note that the Code of Practice which was published together with the Act, although there is no doubt that it is to some extent deficient, generally speaking can only have meaning if the construction which I have considered to be the appropriate construction of ss. 10 and 11 is that which was indeed intended by Parliament.

It follows that I refuse the applications for injunctions in these two actions. I am very grateful to both parties for their arguments.

Note

The method of voting in a ballot, and the content of the voting paper are specified by TULR(C)A 1992, s. 229, as amended.

229. Voting paper

(1)   The method of voting in a ballot must be by the marking of a voting paper by the person voting.

(1A)   Each voting paper must—

(a)   state the name of the independent scrutineer,

(b)   clearly specify the address to which, and the date by which, it is to be returned,

(c)   be given one of a series of consecutive whole numbers every one of which is used in giving a different number in that series to each voting paper printed or otherwise produced for the purposes of the ballot, and

(d)   be marked with its number.

This subsection, in its application to a ballot in which merchant seamen to whom section 230(2A) applies are entitled to vote, shall have effect with the substitution, for the reference to the address to which the voting paper is to be returned, of a reference to the ship to which the seamen belong.

(2)   The voting paper must contain at least one of the following questions—

(a)   a question (however framed) which requires the person answering it to say, by answering 'Yes' or 'No', whether he is prepared to take part or, as the case may be, to continue to take part in a strike;

(b)   a question (however framed) which requires the person answering it to say, by answering 'Yes' or 'No', whether he is prepared to take part or, as the case may be, to continue to take part in industrial action short of a strike.

(2A)   For the purposes of subsection (2) an overtime ban and a call-out ban constitute industrial action short of a strike.

(3)   The voting paper must specify who, in the event of a vote in favour of industrial action, is authorised for the purposes of section 233 to call upon members to take part or continue to take part in the industrial action.

The person or description of persons so specified need not be authorised under the rules of the union but must be within section 20(2) (persons for whose acts the union is taken to be responsible).

(4)   The following statement must (without being qualified or commented upon by anything else on the voting paper) appear on every voting paper—

'If you take part in a strike or other industrial action, you may be in breach of your contract of employment. However, if you are dismissed for taking part in strike or other industrial action which is called officially and is otherwise lawful, the dismissal will be unfair it it takes place fewer than eight weeks after you started taking part in the action, and depending on the circumstances may be unfair if it takes place later.'.

Notes

1.   Section 229(2) of the 1992 Act provides that the voting paper in an industrial action ballot must contain either or both of two questions asking whether the voter is prepared to take part in a 'strike' or in 'industrial action short of a strike'. In some cases it has been unclear whether overtime bans and call-out bans were strikes or industrial action short of a strike, and court action has ensued. In *Connex South Eastern Ltd* v *National Union of Rail Maritime and Transport Workers* [1999] IRLR 249, the Court of Appeal held that the definition of 'strike' encompasses any refusal by employees to work for periods of time for which they are employed to work, provided it is 'concerted', in the sense of being mutually planned. It was not restricted to stoppages of all work, but also includes stoppages of particular days and particular hours. Therefore, both an overtime ban and a ban on rest-day working would fall within definition as they entail employees not working when they otherwise would have worked. Paragraph 6(2) of Sch. 3 to the 1999 Act reverses this decision and clarifies the status of call-out bans by defining both these forms of industrial action as 'industrial action short of a strike' for the purposes of s. 229(2).

2.   Section 229(4) of the 1992 Act required the following statement to appear on all ballot voting papers: 'If you take part in a strike or other industrial action, you may be in breach of your contract of employment'. Paragraph 6(3) of Sch. 3 to the 1999 Act amends this statement by adding words which describe the main features of the new protections against the unfair dismissal of workers taking industrial action contained in Sch. 5 to the 1999 Act.

Post Office v *Union of Communication Workers*
[1990] IRLR 143
Court of Appeal

In late 1987, the Post Office began to formulate a policy to convert a large number of post offices to 'agency status', leading to the closure of Crown Office counters. The Union of Communication Workers (UCW) was opposed to the policy, and in August 1988 it decided to ballot its members who were postal officers or postal assistants on whether they were 'willing to take industrial action up to and including strike action in support of the UCW decision to oppose all aspects of the Post Office board's decision to close up to 750 Crown Office counters'.

The union received 51 per cent support for the question it put in the ballot and between October and December called a series of selective

24-hour strikes. This culminated in a national one-day strike on 12 December.

Between January and April 1989, no industrial action was taken but the union mounted a public relations campaign in opposition to the policy. Closures of offices commenced in April 1989, and in May the union's assistant general secretary told the union's annual conference that the industrial action would continue. In September there was a one-day strike in Harrow, and there was a half-day strike in Aldridge in October.

In January 1990, the union called a 24-hour strike in London South-East. The Post Office applied for an interlocutory injunction, maintaining both that the wording of the ballot question had been defective and that the result of the ballot in August 1988 no longer legitimised industrial action. The application was refused by Turner J, but the Court of Appeal allowed the employers' appeal.

LORD DONALDSON MR: Prior to the passing of the Trade Union Act 1984, trade unions which, in furtherance or contemplation of an industrial dispute, took industrial action which induced a breach of the contracts of employment of its members were protected from claims for damages or injunctive relief by s. 13 of the Trade Union and Labour Relations Act 1974. The 1984 Act introduced the further requirement that this protection only subsisted if the action was supported by a ballot. This was achieved by s. 10 subsections (1) and (3) which were (and are) in the following terms:

Industrial action authorised or endorsed by trade union without support of a ballot.
10.(1)   Nothing in s. 13 of the 1974 Act shall prevent an act done by a trade union without the support of a ballot from being actionable in tort (whether or not against the trade union) on the ground that it induced a person to break his contract of employment or to interfere with its performance.
. . .
(3)   For the purposes of subsection (1) above, an act shall be taken as having been done with the support of a ballot if, but only if—
(a)   the trade union has held a ballot in respect of the strike or other industrial action in the course of which the breach of interference referred to in subsection (1) above occurred;
(b)   the majority of those voting in the ballot have answered 'Yes' to the appropriate question;
(c)   the first authorisation or endorsement of any relevant act, and in the case of an authorisation the relevant act itself, took place after the date of the ballot and before the expiry of the period of four weeks beginning with that date; and
(d)   s. 11 of this Act has been satisfied in relation to the ballot.

This section was followed by subsection (4), which has since been amended by the Employment Act 1988. This, in its unamended form, provided that:

(4)   In subsection (3)(b) above 'appropriate question' means—
(a)   where the industrial action mentioned in subsection (3)(a) above is, or includes, a strike, the question referred to in subsection (4)(a) of s. 11; and
(b)   in any other case, that referred to in subsection (4)(b) of that section.

The key word here was the word 'includes'. As in the present case the union was seeking support for industrial action which *included* strike action, although it also extended to industrial action short of a strike, it may not unreasonably have thought that it was required to base the question which it put to its members in the ballot on s. 11(4)(a). Paragraphs (a) and (b) of s. 11(4) were in the following terms:

(a) a question (however framed) which requires the voter to say, by answering 'Yes' or 'No', whether he is prepared to take part, or as the case may be to continue to take part, in a strike involving him in a breach of his contract of employment;

(b) a question (however framed) which requires the voter to say, by answering 'Yes' or 'No', whether he is prepared to take part, or as the case may be to continue to take part in industrial action falling short of a strike but involving him in a breach of his contract of employment.

I am not entirely sure that the question as framed by the union would have passed muster under the unamended Act but the union could certainly have been forgiven for thinking that it would. This may indeed have been the position when the question was framed. Most unfortunately, from the point of view of the union, the 1988 amendment of the 1984 Act took effect on 26 July 1988, only a few days before the ballot was held. We have therefore to consider whether the 1984 Act as amended, and in particular the slightly amended s. 11, was satisfied in relation to the ballot which took place in the following month. The amendments were of crucial importance.

The first relevant amendment consisted of replacing s. 10(4), which I have already set out, with a new subsection and adding a new subsection (4A). These read:

(4) Subject to subsection (4A) below, in this section and s. 11 of this Act references to the appropriate question are references to whichever of the questions set out in subsection (4) of s. 11 of this Act is applicable to the strike or other industrial action.

(4A) Where both the questions mentioned in subsection (4) above are applicable in relation to any industrial action, an act inducing a breach or interference such as is mentioned in subsection (1) above shall be treated as an act for the purposes of which the requirement of para. (b) of subsection (3) above is satisfied if but only if that paragraph (or, as the case may be, that paragraph as it has effect by virtue of subsection (3A) above) is satisfied in relation to the question applicable to that part of the action in the course of which the breach or interference occurred.

The questions set out in s. 11(4) were amended so that they read:

(4) The voting paper must contain at least one of the following questions—

(a) a question (however framed) which requires the person answering it to say, by answering 'Yes' or 'No', whether he is prepared to take part or, as the case may be, to continue to take part in a strike;

(b) a question (however framed) which requires the person answering it to say, by answering 'Yes' or 'No', whether he is prepared to take part or, as the case may be, to continue to take part in action short of a strike.

The combined effect of these amendments, read with the unamended subsection (3)(b) was to require that the majority of those voting should have answered 'Yes' to the strike question set out in s. 11(4)(a) if the union was calling for a strike and should have answered 'Yes' to the question set out in 11(4)(b) if the union was going to call for a strike and should have answered 'Yes' to the question set out in 11(4)(b) if the union was going to call for industrial action short of a strike. If, as was the case here, the union contemplated both types of action, it had to secure a 'Yes' vote in response to both questions. No longer was it even arguable that a majority 'Yes' vote for strike action would authorise industrial action falling short of a strike upon the grounds that the greater included the less.

If an Act of Parliament is unambiguous, as this one now is at least in this respect, the policy underlying it may not be directly relevant. However, it is reasonably clear that Parliament took account of the fact that some union members who might be prepared to take action short of a strike might not be prepared to take strike action or vice versa and it considered that the union should be required to respect their wishes.

The single question, as framed by the union – 'are you willing to take industrial action up to and including strike action?' – does not permit its members to make this distinction. In effect, they have to say 'Yes' or 'No' to both the questions set out in s. 11(4) and this is contrary to the requirements of the amended Act, which clearly contemplate that, where both questions are asked, the members should be in a position to answer 'Yes' to one and 'No' to the other.

It follows from the fact that the majority of those voting in the ballot answered 'Yes' to an inappropriate and not to the appropriate question (s. 10(3)(b)) that the action of the union in calling for strikes was not in law an act done with the support of a ballot. As a result, the union is unable to rely upon s. 13 of the Trade Union and Labour Relations Act 1974 as a defence to the Post Office's complaint.

Notes

1. In this case, the Court also took the view that the second strike campaign constituted new and disconnected industrial action which needed the support of a fresh ballot.

The question the court has to ask itself is whether the average reasonable trade union member, looking at the matter shortly after the interruption in the industrial action would say to himself, 'the industrial action has now come to an end', even if he might also say, 'the union may want us to come out again if the dispute continues'. (per Lord Donaldson MR at p. 147)

In *Monsanto plc* v *Transport and General Workers' Union* [1986] IRLR 406, CA, the union took industrial action following a ballot. The action was suspended for two weeks in order to allow for negotiations to take place. When the talks broke down, the industrial action was resumed more than four weeks after the date of the ballot. The Court of Appeal held that a fresh ballot was not necessary when there was a resumption of lawful industrial action, temporarily suspended in order to try to reach a settlement of the dispute.

2. Conduct of the ballot is now laid down by TULR(C)A 1992, ss. 227 and 230.

Trade Union and Labour Relations (Consolidation) Act 1992

227. Entitlement to vote in ballot

(1) Entitlement to vote must be accorded equally to all the members of the trade union who it is reasonable at the time of the ballot for the union to believe will be induced to take part or, as the case may be, to continue to take part in the industrial action in question, and to no others.

(2) [repealed]

230. Conduct of ballot

(1) Every person who is entitled to vote in the ballot must—

(a) be allowed to vote without interference from, or constraint imposed by, the union or any of its members, officials or employees, and

(b)   so far as is reasonably practicable, be enabled to do so without incurring any direct cost to himself.

(2)   Except as regards persons falling within subsection (2A), so far as is reasonably practicable, every person who is entitled to vote in the ballot must—

(a)   have a voting paper sent to him by post at his home address or any other address which he has requested the trade union in writing to treat as his postal address; and

(b)   be given a convenient opportunity to vote by post.

(2A)   Subsection (2B) applies to a merchant seaman if the trade union reasonably believes that—

(a)   he will be employed in a ship either at sea or at a place outside Great Britain at some time in the period during which votes may be cast, and

(b)   it will be convenient for him to receive a voting paper and to vote while on the ship or while at a place where the ship is rather than in accordance with subsection (2).

(2B)   Where this subsection applies to a merchant seaman he shall, if it is reasonably practicable—

(a)   have a voting paper made available to him while on the ship or while at a place where the ship is, and

(b)   be given an opportunity to vote while on the ship or while at a place where the ship is.

(2C)   In subsections (2A) and (2B) 'merchant seaman' means a person whose employment, or the greater part of it, is carried out on board sea-going ships.

(3)   [repealed]

(4)   A ballot shall be conducted so as to secure that—

(a)   so far as is reasonably practicable, those voting do so in secret, and

(b)   the votes given in the ballot are fairly and accurately counted.

For the purposes of paragraph (b) an inaccuracy in counting shall be disregarded if it is accidental and on a scale which could not affect the result of the ballot.

British Railways Board v NUR
[1989] IRLR 349
Court of Appeal

In a dispute with BR over pay and proposed changes to collective bargaining arrangements, the NUR balloted some 70,000 of its members on support for a series of 24-hour strikes. 63,719 ballot papers were issued and 51,628 returned in a ballot which involved the distribution and return of papers by a variety of methods. BR's challenge to the validity of the ballot rested on evidence that some 200 members never had an opportunity to vote and the fact that some 6,000 members did not receive a ballot paper.

The employers appealed against the decision of Vinelott J dismissing an application for an interlocutory injunction. The Court of Appeal dismissed the appeal.

LORD DONALDSON MR: [T]he question which then arises is: Is there sufficient evidence to justify us in either holding or considering it likely that it would be held hereafter that there was a failure 'so far as reasonably practicable' to provide all the members entitled to vote with an opportunity of voting? I am bound to say that I do not think there is. It seems inevitable where you have a balloting operation of this size conducted in an industrial context that there will be a few people whose names ought to be on a list but which are not on a list, perhaps because they have changed jobs: there will be a few people who have not notified changes of address or whose ballot papers, if sent by post, may go astray; there will be a number of things which inevitably will go wrong. Indeed, if the situation had been that the NUR claimed to produce evidence that every one of the entitled members had received a ballot paper and returned it, I think that the Court would have been justified in looking very carefully at that evidence to see whether something had not been fiddled. It just does not happen like that in real life, and that, of course, was recognised by Parliament when it used the words 'so far as reasonably practicable'.

Under the balloting system which was adopted and which, as I say, has not been criticised by the Electoral Reform Society, the giving of the ballot papers to the members was decentralised to branch secretaries and others, the intention being that, where you had a group of people, perhaps 100 men, perhaps smaller units, gathering at one place, the ballot papers would be made available at that place. However, it was recognised that that would not cover all the NUR members because some of them work in very isolated conditions – signalmen, for instance. Others may be on leave so that they are not attending at British Rail premises at all during the period. The union and its officials went to great lengths on a decentralised basis to try and find out who those people were and to make alternative arrangements. To give an example, in one instance, and there were probably more, a branch secretary went up the line visiting signalmen, giving them their ballot papers and leaving ballot papers for the succeeding shift. In other cases where it was thought that there would be difficulty in members returning their completed ballot papers these were left at an appropriate place together with an envelope so that it could be posted back. In other cases ballot papers were posted to members, again containing an envelope which enabled the completed ballot paper to be posted back.

For my part, I cannot see that, against that background, there is any evidence at present available that so far as was reasonably practicable, every person who was entitled to vote did not have an opportunity of voting, subject always to what the lawyers describe as 'de minimis' – in other words, trifling errors which should not be allowed to form a basis for invalidating the ballot.

Note
Bob Simpson observes (18 ILJ 236):

If the NUR had lost the *British Rail* case it would have been demonstrably impossible for trade unions to satisfy the requirement of ss. 10 and 11 [now TULR(C)A 1992, ss. 227 and 230] in ballots involving large numbers of workers. But the case still points up the existence of an avenue for challenge to ballots through labour injunction proceedings because of the imprecise nature of the obligations imposed.

In order to provide greater scope for such errors to be disregarded, provided they are accidental and on a scale which is unlikely to affect the outcome of a ballot, the Employment Relations Act 1999, Sch. 3, para. 9 introduces a new s. 232B into the 1992 Act, defining where failures to meet the requirements of s. 227(1) and parts of s. 230 can be disregarded.

Trade Union and Labour Relations (Consolidation) Act 1992

232A. Inducement of member denied entitlement to vote
Industrial action shall not be regarded as having the support of a ballot if the following conditions apply in the case of any person—

(a) he was a member of the trade union at the time when the ballot was held,

(b) it was reasonable at that time for the trade union to believe he would be induced to take part or, as the case may be, to continue to take part in the industrial action,

(c) he was not accorded entitlement to vote in the ballot, and

(d) he was induced by the trade union to take part or, as the case may be, to continue to take part in the industrial action.

232B. Small accidental failures to be disregarded
(1) If—

(a) in relation to a ballot there is a failure (or there are failures) to comply with a provision mentioned in subsection (2) or with more than one of those provisions, and

(b) the failure is accidental and on a scale which is unlikely to affect the result of the ballot or, as the case may be, the failures are accidental and taken together are on a scale which is unlikely to affect the result of the ballot,

the failure (or failures) shall be disregarded.

(2) The provisions are section 227(1), section 230(2) and section 230(2A).

London Underground Ltd v *National Union of Rail, Maritime and Transport Workers*
[1995] IRLR 636
Court of Appeal

In furtherance of a trade dispute with London Underground over pay and conditions, the National Union of Rail, Maritime and Transport Workers (RMT) decided to ballot its members on industrial action. The ballot resulted in a vote in favour of industrial action. When the union informed the employer of the result of the ballot and, pursuant to s. 234A, served notice of its intention to call for industrial action on various dates, the list of members who were to be asked to take part in the action included 692 new members who had joined the union since the date of the ballot and, therefore, had not voted in the ballot or been included in the s. 226A notice.

The employer applied to the High Court for injunctive relief. The High Court granted an injunction restraining the union from inducing employees of London Underground who became members of the union after the date of the ballot to break their contracts of employment.

The Court of Appeal allowed the RMT's appeal.

MILLETT LJ: . . .

The appeal: the 692
The question here is whether a trade union, without losing its immunity from suit, can call on a significant number of members to take part in industrial action who have

joined the union since the date of the ballot and who have therefore not had an opportunity to vote in the ballot. A subsidiary question is whether it makes any difference that the new members have not joined the union by natural accretion during a long dispute, but have been actively recruited in order to make the industrial action more effective. The plaintiff insists that those who have been balloted represent the constituency of those who can be called on to take part in the action. If more than a de minimis number of members who have not been balloted are called upon to take part in industrial action, it is submitted that the action does not have the support of a ballot and the immunity is lost. It does not matter that the members in question joined the union after the ballot and so could not have been balloted. The union must take care to confine its call to take part in industrial action to those of its members who were balloted.

It is to be observed that the statutory immunity is conferred by s. 219 in wide and general terms. It is not limited to trade unions and their members, but extends to *any person* who induces *another person* to commit a breach of contract. The withdrawal of immunity for want of a ballot, however, is in more limited terms. It is withdrawn only in respect of acts done *by a trade union,* and only in respect of acts to induce a person *to take part or continue to take part in industrial action.*

The question turns on the meaning of the critical words in s. 226:

> (1) An act done by a trade union to induce a person to take part, or continue to take part, in industrial action—
> (a) is not protected unless the industrial action has the support of a ballot . . .

The judge rightly concentrated on these words. He said:

> The key to all this lies in s. 226(1), which provides that, for a trade union to be protected in respect of inducement to a person to take part in industrial action – which I read as meaning 'by the particular person induced' – must have the support of the ballot. The question is whether it can fairly be said that a particular industrial action *by a particular person* does have the support of a ballot [my emphasis].

With respect, this is not only an unwarranted gloss on the words of the section but is syntactically incorrect and flies in the face of the plain meaning of the statutory language. What must have the support of a ballot is 'the industrial action', that is to say, the industrial action referred to in the preceding line. That is not industrial action by a particular person (assuming for the moment that that is capable of being an accurate expression), but the industrial action *in which a particular person has been induced to take part.* If the opening words of s. 226(1) are fully expanded, they read as follows:

> (1) An act done by a trade union to induce a person to take part, or continue to take part, in industrial action—
> (a) is not protected unless the industrial action in which he has been induced to take part, or continue to take part, has the support of a ballot.

Industrial action is collective action. An individual does not take collective action; he takes part in it. Those who take part in it will normally be in breach of their contracts of employment. By inducing them to take part in it the union would be liable for the tort of inducing a breach of contract but for the immunity conferred by s. 219. That immunity is withdrawn by the combined effect of s. 219(4) and s. 226(1) if the industrial action does not have the support of a ballot. But the participation of a particular individual in collective industrial action and the industrial action itself are two different things. It is the industrial action which must have the support of a ballot, not the participation of those who have been induced to take part in it.

This construction of the section is supported by the text of other provisions to be found in this part of the Act. Every person taking part in the ballot, for example, must be asked whether he is prepared to take part, or continue to take part, in industrial action (s. 229(2)). If a majority of those who vote in the ballot answer 'Yes', and the other requirements of the Act are satisfied, then 'the industrial action shall be regarded as having the support of a ballot' (s. 226(2)). The industrial action which is to be regarded as having the support of a ballot is not the industrial action of any particular individual, nor is it the action of those who voted 'Yes'. Even those who voted 'No,' but were outvoted, may be called upon to take part in the industrial action without the union losing its immunity. It is the industrial action in which a majority of those voting in the ballot have declared themselves prepared to take part. The collective action is treated as distinct from the participation of the individuals who are prepared to take part in it.

There is nothing in the very detailed requirements which Parliament has laid down for the conduct of the ballot which compels the union to restrict its call for industrial action to those of its members who were members at the date of the ballot and were given the opportunity to take part in it. Parliament must be taken to have appreciated that there would be constant changes in the membership of a large union, and that by normal accretion alone significant numbers of new members might join the union between the date of the ballot notice given to the employer under s. 226A and the holding of the ballot, and between the holding of the ballot and the taking of industrial action. In the case of a lengthy dispute, the numbers in the latter case could be very large indeed.

But all this is expressly catered for. Section 226A requires the union to notify the employer of those of his employees who it is reasonably for the union to believe *at the time when it takes steps to give them notice* will be entitled to take part in the ballot. When the ballot is held s. 227(1) requires the union to ballot all those *of its members* who it is reasonable *at the time of the ballot* for the union to believe will be called upon to take part in the industrial action proposed and no others. If new members have joined since the service of the s. 226A notice, they *must* be included in the ballot. There is nothing in s. 227 which precludes the union from calling on them to take part in the industrial action. Non-members *must not* be included in the ballot.

If the union intends to call out signalmen but not train drivers, the signalmen *must* be balloted; the train drivers *must not*. The object is to prevent the union from distorting the result of the ballot by including militant members whom it does not intend to call upon to take part in industrial action. This is reinforced by subsection (2) which prevents the union from confining the ballot to militant members whom it does intend to call out and then changing its mind and calling out other less militant members. If it changes its mind and decides to extend the industrial action to members *who were members of the union at the time when the ballot was held* but who were not balloted, then it must hold a fresh ballot. But there is nothing in the section to preclude the union from including in the industrial action new members who were not balloted (and who could not lawfully be included in the ballot) because they were not members of the union at the time when the ballot was held.

What may have been a contrary view of what is now s. 227 was expressed by Lord Donaldson of Lymington MR in *Post Office* v *Union of Communication Workers* [1990] IRLR 143 at p. 147, 37. He said:

The union clearly cannot identify and ballot those of its members who are not employees of the employer at the time of the ballot, but who will, in the event, join the workforce at a later date. It would seem to follow that any call for industrial action following a ballot should expressly be limited to those who were employed by the employer, and given an opportunity of voting at the time of the ballot. For the avoidance of doubt, let me say at once that I am not concerned, I do not think that any court would be concerned, at small changes in the workforce but, de minimis apart, this point may repay consideration.

Lord Donaldson appears to have been considering changes to the *workforce*, not to the membership of the union. The persons he appears to have had in mind are persons who *were* members of the union at the time of the ballot (and who should have been balloted) but who were not then employed by the employer. However, neither s. 227 nor its predecessor contain any reference at all to the employer. It is possible, therefore, that Lord Donaldson was intending to refer to changes in union membership rather than in the workforce. Whether this be so or not, his reasoning, if correct, would have even greater force in relation to persons who have become members of the union after the date of the ballot since, as I have already pointed out, the union is not only unable to identify them but is precluded from balloting them by the terms of the section itself.

Lord Donaldson's remarks were obiter and did not receive the support of the other members of the court. They are worthy of respect but are not binding upon us. I am satisfied that in relation to changes in union membership they are unsustainable. The conclusion at which he arrived does not follow from the section; indeed, the section points in the opposite direction. The union is required to ballot those, *and only those, of its members* who *at the time of the ballot* it is reasonable to believe will be called upon to take part in the industrial action. It cannot identify future members, but even if it could it must not ballot them, since the ballot is confined to persons who were members at the time of the ballot. If the section had been intended to preclude the union from calling out persons who were not balloted because they became members of the union after the ballot, subsection (2) would not have been confined to persons who were members of the union at the time of the ballot. In my view, the section makes it clear that a trade union does *not* lose its immunity if it induces members to take part in industrial action, so long as those persons were not members when the ballot was held. . . .

The judge thought that there would be strange consequences if the union were permitted, without losing its statutory indemnity, to induce persons to break their contracts of employment who could not and did not fall within the constituency of those balloted. A small union, he pointed out, could hold a ballot of its own members and then set about inducing all the employees of a much larger constituency who had never been balloted to break their contracts of employment.

So it could; but with respect to the judge, there is nothing in the slightest strange in that. There has never been any identity between the constituency of those to be balloted and the constituency of those whom in contemplation or furtherance of a trade dispute the union may with impunity induce to break their contracts. As I have already pointed out, the immunity is in wide terms. It extends to anyone whom the union induces to break his contract; it is not confined to members. To this extent the immunity is commensurate with the tort. A union may in contemplation or further-ance of a trade dispute with impunity induce non-members to break their contracts.

This was plainly the law before 1984. In my view it is still the law. The immunities conferred by ss. 219 and 220 are still in the widest terms. Sections 226–235, which introduce the balloting requirements, are concerned exclusively with the relationship between a union and its members and are intended for the protection of members. Non-members have no right to be consulted before a union calls on its members to take industrial action; indeed, as we have seen, the union must not include them in the ballot. But there is nothing in ss. 226–235 to limit the union's right to seek to persuade non-members to support it by abstaining from work.

The language of the statute is striking. The immunity is from liability 'for inducing another person to break a contract' (s. 219) or from 'peacefully persuading any person . . . to abstain from working' (s. 220). These expressions are equally applicable to members and non-members. Immunity is withdrawn, however, in narrower circumstances. In describing them, the draftsman has carefully eschewed the use of the expression 'induce a person to break his contract'. Instead, he has throughout used the expression 'induce a person to take part in industrial action'. As a matter of ordinary language, no doubt, a non-member who stops work in support of his colleagues can be said to be taking part in their industrial action. But I am inclined to think that this is not the way in which the expression is used in ss. 226–235. The industrial action there referred to is collective action by members of the union which has called the action with the support of a ballot of its members, a majority of whom have declared that they are prepared to take part in the action. The action must be called by a person specified in that behalf on the ballot paper. There are numerous indications which support the view that the draftsman is drawing a sharp distinction between the act of a union in calling on its own members to take part in industrial action and its acts in calling upon non-members for support by breaking their contracts of employment. The distinction would also help to make sense of an otherwise difficult and perhaps unworkable s. 234A. As, however, we have heard no argument on this section, I prefer to express no view on this.

If inducing non-members to support industrial action by withdrawing their labour is to be distinguished from inducing members to take part in the industrial action called by the union, then it is an activity which attracts immunity under ss. 219 and 220 but falls outside the withdrawal of the immunity in s. 226(1). But even if the premise is not right, I think that the same conclusion is nevertheless correct. It would be astonishing if a right which was first conferred by Parliament in 1906, which has been enjoyed by trade unions ever since and which is today recognised as encompassing a fundamental human right, should have been removed by Parliament by enacting a series of provisions intended to strengthen industrial democracy and governing the relations between a union and its own members.

I conclude, therefore, that there is nothing in ss. 226–235 which curtails a union's long-accepted right to induce non-members to support the industrial action called by the union by breaking their own contracts of employment. But if this is so, then there is no reason to deny the same right in respect of non-members who have subsequently joined the union. There is simply no objection to a small union, which has the support of a ballot of its own members, seeking to attract support from non-members.

The judge may also have been influenced by the fact that the union has obtained a large influx of new members by an active recruiting campaign. I am unable to see what objection there can be to such activity. A union is plainly free to campaign actively for new members before it holds the ballot in the hope that such members will support industrial action. If they become members before the ballot, they *must* be balloted, even though their views may affect the result of the ballot. I am unable to see why activity which is unobjectionable before the ballot is objectionable after it.

I would allow the appeal.

Note

This is an important decision which addresses hitherto unresolved questions relating to the balloting requirements and holds that newly recruited

members can take part in strike action without the need for a further
ballot to be held. Note that the Court of Appeal disagrees with the *obiter*
statement of Lord Donaldson in *Post Office* v *Union of Communication Workers*
[1990] IRLR 143, CA that, *de minimis* apart, 'any call for action for industrial
action following a ballot should expressly be limited to those who were
employed by the employer, and given an opportunity to vote at the time of
the ballot'.

London Borough of Newham v National and Local Government Officers Association
[1993] IRLR 83
Court of Appeal

A dispute arose between NALGO and the London Borough of Newham
over redundancies which occurred at the end of 1991. Those made
redundant included three officers in the poll tax section of the finance
department. On 7 January 1992, a majority of the officers in that section
went out on strike in protest at those redundancies. A ballot in accordance
with the statutory requirements was not held until the strike had commenced. On 11 May, strike action was taken by officers in the rent and
benefits department, and this was followed on 22 June by a strike of officers
in the central grant unit. Both these stoppages had been authorised by a
ballot.

The poll tax officers returned to work on 22 June, following a threat by
the borough to dismiss them if they remained on strike. As a consequence
of this threat the union's national emergency committee met on 18 June
and agreed to a 'massive escalation' of industrial action. On the following
day, the union's general secretary wrote to the leader of the council
informing him of this decision and expressing the wish that a settlement
could be reached in order to prevent the escalation. At the same time, the
union wrote to all its members employed by the council informing them
that there would be a branch-wide ballot on indefinite strike action. The
letter stated that the national emergency committee had agreed to fund
publicity and organise speakers from the national executive committee 'to
help publicise the issues involved and the importance of a "Yes" vote in
the ballot. It is envisaged that the ballot will take a month to carry out . . .
Therefore, it is vital that all members of Newham NALGO become
involved in the campaign and that we send a clear and unambiguous
message to our employers: "Reinstate our sacked colleagues, and hands off
our union".'

The ballot paper posed the single question to members: 'Are you
prepared to be instructed to take indefinite strike action, on strike pay
equivalent to full take-home pay in opposition to compulsory redundancies
in the poll tax section and the council's threat to sack workers?' The ballot
resulted in a majority in favour of the strike, and on 3 August a general
strike began of all NALGO members employed by the council.

In the course of subsequent negotiations, the council offered to re-employ the three redundant poll tax officers and a commitment not to take action against individuals involved in industrial action 'that is authorised or endorsed by their trade union'. However, the union became dissatisfied with the terms of the offer of re-employment and the strike action continued.

The employers sought an injunction alleging that the union had contravened what is now TULR(C)A 1992, s. 233(3)(a). This provision requires that: 'There must have been no call by the trade union to take part or continue to take part in industrial action to which the ballot relates, or any authorisation or endorsement by the union of any such industrial action, before the date of the ballot.' The High Court granted an injunction restraining the strike action. The Court found, first, that 'it seems clearly arguable' that there had been a call for, or endorsement of, industrial action by the union on a matter to which the indefinite strike ballot related, and that the union had decided on a course of action and were promoting it before the ballot.

However, the judge rejected the employers' alternative submission that the dispute to which the ballot related had already been resolved. The union appealed to the Court of Appeal on the first question, and the employers cross-appealed on the second point.

WOOLF LJ: On the first argument of the borough the answer to this issue depends upon ascertaining the effect of the two documents of 19 June when considered in the context in which they were written. Is it, at least, arguable on the documents read in their context, that the union was calling on its members to take part or to continue to take part or authorising or endorsing the members taking part or continuing to take part in industrial action to which the ballot relates so as to contravene the condition set out in s. 7(3) of the 1990 Act? Here I differ from the conclusion of the judge. Read in their context, it is clear to me that while the union were demonstrating that they wanted industrial action to be extended to other members in addition to those who were already on strike, they were not then calling on them to strike or authorising or endorsing their striking but communicating the decision of the union to authorise a ballot of all their members with a view to more extensive industrial action being taken and indicating the manner in which the ballot was going to be carried out. In other words, so far as those employees who were not already on strike was concerned, the effect of the documents in this context was to indicate that the union were intending to comply with the conditions in s. 7(3) of the 1990 Act and will not contravene those conditions. While the documents made it clear that the union was not adopting a neutral stance, not surprisingly the legislation does not make such an unreal requirement of the union. The union, as long as it complies with the legislation, is perfectly entitled to be partisan.

. . .

Held: The Court of Appeal allowed the union's appeal.

Note

The TULR(C)A 1992, ss. 231–231B set out the requirements to be met following a ballot.

Trade Union and Labour Relations (Consolidation) Act 1992

231. Information as to result of ballot

As soon as is reasonably practicable after the holding of the ballot, the trade union shall take such steps as are reasonably necessary to ensure that all persons entitled to vote in the ballot are informed of the number of—

(a)   votes cast in the ballot,

(b)   individuals answering 'Yes' to the question, or as the case may be, to each question,

(c)   individuals answering 'No' to the question, or, as the case may be, to each question, and

(d)   spoiled voting papers.

231A. Employers to be informed of ballot result

(1)   As soon as reasonably practicable after the holding of the ballot, the trade union shall take such steps as are reasonably necessary to ensure that every relevant employer is informed of the matters mentioned in section 231.

(2)   In subsection (1) 'relevant employer' means a person who it is reasonable for the trade union to believe (at the time when the steps are taken) was at the time of the ballot the employer of any persons entitled to vote.

231B. Scrutineer's report

(1)   The scrutineer's report on the ballot shall state whether the scrutineer is satisfied—

(a)   that there are no reasonable grounds for believing that there was any contravention of a requirement imposed by or under any enactment in relation to the ballot,

(b)   that the arrangements made with respect to the production, storage, distribution, return or other handling of the voting papers used in the ballot, and the arrangements for the counting of the votes, included all such security arrangements as were reasonably practicable for the purpose of minimising the risk that any unfairness or malpractice might occur, and

(c)   that he has been able to carry out the functions conferred on him under section 226B(1) without any interference from the trade union or any of its members, officials or employees;

and if he is not satisfied as to any of those matters, the report shall give particulars of his reason for not being satisfied as to that matter.

(2)   If at any time within six months from the date of the ballot—

(a)   any person entitled to vote in the ballot, or

(b)   the employer of any such person,

requests a copy of the scrutineer's report, the trade union must, as soon as practicable, provide him with one either free of charge or on payment of such reasonable fee as may be specified by the trade union.

Note

Section 234 of the 1992 Act covers the timing of the industrial action.

Trade Union and Labour Relations (Consolidation) Act 1992

234. Period after which ballot ceases to be effective

(1)   Subject to the following provisions, a ballot ceases to be effective for the purposes of section 233(3)(b) in relation to industrial action by members of a trade union at the end of the period, beginning with the date of the ballot—

(a) of four weeks, or

(b) of such longer duration not exceeding eight weeks as is agreed between the union and the members' employer.

(2) Where for the whole or part of that period the calling or organising of industrial action is prohibited—

(a) by virtue of a court order which subsequently lapses or is discharged, recalled or set aside, or

(b) by virtue of an undertaking given to a court by any person from which he is subsequently released or by which he ceases to be bound,

the trade union may apply to the court for an order that the period during which the prohibition had effect shall not count towards the period referred to in subsection (1).

(3) The application must be made forthwith upon the prohibition ceasing to have effect—

(a) to the court by virtue of whose decision it ceases to have effect, or

(b) where an order lapses or an undertaking ceases to bind without any such decision, to the court by which the order was made or to which the undertaking was given;

and no application may be made after the end of the period of eight weeks beginning with the date of the ballot.

(4) The court shall not make an order if it appears to the court—

(a) that the result of the ballot no longer represents the views of the union members concerned, or

(b) that an event is likely to occur as a result of which those members would vote against industrial action if another ballot were to be held.

(5) No appeal lies from the decision of the court to make or refuse an order under this section.

(6) The period between the making of an application under this section and its determination does not count towards the period referred to in subsection (1).

But a ballot shall not by virtue of this subsection (together with any order of the court) be regarded as effective for the purposes of section 233(3)(b) after the end of the period of twelve weeks beginning with the date of the ballot.

Notes

1. The normal rule is that the action must be called within four weeks, beginning with the date of the ballot (s. 234(1)(a)). However, the 1989 docks dispute and the litigation surrounding it showed the harsh effect of this time limit where the union was prevented from calling industrial action during the four-week period because of an injunction. The TGWU succeeded in getting the injunction lifted but then had to re-ballot because it was outside the four-week limit. Under s. 234(2), a union may now apply for an extension of time to allow for the period during which it was prohibited from calling the action.

2. A case which illustrates the major complexities in this area is *RJB Mining (UK) Ltd* v *NUM* [1995] IRLR 556, CA. A ballot for industrial action closed at 10 a.m. on 16 May 1985, with a majority in favour of a series of one-day strikes. On 6 June, the union gave the employers written notice that 24-hour action would take place at the commencement of the day shift on 13 June, to the end of the night shift on the morning of 14 June, with more stoppages to follow.

Under the unamended TULR(C)A 1992, s. 234, 'a ballot cease[d] to be effective . . . at the end of the period of four weeks beginning with the date of the ballot'. In this case, the union was initially wrongly advised that the four weeks did not start running until the time during the day the ballot closed and that, therefore, so long as the industrial action was called to commence before 10 a.m. on 13 June, it was within the time-limit. The employers contended that the ballot of Tuesday, 16 May ceased to be effective at midnight on Monday, 12 June and the action called by the union to commence on 13 June fell outside that period. They applied for, and were granted, an interlocutory injunction restraining the union from calling the proposed strikes.

On appeal, the union contended that the day shift of 13 June commenced at midnight on 12/13 June, that midnight is included in both days and that, therefore, the ballot was still effective in respect of a strike called for the commencement of the day shift on 13 June. This argument was rejected by the Court of Appeal, holding that the four-week period ends at the stroke of midnight on the last day of the fourth week. In the words of Butler-Sloss LJ:

> No part of a day can be both Monday and Tuesday . . . As a matter of legal precedent, midnight finishes one day and starts another, but conceptually they are different days and must remain so, otherwise we should be in cloud-cuckoo land.

(Given the nit-picking complexity of these provisions, there are those of us who were under the distinct impression that we had already arrived!)

3. The Employment Relations Act 1999, Sch. 3, para. 10 amends s. 234(1) of the 1992 Act so that the four-week period may be extended by up to a maximum of four more weeks if both the union and the employer agree to the extension. The purpose of the amendment is to avoid circumstances where a union feels obliged to organise industrial action within the four-week period before a ballot becomes ineffective, even though the parties might be able to reach a settlement through further negotiation.

Trade Union and Labour Relations (Consolidation) Act 1992

233. Calling of industrial action with support of ballot

(1) Industrial action shall not be regarded as having the support of a ballot unless it is called by a specified person and the conditions specified below are satisfied.

(2) A 'specified person' means a person specified or of a description specified in the voting paper for the ballot in accordance with section 229(3).

(3) The conditions are that—

(a) there must have been no call by the trade union to take part or continue to take part in industrial action to which the ballot relates, or any authorisation or endorsement by the union of any such industrial action, before the date of the ballot;

(b) there must be a call for industrial action by a specified person, and industrial action to which it relates must take place, before the ballot ceases to be effective in accordance with section 234.

(4) For the purposes of this section a call shall be taken to have been made by a trade union if it was authorised or endorsed by the union; and the provisions of section 20(2) to (4) apply for the purpose of determining whether a call, or industrial action, is to be taken to have been so authorised or endorsed.

Notes
1. The courts have taken a realistic view of the requirement that the 'call for industrial action' must be by a 'specified person' and have held it to include the case where the specified person authorises a subordinate (e.g. regional or local officials) to call for industrial action if a final 'make or break' negotiation fails (*Tank and Drums Ltd* v *Transport and General Workers' Union* [1991] IRLR 372, CA).
2. In the Green Paper, *Industrial Relations in the 1990s*, the Government proposed that, once a ballot produced a majority in favour of (or continuing with) industrial action, a union should be required to give the employer seven days' written notice of any industrial action to which the ballot related. The notice would have to identify which workers were to be called upon to take industrial action, and on what specific date the industrial action would begin. Where a union proposed to call for intermittent action, such as a series of one-day strikes, it would be required to give at least seven days' notice of each day or other separate period of industrial action. Moreover, if the union suspended or withdrew its support for the action, further notice would be required before any subsequent call to resume the action.
TURERA 1993 enshrined these proposals in TULR(C)A 1992, s. 234A.

234A. Notice to employers of industrial action
(1) An act done by a trade union to induce a person to take part, or continue to take part, in industrial action is not protected as respects his employer unless the union has taken or takes such steps as are reasonably necessary to ensure that the employer receives within the appropriate period a relevant notice covering the act.
(2) Subsection (1) imposes a requirement in the case of an employer only if it is reasonable for the union to believe, at the latest time when steps could be taken to ensure that he receives such a notice, that he is the employer of persons who will be or have been induced to take part, or continue to take part, in the industrial action.
(3) For the purposes of this section a relevant notice is a notice in writing which—
(a) contains such information in the union's possession as would help the employer to make plans and bring information to the attention of those of his employees whom the union intends to induce or has induced to take part, or continue to take part, in the industrial action ('the affected employees'),
(b) states whether industrial action is intended to be continuous or discontinuous and specifies—
(i) where it is to be continuous, the intended date for any of the affected employees to begin to take part in the action,
(ii) where it is to be discontinuous, the intended dates for any of the affected employees to take part in the action, and
(c) states that it is given for the purposes of this section.
(4) For the purposes of subsection (1) the appropriate period is the period—
(a) beginning with the day when the union satisfies the requirement of section 231A in relation to the ballot in respect of the industrial action, and

(b)   ending with the seventh day before the day, or before the first of the days, specified in the relevant notice.

(5)   For the purposes of subsection (1) a relevant notice covers an act done by the union if the person induced is one of the affected employees and—

(a)   where he is induced to take part or continue to take part in industrial action which the union intends to be continuous, if—

(i)   the notice states that the union intends the industrial action to be continuous, and

(ii)   there is no participation by him in the industrial action before the date specified in the notice in consequence of any inducement by the union not covered by a relevant notice; and

(b)   where he is induced to take part or continue to take part in industrial action which the union intends to be discontinuous, if there is no participation by him in the industrial action on a day not so specified in consequence of any inducement by the union not covered by a relevant notice.

(5A)   These rules apply for the purposes of paragraph (a) of subsection (3)—

(a)   if the union possesses information as to the number, category or work-place of the employees concerned, a notice must contain that information (at least);

(b)   if a notice does not name any employees, that fact shall not be a ground for holding that it does not comply with paragraph (a) of subsection (3).

(6)   For the purposes of this section—

(a)   a union intends industrial action to be discontinuous if it intends it to take place only on some days on which there is an opportunity to take the action, and

(b)   a union intends industrial action to be continuous if it intends it to be not so restricted.

(7)   Subject to subsections (7A) and (7B), where—

(a)   continuous industrial action which has been authorised or endorsed by a union ceases to be so authorised or endorsed, and

(b)   the industrial action has at a later date again been authorised or endorsed by the union (whether as continuous or discontinuous action),
no relevant notice covering acts done to induce persons to take part in the earlier action shall operate to cover acts done to induce persons to take part in the action authorised or endorsed at the later date and this section shall apply in relation to an act to induce a person to take part, or continue to take part, in the industrial action after that date as if the references in subsection (3)(b)(i) to the industrial action were to the industrial action taking place after that date.

(7A)   Subsection (7) shall not apply where industrial action ceases to be authorised or endorsed in order to enable the union to comply with a court order or an undertaking given to a court.

(7B)   Subsection (7) shall not apply where—

(a)   a union agrees with an employer, before industrial action ceases to be authorised or endorsed, that it will cease to be authorised or endorsed with effect from a date specified in the agreement ('the suspension date') and that it may again be authorised or endorsed with effect from a date not earlier than a date specified in the agreement ('the resumption date'),

(b)   the action ceases to be authorised or endorsed with effect from the suspension date, and

(c)   the action is again authorised or endorsed with effect from a date which is not earlier than the resumption date or such later date as may be agreed between the union and the employer.

(8)   The requirement imposed on a trade union by subsection (1) shall be treated as having been complied with if the steps were taken by other relevant persons or committees whose acts were authorised or endorsed by the union and references to the belief or intention of the union in subsection (2) or, as the case may be, subsections (3), (5) and (6) shall be construed as references to the belief or the intention of the person or committee taking the steps.

(9)   The provisions of section 20(2) to (4) apply for the purpose of determining for the purposes of subsection (1) who are relevant persons or committees and whether the trade union is to be taken to have authorised or endorsed the steps the person or committee took and for the purposes of subsections (7) to (7B) whether the trade union is to be taken to have authorised or endorsed the industrial action.

Notes

1.   Section 234A of the 1992 Act provides for a trade union to send a notice to a person's employer informing him that the union intends to call upon all or some of his employees to take industrial action. The notice must be received at least seven days in advance of the commencement of the action. The notice must specify if action is continuous or discontinuous.

Section 234A(7) deals with the position where continuous industrial action which has been authorised or endorsed by the union ceases to be so authorised or endorsed and is later authorised and endorsed again. It has the effect that the notice issued before the action ceased to be authorised or endorsed does not usually cover any action pursuant to the later authorisation or endorsement. This arrangement discourages unions from suspending industrial action to negotiate a settlement of the dispute because, if the negotiations fail, action cannot resume promptly because a fresh notice has to be issued at least seven days in advance.

The Employment Relations Act 1999, Sch. 3, para. 11(5) inserts new subsection (7B) into s. 234A, which defines the circumstances where, following a specified period in which the industrial action has been suspended by joint agreement between the union and the employer, the action can be resumed without the need to issue a fresh notice. The specified period of the suspension can be extended by joint agreement.

2.   TULR(C)A 1992, s. 62, provides the member's statutory right to prevent unballoted action.

62.   Right to a ballot before industrial action

(1)   A member of a trade union who claims that members of the union, including himself, are likely to be or have been induced by the union to take part or to continue to take part in industrial action which does not have the support of a ballot may apply to the court for an order under this section.

(2)   For this purpose industrial action shall be regarded as having the support of a ballot only if—

(a)   the union has held a ballot in respect of the action in relation to which the requirements of sections 227 to 232 were satisfied and in which the applicant was accorded entitlement to vote,

(b)   the majority voting in the ballot answered 'Yes' to the question applicable in accordance with section 229(2) to industrial action of the kind which the applicant has been or is likely to be induced to take part in, and

(c)   the requirements of section 233 (calling of industrial action with support of ballot) are satisfied.

(3)   Where on an application under this section the court is satisfied that the claim is well-founded, it shall make such order as it considers appropriate for requiring the union to take steps for ensuring—

(a)   that there is no, or no further, inducement of members of the union to take part or to continue to take part in the industrial action to which the application relates, and

(b)   that no member engages in conduct after the making of the order by virtue of having been induced before the making of the order to take part or continue to take part in the action.

(4)   Without prejudice to any other power of the court, the court may on an application under this section grant such interlocutory relief (in Scotland, such interim order) as it considers appropriate.

(5)   For the purposes of this section an act shall be taken to be done by a trade union if it is authorised or endorsed by the union; and the provisions of section 20(2) to (4) apply for the purpose of determining whether an act is to be taken to be so authorised or endorsed.

Those provisions also apply in relation to proceedings for failure to comply with an order under this section as they apply in relation to the original proceedings.

(6)   In this section—

'inducement' includes an inducement which is or would be ineffective, whether because of the member's unwillingness to be influenced by it or for any other reason; and

'industrial action' means a strike or other industrial action by persons employed under contracts of employment.

(7)   Where a person holds any office or employment under the Crown on terms which do not constitute a contract of employment between that person and the Crown, those terms shall nevertheless be deemed to constitute such a contract for the purposes of this section.

(8)   References in this section to a contract of employment include any contract under which one person personally does work or performs services for another; and related expressions shall be construed accordingly.

(9)   Nothing in this section shall be construed as requiring a trade union to hold separate ballots for the purposes of this section and sections 226 to 234 (requirement of ballot before action by trade union).

Notes

1.   While the failure to hold a ballot will result in the loss of immunities, the EA 1988 created the additional legal consequence set out above.

2.   The precise scope of the phrase 'industrial action' is unclear, but interpretation of that phrase under what is now TULR(C)A 1992, s. 238 (dealing with the dismissal of those taking part in a strike or other industrial action) would suggest it encompasses action which does not necessarily involve a breach of contract (see *Power Packing Casemakers* v *Faust* [1983] QB 471). The practical significance of this is not lost on the editors of *Harvey on Industrial Relations and Employment Law*:

One purpose of balloting members over industrial action is to preserve the union's statutory immunity from a suit in tort brought by a plaintiff *employer*. The tort concerned will be or involve the tort of inducing a person to *break* a contract; and there is no need for any tort immunity. Therefore, for the purposes of the 1984 Act, the union does not need to ballot the members unless there is going to be a *breach* of contract. However under the 1988 Act, a member of the union can ask the court to restrain unballoted industrial action whether that industrial action involves breaches of contract or not. Ergo, the union, to be safe, needs to ballot *all* industrial action, whether or not there is going to be any breach of the member's contracts of employment. (IV[1131])

(v)   Industrial Action in Support of Dismissed 'Unofficial Strikers'

Trade Union and Labour Relations (Consolidation) Act 1992

223.   Action taken because of dismissal for taking unofficial action

An act is not protected if the reason, or one of the reasons, for doing it is the fact or belief that an employer has dismissed one or more employees in circumstances such that by virtue of section 237 (dismissal in connection with unofficial action) they have no right to complain of unfair dismissal.

Note

Earlier in this chapter we described how the EA 1990 removed the limited unfair dismissal protection to 'unofficial' strikers (see now TULR(C)A 1992, s. 237). In order to strengthen the employer's position in such a situation, the 1990 Act removed the statutory immunity from any industrial action taken in protest against such dismissals (now TULR(C)A 1992, s. 223).

10 INDUSTRIAL CONFLICT II

I Picketing

A: *The Freedom To Picket*

As with strike action, English law provides no right to picket. Instead it offers an extremely limited immunity from civil and criminal liability.

Trade Union and Labour Relations (Consolidation) Act 1992

220. Peaceful picketing

(1)   It is lawful for a person in contemplation or furtherance of a trade dispute to attend—

   (a)   at or near his own place of work; or

   (b)   if he is an official of a trade union, at or near the place of work of a member of that union whom he is accompanying and whom he represents,

for the purpose only of communicating information or peacefully persuading any person to work or abstain from working.

(2)   If a person works or normally works—

   (a)   otherwise than at any one place, or

   (b)   at a place the location of which is such that attendance there for a purpose mentioned in subsection (1) is impracticable,

his place of work for the purposes of that subsection shall be any premises of his employer from which he works or from which his work is administered.

(3)   In the case of a worker not in employment where—

   (a)   his last employment was terminated in connection with a trade dispute, or

   (b)   the termination of his employment was one of the circumstances giving rise to a trade dispute,

in relation to that trade dispute his former place of work shall be treated for the purpose of subsection (1) as being his place of work.

(4)   A person who is an official of a trade union by virtue only of having been elected or appointed to be a representative of some of the members of the union shall be regarded for the purposes of subsection (1) as representing only those members;

but otherwise an official of a union shall be regarded for those purposes as representing all its members.

Note

Picketing will receive the protection of the immunities only if the pickets are attending at or near their own workplace. So-called 'secondary picketing' was rendered unlawful by the amendments made by the EA 1980.

There is no statutory definition of 'place of work'. However, the Code of Practice on Picketing, published in 1980 to accompany the amendments to the statute and revised in 1992, offers the following guidance:

The law does not enable a picket to attend lawfully at an entrance to, or exit from any place of work other than his own. This applies even, for example, if those working at the other place of work are employed by the same employer, or are covered by the same collective bargaining arrangements as the picket. (para. 18)

Rayware Ltd v *TGWU*
[1989] IRLR 134
Court of Appeal

Pickets assembled on the public highway at an entrance to an industrial estate which included the factory unit where they worked. They were actually ¾ mile from their factory unit, but this was the nearest practicable point to picket without committing a trespass.

At first instance, Judge Nance awarded the employers an injunction on the ground that the picketing was not 'at' or 'near' their premises. The Court of Appeal allowed the union's appeal.

MAY LJ: In my judgement the phrase 'at or near' in section 15(1) of the 1974 Act [now TULR(C)A 1992, s. 220(1)] must be considered in a geographical sense. We must bear in mind the intent and purpose of the legislation with which one is dealing. We are dealing with a statutory provision giving the right to picket. The context is the conduct of industrial relations in a dispute situation: a situation in which perhaps common sense has a greater part to play than in many others. The mere fact that the plaintiffs are on a private trading estate and that other concerns also lease properties on that estate is not in my view of itself sufficient to prevent the nearest point where pickets can lawfully stand from being at or near the plaintiffs' premises.

I do not accept, as I have already indicated the view of Judge Nance that Parliament intended that the picketing should be at a point where those in the factory would be informed or know of it by sight or sound that picketing was taking place.

In the end it is solely a question of fact and degree in each case, and I make no apologies for saying for the third time, perhaps a good dose of common sense.

NOURSE LJ: The words 'at or near', not being terms of art, must be construed with due regard for the purpose of the provision in which they are found. No experience of unlawful picketing, however grave, can obscure the clear purpose of section 15, which, broadly speaking, is to confer on an employee or group of employees a liberty to exert peaceful persuasion over fellow employees. It is not consistent with that purpose to construe the section so as to make it impracticable, in the conditions which many industrial and commercial developments are now found to exist, for many

groups of employees to maintain pickets at all. That would be the result of the learned
judge's decision, if it is held to be correct, is not in doubt. . . .

Accordingly, adopting the view of Byles J [in *Guardians of the Society of Keelman on
the River Tyne* v *Davison* (1864) 16 CBNS 612 at p. 622], that the word 'near' is not
a restraining but an expanding word, to be extended so far as to give effect to the
intention of the legislature, I think that on the facts of this case, as I have stated them,
the plaintiff's employees have been attending near their own place of work within the
meaning of section 15. For this purpose I assume, without deciding, that their place
of work is limited to the plaintiff's premises and does not include the service road. If
this conclusion establishes a precedent for other comparable industrial and commercial developments, we should not flinch from that result in an area of the law where
it is especially desirable that rights and duties should be certain.

Note
The legislation restricts a dismissed employee to picketing 'his former place of
work'. The impact of this restriction was clearly seen in *News Group
Newspapers Ltd* v *SOGAT '82* [1986] IRLR 337, where the dismissed
employees' work had been transferred from Gray's Inn Road and Bouverie
Street to Wapping. Picketing by the dismissed employees at the Wapping plant
was unlawful. According to Stuart-Smith J, 'place' refers to geographical
location, and a place where an employee has never worked cannot become one
where he does. (Other aspects of this case are presented later in the chapter.)

B: Civil Liabilities for Picketing

(i)   The Economic Torts

Trade Union and Labour Relations (Consolidation) Act 1992

219.   Protection from certain tort liabilities
(3)   Nothing in subsections (1) and (2) prevents an act done in the course of
picketing from being actionable in tort unless it is done in the course of attendance
declared lawful by section 220 (peaceful picketing).

(ii)   Private Nuisance
Private nuisance is an unlawful interference with an individual's use or
enjoyment of his or her land. Unreasonable interference with that right by,
for example, blocking an access route to the employer's property, may give
rise to a cause of action. So, even though the pickets stand outside the
employer's premises they may be liable for the tort of private nuisance.

Picketing which exceeds the bounds of peacefully obtaining or communicating information may involve liability for private nuisance. However,
there is still doubt whether peaceful picketing *itself* amounts to a nuisance
when not protected by the trade dispute immunity.

Lyons* v *Wilkins
[1899] 1 Ch 255
Court of Appeal

There was a peaceful picket of two men in connection with a strike at
Lyons. A picket was also posted at the home of one of Lyons outworkers.

No violence, intimidation or threat was alleged. The employers sought an interlocutory injunction to restrain what they alleged was a wrongful watching and besetting of property under the Conspiracy and Protection of Property Act 1875, s. 7 (now TULR(C)A 1992, s. 241).

LORD LINDLEY MR: The truth is that to watch or beset a man's house with a view to compel him to do or not to do what is lawful for him not to do or do is wrongful and without lawful authority unless some reasonable justification for it is consistent with the evidence. Such conduct seriously interferes with the ordinary comfort of human existence and ordinary enjoyment of the house beset and such conduct would support an action on the case for a nuisance at common law . . . Proof that the nuisance was 'peaceably to persuade other people' would afford no defence to such an action. Persons may be peaceably persuaded provided the method employed is not a nuisance to other people.

Ward Lock & Co. v Operative Printers' Assistants' Society
(1906) 22 TLR 327
Court of Appeal

Members of the union picketed the plaintiffs' printing works with the aim of persuading the employees to join the union so as to create a 'closed shop'. There was no evidence of violence, obstruction or common law nuisance and the pickets were found not to have induced the employees to breach their contracts of employment.

MOULTON LJ: . . . I am therefore of the opinion that in support of the plaintiffs' claim with regard to picketing, it must be shown that the defendants or one of them were guilty of a wrongful act, i.e., that the picketing constituted an interference with the plaintiffs' action wrongful at common law, or, as I think it may accurately be phrased, were guilty of a common law nuisance . . . I wish to add, that, in my opinion there is throughout a complete absence of anything in the nature of picketing or besetting which could constitute a nuisance.

Hubbard v Pitt
[1975] ICR 308
Court of Appeal

A tenants' association had mounted a weekly picket of between six to eight people outside the offices of an Islington firm of estate agents. The association was opposed to the practices of the estate agents and the property developers whom they represented. The pickets stood in line with placards and handed out leaflets to passers-by. They did not obstruct the highway and behaved in a peaceful manner. The employers sought and obtained an interlocutory injunction. The defendants appealed from this decision.

LORD DENNING MR: Picketing is not a nuisance in itself. Nor is it a nuisance for a group of people to attend at or near the plaintiff's premises in order to obtain or communicate information or in order to peacefully persuade. It does not become a nuisance unless it is associated with obstruction, violence, intimidation, molestation or threats.

Note

The majority of the Court of Appeal, on the other hand, merely affirmed the exercise of the High Court judge's discretion to grant an interlocutory injunction to the plaintiffs whose premises were being picketed, and had little to say on the substantive issue. However, Orr LJ did feel that the defendants' intentions and states of mind formed what he called 'a crucial question' in this matter, and he was satisfied that in this case the pickets intended to interfere with the plaintiffs' business.

This sort of reasoning was applied subsequently in *Mersey Dock & Harbour Co. Ltd* v *Verrinder* [1982] IRLR 152, where the High Court held that the picketing of the entrances to container terminals at Mersey Docks amounted to private nuisance despite the fact that the picketing was carried out in an entirely peaceful manner by a small group of pickets. On the basis of this approach, it would appear that if the intention of the pickets is to achieve more than the mere communication of information and actually to interfere with the picketed employer's business, then the picket will be tortious.

As can be seen, the conflict between the *Lyons* and the *Ward Lock* approaches is unresolved, though the weight of academic opinion favours the *Ward Lock* approach (see, for example, Lewis, R. (ed.) *Labour Law in Britain* (Oxford: Blackwell, 1986) at p. 199; Davies, P., and Freedland, M., *Labour Law Text, Cases and Materials*, 2nd ed. (London: Weidenfeld and Nicolson, 1984) at p. 852).

Thomas v NUM (South Wales Area)
[1985] IRLR 136
Chancery Division

This was a case arising out of the protracted miners' strike of 1984/5. A group of working miners obtained injunctions restraining the area union from organising mass picketing at the collieries where they worked.

SCOTT J: The position seems to me to be this. Some 50 to 70 striking miners attend at the colliery gates daily. Six of them are selected to stand close to the gates. The rest are placed back from the road so as to allow the vehicle conveying the working miners to pass. Abuse is hurled at the vehicle and at the men inside. Police are in attendance. This picketing or demonstrating is taking place against a background of high community tension and known anger by the pickets or demonstrators against the working miners. It is taking place not on isolated instances but on a daily regular basis. Whether there is thereby committed an infringement of the rights of the working miners I have yet to consider. Whether this picketing or demonstrating is within the rights of those taking part or is such as a trade union is entitled to organise or encourage is also for argument. But I really do not think it can be sensibly suggested that picketing or demonstrating of this sort and in the circumstances revealed by the evidence in this case would be otherwise than highly intimidating to any ordinary person. Why is it necessary for the working miners to be brought into their workplace by vehicles? Why is it necessary for police to be in attendance? Are the apprehensions of violence, intimidation or unruly conduct that prompt these precautions without foundation? On the evidence adduced in the present case I cannot think so.

I must not be taken to be doubting the sworn evidence of those lodge officers who have deposed to their personal abhorrence of violence and to their firm lodge policy that there should be no violence on the picket lines. But where, as in this industrial dispute, feelings run high, substantial numbers of pickets are, in my view, almost bound to have an intimidatory effect on those going to work. I was struck by a remark of Mr Scrivener in this connection. He invited me to imagine a large number of sullen men lining the entrance to a colliery, offering no violence, saying nothing, but simply standing and glowering. That, he said, would not be intimidating to a working miner. I disagree. It would, in my opinion, be highly intimidating.

. . .

The law

The right of the plaintiffs to relief in respect of the picketing at colliery gates raises three questions. First, there is the question whether the picketing sought to be restrained would represent the commission of a tort against a particular plaintiff or plaintiffs. As to this, I regard the phrase 'unlawful picketing' as unhelpful and misleading. It is frequently used. Sometimes it is used to describe picketing in the course of which criminal offences are committed. Sometimes it is used to describe picketing which is tortious. And often it is used to describe picketing which is both tortious and criminal. This is a civil action in which the plaintiffs are asserting their private rights under the civil law. They can complain in a civil action of picketing which is tortious but not of picketing which is criminal. It is for the public prosecuting authorities or for the Attorney-General to control the commission of criminal offences in the course of picketing. It is not for these plaintiffs to do so. The question for me, therefore, is whether the picketing is tortious. The question is not whether the picketing is criminal.

The second question is whether the defendants or any of them are responsible in law for the tortious picketing complained of.

The third question, assuming answers favourable to the plaintiffs on the first two questions are reached, is whether an interlocutory injunction should be granted, and if so, what its terms should be. I will take these three questions in turn.

. . .

The position, therefore, is that the picketing in the present case of which complaint is made will not be actionable in tort if it can be brought within [TULR(C)A 1992, s. 220]. In my judgment, on any reasonable view of the defendants' own evidence, the immunity of this provision cannot be claimed for the persons who regularly assemble at the colliery gates. It may be that the six persons who are selected to stand close to the gates could bring themselves within the provision, but the many others who are present cannot do so. What is their purpose in attending? It is obviously not to obtain or communicate information. Is it peacefully to persuade the working miners to abstain from working? If that is the case what is the need for so many people, what is the need for the police, and what is the need for vehicles to bring the working miners safely into the collieries? It is fair to say that Mr Scrivener, realistically, did not invite me to deal with this application on the footing that the colliery gate picketing could claim immunity under [TULR(C)A 1992 s. 220]. And, of course, picketing at people's houses or places of education cannot qualify for immunity under the section.

It does not, however, follow that because picketing cannot be brought within [TULR(C)A 1992, s. 220], the picketing is therefore tortious. In order to decide whether or to what extent picketing that falls outside the section is tortious, recourse must be had to the general law of tort.

. . .

The working miners are entitled to use the highway for the purpose of entering and leaving their respective places of work. In the exercise of that right they are at present having to suffer the presence and behaviour of the pickets and demonstrators. The law has long recognised that unreasonable interference with the rights of others is actionable in tort. The law of nuisance is a classic example and was classically described by Sir Nathaniel Lindley MR in *Lyons* v *Wilkins* [1899] 1 Ch 255 at page 267. I have already cited the passage. It is, however, not every act of interference with the enjoyment by an individual of his property rights that will be actionable in nuisance. The law must strike a balance between conflicting rights and interests. The point is made in Clark & Lindsell, 15th edition, at paragraph 23/01:

> A variety of different things may amount to a nuisance in fact but whether they are actionable as the tort of nuisance will depend upon a variety of considerations and a balance of conflicting interests.

Nuisance is strictly concerned with, and may be regarded as confined to, activity which unduly interferes with the use or enjoyment of land or of easements. But there is no reason why the law should not protect on a similar basis the enjoyment of other rights. All citizens have the right to use the public highway. Suppose an individual were persistently to follow another on a public highway, making rude gestures or remarks in order to annoy or vex. If continuance of such conduct were threatened no one can doubt but that a civil court would, at the suit of the victim, restrain by an injunction the continuance of the conduct. The tort might be described as a species of private nuisance, namely unreasonable interference with the victim's rights to use the highway. But the label for the tort does not, in my view, matter.

In the present case, the working miners have the right to use the highway for the purpose of going to work. They are, in my judgment, entitled under the general law to exercise that right without unreasonable harassment by others. Unreasonable harassment of them in their exercise of that right would, in my judgement, be tortious . . .

From the comments I have already made earlier in this judgment it will be apparent that I think it plain from the evidence before me that the picketing at the colliery gates is of a nature and is carried out in a manner that represents an unreasonable harassment of the working miners. A daily congregation on average of 50 to 70 men hurling abuse and in circumstances that require a police presence and require the working miners to be conveyed in vehicles do not in my view leave any real room for argument. The working miners have the right to go to work. Neither they or any other working man should be required, in order to exercise that right, to tolerate the situation I have described. Accordingly in my judgment the colliery gates picketing is tortious at the suit of the plaintiff or plaintiffs who work at the collieries in question.

I can deal more shortly with the picketing at Mr Lock's home and the picketing at the entrance to the estate where Mr Fjaelberg lives. Regular picketing at the home of a working miner would represent, in my opinion, regardless of the number of people involved and regardless of the peaceful nature of their conduct, *per se* common law nuisance. The *Ward Lock* case was a case of picketing at business premises, which is a very different matter. Indeed, the bulk of the deponents on the defendants' side very properly recognise the unreasonable character that picketing at someone's home would have. They dissociate themselves from it.

. . .

The grant of an injunction
This is an interlocutory application and it is usual on such applications to pay particular attention to the balance of convenience until trial, and to require of a

plaintiff no more than that an arguable case be shown. Mr Scrivener, however, invited me on this application not to adopt that usual approach, but to apply a more strict test to the plaintiffs' case before supporting it by the grant of interlocutory relief. He put forward two reasons why I should do so. First, he emphasised that the action was brought against the background of a bitter industrial dispute. The strike is, in South Wales, an official one. The striking miners are entitled to be on strike and entitled to picket in support of their strike. I should avoid, he said, so impeding the right to picket as might prejudice the continuance of the strike. I do not think this is a point of weight. The right to picket is, unless the case can be brought within [TULR(C)A 1992, s. 220], no more than the general right which everyone has to do what he or she wants to do, if it can be done without infringing the rights of others. The striking miners have no right, whether by picketing, demonstrating or otherwise, unreasonably to harass the working miners in going to or leaving their workplace.

. . .

I have already expressed the view that given the temper of the local communities and the strong feelings that have plainly been raised by the return to work of some of the members of the union, sheer weight of sufficient numbers on the picket lines would be sufficient by itself to be intimidatory. It is, in my judgment, tortious for the South Wales Union by its lodges to organise or participate in picketing on an intimidatory scale. So the injunction must, in my view, restrain the union from organising or participating in picketing by more than some specified number of persons. What should that number be? Mr Scrivener pointed out that two or three might by their words and gestures intimidate, whereas a dozen might, by the calmness and reasonableness of their behaviour, not be intimidatory at all. I agree with that. Any number chosen is necessarily arbitrary. I am, however, given some statutory guidance.

. . .

A Code of Practice has been issued by the Secretary of State under s. 3 [of EA 1980], and has been approved by both Houses of Parliament. It came into force on 17.12.80 under the Employment Code of Practice (Picketing) Order 1980, Statutory Instrument 1980/1757. Section E of the Code is headed 'Limiting numbers of Pickets'. Paragraph 29 is in these terms:

> The main cause of violence and disorder on the picket line is excessive numbers. Wherever large numbers of people with strong feelings are involved there is a danger that the situation will get out of control and that those concerned will run the risk of arrest and prosecution.

I need not read paragraph 30, but paragraph 31 is important.

> Large numbers on a picket line are also likely to give rise to fear and resentment amongst those seeking to cross that picket line, even where no criminal offence is committed. They exacerbate disputes and sour relations not only between management and employees but between the pickets and their fellow employees. Accordingly pickets and their organisers should ensure that in general the number of pickets does not exceed six at any entrance to a workplace. Frequently a smaller number would be appropriate.

Paragraph 31 [see now para. 51 of the revised Code of Practice] does not make it a criminal offence or tortious to have more than six persons on a picket line. Nor is less than six any guarantee of lawfulness. The paragraph simply provides a guide as to a sensible number for a picket line in order that the weight of numbers should not intimidate those who wish to go to work. I am directed by subsection (8) of s. 3 of the 1980 Act to take this guidance into account.

I do so and propose, therefore, to restrain the South Wales Union, by its lodges, from organising picketing or demonstrations at colliery gates by more than six persons. I should make it clear that there is, in my judgment, no legitimate distinction to be drawn between so-called pickets who are stationed close to the gates of the colliery and the rest, so-called demonstrators, who stand nearby.

. . .

Picketing at premises other than collieries

Picketing by striking miners at premises other than collieries (which I shall refer to as 'secondary picketing') is bound to be picketing which does not qualify for immunity under [what is now TULR(C)A 1992, s. 220]. Mr Blom-Cooper argued from this premise that such picketing was bound to be tortious. I think this is probably so. It is difficult to think of any picketing that does not involve some species of tortious interference with contract. He argued also that such picketing was bound to constitute common law nuisance and so was bound to be criminal under s. 7 of the 1875 Act. Here I do not agree. His proposition was that all picketing involves a 'watching and besetting' of someone's place of business with a view to compelling either the workmen or the proprietor of the business to act or abstain from acting in a certain way. If immunity, now to be found in substituted s. 15 of the 1974 Act, cannot be claimed, he relied on *Lyons* v *Wilkins* as establishing that the conduct was tortious and criminal.

In my opinion, the *Ward Lock* case provides the answer to this submission. Picketing is not a criminal 'watching and besetting' under s. 7 unless it is at least a tortious watching and besetting. And the Court of Appeal held in the *Ward, Lock* case that the picketing did not represent common law nuisance. Further, common law nuisance requires a balance to be struck between the respective rights and interests of the plaintiff and of the defendant. Where the balance should be struck may depend upon prevailing ideas as to the desirability of and justification for certain types of conduct. It may have been right in 1896, when *Lyons* v *Wilkins* was decided, to regard picketing in an industrial dispute as *per se* common law nuisance, no matter how peaceably and responsibly conducted. If so, it seems that a change had come about by 1906 when the *Ward, Lock* case was decided. But this is 1985, and prevailing ideas about strikes and picketing are nothing like what they were in 1896. If picketing in pursuance of an industrial dispute is peacefully and responsibly conducted at or near business premises I can see no reason at all why it should be regarded *per se* as a common law nuisance. Nor, in my view, does the fact that the picketing is secondary picketing invalidate this conclusion. If the picketing is secondary and involves the commission of tort, there is now, under [TULR(C)A 1992, s. 220], no immunity from tortious liability. But there is no statutory provision which makes secondary picketing *per se* a common law nuisance, and in my judgment it is not one. It follows that, in my judgment, secondary picketing will not necessarily constitute an offence under s. 7 of the 1875 Act.

On the other hand, Mr Scrivener submitted that mass picketing – by which I understand to be meant picketing so as by sheer weight of numbers to block the entrance to premises or to prevent the entry thereto of vehicles or people – was not *per se* tortious or criminal. In my judgment, mass picketing is clearly both common law nuisance and an offence under s. 7 of the 1875 Act.

. . .

Note

Two important points arise from this decision. First, private nuisance is concerned with interference with the use of or enjoyment of land in which the claimant has an interest. In this case, a species of the tort was held to extend to interference with the right to use the highway. The terms of the injunction granted by the court restricted picketing at the collieries to peacefully communicating and obtaining information and in numbers not exceeding six. This number is not a purely arbitrary figure, it comes from the Code of Practice on Picketing, which at para. 51 advises that 'pickets and their organisers should ensure that in general the number of pickets does not exceed six at any entrance to a workplace; frequently a smaller number will be appropriate'. The judge was using the guidance in the Code to fix the parameters of lawful picketing. If this view is correct, then any picketing numbering more than six will lose the immunity offered by s. 220 and will be tortious.

News Group Newspapers Ltd v SOGAT '82
[1986] IRLR 337
Queen's Bench Division

The plaintiffs' action was to restrain unlawful picketing at their Wapping plant and elsewhere in connection with a dispute over the printing of News International's newspapers at the plant. The dispute arose following a breakdown in negotiations between the plaintiffs and the unions over the employment of union members at the plaintiffs' new plant in Wapping on a proposed new title, the *London Post*. In January 1986, following a ballot, SOGAT and the NGA called out on strike their members employed at the *Sun*, *News of the World* and *Sunday Times*. All the strikers were then served with dismissal notices and production of all the newspapers concerned was switched to the Wapping plant.

In addition to the official pickets, there were daily demonstrations at Wapping of between 50 and 200 people, mainly dismissed print workers and their families. Every Wednesday and Saturday nights, as well as on other occasions, there were rallies, marches and demonstrations involving numbers between 700 and 7,000. Similar actions took place at Gray's Inn Road and Bouverie Street, where the plaintiffs' newspapers were formerly printed. Picketing also took place at the depots used by TNT Roadfreight, the company which was contracted to transport the plaintiffs' newspapers.

The plaintiffs contended that the conduct complained of involved the torts of nuisance, intimidation, harassment and interference with the performance of their commercial contracts and sought injunctive relief.

STUART-SMITH J:

The law
It is common ground between the parties that picketing *per se* is not actionable. Moreover, this is so even if the picketing is secondary picketing and does not become actionable simply because it does not comply with the provisions of s. 15(1) of the Trade Union and Labour Relations Act 1974 [now TULR(C)A 1992, s. 220] . . .

So too with marches and demonstrations. They are, so long as they are peaceful and orderly, not actionable, even though they may cause some inconvenience to others. The plaintiffs must prove tortious conduct for which the defendants are responsible.

The plaintiffs contend that the conduct complained of involves the commission of four separate torts – that is to say, nuisance, intimidation, harassment and interference with the performance of their commercial contracts. They then contend that the defendants are liable in respect of some or all of these torts. Finally they submit that on balance of convenience and in the exercise of the court's discretion injunctive relief should be granted.

The defendants submit that the torts alleged are not made out; that even if they were, the defendants are not responsible for them and cannot be liable; finally, that the plaintiffs have not made out a case on the balance of convenience and additionally as against the first to sixth plaintiffs they allege that they do not come to court with clean hands and the court should refuse equitable relief for that reason, if all else fails. I must, therefore, examine these propositions.

Nuisance

A nuisance may be a public nuisance actionable at the suit of a particular plaintiff or a private nuisance.

(a) Public nuisance

Public nuisance is a criminal offence which for the purpose of this case may be defined as an unlawful act which endangers lives, safety, health, property or comfort of the public or by which the public are obstructed in the exercise or enjoyment of any right common to all Her Majesty's subjects. It must materially affect the reasonable comfort and convenience of a class of Her Majesty's subjects who come within the sphere or neighbourhood of its operation (see *per* Romer LJ in *Attorney General* v *PYA Quarriers Ltd* (1957) 2 QB 169 at p. 184). It is only actionable as a civil wrong if the plaintiff can show particular damage other than and beyond the general inconvenience suffered by the public. Such particular damage must be substantial, but it is not limited to special damage in the sense of provable pecuniary loss.

Every member of the public has the right of free passage along every part of the highway, including the pavement. Obstruction of the highway is a form of public nuisance. But not every obstruction is a nuisance. There must be in addition an unreasonable use of the highway by the defendant (see *Lowdens* v *Keavney* (1903) 2 IR 82 and *R* v *Clark (No. 2)* (1964) 2 QB 315). And the court must balance the rights of those who wish to demonstrate with those who wish to exercise their rights of passage. Thus a march or procession, which is conducted in an orderly way, is not actionable, even though it may amount to an obstruction. Nor is a meeting or demonstration on the highway necessarily an obstruction (see *Burden* v *Rigler* (1911) 1 KB 337), although it is more likely to be than a procession; and in any event to be actionable as a nuisance it must be an unreasonable use of the highway.

If, therefore, there is an unreasonable obstruction of the highway resulting from the events at Wapping and the seventh plaintiff can establish particular damage, she can sue those responsible for the nuisance. Equally the first to sixth plaintiffs can sue if they can prove particular damage. The defendants contend that if there is any obstruction it does not affect the public at large but only a small number of people, namely the plaintiffs' employees and TNT's drivers. I reject this argument. I am doubtful if it can ever apply to obstruction of the highway, where it may be presumed that those who may wish to pass are obstructed. But, in any event, I am satisfied that it does affect the public at large (see pp. D104, A331–33) and in any event I think that the plaintiffs' employees and TNT's drivers are a sufficient class within Romer LJ's proposition.

(b) Private nuisance

The owner of land adjoining the highway has a right of access to the highway from any part of his premises. Interference with this right is actionable; but where the interference is as here, alleged obstruction, it is subject to the same qualification that the obstruction must be an unreasonable use of the highway. It is submitted that the third plaintiffs as owners of the land are entitled to sue at Wapping, the first and second at Bouverie Street and Gray's Inn Road, respectively, if the nuisance is thus made out.

How are these principles to be applied to the facts at the various places in question?

Wapping

I have no doubt that the conduct of the pickets and the daily demonstrators as described in the evidence amounts to an unreasonable obstruction of the highway. Moreover, it seems to me that unlike the working miners in *Thomas and ors v National Union of Mineworkers (South Wales Area) and ors* [1986] Ch 20, who were unable to establish special damage because they were driven into the pit in a bus provided by their employer and there was no other evidence of damage, both the seventh plaintiff and the other plaintiffs can establish damage peculiar to them. The seventh plaintiff describes how she no longer feels able to leave the plant during the day for a meal or similar break. She has to go by taxi or minicab instead of on foot and how she feels drained by the constant pressure of having to come to work through the picket line. These are all matters in my view capable of being regarded as substantial damage.

So far as the other plaintiffs are concerned, although it is not entirely clear who incurs the expense, the cost of busing their employees is £100,000 per month – by no means insubstantial damage. Moreover, Mr Wilson, the editor of the Times, has made it clear that the second plaintiffs have both lost some journalists and failed to attract others because of the conduct of the pickets and daily demonstrators. Journalists are the life-blood of a newspaper, and, in my view, this is very serious damage.

The third plaintiffs' cause of action in private nuisance is also established, it not being necessary to establish peculiar damage in that case.

So far as the twice-weekly marches, rallies and demonstrations are concerned, when they are peaceful and orderly no nuisance is created. But it is quite clear that on those occasions when the marches or demonstrations get out of control, attack the police, the employees of the plaintiffs and TNT and obstruct the highway by masses of people that is not a reasonable use of the highway and amounts to a nuisance.

. . .

Intimidation

The tort of intimidation is committed when 'A' delivers a threat to 'B' that he will commit an act or use means unlawful against 'B', as a result of which 'B' does or refrains from doing some act which he is entitled to do, thereby causing damage either to himself or 'C'. The tort is one of intention and the plaintiff, whether it be 'B' or 'C' must be a person whom 'A' intended to injure (see Clerk and Lindsell, p. 729).

. . .

The defendants submit, rightly in my view, that abuse, swearing and shouting does not amount to a threat of violence. They further submit that the threat has to be expressed or implied that if the person threatened does not do what is required he will be subjected to violence and that such threats as have been made do not amount to this. I disagree. The words, 'Scab, we will get you', or words to the same effect, could mean, 'We will assault you because you have been working for the plaintiffs'. But, since the obvious intention is to dissuade people from continuing to work, the more likely meaning is, 'We will get you if you do not stop working for the plaintiffs'. There is ample evidence of such threats at Wapping from both the pickets and daily demonstrators. There is also some evidence to this effect in relation to those who attend at Bouverie Street and Gray's Inn Road.

If a threat is little more than idle abuse and is not to be taken seriously, then it would not be sufficient to found an action for intimidation. Indeed, the tort is not complete unless the person threatened succumbs to the threat and damage is suffered. But it is clear that injunctive relief can be granted to restrain the unlawful act and also threats to commit the unlawful act (Clerk and Lindsell, p. 743, footnote 42). But in order for an injunction to be granted the threat or threats must be serious and taken seriously by those who receive them. It is in this context that, in my view, the evidence of what has happened away from the plaintiffs' premises is material. Where there is such an abundance of evidence of the employees being followed, molested, assaulted and subject to criminal damage to their cars and houses, to say nothing of the treatment meted out to TNT drivers, it is idle to suggest that the threats are not serious or to be taken seriously. The taking of photographs of employees, noting of numbers of their cars and the distribution of so-called rolls of dishonour is particularly significant in this context.

There is, in fact, some evidence from Mr Wilson, to which I have already referred, that the second plaintiffs have already lost employees because of the threats. But even without such evidence, where the threats are serious and there is a real risk that some to whom they are made will succumb to them, the court can grant injunctive relief. Such relief can be granted to an individual employee who has been so threatened or to the plaintiff employer who is at risk of losing his employees. It follows that I do not accept the defendants' submission that this relief can only be granted to the employee in the form of an injunction to restrain assault. It is both the threats and the assault that should be restrained.

So far as the seventh plaintiff is concerned, she speaks of the pickets shaking their fists at her, of being photographed at the gate, of the registration number of her car being taken and pinned up opposite the end of Virginia Street. All this is in addition to the most obscene abuse. Not surprisingly, she speaks of feeling frightened and unsafe. In my judgment these actions are in the circumstances of this case, coercive threats designed to persuade her to cease working for the plaintiffs.

Harassment

In *Thomas and ors v National Union of Mineworkers (South Wales Area) and ors* Scott J, after holding that the conduct of the pickets at the colliery gates was intimidating in the ordinary sense of the word, said at p. 64A–G:

Nuisance is strictly concerned with, and may be regarded as confined to, activity which unduly interferes with the use or enjoyment of land or of easements. But there is no reason why the law should not protect on a similar basis the enjoyment of other rights. All citizens have the right to use the public highway. Suppose an individual were persistently to follow another on a public highway, making rude gestures or remarks in order to annoy or vex. If continuance of such conduct were threatened no one can doubt but that a civil court would, at the suit of the victim, restrain by an injunction the continuance of the conduct. The tort might be described as a species of private nuisance, namely unreasonable interference with the victim's rights to use the highway. But the label for the tort does not, in my view, matter.

In the present case, the working miners have the right to use the highway for the purpose of going to work. They are, in my judgment, entitled under the general law to exercise that right without unreasonable harassment by others. Unreasonable harassment of them in the exercise of that right would, in my judgment, be tortious.

A decision whether in this, or in any other similar case, the presence or conduct of pickets represents a tortious interference with the right of those who wish to go to work to do so without harassment must depend on the particular circumstances of the particular case. The balance to which I have earlier referred must be struck between the rights of those going to work and the rights of the pickets.

The defendants criticise this statement of the law. They submit that Scott J should not have invented a new tort and that it is not sufficient to found liability that there has been an unreasonable interference with the rights of others, even though when a balance is struck between conflicting rights and interests the scale comes down in favour of the plaintiffs, unless those rights are recognised by the law and fall within some accepted head of tort.

I am bound to say that, with all respect to Scott J, I think there is force in these criticisms, especially where it does not appear that damage is a necessary ingredient of the tort. If, of course, damage peculiar to the plaintiff is established, then the tort is that of nuisance.

Since, in my view, the tort of nuisance is established and the tort of intimidation is threatened, it is unnecessary for me to express a final view on the question of harassment.

In any event it seems to me that it would only lie at the suit of the seventh plaintiff at Wapping.

Interference with contract

. . .

In my view it is clear that from a short time after production began at Wapping all those in the trade unions' side have known that TNT were performing a contract of distribution of the plaintiffs' newspapers and it has been the clear purpose and intent of those who have committed these torts to obstruct by nuisance or intimidation the departure of TNT's lorries, to inflict delay and so interfere with what must obviously be a primary obligation of that contract. (ii) The unlawful means relied upon here is not interference with the drivers' contracts of employment with TNT, but the commission of the torts of nuisance and intimidation. For the reasons I have already indicated the plaintiffs have established a sufficient likelihood of these torts being established at trial, in the vicinity of the premises at Wapping.

But the plaintiffs also seek relief in relation to the picketing of TNT's depots and their cause of action in relation to such picketing must, it seems to me, rest upon the tort of interference with their contracts with TNT. It may well be that some of this picketing has been tortious in the sense of being a nuisance or intimidation, and it may also have caused delay to the delivery of newspapers. But in my judgment there is insufficient evidence before me to establish this. This is really a matter for which TNT should, if they think fit, seek relief; and I understand that they have in fact done so.

(iii) That as a necessary consequence of the unlawful means TNT were prevented or hindered from performing a primary obligation of the contract, namely, the distribution of the newspapers as and when the first and second plaintiffs required so as to comply with the obligation to deliver by 6.30am.

Mr Tabachnik pointed out that not all delays in the departure of TNT's lorries can be attributed to this cause. Reference to Exhibit PDR1 at p. 588 shows that on occasions the lorries were not ready for their scheduled time of departure, perhaps through internal problems at the plant. Be that as it may, in my view there is evidence that on occasions, usually Wednesdays and Saturdays and caused by the marching, demonstrations and rallies, when these have deteriorated into disorderly conduct and violence so as to give rise to nuisance and intimidation, that substantial delays have been occasioned to the departure of TNT's lorries, such that the plaintiffs have a likelihood of establishing this element of the tort at trial. But it is to be noted that there is no evidence of this after 17 May, although it is possible that it occurred on 23 July.

Note
The existence of a separate tort of harassment was doubted by Stuart-Smith J.

(iii)   Trespass

In *Larkin* v *Belfast Harbour Commissioners* [1908] 2 IR 214, strikers picketed on the quayside which was the property of the harbour authority. It was held that the statute (the Trade Disputes Act 1906, s. 2) did not authorise a trespass on private property.

In *British Airports Authority* v *Ashton* [1983] IRLR 287, a picket line was established within the parameter of Heathrow Airport, the property of BAA. It was held that TULRA 1974 did not authorise a picket line on private property. Mann J thought it would be 'astonishing' if Parliament had intended to imply a right to attend on land against the will of the land-owner.

C: Criminal Liability for Picketing

While it is important to grasp the range of possible civil liabilities which may attach to certain types of picketing, it is the criminal law which is of the greatest practical significance in terms of control of the activity. This can clearly be seen from the employment of the criminal law during the miners' strike, where over 11,000 charges were brought in connection with incidents arising out of the dispute. These ranged in gravity from the serious offences of riot and unlawful assembly to the less serious charges of obstruction of the highway. Additional criminal offences which may be relevant to the conduct of picketing have been created by the Public Order Act 1986.

(i)   Obstructing a Police Officer in the Execution of His Duty

Piddington v Bates
[1960] 1 WLR 162
Divisional Court

As a result of a telephone call for assistance, the police went to the picketed premises of Free Press Ltd. At the request of the police, the number of pickets at a factory was limited to two at the front entrance and two at the rear. Piddington went to join the picket at the rear entrance, but the police told him repeatedly that two were enough. Piddington pushed gently past the police officer and was gently arrested. There had been no obstruction of the highway, no disorder, nor any violence or threats of violence by the pickets. Piddington was convicted of obstructing a police officer in the execution of his duty.

LORD PARKER CJ: . . . It seems to me that the law is reasonably plain. First, the mere statement by a constable that he did anticipate that there might be a breach of the peace is clearly not enough. There must exist proved facts from which a constable could reasonably anticipate such a breach. Secondly, it is not enough that his contemplation is that there is a remote possibility; there must be a real possibility of a breach of the peace. Accordingly, in every case, it becomes a question of whether, on the particular facts, it can be said that there were reasonable grounds on which a constable charged with this duty reasonably anticipated that a breach of the peace might occur.

As I have said, every case must depend upon its exact facts, and the matter which influences me in this case is the matter of numbers. It is, I think, perfectly clear from the wording of the case, although it is not expressly so found, that the police knew that in these small works there were only eight people working. They found two vehicles arriving, with 18 people milling about the street, trying to form pickets at the doors. On that ground alone, coupled with the telephone call which, I should have thought, intimated some sense of urgency and apprehension, the police were fully entitled to think as reasonable men that there was a real danger of something more than mere picketing to collect or impart information or peaceably to persuade. I think that in those circumstances the prosecutor had reasonable grounds for anticipating that a breach of the peace was a real possibility. It may be, and I think this is the real criticism, that it can be said: Well, to say that only two pickets should be allowed is purely arbitrary; why two? Why not three? Where do you draw the line? I think that a police officer charged with the duty of preserving the Queen's peace must be left to take such steps as on the evidence before him he thinks are proper. I am far from saying that there should be any rule that only two pickets should be allowed at any particular door. There, one gets into an arbitrary area, but so far as this case is concerned I cannot see that there was anything wrong in the action of the prosecutor.

Question
While there must be an objective apprehension that a breach of the peace is a real as opposed to a remote possibility, do you think it likely that a court would reject a police officer's assessment of the situation?

Note
The Code of Practice on Picketing makes it clear that the recommended number of six pickets does not affect in any way the discretion of the police to limit the number of people on any one picket line (para. 51).

Moss v McLachlan
[1985] IRLR 76
Queen's Bench Division

Striking miners from other parts of the country travelled to Nottinghamshire in order to picket the pits which were still working. Four of the striking miners were stopped by a police cordon at a junction within one and a half miles of a working colliery. When the miners refused to accept a police instruction to turn back, they were arrested and convicted of wilfully obstructing a police officer in the execution of his duty. Their appeal was rejected.

SKINNER J: . . . If a constable reasonably apprehends, on reasonable grounds, that a breach of the peace may be committed, he is not only entitled but is under a duty to take reasonable steps to prevent that breach occurring . . .

The possibility of a breach must be real to justify any preventative action. The imminence or immediacy of the threat to the peace determines what action is reasonable. If the police feared that a convoy of cars travelling towards a working coal field bearing banners and broadcasting, by sight or sound, hostility or threats towards working miners, might cause a violent episode, they would be justified in halting the convoy to enquire into its destination and purpose. If, on stopping the vehicles, the police were satisfied that there was a real possibility of the occupants causing a breach of the peace one-and-a-half miles away, a journey of less than five minutes by car, then in our judgement it would be their duty to prevent the convoy from proceeding further and they have the power to do so.

Notes
1.   For a detailed commentary on this case, see Morris, (1985) 14 ILJ 109.
2.   Under the Police and Criminal Evidence Act 1984, s. 4, police officers may also operate 'road checks' for purposes which include ascertaining whether a vehicle is carrying a person intending to commit an offence which a senior officer has reasonable grounds to believe is likely to lead to serious public disorder.

(ii)   Obstruction of the Highway
The offence of obstruction of the highway is contained in the Highways Act 1980, s. 137.

Tynan v *Balmer*
[1966] 2 All ER 133
Divisional Court

Tynan, a union official, was in charge of a group of 40 pickets assembled on an access road to a factory which formed part of the highway. He had organised the pickets into a continually moving circle. A constable ordered the defendant to stop the moving circle, and when he refused he was arrested and charged with wilfully obstructing the constable in the execution of his duty. He was convicted and appealed.

WIDGERY J: . . . In my judgement, the proper way to approach this question, and it is a way which may well have commended itself to the recorder also, is to ask whether the conduct of the pickets would have been a nuisance at common law as an unreasonable user of the highway. It seems, in my judgement, that it clearly would have been so regarded. One leaves aside for the moment any facilities enjoyed by those acting in furtherance of a trade dispute, and if one imagines these pickets as carrying banners advertising some patent medicine or advocating some political reform, it seems to me that their conduct in sealing off a part of the highway by this moving circle would have been an unreasonable user of the highway . . .

   In my judgement, therefore, if one ignores section 2 of the Trade Disputes Act 1906, for the moment and considers the position at common law, this action would have been an unreasonable user of the highway, admittedly a nuisance, and a police officer would have been fully entitled to take action to move the pickets on.

   . . . But what in my view one must do is to look carefully at section 2 and see exactly what it authorises. It authorises in its simplest terms a person to attend at or near one of the places described if he does so merely for the purpose of peacefully obtaining or communicating information or of peacefully persuading any person to work or abstain from working.

The recorder has found as a fact that the pickets in this case were not attending merely for the purposes described in the section. He has found as a fact that their object at any rate in part was to seal off the highway and to cause vehicles approaching the premises to stop. In my judgement that finding of fact is quite enough to require this court to say that as a matter of law the recorder's judgment in this case should be upheld.

Broome v *Director of Public Prosecutions*
[1974] IRLR 26
House of Lords

Broome was picketing a building site. He stood with a poster in front of a lorry trying to enter a factory. Broome was requested by a police officer to move, and on his refusal was arrested and charged with wilfully obstructing the highway. Throughout the whole incident there were no angry words or violent actions and the whole episode lasted only nine minutes. The House of Lords dismissed his appeal against conviction.

LORD REID: . . . I see no ground for implying any right to require the person whom it is sought to persuade to submit to any kind of constraint or restriction on his personal freedom. One is familiar with persons at the side of a road signalling to a driver requesting him to stop. It is then for the driver to decide whether he will stop or not. That, in my view, a picket is entitled to do. If the driver stops, the picket can talk to him but only for so long as the driver is willing to listen.

That must be so because if the picket had the statutory right to stop or to detain the driver that must necessarily imply that the Act had imposed on those passing along the road a statutory duty to stop or to remain for longer than they chose to stay. So far as my recollection goes it would be unique for Parliament to impose such a duty otherwise than by express words, and even if one envisages the possibility of such a duty being imposed by implication the need for it would have to be crystal clear. Here I can see no need at all for any such implication.

Without the protection of the section merely inviting a driver to stop and then, if he is willing to stop and listen, proceeding to try and persuade him not to go on, would in many cases be either an offence or a tort or both, particularly if more than a very few pickets were acting together. I see no reason to hold that the section confers any other right.

Questions
1.   In the modern context, can it be said that there is an effective right to picket when pickets are not allowed to 'flag down' motor vehicles?
2.   What difficulties would be encountered in drafting a provision providing a right for pickets to stop vehicles?

Note
The Labour Government did seek to amend the law in 1975 by 'declaring' that pickets had the right to seek to persuade people to stop for the purpose

of exercising their rights of persuasion, whether the person sought to be stopped was in a vehicle or not. The amendment was defeated by the unlikely alliance of the Conservative Opposition and left-wing MPs. The latter thought that the provision did not go far enough because it did not authorise obstruction of the highway and so would not have helped a picket in Broome's situation.

In essence, the effective right to picket is wholly dependent on whether the police exercise their discretion to require vehicles to stop in order to allow the pickets to speak with the drivers.

(iii)   Public Nuisance

This offence derives from the common law and is committed where members of the public are obstructed in the exercise of rights which are common to all Her Majesty's subjects, including the right of free passage along the public highway. As with the more frequently charged offence under the Highways Act 1980, it is necessary for the prosecution to prove unreasonable user.

Where an individual suffers special damage, over and above that suffered by the rest of the public, an action in tort for public nuisance may also be brought.

(iv)   Intimidation or Annoyance by Violence and Otherwise

Trade Union and Labour Relations (Consolidation) Act 1992

241.   Intimidation or annoyance by violence or otherwise

(1)   A person commits an offence who, with a view to compelling another person to abstain from doing or to do any act which that person has a legal right to do or abstain from doing, wrongfully and without legal authority—

(a)   uses violence to or intimidates that person or his wife or children or injures his property,

(b)   persistently following that person about from place to place,

(c)   hides any tools, clothes or other property owned or used by that person or deprives him or hinders him in the use thereof,

(d)   watches or besets the house or other place where that person resides, works, carries on business or happens to be, or the approach to any such house or place, or

(e)   follows that person with two or more other persons in a disorderly manner in or through any street or road.

Notes

1. These offences first appeared in the Conspiracy and Protection of Property Act 1875, s. 7. Until relatively recently, it was assumed that this quaintly worded Victorian provision was only of historical interest and virtually obsolete in practical terms. During the miners' strike of 1984/5, however, at least 643 charges were brought under what is now TULR(C)A 1992, s. 241, mainly to deal with 'watching and besetting' working miners' homes. In the view of the Government, the section had demonstrated its continued efficacy in the circumstances of the strike and should not only be retained but strengthened (see Review of Public Order Law (Cmnd. 9510),

May 1985). Consequently, the Public Order Act 1986 increased the maximum penalty of three months' imprisonment and a £100 fine to six months' imprisonment and/or a fine (currently £5,000). The Act also made breach of what is now s. 241 an arrestable offence (see now TULR(C)A 1992, s. 241(2) and (3)).

2. Of the five offences listed in s. 241, watching or besetting is the one which is most likely to arise out of the course of picketing. In *Ward Lock & Co. Ltd v Operative Printers' Assistants' Society* (1906) 22 TLR 327, it was said that the Conspiracy and Protection of Property Act 1875, s. 7, 'legalises nothing, and renders nothing wrongful that was not so before' (per Fletcher Moulton LJ). So the watching or besetting must be of such a nature as to amount in itself to a tortious activity before it can give rise to liability under s. 241. If peaceful picketing is not tortious, then it cannot amount to a criminal watching or besetting either.

3. One final point on this section concerns the question whether mass picketing amounts to intimidation. In *Thomas v NUM (South Wales Area)* (above), Scott J was of the view that not only was mass picketing a common law nuisance but it also amounted to intimidation under what is now s. 241, even where there was no physical obstruction of those going to work.

(v) The Public Order Act 1986

In putting forward the proposals which were later largely translated into the provisions of the Public Order Act 1986, the White Paper of 1985 stated:

The rights of peaceful protest and assembly are amongst our fundamental freedoms: they are numbered among the touchstones which distinguish a free society from a totalitarian one. Throughout the review the Government has been concerned to regulate those freedoms to the minimum extent necessary to preserve order and protect the rights of others. (Review Of Public Order Law (Cmnd. 9510), May 1985)

A number of commentators, however, have expressed a general concern that the provisions contained in the 1986 Act impose a dangerous restriction on the civil liberties of assembly and protest and, particularly in the light of events during the 1984/5 miners' strike, make it increasingly more difficult for the police to be seen to maintain a position of neutrality in the policing of industrial disputes (see Lewis (1986) op. cit., pp. 216–219; Lord Wedderburn, *The Worker and The Law*, 3rd ed. (Harmondsworth: Penguin, 1986), pp. 550–553).

Part I of the Public Order Act 1986 contains five statutory offences which may have a relevance in the context of picketing. Sections 1–3 of the Act contain the offences of riot, violent disorder and affray, and replace the common law offences of riot, rout, unlawful assembly and affray whose ambit was confused and uncertain. Sections 4 and 5 contain the more minor offences of causing fear or provocation of violence and causing harassment, alarm or distress. Section 154 of the Criminal Justice and Public Order Act 1994 inserted s. 4A in the Public Order Act 1986 and creates the more serious offence of causing *intentional* harassment, alarm or distress.

Part II of the 1986 Act imposes controls over the conduct of marches or processions and static assemblies. Section 11 imposes a national requirement for organisers of 'public processions' normally to give at least six clear days' notice of their intention to the police. The notice must specify the date of the procession, its proposed starting time and route, and the name and address of one of the organisers.

Picketing, by definition, is a static assembly outside the entrance of a workplace. However, protest marches are now a relatively frequent feature of larger industrial disputes, e.g. the protest marches held in support of the striking miners in 1984/5 and the marches, culminating in a mass picket outside the Wapping plant of News International, during 1986 in protest at the dismissal of some 5,500 printworkers (see *News Group Newspapers Ltd* v *SOGAT '82* [1986] IRLR 337). In future such marches will have to comply with the terms of s. 11, though it should be noted that the notice requirement does not apply to processions 'commonly and customarily held', e.g. by trade unionists on May Day.

Section 12 enables the *most senior police officer present* to impose conditions, including route and timing, on processions when the officer reasonably believes that they may result in serious public disorder, serious damage to property or serious disruption to the life of the community, or where the purpose of the organisers is to intimidate others. Where a march or procession is *intended* to be held, 'the senior police officer' with the power to impose conditions is the chief officer of police.

The power to ban marches for up to three months under the Public Order Act 1986 on the ground of reasonable belief that it will result in 'serious public disorder' is retained. The major change is that the 1986 Act makes it an offence to participate in a banned march, punishable with a maximum fine, in addition to organising or inciting others to participate in one.

The Act provides the police for the first time ever with a clear *statutory* power to impose conditions which prescribe the location, size and maximum duration of 'public assemblies' (defined as assemblies of 20 or more people in a 'public place' which is wholly or partly open to the air). As with processions, the most senior officer present will be able to impose such conditions where he or she reasonably believes that an assembly may result in serious disorder, serious damage to property, serious disruption of the life of the community, or the 'intimidation of others with a view to compelling them not to do an act they have a right to do, or to do an act they have a right not to do'. This provision has the clearest relevance for pickets and provides a potent additional weapon of control for the police. As the White Paper observed, 'at Grunwick's or Warrington, for example, the police could have imposed conditions limiting the numbers of demonstrators, or moving the demonstration in support of the pickets further away from the factory' (para. 5.7).

Where conditions are imposed *in advance* of the assembly, then they may only be imposed by the chief officer of police, or his deputy or assistant. The organisers of a static assembly who fail to abide by the conditions, or those who incite disobedience, face a maximum penalty of three months' imprisonment and/or a £2,500 fine. The participants in such an assembly risk a £1,000 fine.

See also the Criminal Justice and Public Order Act 1994, s. 68 which creates the offence of aggravated trespass and s. 70 which empowers chief police officers to seek an order from the district council prohibiting the holding of trespassory assemblies in the district for a specified period.

II Industrial Action: Civil Remedies and Enforcement

Currently, if a trade union organises industrial action which is unlawful, it can be restrained by an injunction from the courts on an application from the employer involved in the dispute, or any other party whose contractual rights have been infringed. Union members also have the right to restrain industrial action if they are, or are likely to be, induced to participate in industrial action which does not have the support of a ballot. TURERA 1993 extends the right of action to members of the public who suffer, or are likely to suffer, disruption from unlawful industrial action (see page 818).

A: An 'Act done by a Trade Union'

The individuals organising unlawful industrial action will be personally liable. Prior to 1982, trade unions themselves enjoyed a wide immunity from actions in tort. This position was radically changed by the EA 1982, which made unions liable in tort, made them vicariously liable for the unlawful actions of their officials, and which set out a scale of maximum damages depending on the size of the union. As a result, it is crucial to be able to identify an 'act done by a trade union'.

Trade Union and Labour Relations (Consolidation) Act 1992

20. Liability of trade union in certain proceedings in tort
(1) Where proceedings in tort are brought against a trade union—
(a) on the ground that an act—
(i) induces another person to break a contract or interferes or induces another person to interfere with its performance, or
(ii) consists in threatening that a contract (whether one to which the union is a party or not) will be broken or its performance interfered with, or that the union will induce another person to break a contract or interfere with its performance, or
(b) in respect of an agreement or combination by two or more persons to do or to procure the doing of an act which, if it were done without any such agreement or combination, would be actionable in tort on such a ground,
then, for the purpose of determining in those proceedings whether the union is liable in respect of the act in question, that act shall be taken to have been done by the union if, but only if, it is to be taken to have been authorised or endorsed by the trade union in accordance with the following provisions.
(2) An act shall be taken to have been authorised or endorsed by a trade union if it was done, or was authorised or endorsed—
(a) by any person empowered by the rules to do, authorise or endorse acts of the kind in question, or
(b) by the principal executive committee or the president or general secretary, or

(c) by any other committee of the union or any other official of the union (whether employed by it or not).

(3) For the purposes of paragraph (c) of subsection (2)—

(a) any group of persons constituted in accordance with the rules of the union is a committee of the union; and

(b) an act shall be taken to have been done, authorised or endorsed by an official if it was done, authorised or endorsed by, or by any member of, any group of persons of which he was at the material time a member, the purposes of which included organising or co-ordinating industrial action.

Notes

1. By virtue of amendments originally introduced by the EA 1990, the scope of union liability was further extended. What is now TULR(C)A 1992, s. 20(2)(c), means that a shop steward could render a union liable where he or she authorises or endorses action without a ballot. Moreover, by virtue of s. 20(3)(b), it is sufficient that such an official is a member of a group, the purpose of which includes organising or coordinating industrial action, and that *any member of that group* has authorised or endorsed the action. The insidious nature of this provision was highlighted by Lord Wedderburn during the House of Lords debates on the Bill that became the EA 1990:

. . . under this Bill the union is at risk from an act of an unknown person, some mysterious stranger acting unilaterally after the gathering of an unknown, shadowy group to which the official, at a material time, at some point entered and became, for a few moments, a member. (Hansard HL, 23 July 1990, col. 1272)

2. A union may repudiate the purported authorisation or endorsement by the third group, i.e. other committees and officials, but can *never* repudiate the actions of the principal executive committee, president, general secretary or those acting under the rules. The requirements for an effective repudiation are far more stringent and complicated as a result of changes introduced by the 1990 Act.

Trade Union and Labour Relations (Consolidation) Act 1992

21. Repudiation by union of certain acts

(1) An act shall not be taken to have been authorised or endorsed by a trade union by virtue only of paragraph (c) of section 20(2) if it was repudiated by the executive, president or general secretary as soon as reasonably practicable after coming to the knowledge of any of them.

(2) Where an act is repudiated—

(a) written notice of the repudiation must be given to the committee or official in question, without delay, and

(b) the union must do its best to give individual written notice of the fact and date of repudiation, without delay—

(i) to every member of the union who the union has reason to believe is taking part, or might otherwise take part, in industrial action as a result of the act, and

(ii) to the employer of every such member.

(3) The notice given to members in accordance with paragraph (b)(i) of subsection (2) must contain the following statement—

'Your union has repudiated the call (or calls) for industrial action to which this notice relates and will give no support to unofficial industrial action taken in response to it (or them). If you are dismissed while taking unofficial industrial action, you will have no right to complain of unfair dismissal.'

(4) If subsection (2) or (3) is not complied with, the repudiation shall be treated as ineffective.

(5) An act shall not be treated as repudiated if at any time after the union concerned purported to repudiate it the executive, president or general secretary has behaved in a manner which is inconsistent with the purported repudiation.

(6) The executive, president or general secretary shall be treated as so behaving if, on a request made to any of them within three months of the purported repudiation by a person who—

(a) is a party to a commercial contract whose performance has been or may be interfered with as a result of the act in question, and

(b) has not been given written notice by the union of the repudiation, it is not forthwith confirmed in writing that the act has been repudiated.

(7) In this section 'commercial contract' means any contract other than—

(a) a contract of employment, or

(b) any other contract under which a person agrees personally to do work or perform services for another.

B: Injunctions

An injunction is an order either requiring the defendant to cease a particular course of action (a negative injunction) or, in its mandatory form, an order requiring the defendant to do something. The most frequent form of order in industrial disputes is the interim injunction requiring the organisers to call off the industrial action pending full trial of the action. Employers who succeed at this stage rarely proceed to full trial: they have achieved their aim of halting the action. They know the suspension of the industrial action, although theoretically on a temporary basis, will defeat the strike in practical terms because the impetus will be lost. Given the crucial effect the obtaining of injunctive relief will have on the outcome of a dispute, the principles on which the court's discretion is based are of great importance.

Trade Union and Labour Relations (Consolidation) Act 1992

221. Restrictions on grant of injunctions and interdicts

(1) Where—

(a) an application for an injunction is made to a court in the absence of the party against whom it is sought or any representative of his, and

(b) he claims, or in the opinion of the court would be likely to claim, that he acted in contemplation or furtherance of a trade dispute,

the court shall not grant the injunction or interdict unless satisfied that all steps which in the circumstances were reasonable have been taken with a view to securing that notice of the application and an opportunity of being heard with respect to the application have been given to him.

(2) Where—

(a) an application for an interlocutory injunction is made to a court pending the trial of an action, and

(b)   the party against whom it is sought claims that he acted in contemplation
or furtherance of a trade dispute,
the court shall in exercising its discretion whether or not to grant the injunction, have
regard to the likelihood of that party's succeeding at the trial of the action in
establishing any matter which would afford a defence to the action under section 219
(protection from certain tort liabilities) or section 220 (peaceful picketing).

Notes
1.   In *NWL* v *Woods* [1979] 3 All ER 614, Lord Diplock was of the view that
the provision was intended as a reminder to judges that, in exercising their
discretion, they should consider a number of 'practical realities', particularly
the fact that the interlocutory injunction stage generally disposes of the whole
action. However, in *Dimbleby & Sons Ltd* v *NUJ* [1984] ICR 386, his
Lordship revised his view of the practical realities, given that in the interim
period the EA 1982 had made it possible to pursue actions for damages
against trade unions themselves and therefore it was wrong to assume that
the matter would be disposed at the interlocutory stage. Lord Diplock
appears to suggest that this should make a judge more willing to grant an
interim injunction. But surely this factor should weigh the balance of
convenience *against* the grant of an injunction, given that the employer is now
able to recover damages and costs at full trial from a solvent defendant.
2.   There are suggestions in several cases (*NWL Ltd* v *Woods*; *Express
Newspapers Ltd* v *MacShane* [1980] AC 672 and *Duport Steels Ltd* v *Sirs*
[1980] ICR 161) that the courts have a residual discretion to grant an
injunction. Consequently, in cases where a strike posed serious consequences
to the employer, a third party or the general public, what is now TULR(C)A
1992, s. 221(2) might be overridden. This possibility is of much less practical
importance since the 1980s, given the considerable narrowing of the scope of
the immunities which has taken place (for a detailed discussion of this highly
complex area see Wedderburn, *The Worker and the Law*, pp. 681–717).

Mercury Communications Ltd v *Scott-Garner*
[1983] IRLR 494
Court of Appeal

(The facts of this case are set out at p. 748.)

SIR JOHN DONALDSON: . . . Proceeding by the appropriate stages, the questions
and my answers are as follows:
(i)   Q. Has Mercury shown that there is a serious issue to be tried?
          A. Yes.
(ii)   Q. Has Mercury shown that it has a real prospect of succeeding in its claim
for a permanent injunction at the trial?
          A. Yes.
(iii)   Q. If Mercury succeeded, would it be adequately compensated by damages
for the loss which it suffered as a result of the union being free to continue to take
industrial action pending the trial?
          A. No. Mercury is in a relatively frail condition as a newcomer to the field
and has very large sums of money invested in the project. New customers cannot be

attracted, whilst industrial action is threatened and the losses will vastly exceed the maximum liability which can be imposed upon the union, namely £250,000 [see now TULR(C)A 1992, s. 22].

(iv)   Q. If the union were to succeed at the trial in establishing its defence under [TULR(C)A 1992, s. 219], would it be adequately compensated by an award under the cross-undertaking?

A. Yes. The union would suffer no loss since, on this hypothesis, the dispute is wholly or mainly about redundancy and there is no suggestion that a temporary cessation in the industrial action would cause or hasten the redundancy.

(v)   Q. Where does the balance of convenience lie?

A. It lies in protecting Mercury pending the trial of the action.

Question

Do you agree with the reasoning of Sir John Donaldson in determining the balance of convenience? Have the commercial interests of the company been given a disproportionate weighting relative to the less tangible and unquantifiable interests of the union members?

C: Damages

Trade Union and Labour Relations (Consolidation) Act 1992

22.   Limit on damages awarded against trade unions in actions in tort

(1)   This section applies to any proceedings in tort brought against a trade union, except—

(a)   proceedings for personal injury as a result of negligence, nuisance or breach of duty;

(b)   proceedings for breach of duty in connection with the ownership, occupation, possession, control or use of property;

(c)   proceedings brought by virtue of Part I of the Consumer Protection Act 1987 (product liability).

(2)   In any proceedings in tort to which this section applies the amount which may be awarded against the union by way of damages shall not exceed the following limit—

Number of members of union	Maximum award of damages
Less than 5,000	£10,000
5,000 or more but less than 25,000	£50,000
25,000 or more but less than 100,000	£125,000
100,000 or more	£250,000

Note

These limits apply in 'any proceedings in tort brought against a trade union'. The effect of this phrase is that where a union is sued by various claimants (e.g., the employer in dispute, customers, suppliers, etc.) for the damages caused to them by the unlawful action, then the maximum will be applied to them separately. In this way, a large union, such as the T&GWU, could find it will be liable to pay well over the £250,000 in damages arising from any one dispute. You should also note these maximums do not apply in respect of the size of any fine imposed for contempt of court where there is a failure to comply with the terms of the injunction. Nor do the limits on damages include the legal costs the defendant union may have to pay. Hepple and Fredman cite the example of the *Stockport Messenger* action in 1983 against the National Graphical Association, as a result of which the union lost one-tenth of its assets.

The damages against the union were assessed at £131,000 plus interest (which included aggravated and exemplary damages in relation to proved losses). When this was added to the £675,000 fines for contempt of court for non-compliance with an injunction, and legal costs of sequestration, it was estimated in December 1985 that the union had lost over £1 million. (*Labour Law and Industrial Relations in Great Britain*, p. 212; see also *Messenger Newspapers Group Ltd* v *National Graphical Association (1982)* [1984] ICR 345.)

D: The Citizen and the Control of Industrial Action

Trade Union and Labour Relations (Consolidation) Act 1992

235A.   Industrial action affecting supply of goods or services to an individual
(1)   Where an individual claims that—
   (a)   any trade union or other person has done, or is likely to do, an unlawful act to induce any person to take part, or to continue to take part, in industrial action, and
   (b)   an effect, or a likely effect, of the industrial action is or will be to—
      (i)   prevent or delay the supply of goods or services, or
      (ii)   reduce the quality of goods or services supplied,
to the individual making the claim,
he may apply to the High Court or the Court of Session for an order under this section.
   (2)   For the purposes of this section an act to induce any person to take part, or to continue to take part, in industrial action is unlawful—
   (a)   if it is actionable in tort by any one or more persons, or
   (b)   (where it is or would be the act of a trade union) if it could form the basis of an application by a member under section 62.
   (3)   In determining whether an individual may make an application under this section it is immaterial whether or not the individual is entitled to be supplied with the goods or services in question.
   (4)   Where on an application under this section the court is satisfied that the claim is well-founded, it shall make such order as it considers appropriate for requiring the person by whom the act of inducement has been, or is likely to be, done to take steps for ensuring—
   (a)   that no, or no further, act is done by him to induce any persons to take part or to continue to take part in the industrial action, and
   (b)   that no person engages in conduct after the making of the order by virtue of having been induced by him before the making of the order to take part or continue to take part in the industrial action.
   (5)   Without prejudice to any other power of the court, the court may on an application under this section grant such interlocutory relief (in Scotland, such interim order) as it considers appropriate.
   (6)   For the purposes of this section an act of inducement shall be taken to be done by a trade union if it is authorised or endorsed by the union; and the provisions of section 20(2) to (4) apply for the purposes of determining whether such an act is to be taken to be so authorised or endorsed.
   Those provisions also apply in relation to proceedings for failure to comply with an order under this section as they apply in relation to the original proceedings.

Notes
1. The Green Paper, *Industrial Relations in the 1990s,* while not proposing an outright ban on strikes in the public services, did advocate further legal constraints. It proposed that customers of public services within the scope of the so-called Citizen's Charter should have the right to bring proceedings to prevent or restrain the unlawful organisation of industrial action in, or affecting, any such service.

While the Green Paper concerned itself solely with industrial action in the public services, TURERA 1993 extended the right to cover *all* industrial action, whether it takes place in the public sector or the private sector. Moreover, unlike the Green Paper, the Act does not make the exercise of the right conditional on the fact that no employer or union member had sought to challenge the legality of the industrial action in the courts.

2. The 1993 Act also created a new Commissioner for Protection Against Unlawful Industrial Action, who would have the power, on application, to grant assistance for proceedings against a trade union under the right in TULR(C)A 1992, s. 235A. In 1996–97 only two formal applications for assistance were received. Of these, one was granted assistance. In addition, the Commissioner's office issued 1,027 information sheets, 233 guides and 369 reports at a cost to the taxpayer of £91,388. The office is abolished by the Employment Relations Act 1999, s. 28.

Question
Why do you think the Conservative Government has deemed it appropriate for individuals who wish to sue trade unions to be provided with legal assistance?

E: Workers Whose Right Lawfully to Withdraw their Labour is Wholly or Partly Restricted

(i)   The Armed Forces

Incitement to Disaffection Act 1934

1.   Penalty on persons endeavouring to seduce members of His Majesty's forces from their duty or allegiance
If any person maliciously and advisedly endeavours to seduce any member of His Majesty's forces from his duty or allegiance to His Majesty, he shall be guily of an offence under this Act.

Note
Those taking the industrial action could be charged with desertion or mutiny.

(ii)   The Police

Police Act 1996

91.   Causing disaffection
(1)   Any person who causes, or attempts to cause, or does any act calculated to cause disaffection amongst the members of any police force, or induces or attempts

to induce, or does any act calculated to induce, any member of a police force to withhold his services, shall be guilty of an offence and liable—

(a) on summary conviction, to imprisonment for a term not exceeding six months or to a fine not exceeding the statutory maximum, or to both;

(b) on conviction of indictment, to imprisonment for a term not exceeding two years or to a fine or to both.

(2) This section applies to special constables appointed for a police area as it applies to members of a police force.

Note Following an abortive strike in 1919, it was made a criminal offence to take any actions likely to cause disaffection or breach of discipline by members of the police force. This law is now contained in the Police Act 1996, s. 91. This statute also forbids police officers the right to join a trade union, though, if they are already union members when they enlist, permission may be granted to retain that membership. The police may join the Police Federation, but that is not a trade union as such and is not affiliated to the TUC.

(iii) Prison Officers
As a result of the Criminal Justice and Public Order Act 1994, s. 127, it is unlawful to induce a prison officer to take industrial action. As in other, similar torts, it is the inducement that is unlawful: actually withholding services or committing breaches of discipline will not be within the section. The tort created by this section is only actionable by the Home Secretary. S/he is entitled to apply for an injunction to present an apprehended breach of duty without the need to show that he would suffer any actual loss or damage.

(iv) Communications Workers

Post Office Act 1953

58. Opening or delaying of postal packets by officers of the Post Office
(1) If any person engaged in the business of the Post Office, contrary to his duty, opens, or procures or suffers to be opened, any postal packet in the course of transmission by post, or wilfully detains or delays, or procures or suffers to be detained or delayed, any such postal packet, he shall be guilty of a misdemeanour and be liable to imprisonment for a term not exceeding two years or to a fine, or to both.

Note
See also the Telecommunications Act 1984, ss. 44 and 45, which created similar offences in relation to telecommunications. The 1984 Act also created a new civil liability of inducing a breach of the licensed operator's duty to operate the telecommunications system or to interfere with the performance of that duty. Liability is established when the action is taken wholly *or partly* to achieve such a result (s. 18(5)–(7)). Industrial action by telecommunication workers could clearly fall foul of this form of liability and, in this context, it will be irrelevant that they are acting in contemplation or furtherance of a trade dispute.

(v)   Merchant Seafarers
The Merchant Shipping Acts create a variety of criminal offences which could be used against those who organise or take part in industrial action *while the ship is at sea*, e.g. in breach of duty endangering a ship, life or limb (Merchant Shipping Act 1995, s. 58); concerted disobedience and neglect of duty (s. 59).

(vi)   Aliens
The Aliens Restriction (Amendment) Act 1919, s. 3(2), makes it a crime punishable by three months' imprisonment for an alien to promote industrial unrest unless engaged *bona fide* in the industry for at least two years. This piece of xenophobic legislation owes its place on the statute book to the panic which followed the Russian Revolution and the fear that foreign agitators were plotting a similar insurrection in Britain.

(vii)   Endangering Life

Trade Union and Labour Relations (Consolidation) Act 1992

240.   Breach of contract involving injury to persons or property
   (1)   A person commits an offence who wilfully and maliciously breaks a contract of service or hiring, knowing or having reasonable cause to believe that the probable consequence of his so doing, either alone or in combination with others, will be—
   (a)   to endanger human life or cause serious bodily injury, or
   (b)   to expose valuable property, whether real or personal, to destruction or serious injury.
   (2)   Subsection (1) applies equally whether the offence is committed from malice conceived against the person endangered or injured or, as the case may be, the owner of the property destroyed or injured, or otherwise.
   (3)   A person guilty of an offence under this section is liable on summary conviction to imprisonment for a term not exceeding three months or to a fine not exceeding level 2 on the standard scale or both.
   (4)   This section does not apply to seamen.

Note
Originally enacted as the Conspiracy and Protection of Property Act 1875, s. 5, this offence might be relevant to a wide range of occupations engaged in industrial action, e.g. hospital workers, firemen, dustmen, etc., but there is no record of this mid-Victorian provision ever being used.

F: Emergency Powers

In the event of a national emergency, the Government possesses extremely wide powers to intervene in an industrial dispute. Under the Emergency Powers Acts of 1920 and 1964, the Government may proclaim a state of emergency and make regulations where there have occurred 'events of such a nature as to be calculated, by interfering with the supply and distribution of food, water or light, or with the means of locomotion, to deprive the community, or any substantial portion of the community, of the essentials of life'. The proclamation must be renewed after one month and Parliament must approve the regulations made by the Government.

While the Act gives almost unlimited power to the Government to make regulations, it cannot make it an offence to take part in a strike or to persuade others to do so, and it cannot introduce military or industrial conscription.

An emergency has been proclaimed 12 times since 1920 (including the seamen's strike in 1966, the docks strike in 1972, the miners' strike in 1972 and coal and electricity in 1973).

In addition, the Government has the power to call in the armed forces to be used on 'urgent work of national importance', and this power may be exercised without any proclamation or consultation with Parliament (see the Defence (Armed Forces) Regulations 1939, now made permanent by the Emergency Powers Act 1964, s. 2).

More recently, the legislation which privatised the electricity and water industries provides ministers with wide powers to issue confidential directions to the relevant operators for purposes which include 'mitigating the effects of any civil emergency which may occur'. The Secretary of State must lay a copy of every direction he or she gives before Parliament unless he or she 'is of the opinion that disclosure of the direction is against the interests of national security' or, in the case of electricity supply, he or she considers that it would be against the commercial interests of any person (Electricity Act 1989, s. 96; Water Act 1989, s. 170). (The Telecommunication Act 1984, s. 94, provides powers of direction.)

On the assumption that industrial action could come within the definition of a 'civil emergency', Gillian Morris has observed:

In the event of industrial action taking place the powers to regulate supplies which previously would have required approval under the Emergency Powers Act 1920 may now be exercised without the need for parliamentary involvement. At the same time as privatising these services, therefore, the Government has increased considerably its scope for taking measures on a wholly unaccountable basis to counter the impact of industrial action. ('Industrial Action in Essential Services' (1991) 20 ILJ 89, at p. 82.)

11 HEALTH AND SAFETY AT WORK

I Introduction

Health and safety can be divided into two distinct subject areas, the common law and statute, although there is naturally some overlap between the two. The prime example of the common law is the tort of employer's liability. This, with the civil claim for breach of statutory duty, may be studied within the remit of a tort law syllabus. However, although the scope of this book may not extend to an in-depth study of those areas, and will certainly exclude vicarious liability, key cases which are part of the recent development of this area will be considered.

The legislative intervention in this area is enormous and continues to grow as more and more European Directives are put into effect. To consider all of the legislation in detail would not be practical or realistic. However, reference will be made to the relevant case law under the Health and Safety at Work etc. Act 1974, as well as to materials highlighting the development of this statute into the more esoteric areas of health and safety, such as violence, smoking, etc.

II Employer's liability

The tort of employer's liability arises where the employer has failed to take reasonable care for the safety of his employees while they are acting within the course of their employment. This is a personal duty owed by the employer to each individual employee, and is non-delegable in that ultimate responsibility remains with the employer. The tort is negligence based. Liability is dependent upon proof of the breach of the duty and resultant damage.

A: Duty of Care

The establishment of the duty of care is based on the existence of an employer/employee relationship. The case law relating to the tests for establishing this can be found in Chapter 2. The scope of the duty of care has gradually developed over the years so that it is now a four-fold duty to provide competent fellow employees, a safe place of work, safe plant and appliances, and a safe system of work. As the case law continues to develop the relationship of express terms in the contract of employment to the common law duty has had to be considered. The original scope of the duty was established in the following case.

Wilsons and Clyde Coal Co. Ltd v *English*
[1938] AC 57
House of Lords

The respondent was employed underground in repairing an airway leading off the Mine Jigger Brae, one of the main haulage roads, and while he was proceeding, at the end of the day shift, between 1.30 and 2 p.m., to the pit bottom by way of the Mine Jigger Brae, the haulage plant was put in motion and, before he could reach one of the manholes provided, he was caught by a rake of hutches and crushed between it and the side of the road.

The respondent's case was that the time fixed by the appellants for raising the day shift men up the pit was between 1.30 and 2 p.m., and that it was a necessary part of a safe system of working that the haulage should be stopped on the main haulage roads during this period, and that this was in accordance with usual and recognised mining practice in Scotland.

It was held, dismissing the company's appeal, that the duty to provide a safe system of work was a personal one, and ultimately responsibility for any negligence in the performance of that duty remained with the employer even where the duty had been lawfully delegated to an agent.

LORD THANKERTON: Counsel for the appellants admitted that primarily the master has a duty to take due care to provide and maintain a reasonably safe system of working in the mine, and he stated the question in the appeal as being whether a master, who has delegated the duty of taking due care in the provision of a reasonably safe system of working to a competent servant, is responsible for a defect in the system of which he had no knowledge; and he submitted the following general propositions in law:

First — If the master retains control, he has a duty to see that his servants do not suffer through his personal negligence, such as (1) failure to provide proper and suitable plant, if he knows, or ought to have known, of such failure; (2) failure to select fit and competent servants; (3) failure to provide a proper and safe system of working; and (4) failure to observe statutory regulations: but,

Second — If he delegates his duty to take care of the safety of his servants to competent subordinates, his responsibility in respect of his primary common law duty ceases, unless there is proof of knowledge by him not acted upon; so that the master's liability in respect of his common law duty may be said to depend on the extent of his interference.

The appellants maintain that the present case is covered by the second proposition, in that they have delegated to a competent agent and manager the duty of providing a reasonably safe system of working, and that any negligence in the provision of such a system is the negligence of these delegates, and, under the doctrine of common employment, that the appellants are not liable therefor.

It seems to me that the fallacy in the appellant's argument lies in the view that the master, being under a duty to take due care in the provision of a reasonably safe system of working, is absolved from that duty by the appointment of a competent person to perform the duty. In my opinion the master cannot 'delegate' his duty in this sense, though he may appoint some one, as his agent in the discharge of the duty, for whom he will remain responsible under the maxim *respondeat superior*. . . .

LORD WRIGHT: . . . In *Rudd's case* [1933] 1 KB 566 the Court of Appeal, applying their general views which I have just stated, held that the employers could escape liability by showing that they had appointed competent servants to see that the duty was fulfilled. This House held that, on the contrary, the statutory duty was personal to the employer, in this sense that he was bound to perform it by himself or by his servants. The same principle, in my opinion, applies to those fundamental obligations of a contract of employment which lie outside the doctrine of common employment, and for the performance of which employers are absolutely responsible. When I use the word absolutely, I do not mean that employers warrant the adequacy of plant, or the competence of fellow-employees, or the propriety of the system of work. The obligation is fulfilled by the exercise of due care and skill. But it is not fulfilled by entrusting its fulfilment to employees, even though selected with due care and skill. The obligation is threefold – 'the provision of a competent staff of men, adequate material, and a proper system and effective supervision' . . .

There is perhaps a risk of confusion if we speak of the duty as one which can, or cannot, be delegated. The true question is, What is the extent of the duty attaching to the employer? Such a duty is the employer's personal duty, whether he performs or can perform it himself, or whether he does not perform it or cannot perform it save by servants or agents. A failure to perform such a duty is the employer's personal negligence. This was held to be the case where the duty was statutory, and it is equally so when the duty is one attaching at common law. A statutory duty differs from a common law duty in certain respects, but in this respect it stands on the same footing. . . .

Johnstone v *Bloomsbury Health Authority*
[1991] IRLR 118
Court of Appeal

The plaintiff was employed by the defendants as a senior house officer in University College Hospital. His contract of employment provided that he had a standard working week of 40 hours and that, in addition, he would be 'available', on call, for a further 48 hours a week 'on average'. He alleged that in some weeks he had been required to work in excess of 100 hours, with inadequate periods of sleep and that, as a result, he suffered from stress, depression, lethargy, diminished appetite and inability to sleep, exhaustion and suicidal feelings.

The plaintiff claimed that the employers were under a duty to take all reasonable care for his safety and well-being and that they were in breach of that duty by requiring him to work intolerable hours with such deprivation of sleep as to damage his health and put at risk the safety of his patients. He sued for damages and applied for a declaration that he could not lawfully be required to work under his contract of employment for more than 72 hours per week or for a continuous period of more than 24 hours without a break of not less than 8 hours.

It was held, dismissing the employers' appeal, that the employers could not lawfully require the plaintiff to work so much overtime in any week as was reasonably foreseeable would damage his health, notwithstanding the express terms of his contract of employment which required him to work for 40 hours and be available for a further 48 hours of overtime on average each week. The plaintiff was allowed a declaration to that effect.

BROWNE-WILKINSON V-C: In my judgement the approach adopted in *Tai Hing* [1986] AC 80 case shows that where there is a contractual relationship between the parties their respective rights and duties have to be analysed wholly in contractual terms and not as a mixture of duties in tort and contract. It necessarily follows that the scope of the duties owed by one party to the other will be defined by the terms of the contract between them. Therefore, if there is a term of the contract which is in general terms (e.g. a duty to take reasonable care not to injure the employee's health) and another term which is precise and detailed (e.g. an obligation to work on particular tasks notwithstanding that they involve an obvious health risk expressly referred to in the contract) the ambit of the employer's duty of care for the employee's health will be narrower than it would be were there no such express terms. In the absence of such express term, an employer would be in breach of the normal obligation not knowingly to put the employee's health at risk. But the express term postulated would demonstrate that, in that particular contract, the duty was restricted to taking such care of the employee's health as was consistent with the employee working on the specified high risk tasks. The express and the implied terms of the contract have to be capable of co-existence without conflict. (I am of course ignoring the effect of the Unfair Contract Terms Act or any statutory duties overriding the contract.)

Therefore I agree with Legatt LJ and disagree with Stuart-Smith LJ that in the present case the scope of the duty of care for the plaintiff's health owed by the Authority falls to be determined taking into account the express terms of clause 4(b) of the contract. If the contract, on its true construction, were to impose an absolute obligation to work 48 hours' overtime per week on average, it would, in my judgement, preclude an argument by the employee that the employer, in requiring 48 hours per week overtime, was in breach of his implied duty of care for the employee's health.

But this case is not the same as the example I have used above. Although clause 4(b) imposes an absolute duty on the plaintiff to work for 40 hours and in addition an obligation 'to be available' for a further 48 hours per week on average, the Authority has a discretion as to the number of hours it calls on the plaintiff to work 'overtime'. There is no incompatibility between the plaintiff being under a duty to be available for 48 hours' overtime and the Authority having the right, *subject to its ordinary duty not to injure the plaintiff*, to call on him to work up to 48 hours' overtime on average. There is, in the present contract, no incompatibility between the plaintiff's duty on the one hand and the Authority's right, subject to the implied duty as to health, on the other. The implied term does not contradict the express term of the contract.

In my judgement there must be some restriction on the Authority's rights. In any sphere of employment other than that of junior hospital doctors, an obligation to work up to 88 hours in any one week would be rightly regarded as oppressive and intolerable. But even that is not the limit of what the Authority claims. Since the plaintiff's obligation is to be available 'on average' for 48 hours per week, the Authority claims to be entitled to require him to work more than 88 hours in some weeks regardless of possible injury to his health. Thus the plaintiff alleges that he was required to work for 100 hours during one week in February 1989 and 105 hours during another week in March 1989. How far can this go? Could the Authority demand of the plaintiff that he worked 130 hours (out of the total of 168 hours available) in any one week if this would manifestly involve injury to his health? In my judgement the Authority's right to call for overtime under clause 4(b) is not an absolute right but must be limited in some way. There is no technical legal reason why the Authority's discretion to call for overtime should not be exercised in conformity with the normal implied duty to take reasonable care not to injure their employee's health.

Reid v *Rush & Tomkins Group plc*
[1989] IRLR 265
Court of Appeal

Mr Reid suffered severe injuries in a road accident which occurred whilst he was working for the defendants in Ethiopia. The accident was the fault of the other driver, for whom the defendants were not responsible, but because there is no requirement in Ethiopia for third party insurance or any system of claiming compensation from an unidentified or uninsured driver, Mr Reid received no compensation for his injuries. He therefore claimed damages from the defendants in respect of the financial losses he sustained.

Before the Court of Appeal, Mr Reid based his claims for damages both in contract and in tort. He submitted that there was an implied term in his contract of employment that the defendants would take out appropriate insurance cover indemnifying him against the risk of death or injury occasioned by the fault of a third party resulting from a road traffic accident in Ethiopia whilst the plaintiff was driving in the course of his employment. The second and alternative implied term alleged was that, prior to his departure for Ethiopia, the defendants would give him all necessary advice relating to working conditions there, including any special risks such as a road accident involving an uninsured driver, and would advise him accordingly to obtain appropriate insurance cover himself.

It was further submitted that the general duty in tort owed to Mr Reid by the defendants as his employers required them to take all reasonable steps as were necessary in the light of any special risks arising from his working in Ethiopia, properly to protect his economic welfare whilst he was acting in the course of his employment and, therefore, in particular either to provide the appropriate insurance cover or to inform him of the special risk and advise him to obtain that cover himself.

It was held, dismissing Reid's appeal, that the duty of care did not extend to the provision of insurance cover against special risks which might be encountered while working overseas; nor did it extend to informing the plaintiff of those risks or advising him to obtain cover.

GIBSON LJ: . . . It is first necessary to examine the plaintiff's claim, which Mr Smith has acknowledged to be a claim for pure economic loss as against the defendants, with reference to the ordinary duty of care owed by a master to his servant. The duty has for very many years always been referred to in terms of the physical safety and well-being of the servant: see *Smith* v *Baker* [1891] AC 325 and *Wilsons and Clyde Coal Co.* v *English* [1938] AC 57. No case has been cited in which it has been held to extend to protect the servant from economic loss. . . .

The law, however, requires the master to use all reasonable care to diminish any danger, if he cannot eliminate it: Glyn Jones J [1955] 1 AER 833 at 836; and, if he cannot effectively eliminate it so that significant risk remains, he may be required to give to the servant such information which he has to help the servant to evaluate properly the benefit of the job against the risk: see per Devlin LJ in *Withers* v *Perry Chain Co. Ltd* [1961] 1 WLR 1314 at 1320. The point was expressed more firmly some 24 years later by this court (Lawton, Fox and Robert Goff LJJ) in *White* v *Holbrook Precision Castings Ltd* [1985] IRLR 215 where, in upholding the dismissal of the plaintiff's claim on the facts, it was held that an employer had a duty to tell a prospective employee about the risks he would expose himself to if he took the job but the risks referred to were those to physical safety or well-being. Lawton LJ said at p. 218:

> Generally speaking, if a job has risks to health and safety which are not common knowledge but of which an employer knows or ought to know and against which he cannot guard by taking precautions, then he should tell anyone to whom he is offering a job what those risks are if, on the information then available to him, knowledge of those risks would be likely to affect the decision of a sensible, level-headed prospective employee about accepting the offer.

The position is, accordingly, that although the duty of a master to his servant may extend to warning him of unavoidable risks of physical injury, it has hitherto not been extended to the taking of reasonable care to protect the servant from economic loss. Apart from the cases of *Deyong* v *Sherburn* [1946] 1 KB 236and *Edwards* v *West Herts Hospital Management Committee* [1957] 1 WLR 415, which were mentioned in argument, we were not referred to any case in which the court has considered and rejected any such claim and no doubt the reason for that is not only the limitation of the duty, as stated, to personal safety but also the fact that it must be rare for any matter of economic loss to have been arguably caused by a breach of duty of the master without it being a breach of contract. If a servant is to have a claim in tort against his employer in respect of economic loss it must be based upon some special factor in the circumstances or in the relationship between them which justifies the extension of the scope of the duty to cover such a claim or upon a separate principle of the law of tort which imposes such a duty.

. . . The next submission, based upon the two cases of *Tai Hing Cotton Mill Ltd* [1986] AC 80 and *Greater Nottingham Co-operative Society Ltd* [1988] 3 WLR 396 was that, since there was between the parties the contract of employment, the plaintiff can only recover damages for economic loss if a term in that contract so provides and not in tort. It is necessary first to determine whether there was any implied term in the contract of employment to the effect that the defendants would give to the plaintiff all necessary advice relating to the special risk and would advise the plaintiff that he should himself obtain appropriate insurance cover. The alleged implied assumption of responsibility gave rise, it is alleged, to a similar duty.

In my judgment it is impossible to hold on the facts pleaded that an implied term arose on the particular relationship of this plaintiff to these defendants as his employers. The only facts are the offer and acceptance of the employment and the defendants' knowledge both of the circumstances in which the plaintiff would in Ethiopia be exposed to the special risk and of the plaintiff's ignorance of that risk. If the parties had been asked what the position was with reference to the risk of the plaintiff suffering injury in the course of his employment by the negligence of another driver, for whom the defendants were not responsible, and from whom the plaintiff could recover no damages, it is impossible to be confident, on the facts pleaded, that either side would have answered that the defendants had undertaken a duty to deal specifically with the matter, whether by advice or otherwise. Both parties must have expected and intended that the plaintiff and the defendants would respectively perform the express terms set out in the contract and would comply with any other obligations arising out of their mutual relationship as master and servant. As in *Lister* v *Romford Ice and Cold Storage Co. Ltd* (1957) AC 555, according to the view of the majority, Lord Simonds, Lord Morton and Lord Tucker, the term on which the plaintiff in this case claims to rely cannot, in my judgment, be implied as a term agreed between the two individuals, and, if it is to be implied at all, must be implied by law. That means that it is to be implied in any contract of employment where the master engages the servant to work abroad in a country where, in doing his work, the servant will face a special risk of the nature relied on in this case and the servant is to the knowledge of the master ignorant of that risk. It is clear, I think, that a new term can be implied by law into contracts of employment: the case of *Lister* v *Romford Ice* is an example of differing opinions held by judges as to whether a new term should on the facts be held to arise by law; and the majority in the House of Lords gave reasons to explain why on the evidence in that case the term then contended for could not be accepted.

It is, however, impossible, in my judgment, to imply in this case a term as a matter of law in the form contended for, namely a specific duty to advise the plaintiff to obtain specific insurance cover. Such a duty seems to me inappropriate for incorporation by law into all contracts of employment in the circumstances alleged. The length of time during which the servant will work abroad and the nature of his work may vary greatly between one job and another and hence the extent to which the servant would be exposed to the special risk. Further, having regard to the many different ways in which a servant working abroad may run the risk of uncompensated injury caused by the wrongdoing of a third party, apart from a traffic accident, it seems to me impossible to formulate the detailed terms in which the law could incorporate into the general relationship of master and servant a contractual obligation to the effect necessary to cover the plaintiff's claim. . . .

Square D Ltd v *Cook*
[1992] IRLR 34
Court of Appeal

Mr Cook was employed by Square D Ltd as a field service electronics engineer. In that position he was sent to Saudi Arabia for two months to complete the commissioning of four computer control systems and ensure that they were working correctly. The premises at which he was to carry out his duties were occupied by Aramco Overseas Co. and the main contractor was Fluor Arabia Ltd. A number of subcontractors were also employed on the site.

Mr Cook's work was carried out in a large control room where the units were installed. The floor consisted of tiles some two and a half feet square. The area beneath the floor contained the wires and cables which connected with the computers. By using a special tool, it was possible to lift the individual tiles to obtain access to that area.

Mr Cook had an accident whilst working on the premises. In what was in effect a relatively narrow corridor, one of the tiles had been lifted so that wiring work could be carried out and left in such a position that there were four sizable triangular holes. In attempting to avoid the holes. Mr Cook slipped and his foot became jammed in one of them. As a result, he suffered injuries to his knee which in due course required surgery. He subsequently claimed damages from his employers in respect of those injuries.

It was held, allowing the employers' appeal, that the duty on employers to take reasonable care for the safety of employees applies where the premises in which an employee is directed to work are occupied by the employer or by a third party. In the latter case, the extent of the employers' responsibility depends upon what is reasonable in all the circumstances. In this particular case it was casting too high a responsibility on home-based employers to hold them responsible for the daily events of a site in Saudi Arabia occupied by a third party.

FARQUHARSON LJ: It is clear that in determining an employer's responsibility one has to look at all the circumstances of the case, including the place where the work is to be done, the nature of the building on the site concerned (if there is a building), the experience of the employee who is so despatched to work at such a site, the nature of the work he is required to carry out, the degree of control that the employer can reasonably exercise in the circumstances, and the employer's own knowledge of the defective state of the premises, as referred to in that last passage of the speech of Lord Denning.

There is no doubt that it is an employer's duty to take all reasonable steps to ensure the safety of his employees in the course of their employment. That has been said again and again, including those cases which I have just cited. There is also no doubt that the duty cannot be delegated, but the authorities show that the considerations which I have just summarised must be taken into account when the employee is injured on premises in the occupation of a third party. As was pointed out in *Wilson's* [1938] AC 57 case, it depends on what is reasonable in all the circumstances.

. . .

In my judgment both the learned deputy judge and Mr Cobb cast far too high a responsibility on the employer. On the facts of the present case there was no delegation by the first defendant of its responsibility to either of the second or third defendants or indeed to anybody else. The first defendant was satisfied – indeed there is no contest – that the second and third defendants (the site occupiers and the general contractors) were both reliable companies and aware of their responsibility for the safety of workers on site. The suggestion that the home-based employer has any responsibility for the daily events of a site in Saudi Arabia has an air of unreality. Neither does it seem to me, as suggested by Mr Cobb, that there is a duty on the appellant to advise the other defendants of the need to take precautions against the kind of hazard encountered in the present case. Circumstances will, of course, vary, and it may be that in some cases where, for example, a number of employees are going to work on a foreign site or where one or two employees are called upon to work there for a very considerable period of time that an employer may be required to inspect the site and satisfy himself that the occupiers were conscious of their obligations concerning the safety of people working there. But one cannot prescribe any rules in this context. It will depend on the facts of individual cases. . . .

Employer's Liability (Compulsory Insurance) Act 1969

1. Insurance against liability for employees

(1) Except as otherwise provided by this Act, every employer carrying on any business in Great Britain shall insure, and maintain insurance, under one or more approved policies with an authorised insurer or insurers against liability for bodily injury or disease sustained by his employees, and arising out of and in the course of their employment in Great Britain in that business, but except in so far as regulations otherwise provide not including injury or disease suffered or contracted outside Great Britain.

Notes

1. The duty imposed on the employer is to take reasonable care in all the circumstances of the case, for the health and safety of each individual employee. The duty is not strict. Once the employer/employee relationship is established the duty comes into play. As can be seen from the case law, there is still some potential for developing the scope of the duty. Regard must also be had to the impact of this duty as an implied duty imposed on employers through the existence of the contract of employment. As *Johnstone's* case clearly illustrates, there may be circumstances where express terms have to be interpreted with reference to the implied duty.

The issue of working hours has been superseded to some extent by the Working Time Regulations 1998 (SI 1998/1833). However, there are specific exemptions under these Regulations, one of which relates to hospital staff including junior doctors. Johnstone would not, therefore, have been able to rely on the Regulations (see below).

2. As the tort is negligence-based, the burden is on the claimant to prove his case by establishing duty, breach and causation – the last two being subject to the established tests to be found in any text on negligence. Liability of the employer for nervous shock or psychiatric injury is based on the *ratio* of *Alcock* v *Chief Constable of South Yorkshire* [1992] AC 310 – see *McFarlane* v *EE Caledonia* [1994] 2 All ER 1.

The extension of the law to provide liability for psychiatric injury suffered by rescuers who give assistance at, or after, a disaster without coming within the range of foreseeable physical injury was discussed at length in *White and Others* v *Chief Constable of South Yorkshire Police* [1999] IRLR 110. It was concluded by the House of Lords, overturning the decision in *Frost* v *Chief Constable of South Yorkshire Police* [1997] IRLR 173, that such an extension was unnecessary and 'probably unacceptable to the ordinary person because it would offend against his notion of distributive justice'.

3. The tests for establishing the existence of an employer/employee relationship and the law relating to the loan of a servant can be found in Chapter 2;

see also Munkman J., *Employer's Liability,* 13th edn (London: Butterworths, 1996).
4. Where the disobedience of a fellow employee is a concurrent cause of the accident regard must be had to the decision in *ICI* v *Shatwell* [1965] AC 656.

Questions
1. If a statute authorises delegation by an employer, would he still be personally liable under employer's liability?
2. What is the significance of the relationship between the common law duty and any contractual duty?
3. Can an employee pursue a claim under this head where he sustains an injury through an inherent danger in the job?

(i) Competent Fellow Employees
In theory this aspect of the general duty of care is wider than the mere duty to provide employees with the ability to do the job, in that it encompasses the provision of supervision and training where necessary. In practice this aspect has been eroded by the principle of vicarious liability, with many claims being based on the fact that an employer is liable for the torts of his employees, avoiding the need to establish 'as a claim under this head must do' that the employer was aware or had notice of the 'incompetency' of the employee concerned.

Hudson v Ridge Manufacturing Co. Ltd
[1957] 2 QB 348
Queen's Bench Division

For nearly four years one of the defendants' employees had made a nuisance of himself to his fellow employees, including the plaintiff, a cripple, by persistently engaging in skylarking, such as tripping them up. Many times he had been reprimanded by the foreman and warned that he would hurt someone, but without effect. No further steps were taken to check this conduct by dismissal or otherwise. On 26 March 1954, this employee, indulging in horse-play, tripped up the plaintiff and injured him.
   It was held that as the potentially dangerous misbehaviour had been known to the employers for a long time, and as they had failed to prevent it or remove the source of it they were liable for failing to take reasonable care for their employee's safety.

STREATFEILD J: This is an unusual case, because the particular form of lack of care by the employers alleged is that they failed to maintain discipline and to take proper steps to put an end to this skylarking which might lead to injury at some time in the future. As it seems to me, the matter is covered not by authority so much as principle. It is the duty of employers, for the safety of their employees, to have reasonably safe plant and machinery. It is their duty to have premises which are similarly reasonably safe. It is their duty to have a reasonably safe system of work. It is their duty to employ reasonably competent fellow workmen. All of those duties exist at common law for the safety of the workmen, and if, for instance, it is found that a piece of plant or part of the premises is not reasonably safe, it is the duty of the employers to cure it, to make it safe and to remove that source of danger. In the same way, if the system of working is found, in practice, to be beset with dangers it is the duty of the employers to evolve a reasonably safe system of working so as to obviate those dangers, and upon principle it seems to me that if, in fact, a fellow workman is not merely incompetent but, by his habitual conduct, is likely to prove a source of danger to his fellow employees, a duty lies fairly and squarely on the employers to remove that source of danger.

I agree with Mr Hodgson, for the defendants, that it is a matter of degree. Nobody would say that if Chadwick had merely tripped somebody up for the first time and had been at once reprimanded by the foreman and then did not do it again, that was such conduct, on an isolated occasion by a man, as would put upon the employers the duty of taking the extreme course of dismissing that workman in case he should do it again. Most people, if they are told not to do a thing, will carry out that instruction. In the same way, nobody would say that employers, after one or perhaps two experiences of that kind, would foresee that danger was likely to result from that particular sort of conduct. . . .

. . . In my judgment, therefore, the injury was sustained as a result of the defendants' failure to take proper steps to put an end to that conduct, to see that it would not happen again and, if it did happen again, to remove the source of it. It was for that reason that this injury resulted.

(ii) Safe Place of Work

'Safe place of work' covers not only the structure and substance of the premises but also any workplace in or on which an employee may be expected to work. In *Bradford v Robinson Rentals Ltd* [1967] 1 All ER 267, for example, a van was found to be a place of work. Whether the place of work is reasonably safe will depend on the circumstances and the nature of the place.

Latimer v AEC Ltd
[1953] AC 643
House of Lords

During an unusually heavy rainstorm the floors of a large factory were flooded and an oily cooling mixture, normally contained in a channel in the floor, along which it was pumped to machinery, rose and mixed with the flood waters, so that, when they subsided the floor became slippery. So far as supplies permitted, sawdust was spread on the floor, but some areas were left untreated. A workman, working in a gangway which had not been treated with sawdust, was attempting to load a heavy barrel on to a trolley when he slipped and injured his ankle. He brought an action against his employers, claiming damages in respect of his injuries.

It was held that the employer had not failed in his duty to provide a safe place of work as he had taken the appropriate steps which a reasonably prudent employer would have taken in the circumstances.

ASQUITH LJ: . . . At common law the question can only be whether, having regard to the nature and extent of the risk created by the slippery patches on the floor, a reasonably careful employer would have suspended all work in this 15-acre factory and sent the night shift home: or whether, having done all he could (and did) do with the sawdust at his disposal, the 40 production service men in the afternoon, and the 24 volunteers between the end of the day shift and the beginning of the night shift, he would have allowed the work to proceed. The learned trial judge concluded that a reasonable employer would have closed down. I agree with practically everything else he said in a most careful judgment. But, of course, this conclusion was crucial. In considering it one cannot but be impressed by the following considerations: (a) it was nowhere specifically pleaded in the statement of claim that the works should have been closed down; (b) no witness for the plaintiff suggested that this should have been done; (c) no question was put to any witness for the defence to that effect; (d) no evidence was directed to the question, which on this issue was fundamental, what degree of dislocation or complication a complete stoppage would have entailed; (e) the point was first taken, after the evidence was closed, by the learned judge himself during the final speech of one of the counsel.

In these circumstances I agree with the observations of Singleton LJ:

> If the test is, as I believe, what would a reasonable employer have done in those circumstances, I fail to see that the employers committed any breach of the duty which they owed, and I fail to see, too, any evidence on which to base a finding that the employers were negligent in not closing down.

What evidence the learned judge had before him suggests to my mind that the degree of risk was too small to justify, let alone require, closing down. The evidence of the plaintiff himself at p. 13C of the appendix to the case is that 'you always get a certain amount of grease about.' Ampstead, his fellow worker, says exactly the same at p. 28H, adding that on 'numerous occasions' (four or five times) he had seen 'mystic' well up from the channels in the floor of the factory owing to flooding. Yet the plaintiff says (at p. 15A) that except for the accident to himself on this occasion in August, he has never known any accident happen to anyone in the factory through these causes. I cannot resist the conclusion that on this occasion, notwithstanding the extent of the flooding, tile risk was inconsiderable, and that the learned judge's conclusion cannot stand. . . .

(iii)   Safe plant and equipment

This involves the provision and maintenance of proper and suitable plant and equipment. To satisfy the duty the employer must not only provide and select the appropriate plant and equipment for that particular job, but also ensure that it is kept in good order. In practice this duty has been put into statutory form by the Employer's Liability (Defective Equipment) Act 1969.

Employer's Liability (Defective Equipment) Act 1969

1.   Extension of employer's liability for defective equipment

(1)   Where after the commencement of this Act—

(a)   an employee suffers personal injury in the course of his employment in consequence of a defect in equipment provided by his employer for the purposes of the employer's business; and

(b)   the defect is attributable wholly or partly to the fault of a third party (whether identified or not), the injury shall be deemed to be also attributable to negligence on the part of the employer (whether or not he is liable in respect of the injury apart from this subsection), but without prejudice to the law relating to contributory negligence and to any remedy by way of contribution or in contract or otherwise which is available to the employer in respect of the injury.

(2) In so far as any agreement purports to exclude or limit any liability of an employer arising under subsection (1) of this section, the agreement shall be void.

(iv) Safe System of Work

In many respects this is the most nebulous duty as its remit is ill-defined. It clearly requires the employer to assess the health and safety hazards of a particular job or task, i.e. the lay-out, method of work and general working conditions, with a view to providing the necessary instructions, training, supervision, warnings and safety equipment to minimise the risks identified. It is a question of fact in each case whether the system devised is sufficient to discharge the duty.

Bux v *Slough Metals Ltd*
[1973] 1 WLR 1358
Court of Appeal

The plaintiff, a die-caster, was employed by the defendants on piece-work in their die-casting foundry. His work consisted of melting ingots of aluminium alloy in a furnace, lifting out the molten metal with a ladle and pouring it into a die. No goggles had been provided during his training or for some two months after he started work. They were then supplied and the plaintiff was told to wear them at work. He found that they misted up, told his superintendent that they were useless and stopped wearing them. No member of the management sought to persuade him to wear them. He had been thus employed for a year when some molten metal splashed up and as a result he lost the sight of one eye and to a large extent of the other. He claimed for breach of statutory duty as well as of the common law duty for failure to instruct him to wear goggles and ensure they were worn.

It was held, allowing the plaintiff's appeal, that the statutory regulations did not supersede the employer's common law duty to take reasonable care for the safety of his employees. Depending upon the facts of each case, this duty could extend to instructing, persuading or insisting on the use of protective equipment.

EDMUND-DAVIES LJ: The question of whether instruction or persuasion or even insistence in using protective equipment should be resorted to is, therefore, at large, the answer depending on the facts of the particular case. One of the most important of these is the nature and degree of the risk of serious harm resulting if it is not worn. Counsel for the defendants retorts that the plaintiff's own evidence showed that he regarded the risk as obvious and that accordingly no further instruction was called for, any more than, as this court held, it was reasonably to be expected on the facts of *Wilson* v *Tyneside Window Cleaning Co.* [1958] 2 All ER 265 where this court drew a distinction between cases where the risk is obvious and those where it is insidious and hidden. I find it difficult to deal with this aspect of the case without also considering the question of causation, for counsel for the defendants submits that the plaintiff's failure to use what the judge held to be suitable goggles indicates that the probability is that he would never have worn them, however much the employers tried (at the risk, testified to by the witnesses, of losing all their die-casters) to establish a rule that they must be. He therefore submitted that, even were there any obligation on the employers to exhort the plaintiff to wear his type 1 goggles, the irresistible inference here – as in *Cummings (or McWilliams) v Sir William Arrol & Co. Ltd* [1962] 1 All ER 623 – was that the plaintiff would not have worn them.

I have found these the most difficult aspects of a somewhat troublesome case. But, basing himself on Mr Bevan's evidence that the prudent employer 'would not do nothing', the learned judge held negligence established. Having seen the type of man the plaintiff is and heard him, and despite his rejection of the plaintiff's evidence on several important points, the judge went on to say:

> He was not the type of man who would have disregarded instructions if they were given personally and in a reasonable and firm manner and were followed up by supervision. I think he would have followed instructions and persistent advice. He was in no way a difficult or obstinate person.

And, as Stamp LJ pointed out during counsel's submissions, a reminder that all die-casters who disobeyed reg. 13(4) were liable to be prosecuted could have fortified the employers' exhortation most effectively. The learned judge held that the plaintiff had discharged the onus of establishing on the balance of probabilities that he would have worn goggles had the sort of system the judge described been instituted and followed. Whether I should have come to the same conclusion I cannot say, so much depending on the view formed by the court of the particular workman who was the plaintiff. This court is in a far less advantageous position in that respect than was Kerr J, and the conclusion I have come to is that we ought not to disturb his finding that the claim in common law succeeds.

Walker v Northumberland County Council
[1995] IRLR 35
Queen's Bench Division

Mr Walker was employed by the Council as an area social services officer, with responsibility for four teams of field workers. His immediate superior was Mr Davison.

The volume of work to be undertaken by Mr Walker and his team gradually rose, but there was no corresponding increase in staffing levels. From 1985 onwards, Mr Walker and others produced reports and memoranda concerning the urgent need to alleviate the work pressures and calling for redistribution of staff or reorganisation. In 1986, Mr Walker suffered a nervous breakdown. Before returning to work in March 1987 he discussed his position with Mr Davison who agreed to provide him with assistance. However, within a month of his return to work, assistance was withdrawn. In September 1987 he suffered a second mental breakdown, and in February 1988 he was dismissed on grounds of permanent ill health.

It was held that the defendants were in breach of the duty of care owed to the plaintiff as his employer in respect of the second mental breakdown which he suffered as a result of stress and anxiety occasioned by his job.

COLEMAN J: . . . There has been little judicial authority on the extent to which an employer owes to his employees a duty not to cause them psychiatric damage by the volume or character of the work which the employees are required to perform. It is clear law that an employer has a duty to provide his employee with a reasonably safe system of work and to take reasonable steps to protect him from risks which are reasonably foreseeable. Whereas the law on the extent of this duty has developed almost exclusively in cases involving physical injury to the employee as distinct from injury to his mental health, there is no logical reason why risk of psychiatric damage should be excluded from the scope of an employer's duty of care or from the co-extensive implied term in the contract of employment. That said, there can be no doubt that the circumstances in which claims based on such damage are likely to arise will often give rise to extremely difficult evidential problems of foreseeability and causation. This is particularly so in the environment of the professions where the plaintiff may be ambitious and dedicated, determined to succeed in his career in which he knows the work to be demanding, and may have a measure of discretion as to how and when and for how long he works, but where the character or volume of the work given to him eventually drives him to breaking point. Given that the professional work is intrinsically demanding and stressful, at what point is the employer's duty to take protective steps engaged? What assumption is he entitled to make about the employee's resilience, mental toughness and stability of character, given that people of clinically normal personality may have a widely differing ability to absorb stress attributable to their work?

. . .

In the result, it is established that by April 1987 Mr Walker was exposed in his job to a reasonably foreseeable risk to his mental health which materially exceeded the risk to be anticipated in the ordinary course of an area officer's job. Was it in those circumstances reasonable for the council to take action to alleviate or remove that risk? In my view, the only course which would have had a reasonable probability of preventing another mental breakdown was the provision of continuous or at least substantial backup for Mr Walker in the Blyth office from Mr Robinson or somebody of equal experience who could in effect have acted as Mr Walker's deputy. However, in deciding what was reasonable conduct I must have regard to the acute staffing problems which at the relevant time confronted the council.

. . .

In my judgment the policy decision/operational decision dichotomy has no more part to play in the context of the duty of care to an employee with whom a statutory body has a contract of employment than it would have in the context of any other contract made by such a body. Just as it would be no defence to a claim for non-performance of a contract for the sale of goods that the local authority had resolved as a matter of policy that the use of its scarce resources for the performance of the contract was inexpedient, so it would be no defence to a claim for breach of the implied term in a contract of employment that the employer would exercise reasonable care for the safety of his employee that its failure to do so was the result of a policy decision on the exercise of its statutory powers. Since the scope of the duty of care owed to an employee to take reasonable steps to provide a safe system of work is co-extensive with the scope of the implied term as to the employee's safety in the contract of employment, see for example, *Johnstone* v *Bloomsbury Health Authority* [1991] IRLR 118, to introduce a ring fence round policy decisions giving rise to unsafe systems of work for the purposes of claims in tort which was not available to the defendant statutory body in defences to claims in contract would be to implant into employment law a disparity which, in my judgment, would be wholly wrong in principle. Whereas the mutual intention to be imputed to the parties to a contract of employment with a public body could be expected to qualify the employer's duty of safety by requiring the employer to do no more than take reasonable steps to procure the employee's safety at work, it is inconceivable that such mutual intention would require the employer to take only such steps for the employee's safety as political expediency from time to time permitted if the exercise of statutory powers were involved. In the absence of authority to the contrary or of compelling common law principle, there can be no sustainable basis for subjecting the duty of care in tort to such a qualification.

That said, the duty of an employer public body, whether in contract or tort, to provide a safe system of work is, as I have said, a duty only to do what is reasonable, and in many cases it may be necessary to take into account decisions which are within the policy-making area and the reasons for those decisions in order to test whether the body's conduct has been reasonable. In that exercise there can be no basis for treating the public body differently in *principle* from any other commercial employer, although there would have to be taken into account considerations such as budgetary constraints and perhaps lack of flexibility of decision-taking which might not arise with a commercial employer.

Having regard to the reasonably foreseeable size of the risk of repetition of Mr Walker's illness if his duties were not alleviated by effective additional assistance and to the reasonably foreseeable gravity of the mental breakdown which might result if nothing were done, I have come to the conclusion that the standard of care to be expected of a reasonable local authority required that in March 1987 such additional assistance should be provided, if not on a permanent basis, at least until restructuring of the social services had been effected and the workload on Mr Walker thereby permanently reduced. That measure of additional assistance ought to have been provided, notwithstanding that it could be expected to have some disruptive effect on the council's provision of services to the public. When Mr Walker returned from his first illness the council had to decide whether it was prepared to go on employing him in spite of the fact that he had made it sufficiently clear that he must have effective additional help if he was to continue at Blyth Valley. It chose to continue to employ him, but provided no effective help. In so doing it was, in my judgment, acting unreasonably and therefore in breach of its duty of care.

I understand it to be accepted that if there was breach of duty, damage was caused by that breach. However, in view of the fact that I have decided this case on the second breakdown alone, it is right to add that I am satisfied on the evidence that had the further assistance been provided to Mr Walker, his second breakdown would probably not have occurred.

Pickford v *Imperial Chemical Industries plc*
[1998] IRLR 435
House of Lords

Miss Pickford was engaged by ICI in January 1984 as a full-time secretary at their Pharmaceutical Division in Macclesfield. She acted as secretary to three section managers and a part-time consultant and was also available to do typing work for a number of other members of staff. She planned and organised her own workload and was recognised as being a very conscientious worker producing an excellent standard of work.

When preparing a job assessment in November 1986, Miss Pickford estimated that she spent 50 per cent of her seven and a half hour working day on typing, which she did on a word processor, and the remaining 50 per cent on other secretarial duties, such as answering the telephone and arranging travel and meetings for those for whom she acted as secretary. However, the typing work gradually increased so that by the end of 1988, she maintained that it was taking up as much as 75 per cent of her time.

According to an entry in her diary for 23 May 1989, it was in late 1988 that she began to experience strange feelings in her hands by the end of the week, but they recovered with rest over the weekend and she did not think that there was anything seriously wrong. The condition then became more acute and on 25 May she went to see her doctor. On examination he found no abnormality. Later that month she was seen by the works' doctor. He also could find no physical signs on examination but after a further consultation expressed the opinion that her complaints and symptoms were caused by excessive typing and recommended that she be redeployed. Her GP then referred her to an orthopaedic surgeon who told her that her symptoms were work-related but there was nothing he could do for her and she should either put up with it or get another job.

After seeing one of their publications, Miss Pickford contacted the Repetitive Strain Injury Association. On their recommendation, she was seen by a number of specialists, only one of whom suggested that her condition might not be related to or caused by her typing but more psychological in origin.

Eventually, the condition rendered her incapable of working as a secretary. She tried working as a filing clerk but her hands became sore and painful after three days and she could not continue. The employers were unable to offer her alternative work and her employment was terminated on 14 September 1990. She subsequently made a claim for damages against her former employers.

It was held that the deputy High Court judge had been entitled to hold that the cramp in her hand which the plaintiff secretary suffered had not been caused by repetitive movement of the fingers while typing for long periods without proper breaks or rest pauses, as opposed to being associated with it. The majority of the Court of Appeal had erred in reversing that decision.

LORD HOPE OF CRAIGHEAD: . . . **The medical issues**
The judge described the three issues which fall under this heading in this way: firstly, whether PDA4, cramp of the hand due to repetitive movements, has an organic cause; secondly, whether the respondent has had PDA4; and thirdly, if she has had it, whether her PDA4 has an organic cause. I have placed them all under the heading of medical issues. But it is clear from his judgment that the judge was unable to resolve all of them without taking account of a substantial body of evidence from the lay witnesses about the work which the respondent was doing during the critical period.

As to the first issue, the judge said that the most that he could find on the whole of the medical evidence was that the condition of cramp of the hand due to repetitive movements may have an organic cause or a psychogenic cause or a combination of both causes, and that this was a matter for the court to consider on the evidence before it in each case. In the Court of Appeal Stuart-Smith LJ described this conclusion as entirely unexceptional. But he then went on to make some comments about the state of the controversy which reveal that his approach to it was very different from the position of neutrality which the judge had decided to adopt at this stage in his examination of the evidence.

. . .

This difference of view between the majority in the Court of Appeal and the judge on this initial question has an important bearing on the way in which, from different starting points, they approached the other issues in the light of the medical evidence. I do not think that I am being unfair to the majority when I say that it seems to me that they were, from the outset, sceptical about the suggestion that the condition was anything other than organic in origin. The judge, on the other hand, was much more circumspect. As to the second issue, he was careful to say that, while he was disposed to find that the respondent had a cramp of the hand, he was not satisfied that it was due to the repetitive movements of typing in the sense that such movements were an effective cause of it. His choice of words was important, because PDA4 has been defined as 'cramp of the hand due to repetitive movements'. To accept without qualification that her cramp was PDA4 might be taken as resolving the next issue, as to whether there was an organic cause in this case. That, the most controversial medical issue in the case, the judge wished to examine separately. The majority in the Court of Appeal said that the judge had concluded, without saying so, that the respondent had PDA4. They omitted to add the qualification which the judge had made. By implication they were criticising his finding as lacking in clarity. I think that they were wrong to do so, as the judge made it clear that the question whether this was cramp due to repetitive movements was one which, at this stage, was still unresolved. Their difference of view from the judge on this point provides the explanation for the further and more fundamental differences between them about the proper approach to be taken to the third issue.

The judge said, in regard to the third issue as to the cause of the cramp, that the appellants did not have to satisfy him that the cause was psychogenic: the onus was on the respondent to establish that the cause was organic. Stuart-Smith LJ said ([1996] IRLR 622, at 626, 31) that this was a misdirection:

> Having established that she had PDA4 there were two alternative explanations for it advanced by the medical experts. One, supported by the evidence of Mr Stanley and Dr Hay, was that it was organic; the other, supported by Dr Lucire, that it was psychogenic being a conversion hysteria. No other hysterical or psychogenic explanation was advanced. It seems to me that what the judge had to do was simply to decide upon the evidence which of these two explanations was the most likely. In the result the judge said that he was not satisfied that it was organic: therefore by inference it must be psychogenic; but he did not accept Dr Lucire's explanation that is was conversion hysteria.

The position which the judge reached after reviewing the medical evidence was that he was unable to decide on that evidence alone whether the organic explanation was the more probable. That was why, after saying what he did about onus, he proceeded to examine the other evidence in order to see whether the onus had been satisfied. This included the respondent's evidence, some of which he thought was exaggerated, and the evidence of two ergonomists. They were agreed that repetitive movements were unlikely to cause injury unless accompanied by other factors, none of which were found by the judge to have been present in this case, He also took into account the findings which he had made about the speed, duration and amount of the respondent's typing work after testing her evidence against that of other witnesses for whom she worked during the critical period. It was only after completing this review and making his findings in the light of all this other evidence that he reached his decision that the respondent had failed to satisfy him that her cramp had been caused by the typing work.

. . .

Foreseeability and negligence

The judge held that it was not reasonably foreseeable, in the state of knowledge about the condition in 1988 and 1989, that the work which the respondent was required to do as a secretary would be likely to cause her to contract PDA4. As he put it, while it was technically foreseeable that a typist might suffer from this condition, it was not reasonably foreseeable that this would happen to a secretary who was typing to the extent which he found established by the evidence. He also held that the respondent had not established the grounds on which she had claimed that the appellants were negligent.

In her particulars of negligence, the respondent had alleged that the appellants were negligent because they had failed .to warn her of the risk of developing the condition from typing at a fast speed all day without respite apart from her lunch break. At the trial, the allegation was that they had failed to take steps to ensure that she was given the same instruction, warnings and advice as were given to the typists in the accounts department. The judge did not think that the appellants were under a duty to prescribe for the respondent rest periods from her typing work, as she had ample non-typing secretarial work to intersperse with it. He said that her work lent itself naturally to rotation and interspersement. He pointed out that the respondent herself had rejected the notion that a regime might be imposed upon her which, as a secretary and not a typist, she would have regarded as unsuitable. This was, he said, a matter of common sense. He rejected the allegation that a warning should have been given to her, on the grounds that the condition was uncommon and, on the evidence, very rare in the case of typists, that it was not the practice in the industry to give such a warning and that to do this, in the case of such a vague condition which was not easily identifiable, might well be counterproductive.

Notes

1. Whether the employer has fulfilled the duty to provide competent employees will depend on the knowledge he has about the employee concerned, i.e. his work record, whether he is a known practical joker etc. Where the employer has this knowledge there is a foreseeable risk of injury and the employer may be liable if an accident occurs (*Coddington* v *International Harvester Co. of Great Britain Ltd* [1969] KIR 146; *O'Reilley* v *National Tramway Appliances* [1966] 1 All ER 499). Even where there is no primary liability on the part of the employer the employer may still be found to be vicariously liable for the tortious actions of one of his employees in respect of an accident to a fellow employee (*Harrison* v *Michelin Tyres Ltd* [1985] 1 All ER 918 and *Aldred* v *Nacanco* [1987] IRLR 292).

2. The provision and maintenance of a safe place of work extends to access as well as to egress and ingress. There is an overlap with the Occupiers Liability Act 1957 which covers visitors in general, employees falling within

this interpretation. However, the duty in the statute is to take reasonable care to ensure that the visitor is reasonably safe (s. 2(2)), not the premises.

3.   Protecting staff from the risks of passive smoking falls within the heading of a safe place of work – see *Waltons and Morse* v *Dorrington* [1997] IRLR 489, in which it was stated that there is an 'implied term that the employer will provide and monitor for employees, so far as is reasonably practicable, a working environment which is reasonably suitable for the performance by them of their contractual duties. This extends to the right of an employee not to be required to sit in a smoke-filled atmosphere'.

The Health and Safety Commission (HSC) is considering the possibility of introducing an approved Code of Practice on passive smoking at work.

4.   Whether the provision of equipment alone will suffice to fulfil the duty to provide safe plant and equipment is doubtful as the duty requires some positive action on the part of the employer, i.e. he should ensure that the equipment is sufficient and suitable to meet the demands of the job (*Machray* v *Stewarts & Lloyds Ltd* [1964] 3 All ER 716). There is some overlap with the duty to provide a safe system of work in that again it may not suffice to make equipment available without giving instructions as to its use (*Crouch* v *British Rail Engineering Ltd* [1988] IRLR 404). This depends on the facts of each case. The maintenance of plant is also of importance. The duty extends to routine, regular safety checks and necessary replacement of defective equipment (*Pearce* v *Round Oaks Steel Works Ltd* [1969] 3 All ER 680).

5.   A ship was held to be 'equipment' falling within the provisions of the Employer's Liability (Defective Equipment) Act 1969 (see *Coltman* v *Bibby Tankers Ltd* [1988] AC 276). 'Equipment' also includes 'materials', according to the Court of Appeal in *Knowles* v *Liverpool City Council* [1993] IRLR 588, in determining that flagstones were covered by the Employer's Liability (Defective Equipment) Act 1969.

6.   A safe system of work requires an assessment by the employer of a wide variety of activities, e.g. the way in which a job is done, precautions to be taken, instruction and training, supervision, warning notices, protective clothing. If the risks of injury are high then a greater standard of care is demanded of the employer (*Paris* v *Stepney Borough Council* [1951] 1 All ER 42; *Nolan* v *Dental Manufacturing Co. Ltd* [1958] 2 All ER 449. However, where the risk is obvious and the foreseeable injury not serious the employer may fulfil the duty by doing no more than providing equipment as opposed to ensuring its use (*Qualcast (Wolverhampton) Ltd* v *Haynes* [1959] AC 743). The system of work extends to protecting the employee from acts of violence if there is a foreseeable risk given the nature of the task (*Charlton* v *The Forrest Printing Ink Co. Ltd* [1978] IRLR 559). A further development relating to claims for work related upper limb disorder can be seen from the decision in *Alexander* v *Midland Bank plc* [1999] IRLR 724. The CA concluded that where upper limb disorder is physical rather than psychogenic in origin and can be linked to an unsafe system at work, a personal injury claim will succeed.

7.   In *Lancaster* v *Birmingham CC* (unreported 5 July 1999) the county court awarded damages of £67,000 for mental injury as a result of work-related

stress. Whilst this case did not break legal ground *per se*, it was the first time an employer had admitted liability. The employee in this case was able to establish each element of the negligence claim against her employer and show that she had a recognised illness, which was caused by the work-related stress. As Ms Lancaster had persistently asked for training and administrative support, which had not been forthcoming, she was able to show that the injury was foreseeable.

Questions
1. Will a practical joke by an employee against a fellow employee render the employer vicariously liable, or will he have primary liability?
2. How far does the duty to provide a safe place of work apply to the employee while he is working away from his employer's premises? See *Wilson v Tyneside Window Cleaning Co.* [1958] 2 QB 110.
3. What are the limitations of the Employer's Liability (Defective Equipment) Act 1969, and how may they be overcome by the Consumer Protection Act 1987?

(v)   Breach of Duty
The standard of care in assessing whether there has been a breach of duty is that of the reasonably prudent employer. Numerous cases may be found in any textbook or casebook on tort containing a chapter on employer's liability. However, the following cases add weight to the rule that the 'disabled', 'inexperienced' or 'disadvantaged' claimant is owed an increased standard of care and furthermore that employers should be aware of their employees' inadequacies.

James v Hepworth & Grandage Ltd
[1968] 1 QB 94
Court of Appeal

The plaintiff was a Jamaican immigrant who could not read or write. The defendants, his employers, did not know of, and had no reason to be aware of his illiteracy. He had been employed by them for three-and-a-half years when he applied to work in their foundry as a metal spinner. He was given a four-week course of training, after which he worked for six months as a metal spinner. He was supplied with safety goggles, gloves and boots but had never been told anything about safety spats. His work as metal spinner involved pouring molten metal into a channel or guide so as to feed it into a rotating or spinning machine. There were two prominent notices in the workshop stating that goggles, safety spats, gloves and aprons were available to all employees free of charge and should be worn for their personal safety. Although the plaintiff knew that the notices were there, he never paused to inquire of his fellow-workmen what the notices said. Some 24 men were employed in the workshop, of whom only two wore safety spats: the remainder considered them inconvenient, uncomfortable and no safer than trousers.

While the plaintiff was pouring molten metal from a ladle into the guide
to feed into the machine there was a splash of molten metal, as a result of
which he burnt his right foot and leg.

It was held, allowing the defendants' appeal, that there was no duty on
the employers to ascertain whether their employees were literate where they
had no reason to believe otherwise. They had therefore fulfilled their duty
by making spats available to the plaintiff and displaying notices urging the
wearing of spats.

SELLERS LJ: . . . The employers did not know, and I cannot see any reason why they
should have known, that the workman could not read. For the four years he had been
in the factory that apparently had been undetected. He could speak and understand,
and no one had noticed that he was not able to communicate in the ordinary way.

It is on that aspect of the case that the judge found in the workman's favour. The
judge found that the spats were provided – there is no doubt that they were available
– but he thought that the workman was in a peculiar position because of his illiteracy;
and because of that the judge discriminated in his favour. In my view, that was to
impose a higher standard and a greater duty of care than the common law requires.
The employers gave adequate notice of the availability of the spats to those working
in the factory by reason of that particular notice-board. Not only that: the position in
the factory was that there were probably, at the most, some 24 people, sometimes less,
working there and the majority did not wear spats; on the other hand, at least two
men did. The spats, which have not been produced on appeal, although they should
have been (having been exhibited in the court below), are of such a distinctive type
that nobody could be unaware that they were a form of protective clothing. The
workman was there: they were available for him to see them and he said that he had
seen them, and I cannot think that they did not convey to his mind that that was yet
another item of clothing which he could have had if he wished it. He could have made
some inquiry about it. In fact, he provided himself with the safety boots, and he was
supplied with goggles and gloves.
. . .

Assuming that there had been a breach of duty, the question would then arise: if
everything had been done that could possibly have been done, if individual attention
had been given to the workman and he had been asked to make his choice expressly
whether he would wear spats or not, what are the probabilities as to what he would
have done? Looking at the evidence as charitably as I can, and having regard to what
others were doing and the fact that the workman himself did not inquire as to what
the notice, which was there, said and whether it had anything to do with him or his
work, and did not make any inquiries of his fellow-workmen who were wearing spats
as to what they were for and why they wore them, and having regard to the large
number who did not wish to wear spats, I think that on the probabilities that it is
unlikely that the workman would have been wearing spats at the time. In those
circumstances, there can be no claim for damages in the present case.

Pape v *Cumbria County Council*
[1991] IRLR 463
Court of Appeal

Mrs Pape was employed by Cumbria County Council as a cleaner. Her
work involved regular use of chemical cleaning materials and detergents.

The cleaners were provided with rubber gloves but they rarely used them. At no time were they warned of the dangers of irritant contact dermatitis arising from frequent contact of the skin with chemical cleaners. Nor were they warned to avoid such contact by wearing gloves or directed to wear gloves in the course of their duties.

In 1982, after working as a cleaner for the council for a number of years. Mrs Pape began suffering from eczema on her hands and wrists. When her condition did not improve, she was referred to a consultant dermatologist. He diagnosed a primary irritant dermatitis and advised her in future to always protect her hands at work by wearing cotton gloves under rubber gloves.

On her return to work. Mrs Pape followed that advice but the eczema on her hands remained active and then started spreading to her face. Eventually, the condition became so serious and so widespread that she was admitted to hospital for an intensive course of treatment. She subsequently developed erythroderma, a generalised inflammatory condition affecting the entire skin. After a lengthy period of treatment, that condition cleared up but the medical prognosis was that her eczema would persist.

At the onset of the aggravated symptoms, the consultant dermatologist told Mrs Pape that in his view her problems were caused by something at work. He advised her to give up her job and her employment was terminated on grounds of ill health in November 1986.

It was held that the plaintiff was entitled to damages from the defendants in respect of the dermatitis which resulted from exposure of her hands to chemical cleaning agents during the course of her employment as a cleaner.

WAITE J: . . . The dangers of dermatitis or acute eczema from the sustained exposure of unprotected skin to chemical cleansing agents is well known, well enough known to make it the duty of a reasonable employer to appreciate the risks it presents to members of his cleaning staff but at the same time not so well known as to make it obvious to his staff without any necessity for warning or instruction.

There was a duty on the defendants to warn their cleaners of the dangers of handling chemical cleaning materials with gloves at all times. It is common ground that no such warning or instruction was given and that is sufficient to place the defendants in breach of their duty of care. . . .

(vi) Course of Employment
The duty of care is owed only while the employee is acting within the course of his employment, i.e. doing the job he is employed to do or something reasonably incidental to it (see *Davidson* v *Handley-Page Ltd* [1945] 1 All ER 235).

Smith v *Stages & Darlington Insulation Co. Ltd*
[1989] IRLR 177
House of Lords

Mr Machin was employed by Darlington Insulation as a lagger at Drakelow Power Station. He and Mr Stages were instructed to go and carry out urgent work at a power station in Pembroke. A normal working day, Monday 22 August 1977, was set aside for their journey to Pembroke; they were paid their normal wages for an eight-hour day and in addition they each received the equivalent of the rail fare as travelling expenses. The employers made no direction as to the means by which the men should travel and they decided to go in Mr Stages' car.

The work at Pembroke was to start at 8.30a.m. on Tuesday 23 August 1977 and had to be completed by 8.30a.m. the following Monday. Since there was still a great deal of work to be done by the time the weekend arrived, both men worked about 13 hours on the Saturday. Between 8.30a.m. on the Sunday and 8.30a.m. Monday, they worked a total of 19 hours without sleep. Consequently, they were entitled to eight hours' sleeping time on the Monday, which happened to be a bank holiday for which they were also paid holiday time. They were then entitled to be paid for a further eight hours to cover the journey home, plus travelling expenses. They were required to report for their usual work at Drakelow at 8.00a.m. on Wednesday 31 August 1977.

Instead of taking time to rest, however, Mr Machin and Mr Stages set off immediately for home on the Monday morning. In the course of that journey, an accident occurred due to Mr Stages' negligence, brought on by fatigue, which resulted in Mr Machin receiving injuries which prevented him from ever working again.

It was held, dismissing the employers' appeal, that the car journey between the employees' temporary place of employment and their homes was undertaken in the 'course of employment'. An employee who is paid wages to travel in his employer's time from his residence to a workplace other than his regular place of work prima facie will be acting in the course of his employment during that journey.

LORD LOWRY: . . . The judge went on:

The allowance in working hours and pay for such hours for travelling does not, in my view, necessarily bring such travel within the ambit of a man's work.

Not *necessarily,* it may be but the payment of wages makes a prima facie case which is uncontradicted. It is, moreover, important that the employers (who had 20 or 30 men engaged at Drakelow) 'withdrew' the deceased and Stages from there and 'sent them to Pembroke'. They were paid eight hours' travelling time there and back as well as eight hours' sleeping time. They were not regarded as having a day off when travelling but were 'receiving time'. The employers knew that they were travelling in Stages' car and were paying their wages during the time spent travelling to Pembroke and back. All this is taken directly from the employers' evidence.

. . .

The paramount rule is that an employee travelling on the highway will be acting in the course of his employment if, and only if, he is at the material time going about his employer's business. One must not confuse the duty to turn up for one's work with the concept of already being 'on duty' while travelling to it.

It is impossible to provide for every eventuality and foolish, without the benefit of argument, to make the attempt, but some prima facie propositions may be stated with reasonable confidence.

1. An employee travelling from his ordinary residence to his regular place of work, whatever the means of transport and even if it is provided by the employer, is not on duty and is not acting in the course of his employment, but, if he is obliged by his contract of service to use the employer's transport, he will normally, in the absence of an express condition to the contrary, be regarded as acting in the course of his employment while doing so.

2. Travelling in the employer's time between workplaces (one of which may be the regular workplace) or in the course of a peripatetic occupation, whether accompanied by goods or tools or simply in order to reach a succession of workplaces (as an inspector of gas meters might do), will be in the course of the employment.

3. Receipt of wages (though not receipt of a travelling allowance) will indicate that the employee is travelling in the employer's time and for his benefit and is acting in the course of his employment, and in such a case the fact that the employee may have discretion as to the mode and time of travelling will not take the journey out of the course of his employment.

4. An employee travelling *in the employer's time* from his ordinary residence to a workplace other than his regular workplace or in the course of a peripatetic occupation or to the scene of an emergency (such as a fire, an accident or a mechanical breakdown of plant) will be acting in the course of his employment.

5. A deviation from or interruption of a journey undertaken in the course of employment (unless the deviation or interruption is merely incidental to the journey) will for the time being (which may include an overnight interruption) take the employee out of the course of his employment.

6. Return journeys are to be treated on the same footing as outward journeys.

All the foregoing propositions are subject to any express arrangements between the employer and the employee, or those representing his interests. They are not, I would add, intended to define the position of salaried employees, with regard to whom the touchstone of payment made in the employer's time is not generally significant.

Note

There are no hard and fast rules for deciding breach; it is clearly a question of fact in each case. The degree of care depends on the nature of the employment and the risks inherent in this. The employer need not necessarily eliminate the risk, but he must minimise it as far as possible. The factors to be taken into account can be found in all tort textbooks. What is clear is that as safety standards continue to develop and improve the employer will have to do more to fulfil his duty (see *James* v *Hepworth & Grandage Ltd* (above) and *Baxter* v *Harland & Wolff plc* [1990] IRLR 516).

Questions

1. What is the effect of known infirmities or disabilities on the assessment of breach?

2. Is it ever reasonable to say that an employee must rely on his own skill and judgement?

3. When is an employer liable for accidents to peripatetic workers?

4. Is it likely that the more experienced the employee the less the standard of care required on the part of the employer?

III   Breach of Statutory Duty

A civil claim may arise where there has been breach of a statute imposing criminal liability. The burden is on the claimant to show that the statute and section in question give rise to such a claim. Many statutes do not give any indication as to the availability of a civil claim, and in these circumstances the criteria expounded by Lord Diplock in *Lonrho* v *Shell Petroleum* [1981] 2 All ER 456, at p. 461, should be applied. Some statutes state clearly their position on this issue, e.g. HASAWA 1974, s. 47 provides that a civil claim is not available for breaches of ss. 2–9; in comparison a civil claim is permitted for a breach of the Factories Act 1961.

In most claims for breach of statutory duty one advantage may be that it is not necessary to establish actual fault on the part of the defendant, although the onus is on the claimant to show not only that a breach of the statute should give rise to a civil claim but also that the claimant, the defendant and the injury come within the wording of the section allegedly breached.

Groves v *Wimborne*
[1898] 2 QB 402
Court of Appeal

The plaintiff was a boy employed in the service of the defendant at the Dowlais Iron Works of which the defendant was the proprietor. Amongst the machinery in the works was a steam winch with revolving cog-wheels, at which the plaintiff was employed. These cog-wheels were dangerous to a person working the winch unless fenced. There was evidence that there had originally been a guard or fence to these cog-wheels, but it had for some reason been removed, and there had been no fence to the wheels while the plaintiff was employed at the winch, a period of about six months. While the plaintiff was so employed, his right arm had been caught by the cog-wheels, and was so much injured that the forearm had to be amputated.

It was held that a personal injury action will lie for a breach of a duty imposed under the Factory and Workshop Act 1878, s. 5, even though the statute in question imposes a penalty in the event of a breach as this penalty is not necessarily awarded to the injured party.

SMITH LJ: . . . Could it be doubted that, if s. 5 stood alone, and no fine were provided by the Act for contravention of its provisions, a person injured by a breach of the absolute and unqualified duty imposed by that section would have a cause of action in respect of that breach? Clearly it could not be doubted. That being so, unless it appears from the whole 'purview' of the Act, to use the language of Lord Cairns in the case of *Atkinson* v *Newcastle Waterworks Co.* (1877) 2 Ex D 441 that it was the intention of the Legislature that the only remedy for breach of the statutory duty should be by proceeding for the fine imposed by s. 82, it follows that, upon proof of a breach of that duty by the employer and injury thereby occasioned to the workman, a cause of action is established. The question therefore is whether the cause of action which prima facie is given by s. 5 is taken away by any provisions to be found in the remainder of the Act. It is said that the provisions of ss. 81, 82, and 86 have that effect, and that it appears thereby that the purview of the Act is that the only remedy, where a workman has been injured by a breach of the duty imposed by s. 5, shall be by proceeding before a court of summary jurisdiction for a fine under s. 82, which fine is not to exceed 100*l*. In dealing with the question whether this was the intention of the Legislature, it is material, as Kelly CB pointed out in giving judgment in the case of *Gorris* v *Scott* (1874) LR 9 Ex 125, to consider for whose benefit the Act was passed, whether it was passed in the interests of the public at large or in those of a particular class of persons. The Act now in question, as I have said, was clearly passed in favour of workers employed in factories and workshops, and to compel their employers to perform certain statutory duties for their protection and benefit. It is to be observed in the first place that under the provisions of s. 82 not a penny of the fine necessarily goes to the person injured or his family. The provision is only that the whole or any part of it may be applied for the benefit of the injured person or his family, or otherwise, as a secretary of state determines. Again, if proceedings for the fine are taken before magistrates, upon what considerations are they to act in determining the amount of the fine? One matter to be considered clearly would be the character of the neglect to fence. This neglect might be either of a serious or of a venial character. Suppose that it was of the latter character, but a person was unfortunately killed or injured in consequence of it. What fine are the magistrates to impose? Are they to impose a fine of the same amount as if it were a flagrant case of neglect to fence? The first thing one would say that they would have to consider would be whether the offence was of a grave character or otherwise. It may be said that in determining the amount of the fine the character of the injury sustained by the workman would be considered, but I am not sure that that is the meaning of the section. It seems to me that the fine is inflicted by way of punishment of the employer for neglect of the duty imposed by the Act, and must be proportionate to the character of the offence. This consideration and the fact that whatever penalty the magistrates inflict does not necessarily go to the injured workman or his family lead me to the conclusion that it cannot have been the intention of the Legislature that the provision which imposes upon the employer a fine as a punishment for neglect of his statutory duty should take away the prima facie right of the workman to be fully compensated for injury occasioned to him by that neglect. Another observation which makes the matter still clearer arises from the fact that, having regard to the provisions of s. 87, it may not be the employer, presumably a person of means and capable of paying a substantial fine, who would have to pay the fine. Under that section the employer may be exempted from the penalty, and the fine may be imposed upon the actual offender, who may be a workman employed at weekly wages; and yet it is said that a fine payable by such a person is the only remedy given by the statute to the injured workman for breach by the occupier of the imperative statutory duty. I cannot read this statute in the manner in which it is sought to be read by the defendant. I think that s. 5 does give to the workman a right of action upon the statute for injury caused by a breach of the statutory duty thereby imposed, and that he is not relegated to the provisions for the imposition of a fine on the employer, or it may be a workman, as his sole remedy.

Close v *Steel Company of Wales*
[1962] AC 367
House of Lords

By the Factories Act 1937, s. 14: '(1) Every dangerous part of any machinery . . . shall be securely fenced . . .'

The appellant was operating an electric drill when the bit shattered and he was struck and injured in the left eye by one or more pieces which flew out. In an action against the respondents, his employers, for damages for breach, *inter alia*, of their statutory duty under s. 14(1) of the Factories Act, 1937 it was held that the risk of injury was not reasonably foreseeable and therefore the bit was not a dangerous part of machinery within the scope of the statutory duty.

LORD MORRIS: The question as to whether there was a dangerous part is one of degree and of fact, and one which must be resolved by considering the relevant evidence. In *Hindle* v *Birtwistle* [1897] 1 QB 192 Wills J said:

It seems to me that machinery or parts of machinery is and are dangerous if in the ordinary course of human affairs danger may be reasonably anticipated from the use of them without protection.

A part of a machine might be dangerous which might be a reasonably foreseeable cause of injury to anybody acting in a way in which a human being might be reasonably expected to act in circumstances which might be reasonably expected to occur (see *Walker* v *Bletchley Flettons Ltd* [1937] 1 All ER 170 and *John Summers & Sons Ltd* v *Frost* [1955] 1 All ER 870).

My Lords, if there were some machine which when being operated had a part which constantly emitted fragments of itself with such force as to be likely to injure anyone who was operating the machine, I would deem such part to be dangerous. The tests denoted by the cases above referred to, as also plain ordinary common sense, would alike point to such a conclusion. So also if there was some part of a machine which was known to have a propensity from time to time, but at unpredictable moments, to cast off fragments of itself in such manner as to be likely to injure anyone operating the machine, I would consider that such part could and ought reasonably to be called a dangerous part. It would be dangerous for any operator if he were not kept out of the area within which there were flying fragments which could injure.

. . . There was evidence that at the respondents' works there might be one bit each week that would shatter. Though this was the case no one had ever been hurt before. This was because fragments had never had force or speed. There was no evidence that anyone had ever sustained a scratch or even a minor penetrating wound. The appellant's injury was an exceptional happening and an entirely unexpected mischance. The facts did not establish that any operator of one of the drills had been subjected to any significant risk of injury. In agreement with the Court of Appeal I consider that if anyone had closely reflected he would have said that the chance of the occurrence of the appellant's accident was extremely remote. In these circumstances I am not persuaded that the bit ought to be characterised as 'dangerous part.'

If the position had been that the bit was a dangerous part then there was a positive requirement that it should be securely fenced. . . . there is a duty to fence so as to prevent an operator from coming into contact with any dangerous part. In very many cases a part of a machine is dangerous for the reason that if the operator touches that part, or if his body comes into contact with it, some personal injury may result. There may be some cases, as those now being considered (though, on the facts, not the present case), where a part of a machine is dangerous for the reason that while the machine is being operated such part either emits fragments of itself with force or disintegrates so as to emit its fragments with force. There would in such circumstances be a radius of danger and the obligation securely to fence the dangerous part would necessitate keeping the operator away from the danger. The extent of the exclusion would naturally be limited if the fencing to exclude the operator was designed closely to contain the danger. . . .

Whitfield v H & R Johnson (Tiles) Ltd
[1990] IRLR 525
Court of Appeal

The plaintiff was employed by the defendant tile manufacturers for over 11 years in the sorting and packing department. Part of that job involved unloading stacks of tiles from a trolley onto a conveyor belt. The work of sorting and packing was done by teams of five workers who took it in turns to do the unloading. Although the member of the team doing the unloading was expected to keep pace with the rest, it was left to the unloader to select a comfortable and convenient number of tiles to lift at a time.

The plaintiff had a congenital back condition of which her employers were unaware. In spite of that condition, she had experienced no difficulty in lifting the tiles and had suffered no problems with her back because of the lifting. She picked up the number of tiles that suited her and she knew that she could cope with. If the load was too heavy she would put it back on the trolley and take a smaller quantity.

In December 1984, however, as she was unloading the last stack of tiles from the trolley, she suffered severe pain in her back and right leg and was unable to carry on working. After a period of rest she felt sufficiently recovered to return to her job but it soon became clear that she was no longer able to do the work involved. She consequently left the defendants' employment.

She claimed that the accident and onset of pain which she had suffered was caused by the employers' negligence and breach of statutory duty. She contended that in employing her to lift and carry tiles from the trolley to the conveyor belt, the employers were in breach of s. 72 of the Factories Act 1961 which provides that: 'A person shall not be employed to lift, carry or move any load so heavy as to be likely to cause injury to him'. The High Court dismissed her complaint.

On appeal to the Court of Appeal it was held, dismissing the employee's appeal, that the defendants were not liable for a breach of s. 72 in circumstances in which the likelihood of the plaintiff being injured was not due to the weight of the load but to a congenital back condition of which the employers were unaware.

BELDAM LJ: The difficulty caused by the further observations suggesting that the likelihood of injury has to be assessed having regard to any individual weakness or predisposition of the employee is that the more severe the inherent and latent weakness, the more likely it is that any risk in lifting or moving any load will cause injury to him. On the hypothetical case referred to by Slade LJ, and on the facts of the case before us, the likelihood of injury does not arise from the weight of the load at all. Lifting or moving an object of virtually any weight would have been likely to cause injury to the plaintiff sooner or later. So it is said that because of the use of the words 'to him', the occupier of a factory or an employer would be in breach of s. 72 if he employed a person on work which involved lifting even the lightest of loads if, for example, the employee suffered from an unsuspected aneurism and the strain of lifting caused it to burst. Thus a breach would be established in such circumstances, whatever the weight of the load, because it would be likely to cause injury 'to him'. So, too, an employee may be employed one week to lift or move a load without any risk of injury but on the following Monday, due to a strain sustained by him over the weekend which diminished his ability to withstand the strain imposed by lifting, the same load could on this hypothesis be said to be likely to cause injury to the employee. I am unable to agree that Parliament, by adding those two words, intended so unreasonable or unlikely a result. I consider that full meaning can be given to those words read in the context of the section as a whole by holding that they were intended to make sure that the weight of the load was appropriate to the sex, build and physique, or other obvious characteristic of the employee in question. To construe the section in this way does not detract from the strict nature of the prohibition against employing persons to lift loads which are so heavy that they are likely to cause injury. Nor does it depart from an objective standard. Once it is shown that the weight of the load he is employed to lift is likely to cause injury to the particular employee, having regard to his obvious characteristics, a breach would be established. It would be no defence to an occupier or employer to argue that he did not foresee the likelihood of injury.

In short, it seems to me clear from the language of this section that the mischief at which it was aimed was employing persons to lift or move objects of excessive weight, or, put in another way, that the likelihood of injury to the employee must arise from his being employed to lift an object of a weight which in all the circumstances, including the nature of the object, the grip he can take of it, the foothold he has, the space available and all the other relevant circumstances, is excessive for him.

Notes

1. Whether a claim for breach of statutory duty will succeed is a question of statutory interpretation. The claimant must show (i) that the section in question places a duty on the defendant and that it is owed to the claimant (*Wigley* v *British Vinegars Ltd* [1964] AC 307 and *Hartley* v *Mayoh & Co.* [1954] 1 QB 383); (ii) that there is a breach of duty which is of the type contemplated by the statute (*Gorris* v *Scott* (1874) LR 9 Exch 125 and *Chipchase* v *British Titan Products Co.* [1956] 1 QB 545); (iii) that the breach caused the harm to the claimant (*Ginty* v *Belmont Building Supplies Ltd* [1959] 1 All ER 414).

The case of *Larner* v *British Steel plc* [1993] IRLR 278 which involved a breach of the Factories Act 1961, s. 29, raises two important issues. First, where the statute in question provides a defence (in this particular case 'so far as is reasonably practicable') it must actually be pleaded by the defendant before it can be considered in the judgment. Secondly, where the words of the statute make no reference to 'reasonable foreseeability', then the test for breach is a strict one, i.e. the claimant does not have to prove that the danger was 'reasonably foreseeable' and the court is under no duty to apply such a test. The decision in *Mains* v *Uniroyal Englebert Tyres Ltd* [1995] IRLR 544 further confirms that the claimant does not have to establish that the risk of injury was reasonably foreseeable in allowing a breach of s. 29 of the Factories Act 1961. The Court of Session concluded that 'There is nothing whatever in the section to suggest that the obligation is only to prevent any risk arising if that risk is of a reasonably foreseeable nature'.

2.   Failure to comply with the Employer's Liability (Compulsory Insurance) Act 1969 does not give rise to a civil claim for breach of statutory duty; so ruled the Court of Appeal in *Richardson* v *Pitt-Stanley* [1995] 2 WLR 26.

3.   The whole of the Factories Act 1961 will eventually be repealed and replaced by regulations made under the Health and Safety at Work etc. Act 1974 but emanating from EC Directives. When this occurs, whether a civil claim for breach of statutory duty will be of any real importance must be open to debate as the majority of cases are pursued because of the strict liability aspect of the current legislation. If liability under the new regulations is fault-based there may be little point in pursuing an action for breach of statutory duty. In addition, it will have to be determined whether the new regulations give rise to a civil claim for breach of statutory duty.

Questions
1.   Must the breach be the sole cause of the injury to the claimant?
2.   Will the breach of a statutory power give rise to a civil claim? See *Watt* v *Kesteven CC* [1955] 1 QB 408.

IV   Health and Safety at Work etc. Act 1974

The Health and Safety at Work etc. Act 1974 (HASAWA 1974) was passed as a direct result of the Robens Report (Report of the Robens Committee on Safety and Health at Work 1972, Cmnd 5034), which recognised that, amongst other things, over 7 million people had no health and safety protection while at work. Furthermore, for a variety of reasons, the Factories Act 1961 was ceasing to have the required impact in those premises to which it applied. This may have been due to the dependence upon the 'policing' approach taken by HM Inspectors of Factories for its enforcement. The recommendations of the Robens Committee were put into effect both quickly and virtually in total.

ROBENS REPORT
CHAPTER 18

SUMMARY

451.   In our preface we drew attention to the fact that the various topics within our terms of reference are heavily interrelated, and that the nature of the solution to one problem tends to depend upon the nature of the solutions adopted for others. We begin this final chapter of our report with a short general summary of the essence of our proposals, followed by a rather more detailed – but by no means exhaustive – chapter by chapter summary.

General summary

452.   We need a more self-regulating system of provision for safety and health at work. The traditional approach based on ever-increasing, detailed statutory regulation is outdated, over-complex and inadequate. Reform should be aimed at creating the conditions for more effective self-regulation by employers and workpeople jointly.

453.   The efforts of industry and commerce to tackle their own safety and health problems should be encouraged, supported and supplemented by up to date provisions unified within a single, comprehensive framework of legislation. Much greater use should be made of agreed voluntary standards and codes of practice to promote progressively better conditions.

454.   This broader and more flexible framework would enable the statutory inspection services to be used more constructively in advising and assisting employers and workpeople. At the same time it would enable them to be concentrated more effectively on serious problems where tighter monitoring and control might be needed.

455.   A single centre of initiative is needed to replace the present heavily-fragmented administrative arrangements. A national Authority for Safety and Health at Work should be established.

Chapter summary

456.   **Chapter 1 – What is wrong with the system?** The toll of death, injury, suffering and economic waste from accidents at work and occupational diseases remains unacceptably high. New hazards and problems are emerging. Apathy is the greatest single obstacle to progressive improvement; it can only be countered by an accumulation of deliberate pressures to stimulate more sustained attention to safety and health at work.

457.   There is a lack of balance between the regulatory and voluntary elements of the overall 'system' of provision for safety and health at work. The primary responsibility for doing something about present levels of occupational accidents and diseases lies with those who create the risks and those who work with them. The statutory arrangements should be reformed with this in mind. The present approach tends to encourage people to think and behave as if safety and health at work were primarily a matter of detailed regulation by external agencies.

458.   Present regulatory provisions follow a style and pattern developed in an earlier and different social and technological context. Their piecemeal development has led to an haphazard mass of law which is intricate in detail, unprogressive, often difficult to comprehend and difficult to amend and keep up to date. It pays insufficient regard to human and organisational factors in accident prevention, does not cover all workpeople, and does not deal comprehensively and effectively with some sources of serious hazard. These defects are compounded and perpetuated by excessively fragmented administrative arrangements.

459.   A more effectively self-regulating system is needed. Reform should be aimed at two fundamental and closely related objectives. First, the statutory arrangements should be revised and reorganised to increase the efficiency of the state's contribution to safety and health at work. Secondly, the new statutory arrangements should be designed to provide a framework for better self-regulation.

460.   **Chapter 2 – Safety and health at the workplace.** Safety and health activity at the workplace needs a central focus. Employers should be required to set out written statements of their safety and health policy and provisions. These statements should be made available to all employees.

461.   Within firms, safety and health objectives and responsibilities should be clearly defined at the level of the boardroom, middle management, safety advisers, supervisors and operatives; and systematic prevention techniques should be employed.

462. Safety and health at work is a matter of efficient management. But it is not a management prerogative. Workpeople must be encouraged to participate fully in the making and monitoring of arrangements for safety and health at their place of work. There should be a general statutory obligation on employers to consult with their workpeople on measures for promoting safety and health. Guidance on methods of consultation and participation should be provided in a code of practice.

463. Annual reports of registered companies should be required to include prescribed information about accidents and occupational diseases suffered by the company's employees, and about preventive measures taken by the company.

464. **Chapter 3 – Action at industry level.** Industry-level organisations, with their knowledge of the special problems of their own industries, have an extremely important part to play in the promotion of safety and health at work. A better mechanism is needed for linking up the efforts of the industry-level safety bodies with the work of the statutory services.

465. There is scope for more collaboration between the CBI and TUC on this subject. Both should devote more resources to the promotion of safety and health activities by employer associations and trade unions.

466. **Chapter 4 – A new statutory framework.** A national Authority for Safety and Health at Work should be set up. Present safety and health legislation dealing separately with factories, mines, agriculture, explosives, petroleum, nuclear installations and alkali works should be revised, unified, and administered by the new Authority.

467. The Authority should have a distinct, separate identity, with its own budget, and full operational autonomy under the broad policy directives of a departmental Minister. It should have a comprehensive range of executive powers and functions. Statutory provisions formulated by the Authority should be laid before Parliament by the sponsoring Minister.

468. The Managing Board of the Authority should be composed of people drawn from relevant fields of experience and interest, so that the Authority can be seen as institutionalising a new policy for greater self-government in this field.

469. **Chapter 5 – The form and content of new legislation.** The existing statutory provisions should be replaced by a comprehensive and orderly set of revised provisions under a new enabling Act. The new Act should contain a clear statement of the basic principles of safety responsibility. It should be supported by regulations and by non-statutory codes of practice, with emphasis on the latter.

470. A determined effort should be made to revise, harmonise and up-date the existing large body of detailed statutory regulations, to simplify their style and to reduce their number. A simplified consultation procedure is recommended.

471. As a general rule, voluntary standards and codes of practice provide the most flexible and practical means of promoting progressively better (rather than minimum) conditions of safety and health at work. in future, they should be used more extensively in supplementation of – and wherever possible in place of – statutory regulations. This change in emphasis should be accompanied by arrangements for increasing the impact and effectiveness of such standards and codes. Voluntary standards and codes approved by the Authority should be taken into account in inspection work and should be admissible in evidence in enforcement proceedings.

472. Statutory regulations and approved voluntary codes and standards should be kept under constant review with the assistance of an Advisory Committee on Regulations and Codes. Expert technical working parties should be established ad hoc to undertake the detailed work.

473. **Chapter 6 – The application and scope of new legislation.** The scope of the new legislation should extend to all employers and employees, except for a limited range of specific exclusions.

474. The scope of the new legislation should also extend to the self-employed in circumstances where their acts or omissions could endanger other workers (employed or self-employed) or the general public.

475. The legislation should not apply to the normal use of the highway, to domestic service, or to transport workers whilst actually engaged in transport operations. Special provision is needed for hospitals, schools and other educational establishments, and research laboratories.

476. **Chapter 7 – The inspectorates.** The existing separate safety and health inspectorates for factories, mines, agriculture, explosives, nuclear installations and alkali works should be amalgamated to form a unified service within the new Authority. As a matter of explicit policy, the provision of expert and impartial advice and assistance to industry should be the basic function of the unified inspectorate. At the same time, tighter control over serious problems should be exercised through the more effective deployment and use of inspection personnel.

477. Present inspection activities are too widely dispersed, and depend too much on routine visitation. The attempt to watch over everything means that the more serious problems may get less attention than they deserve. The resources of the inspectorates should be used more selectively. They should be concentrated on those areas where they are most needed and most likely to be effective. Priorities should be established by systematic appraisal and planning.

478. This problem-oriented approach calls for a field structure of about 30 or so large Area Offices, each providing a wide range of skills and expertise corresponding to the needs of the particular area.

479. **Chapter 8 – Inspection by local authorities.** Local authorities have a very important part to play. Their work should be more effectively co-ordinated and integrated with the work of the Area Offices of the new national Authority.

480. **Chapter 9 – Sanctions and enforcement.** Where the pressure of sanctions is needed to ensure rectification of unsatisfactory conditions, a range of alternatives should be available to the safety and health inspector. In the majority of cases, administrative sanctions of a constructive nature are to be preferred. These should take the form of Improvement Notices and conditional Prohibition Notices issued by inspectors and subject to appeal before industrial tribunals. Higher fines should also be provided for.

481. **Chapter 10 – Public safety.** The new legislation should be so formulated as to ensure that the interests of the public as well as of employees are taken fully into account in measures dealing with hazards at workplaces. Special arrangements are needed to ensure adequate control over large-scale hazards to the public.

482. **Chapter 11 – Additional comments on particular topics.** *General fire precautions* applicable to workplaces should be dealt with under the Fire Precautions Act, with enforcement based on the issue of fire certificates by the fire authorities Special fire safety provisions against particular process risks should be made under the legislation administered by the Authority for Safety and Health at Work. Arrangements should be made for close liaison between the local fire authorities and the Area Offices of the central Safety Authority (paragraphs 311–317).

483. The Authority for Safety and Health at Work should administer comprehensive provisions dealing with *explosive and flammable substances*. There should be a special 'major hazards' unit within the unified inspectorate, and guidance from

a standing Advisory Committee on Explosive and Flammable Substances (paragraphs 318–321).

484.   There should be comprehensive powers of control over *toxic substances,* allied to a general statutory obligation on manufacturers to ensure adequate safety testing of new substances before marketing them for industrial use. Anyone marketing a new chemical or other potentially harmful substance for industrial and commercial use should be required to supply basic information to the Authority for consideration by a standing Advisory Committee on Toxic Substances (paragraphs 322–333).

485.   There should be an institutional link between the new Authority and the National Board for Radiological Protection (paragraphs 334–339).

486.   Basic requirements on *noise control* should be included in the new legislation. Within the unified inspectorate there should be a specialist branch dealing with noise (paragraphs 340–345).

487.   There should be a general statutory obligation to ensure that *plant, machinery and equipment* manufactured for industrial and commercial use is designed and constructed to comply with safety requirements; and powers to require compliance with particular standards and approval arrangements established by independent quality control bodies (paragraphs 346–354).

488.   **Chapter 12 – The organisation of occupational medicine.** The new Employment Medical Advisory Service should function as part of the Authority for Safety and Health at Work, and should maintain close operational liaison with the National Health Service.

489.   **Chapter 13 – Training.** The new Authority should play a promotional and co-ordinating role in safety training. It should actively participate in some neglected areas such as safety training in management courses. New legislation should contain broad powers for making regulations on safety training.

490.   **Chapter 14 – Research and information.** The Authority should seek to promote a more co-ordinated research effort in occupational safety and health. It should have an adequate research capacity of its own, and powers to sponsor and support relevant external research. It should seek to ensure better dissemination of research results as part of an effective general information service.

491.   **Chapter 15 – Statistics.** The new Authority should review the bases and purposes of the statistics currently published. Priority should be given to the task of devising a common report form so that employers would need to report an accident only once.

492.   **Chapter 16 – The costs of accidents.** Study of the costs of occupational accidents has been relatively neglected. The new Authority should be suitably equipped to pursue research into costs and benefits in order to assist the development of a more cost-effective approach to the deployment of public resources for accident prevention, as well as to encourage and assist similar work by industry-level organisations and individual firms.

493.   **Chapter 17 – Compensation and prevention.** There should be a detailed study of possible ways of amending the statutory industrial injuries scheme so as to provide for differential rates of contribution from employers, based on the claims experience of their employees.

494.   There should be an Inquiry into the present system of actions at common law for damages for injuries sustained at work, with particular reference to the deleterious effects of the present system upon accident-prevention provisions and activities.

A: Duty Owed by Employers to their Employees

Health and Safety at Work etc. Act 1974

2.   General duties of employers to their employees

(1)   It shall be the duty of every employer to ensure, so far as is reasonably practicable, the health, safety and welfare at work of all his employees.

(2)   Without prejudice to the generality of an employer's duty under the preceding subsection, the matters to which that duty extends include in particular—

(a)   the provision and maintenance of plant and systems of work that are, so far as is reasonably practicable, safe and without risks to health;

(b)   arrangements for ensuring, so far as is reasonably practicable, safety and absence of risks to health in connection with the use, handling, storage and transport of articles and substances;

(c)   the provision of such information, instruction, training and supervision as is necessary to ensure, so far as is reasonably practicable, the health and safety at work of his employees;

(d)   so far as is reasonably practicable as regards any place of work under the employer's control, the maintenance of it in a condition that is safe and without risks to health and the provision and maintenance of means of access to and egress from it that are safe and without such risks;

(e)   the provision and maintenance of a working environment for his employees that is, so far as is reasonably practicable, safe, without risks to health, and adequate as regards facilities and arrangements for their welfare at work.

Edwards v *National Coal Board*
[1949] 1 KB 704
Court of Appeal

A colliery timberman, while walking along a travelling road in a South Wales coal mine, in the course of his duties, was killed by the fall of a considerable portion of the side of the road. The plaintiff, his widow, claimed damages from the National Coal Board, as owners and occupiers of the mine, for breach of their statutory duty under s. 49 of the Coal Mines Act 1911, to make secure the roof and sides of 'every travelling road and working place.' The defendants contended that having regard to the impossibility of knowing when and where a fall was likely to occur and to the expense and labour and other difficulties involved in propping and lining the sides of every travelling road in all their mines, it was 'not reasonably practicable to avoid a breach' of s. 49, and therefore they were excused from liability by s. 102 (8) of the Act.

It was held, allowing the plaintiff's appeal , that the words 'reasonably practicable' in s. 102 involved weighing the risk of an accident against the measures necessary to eliminate the risk. The greater the risk the less would be the weight to be given to the factor of cost. The defendants had failed to provide sufficient evidence to establish this defence.

ASQUITH LJ: . . . The onus was on the defendants to establish that it was not reasonably practicable in this case for them to have prevented a breach of s. 49. The construction placed by Lord Atkin on the words 'reasonably practicable' in *Coltness Iron Co.* v *Sharp* [1938] AC 90 seems to me, with respect, right. 'Reasonably practicable' is a narrower term than 'physically possible' and seems to me to imply that a computation must be made by the owner, in which the quantum of risk is placed on one scale and the sacrifice involved in the measures necessary for averting the risk (whether in money, time or trouble) is placed in the other; and that if it be shown that there is a gross disproportion between them – the risk being insignificant in relation to the sacrifice – the defendants discharge the onus on them. Moreover, this computation falls to be made by the owner at a point of time anterior to the accident. The questions he has to answer are: (a) What measures are necessary and sufficient to prevent any breach of s. 49? (b) Are these measures reasonably practicable? . . .

R v *Swan Hunter Shipbuilders Ltd*
[1981] ICR 831
Court of Appeal

The appellant shipbuilders were aware of the danger of fire in a ship under construction if the air became oxygen enriched. They instructed their employees of that danger and had a system by which at the end of the day's work all oxygen supply valves at the cylinder or manifold were shut off and all hoses returned to the upper deck. They were the main contractors for the building of a ship. A sub-contractor contracted work to a company, T. An employee of T left the end of an oxygen hose on a lower deck at the end of a day's shift. On the following day, it was not appreciated that the hose attached to the manifold was discharging oxygen into a badly ventilated compartment. A welder in the compartment struck his arc with his welding torch and immediately a fire broke out. The fire burnt with such ferocity that only three of the 11 men in the compartment were able to escape. At the time of the fire, about 1,000 men employed by the appellants and other contractors were working in the ship.

The appellants were charged, *inter alia*, with failing to provide and maintain a system of work for their employees that was, so far as was reasonably practicable, safe and without risks to health, contrary to ss. 2(2)(a) and 33(1) of the Health and Safety at Work etc. Act 1974; failing to provide such information and instruction as was necessary to ensure, so far as was reasonably practicable, the health and safety of their employees, contrary to ss. 2(2)(c) and 33(1); and with failing to conduct their undertaking in such a way as to ensure, so far as was reasonably practicable, that persons not in their employment who may have been affected thereby were not exposed to risks to their health and safety, contrary ss. 3(1) and 33(1) of the Act. At the close of the prosecution case, the appellants submitted that they had no case to answer as they were under no duty by reason of those sections to provide the employees of other companies, in particular T, with information as to the dangers of an oxygen enriched atmosphere or with such instructions as might be necessary to ensure the safety of the workmen in the ship. The judge rejected the appellants' submission and subsequently directed the jury that the appellants were under a duty to provide such information and instruction to the employees of other contractors. The jury convicted the appellants.

Dismissing the appeal, it was held that in order to fulfil the duty under s. 2(1) of the 1974 Act to provide a safe system of work for one's employees, not only must the necessary information and instruction as to potential dangers be given to those employees but also, as the safety of one's own employees was dependent upon it, to the employees of other contractors.

DUNN LJ: . . . In our view the duties are all covered by the general duty in subsection (1) of section 2: 'It shall be the duty of every employer to ensure, so far as is reasonably practicable, the health, safety and welfare at work of all his employees.' As the judge said, that is a strict duty. If the provision of a safe system of work for the benefit of his own employees involves information and instruction as to potential dangers being given to persons other than the employer's own employees, then the employer is under a duty to provide such information and instruction. His protection is contained in the words 'so far as is reasonably practicable' which appear in all the relevant provisions. The onus is on the defendants to prove on a balance of probabilities that it was not reasonably practicable in the particular circumstances of the case.

R v Gateway Foodmarkets Ltd
[1997] IRLR 189
Court of Appeal

Mr Finn was employed by the appellants as a section manager at their supermarket in Broomhill, Sheffield. There was a lift at the store, in respect of which an experienced and highly reputable firm of lift contractors was employed under contract with the company to provide regular maintenance and a call-out service. Those arrangements were made by the company's head office and were in accordance with its policy for all its stores.

However, for some time there had been a persistent problem with the lift at the Broomhill store. A faulty electrical contact meant that the lift jammed frequently. The defect could be cured by freeing the contact manually and, in order to avoid having to call them out each time the lift jammed, the contractors had told the store personnel how to do it. It became the regular practice for the store manager or one of the section managers to go to the lift control room, which was situated on the flat roof of the building, and free the contact. That practice was unauthorised by head office and no one there was aware of it.

On 1 April 1993, the contractors had carried out routine maintenance of the lift and, for no good reason, had left open the trapdoor in the control room floor. The following day, Mr Finn was acting as duty manager in the absence of the store manager and, when the lift jammed, he went up to the control room in order to free the contact. Going from sunshine into darkness, he did not see that the trapdoor was open and fell about 26 feet to the floor of the lift shaft. He died in hospital that afternoon.

On appeal, it was held that the Crown Court judge had not erred in ruling that the appellant company could be liable for a breach of duty under s. 2(1) of the Health and Safety at Work Act in respect of a fatal accident to one of its supermarket employees which resulted from a failure at store management level to take all reasonable precautions to avoid the risk of injury notwithstanding that, at senior management or head office level, all reasonable precautions had been taken to avoid the risk.

EVANS LJ: . . . As regards the legal concepts referred to above, it is said first that s. 2(1) imposes a 'strict' liability on the employer, subject only to the defence contained in the sub-section itself ('so far as is reasonably practicable'). This means 'strict' as distinct from offences which require proof of mens rea, meaning broadly that the wrongdoer was blameworthy or at fault.

It is said, secondly, that the issue is whether s. 2(1) imposes 'vicarious liability' for the acts or omissions of another person. The phrase is used to mean that one person, the defendant, is guilty of a criminal offence even though the relevant acts and omissions, including mens rea where appropriate, were those of another person. *Mousell Brothers Ltd* v *London & North Western Railway Co.* [1917] 2 KB 836 was an example of this.

These two concepts may overlap. A company can only act through persons who are its servants or agents. If the individuals concerned were those whose acts can be regarded as those of the company itself, then no question of vicarious liability is involved. But if the terms of the statute are such that the company has committed an offence, even though the acts or omissions which make it liable were those of persons outside that category then it may be said that the company incurs a vicarious liability, although in our judgment that is not strictly correct. The liability, in such a case, is the company's own.

. . . In our judgment, the significance of Lord Hoffman's speech in *[R* v *] Associated Octel [Co. Ltd* [1997] IRLR 123] for present purposes, is that it emphasises in relation to s. 3(1) the need to avoid 'confusion between two quite different concepts: an employer's vicarious liability for the tortious act of another and a duty imposed upon the employer himself' (125, 12). The former depends generally on the contractual relationship between the employer and the other person, the latter does not. The duty under s. 3 is imposed on the employer himself, 'by reference to a certain kind of activity, namely, the conduct by the employer of his undertaking' (125, 12). The question, therefore, (the statutory defence apart) was simply 'whether the activity in question can be described as part of the employer's undertaking' (125, 16).

I would respectfully adopt the same approach to s. 2(1). The structure of the two subsections is the same. The duty is imposed on the employer. It is a duty to 'ensure . . . the health, safety and welfare at work of all his employees'. If the duty is broken, the employer is guilty of an offence (s. 33(a)). This approach is consistent with what was said in two earlier authorities on s. 3(1), where passing reference was made to s. 2(1): *HM Inspector of Factories* v *Austin Rover Group Ltd* [1989] IRLR 404 at 409, per Lord Jauncey of Tullichettle, and *R* v *British Steel Plc* [1995] IRLR 310 per Steyn LJ at p. 313.

There is no reference in s. 2(1) to the conduct of the undertaking, which is the basis for liability under s. 3(1), and so it is manifest that the content of the duty under s. 2(1) is different from that under s. 3(1). But in our judgment it is the same kind of duty: the company, as employer, is liable when the necessary conditions for liability are fulfilled. Having regard to the statutory qualification ('so far as is reasonably practicable'), the interpretation of s. 2(1) in this way seems to us to be entirely consistent with the principle identified by Lord Reid in *Tesco Supermarkets Ltd* v *Nattrass* [1972] AC 153. Parliament can be assumed to have balanced the need for regulation, achieved by making the employer liable, against the injustice of convicting a person who is blameless, hence the statutory defence (see p. 169).

If s. 2(1) stood alone, then it might be possible to contend that its wording 'the duty of every employer' meant that the duty imposed on the employer was personal to him, so that no breach was committed unless the individual or, the employer being a company, its 'directing mind' had 'failed to ensure' the health etc of its employees. However, the same wording appears in s. 3(1), and in my judgment the general considerations referred to in the authorities, including the purpose and object of the legislation, make it overwhelmingly clear that s. 2(1), like s. 3(1), should be interpreted so as to impose liability on the employer whenever the relevant event occurs, namely, a failure to ensure the health etc. of an employee.

B: Safety Policies

The Robens Committee envisaged a change in approach to health and safety at work which placed a greater onus on the employer working together with his workforce to improve the whole health and safety environment. This is dependent upon the employer adopting a self-regulatory approach, which is critical to the effective implementation of the 1974 Act. This is recognised in HASAWA 1974, s. 2(3).

Health and Safety at Work etc. Act 1974

2.   General duties of employers to their employees
(3)   Except in such cases as may be prescribed, it shall be the duty of every employer to prepare and as often as may be appropriate revise a written statement of his general policy with respect to the health and safety at work of his employees and the organisation and arrangements for the time being in force for carrying out that policy, and to bring the statement and any revision of it to the notice of all of his employees.

Note
The Health and Safety Executive have always stressed that it is not a part of their role to write safety policies for employers. Each policy should in theory be different, as every employer must assess the risks, precautions and needs of his workforce. However, some guidance can be found in the following publication.

Health and Safety Executive, *Successful Health and Safety Management* (1992)

Written communication

The most important written communications are: health and safety policy statements; organisation statements identifying health and safety roles and responsibilities; documented performance standards; and supporting organisational and risk control information and procedures. These may be supplemented by mission statements, codes of ethics or statements of philosophy. . . . An outline of what might be contained in a statement of health and safety policy is given [below].

AN OUTLINE FOR STATEMENTS OF HEALTH AND SAFETY POLICY

Written statements of health and safety policy should at the very least:

• set the direction for the organisation by communicating senior management's values, beliefs and commitment to health and safety;
• explain the basis of the policy and how it can contribute to business performance (eg by reducing injuries and ill health, protecting the environment and reducing unnecessary losses and liability);
• establish the importance of health and safety objectives in relation to other business objectives;
• commit the organisation to pursuing progressive improvements in health and safety performance, with legal requirements defining the minimum level of achievement;
• explain the responsibilities of managers and the contribution that employees can make to policy implementation outlining the participation procedures;
• commit the organisation to maintaining effective systems of communications on health and safety matters;
• identify the director or key senior manager with overall responsibility for policy formulation, implementation and development;
• commit the leaders of the organisation to supporting the policy with adequate financial and physical resources and by ensuring the competence of all employees and by the provision of any necessary expert advice;
• commit the leaders to planning and regularly reviewing and developing the policy;
• be signed and dated by the director or chief executive of the organisation.

Such written statements of policy will need to be supplemented by statements of organisation and arrangements necessary to implement it.

These documents have to be tailored to the needs of each organisation but generally the degree of detail should be in proportion to the level of complexity and risk: in particular, the greater the risk the more specific instructions need to be. The style of presentation should reflect the needs of the users, whether they be managers, supervisors or other employees.

In addition to permanent documents, organisations use notices, posters, hand bills, and health and safety newsletters to inform employees about particular issues or about progress in achieving objectives, e.g. results of inspections, compliance with standards, results of investigations.

The use of notices or posters to support the achievement of specific targets or to improve knowledge of particular risks is more effective than general poster campaigns. Posters can also refer to specific weaknesses which have been identified, for example by accident or incident analysis. The subjects can also be addressed at the same time in 'tool box' talks and other initiatives designed to promote face-to-face discussion and involvement.

Face-to-face discussion

Face-to-face discussion, with an emphasis on the open and honest exchange of views, supports other communication activities by enabling employees to ask questions and make a personal contribution.

Health and safety tours and formal consultative meetings are important opportunities but other systems are used to ensure a good level of communication and participation. These include:

• planned meetings, sometimes known as 'team briefings', at which information is cascaded down the organisation and performance information is given;

• putting health and safety issues on the agenda at all routine management meetings (possibly as the first item);
• monthly or weekly 'tool box talks', or 'tailgate meetings' at which supervisors can discuss health and safety issues with their teams, remind them of critical risks and precautions, and supplement the training effort. These meetings also enable individuals to make their own suggestions about improving safety arrangements.

Flows of information from the organisation

Health and safety information may need to be communicated outside the organisation. For example, it is necessary to supply enforcing agencies with certain accident and ill health data and under Section 6 of the Health and Safety at Work etc Act information must be provided about the safe use of articles and substances supplied for use at work. It may be necessary to communicate with the planning authorities, the emergency services and local residents. On sites where the Control of Industrial Major Accident Hazards (CIMAH) Regulations 1984 apply, these groups must be involved in aspects of emergency planning. In all such cases openness is important and the information given needs to be relevant and to be presented in a form which can be readily understood. Professional advice can be sought on how best to present information so that it can be understood by the audience to whom it is addressed.

Maintaining means of communication in times of emergency is also important and special contingency arrangements may be necessary.

C: Duty Owed to Persons other than Employees

Health and Safety at Work etc. Act 1974

3. General duties of employers and self-employed to persons other than their employees

(1) It shall be the duty of every employer to conduct his undertaking in such a way as to ensure, so far as is reasonably practicable, that persons not in his employment who may be affected thereby are not thereby exposed to risks to their health or safety.

(2) It shall be the duty of every self-employed person to conduct his undertaking in such a way as to ensure, so far as is reasonably practicable, that he and other persons (not being his employees) who may be affected thereby are not thereby exposed to risks to their health or safety.

(3) In such cases as may be prescribed, it shall be the duty of every employer and every self-employed person, in the prescribed circumstances and in the prescribed manner, to give to persons (not being his employees) who may be affected by the way in which he conducts his undertaking the prescribed information about such aspects of the way in which he conducts his undertaking as might affect their health or safety.

Carmichael v Rosehall Engineering Works Ltd
[1983] IRLR 482
Sheriff Court

Sean O'Brien and John Trodden were seconded to Rosehall Engineering Works for a period of work experience as part of a course organised by the Manpower Services Commission. The two youths were interviewed briefly by Mr Hargreave, a director of the company, and then put in the care of

Mr McGivern, a foreman. Mr McGivern gave them a general talk and instructions together with leaflets containing advice about health and safety.

About three weeks after they started, the youths were instructed by Mr McGivern to assist two experienced platers, Mr Larkin and Mr McFarlane, in cleaning two parallel sets of rollers. The two rows of rollers were situated one above the other. The upper set required to be cleaned by clambering onto them; the lower set were cleaned from below in somewhat cramped conditions. The rollers were first of all cleaned with paraffin applied with rags and then rust-proofed by the application of a liquid substance known as 'temporary coating red'. During the cleaning operation the youths and the platers all wore their normal blue boilersuits.

On the first day of the cleaning operation, all four worked together. On the second day, Mr Larkin, the more experienced of the two platers, was not at work and the boys continued the job with Mr McFarlane. He was more liberal in his use of paraffin than Mr Larkin and at the end of the day, the boys' boilersuits were soaking. They left them out to dry but the following day they were still wet and clean suits had to be borrowed from another employee. On this third day, the boys were left to complete the cleaning of the lower set of rollers by themselves. Their replacement boilersuits were gradually impregnated with excess paraffin.

At about 11.15, they stopped for a few minutes break and, since it was a cold day, went and stood beside a free standing paraffin heater, one of 16 used to heat the factory. Whilst they were standing there, they both noticed what was described as steam coming off their overalls. The paraffin impregnating the cotton material was vaporising in the heat and condensing again in the air. The paraffin then ignited on the surface of Sean O'Brien's boilersuit. He tried to beat the flames out with his hands but suddenly he was completely engulfed. He sustained burns from which he died five days later.

The charge against the company was twofold: (i) that there was a failure to provide the two youths with appropriate protective clothing; and (ii) that the company failed to provide them with information and instruction as to the risks to their health and safety, including the risks of contamination to their clothing from flammable liquids and the risks of ignition of such contaminated clothing from unguarded heaters.

It was held that the employers had failed to fulfil the duty placed on them by virtue of s. 3. It could not be accepted that since the employers were totally unaware of the risks involved, it was not reasonably practicable to guard against them.

BOYLE S: The point at issue centred on the argument that neither Mr Hargreave, the company Director, nor Mr McGivern, the supervisor with direct responsibility for the boys and third in the company's chain of command, were aware of the state of the boys' clothing. They claimed, and I believe them, that they did not know that the manner in which the work was being done was leading to serious impregnation. Both told me that if they had known they would have taken steps to correct what was happening. It is clear that no one suspected that standing in front of the heater could be dangerous. That of course is understandable. It was *not* dangerous to do so. It only became dangerous when one was soaked in flammable liquid. The risk that *then* arose would and should have been obvious to any mature person.

The company prayed in aid the loophole provided by the statute. They were only to ensure that the boys were not exposed to risk so far as that was reasonably practicable. As they were totally unaware of the risks, it was not reasonably practicable to guard against them. This work had been done before without any problem and it was quite unforeseeable that the accident would happen in the way it did.

I am unable to accept that argument. These two young men were placed in the company's care for work experience. They had had none before. They were not mature persons. They were expected to take instruction and follow example; to observe and absorb the practices of the company's undertaking. Considering their youth and inexperience, mistakes, carelessness and imprudence, even a degree of irresponsibility were to be anticipated. Adequate supervision was obviously necessary.

. . . It will not do for the company to say through Mr Hargreaves and Mr McGivern 'We did not know'. They plainly should have known. Their state of ignorance was directly attributable to a failure in the company's arrangements for supervising the boys' work. It accordingly follows that the company have not satisfied me, in the words of s. 40 of the Act, that it was not reasonably practicable to do more than was in fact done to satisfy the duty imposed by s. 3. The charge is proved and I find the company guilty.

R v British Steel plc
[1995] IRLR 310
Court of Appeal

In July 1990, British Steel wanted to reposition a section of steel platform at one of their plants. The operation involved cutting the platform free of its supports and moving it by crane to the new position. The task of repositioning the platform was put out to subcontractors on a labour only basis, with equipment and supervision being provided by British Steel.

The subcontractors provided two men to do the job, Mr Coullie, a welder, and Mr Gascoigne, a plater. British Steel appointed Mr Crabb, a section engineer, to supervise the operation. According to Mr Crabb, he told the two men to fit brackets to the main building and not to remove the four main supporting columns until the crane had taken the weight of the platform.

In the event, the platform was cut free of nearly all its supports without being secured to the crane or to temporary supports. While the platform was in such an unstable position, Mr Gascoigne stepped on to it and it collapsed, causing fatal injuries to Mr Coullie who was working underneath.

British Steel were charged with a breach of HASAWA 1974 s. 3(1).

It was held that British Steel were in breach of their duty under s. 3(1), notwithstanding that, at 'directing mind' level, the company had taken all reasonable care to delegate supervision of the operation to a responsible and competent person. The duty under s. 3(1) was not delegable.

STEYN LJ: . . .

The proper construction of s. 3(1)

Counsel for British Steel submitted that properly construed s. 3(1) permits a corporate employer to escape criminal liability if at 'directing mind' level the company has taken reasonable care. He asked us to read the words 'it shall be the duty of every employer to conduct his undertaking in such a way as to ensure' in s. 3(1) as if the words 'through senior management' appear immediately after the word 'employer'. We are conscious that there are perhaps some ambiguities in the way in which we have summarised counsel's submission. But that is inherent in the submission. When pressed to explain the foundation of the submission in the language of s. 3(1), or its contextual setting, counsel said it derived from the very concept of a corporate employer, who can only act through directors and senior management, or from the words 'conduct his undertaking', which have similar overtones. He relied strongly on the decision of the House of Lords in *Tesco Supermarkets Ltd* v *Nattrass* [1972] AC 153, supra. That case involved a charge against a supermarket chain under the Trade Descriptions Act 1968. Section 20(1) of the 1968 Act provides that if an offence has been committed with the connivance of a director, manager, secretary or other similar officer of the company, he as well as the company will be guilty of the offence. Section 24(1) provides as follows:

> In any proceedings for an offence under this Act it shall . . . be a defence for the person charged to prove (a) that the commission of the offence was due to . . . the act or default of another person . . . and (b) that he took all reasonable precautions and exercised all due diligence to avoid the commission of such an offence . . .

The company's defence was that the commission of the offence was due to an act of another person, namely the manager of the store at which it was committed, and that the company had taken all reasonable precautions and exercised all due diligence to avoid the commission of such an offence. The question arose whether the acts of the shop managers were the acts of the company itself. Lord Reid concluded at 175-A:

> They (the board of directors) set up a chain of command through regional and district supervisors, but they remained in control. The shop managers had to obey their general directions and also take orders from their superiors. The acts or omissions of shop managers were not acts of the company itself.

There were five speeches. Lord Reid's observations reflected the ratio decidendi of the case. Once that decision was reached, the company was able to establish a defence that the commission of the offence was due to a mistake or to the act or default of another person, namely the store manager himself an employee. The presence of such a 'due diligence' provision was a powerful indication that the purpose of the Trade Descriptions Act 1968 must indeed 'have been to penalise those at fault, not those who were in no way to blame'. Significantly, there is no due diligence defence in the 1974 Act. It is worth noting that s. 161 of the Factories Act 1961, which did provide such a defence, has been repealed with effect from 1 January 1977 and has no part in the new regime. Thus quite apart from the fact that *Tesco* involves consumer protection, whereas the present case involves health and safety, which prima facie requires more stringent protection, the legislative techniques of the two statutes are quite different, as is apparent from a comparison of ss. 20(1) and 24(1) of the Trade Descriptions Act 1968 and s. 3(1) of the Health and Safety at Work etc Act 1974. Subject to the qualifying words 'so far as is reasonably practicable', which have been taken from s. 29(1) of the Factories Act 1961, s. 3(1) of 1974 Act is prima facie cast in absolute terms. The words 'so far as is reasonably practicable' are simply referable to measures necessary to avert the risk (see *Taylor* v *Coalite Oil and Chemicals Ltd* [1967] Knights Ind 315, and Redgrave, Fife and Machin, *Health and Safety*, 2nd edn, Introductory Notes lxxxii). In our judgment the decision in *Tesco* does not provide the answer to the problem of construction before us. The answer must be found in the words of s. 3(1) of the 1974 Act read in its contextual setting. It is on the 1974 Act and in particular s. 3(1) that we will concentrate. On the other hand, we recognise that our construction of s. 3(1) must have relevance to the interpretation of s. 2(1) which provides for the employer's duty to his own employees.

We have observed that prima facie, and subject to the stated qualification, s. 3(1) created an absolute prohibition. The point is, in fact, covered by the direct authority of two decisions in this Court. In *R* v *Board of Trustees of the Science Museum* [1994] IRLR 25, this court considered the provenance of s. 3(1) as well as the assistance to be gained from a consideration of other provisions of the Act. Subject to repeating that it is right to consider the interpretation of s. 3(1) against the spectrum of risks contemplated by s. 3(1), we do not propose to cover that ground again.

. . . If we had to consider the matter de novo we would have still concluded that the words of s. 3(1) are in context capable of one interpretation only, namely that subject to the defence of reasonable practicability, s. 3(1) creates an absolute prohibition. The defence is a narrow one, analogous to the defence under s. 29(1) of the Factories Act 1961, which simply comprehends the idea of measures necessary to avert the risks to health and safety.

Given the interpretation which prevailed in *Science Museum* and *R* v *Associated Octel Co. Ltd* [1995] ICR 281, and which we have adopted, counsel for British Steel concedes that it is not easy to fit the idea of corporate criminal liability only for acts of the 'directing mind' of the company into the language of s. 3(1). We would go further. If it be accepted that Parliament considered it necessary for the protection of public health and safety to impose, subject to the defence of reasonable practicability, absolute criminal liability, it would drive a juggernaut through the legislative scheme if corporate employers could avoid criminal liability where the potentially harmful event is committed by someone who is not the directing mind of the company. After all, as Stuart-Smith LJ observed in *Octel*, s.3(1) is framed to achieve a result, namely that persons not employed are not exposed to risks to their health and safety by the conduct of the undertaking. If we accept British Steel's submission, it would be particularly easy for large industrial companies, engaged in multifarious hazardous operations, to escape liability on the basis that the company through its 'directing mind' or senior management was not involved. That would emasculate the legislation.

That brings us to a point raised by counsel for British Steel which has proved troublesome. He argued that the interpretation which we have preferred would lead to manifestly absurd consequences. Postulate, he said, the employee who drops a spanner or an employee who drives without due care and attention. Both could be within the scope of s. 3(1). He submitted that in neither case would the corporate employer have a defence of reasonable practicability. But we think that the suggested absurdities are unlikely to arise in practice. An action such as the dropping of a spanner will only be relevant if it exposes a person not in the employer's employment to a risk to his health or safety. That will only occur if he is, as it were, in the danger zone. Thus he will only be exposed to the risk if the system (if any) designed to ensure his safety has broken down and it does not matter for the purposes of s. 3(1) at what level in the hierarchy of employees that breakdown has taken place. Similarly, the driver's carelessness may have resulted from something for which his employer is to be regarded as responsible, such as trying to meet excessively tight delivery schedules or tiredness due to over-long hours of work. We do recognise that there may be circumstances in which it might be regarded as absurd that an employer should even be technically guilty of a criminal offence. An example might perhaps be the driver who is guilty of an error of judgment when driving his employer's lorry on his employer's business. But, in any event, so-called absurdities are not peculiar to this corner of the law: at the extremities of the field of application of many rules surprising results are often to be found. That circumstance is inherent in the adoption of general rules to govern an infinity of particular circumstances. Fortunately, the cases to which counsel referred will in practice cause no real difficulty in relation to s. 3(1) of the 1974 Act. Nobody has suggested that there has ever been a prosecution in such a case, and it is most unlikely that there would in future be a prosecution in such cases. Moreover if such prosecutions are brought, they are not likely to be viewed sympathetically by a judge and jury or by magistrates. In the most unlikely event of a conviction, the judge would be entitled to impose an absolute discharge and refuse to order costs in favour of the prosecution. Despite the intellectual difficulties created by counsel's examples, they do not deflect us from the firm conclusion at which we have arrived.

We believe that s. 3(1) as we have interpreted it is a satisfactory measure for the attainment of the aim of the legislation. On this interpretation the law will also be simplified. . . .

R v *Associated Octel Co. Ltd*
[1997] IRLR 123
House of Lords

Associated Octel operate a large chemical plant at Ellesmere Port which was designated as a 'major hazard site' by the Health and Safety Executive. It was the company's practice to shut down the plant annually for preplanned maintenance and repair. Amongst the work planned for the 1990 shutdown was the repair of the lining of a tank within the chlorine plant. That work was entrusted to a firm of specialist contractors (RGP), who regularly carried out work for the company.

The task, which required the grinding down of damaged areas within the tank and cleaning the surfaces by brushing and washing off with acetone prior to patching, was assigned by the contractors to their employee, Mr Cuthbert. Whilst he was inside the tank, the bulb of the light he was using broke and the electric current caused the acetone vapour to ignite. Mr Cuthbert was badly burned in the flash fire and explosion which followed.

It was held that the appellants had rightly been convicted of a breach of duty under s. 3(1) of the Health and Safety at Work Act in respect of injuries sustained by an employee of a firm of independent contractors whilst carrying out maintenance and repair work to a chlorine tank at the appellants' chemical plant. The work fell within the scope of the employer's duty under s. 3(1) 'to conduct his undertaking in such a way as to ensure, so far as is reasonably practicable, that persons not in his employment who may be affected thereby are not thereby exposed to risks to their health and safety', notwithstanding that it was carried out by independent contractors and the appellants did not control the way in which it was done.

LORD HOFFMAN: . . . At the close of the prosecution's case, Mr Walker QC submitted on behalf of Octel that there was no case to answer. He said that on the evidence the injury to Mr Cuthbert was not caused by the way in which Octel had conducted its undertaking within the meaning of s. 3(1). RGP were independent contractors and the cleaning of the tank was part of the conduct of their undertaking. Control was essential to liability under s. 3(1) and Octel had no right to control the way in which its independent contractors did their work.

His Honour Judge Prosser rejected the submission. He said that Octel's undertaking was the chemical business which it conducted on the site. The conduct of the undertaking included having the tank repaired, whether by employees or contractors. After this ruling, Octel closed its case without calling evidence. By s. 40, the burden is upon the employer to prove that it was not reasonably practicable to take the precautions which would have avoided the risk. In summing up, the judge directed the jury that Octel conducted its undertaking by having the tank repaired by RGP. He drew attention to the fact that this had been done in a way which caused risk to Mr Cuthbert – a risk which had materialised – and that Octel had called no evidence in support of a defence that it had not been reasonably practicable to ask whether he would be using inflammable substances or to take appropriate precautions. Not surprisingly, the jury convicted. The judge fined Octel £25,000.

Octel's main ground of appeal to the Court of Appeal was that the judge had been wrong to reject its submission of no case to answer. The Court of Appeal rejected this argument and so would I. It is based on what seems to me a confusion between two quite different concepts: an employer's vicarious liability for the tortious act of another, and a duty imposed upon the employer himself. Vicarious liability depends (with some exceptions) on the nature of the contractual relationship between the employer and the tortfeasor. There is liability if the tortfeasor was acting within the scope of his duties under a contract of employment. Otherwise, generally speaking, the employer is not vicariously liable. But s. 3 is not concerned with vicarious liability It imposes a duty upon the employer himself. That duty is defined by reference to a certain kind of activity, namely the conduct by the employer of his undertaking. It is indifferent to the nature of the contractual relationships by which the employer chooses to conduct it.

What, then, amounts to the conduct by the employer of his undertaking? Mr Walker said that it meant carrying on activities over which the employer had control. In *HM Inspectorate of Factories* v *Austin Rover Group Ltd* [1989] IRLR 404, at 410, 30, Lord Jauncey of Tullichettle said:

> Sections 2 and 3 impose duties in relation to safety on a single person, whether an individual or a corporation, who is in a position to exercise complete control over the matters to which the duties extend. An employer can control the conditions of work of his employees and the manner in which he conducts his undertaking.

Mr Walker says that the absence of a right to control the way in which the work is done is traditionally the badge of an employer's relationship with an independent contractor. So, as RGP were independent contractors, it must follow that Octel were not in a position to exercise that complete control which is the basis of liability under s. 3.

This again seems to me a confusion of thought. Lord Jauncey was stating what is, if I may respectfully say so, the self-evident proposition that a person conducting his own undertaking is free to decide how he will do so. Section 3 requires the employer to do so in a way which, subject to reasonable practicability, does not create risks to people's health and safety. If, therefore, the employer engages an independent contractor to do work which forms part of the conduct of the employer's undertaking, he must stipulate for whatever conditions are needed to avoid those risks and are reasonably practicable. He cannot, having omitted to do so, say that he was not in a position to exercise any control. This is precisely why Octel insisted that its contractors adhere to the 'permit to work' system.

The concept of control as one of the tests for vicarious liability serves an altogether different purpose An employer is free to engage either employees or independent contractors. If he engages employees, he will be vicariously liable for torts committed in the course of their employment. If he engages independent contractors, he will not. The law takes the contractual relationship as given and in some cases the control test helps to decide the category to which it belongs. But for the purposes of s. 3, the category is not decisive.

. . . The employer is under a duty under s. 3(1) to exercise control over an activity if it forms part of the conduct of his undertaking. The existence of such a duty cannot therefore be the test for deciding whether the activity is part of the undertaking or not. Likewise, the question of whether an employer may leave an independent contractor to do the work as he thinks fit depends upon whether having the work done forms part of the employer's conduct of his undertaking. If it does, he owes a duty under s. 3(1) to ensure that it is done without risk – subject, of course, to reasonable practicability, which may limit the extent to which the employer can supervise the activities of a specialist independent contractor. Although the case was very much on the borderline, I think that there was evidence upon which the justices were entitled to find in the particular circumstances of the case that having the asbestos sheets removed was part of the employer's undertaking. The facts were a matter for them and their decision should not have been disturbed.

Notes

1.   The House of Lords placed great emphasis on the fact that under s. 3 of HASAWA 1974, the employer is required to conduct his undertaking in a way which, subject to reasonable practicability, does not create risks to people's health and safety. The onus is on the employer who engages an independent contractor to stipulate the conditions needed to avoid the risks. The employer cannot abrogate responsibility to the independent contractor in these circumstances. See Barratt, B, 'Employer's Criminal Liability Under HSWA 1974', (1997) 26 ILJ, No. 2, p. 149.

2.   Following *Octel*, employers may be liable under the HASAWA 1974 for the conduct of their independent contractors where that work is part of the conduct of the employer's undertaking.

For further consideration of s. 3 see *R v Nelson Group Services (Maintenance) Ltd* [1999] IRLR 646, in which the Court of Appeal, allowing the employer's appeal concluded that a defence is proven under s. 3 where the employer can 'show that everything reasonably practicable has been done to see that a person doing the work has the appropriate skill and instruction, has had safe systems of doing the work laid down, has been subject to adequate supervision, and has been provided with safe plant and equipment for the proper performance of the work'.

D: Duties of Persons Concerned with Premises

Health and Safety at Work etc. Act 1974

4.   General duties of persons concerned with premises to persons other than their employees

(1)   This section has effect for imposing on persons duties in relation to those who—

(a)   are not their employees; but

(b)   use non-domestic premises made available to them as a place of work or as a place where they may use plant or substances provided for their use there,

and applies to premises so made available and other non-domestic premises used in connection with them.

(2)   It shall be the duty of each person who has, to any extent, control of premises to which this section applies or of the means of access thereto or egress therefrom or of any plant or substance in such premises to take such measures as it is reasonable for a person in his position to take to ensure, so far as is reasonably practicable, that the premises, all means of access thereto or egress therefrom available for use by persons using the premises, and any plant or substance in the premises or, as the case may be, provided for use there, is or are safe and without risks to health.

(3)   Where a person has, by virtue of any contract or tenancy, an obligation of any extent in relation to—

(a)   the maintenance or repair of any premises to which this section applies or any means of access thereto or egress therefrom; or

(b)   the safety of or the absence of risks to health arising from plant or substances in any such premises;

that person shall be treated, for the purposes of subsection (2) above, as being a person who has control of the matters to which his obligation extends.

HM Inspector of Factories v Austin Rover Group Ltd
[1989] IRLR 404
House of Lords

The respondents' car assembly plant contained a spray painting booth beneath which was a large sump which was used to collect excess paint and thinners during painting operations. The booth contained a piped supply of highly inflammable thinners for use in painting. Thinners were also used as solvents to clean the booth. The respondents employed an independent contractor to clean the booth at times when there was no production. The contractor's system of work required that nobody should be in the sump when anyone was working in the booth above, that the contractor's employees should not use the piped supply of thinners in the booth but should use their own supplies, that thinners used in the course of cleaning the booth should not be tipped into the sump but should be dumped outside the booth, and that only a safe electric lamp should be taken into the sump. In the course of cleaning the booth one of the contractor's employees entered the sump to clean it while another employee was cleaning the booth above. A flash fire occurred in the sump and the employee cleaning it was killed. After the fire it was discovered that the employee in the booth above had been using the respondents' piped supply of thinners and had allowed it to overflow into the sump, that he had also been dumping used thinners into the sump instead of outside the booth and that the employee in the sump had been using an unsafe lamp. The contractor was prosecuted and convicted of failing to provide a safe system of work for its employees. The respondents, as the person in control of the non-domestic premises where the deceased was working at the time of the accident, were also prosecuted by an inspector of factories with failing to take such measures as were reasonable for them to take to ensure so far as reasonably practicable that the sump and piped thinners were safe and without risks to health, contrary to s. 4(2) of the Health and Safety at Work etc. Act 1974. They were convicted by the magistrates and fined £2,000. They appealed by way of case stated to the Divisional Court which allowed their appeal. The inspector appealed to the House of Lords.

It was held that the respondents were not in breach of their duty under s. 4(2) as it had not been established that the respondents could reasonably have foreseen the misuse of their premises which caused the accident.

LORD GOFF: Subject to the limited qualification embodied in the phrase 'so far as is reasonably practicable', it seems to me that the duty imposed on the defendant to ensure that the relevant premises are safe and without risk to health for any use for which they are made available is prima facie absolute. In other words, the complainant has only to prove that the defendant has failed to ensure (so far as he can reasonably do so, having regard to the extent of his control) that the relevant premises are safe and without risks to health in the sense I have described: the onus then passes to the defendant to prove, if he can, that it was not reasonably practicable for him to eliminate the relevant risk. It is at this stage that reasonable forseeability becomes relevant, in the sense that there has to be an assessment of the likelihood of the incidence of risk. I wish to add that this reading of s. 4(2) renders it, in my opinion, consistent with the general duties imposed under the immediately preceding ss. 2 and 3 of the Act (concerned respectively with general duties of employers. to their employees, and general duties of employers and self-employed to persons other than their employees), and the immediately succeeding ss. 5 and 6 (concerned with general duties of persons in control of certain premises in relation to harmful emissions into the atmosphere, and general duties of manufacturers and others as regards articles and substances for use at work). This I regard as significant. The duty under s. 4 is concerned only with non-domestic premises made available to persons as a place of work, and the duty is imposed only on a person who has to any extent control of the premises 'in connection with the carrying on by him of a trade, business or other undertaking (whether for profit or not)' (see s. 4(4)). In these circumstances, there is no discernible reason why, as a matter of policy, any less heavy a duty should be imposed under s. 4 than is imposed under the other sections.

Notes

1. Section 40 of the 1974 Act places the onus on the employer to prove that it is not reasonably practicable to do more to satisfy the duties imposed under ss. 2–4. It is firmly established that a plea of 'universal practice' in the industry concerned cannot discharge the onus. However, such a plea is an important consideration in assessing whether a safer method should have been used (*Martin v Boulton & Paul (Steel Construction) Ltd* [1982] ICR 366).

2.   A good example of the use of the test in *Edwards* v *National Coal Board*, i.e. cost outweighing risk, can be seen in *Associated Dairies Ltd* v *Hartley* [1979] IRLR 171.

3.   Traditionally health and safety legislation has been thought of in terms of protection from dangerous machinery, chemicals, etc. where the hazards are more obvious. However, it is clear that more esoteric areas fall within its remit. It offers protection for employees against the well-documented risks of passive smoking, violence, drug abuse, alcoholism and AIDS, where both the direct and indirect effects of these have an impact on health and safety in the workplace. See Painter, R., 'Smoking Policies: The Legal Implications' (1990) *Employee Relations*, vol. 12, no. 4, p. 17; and *Dryden* v *Greater Glasgow Health Board* [1992] IRLR 469, in which it was held that there was no implied term in the contract of employment which entitled the employee to facilities for smoking. As a result, the introduction of a no smoking policy did not entitle an employee to treat himself as constructively dismissed. For consideration of violence at work, see Painter, K., 'It's Part of the Job: Violence at Work' (1990) *Employee Relations*, vol. 9, no. 5, p. 30.

The case law recognises that protection from violence at work is part of the duty to provide a safe system of work. However, an early prosecution in this area failed because although the court accepted that the risk was real and substantial it would not accept that there was a prescribed way of dealing with it and felt that effective measures should be left to the employer (*West Bromwich Building Society* v *Townsend* [1983] IRLR 147).

4.   It is clear from *R* v *Gateway Foodmarkets Ltd* [1997] IRLR 189, that the employer will be liable under s. 2 even where the 'directing mind' of the company was unaware of the failure to ensure the safety of the employees.

5.   The application of HASAWA 1974, s. 3 is not confined to situations when an undertaking is in the process of actively being carried on. It clearly applies when there is a shut down for repairs or cleaning (see *R* v *Mara* [1987] IRLR 156). In establishing guilt under s.3, it is sufficient to show that persons other than employees have been at risk, i.e. the possibility of danger. There is no need to show actual exposure by individuals (see *R* v *Board of Trustees of the Science Museum* [1994] IRLR 25). Further clarification has been made with respect to s. 3 by the decision in *RMC Roadstone Products Ltd* v *Jester* [1994] IRLR 330 in which it was held that:

> . . . In order to establish prima facie liability under s. 3(1), three elements must be proven. First, that the defendant was an employer within the meaning of the Act. Second, that the activity or state of affairs which gave rise to the complaint fell within the ambit of the defendant's conduct of his undertaking. And third, that there was a risk to the health and safety of persons, other than employees, who were affected by the conduct of that aspect of the undertaking. If these three are proven conviction will follow unless the defendant is able to satisfy the court on the balance of probabilities that it did all that was reasonably practicable to comply with the duty imposed.

6.   As many of the duties apply while a person is at work, the issue of whether a person was within the course of employment when the accident

occurred may be relevant (see *Coult* v *Szuba* [1982] ICR 380). Section 2 applies even where, for example, plant and systems of work have not yet been used due to the fact that work has not commenced (*Bolton MBC* v *Malrod Insulations Ltd* [1993] IRLR 274). It would create an anomaly to confine application of the Act to situations where 'at work' meant actually carrying out the job. In addition, this case confirmed that the employer's duty is not confined to employees who are engaged in a specific process. As a result there is a breach of duty where an employee is exposed to risk of injury from unsafe plant even though he is not engaged on the work in question.

7. Consultation by employers with employees is now mandatory, either through the Safety Representatives and Safety Committee Regulations 1977 or by virtue of the Health and Safety (Consultation with Employees) Regulations 1996.

8. Section 100 ERA 1996 provides protection from dismissal by allowing an employee to claim unfair dismissal if the reason is connected with health and safety as specified in the section – see *Harris* v *Select Timber Frame Ltd* (1994) COIT 57214/93. A wide interpretation of s. 100 can be found in *Harvest Press Ltd* v *McCaffrey* [1999] IRLR 778 in which dangers caused by the behaviour of fellow-employees fell within the scope of s. 100(1)(d). Further protection is provided by the Public Interest Disclosure Act 1998, which entitles 'whistleblowers' to claim compensation for unfair dismissal and victimisation if the dismissal etc., is connected *inter alia*, with health and safety matters.

9. The Government is expected to issue a consultative document recommending an offence of corporate killing. Also the Company Directors Disqualification Act 1986 has been used successfully to disqualify a managing director, following a breach of the Provision and Use of Work Equipment Regulations 1992 (SI 1992/2932) which had resulted in a severe injury to an employee.

For an analysis of the Law Commission proposals and the current state of play under the HASAWA 1974, see Ridley, A., and Dunford, L., 'Corporate Killing – Legislating for Unlawful Death?' (1997) 26 ILJ, No. 2, p. 99.

10. Enforcement of the legislation is carried out by the Health and Safety Executive or Environmental Health. The powers given to inspectors to aid their investigations can be found in HASAWA 1974, s. 20. The enforcement action may take the form of an improvement notice, a prohibition notice or prosecution (ss. 21–23 and s. 33). The fine at present in the magistrates' court (where the majority of prosecutions are brought) is £20,000 maximum. The Government is currently considering raising the fine and extending imprisonment as a punishment to all courts dealing with health and safety offences.

There have been a number of criticisms of the lack of enforcement (i.e. the number of prosecutions) and the nature of the enforcement with particular reference to fatalities at work, manslaughter charges being a rarity. This problem is magnified by the insignificant fines which have been awarded for breaches of the Acts. See Bergman, D., *Deaths at Work; Accidents or Corporate Crime* (WEA, 1991); Harrison, K., 'Manslaughter by Breach of Employment

Contract' (1992) 21 ILJ, No. 1, p. 31; Slapper, G. 'Where the buck stops', (1992) 144 NLJ 1037; Criminal Law Involuntary Manslaughter: A Consultation Paper No. 135 (1994) HMSO. Enforcement statistics can be found in HSE's annual report.

11.   The impact of EC law cannot be overlooked. A number of regulations arising out of EC Directives have already reached the statute book, e.g. the Health and Safety (Display Screen Equipment) Regulations 1992; the Management of Health and Safety at Work Regulations 1992; the Workplace (Health, Safety & Welfare) Regulations 1992; the Manual Handling Operations Regulations 1992; the Personal Protective Equipment at Work Regulations 1992; the Provision and Use of Work Equipment Regulations 1998. These regulations, known as the six pack, came into force on 1 January 1993 with a few exceptions. One contentious legal issue is likely to be whether the regulations actually comply with the Directives and may therefore be challenged by an individual following the ruling in *Francovich* v *Italian Republic* [1992] IRLR 84. See Holmes, A.E.M. & Slapper, G., *New Pressures from Europe and the Criminal Law: Companies in the 1990s* (Cavendish, 1995).

There has been little case law of note arising from the 'six pack' regulations. However, the importance of carrying out a risk assessment was noted in *Day* v *Pickels Farm Limited* [1999] IRLR 217. It was held that a risk assessment in relation to pregnant women should have been carried out under the Management of Health and Safety at Work Regulations 1992 as soon as a woman of child-bearing age was employed. It was insufficient to wait until an employee became pregnant.

12.   Lastly it should be noted that s. 27 of the Deregulation and Contracting Out Act 1994 contains a power to repeal or revoke certain health and safety legislation by regulations. Use of this power is subject to consultation with the HSC and other appropriate persons, and to the affirmative resolution procedure. See Walters, D., James, P., *Robens Revisited – The Case for a Review of Occupational Health and Safety Legislation* (Institute of Employment Rights, 1998) for an interim report on the Working Party established by the Institute to consider the ethicacy of current health and safety legislation and to make recommendations for improvement.

V   Working Time Regulations 1998

The Working Time Regulations 1998 (SI 1998/1833) implement the Working Time Directive (93/104). They warrant specific treatment as they are likely to generate a significant amount of case law. The main purpose of the Regulations is to prevent people working excessively long hours without adequate rest periods. The Regulations are to be enforced by the Health and Safety Executive. However, many of the provisions can be contracted out of by written agreement.

The UK Government originally challenged the adoption of this Directive as a health and safety measure on the basis of Article 118a (now 138). In the UK's view, the Working Time Directive was not a measure the essential purpose of which was to put in place minimum health and safety requirements. As a result, it should not have been adopted under Article 118a (now 138) but on the basis of Article 100 (now 94) or Article 235 (now 308), both of which require unanimity within the Council. (See *United Kingdom of Great Britain and Northern Ireland* v *Council of the European Union* [1997] IRLR 30.) The ECJ concluded that the Directive had been adopted correctly as a health and safety measure on the basis of Article 118a and that, as a result, the qualified majority procedure applied. The impact of this decision not only resulted in the Working Time Regulations 1998 but also provided a foundation for claims for damages from private sector workers who suffer a loss as a result of the failure to transpose the Directive into UK law (as per *Francovich* v *Italian Republic* [1992] IRLR 84).

The key elements of the Regulations are as follows:

(a) *48-hour week.* This is to be averaged over a 17-week period; records must be kept for each employee. In *Barber* v *RJB Mining (UK) Limited* [1999] IRLR 308, the High Court held that reg. 4(1) imposed a contractual obligation on an employer not to require an employee to work more than an average 48 hours per week during the reference period. All contracts of employment should be read so as to provide that an employee should work no more than the permitted number of hours. As reg. 4(1) imposes the contractual obligation, the civil courts have jurisdiction to consider such cases. Employees may therefore seek a declaration of rights and/or an injunction barring the employer from requiring them to work additional hours.

(b) *Daily Rest Breaks.* Every worker is entitled to a break of at least 11 consecutive hours between finishing work one day and starting work the next day.

(c) *Weekly rest periods.* Every worker is entitled to an uninterrupted weekly rest period of not less than 24 hours in each seven day period, in addition to the 11-hour daily rest entitlement. This rest period may be averaged over seven or 14 days.

(d) *Rest breaks.* Where the daily working time exceeds six hours, workers are entitled to a rest break away from the work station. This break must be not less than 20 minutes.

(e) *Monotonous work.* Where work is monotonous or the work rate pre-determined, the employer is required to provide the worker with adequate rest breaks where there is a health and safety risk to the worker.

(f) *Night work.* There are special provisions for night workers. 'Night worker' is defined as anyone who works at least three hours of their working time during night-time as a normal course, or anyone who is likely, during night-time, to work a certain proportion of their working time as defined by a collective or workforce agreement. In *R* v *Attorney-General for Northern Ireland, ex parte Burns* [1999] IRLR 315, the Northern Ireland Court of Appeal held that as a 'normal course' simply means that night work should be a regular feature of employment. A worker who spent one week in three of a rotating shift, working at least three hours during the night, was a night worker for the purposes of the Directive. As the case was brought before the Working Time Directive had been transposed into UK law, it was also concluded that the Member State would be liable for an injury sustained by an individual who suffered loss and damage in consequence of the failure to transpose (see also *Dillen Kofer* v *Federal Republic of Germany* [1997] IRLR 60). The normal working hours for night workers shall not exceed an average of eight in each 24-hour period (averaged over a 17-week period). Where the work involves special hazards, the normal working hours must not exceed eight in any particular 24-hour period with no averaging out. Night-time is defined as a period of not less than seven hours, including the period between midnight and 5.00 a.m. and, by default, 11.00 p.m. to 6.00 a.m. Before workers are assigned to night work, they must be given the opportunity of a free health assessment, which must then be carried out at appropriate regular intervals.

(g) *Collective or workforce agreements.* Provisions relating to rest breaks may be modified or excluded either by a collective agreement or by a workforce agreement. However, an equivalent period of rest should be allowed wherever possible.

(h) *Annual leave.* Workers are entitled to four weeks' paid leave in each holiday year. In *Gibson* v *East Riding of Yorkshire Council* [1999] IRLR 359, it was held that Article 7, which related to paid annual leave, had direct effect and, as a result, an employee of an emanation of the State was able to take direct action against his employer.

Notes
1.   There has been some debate around the adoption of the Working Time Directive as a health and safety measure (see Fitzpatrick, B., 'Straining the Definition of Health and Safety?' (1997) 26 ILJ, No. 2, p. 115). However, this should be resolved by the decision in *UK and MN* v *Council of the European Union* [1997] IRLR 30.
2.   For a review of the Working Time Regulations 1998, see Barnard, C., 'The Working Time Regulations 1998' (1999) 28 ILJ, No. 1, p. 61.

INDEX